THE NEW YORK TIMES ON
CRITICAL ELECTIONS, 1854–2008

GERALD M. POMPER

with research assistance by
David J. Andersen

CQ PRESS

A Division of SAGE
Washington, D.C.

CQ Press

2300 N Street, NW, Suite 800

Washington, DC 20037

Phone: 202-729-1900; toll-free, 1-866-4CQ-PRESS (1-866-427-7737)

Web: www.cqpress.com

Cover and interior design: Matthew Simmons, www.myselfincluded.com
Compositor: C&M Digitals (P) Ltd.

∞ The paper used in this publication exceeds the requirements of the American National Standard
for Information Sciences—Permanence of Paper for Printed Library Materials, ANSI Z39.48-1992.

Printed and bound in the United States of America

13   12   11   10   09   1   2   3   4   5

Library of Congress Cataloging-in-Publication Data

Pomper, Gerald M.

The New York Times on critical elections, 1854-2008 / Gerald M. Pomper ; with research assistance
by David J. Andersen.

    p. cm. — (TimesReference from CQ Press series)

    Includes index.

    ISBN 978-0-87289-959-9 (hardcover : alk. paper) 1. Elections—United States—History.
2. Elections—United States—History—Sources. 3. Presidents—United States—Election—History.
4. Presidents—United States—Election—History—Sources. 5. United States. Congress—
Elections—History. 6. United States. Congress—Elections—History—Sources. 7. United States—
Politics and government. 8. United States—Politics and government—Sources.
9. New York times. I. Andersen, David J. II. Title. III. Series.

    JK1965.P66 2010

    324.973—dc22

                                                                        2009035692

TITLES IN THE
TIMESREFERENCE FROM
CQ PRESS SERIES

2008

2009

2011

CONTENTS

ABOUT TIMESREFERENCE
FROM CQ PRESS

The books in the TimesReference from CQ Press series present unique documentary histories on a range of topics. The lens through which the histories are viewed is the original reporting of *The New York Times* and its many generations of legendary reporters.

Each book consists of documents selected from *The New York Times* newspaper accompanied by original narrative written by a scholar or content expert that provides context and analysis. The documents are primarily news articles but also include editorials, op-ed essays, letters to the editor, columns, and news analyses. Some are presented with full text; others, because of length, have been excerpted. Ellipses indicate omitted text. Using the headline and date as search criteria, readers can find the full text of all articles in *The Times'* online Archive at nytimes.com, which includes all of *The Times'* articles since the newspaper began publication in 1851.

The Internet age has revolutionized the way news is delivered, which means that there is no longer only one version of a story. Today, breaking news articles that appear on *The Times'* Web site are written to provide up-to-the-minute coverage of an event and therefore may differ from the article that is published in the print edition. Content could also differ between early and late editions of the day's printed paper. As such, some discrepancies between versions may be present in these volumes.

The books are illustrated with photographs and other types of images. While many of these appeared in the print or online edition of the paper, not all were created by *The Times,* which, like many newspapers, relies on wire services for photographs. There are also editorial features in these books that did not appear in *The Times*—they were created or selected by CQ Press to enhance the documentary history being told. For example, in *The New York Times on Critical Elections, 1854–2008,* electoral and popular vote return boxes help readers crunch the numbers as they read about the highlights of each election.

Readers will note that many articles are introduced by several levels of headlines—especially in pieces from the paper's early years. This was done to emphasize the importance of the article. For very important stories, banner headlines stretch across the front page's many columns; every attempt has been made to include these with the relevant articles. Over the years, *The Times* added datelines and bylines at the beginning of articles.

Typographical and punctuation errors are the bane of every publisher's existence. Because all of the documents included in this book were re-typeset, CQ Press approached these problems in several different ways. Archaic spellings from the paper's early days appear just as they did in the original documents (for example, "employe" rather than "employee"). CQ Press corrected minor typographical errors that appeared in the original articles to assist readers' comprehension. In some cases, factual or other errors have been marked [*sic*]; where the meaning would be distorted, corrections have been made in brackets where possible.

ABOUT THE AUTHOR

Gerald M. Pomper is the Board of Governors Professor of Political Science (emeritus) at the Eagleton Institute of Politics at Rutgers University. He also held visiting professorships at Tel Aviv, Oxford, Northeastern, and Australian National Universities. Among his twenty books and many articles, he was editor and coauthor of a quadrennial series on national elections from 1976 to 2000, and he contributed chapters on the presidential election to CQ Press's books *The Elections of 2004* and *The Elections of 2008*. A new edition of his book *On Ordinary Heroes and American Democracy,* nominated for the Pulitzer Prize, was reissued in 2007. Pomper has been honored for career achievement by the American Political Science Association; has served as an expert witness on campaign finance, reapportionment, and political party regulation; and provided commentary for CBS radio at the national party conventions in 2008.

The second American party system emerged in 1824–1828, reflecting the extension of mass suffrage among white men. [2] The Democratic Party's successors to Jefferson competed vigorously with the new Whig Party, and both factions were active throughout the expanding nation. Although Democrats won most presidential elections, the results were close, and power alternated frequently between the two major parties.

This party system was fated to die as the nation faced "irrepressible conflict" on the issue of slavery, just as *The Times* began publication. Soon a new Republican Party—whose leaders included the paper's first editor, Henry Raymond—would challenge the extension of slavery to western territories and, with Abraham Lincoln in the White House, lead the nation in the causes of union and emancipation.

Since then, the history of American elections has been the story of the Republican and Democratic Parties and how, over time, voters created different party balances between these opponents. For the rest of the nineteenth century, amid intense competition, Republicans won all the presidential elections, except for Grover Cleveland's two victories, and they usually controlled Congress. A new party alignment emerged in 1896, leading to another streak of Republican victories interrupted by Progressives' successes, most notably in the presidency of Woodrow Wilson.

Party fortunes reversed with the onset of the Great Depression in 1929, as Democrats became the country's majority party and defined a new national agenda. Led by Franklin D. Roosevelt and his New Deal, the Democrats won seven of the next nine presidential elections and held majorities in Congress in all but four years from 1930 to 1994. During those decades, national policy continued to reflect the Democratic heritage of the New Deal and the turn of the United States to world leadership.

Eventually, Democratic dominance faded.[3] Republicans began to win the White House again in 1968 and regained congressional control in 1994. New issues, new voting alignments, and new leaders, such as Ronald Reagan, repainted the political landscape during this era. But neither party could fully dominate politics. After each presidential contest or congressional overturn, observers would see the emergence of a new long-term majority party, only to witness the vanquished soon reclaim the seats of power. As the twenty-first century began, the only certainty was continued and vigorous competition.

Even as they have alternated in power, the parties also have changed their character considerably. In their prime, the nineteenth century, party organizations dominated elections. In almost militaristic fashion, they selected candidates, raised funds, organized campaigns, spread party messages, and herded devoted voters to the polls.

During the twentieth century, parties became weaker in some respects. Altered electoral laws and the adoption of primary nominations loosened their control over candidate selection. New funding developed from interest groups, individual contributors, wealthy aspirants, and through public financing, even from government. Campaign communication came to be dominated by mass media independent of the parties. Elections centered on candidates, who still shared their party's identity, but who bore their allegiance as voluntary obligations, not as compulsory fealty.

Nevertheless, the parties continued to be the major institutional drivers of electoral combat and have even strengthened as the nation entered its third century of competitive elections. The parties have become more centralized in contrast to past loose alliances of state organizations. They raise large amounts of money and provide campaign expertise for candidates running on their tickets. Voters have become more open-minded but also more committed to their chosen party's doctrines, and representatives evidence strong cohesion in their legislative votes and programs. American politics remains party politics.

THE PATTERNS OF AMERICAN ELECTIONS

American political history is diverse. It evidences combinations of bedrock stability, long-term changes, and rapid transformations.

Stability is particularly characteristic of the formal electoral system. As laid out in the Constitution, the president is chosen by electoral votes distributed among the states, each allotted the number of votes equal to its combined representation in the Senate and House. Each state decides the method of determining its electoral vote. For almost all presidential contests, each state casts its ballots for the candidate who receives a plurality of its statewide popular votes. A majority of all the states' ballots is required to choose the president; if no candidate receives a majority, the president is chosen by the House of Representatives.

This electoral system has been the foundation for the stability of party competition. To win the single national office of the presidency—to gain the required electoral majority—politicians must form multistate coalitions. Their best chance of success comes when they consolidate in only two competing parties; defections and splits are punished by the electoral math. A similar effect is seen in congressional elections, which have long required single-member districts with winners chosen by plurality vote.

These structural constraints have made the history of U.S. elections principally the story of two strong, competitive, and skilled political parties. Every one of the campaigns presented in this volume was primarily a contest between the Republican and Democratic Parties. In the fifteen reported races for president, Republicans won six outright and two in dubious circumstances (1876 and 2000), and Democrats won seven. The parties evenly split the six congressional contests. Although the record is less balanced over all elections (Republicans have won twenty-one of forty presidential elections outright, as well as two disputed contests), the two major parties have consistently split the spoils of power. Their matched success over the long run testifies to the stability and equilibrium of the American political system.

But American elections also reflect the accumulated effects of underlying trends. The United States has always been a dynamic nation, its history marked by economic development, racial and ethnic divisions, and its emergence during the twentieth century as the most powerful nation in the world. This turmoil has often led to political transformations, particularly evident in the contests reported in this volume.

Some political change has been gradual. Over the years, the voting population has grown exponentially but steadily, both through natural increase and massive immigration, and through the extension of the franchise to new groups—women, racial minorities, and youth. In the years of *The Times* publication the popular vote has grown from 3 million in 1852 to 131 million in 2008, with the number of participating states increasing from thirty to fifty. Partisan loyalties have shifted, eroded, and strengthened as Republicans and Democrats have traded their positions in the competition for ballots.

Elections in the United States sometimes have marked rapid and major departures in national politics, but these "critical elections" in American history are not always self-evident. Every election has consequences, at least for the candidates, and often for the paths the country takes in domestic and foreign policy. The contests reported here stand out because of some distinctive characteristics.

The most common feature of critical elections is economic upheaval. The cyclical downturns in the U.S. business cycle are often paralleled by the altered fortunes of the political parties. The connection between the economy and politics can be seen in these chapters as early as the congressional elections of 1874. This connection is dramatically evident in the triumph of FDR's New Deal in 1932–1936 during the Great Depression and as a major reason for Barack Obama's victory in 2008.

Critical elections also come from national trauma. Clearly the greatest ordeal in U.S. history, the Civil War made Lincoln's two elections crucial for the Union's survival. Tensions between North and South based on racial antagonisms affected the first election considered here, the congressional contest of 1854, as well as later presidential elections from 1876 to the 1960s and on to the present day. Foreign wars also have affected American politics, as in the elections following World War II (1946 and 1952) and during Vietnam in 1968 and the Iraq and Afghanistan conflicts in 2008.

Other changes have been less violent but still wrenching. Economic and social transformations of the United States were reflected at the turn of the centuries in the elections of 1896 and 2000. Political mobilizations, such as the Progressive movement in 1910 and 1912 and the civil rights movement in 1960 and 1964, spurred electoral change. Sometimes the American electorate is simply eager for change in its leadership and chooses new but inconsistent paths, as in the successive victories from 1974 to 1994 of congressional Democrats, Ronald Reagan, Bill Clinton, and congressional Republicans.

Scholarly Analysis

We use the term *critical elections* to designate major turning points in American history. In academic research, that term is used more precisely and has given rise to disputatious studies.

Scholarship on the subject began with an influential article by the distinguished political scientist, V. O. Key. He called attention to unusually significant elections when "the decisive results of the voting reveal a sharp alteration of the pre-existing cleavage within the electorate" and "the realignment made manifest in the voting in such elections seems to persist for several succeeding elections." [4] Illustrating the concept, Key pointed to the transformation of voting alignments in New England before the New Deal and in the presidential election of 1896.

Decades of research by other scholars extended the concept, including attempts to find statistical markers of critical elections,[5] to determine whether critical realignments extended over one or multiple elections,[6] and to describe the varieties of electoral change.[7] In later works, scholars developed theories to connect election transformations to political issues and leadership[8] and to broader social cleavages and social changes, particularly race.[9]

Analysts have devoted considerable attention to locating regular cycles during the history of elections, often seeing patterns of periodic changes. The most prominent exponent of periodic change is Walter Dean Burnham, who attributes the cyclical transformations of national politics to the inability of inflexible American governmental institutions to deal with the tensions of economic development and social change. Because of these tensions, Burnham argued, major transformations in the political system have occurred about every thirty years, once in each generation, throughout American history.[10] The same pattern is found by Paul Beck, who attributes this regularity more directly to generational turnover in the electorate.[11]

Relying on the idea of regular electoral realignment, analysts have divided American history into a succession of party systems. Beginning with the early patterns of Federalists versus Republicans and Whigs versus Democrats, they have sketched as many as six distinct systems, including the close party competition after the Civil War, Republican ascendancy at the onset of the twentieth century, the New Deal Democratic hegemony, the return of Republican dominance after 1968, and a possible new Democratic majority in the new century.[12]

Recently, some scholars have moved away from the concept of party realignment in critical elections. They see the research as fruitless because of the imprecision of the concept; others think that parties have become too weakened as autonomous institutions to be the carriers of major political change.[13] The broadest critique has come from David Mayhew, who applies precise statistical measures to test the theory. Finding it inadequate, he writes a concluding epitaph for the genre: "The realignments perspective had its fruitful days, but it is too slippery, too binary, too apocalyptic, and it has come to be too much of a dead end."[14]

THE CRITICAL ELECTIONS

The elections included in this volume do not fit a pure pattern of periodic realignments. They reflect not only shifts in electoral coalitions but also changes in other aspects of American political history. New campaign methods, the social changes in the population, and the impact of issues as diverse as race, war, and economic trauma all contribute to political realignments.

Although the formal electoral system remains stable, campaigning has evolved in radical ways. When communication and travel were difficult, campaigning was local and interpersonal, featuring street rallies, torchlight parades, and shouted oratory. As literacy spread and printing costs fell, the parties turned to print media to spread their messages. As railroads engirded the nation and airplanes shrank continental distances, candidates abandoned their front porches to barnstorm in whistle-stops and rallies among the growing electorate. When new mass media entered voters' homes, politics came to radio and television. When the Internet displaced communications on paper, campaigners made their appeals by e-mail and blogs. As dizzying technological innovations threaten to make print newspapers obsolete and political parties irrelevant, candidates, supporters, and foes will make greater use of instant messaging, twittering, and innovations still unknown.

Significant elections are not uncommon; they appear at least once in all but three of the decades covered by *The Times*. The interval between these major events has been as few as four years but not more than twenty. As would be expected, political changes coincide most often with the election of a new president, but major impacts have also come from the reelection of three incumbents—Lincoln, FDR, and Lyndon Johnson. Party turnover has been a hallmark of the major contests, occurring in all but one presidential and one congressional balloting.

The contests designated here as critical elections are listed in the table below and then presented in chronological order in the specific chapters of this book. The essays, headnotes, and extensive excerpts of articles reprinted from *The Times* present a tableau of American history in a format designed to combine modern retrospective analysis with the immediate reports on contemporary politics by the nation's premier newspaper.

This history of American elections is a continuing, uninterrupted story; its chapters are soundings in an ever-flowing stream. Yet there are markers of distinct pools in U.S. electoral periods. The chronological sequence of the following chapters comprises the onset of the Civil War and its conclusion (1854, 1860, 1864); the waning of Reconstruction and the emergence of national Republican dominance (1874, 1876, 1896); the triumph of reform culminating in the New Deal (1910, 1912, 1932, 1936); American turbulence after World War II and the travails of the 1960s (1946, 1952, 1960, 1964, 1968); and the divisions of an increasingly ideological politics (1974, 1980, 1992, 1994, 2000, 2008). These pools sometimes have been murky, sometimes stagnant, sometimes refreshing. But the currents of American politics have always found a way to continue their course. Competitive elections are the hallmark of democratic politics. Americans take the system for granted as their unquestionable national inheritance. But the peaceful assumption and transfer of power is as precious and as rare in the world today as it was in the past. The United States, uniquely and longer than any other nation, has held to its founding premise, that governments derive "their just powers from the consent of the governed." To grasp the sweep and wonder of democracy, read on to the stories of America's political life.

PRESIDENTIAL ELECTIONS

YEAR (CHAPTER)	WINNER	PARTY	ELECTORAL VOTE	LOSER	PARTY	ELECTORAL VOTE
1860 (2)	Lincoln	Republican	180	Breckinridge	Democratic	72
				Bell	Constitutional	39
				Douglas	Democratic	12
1864 (3)	Lincoln	Republican	212	McClellan	Democratic	21
1876 (5)	Hayes	Republican	185	Tilden	Democratic	184
1896 (6)	McKinley	Republican	271	Bryan	Democratic	176
1912 (8)	Wilson	Democratic	435	Taft	Republican	8
				Roosevelt	Progressive	88
1932 (9)	Roosevelt	Democratic	472	Hoover	Republican	59
1936 (10)	Roosevelt	Democratic	523	Landon	Republican	8
1952 (12)	Eisenhower	Republican	442	Stevenson	Democratic	89
1960 (13)	Kennedy	Democratic	303	Nixon	Republican	220
				Byrd	Unpledged	14
1964 (14)	Johnson	Democratic	486	Goldwater	Republican	52
1968 (15)	Nixon	Republican	301	Humphrey	Democratic	191
				Wallace	Independent	46
1980 (17)	Reagan	Republican	489	Carter	Democratic	49
1992 (18)	Clinton	Democratic	370	Bush	Republican	168
2000 (20)	Bush	Republican	271	Gore	Democratic	267
2008 (21)	Obama	Democratic	365	McCain	Republican	173

CONGRESSIONAL ELECTIONS

YEAR (CHAPTER)	WINNING PARTY	HOUSE SEATS WON	HOUSE SEATS GAIN	SENATE SEATS TOTAL	SENATE SEATS GAIN
1854 (1)	Republican	151[1]	108	20[1]	15[1]
1874 (4)	Democratic	181	93	29	10
1910 (7)	Democratic	228	56	42	10
1946 (11)	Republican	246	56	51	13
1974 (16)	Democratic	291	43	61	3
1994 (19)	Republican	230	52	53	8

1. Includes Republicans, American Party, unspecified "Opposition."

Notes

1. John Aldrich, *Why Parties?* (Chicago: University of Chicago Press, 1995).
2. Richard P. McCormick, *The Second American Party System* (Chapel Hill: University of North Carolina Press, 1966).
3. David Lawrence, *The Collapse of the Democratic Presidential Majority* (Boulder: Westview Press, 1996).
4. V. O. Key Jr., "A Theory of Critical Elections," *Journal of Politics* 17 (February 1955): 3–18.
5. Gerald M. Pomper, *Elections in America* (New York: Dodd, Mead, 1968), ch. 5.
6. V. O. Key Jr., "Secular Realignment and the Party System," *Journal of Politics* 21 (May 1959): 198–210.

7. Jerome M. Clubb, William H. Flanigan, and Nancy H. Zingale, *Partisan Realignment* (Beverly Hills: Sage, 1980).

8. James L. Sundquist, *Dynamics of the Party System* (Washington, D.C.: Brookings Institution, rev. ed., 1983).

9. Edward G. Carmines and James A. Stimson, *Issue Evolution: Race and the Transformation of American Politics* (Princeton: Princeton University Press, 1989).

10. Walter Dean Burnham, *Critical Elections and the Mainsprings of American Politics* (New York: Norton, 1970); "Realignment Lives: The 1994 Earthquake and Its Implications," in Colin Campbell and Bert A. Rockman, eds., *The Clinton Presidency: First Appraisals* (Chatham, N.J.: Chatham House, 1996), 363–395.

11. Paul Beck, "A Socialization Theory of Partisan Realignment," in Richard Niemi et al., *The Politics of Future Citizens* (San Francisco: Jossey-Bass, 1974), ch. 10.

12. William N. Chambers and Walter Dean Burnham, eds., *The American Party Systems* (New York: Oxford University Press, 1967); John H. Aldrich, "Political Parties in a Critical Era," *American Politics Quarterly* 27 (January 1999): 9–32.

13. Byron E. Shafer, ed., *The End of Realignment?* (Madison: University of Wisconsin Press, 1991), particularly chapter 2, Everett C. Ladd, "Like Waiting for Godot: The Uselessness of 'Realignment' for Understanding Change in Contemporary American Politics."

14. David Mayhew, *Electoral Realignments: A Critique of an American Genre* (New Haven: Yale University Press, 2002), 165.

THE CONGRESSIONAL ELECTIONS OF 1854

NEW REPUBLICAN PARTY CHALLENGES THE SLAVE POWER

After declaring its independence in 1776 and writing its Constitution in 1787, the United States prospered and grew. But the young nation was cursed with a schizophrenia that had been evident from the beginning—its split mind on the issue of slavery. The disease would reach a critical stage with the congressional elections of 1854. The forced birth of the new Republican Party that year would transform the American political body.

Even in the very founding of the new country, adoption of the Declaration of Independence was achieved only by evading the issue of slavery. When Thomas Jefferson submitted his draft of the document to the rebellious Continental Congress, it included a condemnation of the slave trade under King George III:

> he has waged cruel war against human nature itself, violating its most sacred rights of life & liberty in the persons of a distant people who never offended him, captivating & carrying them into slavery in another hemisphere, or to incur miserable death in their transportation.

Upon the objection of southern delegates, the reference to human bondage was removed from the document that magnificently began with the "self-evident truth" that "all men are created equal."

The equivocations of compromise continued in writing a new constitution at the convention of 1787. The major controversy there concerned representation of the states. Slaveholding states, erroneously expecting to be a majority of the total black and white population, sought proportional representation to increase their influence in the national legislature. Eventually, the other states won equality of states in the upper house, the Senate. But slave interests achieved many protections in the Constitution; three-fifths of slaves were counted for purposes of representation, although they obviously could not vote; all states were required to return escaped slaves to their masters; and continuation of the foreign slave trade was guaranteed for twenty years. Still, the issue festered, as Jefferson himself feared, writing even before the Constitution

Source: The Granger Collection, New York

Senator Stephen Douglas (D-IL), sponsor of the legislation that became the Kansas-Nebraska Act, is caricatured as a "squatter sovereign" prepared to defend slavery in Kansas.

1854 MIDTERM ELECTION RESULTS

HOUSE

ELECTION YEAR	CONGRESS	MEMBERS ELECTED		GAINS/LOSSES	
		DEM.	REP.	DEM.	REP.
1854	34th	83	151[1]	−73	+108[1]

SENATE

ELECTION YEAR	CONGRESS	MEMBERS ELECTED		GAINS/LOSSES	
		DEM.	REP.	DEM.	REP.
1854	34th	40	20[1]	+2	+15

1. Includes Republicans, American Party, unspecified "Opposition."

was adopted, "I tremble for my country when I reflect that God is just: that his justice cannot sleep forever."

The Missouri Compromise of 1820 was another attempt to resolve the slavery issue, in particular the extension of the institution beyond the existing states. While admitting Missouri to the Union as a slave state, this act appeared to limit further extension, admitting Maine as a free state to balance Missouri, and prohibiting slavery in most of the western territories.

The expansion of the United States after the Mexican-American War of 1846–1848 reopened the slavery issue and brought another attempted compromise in 1850. Extension of slavery to the new territories was made possible by a new doctrine, "popular sovereignty," meaning that settlers in these lands would decide the issue as new states were admitted. The prior exclusion of slavery, however, continued in the Northwest (the present Midwest). At the same time, California was admitted to the Union, giving the free states a majority in the Senate. Although the South had gained some advantages from the Compromise of 1850, particularly a severe Fugitive Slave Act—it quickly saw itself as a beleaguered minority.

SETTING OF THE ELECTIONS

The attempt at conciliation in the Compromise of 1850 soon foundered. In 1854 Sen. Stephen Douglas, a Democrat from Illinois, sought southern support for two goals. Now expanding to the Pacific Ocean, the nation began planning a transcontinental railroad. Douglas, like other visionaries, saw the railroad as critical to American economic development and wanted it routed from Chicago, rather than alternative southern sites, New Orleans or St. Louis.

Douglas also had a personal ambition: he wanted to be president. With a striking intellect and oratorical power,

the "little giant" had been a principal contender for the Democratic nomination in 1852, even leading the convention count at one point. But his previous opposition to the expansion of slavery denied him the southern support he needed to achieve the required two-thirds majority.

To achieve both goals, Douglas sponsored legislation that would in 1854 become the Kansas-Nebraska Act. Under this statute, the unorganized areas remaining in the Great Plains would become the territories of Kansas and Nebraska, providing the pathway for the transcontinental railroad from Chicago. To win southern support for this route, the legislation opened all of the western territories to slavery by repealing the Missouri Compromise and allowing popular sovereignty everywhere. In effect, slavery could now expand to any new state—eventually the area would add sixteen to the Union.

The legislation permitting slavery's growth transformed the nation's politics. For the previous six elections, presidential contests had been conducted by two coalitional parties, the Democrats and the Whigs. Both had significant support across regional lines and conducted close contests throughout the nation, while evading conflict over slavery. Democrats won four of the six races, but averaged only 49 percent of the popular vote, and significant third parties added uncertainty to the close contests.

This delicate equilibrium was unstable. North and South were drawing apart economically, one region developing an industrial economy, the other remaining agricultural. The racial differences between these regions' labor forces were becoming politically significant—the North building on a base of white workers with a sprinkling of free blacks, the South dependent on slave labor.

The Kansas-Nebraska Act crystallized these emerging sectional differences, completed the erosion of the Whig

Party, and precipitated the emergence of the Republican Party. It made slavery the dominant issue, soon framed by Abraham Lincoln as a stark choice: "Either the opponents of slavery will arrest the further spread of it, and place it where the public mind shall rest in the belief that it is in the course of ultimate extinction; or its advocates will push it forward, till it shall become alike lawful in all the States, old as well as new—North as well as South."

As the extension of slavery redefined American politics along regional lines, another social change—immigration—had a special effect on the northern states. In the ten years before the 1854 election, 3 million immigrants entered the country, which contained a total white population of only 20 million (and nearly 4 million blacks), the greatest proportionate increase of aliens in American history. Where the flood crested, in New York City, the foreign-born became an actual majority of the population.

The new Americans were not only numerous, they were different. Fleeing hunger and persecution, primarily from Ireland and Germany, they were poor, uneducated, and overwhelmingly Catholic—strikingly unlike the dominant white Anglo-Saxon Protestants already in the United States. Northern cities endured social unrest from larger populations, crowded and squalid housing, burgeoning crime, and competition for jobs between the impoverished immigrants and the impoverished native working class. Liquor brought moralistic spice to the cauldron of economic problems, as the largely Protestant temperance movement, repulsed by alleged Catholic drunkenness, sought legislation to prohibit the sale of alcoholic beverages. Regional disparities had already split the North and South into virtually different nations. Now the dissimilarity of ethnic lives brought the threat of a clash of cultures.

New issues and new populations led to a new politics, expressed in a complicated partisan tangle. The Whig Party disintegrated, unable to bridge the widening gap between its regional factions. The proud party of Henry Clay and Daniel Webster was quickly torn asunder in different directions. In the South, Whigs lost ground to the slavery advocates of the Democratic Party. In the North, realignment was more complicated.

In the Northwest, the Kansas-Nebraska Act brought disdain for Democrats and Whigs alike. To white workers, the extension of slavery threatened their opportunities for land in the frontier territories. Douglas visibly described the voters' reaction: "I could travel from Boston to Chicago by the light of my own effigy." Vainly, he tried for four hours to justify his position to a crowd of ten thousand in Chicago, but gained only hooting ridicule. Whig compromises were equally unacceptable.

The slavery issue brought the quick challenge of a new party, created almost overnight by former Whigs—later including a young ex-representative from Illinois, Abraham Lincoln—as well as dissident Democrats. Formally established by conclaves in Wisconsin and Michigan, the new party spread so rapidly in the region that at first it lacked a definitive name. It was years before the party completely took on the Republican label.

In the Northeast, concerns over slavery competed with concerns over the new immigrants. The slavery issue did spur some defections from the Whigs, eventually leading men such as Sen. William Seward of New York, and *The New York Times* editor Henry Raymond, to organize as Republicans. Nativists, however, gave less attention to slavery. They were distressed both by the relatively tolerant attitudes of Whigs toward immigration and by the Democratic voting habits of enfranchised Irish Catholics. They, too, started a new political movement, the American Party. To keep its activity secret, its adherents would refuse to answer political questions, which led to its unofficial but enduring label, the Know-Nothing Party.

The 1854 campaigns took different forms in different states, with contests between varying numbers of parties and candidates, fusion tickets sometimes uniting disparate factions and sometimes splitting the opponents of Kansas-Nebraska. The Democrats' only secure region was the South, where the party had become dominant on the basis of its advocacy of slavery. In the North, it faced the opposition of anti-slavery Whigs, the new Anti-Nebraska or Republican Party, temperance crusaders, and the nativist Know-Nothings.

The 1854 congressional elections took place at a time when politics was conducted entirely at the state and local levels, reflecting the political dispersions of federalism and the incomplete economic development of the United States. Even news was decentralized. *The New York Times,* founded only three years earlier, carried very few articles on elections outside of its immediate market, and telegraph transmissions were still novel, their commercial use begun only in 1851. The balloting was inconsistent, with polling held on varying dates among the states, some even waiting until the following year.

THE RESULTS AND EFFECTS

Though decentralized, the congressional elections wrought an electoral transformation. The Democrats certainly lost the congressional elections of 1854; the winners were harder to identify. Of the 234 seats in the U.S. House of Representatives, Democrats won only 83, almost all in the South. Deposed from 71 seats in the North, they lost the majority control they had held for all but four years since the presidency of Andrew Jackson.

But no party had a clear majority in the new House. Many representatives grouped together under the ambiguous label of "The Opposition," with 108 eventually identified as Republicans and 43 with the Know-Nothings or other factions. With no group in control, the House was paralyzed from the beginning, unable at first even to choose its leader, the Speaker. Wrangling and bargaining went on for two months and 133 ballots. Eventually, the Republicans backed Nathaniel Banks of Massachusetts. Reflecting the shifting party tides, Banks was a former Democrat and Free Soiler, had been elected as a candidate of the American Party, and would soon declare himself a Republican. In the even more confused selection of U.S. senators by the state legislatures (direct election of senators did not occur until the 1914 election, after passage of the Seventeenth Amendment), Democrats continued to hold a majority with forty seats, but were now confronted by an opposition of twenty senators that included fifteen self-identified Republicans. Lincoln, still nominally a Whig, was defeated for a Senate seat by an anti-Nebraska Democrat.

The new Congress did little to resolve the nation's emerging conflict. With the two chambers controlled by opposing parties, and the presidency held by proslavery Democrat Franklin Pierce, there was no possibility of reversing the Kansas-Nebraska Act. In the next presidential election, in 1856, Democrat James Buchanan was elected with a popular minority in a three-man race, and his party won control of both House and Senate. But

neither the weak president nor the contentious Congress provided any leadership as the sectional antagonisms escalated to armed combat among settlers in Kansas and violence even on the floor of Congress. Eventually, any possibility of new compromise was closed, when the Supreme Court, in the 1857 *Dred Scott* decision, ruled that slavery could not be constitutionally excluded from the western territories.

The lasting political impact of the congressional elections of 1854 was the formation of the Republican Party. The new party would lead the nation in the Civil War, preserving the Union and ending slavery. Politically dominant for decades, Republicans would also sponsor programs of economic development, including a national banking system, the distribution of public lands to homestead settlers, and the transcontinental railroad—ironically, fulfilling Douglas's vision of a northern route.

But these achievements lay in the future. The new Republican Party did not, and could not, resolve the nation's immediate problems. As a purely regional party, its emergence foretold the oncoming sectional conflict. The failures of elected leaders soon moved decisive power from political arenas to bloody battlefields. The American disease of slavery was to be healed only through the radical surgery of fratricidal conflict.

THE INTRACTABLE ISSUE

The United States survived its first seventy-five years by repeatedly sidestepping the polarizing issue of slavery. Each time the nation confronted the extension of slavery, northern opponents and southern proponents produced tenuous compromises to maintain national unity. In 1854 Democratic senator Stephen Douglas of Illinois wrote the "Nebraska Bill," undoing all previous compromises by leaving decisions on the spread of slavery to "squatter sovereignty" in the individual territories. The conflict threatened to shred the fragile Union.

[President Pierce's] Administration has taken the first step towards plunging the country into a renewed agitation of the question of Slavery, which will prove more formidable and more fatal to the public peace, than any similar contest through which the country has thus far passed.

JANUARY 24, 1854
RENEWAL OF THE SLAVERY AGITATION—THE NEBRASKA BILL.

President PIERCE, in his late Message, after exulting in the profound repose which had followed the enactment of the Compromise Bills of 1850, gives the country the

solemn assurance, that "this repose shall suffer no shock during his official term if he has the power to avert it." The President has either changed his mind upon this subject, or his "power" over it proves to be far less than he supposed. At all events, his Administration has taken the first step towards plunging the country into a renewed agitation of the question of Slavery, which will prove more formidable and more fatal to the public peace, than any similar contest through which the country has thus far passed.

Senator Douglas has reported a bill, organizing a Territorial Government for Nebraska, which permits the establishment of slavery within its limits. But Nebraska is part of the original territory ceded by France to the United States, under the name of Louisiana; and it all lies north of the parallel of 36° 30.' And over all that territory Henry Clay's great Missouri Compromise Act of 1820 expressly declares that "Slavery and involuntary servitude, otherwise than as the punishment of crime, *shall be and is hereby forever prohibited.*" Senator Douglas therefore proposes indirectly to abolish this clause of the Missouri Compromise; and to avoid all possibility of doubt upon this point, Senator Dixon, of Kentucky, has offered an amendment, declaring, in explicit terms, that this prohibition of slavery "shall not be so construed as to apply to the territory contemplated by this act, *or to any other territory of the United States.*" The proposition, therefore, is simply *to repeal the Missouri Compromise,* or at least so much of it as secures *freedom* to any portion of the territory of the United States. The Administration, through all of its recognized organs, has pronounced in favor of the plan. The organ of the "Soft" section of the party in the State of New York has given in its adhesion. Everything indicates that this is to be adopted and pressed as the platform of the Administration—as the test of loyalty to the Democratic party. And this is the first step taken by the President in fulfilment of his solemn pledge, uttered in presence of the nation, and under the full obligation of an official oath, that all the power of his office should be used to preserve the public repose from suffering any shock from a renewed agitation of the question of Slavery! . . .

This repeal of the Compromise of 1820, and this violation of the Compromise of 1850, are in the interest and for the extension of Slavery. Their sole aim is to establish it in new territory from which it is now excluded,—to provide for a future increase in the number of Slave States,—to add to the power of Slavery in Congress,—and to restore to the Slave States that preponderance in the Federal legislation, of which they have been deprived by the laws of national growth and the natural development of population. It is worthy of notice, however, that *it does not come from the South.* It is not the growth of Southern sentiment;—it is not prompted by Southern ambition;—we do not believe it is sustained by the sober judgment of the Southern people. It is the hellish spawn of demagoguism and partisanship. It comes from a quarter which recognizes no public good that is not identical with private interest. We have no doubt that Senator Douglas would, at any moment, sacrifice any public principle, however valuable, and plunge the country into foreign war or internal dissension, however fatal they might prove, if he could thereby advance himself a single step towards the Presidential chair. President Pierce seems willing to play a similar desperate and hazardous game, for the retention of power. Both undoubtedly assume that when the issue is once presented, the ultra pro-slavery fanatics in the Southern States will force the whole South into its support, and that party drill will control the North. The calculation may be shrewd and cunning, and as a party plot the scheme may be successful. But its very success will sow the seed of a future contest which will admit of no compromise, and which may rend the Union into contending parts. The passage of this Nebraska bill, in the form Senator Douglas has seen fit to give it, will root out from the Northern mind the last vestige of confidence in the good faith of the advocates of Slavery, and create a deep-seated, intense and ineradicable hatred of the institution which will crush its political power, at all hazards, and at any cost.

Parties Divided

The debate over the "Nebraska Bill" began heatedly, with Sen. Stephen Douglas of Illinois hurling incendiary attacks upon the opposition, and President Franklin Pierce providing support for the bill from the White House. The issue of slavery's extension into the territories quickly dominated Congress and the nation. Both of the two major national parties, the Democrats and the Whigs, fractured into northern and southern wings. In the ensuing clamor, party ties weakened and then broke, as politicians and voters sought new coalitions.

FEBRUARY 2, 1854
THE NEBRASKA BILL.

If we are to judge from the manner in which they have commenced their operations, the advocates of the Nebraska bill are determined to force it through Congress as rapidly and with as little debate as possible. Mr. Douglas opened the campaign with a display of violence and bad manners seldom witnessed in the Senate, since Gov. Foote of Mississippi ceased to be a member of it. His attack upon Mr. Chase was coarse and vulgar to the last degree; and the passion which prompted it was needless and discreditable. His attempt the next day to prevent a postponement of the debate until Friday, evinced an unmanly discourtesy and an eagerness to force the measure through the Senate, indicative of anything but a reliance upon its merits and upon the judgment of the country in its support. Fortunately, the dignity of the Senate defeated his endeavor. The debate was postponed in spite of Mr. Douglas. If there were such a thing as the previous question in the Senate, it would doubtless be used to stifle debate and drive this measure to an instant consummation. As it is, however, it will be discussed to some extent:—but it is not at all likely that any general demonstration of public sentiment through the country at large will be permitted to precede the passage of the bill. Its friends are evidently afraid of the public judgment upon it. They express great apprehension that a popular excitement may spring up in regard to it, and are, therefore, anxious to *force* it through Congress in advance of any discussion of its merits, and then to demand acquiescence in its provisions for the safety of the Union.

It is becoming apparent that the Administration is determined to use all its power for the consummation of this measure. It is relied upon as the sop that is to appease the Southern Cerberus. The Southern Democracy, it is hoped, will be reconciled to the alliance with the Softs of the North, when it sees *them* also rallying to the support of this bill. And their favor will undoubtedly be purchased by a lavish use of the public patronage. There is a large number of Missions, Chargéships, Consulships, Collectorships, secret agencies, contracts, &c., &c., at the Executive disposal. And, after the shameless manner in which Polk, Tyler, and Fillmore, distributed these offices among members of Congress, in payment for votes and other party services, there is little ground to hope that moral scruples or considerations of justice will have any greater weight with President Pierce.

Under these circumstances the probabilities are in favor of the passage of the bill. It will, doubtless, be made a Democratic measure, and as such forced upon Congress, and the country, by party pressure. The expectation is that, after it has been passed and is beyond reach, public sentiment will settle down into its accustomed apathy on the subject and that no further mention of it will be made. A fresh claim will have been established for the Southern vote, and the way will have been prepared for another pro-Slavery movement whenever it shall become expedient to make one. The Administration is clearly acting upon the spirit of Mr. Webster's declaration at Marshfield, in 1848, that "there is no North." Whether there ever will be any united, resolute, Northern sentiment on this subject, depends, in our opinion, to a very great extent on the action of the South upon this subject now.

FEBRUARY 8, 1854
THE NEBRASKA BILL—THE GAME EXPOSED.

The Washington Correspondent of the *Journal of Commerce,* one of the boldest and firmest advocates of the repeal of the Missouri Compromise, thus frankly discloses the real scope and ultimate objects of the movement now in progress at Washington:

Washington, Saturday, Feb. 4

It is objected to the Nebraska bill that it will establish a principle of extensive application, and will invoke the application of the same provisions to Oregon and Washington. *Certainly it will.* That is its main object. The principle was established in 1850, now it will be confirmed in 1854. Next year it will be declared that *the ordinance of* 1787 *is inoperative,* and that the slavery resolution in the Oregon bill, which Mr. Polk hesitatingly signed, is *superseded.*

Therefore, if slavery be a universal necessity, it will be allowed universally to prevail. But, probably, it will be found that its limits will be fixed by climate and commerce—by laws above the action of Congress.

The political effect of the passage of this bill will be important, and, on the whole, highly favorable. It will put an end to the old parties, and "crush out" the coalition of the Democracy. It will organize parties into two divisions, and both of them based on the slavery question. One party will be the Non-Intervention party, and the other the Abolition party. It is not quite certain which will finally prevail. But the struggle is, at length seriously begun. All that has ever happened on this question, all the combats from 1820 down, were mere child's play in comparison with what we shall see next Fall, and next year, and for years to come. *There will be no more Compromises.* The old ones will be contemned and set aside. Non-Intervention on one side, and Abolition on the other, are the only two principles upon which the contract is to be made.

This is a valuable disclosure of the purposes of the crusade which the Administration has started for the extension of Slavery. Instead of intending simply to give full play to the Compromise of 1850, its object is to put an end to *all* Compromise on the subject of Slavery. All those which have hitherto been made, will be set aside. The next step will be to repeal the restrictions applied to Oregon and Washington. Then a movement will be made to repeal the ordinance of 1787. And the grand end aimed at, is to secure a *direct, final and decisive struggle* upon the general question of Slavery. This is the plot, as discovered by one of the plotters.

FEBRUARY 24, 1854
THE NATIONAL WHIGS AND THE NEBRASKA BILL.

From the Albany Register.

The National Whigs of the North stand by the Compromises of 1850, and are willing to stand by them always, provided the South is true to itself, its own honor, and its faith. But if the "Whigs in the Southern States" insist upon more than this, if they insist upon removing the ancient landmarks—upon abrogating the law of 1820, and pushing the institution of Slavery beyond the line of 36° 30,' *then the Whigs of the North and the Whigs of the South will have to part company.* The Whigs of the South in that case will *per force* have to rely upon what the *Union* is pleased to call "the great and growing party of the Democracy." But the "Whigs of the Southern States" should calculate the results that are sure to follow such an act of folly. They should remember that *opposition to the extension of Slavery towards the North, is a principle common to all parties of the North.* That it pervades the Democratic as well as the Whig party. That it is just as deep seated, firm, persevering and determined among the people of the North, the masses that make and unmake Presidents and Members of Congress, as the converse is at the South. If the South of all parties unite, in favor of the Nebraska project of Senator Douglas, sending Slavery into territory consecrated to freedom, by ancient laws, and solemn compacts, *they will drive all parties at the North to unite in opposition to the extension of Slavery.* They deceive themselves if they suppose the people of the North are divided on this subject. Presidential aspirants, spoilhunters, the sycophants that gather around existing Administrations, may seek to curry favor by the abandonment of their principles, and the betrayal of their constituency; but the great body of the people, of the men that vote, are united in this matter, and they will crush every man who votes for or advocates the abrogation of the Compromise of 1820. If "the Whigs of the Southern States" choose to rely upon the "growing party of the Democracy," they will have to ally themselves with the "party of the Democracy" of the Southern States alone; they will find neither aid nor comfort from any party at the North. Let this Nebraska measure be pressed to a consummation and there will be no such fact as Democracy in the North. There may not be a Whig party. The cohesiveness of party affinities may be destroyed, but there will be a great, united, resistless Northern party, by whatever name it may be called, based upon the principle of opposition to the extension of Slavery. A party whose watchword will be repeal, not of the Nebraska enactment alone, *but of all the other measures that have been accorded for the protection of Southern institutions.* We desire to see no such state of things. We deprecate this array of one section of the Union against another. We have struggled against it for years. Those with whom we have acted have suffered somewhat in endeavoring to prevent it. But if "Whigs of the Southern States," uniting with "the growing party of the Democracy" of the Southern States, *will have it so,* then so be it. If the great conservative principles to which the great body of the Northern Whigs have so steadily adhered for the sake of the South, are abandoned and abrogated by the South itself, then there will be neither sense nor policy in their making any farther sacrifice. If "the Whigs of the Southern States" will unchain the whirlwind, let them see to it, that they are not the first sufferers by its fury. The National Whigs of the North have gone as far as they can or will go for the protection of the institution of Slavery. If the South is false to itself, *they* will be true to their instincts and their honor. If the old battle between free labor and slave labor; between free institutions and slave institutions is to be fought over again, they will be found on the side of free labor and free institutions, exerting themselves just as earnestly, and as firmly too, as they have heretofore done to prevent strife, and to preserve the harmony of the States. The Whigs of the Southern States, and the Democracy of those States also, should understand and lay these things to heart. They should reflect upon them carefully before they swing out upon the ocean of agitation, of which they have no chart, and without knowing where they may be drifted by the currents or the storm.

MARCH 8, 1854
THE LINES DRAWN.

The Washington *Union* issues an official pronunciamento, which will be found in another column, substantially declaring that the Nebraska bill is to be made a *party test*. It gives, with an edifying minuteness, the view which the President proposes to take of the matter, and the extent to which he will permit members of the Democratic party to withhold their support from the bill. It must be a comfort to the gentlemen of that party to know that "the President does "not [sic] *say* that he shall regard every man as "an [sic] Abolitionist or a Whig, who refuses his "assent [sic] to the *details* of this bill:"—and those who intend to vote for it in the House will undoubtedly be comforted by the assurance, that the President will not *"allow"* his office holders to "wield the public patronage" against them. The article, speaking as it does by authority, affords a lamentable index of the degradation into which our polities have betrayed us. How President PIERCE will thrive in his attempts thus to bestride the Democratic party, we cannot say. Many of its weaker members, who believe that they were created simply to be its tools, will doubtless walk, with more or less complacency, under his huge legs, and "peep about to find themselves dishonorable graves." There have been men, however, in the Democratic ranks, who "would have brooked the eternal devil to keep such state," and hold such tone as this, as easily as a President whom they had placed in power. But this age is not famous for its Brutuses.

An Electorate Realigning

The Kansas-Nebraska Act passed Congress in late May 1854, the only major legislation completed that year. The conflict deeply divided parties, members of Congress, and their constituencies, forging new cleavages in American politics. Historic ties between northern and southern Whigs, and between northern and southern Democrats loosened, and would soon fully erode.

MAY 24, 1854
PASSAGE OF THE NEBRASKA BILL—WHAT IS TO BE THE RESULT.

From the Albany Evening Journal.
The crime is committed. The work of MONROE, and MADISON and JEFFERSON is undone. The wall they erected to guard the domain of Liberty, is flung down by the hands of an American Congress, and Slavery crawls, like a slimy reptile, over the ruins, to defile a second Eden.

They tell us that the North will not submit. We hope it will not. But we have seen this same North crouch lower

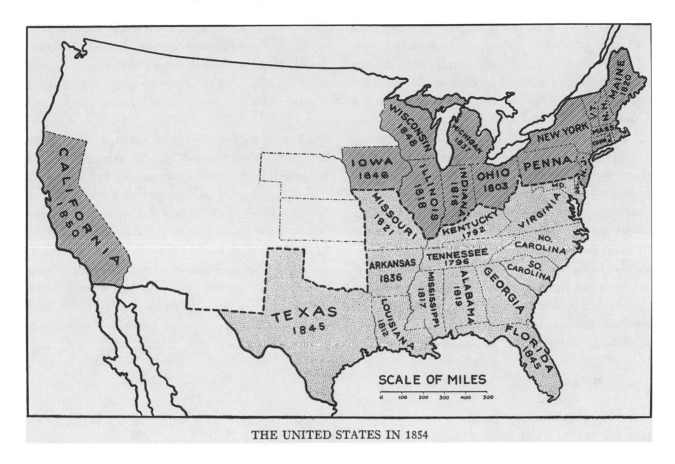

THE UNITED STATES IN 1854

The United States at the time of the Kansas-Nebraska Act of 1854, showing slave states (shaded lightly) and free states, with outlines indicating the future states of Kansas and Nebraska. The act repealed the Missouri Compromise and opened the West to slavery.

Source: The Granger Collection, New York

and lower each year under the whip of the slave driver, until it is hard to tell what it will not submit to now. Who, seven years ago, would not have derided a prophecy that Congress could enact the kidnapping of free citizens, without judge or jury? Who would have believed that it could enact that white men have a right to hold black in slavery wherever it is their sovereign will and pleasure? And yet, who now will deny that that prophecy is more than realized?

It was fitting that the law should be passed as it was. It was in accordance with its spirit that it should be conceived in treachery, sprung upon the House by a fraud, and forced through it by a parliamentary lie. It was appropriate that one member should be bribed and another bullied, and another bought, until the ranks of Slavery were full. Had Law, or Order, or Honesty had aught to do with its passage, there would have been a strange incongruity between the means and the end.

We cannot read the future. We cannot predict what will be the consequences of this last and most fatal blow to

Liberty. But we can see what the duty of freemen is and we mean it shall be through no fault of ours if it be left undone.

If the North is what it claims to be, and what we have of late had gratifying assurance that it will be, this day ends the era of compromise. With the band of representatives that have boldly resisted the consummation of this iniquity for its standard-bearers, it will declare that there shall be no more new Slave States. That there shall be no more Slave Territories. That there shall be no more Northern Congressmen with Southern principles. It will seek the immediate colonization of Nebraska by those who can yet save it from the impending curse. It will take a solemn pledge of the men it sends to Washington that their first and last vote there shall be cast for repeal and freedom. It will send no more fugitives back without a legal trial. It will sweep Slavery out of every nook and corner where the general Government has jurisdiction, imprison it within its fifteen States, and surround it there with triple bands of steel. It will "establish justice, promote tranquility, and secure the blessings of liberty to itself and to its posterity." This the United States will do, if they have reclaimed the spirit of their founders. If not, then God help the Republic, for its days are numbered. Such a gigantic confederacy of crime as it must otherwise become, never exited elsewhere, cannot exist here, and ought not to exist anywhere.

On the other hand, those who have passed the bill, flushed with success, already announce new schemes. They will send mercenary Governments to the Territories to establish Slavery there, if hasty the will of the settlers should oppose it. They count upon the Slave State of Kansas within the next Congress, and the Slave State of Nebraska before the next Presidential election. They are planning an unprovoked and unjustifiable war for the sole purpose of forming Slave States of Cuba. They will send emissaries to Texas and New-Mexico with instructions to form Slave States there. They will demand as the natural consequence of the recognition of Slave property in all the Territories, the recognition of it in all the States. They believe that popular discontent with this bill will die out before November, and they know that if it does, not only office and power, but the whole future policy and destiny of the country will be in the hands of slaveholders and their tools.

This is the struggle before us. It is fraught with results of momentous consequence. From the tone and temper of the people, we have everything to hope. From the unbridled folly and unscrupulous power of party-leaders, we have everything to fear. Believing as we do, that the purposes of Eternal Justice are not to be cast down by men's hands, we have no fear of the ultimate triumph of Right. But whether that triumph shall be slow or speedy, whether it shall come in our day, or be postponed until the Nation itself shall be consumed by the disease that is beginning to gnaw at its vitals—is for the decision of the Freemen, North and South, of the Union.

JUNE 10, 1854
THE POLITICAL FUTURE.

Speculation is busy concerning the political movements of the immediate future. It is widely felt that the passage of the Nebraska bill, and the repeal of the Missouri Compromise, have seriously affected the integrity of existing political parties: and schemes are already rife for new organizations and alliances. It has been proposed by the more ardent opponents of the Nebraska bill, that all party lines be disregarded, and that hostility to Slavery be made the sole basis of a new organization throughout the Free States. The *Tribune* is the most prominent political journal which has urged this policy: but it has been seconded and approved by many others in various sections of the Northern States. In some of the Democratic papers the proposition has also been mentioned with favor:—and a correspondent of the *Evening Post* has gone so far as to propose that Messrs. BENTON and SEWARD be the candidates of the new party for President and Vice-President, at the coming general election.

Of course, under the excitement which so great a wrong as the repeal of the Missouri Compromise may well arouse, the most direct means of seeking redress is very likely to be deemed the most feasible. We apprehend, however, that a little reflection will lead to different conclusions. It is never an easy matter to break down old established party lines. The great mass of the people always cling with tenacity to their party alliances; and even when the pressure of some great emergency may disorganize existing parties and detach individual members from them, this result falls far short of their destruction. The position of the two great parties in the Free States is not essentially changed by the passage of the Nebraska bill; indeed, that measure has only served to define, with greater accuracy, their respective relations to the extension of Slavery. For years past the Whigs as a party have been opposed to it. They have protested against it through State Conventions and Legislatures, at district, town and county meetings, and by all the usual agencies of political action. Individuals among them have wavered at times, and the position of the party has been still further discredited by the refusal of the Southern Whigs to assent to its adoption as the party creed. At National Conventions of the Whig party the Southern Whigs have had the address hitherto to exclude it from the resolutions, and even to compel the adoption of opposite sentiments. Now, however, the Whigs of the Free States present a perfectly clear record upon this subject. Every Whig vote from the North was cast against the Nebraska bill. The position of the Whigs, therefore, upon this subject is clearly defined. There is no reason why they should seek new party alliances or desert their own. No party could be found or formed which would represent a firmer and more unmistakable hostility to the aggressions of the Slaveholding interest, than does the Whig party of the Free States at this moment.

The Democratic party of the North, on the other hand, is no longer the ally of Slavery it has always been hitherto. It is radically divided and disorganized on that subject. A very large body of its members will not be dragooned into any further submission to the behests of the interest which has ruled them, and through them the country, so long. The party will inevitably be divided upon any issue that may arise in which this question is involved; and those who agree with the Whigs in sentiment will either vote for their candidates, or secure their election, by making independent nominations of their own.

We presume, therefore, that the existing political parties will be maintained, and that the sense of the country on the aggressions of the Slaveholding interest will be tested through them. In the Congressional elections, in special cases, the Whigs may return Democrats who voted against the Nebraska bill;—but as a general thing, they will doubtless present their own candidates, and elect them. The Presidential election is too far off to warrant any conjecture as to the shape it will assume. But so far as the Whigs are concerned, we see no reason to doubt that the usual course will be pursued. At the proper time, a Whig National Convention will probably be called and held. It may be, that the Southern Whigs will refuse to join in the call, unless preliminary pledges satisfactory to them shall be given on the subject of Slavery;—and it is still more likely that they will exact, at least, *silence* on the subject in the platform of the National Convention. We presume, however, that the majority will have learned from past experience the futility of securing their alliance on such terms;—and that the resolutions adopted will embody the only principles which give the party any degree of vitality and strength. If this should lead to the secession of the Southern Whigs, the party would be divided, but not necessarily weakened. Indeed, as the Democratic party of the Free States will be divided on the same issue, the Free State Whigs would be greatly strengthened by such a movement, and would be almost certain, under such circumstances, to elect their own candidate on their own platform.

Events may of course arise which will give an entirely different aspect to the political future, and speculation on it now can at the best, be of little use. But people *will* speculate nevertheless. Every man forms his opinion of events as they occur, and modifies it only as subsequent events may require. We see no reason yet to believe that the present political organizations are likely to be broken up, and still less that the Whig party will be dissolved or merged in any party based upon one idea. The Whigs have resisted all such temptations hitherto; and they never needed such a resort less than now.

• •

RISE OF THE KNOW-NOTHINGS

The open confrontation over slavery in the 1854 election created an entirely new partisan environment. Voters accustomed to the two traditional parties now had to deal with divisions within the Democrats and Whigs, as well as numerous third parties. The Know-Nothings emerged as the most prominent new party, primarily championing anti-immigrant sentiment, while also opposing the Nebraska bill. The Know-Nothings led the charge, but the electorate remained uncertain of the new faction's policies beyond its unremitting anti-immigrant rhetoric.

NOVEMBER 8, 1854
THE ELECTION—GREAT KNOW-NOTHING VICTORY.

Voluminous returns of the City and State Election will be found in another part of this morning's TIMES. We give the dispatches as they reach us, as any attempt at arrangement or classification, at the late hour of their receipt, would be fruitless. They embrace only a small part of the whole State, but enough to enable us to form an opinion of the general result. The vote for Ullmann and the Know-Nothing State Ticket is very heavy in every district heard from,—embracing not only this City, but the sections of the State generally most reliable for a decided Whig majority. . . .

The general result is that the Know-Nothings have served the Whigs in this State, just as they served the Democrats in Ohio and Pennsylvania. They have very great strength and have cast it without reference to National or State issues, but with exclusive regard to their own position as an independent party. In other States their principal assailants have been Democrats, and they have occupied a position of hostility to the Democratic party. In this State the leading Whig papers have been against them,—and their direct attack has been upon the Whigs. Their nomination of a Whig as an independent candidate was a sufficient indication of their intention to effect the defeat of that party.

We shall receive more full returns during the day. But we expect nothing that will vary the general result.

NOVEMBER 9, 1854
THE VICTORY—THE KNOW-NOTHING MOVEMENT.

We believe we may safely say that men of all parties, except perhaps the Know-Nothings themselves, were astonished at the tremendous vote cast for the Know-Nothing Candidates on Tuesday last. The strength of that party united was estimated upon the basis of their own returns early in September, at about 75,000; and in view of the fact, that from that time forward their traveling agents were organizing councils all over the State, it was supposed that their aggregate numbers might reach 100,000. But it was also believed that the policy of a separate nomination, adopted by the Grand Council in this City, was not universally satisfactory, and that the Convention at Utica was designed and calculated very greatly to diminish the Know-Nothing vote. It seems, however, that this Convention was either a *sham,* or else a mere bolt from the main body of the party not formidable enough sensibly to affect its vote. The ticket nominated in New-York has received the support of the whole Order throughout the State; and the strength of the Order, as thus developed, is much greater than the public at large had generally supposed. It will certainly reach 125,000, and we should not be surprised if it greatly exceeded that number. Nor are the numbers of this party any more surprising than its moral power. For, at a time when the Anti-Slavery sentiment and the Temperance feeling of the State were at the very highest point of intensity—the one goaded and stimulated by the Nebraska bill, and the other by Gov. Seymour's veto of the Prohibitory law;—it has completely *overslaughed* them both;—and that too without public discussion, the aid of public meetings and the press, or any of the ordinary means of arousing and guiding the public mind. True, it has been aided in this work by the overweening confidence and consequent apathy of the public mind; but making all due allowance for this, the results it has accomplished bear abundant evidence to its *moral power*. It is a movement which has great vitality and great elements of popular strength. None of its candidates were very favorably known to the State at large. It had none of the ordinary means of advancing its pretensions. Its secrecy and the mystery which surrounded its movements, did a great deal for it,—for they always have very great influence over the imaginations especially of the young. But something more even than this is requisite to account for the extraordinary strength it has developed.

The Know-Nothing movement rests partly upon hostility to Roman Catholicism, and partly upon jealousy of foreigners. The former element finds ready alliance in the religious feeling of all the great Protestant sects,—the great mass of whose members regard Catholicism as far more aggressive and far more dangerous than Slavery,—and all Catholics as subject in all things, civil and ecclesiastical, to the dictation of an absolute despot,—who has hitherto held all Europe in subjection, and who now seeks similar authority over the American Republic. The latter is strengthened by the growing rivalry of foreigners in all departments of labor. This is felt most sharply in the large cities,—but there is scarcely a considerable village in the State into which the Irish have not penetrated in considerable numbers, and made themselves unpleasantly felt on the labor, religion, morals, and above all, on the politics of the place. For in every town, however small, where ten or twenty Irish votes are to be cast, the leading political wire-puller of both parties bends all his efforts to secure them. He contributes ostentatiously to the Catholic Church; goes there himself and puts money in the poor box; is twice as careful to speak pleasantly to an Irish voter, as he is to an American;—gives him the preference if he has to hire help; promises to sell him wood, or potatoes, or wheat a trifle cheaper than anybody else can buy it;—and in a variety of ways contrives to make manifest his supreme devotion to any religion and any race, but those to which nine out of ten of his neighbors belong. This of itself excites ill feeling, and lays the foundation for a counter movement whenever the opportunity shall arise. And in a secret society, where no risks are run, the temptation to do something that shall "*fix* these Irish," is too strong to be resisted. Those who are governed by religious motives feel that they have given a death blow to the power of the Pope;—and the rest are satisfied with having preserved the liberties of their country against foreign machinations, in a general way.

Besides this, the Catholics themselves have done much to provoke this hostile political movement. They began ten years ago, when FRELINGHUYSEN was nominated with CLAY, by denouncing him, as the *Freeman's Journal* did, as a "spouter" at the religious Anniversaries and Bible Societies at the Tabernacle, and by calling upon all Catholics to vote against him. They defeated the Whigs then, and roused a deep feeling of resentment throughout the country thereby. And in the last Presidential contest, it is perfectly well understood that a meeting of Catholic magnates was held in Boston about a fortnight before the election, at which an understanding was had by which the Catholic vote was turned over *en masse* to Gen. PIERCE. Nor has the fact that a Roman Catholic from Pennsylvania, never known in any way as a public man, was appointed Postmaster General, escaped notice in this connection. The Catholic press and clergy have, moreover, strengthened the representations of those who regard their organization as hostile to Republicanism, by denouncing every liberal movement in Europe, and by allying themselves with Austria, France, and every despotism which shelters their Church. In this State their demands for new tenures of their Church property, and for a modification of our Free School System, have excited a good deal of distrust and some alarm. It is to these influences, aided by the violent and intemperate tone of the Catholic press, met by corresponding violence from the other side, that we attribute that deep and strong general sentiment which has given birth and power to this new and formidable organization. So far as it is proscriptive and intolerant,—so far as it would deprive any citizen of any of the rights and immunities of citizenship, on account of his religion or his birth place, it cannot command general approval nor meet with permanent support. But no one can deny that some of the evils at which it professes to aim, do really exist and need correction. We only hope that it will not create greater evils than it pretends to cure.

NOVEMBER 13, 1854
THE ISSUES.

The results of the late election show that the great issues made at Washington by the Nebraska bill and at Albany by the veto of the Prohibitory Law were not forgotten. Out of thirty-four Congressmen elected (including one for the short term only) only two are strongly claimed by the friends of the present Administration. Three are marked "Soft," but whether at this day that term signifies, as it did two years ago, a disposition to relax from the Spartan devotion of the Hards to the Slave interest, or, as it seemed during the last Congressional term, a mellowing under the persuasives of an Administration that still holds a cornucopia in its right hand, we can only guess. One, marked "Hard," is claimed as a Nebraska man; but whether CLARKE or DOD is to represent the Saratoga district is yet a matter of doubt. This is a very curious demonstration of the strength with which the Anti-Slavery extension sentiment had taken hold of the people. The principle and policy of Prohibition, too, has received a seal from the State that was hardly looked for when we first awoke to see what a furrow had been cut by the new and unknown folks that in excessive modesty profess that they know nothing. We suspect few would have anticipated so strong a vote had they dreamed of the strength of that little Hercules that lay snoozing in its lodge. If their ticket is defeated it will be by so small a vote as may well rather comfort than disconcert the Prohibitionists.

But the people embittered by many grievances, holding that foreigners claim to themselves greater privileges than they are willing to allow to native-born citizens were so bent on testifying their indignation that they were placed in a false position on both these questions. They had in carrying most of their candidates no principle to be shaped into law by their hands. It was a "war of demonstration." They paraded to show a strength that was far beyond all calculation. The Union looked on to hear the answers that the Empire State would make to grave questions which involved immediate interests. The question was, "Shall the Nebraska iniquity be affirmed?" The answer vouchsafed by our Know-Nothing people is, "Paddy O'Brien has been long enough lamp-lighter in our district." The question was put, "Shall the extension of Slavery, which the Administration adopts as its policy, be endorsed by the Empire State?" The intelligent answer is, "Jemmy McGuire can't no longer drive the dirtcart in our Ward." The world was agape to learn whether we would adopt the principle of Prohibition of poisonous drinks, but to the all-absorbing question came back through the votes of the rural districts the response, "Jacob Scrockenberger is a humbug for working cheaper than our folks—we'll show him that he is one of a meagre minority." The Know-Nothings were like the witty boy at school. Master PIERCE puts out "Nebraska," they spell "Down with the Irish." But there were attentive boys who spelled the word that was put out, and they must go to the head.

● ●

BEYOND 1854

Northern sentiment turned against the Democratic Party in 1854, giving control of Congress to a union of "Opposition" parties combining Know-Nothings and Republicans. Kansas, preparing to vote upon territorial slavery, deteriorated into a bloody fratricidal conflict fueled by partisan nonresidents who flocked to the territory seeking to sway the vote, while the irresolute federal government stood aloof. In Congress, the opposition parties remained united in countering the Democrats, but divided otherwise, unable to present coherent policies, even struggling to select congressional leadership. The two opposition parties vied to determine whether immigration or slavery would emerge as the dominant issue.

MAY 14, 1855
THE KNOW-NOTHINGS.

The Know-Nothing State Convention, held at Syracuse last week, afforded additional proof of the tendency we have already noticed, in the Order, to a radical division of sentiment on the question of Slavery. The Know-Nothing movement originally had no connection with that subject and was not intended to affect it, or to be affected by it. But the course of events has driven the new craft upon that rock, and without much more skillful navigation than has yet been exhibited, shipwreck is very likely to be the result.

In New-England the rapidly developed strength of the new order encouraged hopes of being able, through its agency, to elect the next President; and this hope, as it has done in so many other cases, at once stimulated the leaders to conciliate Southern sentiment and secure Southern votes. For the South, the movement, while it had this shape, was timely and welcome; for it offered means of breaking the force of that resolute resistance to the aggressions of the Slave power, which the repeal of the Missouri Compromise had developed throughout the Free States. For a time it seemed likely to be effectual in accomplishing that result; at the elections last Fall it seemed as if the issues growing out of Slavery had been entirely forgotten in the new crusade. This, however, was but temporary. No sooner was it distinctly perceived that the organization in the North was to be used for such a purpose, than a reaction took place; and the result in Massachusetts was the election of Mr. WILSON United States Senator, a strong Free-Soil delegation to Congress and a Legislature which urged the removal of a Judge because he had returned a fugitive slave.

In this State similar endeavors led to similar results. The leaders of the Silver Grays, aided by the Hunker Democrats, assumed the leadership of the Know-Nothing party, and supposed they had elected a Legislature which they could control for their own ends. The reelection of Mr. SEWARD and the subsequent passage of very strong resolutions against the aggressions of Slavery, undeceived, though it did not discourage, them. Under the immediate inspiration of ex-President FILLMORE and other distinguished gentlemen, the effort to place the Order upon a platform which should meet the views of the South was renewed; members who had proved "recreant" to alleged obligations on this subject were expelled;—new tests were devised and fresh oaths imposed;—and a "national platform" was presented for action and adoption at Syracuse. But, as will have been seen from the letters of our correspondent, the effort failed. The platform was quietly but emphatically laid aside. The representatives of the Know-Nothing Order in this State refuse to render the movement subordinate or tributary in any way to the aggressive purposes and projects of the Slave power.

The truth is the repeal of the Missouri Compromise, the events attending the recent elections in Kansas, and the movements in various quarters which demonstrate the determination of the Slave States to extend the political power of Slavery indefinitely, have aroused a feeling in this State and throughout the North which will not be thwarted or stifled. If those who are sincere in desiring fresh guards against dangers apprehended from foreign influence, would secure that result, they must not permit themselves to be arrayed in opposition to that popular sentiment which demands protection against the more imminent and portentous perils involved in the bold, lawless and desperate aggressions of Slavery.

SEPTEMBER 11, 1855
THE CRISIS IN KANSAS.

No one who has carefully watched the course of events in Kansas can doubt that a conflict is impending there of momentous interest and importance. The wrongs and outrages to which the settlers of that Territory have been subjected are such as Americans cannot submit to without changing their nature, and abjuring all the lessons of their history. Having gone thither with their families and their property, to settle and subdue a new region, to found institutions and build up a society and a State, they have been invaded by armed bands from a neighboring State, who have imposed upon them laws more bloody and tyrannical than any despot in Europe dare promulgate, and deprived them of all voice in the management of their own affairs.

American history offers nothing to compare with the proceedings in Kansas. Never before were armed men marched from a neighboring State, and permitted to seize upon the polls, and elect the law-makers for any community. Never before did the advocates of any line of policy eject from a Legislature all who differed from them, simply and exclusively because of that difference. Never before, in our history, were the inhabitants of any State or territory thus openly and entirely disfranchised, deprived of all voice in their own government, and subjected to the dictation and tyranny of an armed invasion.

The character of its enactments are strictly in keeping with the character of the Legislature thus installed. As the forcible imposition of Slavery upon Kansas—whether its inhabitants desire it or not—is the great end and purpose of all these movements, so the laws they pass are aimed solely at its accomplishment. Enactments have been passed outraging common sense and doing violence to every conception of popular rights and political freedom. A conscientious opposition to Slavery has been legislated into a crime, and punished by exclusion from rights essential to the very idea of citizenship. Printing, writing or uttering sentiments which can be construed into encouragement to slaves to escape from their masters, is made punishable by death. Violence the most extreme has been inflicted upon men for the mere suspicion of disapproving Slavery. Laws have been passed suppressing all freedom of action, speech and even thought upon this subject. And to perpetuate the power thus usurped, the Legislature has appointed officers to execute these laws throughout the Territory *for six years to come*—thus depriving their successors, and the people themselves, for all that time, of the power to change their rulers or elect other men to administer justice and enforce the law. And as a consummation of this crusade against the liberties of this new community, the Legislature has decreed that *any man,* on payment of one dollar, and taking an oath *to sustain these iniquitous Kansas laws, and the Fugitive Slave Law,* shall have the right *to vote*—whether he be a citizen, a resident or not!

It is madness to suppose that any community of American citizens will submit to such tyranny as this. If the settlers in Kansas do not resist the enforcement of such laws *to the last extremity,*—if they hesitate an instant to take up arms, if need be, against the dastardly tyrants who seek thus to trample their freedom under foot,—and to spill the last drop of their blood rather than be thus degraded and conquered, they are unworthy of their name and their descent. The provocation of our forefathers to Revolution was trifling compared with that which these Kansas settlers have experienced. And to this issue the matter must come, if the Pro-Slavery madmen persist in the measures by which they have thus far sought the accomplishment of their schemes. We are confident the people of Kansas will not submit to the domination of their invaders. They will resist the execution of their pretended laws. They will not permit their enforcement against a single inhabitant. And if their execution be attempted *by force,* it will be resisted by force; and then the issue will be one of simple strength.

Under such a menacing state of affairs, it would seem natural to invoke the interposition of the Federal Executive. But the Administration at Washington seems to have been as thoroughly conquered by the Missouri invaders as the people of Kansas themselves. President PIERCE seems to be as completely under the control of ATCHISON and STRINGFELLOW as the myrmidons they marshal to the Kansas polls. It is idle, therefore, to hope for aid from this quarter. The people of Kansas must rely upon themselves for the defence of their liberties and the protection of their rights. And if they are compelled to encounter the weight of the Federal Government in their contest, they must appeal from that to the people. They can trust to the justice of their cause for final victory.

DECEMBER 15, 1855
CONGRESS.

The House of Representatives makes no progress in the work of organization. BANKS continued to be the leading Opposition candidate yesterday, but gained nothing on his previous votes. FULLER'S vote was increased: but he has, evidently, no chance of an election, unless the Democrats should finally vote for him, which is not at all likely they will ever do. If JOHN WHEELER, of this City, and ten or a dozen others from different States, could be convinced that they will not be Speaker in any event, the House would be organized without difficulty. There was a call yesterday for a caucus of all the members opposed to the Administration. It is not at all likely, however, that any such caucus can be held, or that any union can now be effected upon that basis.

It is impossible to predict the result of this *imbroglio.* We do not know whether PENNINGTON, of New-Jersey, is Conservative enough to satisfy the friends of FULLER, or Radical enough for the taste of that recent and specially zealous Anti-Slavery convert, JOHN WHEELER. But he is a man who ought to be satisfactory to all the opponents of the Nebraska bill. There is little prospect, however, that either he, or any other man will be taken up, while personal feelings and paltry jealousies are allowed so much weight.

We can scarcely expect any united and patriotic action during the session, from a body of men who evince so little devotion to the public good as the Opposition have thus far shown. We presume that no party has a working majority in the House. The session is likely, therefore, to be spent in factious wrangling, as discreditable to the parties as it is to the country.

MARCH 1, 1856
THE AGGRESSIONS AND USURPATIONS OF THE SLAVE POWER.
Declaration of Principles and Purposes of the Republican Party.
Address of the Republican Convention, At Pittsburg, Feb. 22, 1856.

To the People of the United States:

Having met in Convention at the City of Pittsburg, in the State of Pennsylvania, this 22d day of February, 1856, as the representatives of the people in various sections of the Union, to consult upon the political evils by which the country is menaced, and the political action by which these evils may be averted, we address to you this Declaration of our Principles, and of the Purposes which we seek to promote.

We declare, in the first place, our fixed and unalterable devotion to the Constitution of the United States, to the ends for which it was established, and to the means which it provided for their attainment. We accept the solemn protestation of the People of the United States, that they ordained it, "in order to form a more perfect Union, establish justice, insure domestic tranquility, provide for the common defence, promote the general welfare, and secure the blessings of liberty to themselves and their posterity." We believe that the powers which it confers upon the Government of the United States, are ample for the accomplishment of these objects; and that if these powers are exercised in the spirit of the Constitution itself, they cannot lead to any other result. We respect those great rights which the Constitution declares to be inviolable, freedom of speech and of the Press, the free exercise of religious belief, and the right of the people peaceably to assemble and to petition the Government for a redress of grievances. We would preserve those great safeguards of civil freedom, the *habeas corpus,* the right of trial by Jury, and the right of personal liberty unless deprived thereof for crime by due process of law. We declare our purpose to obey, in all things, the requirements of the Constitution and of all laws enacted in pursuance thereof. We cherish a profound reverence for the wise and patriotic men by whom it was framed, and a lively sense of the blessings it has conferred upon our country and upon mankind throughout the world. In every crisis of difficulty and of danger, we shall invoke its spirit and proclaim the supremacy of its authority.

In the next place, we declare our ardent and unshaken attachment to this Union of American States, which the Constitution created and has thus far preserved. We revere it as the purchase of the blood of our forefathers, as the condition of our national renown, and as the guardian and guarantee of that Liberty which the Constitution was designed to secure. We will defend and protect it against all its enemies. We will recognize no geographical divisions, no local interests, no narrow or sectional prejudices, in our endeavors to preserve the Union of these States against foreign aggression and domestic strife. What we claim for ourselves, we claim for all. The rights, privileges and liberties which we demand as our inheritance, we concede as their inheritance to all the citizens of this Republic.

Holding these opinions and animated by these sentiments, we declare our conviction that the Government of the United States is not administered in accordance with the Constitution, or for the preservation and prosperity of the American Union; but that its powers are systematically wielded FOR THE PROMOTION AND EXTENSION OF THE INTEREST OF SLAVERY, in direct hostility to the letter and spirit of the Constitution, in flagrant disregard of other great interests of the country, and in open contempt of the public sentiment of the American people and of the Christian world. We proclaim our belief that the policy which has for years past been adopted in the administration of the General Government, tends to the utter subversion of each of the great ends for which the Constitution was established,—and that, unless it shall be arrested by the prompt interposition of the People, the hold of the Union upon their loyalty and affection will be relaxed,—the domestic tranquility will be disturbed, and all constitutional securities for the blessings of liberty to ourselves and our posterity, will be destroyed. The Slaveholding interest cannot be made permanently paramount in the General Government, without involving consequences fatal to free institutions. We acknowledge that it is large and powerful; that in the States where it exists it is entitled, under the Constitution, like all other local interests, to immunity from the interference of the General Government, and that it must necessarily exercise through its representatives, a considerable share of political power. But there is nothing in its position, as there is certainly nothing in its character, to sustain the supremacy which it seeks to establish. There is not a State in the Union in which the Slaveholders number *one-tenth* part of the free white population—nor in the aggregate do they number *one-fiftieth* part of the white population of the United States. The annual productions of the other classes in the Union, far exceed the total value of all the slaves. To say nothing, therefore, of the questions of natural justice, and of political economy which Slavery involves, neither its magnitude nor the numbers of those by whom it is represented, entitle it to *one-tenth* part of the political powers conferred upon the Federal Government by the Constitution. Yet we see it seeking, and at this moment wielding, all the functions of Government—executive, legislative and judicial—and using them for the augmentation of its powers and the establishment of its ascendancy.

From this ascendancy the principles of the Constitution, the rights of the several States, the safety of the Union, and the welfare of the people of the United States, demand that it should be dislodged.

RISE OF THE REPUBLICANS

As the Know-Nothings faded, the Republican Party took center stage as the viable alternative to the Democrats. Strongly opposing the extension of slavery, Republicans united former Whigs, dissident Democrats, and Know-Nothings on a common national platform. In 1858 the Republican Party swept into congressional control (although Lincoln lost his bid for a Senate seat after historic debates with Douglas), united the northern states, and clearly challenged the political power of the South.

NOVEMBER 6, 1856
RESULT OF THE ELECTIONS.

JAMES BUCHANAN, President.

JOHN C. BRECKINRIDGE, Vice-President.
Fifty Thousand Majority for Fremont in New-York.

FORTY THOUSAND MAJORITY FOR BUCHANAN IN PENNSYLVANIA.
Indiana, Kentucky and Tennessee for Buchanan.

ILLINOIS REPORTED FOR BUCHANAN.
The Whole South Except Maryland for Buchanan.
California and Florida to Hear From.

NOVEMBER 6, 1856
THE RESULT AND THE PROSPECT.

This election offers sundry curious matters for speculation. When the returns are all in,—the columns footed, and the philosophy of the whole canvass clearly developed, it will be very easy to see why the Pro-Slavery Party has carried the day, and how such a result can be prevented hereafter.

In the first place, the whole foreign vote—Irish and German—has been cast for BUCHANAN. There may have been here and there some scattering German votes given for FREMONT. In this City and in one or two of the Western States, this has probably been the case:—but on the whole we do not believe that *one tenth* part of the German vote has been given to the Republican ticket. As for the Irish, they have gone in a drove,—as they always do go,—for the regular Democratic ticket. They will probably never do anything else, as long as they remain Irish,—and it takes at least two generations to convert them into Americans. They seem to lack the faculty of individual action, or of exercising a personal judgment on public affairs. They vote in herds,—and are of course, managed like other herds, under the control of skillful and experienced drivers.

Besides this, there is nothing that an Irishman loves like the opportunity to tyrannize over somebody:—and nothing that he hates like a negro. Having been the victim of oppression, as he supposes, all his life at home, his only notion of liberty here is that he can treat somebody else in the same style. The Irish have been told all through the late canvass, by the leaders of the Buchanan Party, that Col. FREMONT if elected would immediately set all the slaves free and bring them North to take the bread out of the mouths of the laboring Irish! They believed it, of course. Their ignorance and credulity make them the ready dupes of every cock-and-bull story that jumps with their inclinations. They care no more for the principles of Freedom, or for any other principle, than they do for anything else of which they have no conception. They care nothing for Slavery,—except that they are rather in favor of it for negroes, and are resolutely opposed to anything that looks like making negroes free and thus their equals. They never look ahead:—both at home and here, foresight,—the prevention of future evils of any kind,— seems to be beyond their capacity. They look out only for themselves, and that only for to-day. Everything else must take care of itself. In our political contests, they neither read nor think. If they attend political meetings, it is to hurrah to order—not to listen or to learn. They follow throughout their instincts, their prejudices, their hatreds and their leaders.

While the Buchanan Party thus had the whole strength of the foreign vote, its opponents were divided by the adroit use of the anti-sovereign sentiment. Thousands and tens of thousands of our best citizens, who have watched the political movements of the past ten or fifteen years, have become utterly disgusted and alarmed at the unity and compactness with which the foreign element in our politics is wielded:—and they have keenly felt the necessity of breaking up this foreign phalanx, or of preventing the increase of its political power. The great body of the American Party in the Northern State is thoroughly hostile to the extension of Slavery, and heartily in sympathy with the great cardinal principles of the Republican movement. And if they had been left to their own free action in this canvass, they would have acted upon that sentiment and joined in the movement for the defeat of BUCHANAN. *But they have been betrayed and sold by the men in whom they trusted.* In this State they have been cheated by the Democrats, who had given them to understand that they would not seriously contest it. They have been deserted by thousands of the Old Whigs, and of their own men, who voted openly at the last moment for BUCHANAN. And in Pennsylvania they have been unconsciously mere tools in the hands of Buchanan men, who obtained ascendency and control in their Councils, for the sole and exclusive purpose of electing BUCHANAN. All these facts are plain enough. BUCHANAN has succeeded solely in consequence of the *division* in the ranks of his opponents.

We presume that the great mass of the American and Republican parties will now be consolidated. The leaders of both may resist. Prominent nations in one or the other may hold out for a price. But the conviction of a common defeat,—the sense of a common danger, and the feeling that substantially, and at bottom, their principles of public policy are the same, will override all the dictation of leaders, and all the intrigues of designing men. The Government of the country may remain in the bands of the Pro-Slavery Democracy. But the popular sentiment,—the moral strength,—the vast majority of the popular votes, will be with the AMERICAN REPUBLICANS of the Union;—and the triumph of that party and its principles is merely a question of time.

NOVEMBER 3, 1858
THE ELECTIONS.

Republican Ticket Probably Elected.

Loss of Five Congressmen to the Administration in New-York.

MASSACHUSETTS REPUBLICAN.

ILLINOIS YET UNCERTAIN.

> [T]he Southern ultraists seem to understand the emergency of the case, and have no disposition to be thus crushed between the sectional millstones which threaten their destruction.

NOVEMBER 10, 1858
THE POLITICAL HORIZON.

There is always a lull after a tempest:—and so the political world has subsided into an unwonted calm since the elections. All parties are trying to devise what consolation the result may be made to yield. The Republicans are naturally and excusably exultant over their sweeping victories, to which the only drawback comes from the brilliant triumph of DOUGLAS in Illinois, with the unpleasant suspicion which it seems to authorize, that he has stolen just enough of their thunder to spoil their chances for 1860. They are, accordingly, scrutinizing the case with special care. One Republican journal comforts itself by thinking of the herculean efforts made by DOUGLAS, and the enormous sums of money he must have spent, very justly supposing that

these exertions cannot be renewed *ad infinitum*. Another is endeavoring to convince itself that his triumph is not very complete after all, and that if the districts of Illinois were only differently constituted he could not be returned to the Senate in spite of his apparent success. And a third predicts that his misdeeds in the past have been so manifold and so wicked, that he will find it impossible to command the confidence of the North to any dangerous extent.

The Administration organs find it still more difficult to derive consolation or hope from any aspect of the political heavens. They are sour and out of temper, and find their chief solace in denouncing the doctrines put forth by Mr. SEWARD in his Rochester speech as involving the height of treason to the country and danger to the Union. They ring the charges upon it as if it were some new revelation of the distinguished Senator's opinion,—as if he had just now for the first time proclaimed his hostilities to Slavery and his hope of its extinction. This is somewhat absurd. Everyone who knows anything of his political history understands perfectly that there was nothing new in the speech, except possibly a stronger imputation of his own views to the Republican Party than that party has ever hitherto been willing to allow. A correspondent of the *Tribune* yesterday shows very clearly, by a collation of Mr. SEWARD's speeches, that he has always held and expressed the very sentiments which now excite so much alarm. This, however, does not amount to a vindication of anything but Mr. SEWARD's personal consistency, and it cannot escape observation that a good many Republicans, in various sections of the country, shrink from the task of maintaining these views and vindicating these opinions of our Senator in a Presidential canvass.

The Washington *Union* evidently considers its own peculiar party *in extremis*. We have heard a rumor—from what ought certainly to be good authority—that the *Union* has been sold to the friends of DOUGLAS, and that they will enter upon its active management soon after the opening of the session of Congress. If so, its temporary editors are evidently inclined to improve the brief remnant of power that still remains to them. They are unusually vehement in their abuse of DOUGLAS, imperative in excluding him from any position of influence in the Democratic Party, and zealous in their endeavors to rally the old Southern State-Rights Party to their support. They join this wing of the Democracy in rejecting the doctrine of popular sovereignty in the Territories, upon which DOUGLAS has taken his stand, and invoke the Southern ultraists to assume their wonted control over the policy and action of the party. Unfortunately for them, however, the Southern ultraists seem to understand the emergency of the case, and have no disposition to be thus crushed between the sectional millstones which threaten their destruction. Senator HAMMOND's speech has created a marked sensation throughout the country, and is regarded as the symptom of a general abandonment, by the Southern Democracy, of the extreme position which they find they can no longer hold. The sentiments of that speech, so far as they relate to practical political issues, meet a very general concurrence from the people of the Free States.

Indeed the general impression seems to be that Senator DOUGLAS and Senator HAMMOND have devised a platform upon which the National Democratic Party can be reconstructed, and by which it can regain the *prestige* and moral power which it lost by the disastrous victory of 1856. The Republicans, who have all along considered their success in 1860 as nearly certain, are puzzled and a little dismayed by the new prospect—while the Democrats are one and all listening anxiously for the recruiting drum which is to give the signal for enlistment under their new commander.

THE PRESIDENTIAL ELECTION OF 1860

LINCOLN'S VICTORY CREATES FEAR OF NATIONAL DIVISION

It might have been the last presidential election in the history of the United States. When Abraham Lincoln won a majority of electoral votes, the threat of secession loomed, then became reality. Only after the trauma of the Civil War would the nation reunite and restore its electoral process.

The election of 1860 culminated the conflict over slavery that had divided the nation long before it brought opposing armies to the battlefield. Decades of compromise failed to end its moral evil or to resolve the issue politically. As recounted in the previous chapter on the congressional elections of 1854, the issue had recurred in the Missouri Compromise of 1820, the Compromise of 1850, and the Kansas-Nebraska Act of 1854. Then, in 1857, the Supreme Court closed off all compromise by ruling, in *Dred Scott v. Sandford,* that slavery could not be prohibited anywhere by federal action.

By the 1856 presidential election, partisan lines had hardened. The new Republican Party, lacking any southern representation, nominated Gen. John Fremont, and the Democrats made a last attempt at sectional alliances by selecting James Buchanan, a Pennsylvanian who supported the slave states' positions. A third party, officially named "American," but widely called the "Know-Nothings" because of their covert opposition to immigration, presented Millard Fillmore, the former Whig president. Buchanan won 45 percent of the popular vote to Fremont's 33 percent and Fillmore's 21 percent, the electoral vote dividing 174–114–8. Buchanan became president, but he lacked both the political mandate and the political skills to repair the widening breach.

THE PARTIES AND THE CANDIDATES

As the 1860 presidential election approached, the slavery conflict split the parties, as it would soon rip the nation. Four major political parties emerged, holding five national conventions.

A political cartoon depicts 1860 Republican presidential candidate Abraham Lincoln about to devour his Democratic rivals, Stephen A. Douglas and John C. Breckinridge.

The Democrats began the process, meeting in Charleston, South Carolina, in April. South and North divided on every issue—rules, platform, and candidates. They clashed repeatedly on the slavery plank of the platform, with the South insisting on the unreserved right to hold slaves throughout all the territories. The adopted position accepted the *Dred Scott* decision favoring slavery's extension, but left future policy on the territories "as the same has been, or shall hereafter be finally determined by the Supreme Court of the United States." Upon the adoption of this ambiguous position, forty-five delegates from nine southern states (of the convention total of 303) withdrew from the convention.

The bolt also led to party paralysis. The Democrats' rules already required a two-thirds majority of delegates to win nomination, but a decision became virtually impossible when the chairman ruled, with the remaining delegates' approval, that the required two-thirds would be based on the number of votes in the original convention allocation,

1860 ELECTORAL VOTE

STATE	ELECTORAL VOTES	LINCOLN	BRECKINRIDGE	BELL	DOUGLAS	STATE	ELECTORAL VOTES	LINCOLN	BRECKINRIDGE	BELL	DOUGLAS
Alabama	(9)	–	9	–	–	Mississippi	(7)	–	7	–	–
Arkansas	(4)	–	4	–	–	Missouri	(9)	–	–	–	9
California	(4)	4	–	–	–	New Hampshire	(5)	5	–	–	–
Connecticut	(6)	6	–	–	–	New Jersey	(7)	4	–	–	3
Delaware	(3)	–	3	–	–	New York	(35)	35	–	–	–
Florida	(3)	–	3	–	–	North Carolina	(10)	–	10	–	–
Georgia	(10)	–	10	–	–	Ohio	(23)	23	–	–	–
Illinois	(11)	11	–	–	–	Oregon	(3)	3	–	–	–
Indiana	(13)	13	–	–	–	Pennsylvania	(27)	27	–	–	–
Iowa	(4)	4	–	–	–	Rhode Island	(4)	4	–	–	–
Kentucky	(12)	–	–	12	–	South Carolina	(8)	–	8	–	–
Louisiana	(6)	–	6	–	–	Tennessee	(12)	–	–	12	–
Maine	(8)	8	–	–	–	Texas	(4)	–	4	–	–
Maryland	(8)	–	8	–	–	Vermont	(5)	5	–	–	–
Massachusetts	(13)	13	–	–	–	Virginia	(15)	–	–	15	–
Michigan	(6)	6	–	–	–	Wisconsin	(5)	5	–	–	–
Minnesota	(4)	4	–	–	–						
						TOTALS	(303)	180	72	39	12

including the southern defectors. A nominee would require overwhelming support from the remaining delegates (equivalent to 78 percent), a result inconceivable in the heated political environment.

Sen. Stephen Douglas was the leading Democratic contender, but certainly no consensus candidate. His advocacy of "popular sovereignty," originally intended to win southern support, was now disdained by the slave states as an infringement on their "peculiar institution." Douglas led on the first convention ballot, with 145 and a half votes, far below the 202 required by the adopted rules. After three days and fifty-seven ballots, nothing changed, with Douglas receiving only six new votes. Deadlocked, the Democrats voted to adjourn the convention, to meet again in six weeks, and in a more neutral site, Baltimore.

Time and travel failed to heal the party wounds. The reconvened Democrats allowed some of the southern bolters to resume their seats, but others were kept out, and defection spread to the remaining southern and border states, as well as to some individual delegates from the free states. By the time the convention had held ten roll calls to resolve its credentials contests, almost no slave state delegates remained. With these losses, the convention had only 190 delegates left, making a nomination mathematically impossible. On the second ballot, Douglas won unanimous support from the depleted group of delegates, who then legitimated his selection by a voice vote declaring him the nominee of the Democratic Party. The remaining southerners were authorized to pick the vice-presidential nominee, selecting Sen. Benjamin Fitzpatrick of Alabama. He declined the nomination and was replaced later by former Georgia governor Herschel Johnson.

The southern wing of the party now held its own convention, in Richmond. A mirror image of the northern Democrats, the convention was dominated by its southern delegates, with only a minority from the northern states. While endorsing most of the previous Democratic platform, this convention took a firm proslavery position, declaring that in any of the territories, "all citizens of the United States have an equal right to settle in the Territory, without their rights, either of person or property, being impaired or destroyed by Congressional or Territorial legislation." In their nominations, the delegates made a nod toward sectional comity. The incumbent vice president, John Breckinridge, was nominated for president, with Oregon senator Joseph Lane as running mate.

The divisions of the Democratic Party, which had spanned the sections, presaged the division of the nation. One attempt to repair the breach came in the emergence of the Constitutional Union Party, a remnant of the older Whig Party and some elements of the 1856 American Party. Intending to be a moderating influence, it met in May, between the major party conventions, and in the border city of Baltimore. There, the new party attempted to appeal to national unity by nominating Sen. John Bell of Tennessee for president and Edward Everett of Massachusetts for vice president. Refusing to take sides on slavery, the Unionists simply endorsed "the Constitution of the Country, the Union of the States, and the Enforcement of the Laws." But the time for such empty rhetoric was quickly passing.

The most important of the party conventions proved to be the May Republican conclave, held in Chicago. Meeting for only their second national convention, the new party sensed victory through its northern appeal against the divided Democrats.

On the central issue of slavery, the Republicans were not abolitionists. They did accept the continued existence of bondage in the existing states, but they were firmly against any extension to the territories. The party platform denounced the *Dred Scott* decision as "a dangerous political heresy, at variance with the [Constitution] . . . revolutionary in its tendency, and subversive of the peace and harmony of the country." It then proclaimed that "the normal condition of all the territory of the United states is that of freedom. . . and we deny the authority of Congress, of a territorial legislature, or of any individuals, to give legal existence to slavery in any territory of the United States."

The party attempted to broaden its appeal beyond the issue of slavery. Echoing the older appeal of the Whig Party, it also looked toward active government involvement in national economic development, favoring protective tariffs for industry, homestead legislation to spur western settlement, extensive public works, and construction of a transcontinental railroad. Disavowing the former "Know-Nothings," it supported the rights of immigrants to full citizenship.

The Chicago convention was memorable not only for philosophy and program. It was also a contest of men for the stakes of power, resolved through the classic political techniques of bargaining and dealing.

Five major contestants sought the presidential nomination. The leading prospect was William Seward, former governor and senator from New York. One of the principal founders of the party, Seward had been prominent in the antislavery movement, a role that brought him support among Republicans but also stoked their fear that his positions would alienate moderate voters and lose the election. Lincoln was the most significant of the other candidates, having achieved attention though his debates with Douglas in the Illinois Senate contest in 1858. Other contestants included Simon Cameron of Pennsylvania, Salmon Chase of Ohio, and Edward Bates of Missouri. All would later become members of Lincoln's cabinet during the Civil War.

A noted journalist, Murat Halstead, telegraphed this dramatic account of the maneuvers before the next day's presidential balloting:

> There was much to be done after midnight and before the convention assembled on Friday morning. There were hundreds of Pennsylvanians, Indianans and Illinoisans who never closed their eyes that night. . . . Henry S. Lane . . . had been operating to bring the Vermonters and Virginians to the point of deserting Seward. . . . This was finally done, the fatal break in Seward's strength . . . destroying at once, when it appeared, his power in the New England and the slave state delegations. . . . The Cameron men, discovering there was absolutely no hope for their man, but that either Seward or Lincoln would be nominated, and being a calculating company, were persuaded to throw their strength for Lincoln at such a time as to have credit of his nomination

Only a simple majority of the 466 delegates was required for victory. Seward led on the first convention ballot, with 173 votes, followed by Lincoln with 102. On the second ballot, as the previous night's promises were redeemed, the field narrowed to Seward, with 184 and a half, and Lincoln behind by only 3 and a half votes. On the third ballot, Lincoln needed only a last switch of four Ohio votes to become the convention's and, ultimately, the nation's, choice. The vice-presidential selection followed in an open contest, won in two ballots by Sen. Hannibal Hamlin of Maine. (He defeated Cassius Clay of Kentucky, the namesake of a more famous competitor a century later.)

THE ELECTION CAMPAIGN

The campaign defied the customary rules of American politics. The usual pattern of presidential elections was a two-man race, as factions combined to gain the required majority of electoral votes. Now, there were four contestants, whose sharp differences in program, regional loyalties, and personal antagonisms prevented compromise.

In these circumstances, the weaknesses of the Electoral College system became evident. The constitutional system did not provide for a national election, but for selection by combinations of states. Candidates who had strong support in particular states gained an edge, but those whose support was diffused among the states at lower levels were disadvantaged. Only unified, cross-sectional parties could make the system work—but their unifying strengths had disappeared in 1860.

In effect, there were different campaigns in the two sections of North and South. It was clearly impossible for Breckinridge or Bell to win a national majority, but they were the leaders in the South. In the North, the contest was between Lincoln and Douglas, whose prospects depended on completely different strategies. Douglas, on the surface, was a national candidate, who might have some chance of winning electoral votes in all areas. In fact, however, the division of the Democratic Party destroyed his chances of southern electoral votes, and his northern support was spread too thin to gain a majority.

Lincoln's appeal was clearly confined to the North. He was not even on the ballot in ten southern states (including South Carolina, which still lacked popular elections), and was virtually invisible in three of the other five southern and border states. Lincoln would later achieve immortality by standing for the union of the states. But, ironically, his election success required division—a division between the sections to emphasize his northern appeal, and a division among his competitors to gain the northern states' electoral votes with only a plurality, not an absolute majority, of the popular votes.

Mobilization was the hallmark of the campaign, with extensive efforts to rally support from all groups, resulting in a 15 percent increase in turnout over 1856 in the thirty states participating in both elections. Lincoln followed tradition and stayed at home in Illinois, while other Republicans toured extensively, with Seward particularly active, serving virtually as a surrogate candidate. In Michigan on September 15, the New Yorker gave one of his many extravagant speeches, combining the lofty appeals of patriotism with the self-interest of his audiences:

> What kind of a nation then do you want? Just such a nation as the State of Michigan; a land where every man may sit, happy and free, not under his own vine and fig-tree, but under his own apple, peach, and shade trees, with none to molest or to make him afraid; a land where all the citizens are free to exercise the spontaneous will of freemen. . . .

> If I take out a freeman and put in a slave, what happens? More than the loss of an enterprising and useful citizen—the loss of virtue—the loss of the spirit and energy that exists only with entire freedom. Let it once be understood that Slavery may exist here, and all the emigrants would desert Michigan at once. The two systems of labor cannot exist as a permanent form of civilization together. *There is* an irrepressible conflict. [Loud and long-continued cheers.]

Douglas faced both the likelihood of defeat and failing health. Nevertheless, he broke with tradition and took his cause directly to the voters in the South and the North. As the likelihood of Lincoln's triumph increased, so did his efforts, directed now to convincing the South to accept the coming national verdict against slavery.

The battleground in the election was the moderate states of the Mid-Atlantic and Midwest regions. Although slavery was clearly the major issue, Republicans tried for broader appeals. They enlisted votes from workers, portraying slavery as an economic threat as much as a moral cause, asking "How can the free labouring man ever get two dollars a day when a black slave costs his master only ten cents a day?" They offered the prospect of new lives for poor farmers and city dwellers by pledging free land in the West through government homesteads, urging the electors to "Vote yourself a farm." To businesses and employees hurt by the recent depression, they promised that high tariffs and public works would revive the economy. To the growing numbers of immigrants, particularly Germans, they promised nondiscrimination and easy naturalization.

To gain these voters, Republicans were eager to separate Lincoln from abolitionists and to portray, as did a September 4 editorial in *The New York Times*, the "conservatism of the Republican candidate." Quoting Lincoln in his earlier debates with Douglas, they argued:

> This is not the language, nor are these the sentiments, of an ultra Anti-Slavery radical. Nor do they give the slightest countenance to the charge that, if elected President, Mr. Lincoln would trespass, in any degree or to any extent, on the constitutional rights of the Southern States. On the contrary, they give every guarantee which reasonable men could ask of a wise, considerate and conservative administration of the government—one which would put an end to that *political power* by which Slavery has hitherto tyrannized over the Government of the country, but which should, at the same time, secure to it all its rights. We believe this is the only basis on which the country can hope for peace upon this disturbing and difficult question.

Threats of violence and disunion permeated the campaign. Southern orators warned that Lincoln's election would bring slave revolts, invasion, and the forcible end of the region's distinctive culture. Republicans tried to calm these anxieties, presenting Lincoln as a moderate, while also disdaining the warnings of secession as the bluff of a weak Dixie. At the same time, Republicans added to the militaristic atmosphere. The party campaign featured the "Wide Awakes," legions of young men who dressed in prescribed uniforms, conducted torchlight parades of tens of thousands, and acted as official escorts for Republican orators at party rallies. Although the Wide Awakes were primarily social clubs, their activities were often enlivened by drinking and street fights. In reaction, southerners developed similar groups of "Minute Men." Soon, the boys playing soldiers would be men dying in a real war.

As the election neared, Lincoln's opponents tried to create fusion tickets in the competitive northern states to deprive him of electoral votes won only by plurality. While still not expecting to win an electoral majority, the fusion groups hoped that they could deny Lincoln the majority as well, and thereby move the presidential decision to the House of Representatives. Fusion tickets were created in five Northeast states; the most important effort came in New York, whose 35 electoral votes could prove decisive. After months of negotiations, the contenders agreed on a common ticket with 18 electors for Douglas, 10 for Bell, and 7 for Breckinridge. It would come close, but still lose the state. In New Jersey, the effort did succeed, and Lincoln lost the popular vote to Douglas on a fusion ticket.

THE ELECTION RESULTS

Election day was peaceful, even solemn, with participation setting a new record for votes cast, 4.7 million. Most observers expected a Republican victory, but none could foresee the ultimate outcome of the sectional division evident in the campaign.

On November 7, *The Times* reported, with little effort at neutrality, an "Astonishing Triumph of Republicanism," with "The North Rising in Indignation at the Menaces of the South." Even the weather cooperated, according to a poetic reporter: "The clouds were dispelled; the sun shone forth as a beneficent sun should shine on such an occasion, and a general good time was the result."

Lincoln and the Republicans won an overwhelming victory in the Electoral College, gaining 180 electoral votes and carrying every state north of the Mason-Dixon line except New Jersey (part of which actually lay below this boundary of free and slave states). Breckinridge followed with 72 electoral votes from the Deep South and border states; Bell with 39

from Virginia, Tennessee, and Kentucky; and Douglas with 12 from Missouri and the fusion vote in New Jersey.

In the congressional elections, Republicans gained a split, losing seven seats in the House, while gaining five in the Senate. In neither body, however, would they hold a working majority until southern Democrats resigned after the secession of their states.

Lincoln won with only a 39.9 percent plurality—the lowest of any elected president in U.S. history. Even with this diminished share, Lincoln's victory was definitive. He won seventeen of the thirty-three states, with absolute majorities in every northern state other than New Jersey, California, and Oregon, and an absolute overall majority in the twenty-one states where he had any viable campaign. But it was no mandate: a shift of only thirty thousand votes in four close states—or the loss of New York alone—would have brought his electoral share below the required majority and cast the presidential choice into the House of Representatives.

Now outside the winner's circle, the South was not ready to accept its loss. As the election outcome became clear, South Carolina declared its secession from the Union, and six others followed. In February, the dissident states met in Montgomery, Alabama, to form a new, if short-lived nation, the Confederate States of America. Federal fortifications in the South were seized by these states, and a fateful siege began at Fort Sumter in the Charleston harbor.

Southern threats of secession had been a central topic in the campaign, expressing the region's fears of Lincoln, raising defiance among some northerners and stimulating searches for compromise among others. With secession actually under way after the election, both reactions continued in the North, some bidding the slave states "good riddance," others seeking a new regional settlement to preserve the Union. The plan receiving most attention was to revive the Missouri Compromise and extend the line dividing free and slave states to the Pacific.

But no compromise could succeed. The incumbent president, James Buchanan, deplored secession yet refused to take any action. Lincoln, elected but not to hold the presidency until his March inauguration, had no power—and no intention of accepting either disunion or the extension of slavery to the territories. Publicly silent, he let it be known that he would accept a constitutional amendment to ensure the continuance of slavery where it already existed, but that proposal was insufficient appeasement for the South.

As the crisis deepened, Lincoln embarked on a twelve-day railroad "whistle-stop" tour to Washington. In a final attempt at conciliation and maintenance of the Union, he said in his inaugural address:

In your hands, my dissatisfied fellow-countrymen, and not in mine, is the momentous issue of civil war. The government will not assail you. You can have no conflict without being yourselves the aggressors. You have no oath registered in heaven to destroy the government, while I shall have the most solemn one to "preserve, protect, and defend" it.

We are not enemies, but friends. We must not be enemies. Though passion may have strained, it must not break our bonds of affection.

His earnest plea was futile. Looking back as he took the oath of office again in 1864, Lincoln tragically recounted the course of his nation:

[F]our years ago all thoughts were anxiously directed to an impending civil war. All dreaded it, all sought to avert it. While the inaugural address was being delivered from this place, devoted altogether to saving the Union without war, insurgent agents were in the city seeking to destroy it without war, seeking to dissolve the Union and divide effects by negotiation. Both parties deprecated war, but one of them would *make* war rather than let the nation survive, and the other would *accept* war rather than let it perish, and the war came.

Lincoln's term in office coincided almost entirely with that war between friends turned to enemies. The election of 1860 named a president, but only blood would ratify his selection.

COMPROMISE OVER SLAVERY BEGINS TO FALTER

The 1860 presidential election brought any country's greatest possible discord, civil war, to the United States. Slavery, the institution that divided the nation, came to America long before 1860, and the results of the election forced its extinction. Conflict over the issue had erupted regularly in American politics since the founding, but confrontations were periodically quieted by compromises that allowed expansion of slavery into new territories. When the newly created Republican Party stormed into Congress, the slavery issue could be put off no longer. Both northern Republicans and southern Democrats anticipated that the 1860 election would bring a final resolution, one way or another.

NOVEMBER 16, 1859
POPULAR SOVEREIGNTY.

Congress meets three weeks from yesterday. Its session will end on the 4th of March. If the whole interval is not spent in debating the Slavery question, adjusting platforms and preparing for the Presidential contest of 1860, it will not be the fault of politicians and party leaders. Every prominent man of every party has already a pocket full of resolutions, bills, &c., designed to define somebody's position or test somebody's fidelity to some party shibboleth. The Republicans, it is said, will move to abolish the English bill of last session, so as to admit Kansas whenever she may choose to apply, without regard to the number of her population. The repeal, it is acknowledged, can have no practical importance until Kansas actually makes application; and then it will be of no consequence, because Kansas can be admitted in spite of the law just as well as if the law itself had been repealed. But it will afford a party *test:*—it

will compel men to define their positions,—and will thus help forward the great Presidential campaign in which our domestic politics find their beginning and their end.

Of course, so prominent and formidable a candidate as Senator Douglas must not be suffered to escape. He will have all sorts of tests offered for his action, by all sections and all parties, and it will be miraculous if he avoids shipwreck on some of them. If he were to consult his own political safety he would decline a reelection to the Senate, and withdraw for a time into private life. Silas Wright never was so strong as a Presidential candidate as after his defeat in the canvass for Governor of this State. Douglas, however, is a different sort of a man, and is much more likely to take counsel of his courage and his hopes than his discretion and fears. He will go to the Senate and face the issues which his foes, of all complexions, are concocting for him. We wish him a safe deliverance.

The Richmond *Enquirer* exposes one of these rods which are held in pickle for him. The principle of Popular Sovereignty was incorporated into the Democratic creed at Cincinnati, having been previously embodied in the Kansas bill. Its main drift was to deny the right of Congress to interfere in any way with the question of Slavery, either in the States or the Territories,—and to leave the people of both at perfect liberty to decide whether it should exist among them or not. This principle proved highly acceptable to the people of the whole Union. It was recognized as eminently just in itself, and as affording a satisfactory and very welcome method of avoiding future controversies between the North and South on this vexed question. The Supreme Court indorsed the principle so far as to deny the right of Congress to prohibit Slavery in the Territories. That point, therefore, must be considered as settled. No party in the country, we presume, will be foolish enough to assert this right hereafter as a fundamental article of political faith. All parties will fall back upon the principle of popular sovereignty; but to console themselves under the necessity of so doing, they will immediately begin to differ as to the *meaning* of that principle. And here is a chance for new definitions and consequently for new party tests.

The Richmond *Enquirer* says that although Congress cannot interfere *against* Slavery in the territories, it must interfere in its favor:—that slaves as property must be protected *by law of Congress* against the possible interference of Territorial Legislatures,—or rather against the possible neglect of those Legislatures to make any law upon the subject. This is to be brought forward as a fundamental principle of political faith. No candidate will be considered "sound," according to Southern quarantine regulations, who does not come up to Virginia high-water mark upon this point. The device is ingenious and is clearly aimed at Douglas. In his canvass of Illinois he took the ground clearly and distinctly that, although slaves would be property in the Territories under the decision of the Supreme Court, yet when there they would be subject, like all other property, to the local law of the Territorial Legislatures. Jefferson Davis in his speech in Maine asserted the right of those legislatures to refrain from protecting slave property by positive enactment, and said that it would in consequence become of little value. The point now is to require Mr. Douglas to vote upon the proposition that *Congress* shall legislate upon this subject, for the protection of slave property within the limits of the federal territories. And the *Evening Post* and other Republican papers are already chuckling over the dilemma in which the Illinois Senator will then find himself involved.

It certainly is not safe to predict what course he will adopt in such a case. But the dilemma will not be half so perplexing as that offered to him by the Lecompton bill. Nor is it easy to see why he, or any other Northern Senator, should go to Washington this winter with less confidence in the North or more dread of the South than they experienced at the last session. The events and elections of this Fall have strengthened them immensely in the positions they have held hitherto.

In our judgment, the great body of the people of all sections and of all parties are prepared to stand by the principle of Popular Sovereignty, in the simple and straight-forward meaning of the word. They are disposed to permit the people of every State and every Territory to decide for themselves whether Slavery shall exist among them or not,—and they will resist any attempt, from any quarter, to revive the exploded doctrine of Congressional intervention, upon either side, or for the benefit of either party. They do not want the Slavery question in Congress at all. So far as the National Government is concerned, they do not wish the subject even to be mooted or mentioned in the halls of legislation. They regard it as a matter with which the Federal Government has no concern, and with which it cannot meddle in any way, without damage to the best interests of the whole country and danger to the stability of the Union itself.

If the South is wise it will accept this basis for a permanent truce. It will ponder and act upon the sensible declaration of Senator Hammond, that "if the South *offer* no issue," it is not easy to see upon what question the Republicans of the North can again rally in a contest for sectional supremacy. We commend this suggestion to the Richmond *Enquirer.* Unless its zeal for some special candidate for the Presidency outweighs its desire for the success of its party and the peace of the country, or will waive all new refinements of the party creed, and admit the principle of Popular Sovereignty as the basis of all future political action, that principle is much more likely to be enlarged than restricted; and if the attempt is made to revive the doctrine of Congressional intervention, it will be very likely to end in the abolition of all intervention, on the part of the President as well as of Congress, in the affairs of the Territories. We advise the *Enquirer* to let well enough alone.

The Public Believes the Union Will Persevere

Although the rumblings of secession were sounded even before the 1860 presidential nominees were selected, many Americans remained optimistic that the Union would persist. The fiery rhetoric on both sides of the slavery question had been heard before, and a great deal of the population believed that the nation would also survive this latest crisis. Some northern abolitionists trusted that slavery faced inevitable extinction, even if another Democrat won a presidential term, and some southerners similarly believed that even a Republican president would be bound to uphold the constitutionality of slavery. As the campaign moved on, such optimism dwindled and the inescapability of a major conflict gripped the nation.

APRIL 17, 1860
POLITICAL.
A REPUBLICAN PRESIDENT—WOULD HE BE SUSTAINED BY THE SOUTH?

Louisville, Ky., Tuesday, April 10

Correspondence of the New-York Times.

I cannot agree with your Mobile correspondent, that everybody in this and all the Southwestern States is ready, in a certain contingency, to break out of the Union. The successful inauguration of a Black Republican, or another Slave Democratic, Administration, in the opinion of very many North and South, will not be enough to dissolve us.

I know the question is often mooted,—Suppose the deplorable event of an extreme Republican's nomination and election on an extreme Anti-Slavery platform shall occur, (which is not at all probable,) will the South, or any portion of her, march under Henry A. Wise, Howell Cobb, Clement C. Clay, or any other Southron, to Washington, and attempt to seize the Government and all its archives, treasures and munitions, before or after such a Republican's installment? The more prevailing popular answer in these parts is, No! The national conservatism, the common sense, the sanity in her midst, will forbid it. Her Sam. Houstons will rise up and cry out, No! And her Jeff. Davises, at the pinch, will probably turn out, as in other instances, non-resistants.

The Southwest in any "contingency" revolt and tear a way from the Northwest? It cannot be. The States of the Mississippi Valley are indissoluble. The folly and madness of Northern Lovejoys and Southern Barksdales will not sunder them. The far-reaching and magnificent destiny of this Valley is not to be cut short and blasted by fanaticism.

Indeed, numerous Southerners and Southwesterners, who will ever oppose all Federal Anti-Slaveryism, trust that no Republican President's actual Administration would be the bug-bear, raw head and bloody-bones, talked of. He would be bound, more or less, to feel the necessities of his position, and to adapt himself to them. They have faith that his conduct would be at least as wise as President Buchanan's, whose inauguration was acquiesced in by all; whom nobody talked of forestalling, or has dreamed of ousting out of his chair till the 4th of March, 1861. . . .

Southern oppositionists and sober Southern Democrats really do not consider the success of the Democratic party of such vital consequence and infinite moment as represented by the Times' Mobile correspondent. The Union will survive its defeat. At least the former are disposed to regard those as public enemies who aim to hold on to power by a terrorism,—by impressing the country that its fate hangs upon theirs. Partisans who can no longer rule through conceded public confidence, merit the punishment suggested by Gov. Seward. Such "cannot be dismissed from power too soon."

Of course, the Southern opposition, if they had not a man of their own like John Bell, would take Judge Douglas before Gov. Seward; but, I apprehend, even Mr. Seward, as President, would not only deserve but receive much less rebuke from them than, such a Southern extremist and secessionist as Mr. Iverson or Mr. Wigfall.

At all events, whoever, of whatever party or section, is constitutionally elected, will, as heretofore, be sustained in the Chair of State by the country at large, until the expiration of his constitutional term.

PONTIAC.

CONFLICT AT THE DEMOCRATIC NATIONAL CONVENTION

The bitter conflict of the 1860 election began in earnest in Charleston, South Carolina, at what turned out to be the first of two Democratic conventions. Southern delegates insisted that the party finally come out and proclaim clearly that slaves were property and therefore incapable of emancipation under the Constitution by either presidential or congressional action. Northern delegates recognized that such a declaration would doom the party's hopes in the free states and throw the election to the Republican Party. Northern voters could accept a Democratic tolerance of slavery for the present, so long as hope remained of a future end of the practice. The conflict in Charleston set the stage for further—and more violent—turmoil to come.

APRIL 28, 1860
EDITORIAL
THE CHARLESTON CONVENTION.

The Democratic bark is fairly launched upon the troubled waters. The Convention is engaged in discussing the Platform; it commenced this task yesterday, but when it will finish it, we shall not venture to predict. The temper and scope of the opening speeches, so far as they can be inferred from the meagre reports received by telegraph, indicate a protracted and an angry debate, without much hope of any substantial and cordial agreement. It is not at all unlikely that an apparent harmony may be reached;—but we see little chance for anything more, for the differences between the two sections are radical and incapable of compromise.

The South and North are at least brought face to face in this Convention. The South demands a distinct declaration, on the part of the entire Democratic Party, that *slaves are recognized as property by the Federal Constitution.* The Pro-Slavery leaders,—those of them who have made up their minds to force a clear and unmistakable issue—know that if they can secure this, they secure everything. If slaves are property, they are to be treated as property, they are to be protected as property:—the rights of their masters are complete, and must be guaranteed at all times and everywhere. If they are property by Federal law,—under the Federal Constitution,—that property is entitled to protection wherever that fundamental law has effect. They are as much property in Kansas, in New-York and upon the high seas when under the American flag, as in South Carolina or Mississippi.

The Northern delegates seem dimly to comprehend the force of such an admission, and refuse to stake their political existence upon it,—they dare not meet it, so they hope to dodge it. Mr. BUTLER, of Massachusetts, suggests that it would be "misunderstood." Not in the least. On the contrary, the fact that it could not be either misunderstood or misrepresented makes it fatal to the party in the Northern States. Mr. COCHRANE knows that it must be evaded. Somebody else desires to turn it over to the Judiciary. Nobody from the North, who represents the North, dare make the admission a plank in the platform.

Northern men, hitherto, have hastily and flippantly conceded that slaves are property, under and by virtue of the Constitution of the United States. Mr. CORWIN has admitted it. Mr. DOUGLAS has conceded it. But it will not answer:—such concessions involve all the consequences drawn from them by the Southern ultraists. The people of the North will never sanction the position. The Constitution does not recognize slaves as property, directly or by implication, in any clause or phrase of its provisions. It recognizes them, solely and exclusively, as "PERSONS *held to service or labor,"* and that only *"by the laws and regulation of certain States."* That is the definition of "slaves" given in the Constitution;—that is the only recognition which it makes of their legal *status;* and it is upon that position that the people of the whole country will take their stand, whenever the question shall be removed from the area of party controversy and taken to the tribunal of reason and common sense.

Moreover, it is the view which the people of the North, with very little distinction of party, will take of the subject in the impending contest. If the Northern Delegates at Charleston are at once wise and firm, they may have the credit and the profit of settling the question on this basis themselves. If not, they will have the satisfaction of seeing the Republicans do it for them.

SOUTHERN DEMOCRATS BOLT THE CONVENTION

The Democratic approach to slavery was finally decided. Northern delegates persuaded the convention to adopt a slavery stance that stopped short of proclaiming a constitutional protection of the practice. Outraged southern delegates refused to accept the decision and stormed out of the convention intending to write an independent proslavery platform. Northern Democrats coalesced around their preferred candidate, Stephen Douglas, but they had lost the southern states that traditionally provided the bulk of their vote support. The national prospects for the Democratic Party in the upcoming election looked bleak.

MAY 1, 1860
CHARLESTON CONVENTION.

Adoption of the Minority Report.

Secession of the Southern Delegations.

Davis and Everett Proposed by the Bolters.

Special Dispatch to the New-York Times.

CHARLESTON, Monday, April 30.

Upon the adoption of the Minority Platform, the delegations from Alabama, Louisiana, South Carolina, Mississippi, Texas, Arkansas and Florida, embodying 37 1/2 votes, retired from the Convention, after filing with the Clerk protests which had evidently been prepared with great care in advance.

Great confusion attended their departure. The Delegates, forgetful of all the proprieties of the place, and the solemnity of the crisis, hooted and shouted in deafening uproar.

The Delaware, Georgia and Virginia members withdrew to consult.

It is thought a portion of the California delegation will join the seceders; among whom the ticket most favorably bruited is Gen. DAVIS for President, and EDWARD EVERETT for Vice-President. The Bolters meet in St. Andrew's Hall.

The Douglas men are greatly elated.

An immense throng gathered at St. Andrew's Hall. All were requested to leave but Delegates and reporters. Mr. PRESTON of South Carolina, led off in a conservative speech, counselling unity of action on a thoroughly consistent platform. He was followed by other speakers, and all in the same strain.

After three hours' session, they adjourned, to hold a mass meeting in front of the City Hall, where thousands are cheering and hurrahing in their honor.

An enthusiastic meeting of the Douglasites was held this evening. Mr. PATTON, of Connecticut, presided. Messrs. FLOURNOY of Arkansas, KING of Mississippi, BRENT and HENDERSON addressed then.

Meetings, sustaining the seceders, were held in the streets. The Bolters were serenaded.

HOWARD.

From the Associated Press.

CHARLESTON, Monday, April 30—A. M.

President-making has been quiet to-day.

The friends of DOUGLAS express great confidence in his nomination on the third ballot.

DICKINSON's friends are equally confident, and it is now thought the South will rally on him.

The weather is very cool.

The Charleston Convention Collapses with No Nominee

The Democratic convention in Charleston concluded without a successful resolution. Southern delegates seceded from the convention, unable to get their proslavery platform adopted. The northern delegates, still hoping to draw their southern compatriots back into the party, refused to nominate a presidential candidate until two-thirds of all the original delegates agreed upon a nominee, something that was impossible after the southerners fled. The party was now split along regional lines, much as the nation was fracturing between Republicans and Democrats. The hobbled Democratic Party limped out of Charleston with neither a nominee nor a truly national party.

MAY 4, 1860
THE DISRUPTION OF THE DEMOCRATIC PARTY.

The Charleston Convention has abandoned the attempt to nominate a Democratic candidate for the Presidency. The failure is due partly to the disorganized condition of the party, and partly to the blind blundering of the Convention itself. The contest between the two sections of the Union has at last penetrated the Democratic Party, and rendered it impossible for the two wings to agree upon a declaration of principles. When the majority adopted its platform the minority seceded. Thereupon the delegates who remained, and who constituted the rightful Convention, resolved that a vote of two-thirds, not of the actual body, but of the whole original number, should be essential to a nomination. In other words, the seceders were still to be counted, and to have all their original weight as members of the Convention! Upon what ground of reason or of common sense, the majority, and especially the delegates from this State, thus put themselves, bound hand and foot, into the power of the seceding minority, it is not easy to conjecture. The result was to give the South the victory. They have controlled the Convention, and prevented the nomination of any candidate. Whether, on reassembling at Baltimore, they will harmonize their differences, remains to be seen.

The disruption itself is a fact of very marked importance, not only in the history of political parties but of the country itself. It seems to sever the last link of nationality in the political affairs of the Union. When all other organizations have been gradually giving way, one after another, to the pressure of sectionalism, timid and conservative men have fallen back upon the national position of the Democratic Party, and felt that so long as this was maintained the Union would be secure. The first effect of this Charleston split will be to alarm this class by the dread of immediate dissolution.

Some of the Republican journals refer to this incident as only another proof of the "irrepressible conflict" between Freedom and Slavery,—and as showing that the contest must go on until one or the other is extirpated. If we believed this to be the true view of the question, we too should despair of the Union. But we do not. We do not believe that the conflict is between Slavery and Freedom, or that the existence of either will be affected by the result. We regard the struggle as one for political power,—and Slavery as playing merely a secondary and subordinate part on either side. Unquestionably, thousands of Northern men seek the overthrow of Slavery, and thousands of Southern men seek its permanence and extension, as the aim of their political contests. But both would be disappointed. Neither class would reap the advantage which it anticipates from victory. The Slave States have substantially controlled the policy of the Federal Government for the last fifty years. Upon all questions—tariff, currency, foreign relations—their views and sentiments have guided the action of the nation. For a long time they held this power by the legitimate tenure of numbers, weight and influence. Then came a period when they held it by alliances with Northern politicians. And for the last few years they have held it by coercion,—by menaces, by appeals to the fears of the timid, the hopes of the ambitious, and the avarice of the corrupt, in the Northern States. The time has come when they must relinquish their grasp. Power is passing into the hands of the majority—into the hands which hold the numbers, the wealth, the energy, the enterprise of the Confederacy. There is no help for it. It is among the inevitable events of political history. It can no more be arrested than the revolution of the earth around the sun, or the rising and falling of the tides of the sea.

Naturally, however, it excites a commotion. All great changes,—especially all restorations of disturbed balances of power,—are attended with more or less of turmoil and alarm. Righting a ship, which has long been so careened as to make it impossible to walk across her deck, throws everything into confusion, and the unaccustomed passenger who has valuables on board, is quite certain she is capsizing. He sees his mistake only when she stands upright, and with full sail makes direct for her destined port.

The South believes sincerely, we doubt not, that the North *seeks power in order to crush Slavery.* In our opinion it denounces Slavery mainly *that it may acquire power.* In many respects the policy of the Federal Government in Northern hands would be different from what it has been hitherto. Men would no longer be excluded from office for doubting the wisdom or the justice of the system Slavery. Federal power would not be used to force it upon unwilling communities. We should no longer be represented abroad by active apostles of Slavery, nor would that be held up to the world as the cherished glory of American institutions. But there would be no interference with Slavery in any Southern State,—no refusal to execute the constitutional provision for the rendition of fugitives,—no attempt to coerce the population of new Territories. A Northern President,—Northern in sentiment as well as geographical position,—would have a degree of influence over his own section, which would disarm the hostility which a Southern sectionalist would be sure to encounter.

One thing is very certain:—the South must make up its mind to lose the sway it has exercised so long. The sceptre is passing from its hands. Its own imprudencies have hastened the departure of its power, but it has always been merely a question of time. The South can either accept it as inevitable and make the best of it,—or plunge the whole country into turmoil, and bring down swift ruin upon its own borders, in the vain contest against national growth and development.

· ·

THE CONSTITUTIONAL UNION PARTY NOMINATES JOHN BELL

Directly following the Democratic implosion in Charleston, a new Constitutional Union Party assembled in Baltimore and selected its own candidate, John Bell. While the Democratic and Republican Parties debated the future of slavery, the Constitutional Union Party focused upon national unity, largely ignoring the slavery debate. With the North and South moving steadily apart, the Constitutional Unionists worked mainly within the central border states to try and maintain a peaceful national coexistence. Despite the admirable intentions, the Unionists had little to offer for most Americans who viewed the 1860 election as a long-awaited decision on the extension of slavery.

MAY 11, 1860
EDITORIAL
BALTIMORE UNION CONVENTION.

A PLATFORM ADOPTED.

Hon. John Bell, of Tennessee, Nominated for President.

Hon. Edward Everett, of Massachusetts, for Vice-President.

Entire Harmony and Unbounded Enthusiasm.

The Presidential Contest.

After much tribulation, we have at last one Presidential Candidate fairly in the field. The Union Convention at Baltimore yesterday nominated JOHN BELL, of Tennessee, for President, and EDWARD EVERETT for Vice-President. Two more respectable names could not be found in the country,—nor will any one doubt that in their hands the Government would be administered with ability, dignity and the most conscientious devotion to the honor and welfare of the whole country.

JOHN BELL has acted a prominent part in public life for many years. A lawyer by profession, he entered Congress first in 1827, and continued to represent his district in the House for fourteen years. At the outset he was a warm admirer and a political supporter of Mr. CALHOUN. In 1832 he was opposed to the protective system, but soon afterwards changed his views on the subject. He resisted Mr. CALHOUN's policy of nullification, and was a zealous supporter of Gen. JACKSON until the removal of the deposits, when he left the Democratic Party. In 1834 he was elected Speaker of the House, receiving the Whig vote, and that of those Democrats who were opposed to Mr. VAN BUREN. In 1835 he openly advocated the election of Judge WHITE in opposition to Gen. JACKSON, and thenceforward acted with the Whigs.

In 1836, Mr. BELL alone of the Tennessee delegation advocated the reception of Abolition petitions, and was sustained by his constituents. In 1841, he became Secretary of War under President HARRISON, but retired after his death, and remained in private life until 1847, when he was elected United States Senator, and reelected in 1853. He opposed the Mexican War,—supported the Compromise measures of 1850, opposed the Nebraska bill and the repeal of the Missouri Compromise in 1854, and denounced the Lecompton policy of the Administration in 1858.

This is the record of the Union candidate for the Presidency. It is a good one throughout. He has decided ability, and is, in the best sense of the word, a statesman. The Platform adopted by the Convention evades all the points of principle and policy now before the country. The position taken is, that, inasmuch as platforms are generally intended to mislead the public, it is best not to adopt any at all. No one can suppose that such a position as this will be regarded as satisfactory by any considerable body of the people in any section of the country. Issues cannot be settled by being ignored; and the controversy growing out of Slavery has reached such a point that both North and South feel the absolute necessity of coming to some distinct and definite understanding in regard to it.

It is quite evident that some, at least, of the leading members of the Convention did not nominate this ticket for the special purpose of electing it, nor indeed with a settled intention of voting for it themselves. Their object is primarily the defeat of the Republican ticket. If this can be done better by voting for BELL, they will vote for him: if not, they will vote for somebody else. Ex-Gov. HUNT, on behalf of the party in this State, distinctly announced that he should not bind himself to this nomination. He should preserve his independence, and remain perfectly free to vote as emergencies hereafter to arise might require.

No judgment can be formed as to the effect of this nomination upon other parties, until their nominations shall have been made. Mr. BELL will command a good deal of strength in the Southern States, and will receive a heavy conservative vote in all those which were formerly Whig. At the North he will be less formidable,—not from any lack of personal popularity, but because his party position does not represent any strong and earnest sentiment of the Northern people.

• •

A DARK HORSE IS NOMINATED AT THE REPUBLICAN CONVENTION IN CHICAGO

In May the Republican Party met in Chicago to select its nominee for president. Having witnessed the fracturing of the Democratic Party, the Republicans aimed for a show of unity to enliven their electoral hopes. The party narrowly avoided conflict of its own, as the front-runner, William H. Seward, failed to gain the necessary votes to win the nomination. Instead, the party formed behind the relatively untested Abraham Lincoln, a candidate best known for losing a Senate seat in Illinois to Stephen Douglas after a highly publicized series of debates. Skillful deals by Lincoln's convention managers brought the party together behind its unified ticket.

MAY 19, 1860
THE REPUBLICAN TICKET FOR 1860.

Abram Lincoln, of Illinois, Nominated for President.

The Late Senatorial Contest in Illinois to be Re-Fought on a Wider Field.

Hannibal Hamlin, of Maine, the Candidate for Vice-President.

Disappointment of the Friends of Mr. Seward.

INTENSE EXCITEMENT AND ENTHUSIASM

Reception of the Nominations in this City.

How They are Hailed Throughout the North.

Special Dispatch to the New-York Times.

CHICAGO, Friday, May 16.

The work of the Convention is ended. The youngster who, with ragged trousers, used barefoot to drive his father's oxen and spend his days in splitting rails, has risen to high eminence, and ABRAM LINCOLN, of Illinois, is declared its candidate for President by the National Republican Party.

This result was effected by the change of votes in the Pennsylvania, New-Jersey, Vermont, and Massachusetts Delegations.

Mr. SEWARD'S friends assert indignantly, and with a great deal of feeling, that they were grossly deceived and betrayed. The recusants endeavored to mollify New-York by offering her the Vice-Presidency, and agreeing to support any man she might name, but they declined the position, though they remain firm in the ranks, having moved to make LINCOLN'S nomination unanimous. Mr. SEWARD'S friends feel greatly chagrined and disappointed.

Western pride is gratified by this nomination, which plainly indicates the departure of political supremacy from the Atlantic States.

The prominent candidates for Vice-Presidency were Messrs. HICKMAN, BANKS, CLAY and REEDER. Pennsylvania desired HICKMAN. New-York, in order to resent the conduct of Pennsylvania, Massachusetts and Kentucky, favored Mr. HAMLIN, of Maine; and on the second ballot, cast her whole strength for him, and it was owing to this, and the desire to conciliate New-York, this his nomination was so promptly secured.

Immense enthusiasm exists, and everything here would seem to indicate a spirited and successful canvass. The city is alive with processions, meetings, music and noisy demonstrations. One hundred guns were fired this evening.

The Convention was the most enthusiastic ever known in the country, and if one were to judge from appearances here, the ticket will sweep the country.

Great inquiry has been made this afternoon into the history of Mr. LINCOLN. The only evidence that he has a history as yet discovered, is that he had a stump canvass with Mr. DOUGLAS, in which he was beaten. He is not very strong at the West, but is unassailable in his private character. . . .

The "Wide-Awakes," numbering about two thousand men, accompanied by thousands of citizens, have a grand torch-light procession. The German Republican Club has another. The office of the *Press and Tribune* is brilliantly illuminated, and has a large transparency over the door, saying, "For President, Honest Old ABE." A bonfire thirty feet in circumference burns in front of the Tremont House, and illumines the city for miles around. The city is one blaze of illumination. Hotels, stores and private residences, shining with hundreds of patriotic dips. ENOUGH.

HOWARD.

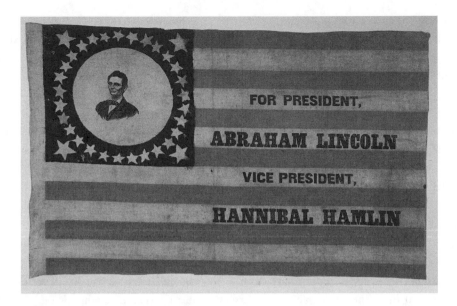

An American flag banner promotes Abraham Lincoln as the Republican Party candidate for president in 1860.

Source: The Granger Collection, New York

THE CANDIDATES ON THE SLAVERY QUESTION

With the nomination of Lincoln, the nation had two official candidates for president, and a presumptive third in Stephen Douglas for the Democrats. The campaign for office now clearly was pinned upon a single crucial question: What to do about slavery? All parties began with nominally moderate positions, but with radical undertones. The Republican Party officially suggested the limitation of slavery, but maintained that they did not aim to abolish it outright, at least not yet. The Democratic Party seemed poised to declare slavery a matter of popular choice at the state level, but also stopped short of declaring it a constitutionally protected practice. The Constitutional Union Party took the only moderate position left and attempted to avoid the issue entirely in the hopes of prolonging coexistence between North and South.

MAY 19, 1860
EDITORIAL
THE PRESIDENTIAL CONFLICT.

Two at least of the three candidates whose claims are to plead for the suffrages of the American people, in the canvass of 1860, now stand before the country. The Union Conservatives, as they style themselves, having nominated Mr. BELL, of Tennessee, on the ground of his integrity, the Republicans have now put forward Mr. LINCOLN, of Illinois, on the ground of his availability. The proceedings of the Democracy at Charleston, and their subsequent movements in the most important sections of the South, indicate with tolerable clearness that Mr. DOUGLAS will be selected by this party at Baltimore, on the 18th of June, as its standard-bearer.

Within a month the only three men who can reasonably be regarded as active competitors for the highest office in the gift of the American people, will be fairly in the field. Should Mr. DOUGLAS be the choice of the Democracy, the contest will define itself very sharply and clearly. The only vital question upon which its issue will depend, is undoubtedly the question of the relations which Slavery as an institution is henceforth to sustain to the Federal Government. This question, lying at the root of all the political excitements and inter-sectional conflicts which have of late years harassed our public life and disturbed our commercial affairs, must be virtually decided in the coming election. By their nomination of Mr. LINCOLN, and by the platform which they have adopted, the Republicans have declared their wish and purpose to deal with this question, if possible, in a spirit of moderation, and to maintain the characteristic position of the Republicans North with as little offence as may be to the rights, the feelings or the interests of the South. They have not asserted in any hostile fashion their cardinal doctrine of the right of Congress to interfere for the exclusion of Slavery from the Territories, though the fanatical violence with which the opposite doctrine, of the duty of Congress to intervene for the protection of Slavery in the Territories, was put forth by Mr. YANCEY and his friends in the Convention at Charleston, might well have tempted them into doing so. Still they have not disowned, and cannot disown, that doctrine, and their triumph will involve the probability of its positive though pacific assertion, when once the power of the country shall pass into their hands. Few Northern men, few Republicans at least, believe that such an assertion would be followed by any formidable resistance on the part of the South; still less by anything like secession or disunion. Even the most conservative of Southern men declare this skepticism to be a fatal mistake. Still it exists, and must be taken into the account in estimating the motives and probable course of the Republican Party. Their answer to the question of the day is peaceful interference against the extension of Slavery.

The supporters of Mr. BELL make quite another reply to this momentous question. They desire to vote that we are living not in 1860, but in 1840, and to settle the agitation of Slavery and Anti-Slavery by a general abstinence from all allusions to the subject in or out of Congress.

The Democratic Party, as represented by Mr. DOUGLAS, have still a third solution of the problem to offer to us. This is the exclusion of the question of Slavery from the discussions of Congress, by relegating it, whenever it shall come up in a practical form, to the decision of the people of the different Territories, as they may be successively called into corporate being. The objections raised to this solution are mainly theoretical and historical. Should it be acquiesced in by a majority of the people; it would at least relieve us from the immediate pressure upon our body politic of those fierce debates between philanthropy and the patriarchal system, in which the time of Congress and the temper of the country have so long been consumed. Whether it will be offered by the Democracy to the popular judgment at all, remains, as we have already said, to be determined at Baltimore on the 18th of June. Should the "Secession movement," begun at Charleston, in favor of still a fourth and notably impracticable scheme, the protection of Slavery as pure and simple property everywhere and by all authorities, State and Federal, spend its force and fall away before the power of the old national Democratic organization at the South, as now appears by no means unlikely, we shall have three united parties pressing three panaceas upon us for the relief of our great national system from the present trying crisis.

. . . .

DEMOCRATS NOMINATE STEPHEN DOUGLAS IN BALTIMORE AND JOHN BRECKINRIDGE IN RICHMOND

In June the Democratic Party reassembled in Baltimore for a second convention to finally complete a platform and nominate a presidential candidate. They wound up with two of each. The northern delegates chose, as anticipated, Stephen Douglas. The southern states that had fled the Charleston convention met separately in Richmond, selecting John Breckinridge. Although few anticipated that he could win, at least, they hoped, a southern candidate would unify the region. At most, the southern Democrats hoped, the election would split so closely among the four candidates that the decision would be left to the House of Representatives, where the slave states held the balance of power.

JUNE 25, 1860
PRESIDENTIAL.
THE PROCEEDINGS OF THE DISUNITED DEMOCRACY.

TWO TICKETS NOMINATED.

Nomination of Douglas and Fitzpatrick by the Regulars.

Breckinridge and Lane the Candidates of the Seceders.

What is Thought of the Nominations.

Special Dispatch to the New-York Times.
BALTIMORE, Sunday, June, 24.

We have assurances from persons who ought to know that both BRECKINRIDGE and LANE will accept their nominations by the Convention of seceders.

It is the game of the Southern wing to defeat an election by the people and carry it into Congress, where they think they are reasonably certain of electing BRECKINRIDGE. The Douglas men here speak openly of preferring LINCOLN'S election to such a result.

YANCEY and other extremists are delighted at the prospect. They say that can either elect BRECKINRIDGE in the House and thus perpetuate their control over the Government, or else elect LINCOLN, which will give them an opportunity to rally the South in factor of dissolution.

The city is entirely deserted.

JUNE 25, 1860
EDITORIAL
THE BALTIMORE CONVENTION—THE DEMOCRATIC CANDIDATES.

The Baltimore Convention has closed its labors. It met to nominate a Presidential candidate, and to adopt a platform; it has ended by giving the party two of each. Its ostensible object was to harmonize the party,—to compromise points of difference,—to reconcile sectional jealousies and distrusts,—and to nominate a candidate who should unite the sentiment and support of the party, and thus secure a victory in the coming canvass. It has accomplished exactly the opposite of all these things. It has divided and demoralized the party,—sharpened and made more prominent its differences of principle,—aggravated its sectional and personal hatreds, and nominated two candidates, each of whom will aim, specially and primarily, to defeat the other. The Convention was not in fact a deliberative assembly at all. It was not a conference of delegates having common interests, common hopes and common aims. It was, from the outset, a duel of hostile sections. The South came into the Convention hoping to rule it, and determined, failing in that, to break it up. The Administration shared alike its ambition and its hatred, and lent it what little aid its enfeebled condition would permit. The North came, goaded by long years of suffering servitude, superior in force and

resolute in its purpose to use it. There were some among them who hoped a chance would arise for compromise,—but the great body of the Northern delegates were determined upon the nomination of DOUGLAS at every hazard and at whatever cost. Finding that this could not be prevented, the South and the Administration resolved as the next step to defeat him at the polls; and it is for this specific object that their ticket has been put in nomination.

Their belief is that BRECKINRIDGE will carry most of the Southern States, and that he will draw off enough votes in doubtful Northern States to prevent their voting for DOUGLAS. They hope in this way to carry the election into Congress, and failing in that, to secure the success of LINCOLN—for unquestionably they would prefer that result to the election of DOUGLAS. Many of them are open Disunionists, and look to the success of the Republicans as the opportunity which will enable them, in Mr. YANCEY's phrase, "to plunge the cotton States into revolution." Others, who are not prepared for such an issue, deem a temporary defeat and exclusion from office the best medicine for the Democratic party, and will look to 1864 as certain to bring them united councils and renewed success. They will spare no effort, therefore, to defeat DOUGLAS, and whatever of influence may remain to the Administration will be remorselessly and unscrupulously used in aid of the same object. Mr. BUCHANAN is not a man of strong passions, but all the hatred of which his cold and clammy nature is susceptible is concentrated upon Mr. DOUGLAS. His ambition when he came into office was to annex Cuba. Time and grief have modified his aspirations—and he will leave his post contented, if he can secure the defeat of his hated rival. . . .

The Seceders have acted with a good deal more malice than wisdom. It was supposed that they would select a candidate from the extreme South, in order to carry beyond peradventure the Cotton States, leaving DOUGLAS to make such fight as he could in the North, and thus to carry the election into Congress. But they have taken a candidate too thoroughly identified with the Administration to be popular anywhere, and not sufficiently strong at the South to be certain of any Southern State. Their object plainly is to insure the running of their electoral ticket at the North, for the sake of rendering the defeat of DOUGLAS all the more secure.

It is not quite certain that they have succeeded even in this. DOUGLAS has a very strong position at the North, made all the stronger by the hatred and persecution of the South; and he may gain as much from this sentiment as he can lose by the hostility of the Administration.

His chances of success, however, are not brilliant. The proceedings at Baltimore,—the factious character of both Conventions, the recklessness of principle, and the selfish devotion to men, which marked their action, have demoralized the party and disgusted the country. There will be at the outset some little enthusiasm at the nomination of DOUGLAS,—but it will not be backed up by any earnest conviction of his superior qualifications for the place, or any confident expectation of his success in reaching it. The action at Baltimore has very greatly increased the chances of LINCOLN's election, by convincing the country that the Republican Party, while it is no more sectional, is much more compact, and better able to assume the responsibilities of administering the Government than any other.

THE CAMPAIGN OF 1860 COMMENCES

By late June the presidential election of 1860 had a full slate of four candidates. The campaign that followed brought little change but increasing anxiety. Each candidate had staked out a distinct position on the slavery issue, with little possibility of drawing voters across the firm party lines. Lincoln's election seemed quite likely, but the future of the nation as a whole appeared ever more precarious.

 Strong in the public sentiment of the Free States, the Republican Party derives an immense advantage from the disruption and utter demoralization of its opponents.

JUNE 26, 1860
EDITORIAL
THE PRESIDENTIAL ELECTION.

The Presidential canvass has at last fairly opened. The several political parties have taken their ground,—all the candidates are in the field,—and it is not difficult to foresee the result. The Republican ticket is morally certain to be elected. Strong in the public sentiment of the Free States, the Republican Party derives an immense advantage from the disruption and utter demoralization of its opponents.

The heat of the battle, it is easy to see, is to be in the Southern States. The question of protecting Slavery by act of Congress—of using the power of the Federal Government for its extension—is to be contested and decided on Southern ground. For the first time in our political history, the slaveholding States will be divided. Hitherto the contest has been mainly sectional: the North has taken one side and the South the other. Now, the South finds the "irrepressible conflict" in the bosom of its own society. Douglas will actually represent in the South that hostility to Slavery extension which is already the unanimous sentiment of the North. He will contest upon slave soil the power of the Federal Government to extend Slavery: and while his position on this question is, in our judgment, unsound and untenable, it is probably the only ground upon which any contest whatever could be maintained in the Southern States. He concedes that slaves are property, recognized as such by the Federal Constitution:—but claims that in the Territories it must be dependent entirely, for protection and existence, upon the local law. Few, if any, of the Southern States will endorse his views;—but if he were more nearly right, they would not tolerate him an hour.

In the Northern States Mr. Douglas is strong, partly on account of his political position and partly from his personal qualities. He represents more thoroughly than any other public man that quickness of intellect, vigor of will and pushing restlessness of temper which characterize American life. Without any large, general culture, he has the useful faculty of studying a particular subject rapidly, and of mastering its leading facts and principles. Whatever he knows is always at his command. He has indomitable industry, an insolent courage, and a tenacity of purpose, born partly of conviction and partly of self-will, which nothing can defeat. These are qualities which in our society, or indeed in any other, give a politician a strong hold upon the popular admiration; and Mr. Douglas adds to them just enough of that irresponsible, good-natured recklessness which characterizes the indigenous American rowdy, to make him the decided idol of a very large and influential class of our political society.

But aside from these personal characteristics, Mr. Douglas is the champion of Popular Sovereignty;— and whether that doctrine finds any warrant in the Constitution, in legal precedents, in the opinions of the Fathers, or not, it has a very strong hold upon the popular instinct. The great mass of the people in all sections, whatever may be their opinions upon its legal validity, recognize it as a fair, just and safe way of solving a very difficult problem. Let the people of every territory decide for themselves whether they will have Slavery among them or not;—let Congress and the Federal Government abandon all attempts, either to force it upon them, or to prohibit them from admitting it;—this, if not the highest Constitutional ground, is ground which satisfies the instinct of nine-tenths of the American people. If it were generally felt that the adoption of this policy depended upon the election of Mr. Douglas, he would be a very formidable candidate. But it is not. The truth is, the Slavery question *will* be settled on this basis, whatever party may come into power. This is, under any circumstances, to be the practical solution of the difficulty. The Republican Party has asserted, though in a modified form, the abstract power of Congress over Slavery in the Territories; but it is not committed to its exercise, nor is there one chance in twenty that any occasion will arise where its exercise would be of service to the cause of freedom.

Mr. Douglas will not have, therefore, in the North, all the support which this principle, distinctly and nakedly presented, would give him. Thousands and tens of thousands, who believe in the practical wisdom of Popular Sovereignty, will vote the Republican ticket,—because they recognize in that party the only compact, responsible and effective political organization of the day. It is the only party in a position to achieve success, or to use it wisely when it has been won. It represents and embodies to-day, far more thoroughly than any other, the democratic conservatism of the country. It stands midway between the Pro-Slavery-ism which has ruled the Federal Government so long, and the Anti-Slavery-ism which would overthrow it altogether. It holds the Constitutional ground and doctrine on the subject of Slavery, and respects, thoroughly and rigidly, the limitations which the Constitution imposes upon its action. It holds the absolute majority of nearly all the Northern States already; while in those which are doubtful it will be substantially aided by the nomination of Breckinridge. In Illinois and Indiana Mr. Breckinridge has a positive strength which will give him twenty or thirty thousand votes in each; in Pennsylvania the power of the Administration is sufficient to give him quite as many, and in New-York we believe it safe to predict that he will withdraw fifty thousand votes from the support of Douglas.

The action of the Democracy at Baltimore seems, with reasonable diligence on the part of the Republicans, to have insured the success of the Republican ticket.

THE WIDE AWAKES CAMPAIGN FOR LINCOLN

The Republican campaign effort was dominated by groups known as "Wide Awakes," quasi-paramilitary organizations that rallied behind the Lincoln candidacy. The Wide Awakes urged northerners to keep their eyes open and maintain awareness of the importance of the Republican cause. They organized torch-lit marches, bonfires, oratory, and all manners of demonstrations to bring attention to their cause and rally supporters for Lincoln and against all possible rivals, including the potential fusion of rival parties.

JULY 28, 1860
THE CAMPAIGN IN CONNECTICUT.

The Great Demonstration of the Wide-Awakes at Hartford.
SPEECHES, MUSIC AND PROCESSIONS.

From Our Own Correspondent.
HARTFORD, Friday, July 27.

No one, who has received from the Creator even the slimmest of perceptive faculties, can have failed to observe the remarkable absence of enthusiasm and spirit which has so far characterised the progress of this political campaign. There are various reasons for it. The Republicans have not cared to expend any money, strength or influence, because they have felt perfect confidence in the result of the election; thinking that the Democracy are totally broken up and they have anticipated an easy victory.

The Democrats have abstained from jubilation for the best of reasons—they have nothing to jubilate over. DOUGLAS has half and BRECKINRIDGE has half, but a true Democrat wants to go the whole hog or none. "Entirety" is a great and favorite word with the Democracy; and, until a fusion is made, or some dirty combination is exposed, which will frighten the Republicans, and cast a ray of hope into the ranks of the no more "unterrified," there will be but few tar-barrels burned, few five-mile processions, and less enthusiastic shoutings from the hosts of the faithful.

In the States of Connecticut and Rhode Island the dissensions between the straight-out Republicans and the conservative Republicans have led certain timid Lincolnites, and certain overeager Douglasites, to imagine that a Democratic victory might be won, even with the present divided vote of the Democratic Party, and an undoubted success if by any possibility the Douglas and Breckinridge wings might be brought together. Hence, no effort is being left untried by which this consummation may be effected. Consultations are frequently held and every inducement offered to accomplish the desired end.

This movement is well understood by the Republicans of Connecticut, and they have at last awoke to a perfect realization of the fact that, if they desire to see their banner in the van of a victorious host in November next, they must work early and late, and not leave a stone unturned or a point unassailed, the removal of the one or the carrying of the other of which can have the least bearing upon the all important end.

Probably in no State, certainly in no Eastern State, are the details of the campaign so well arranged as here. In every school district, in every village, town and city, associations are organized, meetings are held, documents are distributed, and voters canvassed. A list is in preparation which will show the political proclivities of every voter in the State, which indicates his past and present positions, and give data which will enable the "workies" of the party to comprehend exactly their *status*. This energetic working-power has produced its legitimate effect. Already the camp-fires of the Republican host are brightly burning throughout the commonwealth, and the enthusiastic shouts for freedom and for victory are heard in every street. This feeling is not confined to politicians: old and young seem animated by a common desire of ridding the country of the "old man of the sea" who has so long strode its neck and so outrageously abused its confidence. The young men are especially active, and have formed themselves into Republican Associations, Lincoln Battalions, Rail Columns, and Freedom Clubs. Many of them retain the names under which they fought so gallantly in 1856. The familiar banners of the Rocky

Mountain Clubs, the Fremont and Dayton Associations, and the old-time transparencies bearing the inscription of Free speech, Free-men, Fremont and Freedom are seen in front of many a symposium of the gallant young Republican voters The good old songs, too, are once more wafted through the air, and the choruses which so certainly promised the desired victory in the last fight between "Freedom national and Slavery sectional," come cheeringly to our ears and are welcomed heartily, even though they deceived us before.

There is no doubt about it. The campaign has opened in Connecticut. From this time on, until the polls shall be closed at sundown on the 7th of November next, the fight will wage fiercer and the contest grow more desperate, terminating, doubtless, in the triumphant success of the Republican ticket.

Every one must remember

THE WIDE AWAKES OF CONNECTICUT,

who sprang so suddenly into existence at the last elections, taking everybody and everything by surprise, kindling enthusiasm, raising drooping spirits and giving the final impulse to the movement which placed a staunch Republican at the head of the State Government and sent two members of the same party to the United States Senate. Since that time the organization has steadily increased and has extended its ramifications into all the neighboring States. In brief, the Wide-Awakes are a body of young men, of Republican principles, ready at a moment's warning for duty. Each man has a uniform, consisting of cap and cape, and owns a torch which is constantly filled, trimmed, and ready for burning. The ease and readiness with which an *impromptu* torch light procession is gotten up can be imagined. The word being given, each man dons his cap and cape, seizes his torch, and at the appointed rendezvous meets his fellows all equipped like himself; the line is formed, torches are lighted and the torch-light procession moves on in twenty minutes or less after the first notification.

DIVIDED DEMOCRATS FACE AN UPHILL BATTLE

The split of the Democratic Party clearly damaged any hopes it had of winning the 1860 election. Breckinridge seemed poised to win the southern states, but would receive no support in the North. Douglas expected to gather more popular votes than Breckinridge because he had greater nation-wide appeal, but it appeared unlikely that he would be able to defeat either Lincoln in the North or Breckinridge in the South. Douglas was also hampered by his anti-Irish stance on immigration, alienating a constituency that provided massive turnout in northern cities.

AUGUST 6, 1860
PRESIDENTIAL.
PROGRESS OF THE CAMPAIGN.

Mr. Douglas Gaining in the South—The North Carolina Election—The Questions at Issue—The Washington Clubs.

From Our Own Correspondent.
WASHINGTON, Wednesday, Aug. 1.

Recent developments indicate that DOUGLAS is much stronger in the South, and particularly in Virginia and other border States, than I had supposed. I hear, indeed, that his friends in the gulf States are far more numerous than the public at a distance had been induced to believe. But whatever be the fact, one thing is clear, viz: that the power of DOUGLAS in the South is only for evil to the Breckinridge Party, just as the power of BRECKINRIDGE in the Free States is only for evil to the Douglas Party. In the one case the Democratic feud will enure to the benefit of the Bell and Everett ticket, and in the other to that of LINCOLN. It is probably that DOUGLAS will poll more individual votes in the nation at large than his Democratic rival; but BRECKINRIDGE will carry several States, while there is nothing that amounts to a probability that Douglas will receive an electoral vote. The strength of Douglas in Virginia is indicated by the readiness of the Breckinridge faction to unite upon a common electoral ticket, pledged to cast the vote of the State for the candidate who could thereby be elected. Nothing but a quaking sense of weakness could so humble the negro Democracy as to suggest this compromise with a man whom they regard as a factious traitor. Douglas' strength lies in the Valley and the West. Among the F. F. V.'s of the negro-holding region his name is scarcely less odious than that of Lincoln. The strength of Douglas, therefore, only goes to the extent of enabling him to make his enemies "esteem and hate" him, as Gibbon would say, but no farther. So with all the Slave States, except Missouri, where he is conceded to be stronger than his opponent; but the division of the party is so nearly equal that the plurality of votes will, in all probability be given to Bell and Everett.

I am informed by intelligent Democrats that the Catholic population of this city are for Douglas, a fact of no consequence in itself, except so far as it denotes the feelings of that class of citizens. But from this classification, the Catholics connected in any way with the Government must be excepted. They are all true to Breckinridge, and it would be singular if the Irish Catholics should be opposed to the powers that be. They depend upon Government, local or general, for jobs of pipe-laying, and street-making, and generally side with the party that employs them. Among those in a better condition, and not dependent upon Government, it is probably true that they are for Douglas. But this class is by no means considerable in Washington. The Douglas ratification meeting here was a sad failure, while those of Lincoln and Breckinridge were large and enthusiastic. This fact shows that Mr. Douglas cannot have the hearty support of even the Catholic population, which is very considerable in numbers of itself. The open league of Mr. Douglas with the Know-Nothing rump must disgust the Catholics, as well as the foreigners. Certainly all remembrance of the proscriptive spirit of that secret organization cannot be effaced from the memory of the Irish; and it will be surprising if they forgive Mr. Douglas for making an unholy alliance with their sworn enemies. Breckinridge has been placed in the same position by his friends in New-Jersey, to say nothing of his Cynthiana speech; so that the Catholics and foreigners will have no alternative but to go for Lincoln, upon his broad platform of justice and equality.

Observer.

- -

Fusion Tickets Make Last Ditch Effort to Defeat Lincoln

In a late attempt to prevent Lincoln from entering the White House, the northern Democrats, southern Democrats, and Constitutional Union Party began proposing "fusion tickets," offering voters the opportunity to vote for combined tickets of their candidates. These tickets melded slates of candidates with little in common other than an antipathy toward the Republican Party. The fusionists sought to unite the anti-Republican opposition, preventing Lincoln from winning outright in the Electoral College, but had no coherent message of their own. Their ultimate goal was to bring the election into the House of Representatives for a negotiated final resolution.

OCTOBER 8, 1860
THE FUSION MOVEMENT.

The Danger of taking the Election of President from the People, and giving it to Congress.

The Fusionists Playing into the Hands of the Disunionists.

Speech of Mr. H. J. Raymond on the Character and Perils of the Coalition.

Mr. H. J. Raymond made a speech on Friday night at the Republican Head-quarters of the Sixth Ward, in Brooklyn, to a large and intelligent meeting, upon the perils and prospects of the pending Presidential canvass. A considerable portion of his remarks were devoted to a critical analysis of the attempted Coalition of the three parties opposed to Lincoln in this State,—and a presentation of the danger which this Coalition, if successful, threatens to bring upon the country. As this topic just now engrosses a large share of public attention, we publish below an extended report of that part of Mr. RAYMOND's speech.

Mr. RAYMOND said he did not propose on this occasion to enter upon any statement or vindication of the principles of the Republican Party. That had already been done so often and so clearly by the eminent gentlemen who had preceded him in this series of meetings, that it was comparatively unnecessary. He should ask their attention to a single feature of the pending canvass which was peculiar to it,—which distinguished it, in a marked and not very creditable manner, from all the Presidential contests that have taken place in the past history of our Republic.

Hitherto, said Mr. R., all our Presidential contests have been contests of principle. The country has been divided into two or more political parties, each having its own platform of principles with its candidates representing them,—and each striving earnestly and honestly to elect those candidates, for the sake of giving its principles the ascendancy in the national councils. In the last canvass, that of 1856, we had on the one side Mr. BUCHANAN, representing the principles and policy of the united Pro-Slavery Democracy as it then existed, including the extension of Slavery into free Territories of the Union. We had on the other side Col. FREMONT, [loud applause,] representing the principle of opposition to the extension of Slavery; and we had Mr. FILLMORE, representing the party which regarded foreign Catholic influence as threatening the most imminent danger to the country, and which made resistance to it the cardinal principle of their creed and the leading object of their political efforts. Each party was true to its candidates, its principles, and itself. The lines were clearly and distinctly drawn, and every man knew precisely what and whom he was voting for, when he voted for this or that electoral ticket.

THE FUSION A COALITION AND NOT A COMPROMISE.

But now this has all been changed. The political battlefield presents an entirely different array of contending forces. We have, it is true, four parties with four candidates and four platforms; but the Republican Party is the only one of them all that stands its ground and maintains the honor of its flag. [Applause.] The leaders of all the others are busy in cheating their opponents, or in betraying their followers. [Applause.] The whole aim of the three opposition parties in this State is to form a Coalition,—to *fuse,* in support of one electoral ticket. We hear nothing of their principles,—no vindication of their distinctive opinions

and purposes,—nothing but a clamorous cry, the offspring partly of fear and partly of hate,—the ignoblest passions of the human heart,—for a union of their forces and their votes. Yet these three parties have each a distinctive platform. One asserts the principle that the Constitution carries Slavery into every Territory, and that when there the Federal Government must protect it. The other denies and denounces this doctrine, and asserts the right of the people of the Territories to admit or exclude it at pleasure. The third asserts the supreme, paramount duty of having no opinion on the subject, and of ignoring utterly every political question important enough to create a difference of opinion among the people. [Cheers.] There is not a solitary political principle on which these parties do not hold sentiments utterly hostile to each other. They are not agreed upon a single measure of government or a single feature of public policy. Yet their great endeavor, the sole object of their efforts and their ambition thus far in the canvass has been,—not to convince each other or the country of the truth of their principles, but so to assign the places on the electoral ticket, that each party should be content with its share of the spoils, and that all might vote together! Has not this been the burden of their song? Have not their organs, day after day and week after week, insisted upon this as the great object of their efforts? ["Yes," "yes."] Now a coalition is always a suspicious proceeding, when questions of principle are involved,—for it always implies to some extent a sacrifice of principle. But emergencies may arise in which compromises are necessary for the public good. But they must be compromises *based* upon something,—having some common principle for their foundation. The parties to them may waive for the moment some of their differences, on minor points. They may safely and honorably stand together, provided they find some common ground to stand upon. We had an instance of this in 1850, when dangers supposed to be impending over the country led the leading public men of that day to lay aside their peculiar views, and unite to pass what have since been known as the Compromise Measures. But statesmen, instead of political gamblers, were at the head of that great movement. WEBSTER and CASS and HENRY CLAY [loud and prolonged applause,] were the leaders then. They did not base their compromise upon a distribution of honors or of office. The question with them was, not how to divide an electoral ticket among opposing claimants,—not whether this party should have six electors and the other seven, or this should have seven and the other six. They compromised *upon principle.* They drew up a Declaration of Principles upon which all could unite without a surrender of their own convictions, or a violation of their political integrity. [Cheers.] And whatever may be thought of the wisdom of their action, no man can impeach the honor or the patriotism of the actors themselves. But what do we see now? Does any one of the parties to this Coalition abate anything of its peculiar pretensions? Have they drawn up any programme of principles on which, for the sake of saving the country, they are willing to unite, and by which they have solemnly agreed that the country shall be governed in the event of their success? Nothing of the kind! Not only has nothing of the kind been done, but nothing of the kind has even been attempted! [Cheers.] Retaining each its peculiar views—hating each other with all the ancient cordiality—and watching each other all the time, as gamblers at the card table watch each other for fear of being cheated, these volunteer saviours of the country have simply agreed that one shall have *seven,* another *eighteen,* and the other *ten,* Electors—as the prize of their mutual support! They have divided up the vote of the Empire State for the Presidency, precisely as . . . gamblers might share the hazards of the faro-bank. [Applause.]

. . . .

LINCOLN IS THE FAVORITE TO WIN THE PRESIDENCY

As election day approached, a Lincoln victory became probable. He was not expected to carry huge majorities in every northern state, but it was expected that he would gain enough state-wide majorities to win in the Electoral College over the split Democrats and the largely ineffectual Constitutional Unionists. The other parties competed for each other's votes, rather than for the Republican electorate, bolstering Lincoln's strength. With Lincoln's election looming, southern reaction to his likely victory became a concern throughout the nation.

OCTOBER 12, 1860
PRESIDENTIAL.
THE CANVASS IN THE NORTHWEST.

Prospects of the Election in Indiana, Illinois, Ohio and Michigan.

From Our Own Correspondent.
LOGANSPORT, Indiana, Friday, Sept. 28.

Since I wrote last, I have been watching with a pleasurable interest a phenomenon common, I doubt not, in all campaigns, and a thing to be regularly counted upon and allowed for by older and more experienced politicians, but to me both new and full of ever fresh surprise. I mean *the turn of the tide.* I have hesitated to realize the fact—I have told myself again and again that I was a prejudiced observer—but I cannot disguise from myself the truth that the vast Douglas wave is rapidly ebbing. The Democrats have made their push, and the final charge of the battle is wholly Republican. There is a sudden falling off of enthusiasm and confidence—an epidemic chill—among the followers of the "Little Giant;" and an impression daily gains ground that the Douglas fires are burning out, and that LINCOLN is sure to carry the day.

In this State the change is really astonishing. Indiana politics are so mixed as to be very difficult of estimation. The State is all "in spots," so to speak. You speak in a village where every man, woman and child seems to have little to do except to hurrah for LINCOLN; and in the very next village, fifteen miles distant, perhaps, you cannot repeat your former speech without danger of a riot. All through the central portion of Indiana you come upon little communities of Southern people, principally Kentuckians and Tennesseeans, and, generally speaking, Republican doctrines find little favor with them. They are a singularly gross and ignorant class of the population, retaining the Southern carelessness and roughness, without the Southern grace, frankness and generosity. Most of them look upon it as a grievance that Indiana is not a Slave State; and the mildness and lukewarmness with which Republican orators advocate their cause in such localities is positively laughable. CASS. CLAY is almost the only man who ventures upon a really vigorous Republican speech among them.

Then, again, the Bell-Everett Party is strong in Indiana. When I say "strong," I mean, of course, considering the weakness, the almost nonentity, of the party in the Northwest generally. They are strong for mischief. But even these differ as much among each other as in your own State James O. Putnam and Erastus Brooks. Some are most bitter haters of Republicanism,—some are already half Republican. So that you may see that the Indiana politics are difficult to see through. They are further complicated by the savage warfare which Senator Bright wages on the Douglas men. Bright is a man greatly overrated, coarse and of very ordinary ability. But he has been long enough a political leader to have acquired a good deal of influence— that is to say, a good many adherents—and he is thought to be a pretty shrewd political prophet. His loud and confident declarations that Douglas will not have a single electoral vote, have accordingly considerable weight, and are very discouraging. He is not likely to draw off many votes; but Mr. Douglas has none to spare.

Many of the Bell men, who will not support Lincoln, will support Henry S. Lane for Governor, while the Breckinridge men unite with the Douglasites under the banner of Thomas A. Hendricks. I am rather inclined to think the result will be that Lane will come out of the confusion with a small majority, and that the moral effect of this victory in October will be so great upon the undecided class of voters that Indiana will join the Lincoln column in November. Independently of the value of a victory in Indiana, I should rejoice in such a result for the sake of Lane himself, who is the most jovial and effective popular orator I have ever listened to. He is a superb actor; and nothing can be more amusing than his inimitable way of introducing himself to his audience, with frequent obeisances, as, "Ladies and gentlemen, the next Governor of Indiana." Notwithstanding his comic performances, which never degenerate into buffoonery, he is a keen and powerful reasoner, and his speeches not only please a crowd of hearers, but bear the severer test of reading uncommonly well. He is peculiarly powerful in denunciation, and some of his sarcastic sentences sting like a hornet. His transitions are wonderfully rapid and dramatic, and when he attempts an eagle's flight of eloquence, you may be pretty sure it is only that he may pounce on an opponent as an eagle drops upon his prey. It will express my meaning (better than it will harmonize with my previous comparisons) to call him the Zouave of popular orators.

In Illinois the skies are bright. Lincoln's majorities in the northern counties will about counterbalance Douglas' majorities in the Southern portion of the State, (supposing that the colonizing of votes from Missouri, Kentucky and Tennessee will be confined within reasonable limits,) and the centre will give a small but decisive majority for Lincoln. I think his majority in the State cannot fall below ten thousand.

· ·

VOTERS PONDER THE RESULT OF A LINCOLN VICTORY

Just before ballots were to be cast, the consequences of a Republican victory incited worry among many voters. The vote would be made primarily on the slavery issue, and the possibility of secession suddenly seemed real. Voters pondered whether the United States could survive, and who would be at fault for its destruction. Some blamed the Republicans for pressing the issue; others blamed the Democrats for being unwilling, or unable, to compromise. The election of 1860 might be resolved by the counting of ballots, but its critical significance would come from the reactions of the losing states.

NOVEMBER 5, 1860
EDITORIAL
DEMOCRATIC DILEMMAS.

The leaders of the Democracy believe, or affect to believe, that the triumph of the Republican Party in the elections of to-morrow will be followed by the dissolution of the American Union. They accordingly charge it upon the Republicans that they, and only they, are to be held responsible for this fearful and imminent catastrophe. Like the timid Lord Mayor of London in the time of the Gordon riots, who complained to the affrighted Catholics that "if they would only have been Protestants the mob wouldn't have burnt their houses," these excellent patriots profess that if the Republican Party would only have ceased to be Republican the Union would be safe.

This is all very well so far as it goes. But it is an old prejudice of honest people, that a man who has it in his power to prevent a wrong from being perpetrated and fails to do so, is at least as guilty as the perpetrator. If we take the Democracy at their word, and believe that the Union really is to perish on account of the election of Mr. LINCOLN, we have still a right to doubt whether the Republicans are to be made responsible for this result, for the same Democracy assure us that it is only the demoralization of their own party which has made Mr. LINCOLN's election certain.

This leaves them to choose between the following dilemmas:

Either the Democrats in council at Charleston and at Baltimore knew that the election of the Republican candidate for the Presidency would dissolve the Union or they did not. If they knew this, and in the face of this knowledge preferred the gratification of their party feuds, and a divided loyalty to their contending chieftains to the general interest of the nation, then they are themselves the makers of the mischief they deplore. On their own showing they could have beaten Mr. LINCOLN, but they preferred to have Mr. LINCOLN beat them. And they must therefore be content to be regarded either:

1. As impostors who care nothing for the Union which they pretend to adore, and of which they assume to be the sole defenders; or.

2. As incapables who did not foresee in June the results which are staring them in the face in November.

In the first case, their present outcries may well be treated with sovereign contempt. In the second case, sensible men may be pardoned for believing that the Union is in no more danger now than it was in June, and that those who proclaim its impending dissolution are just as poorly informed on the subject, and as far from being conjurors now as they were then.

. . . .

ABRAHAM LINCOLN IS ELECTED PRESIDENT

When all the votes were counted, Abraham Lincoln and the Republican Party stood ascendant. They had trounced their three rivals both in electoral votes and in popular votes though, contrary to *The New York Times* headline, they fell far short of a majority in the popular vote because of the four-way race. With the decisive victory of the Republicans, all eyes turned to the South and the threats of secession.

NOVEMBER 7, 1860
ASTOUNDING TRIUMPH OF REPUBLICANISM.

The North Rising in Indignation at the Menaces of the South.

Abraham Lincoln Probably Elected President by a Majority of the Entire Popular Vote.

Forty Thousand Majority for the Republican Ticket in New-York.

One Hundred Thousand Majority in Pennsylvania.

Seventy Thousand Majority in Massachusetts.

Corresponding Gains in the Western and North-Western States.

Preponderance of John Bell and Conservatism at the South.

Results of the Content upon Congressional and Local Tickets.

RE-ELECTION OF GOV. MORGAN.

The canvass for the Presidency of the United States terminated last evening, in all the States of the Union, under the revised regulation of Congress, passed in 1845, and the result, by the vote of New-York, is placed beyond question at once. It elects ABRAHAM LINCOLN of Illinois, President, and HANNIBAL HAMLIN of Maine, Vice-President of the United States, for four years, from the 4th March next, directly by the People: These Republican Candidates having a clear majority of the 303 Electoral votes of the 33 States, over all three of the opposing tickets. They receive, including Mr. LINCOLN's own State, from which the returns have not yet come, in the

New-England States	41
New-York	35
Pennsylvania	27
New-Jersey	7
And the Northwest	61
Total Electoral for LINCOLN	171

Being 19 over the required majority, without wasting the returns from the two Pacific States of Oregon and California.

The election, so far as the City and State of New-York are concerned, will probably stand, hereafter as one of the most remarkable in the political contests of the country; marked, as it is, by far the heaviest popular vote ever cast in the City, and by the sweeping, and almost uniform, Republican majorities in the country.

- -

SLAVE REBELLION FEARED IN THE WAKE OF LINCOLN'S ELECTION

In addition to the threat of secession, another danger loomed in the South following Lincoln's election, that of slave rebellion. Such fear was common in the South, and, even if exaggerated, the threat of black insurrection put whites constantly on guard. Following Lincoln's victory, many in the South anticipated a large-scale uprising by slaves who had learned from the southern Democrats' campaign that Lincoln's goal was to free them. Despite the inaccuracy of that message, many feared that slaves would act upon the hope of freedom and begin violent struggle. But the southern states gave slaves little time to organize rebellions, soon separating from the Union.

NOVEMBER 7, 1860
EDITORIAL
A REAL DANGER AT THE SOUTH.

We regard the result in Virginia, Kentucky and Tennessee, as having substantially dispelled all the danger of disunion which the election of LINCOLN was supposed to involve. But another peril of a still more fearful character may arise in its place. There is reason to apprehend *negro insurrections,* more or less extensive, in various portions of the South. How far they will spread, or with what circumstances of horror and atrocity they may be attended, it is impossible to predict. But we fear that they will take place in many sections of the South, and that very considerable inconvenience and suffering may result from them.

There can be no doubt at all that the negroes in every portion of the Southern States have been taught to believe that Mr. LINCOLN, if elected President, would set them free. They have heard this asserted, over and over again, by stump speakers,—and in political conversations,—and read from partisan newspapers from one end of the country to the other.

This assertion has been the whole staple of the warfare waged against the Republicans in the Southern States. The orators of the Breckinridge Party have made the charge in the most open and explicit manner, and the other parties have felt that they had no special interest in contradicting it. It is impossible that the slaves should not have heard it incessantly, and equally impossible for them to know that it was utterly untrue.

It will be remembered that precisely such outbreaks followed the election of 1856, although the Republican candidate was not elected:—in Tennessee, particularly, they were numerous and alarming. Various statements, which have recently met our eye, show that the negroes have imbibed the same notions concerning LINCOLN as prevailed concerning FREMONT,—and it would not be at all strange if they were to lead to the same and even worse results.

The responsibility for these outbreaks cannot be laid at the door of the Republican Party. Its orators and

1860 POPULAR VOTE

STATE	TOTAL VOTE	ABRAHAM LINCOLN (REPUBLICAN) VOTES	%	STEPHEN A. DOUGLAS (DEMOCRAT) VOTES	%	JOHN C. BRECKINRIDGE (SOUTHERN DEMOCRAT) VOTES	%	JOHN BELL (CONSTITUTIONAL UNION) VOTES	%
Alabama	90,122	—	0.0	13,618	15.1	48,669	54.0	27,835	30.9
Arkansas	54,152	—	0.0	5,357	9.9	28,732	53.1	20,063	37.0
California	119,827	38,733	32.3	37,999	31.7	33,969	28.3	9,111	7.6
Connecticut	74,819	43,488	58.1	15,431	20.6	14,372	19.2	1,528	2.0
Delaware	16,115	3,822	23.7	1,066	6.6	7,339	45.5	3,888	24.1
Florida	13,301	—	0.0	223	1.7	8,277	62.2	4,801	36.1
Georgia	106,717	—	0.0	11,581	10.9	52,176	48.9	42,960	40.3
Illinois	339,666	172,171	50.7	160,215	47.2	2,331	0.7	4,914	1.4
Indiana	272,143	139,033	51.1	115,509	42.4	12,295	4.5	5,306	1.9
Iowa	128,739	70,302	54.6	55,639	43.2	1,035	0.8	1,763	1.4
Kentucky[1]	146,216	1,364	0.9	25,651	17.5	53,143	36.3	66,058	45.2
Louisiana	50,510	—	0.0	7,625	15.1	22,681	44.9	20,204	40.0
Maine	100,918	62,811	62.2	29,693	29.4	6,368	6.3	2,046	2.0
Maryland	92,502	2,294	2.5	5,966	6.4	42,482	45.9	41,760	45.1
Massachusetts	169,876	106,684	62.8	34,370	20.2	6,163	3.6	22,331	13.1
Michigan	154,758	88,481	57.2	65,057	42.0	805	0.5	415	0.3
Minnesota	34,804	22,069	63.4	11,920	34.2	748	2.1	50	0.1
Mississippi	69,095	—	0.0	3,282	4.7	40,768	59.0	25,045	36.2
Missouri	165,563	17,028	10.3	58,801	35.5	31,362	18.9	58,372	35.3
New Hampshire	65,943	37,519	56.9	25,887	39.3	2,125	3.2	412	0.6
New Jersey[1]	121,215	58,346	48.1	62,869	51.9	—	0.0	—	0.0
New York	675,156	362,646	53.7	312,510	46.3	—	0.0	—	0.0
North Carolina	96,712	—	0.0	2,737	2.8	48,846	50.5	45,129	46.7
Ohio	442,866	231,709	52.3	187,421	42.3	11,406	2.6	12,194	2.8
Oregon	14,758	5,329	36.1	4,136	28.0	5,075	34.4	218	1.5
Pennsylvania	476,442	268,030	56.3	16,765	3.5	178,871	37.5	12,776	2.7
Rhode Island	19,951	12,244	61.4	7,707	38.6	—	0.0	—	0.0
Tennessee	146,106	—	0.0	11,281	7.7	65,097	44.6	69,728	47.7
Texas	62,855	—	0.0	18	0.0	47,454	75.5	15,383	24.5
Vermont	44,644	33,808	75.7	8,649	19.4	218	0.5	1,969	4.4
Virginia	166,891	1,887	1.1	16,198	9.7	74,325	44.5	74,481	44.6
Wisconsin	152,179	86,110	56.6	65,021	42.7	887	0.6	161	0.1
TOTALS	**4,685,561**	**1,865,908**	**39.9**	**1,380,202**	**29.5**	**848,019**	**18.1**	**590,901**	**12.6**

1. Figures from Svend Petersen, *A Statistical History of the American Presidential Elections* (Westport, Conn.: Greenwood Press, 1981), 37.

OTHER VOTES	%	PLURALITY	
—	0.0	20,834	SD
—	0.0	8,669	SD
15	0.0	734	R
—	0.0	28,057	R
—	0.0	3,451	SD
—	0.0	3,476	SD
—	0.0	9,216	SD
35	0.0	11,956	R
—	0.0	23,524	R
—	0.0	14,663	R
—	0.0	12,915	CU
—	0.0	2,477	SD
—	0.0	33,118	R
—	0.0	722	SD
328	0.2	72,314	R
—	0.0	23,424	R
17	0.0	10,149	R
—	0.0	15,723	SD
—	0.0	429	D
—	0.0	11,632	R
—	0.0	4,523	D
—	0.0	50,136	R
—	0.0	3,717	SD
136	0.0	44,288	R
—	0.0	254	R
—	0.0	89,159	R
—	0.0	4,537	R
—	0.0	4,631	CU
—	0.0	32,071	SD
—	0.0	25,159	R
—	0.0	156	CU
—	0.0	21,089	R
531	0.0	485,706	R

journalists have had no access to the ears of the Southern slave. They have had no opportunity, if they had had the least desire, to instill into his mind false and delusive hopes of emancipation as the result of LINCOLN's election. All this has been done by Southern men,—by slave-holders themselves. The *Missouri Democrat* puts the case very clearly and justly in an article published some days since, in which it says:

> "We deliberately assert that the Southern assailants of the Republican Party are the authors of this grievous delusion, and the overt acts which have followed or may follow in its train. The slave has heard strange noises in the air whenever he has heard the Republican Party spoken of by its opponents. *He has heard the white man, his owner, declare at public meetings that the sole object of that party is the abolition of Slavery.* It has been dinned into his ears so often—the Press and the stump have so rung with it—that he believes it at last. To confirm him in his error, *the incendiary speeches of the Abolitionists are republished in the papers which his master reads, as the authorized expression of Northern sentiment.* No wonder that he believes the prophetic day of universal emancipation is at hand. Such is the meaning of the declarations he has heard from the lips of those to whom he looks for instruction and information. If pious, he chants the more popular of the hymn-book melodies with a new emphasis, imagining that he is already transported to Canaan, Happy Land; and if he is otherwise disposed, he probably sets about concocting plots to accelerate the great event. That disturbances should result from the bitter disappointment he is doomed to suffer, comports with the very nature of things. The recoil and agony in his case must be as great as that experienced by the God-forsaken Millerite, whom no chariot of fire or cloud bears away from the housetop to the happy realms of light."

We trust that Southern men will act with better judgment now than they have shown during the canvass in this respect,—and that they will do whatever may lie in their power to prevent their falsehoods from bearing their proper fruit. But whatever may happen, they cannot, with any show of justice, hold the Republicans responsible.

SOUTH CAROLINA SECEDES FROM THE UNITED STATES

In late December 1860, just six weeks after the presidential election but three months before Lincoln would assume office, the eighty-four-year-old union of states came to an end. South Carolina was the first state to declare independence from the United States, citing irreconcilable differences over slavery. Immediately, discussions erupted throughout the nation about the claimed right of secession. In the South, the question was whether to join South Carolina, as six more states did before Lincoln's inauguration in March. In the North, the issue was how to best deal with the secessionists, whether through acceptance, negotiation, or outright war.

DECEMBER 21, 1860
EDITORIAL
THE DISUNION CRISIS.

The Formal Secession of South Carolina.

Unanimous Adoption of the Ordinance Declaring the Union Dissolved.

Interesting Discussions in the Convention.

Highly Important from the Federal Capital.

Reception of the News of the Action of South Carolina.

The Commander of Fort Moultrie Instructed to Surrender.

The U. S. Arms in Charleston Arsenal Delivered to the City Authorities.

CONGRESSIONAL PROCEEDINGS.

Our Washington Dispatches.

The Secession Movement.

South Carolina passed the ordinance of secession yesterday a 1 o'clock p.m., by the unanimous vote of the Convention; and her action was greeted with a salvo of a hundred guns. As this step was universally anticipated, it will create no special uneasiness. It does not change the relations of South Carolina to the Union in the slightest degree, though it will very possibly be followed by acts that will have that effect. . . .

Whatever the movement has lost in recklessness and haste, it may have gained in steadiness and strength. There is thus far no *Union* Party in the South; the only divisions are upon minor points. Some are for seceding now, while others would wait for the cooperation of other States. Some would secede without condition, while others would remain in the Union if their demands should be conceded. What these demands will be we can, of course, conjecture;—and we are bound to add that we see very little prospect that they will be granted.

If the South were in the mood to discuss the subject with candor and fairness,—if they were "open to conviction," or willing even to have their palpable mistakes in matters of fact corrected, we should have little fear of the result. But it is not so,—nor do we see any immediate prospect of their becoming so.

REPUBLICANS SEEK COMPROMISE TO HALT SECESSION

As some southern states withdrew from the Union, others proclaimed their desire to remain, if possible. Their stark declarations that an abolition of slavery would result in secession caused the abolitionist push to stumble, and Congress passed a series of conciliatory measures. Given the choice between a dissolved Union and conciliation between slave and nonslave states, the new Republican government seemed willing to compromise.

FEBRUARY 21, 1861
THE BORDER STATES AND THE UNION.

The general reply to all propositions for conciliation has been, "We cannot compromise with traitors." It was assumed that the whole South had resolved to repudiate the General Government, and it seems useless as well as degrading to offer terms to men who had decided in advance upon their rejection.

This plea was not without force at the outset of the secession movement. So long as there was no party in the Southern States prepared to avow its devotion to the Union, it certainly did seem worse than idle to discuss terms of compromise and conciliation. But the elections in the Border States have changed all that. First, Virginia pronounced her desire to remain in the Union if she could do so with honor. Tennessee next declared her devotion to the Union by an overwhelming majority, and now Missouri adds her voice to that of her sister States. There can be no doubt, therefore, that *all the Border States* are in favor of preserving the Union, are determined to adhere to it against all its enemies, and will, unless driven off by unfriendly action, stand by the Government in its efforts to maintain it.

These elections and the state of Southern sentiment which they reveal, present an entirely new basis for the action of Congress. They are entitled to attention and respect, especially from the Republican Party, which is soon to assume all the responsibility of conducting the Government. They certainly negate and nullify utterly the plea that there can be no compromise with traitors and rebels. No one asks such a compromise. The "traitors and rebels" of the seceding States repudiate all thought of compromise or conciliation. Nothing can suit them better than the *Tribune's* policy of contempt and coercion. It serves their ends, by driving the Border States into rebellion with them, and thus strengthening their Southern Confederacy.

What we are asked to do is to make common cause with *our friends* in the Border States,—to invite them to join us, on common ground, in sustaining the Government, and in perpetuating the Union which our Fathers formed. They ask at our hands no sacrifice of principle,—they exact no terms inconsistent with loyalty to our own convictions. They simply ask that we will give them guarantees for the truth of our own declarations, and take some steps to end the Territorial dispute which has been at the bottom of our sectional differences for the last ten years. A declaration, such as the House of Representatives has just adopted almost unanimously, against interference with Slavery in the States;—an Enabling act for New-Mexico, which will settle the whole controversy concerning Slavery in the Territories, without violating any principle of the Chicago Platform, and some provision concerning the future acquisition of territory,—these points, frankly proclaimed by the Republican Party and made the basis of their action, would create a platform on which *every Border State* could join them in maintaining the Union and supporting the Government which is to have control of its destinies for the next four years.

We find it not easy to understand why any Republican should resist a policy so thoroughly in harmony with the professions of the party, and so imperatively demanded by the exigencies of the times. Every Republican is now more than ever interested in preserving the Union and in securing for the Government a successful and satisfactory Administration. We must repeat, therefore, what we said the other day, that none but those who are *at heart* Abolitionists or Secessionists, or both, will resist every endeavor to retain the Border States in the Union by such acts of friendly conciliation as involve no sacrifice of principle, but only indicate a love of the Union and a desire to preserve it on its original basis. The Union men of the

Border States have a right to ask so much at the hands of the North;—and if the Republican Party is stolid enough to reject the proffered friendship, they may rely upon it their opponents will profit by their folly, and speedily expel them from places of power which they were unfit to wield and unable to hold.

• •

The Civil War Begins

On April 12, 1861, all efforts at peaceful reconciliation ended. South Carolina's military forces opened fire on a federal military base that had defied orders to vacate and had instead attempted to resupply its armaments. With the first shots on Fort Sumpter, as it was then known, the northern and southern states replaced politics with war. Border states that had attempted to remain in the Union now also seceded, leading to a cruel conflict that would determine the very fate of the nation. The American Civil War—the bloodiest conflict in the nation's history—had begun.

The ball has opened. War is inaugurated.

APRIL 13, 1861
THE FIRST GUN FIRED BY FORT MOULTRIE AGAINST FORT SUMPTER.

THE BOMBARDMENT CONTINUED ALL DAY.

Spirited Return from Major Anderson's Guns.

The Firing from Fort Sumpter Ceased for the Night.

Hostilities to Commence Again at Daylight.

The Correspondence which Preceded the Bombardment.

The Demand for a Surrender and Major Anderson's Refusal.

THE RELIEF FLEET OFF THE HARBOR.

How the News is Received in Washington.

OUR CHARLESTON DISPATCHES.
CHARLESTON, Friday, April 12.

The ball has opened. War is inaugurated.

The batteries of Sullivan's Island, Morris Island, and other points, were opened on Fort Sumpter at 4 o'clock this morning.

Fort Sumpter has returned the fire, and a brisk cannonading has been kept up. No information has been received from the seaboard yet.

The military are under arms, and the whole of our population are on the streets. Every available space facing the harbor is filled with anxious spectators.

THE PRESIDENTIAL ELECTION OF 1864

LINCOLN'S REELECTION PORTENDS THE END OF REBELLION AND SLAVERY

The ordinary can be extraordinary. That is the basic characteristic of the presidential election of 1864.

In a historical list, it looks ordinary. An incumbent president wins reelection, with a substantial majority of the popular vote. His victory is seen as an endorsement of his record in office, and he employs that mandate to complete the major task of his administration.

But the reality is quite extraordinary. The incumbent president was Abraham Lincoln, the most revered figure in American history. At the time, the reelection of an incumbent president was unusual, an achievement previously accomplished only once—by Andrew Jackson—since the passing of the founding generation.

Lincoln's reelection came in the extraordinary, wrenching time of the Civil War, after four years of secession, fratricidal conflict, and the partial emancipation of slaves. Nine states of the Confederacy did not participate in the 1864 election and the electoral votes of reconstructed Louisiana and Tennessee were excluded by congressional advocates of more radical policies, while the Union had been enlarged by the new states of Kansas, Nevada, and West Virginia. The war's bloodshed took the lives of more than 600,000 soldiers and uncounted civilians, 2 percent of the total population and more soldiers than have died in any subsequent war. The toll would equal two hundred of the future terrorist attacks of September 11, 2001.

Yet, among this carnage and national fission, the presidential election took place. Despite some scattered suggestions that the election be postponed or that a dictatorship be installed for the duration of the emergency, 4 million Americans voted. Although despairing of his own chances, Lincoln insisted on maintaining the established democratic republic, and on conducting balloting that seemed likely to end his presidency and his mission to preserve the Union.

Source: *The Granger Collection, New York*

Long Abraham Lincoln a Little Longer.

Unusually tall for his era, Abraham Lincoln's reelection as president in 1864 is caricatured in a cartoon called "Long Abraham Lincoln a Little Longer."

Benefiting in part from timely military successes, Lincoln did win a second term over his Democratic opponent, Gen. George B. McClellan, whose candidacy held the promise of a negotiated peace with the South. But Lincoln's second term would last barely a month before his assassination in April 1865. Nevertheless, his victory facilitated the

1864 ELECTORAL VOTE

STATE	ELECTORAL VOTES	LINCOLN	McCLELLAN	STATE	ELECTORAL VOTES	LINCOLN	McCLELLAN
California	(5)	5	–	Missouri	(11)	11	–
Connecticut	(6)	6	–	Nevada	(3)	2	–
Delaware	(3)	–	3	New Hampshire	(5)	5	–
Illinois	(16)	16	–	New Jersey	(7)	–	7
Indiana	(13)	13	–	New York	(33)	33	–
Iowa	(8)	8	–	Ohio	(21)	21	–
Kansas	(3)	3	–	Oregon	(3)	3	–
Kentucky	(11)	–	11	Pennsylvania	(26)	26	–
Maine	(7)	7	–	Rhode Island	(4)	4	–
Maryland	(7)	7	–	Vermont	(5)	5	–
Massachusetts	(12)	12	–	West Virginia	(5)	5	–
Michigan	(8)	8	–	Wisconsin	(8)	8	–
Minnesota	(4)	4	–				
				TOTALS	(234)	212	21

end of the Civil War, the full restoration of the Union, and the eradication of the national shame of slavery. The greatest triumph of his reelection was that of the ordinary political process itself—the continuity of free elections in a time of extraordinary travail.

THE PARTIES AND THE CANDIDATES

The Republican Party no longer formally existed in 1864. Emerging only in 1856 and winning in 1860, it had been reborn as the Union Party. The new, temporary name was adopted to gain votes from war supporters among Democrats and erstwhile Whigs.

Lincoln wanted to run for reelection, but his nomination for a second term was uncertain. Rivals for power within his own party were active even in the cabinet, particularly Salmon Chase, the secretary of the Treasury, who was among those defeated in the Republican convention of 1860. Chase used his considerable sway in the disposition of federal spending and patronage to develop strength among those seeking office and contracts, and attempted

to increase his popularity by printing his own picture on federal banknotes. Other boomlets developed in favor of John Fremont, the 1856 Republican candidate, and Ulysses Grant, the rare successful Union general. The president also had to cope with the uncertain loyalties of the media giants of the day, particularly Horace Greeley, editor of *The New York Tribune,* and James Gordon Bennett, editor of *The New York Herald.*

The war obviously set the political scene. It was long—already almost as long as the time of active military engagement in the Revolution, bloodier than any previous conflict in human history, and—the vital political point—apparently unsuccessful. Union armies lost most early battles with the Confederates, and even the successes, such as Gettysburg, were subverted by what Lincoln considered timid generalship in pursuing the defeated enemy. The doom of the rebellion was already becoming evident in 1863, with the federal conquest of the Mississippi valley, severing five states from the Confederacy. But the struggle continued.

In its secondary effects, the war brought a staggering national debt, dislocation in all aspects of civilian life, inflation, restrictions on civil liberties including suspension of constitutional rights, and internal riots after the imposition of a military draft. Its greatest moral achievement, the Emancipation Proclamation, satisfied neither the advocates of total abolition nor those who still hoped for reconciliation with a slave-owning South. The combination of problems had led to significant Republican losses in the 1862 congressional elections, with the party barely holding control of both the House and Senate.

Beset on all sides, Lincoln and his political allies still ably maneuvered to win his renomination. The Union Party convention was called early, for June in Baltimore, to limit the time for opposition to organize. Endorsement came from Republican-controlled state legislatures and from state party conventions packed with Lincoln supporters. A supportive resolution passed early in Chase's home state of Ohio, destroying his insurgency. Then, unanimous support was gained in party conclaves in the critical state of New York, through the rough tactics of state political boss Thurlow Weed.

When the Unionist convention met, there was little opposition. Lincoln won unanimously among all states attending (494 of 519 votes), as well as from nonvoting delegations from three Confederate states, with the exception of Missouri's 22 votes for Grant. For vice president, although Lincoln was officially neutral, he empowered his allies to work successfully for the second ballot selection of Andrew Johnson, former senator and military governor of occupied Tennessee, a Democrat who might broaden the new party's appeal. The platform pledged unequivocal support for prosecution of the war and insisted that peace with the Confederacy must be "based upon an unconditional surrender of their hostility and a return to their just allegiance to Constitution and laws of the United States." While praising Lincoln's war policies, the convention went further, pledging abolition, through a constitutional amendment to "terminate and forever prohibit the existence of Slavery" in the United States.

Choosing the ticket did not end dissent among Republicans. The Radical wing of the party feared Lincoln's defeat but considered him too conciliatory on the issue of Negro emancipation. Meeting in Cleveland in May, dissidents created a temporary Radical Republican Party, naming Fremont as its presidential candidate on an abolitionist platform, with Gen. John Cochrane of New York as his running mate.

Fremont's candidacy and continuing bad news from the battlefronts convinced many Unionists that Lincoln would lose the election. To avert the disaster of a Democratic—and, essentially a Confederate—victory, they made a late summer attempt to force Lincoln to withdraw. Radical Republicans in

Congress, editor Greeley, and other party leaders looked to convene the party convention to replace him with a more popular figure. But, on August 29, the very day the dissidents were to ask Lincoln to withdraw, the war news turned positive, and they abandoned the effort.

Democrats were clearly the largest threat. Buoyed by the 1862 congressional election results, and reaping the harvest of war dissatisfaction, Democrats advocated conciliation of the Confederate states. Yet they also tried to capture the emotional fervor of the war by nominating a popular general, George McClellan. He had commanded the Union army, gaining the admiration of his troops and the press even as he repeatedly failed to drive offensives against the rebel forces when aggressive tactics might have hastened victory. Twice dismissed from command by Lincoln, who said McClellan had a "case of the slows," he was the most attractive candidate for the opposition, easily gaining the Democratic nomination on the first ballot (with 174 of 226 votes) in its convention in Chicago at the end of August. A conservative Democrat, Rep. George Pendleton of Ohio, was chosen for vice president.

The dominant peace faction of the Democrats—denigrated by their foes as "Copperheads," the human embodiment of poisonous snakes—was unsure of McClellan's views about negotiation with the South, but staked its hopes on his personal popularity and the nation's war weariness. Implicitly accepting the continuation of slavery, the party platform demanded "that immediate efforts be made for a cessation of hostilities, with a view of an ultimate convention of the States, or other peaceable means, to the end that, at the earliest practicable moment, peace may be restored on the basis of the Federal Union of the States."

Torn between ambition and patriotism, McClellan ultimately would not agree to the call for an armistice that would continue the separation of the nation. In his acceptance of the nomination, he declared, "The reestablishment of the Union, in all its integrity is, and must continue to be, the indispensable condition in any settlement," deferring any peace until this condition was met by the Confederacy. At the same time, he made no mention of slavery, thereby implicitly agreeing to its continuation in a restored Union.

THE ELECTION CAMPAIGN

As the campaign began, Democrats still hoped and many Republicans feared that Lincoln would lose to McClellan. Indeed, as late as August 23 of the election year, the president agreed with these pessimistic predictions of the election results. He made his dire forecast in a memorandum he circulated to the cabinet, requiring each member to sign it unread: "This morning, as for some days past, it seems exceedingly probable that this Administration will not be re-elected. Then it will be my duty to so co-operate with the President elect, as to save the Union between the election and the inauguration; as he will have secured his election on such ground that he can not possibly save it afterwards."

Lincoln's fortunes were tied to the course of the war, and both would soon change. In the last week of August, pre-cisely when the Democrats were nominating McClellan and Radicals were boosting Fremont, a new military hero turned the political tide. On September 1, Gen. William Tecumseh Sherman captured the hub of the South, Atlanta, Georgia, thereby severing the Confederacy—already fragmented by Union conquest of the Mississippi valley. Parallel victories came in the Shenandoah approaches to Washington, and in the Deep South with naval victory at Mobile, Alabama. On the central front in Virginia, Grant had pinned Robert E. Lee's Army of Northern Virginia into the last entrenchments before Richmond, Virginia, the Confederate capital. With military victory finally in sight, even critics of the president endorsed the logic of the Unionists—"Don't change horses in the middle of the stream"—a slogan new in 1864 that would be repeated in many later elections, even in years when few voters knew how to mount a steed.

The ambivalence of Lincoln's critics was expressed well by Thurlow Weed, the former Whig and Republican "boss" of New York state in a *New York Times* letter of October 17. Although he was still opposed to abolition of slavery and criti-cal of the conduct of the war, Weed concluded with hesitant support of Lincoln:

> While the people have not had, in results, the worth of treasure and blood; though our armies, especially of the Potomac, have not been ably handled; . . . much has been accomplished in the right direc-tion. . . . We know that Mr. LINCOLN is loyal, persevering and devoted, and that he is doing all he can do to *conquer* a peace. This is not *all* we desire, but it is vastly more than we should get from a Peace Party Administration.

With the changing winds of war now at his back, Lincoln swiftly sailed forward. Plotting for a new convention was dropped, as Greeley's *Tribune* endorsed the president, joined by other Radicals who gave Lincoln their support, albeit grudgingly. Remaining Republican discontents were minimized by bargains and unsubtle inducements. Lincoln won endorse-ments from Chase, who was promised appointment as chief justice of the United States, and from Fremont, who withdrew from the contest, conciliated by a renewed minor military com-mission and the resignation of his political rival, the moderate Montgomery Blair, from the cabinet position of postmaster-general. Editor Bennett's published support of Lincoln came after hints that he would be named ambassador to France; another former Lincoln rival, Simon Cameron, had been removed from the cabinet by appointment as ambassador to Russia.

Still, the election remained competitive. Democrats continued to criticize the conduct of the war, to hold out hopes for its early end through diplomatic conciliation, and to frighten the electorate with the specter of emancipated negroes competing for white workers' jobs. Secret envoys and some public feelers came from the Confederacy, giving some credence to the Democratic peace position. In state elections in October—in those years held separately from the national ballot—Democrats came within 400 votes of victory in the critical state of Pennsylvania, and showed strength in other major states. The Unionists were cheered, however, by deci-sive successes in Ohio and Indiana.

In the heated environment of 1864, the presidential campaign focused on mobilizing the parties' masses, not on persuasive argument. As was common in the nineteenth cen-tury, the candidates stayed out of public view, confining them-selves to directing strategy and conciliating their factional leaders. The active work of the campaigns was conducted by party activists, from ward heelers to orators. Torchlight parades, rallies, sermons, and speeches stoked partisan ardor as Democrats and Unionists rallied behind the nominees. The printed press, the only mass medium available, added to the fervor, through its editorials, slanted news coverage (also a nineteenth-century norm), and advertisements. Politics also became business, as entrepreneurs wooed devoted voters with "THE NEW CAMPAIGN LANTERNS (patented,) with fine illuminated portraits and mottoes of the Presidential candidates, candles, rockets, bombs, batteries, flags &c."

The campaign and war fervor brought a high turnout, estimated at 85 percent of the eligible electorate, almost all male and white. The total number of votes declined 15 percent from 1860, due to the absence of southern voters who lived in seceded states. Yet, even in the throes of war, turnout increased in 17 of the 22 states that participated in both elections. Adding to the turnout was the participation of soldiers, mobilized by the Union Party and army. Many soldiers were able to vote by absentee ballot, newly authorized in many states. Voting lines formed on the battlefields, and other soldiers were furloughed to return home on election day. They provided a stirring simultaneous defense, by arms and by ballots, of the democratic process. An estimated 80 percent of the military vote went to Lincoln, constituting the margin of victory in the closer states.

The New York Times played an unusual role in 1864, its influence extending far beyond its printed pages of news and commentary. Henry Raymond, its editor, was a founder of the Republican Party and its convention keynoter in 1856. He frequently advised Lincoln on policy issues, urging caution on emancipation; he held a seat in Congress and was an active participant in the election campaign. Helping to consolidate party support for Lincoln, Raymond held secret negotiations with envoys from the rebel Confederate government, and served as chair of the party's National Union Executive Committee. Not surprisingly, Lincoln won vigorous backing in the editorial columns of The Times.

The Election Results

Lincoln won the presidency with a strong victory. He carried 22 of the 25 states remaining in the Union, resulting in an overwhelming electoral vote majority of 212–21, with a popular vote margin of 55 percent to 45 percent, and a plurality of 400,000 votes (2.2 million to 1.8 million). McClellan carried only the Border states of Delaware and Kentucky, and his home state of New Jersey, some of which was actually below the Mason-Dixon line and home to substantial numbers of Copperhead sympathizers.

Deeper analysis, however, would show the election to be far closer. The contest was held, after all, only in the loyal Union states, with the eleven formerly Democratic states of the Confederacy excluded, their place taken in part by the three new and loyal states. Even with this limited electorate, McClellan had gained substantial support on a platform that almost advocated treason. He came close to victory in many large states, and the shift of a few thousand votes, as little as 1 percent of the total, would have won the general 5 more states and 77 more electoral votes, bringing him near the ultimate war treasure—the White House.

The Times made no secret of its preferences in its election coverage. The lead article on November 9, the day after the vote, was headlined: "Glorious Result Yesterday. Election of Lincoln and Johnson. Terrible Defeat of McClellan. The Union Triumphant." Its editorial the next day, presumably written by Raymond, interpreted the election as a mandate to continue the war to total victory. It pointed to the enduring significance of the vote for democracy, seeing in the election "the determination and the fortitude, tenacity and self restraint, which freedom develops, for which the friends of popular government all over the world will thank us."

The election of 1864 and the events leading up to it had a tremendous influence on later politics. The Civil War changed American society. Military mobilization had spurred industrialization, the expansion of railroads across the continent, and a strong central government. As many as 3 million men had served in the conflicting armies. Adding slave labor and the women and children left at home, the war directly impacted as much as a third of the total U.S. population.

The military whirlwind inevitably affected the less violent conflicts of political parties. War deaths had brutally reduced the electorate: Of white males aged eighteen to forty-three, who made up most of the eligible voters, 8 percent in the North and 18 percent in the South were killed in combat. The millions who survived were also traumatized. Northerners would respond for decades to the "waving of the bloody shirt" and the plea to "vote as you shot," and southerners to campaign calls to remember "the lost cause." Negroes, so long as their enfranchisement was protected, became reliable Republicans. The Union had been reunited geographically, but not politically.

The political struggle between Republicans and Democrats would continue along the sectional conflict lines established in the Civil War. But the election of 1864 did provide clear mandates. The results provided democratic legitimacy for Lincoln's past conduct; it determined that the war would continue to total victory in the present; and it showed that America's future, however dire, would be grounded in free elections.

In longer historical perspective, the election settled the two major issues at the core of the sectional conflict: preservation of the democratizing nation and the disappearance of slavery. Lincoln posed these questions, and Lincoln's reelection answered them. He asked, at Gettysburg, if a "nation, conceived in Liberty, and dedicated to the proposition that all men are created equal . . . can long endure." It did endure and, with the subsequent quick passage of total emancipation, it realized his vision of "a new birth of freedom." That is the heritage of the presidential election of 1864.

NORTHERN DEMOCRATS DEVELOP STRATEGIES TO DEFEAT LINCOLN

More than a year before the presidential nominees were chosen in 1864, northern Democrats advocating peace with the rebelling states met in New York City to develop campaign strategies for reclaiming the White House. Their attacks focused mainly upon the Lincoln administration's failure to win the war, its alleged abuses of the Constitution, and the administration's support for the abolition of slavery. Fernando Wood, an ardent Peace Democrat and former mayor of New York City, headlined a series of speakers proclaiming Lincoln as a demagogue who was fooling the nation into freeing slaves under the guise of patriotism and reunification with the South.

APRIL 8, 1863
COPPERHEADS IN COUNCIL.

Resolutions Denunciatory of the Administration and its Policy.

Speeches of Fernando Wood, Mr. Carlile, and Others.

Wood's Principles and Plans, his Hopes and Fears, his Wrath and Impotence.

The large hall of the Cooper Institute was densely packed by an audience last evening, who assembled, according to the printed call, to express their opposition to the Conscript Act, the war for the negro, and to the Administration, and to exhibit their favor of the reunion of the States, of the Constitution, and of the rights of the poor. The meeting was highly enthusiastic, and the sentiments, as uttered by the speakers, seemed to be fully and unreservedly indorsed. Amidst the vast concourse, one—and only one—of the gentler sex was observed. Upon the platform were seated several persons who formerly held responsible positions under the State and Municipal Governments, also numerous other individuals of much less note. A band of music was in attendance, which interspersed the proceedings from time to time with patriotic and popular airs. . . .

SPEECH OF FERNANDO WOOD.

FELLOW-CITIZENS: The public man—[confusion, and a voice, "Order, G—d d—n you"]—the public man or man who fails to meet the responsibilities of this crisis, is unfit for public duty. [Applause, and a voice "That's so."] I care not whether the failure comes from timidity or from treachery—in either case he is guilty of infidelity to the public interests. These are no times for hesitation. These are no times for failure to meet the condition of the country as it exists. These are no times for a resort to the base dictates of noncommittalism, or to avoid the responsibilities of the occasion. The country is in a revolution—aye in two

revolutions—a revolution at the South, prosecuted by the sword, and a revolution at the North, prosecuted by legislative and executive usurpation. [Applause, and a voice, "That's so."] The latter is more insidious, more destructive, more to be feared by the people than the former. [Applause.] The South wages war against the Government by open manly, defiant action. The other revolution at the North, under an absolute Government, wages war first by exciting and intoxicating the public mind by appeals to patriotism, and then, when the public mind has committed itself fully and entirely to one cause—that of reunion—it is subverted and used for another purpose, unconstitutional, inhuman, and destructive of the Government under which we live. [Applause.] And it is, my friend, this latter effort to revolutionize our Government and destroy our institutions, that we, in my judgment, are met to-night to resist. [Applause.] . . .

Then we have the Administration—[hisses and groans]—we have the President—[groans]—and the Cabinet, who think they see in the continuance of this war reelection and retention in office, if not for another term, if they would dare to try it on, for a lifetime. And the whole is a power, a great power, a power which, my friends, subverted the elective franchise in our glorious little State of Connecticut yesterday. [Applause.] Then, we have another class, who have been tired of waiting in the Democratic party for their time, who call themselves War Democrats—[applause, hisses and groans]—men who think they see in this great combination to sustain the

Administration an opening for political preferment and of official position—men who have, some of them, grown gray in the Democratic party who have been the recipients of our favors, and whom we have petted and applauded in this hall—these men, in an evil hour for themselves and for their own reputation, sold themselves for less than a mess of pottage. [Applause.] Then again we have the Abolitionists [hisses and groans]—men who always hated the South, and who are for the war because Slavery exists, and who will be for the war so long as Slavery exists, and so long as there is a slaveholder to punish. And, my friends, need we be surprised under all these circumstances, if this powerful combination, all from different motives, operating to act upon one centre—need we be surprised that the men of our opinion should be calumniated, should be persecuted, should be opposed and crushed out when we have nothing to stand upon except our God, our country and our consciences. [Great applause.] My friends, this power that we are to resist is stupendous, but as great as is that power, the majesty of this free and independent people is twenty times greater. ["Good," and applause.] And there are no selfish interests, no selfish combinations, that can put down the American people and, therefore, let us stand by our cause; let us stand by it as we would our heart's blood; let us give property, liberty, life, everything except the glorious cause of our country, and that we will maintain though the heavens fall. [Applause.] Now, gentlemen, what is our position? As I understand the position of the Democratic party—as I understand my own position, and I only speak for myself—I stand upon this rock—the Constitution, the rights of the States, and the rights of the people. [Great applause.] That is my platform, and, if that is treason, let them make the most of it. [Applause.]

I did not conceive, nor do I now conceive that the South had any moral right to secede under the circumstances. She participated in the Presidential election; every Southern State, including South Carolina, voted for a candidate for the Presidency at the last Presidential election. Now I hold that if the South had determined upon secession that was not the time to do it. She had ventured to throw her interests and representation into that election and she lost, and she was bound by all the principles of morality and honor not to have seceded until she had given timely notice. [A Voice—"True," and applause.] I won't stop here to discuss the question as to the rights of one, two or twenty States to secede from the Union. The South claims that she has the right under the Constitution to secede—the South claims that she has the legal right to secede, but I say, admitting that she had, that having participated in the Presidential election, in which she lost, and we lost, she was in honor bound to stand by the result, although that result was the election of ABRAHAM LINCOLN. [Hisses.] Therefore I say this, because I want my principles clearly and distinctly understood. I am speaking here for myself, for no party and no section of a party. The sentiments I utter to-night are the individual sentiments of the speaker, and I ask no man to indorse them if he don't concur in them. [Applause.] I have never, and I do not now— and I desire to be correctly reported and correctly stated—I have never, and do not now, justify the action of the South. ["Bravo."] I go further—I say that I never have at any time— and defy a man to produce evidence to the contrary—I have never declared a sentiment in favor of any course toward the South, except to bring the South back again into the Union. [Applause.] I am opposed to a separation of these States. [Applause.] I am opposed to a recognition of any Southern Confederacy. [Applause.] But I am also opposed to the equally base and oppressive conduct of an Administration which, in my judgment, is far beneath the Administration of the Southern Confederacy. [Deafening and prolonged applause.] Well, my friends, the war went on; the whole American people appeared to rush to the support of the Administration at its origin. We gave them money without stint, we gave them all the men they asked for, and more too. And we have gone on sustaining this Administration—going it blind in its support. [Applause and laughter.] And when we have dared to question its infallibility, when we have dared to exercise these constitutional rights to which I have referred, to criticise the acts of our own servants, and agents into whose nostrils we had breathed the breath of official life, we were called, forsooth, rebels and traitors. [A Voice—"Copperheads."] And when I, who sent one whole regiment to the war, ["Bully"] I, who paid more dollars than these patriots had paid cents; I, in whose veins runs blood of Revolutionary ancestors—to be called traitor because I dared be independent and manly. ["Good."] Ah! my friends, these words have sent me into this fight, and I will never let go of their traitorous throats until they are out of office. [Tremendous applause, stamping, shouting, and three cheers.] Now, my friends, I am for peace. I hold that the war, under this Administration, has proved a failure. ["That's so."]

THE NEW YORK CITY DRAFT RIOTS

On July 11, 1863, names were drawn in New York City for the first military draft since the Revolutionary War. Two days later, riots began. Irish immigrants and poorer residents of the city—enraged by the ability of affluent draftees to avoid service by paying a $300 fine—condemned the conflict as "a rich man's war, and a poor man's fight." They also feared that freeing slaves in the South would further add to the difficulties immigrants faced in finding work. For four days, the streets of New York witnessed the largest civil insurrection the nation has ever witnessed.

JULY 14, 1863
THE MOB IN NEW-YORK.

Resistance to the Draft—Rioting and Bloodshed.

Conscription Offices Sacked and Burned.

Private Dwellings Pillaged and Fired.

AN ARMORY AND A HOTEL DESTROYED.

Colored People Assaulted—An Unoffending Black Man Hung.

The Tribune Office Attacked—The Colored Orphan Asylum Ransacked and Burned—Other Outrages and Incidents.

A DAY OF INFAMY AND DISGRACE.

The initiation of the draft on Saturday in the Ninth Congressional District was characterized by so much order and good feeling as to well nigh dispel the forebodings of tumult and violence which many entertained in connection with the enforcement of the conscription in this City. Very few, then, were prepared for the riotous demonstrations which yesterday, from 10 in the morning until late at night, prevailed almost unchecked in our streets. The authorities had counted upon more or less resistance to this measure of the Government after the draft was completed, and the conscripts were required to takes place in the ranks, and at that time they would have been fully prepared to meet it; but no one anticipated resistance at so early a stage in the execution of the law.

- -

LINCOLN LAYS THE GROUNDWORK FOR RECONSTRUCTION

In December 1863 Lincoln issued his Amnesty Proclamation, offering pardons to southerners who had not held office under the Confederacy or had not abused Union prisoners and who would sign an oath of allegiance to the United States. He was widely criticized by Radical Republicans as too soft on the "southern rebels" and by Democrats as too harsh. The proclamation was a prime example of Lincoln's practical and moderate approach in defiance of more extreme, and perhaps unrealistic, views.

JANUARY 28, 1864
EDITORIAL
RE-ELECTION AND RECONSTRUCTION—THE PRESIDENTIAL QUESTION.

Unquestionably one of the strongest causes of the popular manifestations for the reelection of President LINCOLN, is the fact that he most directly represents an acceptable policy in regard to reconstruction. Every man in the country knows President LINCOLN's method, and the spirit with which it will be carried out. He has disclosed both with a distinctiveness which there is no possibility of mistaking. The good faith and consistency which have marked all his words and actions are taken as a perfect guaranty of his future course. On the one hand, he will not break down State lines or State rights; on the other, he will not surrender the control of States to men whose thoughts and acts are for the rebellion. His Amnesty Proclamation, which treats the loyal men of the State as the only true repositories of State rights under the Constitution, impairs no principle of our system, and yet opens the way to a complete restoration of the Union on its old basis. It is an exponent of his policy, read and understood by all men, and approved by most. It has dissipated a thick cloud of uncertainty, and enabled everyone to look forward with distinctness and confidence.

No other candidates that are named are identified with any particular plan or policy. True, the name of Conservative, or Radical, is applied to some of them with a good deal of pertinacity, as if there were something sufficiently distinctive in that. But the time has passed when it stood for anything definite. Two years ago a Radical was a man who believed in extirpating Slavery root and branch, whatever the consequences. A Conservative was a man who would save it, and shape every military and civil policy to that end. Everybody understood the terms as referring to that institution solely. But since then the institution has perished. The moral influence of the President's Proclamation, and the wear and tear inflicted by the war, have destroyed it beyond all possibility of resurrection. To be conservative toward it now is simply to shield the dead; to be radical is simply to stab the dead. The distinction is worthless and sense-dead. The distinction is worthless and senseless. Yet, with the usual tenacity of party parlance, the names still continue, and much is made of them in some quarters, when the object is to keep up old conservative prejudices or old radical prejudices against the President.

The opponents of Mr. LINCOLN find their chief capital in these obsolete associations. Neither those on the Democratic side, or on the Republican side dare commit themselves to any positive plans of reconstruction essentially different from his. They may carp freely enough at the Amnesty Proclamation, but yet they are very careful to propose nothing definite in its place. Not half of the Democrats in Congress voted for Mr. YEAMAN's proposition to admit the rebels to their old civil rights without delay or restriction, when they should lay down their arms. It is very certain that if a proposition were made on the other side to receive the rebel States back only as territories, it would not secure a quarter of the Republican vote. We know of no proposed candidate for the Presidency who has declared for any distinct plan different from the President's. There stands the President's method in boldest relief, a fixed beacon for every eye; on either side of it are only speculations and shadows. Even if there were no other reason for renominating Mr. LINCOLN, this would suffice. The loyal people of the land are utterly opposed to exchanging a clear straight path, with Mr. Lincoln to lead them, for the unknown ways of new men.

- -

A MEMBER OF LINCOLN'S CABINET OPTS NOT TO CHALLENGE THE PRESIDENT

When the state legislature of Ohio passed a resolution endorsing President Lincoln for reelection, it forced one of his chief rivals, Treasury Secretary Salmon Chase, to pull out of the race. *The New York Times* wrote that his statement made him "a statesman and a patriot, who appreciates the difference between the public duties of this day and the mere political duties of ordinary times." Chase's withdrawal from the race provides a view of the election of 1864 as beyond an ordinary contest, as a battle for the very survival of the nation.

MARCH 12, 1864
EDITORIAL
THE DECLINATION OF MR. CHASE.

Secretary CHASE has done himself new honor in refusing to let his name be longer used in connection with the Presidential nomination. His letter to the member of the Ohio Senate is very timely, and in all respects very appropriate. He defers gracefully to the almost unanimous decision of the Union members of the Legislature of his own State in favor of the reelection of President LINCOLN; and thus, without unduly sacrificing any honorable ambition, prevents all use of his popularity for any purpose calculated to generate discord among loyal men.

We say loyal men, and not Union party, for we agree with Mr. CHASE that "persons and even *parties* are nothing in comparison with the great work to be accomplished." The term Union party is really a misnomer. Strictly speaking there is no such organization. For a party is political, and has to deal with politics. But the saving of the nation from the rebellion that has threatened to destroy it is not a matter of politics, any more than the saving of a man's life is to him a matter of business. A party has to do with the mere administration of a government, not with the vital concern of its life or death. The Union party, so called, is in fact nothing more than the great loyal body of the Northern people, who are opposed to the rebellion, and are loyally sustaining the Government in its efforts to put the rebellion down. It is made up of men of all the former parties; and they still have different opinions in regard to the scanty remnants of the old party issues which the war has now swept out of sight forever. The so-called party lives only in the war which is rescuing the nation; and it will come to an end whenever the war comes to an end.

It acts for the emergency only. When that is over, and the Republic is once more safe, political parties will again form themselves, and contend, as in former time, for certain political principles on which the Government shall be administered. It is grossly wrong to speak of the Union men of the country as constituting a party, in the sense ordinarily attached to the term. They have an infinitely higher purpose and aim than any which either party spirit or party principle can prompt. They work not that the Government should be managed in this way or that, but that we may have a Government to be managed at all.

Mr. CHASE delivers himself in his letter as a statesman and a patriot, who appreciates the difference between the public duties of this day and the mere political duties of ordinary times. Recognizing that the hearts of the great mass of the loyal people are set upon the retention of ABRAHAM LINCOLN at the head of affairs, and that the persistent efforts of a handfull of politicians to put forward his own name, with an adverse political bearing, were engendering dissension where there ought to be completest harmony, he makes an end of every chance of difficulty by this distinct refusal to be longer considered a Presidential candidate. The magnanimous patriotism will be well noted and remembered by all good loyal men; for there never was a time when the public were more keenly appreciative of genuine public devotion.

- -

A CONFEDERATE VIEW ON THE 1864 ELECTION

A common practice of newspapers of this era was to run reprints from other newspapers that provided alternative perspectives. This reprint from a Richmond paper provided the Confederate view on the coming election, referred to as the *canvass*. One of the Republican strategies during the 1864 campaign was to portray the reelection of Lincoln as the southern states' worst fear, and therefore the northern states' best hope.

MARCH 12, 1864
THE PRESIDENTIAL QUESTION.

From the Richmond Enquirer.

The people of the Confederate States cannot be indifferent to the approaching Presidential canvass in the United States. *That canvass will be more important in its ultimate bearings upon the present war, than the military campaign of the ensuing Spring and Summer.* Last Fall, the Northern elections went overwhelmingly for the Abolitionists; but that result was brought about by the

potent agency of bayonets and dungeons. LINCOLN holds himself ready, no doubt, to employ the same expedients at the Presidential election next Fall, and will surely do so if the contest is directly between the Abolitionists and the "Copperheads," as it was at the late State elections. But it is by no means certain that such will be the case.

LINCOLN is anxiously working to secure for himself a renomination and reelection. With the spoils of office and the plunder of rich contracts, he has purchased the support of quite a swarm of adherents. *He has also managed to keep the whip-hand of most, if not all, of his military rivals.* It is even stated that the last Yankee hero—GRANT—refuses the use of his name in connection with the Presidency, and advises his friends to go for LINCOLN. It is quite clear, however, that Old ABE's pretensions to a new lease of power are to be strongly contested. There is a movement on foot to bring out FREMONT; and the movement is so formidable, and at the same time so novel, that it is likely to interfere seriously with the plans of LINCOLN. The "pathfinder" is sharply after the Illinois jester.

● ●

REPUBLICAN OPPONENTS SEEK TO DELAY LINCOLN'S RENOMINATION

Early in April, Republican opponents of Lincoln's renomination proposed to delay the party convention until later in the year. By postponing a choice, they hoped to further weaken support for the president and strengthen the chances of a potential rival. Lincoln supporters feared such indecision might succeed, both damaging Lincoln's own reelection hopes, but also ultimately losing the election for the Union Party. Support for the delay came from one of Lincoln's chief rivals, Gen. John Fremont, the Republican Party's first presidential candidate in the 1856 election, who hoped to resurrect another bid for the presidency.

APRIL 8, 1864
EDITORIAL
THE PRESIDENTIAL NOMINATION.

The *Independent* swells the chorus for a postponement of the Union National Convention. It fears the effect of too long a Presidential canvass. It is afraid *the North* will be divided by a contest lasting from the 7th of June until the 1st of November. But it is quite willing to have *the Union party* divided from June till September, by a sharp, bitter personal controversy about candidates. It sees, or acknowledges, no danger in this.

It is quite needless to say that this is only another part of the machine "pressure" by which the opponents of President LINCOLN hope to compass his defeat. As things are going now they regard his nomination as reasonably certain. The whole drift of public sentiment seems to be in favor of trusting him to finish the work which it was the fate of his administration to begin. His opponents think that in gaining time they gain chances of checking this tendency and turning this tide of opinion in some other direction. They will have more time to arrange for the election of Anti-Administration delegates. They will have the chances of possible defeats in the field, which may damage the Administration, as well as of possible victories, which may help some other candidates. In all this they may or may not reckon wisely. For our own part, we do not believe that President LINCOLN's nomination depends at all on the time of holding the convention. We have very little doubt that he will be the candidate of the Union party, whether the nomination is made on the 7th of June or on the 1st of September. . . .

The sooner this question of candidates is decided the better. It is the right of every man to have his own opinions and his own preferences as to men. But it is not right to insist on making *them* the subject of a prolonged contest among the friends of the Government, to the encouragement and aid of its opponents. Let us have a fair canvass,— full freedom of choice and of action,—an open and free election of delegates, so that every State may express, clearly and fully, its preference, and then let us have an *early decision.* Let us know who is to be our candidate as soon as possible, so that we may all unite in the effort to secure his election. This seems to us the best way, and, indeed, the only way, to prevent divisions in the Union party fatal to its vigorous and effective action.

APRIL 21, 1864
EDITORIAL
FACTIOUS OPPOSITION TO THE UNION NATIONAL CONVENTION.

The *New Nation,* the newly-established organ in this City of the Presidential interests of Gen. FREMONT, says: "We advise every one at once to give up all idea of taking part in the Baltimore Convention, as that convention is a nonentity." Ordinarily, nobody thinks of pricking up the ears at the sound of a little trumpet. But, in this case, it is well to give a little attention, as we have here an outgiving of a spirit which unquestionably animates some, at least, of the supporters of Gen. FREMONT. It discloses the animus of much of the clamor that has been raised against the assemblage of the National Convention in June rather than September. It is from the very extreme wing of the Union party which has been most obstreperous for a postponement of the convention that is now heard the fanfaronade that the convention itself is "a nonentity"— which, being interpreted, means that inasmuch as it is settled that the convention cannot be managed, it shall be repudiated.

MAY 20, 1864
EDITORIAL
GEN. GRANT'S SUCCESSES AND PRESIDENT LINCOLN.

The Copperhead journals have at last found how to extract some comfort from GRANT's success. They are discovering that this success is just the thing to defeat the renomination of President LINCOLN! They feel quite certain that the Baltimore Convention, in view of these victories, will adjourn until September, and then select a more available candidate. . . .

These Copperheads may as well open their eyes to the fact that the success of the war is the success of the Administration. Every advance made in crushing the rebellion is an advance in President LINCOLN's popularity, and in the public determination that, so long as the war continues, its guidance shall not be transferred to new and untried hands. Gen. Grant himself desires no other sphere of action than that which he is now engaged in. His highest earthly ambition is to force the rebellion to its last ditch, and there either exterminate it, or obtain its unconditional surrender. No grander achievement than that is possible, no higher distinction. Yet it is not at all unlikely, if this is accomplished, that the people will at some future period insist upon testifying their admiration and gratitude by according to him the highest civil office in their gift. The time for that, we trust, will come. But, with his consent, this cannot be until his military work is done. Nor will any true friend of either Gen. GRANT or of the cause which he is so splendidly serving, desire that he should be taken from that work for a day until he executes it to the uttermost iota. The very confidence which the people have in Gen. GRANT only binds them the more devotedly to President LINCOLN, who led the way in showing the same confidence, and who, it is certain, will stand by GRANT to the last, in spite of all professional jealousy or party intrigue. There could be no guarantee that Gen. GRANT's career will not be arrested before he deals the rebellion the finishing stroke, but the reelection of President LINCOLN. If Gen. McCLELLAN, or any other man, were in the Presidential chair, Gen. GRANT's present freedom of action would most certainly be restrained, or at least embarrassed. The civil leadership of ABRAHAM LINCOLN and the military leadership of Lieut.-Gen. GRANT are in entire harmony. They stand in the relation to each other of mutual supports, and both make up the completest public service attainable. The people want no change. There will be no change.

• •

RADICAL REPUBLICANS NOMINATE A CANDIDATE TO OPPOSE LINCOLN

In late May the Radical Republicans met in Cleveland to select their nominations for president and vice president. Although derided as a lost cause from the beginning by Lincoln supporters (including *The New York Times*), the Radicals selected the formidable General Fremont to vie for the presidency. Fremont's candidacy threatened to combine sufficient Radical Republicans with others opposed to the progress of the war to turn the election from Lincoln to the eventual Democratic nominee. *The Times* portrays the nominating convention as a lackluster and rather pointless affair.

JUNE 3, 1864
THE CLEVELAND CONVENTION.

The Calls—Sketch of the Proceedings—Who were There—The Nominations.

From Our Own Correspondent.
CLEVELAND, Ohio, Wednesday, June 1.

I have not been able to keep the run of all the various calls under which the people were invited to send delegates to meet in solemn conclave—*i. e.* convention—at Cleveland, on Tuesday, the 31st of May. . . .

Col. Moss, of Missouri, reminded the convention that as it had assembled for business, he moved the nomination of Gen. J. C. FREMONT, for President. Upon this hint the convention was proceeding to set, when GEORGE W. DEMERS, of Troy, obtained the floor, and moved the postponement of such action to what he termed would be a more fitting period. He argued the question rather forcibly and with evidently a leaning for GRANT; but the convention finally choked him down, and the nomination of FREMONT was carried by acclamation, followed by such cheers as only German lungs can give—deep and guttural as a bassoon, and fragrant of the earliest of our Spring esculents.

Somebody then said, let us make Gen. JOHN COCHRANE the candidate for Vice-President, and as the General stood before them, nobody had the face to say no, and so that was carried. . . .

A ratification meeting was called for the evening, but it went over. The people evidently thought the parent who had "borned" the couple, must be too much exhausted to endure the excitement of congratulations, so the people refrained from ratifying, and the next morning Cleveland was again tranquil.

You will think this but a brief recount of a mountain's labors. I have said in its favor all that its bests friends could ask. I have refrained from saying against it all that they could expect me to omit. When there was so little to say in the way of commendation, and no much in omit in the way of censure, no great length of criticism could be expected. To damage slightly an old distich, I might say,

If they had been stronger,
My tale had been longer.

As a spectacle, the convention was pitiful. As a representative body, it was a fraud. As the exponent of principles, it was little better than a humbug—for beyond a half-dozen, the leaders were "the abandoned of all parties." Gen. FREMONT paid the expenses. He may get votes enough to reimburse him for the outlay, by the gratification of his thirst for vengeance; but for all other purposes the convention might as well have been held in Jones' Wood, with the usual Sunday attendance. Such a congregation would have more physical and moral force. Would it not?

LEO.

JUNE 7, 1864
EDITORIAL
THE ACCEPTANCE OF FREMONT.

Of course FREMONT accepts. He laid the plot on purpose to accept. His griefs would run to seed if he did not accept. His "whole charge of ancients, corporals, lieutenants, gentlemen of companies, discarded unjust serving men, revolted tapsters," would all go to the dogs if he didn't accept. It is plainly enough now but an ill venture; yet, being in so far, there was no alternative but to stand to it.

It was needful not only to accept, but to give reasons. FREMONT has given them, in the letter we published yesterday. They are very vague. Words lie so thick about them that it is not easy to make them out. But we gather that his acceptance is necessary because Mr. LINCOLN has violated personal liberty, and the liberty of the press, and especially the right of asylum; because his foreign policy has been feeble and without principle; and because the war has been managed with incapacity and selfishness, with all "the abuses of military dictation, without its unity of action and vigor of execution." These, every one sees at once, are Copperhead reasons, pure and simple. They consist of exactly the stuff faction has been casting at President LINCOLN for the last two or three years, only a little staler. It is evident that FREMONT had his eye on the Copperheads while penning every line of this letter.

• •

An 1864 campaign poster promotes Abraham Lincoln and Andrew Johnson as the Republican Party candidates for president and vice president. Lincoln's reelection ensured the defeat of the Confederacy and the end of slavery.

Source: The Granger Collection, New York

LINCOLN RENOMINATED AT THE UNION PARTY CONVENTION

In sharp contrast to the events in Cleveland, the report of the Union Party's Baltimore convention portrays it as lively and consensual. The party quickly coalesced behind Lincoln, affirming him as the hope of the nation and declaring vast support from loyal patriots around the country. As was customary at the time, Lincoln did not attend the convention, but was informed of his renomination afterwards. In his acceptance, he delivered what became a theme of the campaign, an anecdote about it being "not best to swap horses when crossing streams."

JUNE 9, 1864
PRESIDENTIAL.
LINCOLN & JOHNSON.

Proceedings of the National Union Convention Yesterday.

Unanimous Renomination of President Lincoln.

Gov. Andy Johnson, of Tennessee, for Vice-President.

THE LOYAL PLATFORM.

Slavery Must Perish by the Constitution.

Emancipation, the Monroe Doctrine, Economy and the Pacific Railroad.

Enthusiastic Scenes at the Nomination.

THE FINAL ADJOURNMENT. . . .

JUNE 10, 1864
THE BALTIMORE NOMINATION.

Mr. Lincoln's Acceptance—Address of Gov. Dennison—The Platform—Its Indorsement by the President—Address of the National Union League—The President's Reply.

WASHINGTON, Thursday, June 9.

At 2:30 o'clock to-day the committee appointed yesterday by the National Union Convention at Baltimore to inform President LINCOLN of his nomination by that convention, reached the White House, when they were invited into the East Room, where the President was conversing with members of the delegation who had previously called upon him.

Gov. DENNISON, President of the convention and Chairman of said committee, then addressed the President as follows:

Mr. PRESIDENT: The National Union Convention, which closed its sittings at Baltimore yesterday, appointed a committee, consisting of one from each State, with myself as Chairman, to inform you of your unanimous nomination by that convention for election to the office of President of the United States. That committee, I have the honor of now informing you, is present. On its behalf I have also the honor of presenting you with a copy of the resolutions or platform adopted by that convention, as expressive of its sense and of the sense of the loyal people of the country which it represents, of the principles and policy that should characterize the administration of the Government in the present condition of the country. I need not say to you, Sir, that the convention, in thus unanimously nominating you for reelection, but gave utterance to the almost universal voice of the loyal people of the country. To doubt of your triumphant election would be little short of abandoning the hope of a final suppression of the rebellion and the restoration of the Government of the insurgent States. Neither the convention nor those represented by that body entertained any doubt as to the final result, under your administration, sustained by the loyal people, and by our noble army and gallant navy. Neither did the convention, nor do this committee, doubt the speedy suppression of this most wicked and unprovoked rebellion.

[A copy of the resolutions was here handed to the President.]

I would add, Mr. President, that it would be the pleasure of the committee to communicate to you within a few days, through one of its most accomplished members, Mr. CURTIS, of New-York, by letter, more at length the circumstances under which you have been placed in nomination for the Presidency.

The President said:

MR. CHAIRMAN AND GENTLEMEN OF THE COMMITTEE: I will neither conceal my gratification, nor restrain the expression of my gratitude, that the Union people, through their convention, in the continued effort to save and advance the nation, have deemed me not unworthy to remain in my present position. I know no reason to doubt that

I shall accept the nomination tendered; and yet, perhaps, I should not declare definitely before reading and considering what is called the platform. I will say now, however, that I approve the declaration in favor of so amending the Constitution as to prohibit Slavery throughout the nation. When the people in revolt, with the hundred days' explicit notice that they could within those days resume their allegiance without the overthrow of their institutions, and that they could not resume it afterward, elected to stand out, such an amendment of the Constitution as is now proposed became a fitting and necessary conclusion to the final success of the Union cause. Such alone can meet and cover all cavils. I now perceive its importance and embrace it. In the Joint names of Liberty and Union let us labor to give it legal form and practical effect.

At the conclusion of the President's speech, all of the committee shook him cordially by the hand and offered their personal congratulations.

The members of the National Union League adjourned yesterday from Baltimore to this city and called upon the President this afternoon, by whom they were cordially received in the east room of the White House. The Chairman of the deputation spoke to the President as follows:

MR. PRESIDENT: I have the honor of introducing to you the representatives of the Union Leagues of the loyal States, to congratulate you upon your renomination, and to assure you that we will not fail at the polls to give you the support that your services in the past so highly deserve. We feel honored in doing this, for we are assured that we are aiding in reelecting to the proud position of President of the United States one so highly worthy of it, one among not the least of whose claims is that he was the emancipator of four millions of bondmen.

The President replied as follows:

GENTLEMEN: I can only say, in response to the remarks of your Chairman, that I am very grateful for the renewed confidence which has been accorded to me, both by the convention and by the National League. I am not insensible at all to the personal compliment there is in this, yet I do not allow myself to believe that any but a small portion of it is to be appropriated as a personal compliment. The convention and the nation, I am assured, are alike animated by a higher view on the interests of the country for the present and the great future, and that part I am entitled to appropriate as a compliment is only that part which I may lay hold of as being the opinion of the convention and of the League, that I am not unworthy to be intrusted with the place I have occupied for the last three years. I have not permitted myself, gentlemen, to conclude that I am the best man in the country; but I am reminded, in this connection, of a story of an old Dutch farmer, who remarked to a companion once that "it was not best to swap horses when crossing streams."

The prolonged laughter which followed this characteristic remark should have been heard. It was tumultuous.

. . . .

THE ABOLITION OF SLAVERY BECOMES A WAR AIM

One of the defining pieces of the Union platform was the abolition of slavery. In the 1860 election, Lincoln had been wary of urging the elimination of slavery and instead urged its containment. Prior to 1864 he had preferred urging reconciliation with the South, without pressing the slavery issue, even limiting the scope of the Emancipation Proclamation. During the 1864 election, the push to end slavery throughout the nation became a defining feature of the Union Party's campaign, finally bringing the issue into open national debate.

JUNE 13, 1864
EDITORIAL
THE SLAVERY-EXTERMINATING AMENDMENT.

Among the most gratifying developments of the Baltimore Convention was the unanimity exhibited in favor of a Constitutional amendment making a universal and perpetual end of Slavery. There was a time when such a proposition could not have been pressed without a great risk of making serious, if not fatal, discord in the Union party. We ourselves deprecated its premature agitation. Always recognizing that the unity of the Union party is the prime necessity, we have always been disposed to keep in the background all questions of minor concern calculated to breed strife. The progress of events was far more potent to settle them than any controversy could be. Experience has long since demonstrated that public opinion is shaped mainly by the inaudible and invisible teachings of the war, rather than by any appeals, however urgent, or by any arguments, however forcible.

So far as regards this subject of Slavery, it has been plain enough from the outset that the public mind was detaching itself from its old moorings, and yielding more and more to the Anti-slavery current. This, in fact, was a moral necessity. The rebellion sprang so directly from Slavery, and was so closely connected with Slavery in all of its objects and policies, that it was not possible to make war against the rebellion with a whole heart, and yet remain well affected toward Slavery. Border State influences, in the early stage of the war, did most to check the rising Anti-slavery spirit. All loyal men felt the importance of avoiding anything tending to impel these States to identify themselves with the "Confederacy." As these States became more settled in their position, the Anti-slavery influences of the war became more free to operate; and as the war went on, they continually gained power. They first secured popular sanction to the mere negative policy of not returning fugitive slaves who escaped to our lines; then to the positive confiscation, as "contrabands," of all slaves of rebel masters; then to the issue of an executive proclamation declaring free all slaves in the rebel States, whether belonging to rebel or loyal masters; then to an offer of compensation to the loyal border States as an inducement to emancipation; then to the plan of making negro soldiers, which contributed immensely to break up Slavery in the Border States; and finally they have now had their full consummation in this unanimous adoption by the Union party of the radical measure of making a complete and final extirpation of Slavery, through the whole length and breadth of the land, by a constitutional amendment. Thus the demonstrations against Slavery have all the while been growing stronger and stronger, and the unity of the Union party has at the same time remained unbroken. It is not the invocation of the President, nor debate in Congress, nor agitation by the press or by platform speakers, that has wrought these results, but the logic of the war itself, silent yet irresistible.

This amendment, now regularly adopted as one of the cardinal ends of the Union party, is the logical converse of the peace policy formed by the North before the war. As a last inducement to the leaders of the secession movement to abandon their wicked intent, Congress almost unanimously passed its resolution to submit to the people a constitutional amendment in these words:

"No amendment shall be made to the Constitution which will authorize or give Congress power to abolish or interfere, within any State, with the domestic institutions thereof, including that of persons held to labor or servitude by the laws of said State."

· ·

ANDREW JOHNSON IS NOMINATED FOR VICE PRESIDENT

The nomination of Andrew Johnson of Tennessee as Lincoln's vice president brought balance to the Union ticket. Johnson was a southerner and a Democrat, creating a clear link to the effort to unify the country. His candidacy highlighted the Union effort to promote restoring the nation, while avoiding emphasis on punishing or alienating the southern rebels.

JUNE 22, 1864
EDITORIAL
OUR CANDIDATE FOR THE VICE-PRESIDENCY—POPULARITY OF THE NOMINATION.

The thoroughly unsectional character of the Union party is strikingly evinced in the ardent satisfaction with which the nomination of ANDREW JOHNSON for the Vice-Presidency is hailed by the party throughout the North. We have yet to hear of the slightest murmur. Neither in the Middle nor in the Eastern States is there any complaint that both candidates on the ticket come from the States west of the Alleghanies. All local jealousy is swallowed up in the general sense of the propriety of making special recognition of the peculiar desert of Southern loyalty.

This display of feeling is of much more significance than a superficial glance would discover. Every one who has been in the habit of reading the extracts copied from the Southern newspapers, has seen that the constant effort of the leaders of the rebellion has been to fill the popular heart with rancor against the North, as a geographical division. The term "Yankee" is made the epitome of everything that is odious, and is applied indiscriminately to all who dwell north of Mason and Dixon's line. When Northern parties are spoken of, a certain difference is made between the epithets applied to each. The supporters of the Administration usually get the benefit of the adjectives that express pure hate; while its opponents are more apt to be favored with those that imply contempt. But whatever discrimination there may be in the language used, there is one constant object—and that is the surcharging the Southern heart with the intensest aversion to the Northern people. As the Carthagenian was taught to regard the Roman, as the Frenchman, a half century ago, was taught to regard the Englishman, as his natural enemy, so the Southern man has every influence brought to bear upon him to make him inveterately hostile to the Northern man. This is just what might be expected. The supreme object of the rebellion is separation from the North; and, of course, the more complete the moral separation, the easier becomes the material.

On the other hand, the supreme object of the Union party is to prevent separation and promote union. They are not for fighting the South at all, as a geographical division. They do not even allow the fact that the rebellion is exclusively seated in the South, and that the great majority of the Southern people have given their adhesion to it, to induce upon them anything like an anti-Southern feeling. It is the rebellion alone that they hate. A Southern man who opposes the rebellion, who stands firmly by the old flag, instead of suffering any distrust or prejudice on account of his nativity, in fact is admired and applauded all the more because of his nativity. ANDREW JOHNSON to-day has a far stronger hold upon the great popular heart of the North than he could have had if he had been born in the North. He is no more loyal than hundreds of thousands of others. But the peculiar glory of his loyalty is that it is *Southern* loyalty; and it is because the people are particularly desirous to recognize and honor that loyalty that his nomination to the second office in the gift of the people affords such particular satisfaction. This manifestation is conclusive evidence of the genuine national spirit of the Union party. It is a new proof that the party is truly entitled to the grand name it bears,—a yet further pledge that the party, in its work of restoring the Union, will know no such thing as sectional antipathy.

> Two problems press upon the rebel mind: How to whip Grant and how to defeat Lincoln. The more they are baffled in the first, the more anxiously they set to the second.

LINCOLN PONDERS AN APPROACH TO PEACE NEGOTIATIONS

In July 1864 news broke that a peace delegation had been dispatched by the Confederacy to Canada, where the participants awaited Union representatives to negotiate an end to the war. Lincoln thought such negotiations were unlikely to achieve his two goals, unification and an end to slavery. For the moment, Lincoln had two unpopular options: refuse to negotiate on such terms and appear as a war-minded belligerent to Democrats, or accept the terms and admit the ultimate failure of the war effort, angering Union supporters. Both could prove disastrous to his reelection. The effort collapsed, to Lincoln's benefit, when investigations revealed that that the delegation had no official authority to negotiate for the Confederacy.

JULY 24, 1864
EDITORIAL
THE "PEACE" CORRESPONDENCE—A PRETTY PLOT SPOILED.

Two problems press upon the rebel mind: How to whip GRANT and how to defeat LINCOLN. The more they are baffled in the first, the more anxiously they set to the second. It is plain that to accomplish this latter, any indirect means can be employed. Votes only can defeat LINCOLN and rebels have no votes. The point, then, is: How to secure the votes of others? or, in other words, how to augment the opposition party of the North? The great strength of Mr. LINCOLN is, that he represents the only genuine war spirit of the country. Therefore to prevent his reelection, some device must be found that shall, for a time at least, disconcert this war spirit. The first attempt in this line has just been tried on the Canadian frontier.

Rebels of note show themselves there who pretend that they came on a peace errand. On its face no errand could be more respectable. Every Northern man, who has the feeling of a man, craves peace just as soon as it can be secured with safety to his country. The *quasi* peace agents ask to go to Washington. It is assumed that they are the bearers of propositions, and they have authority to treat upon them. Leave is granted, but they will not assert that they have any propositions, or that they have been authorized to treat!— only that they are "in the confidential employment of their Government," and would be *subsequently* invested with all needful authority. It was calculated that thus an interview by these really irresponsible men could be had with PRESIDENT LINCOLN, without any definite propositions on their part, and with an opening for JEFF. DAVIS afterward to disavow whatever they might say or do. On their own private account they might talk ever so liberally about coming back into the Union, and make ever so fair professions; and yet bind their master to nothing, while at the same time they manage to fix upon Mr. LINCOLN the odium of refusing peace overtures. Out of this would have come excellent electioneering capital for the Copperheads until November. The people will be called upon to pay in the heavy taxes which have been levied, and to meet the heavy quotas on the new draft. If it can be made to appear to the people that the war is needlessly continued, that the rebels are anxious to come back peacefully into the Union, and that Mr. LINCOLN will do nothing to further that object, of course it must tell prodigiously against him at the ballot-box. The Copperhead candidate once elected, JEFF. DAVIS would be master of the situation.

President LINCOLN met this nice little plan with that direct good sense and firm principle that have so often baffled the trickery of his enemies. He declared that "any proposition which embraces the restoration of peace, the integrity of the whole Union, and the abandonment of Slavery, and which comes by and with an authority that can control the armies now at war against the United States, will be received and considered by the Executive Government of the United States, and will be met on liberal terms." There was no room for the play of bad faith here. Peace advances would be welcomed, but must come, if at all, from a responsible quarter, and look only toward the restoration of the Union. Here was an absolute test of the real spirit and purpose of the *quasi* Peace Commissioners. The truth comes out at once. In their labored reply, charged up to the brim with cheap indignation, they say: "Those who control our armies are the servants of the people, not their masters, and they have no more inclination than they have a right to subvert the social institutions of the sovereign States, to overthrow their established Constitutions, or to barter away their priceless heritage of self-government." This is equivalent to saying that there can be no negotiation with JEFF. DAVIS, who is the Commander-in-Chief of "our armies," *except upon the basis of a negotiation of the independence of "the Confederacy."* It discloses that the peace which they seek is a peace issuing only from a division of the Union. A peace of that character is not one which even the Copperheads themselves dare make an issue before the people.

THE DEMOCRATIC CONVENTION

In late August the Democratic Party assembled in Chicago to select their presidential nominee.
The convention matched the energy of the Union Party's convention, but lacked its agreement.
Early bitter arguments divided the party over the seating of delegates from the reconstructed

state of Louisiana and the territories. Attacks upon Gen. George McClellan, the leading candidate, followed quickly. Most damaging for McClellan was that as the commander of Union forces, he had carried out many of Lincoln's war orders that the convention was now vilifying. The discord of the convention boded ill for the party's election hopes.

AUGUST 31, 1864
THE CHICAGO CONVENTION

No Nomination Made Yesterday.

The Platform and How It Was Adopted.

A Piece for the Peace Democrats.

A SOP FOR THE SOLDIERS.

HIGH DUDGEON OF THE PEACE MEN

A Furious Speech by Congressman Harris, of Maryland.

McClellan Denounced As a Tyrant.

He is Nailed to the Wall on Arbitrary Arrests.

A STORMY TIME IN PROSPECT.

CHICAGO, Tuesday, Aug. 30.

The National Democratic Convention reassembled at 10 o'clock this morning.

The attendance both inside and outside the Wigwam is even greater than yesterday.

The proceedings of the convention were opened by Bishop WHITEHOUSE, who first read from the Psalms of David, following with an impressive prayer, the delegates and audience standing.

The Committee on Credentials reported against the admission of delegates from the Territories, Louisiana or District of Columbia; also, to admit both delegations from Kentucky, each delegate to cast half a vote.

The report was adopted. . . .

It was then moved that the Convention proceed to the nomination of a candidate for President.

Mr. JOHN P. STOCKTON, of New-Jersey, in behalf of the delegation of that State, nominated Gen. GEORGE B. McCLELLAN.

Mr. S. S. COX, of Ohio, in behalf of a portion of the Ohio delegation, seconded the nomination.

Mr. SAULSBURY, of Delaware, nominated Gov. POWELL, of Kentucky.

Mr. POWELL returned his thanks to the gentleman, but he firmly believed that the crisis demanded that the candidate of the party should come from a non-slaveholding State. Believing so, he begged the gentleman and his colleagues from the gallant State of Delaware, to withdraw his name.

Mr. STEWART, on behalf of the Ohio delegation, nominated THOMAS H. SEYMOUR.

Mr. WICKLIPP, on behalf of a portion of the delegation from Kentucky, nominated FRANKLIN PIERCE.

Mr. HARRIS, of Maryland, seconded the nomination of THOMAS H. SEYMOUR, and proceeded to eulogize his party services and abilities. Mr. HARRIS continued as follows:

One man nominated here to-day is a tyrant. [Cheers and hisses.] He, it was, who first initiated the policy by which our rights and liberties were stricken down. That man is GEORGE B. McCLELLAN. [Confusion.] Maryland, which has suffered so much at the hands of that man, will not submit to his nomination in silence. His offences shall be made known. This Convention is a jury appointed by the people to pass upon the merits of the public men whose names may be presented for the support of the great Democratic party. Gen. McCLELLAN, I repeat, is a tyrant. [Great confusion.] He stood here to indict him.

A DELEGATE—I call him to order.

The President said that he hoped there was no man present who would deny the right of free speech. Certainly no Democrat will. At the same time he hoped that no delegate would feel called upon to pursue a course of remarks so offensive as to interfere with the harmony of the convention.

Mr. HARRIS read McCLELLAN's order of arrest against the Maryland Legislature, and proceeded to comment upon the same; but the confusion was so great that the speaker could not be heard, except to say that all the charges of usurpation and tyranny that can be brought against Lincoln and Butler he can make and substantiate against McClellan.

[Hisses, cheers, and cries of "Vote for Jeff. Davis."]

The President wished that the convention should come to order. There is no attack made here but can be made elsewhere; and the gentlemen against whom these charges are being made desires that they shall be made now and here, so that he can meet and explain them. These interruptions do injustice to ourselves, to the Speaker, and to the distinguished gentleman against whom they are made. Let the gentleman from Maryland have a full hearing, and afterward hear the other side from a gentleman who is ready and able to make a full explanation.

Mr. Harris proceeded to say, that McClellan was the assassin of State rights, the usurper of liberties, and that if nominated he would be beaten everywhere as he was at Antietam. He added that he could not go home and ask the members of that Legislature to vote for such a man. He would not himself vote for him. [Hisses.] Mr. Carrigan, of Pennsylvania, raised the point of order that the gentleman having said that he would not vote for McClellan, if nominated, he had no right to take part in the proceedings of the convention.

The President decided that the point of order was well taken, and amid the wildest confusion, Mr. Harris retired from the stand.

- -

Gen. George McClellan Nominated for President

After several days of intense argument, the Democrats unified behind George McClellan, former Union general. In a move to match the Union Party's campaign tactics, the vice-presidential nominee, George Pendelton, complemented McClellan well. While McClellan was known for twice commanding the Union forces in war, Pendelton was known for advocating a quick peace. The "war horse and peace horse" were matched against "the horse in mid-stream."

SEPTEMBER 1, 1864
CHICAGO CONVENTION.

McClellan Nominated for President.

Pendleton, of Ohio, for Vice-President.

Vallandigham Moves to Make the Nomination Unanimous.

A PEACE HORSE AND A WAR HORSE.

ADJOURNMENT OF THE CONVENTION.

It is Resolved Into a Permanent Body.

On motion, a committee of one from each State was appointed to inform the candidates of their nomination, and request their acceptance thereof.

On motion, it was resolved that one person from each State, selected by the delegates thereof, be appointed to form the National Executive Committee. On motion, it was resolved that 100,000 copies of the proceedings of the convention be printed.

Mr. TILDEN moved that the same ratio of representation which prevailed at this convention be the ratio of the next convention. Adopted.

On motion, it was resolved that the Democracy of the country be requested to meet in the different cities, and hold mass ratification meetings on the 17th September, the anniversary of the adoption of the Federal Constitution.

A vote of thanks to the officers of the convention, is adopted.

With nine cheers for the ticket, the convention adjourned, subject to the call of the National Committee.

- -

SHERMAN CAPTURES ATLANTA

On September 1, 1864, the city of Atlanta, Georgia, formally surrendered to Union forces under the command of Gen. William Tecumseh Sherman. This victory practically assured the victory of the Union armies in the South, and the reelection of President Lincoln in the North. With Atlanta firmly in Union control, and Union armies making further inroads throughout the South, the rebellion was clearly in retreat. The Democratic candidates who only two days earlier had declared the failure of the administration's war efforts now faced the embarrassment of an inevitable military victory.

SEPTEMBER 3, 1864
FALL OF THE REBEL STRONGHOLD.

A Great Battle on the Macon Railroad.

HOOD'S ARMY CUT IN TWAIN.

THE REBEL GENERAL HARDEE KILLED.

SHERMAN ENTERS THE CITY.

Official Bulletin from the War Department.

A THUNDERBOLT FOR COPPERHEADS.

THE APPROACHING DRAFT

Its Burdens Materially Lightened

Grant Wants but One Hundred Thousand More Men.

These to Finish the Rebellion and Restore Peace. . . .

SEPTEMBER 3, 1864
EDITORIAL
THE NEW AND GREAT VICTORY.

The great rebel stronghold of the Southwest—the position at which the powerful and ever-victorious army of Gen. SHERMAN has been aiming for four months—has fallen, and *Atlanta* is ours. Our forces entered it at noon yesterday.

This is a victory so great in itself, of such wide scope, such far-reaching result, such indisputable importance, that the country will receive the news of it with unbounded exultation. We have shown again and again the immense military value of Atlanta, and all that we have ever claimed on this point has been conceded by the South. The rebel military force in the Southwest can now find no point in all their territory of anything like its strength or value, and their army must soon break up into small and predatory hordes, which also will in due time be exterminated.

This great news comes to us while yet the country is all aglow about the naval triumph of the glorious old sailor, FARRAGUT—while yet we are contemplating GRANT'S vital victory upon the Weldon road. We have had triumphs all around of late—triumphs equal to any ever won by mortal arms or human valor. What an infamy it is that at such an hour croakers should be croaking, and Copperheads hissing, and men actually contemplating a disgraceful surrender to this thrice-accursed rebellion.

McClellan's Candidacy Falters

Following the fall of Atlanta, supporters fled the Democratic Party and embraced the now trium-phant Lincoln. Rumors flew that General McClellan had still not accepted the nomination, and might not, in order to avoid the now seemingly inevitable electoral defeat. The Democrats, once prepared for a jubilant run against a faltering president, now struggled to maintain party unity and faith.

SEPTEMBER 9, 1864
M'CLELLAN MEETING.
A Failure in Numbers and Enthusiasm.
FIREWORKS AND SPEECHES.

The Democracy of the City assembled at Union Square last evening to ratify the nominations of the Chicago Convention. Taking into consideration the fact that neither of the candidates have as yet signified their acceptance of the nomination, there was a considerable display of fire-works and noisy enthusiasm, but the speakers and the audience were evidently embarrassed and puzzled to know whether they had a standard-bearer for the Presidential campaign or not. Loud and numerous were the queries from the crowd. "Has he accepted?" and the answer invari-ably came back, "He has not, but he will." This was very unsatisfactory, but the pyrotechnics were very satisfac-tory, and the large portion of the audience who were drawn together to witness the unusually fine display of rockets, Roman candles and illuminated bombs, cared very little who headed the Democratic ticket or who declined to stand on a peace platform in a Major-General's uniform. Although the speaking was much better and the presence of many distinguished men lent éclat to the meeting, the attendance was not nearly as large as at the McClellan meeting gotten up by Hiram Ketchum several weeks ago. . . .

THE BROADWAY STAND.

Around this, the principal stand, there was a dense crowd early in the evening, which was entertained by a brass band, the firing of cannon and rockets, varied by occasional cheers for "Little Mac." At one period the pres-sure was so great as to threaten that which it remains for the people to do in November—the sweeping of the "plat-form" out of their path.

At 8 o'clock Mr. Luke Cozans organized the meeting by the nomination of Loring Andrews as Chairman.

He was interrupted in his remarks by the inquiry, "What does Mac say?" "McClellan accepts the nomina-tion," was the reply, which elicited a burst of enthusiasm. McClellan (said he) accepts the nomination, feeling that when the nation's life is in danger, no one man should place himself against it. [Cheers.]

SEPTEMBER 18, 1864
POLITICAL.
DEMOCRATIC RATIFICATION MEETING IN UNION SQUARE.
A LARGE CROWD PRESENT,
Plenty of Gas, Lanterns, Small Boys and Copper-heads.

Union Square was witness to another extensive and expensive mass meeting, in honor of the Democratic candidate for the Presidency. It is very doubtful if the distinguished Major-General, whose stolid features illu-minated by tallow candles formed such a feature of the display, ever smelt so much gun-powder in the whole course of his military career. Indeed if the Peace party would find as many ball cartridges at the gunnery as they have blank cartridges for the sake of the noise, the war would soon end; or if all the little boys who were oblig-ing enough to carry Chinese lanterns through the streets last night, would enter the army as musicians, the rebels might be drummed into the Gulf of Mexico in less than a month. This was, undoubtedly, as noisy, numerous, and heterogeneous an assemblage of men, women, little girls and babies, as has been gathered in since the City Fathers gave their annual exhibition of fireworks on 4th of July last. The fact was that the meeting lacked stamina. Instead of earnest men, eagerly seeking instruction upon national topics from the leaders of their party, a crowd of men, women, and children, collected to look at the illuminations and pyrotechnics, eat peaches and oranges, and have a good time. Much gratitude they undoubtedly felt to the managers for the entertainment afforded them, but apparently the last thing thought of was listening to the speakers.

. . . .

ALLEGED SCANDAL WEEKS BEFORE THE ELECTION

Just a month before ballots were to be cast, a scandal broke implicating Gen. F. P. Blair, one of the highest ranking members of the Union army. Blair was alleged to have tried to broker a deal—reportedly on the behest of President Lincoln—that would give General McClellan a high ranking military post in return for declining the Democratic nomination in Chicago. With little else to campaign on, the Democrats pushed the issue, but were quickly stifled by a series of denials and a lack of evidence.

OCTOBER 10, 1864
EDITORIAL
THE PRESIDENT AND GEN. MCCLELLAN.

The Copperhead press has been making a great deal of capital out of an alleged offer made by F. P. BLAIR, Esq., to Gen. McCLELLAN. It has said that Mr. BLAIR had told the General that the President would give him a command in the field, *provided* he would decline being a candidate for the Presidency at the Chicago Convention. It was assumed and charged that in doing this Mr. BLAIR had acted for the President, and that the latter was therefore responsible for the offer.

In another column we publish a letter from Mr. BLAIR on this subject. He states, in the first place, that Mr. LINCOLN not only did not authorize him to make any such proposition to Gen. McCLELLAN, but that he did not know of his intention to see him on that or any other subject, or of his purpose to visit New-York at all. He says, in the next place, that he never made any such offer to Gen. McCLELLAN, or anything which could be construed into an offer of a command in the field on that or any other condition. And, in the third place, he states what he did say to Gen. McCLELLAN on that and other subjects. He *advised* him not to be a candidate for the Presidency, because he was certain to be defeated, and under such circumstances that he could never hope to rise again. He also advised him to apply to the President for a command in the field, because his military knowledge enabled him to be of service to the country in that capacity, and it was due to his friends, who believed he had talent, to evince a willingness to use it.

Now, in all this, we must say Mr. BLAIR showed his usual good sense. His advice was good, and the reasons which he gave for it were good also. Gen. McCLELLAN will see the day when he will regret that he did not follow it. But Mr. BLAIR's positive and explicit statement, that the President had nothing to do with this conversation, that he knew nothing of it or of his interview with Gen. McCLELLAN, ought to put a *quietus* on the story. There is little reason, however, to suppose that it will. The Opposition party and press are too short of material for carrying on the war against President LINCOLN, to afford to throw away so telling a fiction. And when we see the *National Intelligencer* willing to sacrifice its hitherto carefully-nursed reputation for candor and fair-dealing, and laboring through three columns of sophistry to fasten this imputation on the President in the face of Mr. BLAIR's distinct disavowal of all authority, there is not much reason to hope that the less scrupulous organs of that party will take a different course.

The *Intelligencer* is also striving to make a great deal out of a public statement said to have been made by Mr. MONTGOMERY BLAIR to the effect that the President had "concerted with Gen. GRANT to give Gen. McCLELLAN a command *if* the latter would turn his back on the Chicago nomination."

We have no evidence that Mr. BLAIR ever made any such statement. If he did, he made it without authority, for it certainly is not true. President LINCOLN did once ask Gen. GRANT whether Gen. MCCLELLAN would be acceptable to him and useful to the country as commander of a *corps* in the army of the Potomac; but he never said or intimated to Gen. GRANT or any body else, nor did he ever *think* of giving him such a command or of offering it to him on condition of his turning his back on a Presidential nomination. Whatever "conditions," if any, were suggested or thought of in this connection were of a purely military character, and related solely and exclusively to the General's probable usefulness in the field.

NINETEENTH-CENTURY CAMPAIGN REGALIA

Campaigns of the late 1800s utilized the only media available, newspapers, but also heavily relied upon party activists to spread enthusiasm for their candidate. Activists often paraded in complete campaign uniforms, including badges, banners, and torches, all bearing the name and likeness of their favored candidate.

OCTOBER 12, 1864
ADVERTISEMENT.
CAMPAIGN SUPPLY WAREHOUSE.

WAR EAGLE UNIFORMS COMPLETE.

War Clubs, Caps, Eagles, Badges, Aprons, Banners, Torches, Lanterns. Candles, &c.

Out of town orders filled at once. The cheapest house in the City. CAMPBELL & CO. No. 215 New Canal-St.

ANTI-IRISH RHETORIC TARGETS DEMOCRATIC SUPPORTERS

Solid supporters of the Democratic Party included Irish immigrants. Among the most disparaged groups among new citizens, the Irish reportedly registered en masse just prior to elections and cast numerous, and frequently illegal, ballots for their chosen party. Their low status in society, reputed fondness for alcohol, and their alleged use of fraudulent voting combined to make them a reviled group in 1860s New York. This campaign acronym, using a series of popular alcoholic drinks to spell out "Vote for MacClellan" [*sic*] was one of many the disparaging explanations of the loyalty of the Irish to the Democratic Party.

> If the cause can be preserved in alcohol, there is yet hope for it.

NOVEMBER 8, 1864
VOICES FROM THE BOTTLES—A STRONG APPEAL FOR MCCLELLAN.

Travelers by the Erie Railroad who may chance to step into the Lackawaxen House in waiting for the cars, may see some curious specimens, both in life and print, of the sort of allies that now follow the banners of the Democratic leaders. Hanging on the wall of a low rum-drinking tavern, appears the following:

AN ACROSTIC.
V oice of the People.
O tard Brandy,
T om and Jerry,
E xtra Bourbon Whisky.
F rench Brandy,
O ld Ale,
R ye Whisky.
G in Cocktail,
E xtra Old Wine,
N ew Cider.
M ilk Punch,
A pple Jack,
C laret Punch,
C ognac Brandy,
L ondon Porter,
E xtra Old Holland Gin,
L ager Beer,
L ondon Brown Stout,
A mber Ale,
New Ale.

If the cause can be preserved in alcohol, there is yet hope for it.

The friend who communicates the above adds the statement, that when, last week, a large body of clergymen were passing over that portion of the road, and some one passed through the cars to get a vote from the passengers, and the McClellan ticket was found to be at a heavy discount, a Hibernian gentleman aboard was heard to observe: "Ye'll see a different vote from that, when the *dirt train* comes down." Thus will the working men from Ireland go to the polls to vote free labor down, and to give their indorsement to the Southern theory, that the common laborer is in his proper place when under a master.

· ·

Secretary Seward Campaigns for Lincoln on Eve of Election

The day before the election Secretary of State William Seward, a former governor of New York, returned home to cast his vote and address a crowd in Auburn, New York. He described the debate over the aims of the war as it neared its conclusion and as the end of slavery approached. The final evidence of the South's declining ability to resist, he declared, "will appear immediately on the announcement of the reelection of Abraham Lincoln."

NOVEMBER 8, 1864
MR. SEWARD AT AUBURN.

His Views on the Election and the Crisis.

THE POLICY OF THE GOVERNMENT

THE GREAT ISSUE OF THE DAY.

Peace or War—Union or Disunion—Salvation or Ruin.

A Statesmanlike and Philosophical Speech.

Special Dispatch to the New-York Times.
AUBURN, N. Y., Monday, Sept. 7.

Secretary SEWARD, laying aside the duties of the State Department to attend to the higher duty that to-morrow engages the attention of the American people, came home to Auburn on Saturday last to cast his vote for ABRAHAM LINCOLN. This evening he addressed an assemblage of the people of Auburn, who crowded Corning Hall to overflowing to hear the views of their illustrious townsmen on the issue of the hour. It has been Mr. SEWARD'S wont for many years to speak in Auburn on the eve of election, and these free off-hand speeches to his friends and neighbors have frequently been found to convey matters of world-wide importance. The impressive event in our national history on the very eve of which this address was delivered, gave even more than wonted importance to the declarations of the Secretary. It need hardly be added, that speaking to an audience of neighbors and friends, among whom Mr. SEWARD has for many years lived, and with whom acquaintance has ripened into love, he was heard and followed with rapt attention and rapturous applause.

W. S.

FELLOW-CITIZENS: Of course you understand that I have come home to vote. [Cheers, and cries of, "That's what we want now!"] To vote here for the tenth time in ten out of the nineteen Presidential elections which the people of the United States have enjoyed. [Applause.] A change or succession in the executive power of a nation is always vital, and that change in our country constitutes a perpetually recurring crisis. The elector is mortal. I have come home to exercise my suffrage as heretofore, with the conviction, which I suppose you all entertain for yourselves, that this may be my last time. [Cries of, "We hope not." Cheers.]. . .

What remains for me to say, is to warn you against misrepresentations of the issue. There is no question before you of abandoning the war measures against slavery and substituting for them a policy of conservation or concession to slavery. [Cheers.] Those measures are a part of the war. [Cheers.] It is for the nation in a state of war and not for the nation in a future state of peace, that the Government is acting, and of course that we are voting. [Applause.] There is no question before you of changing the object of the war from the maintenance of the Union to that of abolishing slavery. Slavery is the mainspring of the rebellion. The Government necessarily strikes it in the very centre as well as upon every inch of its soil. [Cheers and cries of "It's dying out!"] In my poor judgment the mainspring is already broken, and let the war end when it will, and as it may, the fear that that mainspring will recover its elasticity may give us at present no uneasiness. [Cheers.] Before the war slavery had the patronage and countenance of the United States against the whole world. Its inherent error, guilt, and danger are now as fully revealed to the people of the United States as they have heretofore been to the outside world. Before the calamitous war in which slavery has plunged the country shall end, it will be even more hateful to the American people than it already is to the rest of mankind, while their condemnation of it will remain unchanged. [Applause.] The Opposition will not succeed in misleading you, I am sure, by telling you that you have a question of immediate peace or war involved in the present issue. War, and not peace, you have. Already, God knows that it is severe and painful enough. If I could think of taxes in the face of national death, I should say that our taxes are heavy enough. If I could think of personal interests, affections or sympathies in the face of an insolent public enemy in arms, I should say that men enough have been maimed and slain. But when we shall have said all these things, the actual situation of the country will still be before us, unchanged. It is a state of civil war, and not of peace. [Cheers.]

Persons ask me on every hand, "Is the war to last forever?" "How long is the war to last?" I answer the war will not last forever, but it must continue until we give up the conflict, or the enemy give up the conflict. [Cries of "That's the talk," and cheers.] Are you prepared to give up the conflict? [Cries of "No, never!"] You say, "No, never," Why? Because in that case you give up the national life. [Cheers.] In any and every event. . . .

You have already abundant evidences of the exhaustion of the rebels, but not yet evidence of their consciousness of that exhaustion. Those evidences will appear immediately on the announcement of the reelection of ABRAHAM LINCOLN. [Cheers.] You would have had those evidences earlier if you had rendered this verdict sooner. You will have them all the sooner after the verdict in proportion to the unanimity and determination with which it is spoken. [Loud cheers.]

● ●

LINCOLN WINS REELECTION

The Times proclaimed "Glorious Result Yesterday" as President Lincoln and the Union Party swept to an apparent easy victory. The partisan nature of the era was evident in the headlines, but much of the rhetoric was vindicated, as the next day's editorial discusses. Lincoln's determination, despite accusations of heavy-handedness and unconstitutional actions, ultimately prevailed, and his leadership would ultimately be credited for bringing the Civil War to its imminent conclusion.

1864 POPULAR VOTE

STATE[1]	TOTAL VOTE	ABRAHAM LINCOLN (REPUBLICAN) VOTES	%	GEORGE B. McCLELLAN (DEMOCRAT) VOTES	%
California	105,890	62,053	58.6	43,837	41.4
Connecticut	86,958	44,673	51.4	42,285	48.6
Delaware	16,922	8,155	48.2	8,767	51.8
Illinois	348,236	189,512	54.4	158,724	45.6
Indiana	280,117	149,887	53.5	130,230	46.5
Iowa[2]	138,025	88,500	64.1	49,525	35.9
Kansas	21,580	17,089	79.2	3,836	17.8
Kentucky	92,088	27,787	30.2	64,301	69.8
Maine[3]	115,099	68,104	59.2	46,995	40.8
Maryland	72,892	40,153	55.2	32,739	44.9
Massachusetts	175,493	126,742	72.2	48,745	27.8
Michigan[4]	160,023	88,551	55.3	71,472	44.7
Minnesota	42,433	25,031	59.0	17,376	40.9
Missouri	104,346	72,750	69.7	31,596	30.3
Nevada	16,420	9,826	59.8	6,594	40.2
New Hampshire	69,630	36,596	52.6	33,034	47.4
New Jersey	128,744	60,724	47.2	68,020	52.8
New York	730,721	368,735	50.5	361,986	49.5
Ohio	471,283	265,674	56.4	205,609	43.6
Oregon	18,350	9,888	53.9	8,457	46.1
Pennsylvania[5]	572,707	296,391	51.7	276,316	48.3
Rhode Island	23,067	14,349	62.2	8,718	37.8
Vermont	55,740	42,419	76.1	13,321	23.9
West Virginia	34,877	23,799	68.2	11,078	31.8
Wisconsin	149,342	83,458	55.9	65,884	44.1
TOTALS	**4,030,291**	**2,220,846**	**55.1**	**1,809,445**	**44.9**

1. Eleven Confederate states did not participate in the election because of the Civil War.

2. Figures from *Iowa Official Register, 1913–1914.*

3. Figures from Maine's Executive Council minutes.

4. Figures from *Michigan Manual, 1913,* p. 689.

5. Figures from Pennsylvania's *Manual,* 1865.

OTHER VOTES	%	PLURALITY	
—	0.0	18,216	R
—	0.0	2,388	R
—	0.0	612	D
—	0.0	30,788	R
—	0.0	19,657	R
—	0.0	38,975	R
655	3.0	13,253	R
—	0.0	36,514	D
—	0.0	21,109	R
—	0.0	7,414	R
6	0.0	77,997	R
—	0.0	17,079	R
26	0.1	7,655	R
—	0.0	41,154	R
—	0.0	3,232	R
—	0.0	3,562	R
—	0.0	7,296	D
—	0.0	6,749	R
—	0.0	60,065	R
5	0.0	1,431	R
—	0.0	20,075	R
—	0.0	5,631	R
—	0.0	29,098	R
—	0.0	12,721	R
—	0.0	17,574	R
692	0.0	411,401	R

NOVEMBER 9, 1864
GLORIOUS RESULT YESTERDAY.

Election of Lincoln and Johnson.

Terrible Defeat of McClellan.

THE UNION TRIUMPHANT.

New-England a Solid Phalanx.

New-York for Lincoln and Fenton

Defeat of Governor Seymour and His Friends.

Gain of Five Union Congressmen in the State.

Election of Raymond, Dodge, Darling, Conklin and Humphrey.

Pennsylvania Union on the Home Vote.

HEAVY UNION GAINS.

MARYLAND AND DELAWARE ALL RIGHT.

Heavy Union Gains in New-Jersey.

The Great Northwest Solid for Lincoln.

DETAILS OF THE RETURNS.

THE VOTE OF THE CITY. . . .

NOVEMBER 10, 1864
EDITORIAL
THE GREAT DECISION—THE GLORIOUS RESULT—ITS SIGNIFICANCE AND ITS LESSON.

The country has, after four years' experience of it, given an emphatic adhesion to the policy of President LINCOLN. Any objections to it, grounded on the assumption, which has been so loudly put forward, that he had used the powers of the Government in a way of which the country did not dream when it lodged them in his hands, and of which it has not approved since it has witnessed it, are now completely disposed of. The nation has watched his manner of administering the Government for four years.

It knows all about the confiscation act, the "arbitrary arrests," the emancipation proclamation, the conscription acts, the "bastiles," the public debt, the test oaths, the dismissal of GEORGE B. McCLELLAN, and the employment of negro soldiers; there is hardly any subject upon which it has not heard Mr. LINCOLN'S opinions. There is no charge which his opponents bring against him, with which it is not perfectly familiar. It knows that he tells "little stories" to people who call upon him; that he is not handsome; that his clothes are not well made; that he is unable to prevent our armies from occasionally meeting with reverses in Georgia or elsewhere, when he is in Washington; that he did not prevent the *Alabama* from making her escape from Liverpool; that the roads in Virginia were muddy in the first year of his administration; and that a drought occurred in the last; and yet, knowing all these things, the majority of the people of the loyal States have deliberately, and after full discussion, expressed their desire that he shall continue to hold office during four years more.

We trust, therefore, that the charge of abusing his trust, which has occupied so prominent a place in the vituperations of his enemies during the last three years, will now be abandoned, and that the Copperhead scribes will address themselves henceforward to the somewhat arduous task of proving to the people of the United States, that they neither understand their own interests nor are fit to be guardians of their own honor.

The task before the country now is not to find out some other plan of ending the war, but to end it speedily on the plan at present in use. A large portion of the public has spent their time for the last four years, not in aiding in its prosecution, but in cudgeling their brains to devise some way of escaping from it. The people have now decided that it is to be fought out to the end, and we hope that the gentlemen who will find their occupation gone by this decision, will take up the worthier one of helping their neighbors to bring this disastrous contest to a close in a way that will leave the national authority unimpaired; and no way will leave it unimpaired which involves the smallest concession to the doctrine that the existence of this Government depends on the willingness of a minority of the citizens to live under it; and any attempt at negotiation, or conciliation, or compromise, which concedes in the smallest degree the right of the minority to break up our national political organization, would be just as calamitous, just as much fraught with ruin, as the total defeat of our armies.

We cannot admit this for any purpose, not even for the purpose of bringing about instant peace; for any such admission would leave the cause of the war untouched, and leave us liable at any moment to a convulsion even more terrible than that through which we are now passing; and it is hardly necessary to say, that there is no nation which could live long with such a peril impending over it, without the utter loss of conscience, of dignity, and the utter extinction of the national prosperity.

The voice of the people is, therefore, still for war. We believe that this emphatic declaration of their sentiments will do much to bring the war to a close; but until then they are the best friends of peace and liberty who do most to make the fighting fierce and vigorous. We have in Tuesday's edition afforded a demonstration of the determination and the fortitude, tenacity and self-restraint, which freedom develops, for which the friends of popular government all over the world will thank us. There is no corner of the globe where the manner in which the American people spoke its will on Tuesday, will not give courage and confidence to those who look forward to the time when the people of all civilized nations will administer their own affairs; but to justify their expectations fully, we must follow our brave words with brave deeds; we must be strong and vigilant in war, as we have shown ourselves wise in council.

- -

LINCOLN CELEBRATES VICTORY

Two days after the election, President Lincoln attended a jubilant celebration in Washington. In his typical and incomparable eloquence, he thanked the people and urged them forward in supporting the "brave soldiers and seamen, and their gallant and skillful commanders." His speech highlighted how the ordinary course of an election, even during such tumultuous times as the Civil War, marked the extraordinary character of the American people. The sense of optimism and hope was palpable in Washington, as the newly reelected president prepared for his second term.

NOVEMBER 11, 1864
CONGRATULATING THE PRESIDENT.

A Serenade by the Clubs, and a Speech by Mr. Lincoln.

WASHINGTON, Thursday, Nov. 10.

The several Lincoln and Johnson Clubs of the District of Columbia called on Mr. LINCOLN to-night, and gave him a serenade in honor of his reelection. There was, in addition, an immense concourse of spectators of both sexes in front of the Executive Mansion. The firing of a field-piece was of frequent occurrence, adding to the excitement of the occasion, The President appeared at an upper window, and when the cheers with which he was greeted ceased, he spoke as follows:

"It has long been a grave question whether any Government not too strong for the liberties of the people can be strong enough to maintain its own existence in great emergencies. On this point the present rebellion brought our Republic to a severe test, and a Presidential election occurring in regular course during the rebellion, added not a little to the strain. If the loyal people, united, were put to the utmost of their strength by the rebellion, must they not fall when divided and partially paralyzed by a political war among themselves? But the election was a necessity. We cannot have free Government without elections, and if the rebellion could force us to forego or postpone a national election, it might fairly claim to have already conquered and ruined us. The strife of the election is but human nature practically applied to the facts of the case. What has occurred in this case must ever recur in similar cases. Human nature will not change. In any future great national trial, compared with the men of this, we shall have as weak and as strong, as silly and as wise, as bad and as good. Let us, therefore, study the incidents of this, as philosophy to learn wisdom from, and none of them as wrongs to be revenged." [Cheers.]

"But the election, along with its incidental and undesirable strife, has done good too. It has demonstrated that a people's government can sustain a national election in the midst of a great civil war. [Renewed cheers.] Until now it has not been known to the world that this was a possibility. It shows also how sound and how strong we still are. It shows that even among the candidates of the same party, he who is most devoted to the Union and most opposed to treason, can receive most of the people's votes. [Applause.] It shows also, to the extent yet known, that we have more men now than we had when the war began. Gold is good in its place, but living, brave and patriotic men are better than gold. [Cheers and other demonstrations of applause.] But

the rebellion continues, and now that the election is over, may not all having a common interest reunite in a common effort to save the common country. [Cheers.] For my own part, I have striven and shall strive to avoid placing any obstacles in the way. [Cheers.] So long as I have been here I have not willingly planted a thorn in any man's bosom. While I am duly sensible to the high compliment of a reelection, and duly grateful as I trust to Almighty God for having directed my country to a right conclusion as I think for their good, it adds nothing to my satisfaction that any other man may be disappointed by the result. [Cheers.] May I ask those who have not differed with me to join with me in this same spirit toward those who have? And now let me close by asking three hearty cheers for our brave soldiers and seamen, and their gallant and skilful commanders."

The three cheers were enthusiastically given, accompanied by music and the sound of cannon.

The crowd in part proceeded to the residence of Secretary SEWARD, who in the course of his remarks, said he came on the stage of action some years after the Revolutionary war, and used to hear his parents talk about the vast number of tories who were opposed to the war, and what surprised him was that after twenty-five or thirty years, there was not a tory found in the United States. He could not exactly understand where they had gone to. [Laughter.] During the War of 1812, the Federalists used to carry the intervening elections just as the Democrats carried the election in New-York in 1862, but when the war came to a close, and ended in victory, we had the era of good feeling, and from that time till now, we cannot find an old Federalist. His judgment was, when we all came together, and when the Stars and Stripes again wave over Richmond, in two or three years you will have to look mighty sharp to find a Secessionists or a rebel sympathizer. [Laughter and applause.] After refuting the assertion that the war is a failure he said during the first year of the war the African slave trade in the United States was suppressed; in the second year negroes were brought to be soldiers of freedom; in the third year slavery was abolished in the District of Columbia, and in the fourth slavery was abolished in Maryland. If the Democrats think the war is a failure thus far, when Congress comes together they will adopt a constitutional amendment, to abolish slavery throughout the

United States. [Cheers.] If slavery shall not cease, it will not be the fault of the Administration. Then we shall have an era of good feeling and harmony, and resume our bright career among the nations, and advance the interests of the country and freedom, self-government and humanity. All men will come to see the President a thorough loyal, devoted patriot and benevolent man, and he will take his place with WASHINGTON, FRANKLIN, ADAMS and JACKSON, among the benefactors of the human race. [Applause.]

Secretary WELLES was serenaded, and in the course of his remarks, said the gallant men of the navy, whether in the storm of battle, the night watch or the bivouac, would rejoice with those who had paid him this compliment on the result of the late election which had indorsed the President who had firmly stood by them. In the name of the officers and men of our gallant navy, be heartily joined in these congratulations, and in response to his suggestions three cheers were given for the navy.

Maj.-Gen. ORD being called for, appeared and merely said, while fighting armed rebels, they had achieved a victory over their foes at home, and now with a long pull, a strong pull and a pull altogether, we will soon knock 'em.

The crowd next proceeded to the residences of Secretaries FESSENDEN, STANTON and USHER, but they did not make their appearance.

Attorney-Gen. BATES made a brief congratulatory speech, and thus ended the night's proceedings.

ROBERT E. LEE SURRENDERS

Less than six months after Lincoln's reelection, Confederate general Robert E. Lee surrendered his troops to Union forces under Gen. Ulysses S. Grant at Appomattox, Virginia. The end of the war vindicated Lincoln's controversial wartime decisions and laid the groundwork for his eventual immortalization among the greatest of American presidents. The surrender of the South was treated by Lincoln as a step toward reconciliation among the states, not as the conquering of enemy territory. Even in victory, Lincoln hoped to forge a lasting union of the American people.

APRIL 10, 1865
HANG OUT YOUR BANNERS

UNION

VICTORY!

PEACE!

Surrender of General Lee and His Whole Army.

THE WORK OF PALM SUNDAY.

Final Triumph of the Army of the Potomac.

The Strategy and Diplomacy of Lieut.-Gen. Grant.

Terms and Conditions of the Surrender.

The Rebel Arms, Artillery, and Public Property Surrendered.

Rebel Officers Retain Their Side Arms and Private Property.

Officers and Men Paroled and Allowed to Return to Their Homes.

The Correspondence Between Grant and Lee.

OFFICIAL.

War Department, Washington
April 9, 1865–9 o'clock P. M.

To Maj.-Gen. Dix:

This department has received the official report of the SURRENDER, THIS DAY, OF GEN. LEE AND HIS ARMY TO LIEUT.-GEN. GRANT. on the terms proposed by Gen. GRANT.

Details will be given as speedily as possible.

EDWIN M. STANTON,
Secretary of War.

APRIL 10, 1865
PEACE!
THE SURRENDER OF GEN. LEE—THE END OF THE GREAT REBELLION.

The great struggle is over. Gen. ROBERT E. LEE and the Army of Northern Virginia surrendered yesterday to Lieut. Gen. U. S. GRANT and the Army of the Potomac.

The thrilling word PEACE—the glorious fact of PEACE—are now once again to be realized by the American people.

The profound joy of the nation in this auspicious result, cannot be expressed in effervescent enthusiasm and noisy huzzahs; but will appear in the form in which it is so fitly and opportunely proclaimed by the Secretary of War—ascriptions of Praise to Almighty God and offerings of honor to the great leader of our armies, whom he has used as his instrument to save the nation.

The history of blood—the four years of war, are brought to a close. The fratricidal slaughter is all over. The gigantic battles have all been fought. The last man, we trust, has been slain. The last shot has been fired.

We have achieved, too, that for which the war was begun—that for which our soldiers have so long and grandly fought, and that for which so many thousands of brave men have laid down their lives. We have achieved the great triumph, and we get with it the glorious Union. We get with it our country—a country now and forever rejoicing in Universal Freedom. The national courage and endurance have their full reward.

The event occurred on Palm Sunday—the day which commemorates the triumphal entry of Christ into Jerusalem. It will henceforth be a patriotic as well as a pious holiday in America.

Just four years almost to a day has the war lasted. It was on the 13th of April, 1861, that Sumter was surrendered to the rebels. It was on the 9th of April, 1865, that the great rebel army was surrendered to the power of the Union.

The surrender of the army of Gen. LEE solves a thousand difficulties that but lately threatened us in the future. It simplifies the work of pacification in the South. It gives hope for a speedy restoration of order and fraternity.

The correspondence between GRANT and LEE, which we give in full, is very direct and concise. GRANT proposed the surrender on Friday last, and in three days after LEE accepted the terms.

The terms proposed by GRANT are very simple, and doubtless had the approval of the President, who is at Richmond. We get all the rebel officers and soldiers, all the arms, artillery and public property; but the officers retain their side-arms, private baggage and horses. Each officer and man will be allowed to return to their homes, and will not be disturbed.

We have no idea that Jo. JOHNSTON'S forces or any of the other rebel bodies will be of any trouble after this great event. LEE nominally only surrenders his own immediate army; but he is commander of all the armed forces of the rebellion everywhere, and in one of his letters he speaks about negotiating with reference to the whole of the Confederate States forces under his command. This will undoubtedly be the upshot of the whole affair.

The great rebellion is crushed. The Republic is saved. PEACE comes again. To Heaven be the praise.

LINCOLN IS ASSASSINATED BY JOHN WILKES BOOTH

Just days after the end of the war Abraham Lincoln was assassinated as he watched a play at Ford's Theater in Washington. John Wilkes Booth led a bold plot to assassinate the president, vice president and secretary of state in one night, throwing the government into disarray. Of the three attempts, only Booth's attack on Lincoln was successful, but it was in some ways sufficient for his goal. The loss of Lincoln cast the nation into a protracted struggle over how best to reconstruct the South, turmoil that continued until 1876, the time of another critical election.

APRIL 15, 1865
AWFUL EVENT.
PRESIDENT LINCOLN SHOT BY AN ASSASSIN.

The Deed Done at Ford's Theatre Last Night.

THE ACT OF A DESPERATE REBEL

The President Still Alive at Last Accounts.

No Hopes Entertained of His Recovery.

Attempted Assassination of Secretary Seward.

DETAILS OF THE DREADFUL TRAGEDY.

[Official.]

War Department,
Washington, April 15—1:30 A. M.

This evening at about 9:30 P.M., at Ford's Theatre, the President, while sitting in his private box with Mrs. LINCOLN, Mrs. HARRIS, and Major RATHBURN, was shot by an assassin, who suddenly entered the box and approached behind the President.

The assassin then leaped upon the stage, brandishing a large dagger or knife, and made his escape in the rear of the theatre.

The pistol ball entered the back of the President's head and penetrated nearly through the head. The wound is mortal. The President has been insensible ever since it was inflicted, and is now dying.

About the same hour an assassin, whether the same or not, entered Mr. SEWARD's apartments, and under the pretense of having a prescription, was shown to the Secretary's sick chamber. The assassin immediately rushed to the bed, and inflicted two or three stabs on the throat and two on the face. It is hoped that the wounds may not be mortal. My apprehension is that they will prove fatal.

The nurse alarmed Mr. Frederick SEWARD, who was in an adjoining room, and hastened to the door of his father's room, when he met the assassin, who inflicted upon him one or more dangerous wounds. The recovery of Frederick SEWARD is doubtful.

It is not probable that the President will live throughout the night.

Gen. GRANT and wife were advertised to be at the theatre this evening, but he started to Bulington at 6 o'clock this evening.

All the members of the Cabinet except Mr. SEWARD, are now in attendance upon the President.

I have seen Mr. SEWARD, but he and Frederick were both unconscious.

Edwin M. Stanton
Secretary of War

THE CONGRESSIONAL ELECTIONS OF 1874

DEMOCRATS REVIVED BY CONGRESSIONAL VICTORY

Congressional elections in 1874 marked a transformation of American politics. Most obviously, Democrats won control of the U.S. House of Representatives for the first time since before the Civil War and restored their strong standing in the Senate. The United States again had a competitive two-party system.

But the change went beyond immediate results. The outcome established a new equilibrium between the two major parties and altered the state of party conflict for years to come. Harkening back to the close party competition of Whigs and Democrats before the Civil War, the election of 1874 created a rough balance between Republicans and Democrats that lasted for two decades.

Neither party gained definitive power during the period. In the eleven congressional elections beginning in 1874, the parties switched control six times in the House, four times in the Senate. The same party controlled both chambers only three times, and only twice did the same party hold both the White House and Capitol Hill. The result was a lengthy national stalemate, a time of slim and transient electoral decisions, resulting in inconsistent and incoherent public policies. This static equilibrium persisted until the GOP became a clear national majority in the realigning elections of 1894 and 1896.

SETTING OF THE ELECTIONS

The 1874 election came as the nation suffered the most severe economic crisis of the century, the Panic of 1873. After the Civil War, railroads had expanded rapidly as speculators laid new routes throughout the country, leading to extravagant credit loans to the railroad entrepreneurs. Their debt expanded so rapidly that the bubble burst, credit tightened, and a quarter of the railroads went bankrupt. Adding to the distress, President Ulysses S. Grant and the Republican Congress tightened the money supply by adopting the gold standard, eliminating paper and silver-backed currency, thereby reducing the capital available for loans. With money

Source: Library of Congress

Throughout the South, White Leagues, such as that depicted here in Louisiana, intimidated and disenfranchised black voters. Their efforts returned former Confederates to political power.

scarce, the country entered a six year "long depression." Major banks such as Jay Cooke & Company failed, farmers faced foreclosure, corporate profits disappeared, wages plummeted, and 14 percent of workers lost their jobs.

The consequent political protest was reinforced by reaction to Republican scandals. The most shameful acts involved executive officials, but Congress also shared in the dishonor. Its particular outrage was legislation, in 1873, to increase members' salaries retroactively by 40 percent.

The electoral environment also reflected the cooling fervor of the Civil War. By the 1874 election, nearly ten years after the conclusion of hostilities, the nation had tired of postwar regional and institutional conflict. When the war ended in 1865, the first official response had been conciliation of the

1874 MIDTERM ELECTION RESULTS

HOUSE

		MEMBERS ELECTED			GAINS/LOSSES	
ELECTION YEAR	CONGRESS	DEM.	REP.	MISC.	DEM.	REP.
1874	44th	181	107	3	+93	−96

SENATE

		MEMBERS ELECTED			GAINS/LOSSES	
ELECTION YEAR	CONGRESS	DEM.	REP.	MISC.	DEM.	REP.
1874	44th	29	46	−	+10	−8

North toward the South. Becoming president after Abraham Lincoln's assassination, Andrew Johnson set a soft path to reunion.

Soon after taking office, Johnson issued a proclamation of amnesty to "all persons who have directly or indirectly taken part in the rebellion," restoring their property except for slaves, while requiring only that they take oaths "to defend the Constitution of the United States and the Union of the States," and accept emancipation of slaves. Once these minimal conditions were accepted by a tenth of their prewar electorates, Johnson sought the quick readmission of the southern states to the Union. His efforts gained support from Henry Raymond, editor of *The New York Times,* who held a seat in Congress and chaired the Republican National Committee. But Johnson's indulgent Reconstruction policies soon aroused fervent opposition.

The defeated southerners grudgingly accepted legal emancipation, but showed no willingness to accept any change beyond nominal freedom for blacks as they resisted steps toward true civil and political equality. The new governments of the South tried to maintain past privileges, sending former Confederate officials to Congress and enacting "Black Codes" that virtually reinstituted slavery for emancipated slaves. To retain power, resistant whites organized the Ku Klux Klan and "White Leagues" to terrorize, control, and, when they desired, kill freed bondsmen.

Republicans in Congress would not accept these limited fruits of victory of the bitter Civil War. Instead they created a new and harsher congressional Reconstruction, bent on retribution rather than conciliation. Their goal was not only the absence of slavery, but empowerment and equality for the freedmen. To these ends, they imposed military occupation in place of the new civil governments, refused to seat the southern representatives first elected to Congress, disenfranchised large proportions of the white population, barred former Confederate officials from power, mandated suppression of the KKK, and legislated full Negro civil equality and suffrage in the conquered states.

To make their program permanent, the Republicans passed the sweeping Fourteenth Amendment to the Constitution and required its ratification by newly reconstructed southern state governments as a condition for readmission to the Union. The amendment created national citizenship for all persons born in the United States, required "due process of law" and "equal protection of the laws" for all persons, black or white, threatened the reduction of congressional representation for any state depriving (male) persons of suffrage, and repudiated all Confederate debts. To seal this revolution in national power, the Republican Congress added the Fifteenth Amendment, prohibiting the loss of suffrage on the basis of "race, color, or previous condition of servitude."

The clash between Congress and the executive branch soon led to President Johnson's impeachment by the House of Representatives, although he survived in office by a single vote in the Senate. But the ardor for a harsh Reconstruction soon cooled among northern voters. Instead, they twice elected Grant as president, endorsing his anodyne prescription, "Let Us Have Peace." Federal pressure eased, military forces were withdrawn from most states, and southern whites, their votes restored, turned to "Redeemers" to reclaim power, aided by ballot frauds and extensive intimidation of blacks. As the 1874 elections approached, only four southern states still had Republican state governments, and white resisters would soon also wrest control throughout the region. The Supreme Court contributed to this trend, voiding many of the Reconstruction statutes.

Civil rights for the freed slaves was a major issue in the congressional elections. The Radical wing of the Republican Party attempted to extend equality through legislation that would bar racial discrimination and segregation in places of public accommodation such as hotels, restaurants, and public transportation, and in jury selection, voting, schools, and even cemeteries. Although passed in the Senate, the legislation stalled in the House, its "social equality" opposed not only by Democrats but by President Grant and by less fervent Republicans from southern, border, and midwestern states. They were particularly interested in preserving educational segregation—which was in fact widespread and sometimes required in the North. Beating a retreat from the proposed statute, GOP candidates cautiously ignored the subject or advocated "separate but equal" schools.

Republicans found it easier to condemn the "outrages" of anti-black violence and support federal intervention to protect Negro voters. The Grant administration vacillated, but did intervene in elections in six Dixie states. The most extreme violence came in Louisiana. White vigilantes massacred seventy-one black militiamen in the town of Colfax in 1873 and seized armed control of the state government in September of 1874. For a time, two rival legislatures and governors made fraudulent electoral claims, until Grant tardily ordered federal troops to force the seating of the Republican claimants.

These violent events in the South provided an opportunity for Republicans to again "wave the bloody shirt," and revive Northern loyalties to the Union and the party. But the cause was losing its appeal, as the welfare of blacks became only one of many competing interests, rather than the paramount moral crusade. Northern opinion leaders now showed diminishing concern for racial equality. *The Times* editorialized against the civil rights bill, and editorial cartoonist Thomas Nast drew acidic critiques of Reconstruction. Critics ignored the achievements of the biracial state governments, blaming only blacks for their corruption and extravagant spending— and avoiding obvious comparisons to northern spoilsmen such as New York's Boss Tweed. The shift in public opinion was clear in early elections in 9 states, where Republicans lost 11 of their 62 congressional seats in New England and the Midwest.

The struggles of Reconstruction involved not only moral principles, but a contest for future political power in the entire nation. Republicans envisaged blacks, along with former Whigs, as the key to electoral control of the South

and the foundation for a long-term majority coalition spanning the nation's regions. But Democrats successfully countered, taking control of the South by enlisting business and planter interests, arousing poor whites with racist appeals, and intimidating or corrupting black voters. Northern voters also turned away from the Republicans in 1874, repelled by the economic crisis, government corruption, and their own racial antipathies. The stage was set for a Democratic revival throughout the nation.

THE RESULTS AND EFFECTS

The election resulted in the worst defeat for the Republican Party in its twenty-year history, a loss of 51 incumbents out of a total House membership of 292. The Democrats gained a historic victory, gaining 93 seats in the House, along with 10 new seats in the Senate, giving them a 181–110 House majority and a respectable 29–46 minority in the Senate. Four years later they would gain control of the Senate as well. Outside of the South, the Democrats swept major Republican strongholds in Illinois, Indiana, Massachusetts, New Jersey, Ohio, and Pennsylvania. Overall, the national Democratic congressional vote increased from 45.7 percent in 1872 to 52.2 percent in 1874, while Republicans decreased from 50.9 percent to 43.1 percent.

The 1874 balloting brought the largest party change in Congress of any election up to that time, the greatest party reversal of the nineteenth century, and a turnover virtually unmatched throughout the history of American congressional contests. In the next two decades of balanced party competition, Democrats would win majorities in 7 of 10 Houses, until the transformation of the party system in 1894 and 1896.

The 1874 election ended reconstruction of the South as envisioned by the Radical Republicans. Democratic representation in the new 44th Congress doubled from 28 to 56 of the 73 southern seats, the party moving from its previous minority position in most states to control of the House delegation in all southern states except Florida and South Carolina. Democrats also took over most state governments and gained complete control of the region after the next presidential election. Emblematic of the shift in power was its Confederate heritage: 80 of the 107 incoming representatives from the South and border states had served, and 35 had been generals in the rebel army. Even Andrew Johnson returned, selected as a senator from Tennessee the following year.

The long-term effect of the 1874 party division—ratified in the next presidential election—was the eventual establishment of a purely sectional politics, expressed in the limited competition between two one-party regimes, Republican in the North, Democratic in the South. In 1874 Democrats increased their vote in the southern and border states from 47.8 percent to 57.9 percent; when Reconstruction was fully ended in two years, the South would become politically monolithic. Chased from the region, the Republicans could win the House only with overwhelming victories everywhere else. Founded as a regional party two decades earlier, the GOP reverted to that status in 1874 and 1876, remaining geographically confined for decades.

After losing the 1874 congressional elections, Republicans attempted to limit the Democrats' future actions by passing legislation in the 1875 lame-duck session of the outgoing Congress, before the Democrats assumed control. They provided for a return to the gold standard within four years. Tariffs, which had been lowered slightly, were restored to previous high levels.

In a last-ditch effort toward racial equality, Republicans passed the Civil Rights Act of 1875, banning segregation in public accommodations such as restaurants and railroads, winning passage and Grant's signature by dropping the previous provisions for the desegregation of schools and cemeteries. But even this limited measure was overturned by the Supreme Court in 1883. The end of Reconstruction wrought by the elections of 1874 would institutionalize segregation in schools and public facilities and forestall the civic equality, voting rights, and economic opportunities promised to African Americans by the Civil War. That vision would be realized only after another nine decades of struggle.

The close party balance that followed the 1874 election limited the ability of the national government to develop long-range public policies. For the next two decades, recurrent disputes and party changeovers brought little innovation or consistency amid a national policy stalemate. Congress failed to resolve issues of silver coinage, monopoly corporations, tariffs, and civil service reform. The nation had much unfinished business.

• •

The Republicans Consolidate Power

Following Abraham Lincoln's assassination, Republicans consolidated power in the federal government and sought major social change in the conquered Confederacy. But Lincoln's successor as president, former Democrat Andrew Johnson, sought a quick and conservative reconstruction of the southern states. He argued with, defied, and insulted the Radical Republicans, leading Congress to attempt to remove him from office. Gen. Ulysses S. Grant, hero of the Union army, defeated Democrat Horatio Seymour to take the White House in 1868. Grant, a Republican, worked with a like-minded Congress to enact strong policies on Reconstruction, including the Fifteenth Amendment, which granted the vote to blacks. Invigorated, Republicans reelected Grant in 1872 and strengthened their control of Congress, which proved to be short-lived.

MAY 27, 1868
IMPEACHMENT.

The Final Vote Taken on the Second and Third Articles.

Acquittal of the President on Both Charges.

The Case Abandoned and the Court Adjourned.

Continuation of the Managers' Corruption Investigation.

MAY 27, 1868
CONGRESS AND IMPEACHMENT.

The closing of Impeachment and the adjournment of the Court will, we think, gratify the great body of the people. While there is—as there has been for a long time—a strong desire on the part of the Republican Party for the removal of Mr. JOHNSON from office, there has been no wish, among the people, to have this result brought about by any means that would not be universally recognized as just and fair. And we are inclined to believe that the course of the trial satisfied almost everybody that, however imprudent, overbearing and unjustifiable Mr. Johnson's conduct has been, the evidence did not convict him of such high crimes and misdemeanors as would warrant his conviction and removal from office.

Mr. JOHNSON is now to serve out the remnant of his term, unless he rushes into some renewed extravagance of action which shall provoke a renewal of the impeachment process. We trust he will make no further experiments on the forbearance of the people. He may now very well conclude that it is not for him to force his views of the Constitution, however just they may be, upon Congress and the country. He has certainly relieved himself from all responsibility for its violation.

The House, it will be seen, has ordered the continuance of the inquiry into the corruption by which the President's acquittal has been secured. This is well enough,—though we think it would have been better in every way to hand this whole matter over to the Senate, inasmuch as it is members of that body who are implicated. Enough, however, has already been shown to warrant, and indeed require, the continuance of the investigation; and we hope it will be made as rigid and thorough as possible. If any Senator *did* sell his vote on impeachment, he should be promptly expelled,—and we have no doubt he would be, if the crime were fairly brought home to him.

We hope that Congress will, in spite of all these proceedings, enter vigorously and earnestly upon the business which awaits its action. The Republican Party has adopted a platform of *principles,* but its sincerity in proclaiming them remains to be tested by the attempts it may make during the present session to apply them by practical legislation to the necessities and wants of this country. Let Congress promptly admit the reorganized Southern States, reduce the public expenditures, provide the requisite taxes, relieve the public burdens, and thus prepare the way for a Republican victory in November next.

NOVEMBER 4, 1868
GRANT'S GREAT TRIUMPH.

It is now seen that the assurance which the Republicans have always expressed in GRANT'S election was amply justified.

He has carried three-fourths of all the States of the Union; and he has carried them by larger majorities than were expected even by sanguine calculators.

It is fortunate for the country that the vote for him has been so large as to leave no possibility of dispute, no ground for questioning the validity of the election in any respect, and no necessity for close calculations or close shaving to prove a success.

All the frauds of the Democracy in the North,—all the coercion and intimidation of colored voters in the South,—have failed to give victory to the Democratic Party. They might carry New-York by a reign of fraud, and Louisiana

by a reign of terror;—they might carry Kentucky and Maryland by the votes of men who were lately arrayed in battle against the American flag;—they might have voted in Texas, Mississippi and Virginia, as they are threatened to do, and might have carried these States;—and yet the Republicans would have given them greater odds and still won a decisive success.

The country may well be congratulated on this result.

It has now been shown that the assurance of the Republicans before the election was not mere empty boasting. Their confidence was perfectly intelligible and natural. It was based on the fact that GRANT stood as the representative of the principles that are acknowledged to be of the highest importance to the American people, and for the maintenance of which a million of American citizens were but lately in arms. He represented the supremacy of the Union and the Constitution, the supremacy of liberty and loyalty, the supremacy of law, order and peace. For the past, he represented the triumphant ideas of the war; and for the future, he represented the ideas that constitute the foundation of national well-being. . . .

It was upon the profound appreciation of this matter by the American people that we based our confidence in GRANT's election. Not during this generation, nor during the next, will the people of this country lose sight of the great war, or forget the part played in it by those who have been leaders, or who may aspire to be leaders. To have been false to the Republic in that tremendous crisis, or to have been lukewarm in its service, will be a brand of political ruin for many a year to come. It will be useless during this century for any political party to nominate a Presidential candidate, who cannot show that he battled for the Union with hand and heart when rebellion had the sword at its throat. And in this determination the American people are perfectly justified—even from the highest grounds of conciliation, fraternity and peace.

MARCH 8, 1869
THE AMENDMENT OF THE CONSTITUTION REGARDING SUFFRAGE.

We presume there is little doubt now that the Fifteenth Amendment to the Constitution, regarding suffrage, will be promptly ratified by a sufficient number of State Legislatures to make it part of the fundamental law. Several of the States have already taken the necessary action, and others are evidently prepared to do so at the earliest moment. The strong expression of General GRANT, in his inaugural, in favor of such a course will probably hasten their action upon it.

The adoption of this amendment will put an end to further agitation of the subject, for a long time at least, and thus leave the Government of the country free to deal with its material interests and with the more pressing questions of public policy and administration which will arise from time to time.

We do not concur with those who predict that the question of Suffrage for women will speedily demand public action or engross public attention, or that the right of men to hold office without distinction of color or race, will absorb any great degree of public time or public thought for a long while to come. Until some decided practical advantage is to be gained, by a dominant political party, neither of these questions will be pressed to a decision: and both of them have, in our judgment, commanded more attention already than they will soon command again. With the adoption of the Fifteenth Amendment, we may fairly look upon the suffrage agitation as at an end, for the present political generation at all events:—and that consideration, of itself, affords a very powerful argument in favor of its adoption.

NOVEMBER 8, 1872
THE TIDAL WAVE.

Immense Republican Gains in all the Southern States.

Tennessee, Kentucky, Virginia and Florida all but Certain for Grant.

Great Republican Gains in Congress and the Legislatures.

A Question that is Asked by Everybody Everywhere:

Has Horace Greeley Actually Carried a Single State?

The latest dispatches, given below, increase the Republican victory.

We have more than two-thirds majority in Congress.

The chances are that Tennessee has gone for Grant. She has elected eight Republican Congressmen out of ten, and a Republican governor.

Kentucky is in doubt, and the chances are better for Republican than Democratic success.

Michigan swells her majority to 50,000, and claims the banner on gains, having gained 20,000 on 1868.

NOVEMBER 11, 1872
EDITORIAL
THE INHERENT STRENGTH OF THE REPUBLICAN PARTY.

It suits the purposes of the opposition Press to represent that the recent overwhelming victory of the Republican Party was a victory of a man rather than of a party; that it was the result of the enormous patronage concentrated in the hands of the President, which enabled him to re-elect himself. Further, it is pretended that while the Republican Party has really been weakened by the loss of Sumner, Schurz, Trumball, and others of its former leaders, Gen. Grant has strengthened himself and consolidated his "personal" Government by his hold on the offices and the machinery of the party, until he has virtually embodied it in his own person and made it tributary to his own aggrandizement. A look at the figures brought out by the election returns will entirely demolish this theory. These figures show that the result was purely a victory for Republicanism, and not of men; that Republican principles, now as heretofore, are much stronger with the people than any man who may be put forward to represent them. We have no doubt whatever that Gen. Grant, deservedly popular as he is, would have been as promptly and as unceremoniously dropped by the people, if he had turned traitor to his party, as were Sumner, Schurz, Trumball, or Greeley; and that, in such an event, not all the patronage of the Government, with a tenfold increase in amount, would have enabled him to secure a renomination of a re-election to the Presidency.

It will be found, on an examination of the returns, that the local candidates of the Republican Party everywhere ran very close to, and in some instances ahead of, the Presidential ticket. In this State, Gen. Dix ran ahead of Gen. Grant in Brooklyn and several other localities, while he will fall very little, if any, below the vote for President in the whole State. In New-Jersey, the vote for the Republican candidates for Congress exceeded, on the average, the vote for President. In Massachusetts, the vote for Washburn for Governor is only 1,200 less than that of Grant for President, while in several of the Congressional districts he runs ahead of the President.

And so, in nearly every State of the Union, it will be found that the Republican nominees for local and State offices ran nearly or quite up to the Presidential ticket. It was the inherent strength of the Republican Party, the unswerving faith of the great majority of the people of the United States in the principles and aims of that party, that carried the late election by such unprecedented majorities, and not hero-worship or the power of Government patronage. A majority, even, of the States lately in rebellion have at length come to believe in the wisdom and sound policy of Republican principles, if we are to judge by the recent election; and, with wise and prudent counsels, and a magnanimous course of action, there is no reason why the Republican Party may not retain control of the country and enjoy the confidence of the people for twelve years to come, as it has for twelve years past.

RECONSTRUCTION FALTERS

Reconstruction of the Confederacy comprised different, sometimes clashing goals. One aim was the peaceful reintegration of the defeated southern states into the Union. Another was the social transformation of the South through the implementation of racial equality. To foster the second goal, Republicans in Congress passed amendments to the Constitution banning slavery, granting citizenship to freed slaves, and granting black men the right to vote. They even passed a civil rights bill in the Senate. But these actions did not always produce the desired results. Reacting against Republican policies, southerners worked to return Democrats to power and repressed black citizens in outright defiance of the new laws. The North, tiring of a decade of conflict and facing united southern resistance, contemplated loosening its grip on the South.

FEBRUARY 13, 1870
RECONSTRUCTION—LAND AHEAD.

No American citizen, native or adopted, who values the honor and welfare of the Great Republic, can view with other feelings than those of heartfelt satisfaction the gradual solution of the difficult problem of Reconstruction. It was not to be expected, after the terrible experiences of such a war as that which convulsed the Union during four years, that the cessation of hostilities should be followed by the full sunshine of peace. In the Northern and Western States, indeed, which escaped comparatively unscathed, it is perhaps no marvel that so few traces remain of the stern and sanguinary struggle. But all through the sunny South, where war's desolating blast swept with such terrific violence, where the entire social system underwent so radical a change, it might well be thought that years and years must pass before the public could once more enjoy the blessings of peace, appreciate the benefits of law and order, and frankly acknowledge the boon of liberty and Union. Nor, indeed, if we listened only to the ravings out of that extreme partisan Press, whose main object seems to be to feed and perpetuate the passions and prejudices engendered by the fierce conflict, could we well persuade ourselves that any portion of the South had yet fairly begun to feel the happy influences of Reconstruction.

Such, nevertheless, is the undoubted fact. The South is recovering, and with marvelous rapidity, too, from the effects of the most terrific war that ever laid waste a country. And the South has but to accept the teachings of its own wisest and most unselfish statesmen, to follow the counsels of its most sincere and earnest well-wishers among the people and Press of the North, to insure for itself a career of prosperity hitherto unexampled. It may possibly be thought that the promptings of hope, no less than our interest in the success of Republican policy, have led us to draw a brighter future for the South than the facts themselves will justify. Let us cite a witness, then, whose testimony will not be disputed on either side; who cannot well be suspected of a disposition to exaggerate the promising state of affairs at the South, who certainly will not be charged with any undue partiality for the Republican policy or party. We refer to the *Journal of Commerce,*

"Never did New Year's dawn upon Texas in a more promising condition than on the 1st of January, 1870. An abundant yield of the various products of our soil, for which remunerative prices have been realized, has caused money to be plentiful and times easy. Out of debt, with a surplus in our State treasury of near $300,000, our financial condition is evidently satisfactory. * * The immigration, during the Winter has been unprecedented—coming from almost every State in the Union, and from many foreign countries. Many of these emigrants bring with them capital, character and enterprise. Among all who come to cast in their lots with us, *none are more heartily welcome than Yankees.* * * Recently we have received our first installment of Chinese immigrants, numbering about two hundred and fifty, designed for laborers on the Texas Central Railroad. They have, from both Press and people, met with a cardinal reception. The need of their labor is generally felt and acknowledged. It is the *unanimous* testimony from all sources that the freed people of our State have, during 1869, labored more cheerfully and industriously, and behaved themselves with more general propriety, *than ever before.* They have generally entered into contracts mutually satisfactory for another year."

Here is a pleasing picture, indeed, and one, too, drawn from life. What have our Democratic friends to say to the startling tidings herein communicated? The much-maligned "Yankee," the embodiment of all that is objectionable in Puritanism, Radicalism and Republicanism, made "heartily welcome" in an ultra Southern State. The hard-working, but, unhappily, copper-colored Chinese, whom the liberal and enlightened democracy of California prescribe as Pariahs, meeting with a "cordial reception" at the hands of the Southern chivalry. Above all, the enfranchised negro, that special object of Democratic prejudice and aversion, now made a participator in that "white man's government," and, conscious of his increased responsibility, rising with his new dignity, acknowledged on all hands to be laboring "more cheerfully and industriously," and behaving with more general propriety than ever before! What wonder that with such a condition of affairs the New Year should dawn so brightly upon the "Lone Star State!" And what encouragement, in the results already accomplished, for the Republican Party, upon whom so heavy a responsibility is devolved, to persevere in the good work of reconstruction on the broad basis of amnesty and suffrage.

FEBRUARY 28, 1871
EDITORIAL
IS HOSTILITY TO RECONSTRUCTION A DEMOCRATIC ISSUE FOR 1872?

The Louisville *Courier-Journal* objects to the interpretation the TIMES has placed upon FRANK BLAIR'S speech in the Senate, and the attitude of the Democratic Party toward reconstruction and the Fifteenth Amendment. We have represented hostility to that amendment and to reconstruction, as one of the issues to be presented by the Democracy in 1872; using Senator BLAIR'S declarations as proof of the determination to revive the reactionary and disorganizing policy enunciated in the Brodhead letter. Our Louisville contemporary, on the other hand, maintains that the refusal of the Democracy to indorse what the Republicans have accomplished does not imply a purpose to destroy it—that "no respectable element" in the Democracy disputes the validity of what has been done— that the intention is simply to fasten upon the Republican Party responsibility for its own acts, and that BLAIR'S speech has this significance and no more.

Now, what are the facts? When SEYMOUR and BLAIR were nominated in 1868, the Democratic Party distinctly asserted its ineradicable hostility to the scheme of reconstruction. BLAIR'S letter formed the keynote to the proceedings of the Convention in this respect. That letter pointed to the overthrow by military force of all that the Reconstruction acts had effected, and the Convention itself pronounced these acts null and void. There has not been a single indication of change in regard to these acts on the part of any regular Democratic organization, from that time till now. In not a solitary State have the Democracy formally receded from the ground assumed in 1868. The Democratic Congressional Committee, while calling upon the party to waste no time on "dead issues," carefully abstained from including among such issues either reconstruction or the Fifteenth Amendment.

The Louisville journalist applauds BLAIR'S speech as a forcible presentation of the present views of his party. Well, does BLAIR give evidence of change? On the contrary, he is emphatic in his statement that he is unchanged. As he was on June 30, 1868, so is he now. He professes, indeed, to regard the Fifteenth Amendment as part of the law of the land, but he neutralizes the declaration by remarking that "the Constitutional Amendments"—not the Fifteenth only, but all—"have been obtained by coercion in the South, and

in defiance of the known will of the people of the North." And this is exactly the point at which the opinions of outspoken Democrats, like those of Indiana, possess a peculiar suggestiveness. They cannot at present get rid of the Fifteenth Amendment as a fact. But they contend that it is a fact by reason of ratification which, being in many States compulsory, possesses no real constitutional validity. The whole fabric of reconstruction is menaced in the same way. The National Convention of 1868 condemned the acts on which it rests as "unconstitutional, null, and void." FRANK BLAIR, on the 15th of February, quoted these words as an expression of his unalterable conviction. "I did not, and do not now, regard the reconstruction measures passed by Congress, as any part of the law of the land," he avows. "Although these laws have done their work in subverting the legal Governments of the Southern States," he went on to say, "yet there is a perfectly constitutional mode by which this could be repaired, if we had an Executive who regarded the duties imposed on him by his office." Language of this character is susceptible of but one construction. The loyal Governments of the South are to be recognized only until they can be overthrown. The Republican work is to be endured only until a Democratic president, with the army at his command, had the opportunity of destroying it. If this does not imply reaction and revolution, we should like to know what would.

We appreciate the motives of the *Courier-Journal* in its attempt to show that the party with which it cooperates has grown rational and law-abiding. Our contemporary would gladly believe that the good counsels it has pressed upon its party associates have not been inoperative. Unfortunately, all the facts are against this hypothesis. The good counsel has been wasted. The Kentucky Democracy still exclude negro testimony from the Courts, and doggedly refuse to sanction any measure that would suppress the outrages now so frequent, and bring the disguised perpetrators to punishment. Nor is this all. The Kentucky Democrats not only refuse to listen to the soothing words of the *Courier-Journal,* but have started an opposition sheet, to preach the unadulterated doctrine of the Brodhead letter and the Mobile *Register.* It would be more pleasant to believe otherwise. We have heard so much about reconstruction that we would gladly consider it beyond the range of current political discussion. But we have FRANK BLAIR'S assurance that the Democracy will not allow it to rest. And while the Democrats are preparing to renew their assaults, Republicans cannot afford to be wholly indifferent.

SEPTEMBER 15, 1874
POLITICS IN THE SOUTH.

THE CIVIL RIGHTS BILL.

The Effect on the Republican Vote in North Carolina—The Mixed Schools Question—A Southern View of the Measure.

Raleigh, N.C., Tuesday, Sept. 8, 1874.

To the Editor of the New York Times:

All parties here are agreed as to the cause of the late overwhelming defeat of the Republicans. Ex-Gov. Holden and other leading men of that party are as emphatic as the Democrats in saying that it was mainly due to the passage of the Civil Rights bill by the Republican Senate, and to its probable passage at the next Session of Congress by the Republican House of Representatives. It was in vain that the Republican candidates, almost to a man, declared open opposition to the measure. It was in vain that even their colored supporters, including John Hyman, the colored Representative elect to Congress, opposed it. The Democratic press and politicians urged with irresistible force the fact that the great Republican Party of the North supported it, and that it only failed to become a law at the last session by the Parliamentary rule which requires a two-thirds vote to take up a bill out of its order. They also urged the indisputable fact that the Southern Republicans in Congress, almost to a man, supported the Civil Rights bill, or evaded a direct vote against it; while Wm. A. Smith, of this district, who was a rare exception to the rule, was constrained to withdraw from the candidacy, owing, doubtless, to his avowed opposition to the bill, for at the opening of the campaign the colored voters were all in favor of the measure, and doubtless in their hearts they still cherish the sentiment. But the exigencies of the hour constrained them to follow their white leaders, who saw that defeat was inevitable with that load upon their backs. And even to "unload" in the midst of fight, proved to be ineffectual.

The results of the late election in this State cannot fail to have a purifying effect upon the Republican Party. Not a few bad characters have been defeated, and it may be hoped laid aside as popular leaders forever. The hurricane which has swept over the State has scattered the political miasma and feculence which have been engendered by the hot-house measures of reconstruction, and the field is now clear for legitimate and natural action. If the Republicans of the North would retain or regain the political control of these Southern States; if they would extend over them a Government of opinion in place of a Government of force; if they would win the confidence of the dominant white race without doing the slightest injustice to the blacks, they must abandon forever the idea of enforcing social equality between the races. If they would defeat the Pendleton-Butler scheme of paying off the national debt in Treasury notes—a scheme as disastrous as it would be dishonoring to the nation—they must cease to pass a measure which concentrates every white voter south of the Potomac against them. If they would restore harmony between the races where it has been destroyed, and preserve it where it still exists, they must leave the South to its autonomy, and respect the right of local self-government in this part of the Union as it is respected in Massachusetts, Illinois, and California. There is reason to hope that the lessons of the past will not be lost, and that among the first things which will be done when Congress meets will be the indefinite postponement of the Civil Rights Bill.

G.

- -

REPUBLICANS FACE POLITICAL SCANDAL

As northern capitalism expanded, the Republicans faced a series of public disgraces. Most damning was the Crédit Mobilier scandal, where members of Congress received railroad stock at cut-rate prices in exchange for favorable legislative treatment. As the House of Representatives unsuccessfully struggled to repair its image, the Sanborn Contracts affair revealed that tax collectors in the Treasury had enriched themselves from tax collections. The Republican Congress and executive branch shared the weight of blame, endangering their party's electoral future.

FEBRUARY 19, 1873
EDITORIAL
CREDIT MOBILIER.

Those who anticipated a non-committal, or a "white-washing" report from Judge POLAND'S committee will be disappointed by the document printed in full in our columns this morning. We pointed out, a fortnight since, the fact that the public expected a full and explicit statement from the committee concerning the character of the Credit Mobilier, its relations to the Government, the legislation affecting its value, and the share taken by various members in such legislation, together with the exact nature of the transactions of all members who held the stock.

The report sets forth fully the fact that the Credit Mobilier scheme was, in fact and intent, a fraud upon the Government. It was a device to enable those interested in the Union Pacific Railroad to transfer to their own pockets the bonds and the lands granted by the United States to build the road. We need not here recite the details of this scheme, which are fully set forth by the committee. They clearly sustain the interpretation we have given.

In this fraudulent scheme Mr. OAKES AMES undertook to enlist his fellow-members of Congress by selling them stock at half its value and guaranteeing them large profits on it. His purpose, now avowed, was to advance the interests of the authors of the scheme likely to be affected by legislative action. This purpose he concealed at the time. He even assured those to whom he applied that the owners of the stock would seek no further legislation. This was true, but it was a half truth, intended to mislead. The Credit Mobilier Company was interested not in procuring but in preventing legislation, and it was to this end that AMES used the stock. For so using it, the committee recommends that he be expelled. The recommendation is a sound one. The moral character of AMES' action is obvious. It was an attempt to corrupt, and not the less such an attempt because the motive was withheld and indirectly denied.

FEBRUARY 27, 1873
EDITORIAL
A WORD WITH THE HOUSE OF REPRESENTATIVES.

In order to save a few Republicans, is it worth while to run the risk of ruining the Republican party? That is a practical question which the House of Representatives would do well to consider. The tone of the debate on the Credit Mobilier report suggests the inquiry. We are totally at a loss to understand or justify the temper of the House. We are assured that not only will the resolutions of expulsion fail for want of a two-thirds vote, but that a resolution of censure would hardly obtain even a majority, if the censure included all who were implicated in this miserable business. It is even possible that a declaration of want of jurisdiction—an evasion nothing less than cowardly— would stand a fair chance of adoption. This pitiful and

shameful condition of the House cannot be justly laid to the charge of the Republican party alone. Decided and just action is impossible because Democrats join with Republicans to make it so. But the Republican party, justly or unjustly, will have to bear the responsibility. If there is evasion, it will be charged to Republican cowardice. If there is suspicion that the House is prevented by general demoralization from properly characterizing the offenses of members, it is the reputation of Republicans that will suffer. The Democrats will gain in public esteem by the attitude of Messrs. NIBLACK and MERRICK, in stern condemnation of BROOKS. But the upright position taken by Messrs. POLAND, McCRARY, and HAWLEY will count for nothing in favor of the Republicans, unless it is sustained by the strength of the party. The gentlemen who, putting aside the proven facts and the logical inferences from them, allow their sympathies to lead them from the plain path of duty, are taking a responsibility which they can hardly now measure. They are inviting popular distrust of the Republican Party. They are destroying the power for usefulness of the great organization which has just received the Government in renewed trust from the people. They are sowing the seeds of disintegration, and they will be compelled to reap where they have sown.

This is the view the people take of the question. If Congressmen could meet their constituents in the counting-room and on the farm for five minutes, they would realize that fact. The public believes "the thing looks ugly." If the public were mistaken, we should be glad to say so. We did not hesitate a year ago to denounce those who were trying to raise a false clamor

for selfish purposes. But the public is not mistaken. It has formed deliberately a sober and sincere judgment, based on the evidence, and guided by common sense and sound morals. Such a judgment cannot be safely ignored. Gentlemen who make glowing speeches about mobs may win momentary applause from a gallery full of Washington habitués. But they sadly misinterpret the facts. There is no mob-spirit abroad. But there is a quiet feeling in the public mind that the Credit Mobilier is a bad business, and that a House which will not treat it as such is certainly cowardly, and possibly corrupt. We should be sorry to see this feeling disregarded. It is an honest feeling, and it is strongest where the Republican party is strongest. It is the feeling of that portion of the public which has supported our party in its best work. If the House deals with it dishonestly or evasively, the party will surely be crippled. It will be in danger of being not only crippled, but destroyed.

> The House of Representatives, yesterday, showed that it knew its duty, and did not dare to perform it.

FEBRUARY 28, 1873
EDITORIAL
THE WORK OF YESTERDAY.

The House of Representatives, yesterday, showed that it knew its duty, and did not dare to perform it. It asserted its power to expel AMES and BROOKS by rejecting a resolution containing the negative of that proposition. It acknowledged that these members committed the offenses of which they were accused, and this acknowledgment was made by a more than two-thirds vote. But though the men were guilty, and might be expelled, the House had not the courage to expel them.

This is not a question to be answered at one general election, or immediately. But it is one the people will not readily allow to pass out of mind. The answer will be sought patiently, and the resulting action will be gradual. But the votes of yesterday will be closely scanned by millions of voters bent upon reaching a decision. This much, at least, the people will not slow in perceiving—that the Representatives who can acknowledge the guilt of their associates, yet dare not cast them out, are not to be blindly trusted.

MAY 5, 1874
EDITORIAL
THE PRESIDENT AND THE SANBORN BUSINESS.

The Committee on Ways and Means yesterday presented to the House a careful and compact report of the facts in the Sanborn business, which we publish this

morning. The general conviction will be that it should make it impossible for Messrs. RICHARDSON and SAWYER to remain longer in charge of the Treasury Department. The report leaves but two judgments to be formed of the conduct of these gentlemen—that it was corrupt, or that it was inexpressibly negligent and careless. The committee say, in regard to Mr. RICHARDSON, that they find nothing to impeach the integrity of his action, and they compel us to accept the alternative conclusion. They make no distinct declaration as to Mr. SAWYER, and leave us in doubt as to whether we are to condemn him on one or the other count; but that he is to be condemned they leave no doubt at all. We shall not describe in detail the facts presented by the committee. For these we refer our readers to the report. But we call attention to a few of the most important facts, which show a condition of things in the Treasury Department that cannot be ignored with safety.

Again, it appears from the committee's report that SANBORN had in repeated instances the entire services of officers paid by the Government to "discover" delinquent taxes, of which he then proceeded to get one-half for having "discovered" them himself.

But the fact which most completely establishes the worthlessness, if nothing worse, of the methods of doing business in the Treasury Department is that, though the committee have had before them all the officers whose names can be traced directly or indirectly in connection with these "marauding contracts," they have been entirely unable to find out who is responsible for their origin. We shall not trouble our readers with a recital of the tedious contradictions of the testimony on this point. The point itself is entirely clear, and though we can readily conceive that the Secretary cannot be held directly responsible for all of even the important acts done in his department, he must know who is responsible, or be guilty of gross negligence and inexcusable incapacity.

These, then, are some of the leading features in this Sanborn affair. To us they are both disgusting and discouraging, and they call for immediate and thorough treatment. That treatment cannot now come wholly from Congress. That body can repeal the law that occasioned this miserable business, and can annul the contracts, which ought long since to have been annulled by the Secretary. But they cannot immediately cause the resignation of Messrs. RICHARDSON and SAWYER. That lies, at present, in the power of the President only. If he values the good name of his Administration, and that of the great party which it represents, as he ought to value them, he will lose no time in exercising his power.

- -

THE PANIC OF 1873

Republicans confronted political calamity when the Panic of 1873 struck. Cascading through the financial world, the panic resulted from overspeculation on railroads, culminating with the collapse of the banking giant Jay Cooke & Company and a subsequent crash of the stock market. As the markets disintegrated, government revenues also declined, forcing the Grant administration to meet an economic recession with diminished financial assets. Hobbled economically and tainted by popular perceptions of their corruption, Grant and the Republican Party struggled to respond.

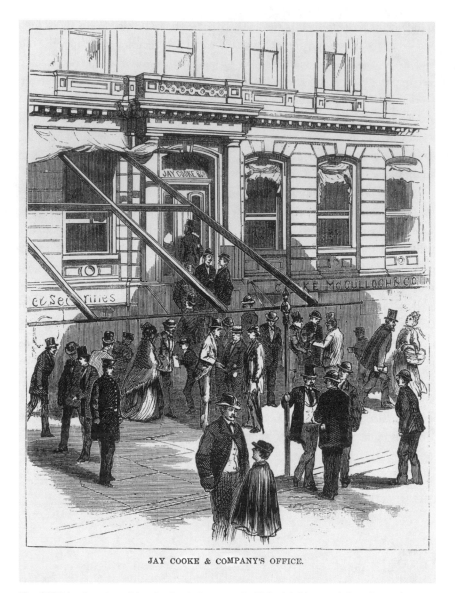

JAY COOKE & COMPANY'S OFFICE.

The 1873 bankruptcy of Jay Cooke & Company in Philadelphia precipitated a major economic crisis. This difficulty, combined with Republican political scandals, led to massive Democratic gains in Congress and state governments and ended Radical Reconstruction.

Source: The Granger Collection, New York

SEPTEMBER 19, 1873
THE PANIC.

EXCITEMENT IN WALL STREET.

SUSPENSION OF JAY COOKE & CO.—WHAT IS THOUGHT OF IT EVERYWHERE—TROUBLES IN OTHER FIRMS.

It was a wild day in Wall street yesterday. The announcements of THE TIMES in the morning prepared the public in a certain degree for the trouble which was to ensue, and many parties were enabled to go in the market early in the morning and protect themselves from loss. While many did this, and so saved themselves from ruin, there were others, and by far the majority, who thought that the trouble was solely brought about by machinations of the bears, and that there would only be a small-sized panic, which would result in a sudden rebound in prices. Those who took this view of the situation held on to their investments as long as possible, and, so soon as their margins gave out, were compelled to go under. Of course, there were many who, by superior strength, were enabled to hold on to their purchases, and so escaped being sold out, at least for the time.

The first opening of the market was altogether in favor of the bull clique. The prices of the Vanderbilt, and nearly all other stocks, advanced. Parties who were frightened the night before by the marked decline in prices became sanguine and predicted an altogether better state of the market. This continued, however, but for a short time. The first intimation which came into the Stock Exchange of any change in the programme was contained in a brief notice, which said authoritatively that Jay Cooke & Co. had suspended payment. To say that the street became excited would only give a feeble view of the expressions of feeling. The brokers stood perfectly thunderstruck for a moment,

and then there was a general run to notify the different houses in Wall street of the failure.

The brokers surged out of the Exchange, tumbling pell-mell over each other in the general confusion, and reached their respective offices in race-horse time. The members of firms who were surprised by this announcement had no time to deliberate. The bear clique was already selling the market down in the Exchange, and prices were declining frightfully.

Of course every one gave orders to sell out holdings as quick as possible, in order to obtain the best prices, and in this way when the brokers returned to the Long Room a fresh impetus was given to the decline, which brought about a fearful panic. There was no one on hand with nerve and money to arrest it either, and so the bear clique, taking advantage of the general demoralization, made confusion worse confounded.

The news of the panic spread in every direction down-town, and hundreds of people who had been carrying stocks in expectation of a rise, rushed into the offices of their brokers and left orders that their holdings should be immediately sold out. In this way prices fell off so rapidly that even Vanderbilt could not have stemmed the tide.

DECEMBER 16, 1873
EDITORIAL

THE NATIONAL FINANCES.

It was inevitable that Congress should take up at an early moment the question of finance. On the one hand, the reports of the Executive Departments, made at the opening of the session, showed that the revenues of the Government had undergone a great and rapid change. Instead of providing all the money that was necessary for current expenditures, and a surplus applicable to the reduction of the debt, the revenues in gold have become barely sufficient to pay the interest on our bonds as it accrues, and the revenues in currency are not sufficient to meet the ordinary demands on the Government already authorized by law, without considering the amount necessary for the sinking fund, which is not only authorized but commanded, and which cannot for a single moment be neglected without dishonor. On the other hand, a portion of our people—happily, we believe, a minority—accustomed for a long period to see the demand notes of the Government taking the place of money, and educated by this unfortunate state of things to look to the Government,

are urgently seeking of the Government a further issue of these notes. The representatives of this view in Congress naturally seize on the wants of the Government as a plausible pretext for complying with this demand.

Under these circumstances three courses appear to be open to Congress. It can reduce appropriations; it can provide money by borrowing, either on bonds or legal tender notes, or it can provide money by taxation. Or it can combine two or more of these plans. The principle difficulty with the plan of reducing appropriations will occur to every one familiar with the way in which the business of the country is necessarily carried on. It is that Congress cannot readily cut down current expenditures till they are no greater than actual current revenues. The appropriations are already made for the year ending June 30, 1874. It is by these appropriations that current expenditures are authorized. The only way in which the expenditures can be diminished is by withdrawing authority for those not yet begun, and suspending some of those already commenced. How far this can be done is a practical question which it is not easy to answer. Those who are best able to answer it—that is, the Chairmen of the Committees on Appropriations and on Ways and Means—we are bound to say, have not answered it in a way to convince the country that a reduction of expenses equal to the reduction already going on in revenue is possible. That some retrenchment is possible is undoubtedly true, and it should be entered on promptly and with the utmost firmness. In this work we make no question that the Executive branch of the Government and the most resolute economists of the House will be found quite in accord.

But if, after all possible retrenchment is discovered and provided for, there remains a deficit, what is to be done with that? This is a practical question, and should be met in a practical way, and the country will both expect and desire that it shall be so met. We have no hesitation in saying that while our people will require rigid economy, they will cheerfully comply with any demands that honor and sound policy may make upon them. In considering how a deficit may be made up, it must be remembered that whatever is done will be doubly effective if is done promptly. To a certain extent it is necessary that it should be done promptly to be effective at all. It is obvious, for instance, that if a tax on tea and coffee is seen to be imminent, but is postponed for a month or more, it will be in the power of importers to accumulate a considerable stock, on which the taxes will be avoided. In like fashion, the manufacturers of spirits would largely avoid a tax on that commodity, and the manufacturers of tobacco could do the same thing, though not so largely. If it should turn out that the deficiency to be met is one likely to be presented in a short time, it is plain that taxes that can thus be avoided are very poor reliance.

Of course, the resort to loans remains. There is no doubt that the Government could borrow, at its ordinary rates, the comparatively small sum it may require. But those who favor borrowing do not favor this plan. Bad as we consider this plan would be, theirs is much worse. It is to pay the Government expenses with legal-tender notes. Anything more extraordinary, worse in policy or in worse faith than this—anything, we may add, more entirely beyond the ascertained powers of Congress, we cannot imagine. When legal-tender notes were last issued, the only justification that was ever pleaded for the act, the only one that was ever thought of, or that would for a moment have been conceded, was the justification of absolute necessity. It has even been doubted whether the necessity which then existed was sufficient. But what have we like it now? What shadow of excuse have we for the assertion of a power that a direct and pressing peril to the national life was barely sufficient to sustain? We have none. The act would be without excuse, and Congress ought not to tolerate the thought of it.

The House of Representatives have asked the president to instruct the heads of departments to revise the estimates for the fiscal year ending June 30, 1875. This is a step good enough in its way, but it does not go far toward meeting the situation. What about the expenditures of the current year? What about the four millions extraordinary expenditures for the navy? Is there no necessity for something different, and something more than a revision of the estimates of a year the beginning of which is more than six months distant? If there is, surely it would be better to face the business fairly and at once.

• •

Resistance in the South

Refusing to comply with constitutional protections granted to blacks or to northern occupation, some whites in the South created "White Leagues" and other associations intended to suppress the political rights of blacks and northern "carpetbaggers." Extremist White Leaguers gained prominent positions within the Democratic Party and quietly condoned violent "outrages" upon black voters. Bloody conflict erupted, expanding to outright insurrection against Republican state governments, destroying hopes that the root causes of the Civil War had been settled.

APRIL 18, 1873
GRANT PARISH.

The Massacre a Most Terrible One—Escape of the Whites—Difficulty in Sending off Troops.

Special Dispatch to the New-York Times.

New-Orleans, April 17.—Later news from the scene of hostilities in Grant Parish show that the massacre of the negroes at Colfax Court-house was even more horrible in all its details and more complete in its execution than was at first reported. It now appears that not a single colored man was killed until all of them had surrendered to the whites who were fighting with them, when over 100 of the unfortunate negroes were brutally shot down in cold blood.

It is understood that another lot of negroes was burned to death in the Court-house when it was set on fire.

The details of the massacre, as they are related by eye-witnesses to the terrible scenes acted at Colfax Court-house, are positively appalling in their atrocity, and would appear to be more like the work of fiends than that of civilised men in a Christian country.

After the butchery of the surrendered negroes the whites scattered in every direction, few of them going to their homes. It is understood that many of them left for the Texas border, in hopes of escaping the consequences of their crime. As yet no arrests have been made.

SEPTEMBER 2, 1874
THE SOUTHERN TERROR.

THE MASSACRE OF NORTHERN MEN IN LOUISIANA.

FRUITS OF THE INCENDIARY SPEECHES OF M'ENERY—SKETCH OF COUSHATTA— THE WHITE LEAGUE ORGANIZATION.

Special Dispatch to the New-York Times.

New-Orleans, Sept. 1.—It is now ascertained through private dispatches that one of the most horrible massacres ever perpetrated in this State has just been committed in the Red River Parish. The accounts which have been received thus far have come through White League sources, and therefore it is but reasonable to suppose that but one-half of the horrible story has been told. So far as ascertained, the following persons have been made victims, as the following statement will show: On Saturday, Aug. 29, H. K. Twitchell, Deputy Postmaster; W. F. Howell, United States Commissioner at Coushatta, La.; Robert A. Dewees, State Supervisor of Registration of Desota Parish; Frank Edgerton, Sheriff; N.C. Willis, Justice of the Peace, and Clark Holland, Supervisor of Registration of Red River Parish, were visited by regularly organized and armed White Leaguers from surrounding parishes at Coushatta, the capital of Red River Parish, who demanded that they should resign their offices. They refused. Shortly after the White Leaguers returned, reinforced, and demanded their surrender. They surrendered in order to save their

women and children from the horrors of a bloody fight, but this was not done until they had been assured by the White Leaguers that they would be protected from further personal violence, and that the women and children would not be molested. They were then made prisoners, together with seven colored men, and placed in the parish jail, where they were guarded by the White Leaguers. On Sunday, the 30th, their captors took them all from the jail, conveyed them beyond the limits of the district, and murdered them in cold blood.

THE INSTIGATORS OF THE TERROR.

This is the work of the White Leaguers, encouraged by the murderous speeches of McEnery and Marr, who, in the late convention at Baton Rouge, in set speeches advised the white people to organize, arm, and drive Republicans from the State, and offered themselves as leaders to resist even United States troops, McEnery going so far as to say that Grant would not dare to use United States troops against them.

THE DEMOCRATS GAIN POWER

Beginning in mid-October, the 1874 midterm elections—which did not all occur on a national election day as they do today—quickly turned against the Republicans. Ohio and Indiana gave early victories to Democrats over Republican incumbents in Congress and state offices. Throughout the nation, voters rebuffed the party in control of the federal government. For the first time since before the Civil War, the Democratic Party appeared poised to retake the reins of power.

NOVEMBER 4, 1874
DEMOCRATIC VICTORY.

GREAT DEFEAT OF THE REPUBLICAN PARTY.

TRIUMPH OF WESTERN IDEAS IN THE EAST—RESTORATION OF TAMMANY IN NEW-YORK—THE "TIDAL WAVE" IN MASSACHUSETTS AND NEW-JERSEY—CONGRESS TO BE DEMOCRATIC.

The tale in the East is one of disaster. Mr. Tilden has been elected Governor of the State of New-York by not less than 30,000 majority. At least sixteen of the thirty-three Congressman are Democrats, and the Assembly has very nearly fallen under the control of the same party. The figures at present stand 67 Republicans, 61 Democrats. In Massachusetts the Democrats have apparently elected their State ticket, and they have gained five Congressmen. From the West cheering news comes, compared with that we are compelled to record in this section. Michigan remains true to the Republican Party, and its Legislature secures a United States Senator as successor of Mr. Chandler. Illinois, also, given comparatively encouraging reports, and Wisconsin, also. For the other States the news is meagre, at the time this edition goes to press.

The Congressman elected yesterday and Monday, according to present figures, are divided: Republicans, 98; Democrats, 115. There had previously been chosen 29 Republicans and 33 Democrats, making the House stand, Republicans, 127; Democrats, 148. Elections are yet to be held in four States, choosing 17 members, of whom 13 are now Republicans, and four Democrats.

> We probably have before us a stormy era, in which many questions which the people imagined were finally settled will be dealt with anew.... The history of the rebellion and its consequences is by no means completed.

NOVEMBER 4, 1874
EDITORIAL
THE DEMOCRATIC VICTORY.

The result of the elections yesterday in this and other Eastern States will not be a surprise to anybody, except perhaps to a few persons at Washington, and it certainly will not surprise any of our readers, who have been kept tolerably well-informed as to the causes which inevitably tended to produce the present overthrow of the Republican Party. All that could be done honorably to avert this defeat has been done by us, but since the last Presidential election, many of the party leaders have been deaf alike to advice and remonstrance. They have apparently believed that the people would quietly submit to anything and everything, and that the party which they represented was indestructible. Nothing short of the events which we record this morning could have opened their eyes to the truth. If a newspaper warned them in a friendly but firm spirit against the policy of blundering which they were pursuing, it was treated with a mixture of the insolence and arrogance which they exhibited toward all opposition. The immediate friends of the Administration possessed themselves of an "organ" at Washington, and filled it with disgusting slanders and with besotted arguments in favor of Gen. GRANT for a "third term." It will be the lot of the President to discover, in common with many great men who have gone before him, that foolish flatterers and venal newspapers cannot turn aside the current of public opinion. The truths which he and his immediate supporters refused to hear from the lips of friends they must now listen to to-day from the people at the polls.

The great and signal defeats of yesterday virtually began last year. The panic did much to injure the Republican Party, but the effects of that disaster might have been greatly lessened had a wise course been adopted by Congress in relation to the finances. All through last Winter we begged Republican Congressman to do something, and to do it quickly, and we pointed out the certain consequences of their mistakes and delays. In return for performing that unpleasant duty, we were simply told that we were "traitors" to the Republican Party, and that we should be instantly stamped out of existence. The mismanagement at the Treasury, the Sanborn frauds, and the general series of blunders in nearly all the public departments, were in the meantime causing incalculable mischief. The first two nominations for Chief Justice were shocking blunders, and disgusted the whole people. The Administration was making enemies and losing friends every day. The party was handed over to the PLATTS and BUTLERS. And just when the disappointment and irritation of the people became most marked, the paper at Washington, which has come to be known as a mere speaking-tube of the White House, was set to work crying out from Gen. GRANT for a "third term." What could any sane man anticipate from such astounding folly except the overwhelming defeats of yesterday? In this State a Republican majority of 55,000 has been turned into a Republican defeat of 42,000, a change of 97,000 votes. The gentlemen who have had the Republican Party in charge during the past two years will be obliged to admit to-day that they have nearly strangled it.

It would be useless to dwell on these obvious lessons except in the hope that they will be thoughtfully pondered at Washington and elsewhere. If the greatest party ever known in this country is to be saved from utter destruction two years hence, and if it is not to pass from history disgraced as well as defeated, the leaders and managers must make a thorough change in their policy. It would be still wiser to change many of the leaders themselves. Fortunately, the people have disposed of BUTLER, as they would have swept away some other prominent persons, in both House and Senate, if their votes could have been brought to bear directly upon them. There is yet time to prevent a still more crushing blow in 1876, but to do that will tax the combined efforts of the best minds in the Republican Party. The opposition will now have an opportunity of producing a policy of their own, and they will find it harder to do that successfully than to attack the measures of Republicans. We shall probably witness the development of ideas which were put forward in the platforms of Ohio and Indiana, and the effect of that upon our entire financial system cannot fail to be very great. The West and South always controlled the Democratic Party, and they will continue to control it. What these sections of the country demand now is inflation, combined with partial repudiation. Whether the people will deliberately approve of that policy when it is submitted to them without disguise remains to be ascertained. When we see the great City of New-York deliberately voting to be put back under the rule of Tammany, it must be admitted that even the cause of common honesty does not appear to be highly popular. We probably have before us a stormy era, in which many questions which the people imagined were finally settled will be dealt with anew, and in a way calculated to the surprise of the world. The legislation which has been carried out since the war, on questions of finance, reconstruction, and the negro, and the constitutional amendments of the same period, are not beyond the reach of the Democratic majority in Congress and the country. The history of the rebellion and its consequences is by no means completed. For the sake of the country, it is to be hoped that the Democrats will use their victory in a spirit of moderation and prudent statesmanship. We doubtless see to-day the Democratic Presidential candidate for 1876; and if the Republican Party is not conducted with greater wisdom and good fortune during the next two years than it has been during the last two, Mr. TILDEN is the most probable successor of Gen. GRANT.

THE CIVIL RIGHTS ACT OF 1875

Defeated at the polls, Republicans still controlled Congress during the lame-duck session until the newly elected members could take office in March 1875. Refusing to concede power silently, Radical Republicans passed the Civil Rights Act of 1875, making it illegal to deny blacks any services, such as hotel rooms and restaurant meals, publicly offered to whites. Revealing the limits of whites' tolerance and social norms, the act drew opposition even from Republicans who normally supported giving political rights to blacks. Out of power and with Democrats eager to roll back Reconstruction's progress, Radical Republicans feared the unraveling of their efforts.

MARCH 2, 1875
EDITORIAL
THE TWO NEW "RECONSTRUCTION" BILLS.

The Civil Rights bill has been signed by the President. The "Force bill," after passing the House by a vote of 135 to 114, is now before the Senate. We reprint it to-day, and it ought not to need much persuasion from us to induce our readers to study it. Under the first of these two bills, if any keeper of a restaurant or inn in this City or any other city refuses to take colored men into his house, he must pay the colored man five hundred dollars, or he may be fined five hundred dollars and imprisoned for one year. If A wishes to injure B, both being engaged in this business, he has only to quietly employ five or six negroes to go to B's house and demand a dinner, bedrooms, or some other accommodation. If B complies, he probably loses his white customers. Seven or eight negroes seated every evening in Mr. DELMONICO'S rooms would not tend to attract general custom, although curiosity might at first draw a crowd outside to stare through the windows. That kind of business, however, does not pay the restaurant keeper. But suppose that B refuses the accommodation in question? In that

case, A proceeds to inform against him, and B is liable to the penalties above stated. Now, few restaurant keepers could afford to be fined $500 a day, perhaps multiplied six or eight times over, or to run the risk of being sent to prison for from thirty days to twelve months for *each offense committed*. Yet that is what Congress and the President have just made the law—*pace* the Supreme Court.

The part of the bill—section 4—which prescribes a new jury-law for all the states—for that is what it amounts to—has clearly been shown to be unconstitutional by Senator CARPENTER. The bill can never stand to the review of the Supreme Court, and the first case which occurs under it will, of course, be taken to that court, and the wisdom of Congress will be subjected to a revision, without which, in these days, it is difficult to imagine what sort of a Republic this might eventually be turned into. The Supreme Court, in such instances as this, is the last hope of all who still attach any value to that somewhat despised instrument, the Constitution of the United States.

MARCH 6, 1875
EDITORIAL
CAN THE CIVIL RIGHTS LAW BE ENFORCED?

Already several of the Southern cities have had a foretaste of the troubles which it was expected would follow the passage of the Civil Rights bill. In Washington, D.C., a barber, and a colored one, too, has been threatened with

persecution because he refused to shave a negro, and in Wilmington, N.C., the keeper of a liquor saloon was arrested for refusing to give drinks to a colored man. The Commissioner before whom the case was tried dismissed the complaint, deciding that the Civil Rights bill did not apply to bar-rooms. In Richmond, Va., colored men have twice been ejected from one of the best hotels, and others who attempted to obtain drinks at bars frequented by the whites were threatened with violence. In Alexandria, Va., the colored people are announced as having given notice that they would profit to the utmost by the privileges which they have a right to claim under the new law. The result was that the proprietors of the two principal hotels abandoned their licenses, and closed the doors of their houses. The same action has been taken by hotel proprietors in other parts of the South, and it will be well if still more serious difficulties do not occur.

We do not believe, however, that it will be possible to generally enforce the new law. That part of it which very justly stipulates that men and women, whether white or black, who pay the same fare on railroad trains, shall have equal accommodations, is not objected to by the sensible people of the South, but the hotel and theatre clauses meet with bitter and universal opposition. Throughout Virginia, the proprietors of hotels under a peculiar State law are taking out licenses as private boarding-house keepers, and in this way will be enabled to evade the law. In other parts of the South a determination is expressed to resist it by force if necessary. Ex-Chief Justice LUCHRANE, of Georgia, who is regarded as one of the most liberal men in the South, recently spoke as follows regarding the matter:

"Congress in emancipating the blacks has not made the white people slaves. An acquaintance of over one-fourth a century makes me know the people of the South, and a thousand Federal lawsuits or fines cannot establish among them negro equality. We would ride in wagons or walk, live in boarding-houses or starve, live without a laugh or public entertainment, rather than be dictated to, and forced to mingle with an element inferior, ill-bred, ignorant, and forced by law upon us."

It is much easier to force a caucus bill through Congress than it is to put into execution a law which is obnoxious to a majority of the people of the South. And it is a great mistake to seek to impose new social customs on a people by act of Congress. These facts may soon become apparent to some of the gentlemen who advocated the Civil Rights bill.

AN EARLY DEATH FOR CIVIL RIGHTS

Not enforced in practice, the Civil Rights Act of 1875 was declared unconstitutional by the Supreme Court in 1883. Ruling on a series of cases dealing with discrimination, the Court found that the Fourteenth Amendment limited only government-sanctioned discrimination based upon race and could not be used to prevent discrimination by private citizens. With a new understanding of the Fourteenth Amendment, and armed with Justice John Marshall Harlan's concept of "state action," the nation nearly one hundred years later would once again confront the issue of civil rights for blacks.

OCTOBER 16, 1883
EDITORIAL
CIVIL RIGHTS CASES DECIDED.

The Supreme Court of the United States has finally decided against the constitutionality of the Civil Rights act of March 1, 1875, in a number of cases submitted to the court a year ago on written arguments. The act provided that all persons within the jurisdiction of the United States should be entitled to equal accommodations and privileges in inns, public conveyances on land and water, and in theatres and other places of public amusement, subject only to conditions established by law and applicable alike to persons of every race and color. Penalties were provided for violations of the rights defined, and provisions were made for their enforcement in the Federal courts. The act was intended to enforce equal civil rights in respect to the matters referred to in behalf of the colored citizens of the

United States, and was based on the power of Congress to enforce the provisions of the fourteenth amendment of the Federal Constitution by "appropriate legislation."

In the temper which the people have now reached in dealing with questions that formerly had a sectional significance and that pertain to the relations of the races in this country it seems as though nothing were necessary but a careful reading of the amendment to show that it did not authorize such legislation as the Civil Rights act, and yet Judge HARLAN is to file a dissenting opinion which may present considerations that do not occur to the ordinary mind. The prohibition of the amendment is specifically directed against the making and enforcing of laws by the States which shall abridge the privileges and immunities of citizens. Assuming that these include the right to equal accommodations in public conveyances and places of entertainment, it does not appear in any of these cases that any State has in its legislation or the enforcement of its laws made the discriminations complained of. The amendment does not give Congress the power itself to legislate in regard to these rights except so far as it may be necessary to counteract the prohibited legislation of the States. This is the exact ground taken by the Supreme Court in the decision just rendered.

The decision is not likely to have any considerable practical effect, for the reason that the act of 1875 has never been enforced. Spasmodic efforts have been made to give it effect, and occasional contests have been made in the courts, but the general practice of railroads, hotels, and theatres has remained unchanged and has depended mainly on the prevailing sentiment of the communities in which they are located. The question of absolute right is not affected by the Constitutional amendment or the decision of the Supreme Court. There is a good deal of unjust prejudice against negroes, and they should be treated on their merits as individuals precisely as other citizens are treated in like circumstances. But it is doubtful if social privileges can be successfully dealt with by legislation of any kind. At any rate, it is not certain that they are beyond the jurisdiction of the Federal Congress. If anything can be done for their benefit it must be through State legislation. They are guaranteed against adverse and discriminating action by the States, and favorable action can only be secured through State authority. This remands the whole matter to the field in which it rightly belongs and in which alone it can be effectually dealt with.

THE PRESIDENTIAL ELECTION OF 1876

AFTER A DISPUTED CONTEST, HAYES ENDS RECONSTRUCTION

It might have started a new violent conflict within the United States. It might have been the first Democratic presidential victory in twenty years. It was surely the most corrupt election in American history. In historical perspective, it became the negotiated final chapter of the Civil War, ending federal efforts to "reconstruct" the South and restoring whites to political rule in the former Confederacy.

The election of 1876 resulted in the presidential inauguration of Rutherford B. Hayes, the Republican governor of Ohio. The oath of office was administered just hours after the final tally gave him a bare majority of 185 electoral votes, only one more than the total credited to his opponent, Samuel J. Tilden, the Democratic governor of New York. Hayes won the White House even though he had a minority of the popular vote, 48.0 percent of 8.4 million votes, compared to Tilden's 51.0 percent.

This election took place during a period of immense national change. As it approached the centennial of its independence, the United States was well on the way to becoming a leading industrial power, with its population growing rapidly due to swelling immigration. Railroads were spanning the continent, American oil had become the world's dominant fuel, and capitalist entrepreneurs were accumulating fortunes in the new "gilded age."

Political change was also evident and likely to lead to a Democratic victory. Financial excesses led to the Panic of 1873, throwing a quarter of the country's railroads into bankruptcy and 14 percent of its workers out of jobs. In reaction, the voters in 1874 gave Democrats control of the House of Representatives, their first national victory since the onset of the Civil War (see The Congressional Elections of 1874).

The rejection of the Republicans, the Grand Old Party of the war years, followed a series of scandals. In one, the Crédit Mobilier scam, large sums intended for railroad construction were stolen from stockholders and the U.S. Treasury, with the aid of Vice President Schuyler Colfax and members of Congress bribed with shares in the transcontinental Union

Source: The Granger Collection, New York

A Thomas Nast cartoon depicts a battered Republican elephant licking its wounds after a Pyrrhic victory in the presidential election of 1876. Republican victor Rutherford B. Hayes was derisively called "Rutherfraud" and "His Fraudulency." Soon after taking office, Hayes removed the remaining federal occupation troops from the former Confederacy.

Pacific railroad. In another scandal, the "Whisky Ring" corrupted more than a hundred Treasury officials to avoid paying liquor taxes. In a third shame, Secretary of War William Belknap was impeached for accepting bribes from companies seeking trading licenses on Indian reservations. Scandal even tainted President Ulysses S. Grant's brother and his personal secretary as well as four members of his

117

1876 ELECTORAL VOTE

STATE	ELECTORAL VOTES	HAYES	TILDEN	STATE	ELECTORAL VOTES	HAYES	TILDEN
Alabama	(10)	–	10	Mississippi	(8)	–	8
Arkansas	(6)	–	6	Missouri	(15)	–	15
California	(6)	6	–	Nebraska	(3)	3	–
Colorado	(3)	3	–	Nevada	(3)	3	–
Connecticut	(6)	–	6	New Hampshire	(5)	5	–
Delaware	(3)	–	3	New Jersey	(9)	–	9
Florida	(4)	4	–	New York	(35)	–	35
Georgia	(11)	–	11	North Carolina	(10)	–	10
Illinois	(21)	21	–	Ohio	(22)	22	–
Indiana	(15)	–	15	Oregon	(3)	3	–
Iowa	(11)	11	–	Pennsylvania	(29)	29	–
Kansas	(5)	5	–	Rhode Island	(4)	4	–
Kentucky	(12)	–	12	South Carolina	(7)	7	–
Louisiana	(8)	8	–	Tennessee	(12)	–	12
Maine	(7)	7	–	Texas	(8)	–	8
Maryland	(8)	–	8	Vermont	(5)	5	–
Massachusetts	(13)	13	–	Virginia	(11)	–	11
Michigan	(11)	11	–	West Virginia	(5)	–	5
Minnesota	(5)	5	–	Wisconsin	(10)	10	–
				TOTALS	**(369)**	**185**	**184**

cabinet. The series of criminal excesses led to new terms for official corruption: "the great barbecue" and "Grantism," a sorry title for Grant's two terms. The superb general of the Civil War would be remembered as one of the worst presidents in U.S. history.

The country wanted to move on, politically and socially. Legal rights for blacks had theoretically been achieved through the postwar constitutional amendments abolishing slavery, providing equal protection of the laws, and enfranchising blacks. Now, the idealism that had energized the struggles for preserving the Union and bringing about emancipation had faded. Reconstruction of the South and the freeing of slaves had brought gains for African Americans in many states, particularly the creation of a public school system. But some black and many white politicians from the North, known as Carpetbaggers for the luggage they brought to Dixie, and regional natives known as Scalawags, combined to bring widespread corruption and extravagant state debts to the region.

As memories of combat receded, the northern states turned from their wartime crusades to the materialism of new wealth. To end the sectional tensions, they sought reunion in place of rebellion. Ready to return power in the conquered provinces to southern whites, Congress supported amnesty for the former rebellious soldiers and leaders (with the exception of former Confederate president Jefferson Davis).

The South obviously welcomed this change of heart. Some of the region's politicians forthrightly called for "white supremacy" and pursued that goal through the violence of the Ku Klux Klan and the forceful exclusion of black freedmen from polling places and jobs. Others were more discreet, invoking the polite principles of states' rights and home rule to restore control to the planters and merchants who had dominated the South before the war. However phrased, the self-styled "Redeemers" regained white rule. By the time the presidential election of 1876 began, federal troops remained in only two states, Louisiana and South Carolina. When the election ended, troops disappeared from the South completely.

THE PARTIES AND THE CANDIDATES

As the election year opened, the Republican Party feared its first presidential loss after the tenures of Abraham Lincoln and Ulysses Grant. The early outlook was dim. The economy remained bad after the Panic of 1873. The scandals of the Grant administration brought calls for reform throughout the nation. The previous congressional elections had unseated eight senators and nearly half of Republican representatives, 96 of 203. The Democrats' control of the House foreshadowed a likely presidential victory.

Moreover, the GOP had few attractive leaders. Many of its possible candidates had been tarred by one scandal or another. Some in the party even championed a third term for Grant, despite the low repute of his administration. A third term ran against the tradition of a voluntary two-term limit, a practice established by George Washington—and even a second term had been denied to every president after Jackson until Lincoln. Republican aspirants for the presidency combined with Democrats to destroy the Grant boomlet. A House resolution of December 15, 1875, reaffirmed the two-term tradition "as part of our republican system of government" and declared a third-term "would be unwise, unpatriotic, and fraught with peril to our free institutions."

Republicans turned to other possibilities at their June convention in Cincinnati. The leading candidate was James G. Blaine of Maine, the previous Speaker of the House, who had many friends among party patronage appointees and officials. Blaine, however, had been touched by the railroad scandals, making him vulnerable to criticism from reformers. Their spokesman was Grant's former secretary of the Treasury, Benjamin Bristow of Kentucky, whose integrity had been shown by his efforts against corruption—efforts that led to his dismissal from the administration. Two senators, Roscoe Conkling of New York and Oliver Morton of Indiana, led the diminishing Radical wing of the party. Waiting off-stage was Hayes, who had established a record for probity and efficient administration in his three terms as governor of Ohio.

Blaine came close, aided by the seating of a challenged delegation from Alabama and a ruling that no delegates would be bound by a unit rule, requiring all state delegates to vote for the candidate leading in the delegation. Blaine began with 285 votes on the first ballot, but could get no higher than 308, still short of a majority of the 756 delegate total. On the seventh ballot, having tested their own strength, his foes coalesced around Hayes, who leapfrogged to a slim majority of 384. For vice president, only one ballot was required to select Rep. William Wheeler of New York.

The party platform revealed large partisan differences on the year's major issues. It was more striking for its virulent attack on the Democratic Party. Not only "waving the bloody shirt" but flaunting it by reminding citizens of the Democrats' association with the former Confederate states, Republicans resolved:

We charge the Democratic party with being the same in character and spirit as when it sympathized with treason; with making its control of the house of representatives the triumph and opportunity of the nation's recent foes; with reasserting and applauding in the national capitol the sentiments of unrepentant rebellion; with sending Union soldiers to the rear and promoting Confederate soldiers to the front; . . . and we warn the country against trusting a party thus alike unworthy, recreant, and incapable.

Democrats, meeting in St. Louis in June, were less contentious, perhaps because they were more confident. Tilden, a conservative lawyer, was the leading candidate, based on his record as a reform governor and his investigations of New York City's notorious Tammany Hall machine and its corrupt leader, "Boss" William Tweed. Establishing a wide lead on the first convention ballot, Tilden was easily nominated on the second, with 535 of 738 votes. Seeking unity, the party harmoniously selected his principal opponent, Indiana senator Thomas Hendricks, for vice president.

In their platform, the Democrats answered the Republicans with equal vehemence. They sought to cleanse the "bloody shirt" by pledging "our faith in the permanence of the Federal Union, our devotion to the Constitution of the United States, with its amendments universally accepted as a final settlement of the controversies that engendered civil war." Then, they went on the attack, denouncing the Republican record and waving their own banner of reform:

All these abuses, wrongs, and crimes, the product of sixteen years' ascendancy of the Republican party, create a necessity for reform, confessed by Republicans themselves. . . . The party's mass of honest voters is powerless to resist the eighty thousand office-holders, its leaders and guides. Reform can only be had by a peaceful civic revolution. We demand a change of system, a change of administration, a change of parties, that we may have a change of measures and of men.

The Greenback Party was a third entrant in the election, nominating Peter Cooper of New York for president. Gaining less than 1 percent of the national vote, it apparently did not affect the outcome in any state. But the Greenbackers drew their votes primarily from Democrats and nearly cost Tilden the critical state of Indiana. Had Hayes gathered 7,000 more of Indiana's 430,000 popular votes, he would have won the state's fifteen electoral votes and an undisputed national victory.

THE ELECTION CAMPAIGN

New institutional rules for the presidential election proved critically important in 1876. Ironically, Democratic prospects had been increased by the outcome of the Civil War. With the abolition of slavery, the black population was now fully counted in the distribution of representatives and electoral votes, rather than only partially, as under the original Constitution's three-fifths rule. The South therefore had more electoral votes than previously—and the Democrats thought these votes, cast in the "redeemed" white South, would be theirs.

But the Republicans gained a countervailing, although little noticed, advantage. In August, Colorado was admitted to the Union, adding three votes to the Electoral College. Democrats had hoped to win the new state, but there was too little time to organize a popular vote, so the new state's electoral votes would be cast by the legislature. It chose three Republican electors, a decisive addition in the eventual national count.

The parties were sharply different from one another. Regional differences were obvious, with the prospect of a newly solid Democratic South reviving memories of the sectional division that had led to the Civil War. Policy differences were also clear. Republicans favored high tariffs to provide a protected market for domestic industry; Democrats supported lower tariffs to aid farmers. Republicans wanted to restore gold as the national currency; Democrats would continue the use of paper greenbacks. Republicans insisted on "the permanent pacification of the Southern section of the Union"; Democrats denounced "a corrupt centralism . . . inflicting upon ten States the rapacity of carpet-bag tyrannies."

Differences existed even in the parties' targets of ethnocentric bigotry. Republicans struck an anti-Catholic note in urging a constitutional amendment to forbid "the application of any public funds or property for the benefit of any school or institution under sectarian control." Democrats in turn scorned Chinese immigration, "the coolie-trade in Mongolian women for immoral purposes, and Mongolian men held to perform servile labor contracts."

The parties were also divided internally. The Democrats were an uneasy alliance of conservative business interests located in the Northeast, urban ethnic groups mobilized by machines such as Tammany Hall, southern planters, and midwestern farmers. Republican strength was partially based on the historical heritage of the abolitionists and Radicals who had led the antislavery effort, vastly enlarged by support from veterans of the Union army and black freedmen of the South. Other party factions looked to a different politics. Liberal "Mugwumps," emphasizing reforms such as civil service, sat on the fence, their "mug" faces on one side and their "wump" posteriors on the other. More conservative interests, such as the ascendant industrial capitalists, looked to revive the former Whig alliance of economic interests across the sectional divisions of North and South.

Governor Hayes personally exemplified this potential alliance; within the constraints of traditional campaigning, he courted white southern conservatives. In ambiguous but still meaningful language (characterized by *The New York Times* on July 10 as "an able and manly state paper"), he hinted at the final removal of federal control from the region, pledging: "It will be practicable to promote, by the influence of all legitimate agencies of the General Government, the effort of the people of these states to obtain for themselves the blessings of honest and capable local government. If elected I shall consider it not only my duty, but it will be my ardent desire to labor for the attainment of this end." In private letters, he was more frank and more materialistic, promising federally funded public works in the South for "internal improvements of a national character."

Party strategies were based on the obvious regional bases of support. Democrats were expected to carry most of the South, now "redeemed," as Republicans would easily win in New England, the Midwest, and far West. The election would be decided, as was common at the time, in the closely competitive "middle" states of New York (with Tilden having the advantage of a favorite son), Ohio (where Hayes held the same advantage), Indiana, New Jersey, and Pennsylvania.

With the nation celebrating its hundredth year, Democrats and Republicans alike marked the birthday with rhetorical paeans to national glory, reconciliation, and friendship. The reality of the campaign was very different. Republicans, bearing the heavy political burdens of a depressed economy and government scandals, returned to their tried-and-true emotional appeal, the "bloody shirt." A Republican orator, Col. Robert Ingersoll, captured the tenor of the campaign in a September 12 New York speech, often repeated on the campaign circuit:

> Recollect, my friends, that it was the Democratic Party that did these devilish things when the great heart of the North was filled with agony and grief. Recollect that they did these things when the future of your country and mine was trembling in the balance of war; recollect that they did these things when the question was liberty, or slavery and perish; recollect that they did these things when your brothers, husbands and dear ones were bleeding or dying on the battle-fields of the South,

lying there alone at night, the blood slowly oozing through the wounds of death; when your brothers, husbands and sons were lying in the hospitals dreaming of home-pictures they loved.

Eventually, to counter these charges and demonstrate the Democratic Party's loyalty, Tilden felt it necessary to publicly oppose any scheme for repayment of the Confederate war debt or any compensation for Confederate veterans to match the generous pensions accorded the Union soldiers. Otherwise, the New York governor did little electioneering. He ignored insinuations about his status as a bachelor and contributed little of his time or substantial fortune to the polling. The national party published extensive campaign fodder, including two biographies, joke collections, and song sheets. It concentrated its spending on the decisive states of New York and Indiana, but gave insufficient attention to potential defections by southern conservatives who were in fact conducting secret negotiations with Hayes.

THE ELECTION RESULTS?

On election night the Democratic strategy seemed to work. Tilden carried the pivotal states of New York and Indiana, as well as Connecticut and New Jersey, and appeared to have swept the former Confederacy and all of the border states. Hayes conceded defeat in his own diary, and Zach Chandler, the Republican national chairman, went to bed convinced his party would soon leave the White House.

The Times—then staunchly Republican—and its managing editor, John C. Reid, had a different interpretation. On November 8 its lead morning story declared "Results Still Uncertain," with Hayes holding 181 electoral votes, only four short of victory. Reid hurried to awaken Chandler, who then telegraphed urgently to Republican officials in three southern states to "hold" until an official canvass could win their electoral votes for Hayes. Later in the day, he boldly claimed all three states for the Republicans, giving Hayes a bare majority of 185.

The next day, in support of the Republican cause, *The Times* reported "The Battle Won," citing "encouraging" dispatches that credited Hayes with Louisiana (8 electoral votes), South Carolina (7), Florida (4), and Oregon (1 of 3 votes in dispute). If Hayes could run the table and win all of the 20 votes still–despite the paper's report—uncertain, he would have a winning total of 185.

To back up the Republican claim, Chandler sent party teams of "visiting statesmen" south, carrying large sums of money. Abram Hewitt, the Democratic chair, soon took

parallel actions. In some respects, the consequent events would foreshadow the later controversial presidential election of 2000. But the 1876 election was far more disorderly.

The outcome would clearly depend on the counting of southern votes. The elections in the three contested states were not stirring scenes of peaceful democracy. In Louisiana and South Carolina, the authority of state government was divided between two contesting governors—the Republican holding the physical site of the state capitol with the protection of federal troops, the Democrat claiming the legitimacy of the most recent polling. In all three states, Negroes—a majority of the population in Louisiana and South Carolina and predominantly supporters of the party of Lincoln—had been intimidated, fraudulently removed from the voting rolls, violently prevented from casting their ballots; some had been murdered. Both parties engaged in various frauds at the polls and in the reporting of their votes. The state boards of elections, which held the power to certify the results, were themselves corrupt and reportedly available for sale, the rumored price being $50,000 to $200,000 for each electoral vote.

The contending parties reported conflicting results from each of the states and three different tallies from Florida. Republicans were particularly ingenious. In Louisiana, a significant initial Democratic victory was reversed by the state board, which excluded 13,000 votes for Tilden, but only 2,000 for Hayes, giving the Republican a 4,800 margin out of 145,000 votes. Similar tactics gave Hayes a razor-thin margin of 922 of 47,000 votes cast in Florida and 889 of 183,000 in South Carolina. In the remaining state, Oregon, only one electoral vote was in dispute. Hayes had admittedly carried the state, but one of the three Republican electors was a postmaster; as a federal officeholder, he was ineligible under the federal Constitution. To replace him, the Democratic governor appointed a Democratic elector, potentially giving ultimate victory to Tilden.

It would now be the responsibility of Congress to settle the controversy, choosing among the conflicting certifications of the electoral votes. The presidential division was reflected in Congress, where Democrats held the House and Republicans, the Senate. In the fall's congressional elections, the Democrats had lost 25 seats while maintaining a majority in the House and gained 7 in the Senate but still were a minority in the upper chamber. Because the new legislature would not be called to order until late in 1877, the presidential succession would be determined by the sitting, lame-duck Congress.

Each party had a favored scenario. The Republicans, dominant in the Senate, relied on the constitutional provision that the electoral votes of the states would be reported to the "President of the Senate [who] shall, in the presence of the Senate and House of Representatives, open all the Certificates and the Votes shall then be counted." They expected the Senate's Republican president would then assign the disputed votes to Hayes.

The Democrats instead relied on an existing rule that allowed either chamber to object to counting the vote of any state. Deadlock would follow, as the Senate would support Republican claims and the House the Democratic. Another proposal was to count neither of the disputed claims from Louisiana, and thereby deprive both Hayes and Tilden of the required electoral vote majority. In that case, the Constitution provided for the House to choose the president, as it had done in 1800 and 1824. With Democrats in control, the likely result would be Tilden's ticket to the White House. But Democrats could not be sure their ranks would hold in the House. Secret negotiations were already under way to provide Democratic House votes for Hayes in return for his support of a southern route for a transcontinental railroad. Tilden Democrats were also wary of any appeal to the Supreme Court, where Republicans held six of nine seats.

Seeking consensus, the parties appeared to strike an acceptable compromise in January. They established a commission consisting of five senators (three Republicans and two Democrats), five representatives (two Republicans and three Democrats), and five justices of the Supreme Court. Specific justices were named in the legislation, two Republicans and two Democrats, with the fifth to be selected by their judicial colleagues. The expectation was that this final member of the Electoral Commission would be David Davis, an independent. But in an unexpected, even inexplicable, surprise, the Illinois legislature, led by Democrats, selected Davis as the state's U.S. senator, leading to his resignation from the commission. Justice Joseph Bradley, a conservative Republican, took Davis's place. Although Bradley had a reputation for judicial fairness, he proved to be the decisive vote for Hayes.

The commission's legislated rules provided that its decisions would be final, unless overruled by votes of both the Senate and House. Soon, an electoral ritual played out. The commission decided that it would not examine the actual elections in the disputed states, but would only choose between the competing sets of reported electoral votes. Next, in repetitive 8–7 votes, all Republicans including Bradley validated the Hayes electors in each state, and all Democrats vainly endorsed those for Tilden. The House of Representatives then objected, but the Senate concurred in the ruling, and the commission vote for Hayes became final.

Still, peaceful resolution of the dispute was not certain. Democrats threatened a filibuster in the House to prevent final action. Without a president declared by the constitutionally established inaugural date of March 4, new perils became possible: the new vice president might still be chosen by the Senate and take over a vacant presidential office, or the Grant administration might attempt to stay in power. Congress might legislate an entirely new election. The greatest fears were that a new civil war would break out, both within and between sections of the country. Many governors, in fact, threatened to mobilize their state guards.

Some southern Democrats were prepared to accept Hayes as president, particularly as he had promised to serve only one term. But they exacted a price, and it was paid. Democrats wanted federal troops removed from Dixie. President Grant ordered the last troops to return to their barracks, the Redeemers took control of the state capitols, and President Hayes soon sent the last troops home. Democrats wanted a share of national power and political appointments. Hayes appointed a Tennessee Democrat and former Confederate general as postmaster-general, the office for patronage, and a third of southern appointments went to Democrats. The new administration also provided the rewards of office to members of the election boards that had certified the Hayes electors in the disputed states.

Democrats also wanted—and received—federal funds for "internal improvements" such as new levees on the Mississippi River. Even earlier, Hayes had promised to support a major goal of the Pennsylvania Railroad and southern capitalists: federal land grants and guarantees of $200 million for bonds of the Texas and Pacific Railroad to build a new transcontinental railroad through the South. Conflict among railroad interests, however, terminated the deal. Without subsidy, the route was completed in 1883.

These arrangements, long in negotiation, became final in late night conferences at Wormley's Hotel in Washington, thwarting continuing opposition from House Democrats to Hayes's selection. Southern defections brought an end to the attempted filibuster. The electoral count was finally completed at 4 A.M. on March 2; Hayes took the oath of office in private the next day, Saturday, and then again publicly on Monday. Frustrated, House Democrats passed a meaningless resolution that Tilden had been "duly elected President of the United States for the term of four years." More substantially, they blocked any appropriations for the army until troops were withdrawn from Louisiana, leaving the nation's soldiers unpaid for some months as they fought Indians in the territories and strikers on the railroads.

It was a messy outcome. Democrats submitted to a Hayes presidency, but sarcastically dubbed the new chief executive "Rutherfraud" and "His Fraudulency"; in the next election they would denounce his ascension as "a deadly blow at our system of representative government." Most of the nation, however, accepted the terms of the "Compromise of 1877." The bargain was partially corrupt, patently unfair, and certainly disruptive. But it was also a peaceful outcome for a nation still torn by a bitter conflict and loath to see its sons fight again. As the treaty that brought Reconstruction to an end, it bore the marks of compromise and moral ambiguity that characterize all political settlements.

The presidential election of 1876 had significant consequences for future politics in the United States. The Democrats gained undisputed control of the South. For a time, the Redeemers kept many of their promises of formal racial equality, and freedmen continued to vote in many places, although blacks were pushed into an inferior political and social condition. Nationally, the intense party competition would continue for twenty years, Republicans and Democrats each winning two whisker-thin presidential contests, while Congress was typically divided between a Democratic House and a Republican Senate. Economic conditions eventually improved, and the quickening pace of industrialization and immigration brought renewed growth, but also rural distress and widening class differences. Life and politics, with their inevitable imperfections, continued.

Trying Times as America Celebrates the Centennial

The election of 1876 occurred during a time of national malaise. A severe economic depression had followed the Panic of 1873. America still struggled to recover from the horrors of the Civil War while also coping with a seemingly endless series of government corruption scandals. Reconstruction had gone on for nearly a decade, and the southern states were chafing under what they perceived as hostile occupation by northern soldiers. The North also had grown weary of Reconstruction, yearning for the South to finally accept the freedom of former slaves and a restored Union. Amidst this scene the nation celebrated its one hundredth anniversary. Witnessing both rising industrialism and ongoing internal conflict, the country braced for a presidential election that would prove to be pivotal in the annals of history.

> We have a right to think . . . that the integrity of the National Union is not to be threatened for many years to come by any danger more formidable than that over which it has recently triumphed.

JULY 4, 1876
EDITORIAL
A GLANCE FORWARD.

There are many warnings against endeavoring, even in a general way, to forecast the future of a country like ours. Both in its successes and its reverses the nation has had an experience very different from that which was expected for it by the wise and earnest men who started it on its way. Their most sanguine hopes never embraced such progress as has taken place in population, in extent of settled territory, and in dignity and influence among the nations of the earth. Their gloomiest forebodings hardly touched the terrible civil war, in which armies more numerous than the entire population of the States a century ago struggled for supremacy. And in many minor matters, for good and for ill, we have not traveled the road which the founders of the Republic thought they saw stretching before them.

Yet it is impossible to avoid reflection on the more prominent features of our probable career as we are celebrating our entry on a second century of national existence. In doing so we are not wholly without guidance which we can reasonably trust. A nation which has attained a strong momentum within its first hundred years in certain defined directions will not immediately change its course. There are some things which we can predict, if not absolutely, yet with a confidence which is not foolish. We have a right to think, for instance, that the integrity of the National Union is not to be threatened for many years to come by any danger more formidable than that over which it has recently triumphed. It is not likely, it is scarcely possible, that there lie within our national system the germs of any disorder so insidious, so powerful, so obstinate, or so violent as slavery. We cannot now point to a single element in the body politic which conflicts as slavery did with the spirit of our institutions. We have, it is true, a serious difficulty to contend with in the race-differences of the Southern States; but this is neither ineradicable nor increasing, nor relatively threatening. It is, in a sense, local, the consequence of a cause forever done away with, and sure itself to yield to the more powerful and enduring influences proceeding from the springs of our national life. We have yet, also, some traces of sectional jealousies, but they are disappearing under the steady operation of the forces of rapid communication and the pursuit of common interests by co-operating means.

It is not unreasonable to expect, too, that our institutions will be still further perfected in the future, and will rid themselves by process of development of the incongruous and incomplete features which may still mark them. It is not too much to say that, tested by the past, the essential portions of our political framework are sound and likely to last, and that the defects, which are undoubted and conspicuous, are mostly in administration, and are due in part to rapid growth and in part to want of experience. We have, for instance, an imperfect system of Government finance, crude taxation, costly collection, and a vicious and vitiating currency. But, bad as our lot is, it is not so bad as that of older nations has been, and the evils we suffer from are noticeable quite as much on account of the extent of the country which they affect as on account of their novelty in the present or in the past. We have no more reason to doubt that we shall make our way out of our troubles in an honorable and safe manner than we have to doubt the continuance of seed-time and harvest in such recurring intervals as the welfare of the race shall demand. And the country will not only survive its apparent defects in government, but it will discover and remedy those more subtle evil influences which have produced the hateful corruption and the detestable perversion of politics that have lately been disclosed to us.

Whatever our fortune may be as a people, it is difficult to imagine that it can be in any serious degree interfered with by foreign complications, or that the influence of the nation on the world at large will not be in the main, helpful to the reign of general peace. We have outlived, in our first century, many possibilities of foreign war. We have seen withdrawn, one after another, all European occupants of the territory which lay within the natural and well-defined boundaries of the country dominated by the thirteen Atlantic colonies. We have seen the neighboring lands from which foreign interference could have been expected, surrendered to their own people, until, except in Cuba, no Government of Europe has an important or possibly threatening footing within reach of our country. We have settled one of the most aggravated and bitter quarrels of modern times between ourselves and the mother country without war, and without any important residuum of unpleasant feeling. We have seen established certain principles of international law governing the maritime intercourse of neutrals with belligerents, which go far toward lessening the danger of our becoming entangled in a European war. It is true that nothing is more uncertain than the course of that force in human history which we may call national temper, and it is not impossible that against reason and without just provocation a people as rational and fair as our own may rush into a conflict of arms; but it is not probable, and we have a right to indulge in calm expectation of a comparatively peaceful future.

With these immense advantages, what do we dare to predict of the national character? Very little that is definite. We are becoming more and more a commercial people. We are driving to the utmost the eager activity and remorseless competition of modern trade. The changes which have occurred within the last hundred years, in the conditions of commercial life, make all prophecy vain. But of this we may be sure, that as the tremendous stimulation by steam and electricity of the energies of business men has not rendered honesty, fidelity, and patient industry less necessary, so no future changes can do so. We may become a relatively greater or less commercial people; but we cannot by any success escape from those supreme obligations to general virtue which have outlived all the mutations that history records, and must survive all that can occur in the future.

THE 1876 REPUBLICAN CONVENTION

As the 1876 Republican convention gathered in Cincinnati, the party faced two main problems: economic distress and a series of corruption scandals that had occurred under President Ulysses Grant. James Blaine, senator from Maine, was the early favorite. Blaine had a strong record of leadership in the Senate, but was also tarred by rumors of his association with railroad corruption schemes, the inevitable target of Democratic campaign attacks. At stake was the long-standing Republican control of the presidency and the future of Reconstruction.

JUNE 15, 1876
EDITORIAL
THE CONVENTION.

The National Convention, which has in its hands the success if not the very existence of the Republican Party, began its formal proceedings yesterday. Much of the real work of the Convention had been done before ex-Gov. MORGAN called the assemblage in the Cincinnati Exposition Building to order, but from that moment the delegates probably began to have a new sense of their responsibilities, and, let us hope, a clearer perception of their duties. The opening address of the Chairman of the Republican National Committee was terse, pungent and admirably suited to the occasion. The speaker showed himself as much alive to the demands which the present makes upon the Republican Party as to the achievements which have made its past illustrious. Hard money, an honest reform of the civil service and the one-term tenure of the Presidency were the principles which ex-Gov. MORGAN commended to the strenuous support of the party. Certainly, no one who listened to him failed to appreciate his references to the party's services in the cause of freedom. We wish we could affirm, with equal certainty, that his audience were equally responsive to his estimate of their duty to the cause of reform. The party certainly needs a candidate "clearly committed on this question, not only by his expressed opinions, but also by his public life and conduct." The question which tens of thousands of Republicans are somewhat dubiously asking themselves to-day is, will it get such a candidate?

With such a nomination as that of Mr. BLAINE the Convention would probably pave the way for defeat in November, but the majority of the party would certainly not be prepared to accept that as a certainty in advance of the election. There are many and obvious reasons which make the worst nomination which the Republican Convention can make a better one than the best which is likely to be made by the Democrats. No one, for example, who appreciates how absolutely the maintenance of free institutions in the South depends upon the existence of a Republican Administration, would hesitate to take the risk even of such a President as Mr. BLAINE in preference to a President who should be under the influence of such men as those who control the present House of Representatives. If we are to be reduced to a mere choice of evils, let us by all means choose the least.

We say this not for the purpose of making any less the outrage on the party and the breach of faith with the people which would be involved in the nomination of such a candidate as the one who still controls the most votes in the Convention. We merely wish to remind that numerous section of the Republican Party whom the present attitude of their delegates fills with unmitigated disgust that on party fealty depends still graver matters than even administrative purity and the elevation of the standards of public life. Fidelity to constitutional guarantees is as absolutely bound up with Republican success as fidelity to the plighted faith of the nation. A Democratic Administration of almost any conceivable type would be an unmixed misfortune for the Southern States and for the Union of which they form a part, because, while leaving untouched the nominal integrity of the recent amendments to the Constitution, it would afford the coveted opportunity to trample them, in practice, under foot. The moderate men in the South have a chance of being listened to now, which in the event of a Democratic victory in November they would no longer enjoy. The rashness and the violence which have been imperfectly restrained in Congress would be unloosed for such a career of mischief as would set back the progress of the country and erect fresh barriers toward the attainment of perfect unity. Democracy in power would mean the revival of smouldering antipathies, the repudiation of solemn promises, and the degradation of the public credit. While considerations like these might save the Republican Party from hopeless schism as the result of a discreditable nomination at Cincinnati, they only help to intensify the folly of those Republicans who are recklessly and blindly striving to make the prospect of a Democratic triumph really formidable.

. . . .

REPUBLICANS SELECT A PRESIDENTIAL NOMINEE

The Republican presidential nomination process began as expected, with Senator Blaine mustering enough votes to gain front-runner status on the first ballot. For several ballots, Blaine's support crept up until it reached 308 of the 756 votes, still short of the required majority. With Blaine blocked, Republicans searched for a candidate capable of uniting the party while presenting a corruption-free image to the general public. Rutherford B. Hayes, governor of Ohio, began garnering attention as a viable and attractive alternative. On the seventh ballot, support coalesced behind Hayes, making him the Republicans' choice for president.

JUNE 16, 1876
THE CINCINNATI CONTEST.

SEVERE REVERSES TO MR. BLAINE.

SENTIMENT OF THE DELEGATIONS MODIFIED BY THE FISHER LETTERS— ENTHUSIASM COOLING AND NO INCREASE OF VOTES—HAYES STOCK MUCH IMPROVED—CONKLING VIRTUALLY OUT OF THE RACE.

Special Dispatch to the New York Times.

CINCINNATI, June 15.—The tone of the Convention was reasonably improved to-day toward the suggestions of reform in administration and toward sound principles in finance. The situation is altogether more hopeful, though not yet free from doubt and anxiety. The reception of the name of Bristow in the Convention was so enthusiastic as to put to shame such utterances as were heard from Gen. Logan yesterday, and the machine men found a sentiment existing against which they did not deem it prudent to display open opposition. The feeling to-night is that Blaine is practically beaten. The emotional features of the canvass for Blaine are less prominent, and the delay has given time for thought and consideration. The letters to Fisher are becoming familiar to delegates who had never read them before coming here. The letters have influence, now that Blaine is announced as safely recovering, which they had not while his physical condition demanded sympathy. The Blaine votes do not increase, and the enthusiasm does not spread, though intense in the localities to which it is confined. The feeling that Blaine is not to be nominated arises from the security that all feel in the holding together of the Conkling forces, the Bristow men, the Pennsylvania delegation, and Ohio. There has been no croak whatever in favor of Blaine, and for the first ballot the estimates are not changed from yesterday or the day before. There will be some changes on the second ballot, but in what direction cannot possibly be learned. The best private estimates made by the canvassers for the different candidates do not disclose any trustworthy information, the fact being that changes are not anywhere definitely arranged, but are dependent upon events and disclosures in their first ballot.

There should not be left out of any statement the fact that there are claims for Blaine of assurances of strength to secure his nomination on the second ballot, which, however, nobody else will admit, and which I fail entirely to discover. Neither can there be found any prospect of a dissolution of forces on the third ballot, though unforeseen occurrences may lead to action in some delegations now unexpected.

Such of the Blaine forces as have been secured to him for complimentary reasons and are fastened only by a slender tenure, will begin to desert, and when he begins to decline he will speedily pass out of sight. Then, if ever, will come the opportunity for combinations, and the possible permutations are not easily computed. The prospect is that the forces opposing Bristow will unite on Hayes. Efforts to such an end are making to night. The New-York delegation is demoralized, and while no formal action is taken there is strong probability of their leaving Mr. Conkling if anything like a unanimous vote can be carried over to Hayes. The Bristow men are urging anew this evening the claims of their candidate on the ground taken in Gen. Harlan's happy speech, and are hopeful of attracting sufficient strength to nominate him. The Bristow men will not go to Hayes, but will make a gallant contest to the end. It is, of course, quite impossible to forecast the action of tomorrow accurately, and the event will be soon enough known. The situation appears, however, as here briefly outlined: Conkling out of the race; Blaine probably beaten from the beginning; the prospects of Hayes excellent; Bristow's chances increased considerably, with the fear still existing that the elements of opposition are too strong to be overcome, and after all the springing of a new name possible but not probable.

JUNE 17, 1876
AN INVINCIBLE COMBINATION.

EXCELLENT WORK OF THE NATIONAL CONVENTION—NOMINATION OF RUTHERFORD BIRCHARD HAYES, OF OHIO, FOR PRESIDENT, AND WILLIAM A. WHEELER, OF NEW-YORK, FOR VICE PRESIDENT—ENTHUSIASTIC RECEPTION OF BOTH NAMES BY THE CONVENTION AND THE NATION.

The Republican National Convention completed its labors yesterday by nominating Gov. Rutherford B. Hayes, of Ohio, for the Presidency, and Hon. William A. Wheeler, of New-York, for the Vice Presidency. The balloting began as soon as the Convention met in the morning. Before the result of the first ballot was announced, Mississippi wished to correct her vote, which raised a question whether this could be done under the rules adopted the day before on this subject. After a brief explanation, the correction was allowed, and the result of the ballot was announced by the Secretary. There was no choice, the highest number of votes being given for Mr. Blaine, which was 285. Gov. Hayes had 61. The second ballot being taken, a protracted debate occurred on the right of four Pennsylvania delegates to vote independently, the rules under which the delegation acted requiring them to vote as a unit. In the end, the Convention sustained the decision of the Chair, allowing the delegates to vote as they pleased. The result of the ballot was then announced, which still showed no choice. The balloting still went on, until; on the sixth ballot, Blaine had 308 votes. The names of Morton and Bristow were then withdrawn, and the seventh and decisive ballot gave Gov. Hayes 384 and Mr. Blaine 351. Gov. Hayes was then declared the nominee of the Convention amid the wildest enthusiasm. For Vice President Hon. William A. Wheeler, of New-York; Stewart L. Woodford, of New-York; Joseph R. Hawley, of Connecticut; Theodore Frelinghuysen, of New-Jersey; and Marshall Jewell, of Connecticut, were successively nominated. The roll was called, and about half the States had responded, giving Mr. Wheeler 366 votes, when, on motion, his nomination was made unanimous. This completed its work, and the Sixth National Republican Convention adjourned with cheers for the ticket.

. . . .

DEMOCRATS SELECT A PRESIDENTIAL NOMINEE

The 1876 Democratic convention met in St. Louis. The expected nominee, New York governor Samuel Tilden, stormed to an early lead on the first ballot, winning the nomination on the second. The Democrats exhibited less division and uncertainty than the Republicans as the party sought its first presidential victory in two decades. *The New York Times,* still a partisan paper, moved to dispel Democratic hopes by portraying Tilden as an unprincipled leader of an incohesive party. The stage was set for an epic election.

JUNE 19, 1876
TILDEN NOMINATED.

A RAILROAD LAWYER AND A REPUDIATION PLATFORM.

THE DEMOCRATIC MACHINE AND ITS WORK AT ST. LOUIS—THE REPUTABLE ELEMENT IN THE PARTY IGNORED AND INSULTED—DISGRACEFUL SCENES—DEMOCRATS GAGGED IN A DEMOCRATIC CONVENTION.

The Democratic National Convention reassembled yesterday morning at 11 o'clock. The first business in order was the report of the Committee on Resolutions, but the committee were not ready to report, and a variety of resolutions concerning the order of business and other matters were offered and disposed of. John Kelly offered a memorial from influential Democrats in New-York, protesting against the nomination of Tilden, but it was declared out of order. Much wrangling took place, but it was finally ended by the announcement that the Committee on Resolutions would be ready to report at 2 o'clock. A recess was taken until that hour. On reassembling the Committee made a majority and minority report, the point of difference being the financial plank of the platform. The majority report condemned the Republicans for their imbecility in not returning to specie payment, accused them of placing hindrances in the way of resumption, denounced these hindrances, and demanded the repeal of the Resumption act. The minority report declared that this act was injurious to the country and demanded its unconditional repeal. After great confusion on motions and counter-motions, the majority report was adopted by a decisive vote. The nomination of candidates then commenced. Thomas Francis Bayard, of Delaware, was the first nominee; Thomas A. Hendricks, of Indiana, came next; Joel Parker, of New-Jersey, followed; then came Samuel J. Tilden, of New-York, who was followed by William Allen, of Ohio; and Gen. Winfield Scott Hancock, of Pennsylvania. This completed the list of nominees, and the balloting ensued. On the first ballot there was no choice; on the second Samuel J. Tilden received more than the necessary two-thirds of the votes, and was declared the candidate of the Democratic Party.

JUNE 26, 1876
EDITORIAL
THE ST. LOUIS CONVENTION.

One of the most curious circumstances attending the meeting of the Democratic Convention at St. Louis is the quiet, not to say indifferent, manner in which its probable action is discussed by the public generally, and even by the Democratic papers. It is no exaggeration to say that the interest felt in the matter is, except in a very limited circle, but languid. All eyes see most easily what they would most like to see, but we are much mistaken if there is not a very general public impression, among Democrats as well as Republicans, that the next President was named at Cincinnati, and that the work of the St. Louis body is superfluous. It is not impossible that this impression may be removed by the action of the Democratic Convention. We are not foolish enough to suppose that it is impossible to nominate a Democrat who would make the contest this Summer and next Fall an earnest one, and would compel the Republican managers to do their work carefully and thoroughly in order to succeed. But it remains true that at the present moment the St. Louis Convention stirs very lightly the popular curiosity.

One reason for this state of things is the degree to which the preliminary discussions at St. Louis have been made purely personal and factional. The quarrel over Gov. TILDEN, carried on as it is mainly on both sides by New-York men, is bitterly personal. Some of the soft-money men oppose him, but others, whose opinions are by no means favorable to specie resumption, favor him. On the other hand, many of the hard-money men support him, but some of these oppose him. The financial question, though not entirely ignored, is a subordinate matter. The principal issue is a personal one. The Convention, therefore, while having a *quasi* national character, has so far been treated by those engaged in it as a private concern, and public opinion has naturally treated it in the same way.

Another feature which goes a great way to account for the slight interest taken in the Convention is the feeling that it will result in a meaningless compromise, presenting no candidate who fairly represents the party, or presenting him hampered with a declaration of policy which will deprive him of all influence. This has always been a favorite practice with the Democrats. It accords well with the narrow and insincere political traditions by which they are governed. The country owes to the Democratic Party many of the most demoralizing elements in our politics—the spoils system, the tyranny of the caucus, the insolent assertion of mere party discipline, the subordination of ends to means, and the control of the party machinery by chicane [sic] and corruption. But of all the evils for which that party is responsible none is greater than the doctrine that the first consideration in a candidate is a low form of availability. It is now twenty years since the Democrats fought a fair fight, with a candidate whose views and purposes were in accordance with those of his party. After Buchanan came the campaign of 1860, which was the secession movement, thinly masked. In 1864 they put a Union General on a treasonable platform. In 1868 they made a repudiation platform for Gov. Seymour, whose sole financial policy was one in support of hard money. In 1872 occurred "the surrender" to Greeleyism, with a sole view to catching votes, and with not a sign of conversion from their own views, which have been more vigorously asserted since that event than before; and this year there is every probability that we shall have a platform of the most double-faced character, and a candidate willing to accept such a platform. Those who suppose that this precludes the nomination of Mr. Tilden mistake the man. He is incapable of refusing a nomination on any platform, and capable of bargaining for it at any sacrifice of consistency and principle.

The scenes which are described in our dispatches this morning, as having occurred at St. Louis during the Sabbath, are calculated to turn the indifference of decent people toward the gathering there into disgust. The turbulence, wrangling, drunkenness, and violence which prevailed throughout the day are unpleasant, but, unfortunately, not insignificant. The reckless crowd which made Sunday the opposite of a day of rest to the people of St. Louis are of a class from which a great many of the managers of the Democratic Party are drawn, and their conduct now is quite in accordance with their general behavior when bent on an important piece of political "work." They have not found the characteristics which make them displeasing to decent people at all in the way of their advancement in their own party, and they are only using now methods which have the sanction of long practice. It is not impossible that Mr. Tilden is to-day, opposed or supported by the gentlemen who, a few years since, stole his watch on his way home from one of his "dear friend" Tweed's conventions, and the tactics employed for and against him are those with which he has long been familiar. It is not unfair, either, to point out that in point of order and decency the St. Louis crowd presents a strong contrast to the Convention recently held at Cincinnati.

THE CANDIDATES ISSUE LETTERS OF ACCEPTANCE

Presidential candidates did not actively campaign for office during the middle 1800s. Campaigns officially began when candidates released "acceptance letters" announcing that they accepted the invitation to become the party's nominee. These letters introduced the candidates to the general public, explaining their ideas and plans for governing. The pro-Republican *New York Times* responded to the acceptance letters of 1876 with glowing praise for Governor Hayes, but sharp rebukes for Governor Tilden. Both candidates focused on the pressing problems of finance and reform.

JULY 10, 1876
EDITORIAL
GEN. HAYES' LETTER OF ACCEPTANCE.

The letter of Gen. Hayes accepting the Republican nomination leaves nothing to be desired. It is the manly, frank, and explicit declaration of a sincere and able man. If there are any who have had doubts as to Gen. Hayes's possession of the pronounced characteristics required in the leader of the Republican Party at this juncture, this letter ought to go far to cause them to dismiss such doubts. It is not the letter of a partisan, a trimmer, an aspirant for office who wishes to avoid criticism by evading an expression of his views and purposes, or, in any sense, the letter of a negative man.

Gen. Hayes shows that he appreciates and respects the right of the people to know what they may expect from him if he shall be placed in the Executive office. He professes nothing, conceals nothing, shuns nothing for the purpose of winning support or propitiating possible opponents. Such as he is he paints himself, and without any pretensions to sincerity, stamps every word with the cogent emphasis of simple and unreserved honesty. There is no more trace of double-dealing than of timidity in what he says. He would not deny that he desires an election with the earnestness which an honorable ambition kindles in every man conscious of capacity for public service; but the election must come to him from a constituency which is neither uninformed nor misinformed concerning the principles he holds and the general objects he would, if elected, pursue. Modestly but fully he lays these before his fellow-citizens, and leaves with them the duty of choice, which cannot, so far as he is concerned, be a blind one. This unfeigned fearlessness will be the first thing in his letter to strike public attention. Whether Republican or Democrat, we do not believe there is an honest man in the country who will not acknowledge it with hearty respect.

Gen. Hayes gives prominence to four points. First of these in order and in importance is civil service reform. His analysis of the evils of the system for which reform is required is clear, exact, and complete, and shows that he has mastered the question with extraordinary thoroughness. He goes further in regard to it than does the Republican platform.

He traces the origin of existing defects to appointments for political services, or, what is worse, for services to political leaders and to the control of members of Congress over such appointments. He points out that the only remedy is to restore the system of the founders of the Government, making appointments for fitness, and rendering every "officer secure in his tenure as long as his personal character remains untarnished and the performance of his duties satisfactory." To this end legislation should be supplied as far as necessary, and he will himself, if elected, employ all the constitutional powers vested in the Executive to establish the reform. Nothing more distinct and comprehensive on this subject could be asked,

and the most ardent believers in the supreme importance of civil-service reform could supply nothing to it. But Gen. Hayes adds to its force by a declaration, couched in the most appropriate terms, of his "inflexible purpose, if elected, not to be a candidate for election to a second term."

On the question of the currency, which ranks next to, if not with, that of reform, the language of Gen. Hayes is unmistakable. He "stands by his record," made in that momentous battle in Ohio last Fall, when he wrested the greatest of the Western States from the hands of the professed inflationists and repudiators, and made the victory a significant and valuable one by the boldness and clearness of his advanced position. "I regard," he says, "all the laws of the United States relating to the payment of the public indebtedness, the legal tender notes included, as constituting a pledge and moral obligation of the Government, which must in good faith be kept." A more succinct statement of sounder doctrine it would be difficult to imagine. He points out that the feeling of uncertainty inseparable from the existence of an irredeemable currency is in itself the greatest obstacle to the revival of confidence and of business. "That uncertainty can be ended in but one way: the resumption of specie payments; but the longer the instability of our money system is permitted to continue, the greater will be the injury inflicted upon our economical interests and on all classes of society. If elected," he concludes, "I shall approve every appropriate measure to accomplish the desired end, and shall oppose any step backward."

We can conceive of no true friend of sound money failing to find satisfaction in this declaration of principles and purposes. There is neither uncertainty nor ambiguity about it. Gen. Hayes knows why resumption is necessary, and will, so far as his power goes, tolerate, neither evasion nor unnecessary delay in securing it. While he will impose on Congress no specific policy of his own, he shows distinctly that the weight of his influence will be in the right direction, and that he will not consent that the pledges of the Government shall be in any way revoked, postponed, weakened, or trifled with. We know of no man whose name has at any time been mentioned in connection with the nomination for the Presidency who could be relied on for a more complete or a sounder declaration of financial policy.

AUGUST 5, 1876
EDITORIAL
THE ESSENCE OF "REFORM."

Gov. Tilden's letter of acceptance, so far as it relates to finance and "reform," is a mere rehash of his last annual

Message. The St. Louis platform was also a rehash of the same document by the same hand. Here we have three documents, all from the same pen, all containing the same barren ideas, and overflowing with cant about reform and exaggerated and untruthful charges against the Republican Party. For that organization, as our readers well know, we do not claim perfection, but we are ready to defend it from slander, and slander is the weapon with which Gov. Tilden assails its financial record and policy.

The present depression in the mercantile and trading community, and the partial disorganization of certain industries giving employment to labor, are facts to be lamented and evils to be patiently endured and outgrown. We experienced as intense a degree of distress about forty years ago, after ten years of Democratic rule under Jackson and Van Buren. We had no war debts then, and were lightly burdened with taxation. "Reform was necessary" in the administration of the General Government then as it is now, but has any sober reasoner ever sought to shift the load of responsibility for the hard times between 1838 and 1845 from the shoulders of individuals to those of the Government? Abuses of credit and paper money, recklessness in contracting debts, the speculative spirit of the preceding years, and other offenses against economical laws, account for the commercial distress of 1840 as they do for that of 1876. But Gov. Tilden has the assurance to put before the sober-minded and thinking portion of the voters of the State, without whose suffrages he has no hope of securing the object of his ambition, such misstatements as these, which follow each other consecutively:

"The present depression in all the business and industries of the people, which is depriving labor of its employment, and carrying want into so many homes, has its principal cause in excessive Governmental consumption. Under the illusions of a specious prosperity engendered by the false policies of the Federal Government a waste of capital has been going on ever since the peace of 1865, which could only end in universal disaster. The Federal taxes of the last eleven years reach the gigantic sum of four thousand five hundred millions. Local taxation has amounted to two-thirds as much more. The vast aggregate is not less than seven thousand five hundred millions."

The railway mania, the speculations in all sorts of securities and in real estate, the losses sustained by hundreds of thousands of people of saving habits through their too confiding investments in worthless bonds and stocks, the facilities of credit unwisely extended by banks and other lenders, the universal inflation which followed the failure of Secretary McCulloch's attempt to withdraw the legal-tender notes, are nothing. "Excessive governmental consumption" is everything. Are men who think for

themselves to be imposed on by such transparent quackery as runs through the sentences we have quoted?

The Democratic candidate then assures us that he said to the Secretary of the Treasury in 1865, "live within your income." But his eyes are closed to the fact that the Government has lived within its income, and has diminished that portion of the public debt bearing interest in coin in no less than $410,000,000 since March, 1869, and in the same interval has reduced the annual interest charge $29,600,000. He does not tell us this. He does not say to his model reformers that without a single exception for every year since 1868 the national Treasury has shown a surplus of income over expenditure. But he drops the subject with the base insinuation that the Government has not lived within its income, and has disregarded his sage advice of eleven years ago.

We are so accustomed to false statements of a statistical nature from Mr. Tilden that we content ourselves with remarking that the total revenue of the Government from June 30, 1864, to June 30, 1875, has been $4,072,000,000, and not $4,500,000,000. Of this sum of $4,072,000,000 at least $600,000,000 was applied to the payment of indebtedness contracted previous to 1865, and $1,309,000,000 was paid for interest on the debt, which leaves a "governmental consumption" of less than one-half the amount given by the author of the platform, the letter, and the Message.

On the subject of the currency the candidate has absolutely nothing new to say. It appears that the denunciations of the act of 1875 embodied in the platform are entirely in accordance with his present professions. More than one-half the letter is devoted to a foggy and ambiguous presentation of the specie payment problem and the methods to be applied to its solution. We have already criticised the barren generalities in which the Governor invariably loses himself when he attacks the currency question. In his last compilation he adds nothing fresh to his old stock of them. We still have the changes sounded on "public economies, official retrenchments, and wise finance." We hear again the twaddle about providing a "central reservoir of coin, adequate to the adjustment of the temporary fluctuations of international balances," and the "payment in coin of such inconsiderable portions of the legal tenders as individuals may, from time to time, desire to convert for special use or in order to lay by in coin their little stores of money." But of contraction, of the necessity of diminishing the number of the paper dollars in order to raise their value, we hear nothing. We defy anyone to frame in his own mind a clear conception of the exhilarating process by which Mr. Tilden professes to be able to make greenbacks worth a dollar in gold which are now worth only ninety cents.

Nothing could more forcibly illustrate the barrenness, the timidity, and the inborn craftiness of Mr. TILDEN than the shuffling and delay which have attended the ushering into the world of this abridgement of last January's Message. It is absurd to suppose that men of cultivated intelligence and moral sense can be the victims of such a charlatan as Mr. TILDEN shows himself to be by his treatment of questions so vital that on the right solution of them the continued existence of our Government in its present form not improbably depends.

- -

THE NEW YORK TIMES BACKS HAYES

The Republican Party relied upon "waving the bloody shirt" for years following the Civil War, portraying itself as the party that had freed the slaves and preserved the Union. In 1876 the party highlighted differences between the two presidential candidates. Hayes had fought for the Union in the Civil War, while Tilden had supported Democratic efforts to conclude a quick peace with the Confederacy at any cost. Hayes had served three terms as governor, achieving an image as honest and above corruption. Tilden had worked as an attorney for railroad interests and as governor was linked with New York's infamous Tammany Hall boss, William Tweed. According to *The Times,* only the Republican Party and its nominee would protect the national interest and root out corruption.

JULY 25, 1876
HAYES AND TILDEN.

AN IOWA GERMAN CONTRASTS THE TWO CANDIDATES, AND SHOWS THAT THE REPUBLICAN IS THE ONLY MAN TO BE TRUSTED.

We mentioned, the other day, a letter written to the Davenport (Iowa,) *Gazette* by ex-Senator Claussen, as influential a German as Iowa contains; and hitherto a Republican, except in 1872, when he supported Greeley. In this letter he discusses the two candidates for President, and his views will be found good reading by all intelligent men. He says:

"Hayes is evidently an honest man. He entered the Army against the rebellion at the commencement of the war, and remained in the Army to the end of the struggle. He had been wounded four times, four horses had been shot under him, but still Hayes valiantly persisted in fighting the rebels until they were subdued. He risked his life for the welfare of his country. And in his letter of acceptance he declares that, if elected, he will not be a candidate for a second term to avoid the temptation of misusing the office for the satisfaction of his personal ambition. These points, it seems to me, are strong evidences of an honest mind, which is mainly guided by a keen sense of duty. Hayes, three times elected Governor against the strongest candidates in the Democratic Party—Thurman, Pendleton, and Allen—has shown good executive abilities. What better guarantees can we have that he will carry out the principles proclaimed in the Republican platform and in Hayes' letter of acceptance, in relation to civil service reform? Hayes undoubtedly is aware that in his declaration respecting specie resumption by yielding nothing to the friends of soft money he has offended many voters, particularly in Ohio and Indiana, and that his expressed opinions in relation to civil service reforms are generally at war with the ambition and aspirations of numerous influential politicians. But Gov. Hayes has the candor and courage to be perfectly open and frank, a virtue quite rare among candidates for offices. It seems to me, that from the examination of the character of the Republican candidate and from the principles announced in his letter of acceptance, the friends of civil service reforms can be satisfied that the appointments by Hayes, if elected President, will be guided by a strong sense of his duty to the country, and by a good sound judgment, qualities which have made the administration of Emperor William highly distinguished. There is no cause whatever to fear that any kind of Grantism will be repeated in Hayes's administration and in his appointment to offices.

Now, let us see what we may reasonably expect from Tilden. What evidences has the country of his character?

Tilden is an attorney for railroad companies, and by his speculations has made a vast amount of money. His means are valued at several millions of dollars. Before his election as Governor, in 1874, he had been a member of the Legislature, and of the Constitutional Convention, in the State of New-York. He has never been in Congress. During the war Tilden was active in publishing Copperhead pamphlets, and in 1865 he was a member of the committee of the Democratic National Convention which declared the war a failure, and required a cessation of hostility and a peaceable settlement, though such was then impossible without yielding to the Southern States a separation from the Union. There is a clear proof against Tilden that he was a friend and political associate of William M. Tweed in the management of the Democratic Party in the State of New-York. Tweed was convicted, but escaped out of his prison. Has the Governor [Tilden] instituted prosecutions against the guilty guardians of the imprisoned great rascal? Tilden's connivance at the escape of Tweed can hardly be doubted. What just expectations can be maintained by reasonable voters, that such a man as Tilden will carry out the Democratic platform respecting civil service reform? That platform is really a surprise; it abandons the maxim, 'To the victor the spoils.' If Tilden should be elected and would strictly adhere to the Democratic platform, he would be bound to leave nearly all honest and able Republican officers in their places. Is anyone so green as to believe that he would do it? Will he not reward the many thousand agents who are now very active for his election, and who have worked eagerly for his nomination? Will he, therefore, not oust nearly all honest and experienced Republican officers to make room for his political friends, the Southern Confederates and their supporters and sympathizers in the North? Nothing else can be reasonably expected from a man who has shown so strong a sympathy for the South during the rebellion. The Democratic civil service reform under Tilden would be a palpable fraud. About eighty thousand civil officers, however trustworthy, competent, and experienced, would be turned out to make room for new men without experience, and for such persons as were the associates and political friends of Tilden during the time when he, with Tweed, managed the Democratic Party, and saw in the war for the Union only a failure. If we know the nature of the tree we cannot be disappointed as to its fruits."

• •

An Election Too Close to Call

The nation voted on November 7, 1876, but the results were not certain the following day. Voter turnout had surged, delivering more votes than had ever previously been counted. The high turnout did not produce a clear winner in many states, leading each party to accuse the other of massive voter fraud and intimidation. Tilden appeared to have won the national popular vote, but the results in a few states were so close that an Electoral College winner could not easily be determined. The nation hung on the announcement of Florida, the only state that had not yet allocated its electoral votes. Throughout the day updates poured in, but failed to conclusively settle the national contest. Both parties optimistically predicted victory.

NOVEMBER 8, 1876
EDITORIAL
A DOUBTFUL ELECTION.

At the time of going to press the result of the Presidential election is still in doubt. Enough has been learned to show that the vote has been unprecedentedly heavy. Both parties have exhausted their full legitimate strength, while the peculiar Democratic policy, for which such extensive preparations were made in the large registry in this city and in the enormous registry in Brooklyn, has had its effect.

In this State, two hundred and fifty-six voting districts outside the Cities of New-York and Brooklyn show a net Democratic gain over 1872 of 6,427. In that year the Republican majority, excluding the two cities named, was 79,720. This year New-York City has given 53,500 Democratic, while the returns from Brooklyn represent a majority of 17,792, the combined majority being 71,292. On the basis of the returns from the remainder of the State, there is little hope of overcoming this majority, and the Electoral vote of New-York will be cast for Mr. TILDEN. That this is largely due to fraud in New-York and Kings County, and that an honest vote in these counties might have changed the result, are conclusions which no intelligent and fair observer can refuse to consider. The exact truth in regard to them cannot now be stated, but it will be ascertained, and it must have its weight.

Conceding New-York to Mr. TILDEN, he will receive the electoral votes of the following States:

Alabama	10
Arkansas	6
Connecticut	6
Delaware	3
Georgia	11
Indiana	15
Kentucky	12
Maryland	8
Mississippi	8
Missouri	15
New-Jersey	9
New-York	35
North Carolina	10
Tennessee	12
Texas	8
Virginia	11
West Virginia	5
Total	184

Gen. HAYES will receive the votes of the following States:

California	6
Colorado	3
Illinois	21
Iowa	11
Kansas	5
Louisiana	8
Maine	7
Massachusetts	13
Michigan	11
Minnesota	5
Nebraska	3
Nevada	3
New-Hampshire	5
Ohio	3
Oregon	22
Pennsylvania	29
Rhode Island	4
South Carolina	7
Vermont	5
Wisconsin	10
Total	181

This leaves Florida alone still in doubt. If the Republicans have carried that State, as they claim, they will have 185 votes—a majority of one.

NOVEMBER 8, 1876
FLORIDA.

THE STATE IN DOUBT.

AUGUSTA, Ga., Nov. 8.—A dispatch from Lake City, Florida, says returns from sixteen counties in Florida, Republican strongholds, show a net Democratic gain over the vote of 1874 of 544. Columbia and Monroe Counties, formerly Republican, elect Democratic tickets. Finley, Dem., for Congress, is probably re-elected. The Democrats claim the State by a small majority.

AUGUSTA. Ga., Nov. 7.—There is nothing further from the Florida election. It will be close. Both sides claim the State.

• •

THE REPUBLICANS CLAIM VICTORY FOR HAYES

On November 8, 1876, a day after results had been expected, the Republican Party declared the election over, with the remaining states in doubt having voted for Hayes. Their final tally awarded Hayes the presidency over Tilden, 185–184 in the Electoral College. The Republican Party had picked up seats in the House of Representatives and retained control over the Senate. Despite the Republicans' optimism, the electoral votes were actually in doubt in four states: Florida, Louisiana, Oregon, and South Carolina. With the most powerful office in the nation still undecided, resolution was elusive.

NOVEMBER 9, 1876
THE BATTLE WON.

A REPUBLICAN VICTORY IN THE NATION.

GOV. HAYES ELECTED PRESIDENT AND WILLIAM A. WHEELER VICE PRESIDENT—THE REPUBLICANS CARRY TWENTY-ONE STATES, CASTING 185 ELECTORAL VOTES—A REPUBLICAN MAJORITY IN THE NEXT CONGRESS.

The dispatches received since our last issue confirm the reports on which THE TIMES yesterday claimed 181 electoral votes for Gov. HAYES. On Wednesday the following States were put down as surely Republican: Colorado, California, Illinois, Iowa, Kansas, Maine, Massachusetts, Michigan, Minnesota, Nevada, Nebraska, New-Hampshire, Oregon, Ohio, Pennsylvania, Rhode Island, Vermont, Wisconsin, Louisiana, and South Carolina. Some of these States were claimed by the Democrats, but all intelligence, thus far received, not only shows that the above estimate was correct, but that Florida, which was left in doubt, has gone Republican by at least 1,500 majority—our latest dispatches say 2,000—and that the two Republican Congressmen are also elected. Encouraging reports were received from Oregon early yesterday morning; and in the afternoon came the decisive news that the Democrats conceded the State, which had given a Republican majority of over one thousand, and gained a Republican Congressman. In Nebraska the same condition of affairs was shown. There the Republican majority rose to 8,000.

Dispatches from Nevada made it certain that the State had gone for Hayes. The latest news from South Carolina shows a Republican victory, the Democrats conceding the State to Hayes and the Republicans claiming 5,000 majority. Louisiana is one of the States which the Democrats have claimed; but our dispatches, coming from various sources in the State, show that it has gone Republican. The latest intelligence points to the certain election of Gov. Rutherford B. Hayes to the Presidency, and a Republican victory in the nation.

All the Congressional districts have not been heard from definitely, but the advices received destroy the Democratic majority in the present House. The indications now are that the Republicans have elected 145 members, (including those chosen in September and October,) and the Democrats 145. In the present Congress the Republicans have but 110 members, to 183 Democrats. There is, therefore, a Republican net gain of 73. All the Representatives have now been chosen except in New-Hampshire, which is now represented by one Republican and two Democrats, and will elect in March, 1877.

> " The colored voters of the South who failed to vote for Hayes Electors did so because they were driven from the polls, or in some other way deprived of the rights conferred on them by the Constitution. "

ELECTION FRAUD AND INTIMIDATION MAR THE VOTE

Both parties resorted to fraud in an attempt to win the election of 1876 and were defended by their supportive partisan presses. Several contested southern states, including Louisiana and South Carolina, were populated by a majority of free blacks, strong supporters of Republican candidates. To block their votes, organized groups favoring the Democratic Party systematically repressed black turnout. Using "rifle clubs" and "citizen patrols," white Democrats threatened, harassed, and attacked potential Republican voters. For their part, Republicans' tactics were less violent, but no less illegal or nefarious. They simply altered the final tally at the polls to inflate Republican support. Ignoring southern suppression of free blacks, Democratic papers such as *The World* defended favorable Democratic returns, while Republican presses such as *The New York Times* focused on the injustice of vote suppression while ignoring Republican attempts.

1876 POPULAR VOTE

STATE	TOTAL VOTE	RUTHERFORD B. HAYES (REPUBLICAN) VOTES	%	SAMUEL J. TILDEN (DEMOCRAT) VOTES	%	PETER COOPER (GREENBACK) VOTES	%
Alabama	171,699	68,708	40.0	102,989	60.0	—	0.0
Arkansas	96,946	38,649	39.9	58,086	59.9	211	0.2
California	155,784	79,258	50.9	76,460	49.1	47	0.0
Connecticut	122,134	59,033	48.3	61,927	50.7	774	0.6
Delaware	24,133	10,752	44.6	13,381	55.4	—	0.0
Florida	46,776	23,849	51.0	22,927	49.0	—	0.0
Georgia	180,690	50,533	28.0	130,157	72.0	—	0.0
Illinois	554,368	278,232	50.2	258,611	46.6	17,207	3.1
Indiana	430,020	206,971	48.1	213,516	49.7	9,533	2.2
Iowa	293,398	171,326	58.4	112,121	38.2	9,431	3.2
Kansas	124,134	78,324	63.1	37,902	30.5	7,770	6.3
Kentucky	259,614	97,156	37.4	159,696	61.5	1,944	0.7
Louisiana	145,823	75,315	51.6	70,508	48.4	—	0.0
Maine[1]	117,045	66,300	56.6	49,917	42.6	662	0.6
Maryland	163,759	71,980	44.0	91,779	56.0	—	0.0
Massachusetts	259,619	150,063	57.8	108,777	41.9	—	0.0
Michigan	318,426	166,901	52.4	141,665	44.5	9,023	2.8
Minnesota[2]	124,119	72,982	58.8	48,816	39.3	2,321	1.9
Mississippi	164,776	52,603	31.9	112,173	68.1	—	0.0
Missouri	350,610	145,027	41.4	202,086	57.6	3,497	1.0
Nebraska	49,258	31,915	64.8	17,343	35.2	—	0.0
Nevada	19,691	10,383	52.7	9,308	47.3	—	0.0
New Hampshire	80,143	41,540	51.8	38,510	48.1	—	0.0
New Jersey	220,193	103,517	47.0	115,962	52.7	714	0.3
New York	1,015,503	489,207	48.2	521,949	51.4	1,978	0.2
North Carolina	233,911	108,484	46.4	125,427	53.6	—	0.0
Ohio	658,650	330,698	50.2	323,182	49.1	3,058	0.5
Oregon	29,873	15,207	50.9	14,157	47.4	509	1.7
Pennsylvania	758,973	384,157	50.6	366,204	48.2	7,209	0.9
Rhode Island	26,499	15,787	59.6	10,712	40.4	—	0.0
South Carolina	182,683	91,786	50.2	90,897	49.8	—	0.0
Tennessee	222,743	89,566	40.2	133,177	59.8	—	0.0
Texas	151,431	45,013	29.7	106,372	70.2	—	0.0
Vermont	64,460	44,092	68.4	20,254	31.4	—	0.0
Virginia	236,288	95,518	40.4	140,770	59.6	—	0.0
West Virginia	99,647	41,997	42.1	56,546	56.7	1,104	1.1
Wisconsin[3]	257,799	130,668	50.7	123,927	48.1	1,509	0.6
TOTALS	8,411,618	4,033,497	48.0	4,288,191	51.0	78,501	0.9

1. Figures from *Maine Register, 1945*.
2. Figures from *Minnesota Votes*.
3. Figures from *Wisconsin Blue Book 1997*, p. 677.

OTHER VOTES	%	PLURALITY	
2	0.0	34,281	D
—	0.0	19,437	D
19	0.0	2,798	R
400	0.3	2,894	D
—	0.0	2,629	D
—	0.0	922	R
—	0.0	79,624	D
318	0.1	19,621	R
—	0.0	6,545	D
520	0.2	59,205	R
138	0.1	40,422	R
818	0.3	62,540	D
—	0.0	4,807	R
166	0.1	16,383	R
—	0.0	19,799	D
779	0.3	41,286	R
837	0.3	25,236	R
—	0.0	24,166	R
—	0.0	59,570	D
—	0.0	57,059	D
—	0.0	14,572	R
—	0.0	1,075	R
93	0.1	3,030	R
—	0.0	12,445	D
2,369	0.2	32,742	D
—	0.0	16,943	D
1,712	0.3	7,516	R
—	0.0	1,050	R
1,403	0.2	17,953	R
—	0.0	5,075	R
—	0.0	889	R
—	0.0	43,611	D
46	0.0	61,359	D
114	0.2	23,838	R
—	0.0	45,252	D
—	0.0	14,549	D
1,695	0.7	6,741	R
11,429	0.1	254,694	D

NOVEMBER 12, 1876
EDITORIAL
THE SOUTH IN THE ELECTION.

The *World* thinks that "no candid Republican who looks at the tremendous majorities for TILDEN in Texas, Arkansas, Kentucky, Mississippi and Alabama can doubt that the Tilden Electors received a great popular majority in Louisiana." In other words, because the shot-gun policy succeeded perfectly in two or three Southern States which are as pronounced in their Republicanism as Iowa and Vermont, it is absurd to suppose that in other States where the negro voters were either better protected or were better able to take care of themselves, the same results did not ensue. We doubt if even the *World* has impudence enough to pretend that on a fair vote Mississippi and Alabama are not overwhelmingly Republican. No wilder assumption could be made than that any appreciable proportion of the negroes of Louisiana and South Carolina voted the Democratic ticket. The colored voters of the South who failed to vote for Hayes Electors did so because they were driven from the polls, or in some other way deprived of the rights conferred on them by the Constitution. The fact is, that over two-thirds of the South the "shot-gun policy" has triumphed to an extent that may well shake our faith in the efficacy of reconstruction. Organized intimidation has overcome the voting power. The main body of the South is on the side of the man who has affirmed the constitutional right of secession, and who had rallied around him conspicuous leaders in the rebellion, struggling to regain under the Government the ground they lost in war.

Of this result there is but one explanation. It cannot be pretended that the immense majorities which twice within four years have declared in favor of the Republicans have been mastered by orderly and legal methods. The change is not the product of discussion, for discussion has been systematically stifled. It has not been brought about by legitimate canvassing to which we of the North are accustomed, for the canvasser not bound hand and foot to the Democracy has opened his lips at the peril of his life. The organizations which worked wonders in behalf of secession in 1860 have in this year of grace been reproduced, with bloody variations, in the interest of TILDEN and HENDRICKS. Oppression and violence have been the arguments most relied upon. The rural districts of the Republican South have been patroled as though the country were in insurrection. By day and by night rifle clubs have ridden through colored neighborhoods, threatening and frightening, whipping and shooting, with the specific purpose of overawing the voters and driving away their local leaders. Meetings have been broken up, white Republicans have been warned that they must leave, and the only systematic work which has been permitted has been that which was subordinate to the one aim of securing the South for the Democratic Party. These tactics have largely succeeded. The ballot has succumbed to the bullet in several of the States, and the great body of the South has sustained TILDEN.

In view of these facts, what bitter irony is in the oft-repeated pretense of the Democrats, that the Federal Government was "invading" the South in the interest of the Republicans! Two or three thousand soldiers, scattered over a vast area, were represented as an aggressive army, doing the bidding of an uncrowned despot at Washington! Its work was to preserve order when called upon by responsible officials, and to maintain peace at the polls—that was all. In South Carolina it has undoubtedly been efficacious; in the other Southern States its existence has been in effect unknown. Louisiana has been the theatre of systematic violence and fraud, as dispatches received thence clearly show. The reconstructed Kuklux, the White Leaguers, and the Rifle Clubs had their own way in Mississippi and other States, as, before now, they had in Alabama, Arkansas, and Georgia. That terrible Federal power which has been the bugaboo of a certain class of Northern citizens, left the South to its fate. It went to the limits of the law when it called upon United States Marshals to do their duty. Beyond that it was powerless. The Democrats snapped their fingers at it, heaped epithets on the Federal Government, and went on their way, bribing and bullying, threatening and killing, with absolute impunity. The effect upon the election we now see.

The spectacle is not one which the loyal citizens of the Union can contemplate with much pride. The war was waged to establish the supremacy of Federal authority; and after all the slaughter and all the expenditure—after all the sacrifices made to sustain a great principle—the Federal authority is overmatched in a struggle for the possession of power, as against the secession principle, backed by armed organizations and a spirit of defiance, which of itself implies legal paralysis at Washington. These Southern Democrats took up arms against the Government and failed; they professed repentance and were pardoned; with a magnanimity which has no parallel, they were restored to political power; and now they use the influence thus conceded to them to strike down the reconstructed Union and to nullify the constitutional amendments. In Alabama, Arkansas, and Mississippi, the emancipated blacks, enfranchised, and guaranteed by the Constitution equality with whites before the law, now discover that the franchise is a mockery, that the guarantee is valueless, and that they are at the mercy of their former owners, intent upon reducing them to vassalage, and upon using their voting privileges as a means of consolidating their own power.

NOVEMBER 19, 1876
A DEMOCRATIC MANIFESTO.

The following document, which on the face of it is a Democratic manifesto, and bears internal evidence of being prepared by the Northern Democrats now in Florida, comes to us through the Associated Press:

TALLAHASSEE, Nov. 18.—The following seems to be the situation in this State: Each party claims the State on the Presidential ticket. It is pretty well conceded that the Democrats carry their State ticket. The Democrats base their claim of the electoral ticket on official returns received here as follows: It is ordered that the count of the votes and the canvass of the same shall be done in public. The Democratic Committee arranged to have sworn duplicates of the official returns made in each county, and forwarded. They have received these from all save five counties, all Democratic. Then estimates based on these unofficial copies of official returns give Drew and Tilden both a clear majority. The Republicans will furnish no figures, stating that they will await the official returns. Many stoutly claim that Hayes has carried the State. However, it is probable that Tilden will have a majority of some 300 or 400 on the returns as made officially by the County Canvassers. The Republicans claim that, even admitting this, they will be able, by proving frauds, to overcome this prima facie majority and establish the State for Hayes. The fight before the State Board will be very bitter; the Democratic leaders, defending their majority for Tilden, will attack the returns in Jefferson, Alachua, and Leon Counties, which are the Republican strongholds. They claim to have discovered a glaring fraud in Alachua, where the returns of the election inspectors were raised 219 votes, and their names forged to a new return.

NOVEMBER 23, 1876
HOW THE VOTING WAS DONE IN EDGEFIELD—GRAPHIC PICTURE OF THE SCENES AROUND THE POLLING-PLACES—RUNNING THE GAUNTLET TO THE BALLOT-BOX—THE WAY TO ROLL UP DEMOCRATIC MAJORITIES.

From an Occasional Correspondent.
COLUMBIA, Monday, Nov. 20, 1876.

Notwithstanding the provision that no man shall be deprived of any political privilege enjoyed by any other man on account of "race, color, or previous condition of servitude," by some tacit understanding on the part of the managers of election, two polling-places were established in the village of Edgefield, one at the Court-house, called No. 1, for the whites; another at Macedonia Church, on the edge of the village, professedly for the colored. The former no colored man attempted to approach until late in the day. Then, it being found that, in consequence of the tactics employed at the church, but a small portion of the colored population would be able to vote there, an attempt was made to vote at No. 1. United States Marshal Beaty succeeded in getting six or eight to the box, but beyond that number all efforts were in vain. Every approach to the Court-house was cut off by horsemen, who formed a cordon across every path, while crowds of white men packed the steps and portico of the Court-house building, preventing the approach of any one suspected of Republicanism. Up to nearly ten o'clock, the hundreds of colored voters, waiting to deposit Republican ballots at poll number two, which they had been made to believe was exclusively their own, the crowds of white men already in the building and voting there.

Amid all the strife and danger of the unequal contest in which they were compelled to engage, not a gun or pistol was to be seen in the hands or on the persons of the outraged but inoffensive blacks. If there was a weapon among that surging mass, it was most skillfully and considerately concealed. A few, it is true, had sticks, but beyond that they were as defenceless as the children of a New-York public school. They never gave expression to a threat, and even desisted, when requested so to do, from indulging in a cheer for the candidates of their choice.

All the previous night the place was in possession of a mob of white men, dancing in the Court-house and yelling everywhere. From daylight until 10 o'clock the black men's polling-place, so called, was surrounded by at least three hundred mounted men, some on horses, some on mules, some with Confederate uniforms trimmed with yellow, all with red shirts, and obeying the commands of "Gen." Gary, who, pistol in hand, yelled his orders to open or close ranks, advance or retreat, as he would have done had he been leading a rebel regiment against the men of the North in 1861. In addition to the mounted men there were a large number dismounted, but all armed, having the same purpose, and obeying the same orders as the mounted force.

At 9:45 o'clock United States Deputy Marshal Beaty obtained a company of United States infantry under the command of Capt. Kellogg, who detailed a squad of four and afterward eight men, under Lieut. Hoyt, to open the way to the poll. This squad pierced the ranks of the "red-shirts" who had packed their horses so closely together that the only approach to the windows, back of which was the ballot-box, was under the bellies of their beasts. An alley, however, was made by the gallant officer, at imminent risk of his life and the lives of his men. Over the heads of the little band innumerable pistols were held. Not a man of that drunken, foul-mouthed crew but had his pistol in hand with his finger on the trigger. Thus eight brave men, representing the United States, opened and kept open a narrow pathway along which the poor but undaunted negro had the dangerous privilege of running the gauntlet.

Every black or brown man that essayed to reach the box through this threatening and furious crowd was greeted with opprobious epithets, such as only South Carolinians can utter, and which they intensified by interjecting every variety of rebel yell. If one unguarded word had fallen from the lips of a colored man, a scene of carnage would have followed frightful to think of. Before the soldiers came on the ground, several colored men had been beaten with bludgeons and the butts of pistols. Their forbearance, however, was beyond all praise. On reaching the box, the fortunate voter found a white man named Shepard standing guard over it, who with his sinister eyes endeavored to look the poor negro into such a state of terror that he began to ask himself whether the poor privilege of acting for a few short moments the part of an American citizen was worth the risk he ran. The gauntlet being safely run, the colored voter was then "put through" a long frivolous catechism—so minute that at the close of the polls several hundred of the colored Republicans had failed even to come in sight of the ballot-box. This was the "Mississippi plan," carried to a degree of perfection not excelled even by Vicksburg itself.

In the afternoon, the whites having done all the voting and repeating at Poll No. 1 which was regarded as necessary to accomplish their ends, it was suggested that the crowd of anxious colored men at No. 2 should go there to vote. Some essayed so to do, but every avenue was so carefully guarded that unless they had crept between the legs of the horses, they would have found no way of approach. In other portions of the district similar and even worse scenes were enacted. At Coopersville the managers were assaulted and run off by 12 o'clock. At another polling place both the manager and the United States Supervisor were put to flight a quarter of an hour

before the time for opening the polls. At another the Democratic manager got exclusive possession of the box, and retained it long enough to bring about the curious result of giving a large Democratic majority at a poll where ten black Republicans had voted to one white Democrat. By these, and similar nefarious ways, the Democrats made a majority of over 3,000 in a district where there are not that number of legal voters all told. It is significant of one of the methods employed, that in the State of Georgia, which this district abuts, there were 30,000 less votes cast at this election than at the last. They were sent into South Carolina and Florida. The villainy of which this is but a poor outline will, I have reason to believe, be fully established by the reports to be made both by the United States Marshals and the officers of the Regular Army on duty at the various points.

G. N.

. . . .

The Electoral College Vote Fails to Settle the Election

A month after the election, the dispute raged on. One by one, each state adopted an official count of their ballots and assigned electors to cast votes in the Electoral College. When the votes were counted, Hayes received the Republican-predicted 185, and Tilden received 184, but that did not settle the matter. The fight then moved into the courts and Congress. The Democrats sued to gain any possible advantage, seeing that the reversal of a single electoral vote would tip the election in their favor. A battle loomed in Congress over whether the sitting Democratic House or the Republican Senate would have the final say in the official count of electoral votes. The election quickly turned into one of the most fiercely contested in American history.

DECEMBER 7, 1876
SOUTH CAROLINA.

THE SUPREME COURT DECIDES THAT WALLACE IS THE LEGAL SPEAKER—THE PRESIDENTIAL ELECTORS MEET AND CAST THE VOTE OF THE STATE FOR HAYES.

Special Dispatch to the New-York Times.

Columbia, Dec. 6.—Two important events have occurred here to-day. The Supreme Court has rendered its judgment that Wallace, of the Democratic House, is the constitutional Speaker on the election of the members having prima facie rights. What action that body will take remains to be seen. It is expected that measures will

at once be instituted to oust the Republican House by force. The Presidential Electors have met and adjourned. The seven votes of the State were cast for Hayes and Wheeler. One of the members informed me he was offered $10,000 for his vote, with $40,000 security put up for its payment.

DECEMBER 7, 1876
HAYES AND WHEELER CHOSEN PRESIDENT AND VICE PRESIDENT.

RESULT OF THE ACTION OF THE ELECTORAL COLLEGES YESTERDAY—EXTRAORDINARY EFFORTS OF THE DEMOCRACY TO DEFEAT THE WILL OF THE PEOPLE—WHOLESALE ATTEMPTS AT BRIBERY—CONSPIRACY IN OREGON—THE REPUBLICAN CANDIDATES RECEIVE 185 ELECTORAL VOTES.

The Electoral Colleges of the several States met yesterday, according to law, and voted for the candidates for President and Vice President as the members had severally been elected to vote. Vacancies were filled in several of the colleges, both Democratic and Republican. The result is that Rutherford B. Hayes and William A. Wheeler have received the 185 votes necessary to election. Several attempts were made to defeat the will of the people, notably in Louisiana, South Carolina, and Oregon. Bribery was the method employed in the two former States, and a conspiracy, to exclude a Republican elector was the method resorted to in the last-named State. . . . The State Board of Canvassers of Florida did not complete their work until 2 o'clock yesterday morning. The result was made public directly after. The majority for Hayes is over nine hundred, the State ticket is elected, and the two Republican Congressmen. The Legislature is Democratic. The board were unanimous in their report on all but a few unimportant points. The concurrence of the Democratic member of the board, in making the report, seems to have been something of a surprise to the visiting Democrats. . . . In South Carolina, the two chief events of yesterday were the meeting of the Republican Electors and the decision of the Supreme Court that Wallace was the legally elected Speaker of the lower house of the Legislature. What the Democrats propose to do is not known. Our dispatch from Washington shows the mistake they made in trying to set up a separate house. They can do nothing now conformably to law. . . . In New-Orleans the chief event was the meeting of the Electoral College, and the statement publicly made by one of its members that he had been offered $100,000 to vote for Tilden. An attempt was also made to buy one of the Republican Electors of South Carolina for $10,000. Both attempts failed, and the votes of the men who had been thus approached, were cast for the man they had been elected to vote for. . . . The President yesterday sent a special Message to Congress, transmitting the report of the gentlemen who went to New-Orleans, on the election in that State, and the work of the Returning Board.

• •

CONGRESS CREATES AN ELECTORAL COMMISSION

In an attempt to resolve the disputed electoral vote, two months after the popular votes had been cast, Congress intervened, creating an unprecedented Electoral Commission that would represent both parties via membership from the Senate, House, and Supreme Court. The commission was given the power to hear cases concerning the disputed states and deliver final judgment, but given broad freedom to develop its rules. The first case heard was Florida. A week later, after secret deliberations, the commission rendered its first decision, in favor of Hayes, by a narrow 8–7 margin, divided precisely by party membership. All subsequent decisions showed the same partisan divide.

A meeting of the Congressional commission created to resolve the twenty disputed electoral votes in the 1876 presidential election between Republican Rutherford B. Hayes and Democrat Samuel Tilden.

Source: The Granger Collection, New York

FEBRUARY 1, 1877
WASHINGTON.

MEETING OF THE NEW COMMISSION.

ALL THE MEMBERS PRESENT—JUSTICE BRADLEY, OF NEW-JERSEY, SELECTED—HOURS ALLOWED FOR ARGUMENT—OPEN SESSIONS TO BE HELD—THE QUESTION OF GOING BEHIND THE RETURNS.

Special Dispatch to the New-York Times.

WASHINGTON, Jan. 31.—The Electoral Vote Commission met to-day in the Supreme Court-room, all the members, including Justice Bradley, who was appointed by the other four Justices, being present. Justice Clifford presided. The Commission determined that eight hours will be allowed for argument in each case presented to them for decision. These eight hours are to be divided equally between such members of the two houses as may be selected to present their cases and the legal counsel of the parties, the first four hours to be given the Congressional managers, and the last four to counsel. In addition, 15 minutes will be allowed counsel for interrogatory argument in respect to points of law that may arise. The presiding Justice was authorized to appoint a Marshal and two Secretaries.

The Commission has decided to sit with open doors during the hearing of arguments, but the consultations will be secret, and the time is not limited. The admissions to the public hearings will be regulated by the President of the Commission, and the number admitted must be small, because the Supreme Court-room, in which the Commission will meet, will hardly hold more than 200 people without packing. This room, by the way, is the old Senate Chamber, the scene of Webster's reply to Hayne, and other

THE PRESIDENTIAL ELECTION OF 1876   143

debates and speeches now historic. The first question to be discussed, that of going behind the returns, will arise when the Florida vote is presented, but as it relates to all the States it will be considered as a distinct question, and if it should be decided to go behind the returns there will be a further hearing allowed upon the case of Florida apart from the preliminary question. The public sessions of the commission will be reported each day in the *Congressional Record.* The meeting adjourned till 2 o'clock to-morrow, when the commission will be ready to go on with any business sent to them.

· ·

THE ELECTORAL COMMISSION NAMES HAYES PRESIDENT

The final decision of the Electoral Commission on February 27, 1877, followed its earlier pattern, awarding victory to Hayes and the Republican Party by an 8–7 margin. The Democratic Party, outmaneuvered at every turn, had no viable options remaining to turn the tide of the election. When Congress reconvened, the Democrats attempted to delay the inevitable through procedural challenges, to little avail. The final electoral votes were awarded to Hayes shortly before 4 A.M., officially granting him the presidency nearly four months after the election.

FEBRUARY 28, 1877
THE ELECTORAL TRIBUNAL

SOUTH CAROLINA FOR HAYES.

DEMOCRATIC LAWYERS AND COMMISSIONERS TALKING TO CONSUME TIME—NO ARGUMENTS ON THE REPUBLICAN SIDE EXCEPT BY THE OBJECTOR, MR. LAWRENCE—THE DEMOCRATIC COMMISSIONERS EVIDENTLY COGNIZANT OF THE ACTION OF THE HOUSE—THE DISPOSITION TO TALK LESS MANIFEST AFTER THE ADJOURNMENT OF THE HOUSE.

Special Dispatch to the New-York Times.

WASHINGTON, Feb. 27.—The Electoral Commission adjourned to-night at 7:30, having completed all the work that is expected to fall to it in the counting of the Electoral vote. Again, the decision was by a majority of 8 to 7, the Democratic Commissioners voting together not to count any Electoral votes from the State of South Carolina, though the majority of Hayes is unchallenged in that State, and the Democratic Committee of the House reported that he was undoubtedly elected. Judge Abbott, one of the Commissioners, was a member of the committee that made the report. The ground upon which the seven Democrats sustained their partisan vote was chiefly that the presence of the military in the State overawed the citizens and prevented the election from being fair and legal. An incidental objection, which was sustained with considerable argument in the Commission, was the failure of the Hayes Electors to certify that they voted by ballot; but it was found on an examination of the statute that this statement is not required in the certificates, which conformed exactly to the law. On the resolution that the Tilden votes were not the lawful and constitutional votes of the State the Commission was unanimous; but there can be no credit claimed by the Democrats for this vote, since the counsel and the objectors and the entire body of the Democratic Party are forced to admit that the Hayes Electors had a majority of votes. This resolution was merely formal, and was not an expression of any opinion on the merits of the South Carolina case which were embodied in the resolution on counting the Hayes Electors.

MARCH 2, 1877
HAYES PRESIDENT.

The Great Contest in Congress Ended.

Unparalleled Obstinacy of the Obstructors.

The Final Joint Convention of the Houses.

Puerile Attempt of the Anarchists to Protest.

After a night session, in which the obstructors of the Presidential count exhausted every pretext, fair and unfair, of delay in reaching a vote, the House, at 3:50 o'clock this morning, voted not to count the vote of the Elector from Wisconsin objected to by the Democrats. This terminated the long struggle to prevent the declaration of the election of the Republican candidate, the Senate having early in the night voted to count the State for Hayes, and notice was sent to that body to meet the House in joint convention to continue the count. The Senators appeared, the President of the Senate took the chair and the action of the two houses was announced. The ten votes of Wisconsin were then counted for Hayes and Wheeler, and these gentlemen were declared President and Vice President of the United States, having received a majority of all the Electoral votes.

MARCH 3, 1877
CLOSING ACTS OF THE COUNT.

THE NIGHT SESSION OF BOTH HOUSES—DECLARATION OF THE RESULT OF THE NOVEMBER ELECTION—THE BLACK EAGLE'S QUILL.

WASHINGTON, March 2.—At 4:05 o'clock this morning, amid an almost breathless silence, which was in marked contrast to the noise and confusion that had prevailed during the day, Mr. Speaker Randall announced that the House was ready to meet the Senate, for the purpose of completing the Presidential count. When the Clerk of the House reached the Senate Chamber to make the announcement, he found it almost deserted. Mr. Ferry, the Presiding Officer, sat in the chair calm, cool, and vigilant as ever, but most of the Senators were either asleep in their seats or dozing in the cloak rooms. Mr. Patterson sat near Mr. Bogy smoking, while Senator Sherman and one or two others wrote letters. After it was announced that the House was ready to go into joint session, the clerks and pages of the Senate were for nearly 10 minutes occupied in waking Senators and getting them in condition to proceed to the other chamber. Then the procession was formed, and five minutes afterward the Sergeant at Arms of the Senate, together with President Ferry, appeared at the entrance to the hall of Representatives. As they did so the Speaker, in conformity with the usages of Congress, rapped once with his gavel and announced the Senate of the United States. Upon this all the respectable members of the House rose and stood in their places. A large number of Democrats, however, with neither respect for themselves nor their associates, left their seats in accordance with a previous agreement and stood outside the bar of the House to protest by their action, as they said, against the consummation of the fraud committed by the Electoral Commission, a tribunal, it will be remembered, which they themselves created. The Senators did not seem to be at all annoyed by this little show of childish spite, and they took their seats with as much apparent satisfaction as if they had been received with the utmost respect by all parties.

Mr. Ferry then took his place beside the Speaker, and in a firm, clear voice, announced that the last joint session of the two houses to complete the Electoral count was then in order. The further proceedings were as brief as they were impressive. The Presiding Officer called upon the tellers to announce the vote of Wisconsin. This duty was performed by Senator Allison, who declared that the 10 votes of the State named should be counted for the Republican candidates. Then the Electoral vote was enumerated by the same Senator, who declared that 185 votes had been cast for Rutherford B. Hayes, of Ohio, and William A. Wheeler, of New-York, and that 184 votes had been cast for Tilden and Hendricks. In accordance with the declaration, Mr. Ferry, in slow and distinct tones, announced that Rutherford B. Hayes and William A. Wheeler, having received a majority of all the Electoral votes cast, were duly elected President and Vice President of the United States. Then, with a trembling hand, which demonstrated plainly the high state of excitement under which he was laboring, he took the black eagle's quill which was sent to him for the purpose, and signed the declaration of the result. Then the houses separated and shortly after adjourned, and the flag was hauled down from the Capitol after flying for 29 days. The declaration is dated Feb. 1, that legislative day under the Electoral bill being constructively continued until 4:30 this morning.

President Hayes Takes Office

Almost four months after the popular vote, Rutherford B. Hayes was sworn in as the nineteenth president of the United States. He quickly took conciliatory action towards the defeated party, appointing Democrats to prominent posts, including the cabinet position of postmaster general, which held large patronage resources. Hayes's stance pleased Democrats, but irritated Republicans, especially in the Senate, who resented his moderate approach and scrutinized each appointment. The election was decided, but the partisan divide remained.

MARCH 6, 1877
THE NEW ADMINISTRATION.

PRESIDENT HAYES TAKES HIS SEAT.

A GRAND POPULAR DEMONSTRATION.

AN EVENT PROMISING PEACE AND PROSPERITY TO THE COUNTRY—WASHINGTON AGLOW WITH ENTHUSIASM OVER THE RESULT OF A BITTER CONTEST—FAREWELL TO THE OLD AND WELCOME TO THE NEW ADMINISTRATION—THE WHITE HOUSE CHANGES TENANTS.

Special Dispatch to the New-York Times.

WASHINGTON, March 5.—The inaugural ceremonies were fortunate and successful beyond the most hopeful anticipations. The weather, which yesterday was warm and balmy with the breath of early Spring, had grown colder this morning, and when the procession began to move there were thick clouds overhead and an occasional fine flake of snow in the air, but, fortunately, there was no wind. The contrast with the 4th of March four years ago, which was the coldest day of the Winter, could not but be remarked by all who recalled the day of President Grant's second inauguration. Then the intense cold and the freezing winds, laden with blinding dust, drove from the streets all but the invincible, and the military escort and companies in the procession suffered intensely. The difference in the weather, no doubt, accounts sufficiently for the fact that many more thousands of people thronged and waited in front of the east portico for a sight of the new President than were gathered there four years ago, when some what unusual pains were taken to organize imposing inaugural ceremonies. The procession that passed from the White House to the Capitol, escorting the Presidential party, was not so large as it has been on some previous occasions, but there were nearly as many men in the military organizations as have ever marched down the avenue together, except in the days of the war. As a spectacle or grand pageant the inaugural ceremonies are never remarkable. They are simple and republican enough for the most puritanical taste. This is illustrated by the fact that one of the features of the day, which the largest number of people are anxious not to miss, is the appearance of the Diplomatic Corps in their gaudy uniforms and jeweled decorations. Not one piece of gold lace, not a badge, or decoration of any kind, distinguished any civil officer. Such insignia being reserved for the military uniforms, some of which, notably that of Gen. Sherman himself, were richly and elegantly ornamented. And yet in spite of its simplicity, in spite of want of drill and discipline which it is impossible to secure when voluntary organizations are brought together under one direction for the first time, the procession itself was a most interesting spectacle.

THE END OF RECONSTRUCTION

Concessions to the losing Democrats continued, as Hayes reduced the presence of northern occupation troops in the South, leaving the former Confederate states unrestricted in making local policy. This return to home rule by southern whites largely abandoned southern blacks to discrimination for the foreseeable future. Within a generation, voting among blacks had dropped to negligible levels as they were expelled from the political process. Following the election, informants reported—but could not prove—that the election had been decided behind closed doors as a secret bargain, exchanging a Hayes presidency for Democratic goals including troop removal. The so-called Compromise of 1877 concluded one of the most tumultuous elections in United States history, but left festering resentment between the parties that would seethe for two decades.

MARCH 17, 1877
WASHINGTON.

THE POLICY TOWARD THE SOUTH.

NON-INTERVENTION TO BE DECIDED AT AN EARLY DAY—TROOPS TO BE REMOVED FROM NEW-ORLEANS AND COLUMBIA—THE CONTENDING GOVERNMENTS TO BE LEFT TO SETTLE THEIR DIFFICULTIES AS BEST THEY MAY—STRICT ACCOUNTABILITY TO BE REQUIRED FOR PEACE, ORDER, AND THE PROTECTION OF THE RIGHTS OF ALL CITIZENS.

Special Dispatch to the New-York Times.

WASHINGTON March 16.—It is more than probable that the Southern policy of President Hayes, about which there has been so much comment, will be developed during the coming week. As has been already intimated, he has, after a careful consideration of the interests involved, decided that the only just course open to the Administration is to remove the United States troops now stationed in Louisiana and South Carolina, thus leaving the contending Governments in those States to settle their own differences in their own way and as similar disputes would be arranged and decided in Northern communities. That this is the President's determination has been definitely known for some days, but there has been some doubt as to when he would carry out his intentions. He has delayed doing so because he desired, before removing the troops, to be fully assured that no violent conflict would follow. He, of course, desires that the contests referred to shall be settled in a peaceable and legal manner, and a number of prominent Southern Democrats have pledged their word that such shall be the case. Trusting to these pledges, and in accordance, as he believes, with the will of the people, it is probable that early next week he will order the removal of the troops now stationed in New-Orleans and Columbia. In doing this, however, he has no intention of allowing the rights of any citizen, of any party, of any color, to be interfered with in any way. The policy of non-interference will be given a fair trial. The Southern whites will be trusted once more. They will be left to settle their own State affairs as the people of other States would do, but they will still be held to the strictest accountability for their acts. Should they violate law, break the peace, or again resort to the acts of violence and bloodshed by which in the past they have been so often disgraced, they may be assured that the present policy of the Administration will be changed at once, the troops will be returned in renewed force, and every precaution taken to keep the peace.

President Hayes desires to harmonize the conflicting elements in the South, and if possible to secure the return of prosperity and good feeling to that section; but, at the same time, he is fully determined that every man, white and black, shall be protected in all the rights which he is entitled to under the law.

THE PRESIDENTIAL ELECTION OF 1896

REPUBLICANS RETURN TO POWER WITH AN ALTERED COALITION

The last presidential election of the nineteenth century marked a major change in the nation's politics. It left behind the heritage of the Civil War and substituted new conflicts of social class based on the growing industrial economy of the United States. Republicans emerged as the clear majority party, their ascendancy based on an altered regional alignment that would dominate elections for a generation and affect politics through much of the twentieth century.

From the ebbing of Reconstruction until 1896, presidential elections were closely contested. Republicans had taken the White House in three of the five preceding contests, but never won in convincing fashion, and no party candidate had achieved a majority of the total national vote. Republicans won only pallid victories, twice with a minority of the two-party popular vote (1876 and 1888) and once by the thinnest of margins (8,000 votes, or 0.1 percent, in 1880). Over the five elections, Democrats had won more total electoral votes and vastly more popular votes than the Republicans.

In the critical election of 1896, the Republican Party finally became the center of the American political universe. Winning a majority of the total popular vote for the first time in a nation undistorted by secession and Reconstruction, it prevailed with an Electoral College margin of 95 votes. This decisive victory gave the party legitimacy and a mandate to govern a nation rising to strategic and economic prominence in the world. For the next three decades, the Republican Party was the "natural party of government," winning six of the next eight elections.

The new Republican majority came to power amid a changing politics. Almost all of the former territories had become self-governing, with forty-five states making up the Union. The military heroes of the Civil War passed party leadership to civilians: William McKinley, an experienced legislator and governor, but a low-ranking officer during the conflict, and William Jennings Bryan, at thirty-six barely old enough to be eligible for the presidency.

A cartoonist depicts the impact of William Jennings Bryan's "Cross of Gold" speech at the Democratic National Convention in Chicago, which won Bryan the party's 1896 presidential nomination.

The nation evidenced major transformation. The western frontier no longer existed as a clear line of settlement and migration. The country's economic base was changing, as agriculture decreased in importance to the national economy, as work shifted toward manufacturing and industry, and as the United States became a world leader in steel, oil, rail, and the emerging technologies of electricity and communications. Manufacturing production in the country had grown larger than that of Britain, Germany, and France combined. Sizable migrations from farm to city followed, making urban areas two-fifths of the total population. Between the census counts of 1890 and 1900, the total population grew by an eighth in

1896 ELECTORAL VOTE

STATE	ELECTORAL VOTES	McKINLEY	BRYAN	STATE	ELECTORAL VOTES	McKINLEY	BRYAN
Alabama	(11)	–	11	Nebraska	(8)	–	8
Arkansas	(8)	–	8	Nevada	(3)	–	3
California	(9)	8	1	New Hampshire	(4)	4	–
Colorado	(4)	–	4	New Jersey	(10)	10	–
Connecticut	(6)	6	–	New York	(36)	36	–
Delaware	(3)	3	–	North Carolina	(11)	–	11
Florida	(4)	–	4	North Dakota	(3)	3	–
Georgia	(13)	–	13	Ohio	(23)	23	–
Idaho	(3)	–	3	Oregon	(4)	4	–
Illinois	(24)	24	–	Pennsylvania	(32)	32	–
Indiana	(15)	15	–	Rhode Island	(4)	4	–
Iowa	(13)	13	–	South Carolina	(9)	–	9
Kansas	(10)	–	10	South Dakota	(4)	–	4
Kentucky	(13)	12	1	Tennessee	(12)	–	12
Louisiana	(8)	–	8	Texas	(15)	–	15
Maine	(6)	6	–	Utah	(3)	–	3
Maryland	(8)	8	–	Vermont	(4)	4	–
Massachusetts	(15)	15	–	Virginia	(12)	–	12
Michigan	(14)	14	–	Washington	(4)	–	4
Minnesota	(9)	9	–	West Virginia	(6)	6	–
Mississippi	(9)	–	9	Wisconsin	(12)	12	–
Missouri	(17)	–	17	Wyoming	(3)	–	3
Montana	(3)	–	3				
				TOTALS	**(447)**	**271**	**176**

the countryside, but much faster, a third, in urban areas, and by 75 percent in cities of more than 1 million inhabitants.

The United States was growing, but it was also in an economic crisis. Wealth was accumulating, but only a few reaped the benefits. Mark Twain called the period the "Gilded Age," when 70 percent of the wealth was held by only a tenth of the population, and half of Americans' money was in the hands of the most fortunate, the top 1 percent, including storied capitalists such as Andrew Carnegie, John D. Rockefeller, and J. P. Morgan.

The condition of most Americans went from modest to disastrous with the onset of the Panic of 1893, the greatest economic downturn to that point in American history. The government imposed a gold standard for the currency, resulting in a severe shrinking of the money supply. Farm prices fell, for some crops to half of their previous levels, but farmers' debts remained at their established levels, leading to bankruptcy and foreclosures on homes and land. In

the cities, wages fell, unemployment rose to 20 percent of the workforce, and poverty spread. When workers attempted collective action through labor unions, employers reacted by imposing economic and political sanctions.

A graphic example of the nation's industrial conflict was the clash between the Pullman Company, manufacturer of the famous railroad sleeping cars, and its employees. Required to live in a "company town" completely controlled by George Pullman, the employees had very little disposable income once they paid compulsory charges for their upkeep. Then, told of a 28 percent cut in these wages, they went on strike, and were soon joined by hundreds of thousands of sympathetic workers throughout the nation. The company brought in strikebreakers, encouraged retaliatory violence, and obtained a court injunction against the strike. When strikers set fire to Pullman property, President Grover Cleveland sent twelve thousand U.S. troops to run the trains, leading to further violence and the death of thirteen workers.

As class conflict loomed, the political system appeared to offer little recourse for those not wealthy. Both major political parties appeared to be in the hands of industrial and financial leaders. A potential means to balance the economic scales, the income tax, was declared unconstitutional by the Supreme Court. The Court also essentially nullified even the weak restrictions on monopolies imposed by antitrust acts. Other courts consistently sided with employers, issuing injunctions against strikes or invalidating social legislation.

Change would require major policy innovations and a major social movement. Political ferment was already evident before the presidential contest of 1896. A dissident third party, the People's Party, or Populists, emerged in the 1892 election, gaining over 1 million votes (8.5 percent of the national total) and 22 electoral votes from six western states. In what was probably the most radical platform ever presented by a significant American party, the Populists called for a graduated income tax, government ownership of railroads and the telegraph and telephone systems, redistribution of land owned by railroads and aliens, restrictions on the banking industry, and an inflationary monetary policy through bimetalism, the unlimited coinage of both gold and silver.

With the onset of the Panic of 1893, the Populists' challenge became still more threatening to the existing parties. Republicans were less worried, expecting the Democratic administration of President Cleveland to bear the blame for tough economic conditions. Their optimism seemed appropriate, given the midterm congressional results in 1894 when Republicans gained 120 seats in the House of Representatives, the largest shift of seats in any congressional election in American history. As an added benefit, the Republicans also won control of the Senate. The presidency seemed to be the inevitable next victory.

For the Democratic Party, populism was a mortal threat. Its advocates, focusing on the silver issue, prepared to take over or replace the party organizations in the plains and mountain states. In the South, the Populist appeal raised the incendiary issue of race. Even after the failure of Reconstruction, blacks managed to continue voting in many parts of the former Confederacy, providing a possible foundation to undermine those in control of the southern states. Upper-income whites feared that blacks would be recruited in a biracial coalition to advance the interests of the poorer classes, while lower-income whites held the reciprocal fear that blacks would be manipulated by the ruling elites. To avoid placing African Americans in the crucial balance-of-power position, the white factions united to disenfranchise them. The result was the elimination of blacks from the southern electorate from the 1890s until the civil rights movement of the 1960s.

THE PARTIES AND THE CANDIDATES

Depressed economic conditions provided the basic frame for the presidential election. The contest was as much a dispute over economic theories as it was between candidates and parties, centering on two different proposed paths to economic recovery.

Republicans, in keeping with their historical stance, argued for high tariffs to provide "protection" for American industry. They claimed that keeping foreign goods out of the United States would mean more jobs for American workers and more sales of domestic goods to American consumers. Democrats countered that a protectionist policy would make it more difficult to sell American goods abroad, especially agricultural products, and would harm consumers by raising domestic prices.

The Democratic solution, adopted from the Populists, was an inflationary currency, putting more money in circulation, making it easier to pay debts—such as land purchases and home mortgages—and to purchase goods in the marketplace. But inflation would work to the disadvantage of lenders, who would be paid back in depreciated money, and employers, who would face pressure to raise wages.

Government policy before the 1896 election was clearly in the conservative direction: Republicans in control of Congress and the presidency had raised tariffs considerably in 1890. The money supply became constricted when Congress, at Cleveland's urging, ended the use of silver as legal tender. With gold in greater demand to redeem the Treasury's paper money, the president borrowed gold from Wall Street financiers, an action attacked as virtually selling the government to the bankers. Cleveland's commitment to the "gold standard" only deepened the economic depression.

As the hard times continued, the parties argued these theories and prepared for the presidential contest. Republicans had the easier course. McKinley was an early favorite. Having served fourteen years in the House of Representatives, he was the primary author of the 1890 tariff, exemplifying his leadership on the defining issue of Republican Party orthodoxy. He left Congress in 1891 to become the governor of Ohio and conducted an efficient, moderate, and corruption-free administration over two terms.

McKinley had many assets as a candidate. His advocacy of protective tariffs gave him a certain attraction to urban workers, fostered by slogans depicting him as "the advance agent of prosperity" whose policies would bring households "a full dinner pail"—welcome contrasts to the nation's ongoing economic misery. While fully orthodox on the currency issue, he downplayed it and avoided attacks from silver advocates inside and outside his party. Coming from Ohio, he seemed likely to win the state, a vital part of a Republican electoral majority.

Most important, McKinley had Mark Hanna, the most celebrated campaign manager in American history. Hanna was a successful industrialist, making his fortune in coal and iron, and saw business support as the basis of long-term Republican dominance. A close friend and financial backer of McKinley, Hanna developed an elaborate plan to win him the Republican presidential nomination. For over a year, Hanna organized McKinley clubs throughout the states and distributed both literature and money to newspapers and convention delegates, as he and McKinley hinted at future patronage for party leaders.

But even with Hanna's inspired aid, McKinley had to face opposition from other Republicans. The most obvious alternative was Thomas Reed of Maine, Speaker of the House of Representatives. Some hoped that Benjamin Harrison, elected president in 1888 but defeated in 1892, would seek a second term. Silver forces in the West backed Sen. Henry Teller of Colorado. Party bosses in New York and Pennsylvania advanced their own favorite sons to increase their bargaining power. McKinley also faced attacks from the American Protective Association, a nativist group that found it suspicious that McKinley had appointed Catholics to public office and credited absurd rumors that his grandmother was buried in a Catholic cemetery. McKinley responded in a defense of religious tolerance and, to avoid Christian controversy, arranged for the opening prayer at the convention to be delivered by a rabbi.

By the time the Republicans met in St. Louis in June, McKinley was the clear front-runner. On the only ballot, McKinley won 661 of the 924 votes, followed by Reed and three favorite son candidates. In a vice-presidential ballot, Garret A. Hobart of New Jersey was selected to provide regional balance to the ticket. The party platform backed high tariffs, pledging "allegiance to the policy of protection, as the bulwark of American industrial independence, and foundation of American development and prosperity." Foreshadowing the emergence of the United States as an international power, Republicans also supported Cuban independence, acquisition of Hawaii, a transoceanic canal in Nicaragua, and expansion of the U.S. Navy.

The only significant convention dissent came on the currency issue. By an 8–1 vote, the convention voted for "sound money . . . the existing gold standard," which it extolled as "the standard of the most enlightened nations of the earth." Tearfully, Teller and other fervent backers of silver coinage left the convention and their historic Republican home, to the taunting chorus of a popular song, "Goodbye, my Lover, Goodbye."

The Democrats had no such harmony, politically or vocally. The currency issue dominated the party's nominating contest. The silver forces won control of virtually all states in the West and South, in the latter region often using racist appeals to prevent a coalition of Populists and Republicans. Pressed by the Populists, they hoped to attract or absorb the third party challenge. On the other side of the issue, President Cleveland and members of his administration gave support to conservatives, and the "gold Democrats" kept control of most eastern and many midwestern delegations.

The silver forces, however, were not united in their candidate preferences. The most prominent possibility among their ranks was Sen. Richard Bland of Missouri. Although his leadership on the matter had earned him the nickname of "Silver Dick," he had limited appeal to Populists. Maneuvering behind the scenes was another silver advocate, a young former member of Congress from Nebraska, William Jennings Bryan. He had received some attention because of his oratorical ability, but few thought a thirty-six-year-old of limited experience could be the nominee. Bryan neither created a formal organization nor announced his availability, but he corresponded with delegates, sent copies of his speeches and his photograph throughout the nation, and spoke wherever he was invited.

The dominance of the silver Democrats was evident from the very beginning of the July convention in Chicago. The delegates overturned leadership recommendations and chose a silver Democrat as chair and seated an insurgent delegation from Nebraska, including Bryan. Then they turned to the platform. Bryan concluded the debate on currency, delivering the most famous speech in the history of conventions. Speaking the language of class conflict, so rare in America, he challenged the dominance of urban industrial capitalism:

> You come to us and tell us that the great cities are in favor of the gold standard; we reply that the great cities rest upon our broad and fertile prairies. Burn down your cities and leave our farms, and your cities will spring up again as if by magic; but destroy our farms and the grass will grow in the streets of every city in the country.

In concluding, Bryan elevated his economic argument to a religious sermon:

> Having behind us the producing masses of this nation and the world, supported by the commercial interests, the laboring interests, and the toilers everywhere, we will answer their demand for a gold standard by saying to them: You shall not press down upon the brow of labor this crown of thorns, you shall not crucify mankind upon a cross of gold.

Frenzied after the oration, Democrats adopted the silver plank by a 2 to 1 margin. Demanding "the free and unlimited coinage of both silver and gold," Democrats held the gold standard responsible for all the nation's ills, including "the enrichment of the money-lending class at home and abroad; the prostration of industry and impoverishment of the people." They added insult to the gold faction's injury when the delegates refused to include a commendation of the Cleveland administration in the platform.

Bryan's speech thrilled the convention, but did not in itself determine the nomination. Bland led on the first ballot, and delegate votes remained scattered for three more tallies. But Bryan steadily increased his vote and became the consensual choice of the silver Democrats on the fifth ballot, winning 652 of the 930 total votes. The gold Democrats refused to formally enter a candidate or to vote on the presidential selection, and soon would reject the convention's choice. Disdaining compromise, the convention went on to nominate Arthur Sewall, a Maine banker, for vice president, in a vain effort to show the ticket's financial acumen.

The major parties now had their candidates, both running against the record of the Cleveland administration, but with strongly divergent economic programs. The arguments went further, as five significant minor parties determined their course. Dissident Republicans formed the National Silver Party to promote silver money, eventually nominating Bryan. Dissident Democrats formed the National Democratic Party on behalf of gold money, and two prohibitionist parties entered the lists. Of most importance was the course of the Populists.

The Populists had advanced their central goal, free coinage of silver, when the Democrats adopted this policy. But many in the People's Party were more ambitious, still wanting to promote their more extensive policy agenda and even hoping to become the new national majority. The party's 1892 nominee, James Weaver, urged it to endorse the Democratic ticket, but other "middle-of-the-road" Populists, particularly from the South, sought to preserve the party's autonomy.

Practicality won out at the People's Party July convention in St. Louis. The Populists reiterated their former radical platform—adding endorsements of direct election of the president and national initiatives and referendums—but the party surrendered its broad reform program, recognizing "that the pressing issue of the pending campaign, upon which the present election will turn, is the financial question." Nominating Bryan as its presidential candidate, it sought a bare degree of distinction by naming its own vice-presidential candidate, Rep. Tom Watson of Georgia—then an advocate of biracial alliances on lines of class, later a virulent racist and anti-Semite. The Populists hoped to maintain their independence by forming joint electoral tickets on behalf of Bryan, but the attempt was largely disdained by the Democrats, and the party itself soon vanished.

THE CAMPAIGN

The 1896 battle was the first modern election campaign, turning the contest into a direct, democratic bond between candidates and the citizenry. In differing ways, McKinley and Bryan each attempted to create a familiar rapport with the electorate. They made their appeals more directly to the voters, relying less on party organizations, surrogates, and newspapers. With these new techniques, they turned campaigning into more of an emotional assessment of the candidates and less of a judgment on the intellectual qualities of party programs.

Mark Hanna led the way in the transformation of campaigning. As the Republican national chairman, he created a centralized headquarters organized like an efficient business, closely controlling party activity throughout the country. Corporations and individual businessmen were solicited for contributions, with suggestions from Hanna on the appropriate amounts, for example, $250,000 from John D. Rockefeller's Standard Oil monopoly. Detailed accounting showed that the party spent about $6 million in the national effort—the modern equivalent of $150 million—in an era without the expense of television and radio ads and airplane travel.

The Republicans relied on words, written and spoken, to define their candidate's character. Newspapers, the only mass medium of the time, were provided with pre-written news stories, editorials, and advertisements. State party organizations received subsidies to mobilize voters. After surveys of public opinion, carloads of freight trains delivered pamphlets, as many as 5 million weekly, to the voters. Speakers were recruited in every state to speak at rallies, both in English and in foreign languages.

In one novel technique, beyond words, Hanna tried literally to wrap McKinley in the American flag, sponsoring rallies in major cities at which the crowd waved thousands of U.S. banners. In what *The New York Times* on November 1 ecstatically called the "Greatest of Parades," 100,000 men "joined in declaring for a gold standard" carried the Stars and Stripes and marched through the city with a hundred bands for seven hours before an estimated 750,000 spectators. *The Times* reported: "Never before in the world's history have so many citizens in time of peace in any country rallied to march under their country's flag." The newspaper's commendation may have been affected by the active participation in the march of its new publisher, Adolph Ochs, and fifty members of his staff.

For his part, McKinley stayed at home in Canton, Ohio, conducting a "front-porch campaign" by greeting visiting delegations. In carefully arranged ceremonies, these visitors came on special trains, heard McKinley speak to their particular concerns, and cheered the candidate. The Ohio governor, usually referred to as Major McKinley to recall the Civil War, emphasized the benefits of the protective tariff law that bore his name, lectured on the virtues of the gold standard, and warned of the dangers of class conflict. The ritual would be repeated many times each day, with McKinley eventually giving three hundred speeches to a total 750,000 people.

Bryan had few financial resources to match McKinley and was outspent by as much as 10 to 1, his only significant donations coming from silver mining interests. Democrats also engaged in the competition of publications, distributing several million copies of a silver tract, *Coin's Financial School.* But Bryan did have one unique resource to deploy, his oratorical ability. In the most notable stump campaign to that date, he conducted a nationwide railroad tour, beginning with a trip to the East—"the enemy's country," as he termed it. Covering 18,000 miles, Bryan gave some six hundred speeches, as many as twenty-seven in a single day.

Bryan was not the first candidate to seek votes through a personal tour—a practice initiated by Stephen Douglas in 1860. But Bryan not only traveled more; he also attempted to make a personal and emotional relationship to the voters the foundation of his campaign, changing the entire basis of electoral judgment. In that effort, he drew huge crowds, in both rural whistle-stops and large cities, seemingly mobilizing the voters in what some saw as a mass movement and others feared as rabble-rousing. The Nebraska orator may have spoken to a total of 5 million people, virtually as many as would eventually cast ballots for him.

Social class was clearly the theme of the election. Bryan hoped to create an alliance of the "producing classes," farmers of the South and West and industrial workers of the Midwest and East. Financial interests saw him as a threat to the entire capitalist system of the United States. *The Times* went so far as to publish a letter (on September 27) from an "alienist" (in today's language, a psychiatrist), who gave his professional opinion that Bryan was, clinically, a "madman . . . [who] suffers from a delusion, and his state is known as that of 'megalomania' . . . an ill-balanced mind—of such minds as with less moral feeling make men who start revolutions and commit crimes." In its own editorial, *The Times* felt justified in asking, "Is Bryan Crazy?" and determined that his behavior "entitles us to say . . . that the man's mind is not sound, and its unsoundness is increasing."

The election eventually depended on more substantial grounds, the loyalties of urban workers. Would they accept Bryan's picture of a national class conflict or the Republican theory that common interests bound them to their employers? Despite his class appeals, Bryan's voice had only limited resonance in the industrial workforce. McKinley in public office and Hanna in his business had been responsive to the needs of workers, and the former head of the Knights of Labor, a major union organization, campaigned for the Republicans. For his part, Bryan found it difficult to relate to the emerging urban nation, industrial economy, and multiethnic population. His vision was more oriented toward the past and an attempt to return to the traditional values of the agricultural hinterland. His retrospective view found little favor as Americans looked forward to the new century and the headlong modernization of the United States.

Business interests pursued their own goals. They pressured voters to support McKinley, sometimes subtly with mandatory lunch-hour lectures and pamphlets included in pay envelopes, sometimes with explicit notices: "Don't bother to come to work Wednesday if Bryan is elected Tuesday." In some instances, farm mortgage extensions and purchase contracts were made contingent on a McKinley victory, and businessmen collected gold to provide safety in a possible revolution. The tactics were justified by the belief, widespread among the upper classes, that Bryan's election would bring socialism, anarchy, and other alleged immoralities to the United States.

THE ELECTION RESULTS

The intense campaign stimulated an outpouring at the polls, a 15 percent increase over 1892, even as southern voting fell with the disenfranchisement of African Americans. Bryan increased the Democratic tally, compared to Cleveland, by more than 1 million votes, mostly by absorbing the support of the Populists, who soon disappeared. McKinley did far better, raising the Republican vote by 1.5 million, more than a fourth of the party total in 1892.

McKinley's triumph was clear—a two-party plurality of 735,000 popular votes (a margin of 5.3 percent), gathered from a majority of the states. The Republican ticket carried every county in New England and every state north of the Ohio River through the western banks of the Mississippi, as well as most of the border states and the Pacific coast. Bryan swept the interior states of the Great Plains and the Rocky Mountains, but their sparse populations could not bring him to the White House either in 1896 or in two subsequent races.

The election results showed a clear split of the agrarian and industrial sectors. The battle for the manufacturing workers had been won by the Republicans, who carried the industrial states by winning in the cities more than on the farms and by gaining the support of immigrant populations, particularly Germans and Scandinavians. The economic solution of protective tariffs had bested the economic solution of currency inflation, at least at the ballot box.

The electoral map of the United States was transformed by the results. In contrast to the previous close contests in most states, the 1896 election created paired one-party systems, the Republicans in the North and Midwest, the Democrats in the South, with meaningful competition restricted to the Far West. Among the sixteen states that had been the battlegrounds of presidential elections—from Maine to Iowa—the Democrats won a popular majority only once in any state in the eight elections from 1896 to 1924 (a political "batting average" of .006). The Republicans did even worse in the old Confederacy, winning not a single state during the same period. In Ohio, formerly the national bellwether, the average Democratic vote fell from 47.5 percent in the five post-Reconstruction elections to 34.9 percent in the period from McKinley to the New Deal.

Republican dominance was the partisan heritage of the 1896 election, but both parties shared the political heritage, the transformation of campaigning. Elections became nationalized contests rather than aggregations of separate state races, focused on the asserted qualities of candidates rather than party loyalties and programs, and grew more expensive as candidates used new technologies to bring their messages directly to the voters. The new century would further develop the campaign innovations of 1896, as airplanes replaced railroads, radio and television spots replaced personal oratory, and the Internet displaced newspapers.

As McKinley entered the White House, events seemed to validate his boastful campaign title as the "Advance Agent of Prosperity." World demand for wheat rose, pushing farm prices up. New discoveries of gold in foreign mines, on the other hand, decreased its price, leading to a larger money supply and higher wages. A year after McKinley's inauguration the country engaged in a war in Cuba against Spain. Winning a virtually bloodless victory, the United States suddenly launched the American empire, dominant in the Western Hemisphere and extended across the Pacific Ocean to the Philippines. Military success aside, the social strains evident in the election continued, and the need for economic and political reform remained. Soon, other presidents—Theodore Roosevelt and Woodrow Wilson—would address these problems more effectively in practice than in the promises of either McKinley or Bryan.

For Americans of the coming century, the election of 1896 became more than a political landmark, living on in the classic novel, film, and television feature, The Wizard of Oz, published in 1900. Although the author, Frank Baum, never claimed (or denied) that the book was other than a children's story, it has often been interpreted as a political allegory.

In this retelling, Dorothy represents the American people, torn from the safety of her past life by the tornado of the Panic of 1893. She enlists the aid of the Tin Woodman (the rusted industrial workers), the Scarecrow (the helpless farmers), and the Cowardly Lion (Bryan). After traveling along the unwelcoming yellow brick road (the gold standard) and facing the opposition of the wicked witches of the East (bankers) and West (Hanna), she unmasks the sham Wizard (deceitful presidents) pulling strings behind a curtain. Now empowered, Dorothy drowns the oppressors (in a transregional tide of votes inspired by the good witches of the North and South). Then, clapping her silver (free coinage) slippers (changed to ruby-colored in this first film in color) together, she is magically transported back to Kansas (Bryan's Nebraska), voicing the moral of the story: "there's no place like home" (traditional values).

This interpretation of the original story is itself controversial, and its conclusion is obviously contrary to the reality of Bryan's defeat. The allegorical interpretation may well be unconvincing, but the continued popularity of The Wizard of Oz underlines the significance of the 1896 election. That contest changed the contours of American politics for a generation, even in some ways for a century. The class conflicts argued then continue, as contending economic theories still differentiate American political parties. And voters still worry that a manipulative Wizard may lurk behind the curtains of the polling booths.

WILLIAM MCKINLEY'S CAMPAIGN USES INNOVATIVE METHODS

Months before the 1896 Republican convention was scheduled to meet in St. Louis, William McKinley began an active campaign for the party's presidential nomination. His campaign's unprecedented methods, changing the face of American electioneering, included early canvassing of delegates, massive contributions from wealthy supporters, and a centralized campaign structure. This new form of politics appalled other candidates, but they were unable to stem the popular tide whipped up by McKinley. Subsequent generations of political candidates were forced to adopt these methods to compete successfully.

MARCH 9, 1896
EDITORIAL
MCKINLEY'S CANVASS.

Certain Republican opponents or rivals of Mr. McKINLEY profess to be surprised by the discovery that the agents of that candidate have been using money to procure support for him in the coming St. Louis Convention, and would have us believe that their suspicions as to the making of such investments in his behalf were not aroused until a few days ago. Senator CULLOM of Illinois, whose political capital consists chiefly of his very slight facial resemblance to ABRAHAM LINCOLN and who hoped to have at least a "favorite son's" complimentary vote from his State, finds that McKINLEY's men have been grabbing Illinois delegates, and is whining because the austere patriotism of contemporary Illinois Republican politicians has succumbed to the allurements of McKinley cash.

One of our contemporaries publishes a letter said to have been written by Mr. CULLOM containing the following remarks: "I am very poor, having no money to spend in the campaign for nomination or election, and I would not solicit financial aid if by doing so I could secure the office. I should feel that I would be placing myself to an extent in the hands of those who furnished it if I should resort to such a course to secure the nomination." Mr. McKINLEY has never been disturbed in mind by such conscientious scruples, and we think that after this advertisement of his poverty Mr. CULLOM may as well take his name from the list of candidates.

There has also been published another letter said to have been written by Senator CULLOM, and bearing his signature. We take from it the following observations, which appear to have been suggested by the successful labors of McKINLEY's opulent emissaries in Illinois:

"The McKinley forces are organized all over my State. They have their agents tramping round, organizing McKinley clubs and doing anything in their power to make the State solid for McKINLEY. They have renewed their efforts since my name was presented at my own home as a candidate for President. There has been a large amount of money spent in Illinois by McKinley workers, and it is not easy to break up the schemes which have been set up for him. They have been at work for more than two years, and have been very active for the past two months. In my opinion, McKINLEY is less qualified for the office than any other conspicuous candidate. He has less courage, less knowledge of National and international affairs than any one of the others."

But he has an abundance of money; not money of his own, for his private business ventures have been as unsuccessful as his administration in the office of Governor of Ohio was weak and inefficient, but money supplied by persons who have for two years been striving to procure his nomination by the Republican National Convention. He, too, is poor, but, unlike Mr. CULLOM, he is willing "to place himself in the hands of those who furnish" the money which the promotion of his political fortunes requires. The generous contributions of protected manufacturers from other States have been used for his benefit in other campaigns, in his Congressional district and in other parts of Ohio. To any one who recalls the history of those campaigns can there be anything surprising now in the operations of McKINLEY's agents in Louisiana, Florida, and other Southern States, or in the beneficent and pervading activity of Mr. HANNA, chief of his lieutenants and organizer of the new Iron Ore

Trust? The leading beneficiaries of the McKinley tariff are subscribing generously to his campaign fund, partly in payment for what that tariff gave them, but chiefly because of their expectation of favors yet to come and dependent in a measure upon the election of the man whose name indicates their tariff platform.

• •

THE REPUBLICAN CONVENTION RUBBER STAMPS MCKINLEY

The Republican convention met in St. Louis, June 16–18, 1896, but with little of the excitement of previous years. William McKinley's nomination was all but certain, and the convention had only to determine the platform and the vice-presidential candidate. The delegates took a strong stand on the currency issue by endorsing the gold standard, alienating some members of the party. A major force throughout the convention and overall campaign was Mark Hanna, the leader of the Republican Party and one of the first important campaign managers in American history. During the campaign, Hanna often appeared to be a more important figure than his candidate, McKinley.

JUNE 18, 1896
MCKINLEY TO BE NOMINATED TO-DAY

He Will Be the Republican Candidate for the Presidency on a Gold Platform.

NOTHING DETERMINED AS TO SECOND PLACE

Indications that a Majority of the Delegates Favor Morton, but Hanna, the Ohio Boss, Seems to be for Hobart.

SILVER SENATORS HAVE FIRMLY DECIDED TO BOLT

Teller, Dubois, Cannon, Mantle, Pettigrew, and Chairman Carter Are to Quit the Party—Whole Delegations and Parts of Delegations Will Follow Their Lead—They Will March Out of the Convention in a Body.

St. Louis, June 17.—The Republican ticket for 1896 will be in nomination by Thursday night. The platform already has been agreed to, and McKinley will be the candidate for President on a gold platform.

There still is reason for expecting that Morton will be the candidate for the second place, but the prediction that he surely will get the nomination would not be a safe one to make. When the fight for gold was being made a day or two ago, and the most courageous men were infusing some of their resolution into the timid straddlers, they were of the belief that they hardly would need to urge upon the gold men the propriety of selecting Morton for the second place. It is a little different now.

Hanna has been begging. His sudden suppression by the imposition upon him of the gold plank that he did not want procured for him the sympathy of a few delegates who were alarmed lest their course on the money question should cast discredit on his boss-ship. He played on this sympathy, using that and the quarrelsomeness of the New-York delegation.

He quietly revived the canvass for his original candidate, Hobart of New-Jersey. It was Hanna also who brought out Evans of Tennessee, but Evans has been retired after an interview with Hanna. Evans is not to have the place. If it be not Morton, it is more likely to be Hobart than "some good Western man." Thurston, Davis, and Allison are talked of, but Hanna has no affection for any of them.

About the tariff there is still absolutely no talk. Discussion runs only on the gold plank and the Vice Presidential nomination.

The silver States waiting for the chance to bolt will be allowed to go and do their worst. And not many of them will take part in the bolt here. Colorado, Idaho, and Nevada will repudiate the gold standard by the withdrawal of the entire delegation from those States. After Mr. Teller shall have made his farewell speech to the Republican Party, Montana and Utah will go in part. Senator Carter hesitates, but there is little doubt that both he and Senator Mantle will get out.

The departure of these mistaken silver men will be the most exciting event of the convention, and it will come close enough upon the nomination of McKinley to mar the delight which otherwise would be felt by Hanna and the McKinley forces.

William McKinley (1843–1901), the twenty-fifth president of the United States, is photographed making his presidential nomination acceptance speech from the front porch of his home in Canton, Ohio, in 1896.

Source: The Granger Collection, New York

HOBART JOINS MCKINLEY IN RUNNING ON THE GOLD PLATFORM

The formal nomination of William McKinley by the Republican Party came as no surprise. He soared through the first ballot with little opposition. Partnered with McKinley for vice president was Garret A. Hobart of New Jersey, a businessman with little experience in politics, but from a vital northeastern state and with credentials in the financial markets that would prove crucial during the campaign. The two ran on a "gold platform," pledging to keep the country's money supply tied to gold, rather than increasing available cash by also using silver to back the dollar.

JUNE 19, 1896
MCKINLEY AND HOBART OF NEW-JERSEY

Nominated at St. Louis by the Republican Party for President and Vice President.

VOTE FOR THE GOLD PLATFORM 812 1-2 TO 110 1-2

Twenty-one Silver Men Bolt the Convention, Led by Teller, Who Weeps Copiously as He Leaves the Hall.

FOUR SENATORS AND TWO REPRESENTATIVES WALK OUT

They Are Going to Chicago to Make an Attempt to Capture the Democratic Nomination for Teller—Chairman Carter Decides to Stick to His Party—Convention Adjourns Sine Die and Delegates Start for Home.

FIRST BALLOT.

McKinley	661 ½
Reed	84 ½
Quay	61 ½
Morton	58
Allison	35 ½
Blank	4
Cameron	1
Total	906

FIRST BALLOT.

Hobart	533 ½
Evans	277 ½
Bulkeley	39
Walker	24
Lippitt	8
Reed	3
Depew	3
Grant	2
Thurston	2
Morton	1
Total	893

St. Louis, June 18.—William McKinley of Ohio was nominated this afternoon as the candidate of the Republican Party for President, and Garret A. Hobart of New-Jersey was named for Vice President.

This outcome, secured in one prolonged session of the convention, the fourth sitting since it was called to order on Tuesday, was more than half expected last night. Gov. Morton's chances were then very doubtful, partly owing to his reiterated disinclination to accept the nomination for Vice President "under any circumstances," and partly because of the bitter opposition to Gov. Morton in his own State—an opposition that was cultivated with complete disregard of the tarnish that it was putting upon the State and its Chief Executive, and which provoked the contempt of Gov. Morton's opponents in other States.

Hanna came to St. Louis, as has been repeatedly stated in these dispatches, determined to make Hobart the candidate with McKinley. He resented the fight made to put "gold" in the financial plank, and he was alarmed when he found that his resentment was not only futile to keep "gold" out, but that the men who were for the use of the word "gold" were disposed to express their thanks to Mr. Platt and the gold people of New-York by voting for Morton for Vice President if he would present him. Morton's dispatch of declination to Mr. Depew helped Hanna. It assisted the protesting anti-Platt men to fix the impression that Morton could not get the unanimous indorsement of his own State.

Battered though his influence was after the fight for a straddle, Hanna was still influential, and his power was fully restored when Mr. Morton to-day telegraphed Mr. Depew that he could only take the Vice Presidency if nominated unanimously. Hanna, Warner Miller, and Bliss had made that impossible.

The ticket is Hanna's. The platform is the work of the convention. At Hanna's request the declaration on the tariff was allowed to come first. Mr. Lodge had promised that, and Foraker was not enough concerned about the order of the paragraphs to assert his contempt for Hanna by insisting that the most important policy should be asserted in the first paragraph of the platform.

To the people the ticket is not likely to be as interesting as the platform. If the Republicans shall be successful in November it will be the money plank, not the tariff plank nor the names of McKinley and Hobart, that will win the victory.

WILLIAM JENNINGS BRYAN AND THE "CROSS OF GOLD" SPEECH

The Democratic convention of 1896 began without a clear front-runner. Sen. Richard Bland of Missouri led early, but there was little enthusiasm for his candidacy. During the platform debate, William Jennings Bryan, a youthful former representative from Nebraska, enraptured the audience with a stirring speech that condemned the reluctance of the nation's political leaders to assist the poor of America. The oratory, which became known as the "Cross of Gold" speech, galvanized many behind Bryan, especially those who favored abandoning the gold standard in favor of "bimetallism," the combined use of gold and silver to support the nation's currency.

> The declaration by him that the people must not be crucified on the cross of gold was the signal for an avalanche of cheers which speedily developed into a measureless outburst.

JULY 10, 1896
BRYAN'S BID FOR FIRST PLACE.

The Silver Men Swept Away by a Flood of Prairie Oratory.

CHICAGO, July 9.—The silverites had their inning when Russell had finished and Bryan, "the boy orator" and general demagogue of Nebraska, took the platform. They yelled and raved, waved flags, threw hats into the air, and acted like wild men for five minutes.

Bryan wore trousers which bagged at the knees, a black alpaca coat, and a low-cut vest. A black stud broke the white expanse of his shirt bosom. His low, white collar was partially hidden by a white lawn tie. Bryan began fishing yesterday for the Presidential nomination. If there was any doubt of his ambition in the minds of the friends of other candidates, that doubt was dispelled to-day by his speech and the events that followed. He dwelt upon the necessity of another Andrew Jackson to rise up and crush the National banks and other agents of the "money kings" and indulged in many like utterances calculated to attract the attention of the silver fanatics to himself. The applause with which his remarks were punctuated attested to the audience's relish for his revolutionary expressions.

Bryan's chief qualification as an orator is his splendid voice. His views on public affairs are those of a wild theorist filled with a desire of personal advancement. No better evidence of the diseased condition of the minds of the silver delegates could be desired than that furnished to-day by their indorsement of Bryan's utterances.

The demonstration at the close of Bryan's speech struck terror to the hearts of the Bland and Boies and McLean and Stevenson boomers. The declaration by him that the people must not be crucified on the cross of gold was the signal for an avalanche of cheers which speedily developed into a measureless outburst. As he started for his seat one policeman stood ready to clear the way and another to prevent the crowd closing in upon him. Their efforts were unavailing.

BRYAN AND SEWALL RUN ON THE SILVER PLATFORM

One day after Bryan delivered his famous "Cross of Gold" speech at the Democratic convention, he was nominated as the party's candidate for president. Despite his youth, Bryan won the populist heart of the party with his strong support of bimetallism and his unrivaled oratorical skills. A short time later Arthur Sewall of Maine, a banker who might give credence to the party's silver platform, was nominated for vice president.

JULY 11, 1896
BRYAN, FREE SILVER, AND REPUDIATION

Chicago Convention Chooses a Fit Candidate to Stand on Its Populistic Platform.

HE IS NOMINATED ON THE FIFTH BALLOT

Tremendous Stampede in His Favor, in Which Practically All Join Except the Sound-Money Delegations.

SELECTION OF MAN FOR SECOND PLACE POSTPONED

Silverites Take an Adjournment Over Night So that They May Have Time to Deliberate—Afraid of Spoiling Their Ticket by Giving It a Weak Tail—Plenty of Candidates.

CHICAGO, July 10.—The Populist Democrats of the United States have chosen William Jennings Bryan as their candidate for President on the fifth ballot, with 162 votes in the convention refusing to consent by participation in the nominations to the revolutionary platform previously adopted or to bind themselves to support the man who was placed upon it. Bryan's nomination was made with a whirl, in the same impetuous manner in which the platform was constructed and put through.

Worn out with excitement the convention took a recess until to-night at 8 o'clock, with the expectation that the ticket would be completed then. At the night session the delegates who had named a Presidential candidate with a rush, paused for reflection. "In order that no mistakes might be made," it was decided to adjourn until Saturday at 10 o'clock to complete the ticket that will be repudiated by all Democrats who have not lost all sense of National honor and credit.

Bryan's nomination was not a surprise to anybody who was in the convention Thursday when Bryan made the speech that stirred the convention so mightily. When Garfield in 1880 rose to name Sherman as the choice of the Buckeye State his eloquence and his presence were a greater recommendation for the speaker than for the man for whom he spoke. So it was with Bryan. But Bryan sways men of the emotional sort more readily and profoundly than Garfield did. Indeed, Garfield never was so superficial, dramatic, sophistical, as Bryan is whenever he speaks. Bryan's bearing is graceful; his face is handsome; his utterance is clear and strong, with something of the McKinley sing-song, and his style is free, bold, picturesque, and brilliant.

No wonder that his oration moved the emotional and enthusiastic silverites, and at once turned the delegates in several Southern States who had declined to pick a man, to the "Boy Orator of the Platte." But the Bland forces, represented by delegates who had insisted that Bland more fitly represented the silver cause than any other man, because he had been identified with it longer and more prominently, hung back. They had built up a boom with great care for the Missouri "Commoner," as they called him when they did not call him "Silver Dick" or "Honest Dick" Bland, and they expected Bland to win as the result of great expenditure for headquarters, bands, uniforms, and singing clubs.

When the convention met to-day the Bryan boom was the popular one. The Bland shouters were on hand, as vociferous as ever. Missouri reinforced its lines by consultation with other States, and was prepared to sweep away Bryan, if possible, by a prodigious lead at the start. . . .

When the fifth call was completed he still needed votes. To recruit the line a common convention expedient was adopted. Amid cheers and frantic demonstrations of delight, the Bryan men made a collection of State banners about Nebraska, organized a march about the body of delegates, and under the inspiration or infection of excitement presently were able to collect near a majority of two-thirds.

Illinois came in to swell the list with her forty-eight votes.

The stampede had come. Bulletins began to fly out of the hall announcing Bryan's nomination. Illinois did not nominate him. It was not until Gov. Stone, speaking for Missouri, hauled down the Bland standard and cast 34 votes for Bryan that the gifted blatherskite was selected as the Presidential candidate of the Democratic-Populist Convention.

Not a gold State had budged.

Campaign Manager Leads the McKinley Campaign

William McKinley's campaign manager, Mark Hanna, was nearly as large a public presence during the election as the candidate himself. Hanna orchestrated McKinley's moves, including his issue positions, the location of campaign headquarters, his vice-presidential partner, and the overall campaign strategy. Hanna soon became known as "the man who made the president." After the 1896 election, all candidates began to rely upon campaign managers, forever changing the nature of campaigns and elections.

JULY 20, 1896
AWAITING HANNA'S COMING.

REPUBLICANS ANXIOUS TO LEARN ABOUT HEADQUARTERS.

Definite Information as to Whether This City or Chicago Will Be the Real Base of Operations Not Expected Until the Arrival of Mr. McKinley's Manager in Chief—Mr. Platt's Sunday Visitors at the Oriental Hotel.

JULY 21, 1896
HANNA SAYS TALK MONEY

McKINLEY MUST ACCEPT THE ISSUE OF THE CAMPAIGN.

The Congressional Campaign Committee of the Republicans Will Keep the Money Question to the Front—Every District in Which There Is a Chance for a Sound-Money Man to Win Will Be Contested with Vigor.

AUGUST 18, 1896
MCKINLEY WILL NOT STUMP.

Mr. Hanna Makes a Final Decision on the Subject.

CLEVELAND, Aug. 17.—Major McKinley and Mr. Hanna were in conference at Mr. Hanna's home all day Sunday. Said Mr. Hanna this morning:

"The outlook throughout the Western States is more promising than two weeks ago, and I construe it as an evidence that the campaign of education is beginning to tell. We have the Chicago headquarters thoroughly organized and up to Saturday night had scattered 15,500 campaign documents in every section of the country. This is a mere handful compared to what will be sent out. There is a healthy and growing demand for Republican literature, which, in my opinion, demonstrates that the people want reliable information and are coming to Republican headquarters to get it.

"Within a week or ten days we will begin to shoot off our oratorical artillery. It will come in good season, as the people then will have had time to digest some of the campaign literature.

"It has been given out that McKinley will not take the stump, and nothing has occurred to cause him to deviate from the original decision. To settle the matter once for all, McKinley will not take the stump. Neither will he address the G. A. R. gathering at Milwaukee.

"At present I cannot justly size up the Eastern situation. All that I will say of Bryan's speech was that it was a skimmer.

"The last member of the Executive Committee has not yet been appointed and the matter is still in abeyance."

OCTOBER 18, 1896
HANNA ORDERS A FLAG DAY.

Final Demonstration in the Interest of McKinley.

CHICAGO, Oct. 17.—Chairman Hanna of the Republican National Committee has suggested a "flag day" in the campaign. He promulgates the following:

"The American flag has been in the political campaign the emblem or insignia of National honor. Its influences have been for great good in the cause of a good people. Its display in many places has been potent in the advancement of the country's battle for the maintenance of its honor at home and abroad.

"I therefore suggest that on Saturday, Oct. 31, all who intend to vote Nov. 3 for the preservation of our National honor, for sound money, and the advancement of our people's interests and general prosperity display the National colors at their homes, their places of business, and wherever they may be seen, in order that their purpose and those who are undetermined may the more patriotically and intelligently conclude how best to perform their duty as citizens."

"M. A. HANNA."

NOVEMBER 1, 1896
GREATEST OF PARADES

100,000 Men March and Shout for Sound Money.

A VAST PEACEFUL ARMY

Carried Stars and Stripes in Flag-Adorned Streets.

MEN OF ALL RANKS IN LINE

Quarter of a Million of Spectators Join Enthusiastic Paraders in Cheering and Singing.

MAYOR AND GOVERNOR REVIEW

Crowds Greater than Famous Armies Splendidly Handled—The City Made a Holiday.

The business men's parade, in behalf of sound money, in this city yesterday, broke the world's record as a civic demonstration.

Never before in the world's history have so many citizens in time of peace in any country rallied to march under their country's flag. Never before in this Nation's history have so many flags been waved as were waved by the army that mustered in the streets of New-York City yesterday.

No such political demonstration has ever been seen on the continent.

BRYAN'S NOMINATION BY POPULISTS LEADS TO "POPOCRAT" CANDIDACY

In July 1896 the People's Party met in St. Louis to formulate its own presidential ticket. After tumultuous quarrels over the party platform, the delegates embraced the financial question as the main issue of the campaign. As virulent "silverites," the Populists viewed Bryan as their natural candidate. To preserve their independence, they rejected the Democrats' choice for vice president and instead selected Rep. Tom Watson of Georgia. Bryan initially had misgivings about the dual selections, but finally accepted the second presidential nomination. This fusion candidacy led some observers to christen Bryan a "Popocrat."

OCTOBER 4, 1896
BRYAN NOW A POPULIST

ACCEPTS THE NOMINATION OF THE ST. LOUIS CONVENTION.

His Formal Letter Recognizes the Influence Which the People's Party Has Exerted in Creating the Free Coinage Sentiment—The Candidate Believes that All the Wings of the Silver Party Can Be Made to Flap Together.

ST. LOUIS, Mo., Oct. 3.—William J. Bryan to-day gave out his letter accepting the Populist nomination. It reads as follows:

LINCOLN, Neb., Oct. 3, 1896.

The Hon. William V. Allen, Chairman, and Others, Members of the Notification Committee of the People's Party:

Gentlemen: The nomination of the People's Party for the Presidency of the United States has been tendered me in such a generous spirit and upon such honorable terms that I am able to accept the same without departing from the platform adopted by the National Convention at Chicago.

Influence of Populists.

I fully appreciate the breadth of the patriotism which has actuated the members of the People's Party, who, in order to consolidate the sentiment in favor of bimetallism, have been willing to go outside of party lines and support as their candidate one already nominated by the Democratic Party, and also by the silver party. I also appreciate the fact that, while during all the years since 1873 a large majority of the Democratic Party and a considerable minority of the Republican Party have been consistent advocates of the free coinage of silver at the present ratio, yet, ever since the organization of the People's Party, its members have unanimously supported such coinage as the only means of restoring bimetallism.

By persistently pointing out the disastrous effects of a gold standard and protesting against each successive step toward financial bondage, the Populists have exerted an important influence in awakening the public to a realization of the Nation's present peril.

Puts Party Aside.

In a time like this, when a great political party is attempting to surrender the right to legislate for ourselves upon the financial question, and is seeking to bind the American people to a foreign monetary system, it behooves us, as lovers of our country and friends of American institutions, to lay aside for the present such differences as may exist among us on minor questions, in order that our strength may be united in a supreme effort to wrest the Government from the hands of those who imagine that the Nation's finances are only secured when controlled by a few financiers, and that National honor can only be maintained by servile acquiescence in any policy, however destructive to the interests of the people of the United States, which foreign creditors, present or prospective, may desire to force upon us.

It is a cause of congratulation that we have in this campaign not only the support of Democrats, Populists, and Republicans who have all along believed in independent bimetallism, but also the active co-operation of those Democrats and Republicans who have heretofore waited for international bimetallism, and who now join with us rather than trust the destinies of the Nation in the hands of those who are holding out the delusive hope of foreign aid while they labor secretly for the permanent establishment of the gold standard.

Difficulties of Fusion.

While difficulties have always arisen in the settlement of details of any plan or co-operation between distinct political organizations, I am sure that the advocates of bimetallism are so intensely in earnest that they will be able to devise some means by which the free-silver vote may be concentrated upon one Electoral ticket in each State. To secure this result, charity toward the opinions of others and liberality on the part of all is necessary, but honest and sincere friends who are working toward a common result always find it possible to agree upon just and equitable terms.

The American people have proved equal to every emergency which has arisen in the past, and I am confident that in the present emergency there will be no antagonism between the various regiments of the one great army which is marching to repel an invasion more dangerous to our welfare than an army with banners.

Acknowledging with gratitude your expressions of confidence and good will, I am very truly yours,

W. J. BRYAN.

BRYAN BUCKS TRADITION OF STAYING HOME

William Jennings Bryan ran an innovative campaign in 1896. Rejecting the tradition of staying home and leaving the campaign to local political organizations, Bryan actively toured throughout the United States in an attempt to rally the masses behind his candidacy. In hundreds of speeches, Bryan urged the repeal of the gold standard and the combined use of gold and silver to back the dollar. Although his oratorical skills were unmatched, reporters speculated whether such an active candidate could survive without exhausting himself completely.

JULY 25, 1896
BRYAN'S CAMPAIGN PLANS
WILL COME TO NEW-YORK EARLY NEXT MONTH.

His Speech at Madison Square Garden Will Be the Effort of His Life—Expects to Take the Stump and Make Several Speeches Each Day—Short Talks to be Made to the People of New-England—A Visit to Sewall's Home.

LINCOLN. Neb., July 24.—The plans of Mr. Bryan for the campaign are gradually shaping into something definite, and when the Committee on Notification shall announce the date of the rally in New-York, at which he will be informed of his selection as the candidate of the Democratic Party, he will prepare a partial programme of his movements.

Senator Jones of Arkansas, Chairman of the National Democratic Committee, is expected in Lincoln within a few days after the adjournment of the two St. Louis conventions, and he will confer with Mr. Bryan as to the conduct of the latter during the campaign.

It is not likely that Mr. Bryan will spend much of his time in Lincoln after he takes the stump. The Democratic managers realize his value as an orator, and want him to take the lion's share of the work for the ticket which he heads. His physical strength is such that he can make several long speeches a day without fatigue, and he has a record of delivering as many as five campaign addresses of an hour each at different places in a Congressional district, and then traveling fifty miles in a buggy to the next place in his itinerary without sleep. Added to his physical endurance is the ability to slumber at all times, and the shortest rest fits him for many hours of work. He does not wish to be spared during the campaign, and his stump-speaking tour is likely to be a record breaker.

From present indications it is probable that Aug. 10 or 12 will be the date of the notification in New-York. Mr. Bryan will start East from Lincoln about five days before the day fixed for that event. He is preparing his speech accepting the nomination and expects it to be the effort of his life, exceeding in eloquence his address to the Chicago Convention July 10.

As contemplated at present, Mr. Bryan will make a through trip to Chicago. From that place he will proceed to Pittsburg and make an address there. From Pittsburg he will go to Washington on an invitation from the delegates of the District of Columbia to the Chicago Convention, and en route to New-York will stop over in Philadelphia and talk there.

From New-York Mr. Bryan will go to Bath, Me., where he will be the guest of Mr. Sewall for a short time. It is probable that he will make some addresses en route. Maine audiences are likely to see something of him, and he will then go westward.

The date of his return to Lincoln has not been arranged, but it is understood here that he will appear in the Nebraska capital Aug. 24, when a reunion of Grand Army men residing in this State will be held. This idea, however, seems hardly feasible, as it will give Mr. Bryan a fortnight only at the utmost to visit Mr. Sewall, make a number of addresses in New-England, and return to his home in the slow fashion incident to Presidential aspirants during a campaign, when invitations to speak at places along the line of their journeys are too pressing to be refused. It is expected that Mr. Bryan will devote most of his time to the States between the Alleghenies and Rocky Mountains, and he is not likely to return to Lincoln for a stay of any length until just before the campaign is over.

Mr. Bryan told a reporter that he had not made any plans for short trips from Lincoln previous to his formal notification. He is devoting his energies to keeping up with his mail, and in this he finds constant employment, even with the assistance of Mrs. Bryan and two clerks. Mrs. Bryan will accompany her husband on his trip to New-York and New-England.

. . . .

CAMPAIGN BOOK OUTLINES HANNA'S CAMPAIGN STRATEGY

William McKinley's campaign was unique in its nationwide structure and massive financial backing. Traditionally, candidates had relied upon party organizations to rally local partisans. Campaign manager Mark Hanna created a highly centralized system to coordinate electioneering across the country. To guide this effort, a campaign book provided the "talking points" Republican supporters would need to counter the arguments of Democrats and Populists and win over the public. This centralized campaign structure facilitated the growth of stronger national parties.

AUGUST 9, 1896
REPUBLICAN CAMPAIGN BOOK OUT.

Instructive Chapters on Money and Special Matter for Democrats.

WASHINGTON, Aug. 8.—The Republican campaign book has been received at headquarters. It forms a volume of 410 pages. The title page contains two quotations—one from Mr. McKinley—as follows:

The Republican Party stands for honest money and a chance to earn it.

The other is from Lincoln, and reads:

That some may be rich shows that others may become rich, and hence, is just encouragement to industry and enterprise. Let not him who is homeless pull down the house of another, but let him labor diligently and build one for himself, thus by example showing that his own shall be safe from violence when built.

The subject matter of the book, so far as it appears in print, deals with a great variety of topics and is presented in an attractive manner. The committee believes that the whole volume will be valuable as a reference book for speakers and as a guide for those who are endeavoring to acquaint themselves with the current questions of the day.

Among the matter thus presented under appropriate heads are strong quotations from leading Democratic newspapers giving the reasons why they do not support the Chicago ticket; an article on American advancement, with arguments against a change in the financial system; quotations from the message of President Harrison of Dec. 6, 1892, on the great prosperity of the country, with particular reference to the farming communities and agriculturalists; Representative Cannon's review of the appropriations of the last session of Congress; historical matter concerning the industries of the country, present and past; essays on special subjects, such as bimetallism and bond issues of the United States, the history of the Bland-Allison act, &c.

The committee is congratulating itself upon what it claims to be the thorough manner in which the book is prepared, and the members say they believe it will be one of the documents most in demand by the people.

Mr. Apsley says its distribution will be largely in the hands of the National Committee. The first edition consists of but 20,000 copies.

In addition to the matters alluded to, the book contains election statistics relative to Presidential elections in the various States, exhaustive chapters on the different phases of the currency question, a history of the demonetization of silver, several chapters on farm products and values, together with tables showing the exports and imports of such articles under the McKinley and the Wilson laws; a chapter showing why the gold standard was adopted, many chapters relating to the labor problem, including tables of wages in this country and elsewhere, with reference to legislation for the advantage of the workmen, which the Republican Party has passed and fostered.

Many quotations from the speeches of McKinley are found throughout the book, and much attention is paid to the statements made by the present Republican candidate on the floor of the House of Representatives on the financial question.

Under the caption of "issues," the following are among the most important set out: "Coin, whether of gold or silver, must be equal to the best; emigrants who are willing to live without robbing other men of employment; financial integrity and money enough to pay all bills; gold and silver; equal dollars for all business; home markets for American products; imports must always be kept below exports; Judiciary of the United States must not be tampered with; ownership of railroads by the National Government is opposed by the Republican Party; tariff to protect American labor and encourage home industry; pensions for the veterans of the war equal to the pledge of the Nation."

· ·

Bryan's Whirlwind Speaking Tour

The Democratic candidate began his campaign tour in late August, speeding from town to town, delivering speeches wherever crowds could be assembled. This frenzied campaigning brought his candidacy directly to the voters, who otherwise might never have encountered his message. During these speeches, Bryan often wore his trademark black alpaca coat, the same that he had worn when giving his famous "Cross of Gold" speech at the national convention one month earlier.

AUGUST 21, 1896
CHALLENGE TO M'KINLEY

BRYAN SAYS HE WILL DEBATE WITH NO-ONE BUT HIS OPPONENT.

Will Attempt No Reply to Bourke Cockran's Arguments—The Chicago Candidate Will Make Several Speeches in This State Before Going West—His Programme Is to Address Several Meetings in Ohio and to Confer with Mr. Jones.

Upper Red Hook, Aug. 20.—William J. Bryan threw down the gauntlet to-day to Major McKinley. It was a dignified challenge, for in it he refused to discuss the issues of the campaign with any person except the one that stands his equal in office-seeking ambition. He was asked if he intended to answer Mr. Cockran, and said in answer that he was receiving many invitations from prominent men to debate the silver question. In order to avoid further invitations of this nature, he said, he would not consider any proposition to debate any question with anybody during the campaign, unless a debate should be arranged between Mr. McKinley and himself, and he added that, so far as he knew, no plan for such a debate was under consideration by either National Committee.

Ex-State Senator Norton Chase and Internal Revenue Collector Louis W. Pratt were here this afternoon to make arrangement for the Albany speech Tuesday night next. At their suggestion, Mr. Bryan will leave an hour or so earlier than he intended, and will arrive in Albany about 4 o'clock, leaving there at 10 o'clock.

Mr. Bryan gave out another itinerary to-day. It contains a programme of his intended movements from Erie to Lincoln, and was dictated in this way by the candidate:

"I will leave Erie Thursday, Aug. 27, for Buffalo, where I will speak in the evening. From Buffalo I will go to Medina, where I will speak Friday afternoon; thence to Niagara Falls, where I will spend the night. I will leave Niagara Falls Saturday morning, passing through Buffalo to Hornellsville, where I will speak in the afternoon; thence to Jamestown in the evening, going to Chautauqua to spend Sunday. I will leave Chautauqua Monday morning for Cleveland, speaking there in the evening of Monday, the 31st. From there I will go to Columbus, Ohio, where I will speak on the evening of Sept. 1; thence to Toledo, Ohio, where I will speak on the evening of the 2d; thence to South Bend, Ind., where I will speak on the evening of the 3d. I will spend the 4th in Chicago at the Democratic National headquarters, and will go to Nebraska over the Burlington route, arriving at Lincoln on the 5th. I will not stop at any point between Chicago and Lincoln."

SEPTEMBER 12, 1896
MCKINLEY TO STAY AT CANTON.

Hanna Says the Major Will Not Debate with Bryan.

CHICAGO, Sept. 11.—Chairman Hanna was asked this morning what would be done about the petition now circulating among organized labor requesting Messrs. McKinley and Bryan to meet in this city in joint debate. Mr. Hanna said: "Mr. McKinley is not going to take the stump. The Democrats undoubtedly would like very much to see him chasing over the country in a wild scramble for votes, as Mr. Bryan has insisted upon doing. Mr. McKinley will continue to conduct himself as a man who appreciates the dignity and importance of the office he seeks. He will not lend himself to any catchpenny scheme for the sake of satisfying the curious or making himself talked about. I have heard this subject discussed, and I think I know what I am talking about when I say Mr. McKinley will continue to address the people who visit him at Canton."

● ●

McKinley Avoids Bryan's Invitation to Debate

As William Jennings Bryan toured the country giving speech after speech, he challenged William McKinley to a debate over the coinage question that was central to the electorate's decision. An open public debate would have been a first for a presidential contest (and not accomplished until 1960), but McKinley, wary of Bryan's powerful command of an audience, wisely avoided such an encounter. Instead, McKinley remained at home in Canton, Ohio, while Bryan continued his whirlwind tour of the eastern United States.

AUGUST 23, 1896
BRYAN TAKES THE STUMP

OPENS HIS CAMPAIGN WITH A SPEECH TO DUTCHESS FARMERS.

Wears His Alpaca Coat and Tries to Duplicate His Chicago Effort—Declares that This Is a Time for Common People to Think—Attacks the Handlers of Money and Draws a Parallel with Demetrius—A Large Crowd Listens.

BARRYTOWN, N. Y., Aug. 22.—William J. Bryan opened the political campaign in earnest to-day at Madalin, a town in Dutchess County. He delivered his first actual campaign speech since his nomination, and showed an earnestness in delivery closely resembling that which brought about the demonstration in his honor at Chicago the day before he was selected as the Democratic standard bearer. Mr. Bryan was in excellent voice and evidently made a good impression on his auditors.

Mr. and Mrs. Bryan and their hosts, Mr. and Mrs. Perrine, drove over to Madalin at 3 o'clock from Upper Red Hook. A number of houses along the five miles of road were decorated with flags, and the town of Madalin and the adjacent village, Tivoli, were also made attractive by a display of bunting. At the outskirts of Madalin a Reception Committee and a brass band greeted the candidate, and, with the band in front, a procession was formed for the entry into the town. Fifteen hundred persons were gathered about the speaker's stand, which was situated in a large pasture, used in all campaigns for political meetings. Mr. Bryan was loudly applauded as he came in sight.

John J. Lenz, candidate for Congress in Ohio on the Democratic ticket, was delivering an address at the time, and he spoke for more than an hour after the Bryan party appeared, devoting himself entirely to the money question, and frequently gaining applause. It had been intended that Senator Stewart of Nevada should follow Mr. Lenz, but the threatening aspect of the heavens and the desire of Mr. Bryan to get back to Upper Red Hook early brought about a change in the programme, and the Democratic

Presidential candidate was allowed to take the place of the venerable "father of the free-silver cause."

Frank S. Orinsbe, who acted as Chairman of the meeting, presented Mr. Bryan in a few words. He called him the "hero of the hour" and the "next President of the United States." There was an outburst of handclapping as the candidate stepped forward, and then a cheer, and more cheers. A small cannon, that had punctuated Mr. Lenz's remarks at irregular intervals, boomed out a salute, the band played, and a delegation from the Bryan and Sewall Club of Saugerties waved transparencies enthusiastically. The people composing the audience were crowded together in front of the stand, and there was a rush forward from those in the rear when Mr. Bryan started to speak. He wore again to-day the old black alpaca coat in which he was attired when he made the famous Chicago speech. His voice, after his long rest, was clear and strong, and he appeared to the best advantage.

- -

Bryan's Speaking Schedule Tests his Endurance

Bryan continued his tour of the country, but focused on the northeastern states he needed to become competitive. Delivering many speeches daily without mechanical amplification, Bryan's endurance wore down and his strong voice began to weaken. The rigors of the tour weakened the youthful candidate, who returned home to Nebraska for a short recuperation.

AUGUST 27, 1896
BRYAN TALKS TO 40,000

NOT ALL AT ONCE, BUT IN LOTS OF FROM 100 TO 10,000.

Talked in Familiar, Straightaway Fashion to Great Assemblages in Syracuse, Rochester, and Erie, Penn., and to Smaller Crowds at Way Stations—Praised Mr. McKinley's Integrity in One Speech and Came to the End of the Day Almost Exhausted.

ERIE, Penn., Aug. 26.—Husky of voice and tired of body after a hard day of campaigning, William Jennings Bryan found himself confronted on his arrival in Erie to-night with a programme calling for three more speeches before he could rest from the weariness that this day of railroad traveling and speechmaking had brought to him.

But he carried out the part of the contract assigned him by the local Committee on Arrangements and performed his triplicate duty with a vigor that spoke well

for his constitution. His reception at the railroad station was hearty in the extreme. Rain was falling when his train arrived at 7 o'clock, but the 2,000 or more persons waiting his coming stood their ground and gave the candidate a royal welcome.

A hard fight was necessary to make a passage for Mr. and Mrs. Bryan through the wall of cheering spectators, and, with a brass band in the lead and members of the local committee in the rear, they were conveyed in a carriage to the Reed House, where another crowd was waiting to echo the station greetings.

Accompanied by Joseph Sibley and other prominent Democrats of Erie, Mr. Bryan started out at 8 o'clock to perform the contract which had been made for him. The three gatherings he addressed repaid him in the potency of their applause for his sacrifice of comfort and rest in their behalf.

Schlosser's Hall, a big, square, low-ceiling place, was the scene of his first speech. It seats 2,500, and to-night not only was every chair supplied with an occupant, but hundreds were obliged to stand, and hundreds more vainly sought admittance.

The annual meeting of Erie County farmers was held near the city to-day. The gathering is always large. It was expected that many of those who were in attendance at the celebration, known as the harvest home picnic, would be at Schlosser's to hear the Democratic candidate.

Whether they were there or not, Mr. Bryan made a stirring speech suitable to an audience of farmers and others who work with their hands. He told a story or two and spoke in a popular, familiar way that had its effect upon his listeners. They howled with laughter when he related a . . . tale of Ignatius Donnelly's to illustrate the silver question and shouted vigorously when he made epigrammatic remarks about his opponents.

From Schlosser's Hall Mr. Bryan was whirled off to carry out another third of his contract. This time he was scheduled to appear at St. Patrick's Auditorium, an exceedingly spacious hall situated in a district largely populated by workingmen. His voice had shown signs of huskiness at Schlosser's. At St. Patrick's he spoke with an effort.

The effect of his two long addresses at Syracuse and Rochester, and his short speeches at a number of places along the route to Erie, had begun to show, and Mr. Bryan's vocal organs appeared to be in the much-weakened state they were after his record-breaking campaign experience from Lincoln to the East.

At the second Erie meeting the 2,300 men and women assembled in the Auditorium were orderly, but on the whole, more enthusiastic than those at the first meeting. The three cheers they gave when the young nominee concluded fairly shook the rafters.

Again the thoroughly fatigued candidate was harried to the waiting carriage. Again he was whirled away, this time to the Park Opera House, where the eighth annual State Convention of Pennsylvania Democratic Clubs was in session. This was the most demonstrative meeting of the evening, and to his audience there Mr. Bryan made the most important speech of the three delivered in the course of two hours.

Mrs. Bryan and Miss Sibley were conspicuous figures in one of the proscenium boxes. It was a meeting seemingly thoroughly in sympathy with the candidate of the party. Some dozen oil paintings of the nominee were suspended from various points about the hall. The orchestra chairs were crowded, but there were vacant seats in the galleries. Many ladies were in the boxes and elsewhere, and the audience was one that suggested refinement and culture.

Various speakers had entertained the delegates and others comprising the audience, but the speaker who was addressing them when Mr. Bryan appeared, was lost to memory and view in the stirring enthusiasm that ensued.

Everybody rose, and the cheering, punctuated with vigorous blasts from the band, handkerchief-waving, hat-throwing crowd of Democratic sympathizers made Mr. Bryan know that he was heartily welcome. When the prolonged shouts of welcome had ended Mr. Bryan was introduced. After he was through the nominee held a handshaking reception, and went back to the Reed House and to bed. Mr. Bryan spoke as follows:

"Mr. Chairman, Ladies, and Gentlemen: I esteem it a great privilege to be permitted to meet to-night with the members of the clubs assembled here from all over the State of Pennsylvania, because I know what these meetings mean. I know the inspiration that they give and of the enthusiasm carried back by those who go forth to prosecute the work of this campaign.

"In my judgment, we are entering upon a campaign which will be memorable in the history of the country, for many reasons; not only because of the issue involved— that would be enough to make it an epoch in the history of nations—but there are other reasons. This campaign demonstrates as no campaign has done within the last generation the capacity of the people for self-government." [Great applause and cheering.]

A Voice—"A Daniel come to judgment."

Mr. Bryan, continuing:

"Is there a man in this land who doubts that the American people can rise to the requirements of any emergency? If so I bid him to cast his eyes upon 70,000,000 of people thinking out their own salvation. [Great applause.]

"Is there a man who believes that party machinery can govern the people? I bid him look until he sees the great common people breaking every machine that stands in their way. [Great applause and cheering.] Is there a man who believes that the age of oratory is gone? I point him to every precinct in this Nation, where he will find a modern Demosthenes. [Great applause.] Oratory will live so long as there are causes which appeal to the human heart. [Applause.] Oratory is the speech of the person who knows what he is talking about and means what he says, and in this campaign you will find the orator everywhere.

"Come to my State and I will show you a banker and a money loaner who will go forth to preach the gospel of bimetallism, and he never preached any other gospel in his life. [Great applause and cheering.] I will show you a brief-less barrister who, armed with right, will meet the attorney of the corporations and crush him before any audience. [Great applause.]

"I will show you the business man who never came from behind the counter before, but he, feeling that the welfare of his family, the welfare of posterity, depends upon the settlement of the cause can come from his store and rise before an audience and make a speech that cannot be answered by any man who would fasten the shackles upon 70,000,000 free men. [Great applause.]

"I will take you to the railroad shops and I will show you men who know more about the money question than the President of the road knows about the subject. [Applause and cheers.] I will take you to a carpenter who as he works at the bench will revolve in his mind these questions and come nearer finding out what is an honest dollar than the man who represents a syndicate and bows to the dictation of Lombard Street. [Great applause.]

"Ah, come with me to the farm and I will show you the man who pushes the plow, and who has studied this money question, and who knows that if the dollars go up his wheat comes down, and you cannot answer the logic of that argument at all. [Great applause.]

"A prominent writer came to this country a good many years ago and wrote a book about Democracy in America and he said that every citizen over here was a public speaker, and he said one of them could not talk five minutes without getting excited and saying; 'Ladies and Gentlemen.' [Laughter.] If he thought that then, what would he think were he here today? [Great applause and laughter.]

"I know Western towns where the people congregated upon the streets and blocked up the sidewalks talking the money question and where they got so numerous they had to push them off the sidewalks and blocked up the streets 100 feet wide, and then in order to allow some business to go on their City Council hired a hall for those people to meet in every day and discuss the money question."

"My friends, when the people come to discuss the money question in that way you cannot drive the tariff question into the campaign with a pile driver. [Continued laughter.] It is not more taxes the people want. It is more money to pay the taxes they already have to-day. [Laughter and applause.]

"I want you to go home and take with you the determination to leave no effort undone to carry out the principles which you espouse. We have a cause that appeals to the hearts of men. There is no sentiment in the human heart that is deeper down than the love of justice.

"It is the love of justice upon which society is built—without there could be no such thing as government—and the sense of justice is offended by any legislation that seeks to give a few people the prosperity that ought to be the heritage of all the people. [Great applause.]

"Now, there is one rule by which we can determine on which side the citizens of this country will light. I remember hearing a sermon preached a good many years ago from the text: 'As he thinketh in his heart, so is he.' The more I have thought of that text the more deeply it has impressed itself upon me. The heart is the place where conduct is determined, and if you want to find out where a man is in this fight, do not look at his brain; that would find a reason for whatever his heart wants to do. Look at his heart." [Long and continued applause.]

● ●

McKinley Campaigns from the Comfort of Home

In contrast to Democrat William Jennings Bryan, the Republican candidate, William McKinley, campaigned in the traditional style. Presidential aspirants during this era were expected to stay home and greet supporters from their front porches, rather than "chasing down voters" on the campaign trail. As the series of headlines below describe, in September and October, McKinley met more than 750,000 supporters who traveled to Canton, Ohio, to hear him speak, cheer their candidate, and possibly shake his hand. This tactic allowed McKinley to enjoy the comforts of home that were denied Bryan on his railroad travels.

SEPTEMBER 6, 1896
THEY CAME IN THOUSANDS

TWO GREAT DELEGATIONS FROM PENNSYLVANIA AT CANTON.

Beaver County Sends Three Special Trains Loaded with Enthusiastic Republicans—Three Other Trains Filled with Citizens of Pittsburg—McKinley Makes Two Speeches, in Which He Enlarges on the Value of Protection.

SEPTEMBER 20, 1896
CANTON IS AGAIN CROWDED

MANY DELEGATIONS OF WAGE WORKERS GREET McKINLEY.

They Come from All Over the Country and Include Many Men Who Have Heretofore Voted the Democratic Ticket—5,000 Railroad Men from Chicago in One Party—Iron Workers, Telegraphers, and Commercial Travelers Represented.

SEPTEMBER 27, 1896
A BUSY DAY FOR M'KINLEY

HE MAKES ELEVEN SPEECHES TO SIXTEEN DELEGATIONS.

Nearly 15,000 Persons Paid Their Respects to the Major at His Home in Canton—Handshaking Was Out of the Question, Which Was a Mercy to Him—Many of the Delegations Were Workingmen.

OCTOBER 18, 1896
MR. M'KINLEY SEES 30,000

THE FIRST SWARM OF VISITORS INTERRUPTED BREAKFAST.

Twenty-five Delegations from West Virginia, Pennsylvania, Maryland, Kentucky, Michigan, and Ohio at Mr. McKinley's Residence—He Makes Eighteen Speeches—Cheered by Students, Old Folks, Railway Men, and Mechanics.

CANTON, Ohio. Oct, 17.—Delegations began to arrive in Canton at 5:30 this morning, the first comers being from Pennsylvania and Michigan. Three hundred voters from Monroe County, Mich., marched up Market Street to Major McKinley's house at 8 o'clock, and caused him to dispatch his breakfast with haste. They were not kept waiting more than ten minutes.

Their spokesman, D. A. Curtis, of Monroe, Mich., made a lively address to Major McKinley, and assured him that his plurality in Michigan would exceed twenty thousand. Major McKinley thanked his Michigan visitors for their call, and urged them to stand firmly for the party of protection and sound money.

Major McKinley's next callers came with drums beating and flags flying at 9 o'clock. There were three delegations in the assemblage that filled the McKinley yard. One was from Altoona, Blair County, Penn., numbering 1,400 men; a delegation of 150 miners from South Fork, and another of 150 miners from Portage, Cambria County, Penn. Major McKinley spoke to them earnestly of protection.

Two hundred citizens of Huntingdon County, Penn., were the next callers. Judge Williamson introduced them to Major McKinley, who made a short address.

The fourth speech was made at 10:30; to a delegation from Grand Rapids and Western Michigan, largely composed of railway men and men engaged in the manufacture of furniture.

A delegation came from Ashtabula County, Ohio, that numbered 2,500 men. There were farmers, mechanics, railroad men, and dock men in the crowd. More than fifty banners with appropriate political inscriptions were borne in the delegation. They greeted Major McKinley with mighty cheers. A delegation of miners and farmers from Perry County, Ohio, came within hearing distance just behind the Ashtabula people. Major McKinley addressed the two delegations at the same time on the loyalty of Ohio to great principles.

College yells from 500 students rent the air. The boys from the Ohio State University and the Ohio Wesleyan University at Delaware marched joyously from the station. Following them was a body of elderly people from Westonville, Ohio, each of more than fifty years of age, and a delegation of students from the Ohio Medical University at Columbus.

The scene about Major McKinley's house at 3:30 in the afternoon cannot be adequately described. The broad street on which the house faces was packed with men four, and often eight abreast, for the distance of three quarters of a mile, and in several side streets delegations were standing waiting their turn to be received.

* *

A Recuperated Bryan Heads South

By mid-September, Bryan had recovered his voice and energy, and he returned to the campaign trail. This time he headed to the southern states, where he reached out to Populists and Democrats. He renewed his campaign's intensity, bouncing from town to town, making speeches wherever he found a crowd willing to listen.

SEPTEMBER 12, 1896
MR. BRYAN AFIELD AGAIN

LEAVES LINCOLN FOR ANOTHER MONTH OF SPEECHES.

The Candidate Will Sweep Around the Southern States from Missouri to Virginia, Speaking from Car Platforms, as Usual, Between the Larger Cities—The Southern Itinerary from Knoxville, Tenn., to Richmond, Va.

LINCOLN, Neb., Sept. 11.—William J. Bryan left Lincoln to-night at 9:15 o'clock over the Missouri Pacific Road for another month of campaigning. He will reach Kansas City at 6:30 to-morrow morning, and proceed on the Wabash to St. Louis, where he is scheduled to make four addresses tomorrow night.

The departure of Mr. Bryan from Lincoln was made the occasion of another demonstration by the local free-silver clubs. They formed a torchlight procession and escorted Mr. Bryan from his residence to the Missouri Pacific station. A brass band headed the parade. Quite a large crowd gathered at the station and cheered Mr. Bryan as his train drew out.

Mr. Bryan made a brief speech from the rear car. He said:

"Ladies and Gentlemen: I don't know whether I shall return to Nebraska again just before the election or not, but I go away from Nebraska feeling that it is not necessary. [Cheers.] I want to say to you, my friends, that from the reports which I have been receiving I do not believe there is a single county in the State that the Republicans are sure of carrying this Fall. [Great cheering.]

"And more than that, every day finds our cause stronger throughout the Union than it was the day before. Every day finds persons who are declaring for free coinage, and I think I am safe in saying that you will not find among all your acquaintances a man who one month ago was in favor of free coinage at 16 to 1 and able to give a reason for it who has changed his mind. But you cannot find any man who was for free coinage who is thinking himself into the gold-standard idea. [Loud cheering.]

"A little over a month ago I went into what I then called the enemy's country, but I found down there just as much enthusiasm as there is in Nebraska. [Great cheers.] To-day some parts of the country are more friendly than others, but there is no enemy's country." [Loud cheering.]

Mr. Bryan's first stop after leaving Lincoln was at Eagle, where a small crowd of persons, a drum corps, and a bonfire composed the elements of his reception. Elmwood, another small place, turned out with torches, and Wabash added red fire to smoky flambeaux.

* *

THE NEW YORK TIMES QUESTIONS BRYAN'S MENTAL CONDITION

The revolutionary nature of William Jennings Bryan's campaign led many people to question his tactics. Bryan suffered obvious exhaustion caused by the rigors of his travels and speaking engagements, but rumors also circulated that he had suffered a mental breakdown. His intense focus on the silver issue led some to suggest that he had become obsessed with the subject. Through September and October, *The New York Times*—which was then a Republican partisan paper—ran a series of articles questioning Bryan's sanity. Numerous leading doctors were consulted, often opining on the Democrat's fitness for the presidency.

SEPTEMBER 27, 1896
BRYAN'S MENTAL CONDITION.

To the Editor of The New-York Times:

I hope you will give me an opportunity in your valuable paper to call attention, and that very seriously, to the mental condition of Mr. William J. Bryan. I am old enough to remember vividly the spectacle of Mr. Greeley stumping the country for the Presidency and confident of his personal power with the people. I remember and, indeed, know well the medical details of his final insanity and pathetic end.

It has been with a professional rather than political interest, therefore, that I have watched Mr. Bryan in his imitation and expansion of the campaign method so disastrous to his predecessor.

And I think I can say now without any bias that Mr. Bryan presents in speech and action striking and alarming evidence of a mind not entirely sound. I say alarming, for, apart from considerations of humanity, what could be more disastrous than a madman in the White House. It would not only be the direct harm that might result from irresponsible acts, but it would forever weaken the trust in the soundness of republics and the sanity of the voting masses.

SEPTEMBER 27, 1896
IS MR. BRYAN A MATTOID

LEADING ALIENISTS ANALYZE THE DEMOCRATIC CANDIDATE.

They Disagree, as Experts Very Often Do—Dr. Sachs Sees a Chance for Physical Breakdown—Drs. Hammond and Dana Think There Is Evidence of Degeneracy— Dr. Spitzka Thinks Lightly of Him—Dr. Collins Wants Fair Play.

OCTOBER 9, 1896
BRYAN'S MENTAL BALANCE.

From The Poughkeepsie Eagle.

THE NEW-YORK TIMES is publishing articles asserting that Mr. Bryan shows indications of unsoundness of mind. We do not believe this, but certainly his manner and style do not indicate that mental balance and soundness of judgment that are necessary for such an office as the Presidency of the United States. Such a man would be dangerous if elected on a sound platform, and with a united and patriotic party behind him. With a platform whose abominations cause it to be rejected by all the best element of Democracy and a party in full sympathy with his most eccentric vagaries his election would be a calamity which even the strength of free government itself would hardly be able to overcome.

OCTOBER 12, 1896
EDITORIAL
WHAT'S THE MATTER WITH BRYAN?

From The Utica Observer.

A correspondent of The New-York Sun recently called attention to the absurd contradictions that Bryan is continually making, and gave it as his opinion that something was the matter with Bryan's mental processes.

Another correspondent in THE NEW-YORK TIMES has also called attention to Bryan's mental condition, and THE TIMES has acted upon the hint, and interviewed many physicians of eminence on the subject. * * * What's the matter with Bryan? Is he all right? We do not believe that he is mad. But in a few weeks we believe that he will be, well—disappointed.

GAMBLERS PREDICT THE OUTCOME OF THE ELECTION

Before the advent of modern surveys and public polling, election predictions came through bookmakers and betting. Wealthy patrons predicted the prospects of their preferred candidate by making large bets, with the proceeds often going to charity. While not entirely scientific, high-profile bets did provide rough indications of public sentiment, at least among the wealthy, and added to the fervor of the campaign.

OCTOBER 17, 1896
$5,000 TO $1,000 ON MCKINLEY.

WASHINGTON, Oct. 16.—Col. Edward Ayres received notice this noon that his certified check sent to Philadelphia to take a bet of $5,000 to $1,000 that McKinley would be elected had been covered.

OCTOBER 30, 1896
BIG ODDS ON MCKINLEY.

CHICAGO, Oct. 29.—The biggest betting proposition that has yet been made around Republican headquarters was submitted today by C. C. Viall & Co., stock brokers, of the Rialto Building, who reported to Perry Heath that they had in deposit in the Union National Bank the sum of $100,000 which they are prepared to bet on McKinley at odds of 3 to 1. They will not bet any sum less than $5,000, and are prepared to bet the entire $100,000 if anybody cares to take them up.

OCTOBER 30, 1896
MR. STRATTON WANTS TO BET.

He Will Support Bryan on a Ratio of One to Three.

COLORADO SPRINGS, Col., Oct. 29.—W. S. Stratton, the rich gold mine owner of Cripple Creek, yesterday made an offer to bet $100,000 against $300,000 that William J. Bryan will be elected President. Mr. Stratton agrees that if he wins he will give the money to the Colorado Springs Free Library, and if the others win they are to have the money. A syndicate of rich men of the city is trying to raise the $300,000. Mr. Stratton says that he does not make the offer through any pointers that he has on the election, but believes their patriotism will arouse the workingmen to the necessity of voting for Bryan. Mr. Stratton is the Colorado Springs carpenter who became a multi-millionaire in Cripple Creek.

He says that the maintenance of the gold standard would be better for him, but not for the masses, and he believes in the masses.

A few days ago Stratton offered to bet $10,000 to $30,000 with Cashier W. S. Jackson of the El Paso County Bank, but Mr. Jackson, although an ardent Republican, declined to wager the money.

RUMORS CONCERNING THE STATE OF BRYAN'S HEALTH

In late October 1896, after two months of frantic campaigning, William Jennings Bryan again began to suffer from exhaustion. His speeches no longer resonated with the same force that had won him acclaim at the Chicago convention, and he no longer exuded a youthful image to his audience. Fears for his health swirled around the Democratic and Populist camps. They maintained slim hopes that he could hold on until the votes were cast in early November.

OCTOBER 29, 1896
FEARS OF BRYAN'S COLLAPSE.

Evidences that He May Break Down Before the Campaign Closes.

CHICAGO, Oct. 29.—Chairman James K. Jones and others connected with the National Democratic headquarters are fearful that Bryan will collapse before the campaign ends.

While he appears robust and insists that he will have no trouble in filling all the engagements he has made, those who have watched him closest since he came to Chicago agree that his throat seems to be swelled beyond its natural proportions; that he is suffering with a severe cold, and that he speaks with great difficulty. Graceful gestures, which once gave force to his orations, are now languid and automatic, and he does not impress those who hear him as a man who could move any number of people by the strength of his eloquence. He is not the same man, physically, that captured the Coliseum Convention.

When a number of ward celebrities crowded around him in Pulaski Hall last night and insisted on shaking hands with him, his face expressed much aversion, and he seemed to reciprocate the attentions with painful reluctance. Indeed, the Democratic candidate's face seemed to reflect physical pain, and while speaking in another Ashland Avenue hall, his voice was scarcely audible beyond the edge of the stage. Men who have traveled with him on his special trains say he has reached the limit of human endurance.

During the early days of his speaking tour they say he was permitted to sleep long hours, and each morning he

appeared refreshed and ready for a repetition of the previous day's task. But since his entry into Illinois, they claim that he has taken less care of his health. He has been unable to get his previous refreshing sleep, and his nights have been disturbed and restless. He appears nervous and easily agitated, and exhibits all the symptoms of a man on the verge of nervous collapse.

Since Mr. Bryan's arrival in Chicago he has had difficulty with his throat, which he did not experience before. During the frequent changes from sweltering halls to the cool outer air, he has several times suffered from chills, and has added to a slight cold contracted several days ago.

His vocal cords are swollen and inflamed, and a number of physicians have expressed the opinion that he was running the greatest risk in continuing the strain on his voice. Mr. Bryan nearly collapsed this morning. He refused to leave his bed until 9 o'clock, and his special train had to be held for him nearly two hours.

"There is a limit to human endurance," said Theodore Nelson, Secretary of the State Committee, who has charge of Mr. Bryan's State tour. "Mr. Bryan is simply used up. He got to bed after 1 o'clock last night, and this morning he simply could not get started in time for his early train. The whole schedule was changed accordingly, and his arrival to-night will be two hours late."

The Republicans Win in a Landslide

When the ballots were counted it became clear that the McKinley-Hobart ticket had won a decisive victory in the election of 1896. The final tally revealed a massive Republican majority in both the popular vote and the Electoral College. The comprehensive victory by McKinley (and campaign manager Mark Hanna) in this critical election signaled a new era in American politics, during which the Republican Party would reign supreme for nearly three decades.

NOVEMBER 4, 1896
MCKINLEY
ELECTED
PRESIDENT UNITED STATES

TIMES OFFICE, Nov. 4.—4 A. M.

William McKinley and Garret A. Hobart, the Republican candidates for President and Vice President of the United States, have been elected by a tremendous majority in the Electoral College and by an enormous plurality of the popular vote.

Out of the 447 Electoral votes, the Democratic-Populist combination of Bryan, Sewall, and Watson was only able to secure 122, as against 313 for their Republican competitors, with one State in doubt.

The victory for sound money is even more strikingly shown in the popular vote. In this, the pluralities from the most trustworthy data make it appear that McKinley and Hobart lead the opposition by more than 1,000,000 ballots.

In the analysis by States, as shown in the adjoining column, the fact is made clear that the attempted coalition of the South and West has been an absolute and thorough failure.

The boasted "Solid South" has been broken. Of the States which formerly made up this mass that was regarded as Democratic under all circumstances, the Republican candidates for the Presidency have carried Delaware,

Maryland, West Virginia, North Carolina, and Kentucky. In nearly all cases, moreover, the pluralities were large.

In the Middle West, which was by common consent made the principal fighting ground, the Republicans have made a clean sweep. Illinois, the pivotal State, has gone Republican by an immense plurality. Ohio, Indiana, Michigan, Wisconsin, Iowa, the Dakotas, Kansas, and Nebraska have followed.

The three Pacific coast States and Wyoming are also to be placed in the Republican list.

In the East, every State from Maine to North Carolina, inclusive, has gone for McKinley and Hobart, with the exception of Virginia, which is in doubt.

Thirty States went Republican and fourteen Democratic and Populist.

Every record for large pluralities in the history of the country has been broken by New-York and Pennsylvania, each of which gives the Republican candidates about 300,000. Of other States in the same column, Illinois gives 150,000, Massachusetts 110,000, and Wisconsin 100,000.

The landslide for honest money came according to prediction.

• •

Vice President Garret Hobart Dies

The 1896 election changed the political landscape of America for the next thirty years, but the men who enjoyed victory that November did not live to see the long-term impact of their accomplishment. Late in 1899 Garret A. Hobart, considered one of the most powerful vice presidents in history, died of heart failure at age fifty-five. His office remained vacant until Theodore

1896 POPULAR VOTE

STATE	TOTAL VOTE	WILLIAM McKINLEY (REPUBLICAN)		WILLIAM J. BRYAN (DEMOCRAT, POPULIST)[1]		JOHN M. PALMER (NATIONAL DEMOCRAT)		JOSHUA LEVERING (PROHIBITION)	
		VOTES	%	VOTES	%	VOTES	%	VOTES	%
Alabama	194,580	55,673	28.6	130,298	67.0	6,375	3.3	2,234	1.1
Arkansas	149,396	37,512	25.1	110,103	73.7	—	0.0	889	0.6
California[2]	299,374	146,688	49.1	123,143	41.2	2,006	0.7	2,573	0.9
Colorado	189,539	26,271	13.9	161,005	84.9	1	0.0	1,717	0.9
Connecticut	174,394	110,285	63.2	56,740	32.5	4,336	2.5	1,806	1.0
Delaware	31,538	16,883	53.5	13,425	42.6	877	2.8	355	1.1
Florida[2]	46,468	11,298	24.3	30,683	66.0	1,778	3.8	656	1.4
Georgia[3]	163,309	60,107	36.8	94,733	58.0	2,809	1.7	5,613	3.4
Idaho	29,631	6,324	21.3	23,135	78.1	—	0.0	172	0.6
Illinois	1,090,766	607,130	55.7	465,593	42.7	6,307	0.6	9,796	0.9
Indiana	637,089	323,754	50.8	305,538	48.0	2,145	0.3	3,061	0.5
Iowa	521,550	289,293	55.5	223,744	42.9	4,516	0.9	3,192	0.6
Kansas	336,085	159,484	47.5	173,049	51.5	1,209	0.4	1,723	0.5
Kentucky	445,928	218,171	48.9	217,894	48.9	5,084	1.1	4,779	1.1
Louisiana	101,046	22,037	21.8	77,175	76.4	1,834	1.8	—	0.0
Maine	118,419	80,403	67.9	34,587	29.2	1,867	1.6	1,562	1.3
Maryland	250,249	136,959	54.7	104,150	41.6	2,499	1.0	5,918	2.4
Massachusetts	401,269	278,976	69.5	105,414	26.3	11,749	2.9	2,998	0.7
Michigan	545,583	293,336	53.8	237,164	43.5	6,923	1.3	4,978	0.9
Minnesota	341,762	193,503	56.6	139,735	40.9	3,222	0.9	4,348	1.3
Mississippi	69,591	4,819	6.9	63,355	91.0	1,021	1.5	396	0.6
Missouri	674,032	304,940	45.2	363,667	54.0	2,365	0.4	2,169	0.3
Montana	53,330	10,509	19.7	42,628	79.9	—	0.0	193	0.4
Nebraska	223,181	103,064	46.2	115,007	51.5	2,885	1.3	1,242	0.6
Nevada[4]	10,314	1,938	18.8	7,802	75.6	—	0.0	—	0.0
New Hampshire[2]	83,670	57,444	68.7	21,271	25.4	3,520	4.2	779	0.9
New Jersey	371,014	221,367	59.7	133,675	36.0	6,373	1.7	—	0.0
New York	1,423,876	819,838	57.6	551,369	38.7	18,950	1.3	16,052	1.1
North Carolina	331,337	155,122	46.8	174,408	52.6	578	0.2	635	0.2
North Dakota	47,391	26,335	55.6	20,686	43.6	—	0.0	358	0.8
Ohio[2]	1,014,295	525,991	51.9	474,882	46.8	1,858	0.2	5,068	0.5
Oregon	97,335	48,700	50.0	46,739	48.0	977	1.0	919	0.9
Pennsylvania[5]	1,194,355	728,300	61.0	427,125	35.8	11,000	0.9	19,274	1.6
Rhode Island	54,785	37,437	68.3	14,459	26.4	1,166	2.1	1,160	2.1
South Carolina	68,938	9,313	13.5	58,801	85.3	824	1.2	—	0.0
South Dakota	82,937	41,040	49.5	41,225	49.7	—	0.0	672	0.8
Tennessee	320,903	148,683	46.3	167,168	52.1	1,953	0.6	3,099	1.0
Texas[6]	515,987	163,413	31.7	267,803	51.9	4,989	1.0	1,797	0.3
Utah	78,098	13,491	17.3	64,607	82.7	—	0.0	—	0.0
Vermont[7]	63831	51,127	80.1	10,179	15.9	1,331	2.1	733	1.1
Virginia	294,674	135,379	45.9	154,708	52.5	2,129	0.7	2,350	0.8
Washington[2]	93,583	39,153	41.8	51,646	55.2	—	0.0	968	1.0
West Virginia	201,757	105,379	52.2	94,480	46.8	678	0.3	1,220	0.6
Wisconsin	447,409	268,135	59.9	165,523	37.0	4,584	1.0	7,507	1.7
Wyoming[2]	21,093	10,072	47.8	10,376	49.3	—	0.0	159	0.8
TOTALS	13,905,691	7,105,144	51.1	6,370,897	45.8	132,718	1.0	125,118	0.9

1. Bryan was nominated by both the Democrats and the Populists but with different running mates. In several states different slates of electors were entered by each party. It is legally incorrect to combine the vote. The separate vote for Bryan usually under the Populist ticket is listed under "Other." In other states it appears that the two slates of electors were the same and it is correct to combine the vote.

2. Figures from Edgar E. Robinson, *The Presidential Vote 1896–1932* (Stanford, Calif.: Stanford University Press, 1934).

3. Figures from Svend Petersen, *A Statistical History of the American Presidential Elections* (Westport, Conn.: Greenwood Press, 1981).

4. Figures from *Political History of Nevada* (Secretary of State).

5. Figures from *Manual, 1897.*

OTHER VOTES	%	PLURALITY	
—	0.0	74,625	D
892	0.6	72,591	D
24,285	8.2	23,545	R
545	0.3	134,734	D
1,227	0.7	53,545	R
—	0.0	3,458	R
2,053	4.4	19,385	D
47	0.0	34,626	D
—	0.0	16,811	D
1,940	0.2	141,537	R
2,591	0.4	18,216	R
805	0.2	65,549	R
620	0.2	13,565	D
—	0.0	277	R
—	0.0	55,138	D
—	0.0	45,816	R
723	0.3	32,809	R
2,132	0.5	173,562	R
3,182	0.6	56,172	R
954	0.3	53,768	R
—	0.0	58,536	D
891	0.1	58,727	D
—	0.0	32,119	D
983	0.4	11,943	D
574	5.6	5,864	D
656	0.8	36,173	R
9,599	2.6	87,692	R
17,667	1.2	268,469	R
594	0.2	19,286	D
12	0.0	5,649	R
6,496	0.6	51,109	R
—	0.0	1,961	R
8,656	0.7	301,175	R
563	1.0	22,978	R
—	0.0	49,488	D
—	0.0	185	D
—	0.0	18,485	D
77,985	15.1	104,390	D
—	0.0	51,116	D
461	0.7	40,948	R
108	0.0	19,329	D
1,668	1.8	12,493	D
—	0.0	10,899	R
1,660	0.4	102,612	R
486	2.3	304	D
171,814	1.2	734,247	R

6. There were two separate Bryan slates in Texas with various sources offering widely different totals. Figures here are from Robinson, *The Presidential Vote*, supplemented with manuscript returns supplied by the Texas secretary of state.

7. Figures from *Vermont Legislative Directory*.

Roosevelt took the position after the election of 1900. Roosevelt had served as vice president for barely six months when, on September 6, 1901, President McKinley was shot by an assassin in Buffalo, New York, moving Roosevelt into the presidency. In 1904 Mark Hanna, by then a U.S. senator and a rumored presidential candidate, succumbed to typhoid fever, dying at the apex of his career.

NOVEMBER 22, 1899
VICE PRESIDENT HOBART DEAD

Surrounded by His Family as He Passes Away.

END FORESHADOWED MONDAY

President McKinley Will Attend the Funeral Saturday.

News of Mr. Hobart's Death Shocks

Washington—Eulogies of Cabinet

Officers and Friends.

Special to The New York Times.

PATERSON, N. J., Nov. 21.—Garret A. Hobart, Vice President of the United States, died this morning. Warning that his long, brave fight with death had been in vain, and that his end was nigh, came yesterday afternoon in the shape of a sharp attack of angina pectoris. He rallied from this for a brief space, but his vitality was exhausted. He sank lower and lower, with full knowledge of his condition, until, as the clock at midnight sounded the passing of another day into the void of unrecallable time, the consciousness of things mundane faded forever from his mind. A few hours later, at 8:30 o'clock, he breathed his last in the presence of his wife, his fifteen-year-old son, Garret A. Hobart, Jr., his physician, Dr. William Newton, Mrs. Newton, who is a cousin of Mrs. Hobart; Private Secretary Frederick Evans, and Miss Alice Waddell, the nurse. The body has been embalmed and the funeral will take place on Saturday.

Mr. Hobart realized that his days were numbered several weeks ago, and with the strength of mind and purpose that had always characterized him in business as in politics, resigned himself cheerfully to the inevitable, bore his suffering without a wince or a murmur, and sought only to lighten the burden of his sickness for those who were near and dear to him, and who, rendered sanguine by his demeanor, were buoyed with hope until death came knocking at the door.

For some days he had been unable to lie down, or even recline, and died in a sitting posture. Yet as late as yesterday, propped up in his bed, he chatted animatedly with his wife and others upon subjects the most diverse. During the day he received a message from Senator Hanna, which he discussed appreciatively. He alluded, among other things, to the elections and the Presidential campaign, and talked generally as though death were the furthest thing from his thoughts.

• •

PRESIDENT McKINLEY IS ASSASSINATED

On September 6, 1901, President McKinley was shot while speaking at a fair in Buffalo, New York. His assassin, anarchist Leon Czolgosz, was apprehended at the scene, and barely escaped being lynched by the crowd. McKinley lay healing from his two gunshot wounds for a full week and seemed to be making a strong recovery, providing the nation with a measure of comfort. A week later, however, he complained of stomach pains and his health quickly deteriorated. McKinley died two days later of gangrene, leaving the nation in shock. He was the third president assassinated while in office, following Abraham Lincoln (1865) and James A. Garfield (1881). After McKinley died, Czolgosz was speedily put on trial, admitted his guilt, and was executed by the state of New York.

SEPTEMBER 7, 1901
PRESIDENT SHOT AT BUFFALO FAIR

Wounded in the Breast and Abdomen.

HE IS RESTING EASILY

One Bullet Extracted, Other Cannot Be Found.

Assassin is Leon Czolgosz of Cleveland, Who Says He Is an Anarchist and Follower of Emma Goldman.

BUFFALO, Sept. 6.—President McKinley, while holding a reception in the Temple of Music at the Pan-American Exposition at 4 o'clock this afternoon, was shot and twice wounded by Leon Czolgosz, an Anarchist, who lives in Cleveland.

One bullet entered the President's breast, struck the breast bone, glanced and was later easily extracted. The other bullet entered the abdomen, penetrated the stomach, and has not been found, although the wounds have been closed.

The physicians in attendance upon the President at 10:40 o'clock to-night issued the following bulletin:

"The President is rallying satisfactorily, and is resting comfortably. 10:15 P. M., temperature, 100.4 degrees; pulse, 124; respiration, 24."

" *Senator Hanna left the house with Harry Hamlin at 2:25 o'clock. As he walked to the corner his head was bowed and shoulders stooped. When he entered the runabout tears were streaming from his eyes.* "

SEPTEMBER 14, 1901
MR. M'KINLEY DIES AFTER A BRAVE FIGHT

End Comes at 2:15 o'Clock This Morning.

MR. ROOSEVELT SUMMONED

President's Touching Farewell to Stricken Wife.

"God's Will Be Done" Were His Last Words—A Remarkable Display of Vitality Marks the Final Hours of Suffering.

Special to The New York Times.

BUFFALO, Sept. 14.—President McKinley died at 2:15 o'clock this morning. He had been unconscious since 7:50 o'clock last night. His last conscious hour on earth was spent with the wife to whom he devoted a lifetime of care. He died unattended by a minister of the Gospel, but his last words were a humble submission to the will of the God in whom he believed. He was reconciled to the cruel fate to which an assassin's bullet had condemned him, and faced death in the same spirit of calmness and poise which had marked his long and honorable career.

For three hours before his death the President apparently suffered no pain. He uttered no connected sentences. Those at his bedside say that the words of the hymn "Nearer, My God, to Thee" were running in his mind, and that occasionally he would murmur a few of the words.

Senator Hanna left the house with Harry Hamlin at 2:25 o'clock. As he walked to the corner his head was bowed and shoulders stooped. When he entered the runabout tears were streaming from his eyes. He bowed his head upon the head of his cane, sobs that were audible shook his frame, he had not a word to say. Abner McKinley and his wife left five minutes after Senator Hanna.

His last conscious words reduced to writing by Dr. Mann, who stood at his bedside, when they were uttered, were as follows:

"GOD'S WILL BE DONE."

"Good bye. All good bye. It is God's way. His will be done, not ours."

THEODORE ROOSEVELT IS SWORN IN AS PRESIDENT

During his 1900 campaign for reelection President McKinley needed a running mate following the death of Garret A. Hobart. The party forced McKinley to accept Theodore Roosevelt, former governor of New York, despite his objections and those of his campaign manager, Sen. Mark Hanna. The Republicans again won in a landslide, but held their positions for only six months before McKinley's assassination. Roosevelt then moved into the presidency, angering many within the party who still opposed him. Despite their doubts, Roosevelt's progressive reforms won much favor from the public.

SEPTEMBER 15, 1901
MR. ROOSEVELT IS NOW THE PRESIDENT

Will Continue Unbroken the Policy of Mr. McKinley.

OATH SOLEMNLY SPOKEN

Simple Ceremony at the Home of Ansley Wilcox.

Members of the Cabinet Asked to Serve in Present Capacities and They Agreed to Do So—Senator Hanna Offered His Services.

Special to The New York Times.

BUFFALO, Sept. 14.—Theodore Roosevelt to-day became President of the United States, with a solemn promise that he would follow out the policy laid down by President McKinley.

His exact words, which produced a most profound impression upon the small company of people to whom he spoke, were: "I wish to say that it shall be my aim to continue absolutely unbroken the policy of President McKinley for the peace and prosperity and the honor of our beloved country."

A more solemn scene would be hard to conceive than was the swearing in of Mr. Roosevelt as President. It occurred in the library of the home of his personal friend, ex-State Senator Ansley Wilcox, which home is a little, old-fashioned Colonial mansion on Delaware Avenue, within a mile of the residence of Mr. Milburn, where the body of the assassinated President is lying.

There was nothing of pomp in the ceremony. It was as simple and as sanctified as a family religious service, such as a wedding. It was hard to realize that it was an event of world-wide import.

Mr. Roosevelt, as Vice President, arrived here at 1:30 o'clock this afternoon. He had been brought on, as fast as the best of horses and the swiftest of special trains could bring him, from his retreat in the Adirondacks, where he went last week, fully satisfied that President McKinley would recover.

· ·

HANNA DIES AT THE HEIGHT OF HIS CAREER

Mark Hanna, the mastermind behind William McKinley's 1896 campaign, continued as a force in American politics, moving into the U.S. Senate in 1897 representing Ohio. After Theodore Roosevelt ascended to the presidency in 1901 upon McKinley's death, party loyalists expected a bitter contest between Hanna and Roosevelt for the 1904 Republican nomination. This clash never came, as Hanna died of typhoid fever early in 1904. He was sixty-eight years old. Unopposed, Roosevelt went on to a landslide victory in the election of 1904 and is now remembered as one of the greatest of American presidents.

FEBRUARY 16, 1904
HANNA'S FIGHT FOR LIFE ENDED

The Senator Died Last Evening at 6:40 o'Clock,

UNCONSCIOUS AT THE END

There Had Been No Hope Since Early Morning—Mrs. Hanna Not with Him When Death Came.

WASHINGTON, Feb. 15.—Senator Marcus Alonzo Hanna died at 6:40 o'clock this evening at his apartments in the Arlington Hotel, after an illness extending over nearly two months, filled with apparent recoveries, followed by relapses, and finally drifting into typhoid fever, which in his weakened condition he was unable to withstand.

When the end came all the members of the Senator's family were in the room except Mrs. Hanna, the Senator's wife, and Mr. and Mrs. Dan Hanna. Mrs. Hanna had left the room only a few minutes before.

THE CONGRESSIONAL ELECTIONS OF 1910

NATION ELECTS A PROGRESSIVE MAJORITY IN CONGRESS

The congressional elections of 1910 marked a major transition in American politics, demonstrating the new dominance of progressive reform philosophy. Progressivism was a diverse movement, coming to the fore in a time of industrialization, urbanization, and teeming immigration. Evident among Republicans, Democrats, and third parties, Progressives held common central concerns. As the United States economy was transformed to an industrial base dominated by giant corporations, Progressives urged regulation of business, trust-busting, and higher taxation of the rich and corporations. They also joined in their attention to the disadvantaged in the United States. They favored government action to alleviate problems of poverty, falling farm prices, and the afflictions of urban factories and slums. They promoted social justice legislation to abolish child labor, protect women workers, and conserve natural resources.

Central to the Progressives' agenda were political reforms to increase the influence of individual citizens, "the people," and weaken entrenched, malevolent "interests." They sought to curb official corruption, eliminate party "machines," and regulate campaign contributions. They hoped to replace these perceived evils with a new politics of active, informed citizens led by expert, objective administrators—exemplified in municipal government by nonpartisan elections and professional city managers.

The social basis of mass involvement was being laid at this time by the growth of interest groups, the burgeoning of inexpensive popular newspapers, union organization, and widening public education. On this base, reformers sought to promote a more egalitarian politics through honest electoral administration, secret ballots, woman suffrage, and measures of "direct democracy," such as primaries, popular election of senators, and direct popular legislation through initiatives and referendums.

SETTING OF THE ELECTIONS

Even before 1910 Progressives had a significant impact on American life, in the administrations of President Theodore

Source: The Granger Collection, New York

THE QUESTION BEFORE THE HOUSE:
"Can he fill them?"

A 1911 cartoon questions James Beauchamp "Champ" Clark's ability to fill the shoes of "Uncle Joe" Cannon, Clark's predecessor as Speaker of the House of Representatives.

Roosevelt and in many states. But old-guard Republicans generally controlled national politics, particularly in Congress as well as in the presidencies of William McKinley and William Howard Taft. The House of Representatives was dominated

1910 MIDTERM ELECTION RESULTS

HOUSE

ELECTION YEAR	CONGRESS	MEMBERS ELECTED			GAINS/LOSSES	
		DEM.	REP.	MISC.	DEM.	REP.
1910	62nd	228	162	1	+56	–57

SENATE

ELECTION YEAR	CONGRESS	MEMBERS ELECTED			GAINS/LOSSES	
		DEM.	REP.	MISC.	DEM.	REP.
1910	62nd	42	49	–	+10	–10

by its Speaker, appropriately characterized as "Czar" Joseph Cannon. In the White House, Taft shifted to the right of Roosevelt, his progressive-leaning predecessor.

Progressives began their road to congressional power after the 1908 election, centering their efforts in opposition to "Uncle Joe" Cannon. The Speaker unabashedly identified his political stance as "stand pat" and defended his minimalist credo, proclaiming, "The country don't need any legislation." To stave off change, Cannon had become increasingly conservative and arbitrary. He opposed or undermined Roosevelt's proposals to regulate corporations, railroads, and banks, tax the income and estates of the rich, limit immigration, extend national parks, and relieve unions of strike-breaking court injunctions. When Taft proposed modest tariff reductions, Cannon maneuvered to maintain the system of high import duties for the protection of industry.

As Speaker, Cannon had extensive powers. He appointed all committees, stacking them with supporters of his policy goals; he chose committee chairs; and he rewarded his favorites in the allocation of offices or perquisites, including staff and stationery. He controlled the course of floor debate to suit his own preferences, thoroughly stifled the voice of the minority Democrats, and cut off campaign funds from dissident Republicans. Often, Cannon would simply refuse to allow bills to come to the floor of the House, ignoring representatives' calls for recognition, burying bills in the Rules Committee, which he appointed, chaired, and controlled, or refusing roll call votes to determine the will of the House majority. Personal ambition turned him against his own party's presidents, Roosevelt and Taft. Although older than seventy in 1908, he had run for the Republican presidential

nomination and resented both Roosevelt's flirting with a third term and Taft's eventual succession.

Cannon drew widespread opposition in the congressional elections of 1908, not only from Democrats and Progressives but also from the growing temperance movement, which saw him as allied with liquor interests. In the polling, Democrats gained 10 House seats and, in coalition with dissident Republicans, neared a majority of the chamber. They expected support from the new president, who personally disparaged Cannon, but Taft took no public stand.

When the new Congress met in 1909, the coalition plotted a revolt against Cannon. They lacked the votes to oust him outright, but did barely pass a resolution to amend the House rules. The Speaker reversed that loss by providing pieces of legislative pork for some Democrats, such as holding the tariff on beer low to gain votes from Tammany Hall.

Cannon lost his edge, however, by pushing through new tariff legislation that, contrary to Taft's campaign promise, actually increased duties on consumer goods. When Congress reconvened in 1910, the insurgents were ready to strike. Taking advantage of parliamentary finesse and absences by the standpatters--those resisting change--the insurgents forced a wearying session extending over three days and two nights to break a conservative filibuster. Although the dissidents still lacked the votes to remove Cannon from office, unanimous Democrats and thirty insurgent Republicans, on a 182 to 163 vote, stripped the Speaker of his power to appoint or serve on the Rules Committee, the gatekeeper of the House, ending his control of the legislative agenda.

In later actions, the House further diminished the reach of Cannon's office. It moved the power to appoint other committees from the Speaker to party committees and provided the means for committees and the minority party to bring legislation to the floor without the Speaker's approval and for the discharge of bills from recalcitrant committees. Cannon's defiant offer to resign as Speaker was refused. For the dissidents it was enough to make Cannon impotent even as he stayed in office and to make the Republicans vulnerable to defeat in the congressional polling. The subsequent Democratic victory removed Cannon himself from the House for one term and ended Cannon's reign when Champ Clark became Speaker.

President Roosevelt had left his office in 1909 to Taft, his chosen successor, and then left the country on a prolonged hunting expedition in Africa and a European tour. Upon his return, he garnered more publicity than the incumbent president and quickly showed his dissatisfaction with his heir both socially, by refusing an invitation to visit the White House, and politically. While Roosevelt called for an expert tariff commission to set and lower rates, Taft defended the latest, protective Payne-Aldrich law as "the best tariff ever." In a major lecture on the "New Nationalism," Roosevelt offered a far more progressive program than Taft's, including federal control of corporations, a "welfare state" to expand social benefits, taxation of the rich, and institutional change as radical as popular recall of judicial decisions. *The New York Times* deemed him so radical that it equated his program with that of William Jennings Bryan, the three-time losing Democratic presidential candidate. (A further cause of estrangement was a controversy on conservation policy, the Pinchot-Ballinger dispute described in the next chapter.)

The two presidents chose different sides in the 1910 Republican campaign. TR entertained insurgents at his New York home and heard pleas that he return to the presidency. He rallied support for Progressives in a vigorous 5,500 mile railroad tour of the West, giving a hundred speeches over three weeks; led the Republican effort in New York; and then resumed campaigning in the Midwest in the last month before the vote, making a particularly vigorous effort on behalf of Indiana's insurgent Republican senator, Albert Beveridge. In contrast, Taft campaigned indifferently, staying immobile in his summer home planning a presidential trip to Panama. Disdaining Progressive legislators, he unsuccessfully attempted to purge them in state party nominating caucuses. But the power of party leaders was slipping. Instead of conventions controlled by the leadership, intraparty nominating conflicts were waged in direct primaries. In the Republican primaries, forty regulars were ousted, but all Progressives were renominated.

Democrats were confident in their campaign. Champ Clark, the Democratic House leader, exemplified their assurance in a Fourth of July speech at Tammany Hall: "Nothing is absolutely sure but death and taxes," he proclaimed, "but the next sure thing is Democratic supremacy in the new House of Representatives." They delighted in the feud between Roosevelt and Taft, some denouncing the Rough Rider equally with Taft, others suggesting that he be chosen again as president in 1912. In the Maine elections, held in September, the Democrats swept almost all races, state and federal—their first victories there since 1880 and a further encouragement for the party. Anticipating the outcome in its election night report, *The Times* planned a series of light flashes from its tower, with a steady beam to the south indicating a Democratic landslide.

THE RESULTS AND EFFECTS

In the election, the conservative Republican regime was replaced by Democratic and Progressive Republican control of both houses of Congress. Following this change, the nation would soon turn to Progressive presidential candidates and the reformist regime of Woodrow Wilson. Other possible portents of the future came in the extension of the vote to women in Washington, the fifth state to endorse female suffrage, and the election of Victor Berger of Milwaukee as the first Socialist member of Congress.

The balloting produced a Democratic and Progressive triumph. Discontent with the Taft administration, particularly in regard to tariffs and conservation, brought widespread change. Democrats took full control of the House, winning 56 new seats for a 228 to 162 majority, their first since 1894. They extended the party's reach into the North, winning congressional seats in eastern cities and midwestern farm areas and, for the first time in two decades, the governorships of New York and New Jersey—where Wilson was elected.

Democrats gained 10 seats in the Senate; with 42 seats, they combined with 11 progressive Republicans to dominate the upper chamber. Most of the Republican losses came among party conservatives, particularly in the East, while virtually every insurgent was reelected. The election was interpreted as a repudiation of the high tariff law. Its author in the House, Sereno Payne, lost his leadership position, and its Senate author, Nelson Aldrich, retired.

The new Congress moved national policy sharply leftward. It sent a constitutional amendment for direct election of senators to the states, established spending limits for congressional elections (which proved ineffective), aided the working class by enacting an eight-hour federal workday and creating the Department of Labor and its Children's Bureau (headed by one of the first women in a high administrative position), extended regulation of drugs, provided federal aid for state roads, increased federal regulation of railroads, and completed the continental Union with the admission of Arizona and New Mexico to statehood.

The split in the congressional Republican Party foreshadowed the party's split in the next presidential election. Commenting on the results, TR set a future challenge, declaring, "The fight for progressive popular government has merely begun, and will certainly go on to a triumphant conclusion." Forming the Progressive Republican League headed by Sen. Robert La Follette of Wisconsin, the insurgents advocated increased regulation of business and opposed the renomination of Taft in 1912. The Roosevelt-Taft rivalry carried over to 1912, when Taft won presidential renomination in a bruising contest with Roosevelt, but trailed far behind him in the eventual three-way general election.

The revolt against Cannon and changes in House rules would affect Congress for the rest of the century. Cannon had stood for a system of party government, compelling loyalty from all Republicans while accepting party responsibility for the results. The revolt against the Speaker undermined this responsibility, shifting power to uncertain alliances across party lines, exemplified by the 8 to 4 lineup of the majority and minority parties' seats in the newly dominant Rules Committee. By these actions, the House diffused power in the chamber, but created new barriers to effective action. In place of the imperfections of accountable party government and sometimes arbitrary leaders, it established the imperfections of unaccountable coalition government and shifting interest groups and party factions.

The Congress elected in 1910 initiated a long period of Progressive reform, extending to Wilson's administration and to the New Deal heritage that is evident even in the contemporary Obama presidency. The Progressive movement permanently changed the nation and its politics. By its regulation of business, it lessened the hardships of American capitalism, in the process probably diminishing the possibilities of socialism in the United States. Through programs to aid disadvantaged groups, it initiated the modern welfare state. Its political reforms opened prospects of greater mass participation and more democratic control of government.

The triumph of progressivism revivified the promise of American life. Yet the movement created its own tensions. The reformers differed in their basic philosophies. Some wanted to revive the agricultural and entrepreneurial economy of the past, others to adapt to the industrial and corporate economy emerging for the future. Wilson and Roosevelt marked these very different directions, in their respective "New Freedom" and "New Nationalism" programs. For all their good intentions, Progressives sometimes supported programs that added new harms to disadvantaged groups, including racial segregation, restriction of immigration, and Prohibition. By weakening political parties and institutional checks in the cause of direct democracy, Progressives unintentionally laid the path to a swollen presidency and bureaucracy. These uncertainties continue to affect American politics a century after the congressional elections of 1910.

THE RISING PROGRESSIVE VOICE

Theodore Roosevelt ended his term as president in 1908, seven years after succeeding the conservative Republican president, William McKinley. Breaking from the past, Roosevelt began the Progressive era, encouraging greater government concern for, and control by, ordinary citizens. TR's anointed successor, William Howard Taft, continued Republican control of the presidency, buoyed by a solid Republican Congress. As their party entered its second decade of holding power, Republicans debated its basic principles. The traditional conservatism still dominant in Congress was being challenged by the new Progressive directions being taken by the early presidents of the twentieth century.

NOVEMBER 4, 1908
TAFT WINS

Falls Only 22 Short of Roosevelt's Electoral Vote.

GETS 187,902 IN THIS STATE

Has 314 Electoral Votes—The House Republican by Increased Majority—But Some Western States Vote for Bryan

William H. Taft will be the twenty-seventh President of the United States, having swept the country by a vote which will give him **314** ballots in the Electoral College against Mr. Bryan's **169**, or only **22** less than Mr. Roosevelt had in 1904. His majority will be 145. William J. Bryan yesterday suffered his third and most crushing defeat in his twelve-year run for President of the United States.

To enforce his policies President Taft will have an overwhelmingly Republican Congress, the Senate being as strongly Republican as before, and the House increasing its Republican majority from **57** to **65**.

About every so-called doubtful State went Republican, though Indiana is still in doubt. It was noticeable that the majorities in the East were greater than those in the West. In New York, for instance, Taft beat the great Roosevelt majority of 1904, getting **187,902** majority, as against Roosevelt's **175,000**.

The greatest surprise of the election was the Republican victory in New York City, where Taft's majority was **9,378**. Never before this has this city gone Republican in a Presidential election except in 1900, when it voted for McKinley as against Bryan. Chanler's plurality in the city was **56,000**.

Taft's plurality on the popular vote is estimated at **1,098,000** as against Roosevelt's plurality of **2,545,515** over Parker.

NOVEMBER 24, 1908
TAFT PLANS FIGHT ON SPEAKER CANNON

Progressives Will Try to Prevent His Re-election and Rout the System He Represents.

NOT TARIFF BATTLE ALONE

But Hastened to Action by Letters Declaring Payne's Investigation Lacks Sincerity—Sherman for Cannon.

Special to the New York Times.

WASHINGTON, Nov. 23.—Authentic information received in Washington to-day from Hot Springs, Va., makes it practically certain that President-elect Taft has made up his mind to have it out with Speaker Cannon right at the outset of the new Administration, which means that the biggest fight the Republican Party has seen for years is impending. By force of circumstances the fight will be over the election of the Speaker of the next House, which will meet in special session under the call of Mr. Taft soon after the inauguration of the new President.

On the surface it will be a fight between Taft and Cannon, but in fact it will be a fight between the progressive, or radical, Republicans, and the conservatives, or reactionaries. It is not against Cannon merely that Mr. Taft will array the power of his Administration, but against the entire system which the Speaker represents, and of which he is the head in the House of Representatives.

Nor is it merely a fight for an honest revision of the tariff. Its purpose embraces all the whole line of progressive policies for which Mr. Taft stands. The fact is that he stands for one tendency in Government and legislation and Mr. Cannon stands for another. The two are radically opposed to each other, and Mr. Taft means to have it settled right at the start, if it is possible for him to do so, which line shall be followed during his Administration. To do that he is willing to join issues with the Speaker now and put it to the crucial test of the Speakership election.

Actually Stirring Up the Row.

This is a brand-new Taft. His friends here have known for years that Mr. Taft is a great fighter when once he becomes involved in a contest. They know of some hard struggles which he has conducted. But they have never before seen him engaged in any great contest on his own behalf. Now he is actually stirring up the row and preparing to lead it in person.

And it is solely in the interest of his own Administration that he is inviting the battle. Moreover, it is primarily in behalf of the one policy he has advocated which more than any other can be said to be entirely his own, as distinguished from the "Roosevelt policies" which he so often during the campaign pledged himself to carry out. Tariff revision of the sort advocated by Mr. Taft was not in the Roosevelt quiver. Mr. Taft has gone well and beyond the point where Roosevelt would have stopped on that line, as even the President would admit.

Republican Insurrection

Immediately following the 1908 election, factional tensions began to split the new Congress. Revolting against the powerful Speaker of the House, "Uncle Joe" Cannon, insurgent Republicans began working with Democrats either to remove Cannon or, at least, to reduce his power in order to advance their own legislation. President Taft, initially expected to side with the insurgents, allied with the Speaker to protect the administration's signature policy, tariff revision. Cannon ultimately prevailed, retaining his powers and ready to use them with enhanced hostility towards his antagonists.

DECEMBER 12, 1908
TO CURB SPEAKER'S POWER.

House Insurgents Confer on Rules—No Fight on Cannon Personally.

Special to The New York Times.

WASHINGTON, Dec. 11.—Twenty-five Republican members of the House conferred for three hours to-night on the subject of changing the Cannon rules and diminishing the power of the Speaker. At the conclusion of the meeting Mr. Hepburn, who acted as Chairman, was authorized to appoint a committee of five to report amendments to the present rules to a larger meeting of the insurgents to be held next Tuesday.

The participants in the conference were anxious to have it understood that they were not in any way lining up to a fight against Speaker Cannon's re-election, but were merely acting in a general way to divide power over legislation.

One of the important suggestions of the evening was made by Mr. Townsend, that a committee on committees be formed in the House to take care of all committee appointments so that the Speaker's friendship shall not play too important a part. Mr. Hays went along the same line in suggesting that the Committee on Rules be a large body elected by the House. One member went so far as to suggest that the Committee on Rules be done away with altogether.

All the participants said the meeting was a great success. A following of fifty was claimed to-night. A number of sympathizers with the movement were not present. Parsons of New York is counted as a radical on the subject of rules, while Mr. Bennet is said to lean in the same direction.

The general declaration of the members of to-night's conference that the feeling toward the Speaker was not the least hostile is taken to mean that unless something unforeseen happens there will be no fight on the Speaker. That was the opinion expressed by Mr. Longworth, son-in-law of the President.

MARCH 7, 1909
FLOOD OF LETTERS AGAINST SPEAKER

Defeat of Cannon Urged Upon the Insurgent Republicans in the House.

BUT SPEAKER WILL STAY

Fight Will Be Made on Changes of the Rules, and Cannon May Be Defeated.

Special to The New York Times.

WASHINGTON, March 6.—As the time draws near for the election of a Speaker of the House of Representatives, a flood of letters from all over the country is pouring in on the so-called rules insurgents. Their general tenor is of antipathy to Speaker Cannon, and nearly every one ends with a plea for the insurgents to combine with the Democrats to defeat the man who, in the opinion of the writers, has retarded the course of legislation for six years.

While the insurgents find in these letters substantial commendation for the course they have pursued so far, they are not inclined to go against the Speaker personally, even if it were possible to get the Democrats to stand in line for an insurgent Republican and support him for the chair. After talking the matter over with the leaders in the movement, Mr. Madison of Kansas, who has fought hard for a revision of the rules, said to-day that he had instructed his secretary to answer the letters, telling his correspondents that there was no chance to defeat Cannon and no intention of getting up any opposition to him.

There are 172 Democrats in the House and, according to the latest count, 24 insurgent Republicans, making in case of a combination a total of 196 votes. That would give a bare majority of one if the combination whip kept every man in line. The difficulty arises, however, in keeping the Democrats and Republican insurgents in harmony.

The insurgents are insurgents simply on the rules. They have no hope of defeating Speaker Cannon, though it is probable that if they saw an opportunity they would put one of their own men in power. On the other hand, the Democrats, while favoring a revision of the rules, will naturally decline to support a Republican, even an insurgent, for the Speakership. They realize that they cannot elect their leader, Champ Clark, but rather than slip their heads into the parliamentary noose of being the opposing minority under a Speaker they have themselves elected they will see Speaker Cannon re-elected over their perfunctory vote for Champ Clark.

MARCH 9, 1909
CANNON TO BE SPEAKER.

But Insurgents Still Hope to Take Away Some of His Power.

Special to The New York Times.

WASHINGTON, March 8.—Suddenly shifting from the Capitol, the struggle against the domination of Speaker Cannon was brought into the White House to-day. Emissaries from the Republican insurgents saw President Taft, as did leaders in the Cannon camp. Mr. Taft held out no encouragement to either faction so far as could be ascertained, but it was taken as significant that he gave more of his time to Representative Mann of Illinois, one of the Speaker's principal lieutenants, than he did to the delegation of insurgents composed of Representatives Gardner of Massachusetts, Nelson of Wisconsin, and Madison of Kansas. These three are the steering committee for the insurgent movement, which hopes to overthrow the Cannon rules through a coalition with the Democrats.

The regular Republicans assert that there is no doubt of the re-election of Speaker Cannon, but they do not speak so confidently of the passage of the old rules that have placed such enormous power in the presiding officer's hands.

The fact is that the insurgents have about abandoned the idea of defeating Cannon, and will confine their efforts to securing a revision of the rules, by which they hope to diminish the power of the Speaker. Their main effort now is to secure the appointment of a committee on committees which shall assign the committee places instead of leaving them in the gift of the Speaker, as at present.

MARCH 11, 1909
TAFT IN THE MIDST OF A CONGRESS FIGHT

Backing Speaker Cannon Against the Insurgents in Order to Save Tariff Bill.

CANNON EAGER TO AID HIM

Insurgents, Unterrified, Still Plan Fight—Threat That Speaker May Herd Them with Democrats.

Special to The New York Times.

WASHINGTON, March 10.—It took President Taft only five days in the White House to get into a Congressional fight which would have delighted the belligerent soul of Theodore Roosevelt. The row raised by the Republican insurrection against the rules of the House is the merriest and fiercest seen in Washington for many a day, and President Taft is squarely in the centre of it. He has taken the side of the regulars, and there is consequently a tremendous relief visible in and about the headquarters of Speaker Cannon. The anxiety so apparent there only a day or so ago had disappeared to-day, and in its place there was easy confidence and an atmosphere of menace toward the insurgents not discoverable yesterday afternoon. It was even intimated this afternoon that as soon as the victory is won next Monday, the insurgents will be lined up for slaughter. The proposition made to-day for disposing of them was to put them willy-nilly, into the ranks of the Democrats, and to emphasize that by assigning them to committees far down the minority list.

The insurgents meantime are talking boldly of the support they are receiving from their constituents and the country in general, and insisting that they have the votes to effect a considerable change in the rules on Monday. But their talk is met from the Speaker's side by a swift and flat rejection to-day of the compromise plans which were taken under consideration yesterday. Mr. Cannon is sure of his ground, now that he has the Administration with him, and he is preparing to put through his own plans by the road roller process as merrily as it was ever done in a National convention.

Cannon Lined Up With Taft.

The Administration is lending itself vigorously to the defeat of the insurgents, not only because success on their part would endanger the Tariff bill, but because President Taft is utterly opposed to any combination with the Democrats. It was reported to President Taft that the insurgents were considering an effort to make it appear to the country that "Taft is lined up with Cannon." The President replied that, for the purpose of this engagement, he is with the Speaker, and there is no other place where he could be. In fact, it is Cannon who is lined up with Taft. The Speaker has come to the Administration for help, and the President is giving it.

MARCH 16, 1909
CANNON STILL HOLDS POWER IN THE HOUSE

Some Democrats, Led by Fitzgerald of Brooklyn, Desert Rules Insurgents.

SPEAKER IS RE-ELECTED

Minor Modifications Made in the Rules by Brooklyn Man's Resolution—Champ Clark Routed.

Special to The New York Times.

WASHINGTON, March 15.—The House insurgents won a partial victory to-day when they succeeded in voting down a resolution presented by Mr. Dalzell of Pennsylvania, making the rules of the Sixtieth Congress applicable to the present Congress. This was offset, however, by the defeat of Champ Clark's resolution amending the rules and providing for a Rules Committee of fifteen to be named by the House instead of five named by the Speaker, and the adoption of a substitute offered by Mr. Fitzgerald, a Democrat, of Brooklyn, which practically leaves Speaker Cannon in as complete control as ever. The vote on the Dalzell resolution was 193 against to 180 for. On the Clark resolution, 179 for, 203 against, and on the Fitzgerald substitute, 211 for, 172 against. Speaker Cannon was re-elected, receiving 209 votes.

• •

The Tariff and Spreading Upheaval

Retaining his power in the House, Speaker Cannon turned his attention to the tariff, the priority legislation of a special congressional session. After limited downward revisions passed the House with Cannon's consent, the Senate took up the measure, pitting Progressive insurgents in that chamber against the conservative Finance Committee chair, Nelson Aldrich. Largely disregarding the growing Republican divide, Aldrich moved tariffs upward in the Senate, then joined with Cannon to force a conservative measure through the House-Senate conference committee. Ignoring the growing appeal of Progressive legislation to voters of both parties, the entrenched Republican leadership wrote their own priorities into the law, sending it to President Taft for his reluctant signature.

JUNE 8, 1909
REPUBLICAN SPLIT WIDENS IN SENATE

Insurgents Taunted as Planning a New Party—MacVeagh's Republicanism Attacked.

OPEN THREATS OF REVOLT

Bryan Criticised on the Democratic Side—Aldrich Wins on Votes, but Withdraws High Schedules.

Special to The New York Times.

WASHINGTON, June 7.—Strong intimations that an open split was coming in the Republican Party as a result of the tariff fight were the feature to-day of one of the liveliest debates of the special session. Senator Aldrich taunted the insurgents with designs of forming a new party and received warm replies that he was forcing matters too far. Senator Bailey openly declared that Republicans would vote against the Tariff bill. Most significant of all, however, was an open attack by Senator Smith on the Republicanism of Secretary of the Treasury MacVeagh, who on Saturday night in Chicago gave warning that President Taft would carry out his pledges and might find it necessary to change the control of the party.

The Democrats did not escape division, and William J. Bryan came in for criticism for attempting to rebuke Senators for their votes on various schedules.

Beveridge Begins the Fight.

The colloquies that kept the Senate and galleries thoroughly awake throughout the afternoon began shortly after noon when Senator Beveridge declared that the small increases in duty—3 cents on a $1.50 shirt, 5 cents on a pair of hose, 10 cents on a dress—became in the end, when added together, the burden of the poor. That burden, he declared, had raised the storm for tariff revision that wrote the tariff plank into the Republican platform in Chicago.

"In the remarks of the Senator," retorted Senator Aldrich, "we have an instance of influences and dangers of association. Never have I heard that doctrine from protectionists, rarely from Republicans. The Senator has been voting so long with the Democratic side that he believes with them that the duty is added to the selling pricing of the article—"

Cummins Warns Aldrich.

Senator Cummins said he had so often been classed with Democrats that such a charge had no terror for him. An intelligent electorate knew how to discriminate in such matters. Referring to a statement by Mr. Aldrich concerning Senators who had shown "loyalty" to the party by upholding the Committee on Finance, he said there was no man in the Senate who could put him out of the Republican Party.

Mr. Aldrich disavowed any intention to reflect upon the Republicanism of Mr. Cummins.

"Unless you want to disintegrate the Republic party," said Mr. Cummins, "there should be an end here to direct or indirect challenges to party faith."

JUNE 11, 1909
EDITORIAL
THE INSURRECTION

With entire and well-justified confidence the hosts of protection have for a generation relied upon the skill, the valor, and the hardihood of their commanders and their legionaries in the Senate and the House. The opposition of the Democrats to high protective duties has been for the most part faint, feeble, and perfunctory. As a matter of party policy the Democrats had to stand for something not in the Republican creed. Rarely has a voice been lifted in disinterested advocacy of the interests of the consumer.

Now there appear to be several such voices. If DOLLIVER, BEVERIDGE, CUMMINS, BORAH, and the other Republican "insurgents" do not represent the consumer, we fail to see what client or interest they do represent. Certainly they do not speak for the Republican Party or its policy. Senator ALDRICH is the official spokesman and representative of that interest. The insurgents are waging their warfare on the Aldrich schedules not as politicians, not for party, but manifestly because they have heard and felt the demand of the people. The pledges of the Republican Party and of the Republican candidate were accepted in the West as having been given in good faith. The insurgents are simply demanding that those pledges shall be kept. They insist that the widespread popular demand for lower duties shall be heard and heeded. They are a

pretty determined band. We do not recall that any former Chairman of the Finance Committee in charge of a tariff bill in the Senate has been talked to as they have talked to Senator ALDRICH. He has been disturbed by their courage and their persistence. The situation within the last few days has become dangerous to the Republican unity. Something has to be done.

It is a new situation for Mr. ALDRICH and for the Republican protectionists. They have been accustomed to obedience. Now insurrection confronts them. Weakened in that way, they suffer a further impairment of strength from the gross immorality and bad faith of their proceeding in attempting to maintain or increase the Dingley rates in the face of the solemn pledges of the campaign that those rates should be lowered. Mr. ALDRICH and his band are held together, sustained and fortified only by the old protectionist principle, which is greed, naked and unashamed. The interests they represent are unwilling to surrender the enormous profits and the great advantage accruing to them from a Government ban upon their foreign competitors. It is a serious situation for them as well as a new one. In view of the often expressed convictions of President TAFT and of his campaign assurances, it is also a serious situation for him.

JULY 16, 1909
ALDRICH AND CANNON HAVE TARIFF FIXED

Conference Deliberations Called Play-Acting and Rates Said to be Cut and Dried.

PROMISE TAFT REDUCTIONS

But Only in General Terms—President Unruffled and Planning Sweeping Corporation Legislation for Winter.

Special to The New York Times.

WASHINGTON, July 15.—There is a growing impression in Washington that the conference discussions on the Tariff Bill now going on conceal the fact that the final

state of the bill is a matter of clear agreement; that there is a distinct understanding between President Taft on the one hand and Senator Aldrich and Speaker Cannon on the other. So far as the President is concerned, the understanding is said to be somewhat vague as to the rates of duties, and specific only on the point that there shall be "reductions in conference." As to the rates, the belief is that Mr. Aldrich and Speaker Cannon have agreed as to just what the conferences shall do in the matter of fixing them. On the spectacularly controversial items, like lumber, coal, hides, and iron ore, it is said, the rate will be a compromise involving a reduction from the Senate rates and an increase over the House rates. This will be exhibited to the President as a fulfillment of the agreement with him that everything should be straightened out in conference, and he will be called upon to sign the resultant bill.

What Mr. Taft will do under such circumstances remains to be seen. He maintains his serene confidence that everything will be made all right in conference.

Corporation Legislative Programme.

The President undoubtedly believes, as a good many shrewd observers of political conditions do, that the Tariff bill, in any case, will not cut much of a figure in the next campaigns. As one Administration official puts it, the country is all set at the starting line waiting for the adjournment of Congress to give the word "go!" to be off on a phenomenal revival of business. That revival alone would be enough to divert attention completely from the tariff, but it will have to help it next Winter a programme of corporation legislation, which, if it had been undertaken by President Roosevelt would have precipitated an uproar such as nothing he did or said evoked.

AUGUST 6, 1909
TAFT SIGNS BILL; IN EFFECT TO-DAY

Tariff Measure Is Finally Passed, Corrected and Signed—Congress Ends Its Session.

SEVEN REPUBLICAN REBELS

Middle Westerners Vote Against Compromise Bill, but it Passes the Senate, 47 to 31.

STATEMENT FROM TAFT

Earnest Attempt at Downward Revision, He Declares, but Intimates He Will Later Demand More.

Special to The New York Times.

WASHINGTON, Aug. 5—President Taft signed his Tariff bill at 5:07 o'clock this afternoon in the President's room adjacent to the Senate Chamber in the Capitol. Later he gave out a statement mildly defending the measure as a "sincere effort" though "not a perfect bill," adding that the authority "to use agents to assist him in the application of the maximum and minimum clauses gives wide latitude for the acquisition of information," and hinting at the use of such information toward a less imperfect tariff. Congress adjourned a few minutes before 6 o'clock.

The new law goes into effect at midnight, so far as most of the rates of duty and the free list are concerned. The chief exception is on hides of cattle "of the bovine species," with the boots, shoes, leather, and harness made of them, in which case it becomes effective on Oct. 1. The maximum and minimum provision becomes effective "from and after March 31, 1910." After that date 25 per cent ad valorem is to be added to the duties on all articles coming from any country which discriminates "unduly" in any manner against American goods.

Whether or not there is discrimination is to be determined by the President. Unless he issues a proclamation to the effect that a country does not discriminate against American goods, the maximum rates will go into effect against that country automatically on April 1, 1910. It thus requires a proclamation affirmatively stating that there is not discrimination to keep the minimum rates, which are those established by the regular dutiable list of the new law, in effect after that date.

A REPUBLICAN HOUSE WAR

As President Taft signed the tariff bill into law, Speaker Cannon turned on the insurgent Republicans he had defeated, stripping them of desirable committee assignments and making it clear that he would tolerate no dissent within his party. Refusing to back down, the insurgents determined to resist "Czar Cannon" and his "stand pat" philosophy, maintaining their public attacks on his obstruction of their Progressive program. By mid-March Cannon's popularity had ebbed low enough for a coalition of Democrats and Republicans to revive the proposed reforms of the House. Stripping Cannon of his dominance on the critical Rules Committee, the Progressive forces effectively ended the reign of the Speaker, leaving him in his formal position, but with only a shadow of his former power.

AUGUST 6, 1909
CANNON DISCIPLINES HOUSE INSURGENTS

Takes Revenge on His Opponents by Giving Them Undesirable Committee Appointments.

VREELAND GETS GOOD PLACE

Made Chairman of Banking and Currency—Weeks Off Agriculture—Alexander Heads Rivers and Harbors.

Special to The New York Times.

WASHINGTON, Aug. 5.—Speaker Cannon drove the steam roller to-day over such of the insurgent Republicans as had acquired prominent committee assignments. With few exceptions members of the House who opposed the Speaker's candidacy at the opening of the session or who opposed the adoption of the Reed rules find themselves to-night in undesirable committee assignments or without the promotion long service on a particular committee entitled them to expect. The Speaker announced the appointments at the close of the session.

NOVEMBER 27, 1909
CANNON IS FOR WAR ON THE INSURGENTS

Classes Cummins and La Follette With Bryan and Will Fight Them, He Says.

CONFIDENT ON PAYNE BILL

Declares in Kansas City Speech That After a Year's Trial the People Will Endorse It.

KANSAS CITY, Mo., Nov. 26.—"When Senators Cummins, La Follette, Bristow, and their so-called 'progressive' following join hands with Mr. Bryan in making war upon the Republican members of Congress who passed the tariff bill, and upon the President, who signed it, in that contest I know but one way to treat them, and that is to fight them just as we fight Mr. Bryan and his following."

Such was the declaration of Speaker Cannon, who delivered the principal address before the Knife and Fork Club here to-night. This speech was announced some time ago, and it was understood that Mr. Cannon would make plain the attitude toward the insurgent Republicans that he would hold in the coming session of Congress.

The Speaker devoted the first part of his address to the great growth of the country, and its many problems, and the need for large revenue that was expected from the Payne bill. He then went on:

"The Senators and Representatives who call themselves 'Insurgents' and who voted against the enactment of the Payne bill, voted to increase or maintain the duties on the industries and products of their own States and sections. They were protectionists for their own people, but they were opposed to protection from other people in other sections."

NOVEMBER 28, 1909
CANNON'S FOES PLAN TO KEEP HIM ANGRY

Insurgents in Congress Hope They Can Bring About an Open Breach With Taft.

THEY CAN'T WIN OTHERWISE

If Speaker and President Work Together, as Taft Desires, They Will Be in a Bad Position.

Special to The New York Times.

WASHINGTON, Nov. 27.—The gathering of the clans for the opening of Congress a week from Monday has set in rapidly with the close of this week, and already the air of Washington is beginning to resound with the preliminary outcries of strife between the regulars and the insurgent Republicans.

The insurgents—who are especially anxious to be called "progressives"—have been doing more or less talking throughout the Summer from their homes and wherever else they found the opportunity. On the regulars' side there has not been much participation in the talk, but the lack of numbers has been more than made up in the language used by Speaker Cannon, who is the main target of the insurgents.

Each side is making its claims already. The insurgents declare that they are going to embarrass the Speaker at every turn and by every political means, and they now have a number of schemes, any one of which will give the "Czar of the House" some trouble to handle. The regulars affect to despise the insurgents and their cause, thus following closely the lead of the Speaker, and those who have come to town are talking in tones of confidence as to what is going to happen during the Winter.

FEBRUARY 13, 1910
CANNON'S WEAKNESS GROWING CLEARER

Evidence Accumulates That He Is Afraid to Face a Test Vote in the House.

ALLOWING THINGS TO DRIFT

Eleven-Hour Debate on Summons of Printing Committee to Court Sign of Changed Status.

Special to The New York Times.

WASHINGTON, Feb. 13.—The serious undermining of Speaker Cannon's personal power in the House and the almost complete collapse of power of the machine he so carefully built up is becoming more and more evident every week. Affairs have already reached such a pass that for almost a month the Committee on Rules has not dared to bring in a "special rule" for expediting such legislation as the Speaker's clique desired.

A striking demonstration of the fact that the House is held now with a loose rein was the eleven-hour debate needed this week to pass a simple resolution deciding whether or not the House members of the joint Committee on Printing should answer a summons of the Supreme Court of the District of Columbia. Such measures are ordinarily put through with brief debate on each side and, though in a non-partisan affair of the sort it has often been considered good policy to allow full discussion, no one can remember when the talk of the House was allowed by the Speaker to run to the length it did on Thursday, when the final vote was not reached until nearly midnight.

The fact is that either the Speaker or his more trusted associates have lost confidence in their strength. The Speaker has been slow to give up hope, but it is thought that at last he has seen the handwriting on the wall. What brought home the changed status in the House to Mr. Cannon was not the long speeches made against him

Speaker of the House of Representatives Joseph G. Cannon's powerful grip on Congress was broken by a coalition of Progressives in 1910.

Source: Library of Congress

by the insurgents or the cry that has gone up against him all over the country. He has heard demonstrations of that sort for years, and has always listened unmoved.

There is but one argument that shakes Mr. Cannon, and that argument is votes. On the question to let the Speaker appoint the House members of the Ballinger Investigating Committee he was defeated after a long fight by a handful of votes. That was immediately following the reconvening of Congress after the holidays, yet the Speaker has not since risked a test of strength with the disorganized House.

MARCH 20, 1910
CANNON, SHORN OF HIS POWER, KEEPS OFFICE

House Removes Him from Rules Committee, but Declines to Elect a New Speaker.

INSURGENTS SEEK PEACE.

Democrats Satisfied with Outcome, as They Wish to Keep Up Cannonism Issue.

A NEW RULES COMMITTEE

Resolution, Adopted 191 to 155, Provides for Ten Members to be Elected on Floor.

GREAT DISORDER IN HOUSE

Succession of Votes Before Final Action is Taken—Big Demonstration When Motion to Remove Speaker Is Defeated.

Special to The New York Times.

WASHINGTON, March 19.—After having beaten Speaker Cannon on six consecutive roll calls to-day by majorities ranging from 17 to 40 and after throwing him off the Committee on Rules, which had been the citadel of his power in the House, the Republican insurgents turned squarely around and helped to give him a tremendous vote of confidence, which was tantamount to re-electing him to the Speakership by a majority of 36, ten more votes than the majority had give him upon his election to the place a year ago.

Only eight insurgents voted against Mr. Cannon on the last roll call. By the other insurgents the result is regarded as a long step towards harmony in the Republican Party and the election of a Republican House next November. By the regulars it is openly hailed as a great victory for the Speaker, and their rejoicing not only filled the House with cheers but is yet resounding everywhere they meet.

The Norris resolution, providing for the election of an enlarged Committee on Rules on which the Speaker should not be a member, after having been amended so as to avoid the division of the House into groups, as at first proposed, and making the membership of the new committee ten instead of fifteen with election by the House within ten days, was adopted by a vote of 191 to 155 after a long and exciting day of roll calls and debate.

MARCH 20, 1910
EDITORIAL
THE END OF CANNONISM

Those members of the House of Representative spoke truly who described the uprising against Cannonism as a revolution, not a revolt. The revolution has been successful so none can call it treason. The king is dethroned. When by a vote of 191 to 155 the House adopted Mr. Norris's resolution providing that the Committee on Rules consist not of five but of ten members and that the Speaker should not be a member of the committee, Mr. Cannon and his supporters saw, of course, that all was lost, they had been beaten. Mr. Cannon has refused to accept the terms of compromise suggested by some of his friends that he withdraw from the Rules Committee and be permitted to continue as Speaker. This is a kind of courage, or obstinacy, that with many will pass for gallantry. At any rate he proceeded forthwith to keep his promise by announcing his willingness to recognize any member who should rise to move that the House proceed to the election of another Speaker.

It had been felt that the insurgents or the Democrats would be content with the fullness of their victory in the adoption of the Norris resolution, and that they would not go to the extreme of attempting to oust Mr. Cannon from the Speakership. The Democrats showed no such consideration for his feelings. Mr. Burleson of Texas promptly offered a resolution that the Speakership be declared vacant and nominated Champ Clark, a Democrat, to be Mr. Cannon's successor. There were great shouts from the Democratic side, but very naturally the resolution did not prevail. Only nine Republicans voted to declare the Speaker's office vacant.

It is indeed a very killing frost that has made an end of Cannonism. All that great power is stripped from the man, all that system of conducting the business of the House of Representatives is discarded and destroyed. A few years ago, when President Roosevelt took a sudden interest in the currency, Mr. Cannon was one of those Republican chiefs who conferred with the President at Oyster Bay. It has always been supposed that upon that occasion he permitted Mr. Roosevelt to believe that he sympathized with the Executive policy of currency reform. But Mr. Cannon spoke his true intention when he declared in this city the day after the conference, "There ain't going to be no currency reform." This was a typical manifestation of Cannonism. There has come an end to all that. The House is once more a deliberative body, not a meeting in vassalage to the Speaker. Majority rule is re-established, and will be maintained so long as the insurgent Republicans act upon their present views of public affairs and the policy of their party. They are actuated by a desire to make their party somewhat more nearly a party of the people. It has been a party of privilege, of bounty, of favor, a party of the interests. It is a most momentous change that they have wrought, and the old conditions will not easily be restored.

It is a great change that these insurgents brought about in the House procedure, it is a still greater change in the Republican Party. Parties have gone to pieces over quarrels of less moment. Of course, this is not exactly a good preparation for the Congressional campaign this Fall, but the result of an appeal to the people of these recent years has depended rather more upon the temper and behavior of the Democratic party than upon the foibles and mistakes of the Republicans. Certainly the Democrats ought to win the next House. Luck is finally on their side. Nothing but the most unheard-of folly and blundering can rob them of the victory. With that victory there are likely to be some notable victories in State elections. Leading Republicans at Washington have not only expected this, they have been inclined to hope for Democratic success in November. In the present condition of their party, they argue, opposition would be safer for them than the possession of power.

They believe, and not without many good reasons, that with the Democrats in possession of the power and responsibility in the House that party will do more to promote Republican success in 1912 than the Republicans could do themselves.

STRUGGLES OVER REPUBLICANISM

Speaker Joseph Cannon's downfall mirrored internal struggles within the Republican Party, as emerging Progressive candidates challenged the ideology and the control of dominant conservative elites. Republicans, already facing a rising Democratic Party, also fought over the future of their party's philosophy and leadership. Nelson W. Aldrich of Rhode Island chose to retire, which left a vacuum in leadership and ensured a shakeup in the Senate. Other standpatters fell in direct primaries. Roosevelt and Taft, the party's national leaders, took opposing sides, with Taft favoring, but doing little for, the regular Republican establishment and Roosevelt embracing the Progressives. The party war that had shaken the House rapidly spread throughout the nation, setting a militant tone for the upcoming 1910 election.

APRIL 8, 1910
EDITORIAL
THE TROUBLESOME INSURGENTS

The Republicans, so the story runs in Washington, would be entirely willing to pass through the fires of defeat in the Congressional elections this Fall if only they could be sure that the insurgents would be scorched and smothered. They are said to desire, even, that Senator BEVERIDGE may lose his seat in the Senate as the penalty of his insurgency. His term expires in 1911. The report has long been current at the National Capital that the Republicans believe it would be a piece of good fortune for them to lose the House of Representatives. With a Republican President and a Republican Senate, a Democratic majority in the House could do no harm, and, reasoning from the recent behavior of the party, it would be very likely to make such ill-judged use of its power that in 1912 the country would gladly turn to the Republicans again, electing a President of that party and restoring its control of the House. In various ways this legend is woven in with the reports concerning President TAFT's reconsideration of his announced purpose to make a speech at Indianapolis May 5. That decision was said to have been the result of his displeasure at the Indiana Republican platform and the speech of Senator BEVERIDGE.

In their wrath men will say many things. Mr. PAYNE and Mr. DALZELL are very angry with the insurgents. They feel, they may have said, that they could get along better with a Democratic majority than with a House in which the Republican majority control is tempered with frequent and triumphant exhibitions of insurgency. But we are of the opinion that the sober-minded and far-seeing leaders of the party are very little in sympathy with the idea of permitting a Democratic triumph this Fall. It is a maxim that parties advance by victories, not by defeats. There would be great and obvious perils in permitting a Democratic majority to come in by default. There is the risk that the Democrats might obstinately refuse to blunder. They might by their Congressional policy win in increased measure public respect and confidence. Something of that kind happened when the Democrats won the House in 1890, just after the enactment of the McKinley tariff. They carried the next House, also, and the Presidency with it. No, the Republican Congressional Committee will not ride for a fall this year. Money will be obtained in some way, and the doubtful districts will be attended to.

Mr. PAYNE, Mr. DALZELL, and the other defenders of the Payne-Aldrich tariff may be amazed this Fall at their remarkable success in reading the insurgents out of the party. The Republicans of the Senate and House who refuse to accept the new tariff as an honest fulfillment of the Republican promise are not the real insurgents. It is the people themselves who are in insurrection. In their present temper, feeling every day the pinch of high prices, they are quite willing to be read out of the party,

they have read themselves out. Hosts of them will vote as Democrats this Fall. If the Republican leaders and those about them persist in their uncompromising adherence to the present tariff, they will vote as Democrats in 1912. A more fatuous policy than that of withdrawing the right hand of party fellowship from members of that wing of the Republicans who have the sympathy and the true representatives of popular sentiment, could not well be imagined.

APRIL 16, 1910
ALDRICH TO RETIRE AT THE END OF HIS TERM

Master of the Senate Said to Be Determined to Lay Down Public Office.

HIS HEALTH THE CAUSE

May Drop All Committee Work This Season Except That on Monetary Reform.

Special to The New York Times

WASHINGTON, April 15.—Information has been received here that Senator Nelson Wilmarth Aldrich of Rhode Island has not only decided definitely to adhere to his previously announced determination to retire from the Senate at the expiration of his present term, on March 4 next, but in preparation for that event will shortly retire from all his committees except, possibly, that on finance, in order to devote the remainder of his time in the Senate to the work of the Monetary Commission of which he is the head.

Consideration of his health is assigned as the reason for this determination on the part of Mr. Aldrich. He has not been enjoying his usual good health this Winter, and it is understood that his physician has at last advised him that unless he gives up his Senatorial labors by next Spring at the latest he "will have a very disagreeable old age."

Senator Aldrich is at his Rhode Island home just now and so nothing authoritative from him can be obtained here on the matter. He is not expected back in Washington until next week.

MAY 25, 1910
ROOSEVELT FAILED TO GET TAFT PLEDGE

Authenticated Story That He Asked Successor to be Neutral in Cannon Fight.

APPROVED INSURGENT PLAN

Said Speaker Had Balked Him—Sounded Taft and Found Him Opposed to the Rebels.

Special to The New York Times

WASHINGTON, May 24.—The hopes of the insurgents that ex-President Roosevelt will come to their aid in the face of President Taft's open alignment with the regulars has brought out a strange but authentic account of the efforts made by the House insurgents to

get endorsement for their fight against Speaker Cannon from the retiring President. This revelation throws an interesting light on Mr. Roosevelt's information concerning his successor's political leanings even before Mr. Taft took office.

Shortly before March 4 the insurgents concluded that Mr. Taft was turning from them in their fight on the Speaker, and Messrs. Madison, Gardner, and Nelson were sent to call on Mr. Roosevelt. They called on March 3—the day before Mr. Taft's inauguration. As to their plans Mr. Roosevelt agreed with them heartily.

"Cannon," he said, "has been the greatest obstacle in the way of my efforts to obtain good legislation for the country throughout the seven years of my Administration."

When it came to his taking an active hand in the fight he hesitated. Throwing himself back in a characteristic attitude he said, looking at the ceiling:

"Now, boys, let me think out loud."

He set forth his relations with the Speaker, and the Speaker's relations to the legislation, but ended by merely promising to sound his successor on the subject.

"I'll tap him and then report," he said.

The next day the retiring and the incoming Presidents were at the Capitol surrounded by a host of politicians and diplomats. Mr. Roosevelt sent a page and summoned the three insurgents. As the insurgents entered the President's room Mr. Roosevelt led them aside.

"I've tapped him," he told them, bluntly, "and he is 'agin' you."

It is said that later that day Mr. Roosevelt led two of the insurgents to Mr. Taft and begged him at least to keep hands off the coming fight. According to this account, Mr. Taft received the plea good-humoredly, and laughed over the earnestness of his predecessor.

JUNE 28, 1910
ROOSEVELT TALKS WITH LA FOLLETTE

Insurgent Legislation Their Theme, Says Senator, and the Colonel Is in Fighting Trim.

OYSTER BAY, N.Y., June 27.—Robert M. La Follette, United States Senator from Wisconsin and the father of Republican insurgency, spent two hours this afternoon talking politics with Theodore Roosevelt. He left Oyster Bay wearing a broad smile.

Senator Elmer Burkett of Nebraska, another out-and-out insurgent, is coming to Sagamore Hill after Col. Roosevelt returns from Boston. He, too, will talk politics.

Representative Madison of Kansas, irreconcilable insurgent and ardent defender of Gifford Pinchot as a member of the Ballinger-Pinchot Congressional Investigating Committee, will be at Sagamore Hill probably later this week. His theme will be politics.

Within the last few days Col. Roosevelt has talked politics with Gifford Pinchot and his ally, James R. Garfield.

Senator La Follette arrived early in the afternoon. He had with him G. E. Roe, a New York lawyer who was formerly his law partner. Col. Roosevelt's chauffeur was waiting for them and whisked them away to Sagamore Hill. The Senator had tried to escape unseen. But he was caught fairly at it by a group of newspaper men who saw the Roosevelt auto. They tackled him on suspicion, although nobody recognized him, for his hat hid his famous pompadour.

"Not a word," he said. "I am going to Sagamore Hill, but I don't want a word said about it."

When he returned just in time to catch a train for New York he looked like a schoolboy who had just won a medal. He was smiling his most expansive, persuasive smile.

"It's all right, boys," he cried jovially.

"The Colonel says I may talk to you."

The train pulled out and the interviewers jumped on the Senator and rode to the next station.

They Talked Politics.

"Did we talk politics?" he replied to the first question.

"We did." And he emphasized the affirmation.

"We talked of the legislation of the present session of Congress, from the attitude of those members of the Republican Party whom the newspapers are pleased to call insurgents."

"Can you go into details?"

"No, I prefer that they come from Sagamore Hill. I am very much pleased with the result of my visit with Col. Roosevelt, very much pleased, indeed."

JULY 15, 1910
ROOSEVELT'S TOURS.

Itineraries for the West and South Given Out—Many Speeches.

Special to The New York Times

OYSTER BAY, L.I., July 14—Theodore Roosevelt made public to-day the itinerary of the two trips he will take this Fall, one through the West and the other down South. Both trips will be political in their nature and the Colonel will make a speech in every town or city in which he will stop. His first trip, starting in the latter part of August, will last about two weeks. He will be back home from his second trip in ample time to take in the State campaign.

The two tours will not be unlike a campaign trip by a Presidential candidate, for Col. Roosevelt will make not only as many set speeches as his traveling card permits, but will probably deliver extempore talks from the rear end of his private car. For the first trip a car has already been chartered.

JULY 30, 1910
TAFT CANCELS TRIP; WILL SEND CRANE

Asks Massachusetts Senator to Tour West and Report on Political Conditions.

HE IS GOING TO PANAMA

Also Finds He Will Have Much to Do in Washington This Fall—Annuls Many Dates.

BEVERLY, Mass., July 29.—President Taft has canceled practically all his engagements, tentative and otherwise, to speak in various parts of the country this Fall and has asked Senator Winthrop Murray Crane of Massachusetts to make a trip through the West and report to him on the political conditions.

These facts were made known to-day after a conference between the President and Senator Crane. The Senator's visit to Burgess Point was surrounded with the greatest secrecy. He did not come by the well-beaten roads, but slipped into Beverly by making a long detour around Manchester. Not until he was seen by the correspondents was it admitted at the executive offices that he had been anywhere in the vicinity of the President's cottage.

Whether the cancellation of the numerous engagements for the Fall means a reversal of the President's travel policy could not be learned. Political considerations may have had a great deal to do with the President's decision. It would be difficult for him to travel through the doubtful States in September and campaign, or at least having his speeches construed into political utterances. In a speech at Rockland, Me., the other day Mr. Taft said he did not believe a President of the United States had a right to talk politics, and that his only platform should be "patriotism, love of country, and prosperity for all."

• •

THE REPUBLICAN COLLAPSE

The Republicans fell from power in the 1910 election, their demise evident from the beginning of the electoral cycle. During early primaries, regular Republicans were swept aside by insurgent challengers, portending the turmoil that conservative party candidates would face from the opposition party. The first general elections, held in heavily Republican Maine, sent shockwaves through Washington, as Democrats replaced Republicans at every level. The trend continued through November, with Democrats ousting scores of Republicans and sweeping into control of the House. In the Senate, ascendant Republican insurgents effectively became the "swing votes," combining with additional Democrats to wrest power from the old guard party establishment. The long dominance of the conservative Republicans came to a decisive end.

AUGUST 3, 1910
INSURGENT SWEEP IN KANSAS PRIMARIES

Four Standpat Congressmen Beaten for Renomination—No Returns on Others.

BIG MAJORITY FOR STUBBS

Republican Progressives Generally Successful in Fight Against Men Who Supported Speaker Cannon.

Special to The New York Times

TOPEKA, Kan., Aug. 2.—At 11 o'clock to-night returns from the primaries showed that six of eight insurgent candidates for nomination as Congressmen from Kansas were successful. Returns from the First District, D. R. Anthony's, were late, and the same condition existed in the Third District. These two were the strongest stand-pat districts, and while the insurgents believed they had a chance to defeat Anthony and Campbell, the districts were not really claimed. They must still be considered in doubt, however, as a result of the landslide to the insurgents in the other districts.

At a late hour reports from the various headquarters showed.

First District—In doubt; no returns.

Second District—Alexander Mitchell, Progressive, defeats Congressmen C. F. Scott, Standpatter.

Third District—In doubt; no returns.

Fourth District—Fred S. Jackson, Progressive, defeats Congressman J. M. Miller, Standpatter.

Fifth District—R. R. Rees, progressive, defeats Congressmen W. A. Calderhead, standpatter.

Sixth District—I. D. Young, progressive, defeats W. A. Reeder, standpatter.

Seventh District—E. H. Madison, insurgent, returned uncontested.

Eight District—Victor Murdock, insurgent, returned uncontested.

Gov. Stubbs, progressive and supporter of Murdock and Bristow, has defeated Wagstaff, stand-pat candidate for Governor by an overwhelming majority.

> It has been years since a Democrat has been sent to Congress from Maine, and members of that party here to-night are confidently predicting that what was done to-day in that State will happen shortly in Illinois, Indiana, and many other doubtful States. "

SEPTEMBER 13, 1910
WASHINGTON IS ASTONISHED.

Apparently Nobody Really Thought Maine Would Go Democratic.

Special to The New York Times

WASHINGTON, Sept. 12.—The Democratic sweep in Maine seems to have caused more excitement among politicians than anything connected with the Roosevelt tour of the West. In spite of the persistent predictions of Democratic victory, which have now been proved correct, no one here seems really to have expected the State to desert the Republican Party. Now the politicians are simply waiting to hear how far the Democratic victory extends. As one man expressed it to-night:

"If the Democrats have got the Legislature and elect a Democrat to succeed Senator Hale the world will come to an end."

Naturally the chief interest here is in the National aspect of the case, the Congressional representatives, and the chances for a Democratic Senator. It has been years since a Democrat has been sent to Congress from Maine, and members of that party here to-night are confidently predicting that what was done to-day in that State will happen shortly in Illinois, Indiana, and many other doubtful States.

The fact that there were really no National insurgents in Maine had the effect apparently, of driving straight into the Democratic fold every one not entirely satisfied with the Republican Party. Dissatisfaction with the tariff has figured in the campaign to an important extent, but the Republicans who disliked the Payne-Aldrich act found no General in their own party to lead them against the Hale following that had fostered the tariff law. The result was they took their opposition to the Democratic camp and there fought against the Republicans instead of trying, like the insurgents in the Middle West, to change the party from within. In a speech delivered in Chicago, when insurgent criticism of the tariff was at its height, Attorney General Wickersham said that men dissatisfied with the Republican party should get out. That is exactly what the malcontents in Maine have done, and Democrats to-night are recalling Mr. Wickersham's advice with every manifestation of glee.

NOVEMBER 10, 1910
60 MAJORITY NOW IN DEMOCRATIC HOUSE

And the Old Guard Standpatters Are Practically Wiped Out of the Senate.

SEVEN CERTAINLY DEFEATED

It's a Republican Rout in Ohio with Eight Seats Captured—Some Districts Close and Majority May Increase.

As the completed returns from the Congressional and legislative elections came in yesterday the size of the Democratic victory in Congress steadily increased. The majority in the House leaped from forty to sixty, with several districts so close that it was still impossible to say definitely whether they had gone Democratic or Republican.

The returns of the day showed Democratic gains in Pennsylvania, Colorado, Michigan, and Ohio. The Republican defeat in Ohio developed into a rout, the Democrats capturing eight Congress districts now held by Republicans and exactly doubling their present representation. The wave of disapproval of the Payne-Aldrich tariff rolled pretty much over the whole country, manifesting its power in the scattered districts in many States.

But far reaching as was the Democratic victory in the House, it is hardly more significant than the gains made in the Senate. The Republican old guard of standpatters practically disappears from the Senate with the results of this election. Three or four of them, foreseeing the storm, had announced their intention of retiring with the expiration of their present terms next March. But of those who fought for re-election seven are certainly defeated, and two or three more were in great danger on the showing of last night's returns. The Old Guard losses include their two great leaders, Aldrich and Hale, both of whom announced voluntary retirement. Maine has already elected a Democratic Legislature, insuring the return of a Democrat in Hale's place, but the Rhode Island Legislature is safely Republican on joint ballot.

Senator Burrows of Michigan, another Old Guard leader, was defeated for renomination, and Charles E. Townsend, a near insurgent, is coming to the Senate in his place. Mr. Piles of Washington retired voluntarily, thus getting out of the way of the insurgent wave that sweeps Miles Poindexter in. Flint of California also retired voluntarily, and an insurgent is taking his place. Now, in addition to these losses to the progressives, the Democrats turn a round half dozen of the Old Guard violently out of the Senate by taking the Legislatures of their States. These are Depew of New York, Dick of Ohio, Kean of New Jersey, Scott of West Virginia, Warner of Missouri, and Burkett of Nebraska. Thus the Democrats gain—with Maine—seven seats in the Senate at the elections, all from the Old Guard. They lose one, in North Dakota, where a Republican Legislature has been chosen that will elect A. S. Gronna, the insurgent Republican, to take the place now held by Senator Purcell on appointment of Gov. Burke.

The Democrats make only one gain from the insurgents, getting the place of Beveridge of Indiana, whom Col. Roosevelt put in a strenuous day helping. This insurgent loss offsets their gain in North Dakota.

The insurgents will retain their present strength in the Senate, even if there should be an upset in Iowa preventing the election of a progressive to the vacancy caused by the death of Senator Dolliver. If a progressive is elected in that place they will make a net gain of one and will hold the balance of power. The present Republican majority is 26. The Democrats have already made a certain net gain of 7, reducing the Republican majority to 12. If they get their men also in Montana and Wyoming the Republican majority will be further reduced to 8, the exact number of the progressives. Thus on any matter on which the Democrats and progressives can get together as they did so often in the House at the last session, they will have their own way. There is small prospect, however, that the insurgents and Democrats can work together on tariff legislation. If they could there might be a prospect of tariff revision in the next Congress. But most of the Senate Democrats are in exactly the same position on the tariff that the standpat Republicans are—the insurgents will not work with them.

The Democratic strength in both House and Senate, with the strong progressive force in each body, is bound, however, to create a situation that will give President Taft and the Administration something to watch all the time.

NOVEMBER 10, 1910
REGULARS LOSE THE SENATE.

Special to The New York Times.

WASHINGTON, Nov. 10—With the certainty established that the House will be overwhelmingly Democratic, interest here has switched to the Senate. In that body it is equally certain that by a small majority—returns to-night make this a majority of 10—the Republicans will be in control. That on the face of things is not close enough to promise trouble, but when it is known how many of the Old Guard—the men who made the organization possible—will stay at home, and that the insurgents are slightly stronger than before, the possibility of any sort of insurgent-Democratic combination becomes important.

On particular subjects, of course, such a combination is certain. In the tariff struggle, for instance, in spite of the jeers of Senator Bailey and Senator Tillman, in the majority of cases the insurgents voted with the majority of the Democrats. The repetition of that condition would depend on the subjects that come up for legislation. What is certain, however, to follow the present great political upheaval, with its retirement of Old Guard leaders, is a change in the organization of the Senate, with the proportionate advance of the insurgents in the control or influencing of committees.

In other words, while the insurgents have gained one man by actual count and have increased their prestige enormously in the defeat of the regulars, the old organization has lost most of its leaders. Furthermore the strength of the regulars has been undermined by the Democrats until the united vote of regular and insurgent Republicans will only give them—according to present returns—51 votes against the Democratic 41. This means that any time a change of 6 votes will give the minority control of the upper house. The seven insurgents then are in the saddle. They hold the power, and if they do not use their power for insisting on concessions they have greatly changed their temperaments since last year.

The suggestion is made that the insurgents might actually ally themselves with the Democrats and assume control of the organization, but the party difficulties in the way are many. What will probably happen as to organization is that the regulars, though still dominating their caucus overwhelmingly, will seek to placate the insurgents by giving them better assignments.

CHANGING POLITICS

Changing faster than the politicians seated in Congress, voters in 1910 transformed the political landscape, providing fuller representation of the palette of American society. New faces and new parties emerged, including Princeton University president Woodrow Wilson, who was elected the Democratic governor of New Jersey. The fringe Socialist Party made a good showing throughout the Northeast. In the West, Washington became the fifth state to grant suffrage to women, reigniting a movement that would sweep the country. In a constitutional amendment to extend democratic principles, the new Congress proposed the direct election of United States senators, which became effective in 1913. Progressive programs to improve the quality of life for average Americans advanced to the forefront of American politics.

NOVEMBER 9, 1910
WILSON ELECTED IN NEW JERSEY

Democrats Make Great Sweep in Republican Counties and Capture the Legislature.

PROBABLY 34,000 PLURALITY

Parker and Wiley Beaten in Essex and Even Gardner in Doubt.

OVER 10,000 IN ESSEX

Returns from Cities and Rural Districts Alike Show Landslide All Over State.

Dr. Woodrow Wilson was elected Governor of New Jersey yesterday by probably 34,000 plurality, sweeping such strong Republican counties as Essex, Middlesex, and Monmouth. The polls did not close until 7 o'clock and the returns from rural districts will not be received until this morning, but at a late hour it was evident that the Democrats had not only carried the Legislature, insuring a Democratic successor to John Kean, but had elected eight of the ten Representatives in Congress. Not in fifteen years have the Republicans been so badly beaten.

At the Republican State Committee rooms in Newark Dr. Wilson's election was conceded at 9 o'clock, and one of the Republican leaders remarked that he had started on his way to the White House.

NOVEMBER 10, 1910
SOCIALIST VOTE TAKES A JUMP

Apparently All the Discontented Did Not Cast Their Ballots for Dix.

BIGGER NOW THAN HEARST'S

Likely to be Between 60,000 and 65,000 in the State, Which Is Double That Cast for Wanhope Two Years Ago.

Local politicians were commenting last night with a great deal of interest on the increase in the Socialist State vote. The incomplete returns available indicated that the total Socialist vote in the State will be between 60,000 and 65,000, probably more than 10,000 over Mr. Hearst's personal vote.

While this increase in the city was large, the gains made by the Socialist ticket up State were equally notable. In many of the labor towns the Socialist vote increased threefold this year; in nearly all the places where the party has any strength at all its vote was doubled.

NOVEMBER 10, 1910
JUBILEE FOR SUFFRAGISTS

They Will Celebrate Their Victory in the State of Washington.

The suffragists of New York will give a thanksgiving jubilee in Cooper Union to-night to express their appreciation of the State of Washington having given women the franchise. Mrs. Chapman Catt, President of the National Suffrage Association, and Miss Mary Garrett May received a telegram at 7 A.M. yesterday announcing the fact that the State had awakened from a sound sleep to receive the news.

"I can stand defeat," she said, "but victory is almost too much for me. This is the first one we have had in fifteen years."

Mrs. O. H. P. Belmont is planning to get out some new "Votes for Women" flags, as all her big blue banners bearing those words have only four stars on them and now there are five States in which women vote.

 The long fight which began in 1826 for an amendment to the Constitution, providing for the popular election of United States Senators, is nearer success to-night than ever before in the country's history.

MAY 14, 1912
SENATORS BY DIRECT VOTE PASSES HOUSE

Proposed Amendment Will Go to the State Legislatures for Approval.

SENATE AMENDMENT WINS

Federal Supervision of Elections Provided For—Agitation for Change Has Lasted 86 Years.

Special to The New York Times

WASHINGTON, May 13.—The long fight which began in 1826 for an amendment to the Constitution, providing for the popular election of United States Senators, is nearer success to-night than ever before in the country's history, as a result of the action of the House of Representatives to-day in accepting the direct elections joint resolution as passed by the Senate with the Bristow constitutional amendment.

This amendment was intended to maintain the status quo of the Federal Government as to supervisors over these elections, and was the snag upon which the direct elections resolution has been hung high and dry in conference since last June. Twice since then the Bristow amendment has been rejected by the House on the theory that it would interfere with the control of Senatorial elections by the states. Southern members, mindful of the malodorous Force bill and reconstruction days, have been bitter and determined in their opposition to the Bristow amendment.

But to-day the House, by vote of 237 to 39, receded from its disagreement to the Senate amendment and concurred in the action of the Senate. This was the final legislative step in proposing this new constitutional amendment to the States and the joint resolution will go at once to President Taft for his signature. Then it will be submitted to the States.

There are forty-eight States, and ratification of the amendment by the Legislatures of thirty-six of them is necessary to make it a valid part of the Constitution. One Legislature, that of Louisiana, meets this month, and thirty-four other Legislatures meet in 1913. It is evident that unless some other State among those whose Legislatures do not meet until 1913 calls a special session the direct election amendment cannot become a part of the Constitution before 1914.

THE PRESIDENTIAL ELECTION OF 1912

WOODROW WILSON'S NATIONAL VICTORY PROMISES MAJOR REFORMS

The United States was experiencing rapid change as it approached the presidential election of 1912. In the second decade of the twentieth century, the population grew 15 percent, passing 100 million for the first time. Almost all of the nation's growth came in urban areas, which, in another landmark change, would house a majority of citizens by 1920. Ethnic diversity also was increasing. Nearly 9 million immigrants entered the country in the first decade of the century—by 1920 those born abroad or of foreign-born parents made up more than one-fourth of the white population, and nonwhites comprised a tenth of the total population.

New lifestyles emerged; their common characteristic was the enlargement of personal freedom. Americans were living longer—the death rate reached a new low in 1912, falling 10 percent during the decade, and life expectancy rose four years, to fifty-four. Automobiles would soon become the preferred, individualistic means of transportation. By the election of 1912, close to a million Americans had become car and truck owners, a forty-fold increase in just ten years. Electricity use expanded, reaching a sixth of all U.S. households. Following soon after the Wright brothers' experimental trials, airplanes were already evident in the skies and promised a vast expansion in the geographical reach of travelers.

Political institutions also evidenced change, adding to individuals' opportunities to affect elections. National party conventions, historically the domain of politicians and party bosses closeted in the proverbial smoke-filled rooms, began to include some delegates chosen in direct presidential primaries. Some states moved toward "direct democracy," enabling voters to write legislation through initiative and referendum procedures, and to oust officials from power through special recall elections. On the federal level, the direct election of United States senators—rather than their appointment by state legislatures—was approved by both houses of Congress and would be ratified by the states as the Seventeenth Amendment shortly after the presidential election.

Source: The Granger Collection, New York

Former president Theodore Roosevelt and President William Howard Taft battle for the Republican presidential nomination in a 1912 political cartoon.

New voters entered the electoral system. Women won the right to vote in nine states, and the national movement toward sexual equality at the ballot box gained momentum. By 1912 all forty-eight states on the U.S. mainland participated in the presidential election, when the last territories, Arizona and New Mexico, joined the Union. All voters, now more concentrated in cities and more literate with the spread of public education, enjoyed greater access to political information. New print technology—the use of wood pulp for newsprint and photoengraving for pictures—made newspapers more attractive and considerably cheaper (1 cent to 5 cents a copy) for the growing readership.

1912 ELECTORAL VOTE

STATE	ELECTORAL VOTES	WILSON	ROOSEVELT	TAFT	STATE	ELECTORAL VOTES	WILSON	ROOSEVELT	TAFT
Alabama	(12)	12	–	–	Nebraska	(8)	8	–	–
Arizona	(3)	3	–	–	Nevada	(3)	3	–	–
Arkansas	(9)	9	–	–	New Hampshire	(4)	4	–	–
California	(13)	2	11	–	New Jersey	(14)	14	–	–
Colorado	(6)	6	–	–	New Mexico	(3)	3	–	–
Connecticut	(7)	7	–	–	New York	(45)	45	–	–
Delaware	(3)	3	–	–	North Carolina	(12)	12	–	–
Florida	(6)	6	–	–	North Dakota	(5)	5	–	–
Georgia	(14)	14	–	–	Ohio	(24)	24	–	–
Idaho	(4)	4	–	–	Oklahoma	(10)	10	–	–
Illinois	(29)	29	–	–	Oregon	(5)	5	–	–
Indiana	(15)	15	–	–	Pennsylvania	(38)	–	38	–
Iowa	(13)	13	–	–	Rhode Island	(5)	5	–	–
Kansas	(10)	10	–	–	South Carolina	(9)	9	–	–
Kentucky	(13)	13	–	–	South Dakota	(5)	–	5	–
Louisiana	(10)	10	–	–	Tennessee	(12)	12	–	–
Maine	(6)	6	–	–	Texas	(20)	20	–	–
Maryland	(8)	8	–	–	Utah	(4)	–	–	4
Massachusetts	(18)	18	–	–	Vermont	(4)	–	–	4
Michigan	(15)	–	15	–	Virginia	(12)	12	–	–
Minnesota	(12)	–	12	–	Washington	(7)	–	7	–
Mississippi	(10)	10	–	–	West Virginia	(8)	8	–	–
Missouri	(18)	18	–	–	Wisconsin	(13)	13	–	–
Montana	(4)	4	–	–	Wyoming	(3)	3	–	–
					TOTALS	**(531)**	**435**	**88**	**8**

These changes formed the background of a period of fervent politics, the Progressive era. Reform causes flourished, often stimulated by the new investigative journalism of "muckrakers" such as Ida Tarbell, who exposed the coercively monopolistic practices of Standard Oil; Lincoln Steffens, who wrote of the corruption of urban political party machines; and Upton Sinclair, who graphically described filthy conditions in the meatpacking industry. Other reformers, such as Jane Addams and Jacob Riis, highlighted urban poverty. Wage laborers became more assertive with the formation of the Industrial Workers of the World, and the temperance movement sought the prohibition of alcoholic beverages. Laws limiting child labor and regulating urban housing began to pass state legislatures. The

federal government developed new powers, its capacity soon enlarged by the income tax, ratified as an amendment to the Constitution in 1913.

Theodore Roosevelt presided over this turbulent period. He had become president in 1901, after the assassination of William McKinley. Roosevelt led major initiatives to reform social conditions. Antitrust lawsuits challenged monopolies, most prominently Standard Oil Company, which eventually was transformed from a single corporation controlling 90 percent of the nation's oil into thirty-eight separate companies. The president intervened in major strikes on behalf of industrial workers, initiated the conservation movement through the creation of major national parks, and sponsored legislation to ban corporate donations to political candidates, protect the nation's consumers through the Pure Food and Drug Act of 1906, and regulate railroads.

Roosevelt also changed the character of the presidency itself, seeing himself as a "steward" of the national welfare who would use the "bully pulpit" and the inherent powers of his office to rally the citizenry to his causes. In foreign policy, he led a growing world power, expanding the navy, claiming the right to intervene in unstable Latin American countries, and aiding in a revolt against Colombia to gain the territory needed to construct the Panama Canal.

The assertive president was hugely popular. After winning reelection in 1904, he probably could have won again in 1908, but he declined to run, citing the tradition of a two-term presidential limit. Instead, he used his domination of the Republican Party to install his chosen successor, Secretary of War William Howard Taft, as the party candidate. Taft went on to win an easy victory in 1908 against a three-time loser, Democrat William Jennings Bryan. Apparently happy with the result, Roosevelt retired to write his memoirs and to explore Africa, where he traveled for a year. But, at age fifty, T.R. was too energetic and too committed to personal renown to leave politics quietly.

THE PARTIES AND THE CANDIDATES

Political conflicts played out principally among Republicans, the dominant party in this period. Soon after his inauguration, President Taft began drawing fire from the party's Progressive wing, on both policy and institutional issues.

Taft first stumbled on the persistent issue of tariffs. Although he favored lowering trade barriers, he eventually had to accept a new protective law, the Payne-Aldrich tariff, disappointing farmers seeking higher prices for farm exports. Progressives then turned to congressional reform, seeking to curb the dominance of Joseph Cannon, the long-ruling Speaker of the House and a Taft ally. With the help of Democrats, they stripped Cannon of his power to appoint committees and the leadership of the Rules Committee, which controlled the flow of legislation. But these reforms did the Republicans little good in the congressional elections of 1910. The party lost 56 seats and control of the House, and 10 seats in the Senate.

Roosevelt was soon back in the political fray, and the dissidents had their magnetic leader. Unhappy from the onset of the Taft administration, T.R. clearly missed power and even felt snubbed at White House functions. More substantively, in contrast to Roosevelt's expansive "stewardship" theory, Taft held a different view of the presidency, seeing the chief executive as limited in his powers. Moreover, Taft had replaced most of his cabinet, although Roosevelt thought he had obtained a promise from Taft of their retention.

Their largest conflict involved Roosevelt's cherished conservation program. Taft initially incurred Roosevelt's suspicions when he named an opponent of public land ownership, Richard Ballinger, to head the Interior Department. Soon, Gifford Pinchot, the head of the Forest Service and a founder of the conservation movement, accused Ballinger of corruption in the disposition of mineral and water rights in the national lands. When Pinchot took his charges to Congress, Taft fired Pinchot, stoking Roosevelt's ire.

Progressives launched a formal effort to deny Taft renomination early in 1911, with Wisconsin senator Robert La Follette seen as their most likely presidential candidate. When his candidacy failed to catch fire, they turned to Roosevelt, who reentered the fray in February 1912 with a major address embracing the Progressive program, including the radical idea of popular recall of judges and judicial decisions.

Roosevelt hoped to win the Republican nomination with the aid of a major innovation in presidential politics, the selection of delegates by direct presidential primaries. By 1912, twelve states held these contests. Roosevelt swept to victory in nine, including the major states of Illinois, Pennsylvania, and Taft's home state of Ohio. The "Rough Rider" of the Spanish-American War won an overall majority of the 2,270,000 votes cast, led Taft by a 3–2 margin and La Follette by more than 3 to 1, and gained 278 of the 362 elected delegates. In language that foreshadowed contemporary nominations, Roosevelt claimed that these victories constituted a mandate that should be followed by the Republican convention.

But it was still 1912, and most delegations were chosen by the state parties, persuaded by the White House and its organizational power, bolstered particularly by delegates from the southern states where the tiny bands of Republican activists were in thrall to administration patronage. Roosevelt came to the June convention in Chicago, the first presidential candidate ever to attend his party's convention, to challenge the Taft delegations. Although he described himself "as strong as a bull moose," his fight did little more than give a name to the dissident faction.

Floor challenges demonstrated Taft's control. In narrow votes, the conventioneers chose Taft's candidate as the presiding officer, allowed disputed delegates to vote on the credentials of all states but their own, and then seated almost all of the Taft supporters, turning back challenges to one fourth of the convention delegates. Rubbing salt into Progressives' wounds, the convention then adopted a sycophantic platform, giving Taft credit that "the country has prospered and been at peace under his Presidency," and lauding "a record on which any administration might appeal with confidence to the favorable judgment of history."

Seeing the inevitable outcome, the Roosevelt forces abstained from further participation. Taft was renominated on the first ballot, with 556 votes, only 52 percent of the delegate total. Vice President James Sherman won renomination by a larger margin. He would never have the chance to be reelected, however. Sherman died just before the general election and was replaced on the Republican ticket by Nicholas Murray Butler, president of Columbia University.

The Republican minority prepared to launch a new Progressive party, inspired by Roosevelt's zealous call, "We stand at Armageddon and battle for the Lord." Convening in August in Chicago, the new party had delegates from all states but South Carolina, including women representatives for the first time—but excluding blacks from southern "lily-white" delegations. Welcomed by Roosevelt in a stirring "Confession of Faith," the convention had more of the air of a religious revival meeting than a political caucus, enlivened by fervent singing of "Onward Christian Soldiers" and "The Battle Hymn of the Republic." Roosevelt was nominated by acclamation, followed by the similar selection of California governor Hiram Johnson, a leading Progressive, for vice president.

Even more than its campaign crusade, the Progressives were notable for their daring platform, which set the American reform agenda for generations. The party urged major change in political institutions, including women's suffrage, nationwide presidential primaries, and direct democracy through initiatives, referendums, recall elections, lobbyist registration, voter referendums on court decisions, and direct election of U.S. senators.

The Progressives looked forward to national direction of the economy through "permanent active supervision over industrial corporations engaged in inter-State commerce," and backed both income and graduated inheritance taxes. On social policy, the new party pledged the prohibition of child labor, minimum wage standards for women and a "living wage" for all, an eight-hour work day, a national health service and—most portentous for the future—social insurance to provide protection "against the hazards of sickness, irregular employment, and old age."

The Democratic Party met in Baltimore in late June, between the meetings of the Republicans and the Progressives. Reveling in the Republicans' quarrels, the party saw its best opportunity for presidential victory in the past two decades. It could not match Taft's incumbency or Roosevelt's glamour, but the prospect of White House occupancy brought many candidates.

The leading Democratic aspirant was Champ Clark of Missouri, the party leader and Speaker of the House. His opponents included Rep. Oscar Underwood of Alabama, the first serious southern candidate since the Civil War, and, most prominently, Woodrow Wilson of New Jersey. Wilson, born in Virginia, had been professor of political science and then president of Princeton University. Embroiled in academic disputes, he left the university to win election as governor of New Jersey, where he defied the state's party bosses to achieve a reform agenda.

None of the Democrats gained an advantage in the new presidential primaries; Wilson and Clark each won five victories, principally in their home regions, with Wilson amassing a slight edge in delegates. A long conflict loomed at the convention, where nomination required a two-thirds vote. Of vital importance was the support of William Jennings Bryan, still the leading figure in the party. Although officially neutral, Bryan came to oppose Clark as allegedly beholden to banking interests and to New York's Tammany Hall, and he worked to halt Clark's bid despite his lead in the early ballots. When Bryan came out openly for Wilson, a bandwagon effect slowly developed, bringing Wilson the required two-thirds on the forty-sixth ballot. Indiana governor Thomas Marshall, an early favorite son, was selected as the vice-presidential candidate. Bryan would be rewarded later with an appointment as Wilson's secretary of state.

The Democratic platform combined the party's established support for lower tariffs and states' rights with new reform proposals. The party pledged vigorous enforcement of antitrust laws, restrictions on antilabor injunctions, and regulation of utility rates. In regard to the nation's political institutions, the Democrats advocated direct senatorial election, state presidential primaries, and most startling, a single term for elected presidents. The party would quickly forget that position after Wilson was elected and ran for a second term in 1916.

As if this three-ring circus were not enough for the voting public to digest, there was an added ring—the Socialist Party, led by Eugene V. Debs, running for the fourth time as its presidential candidate. Socialism never achieved mass support in the United States comparable to that in Europe, where similar parties eventually won control throughout the continent, but it was a rising force in the 1912 election. By that time, Socialists had elected more than twelve hundred public officials, including two members of Congress and the mayor of Milwaukee. It claimed more than 130,000 members and published hundreds of daily and weekly newspapers.

The Socialists adhered to the doctrines of Karl Marx and particularly appealed to urban workers and immigrants. But they were continually riven over tactics, especially their approach to labor issues and political change. Those who advocated gradual change supported unions' taking workplace action, such as the epochal strike in the textile mills of Lawrence, Massachusetts, where women and immigrant workers shut factories for two months to win union recognition. More broadly, they favored "political action," active participation in campaigns, elections, legislatures, and public administration. The more radical Socialists allied with the Industrial Workers of the World in disdain for such "reformism." Following rigidly orthodox Marxism, they looked to the violent overthrow of the government, endorsing sabotage against capitalist industry and revolutionary violence, even assassination.

Seeing opportunity in the tumultuous politics of the election year, the Socialist convention met in Indianapolis, Indiana—Debs's home state—in June. Debs won the presidential nomination over limited opposition, with Milwaukee's Socialist mayor, Emil Seidel, as his running mate. On a crucial platform vote, the party declared for political action as its principal tactic, and repudiated sabotage and violence, leading to the expulsion of extreme radicals from party positions.

Even if officially pacific in its tactics, the party was still radical in its platform, disdainfully declaring "the capitalist system has now outgrown its historical function, and has become utterly incapable of meeting the problems now confronting society." Its program included "collective ownership" of banks, communications, transportation, food distribution, natural resources, patents, and most land; graduated income and inheritance taxes; prohibition of child labor; shortened work days and work weeks; government jobs on public works for the unemployed; minimum wage scales; and noncontributory social insurance. The political program included women's suffrage; direct election of the president; and abolition of the Senate, the president's veto power, all federal district and appellate courts, and the Supreme Court's power of constitutional review; and—to move the revolution still further—a new constitutional convention.

THE CAMPAIGN

With the Republicans divided, a Democratic victory was the clear outlook. But none of the three major candidates accepted that prospect passively. As challengers, Roosevelt and Wilson pursued the active barnstorming that had now become typical in a presidential election. They were joined by Taft, the first incumbent president to campaign actively, although his efforts were much less extensive than his rivals.

Debs, a vivid speaker and personality comparable to Bryan and Roosevelt, added his strong physical effort to the Socialists' radical message. As he had done on the party's "Red Special" in the 1908 election, Debs traveled by railroad throughout the country, speaking four or five times a day, directly reaching perhaps half a million listeners. More than doubling his previous ballot support, he would in 1912 win the largest number of votes ever achieved by an American Socialist.

The candidates exemplified the ideological significance of the election. As much as a contest for power, the campaign was a debate about contending philosophies on the best means to manage the new, triumphant industrial economy of the United States and to control the dominance of the giant, even monopolistic, corporations. Although all of the candidates were reformers to some degree, they differed considerably in their broader ideologies.

Taft leaned toward a traditionally conservative doctrine. Prosperity, in his view, came through the success of business, rather than through government action. Government should safeguard domestic industry with high tariffs, protect working women, and actively promote economic competition through antitrust legislation. For the most part, however, in Taft's view, the country would be better off if government refrained from interference in the free market.

Wilson certainly accepted the basic premise of a capitalist order, but added a reformist direction, which he called "The New Freedom." His goal was to bolster the economic viability of smaller capitalists through antitrust laws, improved management of the banking system, and lower tariffs. Wilson was skeptical of social programs, however, even opposing minimum wage laws. Reflecting traditional southern support of states' rights, Wilson's aim was not a larger federal government but a restoration of an earlier time of smaller more competitive enterprises.

At the furthest extreme, Debs saw capitalism as a failed and wicked system that required not reform, but total replacement. Only government ownership—on national, state, and municipal levels—and government social programs could provide prosperity, economic equality, and simple justice. The economic individualism of capitalism would then be replaced by the "cooperative commonwealth" of socialism.

Roosevelt's Progressives shared some specific proposals with both the Socialists and the Democrats, but they had a distinct vision. Roosevelt championed "The New Nationalism," which saw the United States as an integrated economy. T.R. was willing to accept "good trusts," so long as they were sufficiently regulated by government administrators to serve the public interest. In his convention "Confession of Faith," he attempted to combine "scientific" principles of efficient management with social idealism. Expert bureaucracies would promote a "square deal," promoting both economic growth and social goals such as the abolition of child labor and minimum wages for women.

The presidential candidates presenting these programs were men of unusual talent. Their intellectual qualities were exceptional, probably the highest in any presidential election since the early contests between John Adams and Thomas Jefferson. Among them, they would write more than one hundred books—on topics ranging from constitutional law to big-game hunting. Most of their campaigns added religious overtones to the intellectual debates: Roosevelt inspired the fervor of a new messiah; Wilson sermonized like a Presbyterian prelate; and Debs preached the Socialist gospel like an evangelical Christian.

The contest among the four candidates was violently interrupted in mid-October when a psychotic saloonkeeper attempted to assassinate Roosevelt in Milwaukee. Hit by a single bullet in the chest, the former president luckily had a 50-page manuscript and a steel glasses case under his coat. For once, a politician's wordiness did him good; despite the wound Roosevelt finished his speech before seeking medical care and left the hospital in a mere eight days.

While the shooting apparently removed Roosevelt from the campaign trail, his opponents, after respectfully waiting a week, resumed their pursuits. Roosevelt returned briefly to the hustings on the last weekend, speaking to an overflow crowd at Madison Square Garden. For forty-five minutes, *The New York Times* reported, "They began with cheering, and from that they went on to inventing strange noises. When the possibilities of strange noises were exhausted they would go back again to cheering, and so it went on until it seemed as if noisemaking opportunities had been tested to the limit."

The candidates also developed innovative electioneering techniques. Wilson climaxed his campaign with a giant rally in New York. His message was simultaneously relayed to gatherings throughout the nation, including picnics "at thousands of small country places, far from the populous centres, [where] the Democratic voters will assemble around huge bonfires to listen to the final message from their leader on the eve of election." At a different site, President Taft attended a ceremonial meeting in Boston, where he was serenaded by the Mayor, John F. Fitzgerald, grandfather of another future president, and watched himself in the newest medium of the times, motion pictures. In aid of the Progressive Party, women left the confines of home to campaign, the "Moosettes" holding rallies in New York City parks, where they sold "badges and buttons, newspapers, and other souvenirs."

THE ELECTION RESULTS

As the balloting neared, attempts to predict the outcome included organized betting and straw polls conducted in many states by local newspapers, most of them accurately forecasting a Wilson triumph. Accounts of the campaign and predictions of the outcome in individual states accumulated in the pages of *The Times*. Led since 1896 by its transformative publisher, Adolph Ochs, it had become the nation's authoritative newspaper, clearer in its format and language, objective in its reporting. It illuminated its central position on election night itself, as *The Times* reported the election results through coded electric lights circling its tower, the new landmark of New York City.

Although the campaign had been peaceful, anxieties still arose. Roosevelt particularly worried traditionalists, who feared that a third presidential term would be the gateway to tyranny and even socialism. Debs, the true Socialist, derided Roosevelt's claim to that mantle, but posed no threat of victory on his own. Taft and Wilson were regarded as safe.

Previous elections had repeatedly demonstrated that the Republican Party was the country's normal majority. With the party divided, a Republican success in 1912 required either that one of the party's factions dominate or, improbably, that they somehow repair their breach.

Some Republicans had tried to restore party unity. Most of the party's governors who had originally backed Roosevelt returned to the fold, and other leaders futilely attempted to create fusion tickets of state electors. But other Republicans disavowed Taft, endorsing either Wilson or Roosevelt. The Progressives, too, had problems holding their ranks, with La Follette, still bitter over his displacement by Roosevelt, casting his lot with Wilson.

Roosevelt was clearly a stronger candidate than Taft, but was not able to drive Taft from the field by winning control of the party's state organizations and their slates of electors. The resulting division of the normal majority vote of the GOP virtually guaranteed the election of Wilson, an apparent moderate reformer who aroused little fear of either Socialist revolution, Progressive turmoil, or conservative immobility.

In the balloting, Wilson won an overwhelming electoral victory, carrying 40 of the 48 states, and 435 of the nation's 531 electoral votes. Roosevelt won 88 electoral votes from 6 states—2 in the West, 3 in the Midwest and Plains, and only Pennsylvania in the East. Taft had but 8 electoral votes, from Utah and Vermont. It would be the worst defeat of an incumbent president in American history. Democrats gained 62 seats in the House and 9 in the Senate, bringing them control in both chambers, and securing the support Wilson would use in his innovative administration.

Wilson's victory, however, was more impressive on the map than in the actual ballots. Outside of the South, the Democrat failed to gain a majority in any state. Wilson in fact got fewer votes, and lower percentages, than the Democrats' standard-bearer, William Jennings Bryan, had gained in each of his three losing efforts. Overall, Wilson won less than 42 percent of the popular vote of 15 million, less than the combined shares of the two once-Republican factions. With Roosevelt garnering over 27 percent and Taft over 23 percent, the divided party actually had a national majority. On the left, in the high-water mark of American socialism, Debs gained 900,000 votes, 6 percent of the national total.

Even as a minority president, Wilson, with his party in control of Congress became one of the most significant American presidents. Government regulation of the economy advanced with the passage of tougher antitrust legislation and the creation of the Federal Trade Commission. The nation's banking system was permanently reformed by creation of the Federal Reserve System. The graduated income tax, along with lower tariffs, forever changed the fiscal structure of the federal government. The foundations of the modern welfare state were laid in laws to prohibit child labor and regulate the hours of railroad workers. And, in his second term, Wilson led the United States into the Great War, known today as World War I, and to international prominence.

The election of 1912 changed the character of the nation's political institutions, moving it toward a fuller and more direct democracy. Direct primaries would become the most common means of nominating candidates, even presidents, diminishing the control of party chieftains. Women came closer to equal suffrage, which they would gain in 1920. The Senate changed from an aristocratic body of state ambassadors to a chamber of representatives subject to popular election. Populist procedures of initiative, referendum, and recall spread through many states.

The waves of change would recede after Wilson, but surge again in the New Deal of Franklin Roosevelt, who appropriately was both a distant relative of T.R. and a former member of Wilson's administration. As these tides ebbed and flowed, they would be channeled by the bedrock formations of the Progressive era, solidified into American institutions in the presidential election of 1912.

- -

THE NORTH DAKOTA PRIMARY KICKS OFF THE 1912 PRESIDENTIAL ELECTION

The 1912 election was the first in which voters were given a voice in selecting the candidates for president via widespread presidential primary votes. The first presidential primary of the year came in North Dakota, won by Sen. Robert La Follette of Wisconsin on the Republican side and Gov. John Burke on the Democratic side. President William Howard Taft, the eventual Republican nominee, finished a distant third behind Theodore Roosevelt, and the eventual Democratic nominee, Woodrow Wilson, did not even appear on the ballot. The primary laws were designed to encourage independent voters to vote in either primary, which led many Democratic voters to vote in the Republican primary instead of their own.

MARCH 20, 1912
BEAT ROOSEVELT IN NORTH DAKOTA

Republicans Give La Follette a Lead of 3,000 in 18 Out of 49 Counties.

FIRST PRIMARY BATTLE

The Colonel's Managers Declare La Follette Vote Came from Democrats.

TAFT WAS NOT AN ISSUE

Receives a Small Vote—Roosevelt Carries Medina, His Old Ranch Town, by Only 7 Votes.

Special to The New York Times.

FARGO, N.D., March 19.—Senator La Follette of Wisconsin defeated Col. Theodore Roosevelt to-day in the first State-wide Presidential primary ever held in the United States. At a late hour tonight the Senator was leading by more than 3,000 votes, but his managers freely predict that when all the returns are in he will have a majority of at least 10,000.

Complete returns from 18 counties out of a total of 49 in the State give:

La Follette	6,953
Roosevelt	3,981
Taft	270

The small vote for President Taft is accounted for by the fact that the fight was between the two factions of the Republicans—the La Follette and Roosevelt men.

Frank Talcott, Chairman of the Republican State Committee, and John F. Bass, manager of the Roosevelt campaign in this State, notified Senator Joseph M. Dixon at Washington late to-night that in their opinion Senator La Follette had carried the primaries. Neither made a prediction as to La Follctte's plurality.

Going over the figures from the eighteen counties, where the returns have been counted, the Roosevelt managers conceded ten to La Follette, listed two others as about even, and claimed six counties for the Colonel.

"Our reports indicate that practically all the Democrats have voted for La Follette." said Mr. Bass. "If the Democrats had stayed out of the Republican primary there is no question that Roosevelt would have won." . . .

Analysis of some of the early returns Indicate that La Follette obtained 80 per cent. of the Norwegian vote in six big valley counties. He received a heavy vote at all points at which he spoke last week. His tour came just in time to check the rising Roosevelt strength. La Follette committees had been active for months not only with State and county organizations, but had local representation in practically every precinct.

Roosevelt organizers were slow in establishing headquarters. John F. Bass, a brother of Gov. Bass of Vermont, was sent into the State to manage the campaign. This importation of an outsider did not please some of the Roosevelt supporters.

Among the Democrats there was no contest in the matter of a Presidential choice. Gov. John Burke's name appeared alone on the ticket. Many Democrats, realizing that one vote would be as good as a thousand registered for Burke, cast their ballots in favor of La Follette in order to embarrass Roosevelt and thus widen the breach in the Republican Party.

A storm raged in Western, Southwestern, and Northeastern North Dakota and the vote was not as heavy as in other districts. Cold, clear weather, with a brisk north wind in the Devil's Lake district, following a drop in temperature of more than 35 degrees over night, made country roads hard in that region, and, as a result, voters turned out in large numbers. Weather conditions in Pembina County also were favorable to a heavy vote.

"Here are eight aspirants for the Presidential nominations madly racing over the country, haranguing their fellow-citizens night and day, abusing each other or intriguing against each other, and appealing for votes, to all intents and purposes begging for votes, in favor of delegates who will in turn vote for them in the National Convention."

THE NEW YORK TIMES ARGUES AGAINST THE PRIMARY SYSTEM

The first presidential primaries did not get a warm reception. In an editorial, *The New York Times* called for an end to the practice, citing the many ills that plagued the primary system: the electorate was wearied by the long harsh campaign, the parties were battered by brutal negative campaigning between their own members, and the candidates themselves seemed to fall from the dignified pedestals envisioned for presidential candidates. A later *Times* editorial compared primaries to "a first-rate device for splitting a party wide open and inviting defeat on election-day. It is as if an army before engaging the enemy should divide in two portions and fight a terrific battle, one-half against the other."

APRIL 28, 1912
EDITORIAL
THE FIRST FRUITS.

This is our first Presidential campaign under the preference primary plan. We hope it may be our last. The spectacle presented by the fierce fight for the nomination is one that must be amazing to foreigners, it is one that should bring a blush of shame to the cheek of every American having any pride or patriotism, or any common sense. Here are eight aspirants for the Presidential nominations madly racing over the country, haranguing their fellow-citizens night and day, abusing each other or intriguing against each other, and appealing for votes, to all intents and purposes begging for votes, in favor of delegates who will in turn vote for them in the National Convention. These are the first fruits of our experiment in the direct action of the people upon the affairs of their Government. There has been nothing like it hitherto. The support of district and State delegates has been sought, but by no such method as this. Aspirants to the Presidential office have been content to await the action of the convention. Then the candidate, in a letter of acceptance and in a public address or two, appealed to the electorate for its confidence and its support. That was a rational, a seemly procedure. The people acted with all-sufficient directness, and they acted well and wisely. The present goings-on must give foreign observers the impression that we are no longer a people, but a mob. With mobs, of course, the demagogue has the best chance. That is why Mr. ROOSEVELT is an enthusiastic advocate of the preference primary system.

In Massachusetts, where the strife is now hottest, the primary to be held next Tuesday is of the soap-box variety. Enrollment is not required. The advertisements of Mr. ROOSEVELT's managers instruct the voters that they do not need to be enrolled. In the news columns of the press they are told "that if you are a Democrat and wish to vote for ROOSEVELT or TAFT you can do so unless now enrolled as a Democrat." A Socialist, a Prohibitionist, a voter belonging to any group or faction may at the primary indicate a preference for the Colonel, even though he does it only to disrupt the Republican Party and with no intention of voting for the candidate of that party. Ingenuity could hardly devise a plan better contrived to defeat the true will of a party's majority, or to betray the people and drag politics into the mire.

It is in the attempt to snatch delegates from all this writhing and confusion that THEODORE ROOSEVELT has personally assailed the President, and through him has insulted the American people. It is not a pleasing spectacle, but we cannot complain of Mr. ROOSEVELT on this ground, for Mr. TAFT was compelled to attack him. On grounds of decorum alone it would have been held that Mr. TAFT should not expose the moral delinquencies of Mr. ROOSEVELT. The exigencies of politics, the interests of the party of which Mr. TAFT is the head, and in truth the deliverance of the Nation from the peril of Roosevelt leadership made it necessary that the truth should be told about him. He has attempted to reply. The weight and sufficiency of his answer may without fear be submitted to the judgment of candid men. He did not meet the charge that he had willfully misrepresented the President's attitude toward Senator LORIMER. He could not meet it. The proof confronted him and it was convincing. Mr. ROOSEVELT says that he, on grounds of principle, changed his mind about reciprocity, which he had formerly indorsed with heartiness. If the veracity of Mr. ROOSEVELT had not been successfully and many times impeached, his statement would be accepted. Candid men will not believe him now. It will be the general belief that he attacked what he once indorsed, not from conviction, but for political advantage. Upon the subject of the third-term pledge he says nothing that will change any opinion. He has broken his word. He has been faithless, and the country knows it. Nor will his attack upon Mr. TAFT as being infirm of purpose, as having come under the influence of bad and selfish men, have any weight save with those whose devotion to the Roosevelt interest blinds them to truth and disqualifies them to judge of what is fair and what is foul, what is decent and what is indecent in politics.

The people of Massachusetts are indeed on trial. Senator BOURNE said that to the people of Oregon. But there the choice was between retaining him as Senator or sending another in his place. The decision could make not much difference to the country. The decision of Massachusetts will make a vast difference to the country, it is of immeasurable importance. It is the choice not merely between Mr. TAFT and Mr. ROOSEVELT, although that is a grave matter, it is the choice between a well-ordered Government of laws and Government by a man who has repeatedly shown his impatience of the restraints of law, a man who has contempt for our Constitution, and who has planned and proposed dangerous changes in the forms of Government. When such alternatives confront the voters of a State, the choice they make gives the measure of their judgment and their sobriety. The voters of the Old Commonwealth are not ignorant of what is involved in this primary contest, they have been thoroughly informed. If they do not clearly see the unfitness of Mr. ROOSEVELT, with his unsteadiness of temperament and his moral defects, ever again to hold a great office of power and responsibility, then we should have as the first fruits of the direct-action principle clear proof that the voters of one of the most intelligent States in the Union were the poorest possible judges of their own affairs, and actually incapable of governing themselves wisely and safely. It is plain that matters of great moment are to be determined in Massachusetts next Tuesday.

THE SOCIALIST PARTY ENLIVENS THE ELECTION OF 1912

The Socialist Party, led by the fiery Eugene Debs, recurrently ran as a third party during the early twentieth century The Socialists had the most radical political program of all the parties, advocating a drastic restructuring of American society and government. Some of their ideas, such as women's suffrage and protections for American industrial workers, later became cornerstones of other parties' platforms. But the Socialist platform also included more radical ideas that prevented the party from gaining mainstream acceptance, such as eliminating the U.S. Senate and overthrowing the capitalist economic system in America. Although Debs never posed a serious challenge in the presidential race, the specter of socialism that he represented enlivened American politics for decades.

MAY 18, 1912
THE SOCIALIST CONVENTION.

The Socialist National Convention at Indianapolis is supposed by its members to represent 1,000,000 voters this year. EUGENE V. DEBS, its perpetual candidate for President, polled somewhat more than 420,000 votes in 1908. That his vote will be more than doubled this year is very doubtful, especially as the convention, determined to abide solely by its own issues, has refused to approve either the American Federation of Labor or the anarchistic Industrial Workers of the World. The Industrial Workers were defeated in a vigorous effort to secure recognition and turn the Socialist movement, whatever it may amount to, to their own account. But the convention sagely left to the labor organizations the solution of their own problems, and incorporated in its platform a plank denouncing violence and riot.

The platform of the Socialists charges to existing social and political conditions all such evils as poverty and child labor, and most insanity and crime. Anti-trust laws, with their resultant prosecutions, indictments, and investigations, it condemns as "futile and ridiculous." It is the aim of the Socialists to abolish poverty, crime, insanity, trusts, Government, and courts. Resolutions were adopted yesterday favoring woman suffrage. It is needless to say that this would be a much better world if the real evils these Socialists protest against could be abolished. But their destructive force has thus far been negligible, while their constructive force is purely mythical.

Thus far the Socialists have elected one Representative in Congress, Mr. BERGER of Wisconsin. They assert that they will elect many more this Fall. They maintain a compact and workable political machine, but they will probably encounter new opposition this year. Their largest vote was in 1904. It was then nearly twenty times larger than that obtained by the first Socialist candidate for President in 1892. In 1910 W. J. GHENT estimated the total Socialist vote of the United States at 620,000. It was an optimistic estimate, as the combined vote of the two Socialist candidates for President in 1908, when the Socialist Labor Party, so called, supported GILHAUS, was about 434,000.

REPUBLICANS RENOMINATE WILLIAM HOWARD TAFT

A bitterly fought Republican primary battle between William Howard Taft and Theodore Roosevelt climaxed at the Republican nominating convention. While Roosevelt spent his time and energy rallying voters in the new primary elections, Taft had used more traditional methods to gain control of the party members who ran the convention. With their backing in hand, Taft had his supporters replace Roosevelt's delegates at the convention, purging Roosevelt's candidacy before it could gain momentum. Roosevelt's supporters, realizing their loss, quickly fled the Republican convention to start their own party. Taft meanwhile was renominated by the Republicans for president, along with his vice president, James Sherman.

JUNE 22, 1912
FIGHT OUT OF ROOSEVELT MEN.

Only Faint Protests as the Taft Vote in the Convention Grows.

Special to The New York Times.

CHICAGO, June 21.—When the Republican National Convention met to-day it was manifest from the outset that the fight was out of it. Throughout the afternoon it ground its way monotonously through the reports of the Committee on Credentials, mechanically voting the Roosevelt men down at every step, without excitement, without interest, and without ginger.

The threats of trouble seemed like things of years ago. All the brave Roosevelt talk about making a big fight on everything that came up had vanished. At first ex-Senator Flinn of Pennsylvania, ex-Gov. Fort of New Jersey, and Francis J. Heney of California made a bluff at keeping it up, but only by demanding a roll call on every proposal, and as the afternoon wore on they ceased to do even this. They gave it up and allowed the Taft delegates to be seated by a viva voce vote. The tumult and the shouting had died, the Captains and the Kings had shed their uniforms and laid down their sceptres.

The formula was the same in every case. Some Taft man on the Credentials Committee would read a report seating the Taft delegates, some Roosevelt man would read a statement in opposition, and move the substitution of the Roosevelt delegates, Watson of Indiana would move to lay that motion on the table, it would be tabled, and the majority report passed. The Roosevelt men accepted their fate in gloomy silence.

Only in the California delegation was there any real protest. There those unterrified irreconcilables, Gov. Hiram Johnson and Francis J. Heney, did their best to stir up trouble every time the name of their State was mentioned, by insisting that the two Taft men from California should not be allowed to vote, but the secretaries drowned them out with megaphones, and even these embattled warriors, after shouting impotently for a few moments, would sit down resignedly and wait for the roll call.

Strategic Move by Taft Men.

The convention was to meet at 11 o'clock, but it was 12:25 before the Credentials Committee was ready to make its first report. It had been decided that, instead of making one comprehensive report, the committee should announce its decisions piecemeal, first reporting on Alabama, then on Arizona, and so down the alphabetical roll, the convention voting on each case as it was announced.

There was a strategical reason for this. If the committee had followed the usual custom and reported on all the cases at once Gov. Hadley would have immediately moved the substitution of a comprehensive roll containing the names of Roosevelt contestants. On that motion none of the seated Taft delegates whose seats were contested could have voted, and the Taft army would have been deprived of 78 votes at one fell swoop. But by presenting the report piecemeal the only Taft men disfranchised on each vote were the men whose seats were involved in that particular case. For instance, all the Taft men from Texas could vote on the Alabama report, and so on along the line, but the Alabama contested delegates could not vote on their own case.

Before the first report of the committee was read there was a dull and apathetic crowd sitting gloomily in its place, not cheered or pleased by the dim efforts of an uncomfortable band to arouse it to enthusiasm. Nobody applauded, nobody seemed to take any interest in the proceedings about to begin. The New Jersey delegation and half of that from Massachusetts tried to start a Roosevelt demonstration, but it was the feeblest thing imaginable, and ended in dismal collapse. They cheered and gave imitation college yells, but hardly anybody responded.

"One thing they can't give," remarked a sour-minded Taft man from Ohio, "is the Electoral College yell."

JUNE 23, 1912
TAFT RENOMINATED BY THE REPUBLICAN CONVENTION; ROOSEVELT NAMED AS CANDIDATE BY BOLTERS; WILSON BACKS BRYAN'S STAND AT BALTIMORE

Roosevelt Delegates Go from the Regular to Rump Convention.

GOV. JOHNSON PRESIDES

Scores the National Committee as Thieves and Promises Them a Lesson.

NEW PARTY ON RUINS OF OLD.

Prendergast Makes the Nominating Speech He Had Prepared for Regular Convention.

COMMANDMENT AS PLATFORM

It Is "Thou Shalt Not Steal" Applied to All the Affairs of Life.

WIFE AND DAUGHTERS THERE

News That Bolting Convention Was to be Held Drew a Great Crowd and the Police Reserves.

Special to The New York Times.

CHICAGO, June 22.—Col. Roosevelt has at last openly broken off all connection with the Republican Party as represented in the National Convention.

He was nominated for President on an independent ticket to-night in the dying hours of the Republican National Convention in which he had met a defeat.

The followers of Col. Roosevelt gathered in Orchestra Hall, less than a mile from the Coliseum, and pledged their support to the former President. In accepting the nomination, Col. Roosevelt appealed to the people of all sections, regardless of party affiliations, to stand with the founders of the new party, one of whose cardinal principles, he said, was to be "Thou Shalt Not Steal."

The informal nomination of Col. Roosevelt was said to be chiefly for the purpose of effecting a temporary organization. Beginning to-morrow, when a call is to be issued for a State convention in Illinois, the work of organization will be pushed forward rapidly, State by State. At a later time, probably early in August, it is intended that a National convention shall be held.

Col. Roosevelt, in accepting the nomination to-night, said he did so on the understanding that he would willingly step aside if it should be the desire of the new party when organized to select another standard bearer.

JUNE 23, 1912
SHERMAN AGAIN CHOSEN RUNNING MATE OF THE PRESIDENT.

VOTE FOR TAFT WAS 561

107 for Roosevelt, but 344 Obeyed Him and Refused to Vote.

DELEGATES COME TO BLOWS

Convention on the Verge of Riots Several Times While the Balloting Was On.

ROOSEVELT SENDS DEFIANCE

Through Allen of Kansas the Colonel Repeats His Cry of Fraud and Theft.

WOMAN LEADS TAFT CHEERS

Widow of Gen. Legan Starts Demonstration as Harding of Ohio Ends Nominating Speech.

CHICAGO, June 22.—Amid scenes of turbulence and disorder, which at times bordered upon a riot, the Republican National Convention wound up its labors late to-night by nominating William Howard Taft of Ohio for President and James Schoolcraft Sherman of New York for Vice President.

President Taft was renominated at 9:28 o'clock by the narrow majority of 21 votes. The total vote cast for him was 561. Vice President Sherman did much better. His vote was announced as 597.

The vote on the Presidential candidates was:

Taft	561
Roosevelt	107
Cummins	17
La Follette	41
Hughes	2
Not voting	344
Absent	6
Total	1,078

President Taft's and Senator La Follette's names were the only ones formally presented to the convention. The votes for the others were cast by delegates who insisted on following their instructions and two who favored Justice Hughes.

While this nomination was made Col. Roosevelt had declared himself a candidate for President and announced the organization of a third party to meet in convention in August. The Grand Old Party is for the moment smashed to pieces.

Before it proceeded to its final business Col. Roosevelt informed the convention through Henry J. Allen of Kansas that his delegates would not vote on any proposition that came before it. The reason given was that robbery and fraud controlled the convention and that it was not a Republican convention and more, but an illegal and unofficial body. These unpalatable things were said to the convention in so many words. It howled and protested, but not for long, and the amazing thing about it was that such statements could be made without evoking more of a fight.

Listen to Bitter Attack.

There has always been a tradition that no matter how bitter your feelings may be against the man who is opposing your candidate you must preserve the fiction of its all being a friendly disagreement, your real antagonism being to the party which is to nominate the opposing candidate. To-day that fiction was entirely disregarded. Taft was renominated in the face of a plain declaration to the convention by some of its own members that it was fraudulent and crooked, and that its ticket would be defeated at the polls.

Any other convention would have roared such a speaker off the platform in a tempest of indignation. This one kept silent during most of these assaults and merely barked sullenly at the worst of them.

By the Colonel's orders the Roosevelt men sat mute during the session and refused to vote on any proposition. His name was not presented to the convention. Both the Colonel and Allen explained that this was because, having exhausted every means of protest and finding that they were the victims of plain, ordinary burglary and highway robbery, they refused any longer to take part in or sanction by their participation the proceedings of such an assemblage.

Allen, speaking for the Colonel, and the Colonel, speaking for himself through a printed statement, read by Allen, declared that this was not a convention at all; that it was made up by the seating of men who had no right to sit in it, and that to countenance such performances by taking part in the deliberations of such a body was impossible. Therefore the Colonel ordered his followers not to vote either on the rules, the platform, the nominations, or anything else that might come before this illegal and piratical body. When Allen said these things, with the announcement that he was saying them for Col. Roosevelt, the crowd in the hall—William J. Bryan being one of them—joined heartily in the applause that the Roosevelt men set up.

Disorder at the End.

This convention will go down in political history as one of the most momentous in the annals of the Republican Party. It will surely be remembered as one of the longest drawn out, for it has been in progress for almost a week. The scenes that attended the closing session tonight will render it conspicuous as one of the most rowdy and disorderly of party gatherings.

THE DEMOCRATIC CONVENTION BEGINS WITH A POWER STRUGGLE

The 1912 Democratic Convention in Baltimore ended an era dominated by William Jennings Bryan, the party's candidate in three of the previous four elections, dating back to 1896. The convention began with Bryan seeking selection as the temporary convention chair, which would have enabled him to dominate the action. He was rebuffed, the position instead going to New Yorker Alton B. Parker, the party's presidential candidate in 1904, the only recent year in which Bryan had sat out. House Democratic leader Champ Clark, who claimed responsibility for deposing Bryan, seemed poised to claim the role of new party spokesman. Clark's main opposition was New Jersey governor Woodrow Wilson, who had competed against Clark in the primaries and had supported Bryan at the convention. The party faced a conflict of wills as it turned to the presidential nomination.

JUNE 26, 1912
CONVENTION BEATS BRYAN, 579 TO 510; PARKER, CHAIRMAN, URGES HARMONY

Nebraskan Fails to Stir the Delegates as of Old.

HIS PARTY GRIP BROKEN

Little Fear Now of a Stampede to Make Him the Candidate.

CLARK MEN ARE JUBILANT

Believe Aid They Gave Murphy Must Be Repaid with the Nomination.

NEW YORK LEADER SILENT

Fears Effect of Hearst Stamp in State Campaign—May Switch at Any Moment.

WILSON MEN UNDISMAYED

Count on Getting Many Clark Deserters After the First Ballot—Gaynor Boom Crows.

DISORDER IN CONVENTION

Police Called in Once—Night Session Held to Hear Parker's Speech.

Special to The New York Times.

BALTIMORE, June 25.—William Jennings Bryan made a personal appeal to the Democratic National Convention at its first session to-day to make him its Temporary Chairman instead of Judge Alton B. Parker of New York, whom he designated as the candidate of the "predatory Wall Street interests." It was the last card that Bryan had to play, and he lost by a vote of 570 to 510.

To-night he and his followers, sobered by the blow, are wondering what they can do next to save the progressive Democratic spirit from being entirely eliminated from the results of the convention.

Bryan made an heroic effort to "come back," but he had not the force to do it, nor did he have an audience that he could reach. The delegates that represented the majority were of the sort that Charles F. Murphy and others call "hand-picked." The spectators were not of the partisan sort, but rather a disinterested crowd, largely composed of women and children, who had obtained their seats through the courtesy of local contributors to the convention fund.

The convention itself was utterly unlike the session of any National Convention in twenty years. It was without snap and ginger, without inspiration, seemingly without a man or a cause to cheer for—just a large assemblage of people watching the business-like operation of the machine which had been organized to put the Peerless Leader out of business so far as the control of the Democratic Party was concerned.

Even with this Bryan might have been able to do something had he been the Bryan who carried the Chicago Convention in 1896 off its feet with his great "Cross of Gold" speech; but he was not that Bryan. He had not a battle cry as he had then with which to arouse the delegates and make them forget the ties that bound them to other leaders, and his declaration that "The Democratic song of triumph should on this eve of possible party victory be sung by one who had been steadfast in the fight for the Progressive spirit" did not ring clear. This speech, which he intended to be a war hymn, had the sad cadence of a swan song, so much so that even those who were rejoicing in Bryan's defeat could not help but sympathize with him.

Bryan Passive, Not a Bolter.

From every indication to-night the vanquished Commoner will remain comparatively passive in the convention from now on, even though, as a delegate at large from Nebraska and a member of the Committee on Resolutions, he must be more than a mere on-looker. He does not harbor any plans for a bolt.

In defeat, the Nebraskan was far from a lonesome figure. The hearty regard in which he is held by the Progressive Democrats was amply testified to by the vote and by the great throng that lavished sympathy on him in his hour of defeat. To all such callers Mr. Bryan showed a smiling, happy face. His friends said that they felt convinced that both the platform and the nominees of the convention would be such that Mr. Bryan could give them his support.

Nor was there the slightest disposition in the camp of those who accomplished Mr. Bryan's downfall, and whom he designated in the convention as the "Wall Street Interests," to gloat over his downfall, or if there was such a disposition it was suppressed. It would have been bad policy, and besides, they were too busy trying to bring about a combination of delegates that would result in the nomination of a ticket to their liking.

In their ears is ringing the cry to-night that Champ Clark will surely win now; but he is not the man they want, and he is not the man they will help to win if they can find a way to beat him. They don't like the Hearst stamp on the Clark candidacy. Murphy, particularly, believes it would hurt him in his New York State fight this Fall.

This disposition of the victors of to-day not to arouse the ire of the vanquished by trampling upon them was shown strongly to-night, when Judge Parker urged the Committee on Resolutions to make Col. Bryan its Chairman, which request will undoubtedly be complied with, but the fact that Bryan would preside over the deliberations of the platform constructors does not mean that he would prevail there, as his friends would be in a minority.

Clark Men Claim Victory.

The question arises of how the various candidates for the Presidential nomination stand in the light of to-day's votes in the convention. The analysis of the vote which elected Parker Temporary Chairman to-day justifies the remark that it was a "cross between the Houn' Dawg and the Tammany Tiger" that produced the result. The question is what the result of such a union can be. The Clark men say that the elimination of Bryan leaves only Clark, but less interested observers say that Tammany has simply "taken the B off Bryan and left Ryan," and that Mr. Clark and some others who are looking to Tammany for support will find it out to their sorrow.

The Clark men claim all the tactical advantage of the Parker victory, saying that it was made possible by their votes, although half the Clark delegates could not be delivered by the managers and voted for Bryan. The Clark men expect to gather in the support of the Murphy-Sullivan-Taggart combination, with the uninstructed delegates from the North and East and those nominally for Gov. Marshall of Indiana and Gov. Baldwin of Connecticut as favorite sons. They say the narrow margin by which Parker won makes it clear that Conservatives must help nominate Clark or Bryan would regain control. They hope to nominate Clark on the first ballot, as they will have trouble in a number of the delegations instructed for Clark after that, such as those from West Virginia and Louisiana, where there is much Wilson sentiment.

Hope in the Other Camps.

The Wilson men say their candidate has lost no ground through the outcome of the Chairmanship contest, that many of the delegates feel that they have done quite enough for the Conservatives, and that the elimination of Bryan as a candidate, which they say has been accomplished, leaves Wilson the only Progressive in the field. The ambiguous position of the Clark forces on both sides of the fence, they say, will lead to a concentration of the Progressive vote on their candidate, which, with the thirty or forty Wilson men who voted for Parker, will give them a majority and lead to their getting the necessary two-thirds.

WOODROW WILSON SECURES THE DEMOCRATIC PRESIDENTIAL NOMINATION

Woodrow Wilson emerged from the 1912 Democratic convention as his party's leader. The convention began with the toppling of William Jennings Bryan as the head of the party, but the emergence of Wilson as his successor could not have been accomplished without Bryan's aid. Wilson supported Bryan in his attempt to remain a power broker, while the leading candidate for the nomination, Champ Clark, opposed him. Facing a loss of power, Bryan threw his considerable support behind Wilson, leading to a long battle over forty-six nomination ballots. Ultimately Wilson prevailed, earning the nomination and reminding the party that Bryan still held considerable influence.

JULY 3, 1912
WOODROW WILSON IS NOMINATED FOR PRESIDENT; GOV. MARSHALL OF INDIANA FOR VICE PRESIDENT

Convention Deadlock Is Broken on Forty-sixth Ballot at 3:30 P. M.

ACTION MADE UNANIMOUS

After 990 Votes Had Been Cast for the New Jersey Governor and 84 for Clark.

ILLINOIS STARTS THE SLIDE

Then Underwood Is Withdrawn as a Candidate and Clark Delegates Are Released.

NEW YORK GETS INTO LINE

No Protest from Bryan When Her Ninety Votes Are Cast For Wilson.

CHEERS BY TIRED DELEGATES

Demonstration in Honor of the Nominee Hearty but Not of Long Duration.

JULY 3, 1912
EDITORIAL
WOODROW WILSON FOR PRESIDENT

In the nomination of WOODROW WILSON the Democratic Party regains its ancient estate of worth, of dignity, of power. It escapes the thralldom of little men and ignoble leaders. It takes as its chief a man of that statesmanlike quality which befits the Presidential office. The nomination of Gov. WILSON will unite the party. There is not a Democrat who can find a sound and sufficient reason for withholding his vote from such a candidate. Search for the taints and blemishes, the imprints of subserviency to the selfish and the predatory, of which we have heard so much, and you will not find one of them upon Gov. WILSON. No bargain or understanding with Mr. MURPHY or with Wall Street, nor with any interest, brought about his nomination. He does not owe his nomination to Mr. BRYAN, nor will he be in the slightest degree under Mr. BRYAN's control or guidance; he is too firm, too self-reliant, some would say too obstinate. When the legions of self-appointed advisers converge upon Trenton during the campaign, or upon Washington after the inauguration, obstinacy will be an ever-present help and a distinguishing virtue. Mr. WILSON is not a radical. The radicals of the Democratic Party assailed him ferociously during the campaign of the primaries. He is a Progressive, and so is in sympathy with the widely prevailing sentiment. He will have the support and the votes of Democrats in the Western and Far Western States. His nomination reduces Mr. ROOSEVELT's bolt to the proportions of a purely Republican quarrel. Gov. WILSON is an educated gentleman, he has been President of a university, his knowledge of the policy of nations and of public affairs has been broadened by diligent study, made exact by historical writing, and ripened by close observation and experience. It is a fortunate nomination, a wise nomination, the best the convention could have made.

No nominating convention in our history has presented a finer example of the triumph of individual convictions over the intrigues and the bargains of the bosses and the obstructive tactics of selfish rivals. That WILSON column in the roll-call table, advancing by measured but irresistible gains, mostly of a few votes on each ballot, with only now and then a trifling loss, quickly regained, starting with 324 on the first ballot and rising above 500 on the 30th, is full of teaching and inspiration for men who are loyal to a principle, a cause, and a man. They won, they were bound to win, by their courage, their determination, and their disinterested devotion to the best interests of the party. They had no leader, they needed none, save that spirited Democracy that was common to them all.

We believe Mr. WILSON's nomination to be in the highest degree fortunate for the country. It invites, we may almost say it commands, the return of prosperity. It bids our half-famished industries take their fill of the vitalizing nourishment of activity. It quickens the sluggish currents of trade and enterprise. It does these beneficent things, first, because in the last three months we have cast out so many devils, and second, because whatever may befall on

election day, a gentleman will be in the White House during the next four years, a man of sanity and balance, a man sincerely desiring the welfare of the American people, a man of sobriety and principle, not a savage or a visionary. It is the ideal condition, with a candidate on either side under whose administration the country would be content.

Not long ago some apprehension was felt lest Gov. WILSON was going quite too far along the Progressive path. We shared that feeling ourselves, and we admonished him that some of his later opinions seemed to be too much at variance with those he had formerly held and expressed. But Gov. WILSON, as we have said, is not a radical, he is a moderate Progressive. "Our Constitutions have time out of mind," he said in an interview published in THE TIMES last Winter, "committed us to representative government, and I have not found any thoughtful man anywhere who wanted to get rid of it. The initiative and the referendum, in his judgment, are not for everyday use. They are remedies by which the people may bring Legislatures not properly representative back under their control. And these are necessarily State questions. In that interview Mr. WILSON was asked, "Do you think that war should be made on the combinations?" He prepared this answer:

I do not think that "war" should be made on anything: our problem is one of equitable readjustment. I do not understand that the policy of our law was ever directed against combinations as such, against their mere size, but only against combinations in restraint of trade. Combination has proved an extremely successful means of economy and efficiency; but restraint of trade is another matter and affects the healthful operation of our whole economic system.

In other words, penalties are for those who violate the law, for those who are guilty of inexcusable wrong. Again, Gov. WILSON said:

The whole country depends upon its business. Where will you draw the line between those who are business men and those who are not, between those whom business affects and those whom it does not affect? No one who cares for the welfare of the country as a whole can overlook or do an intentional disservice to its business men, for they are in a sense all of us. The process of tariff revision (which Gov. WILSON declared to be the main question now before the country) like everything else we have to undertake must be a process of readjustment, not revolutionary, but carried carefully forward upon a definite principle. That principle is a tariff for revenue.

For the country the nomination made at Baltimore will be reassuring. For the Democratic Party it means salvation, it means deliverance out of long bondage to delusion and heresy. That in itself, in this land where party government prevails, will be of immeasurable benefit. Both parties must be sound if they are to serve as a check the one upon the other. The Democratic Party in the nomination of Gov. WILSON is reborn. It will be reorganized, it will become efficient, it will have once more the confidence of the people.

• •

THE DEMOCRATS UNITE BEHIND WILSON

The Republican Party split in two, with William Howard Taft receiving his party's nomination and Theodore Roosevelt launching the Progressive Party to continue his candidacy. Meanwhile, the Democrats ran an innovative campaign that united their party, as directed by Woodrow Wilson. Rather than rely upon large business donations or wealthy sponsors, Wilson funded his campaign through numerous small donations, allowing the governor to present himself as free from corruption and independent of wealthy interests. Wilson also took advantage of the hostile campaigns run by Roosevelt and Taft and declared his own campaign to be clean and free of negative attacks. Although the Democrats did engage in negative campaigning, they successfully insulated Wilson from responsibility. Instead, William Jennings Bryan shadowed Roosevelt throughout the country making attacks of his own, freeing Wilson of the distasteful work.

JULY 14, 1912
WILSON FOR CLEAN CAMPAIGN.

He Will Abstain from Personal Attacks on His Rivals, He Declares.

WASHINGTON, July 13.—Gov. Woodrow Wilson intends to make his campaign for the Presidency entirely without attacks on the other candidates, and he will direct personally every detail of the fight. His rule against personal attacks he expects also to enforce on his campaign managers.

Gov. Wilson made these points in the course of a conference with Representative Charles Bennet Smith of Buffalo, who returned to Washington yesterday, after having seen Gov. Wilson.

"I had gone to see Gov. Wilson," said Mr. Smith to-day, "to bring to his attention the need of a well-managed publicity bureau for the campaign. I have gone through four Presidential campaigns as a newspaper man, and I have been impressed with the lack of efficiency which the publicity bureaus evidence. Instead of clearly setting forth the merits of the platform and candidates, the publicity bureaus have seemed to expend their efforts in attacking the opposition forces. The copy put out has never been such as would appeal to a practical newspaper man.

"He assured me that he would at once take up the matter of organizing a press bureau. The choice of Samuel F. McCombs as National Chairman means that Gov. Wilson will listen to everybody, consult with many, and then arrive as his own conclusions as to what is best.

"Though he did not commit himself directly on this point, I gathered from the general trend of his conversation that he would prefer not to make a speech-making tour, preferring to confine himself to published statements. Should he finally decide to make campaign speeches, they will be limited in number."

Woodrow Wilson campaigns for the presidency in Union Square, New York City, on September 9, 1912.

Source: The Granger Collection, New York

JULY 25, 1912
BRYAN, HEAD HUNTER OF THE BULL MOOSE

His Campaign Job Will Be to Follow the Colonel's Trail Into Every Debatable State.

HE'S INVITED TO SEA GIRT

The Only Political Visitor Asked to Spend a Night or Two—Wilson Plans Few Speeches.

Special to The New York Times.

SEA GIRT, N. J., July 24.—The Question as to what is to become of William Jennings Bryan in the Democratic National campaign was seemingly answered here to-day when close political advisers of Gov. Wilson let it be known that Col. Bryan's assignment would be to worry and harass the Bull Moose candidate and to follow him into every debatable state.

The assignment of Bryan to take care of Col. Roosevelt is regarded here as one in which the Nebraskan will take great joy. It is known that Bryan has regarded Roosevelt as a trespasser upon Democratic preserves, and the Wilson forces expect him to make a brave showing as a defender of his party's right to carry out in office the things which Bryan advocated long before Col. Roosevelt decided that he, too, would take them up.

OCTOBER 27, 1912
EDITORIAL
THE FUNDS FOR WILSON.

The campaign managers of Gov. WILSON are to be congratulated if they did not need to depend upon the contributions of a few individuals in gathering the $678,364 of the Democratic campaign fund. This is $158,000 less than was spent by the backers of Mr. ROOSEVELT in his contest for the Republican nomination for the Presidency, money contributed by a few interested individuals. WOODROW WILSON's campaign fund has been raised by 53,303 subscribers, of whom

52,246 contributed under $100. The amounts over $100 were contributed by 1,057 persons, none of whom gave corporation money, and the largest single contribution in the list was that of $13,000, given by Justice GERARD. Mr. MUNSEY and Mr. PERKINS are bearing between them one-third the expenses of the Bull Moose campaign. Unless there has been evasion of the law, and his opponents do not make this accusation, Gov. WILSON's fund is more broadly, more democratically, based.

It is an encouraging showing. It means that Mr. WILSON has inspired confidence in his party and among the independent voters. But the most encouraging symptom of better campaign morality is that the total expenditures and obligations to date, including the amounts incurred before the conventions, are for all parties $2,637,303, but $357,000 more than the Roosevelt fund of 1904.

ROOSEVELT SUPPORTERS FOUND THE PROGRESSIVE PARTY AND NOMINATE THEIR CANDIDATE

The Republicans who fled the Chicago convention with Theodore Roosevelt quickly reassembled under a new party label, Progressives. The Progressive Party blended several elements of the Republican, Democratic, and other third parties, but were particularly characterized by their devotion to reforming government and to their deep religious fervor. The Progressives viewed the campaign as more than an electoral contest. It was instead a battle between the forces of good and evil, the two traditional parties representing the evil of entrenched power and the Progressives representing the virtuous working class.

AUGUST 6, 1912
HAIL NEW PARTY IN FERVENT SONG

"Battle Hymn of the Republic" Sways 1,000 Delegates to the Roosevelt Convention.

NO LEVITY, LITTLE CHEERING

Beveridge, in Opening Speech, Skillfully Plays on Fanaticism of His Audience.

JOHNSON ON THE TICKET

Slated to Run with Roosevelt—Negro Issue Still a Disturbing Factor.

Special to The New York Times.

CHICAGO, Ill., Aug. 5.—About one thousand serious, earnest, almost fanatical men and women met in the Coliseum today at noon to create a new party. Every one of them believed that he or she was a crusader. There was no levity, and there was a solemn gravity that was striking and impressive.

To-day's work was all preliminary. Tomorrow Col. Roosevelt will make his declaration of faith. On Wednesday a platform will be adopted and Col. Roosevelt will be nominated for President. Gov. Johnson of California will probably be named for Vice President.

Let no one mistake the Progressive Party. Theodore Roosevelt may or may not be bitten by personal ambition, but the men who are following him believe sincerely that they are followers of the Lord enlisted for the battle of Armageddon. They may be absolutely wrong about it, but about the strength of their conviction there cannot remain a doubt in the mind of anybody who saw the strange, moving, and compelling spectacle in the Coliseum to-day.

It was not a convention at all. It was an assemblage of religious enthusiasts. It was such a convention as Peter the Hermit held. It was a Methodist camp meeting done over into political terms. From Jane Addams of Hull House fame, sitting in the first rank below the platform, to Judge Ben Lindsey of Denver, sitting half way down the hall, there was an expression on every face of fanatical and religious enthusiasm. Perhaps such men as William Flinn of Pennsylvania may have had a more worldly expression on their faces, but they were lost in the crowd of visionaries who listened to their Chairman, ex-Senator Beveridge, and believed—obviously and certainly believed—that they were enlisted in a contest with the Powers of Darkness.

Mr. Beveridge's speech was a great one in its appeal to the kind of sentiment that he knew to be prevalent in the convention. It was the best speech he ever delivered in his life. He knew the Lutheran and Garrisonian strain in his audience, and he skillfully bent his speech to that element. He is a phrasemaker equal to Col. Ingersoll. He has developed tremendously in the last few years. The sophomoric element has disappeared, and he is as polished and complete an orator as Martin Littleton.

Women Eager and Earnest.

The men and women before him listened with rapt faces. Some of them had their jaws set, and seemed to be biting their lips. Here and there men were seen wiping tears from their eyes. There was little cheering; the men and women were too earnest for it. They sat there, bent forward in their places, many of them with their hands to their ears, anxious to catch every word. When they did cheer it was always for some sentiment in which Beveridge expressed the aspiration of the new party for a better day for humanity. To his talk about details they remained callous.

The women were vastly in evidence. Most of them were old or middle-aged; the gay, half-serious, and brightly dressed crowd that represents woman suffrage in New York was largely absent. Every woman there was one whose name compelled respect. Miss Addams sat in the first row, and for an hour before the convention came to order she held a regular levee. There was not a moment when a procession was not passing in front of her, partly of women and partly of men. Everybody who came stopped to speak to her, and usually lingered for many minutes. Every one who stopped spoke to her with an earnest face and manner. Miss Addams herself acted like a religious devotee. Once, when Mr. Beveridge committed the new party to woman suffrage she smiled and her eyes flashed. But mostly she sat with the same intent and almost reverent look on her face that the shouting Methodists and Presbyterians behind her wore.

The band played such airs as "My Country 'Tis of Thee" and "The Battle Hymn of the Republic," Julia Ward Howe's famous hymn, and when the men and women delegates got up and joined in such songs they did it almost with frenzy. Everybody there, except possibly such calculating and sedate persons as William Flinn, unmistakably regarded himself as a soldier of the Lord.

THE REPUBLICANS AND DEMOCRATS UNITE IN OPPOSITION TO ROOSEVELT

Former president Theodore Roosevelt officially ran as the nominee of the Progressive Party in 1912, a party formed in order to depose Republican incumbent William Howard Taft. For vice president the party selected the highly regarded California governor, Hiram Johnson. The combination of Roosevelt and Johnson pleased Progressives, but gave Republicans and Democrats alike reasons to despise the ticket. Republicans remained furious about Roosevelt's bolt from the party, and Democrats opposed his extreme progressivism. The Progressive Party, despite having wide popular support, was dismissed by many as a party with only one purpose and one program, the glorification of Theodore Roosevelt.

AUGUST 8, 1912
EDITORIAL
ROOSEVELT AND JOHNSON.

It is of happy augury for the Republican Party that it has got THEODORE ROOSEVELT out of its system, that he has gone off and had himself nominated for the Presidency by a new party. The process by which he has divulged himself has been rude and savagely painful. The old party has lost much blood and tissue, but also floods of peccant humors. It will live and be the better for this purification.

Let the Republicans think on their mercies. Sixteen years ago WILLIAM J. BRYAN fell upon the Democratic Party, even as Mr. ROOSEVELT fell upon the Republicans at Chicago. The difference is that he succeeded, while the Colonel was beaten back. BRYAN seized the Democratic banner and smeared it all over with the strange symbols of his crazy creed. He captured the party, he fastened himself upon it, and he has stuck to it ever since, poisoning its counsels, misguiding its impulses, well-nigh plaguing the life out of it. Is it not better, a thousand times better for the Republicans, that, unlike the Democrats, they can fight Mr. ROOSEVELT outside, instead of inside?

Long ago it could have been foretold what manner of convention would nominate Mr. ROOSEVELT for the Presidency. Good men and women, intelligent men and women, but emotional men and women, whose emotions have got the better of their intelligence, listened in that hall to his long address, greeted him and the speeches nominating him with rapturous applause. They nominated him because they only half understand him. They were captivated and thrown altogether off their guard by his appeals in behalf of common humanity, by his pleas for justice, by the thousand things he said at Chicago and has said elsewhere which no man not a cynic or a criminal would dispute. Convinced by the common moralities of his multitudinous discourses and by the many really sound and salutary things he has uttered, that he is a good man, a perfectly righteous man, they have not taken the trouble to analyze his remedies or to picture forth the consequences of what he proposes to do. In their view it all makes for righteousness and justice.

They do not see that his remedial projects are the denial of human wisdom and human experience, that most of them have been repeatedly tried but have failed, and have been rejected. They do not see that his system is at war with all that is best and sound and preservative in our existing system of Government. He preaches contempt for law, defiance of law, Government without law, and they have an ecstatic vision of higher and purer laws. He would set up despotism and tyranny, the unlimited despotism of the majority which is more dangerous than the despotism of one monarch, and they call it

emancipation. He writes whole pages of socialistic doctrine into his address and into the platform, and some of those who sat in his convention did understand, they understand it perfectly. They are Socialists, and they welcome and applaud him as a new and great leader in the Socialist advance. His followers and his worshippers are quite without perception of the moral defects and delinquencies of the dangerous temperamental aberrations of THEODORE ROOSEVELT.

But he and his Progressive Party must be considered seriously. There could be no greater blunder than to dismiss them contemptuously as cranks. They are enthusiasts, many of them are fanatics, most of them are dreamers, a few only are self-seeking and insincere. Above all, they are numerous. Mr. ROOSEVELT may win the electoral vote in a few States. He will be defeated, but that will hardly make an end of him or of his party. It is not improbable that after his defeat Mr. ROOSEVELT will again appear in the political field as an avowed Socialist, as the leader of the Socialist Party in the United States. He has no particular bridges to burn, he has no great advance to make to put him in that position. The return of general prosperity in the country would baffle any plots against the welfare of the people that his fertile mind may contrive, it would upset the plans and check the growth of Socialism. The best way to deal with Mr. ROOSEVELT and his misguided followers is to invite and promote a revival of industrial prosperity.

The platform of the Progressive Convention is pretty stale matter. Its authors under a sense of prodigious solemnity wrote a thousand undisputed things. But why have a platform? If these books of the Alexandrian Library, said OMAR, agree with the Koran, they are superfluous; if they disagree they are heretical and must be burned. Mr. ROOSEVELT is the platform, his innumerable speeches and writings are the platform. The formal resolutions cannot disagree with him, he would not have it. He is the whole campaign of Socialism, but in Gov. JOHNSON of California the convention has given him a fitting associate. Of all the seven Governors, JOHNSON was the wildest. His State has gone further than any other in Progressive adventure. Mr. ROOSEVELT knows what it all means, JOHNSON has no idea what it means, but that makes him a more convenient and manageable running mate.

TAFT RUNS A RESTRAINED REELECTION CAMPAIGN

President William Howard Taft ran a less active campaign than his rivals, relying instead upon his record in office and his stated political stances. He made few rebuttals to Theodore Roosevelt's attacks upon him, yet he believed that simply preventing Roosevelt from reentering the White House was nearly as critical as winning reelection for himself. The bitter divide between these former allies ruptured the Republican Party and ultimately assured a Democratic victory in November.

AUGUST 13, 1912
TAFT TELLS HIS CAMPAIGN VIEWS

Interview with a New York Times Correspondent on the Issues to Be Met.

WHAT HE WILL NOT DO

"Turn Tricks" for Headlines or Make Himself "Part of the Menagerie."

THAT IS DUE TO HIS OFFICE

But He Believes His Record Good and Stands on It—Defends His Tariff Course and the Administration He Has Given.

Special to The New York Times.

WASHINGTON, D. C., Aug. 12.—"I have been told that I ought to do this, ought to do that, ought to do the other; that I ought to say this, ought to say that, ought to say the other; that I do not keep myself in the headlines, that there is this or that trick I might turn to my advantage. I know it, but I can't do it. I couldn't if I would and I wouldn't if I could."

When Mr. Taft was advised to-day that his political interests would be advanced if he would only adopt the tactics of his Bull Moose friend, this or something like it is what he said, and said it with an emphasis which left no doubt of his conviction that something is due to himself and to the office he holds. He is not willing to make himself a part of the menageries.

He was overpersuaded to enter the recent ante-primary campaign. He did not fancy that sort of politics. He stands on the record of his Administration, and is willing to be judged by it, by its promise and performance, by the facts that are readily available to all anxious inquirers, but not by the misrepresentations of those who would encompass his political destruction in order that they might gain some selfish advantage, or pay off some vengeful score.

One of the most proper of his critics who takes no pleasure, usually, in brutal or frivolous speech, protests that the President does not imitate the example of the former President and invent phrases that will stick in the common fancy and serve as rallying cries; that he does not take his stand at Armageddon to battle for the Lord; but this is a gift the President does not possess in a marked degree, and it is not a gift which has been commended in Mr. Roosevelt by those who would condemn Mr. Taft. They have said that it is cheap and vulgar, the style of the clown, the form of the faker, the adventitious speech of the barker in midway shows rather than the speech of the serious-minded statesman respectful of his service.

Says Things and Proves Them.

Yet Mr. Taft has been known to say things about his antagonists sufficiently virile to satisfy the taste of those who affect a certain fancy for invective. For example, in his speech of acceptance he gives the people credit for the ability "to see through the fog of misrepresentation and demagogy" in which Mr. Roosevelt has endeavored to envelop them so that he might work out his plans for personal aggrandizement. He speaks of "the radical propositions of change in our form of government that are recklessly advanced to satisfy what is supposed to be popular clamor." He hopes that "the great majority of voters will be able to distinguish between the substance of performance and the fustian of promise." He declares that "the people" are not alone the unfortunate and the weak, but that they are "the weak and the strong, the poor and the rich, and the many who are neither, the wage earner and the capitalist, the farmer and the professional man, the railroad manager and the manufacturer, the storekeeper and the clerk—they all make up the people, and they have not any of them given into the hands of any one the mandate to speak for them as peculiarly the people's representative." He takes courage in "the clarifying effect of a campaign of education" and "the pricking of the bubbles of demagogic promise" and the "rejection of the injurious nostrums" upon which Mr. Roosevelt relies for the success of his assault upon the established order.

Mr. Taft does not indulge in epithets, he has called nobody liar or thief. He prefers the more decent and altogether better way of proving it. This is what he did on more than one occasion during the recent primary campaign, when over against the clamor of the clown he set out the facts so clearly that the wayfaring man, though a so-called insurgent or Progressive, could not mistake his meaning or be deceived by the "fustian" of the common enemy—the same being Mr. Roosevelt and so aptly described, as he is as much the foe of the Democratic as of the Republican Party.

The Spirit of His Fight.

The true temper of Mr. Taft's spirit in the fight he has been making and will continue to wage until the end in November was never more clearly described than by himself. Speaking to one of his friends while the Republican Convention was in session at Chicago, and at the very moment when the news came by wire that the danger of Mr. Roosevelt's nomination had passed, he exclaimed:

"It does not matter much what may become of me and my political fortunes. If I shall succeed in doing nothing more than to defeat Mr. Roosevelt in this convention, I shall think that I have done the people of this country a great service."

This service will not have been completely performed, however, until he shall have defeated Mr. Roosevelt's election in November, and to this work he will devote, within proper bounds, and always with respect to his office, his best talents. In his opinion, the high-water mark of the Bull Moose movement was reached at Chicago. Hereafter it will grow small by degrees and beautifully less. It did not approach the dignity of tragedy; it was only melodrama of the ten, twent,' thirt' order, and what is to follow will be anti-climax.

Thoughtful people are beginning all over the country to ask what it was all about, and it is on the sober second thought of the people that Mr. Taft is relying for a practically united party and his success at the election in November. The worst he fears—and that would be rather good than bad—is the election of Woodrow Wilson. He does not think for a moment that Mr. Roosevelt stands the ghost of a chance to run himself in again. He still thinks that Roosevelt did not at first have any idea of being a candidate for President, although he has almost reached the point of believing that Roosevelt desired his defeat in order that he might come back four years hence, with the claim that he only could restore the Republican Party to power. Roosevelt cannot do this now since he has cut loose from the Republican Party, and will not be eligible as a Republican candidate in 1916, whatever the result of the present contest.

· ·

ROOSEVELT POSITIONS HIMSELF AS THE CHALLENGER TO WILSON

Theodore Roosevelt viewed the 1912 election as a two-way race between himself and Democrat Woodrow Wilson, discounting the possibility of a victory by President Taft, the Republican incumbent. Roosevelt spared little in his campaigning, conducting a nonstop whirlwind tour throughout the United States. He typically delivered several speeches every day, attacking the policies of Wilson and dismissing Taft's viability. His direct and abrasive political style resonated with those dissatisfied with the political system, but also contrasted sharply with the more traditional, reserved campaign styles of his opponents.

AUGUST 19, 1912
ROOSEVELT DECIDES TAFT ISN'T A FACTOR

A Two-Sided Fight, He Says Now, and He'll Drop the President to Attack Wilson.

BACK HOME MORE CONFIDENT

Big Meetings in Boston and Providence Satisfied Him Things Were Going as in His Primary Fight.

Special to The New York Times.

OYSTER BAY, N.Y., Aug. 18.—Col. Roosevelt returned to Sagamore Hill today more confident than he has been at any time since he bolted the National Republican Convention and started his third-party movement. The big receptions he received in Providence and Boston on his first New England campaign, and the reports that have been coming in from his managers all over the country have led him to believe that the fight may not be a hopeless one after all. He believes President Taft is not going to be a factor in the race.

"It is a two-sided fight," he said today, "not a three-cornered one."

As a result of this decision Col. Roosevelt let it be known that he has about decided to drop President Taft from any further serious consideration, and devote most of his time and energy to attacking the Democrats and their platform. He believes that Gov. Johnson of California, his running mate, is a "bigger" man than either President Taft or Gov. Wilson and is anxiously waiting to see the impression that Gov. Johnson will make in his Eastern campaigns. Gov. Johnson, the Progressives declare, has accomplished much more along progressive lines in California than has Gov. Wilson in New Jersey.

Col. Roosevelt is refraining from direct personal attack upon Gov. Wilson, but it is evident that he is only too anxious to have the Jersey Governor start to "mix things up." That will be the signal for the Colonel to let loose, and if the occasion arises he promises a lively time of it for all concerned.

The Colonel made reference to-day to the address delivered by Gov. Wilson at Sea Girt Saturday.

"We are not saying that we are like the Democrats," he said, "but the Democrats are saying that they are like the Progressives. There could have been no better endorsement of the Progressive Party than that given by Dr. Wilson yesterday. He said that it is the feeling that men have gone into blind alleys and come back often enough, and that they propose to find an open road for themselves.

"He said what was perfectly true, and it is for just that purpose, to lead people out of blind alleys, that the Progressive Party has been formed. And we have led the way in this movement."

The big meetings in Providence and Boston, and especially the mass meeting on the Boston Common last night, which was attended by fully 20,000 people, the Colonel said, had surprised him and given a tremendous impetus to the Progressive movement.

"They were all listening intently," said the Colonel, "and there was sincere purpose in their faces. In my primary fight we reached the people. There were great crowds, and they came out afterward and voted.

"And we won.

"I was glad to answer, last night, the questions about Mr. Perkins and tell about Mr. Flinn. I understand that some one asked about McCormick, too. I did not hear that question, but I am glad to answer it now.

"I suppose they meant to refer to the Harvester Company when they mentioned McCormick. My answer is that the McCormicks who are with me have not a dollar's interest in the International Harvester Company, and that the McCormicks who are interested in the company are, I understand, helping Taft or Gov. Wilson, as they properly should do."

Col. Roosevelt will remain at Oyster Bay until Wednesday evening, when he will go to Wilkesbarre to attend the golden jubilee of Father Curran, who entertained him two years ago when he visited the anthracite coal mining district. He will have no prepared address, but will talk on the subject of moralities and good citizenship.

After his Western trip, which ends at Memphis about Aug. 25, Col. Roosevelt will spend a week touring in the South, and will visit New Orleans, Atlanta, Ga., and other Southern cities.

ROOSEVELT SURVIVES AN ASSASSINATION ATTEMPT

On October 15, 1912, a deranged citizen attempted to assassinate Theodore Roosevelt in Milwaukee, Wisconsin, viewing the former president's candidacy as a violation of the two-term limitation for presidents, a tradition set by George Washington. The attacker fired a single shot at the candidate from only a few feet away, hitting Roosevelt in the chest. Despite the shot, Roosevelt protected his assailant from the enraged crowd and failed to notice his own wound for several minutes. The bullet had penetrated his jacket, but was slowed by the thick speech manuscript he had in his pocket. Rather than receive medical attention, Roosevelt insisted upon delivering his speech and only reluctantly went to the hospital an hour later. The incident became enshrined as an example of Roosevelt's larger-than-life personality.

OCTOBER 15, 1912
MANIAC IN MILWAUKEE SHOOTS COL. ROOSEVELT; HE IGNORES WOUND, SPEAKS AN HOUR, GOES TO HOSPITAL

Bullet in Right Breast, Doctors Say Wound Is Not Serious.

LUNG NOT PENETRATED

Roosevelt Walks from Hospital Unassisted, and Starts for Chicago.

MANUSCRIPT WAS A SHIELD

Assassin's Aim Good, but Papers in the Colonel's Pockets Save Him.

CALM ON OPERATING TABLE

Talks Politics with Physicians While Waiting for X-Ray Machine.

COLONEL CHECKS CROWD

"Don't Touch Him," He Says, as Rush is Made for His Assailant—Secretary Martin Fells Maniac.

Special to The New York Times.

MILWAUKEE, October 14.—Col. Theodore Roosevelt was shot and wounded in the right breast in front of the Hotel Gilpatrick shortly before 8 o'clock to-night. Col. Roosevelt was about to enter his automobile to go to the Auditorium for his evening address, when a man rushed up and fired at close range.

The bullet entered the flesh under the right nipple, but its force was broken by the manuscript of the speech which Col. Roosevelt had prepared for this evening. He at first declared he had not been wounded, but on the way to the hall a hole was noticed in his overcoat and it was found that his shirt was covered with blood. Nevertheless he insisted on delivering his speech, and went on, for fifty minutes, even though his weakness became so apparent that physicians insisted that he should stop.

Talked Politics at Hospital.

After his speech he was taken to the Emergency Hospital to have his wound examined.

At 10:30 o'clock Col. Roosevelt was sitting on the operating table talking politics with the physicians while they were awaiting the arrival of an X-ray machine.

Col. Roosevelt left the hospital at 11:25 P.M. He was able to walk unassisted.

"I am feeling fine," he said.

Surgeons Say Wound Is Slight.

Col. Roosevelt left at 12:50 A.M. for Chicago. Before he left surgeons who had attended him gave out the following statement:

"Col. Roosevelt is suffering from a superficial flesh wound in the right breast. There is no evidence of injury to the lungs. The bullet is probably somewhere in the chest wall. There is only one wound and no sign of injury to the lung. The bleeding is insignificant. The wound has been sterilized externally with gauze by Dr. R. T. Fayle, the consulting surgeon of the Emergency Hospital. The bullet passed through Col. Roosevelt's army overcoat and other clothing and through a manuscript and spectacle case in his breast pocket, and its force was nearly spent before it penetrated the chest. The appearance of the wound also showed evidence of a much-spent bullet.

"Col. Roosevelt is not suffering from the shock and is in no pain. His condition is so good that surgeons did not object to his continuing his journey to Chicago in his private car. In Chicago he will be placed under surgical care.

. . . .

VICE PRESIDENT SHERMAN DIES

On October 30, 1912, just six days before the election, Vice President James S. Sherman died of kidney failure. Sherman had been ill but was renominated in 1912 at the insistence of the Republican Party. Disregarding his doctors' advice, Sherman had delivered a long acceptance speech to the convention, sapping what remained of his strength. He struggled to recover for nearly three months, but ultimately succumbed.

OCTOBER 31, 1912
SHERMAN IS DEAD, HURT BY SPEECH

Vice President Broke Down After Insisting on Long Address on Notification Day.

WANAMAKER MAY BE NAMED

Republican Leaders, However, Doubt if They Can Fill Vacancy on the Republican Ticket

TAFT EXPRESSES HIS SORROW

Hears News While at Navy Yard Dinner—Roosevelt Told as He Leaves Madison Square Garden.

Special to The New York Times.

UTICA, Oct. 30.—The long illness of James Schoolcraft Sherman, Vice President of the United States, ended tonight at 9:12 o'clock, when he succumbed to uraemic poison, caused by Bright's disease. He had been sinking since early morning, and it was realized that death was a question of only a few hours. There was slight relief shortly after 7 o'clock, caused by an apparent improvement in the condition of the kidneys, but at best it gave only temporary hope. At 9 o'clock his temperature rose to 106. From that time his condition rapidly passed from bad to worse until the end. He was unconscious when the end came.

Mr. Sherman's sick room in the last twenty-four hours was without incident of an unusually distressing nature, for he slept most of the time, apparently without pain, growing gradually weaker. At 11 o'clock yesterday morning came the final warning. His physicians then lost hope. It was what Dr. Peck, his family physician, had feared for the last four years. Members of his family were told they must prepare for the worst, and that his death was only a matter of a day or two. His brother, Richard W. Sherman, engineer of the Conservation Commission, was summoned from Albany, and his three sons, Richard U., Sherrill and Thomas M. Sherman, and his youngest brother, Sanford E. Sherman, of this city, assembled at his bedside with Mrs. Sherman, to await the end.

In the campaign of 1904 Mr. Sherman had the first symptoms of kidney trouble. Since then he adhered to a careful diet, and had been warned time and again that he should give up a great part of his work and devote himself to rest and outdoor life. It was known that he did not desire the nomination on the Presidential ticket this year, but the leaders in the party pressed him to run again, declaring that his name would greatly strengthen the ticket, especially among those who were the firmest friends of protection. Mr. Sherman consented with reluctance.

When overwrought beyond his strength by the long session of Congress and tied to his place the Senate, by the failure of that body to choose a President pro tem., he returned here in June a very sick man. He had always found new vigor in the mountains, and he went to Big Moose intending to remain two or three weeks. But he experienced a distressing weakness of the heart on the second day, and it was with difficulty that he was brought from the woods to his home. He recuperated somewhat, and was progressing favorably until the day of his notification on Aug. 21. The extraordinary demands upon his strength on that occasion was the final blow, and from this he did not rally.

Breakdown Since Notification.

Mr. Sherman's rapid decline in health dated from then, according to Dr. Peck. He was warned that the exertion incident to the ceremonies might have an ill effect, but insisted that the programme as arranged be carried out.

"You may know all about medicine," Mr. Sherman told his physician when he urged him to arrange for a brief and informal notification, "but you don't know about politics."

"It was against my advice," said Dr. Peck to-night, "that Mr. Sherman participated in the formalities of the notification ceremonies. I suggested that it would be better for him to receive the committee in the parlor of his home, tell them briefly that while he did not want a renomination he would accept in a spirit of loyalty and let that suffice. When it became apparent that he would not yield to my suggestions, I urged him to make a speech of not more than five minutes. Instead, he spoke for more than half an hour. Two days later the exertions of notification day began to tell on the patient, and he began to fail."

Dr. Peck said the Vice President apparently had not worried over the outcome of the campaign. "His peace of mind has been more disturbed over his illness, as several of his relatives had died from the same disease," continued the physician.

When his name was being considered as a candidate for the Vice Presidency by the Republican National Convention, Mr. Sherman consulted Dr. Peck as to whether he had better accept because of his physical condition, but the doctor told him he did not care to advise him upon so grave a question.

Stages of His Illness.

With the exception of a statement of his position which he issued a few days ago, Vice President Sherman has taken no active part in the Fall campaign.

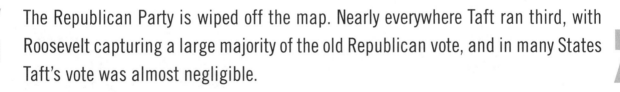

> The Republican Party is wiped off the map. Nearly everywhere Taft ran third, with Roosevelt capturing a large majority of the old Republican vote, and in many States Taft's vote was almost negligible.

WOODROW WILSON WINS THE ELECTION OF 1912

On November 5, 1912, the nation overwhelmingly elected Woodrow Wilson as the twenty-eighth president of the United States. Although he won a minority of the popular vote because he faced three other candidates—Eugene Debs, Theodore Roosevelt, and William Howard Taft—Wilson's victory in the Electoral College was one of the largest in American history. The Democratic Party had clearly seized political power, and the survival of Taft's Republican Party seemed in doubt after Roosevelt's Progressive Party received more popular and electoral votes than the Republicans. President Wilson had an eventful first term in office, emphasizing domestic policy and initially keeping the United States out of the Great War in Europe. In 1916 Wilson narrowly won reelection over a resurgent Republican Party, the Progressive Party having dissolved when Roosevelt refused its nomination for 1916. Involving the United States in World War I during his second term Wilson redefined the office of the president, but it was his first election that stands out as one of the most important of modern history.

1912 POPULAR VOTE

STATE	TOTAL VOTE	WOODROW WILSON (DEMOCRAT) VOTES	%	THEODORE ROOSEVELT (PROGRESSIVE) VOTES	%	WILLIAM H. TAFT (REPUBLICAN) VOTES	%	EUGENE V. DEBS (SOCIALIST) VOTES	%
Alabama	117,959	82,438	69.9	22,680	19.2	9,807	8.3	3,029	2.6
Arizona	23,687	10,324	43.6	6,949	29.3	2,986	12.6	3,163	13.4
Arkansas	125,104	68,814	55.0	21,644	17.3	25,585	20.5	8,153	6.5
California	677,877	283,436	41.8	283,610	41.8	3,847	0.6	79,201	11.7
Colorado	265,954	113,912	42.8	71,752	27.0	58,386	22.0	16,366	6.2
Connecticut	190,404	74,561	39.2	34,129	17.9	68,324	35.9	10,056	5.3
Delaware	48,690	22,631	46.5	8,886	18.3	15,997	32.9	556	1.1
Florida[1]	51,911	36,417	70.2	4,555	8.8	4,279	8.2	4,806	9.3
Georgia	121,470	93,087	76.6	21,985	18.1	5,191	4.3	1,058	0.9
Idaho	105,754	33,921	32.1	25,527	24.1	32,810	31.0	11,960	11.3
Illinois	1,146,173	405,048	35.3	386,478	33.7	253,593	22.1	81,278	7.1
Indiana	654,474	281,890	43.1	162,007	24.8	151,267	23.1	36,931	5.6
Iowa	492,353	185,322	37.6	161,819	32.9	119,805	24.3	16,967	3.4
Kansas	365,560	143,663	39.3	120,210	32.9	74,845	20.5	26,779	7.3
Kentucky[2]	453,707	219,585	48.4	102,766	22.7	115,520	25.5	11,647	2.6
Louisiana	79,248	60,871	76.8	9,283	11.7	3,833	4.8	5,261	6.6
Maine	129,641	51,113	39.4	48,495	37.4	26,545	20.5	2,541	2.0
Maryland	231,981	112,674	48.6	57,789	24.9	54,956	23.7	3,996	1.7
Massachusetts	488,056	173,408	35.5	142,228	29.1	155,948	32.0	12,616	2.6
Michigan	547,971	150,201	27.4	213,243	38.9	151,434	27.6	23,060	4.2
Minnesota	334,219	106,426	31.8	125,856	37.7	64,334	19.2	27,505	8.2
Mississippi	64,483	57,324	88.9	3,549	5.5	1,560	2.4	2,050	3.2
Missouri	698,566	330,746	47.3	124,375	17.8	207,821	29.7	28,466	4.1
Montana	80,256	28,129	35.0	22,709	28.3	18,575	23.1	10,811	13.5
Nebraska	249,483	109,008	43.7	72,681	29.1	54,226	21.7	10,185	4.1
Nevada	20,115	7,986	39.7	5,620	27.9	3,196	15.9	3,313	16.5
New Hampshire	87,961	34,724	39.5	17,794	20.2	32,927	37.4	1,981	2.3
New Jersey	433,663	178,638	41.2	145,679	33.6	89,066	20.5	15,948	3.7
New Mexico	48,807	20,437	41.9	8,347	17.1	17,164	35.2	2,859	5.9
New York	1,588,315	655,573	41.3	390,093	24.6	455,487	28.7	63,434	4.0
North Carolina	243,776	144,407	59.2	69,135	28.4	29,129	11.9	987	0.4
North Dakota	86,474	29,549	34.2	25,726	29.7	22,990	26.6	6,966	8.1
Ohio	1,037,114	424,834	41.0	229,807	22.2	278,168	26.8	90,164	8.7
Oklahoma	253,694	119,143	47.0	—	0.0	90,726	35.8	41,630	16.4
Oregon	137,040	47,064	34.3	37,600	27.4	34,673	25.3	13,343	9.7
Pennsylvania	1,217,736	395,637	32.5	444,894	36.5	273,360	22.4	83,614	6.9
Rhode Island	77,894	30,412	39.0	16,878	21.7	27,703	35.6	2,049	2.6
South Carolina	50,403	48,355	95.9	1,293	2.6	536	1.1	164	0.3
South Dakota	116,327	48,942	42.1	58,811	50.6	—	0.0	4,664	4.0
Tennessee	251,933	133,021	52.8	54,041	21.5	60,475	24.0	3,564	1.4
Texas	300,961	218,921	72.7	26,715	8.9	28,310	9.4	24,884	8.3
Utah	112,272	36,576	32.6	24,174	21.5	42,013	37.4	8,999	8.0
Vermont	62,804	15,350	24.4	22,129	35.2	23,303	37.1	928	1.5
Virginia	136,975	90,332	65.9	21,776	15.9	23,288	17.0	820	0.6
Washington	322,799	86,840	26.9	113,698	35.2	70,445	21.8	40,134	12.4
West Virginia	268,728	113,097	42.1	79,112	29.4	56,754	21.1	15,248	5.7
Wisconsin	399,975	164,230	41.1	62,448	15.6	130,596	32.7	33,476	8.4
Wyoming	42,283	15,310	36.2	9,232	21.8	14,560	34.4	2,760	6.5
TOTALS	**15,043,029**	**6,294,326**	**41.8**	**4,120,207**	**27.4**	**3,486,343**	**23.2**	**900,370**	**6.0**

1. Figures from Svend Petersen, *A Statistical History of the American Presidential Elections* (Westport, Conn.: Greenwood Press, 1981); Edgar E. Robinson, *The Presidential Vote 1896–1932* (Stanford, Calif.: Stanford University Press, 1934).

2. Figures from *Kentucky Directory 1916*, pp. 145–149.

OTHER VOTES	%	PLURALITY	
5	0.0	59,758	D
265	1.1	3,375	D
908	0.7	43,229	D
27,783	4.1	174	PR
5,538	2.1	42,160	D
3,334	1.8	6,237	D
620	1.3	6,634	D
1,854	3.6	31,862	D
149	0.1	71,102	D
1,536	1.5	1,111	D
19,776	1.7	18,570	D
22,379	3.4	119,883	D
8,440	1.7	23,503	D
63	0.0	23,453	D
4,189	0.9	104,065	D
—	0.0	51,588	D
947	0.7	2,618	D
2,566	1.1	54,885	D
3,856	0.8	17,460	D
10,033	1.8	61,809	PR
10,098	3.0	19,430	PR
—	0.0	53,775	D
7,158	1.0	122,925	D
32	0.0	5,420	D
3,383	1.4	36,327	D
—	0.0	2,366	D
535	0.6	1,797	D
4,332	1.0	32,959	D
—	0.0	3,273	D
23,728	1.5	200,086	D
118	0.0	75,272	D
1,243	1.4	3,823	D
14,141	1.4	146,666	D
2,195	0.9	28,417	D
4,360	3.2	9,464	D
20,231	1.7	49,257	PR
852	1.1	2,709	D
55	0.1	47,062	D
3,910	3.4	9,869	PR
832	0.3	72,546	D
2,131	0.7	190,611	D
510	0.5	5,437	R
1,094	1.7	1,174	R
759	0.6	67,044	D
11,682	3.6	26,858	PR
4,517	1.7	33,985	D
9,225	2.3	33,634	D
421	1.0	750	D
241,783	1.6	2,174,119	D

NOVEMBER 6, 1912
WILSON WINS

He Gets 409 Electoral Votes; Roosevelt, 107, and Taft, 15.

206,000 OVER TAFT IN NEW YORK

Illinois and Pennsylvania for Roosevelt, but Close—House Democratic By 157—Maybe Senate, Too—Cannon Beaten

Woodrow Wilson was elected President yesterday and Thomas R. Marshall Vice President by an Electoral majority which challenged comparison with the year in which Horace Greeley was defeated by Grant. Until now that year has always been the standard of comparison for disastrous defeats, but the downfall of the Republican Party this year runs it a close second.

The apparent results at 4 o'clock this morning gave Wilson **409** Electoral votes, Roosevelt **107**, and Taft **15**.

Wilson carried 38 States, Roosevelt 6, and Taft 4.

The Republican Party is wiped off the map. Nearly everywhere Taft ran third, with Roosevelt capturing a large majority of the old Republican vote, and in many States Taft's vote was almost negligible.

New York gave Wilson a plurality over Taft of about 206,000. Wilson's vote in the State was 698,000, Taft's 493,000, and Roosevelt's 419,000.

The Democratic plurality in the House of Representatives will not be less than **157**, and the United States Senate will probably be Democratic also.

The Democrats swept New York, electing Sulzer Governor, with Hedges running second and Straus a poor third.

Throughout the night the most interesting features were the fluctuations in Illinois and Pennsylvania, the returns from which every minute or two put first one candidate and then another in possession of the two States. This morning it is apparently certain that Roosevelt has carried them both.

New Jersey produced a majority of about **50,000** for Wilson over Roosevelt, and the Democrats have apparently gained three Congressmen. The Legislature is overwhelmingly Democratic, insuring the election of a Democrat to succeed Senator Briggs and a Democratic Governor to succeed Wilson.

In Idaho, where Senator William E. Borah is running for re-election as a Republican, though a Progressive at heart, the Legislature is badly split.

There is a close race for the Senate in Oregon, with Senator Bourne, who ran independently, utterly out of it.

Maine went for Wilson by probably 7,500, with Roosevelt second. The indications are that Wilson has 47,500, Roosevelt 40,000, and Taft 27,000.

The returns from California, which Roosevelt has been expected to carry, are naturally meagre, owing to the three hours' difference in time to New York, but Wilson has carried San Francisco by 20,000 and the State seems to have gone for Wilson. The reason, of course, is that the Taft Republicans, having no opportunity to vote for candidates of their own under the California law, have voted in a body for Wilson.

Ohio has gone overwhelmingly for Wilson, electing Cox (Dem.) for Governor. President Taft's defeat in his own State was as complete as Col. Roosevelt's in his State.

Massachusetts not only went for Wilson by a great majority, but for the first time in her history she elected a Democratic State ticket and a Democratic Legislature. This means a Democratic Senator from the Bay State in the place of Winthrop Murray Crane.

One of the features of the election was the heavy vote Roosevelt polled in the South, particularly Alabama and Georgia. At one time it seemed as if Congressman Underwood, the Democratic leader in the House, might be defeated because of the heavy vote for the Bull Moose in his district. The first three counties to be heard from in Georgia reported that Roosevelt had carried them.

Iowa has apparently gone for Roosevelt by between 4,000 and 5,000, despite Gov. Cummins's failure to take any active part in the campaign after Mr. Roosevelt's failure to take his advice about not running a State ticket.

Nebraska, which had been expected to cast an overwhelming majority for the Democrats since Mr. Bryan took an active part in the campaign, did not do so well as had been expected. Wilson has apparently carried the State, but the fight over both the Senatorship and the Governorship is close, and it is possible that Senator Brown, (Rep.,) who was looked upon as a sure loser, may win.

"Uncle Joe" Cannon went down to defeat in the Danville district, and will be missing from the Capitol for the first time since his defeat in 1890, the only other defeat he has ever met with since he began representing that district in the 70's of the last century.

Roosevelt and Taft each carried their home towns handsomely. Oyster Bay went for Roosevelt by a majority of 292, giving him 510, Wilson, 218, and Taft, 67. Gov. Wilson's birthplace, Staunton, Va., gave him 632, Taft, 287, and Roosevelt, 65.

In Vermont Taft won by 924 votes, but Roosevelt is close behind him.

New Hampshire is Democratic. Wilson carried Connecticut by nearly 7,000, and Baldwin was re-elected Governor.

Victor L. Berger, the Socialist Congressman from Milwaukee, is defeated by William H. Stafford, the Republican candidate. His majority was over 2,000.

In New York City Wilson defeated Roosevelt by 123,000, but Roosevelt had 59,000 more than Taft.

Wilson lost 6,000 votes in Erie because of the double ballot. They have voting machines there, and that many voters pushed the knob for Sulzer, but did not push the knob for Wilson, forgetting that both knobs had to be pushed.

THE PRESIDENTIAL ELECTION OF 1932

ROOSEVELT SWEEPS, SEEKS TO END THE DEPRESSION

Coming during one of the deepest economic crises in American history, the presidential election of 1932 marked a massive change in the United States. The election brought transformations of government institutions, the economic order, and the nation's political parties. These transformations began with the election of Franklin D. Roosevelt as president in 1932, and aspects of them continue to affect the country to this day.

Two major developments shaped the 1932 presidential election. The obvious and dominant influence was the Great Depression, the most severe economic downturn in U.S. history.

The Great Depression began on October 24, 1929, when stock market prices collapsed after years of speculative trading. At first, many expected a quick recovery. President Herbert Hoover and New York governor Franklin Roosevelt expressed confidence in the economy. *Variety*, the trade journal of the Broadway theater, made light of the collapse with a jocular headline, "Wall Street Lays an Egg."

But the shock to the economy was no joke. Within four days, stocks had declined 40 percent from their high. By the end of the Hoover administration, they had lost nearly 90 percent and would not again reach the same nominal value for twenty-five years.

The effects of the crash went far beyond Wall Street, even as some investment bankers committed suicide there by jumping from their office windows. Stock market speculation had become a mass entertainment, and millions of Americans who had put their savings into the market saw their money vanish. Even when the decline in stocks stabilized, economic miseries spread, reaching their worst levels as the 1932 election neared.

Unable to raise capital, corporations reduced their output, their payrolls, and their wages. With fewer people at work, a vicious cycle brought lower demand, fewer goods and services made to meet that demand, fewer jobs to create

Source: The Granger Collection, New York

A political cartoon satirizes President Herbert Hoover's optimistic assessment of the state of the country during the presidential campaign of 1932 while an unemployed man shivers in the cold. Hoover's perceived indifference to the difficulties faced by Americans helped to swing the election in favor of Democratic candidate Franklin Delano Roosevelt.

goods, and still lower demand. Eventually, nearly a quarter of the labor force was unemployed, and another quarter was working only part-time.

For two years after the stock market crash, intermittent glimpses of a brighter economic dawn alternated with more darkness. The final plunge into national distress came with the failure of the banking system. An international credit crisis exported from Europe in 1931 made U.S. banks unable to meet their obligations, panicking Americans into making runs—sudden, widespread withdrawals of money—on the banks. By the beginning of 1932, close to a fifth of American

1932 ELECTORAL VOTE

STATE	ELECTORAL VOTES	ROOSEVELT	HOOVER	STATE	ELECTORAL VOTES	ROOSEVELT	HOOVER
Alabama	(11)	11	–	Nebraska	(7)	7	–
Arizona	(3)	3	–	Nevada	(3)	3	–
Arkansas	(9)	9	–	New Hampshire	(4)	–	4
California	(22)	22	–	New Jersey	(16)	16	–
Colorado	(6)	6	–	New Mexico	(3)	3	–
Connecticut	(8)	–	8	New York	(47)	47	–
Delaware	(3)	–	3	North Carolina	(13)	13	–
Florida	(7)	7	–	North Dakota	(4)	4	–
Georgia	(12)	12	–	Ohio	(26)	26	–
Idaho	(4)	4	–	Oklahoma	(11)	11	–
Illinois	(29)	29	–	Oregon	(5)	5	–
Indiana	(14)	14	–	Pennsylvania	(36)	–	36
Iowa	(11)	11	–	Rhode Island	(4)	4	–
Kansas	(9)	9	–	South Carolina	(8)	8	–
Kentucky	(11)	11	–	South Dakota	(4)	4	–
Louisiana	(10)	10	–	Tennessee	(11)	11	–
Maine	(5)	–	5	Texas	(23)	23	–
Maryland	(8)	8	–	Utah	(4)	4	–
Massachusetts	(17)	17	–	Vermont	(3)	–	3
Michigan	(19)	19	–	Virginia	(11)	11	–
Minnesota	(11)	11	–	Washington	(8)	8	–
Mississippi	(9)	9	–	West Virginia	(8)	8	–
Missouri	(15)	15	–	Wisconsin	(12)	12	–
Montana	(4)	4	–	Wyoming	(3)	3	–
				TOTALS	**(531)**	**472**	**59**

banks had failed, locking their doors as customers vainly sought to withdraw their deposits that had now seemingly disappeared. By the next year, the assets of the remaining banks had shrunk 27 percent.

Distress and desperation were evident throughout the nation. Prices and wages fell, so that businesses could not make profits and workers could not buy goods. Industrial output was cut almost in half, automobile production by two-thirds, construction by 80 percent. Among small business, the rate of failure increased by a fifth. Farm products could not be sold: as prices declined by two-thirds, it made more sense to burn crops for fuel than to sell them. A fourth of farmers lost their homes, setting off mass migrations in search of better prospects. Overall, the total economy

contracted 44 percent from 1929 to 1932; even taking lower prices into account, the contraction was still 27 percent.

But these statistics cannot portray the human costs of the Depression. Farmers could not sell their crops, and city dwellers could not buy food. The unemployed millions were forced to compete for scraps in garbage cans. In search of work, some turned to crime, others to charity, others to selling apples on the street. Marriages were less frequent, and the birth rate declined. To stretch resources, families combined into crowded residences. Others resorted to railroad boxcars or constructed flimsy shantytowns, soon known as "Hoovervilles."

Government was overwhelmed by the economic and social catastrophe. President Hoover did, in fact, attempt to meet the crisis. He established a new federal Reconstruction Finance Corporation to make loans to troubled banks, urged employers to hold wages steady, instituted farm market cooperatives, and initiated international agreements to loosen world credit. Nothing worked, but other government bodies were even less effective than these measures. Congress passed the extreme Smoot-Hawley Tariff, hindering world trade. The Federal Reserve raised interest rates, the most harmful policy it could have chosen when easy credit and price inflation were needed. State and local governments had no capacity to meet their citizens' basic needs for survival and provided as little as five cents a day in aid.

The one thing Hoover could not do was change his basic political beliefs. A firm traditional conservative, he held to his commitment to a limited federal government, his opposition to direct relief payments to the unemployed, and his insistence on a balanced federal budget. Concerned but unbending, he became an object of venom and mockery for years. Voters bitterly remembered his campaign promise, "a chicken in every pot and a car in every garage," and recalled the vision in his inaugural address, when he saw the United States "in sight of the day when poverty will be banished from the nation."

With Hoover discredited, the country turned to Roosevelt and his unspecific but hopeful call: "The country needs and, unless I mistake its temper, the country demands bold, persistent experimentation. It is common sense to take a method and try it. If it fails, admit it frankly and try another. But above all, try something."

The Depression provided the framework for the 1932 election, but another story, less obvious but also vital, shaped the contest. This story was the oncoming realignment of the national parties.

The 1928 election had appeared to be no more than the continuation of the Republicans' dominant majority, which, except for Woodrow Wilson's two terms, had prevailed in every presidential election since 1896. Yet the political tides had begun to shift, stirring new waves that the Democratic Party would soon ride to victory.

In 1928 the Democrats began their emergence as the party of urban immigrants and the working class. They nominated Alfred E. Smith, former governor of New York, a Catholic of Irish descent, a son of the sidewalks of New York City, an advocate of economic reform, and an opponent of the Eighteenth Amendment to the Constitution banning the manufacture or sale of alcoholic beverages. Smith's designation—after two earlier efforts blocked by conservative party factions—marked a sharp change from the party's domination by its rural, conservative, and Prohibitionist wing, and its favored southern and western Protestant candidates.

Smith lost the 1928 election overwhelmingly, but his candidacy began a transformation of national political alignments that would become evident in later Democratic victories. For the first time since Reconstruction, the Republicans had cracked the "Solid South," winning five states thanks to votes against Smith's Catholicism. In the other direction, Smith won Massachusetts and Rhode Island, each of which had voted for a Democrat only once since the time of Andrew Jackson.

Change was stirring: national turnout increased by a fourth; in many states it rose by close to 50 percent, and Smith nearly doubled the previous Democratic vote. The largest increases were illuminating, coming either in the Deep South or in eastern industrial states. Both groups were responding to Smith's Catholicism, the South repulsed, even where still grudgingly loyal, and the East attracted. In 1928 the religious cleavage hurt the Democratic cause, but party prospects were much brighter for the future. By 1930 more than 11 percent of the U.S. population was foreign-born, and another 21 percent were the children of foreign-born parents, including 8 million probable Catholics with parents from Ireland, Italy, and Poland. The large stream of immigrants in the early years of the century was now entering the political ranks, and their higher birth rates would in time yield greater numbers of future Democrats.

These population changes foreshadowed an electoral realignment. The dismal circumstances of the Depression provided the opportunity for change in the nation's politics. In combination, long-term trends and immediate circumstances would make the election of 1932 a critical event.

The Parties and the Candidates

By 1932 the Republican Party faced an apparent political disaster as severe as the nation's economic catastrophe. In the 1930 congressional elections, it had lost 53 seats and control of the House of Representatives. In the Senate, after losing 8 seats, it still held a nominal 1-seat majority, but defections by former Progressives made the party's control illusory. In fact, neither political party managed to lead effectively, and neither had a program capable of combating the nation's severe decline.

Despite Hoover's failures and unpopularity, Republicans could not repudiate their president. Hoover ignored the primaries, where he was opposed by former Maryland senator Joseph France, and lost all but one contest. Overall, aside from an unchallenged victory in his home state of California, the incumbent won less than 7 percent of the primary vote. But in 1932 primaries were unimportant for the Republicans. Hoover completely controlled the June convention in Chicago, and the delegates even refused to allow France to nominate former president Calvin Coolidge.

Hoover was dutifully renominated for reelection on the first ballot, gaining 1,126 of the 1,154 delegates. Party anxieties were displaced onto the vice president, Charles Curtis, who failed to gain renomination on the first ballot until switching state delegations carried him over the top.

The only open dispute was on Prohibition. The failure of the moralistic crusade—and the prospect of tax revenue from legal liquor sales—attracted support for repeal of the Eighteenth Amendment. The platform draft waffled, condemning "the evils inherent in the liquor traffic," while endorsing a new amendment to the Constitution to allow each state "to deal with the problem as their citizens may determine." A minority report, calling for outright repeal, was defeated by a 3 to 2 margin.

Otherwise, the platform was uncontested, even complacent. Although sympathetic to the nation's plight, the party was unstinting in its praise of Hoover as "a leader—wise, courageous, patient, understanding, resourceful, ever present at his post of duty, tireless in his efforts and unswervingly faithful to American principles and ideals." The party endorsed the president's programs as well, including a balanced federal budget, the gold standard, high tariffs, and a restriction of relief efforts to state and local governments and private charities.

Democrats were ready for change and eagerly expected it in party control of the presidency. The prospect of victory brought many candidates into a race that seemed inevitably to lead to the White House, including Al Smith, seeking another chance after his 1928 defeat, and Texan John Nance Garner, Speaker of the House. Roosevelt, the clear favorite, had the name of his distant cousin, former President Theodore Roosevelt, experience gained as assistant secretary of the Navy in the Wilson administration and as the party's vice-presidential candidate in 1920, the political skill to win election as governor in 1928 even as Democrats lost the presidential contest, and a progressive record that drew commendation even during the hard Depression years.

Roosevelt had built a considerable lead toward the party nomination. In the limited number of primaries, FDR held a plurality of popular votes, but turnouts were low, contests few, and the results mixed in the seventeen states holding nominating elections. More important in his drive were visits with party leaders and an extensive recruiting trip by his campaign director, James Farley, who gathered support as he traveled across the country.

When the convention met in Chicago in June, Roosevelt was the obvious front-runner. He carried some preliminary votes, but party rules still required a two-thirds majority to win nomination. For a time, the governor's campaign considered forcing a change in the rules to require only a simple majority, which raised the threat of a revolt by southern delegations insistent on preserving their implicit veto power. The Roosevelt forces retreated, postponing the rules change to the next convention in 1936. Democrats were in no mood to relive the historic deadlocks that had wrecked the party before the Civil War or kept it in fruitless combat for 103 ballots in 1924.

As the nominating ballots began before dawn, Roosevelt showed his majority support with 666 of the total 1,154 votes. After two more ballots produced little change by midmorning, the convention adjourned. Some time before evening, the Garner camp shifted its support to Roosevelt, most probably through an explicit bargain. When the convention reconvened, Roosevelt had a solid victory of 945 votes on the fourth ballot. Redeeming the promised deal, Garner was unanimously nominated as vice president. Only Smith remained in opposition, bitter at his own rejection and ever more suspicious of Roosevelt's program.

The party platform occasioned little conflict. Democrats overwhelmingly supported the repeal of Prohibition, but still moralistically urged state governments to enact "such measures as will actually promote temperance [and] effectively prevent the return of the saloon." The Depression was seen as the fault of Republican rule. To meet the economic emergency, the party's first proposal was conservative: a reduction of 25 percent in federal expenditures and a balanced national budget. There were suggestions, however, of the more reformist course that the future Democratic administration would take, including federal funds for unemployment relief and spending on public works, utility and stock market regulation, farm mortgage financing, and old-age insurance.

As the convention neared its end, news arrived that the presidential candidate was flying through heavy winds to Chicago to accept his nomination personally before the delegates. Deliberately departing from the established ritual that he wait weeks to be notified of his nomination, Roosevelt assertively discarded what he termed "absurd traditions," giving promise of an activist president and of substantive changes in governance. In his address, the Democratic candidate stated the basic programmatic goals he offered voters: "work, with all the moral and spiritual values that go with it; and with work, a reasonable measure of security—security for themselves and for their wives and children." In his peroration, Roosevelt gave an identity to the administration he would soon bring to Washington: "I pledge you, I pledge myself, to a new deal for the American people."

In the dire conditions of the time, radical and other third parties abounded. Four different parties advanced socialist programs. The largest, Eugene V. Debs's Socialist Party, nominated Norman Thomas for the second of his six presidential candidacies. The 1932 election would prove to be Thomas's best showing, when he won almost 900,000 votes, more than 2 percent of the national total. Further to the left, the small Communist Party nominated William Z. Foster. Openly urging the creation of the "United States of Soviet America," the party reached its highest support in the turmoil of 1932, a still minuscule 100,000 votes. Despite their harsh living conditions, American citizens and America's major parties remained committed to a capitalist economy in a democratic republic.

THE CAMPAIGN

Given the country's condition, Roosevelt seemed a sure winner. Many policy differences were aired, but not in direct debate between the candidates. The one overriding issue was the Depression. Hoover attributed it to the international finance system and tried to find signs that his efforts would soon turn the corner toward recovery. Roosevelt blamed Hoover and the Republicans for their weak reactions to the crisis, but offered only vague and contradictory solutions.

Hoover's dim chances declined still further as the campaign began. In June a "bonus army" of unemployed veterans marched to Washington, camping on government grounds while pressuring the government for promised cash benefits. On orders from the Army chief of staff, Gen. Douglas MacArthur, the marchers were dispersed by tanks and federal troops wielding bayonets and tear gas. The protestors' shacks were burned, and two of them were killed. Hoover had not ordered the attack on his countrymen, but he still bore the blame for their sufferings.

The campaign was a total mismatch. Hoover was handicapped not only by the realities of economic conditions, but also by his own limitations. An engineer by training, he had never held political office before his election as president.

Dour and dull, his speeches were technical, detailed, and boring. Accepting the traditional constraints on an incumbent, he at first waged his campaign principally in the White House to showcase his efforts to cope with the crisis. In the last month, incredulously hearing reports of Roosevelt's lead, the president took vigorously to the campaign trail, ultimately covering ten thousand miles and engendering false optimism among Republican leaders.

In contrast to Hoover, Roosevelt was possibly the most gifted politician of the century. He had held public offices from the state legislature to the subcabinet to the governorship. He was endowed with a superb voice and used it effectively to reach the national audience. Paralyzed from the waist down by polio, but living in an age before television and the Internet, he hid his disability from the public and press photographers. To demonstrate his physical capacity and his self-confidence, he traveled by rail and plane throughout the country.

He also had the advantage of a modernized Democratic National Committee. In previous elections, the national committees had shut down operations soon after the presidential vote. In an electoral innovation, the Democrats had kept their national organization going over the past four years, setting up a publicity office to distribute the party's propaganda. When Farley took command of the committee after Roosevelt's nomination, he had a functioning operation ready for the campaign.

The campaign made extensive use of the new mass medium, radio. By 1932 the new technology had reached a potential audience in excess of 50 million, including more farm homes than had electricity. Both parties secured time on the era's crystal sets, but Roosevelt was clearly the master of the medium, broadcasting shorter and more frequent speeches in tones warmer and more assured than the president's. Once in office, his "fireside chats" would create the appearance of intimate conversations within the Oval Office and the nation's living rooms.

In newspaper accounts, the leading issue was Prohibition. Roosevelt stood on the Democratic platform, pushing for direct repeal of the Eighteenth Amendment, winning the full support of Smith and other fervent "wets" throughout the country. Hoover, in his August acceptance speech, went beyond the Republican platform, admitted that Prohibition had been a failure despite its "high purpose," and supported a constitutional repeal that would leave each state to determine its own stance.

The distinct difference between the candidates stimulated the campaign's strange focus on drinking alcohol at a time when many Americans did not even have enough to eat. Roosevelt ridiculed Hoover for his "pussycat words," and Democrats pressed local Republicans to get off their party wagon. When the mid-September Maine elections led to the defeat of two "dry" Republican members of Congress, the party wavered. Many suggested the legalization of beer, rather than stronger drink, to slake the nation's thirst; others doubted that the southern Democrats dominant in Congress would actually redeem the repeal promise. The leading Prohibitionist groups saw Hoover's position as an unacceptable straddle and refused to endorse either candidate.

Making the best of the situation, *The New York Times* on August 12 commended Hoover for his new position on the "irrepressible issue" (using language akin to the characterization of slavery before the Civil War), reading it as "witnessing Mr. Hoover's willingness to change his mind, for good reasons shown, and to respond to the needs of the hour and the impatient demands of the great body of our citizens." Even before the presidential inauguration, Congress passed the repeal constitutional amendment and sent it to special state conventions for ratification—the only time this procedure has been used. Tavern taps opened legally in December 1933, amid widespread celebrations.

There were more serious issues than repealing Prohibition. Roosevelt's campaign theme was simple: a negative retrospective judgment of the Hoover administration. The Republican incumbent replied in kind, denouncing the asserted radicalism of the Democratic challenger, while defending his responses to the Depression and relentlessly seeking out any stray signs of recovery. Hoover continued to place the blame for the economic crisis on foreign debts and banks, but gave no attention to looming military threats in Europe and Asia.

As to his own future policies, FDR was inconsistent, if not muddled. He favored extensive federal efforts of unemployment relief and social welfare, yet also advocated the Democratic platform planks of a balanced budget and a 25 percent cut in spending. He spoke on behalf of both high and low tariffs and had no clear farm program. He endorsed the capitalist economic model, yet envisioned national regulatory power to control corporate abuses. Once a spokesman for Woodrow Wilson's internationalist policy, he neglected foreign policy entirely, even as Japan invaded China and Adolf Hitler's Nazis approached power in Germany.

In his campaign, as in his future administration, FDR's basic program was a confident but nonideological pragmatism. His campaign appeal was not his indeterminate program, but his aura of strong leadership. As he would soon say in his inaugural address, he convinced voters that "the only thing we have to fear is fear itself."

Some commentators doubted Roosevelt's intellectual depth; others were troubled by his perceived lack of programmatic convictions. Hoover even considered him a "dangerous demagogue" whose policies would mean that "grass will grow in the streets of a hundred American cities and weeds will overrun the fields of millions of farms." But depicting Roosevelt as a radical had little plausibility, given his patrician family background and moderate demeanor. Two days before the November 8 election, the conservative *New York Times* refuted the conservative President Hoover and endorsed a change in government. Praising Roosevelt, *The Times* wrote: "He has dealt with unemployment as a difficult problem to be solved, not as an incitement to political vengeance. The people have seen that there is nothing of the unscrupulous agitator in Franklin Delano Roosevelt."

THE ELECTION RESULTS

The general expectation in the press was that Roosevelt would win, betting odds running about 4 to 1 and higher in his favor. The emerging science of public opinion research drew considerable attention. The most widely noted poll was that of a popular magazine, the *Literary Digest,* which gathered 3 million straw votes on an unscientific basis across the country. As the balloting neared, it predicted a Roosevelt margin of 7 million votes, a division of 56 percent to 38 percent in the total vote, and Democratic victory in 41 states—very close to the actual results.

In contrast, polls of students at most colleges, including Harvard, Roosevelt's alma mater, put Hoover well in the lead–although most college students actually could not vote because the typical age of suffrage was still twenty-one. Columbia, where Roosevelt attended law school, was an exception, but it also rejected the New Yorker, supporting Socialist Norman Thomas instead.

Roosevelt did win the expected landslide. With 40 million voters casting ballots, he gained 57.4 percent to Hoover's 39.6 percent, led the repudiated president by 7 million, and carried 42 states. The Republican base shrank to northern New England and 3 other eastern states. The electoral count was even more overwhelming, 472 for Roosevelt and a paltry 59 for Hoover. Democrats also rode Roosevelt's coattails to congressional dominance. With 97 new representatives, the party had a 313 to 117 majority in the House. Twelve new senators gave the party a strong 59 to 36 margin in the upper chamber.

The election results showed sharp reversals from 1928 across the nation. Hoover lost more than 1 of every 4 ballots he had garnered earlier, as well as 7 of 8 previous electoral votes. Within the national Democratic deluge, there were some limited regional variations in the electoral tide. The South returned to party orthodoxy, the East showed some pockets of Republican support, and the western states backed Roosevelt.

Despite the nation's economic distress, turnout increased only by 8 percent. The electorate did not storm the polls, but appeared reserved, hopeful of improvement and supporting FDR with their votes rather than mobilizing for radical change. With relatively few new voters, the outcome resulted from changed opinion, 1928 Hoover voters now backing Roosevelt. That apparent conversion was evident as well in the *Literary Digest* poll, which found that a third of FDR's support came from previous Republican voters.

The landslide, expected and large, calmed the nation. Press editorials consistently called for acceptance of the electoral decision, along with hopes for economic recovery in the new administration. But Roosevelt would not take office until March 4; he was the last president elected before the Twentieth Amendment to the Constitution ended the four-month interregnum between terms. The world did not stop to wait, and real conditions deteriorated. The international banking system became frozen, leading to new panic in the United States. As inauguration day drew nearer, governors closed banks in thirty-eight states, the New York Stock Exchange suspended trading, and financial institutions throughout the country were on the brink of failure. Hoover, still in office, clung to the same policies and wanted Roosevelt to back his actions, but the president-elect refused to share responsibility with his failed predecessor.

Another crisis almost ended Roosevelt's term before it could begin. On February 15, he spoke at a public celebration in Miami. As he began to drive away through the surging crowd, an unemployed bricklayer rushed toward the car firing a pistol at Roosevelt, missing him but wounding a notable bystander, Chicago mayor Anton Cermak. Roosevelt stopped his car, ordered Secret Service agents to put Cermak inside, and held him on his lap as they drove to a hospital. Within weeks, Cermak died of his wounds. His assailant was convicted of murder and executed. Roosevelt not only survived, but provided a personal model of bravery and compassion to the nation.

As Roosevelt took the oath of office, the nation knew it had a new leader, but the way forward was uncertain. The election had certainly repudiated the past, but it had not marked a future direction. The political parties still reflected the voting coalitions established first by the Civil War, then realigned in 1896 and the Progressive period. FDR's victory might ultimately mean no more than a temporary deviation from the accustomed Republican dominance. Or it might mean a long-term shift in the partisan alignment or even the major parties' replacement by new social movements.

The Depression had changed America, but neither solutions to the nation's travail nor indications of the new president's program had become clear. There would be a New Deal, but what would that rhetorical slogan actually mean for unemployed workers, ruined bankers, bankrupt farmers, homeless clerks, and ignored African Americans? Would recovery await the turn of the incomprehensible business cycle, or would government adopt a new role in management of the economy? And how would the United States react to the international crises foretold by another change of government that winter, the ascension to power by Adolf Hitler?

Only the future would answer these questions. For now, Americans could but listen cautiously, perhaps hopefully, to their new president. They might take heart from his confident declaration, "This great Nation will endure as it has endured, will revive and will prosper." They might heed his moral lesson, "These dark days will be worth all they cost us if they teach us that our true destiny is not to be ministered unto but to minister to ourselves and to our fellow men." They might respond to his forceful call, "The people of the United States have not failed. In their need they have registered a mandate that they want direct, vigorous action. They have asked for discipline and direction under leadership. They have made me the present instrument of their wishes. In the spirit of the gift I take it."

The transformation of American politics had begun.

THE WALL STREET CRASH OF 1929

On October 24, 1929, the stock market crashed in New York City, beginning an economic crisis that rapidly crippled the nation. The downturn idled businesses and threw millions out of work and out of their houses for years to come. Stunned Americans sought to pinpoint the cause of the collapse and find solutions. Explanations ranged from the impact of isolationist policies and high tariffs to a loss of religious faith and even the rise of feminism. Despite the clamor, answers to the catastrophe proved elusive. Heading into the election of 1932, the nation yearned for a program and a candidate to handle the crisis.

OCTOBER 24, 1929
PRICES OF STOCKS CRASH IN HEAVY LIQUIDATION, TOTAL DROP OF BILLIONS

PAPER LOSS $4,000,000,000

2,600,000 Shares Sold in the Final Hour in Record Decline.

MANY ACCOUNTS WIPED OUT

But No Brokerage House Is in Difficulties, as Margins Have Been Kept High.

ORGANIZED BACKING ABSENT

Bankers Confer on Steps to Support Market—Highest Break is 96 Points.

Frightened by the decline in stock prices during the last month and a half, thousands of stockholders dumped their shares on the market yesterday afternoon in such an avalanche of selling as to bring about one of the widest declines in history. Even the best of seasoned, dividend-paying, shares were sold regardless of the prices they would bring, and the result was a tremendous smash in which stocks lost from a few points to as much as ninety-six.

Loss in Market Values.

The absolute average decline of active and so-called inactive issues yesterday was 2,995, or roughly three points. Using this figure as a base and taking the percentage of shares listed on the Exchange in relation to the percentage of issues traded in, the loss in value of listed securities amounted to $2,210,675,184. This, however, does not measure up to the full value of the loss, for the reason that many lesser-known issues of small capitalization did not figure in the sharp declines. It might be conservatively estimated that the actual loss in market value on the New York Stock Exchange ran to about $4,000,000,000.

Since there are 1,048,359,363 shares listed on the Exchange, a decline of one point a share would mean more than $1,000,000,000. Obviously all issues were not traded in, but those which were not declined in bid and asked representation, so that while no sales were actually recorded the market position of most issues was lowered.

In addition to the situation on the big board there was also the decline on the Curb market, where values were ruthlessly cut, and to this must be added declines in securities in other markets affected sympathetically by the New York Stock Exchange fluctuations and declines in the over-the-counter market. The wiping out of open-market values throughout the country therefore probably ranged as high as $6,000,000,000. The $4,000,000,000 decline on the New York Stock Exchange represented a loss of about one twenty-second in the value of all listed securities, which on Oct. 1 was rated at $87,073,630,423.

Crash in Final Hour.

The collapse of the market in the final hour of trading seemed the more violent because of its suddenness, the mystery which surrounded it, particularly as to the identity of the sellers, and the tremendous volume of the trading, which reached a total of 2,600,000 shares in the hour between 2 and 3 o'clock.

Statistically the market made a sorry showing. The railroad shares, as measured by THE NEW YORK TIMES average of twenty-five representative stocks, were down 5.52 and the industrial shares 30.97. The total combined average of fifty representative issues was down 18.24, marking the largest decline since the start of the compilation of these records in 1911. Sales on the Exchange were 6,374,960 shares, marking the eleventh time the sales on the Exchange have exceeded the 6,000,000-share figure. On the Curb they were 1,793,415 shares.

MAY 12, 1931
SAYS HOOVER SEES SLUMP AS 'MENTAL'

Lord Mayor Thompson Quotes Him as Believing Depression to Be Largely Psychological.

POINTS TO LIVERPOOL GAINS

Honor Guest at British Luncheon Club Stresses Need for Cheerful Attitude Toward Conditions.

President Hoover believes that the current economic depression is due in great part to "the mental condition of business," Alderman Edwin Thompson, Lord Mayor of Liverpool, said yesterday as the guest of honor of the British Luncheon Club, 53 Broadway.

"Last Friday I was received by President Hoover at Washington," Lord Mayor Thompson said. "In the few minutes' conversation that we had, President Hoover said he felt that a great deal of the difficulties of the present commercial situation were due to the mental condition of business."

The Lord Mayor likened the state of business throughout the world today to that of an ill person who, if the doctor tells him he is going to die, probably will.

"If the doctor says 'You are going to get well,'" he continued, "the effect of mind over matter is tremendous and the patient may pull through.

"I think that in the condition of the world today a spirit of cheerfulness does much good. I wanted to make my official visit to New York because the interests of New York and Liverpool are identical, as the interests of the whole world are identical. And I wanted to point out that things are not so bad."

MAY 20, 1931
LINKS DEPRESSION TO FEMINISM HERE

Dr. Welti, Swiss Economist, Finds Our Men Wasting Time and Admiration on Women.

URGES LIBERAL REFORMS

Tariff, Standardized Psychology and "Medieval Lawlessness" Also Blamed for Business Ills.

America's high tariff wall is one of the main causes of the universal economic depression, according to Dr. H. Robert Welti, lawyer and economist of Zurich, Switzerland, who is in New York on a five-day visit to attempt to find the "real reason" for the decline in stock market prices.

Dr. Welti, who headed a Swiss economic commission to this country a year ago, said yesterday that bankers and business men of Zurich had lost at least $10,000,000 in American shares during the past year, and that they were "bewildered as to the real reason for the collapse." For that reason, he said, he had been delegated to interview local bankers and to attempt to make as many observations as possible during his short sojourn here.

Two days of such investigation had convinced him, Dr. Welti said, that there are four main reasons for the financial failure of Wall Street and the consequent influence on business in the rest of the world. These he classified as follows:

1. The high tariff.

2. The standardized mass psychology of the people of America.

3. The "medieval lawlessness, especially as regards methods of administration."

4. A too highly developed cult of the feminine, "resulting in lack of creative, constructive power."

Dr. Welti was outspoken on the last-named subject, declaring that the men of the United States were wasting time and admiration upon the women, who, he said, were not so well equipped mentally as the women of Europe. He declared they did not have much individuality, a lack which he bestowed upon the men of this country as well.

JUNE 3, 1931
EDITORIAL
CART BEFORE HORSE.

When people call an economic depression worldwide they necessarily imply that its causes too are world-wide. But it would be more than human if every country did not manage to suggest that out in the wide, wide world the responsibility for hard times is a little graver than at home. In a single day's news MARK SULLIVAN, at Washington, is impressed by the fact that "much" of the recent liquidation on the New York Stock Exchange had a "European" cause. But Professor CASSEL, addressing the London Institute of Bankers, chooses to stress American responsibility for the ills of the nations, assigning the chief role to the 1929 Wall Street crash. Was that collapse of twenty months ago precipitated by the Hatry failure in London, resulting in a sudden demand for the return of British money on the New York call loan market? Was the Hatry adventure inspired by what was going on in the United States? If a little finger-pointing is in order, one can think of one or two possible directions, and the final effect is like one of THOMAS NAST'S pictures about Tammany Hall.

Even more complicated than who was responsible for the economic depression is what was responsible for it. Did business get its first push downhill from civil war in China, demonetization of silver in India, reparations in Germany, drought in Arkansas, too many automobiles in the United States, too much coffee in Brazil, too much rubber in Sumatra, too much sugar in Cuba and Czechoslovakia, too much nitrates in Chile and Germany, too many soldiers in Europe, too many unemployed in Great Britain, too much real estate on Park Avenue and Central Park West? A list of the causes of world depression mentioned in Parliaments, books and newspapers during the last twenty months would easily run into hundreds. The trouble with the great majority of them is that they are not causes but symptoms. Indigestion, headache, pains in the back and susceptibility to colds are not the causes of a run-down condition, but its results and signs. When a man burns the candle at both ends, he is easy game for disease germs. He catches everything.

When an after-war economic world continues to burn the candle at both ends, when it makes the furious and dangerous life the normal life, when all the old rules of sane, economic living are discarded, the inevitable end is an exhausted system. It becomes a ready victim to infections that it might otherwise throw off easily. When the nations have played fast and loose with their basic economic health, everything will go wrong with them—their Chinese wars and their Indian silver and German reparations and Arkansas drought and Sumatra rubber and Park Avenue real estate.

OCTOBER 5, 1931
DR. RAY ADVOCATES DRY MODIFICATION

Denounces Prohibition as Chief Cause of Depression and as Corrupter of Nation.

ASKS COURAGEOUS THINKING

Worry, He Says, Only Puts Us Into a Funk, but He Warns on 'Pollyanna' Attitude.

Modification of the "pernicious" prohibition law and courageous thinking as measures to cope with the present economic depression were urged by the Rev. Dr. Randolph Ray in his first sermon of the season at the Little Church Around the Corner, Twenty-ninth Street, east of Fifth Avenue, yesterday morning. A special service marked the eighty-third anniversary of the founding of the parish of the Transfiguration in 1848.

"Today the job of living seems supremely difficult," Dr. Ray continued. "We are always inclined to exaggerate our ills and difficulties, yet the stark fact remains that, despite our greatest optimism, times are bad.

"We must face the issue frankly. First of all we must recognize a fundamental truth, that is that our thinking, our attitude of mind, has a great deal to do with our job. I am not intending to dish out 'pollyanna,' but I am emphasizing a great truth that by whining, lamenting, talking about our ills and worries, sooner or later we get thoroughly frightened, a terrible blue funk overtakes us and we lie down on our jobs. Hence a crop of failures, suicides, murders, riots and robberies.

"We must try to help conditions and their causes not only by our thinking but by our actions. This Winter will mean actual want and suffering to more thousands than we can estimate right here in our own city. We must, each one who has more than the one in want, do our best to help. We cannot let men and women starve while we are looking for a remedy; but we must never think that alleviating present suffering is a solution of the problem."

Dr. Ray then declared that prohibition was the outstanding cause of the present situation and that it was our duty as citizens to see that the law was altered. "The millions of dollars now corrupting the country in the bootlegging and illegal distribution of alcoholic drinks over the futile efforts to suppress the manufacture and distribution," he said, "should be properly used in the legal manufacture and distribution of properly taxed beers, wines and liquors."

With the modification of the law, Dr. Ray concluded, legitimate work could be given to thousands of men and many millions of dollars could be saved to the government.

• •

THE REPUBLICANS RENOMINATE PRESIDENT HOOVER

The Republican convention met in Chicago in June 1932 facing two critical decisions. First, the party had to decide whether it would continue to endorse the constitutional prohibition of alcoholic beverages, despite growing frustration with the effort, or whether it would move for outright repeal. Second, the delegates would vote on renomination of the victorious 1928 slate, Herbert Hoover and Charles Curtis. President Hoover deftly managed both decisions, securing a platform plank that would continue Prohibition through state options and retaining his vice president for the upcoming election. Retention of the entire ticket had happened only once before in the history of the Republican Party, in William Howard Taft's failed reelection bid.

JUNE 16, 1932

CONVENTION ADOPTS HOOVER DRY-WET PLANK; REPEALISTS WAGE A FUTILE BATTLE ON FLOOR; UPROAR AMONG DELEGATES AND IN GALLERIES

REPEAL REJECTED, 681–472

Hoover Leaders Keep Grip on Delegates in a Stiff Battle.

EXTREME DRYS ALSO LOSE

Measure Calls for Conventions on New Amendment for State and Federal Control.

FULL PLATFORM ADOPTED

Final Refusal of Dawes to Run Spikes the Guns of the Anti-Curtis Forces.

By ARTHUR KROCK.

Special to The New York Times.

CHICAGO, Thursday, June 16.—Under the pressure of the administration, a reluctant Republican National Convention shortly before 1:30 o'clock this morning voted down the minority's effort to have flat repeal of prohibition submitted to the American people.

The vote on the plank offered for the minority of the resolutions committee by Senator Hiram Bingham of Connecticut was 681 against, 472 for, with one absentee. Only Mississippi broke away from the powerful control of the administration.

After the minority report had been defeated the entire platform was adopted by a viva voce vote and the convention adjourned until 11 A. M. today.

Though the most serious economic problems press for solution, and the platform was full of discussions of these and plans for the reconstruction of the nation, the convention debated only the subject of prohibition.

The Question, as Presented.

The question was whether, as Senator Bingham put it, the party would offer a clean-cut chance for a yes and no vote on the Eighteenth Amendment or whether, as Secretary Mills defined it, a new amendment should be recommended, which would give the Federal Government, should the adoption of the new amendment make prohibition a matter for State instead of national solution, the power to keep dry those States which wished to remain that way and to prevent the open saloon from being established in States which choose to be wet.

The debate began in an atmosphere of heat and emotion, much stimulated by galleries devoted to the idea of flat repeal. Chairman James R. Garfield of the resolutions committee was hissed and booed, and so were other speakers for the compromise plank. But as the night wore on, the galleries wearied, and the epochal decision was taken in a quiet stadium.

Before it ended a personal appeal to the convention to stand by the majority report in the name of President Hoover was made by John McNab, a California delegate, who put Mr. Hoover in nomination at Kansas City in 1928. This is the first time that there has been public admission that the President has been directing the decisions of the convention.

President in Full Control.

Though what was tonight publicly confessed had been well known unofficially for weeks, New York, Pennsylvania, New Jersey, Illinois, Indiana and Michigan, all Republican stalwarts, cast more votes for the Bingham motion than for the proposal sanctioned by Mr. Hoover. It was evident that the sentiment of the convention was overwhelmingly for repeal. But the word had been passed down the line from the White House and, as is the unvarying rule of American politics, a President on renomination eve controlled the declarations of his party.

If it is the wish of the President, tomorrow the Vice President will be renominated along with him, although the sentiment in the convention against Charles Curtis is as strong as it was against the "new amendment" plan. Whatever the result in that matter, the fiction that this convention was to be permitted to work its untrammeled will is gone into limbo.

JUNE 17, 1932
HOOVER, CURTIS RENAMED ON FIRST BALLOTS; DRY-WET PLANK IS DEFENDED BY STIMSON

CHEER HOOVER 27 MINUTES

Delegates Give 1,126½

Votes on First Ballot, 634¼ to Curtis.

NEW YORK FOR HARBORD

France Ejected From Rostrum—Coolidge's Name Fails to Stir Convention.

HOOVER VICTORY COMPLETE

Administration Had 200 Votes in Reserve—Convention Ends After Nominations.

By ARTHUR KROCK.

Special to The New York Times.

CHICAGO, June 16.—Under the disclosed domination of the President, the Republican national convention at its closing session today renominated Herbert Hoover and gave a grudging but safe majority to Charles Curtis of Kansas, renominated as the party candidate for Vice President.

Mr. Hoover received 1,126½ votes on the first ballot, his nomination immediately thereafter being made unanimous. Mr. Curtis, the beneficiary of a last-minute switch of Pennsylvania's 75 votes from its Republican State Chairman, General Edward Martin, to the Vice President, had a first ballot majority of 55¾, with a total of 634¼. His nomination also was made unanimous. Until Pennsylvania responded to the Administration goad, Mr. Curtis lacked 19¼ votes of the sum required for his renomination.

It has been twenty years since the obvious will of a Republican National Committee has been so completely and publicly subordinated to a President's program. In 1912, as today, both President and Vice President were renominated, the only time in its history that the Republican party has repeated its ticket.

But then Theodore Roosevelt bolted the convention and formed the Bull Moose party, badly defeating the regular Republicans under William H. Taft in the election and assuring the victory of the Democratic ticket headed by Woodrow Wilson.

No Prospect of a Bolt.

So far as the political elements of the Republican party are concerned, there were no prospects of a bolt as the result of the defeat of the repeal plank last night and the renomination of Mr. Curtis today. The only menacing element was the insurgency of the New York delegation. Today its members cast ninety-five of their ninety-seven votes for General J. G. Harbord for Vice President, ignoring the plain warning which lay in the fact that the two New Yorkers who voted for Mr. Curtis were the Secretary of State, Henry L. Stimson, and the Secretary of the Treasury, Ogden L. Mills.

Last night the New Yorkers cast seventy-six of their votes for the Bingham repeal plank. The administration, which made that struggle the test of its control, had only twenty-one. Had not Charles D. Hilles, the national committeeman, declined to aid the State chairman, W. Kingsland Macy, in his effort to supplant Representative Ruth B. Pratt as national committee woman, this steadfast friend of the President would have been defeated.

The church drys, and those who are dry before they are Republican or Democratic, will not be heard from until they meet in national conclave in August, after they have examined the prohibition plank which the Democrats will adopt in Chicago the week after next.

It may be that then, as they did against James W. Wadsworth Jr. and Charles H. Tuttle, they will put independent New York State and national tickets in the field. Should this happen, the effect of that action, joined to the demonstrated dissatisfaction with Mr. Hoover's program of New York's regular Republicans, may be as disastrous to the national Republican candidates as was Colonel Roosevelt's third-party movement twenty years ago.

· ·

Franklin Delano Roosevelt Receives the Democratic Nomination

The Democratic convention met in Chicago at the end of June to form a platform, nominate a presidential slate, and propose solutions to the nation's ongoing economic crisis. In contrast to past battles, the party united to promise outright repeal of Prohibition, the first direct attack on a constitutional amendment in American history. Selecting the presidential nominee proved to be more troublesome as Franklin Delano Roosevelt, the leading contender, initially failed to win the necessary two-thirds margin. He clinched the nomination by selecting Texan John Nance Garner for vice president. FDR then broke with tradition, flying to Chicago to accept the nomination in person. The party united behind the ticket, presenting a sharp contrast to their Republican rivals.

JUNE 30, 1932
DEMOCRATS PLEDGE PARTY TO REPEAL OF THE DRY LAW AND QUICK MODIFICATION TO LEGALIZE BEER, 934¾–213¾; PLANK AGAINST WAR DEBT CANCELLATION IS SUBMITTED

BIG MAJORITY FOR REPEAL

Only Seven States Vote in Favor of the Mild Wet Plank.

THREE CANDIDATES DEBATE

All the Contenders Release Their Delegates to Vote Their Own Opinions.

ARENA IN WILD ACCLAIM

Southern and Western States Which Helped Adopt Prohibition Reverse Former Stand.

By ARTHUR KROCK.

Special to The New York Times.

CHICAGO, Thursday, June 30.—Early this morning the Democratic party went as wet as the seven seas at the fourth session of its national convention in the Stadium. By an overwhelming majority the delegates sustained the majority plank in the platform which puts the party on record as favoring outright repeal of the Eighteenth Amendment and immediate modification of the Volstead act to permit the manufacture and sale of beer.

The vote was 934¾ against substitution of the minority report and 213¾ for.

The minority proposal was that the party merely pledge prompt submission of repeal to State conventions and guarantee Federal protection to those which desire to remain dry.

Although Senator Cordell Hull of Tennessee pleaded with the convention not to make prohibition a party question, and W. A. Fitts of Alabama said that the committee action would make doubtful the vote of five States in the election, the majority proposal carried overwhelmingly.

Only from Alabama, Arkansas, Georgia, Kansas, Mississippi, North Carolina and Oklahoma did the minority plank command the support of a majority.

Kentucky was the first State to vote for the dripping wet plank, followed by Louisiana, South Carolina and Texas.

The once dry South and West deserted the amendment which they put in the Constitution in 1919 after fifty years of agitation. California, Florida, Indiana (which had the driest of bone-dry enforcement acts), Iowa, Kentucky, Louisiana, Maine (the first dry State), Michigan, Minnesota, Missouri, Montana, Nebraska, Nevada, North Dakota, Ohio, Oregon, South Carolina, Tennessee, Texas, Utah, Washington—all these gave majorities of their total strength to the party advocacy of repeal.

Debate Thrills Hearers.

The convention action was preceded by a thrilling debate in which three Presidential candidates made their first appearances on the platform, Alfred E. Smith, Governor Ritchie and Governor Murray. The first two were for the majority plank. Mr. Murray was on the other side.

Not since the convention began has there been such a demonstration as was given to Mr. Smith. Galleries and delegates joined in the storm of applause which greeted the candidate of 1928 and roared out approval of a statement by a delegate from Texas who followed him with the statement that it was not prohibition but religious prejudice which lost Texas for Mr. Smith in 1928.

Every seat in the galleries and on the floor was filled and during the four-hour debate few left the hall. The galleries were almost always turbulent, their wet sentiments leading them to give the minority plank orators indifferent attention.

JULY 2, 1932

ROOSEVELT NOMINATED ON FOURTH BALLOT; GARNER EXPECTED TO BE HIS RUNNING MATE; GOVERNOR WILL FLY TO CONVENTION TODAY

ROOSEVELT VOTE IS 945

Smith His Nearest Rival, With 190½ as Four States Stick to End.

McADOO BREAKS DEADLOCK

Casts California's 44 Amid Wild Demonstration After Garner Releases Texans.

RITCHIE MEN FALL IN LINE

Tammany Holds Aloof—Cermak Forced to Appeal to the Booing Galleries.

By ARTHUR KROCK.

Special to The New York Times.

CHICAGO, July 1.—California and Texas, which came to Chicago pledged to Speaker John N. Garner, broke the deadlock on the Presidential nomination in the Democratic National Convention on the fourth ballot tonight by casting their ninety votes for Governor Franklin D. Roosevelt of New York.

This started a bandwagon rush, in which only New York—the nominee's home State—Massachusetts, Rhode Island, New Jersey and Connecticut declined to join, and Mr. Roosevelt was selected by a vote of 945, the convention's two-thirds requirement being 769 1/3. His nearest rival, Alfred E. Smith, received 190½ votes, the four States named sticking to him to the last.

Roosevelt to Fly to Chicago.

Governor Roosevelt, as soon as he heard of his success, sent a message which the permanent chairman, Senator Thomas J. Walsh of Montana, read to the convention. The Governor announced that he will be here tomorrow, coming by airplane from Albany, to address the convention and to receive his formal notification, thus avoiding the expense of a more formal and distant ceremony.

The national committee will also be reorganized under the eye of the nominee tomorrow with his convention manager, James A. Farley of New York, as chairman. A great occasion, led by Senator Walsh, with bands and speeches, is to be made of the notification ceremonies.

Senator Walsh, the permanent chairman, sent the following telegram to Governor Roosevelt:

"The convention extends its greetings and assurance of fealty to our nominee and welcomes the news that he will be here with us tomorrow."

William G. McAdoo, former Secretary of the Treasury, was the voice of Mr. Roosevelt's destiny. When the name of California was called by the reading clerk he took the platform to explain the change of the vote in the Western States. The news of the impending action had spread throughout the delegates.

But the galleries had not heard about it, and, when they sensed what was happening, the boos and yells with which they expressed their anger over the defeat of Alfred E. Smith required the efforts of Mayor Anthony J. Cermak of Chicago, whose presence was demanded by Permanent Chairman Thomas J. Walsh, to restore a measure of quiet.

McAdoo Speaks for West.

Mr. McAdoo said that California had not come to Chicago to deadlock the convention, that Democracy had suffered enough, as in 1924 when he himself had almost polled a majority, by such methods. He said that the opinion of the West, in which Speaker Garner joined, was that Democrats should fight Republicans and not one another.

JULY 3, 1932
ROOSEVELT PUTS ECONOMIC RECOVERY FIRST IN HIS ACCEPTANCE SPEECH AT CONVENTION; GARNER FOR VICE PRESIDENT BY ACCLAMATION

FAMILY FLIES TO CHICAGO

Thundering Cheers Greet the Governor at Airport and in Stadium.

'100%' FOR THE PLATFORM

"Eighteenth Amendment Is Doomed From This Day," He Declares in Speech.

PLEDGES SELF TO 'NEW DEAL'

He Calls for Enlightened International Outlook and Shorter Work Day and Week.

By ARTHUR KROCK.

Special to The New York Times.

CHICAGO, July 2.—Before it adjourned tonight, after unanimously nominating Speaker John N. Garner of Texas for Vice President, the Democratic National Convention saw and heard its Presidential choice of yesterday, Governor Franklin D. Roosevelt of New York.

Mr. Roosevelt confessed that in coming here he was breaking a tradition.

"Let it be from now on," he said, "the task of our party to break foolish traditions. We will break foolish traditions and leave it to the Republican leadership * * * to break promises."

Pledges Aid to "Forgotten Man."

His speech was aggressive. He pledged his aid, "not only to the forgotten man, but to the forgotten woman, to help them realize their hope for a return to the old standards of living and thought in the United States." He would, he said, "Restore America to its own people."

Mr. Roosevelt began with a tribute to Woodrow Wilson. He then described the economic situation from his own viewpoint, saying that swollen surpluses went into the building of "unnecessary plants and Wall Street call money." The government should be "made solvent" again, said Mr. Roosevelt.

The galleries warmed to him when he firmly endorsed the platform plank advocating repeal of the Eighteenth Amendment and modification of the Volstead act, and the Southern delegations noted his pledge to protect the dry States in their wish to keep out intoxicating liquors and to prevent the return of the saloon.

• •

HOOVER AND ROOSEVELT ENACT DIFFERING CAMPAIGN STRATEGIES

Herbert Hoover and Franklin D. Roosevelt, worlds apart politically, approached the 1932 campaign with vastly different strategies. Hoover deferred to tradition. As the incumbent president, he chose to remain in Washington, dealing with presidential responsibilities, and relying on his record and his party supporters to speak for him. Later, facing probable defeat, he took to the stump to vindicate his policies. Roosevelt, defying tradition, began his campaign almost immediately, reaching out to the electorate with his in-person acceptance speech at the party convention. Preaching hope and courage in the face of Republican pessimism, Roosevelt remained vague regarding actual policy proposals.

JUNE 19, 1932
HOOVER TO RESTRICT HIS CAMPAIGN TALKS; BARS TRIP TO COAST

Has Told Republican Leaders He Will Take Little Part in Political Drive.

DUTIES OF OFFICE PREVENT

They Demand 'Undivided Attention'—Trip to Olympic Games Is Now 'Improbable.'

COMMITTEE OFFICE MOVING

Situated Here and in Chicago, It Will Pursue an Independent Course—Sanders in Full Charge.

Special to The New York Times.

WASHINGTON, June 18.—President Hoover announced today that he would limit his part in the Presidential campaign to a few addresses and that the conduct of the campaign would be entrusted entirely to Chairman Everett Sanders and the Republican National Committee.

Mr. Hoover will devote his "undivided attention" to the duties of the Presidency, his statement declared. It was unlikely that he would go to Los Angeles for the opening of the Olympic Games the last week in July.

The President said that the offices of the national committee would be removed to Chicago and New York and that Chairman Sanders was due here in "a few days" to complete arrangements.

Hoover Statement on Plans.

The announcement, which was designed to set at rest reports that Mr. Hoover would conduct the campaign from the White House, read as follows:

I have informed Republican leaders that except for a few major addresses expounding policies of the administration I will not take part in the forthcoming campaign, as my undivided attention must be given to the duties of my office.

The campaign will be conducted and managed entirely by Chairman Sanders and the Republican organization. It has been settled that the offices

of the Republican National Committee should be removed from Washington and established at Chicago and New York. Mr. Sanders will be visiting Washington in the course of a few days to complete these arrangements.

In accordance with the tradition since their beginning that heads of States should open the Olympic Games, I had hoped to avail myself of that pleasure and I had also hoped to spend a few weeks at my home at Stanford University, but at the moment this seems improbable, as my paramount duty is here.

Stays in Capital for Week-End.

President Hoover did not go to his Rapidan camp for the week-end, and this gave emphasis to reports that Mr. Sanders might arrive from Chicago by tomorrow and go to the White House to map campaign plans.

The set-up broadly outlined by the President in his announcement is in line with the political ideas of Mr. Sanders, who, according to views expressed here today, may have influenced Mr. Hoover's decision.

The new national chairman has always felt strongly that solely from a political standpoint the best tactics for a President comprised devotion of energies to the conduct of the government.

The arrangement also fits into Mr. Hoover's ideas in that, according to his close advisers, he is confident that the American people will endorse his administration when they have had an opportunity to apply a calm judgment to his record in office.

His intention is said to be to explain the measures he has taken in the years of economic depression and to lay down his program for the future in the national emergency. Removal of the committee headquarters from Washington, it is felt, will emphasize a singleness of purpose in carrying on the duties of the Presidency.

JULY 3, 1932
ROOSEVELT URGES EARLY CAMPAIGN

He Declares in Interview That Object of Plane Trip Was to Spur Vote Drive.

DISAPPOINTED OVER SMITH

He Had Hoped to See His Rival Soon—Plans to Take Train Home From Chicago Tonight.

From a Staff Correspondent.

Special to The New York Times.

CHICAGO, July 2.—An early and vigorous Democratic campaign throughout the country was urged by Governor Roosevelt tonight as he established himself in the Presidential suite at the Congress Hotel for a brief stay in the convention city.

Holding his first "levee," for a large group of correspondents, Mr. Roosevelt set forth a supplementary reason for making an airplane trip to the convention.

"The whole idea of flying here," he said, "was to bring forward the idea of getting the campaign started. You know that August is usually the month to get stirring. But I believe that some votes can be made in July.

OCTOBER 26, 1932
ROOSEVELT LIKENS THE ADMINISTRATION TO FOUR HORSEMEN

'Destruction, Delay, Deceit and Despair' Pictured at Baltimore as Abroad in the Land.

HOOVER POLICIES BLAMED

Tariff, Foreign Loans and Stock Market Boom Held Causes of Economic Depression.

WET PLANK CALLED FRAUD

Nation Is Urged to Bear in Mind Maryland's Example of Religious Freedom.

By JAMES A. HAGERTY.

BALTIMORE, Oct. 25.—Repeating his promises of a "new deal," Governor Roosevelt declared tonight that he was waging a war in this campaign against the "four horsemen" of the Hoover Administration.

Striking out against President Hoover in fighting fashion, and going to the Book of Revelation for his text, the Governor listed the "four horsemen" as "destruction, delay, deceit and despair." Each, he asserted, had driven through the country under the spur of the leadership of the Republican party, spreading ruin and furnishing no hope to the millions of American citizens hurt by the economic depression.

Twelve to fifteen thousand persons crowded the Fifth Regiment Armory in which Governor Roosevelt made the most belligerent speech of his campaign. Each attack on the Republican leadership and each criticism of the President brought roars of applause until the crowd was wrought up to a high pitch of enthusiasm.

Reply to Hoover's Speeches.

In this speech, which was intended to be a reply to President Hoover's recent addresses, Governor Roosevelt charged Mr. Hoover and his associates with having destroyed American prosperity by the encouragement of speculation before the stock market crash, by lending money to "backward and crippled" countries and by the "Grundy," or Hawley-Smoot tariff act, in other words, with having mounted the "horsemen of destruction."

Pictures "Horseman of Delay."

The "horseman of delay," Governor Roosevelt declared, followed closely the "horseman of destruction." The President was charged with delay in taking action to balance the Federal budget, with delay in providing unemployment relief and with delay in taking steps to restore the country's foreign markets.

"The horseman of deceit rides by night," Governor Roosevelt declared. "He rode when the administration told the public the crash of 1929 was not serious. He rode when he said prosperity was just around the corner. He rode when people were told to buy and invest and continue business as usual. He is riding now when spokesmen of the administration misrepresent what I say and what my associates say."

The "horseman of deceit" also rode, he declared, when the Republican National Convention wrote its plank on prohibition, and President Hoover and his associates attempted to interpret that plank.

"The Republican convention, as you all know, adopted a prohibition statement that was intended to sound wet to the wets and dry to the drys," he asserted. "The trouble was that it ended by deceiving no one. It sounded dry to the wets and wet to the drys. And so the Republican candidate attempted to correct it. He added new elements of confusion. He promised to work for the repeal of the Eighteenth Amendment with a very important reservation."

Assails Rivals on Dry Law.

"Everything went well, but suddenly the Vice President was heard from. He attempted to make provision for a dry interpretation of what the President meant as an appeal to the wets. Thus it looked as if the ticket was facing both ways. But on close examination it was found that the Vice Presidential candidate was indubitably dry, and the Presidential candidate was only half dry.

"The result or this curious attempt to move two ways on a one-way street was to resolve the Republican party into a whirling motion that meant to the voter honestly attempting to make a choice only a dizzy exhibition of uncertainty. Here is where the issue stands, my friends. No honest wet and no honest dry can approve of such political tactics. It is the most palpable attempt to defraud the American people we have seen in our time."

After the storm of applause which greeted this criticism of the Republican prohibition policy had died down Governor Roosevelt continued:

"And now a word as to beer. I favor the modification of the Volstead act to permit States to authorize the manufacture and sale of beer. This is a way to divert $300,000,000 or more a year from the racketeers to the Treasury of the United States."

This renewed declaration for beer brought another outburst.

With the audience shouting approval. Governor Roosevelt continued:

"The horseman of deceit was certainly riding high when the Republican leaders were trying to make up their minds about the Eighteenth Amendment."

Says "Horseman of Despair" Rides.

There was another period of cheering, and the Governor continued:

"Finally, there now rides abroad in stricken country among a people impoverished, confused, sore and weary the fourth horseman. He is the horseman of despair."

The President and his administration, Governor Roosevelt declared, had resorted to "the most plaintive diagnosis of despair that any country has ever heard from a responsible statesman."

The President, he continued, told the farmers in his acceptance speech that he sympathized with their stricken condition, wished he could do something to help them, admitted that his attempt to aid through stabilization of the prices of farm products had been a failure and had come to the conclusion that nothing but a general revival of business could restore the position of the American farmer.

The Governor characterized this as "bitter medicine" for the farmer, and asked how industry, which depends for its restoration upon the recovery of purchasing power by the farmer, could recover prosperity first.

The President, it was contended, also preached the doctrine of despair in his recent speech, when he quarreled with Mr. Roosevelt's statement that it was the responsibility of government to see that workers should be kept on their jobs wherever possible and that, when they were out of jobs, the jobs should be restored.

Says Jobless Gain No Hope.

Governor Roosevelt added that President Hoover seemingly believed that the millions of men and women now out of work in the United States must remain unemployed unless the government provided employment for all of them.

"Despair is written all over this statement of the President," he said, "a despairing cry which says to the ten million or more American unemployed that normal employment is not for them and is not in sight. This is pure, unadulterated despair. There is something worse, my friends, than offering hope. He apparently is opposed to any optimism in the face of present conditions. He apparently feels that the way to restore the spirit of the American people is to tell the unemployed, the vast, weary army of the unemployed, that they are going to remain unemployed."

After another interruption by applause, the Governor continued:

"This, my friends, is pure and unadulterated pessimism. It is, I submit, hair-shirt hypocrisy with a vengeance.

"If my opponents feel that I am to be diverted by puerile criticism I reply by returning to the attack.

"My statements are a matter of public record. They are correct. They are clear. They are directly and clearly addressed to the needs of the country.

"Do not be deceived in these, the last moments of the campaign by false lights on the shore, by smoke screens, by theatrics, by magic, by juggling, by the calling of names, by misrepresentation."

Says Nation's Strength Remains.

"The Four Horsemen have passed on their way."

- -

Radio Transforms Politics

The 1932 presidential election ushered in a new era in American politics—the electronic age. Radio became an inexpensive and easy medium for reaching the public, most of whom had never before personally encountered a candidate for the highest office in the land. With limited income during the Depression, Americans were largely confined to their homes for entertainment; radio enlarged their lives. Both Herbert Hoover and Franklin D. Roosevelt reached out to Americans over the airwaves, but it was Roosevelt who dominated this new form of communication. His powerful voice, conveying messages rich with imagery and hope, quickly overwhelmed Hoover's more business-like tone.

Radio has blown away a certain mist that in former days added to the candidate's mystery. Today he is more in the spotlight. The voters get a better view of him.

JULY 10, 1932
HOOVER, ROOSEVELT AND RADIO

Voice Personality Now Has Dominant Part in Political Campaign—Spoken Words "Paint" Character of the Candidate

By ORRIN E. DUNLAP JR.

VOICES "paint" character on the radio. Now the time has come when politicians and broadcasters alike are studying the microphone technique of Hoover, Roosevelt, Curtis and Garner. They are weighing radio's part in the campaign. They realize that voice personalities overspreading the nation, within range of millions of voters, can play an important role in the fortunes of politics in this electrical age.

The mere sound of a voice, the intonation, inflection and power of delivery can portray sincerity, cheerfulness, self-confidence, shrewdness and other qualities. The voice with a smile on the radio is as popular as on the telephone. The gushing voice is not liked generally but it travels through space and picks up an audience, in fact, so vast is the invisible assemblage, so diversified their interests and judgments, that no matter how lacking in voice personality some sort of an audience is assured. It may not number many millions as the broadcasters often claim, but if a speaker has from 10,000 to 50,000 listening to him out of a possible 50,000,000 he has a large audience compared to the political campaigners of Theodore Roosevelt's day.

* * *

President Hoover's voice betrays deliberate effort, according to John Carlile, production manager of the Columbia Broadcasting System, who labels the Hoover voice "typical of the engineer." He calls Governor Roosevelt's voice "one of the finest on the radio, carrying a tone of perfect sincerity and pleasing inflection."

One advantage both Hoover and Roosevelt have in common is that their voices are not sectional, that is, they are not too Yankee, too Southern or too Western. They are more of the universal type representative of the United States. The words of both are polished.

Radio inspires thought among the people. The candidate must have something worth while listening to, otherwise he may be lost in the maze of wave lengths. It is easy for the radio listener to become bored. There are no torches, gestures, bands in regalia, bunting or mob enthusiasm and emotion to supplement the oratory and help to hold attention.

There was a day not so long ago when Presidential candidates were introduced to the multitudes by large posters on barns, pictures in store and home windows, and by printed matter disclosing the history of their careers, their economic policies, their principles of government, philosophies, hobbies and friendships. Radio supplements all this with an intimate touch. It wafts spoken words across the land to the farm and city, to the valley and the hilltop. The invisible waves that drift through space in quest of a slender wire-like entrance to the home, establish direct contact with the voter, who may be influenced one way or another by the words plucked from above the rooftop.

The microphone is a modern weapon in politics. It calls for new campaign tactics. The candidates are aware that by their voices the people shall know them. They have observed that when a man goes on the air, whether he be a politician, preacher or comedian, he immediately opens himself to far greater criticism and general observation than he would ever encounter if he remained in the theatre or in a radioless rostrum. Radio has blown away a certain mist that in former days added to the candidate's mystery. Today he is more in the spotlight. The voters get a better view of him. And after four months of campaigning in print, radio, talking pictures and by personal appearances a candidate is no mystery man to the nation. He is known personally by deed, by picture and by word. . . .

* * *

RADIO organizations have no information or confirmation of the report that the Republicans and Democrats will take $1,000,000 each from their campaign chests for broadcasting. They assert that no definite plans have been formulated for campaigning on the air, but conferences will be held within the next few weeks to make arrangements for transcontinental rallies and campaign oratory. Radio officials and party chieftains at the Chicago conclaves discussed some phases of the ethereal campaign. They admit that many of the autumnal entertainment programs will be sidetracked as politics again grip the microphone, especially in October and up to election day.

It is the custom of the radio organizations to handle a Presidential address without charge. On that basis Mr. Hoover's campaign talks would be free, but Mr. Roosevelt would receive a bill. Inquiry reveals that the major networks will have a parley on this point, when the question arises, and if Mr. Hoover makes a strictly campaign speech he, too, may be billed for time on the air.

One thing is certain, the Democrats have no notification ceremony to pay for because that went on the air as part of the convention finale. It is expected that the Hoover official notification and acceptance speech will be broadcast to the nation.

The Columbia Broadcasting System spent approximately $100,000 for the convention programs, which were not paid for by either party. That includes engineering, wire lines, personnel and cancellation of commercial programs.

Hoover Begins Campaigning as Republican Worries Mount

President Hoover's reelection hopes dimmed rapidly, as did those of other Republicans. GOP leaders, recognizing the massive electoral momentum building for the Democrats, pleaded with the president to campaign and mobilize support for the party. Maine, which until 1957 held its state elections in mid-September, was regarded as a predictor of party strength heading into the November election. When the Democrats won by a landslide in Maine, Hoover relented and agreed to campaign on his own behalf and for the good of the party. The president belatedly took to the stump against a surging Democratic tidal wave. Ironically, Maine was one of the six states Hoover carried in November, leading James Farley to joke, "As Maine goes, so goes Vermont."

SEPTEMBER 14, 1932
EDITORIAL
MAINE.

The Maine September election may not be a good "political barometer," but it is a pretty efficient seismograph. It accurately records the occurrence of an electoral earthquake. No other description fits the totally unexpected overturn on Monday. To have elected a Governor and two out of three Representatives in Congress must have surpassed the wildest dreams of the Democrats. For it was a hotly contested campaign. The result was not decided by the stay-at-home vote. The total cast was more than 30,000 above that recorded in the corresponding election of 1928. And the shift in the party polling was amazing. The Republican vote fell off 31,000 from four years ago. The Democratic gain was no less than 53,000. The figures are their own eloquent commentary. It is evident that thousands of Maine Republicans abandoned their own party and voted Democratic. This is the great and startling political fact which stands out above all minor explanations or excuses. The prohibition issue may have played its part in Maine; the economic depression doubtless had its influence, although New England has notoriously suffered less from it than other parts of the country; but there is no escaping the inference that a vast discontent with Republican policies and the Republican Administration was the principal cause of the cataclysmic overturn in Maine.

Will not like causes produce like effects all over the country next November? This is the question which will make Republican managers haggard and sleepless from now till election day. They will feel that they have to deal with something imponderable but probably invincible. The State of Maine flies an unmistakable signal of distress. If everything may go wrong in so supposedly firmly anchored a State as Maine, what may not happen elsewhere? The whole nation is admittedly going through the same fit of the blues that was reflected in the Maine election. No politician can now shut his eyes to the fact that a great mass of American voters are cherishing grievances against the Republican party which they are at present disposed to wreak upon its candidates in the Presidential election. This impalpable but real political drift may be unreasonable, illogical and perfectly unfair toward President Hoover. But there it is. It will hereafter enter definitely into all the political forecasts this year. No party managers can leave it out of their reckoning, no matter how put to it they are to know how to deal with it. All the signs are that we are in the midst of a grand national "grouch," and what will come out of it politically no Republican leader can predict, though every Republican leader must fear.

Secretary Mills put the best face possible upon the Republican campaign in Maine, when he asked the voters "Why change?" Their answer came on Monday like the sound of many waters, "We want a change." How long this determination will persist, and how many thousands or millions of Americans will act upon it, it is of course impossible to foretell. But it cannot be denied that the moving finger has written upon the walls of the Republican palace a solemn warning, if not a verdict.

SEPTEMBER 15, 1932
PRESIDENT DECIDES TO TAKE THE STUMP

Roosevelt Farm Speech Spurs His Determination to Make Reply in the West.

LEADERS' URGINGS HEEDED

Five Addresses Planned, With That on Agriculture at His Iowa Birthplace.

Special to The New York Times.

WASHINGTON. Sept. 14.—President Hoover has definitely decided to take the stump and personally carry the "issues at stake" to the electorate. It was learned today after Governor Roosevelt's Topeka speech on the farm problem had been analyzed by administration advisers.

Mr. Hoover and his advisers immediately decided that the views expressed by Governor Roosevelt on farm relief presented a vulnerable spot in the Democratic offense, and that the President was the only person who could adequately reply to the suggestions advanced by his rival.

The reply to Mr. Roosevelt probably will be made early in October in an address at West Branch, Iowa, Mr. Hoover's birthplace.

In the discussion of the President's plan, which took place after Senator Dickinson of Iowa and Secretary Hyde had discussed with the President what they termed the "fallacies" of Governor Roosevelt's farm program, it was intimated that the President probably would make five speeches.

Party Leaders See a Crisis.

In revamping his campaign plans, the President, it is said, was influenced not only by the Topeka speech, but by telegrams that poured in on the White House today from worried party leaders. Some of these counseled him to go on the hustings as the only hope of successfully carrying his economic policies to the country. They urged him to face a situation which they described as critical.

Some leaders who have been watching the progress of the campaign were severe in criticizing the Republican National Committee. They said the committee had been slow in getting under way.

The Maine election had a decided effect on Republican concern over the way the campaign was progressing. Some party workers suggested a conference of chieftains here to discuss ways to combat the electorate's discontent. It is understood that such a conference may be held within a few days, and that the President will see several party war horses this week-end.

The Maine election undoubtedly is responsible in part for the decision of the President to conduct his campaign more aggressively in the next two months. Senator Dickinson, who, among others, advised the President to answer Governor Roosevelt on the farm situation, expressed confidence that with the President going directly to the people, the Republicans could offset the effect of the revolt in Maine through the campaign in the West. He said that sentiment in the corn and wheat regions was swinging to Mr. Hoover, and he did not look for this movement to be deterred by the Maine results.

- -

EARLY PUBLIC OPINION POLLING PREDICTS AN FDR VICTORY

Systematic public opinion polls first appeared during the 1932 election. These early attempts to survey the public's political preferences were simplistic in comparison to modern versions, but captured the attention of candidates and voters alike. Early results showed President Hoover barely ahead, but the numbers quickly moved in FDR's favor. The final polls, indicating a strong Democratic victory, closely matched the final electoral tally. After the 1932 election, polls became a dominant feature of American campaigns.

SEPTEMBER 23, 1932
60,237 VOTE IN POLL; HOOVER LEAD IS 539

President Gets Slight Margin Over Roosevelt in Returns on Literary Digest Survey.

HE IS AHEAD IN NEW YORK

Indiana Also for Him, While Rival Is in Front in Pennsylvania, Ohio and West Virginia.

First returns in the Literary Digest's nation-wide Presidential poll, covering five States and including 60,237 returned "straw" ballots, give President Hoover a slight lead of 539 votes over his Democratic opponent, Governor Franklin D. Roosevelt.

The aggregate vote for Mr. Hoover 28,193, is 46.73 per cent of the total cast for the two major candidates, while Mr. Roosevelt's 27,654, constitutes 45.84 per cent of that total. The remaining 7.43 per cent of returned ballots was cast for five minor candidates with Norman Thomas, the Socialist candidate, leading these.

The first installment of the Presidential poll, designed to comprise 20,000,000 ballots, will be published in tomorrow's issue of the Literary Digest. The five States included are Indiana, New York, Ohio, Pennsylvania and West Virginia. Of these Mr. Hoover received a plurality in two, Indiana and New York, and Mr. Roosevelt in the other three.

Rock-ribbed Republican Pennsylvania gave the Democratic nominee a plurality.

Many Party Shifts.

A comparison of the Literary Digest returns in its Presidential "straw" poll with the actual vote four years ago shows that in these early returns Governor Roosevelt is receiving 39.51 per cent of his strength from persons who voted the Republican ticket in 1928, while President Hoover has drawn to his strength 6.16 percent from voters who cast their ballots for Smith in 1928.

Of Governor Roosevelt's total vote 44 per cent is Democratic, and of President Hoover's, 81.03 Republican, taking the actual vote in 1928 as a basis.

Fifteen per cent of the vote covered by the first returns did not figure in the 1928 election, ascribed by the Literary Digest to the probability that these voters had not then attained voting age.

NOVEMBER 4, 1932
ROOSEVELT IS VICTOR IN FINAL DIGEST POLL

3-to-2 Lead in the Popular Vote Is Revealed in Tabulation of 3,064,497 Ballots.

ELECTORAL TALLY 474 TO 57

37% of Governor's Supporters Were Republican in 1928—55% of All for Him.

PRESIDENT GAINS SLIGHTLY

But Magazine Sees a Possibility Hoover Will Carry Only Maine and Vermont—Some States Close.

Final returns from the Literary Digest's nation-wide Presidential poll give Governor Franklin D. Roosevelt, Democratic nominee for President, a lead over his Republican opponent, President Hoover, in forty-one States and, approximately, a 3-to-2 lead in the popular vote. On the basis of these returns, Mr. Roosevelt would have 474 and Mr. Hoover fifty-seven votes in the Electoral College.

In the semi-final returns, published by the Digest last week, President Hoover was shown to have made a gain of .14 in his percentage of the popular vote, as compared with the quarter-finals, published the week before. At the finish of the Digest poll another and slightly larger, but still fractional, gain of one-fifth of 1 per cent is recorded in Mr. Hoover's favor.

The final vote in the Digest poll covers a total of 3,064,497 tabulated ballots, a new high record for the quadrennial straw vote of the magazine. Ballots were sent out to 20,000,000 voters. The total this year is divided between the Presidential candidates of the three leading parties as follows: Roosevelt, 1,715,789, or 55.99 per cent; Hoover, 1,150,398, or 37.53 per cent; Thomas, Socialist, 148,079, or 4.84 per cent.

Final Vote by States.

The following table shows the final vote for the three major Presidential candidates in the several States, together with the vote of the States in the Electoral College:

State	Electoral Vote	Roosevelt	Hoover	Thomas	State	Electoral Vote	Roosevelt	Hoover	Thomas
Alabama	11	20,161	4,272	402	Nebraska	7	20,952	11,405	950
Arizona	3	4,910	2,574	254	Nevada	3	1,506	701	55
Arkansas	9	16,225	3,712	225	New H'mpshire	4	4,625	6,943	408
California	22	148,832	81,834	7,874	New Jersey	16	58,101	69,828	11,886
Colorado	6	14,304	11,950	1,546	New Mexico	3	1,934	1,270	126
Connecticut	8	16,884	26,469	4,256	New York	47	172,765	164,453	30,568
Delaware	3	2,546	2,384	205	No. Carolina	13	28,153	9,963	571
Dist. of Col.		5,061	3,937	514	North Dakota	4	8,762	4,878	499
Florida	7	23,606	9,302	857	Ohio	26	109,943	81,512	12,275
Georgia	12	31,849	4,823	329	Oklahoma	11	22,848	10,692	1,409
Idaho	4	5,159	3,282	307	Oregon	5	15,433	8,551	994
Illinois	29	105,920	75,414	7,665	Pennsylvania	36	124,675	93,057	17,607
Indiana	14	53,465	40,227	3,546	Rhode Island	4	7,046	8,856	729
Iowa	11	32,956	23,372	1,712	So. Carolina	8	15,657	1,601	162
Kansas	9	29,067	23,529	1,602	South Dakota	4	9,131	5,910	314
Kentucky	11	24,826	13,114	771	Tennessee	11	26,635	11,352	682
Louisiana	10	19,050	4,004	401	Texas	12	74,511	15,317	1,458
Maine	5	8,264	11,462	557	Utah	4	8,274	4,744	558
Maryland	8	26,955	12,854	2,650	Vermont	2	3,301	4,945	271
Massachusetts	17	34,659	60,712	7,125	Virginia	11	34,191	13,440	942
Michigan	19	69,939	49,728	5,453	Washington	8	30,324	16,717	1,624
Minnesota	11	52,233	32,613	4,047	West Virginia	8	23,153	14,365	768
Mississippi	9	9,887	1,051	88	Wisconsin	12	44,054	21,375	4,289
Missouri	15	70,882	39,071	3,254	Wyoming	3	2,913	2,201	248
Montana	4	8,508	5,971	650	Unknown	0	30,749	17,661	2,396
					Grand Totals	**531**	**1,715,789**	**1,150,398**	**148,079**

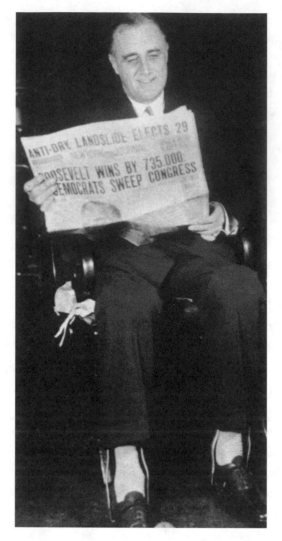

Franklin Delano Roosevelt, the thirty-second president of the United States, is photographed after winning his first presidential election in 1932.
Source: The Granger Collection, New York

A political cataclysm, unprecedented in the nation's history and produced by three years of depression, thrust President Herbert Hoover and the Republican power from control of the government yesterday.

FRANKLIN DELANO ROOSEVELT WINS THE ELECTION OF 1932

On November 8, 1932, the nation decisively elected Franklin D. Roosevelt to be the thirty-second president of the United States. President Hoover received only 59 electoral votes and suffered the largest popular defeat of an incumbent president in U.S. history. Roosevelt carried all but six states, on a national margin of 7 million votes. FDR entered office with the nation rallying behind him and his message of hope. Few presidents have begun their term with such broad support or such high expectations.

NOVEMBER 9, 1932
ROOSEVELT WINNER IN LANDSLIDE! DEMOCRATS CONTROL WET CONGRESS; LEHMAN GOVERNOR, O'BRIEN MAYOR

SWEEP IS NATIONAL

Democrats Carry 40 States, Electoral Votes 448.

SIX STATES FOR HOOVER

He Loses New York, New Jersey, Bay State, Indiana and Ohio.

DEMOCRATS WIN SENATE

Necessary Majority for Repeal of the Volstead Act in Prospect.

RECORD NATIONAL VOTE

Hoover Felicitates Rival and Promises 'Every Helpful Effort for Common Purpose.'

Roosevelt Statement.

President-elect Roosevelt gave the following statement to THE NEW YORK TIMES early this morning:

"While I am grateful with all my heart for this expression of the confidence of my fellow-Americans, I realize keenly the responsibility I shall assume and I mean to serve with my utmost capacity the interest of the nation.

"The people could not have arrived at this result if they had not been informed properly of my views by an independent press, and I value particularly the high service of THE NEW YORK TIMES in its reporting of my speeches and in its enlightened comment."

By ARTHUR KROCK.

A political cataclysm, unprecedented in the nation's history and produced by three years of depression, thrust President Herbert Hoover and the Republican power from control of the government yesterday, elected Governor Franklin Delano Roosevelt President of the United States, provided the Democrats with a large majority in Congress and gave them administration of the affairs of many States of the Union.

Fifteen minutes after midnight, Eastern Standard Time, The Associated Press flashed from Palo Alto this line: "Hoover concedes defeat."

It was then fifteen minutes after nine in California, and the President had been in his residence on the Leland Stanford campus only a few hours, arriving with expressed confidence of victory.

A few minutes after the flash from Palo Alto the text of Mr. Hoover's message of congratulation to his successful opponent was received by THE NEW YORK TIMES, though it was delayed in direct transmission to the President-elect. After offering his felicitations to Governor Roosevelt on his "opportunity to be of service to the country," and extending wishes for success, the President "dedicated" himself to "every possible helpful effort * * * in the common purpose of us all."

This language strengthened the belief of those who expect that the relations between the victor and the vanquished, in view of the exigent condition of the country, will be more than perfunctory, and that they may soon confer in an effort to arrive at a mutual program of stabilization during the period between now and March 4, when Mr. Roosevelt will take office.

The President-elect left his headquarters shortly before 2 A. M. without having received Mr. Hoover's message.

As returns from the Mountain States and the Pacific Coast supplemented the early reports from the Middle West and the eastern seaboard, the President was shown to have surely carried only five States with a total of 51 electoral votes. It is probable that Mr. Roosevelt has captured forty-two States and 472 electoral votes. With two States in doubt he has taken forty States and 448 votes. Only 266 are required for the election of a President. It also appeared certain that the Congress elected by the people yesterday will be wet enough not only to modify the Volstead act, as pledged in the Democratic platform, but to submit fiat repeal of national prohibition.

Votes National Grouch.

The country was voting a "national grouch" against three years of business stagnation, against farm foreclosures, bank failures, unemployment and the Republican argument that "things could have been worse." The President's single-handed fight to sustain his record, his warnings against Democratic changes in the Hawley-Smoot tariff and efforts to impress the country with fear of a change of administration were as futile in the final analysis as straw votes and the reports of newspaper observers indicated that it would be.

Mr. Hoover joins in history Benjamin Harrison and William Howard Taft as the only Republican Presidents who sought and were denied re-election. In the sum, his defeat was greater even than Mr. Taft's in 1912, for while his electoral and popular vote will be greater, he had a united party organization behind him and Mr. Taft was opposed by Theodore Roosevelt and the Bull Moose party.

• •

A DIFFICULT TRANSITION AND AN ASSASSINATION ATTEMPT

The transfer of power in 1932 was turbulent. Early in the transition period, Herbert Hoover and FDR clashed over foreign relations and domestic policy, but especially on proposed renegotiation of debt repayment from Great Britain. The battle, which persisted throughout the four months leading to the March inauguration, was contested bitterly in private but portrayed more benignly to the public. Then, on February 15, 1933, a would-be assassin fired five rounds just as FDR finished a speech in Miami. The attempt on FDR failed, but Chicago mayor Anton Cermak was wounded and died a few weeks later. The shooting rattled the nation, further adding to the tension of the time. Amid the tumult of the Great Depression, it seemed that nothing, not even presidential transitions, could go smoothly.

DECEMBER 23, 1932
EDITORIAL
AGREEMENTS AND DIFFERENCES.

It would be hard to find in our political annals a precedent for the correspondence between President HOOVER and Governor ROOSEVELT, now made public. JOHN ADAMS would have scorned communication with JEFFERSON about the difficulties of the Government which the latter was to take over. There is no evidence that BENJAMIN HARRISON ever consulted with GROVER CLEVELAND about the financial embarrassments of the Administration which were certain to have a cumulative and disastrous effect after March 4, 1893. President TAFT is said to have exchanged views with WOODROW WILSON after the election of 1912, but what subjects were discussed between them, and what conclusions were arrived at, we do not yet know. The telegrams which passed between Mr. HOOVER and President-elect ROOSEVELT reveal an admirable tone and temper on either side. They are courteous and friendly. Neither man shows distrust of the other, nor seems to fear that a political snare was being laid for his feet. The correspondence, as printed, does honor to both sides. It may be helpful to point out wherein they agree and wherein they differ.

First, taking up the agreements, Mr. HOOVER and Governor ROOSEVELT are of one mind in holding that (1) the intergovernmental debts must be revised; (2) no time should be lost in setting about the task, sounding out the debtor nations, ascertaining all the facts; (3) the debtor countries should be approached separately, and the questions of disarmament and tariffs should be kept, if possible, distinct from the war debts; (4) the present Administration should not undertake any commitments which would even seem to have the effect of binding, legally or morally, the Administration which is to take office on March 4.

Where the President and the President-elect differ is, chiefly, in the matter of a new commission to begin an official examination of all the related problems which tie themselves up, despite all efforts to keep them severed, with the war debts. Nor is Governor ROOSEVELT willing to fall in with the President's suggestion that he join in urging some eminent Democrat, like Mr. OWEN YOUNG, for appointment as head of the committee, or delegation, instructed to explore the whole international situation connected with the debts. That would seem to the European nations, argues Mr. ROOSEVELT, as if such a leadership were authorized by him to present his views on "matters of large and binding policy." Such an inference he would not wish to have drawn. But short of any means or measure that tie his hands before he becomes President on March 4, the Governor is more than willing to cooperate in every helpful way open to him with the President in instituting and pushing the preliminary inquiries which must precede any decision that will stand up.

As regards the general policy of disarmament, Mr. ROOSEVELT heartily assures the President: "Your policy is clear and satisfactory." Again and again he reiterates his desire that the advance studies of the debt question should be expedited by such agencies as the President may select. He declares that he will be "happy" to receive reports of progress from time to time, and adds a positive expression of his willingness to "consult with you freely" during all the period when the investigation is under way.

Mr. HOOVER appears now inclined to drop the whole subject. He states that he will "respect the wishes" of Governor ROOSEVELT. But those wishes distinctly favor the idea of proceeding without delay through the established diplomatic agencies, or through specially appointed men, in order to clear the ground as fully as may be before March 4. The President has been compelled to abandon his proposal of a new general commission, or a revival of the old Debt Funding Commission. This he could not have got from Congress, even if Governor ROOSEVELT had joined him in asking for it. But there is no reason why Mr. HOOVER should not go ahead in the ways suggested by Mr. ROOSEVELT, and, without trying to set up that distinctive "machinery" of which he spoke in his message to Congress, see what can be done toward directing and energizing the existing agencies of diplomacy. In any such plan, it is now clear, he would have not merely the assent but the approval of Governor ROOSEVELT.

FEBRUARY 16, 1933
ASSASSIN FIRES INTO ROOSEVELT PARTY AT MIAMI; PRESIDENT-ELECT UNINJURED; MAYOR CERMAK AND 4 OTHERS WOUNDED

ASSASSIN SHOOTS 5 TIMES

Police and Bystanders Leap for Him and Take Him Prisoner.

ACCOMPLICE TAKEN LATER

Cermak and New York Officers Rushed to Hospital—Now in Serious Condition.

ROOSEVELT DELAYS TRIP

Had Been Warmly Welcomed and Intended to Start for North at Once.

By JAMES A. HAGERTY.

Special to The New York Times.

MIAMI, Feb. 15.—An unsuccessful attempt was made to assassinate President-elect Franklin D. Roosevelt just after he ended a speech in Bay Front Park here at 9:35 o'clock tonight, two hours after his return from an eleven-day fishing cruise on Vincent Astor's yacht Nourmahal.

Although the gunman missed the target at which he was aiming, he probably fatally wounded Mayor Anton Cermak of Chicago and four other persons were hit by five shots from his pistol before a woman destroyed his aim on the last shot by seizing his wrist and a Miami policeman felled him to the ground with a blow of his night stick.

1932 POPULAR VOTE

STATE	TOTAL VOTE	FRANKLIN D. ROOSEVELT (DEMOCRAT) VOTES	%	HERBERT C. HOOVER (REPUBLICAN) VOTES	%	NORMAN M. THOMAS (SOCIALIST) VOTES	%	WILLIAM Z. FOSTER (COMMUNIST) VOTES	%
Alabama	245,303	207,910	84.8	34,675	14.1	2,030	0.8	675	0.3
Arizona	118,251	79,264	67.0	36,104	30.5	2,618	2.2	256	0.2
Arkansas	216,569	186,829	86.3	27,465	12.7	1,166	0.5	157	0.1
California	2,266,972	1,324,157	58.4	847,902	37.4	63,299	2.8	1,023	0.0
Colorado	457,696	250,877	54.8	189,617	41.4	13,591	3.0	787	0.2
Connecticut	594,183	281,632	47.4	288,420	48.5	20,480	3.4	1,364	0.2
Delaware	112,901	54,319	48.1	57,073	50.6	1,376	1.2	133	0.1
Florida	276,943	206,307	74.5	69,170	25.0	775	0.3	—	0.0
Georgia	255,590	234,118	91.6	19,863	7.8	461	0.2	23	0.0
Idaho	186,520	109,479	58.7	71,312	38.2	526	0.3	491	0.3
Illinois	3,407,926	1,882,304	55.2	1,432,756	42.0	67,258	2.0	15,582	0.5
Indiana	1,576,927	862,054	54.7	677,184	42.9	21,388	1.4	2,187	0.1
Iowa	1,036,687	598,019	57.7	414,433	40.0	20,467	2.0	559	0.1
Kansas	791,978	424,204	53.6	349,498	44.1	18,276	2.3	—	0.0
Kentucky	983,059	580,574	59.1	394,716	40.2	3,853	0.4	271	0.0
Louisiana	268,804	249,418	92.8	18,853	7.0	—	0.0	—	0.0
Maine	298,444	128,907	43.2	166,631	55.8	2,489	0.8	162	0.1
Maryland	511,054	314,314	61.5	184,184	36.0	10,489	2.1	1,031	0.2
Massachusetts	1,580,114	800,148	50.6	736,959	46.6	34,305	2.2	4,821	0.3
Michigan	1,664,765	871,700	52.4	739,894	44.4	39,205	2.4	9,318	0.6
Minnesota	1,002,843	600,806	59.9	363,959	36.3	25,476	2.5	6,101	0.6
Mississippi	146,034	140,168	96.0	5,180	3.5	686	0.5	—	0.0
Missouri	1,609,894	1,025,406	63.7	564,713	35.1	16,374	1.0	568	0.0
Montana	216,479	127,286	58.8	78,078	36.1	7,891	3.6	1,775	0.8
Nebraska	570,135	359,082	63.0	201,177	35.3	9,876	1.7	—	0.0
Nevada	41,430	28,756	69.4	12,674	30.6	—	0.0	—	0.0
New Hampshire	205,520	100,680	49.0	103,629	50.4	947	0.5	264	0.1
New Jersey	1,630,063	806,630	49.5	775,684	47.6	42,998	2.6	2,915	0.2
New Mexico	151,606	95,089	62.7	54,217	35.8	1,776	1.2	135	0.1
New York	4,688,614	2,534,959	54.1	1,937,963	41.3	177,397	3.8	27,956	0.6
North Carolina	711,498	497,566	69.9	208,344	29.3	5,588	0.8	—	0.0
North Dakota	256,290	178,350	69.6	71,772	28.0	3,521	1.4	830	0.3
Ohio	2,609,728	1,301,695	49.9	1,227,319	47.0	64,094	2.5	7,231	0.3
Oklahoma	704,633	516,468	73.3	188,165	26.7	—	0.0	—	0.0
Oregon	368,751	213,871	58.0	136,019	36.9	15,450	4.2	1,681	0.5
Pennsylvania	2,859,021	1,295,948	45.3	1,453,540	50.8	91,119	3.2	5,658	0.2
Rhode Island	266,170	146,604	55.1	115,266	43.3	3,138	1.2	546	0.2
South Carolina	104,407	102,347	98.0	1,978	1.9	82	0.1	—	0.0
South Dakota	288,438	183,515	63.6	99,212	34.4	1,551	0.5	364	0.1
Tennessee	390,273	259,473	66.5	126,752	32.5	1,796	0.5	254	0.1
Texas[1]	863,406	760,348	88.1	97,959	11.3	4,450	0.5	207	0.0
Utah	206,578	116,750	56.5	84,795	41.0	4,087	2.0	946	0.5
Vermont	136,980	56,266	41.1	78,984	57.7	1,533	1.1	195	0.1
Virginia	297,942	203,979	68.5	89,637	30.1	2,382	0.8	86	0.0
Washington	614,814	353,260	57.5	208,645	33.9	17,080	2.8	2,972	0.5
West Virginia	743,774	405,124	54.5	330,731	44.5	5,133	0.7	444	0.1
Wisconsin	1,114,814	707,410	63.5	347,741	31.2	53,379	4.8	3,105	0.3
Wyoming	96,962	54,370	56.1	39,583	40.8	2,829	2.9	180	0.2
TOTALS	**39,747,783**	**22,818,740**	**57.4**	**15,760,425**	**39.6**	**884,685**	**2.2**	**103,253**	**0.3**

1. Figures from Svend Petersen, *A Statistical History of the American Presidential Elections* (Westport, Conn.: Greenwood Press, 1981); Clerk of the House of Representatives, *Statistics of the Congressional and Presidential Election* (Washington, D.C.: U.S. Government Printing Office, 1932); *Texas Almanac.*

OTHER VOTES	%	PLURALITY	
13	0.0	173,235	D
9	0.0	43,160	D
952	0.4	159,364	D
30,591	1.3	476,255	D
2,824	0.6	61,260	D
2,287	0.4	6,788	R
—	0.0	2,754	R
691	0.2	137,137	D
1,125	0.4	214,255	D
4,712	2.5	38,167	D
10,026	0.3	449,548	D
14,114	0.9	184,870	D
3,209	0.3	183,586	D
—	0.0	74,706	D
3,645	0.4	185,858	D
533	0.2	230,565	D
255	0.1	37,724	R
1,036	0.2	130,130	D
3,881	0.2	63,189	D
4,648	0.3	131,806	D
6,501	0.6	236,847	D
—	0.0	134,988	D
2,833	0.2	460,693	D
1,449	0.7	49,208	D
—	0.0	157,905	D
—	0.0	16,082	D
—	0.0	2,949	R
1,836	0.1	30,946	D
389	0.3	40,872	D
10,339	0.2	596,996	D
—	0.0	289,222	D
1,817	0.7	106,578	D
9,389	0.4	74,376	D
—	0.0	328,303	D
1,730	0.5	77,852	D
12,756	0.4	157,592	R
616	0.2	31,338	D
—	0.0	100,369	D
3,796	1.3	84,303	D
1,998	0.5	132,721	D
442	0.0	662,389	D
—	0.0	31,955	D
2	0.0	22,718	R
1,858	0.6	114,342	D
32,857	5.3	144,615	D
2,342	0.3	74,393	D
3,179	0.3	359,669	D
—	0.0	14,787	D
180,680	**0.5**	**7,058,315**	**D**

Roosevelt Was Target.

The would-be assassin, who was arrested immediately and lodged in the city prison on the nineteenth floor of Miami's skyscraper City Hall, is Giuseppe Zingara [sic] of Hackensack, N. J.

Although early reports were that he intended to kill Mayor Cermak rather than the President-elect, due to his remark, "Well, I got Cermak," it appeared later that Mr. Roosevelt was his target.

"I'd kill every President," he was reported by the police to have said after his arrest.

"I'd kill them all; I'd kill all the officers," he also is reported to have said, indicating that he may be an Anarchist.

Evidence that the attempted assassination of Roosevelt was premeditated was obtained by the police late tonight and Andrea Valemti, [sic] who lived with Zingara, was arrested on suspicion of being an accomplice.

FASCISM AND NAZISM RISE IN EUROPE

The year 1932 was critical on the global stage, as well as within the United States, although foreign policy received almost no attention during the election. The problems that dominated American politics, especially the collapse of the economy, had spread around the world. At the same time that FDR promised the American people a "New Deal" that would expand liberal democracy, other nations embraced different solutions. In Italy Benito Mussolini embraced antidemocratic fascism, and in Germany Adolf Hitler and his Nazi Party took power after Germany's last democratic election. The conflicts between democracy and fascism set nations on a path toward a war that would encompass the globe.

SEPTEMBER 18, 1932
FASCISM DEFINED BY MUSSOLINI AS THE CREED OF THE CENTURY

He Upholds War, Condemns Democracy as an Outworn Doctrine, and Calls the Trend to Empire a Manifestation of Vitality

As originator, developer and administrator of the political regime and doctrine of fascism, Premier Mussolini of Italy recently prepared an exposition of the doctrine for the Encyclopedia Italiana, herewith reproduced with slight abridgement.

By BENITO MUSSOLINI.

FASCISM today has a distinct personality of its own, both as a regime and as a doctrine. The word must be interpreted in the sense that today fascism, exercising its critical faculties on itself and on others, has its own unmistakable points of view and of reference—and, therefore, also of direction—with regard to all the problems which affect the intelligence or the material aspects of the life of the peoples of the world.

In the first place, fascism, as it generally regards the future and the development of humanity, and laying aside all considerations of present-day politics, does not believe either in the possibility or the utility of perpetual peace. It therefore repudiates pacifism, which betrays a tendency to give up the struggle and implies cowardice in the face of the necessity of sacrifice.

Only war raises all human energies to the maximum and gets a seal of nobility on the peoples which have the virtues to undertake it. All other tests are mere substitutes, which never place man face-to-face with himself in the alternatives of life or death. Any doctrine, therefore, which starts from the initial postulate of peace, is foreign to fascism.

Equally unrelated to the spirit of fascism are all those international and League of Nations institutions—even if they are accepted for the usefulness they may have in certain political situations—which, as history proves, may be scattered to the winds when sentimental, ideal or practical elements cause storms to rage in the hearts of peoples. . . .

Dropping Republicanism.

Fascism is radically opposed to the whole mass of democratic ideology and repudiates it, both in its theoretical premises and in its practical applications. Fascism denies that numbers, from the mere fact of being numbers, can play the role of leaders of human communities. Fascism denies that numbers can govern, through a system of periodical consultation of the electorate, but affirms the irremediable, fruitful and beneficial inequality of men, who cannot all be reduced to the same level by an external and mechanical fact such as universal suffrage.

MARCH 6, 1933
HITLER BLOC WINS A REICH MAJORITY; RULES IN PRUSSIA

Stay-at-Homes Turn Out and Give Government 52% of 39,000,000 Record Vote.

NAZIS ROLL UP 17,300,000

Get 44% of Total Poll and Even Wrest the Control of Bavaria From Catholics.

ELECTION IS PEACEFUL

Berlin is Closely Guarded—The Stahlhelm Holds Parade Under Sunny Skies.

By FREDERICK T. BIRCHALL.

Special Cable to The New York Times.

BERLIN, Monday, March 6.—With almost mathematical precision the results in yesterday's German elections for the Reichstag and the Prussian Diet bear out the predictions based on the pre-election campaign. Just as two and two make four, so suppression and intimidation have produced a Nazi-Nationalist triumph. The rest of the world may now accept the fact of ultra-Nationalist domination of the Reich and Prussia for a prolonged period with whatever results this may entail.

At 2 o'clock this morning, when 39,000,000 out of the Reich's eligible vote of 44,000,000 [was] counted and with every indication of a probable total vote of 90 per cent, exceeding all precedents Nazi-Nationalist control of the Reichstag was assured. The Nazis will have at least 288 seats and the Nationalists 53 more, giving them together 341 seats, or a clear 52 per cent in a total of 648. . . .

The so-called stay-at-home vote came out with a vengeance and almost the whole of it went to the Nazis; while, in addition, the Hitlerites gained a full 10 per cent from the other parties.

Gain 4,000,000 Votes.

The Nazis have increased their own vote by more than 4,000,000, or almost 30 per cent over the November total. The Centrists and Socialists throughout the country have almost held their own. The Communists lost more than 20 per cent, but their lost votes did not go to the Socialists, as had been expected. While a few may have gone in that direction to make up for the non-voting Socialists, the greater part of the Communist loss, by some strange psychology, must have gone to the Nazis. Therein is food for international consideration.

After fourteen years under the most democratic Constitution on earth, four weeks of ballyhoo and big-stick tactics sent the German people to the polls in the spirit of the seventeenth century, when in the thirty years' religious war the Catholic Thilly whenever successful over the Protestant Gustavus Adolphus, never lacked Protestant recruits.

To put it another way, the German collectivist leaning, the desire to be commanded rather than be free, has again prevailed. And the result is that the democratic republic the world superimposed on the Germany of 1918 is for the time being as dead as the Pharaohs. Throughout Berlin yesterday among the thousands of Nazi and Nationalist banners waving from apartments, not one flag of the present republic could be seen. The Nazis had announced they disapproved of it.

THE PRESIDENTIAL ELECTION OF 1936

FDR WINS HISTORIC ENDORSEMENT OF HIS "NEW DEAL"

Running for reelection in 1936, President Franklin Delano Roosevelt prophesied, "This generation has a rendezvous with destiny." The Democratic triumph at the polls that followed would indeed affect America's destiny. Roosevelt's New Deal forever changed the character of the country, establishing a permanent role for the federal government in the management of the economy. Later, his guidance of the United States in World War II committed it to an enduring role of world leadership.

Roosevelt's victory in 1932 had been impressive, but not necessarily durable. It remained to be seen whether it had been a temporary reaction to the travails of the Great Depression and only a transient interruption of the long dominance of the Republican majority. As economic miseries had brought Hoover's dismissal, so did Roosevelt's fate hang on the success of his programs.

Initially, FDR attempted to unify the nation in a consensual effort, beginning with restoring confidence in the banking system and creating immediate relief funds for the 13 million unemployed. His core program was to promote cooperative planning to stabilize the industrial sector (the National Recovery Act) and raise farm prices (the Agricultural Adjustment Act). These programs did bring some improvement in the economy, but the limited gains were lost when the Supreme Court declared these laws unconstitutional.

A different—and lasting—New Deal began in 1935, aided by Democratic gains in the 1934 mid-term elections that gave the party majorities of 322 to 103 in the House and 69 to 25 in the Senate. Institutionally, Roosevelt led the executive branch and Congress in creating new agencies to regulate the economy and reform the free market while maintaining the basic capitalist structure. Economically, to increase Americans' income and spur consumer demand, they substantially increased government spending for unemployment relief and public works. Politically, the Democrats formed a new majority coalition based on deliberate class appeals to workers, union members, white ethnic immigrant minorities, and blacks.

In this Clifford Berryman cartoon President Franklin D. Roosevelt tries to heal a Depression-stricken United States with an ever-growing assortment of New Deal agencies and programs.

To revive the economy, Roosevelt abandoned his commitment to a balanced budget. Instead, the federal government became employer of the jobless and builder of the national infrastructure. The most prominent agency was the Works Progress Administration. Before the election, it provided work for more than 3 million and eventually for a total of 8.5 million people, spending $11 billion while paying an average monthly wage of $41.57.

For its money, the country ultimately got much in return: 78,000 bridges and viaducts, 640,000 miles of rural roads and urban streets, 39,000 schools, 2,500 hospitals, 12,800 playgrounds, 800 airfields, 2,500 sports stadiums, and 24 million planted trees. Writers, musicians, and artists also were hired, the latter crafting 20,000 murals and sculptures in public spaces and many hundreds of paintings. The Public Works Administration, a bureaucratic complement and rival, focused on major construction projects, from New York's Triborough Bridge to San Francisco's Bay Bridge, including some that would eventually honor Republican presidents,

1936 ELECTORAL VOTE

STATE	ELECTORAL VOTES	ROOSEVELT	LANDON	STATE	ELECTORAL VOTES	ROOSEVELT	LANDON
Alabama	(11)	11	–	Nebraska	(7)	7	–
Arizona	(3)	3	–	Nevada	(3)	3	–
Arkansas	(9)	9	–	New Hampshire	(4)	4	–
California	(22)	22	–	New Jersey	(16)	16	–
Colorado	(6)	6	–	New Mexico	(3)	3	–
Connecticut	(8)	8	–	New York	(47)	47	–
Delaware	(3)	3	–	North Carolina	(13)	13	–
Florida	(7)	7	–	North Dakota	(4)	4	–
Georgia	(12)	12	–	Ohio	(26)	26	–
Idaho	(4)	4	–	Oklahoma	(11)	11	–
Illinois	(29)	29	–	Oregon	(5)	5	–
Indiana	(14)	14	–	Pennsylvania	(36)	36	–
Iowa	(11)	11	–	Rhode Island	(4)	4	–
Kansas	(9)	9	–	South Carolina	(8)	8	–
Kentucky	(11)	11	–	South Dakota	(4)	4	–
Louisiana	(10)	10	–	Tennessee	(11)	11	–
Maine	(5)	–	5	Texas	(23)	23	–
Maryland	(8)	8	–	Utah	(4)	4	–
Massachusetts	(17)	17	–	Vermont	(3)	–	3
Michigan	(19)	19	–	Virginia	(11)	11	–
Minnesota	(11)	11	–	Washington	(8)	8	–
Mississippi	(9)	9	–	West Virginia	(8)	8	–
Missouri	(15)	15	–	Wisconsin	(12)	12	–
Montana	(4)	4	–	Wyoming	(3)	3	–
				TOTALS	**(531)**	**523**	**8**

such as Boulder (now Hoover) Dam and Washington D.C.'s National (now Reagan) Airport.

The economic stimuli seemed to work. By the time of the 1936 election, unemployment had fallen by two-fifths and 6 million workers were back on the job. Two million homes were rescued from foreclosure by federal mortgage insurance. The gross national product was almost back to its 1929 level, national income had risen 50 percent, and the Dow-Jones stock index had gained 80 percent since FDR's inauguration.

But even as the economy improved, much of the business community did not sing the Democratic campaign song, "Happy Days Are Here Again." The New Deal had changed its political model from cooperation among all groups to mobilization of the less fortunate. Far-reaching legislation redistributed

political power and economic privilege. Social Security established pensions for the aged and benefits for the unemployed. The federal government put its authority behind union organizational drives, now reaching the major manufacturing industries. Holding companies controlling public utilities faced a legislative "death sentence." Banks were subjected to new regulations. The tax laws tilted against the wealthy, through punishing rates on very high incomes, a tax on large inherited estates, and new levies on corporate profits.

These fundamental changes made the election of 1936 much more than a contest of candidates or an argument about policy proposals. Critics of the New Deal abounded. They found it bureaucratic, wasteful, and corrupt. More basically, they saw Roosevelt as a threat to American freedom, a despot who would inevitably transform the United States into a personal dictatorship if not a Soviet communist state. Roosevelt too saw the election in these apocalyptic terms, a battle between the deprived many and the privileged few, a combat of mass democracy against economic elites. Social class inequality—always present but often hidden in the past—had become the focus of American politics.

THE PARTIES AND THE CANDIDATES

The major parties faced little internal controversy, reserving their fire for a fierce clash between united Republicans and united Democrats. Outside of their ranks, significant social movements and third parties challenged the basic economic structure of the country and the dominance of the two-party system.

Republicans saw reasons for optimism, even in the face of Roosevelt's popularity, if they named a candidate from their Progressive wing. Meeting that description were Idaho senator William Borah, long-time dissident and isolationist, and Chicago publisher Frank Knox, a companion of former president Theodore Roosevelt in the famed "Rough Riders." Although they participated in the limited number of presidential primaries, neither developed momentum.

Instead, the party turned to Kansan Alfred Landon, the only Republican governor to win election in both 1932 and 1934. Landon's record combined a balanced state budget with a readiness to use state (and federal) funds in relief projects and a defense of radicals' civil liberties. Hailed by Republican publishers, particularly William Randolph Hearst, as an oxymoronic "liberal Coolidge," Landon came to the June Republican convention in Cleveland as the consensual choice. A brief threat to his nomination arose when former president Hoover enflamed the delegates with an impassioned diatribe against the New Deal. But the party leaders held to their commitments, giving Landon all but 19 of 1,003 votes on the first ballot.

Convention delegates had more doubt about the vice-presidential nomination, due as much to rhyme as reason. One possibility was Gov. Styles Bridges of New Hampshire, but his selection was undone by fears of a potential Democratic sneer of the ticket, "Landon Bridges Are Falling Down." The favored running mate, Michigan senator Arthur Vandenberg, then declined. Finally, the party unanimously chose Knox and formulated its campaign doggerel, "Get Off the Rocks with Landon and Knox."

The party platform condemned the New Deal in general terms, but adopted some of its program. It began with a clarion call of danger: "America is in peril. The welfare of American men and women and the future of our youth are at stake. We dedicate ourselves to the preservation of their political liberty, their individual opportunity and their character as free citizens, which today for the first time are threatened by Government itself."

When it came to specific policies, however, Republicans were more moderate, accepting many New Deal goals while endorsing different methods. Reemployment would come from "encouragement instead of hindrance to legitimate business" and "withdrawal of government from competition with private payrolls." Relief for the jobless would be better provided through "non-political local agencies familiar with community problems" and by grants to the states. Security for aged Americans would be provided not by uniform federal benefits, but by "supplementary payment necessary to provide a minimum income sufficient to protect him or her from want."

The Democrats were united and found no need for even a single roll call at their June convention in Philadelphia. As presaged four years earlier, the delegates abolished the traditional two-thirds requirement for nominations and endorsed by acclamation the reelection of Roosevelt and Vice President John Nance Garner.

Beneath this unity, new voter groups foretold future claims to power and future conflicts. Women, inspired by the activity of the first lady, Eleanor Roosevelt, became politically visible, sending 219 delegates and alternates to the convention. African Americans, shifting from their traditional support of the party of Lincoln, gained recognition when a black preacher, the first African American Democrat elected to the House, addressed the convention—leading to a walkout of segregationist South Carolina delegates.

The Democratic platform lambasted the previous Republican administrations and praised its own policies, defending activist government while making few specific promises for the future. Its rhetorical theme was the Declaration of Independence:

We hold this truth to be self-evident—that the test of a representative government is its ability to promote the safety and happiness of the people.

We hold this truth to be self-evident—that 12 years of Republican leadership left our Nation sorely stricken in body, mind and spirit; and that three years of Democratic leadership have it back on the road to restored health and prosperity. . . .

We hold this truth to be self-evident—that government in modern civilization has certain inescapable obligations to its citizens.

In his acceptance speech, FDR cast the election in combative terms of social class conflict against "economic royalists." Again invoking the American founding, he challenged: "For too many of us the political equality we once had won was meaningless in the face of economic inequality. A small group had concentrated into their own hands an almost complete control over other people's property, other people's money, other people's labor—other people's lives. For too many of us life was no longer free; liberty no longer real; men could no longer follow the pursuit of happiness."

Roosevelt turned to social class appeals to meet radical, not Republican, challenges to the Democrats. In the despair of the Depression, many schemes for economic improvement, many social movements, and many ambitious demagogues arose, including Sen. Huey Long of Louisiana. Long, who had also served as Louisiana's governor, created a "share the wealth" movement that claimed more than 7 million members. It supported confiscatory taxation of individuals' wealth above a million dollars to provide an annual income of $2,500 to every American family, as well as pensions, college education, and homestead allowances. When Long was assassinated in 1935, his mantle was assumed by a radical preacher, Gerald L. K. Smith, who later organized a Nazi political party.

Another movement drawing great support was founded by Francis Townsend, a California physician. National clubs enrolling about 2 million pensioners built support for a simple program: give all persons over the age of sixty $200 a month, on condition that they spend the money to build consumer demand. Funding would come from a 2 percent national sales tax. Another economic program came from Rep. William Lemke of North Dakota. He proposed to spend $8 billion to support farm mortgages, to be financed by issuing new paper money.

A more dangerous advocate was Charles Coughlin, a Catholic priest in metropolitan Detroit. In weekly radio broadcasts reaching as many as 40 million, Coughlin offered a "social justice" solution to the Depression, mixing admiration for Italian Fascism and German Nazism, anti-Semitism, and a populist economic program. A supporter of Roosevelt in 1932, he reversed course in 1936 in bitter attacks against the president and his alleged allies among Wall Street brokers, the Federal Reserve, "international bankers," Jews, and Communists.

When removed from the air by direct intervention of the Vatican, Coughlin turned to politics. Smith and Townsend joined him in a new Union Party, which consolidated the dissident populist movements. In a raucous convention in Cleveland in August, the new organization named Lemke as its presidential candidate and a Boston lawyer, Thomas O'Brien, for vice president and adopted a platform written largely by the "radio priest." The program included a new government central bank to pay off all existing federal debt, the refinancing of the debts of all farmers and all mortgages of city dwellers, congressional assurance of "a living annual wage for all laborers. . . production at a profit for the farmer. . . a reasonable and decent security for the aged," as well as limitations on individual income and inheritance. By comparison, the familiar programs of the older minor parties—whether Prohibitionist, Socialist, or Communist—seemed shopworn and unthreatening.

THE CAMPAIGN

The volatile combination of strident and conflicting ideologies, polarized assessments of Roosevelt, and continuing national economic distress made for a divisive and fervent campaign.

Yet the election season opened calmly. FDR went off on a sea cruise, and Landon stayed close to home in Kansas, ignoring pleas to counter the perceived threat from a continued Democratic administration or to meet with Hoover. When the nominees did speak, the governor was moderate, and the president nonpartisan, traveling to areas devastated by floods, and even declining to endorse some Democratic candidates. In early September, the two candidates met at a conference convened by Roosevelt to develop solutions for the drought-stricken areas of the Dust Bowl. The proceedings were so cordial—each calling his opponent a "fine gentleman"—that some observers almost thought the election had been cancelled.

In October the candidates left the doldrums and set an energetic course. Landon became increasingly strident. In a speech on Social Security, he attacked the new legislation as "a cruel deception. . . . The largest tax bill in history and to call it 'social security' is a fraud on the working man. . . that involves prying into the personal working records of 26,000,000 working Americans." Instead he favored a smaller and less costly plan, administered by the states, providing only for the most needy.

Encouraging Republican effort in Maine's early elections, Landon defined the choice as one between "a system of free competitive enterprise and a system under which the minutest doing of every citizen would be scrutinized and regulated, the privacy of homes would be invaded, fields would lie idle by government edict, and a million government 'keep off' signs would spring up all over America."

Going beyond his earlier critique of the New Deal's extravagance and inefficiency, Landon used the foreboding empowerment of antidemocratic governments in other countries to exhort American voters, "They will determine whether they and their children will remain a free people, capable of self-government, or be dominated by an all-powerful central authority."

FDR tried a calmer tone. A *New York Times* reporter described his approach: "President Roosevelt in his campaign for re-election has assumed the role of a salesman for a single commodity—confidence. Confidence in economic recovery, in social security, in business stability—that is what he is trying to sell as he campaigns energetically up and down the country."

Roosevelt campaigned more vigorously as the balloting neared. He took off on a 5,000 mile journey to the West to defend his record. Even though his legs were paralyzed, he gave up to ten speeches a day, more often from trains and automobiles than from formal platforms, and he occasionally dropped into farmers' homes. He enlisted more tangible aid in the campaign as well, directing that there be no reductions in WPA employment or any decrease in cotton prices before the election.

The minor parties failed to gain much attention, beset by division and extremism among their leaders. Townsend, unenthusiastic about the Union Party, partially defected and endorsed Landon in his own state of California and other states where Lemke was not on the ballot. Coughlin condemned the New Deal as "anti-God" and came very close to advocating violence with this threat: "If and when that day will arrive—and God forbid it—if and when ballots have proven useless, then as one American, imbued with the tradition of Washington, I shall not disdain using bullets for the preservation of liberty of conscience and liberty of Constitution." The self-proclaimed leader of the American Nazi Party also supported Landon, his endorsement repudiated even by Hitler's government.

The campaign featured new communications techniques. Besides his command of the radio in his "fireside chats," Roosevelt held two informal press conferences weekly, giving reporters stories, without direct quotation, that spread the administration's messages. The president gained further public attention by moving the State of the Union speech to the evening, when it would get a national radio audience. Republicans responded by airing the medium's first "spot" advertisements, in which "ordinary" voters told of their woes under FDR.

A critic pointed out differences in the radio styles: "Roosevelt knows tricks about broadcasting that Landon still must learn. Simple straightforward language is not always enough; delivery with oratorical ease counts. To date Landon misses this mark; Roosevelt strikes it." Perceiving their problem, Republicans praised Landon as no "radio crooner." The governor was hurt, however, by his verbal plainness, satirized for one especially infelicitous statement, "Wherever I have gone in this country, I have found Americans."

Use of the mass media drove up campaign costs: Republicans reported spending $14 million, and the Democrats $9 million. Landon had the advantage of predominant support in newspaper endorsements, but Roosevelt had a more important asset—his artful use of the free publicity available to a White House incumbent. FDR also had support among some conservatives. On October 1 *The New York Times* endorsed him because "we believe that Mr. Roosevelt is a keen enough judge of public opinion to make his second Administration more conservative than his first" and "that in a very fundamental way the president's re-election will provide insurance against radicalism of the sort which the United States has most to fear."

Party alignments were shifting. Al Smith, once the embodiment of the Democratic base of urban immigrants and workers, joined with wealthy conservatives to form the American Liberty League. Attacking the programs of the New Deal—and even a constitutional amendment to ban child labor—Smith endorsed Landon and delivered a series of anti-Roosevelt speeches, warning, "There can be only one capital, Washington or Moscow. There can be only one atmosphere of government, the clean, pure, fresh air of free America, or the foul breath of communistic Russia." Other conservative Democrats also left their party—including the publisher of William Jennings Bryan's former newspaper and John W. Davis, its 1924 presidential candidate.

In the other direction, Progressives such as Robert La Follette of Wisconsin and George Norris of Nebraska abandoned the Republican Party to back Roosevelt. The Democrats formed alliances with the previously separate Progressive and Farmer-Labor Parties in Wisconsin and Minnesota. The New Deal program had also submerged the appeal of radical leftists, as backers of the large Socialist and minuscule Communist parties switched to Roosevelt.

New social movements spurred these alignments. Women became visible politically, a generation after the adoption of female suffrage. African Americans received novel attention. Landon acted to keep the party's traditional support among blacks by endorsing antilynching legislation, although he did not explicitly support federal, rather than state, action. Democrats held mass meetings in twenty-six northern cities to proclaim Roosevelt as "the new Lincoln." Aided by the administration's relief efforts, blacks were preparing for a historic turn away from the party of emancipation to the party of the

New Deal. The white South warily noticed the trend, foreshadowing the later decline of the Democrats' traditional base.

Labor became a major new element in the Democratic coalition. With the aid of the New Deal's legislation and administration, union organizers moved into the nation's large industries, enrolling members in coal fields, steel mills, garment-making lofts, and, soon, automobile plants. Union treasuries provided $500,000 to FDR's campaign. In New York, the major unions established a new American Labor Party to give a second line for Roosevelt on the state ballot.

As the campaign ended, the focus became the president himself, as both candidates delivered their final speeches at New York's Madison Square Garden. Landon explicitly challenged FDR, "I leave my gage at your feet. . . . The people of this country will not trust a man who does not trust them. If he trusts them he will answer the questions being asked from one end of the country to the other." Two days later, FDR responded with relish to his opponent's set-up:

> Of course we will continue our efforts for young men and women so that they may obtain an education and an opportunity to put it to use. Of course we will continue our help for the crippled, for the blind, for the mothers, our insurance for the unemployed, our security for the aged. Of course we will continue to protect the consumer against unnecessary price spreads, against the costs that are added by monopoly and speculation.

And then he defiantly threw his own gage at the opposition:

> Never before in all our history have these forces been so united against one candidate as they stand today. They are unanimous in their hate for me—and I welcome their hatred.

> I should like to have it said of my first Administration that in it the forces of selfishness and of lust for power met their match. I should like to have it said of my second Administration that in it these forces met their master.

THE ELECTION RESULTS

As always, predictions of the outcome were numerous, and, as is often the case, many were wrong. Some observers relied on the prestigious samples of the *Literary Digest,* which would become immortalized as a case study of unscientific

public opinion surveys. Persistently relying on reports from rural areas and small towns, the *Digest* poll ultimately gathered 2,377,000 straw votes to predict Landon would gain a 4 to 3 popular majority and an Electoral College victory of 370 to 161, carrying 32 of the 48 states. The Republicans were projected to gain 54 percent of the popular vote, Democrats 41 percent, and the minor parties 5 percent. Wrong on every count, the humiliated *Digest* soon went out of business.

The *Digest* error was spectacular. It did less well than the National Association of Fortune Tellers, which in September correctly predicted Roosevelt's reelection. College students at prestigious institutions, mostly wealthy at this time, continued to prefer Landon, but there were signs of change in the thin Roosevelt majority in a national poll of ninety-two institutions in thirty-four states conducted by the *Daily Princetonian.*

For the future, the most significant assessments came from more scientific pollsters—George Gallup, Archibald Crossely, and Elmo Roper—who predicted FDR would win, although by a relatively small margin. Instead of indiscriminately gathering responses from a large number of respondents, these new analysts developed techniques to poll smaller samples that were representative of the entire electorate. Their success made the new science of opinion polling a major element in all subsequent campaigns as well as in academic research.

The actual elections results constituted a massive Democratic victory. Turnout increased 15 percent. Roosevelt won 60.8 percent, 27,750,000 votes—11 million more than Landon's 36.5 percent, and every state and electoral vote except 8 from Maine and Vermont. He gained the most popular votes, the largest plurality, and the largest number of electoral votes of any presidential candidate up to that point in the history of American competitive elections. As another measure of success, the Democrats added 11 House and 6 Senate seats to amass swollen majorities of 333 to 89 and 75 to 17 over Republicans in Congress. The minor parties collapsed. Together, they won less than 3 percent of the national vote; Coughlin's feared Union Party garnered less than 900,000.

The election showed a basic change in voting patterns, as American politics shifted from geographical attachments to group alignments. Roosevelt's vote created a new and long-term Democratic coalition, based on social class, religion, ethnicity, and residence, forging a winning combination of manual workers, Catholics, Jews, blacks, recent immigrants, and urbanites. For the next decades, the basic divide in American politics would be along class lines, a typical difference of 15 percent to 20 percent between Democratic blue-collar and Republican white-collar workers.

The emergent class division explained the notorious failure of the *Literary Digest* poll, which had relied on mail-in ballots sent to telephone subscribers and automobile owners, relatively affluent groups unrepresentative of the national population. But the atypical character of the sample had not completely skewed the survey in earlier years, when voting was not along lines of social class. In the Depression, however, having a phone or a car became even less common than before, and voting came to be more defined by relative wealth.

The 1936 results combined retrospective and prospective meanings. Retrospectively, the election marked the voters' approval of the New Deal and mandated a permanent change to an activist national government. Prospectively, the ballots created a long-term Democratic majority, placing its leaders in positions of power at every level from president to county commissioners, fusing a bedrock of voter loyalties that would make Democrats the most likely winners in national elections for three decades and beyond.

Yet even at the moment of its greatest triumph, the vigor of the New Deal was uncertain. The large Democratic coalition proved to be too large, and it soon split on regional and ideological lines. Only one more law of future significance was enacted—the Fair Labor Standards Act. Soon, the looming threats of expanding autocracies in Italy, Germany, and Japan compelled Roosevelt to turn his attention abroad. His New Deal had transformed the nation. World crises would soon force even greater challenges upon the United States.

- -

ROOSEVELT DEFENDS HIS POLICIES AS HE PREPARES FOR REELECTION

President Franklin D. Roosevelt followed his 1932 election by transforming American government and greatly expanding its role in the domestic economy. These bold policies rallied the nation, surging the Democratic Party into massive wins in the 1934 midterm elections. By early 1936, support had weakened. Political opponents had savagely attacked the president and his programs, accusing them of violating constitutional and ideological bounds, and the conservative Supreme Court had ruled the major New Deal legislation unconstitutional. FDR answered his critics by personally delivering a combative State of the Union speech to Congress. As the 1936 election year began, little was certain about FDR's future or that of the New Deal.

He was never so dramatic. He read his lines as a great actor would read them—now solemn, now stern, now lightsome, now sly. At times he spoke with such fervor that he seemed breathless.

JANUARY 5, 1936
EDITORIAL
THE PRESIDENT DEFIES CRITICS OF NEW DEAL

Rhetorical Challenge to Foes High Spot in His Largely Political Message to Congress

WAR REFERENCES IMPORTANT

By ARTHUR KROCK.

WASHINGTON, Jan. 4.—"Let them propose to this Congress the complete repeal of these measures. The way is open to such a proposal."

If any one had doubted the political cast of the President's annual message, from which the above is a definitive extract, or of the session which he was opening with a challenge to his foes, these sentences should convince them that little business will be transacted in a legislative mood this Winter and Spring in Washington.

There are always people who doubt the wholly obvious, and these expected Mr. Roosevelt to send down to the Capitol by messenger, and have read by a clerk, a dry and dignified document, listing statistics and calling to the attention of Congress that such things as the Mississippi River need attention. They are the same people who believe there is a startling "inside" to every newspaper item, and they buy private correspondence services and search vaunted "behind-the-news" columns to find it.

But all should now be convinced that a President who is a consummate politician, the best showman of the generation, gifted with a voice and accent that would charm Pluto to set Eurydice free, availed of the radio through which to address his own electors and millions of other people in the world, would turn on his savage critics at his first good opportunity with all the force and arts at his command.

That is what Mr. Roosevelt did in the hall of the House of Representatives last night. That was the natural thing for a man of his temperament, in his position, to do.

An Opportunity Embraced.

In the year which has followed the overwhelming endorsement given to him personally at the polls of 1934 his plans and policies have suffered much adversity. Foes have come out of hiding and attacked him and his helpers with shouts, whispers, sharp-shooting and legal restraints. Straw ballots have attested the waning popularity of the New Deal and presaged a deep drop in his own public esteem. It is re-election year for him, for Congress and for local and State officers the country over. On the scales of justice his major proposals for recovery and reform are being gravely weighed. By the custom of the country, and other countries, it was the time and place for a political address, and that is what the President made.

He is best in challenge. Although Mr. Roosevelt, as he repeatedly proved in the early and exciting days of his tenure, is a master of clear explanation in simple terms, amounting equally to a defense of what he does and proposes to do, his national role has always been that of the reformer. Laissez faire has never been in his line. As President of a normally minority party, mostly out of office during his lifetime, it would be no other. Not until his opponents have prepared and offered to the country a full set of plans to supplement or supplant his own will the President be forced into that position of defense which politicians do not prefer to the slashing offer of battle.

That will and must come in part during the campaign. But the President made it clear in his "message to Congress" that he will not assume a wholly defensive attitude until circumstances—such as re-election with a greatly reduced party representation in Congress—force him to do that.

A Rhetorical Challenge.

It was in pursuit of this tactic that the President uttered his highly theatrical challenge to the opposition to move at once for repeal of the measures they have been criticizing. It was a theatrical challenge because it cannot, in common sense, be accepted for two excellent reasons. One is that the Supreme Court may do the job for the President's opponents in several important particulars. The other is that the Seventy-fourth Congress is so overwhelmingly Democratic in both branches that the defeat on the record would be crushing, giving a political advantage to the administration.

After the Supreme Court has imparted its findings to the public, and this session of Congress has politically orated itself into adjournment, the conventions will assemble, and the challenge will be met. But instead of presenting it to a partisan Congress, chosen with a mandate to support Mr. Roosevelt, his foes will offer their program to the people for a decision not foreordained.

He knows that perfectly well, and he knows further that it is the only sensible political procedure. Therefore, his challenge for a showdown now was merely rhetorical. But it was good and telling rhetoric, and by the rules of the game that is called politics it counted for a score.

Conscious of Effect.

Rhetoric is useful if it is good. But when uttered as the President utters it, and carried by the magic of aerial vibration instantaneously to the entire world, it is a force to sway the minds of men. His complete consciousness of this was the reason for the President's address in person at a night session, and that consciousness animated his delivery in a manner not noted before.

Those of us who sat with the prepared address, following the words as the President spoke them, sensed his pervading realization that the ears of the world were in attendance. He was never so dramatic. He read his lines as a great actor would read them—now solemn, now stern, now lightsome, now sly. At times he spoke with such fervor that he seemed breathless, and there was wonder whether, as he began his next sentence, his voice would be firm and full.

But it rose again, with that musical resonance which is worth countless votes, that clear warmth which must fill his less fortunate listeners with the feeling that the President is their champion against the privileged and entrenched who have so often been the targets of his attack. The slight gasp may have been the result of excitement, of weariness, of intensity, or realization that his words were being heard in the far corners of the earth. It may have been pure elocution. At any rate it was most effective, and new.

• •

THE REPUBLICANS SEARCH FOR AN OPPONENT TO FACE ROOSEVELT

The Republican Party faced a dire test in the 1936 election. FDR was a popular incumbent president, pushing an innovative program during a time of crisis. Moreover, he had received a large vote of confidence in the 1934 midterm elections. Yet the Republicans still saw prospects of victory if they could unite behind an attractive candidate. Alfred Landon, the popular yet relatively inexperienced governor of Kansas, became the early favorite. But Landon faced a strong challenge from former president Herbert Hoover and the "Lion of Idaho," Sen. William Borah, who attempted to unify the other candidates.

MAY 16, 1936
BORAH IS REPORTED BENT ON AVERTING LANDON NOMINATION

Senator Is Said to Be Ready to Join Hoover and Others in Fight on Kansan.

VANDENBERG SEEN IN LINE

He Would Be Acceptable to Idahoan, According to Conjecture in Capital.

By CHARLES R. MICHAEL

Special to THE NEW YORK TIMES.

WASHINGTON, May 15.—Senator Borah is out to defeat Governor Landon for the Republican nomination for President, according to definite reports here today. He is said to be willing to join with former President Hoover and the others to fight the Kansas Governor at the Cleveland convention. It is asserted that he would accept Senator Vandenberg as a compromise candidate.

He is reported to hold that Mr. Landon is not qualified by training for the Presidency and would be attacked as the apparent choice of the "corporation and oil interests," making his election impossible.

In a discussion today of the preconvention situation, Senator Borah made it clear that he had fully made up his mind on his course in the campaign, but declined to give details.

His advisers, however, construed his recent statement attacking the Republican leaders and his Newark speech of last night as leading, if the Senator is not himself nominated, to one of two things:

Refusal to support Landon if he is the nominee, but without actually bolting the ticket.

Denunciation of the Republican party and its control by the corporation interests and tacit support of President Roosevelt if the platform of the Democratic party squares with his views.

JUNE 8, 1936
LANDON'S FOES JOIN IN STRATEGIC MOVE

Hope to Recess the Convention After Blocking Nomination for Several Ballots.

HIS POWER IS CHALLENGED

'Certain' First-Ballot Votes Are Put at 350 in Check-Up—Favorite Sons Boomed.

By JAMES A. HAGERTY

Special to THE NEW YORK TIMES.

CLEVELAND, June 7.—After almost abandoning hope of blocking the nomination of Governor Landon for President, supporters of rival candidates became active today and started a campaign to canvass arriving delegates with a view to preventing his being chosen on the first ballot.

It is the hope of the campaign managers for Senator Borah, Colonel Frank Knox, Senator Vandenberg, Senator Dickinson and others whose names will go before the convention to prevent Mr. Landon's nomination even on the second or third ballots after which a motion would be made to recess the convention.

Those opposed to Governor Landon believe that his defeat is certain if he fails to win the nomination at the session at which the balloting begins.

No formal coalition of the anti-Landon candidates has been formed, but a certain understanding to work to block the Landon nomination has been reached by the managers of their campaigns.

This understanding provides that representatives of each shall confer with delegates on their arrival and urge them to give careful consideration to each of the candidates and try to nominate the man who seems to them to be the best qualified and to have the best chance of election.

Challenge Landon Claims

Every effort will be made to convince a majority of the delegates that the nomination is foreclosed to Mr. Landon, and that the claim of his managers for a first ballot nomination is without foundation.

A check by supporters of Colonel Knox is said to have indicated that Governor Landon has only about 350 certain first ballot votes, as compared with the more than 400 claimed by the Landon forces. It is a matter of record that about 800 of the 1,003 delegates are legally unpledged, although many of the 800 are known to favor the Kansas Governor . . . whose views on vital issues are, they declare, unknown.

An attempt will be made to create a demand that the Kansas Governor be asked in advance of the nomination to state his views on a money plank, social security and the advisability of a constitutional amendment to remedy the situation caused by the Supreme Court's invalidation of New York State's minimum wage law.

The opposition to Landon will declare that the election cannot be won by compromising with the New Deal and call for condemnation of Roosevelt policies.

Another argument to be made to the delegates will concern the political inexpediency of nominating a candidate for President whom Senator Borah will not support. This contention bore fruit today when two North Dakota delegates called on a prominent party leader and informed him that they doubted Mr. Landon or any other candidate could carry that State if Senator Borah was inactive in the campaign. A similar expression from a party leader in Montana was reported.

Hoover Help Is Expected

Help in the block-Landon movement is expected from the devoted followers of Herbert Hoover, who may muster seventy to seventy-five votes in the convention. Some of these delegates are reported ready to vote for Mr. Hoover as a complimentary gesture, whether or not his name is formally presented.

Mr. Hoover in addressing the convention Wednesday night is expected to give something of a description of the type of man whom the convention ought to nominate. It is believed that the picture will not fit Governor Landon.

ALFRED LANDON RECEIVES THE REPUBLICAN NOMINATION

The Republicans met in Cleveland in early June. As expected, Alfred Landon dominated the convention, securing the presidential nomination on the first ballot and nailing his victory with a telegraphed commentary on the party platform. The following day brought a shock to the party. Sen. Arthur Vandenberg, a near certainty for the vice-presidential slot, refused the nomination. The party quickly unified behind another former presidential aspirant, Col. Frank Knox.

JUNE 12, 1936
REPUBLICANS NAME LANDON UNANIMOUSLY; HE ACCEPTS PLATFORM, ADDING OWN IDEAS

LANDON SENDS TELEGRAM

To Back Constitutional Amendment if States' Wage Laws Fail.

FOR GOLD AT PROPER TIME

In His Message to Convention He Specifies Exceptions in Accepting the Platform.

BORAH WINS HIS PLANKS

Vandenberg Is Expected to Be Vice Presidential Choice at Final Session Today.

By ARTHUR KROCK

Special to THE NEW YORK TIMES.

CLEVELAND, Ohio, June 11.—An unbossed Republican National Convention, yet working like a machine, at 11:41 o'clock tonight unanimously nominated Alfred M. Landon of Kansas for President, adopted unanimously a platform embracing certain social welfare ideas of the New Deal (which otherwise is excoriated) and seated party control in a group of young Kansas politicians and editors who entered the national political field less than two years ago.

At a final session tomorrow Arthur H. Vandenberg of Michigan is expected to accept the Vice Presidential nomination.

Eighteen Borah delegates from Wisconsin and the Senator's campaign manager (Delegate Carl G. Bachmann of West Virginia) voted for Mr. Borah on the first ballot, which prevented a nomination by acclamation under the rules. But Wisconsin then moved to make the nomination unanimous, and it was done.

Hamilton Reads Message

Two dramatic events colored the night session. Before John D. M. Hamilton, the chief of staff of the nominee, presented his name to the convention, he read at Mr. Landon's request a telegram from the Governor "interpreting" three planks of the platform and stating reservations. These planks, relating to currency, civil service and State control of wages and hours, had been revised by the resolutions committee from the text submitted by the Governor as a part of the week-long effort to placate Senator Borah and win his support in the campaign.

Governor Landon "interpreted" a "sound currency" to mean a currency eventually convertible into gold, insisted that the civil service should extend as far as the government's under-secretariat and pledged himself to support a constitutional amendment to permit the States to regulate wages and hours if the statutory method were not effective. He said "in good conscience" he must make these intentions known in advance.

The other element of drama was when all the other Presidential candidates but Senator Borah, who had already left for Washington, took the platform and seconded the nomination of Mr. Landon. Mr. Borah is only fairly well-pleased with the platform, and he expects to survey Mr. Landon's speeches and the personnel of his campaign cabinet for a couple of months before deciding whether to support the candidacy. Herbert Hoover, the other eminent Republican whose opposition was feared by the Landon group, phoned here today that he was satisfied with the platform.

Senator Vandenberg was among those seconding the nomination. Colonel Knox, L. J. Dickinson, Robert A. Taft, and Harry Nice, the other aspirants, followed.

Harmony the Landon Goal

Harmony among all Republicans and the support of anti-New Deal Democrats have all along been stated as the twin goals of the Landon managers, and, except for Mr. Borah, the harmony seems to have been effected.

JUNE 13, 1936

KNOX NOMINATED FOR VICE PRESIDENT, HAMILTON CHAIRMAN, CONVENTION ENDS; LANDON PREPARES VIGOROUS CAMPAIGN

VOTE ON KNOX UNANIMOUS

Vandenberg Rejects Bid of Landon Forces and Edge and Nice Quit.

IT'S A BULL MOOSE TICKET.

Both Nominees Bolted in 1912, and Both Are From Midwest, Riding Into Party Control.

HARMONY AIM TO THE FORE

Attempt to Draft the Michigan Senator Dropped When Pennsylvania Swings Away.

By ARTHUR KROCK

Special to THE NEW YORK TIMES.

CLEVELAND, June 12.—Colonel Frank Knox of Chicago appealed to the delegates to the Republican National Convention as the strongest possible nominee for Vice President, after Senator Arthur H. Vandenberg of Michigan formally notified them today that he would not accept the second place on the ticket headed by Governor Alfred M. Landon of Kansas. Therefore, in the same free-will spirit which has characterized this remarkable gathering, the delegates unanimously nominated Colonel Knox and adjourned soon after 1 o'clock this afternoon.

The sentiment for Colonel Knox over ex-Senator Edge of New Jersey, Governor Nice of Maryland and others was made so plain by the seconding speeches for the Illinois publisher that the others, following last night's example, withdrew on the platform, and this time even Wisconsin went along on the first ballot.

When it was over the Republicans had chosen as candidates for President and Vice President of the United States two former Bull Moosers, who bolted the party in 1912; two veterans of the World War; two men from the Mississippi River basin, where party control is now lodged.

That control was sealed, in an organization sense, this afternoon by the unanimous election of John D. M. Hamilton, Governor Landon's pre-convention campaign manager, as chairman of the Republican National Committee to succeed Henry P. Fletcher of Pennsylvania.

West in Saddle, Rides Lightly

Although the West is in the saddle, it is riding lightly, as the process of the Vice Presidential nomination today once more revealed. Governor Landon and his young group of Kansas University classmates, Kansas politicians and Kaw Valley editors very much wanted Senator Vandenberg for second place. They carefully devised a plan to draft him today, feeling sure that he would be obliged to accept.

But Mr. Vandenberg would only consider a draft by acclamation, and did not desire even that. By the time this viewpoint was finally made known to the Landon leaders, Pennsylvania had grown tired of waiting for them to get in touch with the Senator and at 9:30 o'clock this morning pledged itself to Colonel Knox with whom Mr. Vandenberg is understood to have conferred early this morning.

Acclamation being then impossible, the Senator drafted a letter to the convention, once more taking himself out of consideration. The Kansans still insist they could have obtained acclamation if they had been able to reach the Senator by telephone last night. Yet this correspondent had a phone conversation with him as late as 1:30, an hour when the Landonites say they were informed his telephone was shut off.

Roosevelt Is Renominated in a Forward-looking Convention

There was no doubt that President Roosevelt would be renominated at the Democratic convention held in Philadelphia. Both he and his vice president, John Nance Garner, were widely popular within the party and across the nation. The convention focused on stating aims for the next term and building enthusiasm behind its candidates. Roosevelt was strident in his desire to turn the New Deal from simple relief to the lower classes to directly targeting the wealthy of the country.

JUNE 27, 1936
ROOSEVELT NOMINATED BY ACCLAMATION; DEMONSTRATIONS FOR HIM AND LEHMAN

ENTHUSIASM RUNS HIGH

Eight Hours of Oratory Precede Acclamation in Early Morning.

CHEER PRESIDENT AN HOUR

Delegates in Ecstatic Climax When Name Is Presented to Convention by Mack.

LEHMAN TOPS SECONDERS

Received So Enthusiastically as to Leave No Doubt of Desire That He Run Again.

By ARTHUR KROCK

Special to THE NEW YORK TIMES.

THE MUNICIPAL AUDITORIUM, PHILADELPHIA, Saturday, June 27.—After more than eight hours of eulogistic oratory and demonstrations, which kept the Democratic National Convention in session from 1 P.M. yesterday until 12:55 o'clock this morning, Franklin Delano Roosevelt was nominated for re-election by acclamation. Vice President Garner will be similarly honored this afternoon.

Fifty-seven speeches were made by the orators in the seconding talkathon, representing every State, territory, possession and the District of Columbia. They included twelve Governors, eight Senators, one Senator-elect, eight women, a Cabinet officer and the Governor General of the Philippine Islands. Senator McAdoo, when called to the chair, also spoke in favor of the nomination but his was not strictly a seconding speech.

On motion of Governor Berry of South Dakota the rules were suspended and the roll-call was dispensed with, the nomination coming at 12:42 A.M.

Final, Noisy Celebration

Senator Robinson's announcement from the platform that the President had been chosen by acclamation— thus "beating Cleveland"—loosed another and the final demonstration of the all-day, all-night session. It was just like the rest and was still in progress when the chairman heard, put and declared passed a motion to recess until 10 o'clock this morning—an action unknown to nearly all the shouting, parading, horn-tooting demonstrators.

Rarely has the flow of harmonious oratory been equaled in a national political gathering as a few conservatives joined a long parade of New Dealers in extolling the President. Going a step beyond the Republican convention at Cleveland two weeks ago, the Philadelphia delegates cast not a single vote against Mr. Roosevelt. A score of votes from Wisconsin and West Virginia kept Governor Alf M. Landon from enjoying the same distinction.

Much more exciting than the actual nomination was a series of tumultuous uprisings to honor Governor Herbert H. Lehman of New York, who made the chief seconding speech at 10 o'clock last night. The effort was in part prearranged to convince Mr. Lehman that he must stand for re-election. At the same time a great deal of it was spontaneous and sincere. When Mr. Lehman was finally permitted to leave the platform he received a telegram of thanks from the President at Washington. Though beset with importunities, he declined to admit any change in his intention to retire.

JUNE 28, 1936

ROOSEVELT TO WAR ON 'ECONOMIC ROYALISTS'; HAILED BY THRONGS IN ACCEPTANCE CEREMONY; GARNER NAMED AS WEARY CONVENTION CLOSES

CAMPAIGN ISSUE DEFINED

The President Avoids All Personalities in His Philadelphia Speech.

FIGHT FOR FREEDOM SEEN

Battle Today Is Like That of 1776, He Says, With New Set of 'Royalists' in Power.

GARNER RENEWS PLEDGE

Renominated by Acclamation, Vice President Vows His Fealty to New Deal.

By ARTHUR KROCK

Special to THE NEW YORK TIMES.

FRANKLIN FIELD, PHILADELPHIA, June 27.—Under a cloud-veiled moon, in skies suddenly cleared of rain, to a mass of more than 100,000 people gathered in the stadium of the University of Pennsylvania, and by radio to unnumbered millions all over the nation, and world, Franklin Delano Roosevelt tonight accepted the renomination of the Democratic party for President of the United States and, avoiding personalities of any description, defined the issue of this campaign as it appears to him.

The President said that, as the fathers of the Republic had achieved political freedom from the eighteenth-century royalists, so it was the function of those who stand with him in this campaign to establish the economic freedom they also sought to establish, and which was lost in the industrial and corporate growth of the nineteenth and twentieth centuries.

The following is a summary of the President's speech, which was more of a rededication of the New Deal to obtain and secure "economic freedom" than an acceptance speech, outlining a definite program, according to custom:

This occasion is for dedication to a simple and sincere statement of an attitude toward current problems. The speaker comes not only as party leader and candidate for re-election, but "as one upon whom many critical hours have imposed and still impose a grave responsibility."

For loyalty in cooperation thanks are due the people, Democrats everywhere, Republicans in Congress, many local officials and especially those who have borne disaster bravely and "dared to smile through the storm." The rescue was not the task of one party; the rally and survival were made together.

Fear which was the most dangerous foe in 1933, has been conquered. Yet all is far from well with the world. The United States is better off than most, but "the rush of modern civilization" has created problems for solution if both political and economic freedom are finally to be attained.

The eighteenth-century Royalists sought to perpetuate their special privileges from the British Crown. They regimented the people in labor, religion and the right of assembly. The American Revolution was fought to win political freedom, and political tyranny was wiped out at Philadelphia July 4, 1776, when the Declaration was penned.

But modern industry and invention have raised new forces that produced new royalists and new dynasties, with new privileges which they seek to retain. Concentration of economic power pressed every citizen into service, and economic freedom—the twin ideal, with political freedom, of Jefferson and Washington—was lost again.

Small business men, with the worker and the farmer, were excluded from this new royalty. "New mercenaries sought to regiment the people." The average man once more confronts the problem faced by the Minute Men. He is entitled to a living that means something to live for as well as something to live by.

The collapse of 1929 revealed the new despotism for what it was. In the election of 1932 the people gave to the present administration a mandate to end it. It is being ended.

Freedom No Half-and-Half Affair

The modern royalists contend the economic slavery is nobody's business, and certainly not the government's. But the administration contends that freedom is no half-and-half affair; the citizen must be free in the market place as well as in the polling place.

To the complaint of the economic royalists that the New Deal seeks to overthrow American institutions, the President answers that what they really seek to retain is their kind of power, hidden behind the flag and the Constitution. But the flag and the Constitution stand for democracy and freedom, and no dictatorship either by the mob or the overprivileged.

"The brave and clear platform to which I heartily subscribe," sets forth the inescapable obligations of the government: protection of family and home, establishment of equal opportunity and aid to the distressed. The opposition will beat down these words unless they are fought for, as for three years they have been maintained. The fight will go on as the convention has decreed.

Faith, hope and charity are not unattainable ideals, but stout supports of a nation struggling for freedom.

The nation is poor indeed if it cannot lift from the unemployed the fear they are not needed in the world. That accumulates a deficit in human fortitude. The bearers of the standard of hope, faith and charity, instead of privilege, seek daily to profit from experience, to learn to do better.

The sins of the cold-blooded and of the warm-hearted are, as Dante says, weighed in different scales. The overt faults of a charitable government are preferable to the consistent omissions of an indifferent one.

This generation of Americans has a rendezvous with destiny. Some who have long fought for freedom have wearied and yielded their democracy. Success of the New Deal can revive them. The war is for the survival of democracy, to save "a great and precious form of government for ourselves and for the world."

The President accepts the nomination and is enlisted "for the duration of the war."

· ·

ROOSEVELT ADDRESSES HIS STRUGGLES WITH THE SUPREME COURT

Roosevelt faced two major challenges as the incumbent president. First, he had to convince the country that his New Deal programs were successful and desirable. Here he had little difficulty, calling on his unbounded popularity. Second, he had to persuade the Supreme Court that those policies were constitutional. Beginning in 1935 and continuing through the 1936 campaign, the Court repeatedly ruled against the president, declaring that the New Deal programs exceeded the powers of the federal and in some cases state government as well. In response to the Court striking down a New York law establishing a minimum wage for women in *Morehead v. New York ex rel. Tipaldo* (1936), FDR went on the offensive, formulating new constitutional interpretations to legitimate his actions. The debate resonated through the campaign and impacted American judicial philosophies for generations to come.

JUNE 3, 1936
ROOSEVELT SEES A 'NO MAN'S LAND'

He Says Recent Court Rulings Leave a Void Between Federal and State Authority.

HE OFFERS NO SOLUTION

Fish, 'Shocked' by Invalidation, Believes Democrats Can Gain 1,000,000 Votes.

Special to THE NEW YORK TIMES.

WASHINGTON, June 2.—Recent decisions by the Supreme Court, including the one yesterday holding unconstitutional New York State's Minimum Wage Law, were described by President Roosevelt today as seeming to create a "No Man's Land" where neither States nor the Federal Government had the right to legislate.

He made this observation in reply to a question at a press conference as to whether he had any statement to make on how the New Deal's objectives could be brought within the framework of the court's decisions nullifying the National Recovery Act, the Agricultural Adjustment Act, the Guffey Coal Act and, finally, the one yesterday holding that not even the States could impose schedules of minimum wages.

Mr. Roosevelt said deliberately but with a smile that the question should be redrafted to ask whether he cared to comment on the Supreme Court's decision. He then said that the answer was no.

He paused a moment and puffed a cigarette before he made his observation. He thereafter declined on four distinct occasions in the press conference to discuss possible methods of meeting the situation.

This was his first comment of any kind on decisions by the court since the now historic press conference a little over a year ago in which he said that the Schechter decision invalidating the NRA put the United States back in the horse-and-buggy days.

An even temper combined with a determination not to be drawn into a new controversy such as he started with his comment on the Schechter decision marked the delivery of the President's remarks on the Supreme Court decisions.

They appeared to have been thought out with great care, and, while the President may not be quoted directly from his extemporaneous remarks made in press conferences, his observations were substantially as follows:

It will be of great interest to practically everybody in the United States if they will read the three opinions in the New York case—those of Justice Butler, Chief Justice Hughes and Justice Stone—because the combination of the three seems to indicate that at the present time a majority of the court have made clear a fact that aroused special interest in the President because the law under consideration was discussed in his administration as Governor of New York and enacted soon afterward.

It seems to be fairly clear after this decision, using the minimum wage law as an example, that the No Man's Land, where no government can function, is being more clearly defined. The State cannot do some things and the Federal Government cannot do them.

"How will you meet this situation?" the President was asked.

He replied that there was nothing else to be said.

"Do you see a danger in the No Man's Land?" was another question asked in a long series.

To each Mr. Roosevelt replied that there was nothing else to be said.

JUNE 11, 1936
ROOSEVELT CALLS FOR BROADER VIEW OF CONSTITUTION

SEES NO CHANGE NEEDED

Its Breadth Includes Nation's Welfare, He Says in Arkansas.

JEFFERSON'S ACT CITED

No One Took Louisiana Purchase to Supreme Court, He Recalls in Historical Speech.

CROWDS HAIL PRESIDENT

Thousands Pack Little Rock Stadium After Throngs Greeted Him in Tour of State.

By CHARLES W. HURD

Special to THE NEW YORK TIMES.

CENTENNIAL STADIUM, LITTLE ROCK, Ark., June 10.—In a speech which constituted a virtual challenge to the Republican National Convention, President Roosevelt tonight opened a totally unexpected campaign for broadening interpretation of the Constitution to embrace all legislation necessary to safeguard human welfare under modern conditions.

He took the position that amendment of that document is not necessary to safeguard self-government, but argued that the Central Federal Government has authority to control all conditions too widespread to be handled by the individual States.

While Mr. Roosevelt did not criticize directly the numerous adverse decisions on New Deal legislation and

New York's Minimum Wage Law, handed down in the past year by the Supreme Court, he pointed out that the Louisiana Purchase, which brought Arkansas and other States, including Kansas, home of Governor Landon, into the Union was consummated by President Jefferson "without the full and unanimous approval of every member of the legal profession."

He remarked pointedly of that action that "nobody carried the case to the Supreme Court."

Address Held Platform Basis

Although the President's speech, delivered at Centennial Stadium here in commemoration of a century of Statehood for Arkansas, had been described repeatedly in advance by the White House as "historical," it contained general statements woven into a background of historical allusion which observers believed would be restated as the basic policies in the Democratic platform.

While the speech contained no specific recommendations, it was one of the broadest discussions made by Mr. Roosevelt as President, covering the fields of self-government, States' rights, control of predatory groups and related topics in the realm of political discussion.

Mr. Roosevelt stated as firmly as possible his belief in the doctrine of States' rights and the right of self-government by all subdivisions of population, arguing exceptions to this rule only on the basis that there are social and economic problems in modern life which cannot be handled individually by State units.

"The Federal Union itself was organized under a Constitution," he said, "because in the days following the Revolution it was discovered that a mere federation of States was such a loose organization, with constant conflicts between the thirteen States themselves, that a Constitution and a national organization to take care of government beyond State lines was necessary."

Speech Is a Surprise

"The Constitution provided the best instrument ever devised for the continuation of these fundamental principles," he continued, "Under its broad purposes we can and intend to march forward, believing as the overwhelming majority of Americans believe, that it is intended to meet and fit the amazing physical, economic and social requirements that confront us in this generation."

* * * * * * * * * *

LANDON CAMPAIGN STARTS SLOWLY BEFORE GOING ON THE ATTACK

Gov. Alf Landon began his campaign in a traditional manner. He planned to give few speeches, while relying upon his vice-presidential candidate to do most of the "barnstorming." The campaign began on a temperate note, focusing on policy differences between Roosevelt and the Republicans and urging the country to rely upon American individualism to overcome its problems. As the campaign wore on, the rhetoric grew harsher. Landon attacked Roosevelt for wasteful spending and accumulating undue power in the presidency. Finally, he accused FDR of seeking an outright dictatorship. As the two sides clashed, stark distinctions between their political philosophies emerged.

JUNE 21, 1936
EDITORIAL
LANDON-KNOX CAMPAIGN TAKING ORTHODOX FORM

Barnstorming to Be Left to Running Mate, With Kansan Timing Talks On Both Coasts and Between

By WARREN MOSCOW

TOPEKA, Kan., June 19.—The Republican campaign plans, as they have been outlined here this week, indicate the intention of the party leaders to do two things. The first is to have Governor Alf M. Landon and his running-mate, Colonel Frank Knox, wage a fairly orthodox type of campaign. The second is to concede nothing to the enemy.

The fly in the ointment is the versatility of the man they are seeking to dislodge from the White House. They admit that, although campaign tours can be planned now, the Republican strategy may have to be changed from time to time to meet the shifting "quarterback" in Washington. Both the so-called Kansas crowd and the Eastern conservative leaders who still seem to have a fairly important voice in the running of the party appear to have agreed on this.

They are still uncertain as to how Governor Landon, who, they are certain, will make an excellent impression in personal appearances, will register on the radio, and they decline to make the mistake made by the Hoover camp in 1932, when the sudden scrapping of announced plans near the very end of the campaign clearly indicated the panic that existed.

Appeal to Midwest

In the Midwest the Republicans are counting on neighborly Mr. Landon to appeal to the farmer vote. They refuse to think that there is any doubt about Kansas, despite the receipt here of AAA checks from a Democratic administration in Washington. The home State pride is strong, they say, and should more than counterbalance the strength of the Democrats here.

They are hoping that Iowa and other bordering States will also know Mr. Landon well enough before the end of the campaign so that the voters will recognize him as one of their own kind.

They are hoping, too, that the present fairly prosperous condition of the farmers, even though it came into being under a Democratic administration, will lead the men of the soil back into the Republican fold. The story of Democratic extravagance will be spread throughout the farming belt, where cash has always been a sort of luxury.

AUGUST 27, 1936
LANDON ASSAILS ROOSEVELT FOR 'RECKLESS SPENDING'; TAX ON SURPLUS 'COCKEYED'

20,000 CROWD STADIUM

Buffalo Hears Nominee Warn That Corporation Levy Menaces Jobs.

REPEAL OF LAW PLEDGED

Kansan Declares the Rich Are Aided While Little Fellow Must Pay.

APPEAL MADE TO WOMEN

Governor Tells Them Indirect Imposts Are Increasing the Cost of Living.

By JAMES A. HAGERTY

Special to THE NEW YORK TIMES.

BUFFALO, Aug. 26.—Governor Landon tonight arraigned the Roosevelt administration for extravagance and for piling up a huge debt which either will have to be paid by the mass of the people with moderate and small incomes, or be passed on to their children as a staggering burden which will close the door of opportunity to the youth of America.

Governor Landon, who spoke in the Offerman Stadium, the ball park of the Buffalo International League team, received the cheers of an audience of about 20,000 when he was introduced as a "pioneer Progressive" and the next President of the United States by Edwin F. Jaeckle, Erie County chairman.

The crowd, though large, was ten or fifteen thousand less than expected by the local party leaders. The chilly weather and a light rain in the early evening were blamed for keeping many away.

Tax Repeal Pledge Cheered

The audience listened to Governor Landon with close but rather quiet attention until he declared the Surplus Tax Bill was the most "cockeyed piece of legislation" ever enacted in a modern country, and said that, if elected, he would advocate repeal. A spontaneous, long and hearty cheer, the first during the speech, followed this declaration.

The applause for most of the points in the candidate's speech was very slight, although the crowd warmed up a little to his attack upon the Roosevelt administration for failure to balance the budget. The crowd cheered and many waved their hats as the Governor finished.

In his speech Mr. Landon asserted that the Surplus Tax Bill, jammed through Congress by the administration, by forcing payment of profits in dividends prevented a corporation from using these profits for plant improvement and expansion, from building up financial reserves or restoring reserves which have been depleted.

Far from "soaking the rich," as its proponents claim, this law, the Kansas Governor declared, really protects "the big fellow who still has a reserve, and hangs a mill stone around the neck of the little fellow," makes re-employment of those out of work harder and is jeopardizing the job of every man and woman who works for a business corporation.

Would Repeal Surplus Tax

"This is the most cockeyed piece of tax legislation ever imposed in a modern country," Governor Landon said with emphasis, "and, if I am elected, I shall recommend the immediate repeal of this vicious legislation."

SEPTEMBER 19, 1936
LANDON DECLARES A 'FREE AMERICA' IS THE REAL ISSUE

People Would Be Puppets Under New Deal Aims, He Tells Young Republicans.

TRADE 'MANAGEMENT' HIT

As 2,000 Cheer, Governor Says Nation Should Again Give Opportunity to Youth.

By JAMES A. HAGERTY

Special to THE NEW YORK TIMES.

TOPEKA, Kan., Sept. 18.—In a message to the youth of the country, Governor Landon declared today that the real issue of the campaign was whether the Federal Government should "regulate" business or "direct and manage" it, and that the future prosperity and happiness of young Americans depended upon the preservation of a free form of government.

History and experience, he said, showed that America was made over in every generation, not from blueprints in Washington but by the honest toil of the people.

He added that the presence of young men and women from every State showed that the present generation was following in the footsteps of the generations of youth which have built America.

Sees a Graver Issue

Governor Landon said that in the past campaigns had dealt chiefly with how the government should exercise the powers it had. The present campaign, he asserted, cuts across party lines and holds a graver issue; what powers the government shall have and what powers it shall not have.

Expressing sympathy with the young people, whom he characterized as among "the saddest victims of the depression" in that many of them had been unable to find employment, the Governor said he was confident that the young voters would reject the "theory of the Roosevelt administration" that this country had reached its peak, that there would be a permanent army of unemployed and that the government must take an increasingly greater part in regulating the daily lives of its citizens, and would accept the philosophy of the Republican party.

The Republican party, he added, believes that the government should tighten the rules governing business but should not attempt to manage business, so that America once again will become a nation where youth can be confident of its future.

The Governor declared that a dangerous and insidious New Deal argument was that youth had no future under the American system, that American business men were no longer capable of running their own businesses and that the government had to take over the responsibility of making business decisions to assure the maximum good for the greatest number.

Opposes "Business Direction"

On the surface, Mr. Landon said, this appears to be an extension of the policy the American people always have followed.

"But there is a fundamental difference between this argument and the policy we have always pursued," the Governor continued.

"In the past we have had regulation of business by the government, not direction and management of business by the government.

"What is the difference between the two? It is very simple. Under the one—in the policy we have always followed—the government tells us what we cannot do. Under the other, the government tells us what we must do.

"Under the one system, the government is the umpire, enforcing the rules made by the people. Under the other system, the government itself plays the game; the people are mere puppets."

OCTOBER 14, 1936
GOV. LANDON SEES PRESIDENT ON WAY TO DICTATORSHIP

Speaking in Detroit He Cites Great Powers Given Him and Pledges Repeal.

FAVORS FREE ENTERPRISE

10,000 Shiver in Outdoor Stand—Nominee Lunches With Ford, Who Calls on Him.

By JAMES A. HAGERTY

Special to THE NEW YORK TIMES.

DETROIT, Oct. 13.—Asserting that President Roosevelt has started on the road that leads to dictatorship, Governor Landon declared tonight that, if elected President, he would recommend to Congress the repeal of all acts giving what he regarded as autocratic powers to the executive.

The Republican candidate, who spoke at an open air meeting in Navin Field, home of the Detroit American League baseball club, cited the record of the automobile industry to support his contention of the necessity of preserving the American system of free enterprise, which he said the New Deal would destroy.

Traces Downfall of Democracies

We live in a world in which human liberties are falling and ideals of democracy have been swept away. Governor Landon told his audience. Tracing the process of the destruction of popular government, he said that first the Executive sets himself up as a popular leader and in the name of national emergency asks for additional authority; the Legislature gradually yields more and more power until it becomes an instrument of the Executive; the courts are undermined and the judiciary ceases to be a protection to the people.

"When this final stage is reached—when the independence of the courts is destroyed—the rights and liberties of the people are gone," said the Governor, "the people are then at the mercy of the Executive.

"We have seen the results of this process abroad. The first steps have already been taken here. Think back over the last three and one-half years, and see what has happened."

Adding to his charge that the President had obtained autocratic power to control the nation's money and credit on the ground of emergency, Governor Landon said that Mr. Roosevelt had also asked for and received authority to determine how much agriculture and industry could produce and sell, the wages of workers and how many hours they could work, and obtained bank checks from Congress totaling $13,500,000,000 to be spent at his discretion.

"In other words, one President has been given the power to spend almost without restrictions as much as the discretionary spending power given to thirty Presidents over a period of 143 years," said Mr. Landon.

Congress in effect gave up its constitutional powers and surrendered its control over the spending policy of the government, he declared, and continued:

"Yet one of the most important victories in the history of popular government was that which won for the people's representatives control over the public purse. Congress should never abdicate the rights won by the blood of men determined to be free."

The Governor asserted that through this transfer to the Executive of power over the purse strings President Roosevelt had been able to override the rights of local communities and States and to accomplish indirectly what the Constitution forbade him to do directly.

"It is a shameful thing," he added, "when our Mayors and the Governors of our several States must appear before the Chief Executive as suppliants or else lose their share of the Federal handout."

Governor Landon said the President had spoken truly when he declared before Congress last January in his report on the state of the Union:

"We have built up new instruments of public power."

He added that Mr. Roosevelt had also spoken truly when he said these instruments could provide "shackles for the liberties of the people and enslavement for the public."

• •

Reverend Coughlin

As the two major parties formed platforms and selected their candidates, a separate political force coalesced behind the voice of Reverend Charles Coughlin. A fiery Catholic priest with a renowned, nationally broadcast radio program, Coughlin attacked both Democrats and Republicans as beholden to bankers and moneyed interests, urging Americans to look elsewhere for political change. He attempted to convince Americans that the election of President Roosevelt to another term would destroy American democracy and result in a communistic dictatorship, while also suggesting the futility of supporting Republican Alf Landon. Despite his wide audience, estimated as high as 40 million listeners, Coughlin's preferred candidate, Union party nominee William Lemke, ultimately polled fewer than 900,000 votes nationally, below 2% of the total.

JULY 4, 1936
COUGHLIN BATTERS ROOSEVELT PLANKS

Social Justice Article Assails 'Glass Promises' Written Into Democratic Platform.
ATTACKS 'MONEY VULTURE'
Whole New Deal Set-Up Is Hit—Republicans Referred To as Prey of Bankers
Special to THE NEW YORK TIMES.

DETROIT, July 3.—In today's issue of Social Justice, published by the Rev. Charles E. Coughlin, he hotly attacked the Democratic platform. An Editor's note stated that Father Coughlin's inspection of the platform "shatters this brittle structure of glass promises into a thousand slivers of worthless political debris."

"The analysis is plain," the article says. "Both the Republicans and Democrats form the left wing and the right wing of the common bird of prey, the banker. The issue is plain, and the American people are cognizant of the danger that this vulture of private money creation which hovers over the dying carcass of our civilization will pounce upon our liberties and spew out its vomit in the face of posterity.

"There is still want in the midst of plenty and the Republicans and the Democrats both refuse to recognize it. There is still danger of being devoured by the vultures of poverty, and the people recognize this to such an extent that the open hunting season is on not only for the Congressmen but for double-dealing Presidents as well as for New Dealing Presidents.

"No wonder I stated on a former occasion that the New Deal platform is repudiated before it is printed."

• •

Roosevelt Remains the Favorite

President Roosevelt began the campaign with a clear advantage as the popular incumbent. He was not bashful about using this advantage, artfully garnering much media attention, while extolling the successes of his New Deal programs. Spreading his message of hope, FDR accused the Republicans of running a campaign of fear. Roosevelt's charisma and optimism marked a sharp contrast to the Republican attacks on the New Deal. Heading into election day, Roosevelt's reelection seemed likely.

AUGUST 4, 1936
ROOSEVELT PLANS 'AGGRESSIVE' DRIVE TO START AT ONCE

Confers With Leaders for Two Hours on Campaign to Cost $2,000,000.

MAY GO WEST NEXT WEEK

Is Said to Feel, After Seeing Wallace, That Drought Needs Demand Earlier Attention.

HEADQUARTERS ALL READY

States to Have Miniature Setups—Farley Gave President an 'Optimistic Report.'

Plan Democratic Drive

By CHARLES W. HURD

Special to THE NEW YORK TIMES.

HYDE PARK, N. Y., Aug. 3.—An "aggressive" campaign for the re-election of President Roosevelt, to start immediately, was planned this afternoon at a two-hour conference between the President and Democratic leaders at Hyde Park House.

James A. Farley, chairman of the Democratic National Committee, thus characterized the contest to be waged in the three months before election.

He estimated the cost of the campaign at about $2,000,000, and said that the organization now completed in national headquarters in New York City would be duplicated in miniature in each of the States.

President Roosevelt is considering a change in plans, the White House offices here announced, under which he would depart possibly next week for a visit to the drought regions in the Dakotas, Minnesota and other Western States; he would postpone until later an inspection of the flood areas in New York, Pennsylvania and Ohio.

Officials continued to insist that there was no political motive behind the Western trip, originally scheduled for late in the month, but the political advantages of such a visit appeared obvious.

The President discussed his political program with a group of nine persons who sat in a semi-circle facing him in the spacious library of his mother's home here. He received reports on progress in organization made during his recent vacation cruise.

SEPTEMBER 11, 1936
DEPRESSION BEATEN, ROOSEVELT ASSERTS IN CHARLOTTE TALK

He Tells Green Pastures Rally Rights of States Were Not Violated.

35,000 CROWD STADIUM

President Points to Improved Conditions on Farms and in Factories.

DRENCHED ON WAY TO PARK

Executive Is Cheered by 10,000 at Asheville—He Visits the Crippled Children.

By CHARLES W. HURD

Special to THE NEW YORK TIMES.

CHARLOTTE, N. C., Sept. 10.—In a speech addressed primarily to the South, President Roosevelt told thousands of persons at a great "Green Pastures Rally" today that the depression had been conquered without any infringement by the Federal Government on the rights of the States.

The Federal Government, he said, had only exercised the functions which it alone could utilize, and thereby had removed "from the red and into the black," in bookkeeping terminology, most corporations, agriculturists and wage earners and the great majority of State, county and municipal governments.

Speaking in religious phrases, he quoted a portion of the Twenty-third Psalm and stated in allegorical terms that the New Deal had guided the United States back into the "green pastures" of security.

"I speak to you today," he said, "as common-sense American men and women. You will agree that from the material aspect this nation's consuming power has been rapidly restored. I trust that you will likewise agree that better conditions on the farms, in the factories and in the homes of America are leading us to the spiritual figure of the Psalmist, green pastures and still waters."

Political Elements in Speech

While the speech here had been announced as another "non-political" utterance by the President, it contained in it almost every element which is expected to enter into the direct campaign arguments he will begin using soon.

Since the speech was delivered in the South he put the first emphasis on the results of the agricultural program in raising the prices of cotton and tobacco. From there he went on to describe benefits given to workers, principally through the National Recovery Act, and finally he dwelt on the solvency of governmental subdivisions as a result of the upturn in values in business and agriculture.

NOVEMBER 1, 1936
PRESIDENT ENDS CAMPAIGN

'Just Begun to Fight' for His Program, He Tells Throng in Garden.

PUSHES SECURITY DEFENSE

Calls 'Unscrupulous' Enemies 'Alien to American Spirit,' Welcomes Their 'Hatred.'

CONFIDENT OF VICTORY

Gets 13-Minute Ovation From More Than 20,000—State Ticket Also Closes Drive.

By RUSSELL B. PORTER

President Roosevelt closed his active campaign for re-election last night with a fighting speech before an enthusiastic, cheering, flag-waving crowd of more than 20,000 persons, filling Madison Square Garden to capacity.

He expressed confidence in victory and defied his enemies. It was his last word to the voters except for a brief "fireside chat" to be delivered by radio from his study in Hyde Park on election eve.

Scores "Organized Money"

Denouncing the forces of "organized money," of "selfishness," and of "lust for power," whom he characterized as "unscrupulous enemies" resorting to "misrepresentation" and "statistical contortions" in order to seize the government for their own profit, the President declared that they were united in hatred of him as they had never been united against any candidate before.

"I welcome their hatred!" he told the crowd in challenging tones. He went on to assert that he had proved a match for these forces in his first term and to express the hope that he would be able to show himself their master in the next four years.

The President indignantly attacked the current pay-envelope propaganda against the Social Security Act as "below the level of decent citizenship." He declared that the sponsors of this attack were deliberately trying to deceive the workers by stressing their contribution to the cost of old-age insurance under the new law and by omitting mention of the employers' contribution to this and to the employers' full payment of the cost of unemployment insurance. Those who implied that insurance reserves comprised of workers' contributions would be "stolen" by some future Congress, for diversion to some other purpose, he charged, proved themselves "alien to the spirit of American democracy."

"Let them emigrate," he cried, "and try their lot under some foreign government in which they have more confidence."

Without specifically mentioning the NRA, the AAA or any other controversial measure, Mr. Roosevelt asserted that he would continue to carry out the program of his first term in labor legislation, social reform, farm legislation, laws against monopoly, abuses of speculation and finance—in short, practically all the measures which have been associated with the New Deal.

He coined a new refrain in pledging himself to continue on this line. After stating each group of his objectives, he declared:

"For all these we have just begun to fight!"

The President defended his work relief program against those who would substitute "the pauperism of the dole," and who would "purge the rolls by starvation," and announced his intention of retaining it.

"Peace at home and abroad," he declared to be the major purpose of his ideology. He repeated the phrase "I hate war!" which he had used in an earlier speech. What he was trying to do, he explained, was to keep peace at home by removing "the causes of unrest and antagonism," and to resist the efforts of those who "stand to profit by war." His victory, he said, would be the victory of the people and of humanity, and would preserve the democracy which was restored to the American people by the election of 1932.

President Roosevelt pictured himself as engaged in a struggle, which he expected to continue in the future, with "the old enemies of peace—business and financial monopoly, speculation, reckless banking, class antagonism, sectionalism and war profiteering."

Giving an account of his stewardship, the President submitted "a record of peace; and on that record a well-founded expectation for future peace—peace for the individual, peace for the community, peace for the nation, and peace with the world."

He proclaimed his leadership of the millions of people "who never had a chance" in a "crusade" to "restore America to its own people."

ROOSEVELT WINS REELECTION IN A LANDSLIDE

On election day Americans delivered the largest electoral victory in the nation's history to President Roosevelt. Surpassing all expectations, FDR achieved a huge landslide in both the popular and electoral vote. The massive support delivered a mandate for the president, signaling the country's backing for his New Deal programs, whatever the Supreme Court's position on their constitutionality.

1936 POPULAR VOTE

STATE	TOTAL VOTE	FRANKLIN D. ROOSEVELT (DEMOCRAT)		ALFRED M. LANDON (REPUBLICAN)		WILLIAM LEMKE (UNION)		NORMAN M. THOMAS (SOCIALIST)	
		VOTES	%	VOTES	%	VOTES	%	VOTES	%
Alabama	275,744	238,196	86.4	35,358	12.8	551	0.2	242	0.1
Arizona	124,163	86,722	69.8	33,433	26.9	3,307	2.7	317	0.3
Arkansas	179,431	146,765	81.8	32,049	17.9	4	0.0	446	0.2
California	2,638,882	1,766,836	67.0	836,431	31.7	—	0.0	11,331	0.4
Colorado	488,685	295,021	60.4	181,267	37.1	9,962	2.0	1,594	0.3
Connecticut	690,723	382,129	55.3	278,685	40.3	21,805	3.2	5,683	0.8
Delaware[1]	127,603	69,702	54.6	54,014	42.3	442	0.3	172	0.1
Florida	327,436	249,117	76.1	78,248	23.9	—	0.0	—	0.0
Georgia	293,170	255,363	87.1	36,943	12.6	136	0.0	68	0.0
Idaho	199,617	125,683	63.0	66,256	33.2	7,678	3.8	—	0.0
Illinois	3,956,522	2,282,999	57.7	1,570,393	39.7	89,439	2.3	7,530	0.2
Indiana	1,650,897	934,974	56.6	691,570	41.9	19,407	1.2	3,856	0.2
Iowa	1,142,737	621,756	54.4	487,977	42.7	29,687	2.6	1,373	0.1
Kansas	865,507	464,520	53.7	397,727	46.0	494	0.1	2,766	0.3
Kentucky	926,214	541,944	58.5	369,702	39.9	12,501	1.3	627	0.1
Louisiana	329,778	292,894	88.8	36,791	11.2	—	0.0	—	0.0
Maine	304,240	126,333	41.5	168,823	55.5	7,581	2.5	783	0.3
Maryland	624,896	389,612	62.3	231,435	37.0	—	0.0	1,629	0.3
Massachusetts	1,840,357	942,716	51.2	768,613	41.8	118,639	6.4	5,111	0.3
Michigan	1,805,098	1,016,794	56.3	699,733	38.8	75,795	4.2	8,208	0.5
Minnesota	1,129,975	698,811	61.8	350,461	31.0	74,296	6.6	2,872	0.3
Mississippi	162,142	157,333	97.0	4,467	2.8	—	0.0	342	0.2
Missouri	1,828,635	1,111,043	60.8	697,891	38.2	14,630	0.8	3,454	0.2
Montana	230,502	159,690	69.3	63,598	27.6	5,539	2.4	1,066	0.5
Nebraska	608,023	347,445	57.1	247,731	40.7	12,847	2.1	—	0.0
Nevada	43,848	31,925	72.8	11,923	27.2	—	0.0	—	0.0
New Hampshire	218,114	108,460	49.7	104,642	48.0	4,819	2.2	—	0.0
New Jersey	1,820,437	1,083,850	59.5	720,322	39.6	9,407	0.5	3,931	0.2
New Mexico	169,135	106,037	62.7	61,727	36.5	924	0.5	343	0.2
New York	5,596,398	3,293,222	58.8	2,180,670	39.0	—	0.0	86,897	1.6
North Carolina	839,475	616,141	73.4	223,294	26.6	2	0.0	21	0.0
North Dakota	273,716	163,148	59.6	72,751	26.6	36,708	13.4	552	0.2
Ohio	3,012,660	1,747,140	58.0	1,127,855	37.4	132,212	4.4	167	0.0
Oklahoma	749,740	501,069	66.8	245,122	32.7	—	0.0	2,221	0.3
Oregon	414,021	266,733	64.4	122,706	29.6	21,831	5.3	2,143	0.5
Pennsylvania	4,138,105	2,353,788	56.9	1,690,300	40.8	67,467	1.6	14,375	0.3
Rhode Island	310,278	164,338	53.0	125,031	40.3	19,569	6.3	—	0.0
South Carolina	115,437	113,791	98.6	1,646	1.4	—	0.0	—	0.0
South Dakota	296,452	160,137	54.0	125,977	42.5	10,338	3.5	—	0.0
Tennessee[2]	475,533	327,083	68.8	146,516	30.8	296	0.1	687	0.1
Texas[3]	843,482	734,485	87.1	103,874	12.3	3,281	0.4	1,075	0.1
Utah	216,679	150,248	69.3	64,555	29.8	1,121	0.5	432	0.2
Vermont	143,689	62,124	43.2	81,023	56.4	—	0.0	—	0.0
Virginia	334,590	234,980	70.2	98,336	29.4	233	0.1	313	0.1
Washington	692,338	459,579	66.4	206,892	29.9	17,463	2.5	3,496	0.5
West Virginia	829,945	502,582	60.6	325,358	39.2	—	0.0	832	0.1
Wisconsin	1,258,560	802,984	63.8	380,828	30.3	60,297	4.8	10,626	0.8
Wyoming	103,382	62,624	60.6	38,739	37.5	1,653	1.6	200	0.2
TOTALS	**45,656,991**	**27,750,866**	**60.8**	**16,679,683**	**36.5**	**892,361**	**2.0**	**187,781**	**0.4**

1. Figures from Clerk of the House of Representatives, *Statistics of the Congressional and Presidential Election* (Washington, D.C.: U.S. Government Printing Office, 1936). Two sets of Landon electors—Republican and Independent Republican—are combined here.

2. Figures from Svend Petersen, *A Statistical History of the American Presidential Elections* (Westport, Conn.: Greenwood Press, 1981); Clerk of the House, *Congressional and Presidential Election*.

OTHER VOTES	%	PLURALITY	
1,397	0.5	202,838	D
384	0.3	53,289	D
167	0.1	114,716	D
24,284	0.9	930,405	D
841	0.2	113,754	D
2,421	0.4	103,444	D
3,273	2.6	15,688	D
71	0.0	170,869	D
660	0.2	218,420	D
—	0.0	59,427	D
6,161	0.2	712,606	D
1,090	0.1	243,404	D
1,944	0.2	133,779	D
—	0.0	66,793	D
1,440	0.2	172,242	D
93	0.0	256,103	D
720	0.2	42,490	R
2,220	0.4	158,177	D
5,278	0.3	174,103	D
4,568	0.3	317,061	D
3,535	0.3	348,350	D
—	0.0	152,866	D
1,617	0.1	413,152	D
609	0.3	96,092	D
—	0.0	99,714	D
—	0.0	20,002	D
193	0.1	3,818	D
2,927	0.2	363,528	D
104	0.1	44,310	D
35,609	0.6	1,112,552	D
17	0.0	392,847	D
557	0.2	90,397	D
5,286	0.2	619,285	D
1,328	0.2	255,947	D
608	0.1	144,027	D
12,175	0.3	663,488	D
1,340	0.4	39,307	D
—	0.0	112,145	D
—	0.0	34,160	D
951	0.2	180,567	D
767	0.1	630,611	D
323	0.1	85,693	D
542	0.4	18,899	R
728	0.2	136,644	D
4,908	0.7	252,687	D
1,173	0.1	177,224	D
3,825	0.3	422,156	D
166	0.2	23,885	D
136,300	**0.3**	**11,071,183**	**D**

3. Figures from Petersen, *A Statistical History;* Clerk of the House, *Congressional and Presidential Election; Texas Almanac.*

NOVEMBER 4, 1936
ROOSEVELT SWEEPS THE NATION; HIS ELECTORAL VOTE EXCEEDS 500; LEHMAN WINS; CHARTER ADOPTED

POLL SETS RECORD

Roosevelt Electoral Vote of 519 Seen as a Minimum

NO SWING TO THE BOLTERS

'Jeffersonian Democrats' Fail to Cause Rift as Expected.

NEIGHBORS HAIL PRESIDENT.

Landon Concedes Defeat and Sends His Congratulations to Victorious Rival.

By ARTHUR KROCK

Accepting the President as the issue, nearly eight million more voters than ever before had gone to the polls in the United States—about 45,000,000 persons—yesterday gave to Franklin Delano Roosevelt the most overwhelming testimonial of approval ever received by a national candidate in the history of the nation.

Except for the small corner of New England occupied by Maine, Vermont and New Hampshire—which was oscillating between Republican and Democratic in the early morning hours of Wednesday—the President was the choice of a vast preponderance of the voters in all parts of the country, and with him were re-elected as Vice President John N. Garner of Texas and an almost untouched Democratic majority in the House of Representatives. The Democratic national ticket will have a minimum of 519 electoral votes and a possible popular majority of ten millions.

The Republican candidates for President and Vice President, Governor Alfred M. Landon of Kansas and Colonel Frank Knox of Illinois, are the worst-beaten aspirants for these offices in the political annals of the United States, with the exception of William H. Taft in 1912, when Colonel Theodore Roosevelt led a formidable revolt in the Republican party and Mr. Taft carried only Vermont and Utah. Yesterday Utah was also in the President's campaign bag. He had carried forty-five States as contrasted with the forty-two he won from Herbert Hoover in 1932. And to assure his reputation as the greatest vote-getter in the annals of the United States he—a Democrat—had overwhelmingly swept Pennsylvania, unfailingly Republican for generations in national elections.

South Piles Up a Huge Vote

The "Jeffersonian Democrats," led by such well-known and supposedly influential Democrats as Alfred E. Smith, John W. Davis and James A. Reed, and on whose rejection of the New Deal the Republicans had greatly depended to cut into Southern votes and swing the Northeast away from the President, proved as ineffectual foes as did the Republican campaign candidates and management. The South rolled up tremendous Roosevelt pluralities, and the President carried Philadelphia, Chicago, New York City and Boston by large margins.

Labor, the unemployed and the colored voters, on whose support the Democrats had counted, were visible in the stunning returns from Illinois, Pennsylvania, New York, Ohio and Michigan.

Several thousand neighbors, bearing torches and accompanied by a band playing "Happy Days Are Here Again," visited the President at Hyde Park after it appeared that his victory was established. He stood facing them in a light drizzle and said that, "while I can't say anything official, it appears that the sweep is covering every section." The President, on the arm of his son Franklin, urged press photographers to get through with him because "I've got to get back and get the returns from California."

Soon after 11 P. M. Mr. Farley issued a formal statement in which he congratulated the nation on the results of the election and praised the President for his administrative efforts. He said the final results would show that the President had received "probably the greatest vote of confidence" ever accorded in the United States. The victory was in large measure a personal triumph for Mr. Farley himself, who takes rank as the most successful political manager in the history of the Democratic party. Since he was a steady personal target throughout the Republican campaign, his share in the outcome is particularly gratifying to his associates.

> "The votes which have re-elected Mr. Roosevelt are votes cast by large numbers of people who believe that his Administration has helped greatly to restore hope, to equalize opportunity, to prevent the excesses of the recent past and to conserve American institutions by adapting them to changing times."

NOVEMBER 4, 1936
EDITORIAL
MR. ROOSEVELT'S NEW DUTIES

President Roosevelt asked the country for a vote of confidence. He has received it, pressed down and running over. The sweep of his victory crosses sectional lines. It ranges under the Democratic banner many States which are normally regarded as Republican. It leaves no doubt of the President's great personal popularity. A large majority of the American electorate has now looked at the record of the last four years and found it in the main satisfactory.

Even in these first hours of triumph the President must ask himself what is the true significance of the great victory he has won. Plainly, if the result is judged in the light of his own appeal to the electorate, this victory is an endorsement of broad principles he has followed in the past, rather than of specific measures he now advocates.

The votes which have re-elected Mr. Roosevelt are votes cast by large numbers of people who believe that his Administration has helped greatly to restore hope, to equalize opportunity, to prevent the excesses of the recent past and to conserve American institutions by adapting them to changing times. All this the President's victory means. It does not mean that he has been given an order or authority to proceed along the line of a highly centralized government or new and radical policies. The people who have re-elected him have simply been placing in his hands a national trust to be discharged.

No one doubts that there was a great measure of admiration for Mr. Roosevelt in the vote given him on Tuesday. No one can deny him praise for the courage and resolution with which he took up the work of the Presidency three

The New York Times front page on November 4, 1936, announcing the reelection of President Franklin Delano Roosevelt.

Source: The Granger Collection, New York

and one-half years ago. It was a time of acute national crisis, and he faced it without a tremor and with skill. What he did was important, but the way in which he did it was of more value in restoring and bracing the morale of the American people. They have not forgotten these things and are still grateful for them. Nor have they forgotten other things for which they had to forgive the President even while voting for him. Too often, as in his last campaign speech on Saturday night, he has impulsively used words that cause cold chills to run down the backs of his friends and supporters. They do not like to hear the President of the United States declare vehemently that he welcomes the hatred of any group of citizens, whoever they may be. Nor do they like to hear him threaten to subject them in the future to himself as to a "master." Americans call no man master. They admit the supremacy of the law over them, which is perhaps all that the President meant, and certainly all that he should have said. It may be that his last-minute plea on Monday night to take bitterness out of politics was intended in part to still and soften his previous explosive utterance.

Indeed, the natural and patriotic course which lies before Mr. Roosevelt in his second term seems plain. He is facing his last four years as President. In them there is still to be done a great work of repair and restoration.

The spirit required is that, not of the leveler, but the builder. What can be more congenial to Mr. Roosevelt's character than a desire to leave behind him a record of national unifying and strengthening? The opportunity before him is vast and tempting. The forces at his disposal are ample. After taking anew his oath of office he can proceed quietly and steadily to administer his great trust with all fidelity, and in a way to secure the adhesion and cooperation of all sorts and conditions of the people.

Such official conduct seems clearly dictated by the position in which the President now finds himself, and to be what American citizens in their totality desire from him. To meet successfully the conditions which will still confront him President Roosevelt will need a flowing together of minds, North and South, East and West. This he may have if he now exhibits statesmanlike poise and a spirit of devotion to the good of the whole people. Their vote of confidence on Tuesday carries with it the hope that he may prove to be a master-builder for a still damaged and troubled America.

"New occasions teach new duties." The country will expect President Roosevelt to act upon the principle in that line from a poem, famous in its day, which was written by an American who all his life was truly a Liberal.

FDR Leads America into World War II

Franklin D. Roosevelt is remembered as the president who overcame the Great Depression and instituted the New Deal. Roosevelt then faced a new threat after Japanese attacks on the United States pulled the country into World War II, the greatest challenge to democracy and freedom the world has ever faced. Although he died shortly before the war's conclusion, FDR's leadership during these two crises cemented his place in history.

DECEMBER 8, 1941
JAPAN WARS ON U. S. AND BRITAIN; MAKES SUDDEN ATTACK ON HAWAII; HEAVY FIGHTING AT SEA REPORTED

GUAM BOMBED; ARMY SHIP IS SUNK

U. S. Fliers Head North From Manila—Battleship Oklahoma Set Afire by Torpedo Planes at Honolulu

104 SOLDIERS KILLED AT FIELD IN HAWAII

President Fears 'Very Heavy Losses' on Oahu—Churchill Notifies Japan That a State of War Exists

By FRANK L. KLUCKHOHN

Special to The New York Times.

WASHINGTON, Monday, Dec. 8—Sudden and unexpected attacks on Pearl Harbor, Honolulu, and other United States possessions in the Pacific early yesterday by the Japanese air force and navy plunged the United States and Japan into active war.

The initial attack in Hawaii, apparently launched by torpedo carrying bombers and submarines, caused widespread damage and death. It was quickly followed by others. There were unconfirmed reports that German raiders participated in the attacks.

Guam also was assaulted from the air, as were Davao, on the island of Mindanao, and Camp John Hay, in Northern Luzon, both in the Philippines. Lieut. Gen. Douglas MacArthur, commanding the United States Army of the Far East, reported there was little damage, however.

[Japanese parachute troops had been landed in the Philippines and native Japanese had seized some communities, Royal Arch Gunnison said in a broadcast from Manila today to WOR-Mutual. He reported without detail that "in the naval war the ABCD fleets under American command appeared to be successful" against Japanese invasions.]

Japanese submarines, ranging out over the Pacific, sank an American transport carrying lumber 1,300 miles from San Francisco, and distress signals were heard from a freighter 700 miles from that city.

The War Department reported that 104 soldiers died and 300 were wounded as a result of the attack on Hickam Field, Hawaii. The National Broadcasting Company reported from Honolulu that the battleship Oklahoma was afire. [Domei, Japanese news agency, reported the Oklahoma sunk.]

Nation Placed on Full War Basis

The news of these surprise attacks fell like a bombshell on Washington. President Roosevelt immediately ordered the country and the Army and Navy onto a full war footing. He arranged at a White House conference last night to address a joint session of Congress at noon today, presumably to ask for declaration of a formal state of war.

This was disclosed after a long special Cabinet meeting, which was joined later by Congressional leaders. These leaders predicted "action" within a day.

DECEMBER 9, 1941
U. S. DECLARES WAR, PACIFIC BATTLE WIDENS; MANILA AREA BOMBED; 1,500 DEAD IN HAWAII; HOSTILE PLANES SIGHTED AT SAN FRANCISCO

UNITY IN CONGRESS

Only One Negative Vote as President Calls to War and Victory

ROUNDS OF CHEERS

Miss Rankin's Is Sole 'No' as Both Houses Act in Quick Time

By FRANK L. KLUCKHOHN

Special to THE NEW YORK TIMES.

WASHINGTON, Dec. 8—The United States today formally declared war on Japan. Congress, with only one dissenting vote, approved the resolution in the record time of 33 minutes after President Roosevelt denounced Japanese aggression in ringing tones. He personally delivered his message to a joint session of the Senate and House. At 4:10 P. M. he affixed his signature to the resolution.

There was no debate like that between April 2, 1917, when President Wilson requested war against Germany, and April 6, when a declaration of war was approved by Congress.

President Roosevelt spoke only 6 minutes and 30 seconds today compared with Woodrow Wilson's 29 minutes and 34 seconds.

The vote today against Japan was 82 to 0 in the Senate and 388 to 1 in the House. The lone vote against the resolution in the House was that of Miss Jeanette Rankin, Republican, of Montana. Her "No" was greeted with boos and hisses. In 1917 she voted against the resolution for war against Germany.

The President did not mention either Germany or Italy in his request. Early this evening a statement was issued at the White House, however, accusing Germany of doing everything possible to push Japan into the war. The objective, the official statement proclaimed, was to cut off American lend-lease aid to Germany's European enemies, and a pledge was made that this aid would continue "100 per cent."

A Sudden and Deliberate Attack

President Roosevelt's brief and decisive words were addressed to the assembled representatives of the basic organizations of American democracy—the Senate, the House, the Cabinet and the Supreme Court.

"America was suddenly and deliberately attacked by naval and air forces of the Empire of Japan," he said. "We will gain the inevitable triumph, so help us God."

Thunderous cheers greeted the Chief Executive and Commander in Chief throughout the address. This was particularly pronounced when he declared that Americans "will remember the character of the onslaught against us," a day, he remarked, which will live in infamy.

"This form of treachery shall never endanger us again," he declared amid cheers. "The American people in their righteous might will win through to absolute victory."

Then, to the accompaniment of a great roar of cheering, he asked for war against Japan.

THE CONGRESSIONAL ELECTIONS OF 1946

VOTERS SEEK A NEW DIRECTION AS REPUBLICANS TAKE CONGRESS

Republicans had a simple slogan in the congressional elections of 1946. "Had Enough?" they asked. The voters agreed with the challenge and gave the Republicans control of both houses of Congress for the first time since 1928. The outcome ended the Democratic dominance created by the New Deal and the leadership of Franklin Delano Roosevelt during the Great Depression and the Second World War.

SETTING OF THE ELECTIONS

Americans were tired of epic struggles, at home and abroad. In the economic travails of the 1930s, a fourth of the labor force had been unemployed, and millions had suffered the loss of their homes, farms, and savings. Crop failures, hunger, and forced migration in search of jobs added to their woes. Roosevelt's programs had relieved some of these problems and recast American social and political institutions while creating the modern welfare state. But economic distress had not disappeared, and unemployment ended only with the wartime mobilization of workers, business, and resources.

The war brought victory and prosperity, but also great costs to the nation. The U.S. military forces suffered a million casualties, including more than 400,000 deaths. With 16 million men in uniform, social life was restricted, and births declined. Taxes rose, expenditures of the federal government increased to unprecedented levels, consuming nearly half of the nation's total economy, and the national debt increased to 123 percent of the total national product— equivalent to $18 trillion in today's values (twice the actual national debt in 2008).

The necessities of war brought severe constraints on Americans' freedom. Although jobs were plentiful, strikes were outlawed, wage increases were limited by government directive, and overtime hours were mandated in many industries. Consumption was limited by government allotment of basic foods, and personal travel was restricted by severe rationing of gasoline and military requisition of public transportation. Censors controlled news reports from the battlefield areas

Source: The Granger Collection, New York

AT THE HOW-DID-IT-HAPPEN CLUB
NOVEMBER 7, 1948

A D.R. Fitzpatrick cartoon, "At the How-Did-It-Happen Club," depicts surprise over President Harry S. Truman's 1948 reelection which reversed the Republican gains of 1946.

and personal correspondence with servicemen. Dissidents were liable to prosecution, and nearly 120,000 Japanese Americans were forcibly relocated to desert camps.

Americans of "the greatest generation" endured these deaths, costs, and privations with remarkable patience and cooperation. By war's end, however, the nation wanted relief, but economic prospects were uncertain. Remembering the severe conditions of the Depression, voters worried that jobs might not be available as the returning servicemen poured into the labor force. These men sought opportunities for a normal life at home, women left or were pushed out of the labor force, and a "baby boom" exploded, bringing demands for new jobs, homes, and education.

Voters found their pent-up demands frustrated by inflation, lingering price controls, and shortages, as the transition

1946 MIDTERM ELECTION RESULTS

HOUSE

ELECTION YEAR	CONGRESS	MEMBERS ELECTED			GAINS/LOSSES	
		DEM.	REP.	MISC.	DEM.	REP.
1946	80th	188	246	1	–55	+57

SENATE

ELECTION YEAR	CONGRESS	MEMBERS ELECTED			GAINS/LOSSES	
		DEM.	REP.	MISC.	DEM.	REP.
1946	80th	45	51	–	+12	–13

from a war economy delayed revived production of consumer goods. Labor unrest added further discomfort. Unions, now free of wartime constraints, went out on strike to win higher wages to combat inflation, shutting down the major industries, including steel, railroads, coal, maritime trade, automobiles, electrical equipment, and meat-packing. Combined, the strikes included 4.75 million workers and the loss of 110 million workdays. The walkouts did bring workers wage increases of 18 percent to 22 percent, but they also increased inflationary pressures.

The economic troubles led to sharp ideological disputes in Washington, focusing on price controls. Republicans and conservatives argued for the abolition of the wartime regime (when 80 percent of consumer goods had been under government direction), seeing an unfettered market as the best way to achieve prosperity. President Harry S. Truman thought the controls should continue until conditions became more normal. In June 1946 Congress passed legislation to end all price controls, but Truman successfully vetoed the bill. A compromise lifted controls on most food, but reinstituted them for animal products. Shortages followed, with three-fourths of normal meat supplies dropping out of the marketplace. Facing voter revolt in "a beefsteak election," Truman removed all food controls on October 14. Goods reappeared on the nation's store shelves, but prices soared; most galling was a doubling of the cost of meat.

Having defeated the Axis powers and emerging as the most powerful nation in the world, Americans were also dismayed at new international threats. Europe was devastated, its economy destroyed by war and its population hungry and cold. The wartime alliance with the Soviet Union was rent by the imposition of a Communist "Iron Curtain" across the continent and the threat of further Soviet expansion into Greece, Turkey, and even France and Italy.

The voters also lacked confidence in the country's leadership. FDR, the inspiring national leader in Depression and war, had died on the eve of wartime victory. It was inevitable that Truman, the new "accidental" president, would be compared unfavorably with his charismatic predecessor. Truman had been a compromise choice for vice president on the Democratic ticket in 1944. He entered the White House without a political base and with no preparation for the job, not even knowing about the atomic bomb that would soon end the war. As troubles rose at home and abroad, he also lost the public's initial support; only a third of the voters approved of his performance by the time of the congressional elections.

Truman was beset by attacks from both the left and the right. Republicans opposed his domestic programs, while holding him responsible for the nation's economic distress. Within his own party, labor unions were unhappy with his efforts to keep controls on wages and his opposition to strikes in vital industries. When railroad unions threatened a national stoppage, which would effectively halt the entire economy, Truman seized the railroads, prepared to use the military to operate them, and went to Congress for authority to draft strikers—announcing a settlement of the dispute in the middle of his address. Later in the year, he would threaten similar action to prevent a renewed strike of coal miners.

The president's uncertain foreign policy also aroused opposition. Republicans and southern Democrats found him too conciliatory in negotiations with the Soviet Union on the future of Europe. At the same time, left-wing Democrats thought he was too aggressive in dealings with the former ally. Their distemper came to a climax in a September speech by Commerce Secretary Henry Wallace, the former vice president, who had been removed from the party ticket in 1944 in favor of Truman. After first defending Wallace's right to "free speech," Truman forced the resignation of the insubordinate cabinet secretary.

A Democratic Party disaster loomed.

THE RESULTS AND EFFECTS

In November, as *The New York Times* reported, voters "swung this nation sharply right in a left-veering world." Republicans swept the election, picking up 56 seats in the House and 13 in the Senate, giving them majorities of 246 to 189 and 51 to 45. They would never again achieve such dominance in the House and would wait until the administration of Ronald Reagan to do better in the Senate.

The Democratic majority forged in the New Deal was severely damaged. The party lost significantly in its base support, the industrial cities and the working class. The nominal leader of the party, Truman, was seen as the primary cause of the Democratic losses. The unpopular president had stayed away from the congressional campaigns, but his reticence did not win friends among either voters or party activists. Rumors abounded of third party movements among factions as disparate as labor unions and southern segregationists. Some Democratic leaders began to think of replacing Truman as the party's presidential candidate in 1948 and eventually made a futile attempt to draft the hero of World War II, Dwight D. Eisenhower.

The new Congress would have a significant impact on future American politics. It included some first-termers who rose to prominence in later years, such as future presidents John F. Kennedy and Richard Nixon, fated to face each other in the presidential election of 1960. A freshman senator from Wisconsin, Joseph McCarthy, would soon threaten the freedoms of Americans and the stability of the government. And another incoming senator, Arthur Watkins, Republican of Utah, would later chair the investigations that destroyed those threats.

Despite its reputation for inaction, the Eightieth Congress recorded some notable and some controversial achievements. Major changes were made in the structure of government. The National Security Act created the mechanisms that enabled the United States to fulfill its new role as the world's greatest power. The act merged the separate armed services into the Department of Defense, created the National Security Council as the president's agency for coordinating foreign and military policy, and established the Central Intelligence Agency for expert acquisition of the information needed for foreign policy decisions.

The new Congress also changed the presidency politically, giving greater prominence to the legislative branch. It altered the line of succession to the presidency so that after the Vice President (vacant until 1949), succession would fall to the Speaker of the House and the president pro tempore of the Senate, rather than to members of the cabinet. The Republicans controlling Congress also initiated a constitutional amendment to limit presidents to two terms. Ironically, this belated reproach to Franklin Roosevelt for winning four terms later proved harmful to their party, when it prevented Eisenhower or Ronald Reagan from seeking third terms.

In foreign policy, the Republican Congress cooperated with Truman in major new initiatives, including creation of the Fulbright exchange program and the Truman Doctrine to provide aid to combat Communist insurgents in Greece and Turkey. The most important action was the revitalization of Europe, through the Marshall Plan, possibly the most successful program in American diplomatic history.

The war had devastated Europe. Both winners and losers saw their factories and transportation destroyed, their fields barren and unplanted, their capital vanished, their population scattered and jobless. The continent was vulnerable not only to economic distress but to the advance of communism, either through force or voter despair. To meet the problems, Secretary of State George Marshall and Truman proposed a program of economic reconstruction combining American financial aid with the development of new European institutions to implement the aid.

Republicans soon backed the proposal, abandoning their past isolationist positions, with Sen. Arthur Vandenberg of Michigan leading the effort, while insisting that it be directed by a new agency to be led by a Republican. Three months after Marshall first proposed the program, European governments submitted detailed proposals, including a common economic authority. Truman held a large meeting with congressional leaders only a week later, called a special session of Congress in November, and submitted a detailed program before Christmas. On April 2, 1948, the authorizing legislation cleared Congress, committing 12 percent of the federal budget, and 2 percent of the nation's total output to the task. Within four years, the continent was prosperous, safely democratic, and firmly allied with the United States. The cooperation between Truman and congressional Republicans achieved a monumental success.

Domestic programs fared quite differently in the Eightieth Congress and aroused great conflict. The president's budget requests were cut substantially, about 5 percent in each year. In parallel fiscal actions, three tax reductions were passed, each was vetoed, and the last was passed over Truman's objections. Republicans also defeated or ignored Truman's programs to extend Social Security coverage, increase public housing, broaden public health research, and institute universal military service in place of the draft. Southern Democrats further stymied the president by burying proposed civil rights legislation to eliminate poll taxes, combat lynching, support racial equality in hiring, and desegregate the armed forces.

The most contentious issue was labor legislation, with Republicans bent on limiting the power of unions and Truman adamantly defending this core Democratic group. After bitter debate, Congress passed the Taft-Hartley Labor-Management Relations Act over Truman's veto, with most Democrats deserting the president. Alleging abuses of union power, the act outlawed the closed shop, encouraged states to abolish union shops, required supervised strike votes, compelled union officials to swear they were not Communists, and outlawed political expenditures from union treasuries. To deal with strikes that might threaten public safety, such as the postwar railroad stoppage, Taft-Hartley provided for compulsory government intervention and authorized antistrike injunctions.

Unions derided the legislation as a "slave labor law" and made its repeal their primary political goal, repressing their previous disagreements with Truman. The president built on their support, using his conflicts with the Republican legislature to frame the 1948 election as a referendum on the "do-nothing" Congress. Truman ignored the universal prediction that the Democrats faced certain defeat, with dissidents forming both a segregationist States' Rights Party in the South and a left-wing Progressive Party under Wallace in the North. Accepting the party nomination, Truman aroused a dispirited convention by calling Congress into special session and challenging Republicans to enact their platform promises. After three weeks, Congress adjourned without any significant action–further spurring Truman's defiance.

In a historic upset, Truman defied all expectation, beating New York governor Thomas E. Dewey. Truman won almost half of the popular vote and a clear electoral victory. Democrats made large gains in Congress, capturing both houses with 75 new House and 9 new Senate seats. The Democratic victory, however, did not lead to much legislative success for Truman's "Fair Deal" extension of the historic New Deal. The Taft-Hartley Act was neither repealed nor significantly amended, and Truman spent most of his remaining years in office in a rear-guard defense against Republican initiatives.

The congressional elections of 1946 set a pattern for postwar politics. The parties followed common foreign policies, opposing the expansion of Soviet communism and supporting a large military establishment, but there were many differences on domestic issues. Although they often cooperated in practice, the parties followed disparate ideologies, Republicans emphasizing tax reductions, Democrats seeking expanded government programs.

Politically, the parties became more competitive and more contentious. Republicans despaired over the 1948 defeat that had seemed impossible. Democrats, reveling in the unexpected victory, came to see themselves as almost immune from public disapproval. But the wheel of political fortune would turn. For the rest of the century, Republicans and Democrats would move into and out of power, but neither party would achieve long-term majority control of both the presidency and Congress. The nation advanced, but its politics stagnated.

* *

THE NEW PRESIDENT

Amid the horrors of World War II, President Franklin D. Roosevelt won his fourth term in 1944 despite failing health. Fearful of his death in office, the Democrats selected a new vice-presidential candidate, Sen. Harry S. Truman of Missouri, a soft-spoken moderate acceptable to all factions of the party. FDR survived only a few months of his new term. He died suddenly in mid-April of 1945, and Truman became president.

JULY 22, 1944
NAZIS BLOCK PLOT TO SEIZE GOVERNMENT; AMERICANS LAND ON GUAM, PUSH INLAND; TRUMAN NOMINATED FOR VICE PRESIDENCY

JULY 23, 1944
EDITORIAL
THE DEMOCRATIC PARTY ENTERS A NEW PHASE

Truman's Nomination Marks Attempt To Hold Together the Dissidents For the Campaign's Duration

'MAJOR NEW DEAL SURRENDER'

By ARTHUR KROCK

CHICAGO, July 11—In its national convention of 1944, just concluded here, the Democratic Party—as realigned by President Roosevelt—entered upon a new phase which many believe to be the final one under its present leadership. The new phase was an attempt, through the nomination for Vice President of Senator Harry S. Truman of Missouri over Henry A. Wallace, and by the adoption of a platform which in many respects turned its back on the early New Deal, to hold in a common front for the campaign's duration the dissident groups that came into violent conflict during the convention.

On the surface the effort was successful, although it was achieved at the expense (1) of Mr. Wallace's ambition to succeed himself, (2) of the attempt of the CIO to exercise a full affirmative as well as negative power over all the proceedings of the convention and (3) of the hopes of Negro organizations that what the New Deal had so lavishly encouraged would be reflected in the Democratic platform the President dictated, line by line.

It was successful because the warnings of old-line Democrats to Mr. Roosevelt that he would risk his election by dictating to the convention the nomination of Mr. Wallace as his running mate persuaded him to make a series of substitute endorsements that put the Vice President at the mercy of his party opponents. These, by scattering their opposition on the first ballot and thus preventing Mr. Wallace from getting a majority, were able thereby to effect a winning combination with Senator Truman, who was apparently the only rival of the Vice President acceptable to the old-liners and to the CIO who could possibly defeat Mr. Wallace for renomination.

Weakness Revealed

The weakness which, despite the war that made the President the inevitable nominee for a fourth term, was revealed here by concessions in the platform and the permitted sacrifice of Mr. Wallace, compelled the first major surrender of the New Deal. If the political reasoning of the groups that sponsored the Vice President, particularly the CIO, had been accepted by Mr. Roosevelt, the Negro leaders would not now be denouncing the platform for failing even to endorse the Fair Employment Practices Commission by name, as the Republicans did, an omission which was deliberately made to forestall if possible the electoral loss of certain Southern States. And if this reasoning has been accepted, the President, who really preferred to run again with Mr. Wallace, would have dictated his renomination as patently as he did the platform.

If the President had believed his political strength as Commander in Chief in wartime was as sure to win him re-election as it was renomination, the decisions of this convention would have been different. No attempt would have been made, as it was unsuccessfully, to compromise the basic issue between the regular and the contesting delegations from Texas, and Mr. Wallace would not have been the sacrifice to expediency he has become.

APRIL 13, 1945
PRESIDENT ROOSEVELT IS DEAD; TRUMAN TO CONTINUE POLICIES; 9TH CROSSES ELBE, NEARS BERLIN

END COMES SUDDENLY AT WARM SPRINGS

Even His Family Unaware of Condition as Cerebral Stroke Brings Death to Nation's Leader at 63

ALL CABINET MEMBERS TO KEEP POSTS

Funeral to Be at White House Tomorrow, With Burial at Hyde Park Home—Impact of News Tremendous

By ARTHUR KROCK

Special to The New York Times.

WASHINGTON, April 12—Franklin Delano Roosevelt, War President of the United States and the only Chief Executive in history who was chosen for more than two terms, died suddenly and unexpectedly at 4:35 P.M. today at Warm Springs, Ga., and the White House announced his death at 5:48 o'clock. He was 63.

The President, stricken by a cerebral hemorrhage, passed from unconsciousness to death on the eighty-third day of his fourth term and in an hour of high triumph. The armies and fleets under his direction as Commander in Chief were at the gates of Berlin and the shores of Japan's home islands as Mr. Roosevelt died, and the cause he represented and led was nearing the conclusive phase of success.

Less than two hours after the official announcement, Harry S. Truman of Missouri, the Vice President, took the oath as the thirty-second President. The oath was administered by the Chief Justice of the United States, Harlan F. Stone, in a one-minute ceremony at the White House.

Mr. Truman immediately let it be known that Mr. Roosevelt's Cabinet is remaining in office at his request, and that he had authorized Secretary of State Edward R. Stettinius Jr. to proceed with plans for the United Nations Conference on international organization at San Francisco, scheduled to begin April 25. A report was circulated that he leans somewhat to the idea of a coalition Cabinet, but this is unsubstantiated.

President Truman, in his first official pronouncement, pledged prosecution of the war to a successful conclusion. His statement, issued for him at the White House by press secretary Jonathan Daniels, said:

"The world may be sure that we will prosecute the war on both fronts, East and West, with all the vigor we possess to a successful conclusion."

The War Ends

Harry Truman succeeded to the presidency with little preparation, even uninformed about the secret atomic bomb program. But the course of military success continued toward its destined victory. The United States and its allies soon won the war in the European theater, then unleashed the power of two atomic bombs to speed Japan's surrender. The new president faced a new world.

MAY 8, 1945
THE WAR IN EUROPE IS ENDED! SURRENDER IS UNCONDITIONAL; V-E WILL BE PROCLAIMED TODAY; OUR TROOPS ON OKINAWA GAIN

Wild Crowds Greet News In City While Others Pray

By FRANK S. ADAMS

New York City's millions reacted in two sharply contrasting ways yesterday to the news of the unconditional surrender of the German armies. A large and noisy minority greeted it with the turbulent enthusiasm of New Year's Eve and Election Night rolled into one. However, the great bulk of the city's population responded with quiet thanksgiving that the war in Europe was won, tempered by the realization that a grim and bitter struggle still was ahead in the Pacific and the fact that the nation is still in mourning for its fallen President and Commander in Chief.

Times Square, the financial section and the garment district were thronged from mid-morning on with wildly jubilant celebrators who tooted horns, staged impromptu parades and filled the canyons between the skyscrapers with fluttering scraps of paper. Elsewhere in the metropolitan area, however, war plants continued to hum, schools, offices and factories carried on their normal activities, and residential areas were calmly joyful....

 The White House and War Department announced today that an atomic bomb, possessing more power than 20,000 tons of TNT, a destructive force equal to the load of 2,000 B-29's and more than 2,000 times the blast power of what previously was the world's most devastating bomb, had been dropped on Japan.

AUGUST 7, 1945
FIRST ATOMIC BOMB DROPPED ON JAPAN; MISSILE IS EQUAL TO 20,000 TONS OF TNT; TRUMAN WARNS FOE OF A 'RAIN OF RUIN'

NEW AGE USHERED

Day of Atomic Energy Hailed by President, Revealing Weapon

HIROSHIMA IS TARGET

'Impenetrable' Cloud of Dust Hides City After Single Bomb Strikes

By SIDNEY SHALETT

Special to The New York Times.

WASHINGTON, Aug. 6—The White House and War Department announced today that an atomic bomb, possessing more power than 20,000 tons of TNT, a destructive force equal to the load of 2,000 B-29's and more than 2,000 times the blast power of what previously was the world's most devastating bomb, had been dropped on Japan.

The announcement, first given to the world in utmost solemnity by President Truman, made it plain that one of the scientific landmarks of the century had been passed, and that the "age of atomic energy," which can be a tremendous force for the advancement of civilization as well as for destruction, was at hand.

At 10:45 o'clock this morning, a statement by the President was issued at the White House that sixteen hours earlier—about the time that citizens on the Eastern seaboard were sitting down to their Sunday suppers—an American plane had dropped the single atomic bomb on the Japanese city of Hiroshima, an important army center.

Japanese Solemnly Warned

What happened at Hiroshima is not yet known. The War Department said it "as yet was unable to make an accurate report" because "an impenetrable cloud of dust and smoke" masked the target area from reconnaissance planes. The Secretary of War will release the story "as soon as accurate details of the results of the bombing become available."

But in a statement vividly describing the results of the first test of the atomic bomb in New Mexico, the War Department told how an immense steel tower had been "vaporized" by the tremendous explosion, how a 40,000-foot cloud rushed into the sky, and two observers were knocked down at a point 10,000 yards away. And President Truman solemnly warned:

"It was to spare the Japanese people from utter destruction that the ultimatum of July 26 was issued at Potsdam. Their leaders promptly rejected that ultimatum. If they do not now accept our terms, they may expect a rain of ruin from the air the like of which has never been seen on this earth."

AUGUST 15, 1945
JAPAN SURRENDERS, END OF WAR! EMPEROR ACCEPTS ALLIED RULE; M'ARTHUR SUPREME COMMANDER; OUR MANPOWER CURBS VOIDED

YIELDING UNQUALIFIED, TRUMAN SAYS

Japan Is Told to Order End of Hostilities, Notify Allied Supreme Commander and Send Emissaries to Him

MACARTHUR TO RECEIVE SURRENDER

Formal Proclamation of V-J Day Awaits Signing of Those Articles—Cease-Fire Order Given to the Allied Forces

By ARTHUR KROCK

Special to The New York Times.

WASHINGTON, Aug. 14—Japan today unconditionally surrendered the hemispheric empire taken by force and held almost intact for more than two years against the rising power of the United States and its Allies in the Pacific war.

The bloody dream of the Japanese military caste vanished in the text of a note to the Four Powers accepting the terms of the Potsdam Declaration of July 26, 1945, which amplified the Cairo Declaration of 1943.

Like the previous items in the surrender correspondence, today's Japanese document was forwarded through the Swiss Foreign Office at Berne and the Swiss Legation in Washington. The note of total capitulation was delivered to the State Department by the Legation Charge d'Affaires at 6:10 P.M., after the third and most anxious day of waiting on Tokyo, the anxiety intensified by several premature or false reports of the finale of World War II.

Orders Given to the Japanese

The Department responded with a note to Tokyo through the same channel, ordering the immediate end of hostilities by the Japanese, requiring that the Supreme Allied Commander—who, the President announced, will be Gen. Douglas MacArthur—be notified of the date and hour of the order, and instructing that emissaries of Japan be sent to him at once—at the time and place selected by him—"with full information of the disposition of the Japanese forces and commanders."

President Truman summoned a special press conference in the Executive offices at 7 P.M. He handed to the reporters three texts.

The first—the only one he read aloud—was that he had received the Japanese note and deemed it full acceptance of the Potsdam Declaration, containing no qualification whatsoever; that arrangements for the formal signing of the peace would be made for the "earliest possible moment;" that the Japanese surrender would be made to General MacArthur in his capacity as Supreme Allied Commander in Chief; that Allied military commanders had been instructed to cease hostilities, but that the formal proclamation of V-J Day must await the formal signing.

The text ended with the Japanese note, in which the Four Powers (the United States, Great Britain, China and Russia) were officially informed that the Emperor of Japan had issued an imperial rescript of surrender, was prepared to guarantee the necessary signatures to the terms as prescribed by the Allies, and had instructed all his commanders to cease active operations, to surrender all arms and to disband all forces under their control and within their reach.

The President's second announcement was that he had instructed the Selective Service to reduce the monthly military draft from 80,000 to 50,000 men, permitting a constant flow of replacements for the occupation forces and other necessary military units, with the draft held to low-age groups and first discharges given on the basis of long, arduous and faithful war service. He said he hoped to release 5,000,000 to 5,500,000 men in the subsequent year or eighteen months, the ratio governed in some degree by transportation facilities and the world situation.

The President's final announcement was to decree holidays tomorrow and Thursday for all Federal workers, who, he said, were the "hardest working and perhaps the least appreciated" by the public of all who had helped to wage the war.

Mr. Truman spoke calmly to the reporters, but when he had finished reading his face broke into a smile.

- -

TRUMAN'S TROUBLES

Assuming office during tumultuous times in the shadow of one of the most successful presidents ever to hold office, President Harry Truman struggled to forge his own path. Retaining FDR's cabinet and policies enhanced Truman's legitimacy, but did not reflect his own moderate preferences. He clashed with his own party in Congress, vetoing more of that body's legislation than any president in fifty years. Republicans, sensing the Democrats' weakness and their own opportunities after a generation in exile, attacked the president and the Democratic Party's seeming lack of cohesion and tendency toward "extreme liberalism." Conditions appeared ripe for a massive political swing.

APRIL 7, 1946
PRESIDENT PUTS A TROUBLED YEAR BEHIND HIM
A Series of Grave Problems Were Taken Up
By FELIX BELAIR Jr.

WASHINGTON, April 6—As Harry S. Truman rounds out his first year in the White House the periodic auditors of the President's leadership once again are busy with the tally sheets.

Because the debits and credits are seen here at first hand, Washington sometimes is accused of failing to see the forest for the trees.

However that may be, the general conclusion seems to be that the business of the Presidency under Mr. Truman is still operating in the black even if no bonuses are being declared.

To say that the last twelve months gave rise to problems which would have been tremendously difficult of solution even for men better experienced in world leadership than was Mr. Truman would be to paint a picture in half tones.

Probably no President since Andrew Johnson has entered the White House under such trying conditions. Nor was the job any less difficult because the start was from scratch. President Roosevelt was no man to share his responsibilities with a Vice President or to encourage a study of problems which might one day be his successor's.

Mistakes Have Been Made

That there have been mistakes—serious ones—President Truman probably would be the first to admit.

For the most part, these errors stemmed from lack of experience and proved again that no man ever knew how to be President before entering the White House. Happily they were subject to correction.

Had it not already happened, it would be difficult to conceive of a President giving every appearance for a considerable time of pursuing an anti-Russian policy while actually doing nothing of the kind. Yet it was on the front porch of his fishing lodge at Reelfoot Lake, Tenn., that Mr. Truman made the casual observation that the United States did not intend to share the secret of the atomic bomb with Russia or any other country.

Before this episode, the President seemed to encourage by his silence and refusal to interfere in the anti-Russian outbursts of lesser Administration officials who were willing to risk an open break with the Soviets and possible collapse of the United Nations over the issue of Argentina's admittance—a country we were later to condemn formally for playing hand in glove with our enemies of World War II.

Along with others like it, this chapter is a part of history. As the President more than once has said privately to friends, only a hurried trip to Moscow by the late Harry L. Hopkins prevented the collapse of the organizing conference of the United Nations.

Whether he likes it or not, on the other hand, the President is committed to a political and economic policy somewhat left of center, and he will remain so committed until the Democratic convention in 1948.

When it is remembered that law and policy depend for their success on their effective administration, it is not difficult to foresee troubled days still ahead for the President.

But more than by these considerations, the auditors of the President's leadership are influenced by the picture of the country prosperous after having all but completed its perilous transition from war to peace.

Popular With People

He continues popular with the masses of the people, and, that being so, who are the auditors to say that Presidency business is not operating in the black? Seasoned politician that he is, Mr. Truman is not likely to overlook the fact that the same considerations that make for his popularity with the people may account for some of his troubles with Congress.

For history shows that when the people are prosperous, or think they are, they become conservatively inclined. They were already pretty well fed up after twelve years of reform, and if this condition is reflected by a Congressional unwillingness to accept still more reform, perhaps the President can afford to be philosophic.

At least this attitude seems to be borne out in the Presidential disposition of late, for he has had occasion to say recently that he is beginning to like his job in the White House.

APRIL 14, 1946
REPUBLICANS ASSAIL TRUMAN 'CONFUSION'

National Committee Asserts Year Shows Failures at Home and in World

HANNEGAN 'THANKS' REECE

Declares Reply to Challenge Demonstrates Rival Party Lacks Positive Program

By CHARLES E. EGAN

Special to The New York Times.

WASHINGTON, April 13—The end of President Truman's first year in office finds the country suffering from policies which have created confusion in national affairs and in our dealings with foreign powers, according to the Republican National Committee.

In a twelve-page appraisal of the Democratic Administration since President Roosevelt's death, the Republican committee declares today that the confusion is a natural reflection "of the man who didn't wish to be President."

Failure of the Administration to "say what it means and to mean what it says" accounts for the state of Russian-American relations, according to the committee. It asserts that our dealings with South America, particularly

Argentina, have been "incredibly stupid" and that the Administration's handling of international relief problems is accountable for the fact that relief had fallen "scandalously short" of commitments.

In its attack on Administration activities in the foreign field, the Republican committee charges that, while President Truman pays lip service to the United Nations, he simultaneously pursues independent purposes.

Says Aides Go Uninformed

Although the President has called for bipartisan support and had made bipartisan appointments to the United Nations, it adds, he has failed to inform his representatives of official policy on vital matters, such as trusteeships and atomic energy control.

Hits Reconversion "Muddle"

On domestic problems, the Republican committee declares, there has been a bankruptcy of leadership which has made a muddle of reconversion, alienated a cooperative Congress by "preferring to tread the leftward path of radical experimentation" and brought confusion into labor and management relationships.

AUGUST 4, 1946
TRUMAN AND CONGRESS PART AT A CROSSROADS

A 'Veto President' With Own Party in Power, He Faces Hostility Among Legislators for Rest of His Term

COURT SPLIT IS NOT HELPING

By ARTHUR KROCK

WASHINGTON, Aug. 3—The end of the second and final regular session of the Seventy-ninth Congress found the three coordinate branches of the Federal Government in unusual need of coordination. The legislative and executive arms were at cross purposes with each other; the party memberships in Congress were divided on basic matters; and the Supreme Court, head of the judicial branch, was the exposed battlefield of a verbal duel between two of the justices.

Congress and the Executive have come to a stalemate often before in our history. Bitterness between members of the Supreme Court is not new, though its public revelation—such as Justice Robert H. Jackson made in this instance—is unprecedented. But an abiding executive-legislative quarrel is much more rare when the President and the nominal Congressional majority are of the same party. And an open Supreme Court feud among justices appointed from a faction of that party by the same President is rarer still.

The immediate consequence of major differences between a President and a Congress organized by his party is a series of vetoes. That result also follows the capture of Congress, or either branch of it, by the opposition in the middle of a Presidential term, as will appear next January if the Republicans win the House or Senate or both. But when a Chief Executive becomes a "veto President" in the first-named circumstances, as Mr. Truman has, the party split is deep, and the chances of the opposition to carry Congress and the Presidency are enhanced.

Mr. Truman has engaged deliberately in his war with Congress and his party majority there. He has no responsibility for the feud in the Supreme Court, where the ethics if not the integrity of Justice Hugo L. Black have been seriously impugned by Mr. Jackson. But that contributes to the show of Democratic impotence and disorder in government. And our political tradition is that in such circumstances, the President, as party leader and Chief of State, is held accountable.

OCTOBER 18, 1946
SECOND GOP BLAST AIMED AT TRUMAN

Brown of Ohio Labels Address 'Unfair' in Radio Rebuttal, Predicts Nov. 5 Victory

By WILLIAM S. WHITE

Special to The New York Times.

WASHINGTON, Oct. 17—The Republicans returned tonight to the attack on President Truman, accusing his Administration of creating shortages in such essentials as meat and housing by adopting radical economic theories.

Representative Clarence J. Brown of Ohio, campaign director of the Republican National Committee, asserted that Mr. Truman and the Democratic Congress alike had followed the policies of men "who are not interested in preserving either our Constitutional form of Government or our American way of life."

Shortages Laid to Democrats

Going beyond the meat controversy, Representative Brown asserted that President Truman and the Democrats were in fact to blame for scarcities in housing, sugar, shortening, soap, paper tissues "and many other necessities of life," and added:

"The American people are refusing to longer stand for a controlled economy, or to accept it as a permanent part of our national life.

"They are determined that no group of left-wingers, fellow travelers, radicals or communists are going to make this nation over into any sort of a socialized state.

"Yes, on Nov. 5 the American people will vote their own liberation from the tyranny of little men in big jobs. It will be a glorious day in our national history, for the American people have had enough."

• •

PRICE CONTROLS

Inflation and government control of prices were the main issues in the 1946 congressional elections. During World War II the government had instituted rationing and price controls of basic food products in an effort to keep their prices stable amid the limited supply of goods. Now, in peace, producers sought to raise prices to spur production and increase profits in a competitive market, which risked massive inflation. Congress and President Truman clashed on their economic policies, with Congress seeking to end, and Truman seeking to extend, price controls. As the fall elections neared, meat disappeared from grocery stores as farmers, anticipating higher prices, did not bring their stock to market. Facing massive shortages, Truman reluctantly ended price controls on meat. Food became more plentiful, but with huge price increases. Republicans blamed the administration for both restricted supplies and high prices.

JUNE 30, 1946
OPA PRICE CONTROLS END AT MIDNIGHT TONIGHT AS HOUSE 173 TO 142 SUSTAINS TRUMAN VETO; PRESIDENT ASKS NATION NOT TO RAISE PRICES

PRESIDENT IS SHARP

Rejecting OPA Bill, He Tells House It Would Legalize Inflation

ASKS STOP-GAP LAW

Maps 'Effective' Plan for Year of Stabilization to Be Voted Later

By BERTRAM D. HULEN

Special to The New York Times.

WASHINGTON, June 29—President Truman vetoed the OPA bill today in a strong message of 4,000 words to the House, declaring that it presented "a choice between inflation with a statute and inflation without one."

At the same time he put forward in detail recommendations for what he considered a sound law on the subject. With such a measure, he contended, "we can win the war against inflation just as decisively as we won the war against the Axis." Pending passage of such a measure, which he wants now, he requested temporary extension of present controls by resolution.

The vetoed measure, he said in his message to Congress, is one that "continues the Government's responsibility to stabilize the economy and at the same time it destroys the Government's power to do so." It was only

fair, he maintained, to tell the American people "now" that it would not protect them.

Points to Inflation Abroad

"In the end this bill would lead to disaster," he emphasized, adding, "inflation and collapse in this country would shake the entire world."

"I cannot bring myself to believe," he said, "that the representatives of the American people will permit the great calamity which will befall this country if price and rent control end at midnight Sunday."

The fact that inflation has already "gutted the economy of country after country all over the world should shake our comfortable assurance that such a catastrophe cannot happen here," he said.

JULY 26, 1946
TRUMAN SIGNS THE OPA BILL; IF INEFFECTIVE HE INTENDS TO CALL A SPECIAL SESSION

CONGRESS WARNED

President in a Message Says It Must Act if Inflation Threatens

BILL 'FAR SHORT' OF HOPES

But It Is Worth a Trial, Executive Holds—Promises a Fair Decontrol Board

By JOHN D. MORRIS

Special to The New York Times.

WASHINGTON, July 25—President Truman signed the Price Control Bill shortly after it reached his desk today— "reluctantly," he said in a message to Congress, because it fails to assure the maintenance of stable prices.

The President stated in his message that if the combined efforts of the Government and the people under the new law

failed to block inflation, "I shall have no alternative but to call the Congress back into special session to strengthen the price-control laws and to enact such fiscal and monetary legislation as we need to save us from the threat of economic disaster."

In signing the bill Mr. Truman ended a twenty-five-day hiatus in Federal price and rent controls, revalidating Office

President Harry S. Truman appeals for food economies in an address at the White House, October 1, 1947, to the twenty-six-man Food Committee, as Charles Luckman, committee chair, listens at right.

Source: AP Images

of Price Administration regulations and price schedules, with specified exceptions, that existed when the agency expired June 30. The legislation revives the OPA, with drastic restrictions on its powers, until next June 30.

Measure Held Improved

The President told Congress that its bill to revive price control fell "far short" of his hope for a measure under which the Government could assure the people with full confidence that prices would remain generally stable "in these last few months of the transition to a free economy."

He said he was advised, however, that it was the best bill that Congress would now pass and "it is clear,

moreover, that it is a better bill than the one I was forced to veto on June 29."

"If that bill had become law," he stated, "inflation would have been inevitable. While the present measure by no means guarantees that inflation can be avoided, it offers a sufficient prospect of success to warrant the making of a whole-hearted effort to keep our economy on an even keel until a flood of goods makes further controls unnecessary."

The fact that prices and rents have "steadily and ominously" risen during the price control hiatus demonstrates, Mr. Truman said, "that the continuance of effective price control is a vital necessity to our people."

SEPTEMBER 8, 1946
UNPARALLELED MEAT FAMINE PREDICTED FOR THE COUNTRY

Special to The New York Times.

CHICAGO, Sept. 7—Livestock industry spokesmen predicted today a meat famine such as the nation never before has seen. The prediction came as Chicago housewives stormed butcher shops to load up their refrigerators

with the last steaks, chops and roasts they expect to be able to buy for weeks.

Blame for the situation was placed by the livestock men on the reimposition of price controls, ceiling prices at the slaughtering level, which went into effect at midnight Aug. 31, and retail ceiling prices which became effective Tuesday.

Since the slaughtering ceilings were announced livestock receipts at the nation's stock yards have declined daily to new lows.

Stock yards officials offered these reasons for the predicted meat famine:

1. Farmers and cattle raisers are opposed to any form of price or Government control and are holding animals for fattening on grains, which were not returned to price control.

2. Pastures were stripped of almost all grain-fed cattle when prices boomed during the lapse of price control. There are few left to send to market.

3. Grass-fed cattle from the western ranges, which yield only utility cuts and are the principal source of meat at this season of the year, are being withheld from market because of opposition to price control.

By nightfall today, after the rush of buying by housewives here, there was not a pound of meat, except a few cold cuts, on retailers' shelves, retail trade associations reported.

OCTOBER 15, 1946
TRUMAN ENDS ALL PRICE CONTROLS ON MEAT, EFFECTIVE TODAY, AS 'ONLY REMEDY LEFT' TO HIM; WAGE CURBS AND OTHERS WILL BE DROPPED SOON

TALKS TO COUNTRY

President Calls on the Meat Industry to Keep Prices Reasonable

HITS 'SELFISH FEW'

He Promises a Return to Free Economy as Quickly as Possible

By WALTER H. WAGGONER

Special to The New York Times.

WASHINGTON, Oct. 14—President Truman removed tonight all price controls from livestock and meat, effective tomorrow, in resorting to what he described as "the one remedy left" for ending the most critical meat shortage in the country's history.

Mr. Truman handed down his long-awaited decision in a country-wide radio address at 10 P.M. He put the blame for the crisis, which made his action necessary, on "the reckless group of selfish men" who for political gain encouraged sellers of meat to gamble on the end of price controls.

He said that he had studied a number of alternatives before taking the decontrol action. These included a "price control holiday"; a price increase for livestock; Government seizure of packing houses and cattle for slaughter, and importation of dressed meat from foreign countries.

These proposals were "carefully weighed and considered," but they had to be rejected, Mr. Truman said.

Real Story Called Simple

Accordingly, the President added, he had ordered the Secretary of Agriculture, Clinton P. Anderson, and the Price Administrator, Paul Porter, to remove all price controls on livestock, meat, and meat products and feedstuffs derived from livestock.

The questions of why there is a meat shortage, while there are millions of cattle and hogs on farms and in feed lots, and who the people are behind this shortage, are easily answered, Mr. Truman said, adding:

"The real story is a simple one: The responsibility rests squarely on a few men in the Congress who, in the service of selfish interests, have been determined for some time to wreck controls no matter what the cost might be to our people."

Voluntary Price Curbs Urged

The President at the same time called on the livestock and meat industries to hold to their assurances that the removal of price controls would bring meat back to the restaurants and dinner tables "at reasonable prices."

"The American people will know where the responsibility rests if profiteering on meat raises prices so high that the average American cannot buy it," he asserted.

OCTOBER 27, 1946
RETAIL FOOD PRICES UP 19.6% IN 90 DAYS

Levels on Sept. 17, Before End of Many Controls, Showed 24.9% Rise in a Year

Special to The New York Times.

WASHINGTON, Oct. 26—On the basis of final data the Bureau of Labor Statistics of the Department of Labor reported today a 1.7 per cent rise in retail food prices in the period of Aug. 13 to Sept. 17.

The bureau pointed out that the effects of the Oct. 22 order removing meat price controls and other sweeping decontrol orders would not be indicated in the index until November.

Prices for "all foods" except meat rose an average of 2.2 per cent in large cities for the period reported on.

On Sept. 17, according to the bureau, the food price index stood at 174.1 per cent of the 1935–39 average. The figure was 24.9 per cent higher than a year ago, and 86.2 per cent higher than in August, 1939.

In the three months from mid-June to mid-September, retail food prices advanced 19.6 per cent.

THE SOVIET MENACE

An invaluable American ally in fighting and winning World War II, the Soviet Union quickly split from the United States after peace was won, dividing the world between itself and the Western powers and leading former prime minister Winston Churchill of Britain to declare, "An iron curtain has descended over Europe." Policy toward the Soviets divided the administration. Secretary of State James Byrnes, with Truman's backing, pushed a "hard-line" stance. An opposing position came from Commerce Secretary Henry Wallace, vice president during FDR's third term. Wallace urged a less aggressive U.S. approach toward the Communist regime, contradicting Truman's announced policy. Public controversy soon forced Truman to demand Wallace's resignation. The split further weakened Democratic unity, leading many to question the party's future.

MARCH 6, 1946
U.S. SENDS 2 PROTESTS TO RUSSIA ON MANCHURIA AND IRAN ACTIONS; CHURCHILL ASSAILS SOVIET POLICY

BRITON SPEAKS OUT

Calls for Association of U.S., British to Stem Russian Expansion

APPEASEMENT IS OPPOSED

'Iron Curtain' Dividing Europe Is Not What We Fought For, Churchill Says at Fulton, Mo.

By HAROLD B. HINTON

Special to The New York Times.

FULTON, Mo., March 5—A fraternal association between the British Empire and the United States was advocated here today by Winston Churchill to stem "the expansive and proselytizing tendencies" of the Soviet Union.

Introduced by President Truman at Westminster College, Great Britain's wartime Prime Minister asserted that a mere balance of power in the world today would be too narrow a margin and would only offer "temptations to a trial of strength."

On the contrary, he added that the English-speaking peoples must maintain an overwhelming preponderance of power on their side until "the highroads of the future will be clear, not only for us but for all, not only for our time but for a century to come."

Says Curtain Divides Europe

Mr. Churchill painted a dark picture of post-war Europe, on which "an iron curtain has descended across the Continent" from Stettin in the Baltic to Trieste in the Adriatic.

Warsaw, Berlin, Prague, Vienna, Budapest, Belgrade, Sofia and Bucharest are all being subjected to increasing pressure and control from Moscow, he said, adding:

"This is certainly not the liberated Europe we fought to build up. Nor is it one which contains the essentials of permanent peace."

SEPTEMBER 13, 1946
WALLACE WARNS ON 'TOUGH' POLICY TOWARD RUSSIA

He Cautions on Britain Also, Urging U.S. to Guard Own Interests to Avoid War

TRUMAN SUPPORTS VIEWS

Secretary Is Heckled at PAC Rally When He Says Russia Must Understand Us

By JAMES A. HAGERTY

Secretary of Commerce Henry A. Wallace warned last night that the British imperialistic policy in the Near East combined with Russian retaliation would lead the United States straight to war unless we have a clearly-defined and realistic policy of our own.

Secretary Wallace, who spoke in Madison Square Garden at an anti-Dewey, anti-Republican rally, sponsored by the National Citizens Political Action Committee and the Independent Citizens Committee of Arts, Sciences and Professions, declared that the United States could not handle the forces in the world by a "Get tough with Russia" policy.

"The tougher we get, the tougher the Russians will get," he said. "To prevent war and insure our survival in a stable world, it is essential that we look abroad through our own American eyes and not through the eyes of either the British Foreign Office or a pro-British or anti-Russian press."

In Washington, President Truman said at his press conference that he had read and approved Secretary Wallace's speech and that there was nothing in it that conflicted with Secretary of State James F. Byrnes' address at Stuttgart, Germany, a week ago.

Pepper Attacks Truman Policy

Though Secretary Wallace's speech had the approval of President Truman, the address of Senator Claude Pepper could hardly have had such approval, for the Florida Senator, to the accompaniment of applause, criticized the foreign policy of the Truman Administration.

"With conservative Democrats and reactionary Republicans making our foreign policy as they are today, it is all we can do to keep foolish people from having us pull a Hitler blitzkrieg and drop our atomic bombs on the Russian people," Senator Pepper declared. "It is not so far from 'get tough' to 'get rough.' I think we ought to remember, however, that the last two fellows who tried to get rough with the Russians—you may remember them from their first names, Napoleon and Adolf—did not fare so well."

SEPTEMBER 14, 1946
EDITORIAL
MR. WALLACE'S CONTRIBUTION

When President Truman says that he read Secretary Wallace's Madison Square Garden speech in advance of its delivery, and found in it nothing that conflicts with the policies Secretary Byrnes has been following, two explanations are possible. One is that he read the speech hurriedly and superficially, a credible hypothesis in view of the fact that he read it on Tuesday, which was a busy day for him, considering that the whole country was in the grip of a nation-wide shipping strike directed against one of his own Federal agencies. The other hypothesis is more difficult to accept, for it implies that Mr. Truman does not understand the policies which his Secretary of State has been following.

These policies have been directed toward preventing Europe from being divided into two irreconcilable camps separated by an iron curtain; toward reasserting a vital American interest in all parts of Europe and the Near East; toward using every proper diplomatic pressure now available in order to check an expansion of Russian imperialism into these areas, at the expense of the elimination of such democracy or beginnings of democracy as exist in them; and toward allying ourselves to this extent and for this purpose with the British people, whose interests in this matter are parallel with our own. Mr. Wallace dissents in large measure from these policies. That is unquestionably his privilege as a private citizen. It becomes a more questionable practice when he speaks as a fellow Cabinet member of Secretary Byrnes. And the whole matter must become endlessly confusing, not only to the British and the Russians but to everyone else in Europe, when President Truman blithely asserts that he sees no conflict between what Mr. Wallace is saying and what Mr. Byrnes is doing.

In our own judgment, what Mr. Wallace is saying conflicts in a very basic and important way not only with the present policies of Mr. Byrnes, but with the past policies of President Roosevelt, of whose leadership Mr. Wallace believes himself to be a faithful follower. For it is a fundamental premise of Mr. Wallace's Madison Square Garden speech, a premise upon which many of his conclusions rest, that we in this country "should recognize that we have no more business in the political affairs of Eastern Europe than Russia has in the political affairs of Latin America, Western Europe, and the United States."

If that is true and a wise and a proper comment, what business was it of ours when Hitler invaded Poland? What business was it of ours when he invaded Yugoslavia and crushed Greece and overran the Balkans? What business was it of ours, and what business was it of President Roosevelt's, to offer Lend-Lease aid to these very countries, long before Pearl Harbor? What business was it of Mr. Roosevelt's to insist, as he did insist at Yalta, that after the war was won there be created, throughout this Eastern Europe, "governmental authorities broadly representative of all democratic elements in the population and pledged to the earliest possible establishment through free elections of Governments responsive to the will of the people," and when he pledged the good faith of the American Government to achieve this purpose? These are "political affairs" in Eastern Europe. Have we no proper interest in them? President Roosevelt thought differently. So did the Atlantic Charter. When Mr. Wallace talks this way he is not talking as President Roosevelt talked and acted. He is talking as Nye and Wheeler and Borah and Hiram Johnson all used to talk, when they insisted that what happened in faraway places like Poland and Czechoslovakia was "no business" of the United States. This is isolationist talk. And Mr. Wallace's easy acceptance of the idea of separate spheres of political influence, one for Russia in Eastern Europe and one for ourselves and the British in Latin America and Western Europe, leads us remorselessly to a conception not of One World, but two.

SEPTEMBER 21, 1946
WALLACE OUSTED, STARTS A 'FIGHT FOR PEACE'; TRUMAN SAYS HIS VIEWS CLASH WITH POLICY; DECLARES COMPLETE SUPPORT FOR BYRNES

THE PRESIDENT ACTS

Dismisses Commerce Head in Surprise Step to End Policy Split

PRESSURE IS DENIED

Decision 'Independent,' White House Says—Wallace Amazed

By LEWIS WOOD

Special to The New York Times.

WASHINGTON, Sept. 20—President Truman forced Henry A. Wallace, Secretary of Commerce, out of the Cabinet today because the latter's views on foreign policy clashed fundamentally with the Administration's international program, and issued a strong endorsement of that policy as evolved by Secretary of State Byrnes.

The extreme step, announced at a crowded news conference, was a surprise to everyone, including Mr. Wallace. It was an absolute victory, too, for James F. Byrnes, but the White House denied unequivocally that the Secretary of State ever had laid down an ultimatum, either in yesterday's teletype "conversation" with the President or elsewhere.

The dismissal of Mr. Wallace, last of the original Roosevelt Cabinet, strikes from the Truman Administration a prime favorite of Left-Wing forces who had been heavily counted on to win votes in the autumn campaigns and in the Presidential race of 1948. Bruce Catton, Commerce Department information director, said Mr. Wallace would not speak for candidates in the campaign.

SEPTEMBER 21, 1946
WALLACE EXPLAINS

In Radio Address, He Says Peace Is Above High Public Office

BACKS 'ONE WORLD'

Released From Pledge on Talks, but Will Await Paris Finale

By ROBERT F. WHITNEY

Special to The New York Times.

WASHINGTON, Sept. 20—Henry A. Wallace, who resigned from the Cabinet today at President Truman's request, said tonight that "winning the peace is more important than high public office."

Mr. Wallace said in a brief radio speech that the President's action in asking him to quit released him from the promise that he would not talk on foreign policy until the peace conference in Paris was terminated.

But he declared he did not wish to abuse this freedom by saying anything that might interfere with the success of the treaty-making meeting.

The former Secretary of Commerce and Vice President, speaking over the four major broadcasting networks, said he deemed winning the peace more important than party politics.

On the success or failure of United States foreign policy, Mr. Wallace said, will depend the life or death of our children and grandchildren, the life or death of our civilization, the difference between existence or extinction for the human race. Therefore, he added, it is a holy duty that all should join the fight for winning the peace.

SEPTEMBER 21, 1946
ANTI–NEW DEALERS ACCLAIM DISMISSAL

Republicans Also Are Jubilant, but Many Democrats Say They Still Will Win Race

President Truman's action yesterday in dismissing Secretary of Commerce Henry A. Wallace brought a flood of congratulatory comment from Republicans and many anti-New Deal Democrats.

Leftists and some labor groups warned of their opposition as a result of the dismissal.

Republicans in general declared that the situation reflected a basic weakness in the Democratic party, while many Democrats insisted that the incident would not impair party prospects.

● ●

ELECTION RESULTS

On November 5, 1946, voters ended Democratic dominance of the federal government. Unhappy with both foreign and domestic policy, they packed the House and Senate with new Republican members, also handing the Republican Party a majority of governorships. Disbelieving Democrats faced the stark consequences of losing control of the government for the first time in over a decade. President Truman, seeing the nation turn towards conservatism, bowed to the electoral results, pledging to work with the new Republican majorities.

NOVEMBER 6, 1946
DEWEY AND IVES WIN IN A STATE SWEEP; REPUBLICANS SURE OF CONTROL IN HOUSE, MAKE GAINS IN NATION IN TURN TO RIGHT

GOP TREND IS WIDE

Republicans Gain Eight in Senate, Majority Is Indicated

WIN IN CONNECTICUT

Later Returns From West May Turn Victory Into a Landslide

By ARTHUR KROCK

The voters in yesterday's elections for the full membership of the next House of Representatives, for one-third of the Senate and for Governors of many States, swung this nation sharply right in a left-veering world.

They placed the Republican party, the minority opposition in the United States for the last fourteen years, in control of the House by a majority of more than forty.

They put the government of twenty-five States, a majority of the Union, in Republican hands by adding Republican Governors in Ohio and Massachusetts to the twenty-three already belonging to that party.

They exchanged Democrats for Republicans in several key States—notably New York, Delaware, Massachusetts,

Pennsylvania, Nevada, Idaho and Ohio—with indications that the changes will amount to the ten necessary to give the Republicans control of the Senate. Also, a Wisconsin Senate seat changed from Progressive to Republican.

Control will be settled by the trans-Mississippi States of Missouri, New Mexico, Wyoming, Washington, Montana and California. In New Mexico and California the portents favored the Republicans at 2 A.M. today, and Senator Frank Briggs, the Democratic incumbent in Missouri seemed to be marked for defeat.

The voters who turned to the Republicans in great numbers made the race for the Senate in Maryland closer than the Democratic supporters of Gov. Herbert R. O'Conor had expected after he had disavowed the programs of the radicals in the Democratic party. This disavowal will add another conservative to the Senate Democrats, and Virginia, by overwhelming majorities for Senator Harry F.

Byrd and Representative Willis Robertson, nominated to fill out the unexpired term of the late Senator Carter Glass, added two more.

NOVEMBER 10, 1946
DOMINANT CAUSE SEEN FOR REPUBLICAN SWEEP

From New England to Pacific, Voters Seem to Have Turned Against Party With Left-Wing Alliances

SHIFT TO RIGHT OF CENTER

By ARTHUR KROCK

WASHINGTON, Nov. 8—A variety of causes, including the American instinct against letting one party stay too long in power, was responsible for the loss of House and Senate majorities by the Democrats at last Tuesday's elections; and for Republican recapture of a majority of State Governments also. But an analysis of one phase of the results, visible from coast to coast, supports the belief that a single cause was fundamental.

This was public resentment over the dominance of the Democratic leadership by union labor and other pressure-groups, generally radical and some under Communist influence, which was established by President Roosevelt in 1933 and which President Truman sought to maintain by legislative proposals and executive acts.

The voting consequences of this resentment were as impressive as they were tangible, and they extended in a chain reaction from New England to the Pacific. It clearly was an important factor in bringing to the registration counters and the election booths what will probably go on record as the largest vote ever cast in a non-Presidential year in this country. Because of it the Democrats lost great urban industrial areas where they have prevailed for fourteen years, or suffered deep cuts in their followings there.

Only the South Remains

All that remained for the party when the votes were in last Tuesday night was the South—even more strongly

controlled than recently by moderate and conservative Democrats, who share the resentment against the long-held alliance—and an atoll or two in the Republican sea—Rhode Island, Maryland, West Virginia, New Mexico and Wyoming. The net these can produce is twenty-seven of the 521 electoral votes in the so-called college that chooses the President. And so close were the Senatorial contests in West Virginia and Maryland that official counts were required in both, and a contest is threatened in the first-named State.

The effect of this demonstration of public opinion on the Democratic party as a whole will not be apparent for some time. But it certainly will evoke a move among Democrats surviving in Congress to subordinate the radical allies and bring the party leadership much nearer to the middle of the road.

The President may decide to continue to stand with the pressure groups for the program that was rejected so emphatically, but the history of politics and Mr. Truman's own revealed turn of mind make that improbable.

The voters Tuesday moved the United States toward the Right, though other nations have been traveling in the opposite direction. But a move toward the Right is not to it. Perhaps a degree or so to the Right of Center is the course the voters have ordered.

THE DO-NOTHING CONGRESS

The Republican Congress elected in 1946, later called the "Do-Nothing" Congress, challenged President Truman for control of public policy. Wielding the power of his veto, Truman attempted to beat back the Republican resurgence when necessary, but was often overridden. Despite its nickname, the Eightieth Congress passed several major pieces of legislation, including acts limiting the power of labor unions, altering the general foreign policy of the nation, and, through bipartisan consensus, adopting the epochal Marshall Plan. Occasional agreements aside, the two parties revealed stark differences on domestic policy and contrasting visions for the future.

JUNE 24, 1947
BILL CURBING LABOR BECOMES LAW AS SENATE OVERRIDES VETO, 68–25; UNIONS TO FIGHT FOR QUICK REPEAL

TRUMAN PLEA FALLS

Barkley Reads His Letter Opposing Bill, but 20 Democrats Desert Him

FIRST CURBS IN 12 YEARS

Republican Sponsored Measure Is Enacted By Six More Votes Than Needed

By WILLIAM S. WHITE

Special to The New York Times.

WASHINGTON, June 23—The Senate by 68 to 25, or six votes more than the necessary two-thirds, overrode President Truman's veto of the Taft-Hartley Labor Bill today, and at 3:17 P.M., Eastern daylight time, made it the law of this country.

It automatically went on the statute books at that moment as the Senate's presiding officer announced the result of the ballot because the House had voted to override last Friday by 331 to 83.

The Senate cast aside one brief and final appeal from Mr. Truman as, in a warm, hushed and crowded chamber, it took the last decision to turn away from much of the labor policy of the Roosevelt and Truman Administrations. The measure it approved represented the first peacetime Federal restraint on the power of labor unions in a half a generation.

Truman Writes to Barkley

In a letter to Senator Alben W. Barkley of Kentucky, minority leader, Mr. Truman made his third and final effort to sustain his veto, but it caused little change in Senate sentiment as it had been established in previous tests on the bill.

However, two Democrats who had not heretofore been with him voted today to uphold him. They were Senator Scott W. Lucas of Illinois, the party whip, and John J. Sparkman of Alabama, who had for some days been counted with the anti-veto forces.

Twenty Democrats joined forty-eight Republicans in voting to override. Twenty-two Democrats voting to sustain the head of their party were aided by three Republicans, who were Senators William Langer of North Dakota, George W. Malone of Nevada and Wayne Morse of Oregon.

Where Mr. Truman had been unsparing in his denunciation of the bill in his veto message last Friday and his speech to the country that night, he was more restrained today in his letter to Mr. Barkley, who read it to the Senate just before the vote was taken.

APRIL 4, 1948
AID BILL IS SIGNED BY TRUMAN AS REPLY TO FOES OF LIBERTY

Thus America Meets 'Challenge Facing Free World,' President Declares at Ceremony

MARSHALL PRAISES STEP

Hails 'Courage and Wisdom' of Congress—Goods Reported Already on Way to Europe

By HAROLD B. HINTON

Special to The New York Times.

WASHINGTON, April 3—President Truman signed today the Foreign Assistance Act of 1948, which made the long debated European Recovery Program an actuality. "This measure," he said, "is America's answer to the challenge facing the free world."

The Chief Executive affixed his signature shortly after his return to the capital aboard the Presidential yacht, Williamsburg, from a visit to Williamsburg, Va. A number of the chief architects of the measure witnessed the signing.

It took the European Recovery Program ten months to develop from the bare suggestion known as the Marshall Plan to the detailed legislative project signed today. Its originator, George C. Marshall, the Secretary of State, was attending the Inter-American Conference at Bogota, but the following statement was issued on his behalf at the White House:

"The decision of the United States Government as confirmed by the Foreign Assistance Act of 1948 is, I think, an historic step in the foreign policy of this country. The leaders in the Congress and the membership generally have faced a great crisis with courage and wisdom, and with legislative skill, richly deserving of the approval and the determined support of the people."

Witness President's Signature

Mr. Truman, in his own statement, pointed to the efficacy of a Democratic system of free debate under which a bipartisan foreign policy could effectively be enacted into law. Senator Arthur H. Vandenburg, Republican, of Michigan, President Pro Tempore of the Senate and chairman of its Foreign Relations Committee, who is generally credited with guiding the measure to successful passage, witnessed the signature in the president's office.

- -

REPUBLICAN REVERSAL

The gains made by the Republican Party in 1946 proved fleeting, despite wide expectations that it would build on its ascent into power and earn the presidency for New York governor Thomas E. Dewey in 1948. Truman took the offensive in his campaign for reelection, blaming Republicans for the discord between the branches of government, calling Congress into a special session, and challenging Republicans to enact their promised legislation. They did not, and the ploy succeeded. On election night, even as both candidates and the mass media predicted a Dewey victory, the electorate returned Truman to the White House by a slight popular margin and restored the Democrats to power in Congress. The brief Republican resurgence stalled, awaiting a new leader and a new message.

JUNE 20, 1948
EDITORIAL
EIGHTIETH CONGRESS: TO DATE

Yesterday's prolonged uncertainty as to whether the Eightieth Congress should adjourn, recess or keep on going until its work was completed could not change one essential fact. This Congress will not go out of existence until next January. Its books will not be closed until then. But neither could yesterday's confused last-minute pulling and hauling change another essential fact. This is that the record of what the Eightieth Congress has done, and not done, to date, will be a dominant factor in the National Convention opening tomorrow in Philadelphia and a dominant factor in next fall's elections. Neither the Republicans nor the Democrats can escape the Scriptural doom: By their deeds shall ye know them.

I

The results must be measured against the promises and expectations of 1946. The Republicans took control of Congress on the basis of an obvious popular revulsion against some of the policies of the Roosevelt-Truman administrations. There was no landslide but there was a perceptible movement of the political terrain. The new legislators certainly had a mandate to liquidate some war measures, to loosen some New Deal controls, to check some New Deal projects and to effect practicable economies. They did not have a mandate to throw this country back into isolationism, as was done after the First World War.

The letters of fire on the walls of Convention Hall, behind the bunting, may not be too easy to read. There is now a manifest split in the Republican party, and there have been important instances—as during last week's hectic days and nights—in which Democrats have joined with their titular opponents in passing measures over a Presidential veto. In both Houses, however, the Republicans could pass any measure brought to a vote and the Democrats, standing by themselves, could not. The record is a Republican record. It does not show the Eightieth Congress as either the best or the worst that ever happened; it shows this Congress, and its majorities, as often confused, often dilatory, often lacking a sense of direction, often inconsistent in successive votes, magnificently fortunate in some of its leaders, fantastically unhappy in some others. It shows some deterioration in leadership between 1947 and 1948, which we may blame partly but not wholly on the inevitable pressures of an election year.

In the domestic field the Eightieth Congress did much of what was expected of it. It passed a new labor-management act, with Democratic cooperation in overriding Mr. Truman's veto. It cut taxes, again over a veto and therefore with Democratic support. It trimmed the President's budget, in many instances recklessly. It lifted most of the inflation controls. It expanded social security, but not to the full extent asked by Mr. Truman; and Democrats again aided to override his veto.

It arrived at its final pre-convention days with a long list of important measures still to be acted on. This last-minute rush is a defect of our legislative system, and the Republicans cannot be held solely responsible for it. Still, a stronger and more united leadership might have mitigated it and prevented some hasty action and some postponement of important measures.

The final conclusion is that on the basis of the Congressional experience of the past eighteen months one cannot tell what Republicanism now means. The Philadelphia Convention will have to make up its mind. It cannot accept, endorse and nominate candidates on the whole record. To do so simply would not make sense.

JULY 15, 1948
TRUMAN, BARKLEY NAMED BY DEMOCRATS; SOUTH LOSES ON CIVIL RIGHTS, 35 WALK OUT; PRESIDENT WILL RECALL CONGRESS JULY 26

VICTORY SWEEPING

President Wins, 947 ½ to 263, Over Russell on the First Ballot

BARKLEY ACCLAIMED

Nominees Go Before Convention to Make Acceptance Talks

PHILADELPHIA, Thursday, July 15—President Harry S. Truman won nomination for a full term in the Democratic National Convention early today and promptly made the Republican record in Congress the 1948 key issue by calling a special session of Congress to meet July 26 to challenge the GOP to keep its platform pledges.

The President, selected by well over two-thirds of the Democratic delegates, although the Solid South dissented and thirty-five delegates from Mississippi and Alabama walked out, was in a fighting mood as he went before the convention with his running mate, Senator Alben W. Barkley, who was chosen by acclamation.

Confidently predicting his and Senator Barkley's election because "the country cannot afford another Republican Congress," the President said that the special session would be asked to act on legislation of various types.

Cites Republican Platform

He would call on it, he declared, to act to halt rising prices, meet the housing crisis, provide aid to education, enact a national health program, approve civil rights legislation, raise minimum wages, increase social security benefits, finance expanded public power projects and revise the present "anti-Semitic, anti-Catholic" displaced persons law.

The Republicans said they were for all these things in their 1948 platform, the President stated, and, if they really meant it, all could be enacted into law in a fifteen-day session.

President Truman set the convention on fire with his acceptance speech, which came at the end of a long, tiring, tumultuous session in which the north-south party split was deepened appreciably, although only a handful of southern delegates bolted.

NOVEMBER 4, 1948
TRUMAN WINS WITH 304 ELECTORAL VOTES; DEMOCRATS CONTROL SENATE AND HOUSE; EUROPE SEES FOREIGN POLICY CONTINUING

SWEEP IN CONGRESS

Democrats Obtain 54–42 Margin in Senate by Winning 9 GOP Seats

CERTAIN OF 258 IN HOUSE

Republicans Have 167, With 9 Still in Doubt—Shifts in Chairmanships Slated

By WILLIAM S. WHITE

The Democrats swept all of Congress yesterday, recapturing the supposedly impregnable Republican House by a landslide and seizing firm control of the Senate in one of the great political revolutions of American history.

As the story of Tuesday's elections yet unfolded in the late counts from the voting places, the first Republican Congress since 1932 looked out upon a scene of catastrophe as it prepared to relinquish its brief two-year tenure of leadership.

Broken were the great bastions of Republican Congressional strength; vanished was the almost universal presumption that no matter what happened to the Senate, the House would stay in Republican hands.

The labor vote, implacably angry over the Taft-Hartley Act and resentful over Republican tax reductions, had moved with strength and determination against the Republican incumbents.

" As the story of Tuesday's elections yet unfolded in the late counts from the voting places, the first Republican Congress since 1932 looked out upon a scene of catastrophe as it prepared to relinquish its brief two-year tenure of leadership. "

Farm Vote Disappoints GOP

The farm vote had bitterly disappointed the Republicans. Where it did not turn upon them outright, the Democrats made sharp inroads in the grain belts.

President Truman's long campaign against the Eightieth Republican Congress, which he had called either "the worst" or "the second worst" of all time, apparently had a strong appeal at the ballot boxes.

Thus, last night, with all the votes not yet counted, the Democrats had taken in overflowing measure their revenge for their own Congressional rout of 1946.

The clear prospect was that in the Eighty-first Congress of next January the House would be overwhelmingly Democratic with as many as 260 to 270 members against fewer than 200 Republicans.

Late tabulations gave 258 certain Democratic seats; 167 Republican seats; one American-Labor party seat, and nine yet in doubt.

As to the Senate, Democratic members will number 54 and Republican members 42 by virtue of the Democrats' capture of nine Republican seats.

THE PRESIDENTIAL ELECTION OF 1952

EISENHOWER OVERTURNS TWO DECADES OF DEMOCRATIC CONTROL

As the twentieth century passed its halfway mark, the United States seemed a fortunate country.

It had won a global victory in the Second World War, defeating the totalitarian states of Germany, Italy, and Japan, and now was the predominant power on the globe. It was prosperous, holding as much as half of the world's wealth, and the postwar "baby boom" testified to its confidence and its future growth. Its scientific and technological leadership had initiated the atomic age, giving it a temporary monopoly of mankind's most fearsome weapons. Although challenged by the expansion of the Soviet Union, it had fashioned bold initiatives in international relations, including the United Nations, the Marshall Plan to revive Western Europe, and the North Atlantic Treaty Alliance (NATO).

Politically, the Democratic Party still held an electoral majority fashioned by Franklin D. Roosevelt and continued, to many observers' surprise, in Harry S. Truman's underdog victory in the 1948 presidential election. With one two-year exception, Democrats had also controlled both houses of Congress since 1932. Labor unions, enrolling a third of the national workforce, provided money and campaigners, and the party enjoyed strong backing from the rising numbers of Catholic and black voters.

But that majority would prove fragile in 1952. The Democratic majority had already been successfully challenged in the congressional elections of 1946, when a tide of postwar discontent brought the Republicans majorities of the House and Senate for two years. The incumbent Truman administration faced relentless attacks over corruption scandals and fervent charges of communist subversion stoked by the new "cold war" against Soviet expansion, the loss of the U.S. atomic monopoly after the Soviets exploded their own bomb, and the conquest of China by the forces of Mao Tse-tung.

The most serious crisis followed the Communist invasion of South Korea and the subsequent military response of the United States. The new war renewed the trials, but not the

With smiles and waves, President Harry S. Truman, left, and his successor, President-elect Dwight D. Eisenhower, leave the White House for inauguration ceremonies in Washington, D.C., on January 20, 1953.

triumph, of World War II: the military draft, price controls, inflation, and the deaths of 36,000 American soldiers. Although public opinion at first supported Truman's action, a military stalemate soon developed, and the president found his popularity dropping to the lowest levels ever recorded to that time.

Beyond these events, politics was changing. For the first time in a generation, the candidates were completely new, with no incumbent president or vice president on the November ballot (a combination of candidates that would not recur until 2008). The returning veterans of the global conflict had created a new society—more educated because of the postwar G.I. Bill, housed in proliferating suburban developments, procreating in record numbers in a baby boom— that might loosen the ties of inherited party loyalties.

Politics would also soon be transformed by a new mass medium, television. As the 1952 election neared, the nation passed a significant milestone: half of its households became connected to black-and-white television sets. Now voters

1952 ELECTORAL VOTE

STATE	ELECTORAL VOTES	EISENHOWER	STEVENSON	STATE	ELECTORAL VOTES	EISENHOWER	STEVENSON
Alabama	(11)	–	11	Nebraska	(6)	6	–
Arizona	(4)	4	–	Nevada	(3)	3	–
Arkansas	(8)	–	8	New Hampshire	(4)	4	–
California	(32)	32	–	New Jersey	(16)	16	–
Colorado	(6)	6	–	New Mexico	(4)	4	–
Connecticut	(8)	8	–	New York	(45)	45	–
Delaware	(3)	3	–	North Carolina	(14)	–	14
Florida	(10)	10	–	North Dakota	(4)	4	–
Georgia	(12)	–	12	Ohio	(25)	25	–
Idaho	(4)	4	–	Oklahoma	(8)	8	–
Illinois	(27)	27	–	Oregon	(6)	6	–
Indiana	(13)	13	–	Pennsylvania	(32)	32	–
Iowa	(10)	10	–	Rhode Island	(4)	4	–
Kansas	(8)	8	–	South Carolina	(8)	–	8
Kentucky	(10)	–	10	South Dakota	(4)	4	–
Louisiana	(10)	–	10	Tennessee	(11)	11	–
Maine	(5)	5	–	Texas	(24)	24	–
Maryland	(9)	9	–	Utah	(4)	4	–
Massachusetts	(16)	16	–	Vermont	(3)	3	–
Michigan	(20)	20	–	Virginia	(12)	12	–
Minnesota	(11)	11	–	Washington	(9)	9	–
Mississippi	(8)	–	8	West Virginia	(8)	–	8
Missouri	(13)	13	–	Wisconsin	(12)	12	–
Montana	(4)	4	–	Wyoming	(3)	3	–
				TOTALS	(531)	442	89

could see at least the images of the candidates in their own living rooms, foreshadowing the decline of traditional campaign rallies and parades and diluting the impact of print media and newspaper endorsements. In time, interpersonal party canvassing would decline, and, as campaigners turned to television for more immediate contact with the voters, the media consultant would eventually replace the precinct captain as the means to mobilize the electorate. Modern American politics began with the election of 1952.

THE PARTIES AND THE CANDIDATES

The transition to modern politics was evident, albeit retrospectively, in the party nominations. The 1952 conventions were covered in full by television, causing some delegates to play for the cameras, but also soon leading to streamlined deliberations. Party "bosses" were present and powerful, but primary election results took on new significance. As it turned out, these conventions were the last to need more than a single ballot to nominate a presidential candidate, and the following election year would be the last to have a second ballot for vice president.

Republicans approached the election confidently. After twenty years out of the White House, the electoral tides seemed to be running in their favor. As the party soon proclaimed, voters appeared to agree that "Time for a Change" had come. But what kind of change, and who would lead it?

The conservative leadership of the party had its preferred candidate, Ohio senator Robert Taft. Son of the former president and chief justice, William Howard Taft, Bob Taft became the leader of the Senate Republicans. Known as "Mr. Republican," he stood for an isolationist foreign policy; he disdained opposition to Nazi Germany before World War II and rejected the North Atlantic Treaty Organization (NATO) afterward. He attacked many New Deal programs and wrote the anti-union Taft-Hartley Act. Two minor candidates presented more moderate policy stances: former Minnesota governor Harold Stassen and California governor Earl Warren.

The most significant alternative was Dwight D. Eisenhower, familiar to the nation as "Ike." Leader of the American armies in Europe, Eisenhower commanded the largest and most successful armed force in world history. After service as Army chief of staff, he retired from the military to become president of Columbia University, but was then recalled to service as the first commander of the NATO alliance.

Keenly aware of Eisenhower's standing as a victorious hero, Republican moderates—including Thomas E. Dewey, the Republican standard-bearer in 1944 and 1948—began a "draft Eisenhower" movement, urging the general to enter the presidential race to defend an internationalist foreign policy. Eisenhower had previously abstained from politics in deference to the principle of civilian control of the military, and he had declined recruitment to the presidential race from both Democrats and Republicans in 1948. Now, he remained reluctant, but allowed his name to be entered by the moderates in the first contests. Major newspapers, including *The New York Times,* added their support to the draft.

Even in his absence, Eisenhower won the first primary, in New Hampshire, beating Taft 50 percent to 39 percent, and he accumulated 109,000 write-in votes against favorite son Stassen in Minnesota. Eisenhower then decided to take the plunge, resigning his position and returning home on June 1. Although Taft gained more accumulated votes in the primaries, the two principal candidates were formally listed together on the ballots of only three of the thirteen states holding primaries. Eisenhower added New Jersey, and Taft narrowly led in South Dakota, but the decision would be made by the convention delegates.

As the Republicans met in Chicago in early July, the outcome hinged on contested delegations from three southern states, where new groups favoring Eisenhower challenged the established, and largely moribund, pro-Taft forces. The Eisenhower factions won two important procedural battles, first to exclude contested delegates from votes on credentials and then to seat the Eisenhower delegates in the contested races.

These test votes presaged an Eisenhower victory. On the first ballot, he garnered 595 of the 1,206 delegates. Vote switching, led by the small Stassen group, quickly brought Eisenhower a majority, and ultimately 845 declared votes. The Warren votes held firm until a final ritual of unanimity, but California's weight was recognized, to a degree, in the selection of its native son, Sen. Richard Nixon, as the vice-presidential candidate. Nixon had won attention in investigations of alleged Communist infiltration of the government, a theme that Republicans would stress in the campaign.

The party platform strongly attacked the Truman record, in a list of charges that the Democrats "have arrogantly deprived our citizens of precious liberties. . . . [W]ork[ed] unceasingly to achieve their goal of national socialism. . . . [D]isrupted internal tranquility by fostering class strife for venal political purposes. . . . [S]hielded traitors to the Nation in high places and. . . . [P]lunged us into war in Korea without the consent of our citizens through their authorized representatives in Congress, and have carried on that war without will to victory."

Yet, for all their harshness, the Republicans did not propose major reversals in Roosevelt's and Truman's programs, accepting their heritage of the welfare state and U.S. involvement in the international community and the Korean conflict. Eisenhower, in accepting the party nomination, also struck a moderate tone. While dismissing "an Administration which has fastened on every man of us the wastefulness, the arrogance and the corruption in high places," he pledged no radical changes beyond "a program of progressive policies drawn from our finest Republican traditions; to unite us wherever we have been divided; to strengthen freedom wherever among any group it has been weakened; to build a sure foundation for sound prosperity for all here at home and for a just and sure peace in our world."

Democrats entered the 1952 campaign in even greater disarray than the Republicans. The party would campaign without an obvious new leader against an esteemed hero, while carrying the burdens of the unpopular administration and facing the possible defections of its traditional southern base.

For a time, President Truman was considered the likely Democratic candidate. Although the just-ratified Twenty-second amendment to the Constitution limited presidents to two terms, the incumbent was specifically excluded from its provisions, and Truman probably could have gained renomination, despite his low popularity.

If Truman did harbor ambitions to remain in office, he certainly faced a struggle. Television demonstrated its power when Tennessee senator Estes Kefauver gained national celebrity through televised hearings into organized crime and its political influence, telecasts that dominated the limited electronic fare of the time. Adding a homespun personal style to his television fame, Kefauver conducted a vigorous primary campaign, beginning with the surprising defeat of Truman in the New Hampshire contest by 4,000 votes and 11 percentage points.

For the future, the outcomes in the two parties' contests made New Hampshire's primary the most important in presidential nominating contests. The immediate effect was to prompt Truman to declare publicly his previous personal decision that he would not be a candidate for reelection. His surprising withdrawal opened the field to a scrum of Democratic possibilities. The announced aspirants included

Georgia senator Richard Russell, a southern favorite, and Averell Harriman of New York, who had held various positions in the Roosevelt and Truman administrations.

Truman had been considering various potential heirs to the Democratic leadership and gave little weight to the primaries, which he denigrated as "eyewash." Nevertheless, Kefauver continued to gain support throughout the nation, winning 12 of 16 primaries, losing only 1 open contest while accumulating more than 3 million votes, nearly two-thirds of the Democratic total in the primaries.

Kefauver, however, was unacceptable to party leaders, who still controlled the bulk of convention delegates. Truman himself had sought to name his successor, first soliciting Chief Justice Fred Vinson, then attempting to recruit Illinois governor Adlai E. Stevenson II, grandson of Grover Cleveland's 1892 running mate. Stevenson declined the invitation, ostensibly because he had already announced his intention to run again for governor, possibly because he did not want to bear the burden of selection by the unpopular president. In addition, as a divorced man, he might have worried that no previous presidential candidate had that marital status. Truman then encouraged the incumbent vice president, Alben Barkley of Kentucky, to become a candidate. But Barkley, at age seventy-four, was considered too old and too conservative and was rejected in preconvention meetings with party and labor leaders.

As the Democratic convention opened in Chicago in late July, the party first had to deal with the emerging issue of civil rights and the consequent southern disaffection. Truman had set the party on a new path on the issue with his desegregation of the armed forces and support for legislation to protect African Americans against discrimination. Those programs had been backed by adoption of a platform amendment in the 1948 convention, which had in turn brought a walkout by two southern delegations and the Democrats' loss in the fall elections of four "Dixiecrat" states where the Democratic leaders displaced Truman from the ballot.

Northern leaders were determined to prevent another defection in 1952. They insisted that all delegations pledge that the nominees of the convention would be placed on their states' ballots under the Democratic label and wanted to unseat the delegations of three states that refused to take the pledge of party loyalty. Upon verbal but informal promises to honor the commitment, the convention seated the delegations in a close vote.

The presidential nomination remained in dispute, with eleven candidates formally nominated in long proceedings that would ultimately extend the convention to six tedious days. Amateur and professional politicians began a movement to draft Stevenson for president, gaining attention after Stevenson, as the host governor, addressed the convention. Mixing humor and eloquence, he presented a forceful defense of the Democratic Party.

Stevenson allowed his name to be put in nomination, but Kefauver still led in delegate support. On the first ballot, he had 340 votes, far short of a majority of the 1,230 delegates; Stevenson was not far behind, with 273, with the remaining votes scattered among twelve possible contenders. On the third ballot, the industrial states moved to Stevenson as Harriman and Russell withdrew, giving him a bare majority of 617. In conferences held behind the convention rostrum, party leaders selected Sen. John Sparkman of Alabama as the running mate, an effort to conciliate the southern delegations. Although Sparkman was relatively liberal in his positions, his support of racial segregation led fifty black delegates to quit the convention.

The party platform caused no overt dissension, although it endorsed the actions of the Truman administration and maintained the party's liberalized civil rights position. While advocating a variety of future programs, its basic message was a proud retrospective evaluation: "An objective appraisal of the past record clearly demonstrates that the Democratic Party has been the chosen American instrument to achieve prosperity, build a stronger democracy, erect the structure of world peace, and continue on the path of progress."

Far more inspiring was Stevenson's acceptance speech. Modestly conceding, "Better men than I were at hand for this mighty task," the nominee spoke in language that was more a secular sermon than a party celebration:

> Even more important than winning the election is governing the nation. That is the test of a political party, the acid, final test. When the tumult and the shouting die, when the bands are gone and the lights are dimmed, there is the stark reality of responsibility in an hour of history haunted with those gaunt, grim specters of strife, dissension, and materialism at home and ruthless, inscrutable, and hostile power abroad.

> The ordeal of the twentieth century, the bloodiest, most turbulent era of the whole Christian age, is far from over. Sacrifice, patience, understanding, and implacable purpose may be our lot for years to come. Let's face it. Let's talk sense to the American people. Let's tell them the truth, that there are no gains without pains, that we are now on the eve of great decisions, not easy decisions, like resistance when you're attacked, but a long, patient, costly

struggle which alone can assure triumph over the great enemies of man—war, poverty, and tyranny—and the assaults upon human dignity which are the most grievous consequences of each.

The parties had chosen very different candidates, but the nominees evidenced some striking similarities. Both had been reluctant candidates, persuaded to seek the presidency not by personal ambition but by felt duty to programmatic causes. Both were men of independent mind, yet they owed their nominations to the skills of party leaders. Both were committed to maintaining the new international role of the United States, and both accepted the new welfare state. Their similarities might be obscured in the heat of the coming months, and their qualities might not be immediately perceived by partisan observers. But in fact the election of 1952 was a match between moderate and able contestants.

THE CAMPAIGN

The summer was quietly devoted to party building. Stevenson moved control of the Democratic campaign to Illinois, away from Truman's presence and the party establishment in Washington. Eisenhower attempted to conciliate the Republican conservatives by holding a "Morningside Heights summit" at Columbia University with Taft and promising that the senator's supporters and policies would be part of his administration.

Eventually, both candidates would travel more than 30,000 miles, visit almost every state, and give hundreds of speeches locally and dozens on national television. Although the candidates never met in a direct confrontation, the campaign constituted a true debate. Democrats defended their heritage, particularly on economic policy, while Republicans attacked the Truman administration, particularly on foreign policy. Carrying out the extended argument on television drove up campaign costs, resulting in a combined expenditure near $80 million.

Beginning his active campaign at a Labor Day rally in Detroit, Stevenson focused on reinvigorating the Democratic coalition of labor, ethnic minorities, and the South. He focused on domestic policy and the New Deal heritage, urging voters to remember, "You never had it so good." More innovatively, he presented himself in a different style: witty, intellectual, and ready to upset political orthodoxy—as he did in challenging veterans' claims at the American Legion convention, rejecting the characterization of the Taft-Hartley Act as "a slave labor law" at a union rally, and opposing offshore oil drilling in Texas.

The Republicans sensed victory, buoyed by the national admiration of Eisenhower, expressed even in the Broadway

theater song, "I Like Ike." The party also innovated campaign techniques, adopting the methods of business marketing and relying on television "commercials"—including the new thirty-second "spots"—produced by professional advertising agencies. The campaign climaxed with a $1.5 million ad saturation in critical areas during the final three weeks.

But the Republican effort met a severe crisis in early September, when Nixon was found to be the beneficiary of a "secret fund" of $18,000 in contributions from wealthy California businessmen to pay his political expenses. The appearance of corruption brought calls for Nixon's removal from the national ticket until Nixon gave a nationally televised address, reaching the largest audience that had ever watched a single program. Demonstrating the impact of the medium, the vice-presidential nominee defended the fund as necessary for a person of his limited personal income. He added one emotional admission:

> We did get something, a gift, after the election. A man down in Texas heard Pat on the radio mention the fact that our two youngsters would like to have a dog. And believe it or not, the day before we left on this campaign trip we got a message from Union Station in Baltimore, saying they had a package for us. We went down to get it. You know what it was? It was a little cocker spaniel dog in a crate that he'd sent all the way from Texas, black and white, spotted. And our little girl Tricia, the six year old, named it "Checkers." And you know, the kids, like all kids, love the dog, and I just want to say this, right now, that regardless of what they say about it, we're gonna keep it.

Pledging fealty to Eisenhower, Nixon concluded his speech with an appeal to listeners to write their opinions. The public response, expressed in 200,000 telegrams, was overwhelmingly favorable. Eisenhower met and embraced Nixon, absolving him with the words, "You're my boy." The ticket was reunited and back on track, but Nixon would face other television scrutinies in the future, eventually leading to his forced resignation from the presidency itself in 1974.

The theme of the Republican campaign was the failures of the Truman administration, summarized in the alliterative slogan, "Communism, Corruption, and Korea." Of these, the most wrenching was Korea. After the initial invasion of South Korea, American forces had fought up and down the Asian peninsula—repelling the attacking North Korean armies, conquering most of the North, fleeing invaders from Communist China, slogging back to the original dividing line of the two nations, then settling after a year of combat into a prolonged war of attrition.

Eisenhower had been critical of the conduct of the war without presenting any major alternative strategy. At the end of the campaign, he found a dramatic appeal. Blaming the administration for virtually inviting the invasion, Eisenhower pledged "to bring the Korean War to an early and honorable end." Invoking his experience and renown, he asserted his personal ability to meet that goal: "That job requires a personal trip to Korea. I shall make that trip. Only in that way could I learn how best to serve the American people in the cause of peace. I shall go to Korea." The nation could easily believe that the conqueror of Europe would end the bloodshed. As the voters reached their decisions, there was no possible effective response by the Democrats.

THE ELECTION RESULTS

Public interest in the election ran high. Both Eisenhower and Stevenson were new candidates, each attractive in his own way, each engendering fervent attraction by their distinctive personal characteristics and programs. Their extensive campaigning and television coverage brought the campaign directly into Americans' homes. With minor parties proving insignificant, the contest was a straight fight between Republicans and Democrats. The parties developed and financed extensive mobilization efforts, aided by large volunteer organizations.

Opinion polls indicated a close election, with Eisenhower in the lead, but many voters still undecided. The polls, however, were met by skepticism after their egregious failure in 1948, when all had predicted Truman's defeat by Dewey, and some pollsters shied away from predicting the 1952 outcome. Remembering the pollsters' earlier errors, politicians strived to mobilize their supporters, and voters acted to record their decisions where it truly counted, at the voting booths.

Turnout reached a record level, 61,500,000, an increase of 26 percent over the previous election, marking the highest rate of voter participation in the twentieth century since the enfranchisement of women. Eisenhower swept to victory with nearly 34 million ballots, 54.9 percent of the total vote. Although Stevenson lost overwhelmingly, he had the limited satisfaction of gaining the highest vote of any losing candidate in American history, and almost as many votes as Franklin Roosevelt had gained in any of his triumphs.

Eisenhower won nationwide, accumulating 442 electoral votes from 39 states, leaving Stevenson with only 89 electoral votes from 9 southern and border states. In a significant result for future elections, Ike shattered the Democrats' southern base. With the aid of party dissidents, he won 4 of the more moderate states of the region—Florida, Tennessee, Texas, and Virginia—and came close to carrying Louisiana and South Carolina, while more than doubling the party vote in every state of the Confederacy. Unlike previous southern defections based on anti-Catholicism (Al Smith in 1928) or racism (the Dixiecrats of 1948), Ike's southern appeal in 1952 was founded on social class. Just like their counterparts in the North, wealthier southerners backed the Republican ticket, laying the foundations for the party's later dominance in the region.

The Eisenhower tide also inundated other strongholds of the Democratic voting majority. About a quarter of Truman's 1948 voters switched to Ike, but few changed in the other direction, and Eisenhower also won majorities among new voters, young and old. California and the large industrial states of the East and Midwest all went Republican, generally by margins similar to the national figure. The Democratic vote declined significantly in the large cities that had been the core of the New Deal's support, class differences diminished, and Catholics now split their vote almost evenly. In contrast to these movements, only African Americans remained strongly loyal to the party of Roosevelt and Truman.

Analyses of the vote, now extended to university research scholars, would show that the election turned on the personal attraction of Eisenhower and the specific issue of Korea. Even Democrats now regretted the war and could honestly sing "I Like Ike." When combined with the still more positive evaluations of Republicans and independents and the secondary issues of corruption and communism, the Eisenhower victory was certain.

The long-term electoral balance was less clear. Republicans had won slight majorities in Congress, but by unreliable margins—8 seats in the House, only 1 in the Senate. The party's congressional candidates trailed far behind Eisenhower, whose coattails proved to be very short by historical standards. Voters' party identification as Democrats, as measured in scholarly studies, dominated Republican loyalties, by a 58 percent to 35 percent margin, and Democrats were more trusted to deal with the enduring issues of economic prosperity and social welfare.

Eisenhower's election gave the Republican Party the opportunity to change the recent course of American politics, but no guarantee of continued success. The immediate sources of its election victory soon faded: the Korean War ended, the anti-Communist witch hunts abated, and the popular war hero now faced the realities of political choice. America would remain fortunate in the 1950s—prosperous, at peace, and confident. But, as always, the future standing of the parties would depend on unpredictable events.

THE TWO-TERM AMENDMENT

The drama of the 1952 election began early with the ratification of the Twenty-second Amendment to the Constitution, limiting presidents to two terms in office. The amendment specifically exempted the incumbent president, Harry S. Truman, permitting him to run for reelection. Pressure mounted quickly for the president to decide if he would seek a third term, a tenure only Franklin Delano Roosevelt had previously achieved.

FEBRUARY 27, 1951
2-TERM AMENDMENT IN FORCE AS THE 36TH STATE RATIFIES; TRUMAN EXEMPT FROM LIMIT
NEVADA, UTAH VOTE
Proposal Becomes Law Automatically as Two Legislatures Approve
POLITICAL EFFECTS WIDE
President After 2d Election Would Have Less Control—'Changing Horses' Possible
By ROBERT F. WHITNEY
Special to THE NEW YORK TIMES.

WASHINGTON, Feb. 26—The Constitution of the United States was amended tonight to forbid any President from being elected for more than two terms or from being elected more than once if he had served in excess of two years of his predecessor's term.

The amendment will not apply to President Truman. He may run again for his second elected term in the Presidential election of 1952 or in future campaigns, should his party wish to nominate him.

It was the Twenty-second Amendment to the Constitution and its ratification became complete with the approval of the Legislature of the State of Nevada providing the needed thirty-six states, or three-quarters' approval. Earlier in the day Utah's lawmakers had backed it as the thirty-fifth state.

It was eighteen years since the Constitution had been changed. Then the ratification was that of the Twenty-first Amendment repealing National Prohibition Dec. 5, 1933. The dry law repeal was initiated by President Roosevelt and completed in the first year of his first term.

Inspired by Roosevelt

It was President Roosevelt who "inspired" the Twenty-second Amendment by his election four times to the Presidency. The Eightieth Congress, in which the Republicans gained control for the first time since President Hoover's term, started the action on the opening day, the third of January, 1947. . . .

The amendment has great political importance aside from the bare fact that it limits the Presidential tenure.

While President Truman is excepted, the fact that the country has spoken for only two terms may well have an effect on his decision whether to run in 1952.

One astute political observer suggested tonight that Mr. Truman could not ignore that the legislators of three-fourths of the states have said:

"Two terms."

The amendment, of course, would make it mandatory for the United States to change its President at required intervals no matter what peril the country was in.

This would throw overboard Lincoln's old adage, "Don't change horses in midstream." If the amendment had been in effect in 1940 when World War II started Mr. Roosevelt could not have been re-elected.

The fact that he could not have been a candidate might have meant that whoever was nominated by the Democrats could not have beaten the late Wendell Willkie.

Thus not only the person in the Presidency but the party in power might be changed as the result of the operation of the amendment, not only in times of national crisis but in a calm era.

But on the reverse side, students of government believe that the amendment, by stimulating a greater competition for the nomination, might build stronger and more able candidates and perhaps result in the better definition of issues.

Another implication of the amendment would seem to be that the person of the President, as soon as he started his second or last eligible term, might lose a degree of control over his party.

A President in such circumstances would not have the strategical position of being a threat for a third term—whether he wished it or not—right up to the time when he publicly declined to run.

This control might limit the power of a President to choose, or have a weighty influence in the selection of, his party's candidate for the next election.

SPECULATION ON THE CANDIDATES

Both parties had early but aloof favorites to win presidential nominations in 1952. The Democrats saw a chance to keep the office in the hands of Harry Truman. Although limited in popularity, Truman would be able to bring the powers of an incumbent president to the campaign. The Republicans viewed their best hope as five-star general Dwight D. Eisenhower. The hero of World War II, Eisenhower had been offered both parties' nominations in 1948, but remained out of politics. His partisanship was uncertain, but his electoral appeal was immense.

MARCH 4, 1951
THEY ASK: WILL TRUMAN AND EISENHOWER RUN?

Uncertainty as to Candidates Rises In Both of the Major Parties

By CABELL PHILLIPS

Special to THE NEW YORK TIMES.

WASHINGTON, March 3—Two occurrences of the week have brought out fresh and interesting speculations about the biggest political event on the horizon—the Presidential contest of 1952.

The wind-up of the big debate on stationing troops in Europe spotlighted in bold relief both the nature and severity of the split in the Republican party. There are two factions which no amount of compromise, it now appears, will be able to reconcile. Each can be counted upon to put up a slate of candidates at the party convention in the summer of 1952 and to fight to the finish for dominance.

The other significant event of the week was the ratification of the Twenty-second Amendment limiting the tenure of future Presidents to two terms. Technically, this is not applicable to Mr. Truman. But it might be interpreted as imposing a moral obligation upon him which, it is felt here now, may be persuasive. In any event, it does offer him a graceful "out" if, as many believe, he decides he has had enough of responsibility.

These two circumstances, added to others that have accumulated over a somewhat longer period, have brought into the sharp focus of public attention the men and the issues which seem most likely to dominate the political stage next year. . . .

Governor Dewey has anointed General of the Army Dwight D. Eisenhower as his choice for the party's top honor. The General has neither accepted nor rejected the offer, and he remains as great a political enigma today as ever.

Attractive Figure

If he should accede to the pressure, there is nothing visible on the horizon now, including the formidable shadow of Senator Taft, that would stand between him and the nomination—and in all probability the Presidency. He is the most attractive and the most intriguing figure in American public life today.

Speculation Over Truman

On the Democratic side speculation now centers more avidly around the question of whether President Truman will or will not run than on who might be nominated to run in his stead.

Many arguments are being advanced as to why he will elect to return to private life in 1953.

One of these is that he is getting tired of the hammer blows of responsibility, and that he yearns for the quiet of his Independence home, or even the relative calm of his old desk in the Senate.

A second argument is that both Mrs. Truman and daughter Margaret are urging him to retire in order to preserve his health and peace of mind.

A third is—and this seems highly improbable—that Mr. Truman has become convinced of his slipping popularity and reasons that he should step down while his prestige is comparatively intact.

Finally, and most persuasive of all, is the belief that the President would not go against the popular aversion to a third term as manifested in the latest amendment to the Constitution.

In any event, the President cannot, for sound administrative and political reasons, make his decision on this point known until well after the beginning of 1952. In the meantime, those who would inherit his mantle must pursue their mission with tedious and frustrating circumspection.

Other Possibilities

There are others in the Senate who are mentioned in much more casual tones—Lyndon B. Johnson of Texas, for example, Estes Kefauver of Tennessee, Richard B. Russell of Georgia and John J. Sparkman of Alabama, among others. But the name being heard with increasing frequency of late is one which has never graced even a county Democratic ballot. It is—you've guessed it—Eisenhower.

There is much earnest talk that he might just as easily be persuaded to run on the Democratic ticket as on the Republican. After all, he has come out of retirement twice to serve President Truman, and it was another Democrat, Franklin D. Roosevelt, who invested him with the commission in World War II that brought him to fame. It is argued that while his few utterances on domestic politics have had a faintly Republican tinge, they could be interpreted just as easily as being tinged with Democratic conservatism. And as for foreign policy, the argument runs, certainly he has nothing in common with the dominant Taft wing of the Republican party.

So, if not President Truman, why not General Eisenhower in 1952? they are asking. Indeed, some good Democrats seem quite ready to settle for just half of that question.

• •

THE FIELDS NARROW

The fields of presidential candidates slowly became clearer. Eisenhower was officially entered into the Republican nomination process. Hindered by laws barring military officers from active politics, Eisenhower announced that he would accept a Republican nomination from the party as an act of duty, but would not campaign. The election contestants therefore could have been an incumbent commander in chief and his formal subordinate. The problem was resolved when Truman announced that he would neither run nor accept a nomination from the Democrats and Eisenhower resigned his commission. The Republicans now had a popular candidate available, and the Democrats had to scramble.

JANUARY 7, 1952
LODGE TO ENTER EISENHOWER IN NEW HAMPSHIRE PRIMARY; SURE GENERAL IS REPUBLICAN

'IN TO THE FINISH'

Senator Says Candidate Is Not Being Named 'Just for Exercise'

SHAPE HAS NO COMMENT

But Officer Declares 'Silence Is Sometimes More Eloquent Than Any Statement'

By CLAYTON KNOWLES

Special to The NEW YORK TIMES.

WASHINGTON, Jan. 6—Senator Henry Cabot Lodge Jr., manager of the Eisenhower-for-President campaign, announced today that he had authorized entry of the name of General of the Army Dwight D. Eisenhower in the New Hampshire Republican Presidential primary on March 11.

The Massachusetts Senator said he had assured Gov. Sherman Adams of New Hampshire that the general was "in to the finish" and that, upon the general's own word, he was a Republican.

Mr. Lodge, making his announcement at a crowded news conference, said the general was "a candidate to the full limit that Army regulations permit."

"I am speaking for the general and I will not be repudiated," the Senator said, urging reporters who wanted to check further to get in touch with the general's headquarters at Rocquencourt, near Paris. A check made at Supreme Headquarters, Allied Powers in Europe, produced no immediate comment.

Four Points Listed

Life Magazine editorially listed four major points in General Eisenhower's favor: that he understands war and, because of this, is a man of peace; that he has great administrative ability; that he favors "the middle road between the unfettered power of concentrated wealth and the unbridled power of statism or partisan interests," and that he has a gift for leadership and a sense of America's role in history's next turn.

These endorsements represent unusual cases in which leading newspapers and publications have come out for a candidate so far in advance of the political conventions.

In his letter to Governor Adams, Mr. Lodge said that he and Senator Frank Carlson of Kansas had a number of conversations with General Eisenhower while the general was serving as president of Columbia University. These, he said, had convinced them the general was a Republican.

"During these discussions," Senator Lodge wrote "he [General Eisenhower] specifically said that his voting record was that of a Republican. He also pointed out that his political convictions coincided with enlightened Republican doctrine and that the family tradition was Republican."

The Senator said it also was "worth noting" that the general in these conversations "pointed out that he would never seek public office but would consider a call to political service by the will of the party and the people to be the highest form of duty."

The Lodge letter, sent Friday in response to an appeal from Governor Adams for authority to enter the general's name, concluded on the following note:

"Our simple task is to see that the will of the people, as expressed in all the polls from coast to coast, is asserted at the convention as it will be at the election. Failure to secure a true expression of public opinion would constitute a mockery of our free system in this citadel of freedom."

In explaining to the Governor why he could not at this time ask the general directly if he were a Republican, the Senator noted that General Eisenhower "as a member of the Army on active duty, is prohibited by Army regulations from engaging directly or indirectly in a nomination campaign."

"The prohibition includes participation in political campaigns or any other public activity looking to the influencing of any election or the solicitation of votes for themselves or others," he wrote.

The Senator was questioned at some length on this point at his news conference, held in a small, lavishly decorated suite in the Eisenhower-for-President headquarters at the Shoreham Hotel. Barely half of the more than 100 reporters on hand could crowd into the main room, where a dozen television and newsreel cameras ground away.

"Can he ever be a candidate as a five-star general?" asked one reporter.

Senator Lodge started to say that the general could resign, but, when a half dozen reporters broke in to say five-star generals could not resign, he said he was sure the general "can get into a status where he can become a candidate."

Asked whether the general would remain silent until President Truman, his commander in chief, announced his own plans, Senator Lodge replied:

"I don't believe that has the slightest bearing on his plans."

MARCH 30, 1952
TRUMAN ANNOUNCES HE WILL NOT RUN AGAIN; SAYS HE SERVED LONG, FEELS 'NO DUTY' TO STAY; NEWS STUNS DEMOCRATIC LEADERS AT DINNER

HE BARS ANY DRAFT

President Also Maps the Party's Strategy, Says It Can Win Again

ASSAILS G.O.P. DRIVE

Lashes 'Dinosaurs' and 'Loud Talkers' Among the Republicans

By W. H. LAWRENCE

Special to The New York Times.

WASHINGTON. March 29—President Truman dramatically announced tonight that he would not be a candidate for re-election and would not accept the nomination if he were drafted by the Democratic convention.

He made the announcement in almost dead-pan fashion toward the end of his speech before the 5,300 Democrats attending the party's traditional $100-a-Plate Jefferson-Jackson Day dinner in the National Guard Armory here.

Following is the text of the statement interpolated into his prepared speech:

"I shall not be a candidate for re-election. I have served my country long and I think efficiently and honestly. I shall not accept a renomination. I do not feel that it is my duty to spend another four years in the White House."

The audience was taken completely by surprise by the announcement since there had been no indication anywhere in the earlier part of his speech nor in the advance word given to highest officials on his staff that he intended at this point to bow out of the 1952 political campaign.

"Oh no, oh no," shouted a few people on the floor.

MARCH 30, 1952
RACE IS WIDE OPEN

Truman Decision Leaves Time for Intensive Party Contest

STEVENSON TO FORE

Barkley Also Mentioned in Addition to Those Already in Field

By ARTHUR KROCK

Special to The New York Times.

WASHINGTON, March 29—President Truman's announcement at the Jefferson-Jackson Day dinner here tonight that he would not accept renomination threw wide open the contest for the Democratic party choice for the first time since 1932.

Though President Roosevelt in 1940 withheld announcement of his willingness to run again until just before the convention acted, and in 1944 kept the party leaders guessing until a few weeks before the hour of decision, the general belief never failed that he would accept renomination. Consequently nothing like an open contest occurred in either year.

Mr. Truman's withdrawal, however, occurs nearly four months before the Democratic national convention is to meet in Chicago, and this will afford ample time for those Democrats already in the field and others who will enter to make a positive and intensive campaign for the nomination.

Among the added starters the names most prominently mentioned tonight were those of Gov. Adlai E. Stevenson of Illinois and Vice President Alben W. Barkley.

Up to now Senators Kefauver of Tennessee, Russell of Georgia and Kerr of Oklahoma were running under the handicap of the President's silence. The fact that he could at any time cancel all their efforts by announcing that he was again a candidate, and the further fact that no one could be sure that he would not do so, had the effect of making their campaigns seem like shadow-boxing.

But now that the field is open, the more so because the President as yet has offered no public advice as to a successor, the Democratic battle has begun in earnest, and the outcome of the primaries and conventions from now on has become of vital consequence.

Mr. Truman's announcement tonight came too late to make the Wisconsin, Nebraska and Illinois primaries the hard and broad contests they would have been if he had spoken while there was still time for other Democrats to compete in them with Senators Kefauver and Kerr. It came after Governor Stevenson had thrice committed himself to his candidacy for renomination in the state primary—a position he reiterated tonight after the President's notice of withdrawal.

Stevenson Boom Expected

Nevertheless, there will be a rapid increase of activity in these primaries by supporters of the candidates who already have announced, and Democrats who attended the dinner here tonight were predicting that Illinois leaders would now encourage write-in campaigns for Mr. Stevenson in their state and perhaps others with a view to impressing the national party with the backing he has for President.

Since Mr. Truman has not denied a report that he recently offered to help Governor Stevenson get the nomination, and since the Governor has been at the head of the waiting list of many influential Democrats who were standing by for the President's word, predictions were also made that a Stevenson boom of large proportions would shortly appear.

- -

THE REPUBLICAN CONVENTION

The Republican convention met in July to settle a heated contest between Dwight Eisenhower and Sen. Robert A. Taft, son of former president William Howard Taft. Eisenhower had hoped to be "drafted" by a united party, but instead faced a fierce challenge requiring a full campaign. The contentious convention fell into line behind the general, then selected the youthful Richard Nixon to run for vice president. Eisenhower then moved to placate Senator Taft and unite his party forces for the upcoming campaign.

JUNE 1, 1952
EISENHOWER IN A BATTLE THAT HE TRIED TO AVOID

His Plan to Stand Aloof From Party Struggles Has Proved Untenable and He Must Fight to Win Nomination

DISPUTES LIKE THOSE OF 1912

By ARTHUR KROCK

WASHINGTON, May 31—The return of General of the Army Eisenhower to this country and to inactive military status is amid political circumstances from which he hoped, and was unable, to stand aloof. The Republican party, to which he announced allegiance on Jan. 7, 1952, is closely and bitterly divided on whether he or Senator

Taft of Ohio shall be its Presidential nominee this year. Far from being "drafted," Eisenhower can only be chosen by the party convention against the preference of hundreds of delegates. And his determination to do nothing in his own interest that, by any fair definition, could be termed "active" has been shattered by the inevitable consequences of the pre-convention campaign he authorized to be made in his behalf.

Of all his resolutions to keep out of elective politics only one will remain when Eisenhower changes into civilian clothes here next Tuesday. This is his refusal to make a "whistle-stop" tour and take detailed positions on controversial subjects that divide the two major parties and the candidates within each.

Gone is the general's attitude of 1948 that only in a great emergency and in response to an overwhelming party and popular call should a professional soldier seek high office. (The current situation may fit his view of an emergency more than the one that existed in 1948, but the party call to him is far from overwhelming). Gone is his recent statement that the people must seek him out, "they know where to find me." (Before his return, the general's campaign group, with his approval, sent requests to Republican delegations, beginning with Maryland's, to come and see him at places, dates and hours described and discuss what can only be political matters. The not unusual fact that the expenses for these trips are to be met by Eisenhower clubs locally, when they are able, brought outcries from rivals that will accentuate the political aspect of these conferences).

Vanishing Dream

Eisenhower has agreed to make several speeches on public questions, and his spokesmen are saying with confidence that he will make many more before the Republican convention meets on July 7. The dream that he could deny himself to public inquiry and appearance as Generals William Henry Harrison and Zachary Taylor did, and yet follow them into the White House, has vanished at the insistence of his supporters and the realities of the forthcoming convention.

JULY 12, 1952

EISENHOWER NOMINATED ON THE FIRST BALLOT; SENATOR NIXON CHOSEN AS HIS RUNNING MATE; GENERAL PLEDGES 'TOTAL VICTORY' CRUSADE

REVISED VOTE 846 [sic]

Minnesota Leads Switch to Eisenhower and Others Join Rush

BUT SOME HOLD OUT

First Call of the States Gave General 595 to 500 for Taft

By W. H. LAWRENCE

Special to THE NEW YORK TIMES.

CONVENTION BUILDING in Chicago, July 11—General of the Army Dwight D. Eisenhower won a hard-fought first-ballot nomination today as the Republican candidate for President and Senator Richard M. Nixon of California was chosen by acclamation as his running mate for the Vice Presidency.

The former Supreme Allied Commander in Europe went before the 1,206 Republican delegates tonight to accept the nomination and pledge that he would lead "a great crusade" for "total victory" against a Democratic Administration he described as wasteful, arrogant and corrupt and too long in power. He said he would keep "nothing in reserve" in his drive to put a Republican in the White House for the first time since March 4, 1933.

The Republican convention adjourned finally at 8:21 P.M., Central daylight time (9:21, New York time) after it had heard Senator Nixon accept the Vice-Presidential nomination. He pledged a "fighting campaign" to insure election not only of a Republican President, but also a House and Senate controlled by his party.

Bitterly Divided Convention

General Eisenhower won in a bitterly divided Republican convention. In the last week the general had taken leadership in the contest from Senator Robert A. Taft of Ohio, the chief party spokesman in Congress, who was making his third unsuccessful bid for nomination to the office once held by his father, William Howard Taft.

Victory came for General Eisenhower on the first ballot. The official results were 845 for General Eisenhower, 280 for Senator Taft, 77 for Gov. Earl Warren of California, and 4 for General of the Army Douglas MacArthur.

But that figure did not represent truly the voting sentiments of these delegates as they faced the crucial and final showdown between General Eisenhower and Senator Taft.

When the first roll-call of the states was completed, General Eisenhower had 595 votes—nine short of the required majority of 604—and Senator Taft had 500. The balance of power rested with favorite-son candidates, such as Governor Warren, who had 81 votes, and Harold E. Stassen, former Minnesota Governor, with 20. General MacArthur had received only 10 votes.

Others Then Changed

And while Governor Warren's California delegation held firm for him in the hope of a deadlock, Mr. Stassen's Minnesota delegates, no longer bound because he had received less than 10 per cent of the vote, broke away and cast nineteen votes for General Eisenhower before a first ballot result could be announced.

The nineteen, added to the General's previous total, gave him 614, or ten more than a majority. Then other states began to change their votes in order to be recorded on the side of the winner.

Thus, while General Eisenhower's nomination later was made unanimous on the motion of principal backers of Senator Taft and Governor Warren, who pledged the support for their principals to the nominee, it was made clear that General Eisenhower was the choice of a divided convention, and that one of his first tasks would be to restore party unity and heal the deep wounds inflicted during the fierce competition for the nomination.

To that end, General Eisenhower's first act, after he knew he had won, was to call on Senator Taft to ask—and receive—from him assurances that the Ohioan would campaign actively for the Eisenhower-Nixon ticket.

The Republicans who picked the 61-year-old commander of the Allied invasion of Europe and the 39-year-old California Senator believed this to be their best chance of victory over the Democrats in twenty years, and their only fear was that continued bitterness over the outcome would make it possible for the Democrats to run to six their consecutive string of victories in national elections.

Starting his active campaign preparations at once, General Eisenhower asked Republican members of the Senate and House who were in Chicago for the convention to meet with him at 10 A.M. tomorrow in his Blackstone Hotel suite. This group predominantly favored Senator Taft's nomination, and the invitation to its members was one more step by the general toward establishing party harmony.

· ·

THE DEMOCRATIC CONVENTION

The Democrats met in late July amid many concerns. Until the convention, Adlai Stevenson, a new and attractive candidate, held to his pledge to stay out of the race. The party also faced sharp divisions between liberal northerners and southern conservatives, known as Dixiecrats. Southerners unhappy with the party platform had bolted from the 1948 convention, and the threat of another defection loomed. On the third ballot, Stevenson won a contested but calm nomination battle, providing a candidate whom even Eisenhower supporters, such as *The New York Times,* could admire. It took an additional day to gather consensus behind a balancing vice-presidential nominee, Sen. John Sparkman, a moderate from Alabama.

President Dwight D. Eisenhower and Adlai Stevenson shake hands on February 17, 1953, at the White House. Stevenson lunched with the president and a group of congressmen at the Executive Mansion.

Source: AP Images

JULY 26, 1952
STEVENSON IS NOMINATED ON THE THIRD BALLOT; PLEDGES FIGHT 'WITH ALL MY HEART AND SOUL'; TRUMAN PROMISES TO 'TAKE OFF COAT' AND HELP

GOVERNOR ACCEPTS

Humility Marks Speech by Nominee Before Cheering Delegates

HE HAILS PLATFORM

Illinoisan in Tribute to Losing Candidates—Bids for Unity

By JAMES RESTON

Special to THE NEW YORK TIMES.

CONVENTION BUILDING in Chicago, Saturday, July 26—Gov. Adlai E. Stevenson of Illinois, in a speech marked both by humility in the face of the high honor and by a vigorous determination in the face of its challenge, early today accepted the Democratic nomination for President.

"I will fight to win that office with all my heart and soul," he told the cheering delegates. "With your help, I have no doubt that we will win."

Earlier, the "no" man from the Lincoln country, had for the first time said "yes."

"I did not seek it. I did not want it," he said a moment after he had been nominated by the Democratic National Convention.

"But to shirk it would be to repay honor with dishonor," he added.

The call, he continued, "asked of me nothing except that I give such talents as I have to the services of my country. That I will do."

"I feel no exaltation or sense of triumph whatever, nothing but humility. I shall go on my knees and I shall ask my

God to give me strength and courage and to nourish my spirit for this great undertaking in this great hour of history."

At the outset, he said, he had never been "more conscious of the appalling responsibility of office."

He went immediately to the convention hall from the home on Chicago's "Gold Coast" where he made his short statement.

The 52-year-old Governor developed this same solemn theme after he had been driven at breakneck speed through the late night traffic of Chicago to the convention hall.

There he delivered a highly personal address to a jam-packed convention audience.

"I would not seek your nomination for the Presidency,"

he said, "because the burdens of that office stagger the imagination. Its potential for good or evil now and in the years of our lives smothers exultation and converts vanity to prayer."

The Governor added that he had asked "the merciful Father of us all" to "let this cup pass from me." He added that "from such dread responsibility one does not shirk in fear, in self-interest or in false humility."

Governor Stevenson, who was dressed in blue, double-breasted suit; blue-and-white striped shirt and blue-and-white figured tie, paid a moving tribute to those Democrats who, unlike himself, had sought the office and campaigned hard for it over the past weeks and months.

> As a newspaper that is emphatically and enthusiastically in favor of General Eisenhower's election to the Presidency of the United States, we can and do find satisfaction in the nomination of Governor Stevenson.

JULY 27, 1952
EDITORIAL
EISENHOWER VS. STEVENSON

At the Democratic Convention just ended, and at the Republican Convention which preceded it, a striking victory has been won by the people of the United States. Through all the mumbo-jumbo in Chicago, despite all the ritual dances of frenzied politicians before the usual political images, American democracy has proved itself strong and vigorous enough to force the selection of the two best possible candidates in the field.

The Republicans named a man who came into the political picture reluctantly and only at the insistence of others, a man who was deeply opposed by the old-line organization of his party, but who managed to capture the imagination and allegiance of millions of ordinary Americans. The Democrats had the good sense to follow suit. They have selected—almost literally forced into the nomination—a man who was not running for the job. In passing over the candidates who tried so hard for the nomination, and in choosing Governor Stevenson, who did not try at all, the Democrats instinctively turned to the man who could best unite the party and whose ability is undisputed.

As a newspaper that is emphatically and enthusiastically in favor of General Eisenhower's election to the Presidency of the United States, we can and do find satisfaction in the nomination of Governor Stevenson. His selection as Democratic nominee insures that—at least so far as the two protagonists are concerned—the campaign will be conducted on a decent and dignified level. We hope and expect to see the differences of opinion between Democrats and Republicans on many important matters developed, clarified and argued out during the coming months. That is the way a healthy democracy works. But in the state of the world today it would have been exceedingly unhealthy if this campaign had degenerated into a fiercely partisan and demagogic dispute over the past, present and future foreign policy of the United States. Of that we now need have no fear; for Eisenhower and Stevenson both have the character and the understanding that would make such a destructively divisive campaign impossible.

If this newspaper has so high a regard for Governor Stevenson, it may fairly be asked why we continue to argue—now even more intensively than ever before—for the election of General Eisenhower. There are two fundamental reasons, and they are the same reasons on which we based our original plea for General Eisenhower's nomination. One is in the field of domestic policy; the other in foreign policy.

It is this newspaper's belief that a change of Administration is essential to the welfare of this country and to the continuation of the two-party system in the United States. The Democrats have been in office for twenty years—for five Presidential terms—and they have been giving increasing evidence of fatigue, ineptitude and corrosion.

The party has accomplished many fine things during its two decades under Roosevelt and Truman; but, particularly in the realm of economic policies in recent years, it has been willing to follow the course of least resistance, with seriously harmful effects. More important than that, with the years of power there has come a certain complacency, an indifference to the highest standards of public service, a comfortable liaison with special interests, a seamy connivance in petty corruption, an arrogance toward those in disagreement, a distasteful tendency to self-praise and an aversion to self-criticism. Admittedly, Governor Stevenson himself has not been tainted in this way, for he has been busy cleaning up Illinois while Washington basked in the fruits of power; but Stevenson or no Stevenson, it is the

Democratic party that has been in the saddle, and there is an inherent, concrete and important value in the simple fact of change that a Republican victory would bring about.

Much as we desire this change, however, we would only be able to support a Republican nominee who recognized America's position of responsibility in the world. General Eisenhower not only recognizes this responsibility; he is almost the embodiment of it. More than any other living man General Eisenhower stands as the symbol of effective American participation in the global effort to stem the tide of Soviet Communist aggression. He understands the workings and the implications of the North Atlantic Pact, keystone of our foreign policy; and if American leadership is required, as we believe it is, to inspire and unite the rest of the free world in defense of its liberty and its freedom, Eisenhower as President is the man to furnish such leadership in these most difficult times. He has the confidence of America as well as of America's allies; and he has the knowledge and the experience essential to meet the terrible international problems that beset us on every side.

We congratulate the Democratic party on choosing Governor Stevenson; and at the same time we renew our support for General Eisenhower in his campaign for election as the next President of the United States.

JULY 27, 1952
EDITORIAL
SPARKMAN FOR VICE PRESIDENT

In selecting Senator John Sparkman of Alabama for the Vice-Presidential nomination, the Democratic National Convention made a gesture to the Southern branch of the party without capitulating to its extreme right-wing element. Senator Sparkman has a reputation as one of the relatively liberal Democratic leaders of the South, and he is highly regarded in the Congress, where he has ably served for fifteen years.

While Mr. Sparkman adheres to the usual Southern line in respect to civil rights legislation and even supported the Dixiecrat movement four years ago, he nevertheless has gone along with the Administration on most other issues of both foreign and domestic policy. Senator Sparkman was a backer of Senator Russell for the Presidential nomination, but his own voting record is more progressive and more in tune with the needs of the time than is that of the Senator from Georgia.

However, there is not much doubt that Mr. Sparkman was chosen for the Vice-Presidential nomination less for his record than to please the South. The more moderate and more reasonable leaders of the Democratic party were justly alarmed by the divisive tactics pursued almost to the bitter end by the diehards at both extremes—by the Humphrey-Moody-Roosevelt group of Northerners and by the Byrnes-Byrd-Battle group of Southerners. The futile struggle between them that occupied so much of the convention's time and energy threatened for a while to conjure up a Dixiecrat movement of 1952, and even after the fight was settled some bitterness inevitably remained. Some danger of Southern defection persists; and the nomination of Mr. Sparkman is clearly designed to minimize this danger.

THE NIXON FUND

In mid-September a scandal enveloped Richard Nixon, the Republican nominee for vice president. Nixon had maintained a fund of campaign contributions for personal and political purposes. Although the fund was not illegal, many felt the practice to be unethical and called for his removal. Putting his fate in the hands of GOP leadership, Nixon delivered a televised explanation to the electorate. The appeal became known as the "Checkers speech" because of Nixon's reference to his pet dog. It succeeded completely, improving Nixon's stature as a candidate, increasing contributions to the campaign, and solidifying his spot on the party ticket.

SEPTEMBER 24, 1952
NIXON LEAVES FATE TO G.O.P. CHIEFS; EISENHOWER CALLS HIM TO A TALK; STEVENSON MAPS INFLATION CURBS

'I'M NOT A QUITTER'

Senator Says He'll Let Republican National Committee Decide

HE REVIEWS HIS FINANCES

Accepts Bid to Meet General—Cites Legal Opinions on Use of $18,235 Fund

BY GLADWIN HILL

Special to THE NEW YORK TIMES.

LOS ANGELES, Sept. 23—Senator Richard M. Nixon, in a nation-wide television and radio broadcast tonight, defended his $18,235 "supplementary expenditures" fund as legally and morally beyond reproach.

He laid before the Republican National Committee and the American people the question of whether he should remain on the Republican party's November election ticket as the candidate for Vice President.

Rising, near the end of his talk, from the desk at which he had sat, Senator Nixon urged his auditors to "wire and write" the Republican National Committee whether they thought his explanation of the circumstances surrounding the fund was adequate.

"I know that you wonder whether or not I am going to stay on the Republican ticket or resign," he said. "I don't believe that I ought to quit, because I'm not a quitter. . . ."

Decision 'Not Mine'

"But the decision, my friends, is not mine. I would do nothing that would harm the possibilities of Dwight Eisenhower to become President of the United States; and for that reason I am submitting to the Republican National Committee tonight, through this television broadcast, the decision which it is theirs to make. . . .

"Wire and write the Republican National Committee whether you think I should stay or whether I should get off; and whatever their decision is, I will abide by it."

Later he accepted an invitation from General Eisenhower for a conference.

In a half-hour talk that was partly personal, including a frank exposition of his finances, and partly an appeal for support of the Republican ticket such as he has been making in his current whistle-stop tour, the Senator declared of the Southern California supporters' fund disclosed last week:

"I say that it was morally wrong if any of that $18,000 went to Senator Nixon for my personal use.

"I say that it was morally wrong if it was secretly given and secretly handled.

"And I say that it was morally wrong if any of the contributors got special favors for the contributions that they made."

But he declared that, on all three points, the factual answer was negative.

The candidate, clad in a gray suit and a dark tie, delivered his address in a Hollywood radio-television studio—from which the public was excluded—with composure and assurance. His wife, Patricia, was seated close to him, and he made frequent references to her in detailing his career.

His talk also was peppered with barbed references to the Democratic opposition.

Referring to an Illinois political fund with which Gov. Adlai E. Stevenson, Democratic Presidential nominee, has been linked, Senator Nixon, while stipulating that he did not "condemn" this, suggested that both Mr. Stevenson and his running mate, Senator John J. Sparkman of Alabama, should "come before the American people" and report on their incomes.

"If they don't," he said, "it will be an admission that they have something to hide."

* *

STEVENSON

Adlai Stevenson defined his campaign through frequent and well-written speeches. Turning away from passionate politics, Stevenson believed that voters were best swayed by rational personal appeals. He carefully planned his own speeches while on the campaign trail, yet frequently innovated with humorous insertions. His artful blend of humor and reason made him an engaging speaker, admired even by his opponents.

OCTOBER 18, 1952
STEVENSON AS CAMPAIGNER

He is staking his campaign on speeches which make an appeal to the intellect.

By JANE KRIEGER

SPRINGFIELD, ILL.

THERE is one thing about Gov. Adlai E. Stevenson's campaign for the Presidency on which most observers agree: that it is extraordinary among political campaigns in that its appeal has been and still is—despite, some recent deviations—to the mind rather than to the emotions. It is interesting, therefore, to consider the why's and how's of the Stevenson campaign; the criticisms that have been directed against it and the Governor's answer to these criticisms.

In his office at Springfield the other day, Governor Stevenson talked of his theory of the art of politics. He summed it up this way: "One of the first objectives of a candidate for any office—but especially the Presidency—should be to get his views across, show the voters where he stands and where he's going."

The Governor is particularly anxious to get *his* views across because he is painfully aware that until last spring few voters outside of Illinois had ever heard of him. He believes that the best way he can stamp himself in the public mind is through his speeches.

He has an enormous amount of what he calls "faith" in the intelligence of the voters. He said he believed that "people really appreciate it when you talk straight to them." But even if he were beginning to have some doubts, Stevenson could not stage a real pulpit pounding "hellfire-and-damnation" campaign. He said, "I'm just not that kind of person and I can't change my style now. Wouldn't even if I could."

Stevenson is convinced that the country is moving into a new political era and that many of the old rules have become outdated. For example, he thinks a candidate must appeal to people primarily as individuals rather than blocs of voters. He doesn't believe in what he calls "monolithic voting." He said, "A man who belongs to the American Legion may also be a union member and his wife may be in the League of Women Voters. So in what bloc does he vote?"

Finally, Stevenson doesn't think anyone knows for certain what is "smart politics." He said that after he became Governor of Illinois "we used to have great bull sessions about whether this or that was good politics. I got plenty of advice from the professionals—they would say, 'You can't do this, Governor.' Politicians are often the most conventional, hidebound fellows in business. Eventually you discover you can do what you think is best and generally it works out all right. You get into a bottomless pit if you try to figure out the political consequences of every step."

HE concedes that his theory of the art of politics is unorthodox. But he believes that ultimately—if not on Nov. 4—his kind of campaign will win the votes. "Trouble is," he said, "there's always a time lag. It was years before people realized that Wilson was right about the League of Nations. Maybe it will be the same in my case. Maybe I'll be defeated, but this kind of campaign will eventually be accepted. And the reason is that people really want a change—a change not in parties but in the whole approach to public office and politics."

How, then, is Stevenson putting his theories into practice? How is he waging his campaign?

Last August the Governor informed his aides that he was going to discuss the issues and not the personalities of the election and he assumed his opponent would do the same. Stevenson was running on the Democratic record, but he still felt free to criticize parts of that record. Eisenhower was a Republican, but Stevenson respected him and refused flatly on several occasions to attack him.

LATELY the Governor has altered his tactics somewhat. His aides say it is because of Eisenhower's slashing attacks on the whole Administration record and on Stevenson's own integrity. Stevenson says privately that he is angry and deeply disillusioned. He believes he is now being forced to go down the line for the Administration and to hit hard at Eisenhower. But he still intends to adhere to his principles and discuss the issues right up to Nov. 4.

THE Governor's delivery is almost as unorthodox as his speeches. He counts on humor rather than histrionics to get his audience's attention. He makes a speech the same way he plays tennis—serves easily with a series of perfectly timed gags and then rushes the net with the serious stuff.

The Governor really loves his own jokes. Every now and then he will watch a film recording of one of his speeches on his television set at Springfield—which has easily the worst reception in the country. Before the joke comes up Stevenson is trying to hide an expectant grin.

Stevenson's ideal campaign audience is a big indoor crowd and the TV cameras; he is not enthusiastic about whistle-stopping. This may be primarily because of his belief that 1952 is a transition year in campaigning and that the trend is toward television and away from fish fries and whistle-stopping. But there is also the fact that Stevenson is not an informal person and he doesn't believe that whistle-stopping quite suits him.

· ·

It is worth while, in technological as well as political interest, to pinpoint the moment when TV became a major instrument of national politics.

TELEVISION

The 1952 election marked the onset of the television era in American politics. For the first time, a majority of citizens were able to see the candidates instead of just hearing them, a revolution matching that of the transition to radio. Television's impact began early in the year, with Truman's withdrawal and Eisenhower's entrance, soon followed by Nixon's effective "Checkers" speech. The new medium also raised some fears about the theatrical nature of televised politics, fears that have persisted.

JUNE 8, 1952
EDITORIAL
TV AS A POLITICAL FORCE

This year's Presidential campaign will differ from all others that have preceded it in that television will take the voter everywhere, and put him face to face with the candidate. It is worth while, in technological as well as political interest, to pinpoint the moment when TV became a major instrument of national politics. This moment was probably the beginning of General Eisenhower's first political speech, in Abilene, Kan., on June 4, 1952, to be quickly followed by his first press conference.

The TV audience is now nationwide for the first time in a national campaign, and the camera is also newly ubiquitous. Television will watch the political conventions in Chicago. It will examine the spellbinders. It makes a goldfish bowl out of every rostrum. It applies the litmus test to shenanigans, phonies and plain bores. It separates the men from the boys.

Never before has the voter had such widespread opportunity to get the "feel" of the man he may or may not vote for to sit in the White House. Never before has he been able, with his own eyes, to take measure repeatedly of the sincerity, the goodwill and the intelligence of a candidate for high office.

It is one thing for a candidate to mount the platform and read a speech, which he himself may or may not have written. It is another thing for him to face a roomful of newspaper men and submit to informed, critical questioning. In no respect has television made a greater contribution of public service, perhaps, than in putting a press conference on the air. The public is able at first-hand to measure the forthrightness, the courage or the evasiveness of a candidate. It watches while the subject speaks on topics he might prefer to avoid. It catches all the hesitations and the nuances.

We of the newspaper press need not fear or be jealous of this comparative newcomer in the spread of information to the public. TV is a stimulant to fair, complete news reporting, a check on bias, slant and warped selection or emphasis. The camera's grasp is necessarily incomplete and selective, of itself. The public will continue to want the trained newspaper man's report, the black-and-white record of what was asked and what was replied, the background and the editorial page's opinion. But the reading public will also have the advantage of having been there, seeing it happen, and a better, more complete basis of making up its own mind. If we believe in democracy and the ability of the people to choose wisely when they have all the facts this new medium of political education is a welcome arrival.

SEPTEMBER 28, 1952
THE NIXON TELECAST

Personal Story Brings High Drama to TV
By JACK GOULD

AFTER Senator Richard M. Nixon's defense of his personal trust fund of $18,000 last Tuesday evening, there can be no further doubt about television's influence on the political scene. On all major counts his was a remarkable performance peculiar to the video age.

The telecast by the Senator was easily the moment of high drama in the campaign thus far; the plot and setting were a playwright's dream. A handsome and youthful figure, with his pretty wife at his side, sat in a lonely studio before the cameras. He had thirty minutes in which to argue his case before a jury of millions and stave off personal tragedy. Whatever he did was history in the making.

For the initial fifteen minutes the Senator was very effective. Amazingly self-assured under the circumstances, he sat quietly at a desk, looked directly at the camera and with understatement began the recital of his affairs. If he never addressed himself directly to the moral issue of the fund that aroused a national furor, he spoke earnestly and persuasively. He gave his audience a sense of sharing his personal ordeal.

The second half of the program saw Senator Nixon succumb to theatrics. The story of his children's love for their little cocker spaniel which they had received as a gift was an awkward sequence to be injected into a candidate's discussion of his qualifications for the Vice Presidency.

Dilution

Senator Nixon then took a tack which seemed to dilute even further the impact of what had gone before. In launching into a routine campaign speech attacking his opponents and effusively championing General Eisenhower, who was to decide his political fate, there was somehow lost the element of poignancy and personal crisis that was felt during the program's opening.

Even with these limitations, however, there can be no gainsaying that the program had the high emotional content that in television and radio always has won a broad response. The glimpses of Mrs. Nixon, the little details of their family life and the climactic appeal for support were unusual in political broadcasting from a studio, certainly on the level of the campaign for the country's second highest office.

But if Senator Nixon hardly can be blamed for turning to his own advantage the emotionalism and melodrama inherent in his unprecedented situation, the important point to remember is that the extraordinary circumstances are not likely to be duplicated again.

Hence it must be hoped that other political leaders will not regard the Nixon type of program as a pattern for the future use of television under normal campaign circumstances. Because if impetuous partisans should misinterpret the broadcast as merely a magic format worth the copying, the consequences could be perilous to Democrats and Republicans alike.

Box Top Code

There is a very real danger in superimposing the methods of show business on politics. Chiefly, these methods can result in misleading oversimplification of vital issues and the substitution of emotion for information, slogans for reasoning and glamour for understanding. Especially in a visual medium having easy access to the nation's mind, the problems of government must be presented soberly with the hope to inform, not just to divert.

The philosophy of broadcasting that Hooper and Nielsen popularity polls justify the means may have at least a commercial plausibility in the entertainment world. But governmental issues hardly lend themselves to dignified, calm and judicious determination by the code of the returned box top.

There are many legitimate ways in which television can and has contributed wholesomely to the political field. From the voter's standpoint the most rewarding is the televised press conference, where a candidate has to stand on his feet. It still is the most revealing of a candidate's personality, opinions, and knowledge of issues. Other variations on this format may serve much the same purpose.

Where the risk comes is when the world of politics steps over the line into the purely entertainment sphere. Then politicians try to become actors or campaign topics turn up as plays or vaudeville sketches.

At the time such practices may seem harmless in themselves and justified if there is a chance of influencing a few votes. But here the political world could profit from the experience of broadcasting. In radio it was the disheartening truth that once the bars were lowered a little here or there on certain programming practices a whole succession of compromises quickly followed. And the pattern is repeating itself in some phases of television.

Now—not tomorrow—is the time to hold the line against television turning politics into a coast-to-coast vaudeville show or a daytime serial. Because if that happens it would be but a short step for video to become the platform of the irresponsible demagogue. Then television's power could be frightening.

KOREA

The war in Korea was the defining issue of the 1952 election. It exemplified the historic turn of American foreign policy away from isolationism and its new leading role in world affairs. Eisenhower, blaming the Truman administration for waging the war ineffectively, campaigned on a promise to go to Korea to negotiate a peace. Truman swooped in to rebut Eisenhower, releasing a classified document revealing that the Joint Chiefs of Staff, including Eisenhower, had recommended troop reductions early in the conflict. Public and convoluted battles over foreign military policy would recur over the next fifty years.

NOVEMBER 3, 1952
TRUMAN RELEASES SECRET DOCUMENT ON POLICY IN KOREA
Declassifies Chiefs' '47 Note on Troop Withdrawal Quoted in Campaign by Morse
SCORES EISENHOWER ROLE
Stevenson Fears Risk of War in Rival's Plans—Wedemeyer Challenges the President
By ANTHONY LEVIERO
Special to THE NEW YORK TIMES.

KANSAS CITY, Nov. 2—President Truman declassified and made public this evening the controversial top secret document in which the Joint Chiefs of Staff in 1947 had recommended the withdrawal of United States occupation forces from Korea.

The document has been the cause of a continuing political furor since last Monday, when Senator Wayne Morse of Oregon, who has bolted the Republican party, made use of it in an attack on Gen. Dwight D. Eisenhower, the Republican Presidential candidate.

Mr. Truman asserted that he had decided to release the opinion of the Joint Chiefs of Staff, along with the State Department request that had occasioned it, in order to defend military and civilian officials who, he said, had been the victims of General Eisenhower's "false and malicious attacks."

The President also said he would not have released the secret document if General Eisenhower, "who was Chief of Staff of the Army and a member of the Joint Chiefs of Staff in 1947, had not in his campaign misrepresented the contents of this memorandum and made intemperate and unjustified attacks upon the civilian agencies participating in our decisions with respect to Korea."

Gives Reasons for Release

"I hope that the release of these documents will set this controversy at rest," Mr. Truman said, "and will in some measure protect those who have not been able to protect themselves in this debate because of their official positions and because of the secrecy classification which must necessarily cover a great deal of their work."

[In Springfield, Ill., Gov. Adlai E. Stevenson, the Democratic candidate for President, declared that General Eisenhower's plans for handling the Korean war "might well increase the risk of a third world war."

[In a nationwide broadcast, Lieut. Gen. Albert C. Wedemeyer, retired, disputed recent charges by the President and defended General Eisenhower. The Joint Chiefs, he said, "were not asked about global policy."]

The controversy began when General Eisenhower charged in campaign speeches that the Korean war had resulted from the ineptitude and blunders of civilian officials of the Government. The President asserted tonight that "the Republican candidate sought to create the false impression that our civilian officials were solely responsible for our decisions with respect to Korea and that they were guilty of blundering, if not of something worse."

Once General Eisenhower had made his "blunder" charge, Mr. Truman opened an unrelenting campaign in which he told audiences all over the country that the General had failed to explain that he had been one of those who had recommended the troop withdrawal in 1947.

Then Senator Morse brought the controversy to a boiling point by reading the top secret document in a political speech. When the Senator recently resigned from the Republican party, he accused General Eisenhower of surrendering to the Old Guard of the party.

THE CAMPAIGN

The 1952 campaign broke all previous records for speeches given and miles traveled. Television and air travel permitted the candidates to reach more people in more places, opening the campaign to a wider audience. Despite the high tenor of the opening of the campaign, the two presidential hopefuls soon began savage attacks on each other, supplemented by the voices of the vice-presidential candidates and by President Truman and Senator Taft, who eagerly joined the scrimmages. Amid the fray, Eisenhower seemed poised to emerge victorious.

SEPTEMBER 7, 1952
EDITORIAL
'HIGH-LEVEL CAMPAIGN' BEGINS TO GET ROUGH

By JAMES RESTON

Special to THE NEW YORK TIMES.

KASSON, Minn., Sept. 6—Fasten your seat belts, mates. The political weather is getting rough.

Last week, the script called for what was invariably defined as a high-level campaign. The formal campaign is six days old and the two candidates are now trading high-level punches in the nose.

When General Eisenhower came home, he said peace was the great issue of the election; now he says it's the "mess" in Washington.

When he attended that now famous luncheon with the reporters in Denver before the conventions, he resented suggestions that he was making overtures to the Republican Old Guard. Now he is composing whole symphonies for their benefit.

When the delegates visited him in Denver's Brown Palace Hotel last June, he used to give them a little lecture on avoiding half-truths and slogans. Now it looks from here as if he is concentrating on that oldest chestnut of them all: "Kick the rascals out."

Gov. Adlai E. Stevenson of Illinois has also changed his tactics a little.

New View of General

He hesitated to run for the Democratic nomination partly because the prospect of General Eisenhower in the White House did not fill him with mortal terror. Now he sees the general as a captive of the Old Guard and the Old Guard as a menace to every soul in Christendom.

Before the great draft in Chicago he seemed to be impressed with the argument that the defeat of General Eisenhower would deliver the Republican party once more into the hands of the conservatives, perpetuate the acrimonious debates over unreal issues of foreign and domestic policy, and jeopardize the two-party system in America.

Yesterday he raised this argument himself and dismissed it with a wisecrack. "I believe," he said, "that this is the first time it has been contended that now is the time for all good Democrats to come to the aid of the Republican party."

Finally, Mr. Stevenson has modified his public comments about his opponent. If he mentioned him at all right after the Democratic convention he was almost deferential.

This is now out. He still praises him, but usually just before he decapitates him with a phrase. Also, he has taken to feeling sorry for him in public, a stance which will not appeal to the general's sense of humor.

NOVEMBER 2, 1952
EDITORIAL
THE NATURE OF THE CAMPAIGNING

By W. H. LAWRENCE

Special to THE NEW YORK TIMES.

CHICAGO, Nov. 1—Axiomatic as it is for rival campaign managers to claim certain victory for each Presidential candidate three days in advance of the election, there is a truer and deeper significance this year in the assertion from both camps that the electioneering effort now almost over has achieved all that could have been accomplished both for Gen. Dwight D. Eisenhower and Gov. Adlai E. Stevenson.

The verdict of the voters won't be in until Tuesday night, but, as of now, Gov. Sherman Adams of New Hampshire, General Eisenhower's political chief of staff, and Wilson W. Wyatt, Governor Stevenson's personal campaign manager, are satisfied that nothing that could have affected the outcome of the election has been left undone.

Candidates' Travels

Each candidate has traveled farther, talked to more people, visited more states in person and been viewed and heard by larger television audiences than any preceding Presidential aspirant in United States history. The Southern states, as a whole, for example, have seldom seen a Presidential nominee of either party since the Civil War because the Democrats thought those states were certain to vote Democratic and the Republican candidate believed the effort didn't justify the travel expenditure.

But this year General Eisenhower has campaigned in ten of the Southern states, and Governor Stevenson has followed him into five of them. Only Mississippi, which seems certain to vote Democratic, although it backed the States' Rights candidacy of former Gov. J. Strom Thurmond of South Carolina four years ago, has been skipped by both nominees.

Campaign Scorecard

The active campaigning is now over except for Monday's final effort.

The scorecard shows that General Eisenhower has visited forty-four of the forty-eight states, omitting only Nevada, Mississippi, Maine and Vermont, while Governor Stevenson has visited thirty-two states. Each has traveled 30,000 miles or more, and each has made about 200 major and minor speeches.

In addition, both have used television to a greater extent than previous Presidential nominees, and this has brought their images and words into additional millions of homes.

The idea back of all this has been that each candidate show himself to the widest possible audience in order to have a hope of election.

While this general reasoning applied both to General Eisenhower and Governor Stevenson, each had different reasons for taking the stump so intensively.

Advantage for Eisenhower

To begin with, General Eisenhower had a big advantage when he was nominated. His name was a household word all over the United States because of his record as Supreme Allied Commander both in World War II and in the post-war efforts to build an Allied force in Europe to resist Communist expansion.

"I Like Ike" was not only a political slogan, but a fact, in nearly every home in the land. And General Eisenhower's victory over Senator Robert A. Taft of Ohio

at the Republican National Convention in Chicago was stirring in itself.

Governor Stevenson, on the other hand, was not so widely known across the land. He had been Governor of Illinois for four years, which does not bring too many front-page notices, and he had resisted efforts of his friends to form Stevenson clubs throughout the country to win the nomination for him. A large part of the country got its first look at him on the "Meet the Press" program the day after President Truman said he would not run for re-election, and on this occasion Governor Stevenson said he really did not want to run for anything but re-election as Governor.

But when both were nominated both undertook to reach as many voters as possible. Why?

General's Purposes

In General Eisenhower's case, Governor Adams has said that it was important that he campaign on the widest possible scale. He could not, Governor Adams believes, have won if he had stayed in uniform and in Europe and waited for the American public to draft him. The General had to be measured as a political leader, as well as a military hero, so the public could judge for itself what he thought and how he looked and whether at 62 years of age he could withstand the rigors of a tough campaign.

As Mr. Wyatt saw it, the job of his candidate was to make himself known to millions of Americans who had never heard much about him until he was nominated. And the Democratic nominee had to counter the admittedly strong desire for "a change" in Washington by attempting to persuade voters that in his person and policies there was "enough" of a change to satisfy this feeling.

Stevenson Strategy

Governor Stevenson and his advisers decided that his greatest chance rested upon the maximum use of television to bring him into homes across the country that he could not hope to visit in person. This is not to say that Governor Stevenson appeared on TV more than did General Eisenhower, but he deliberately chose another technique.

To a substantial degree, Governor Stevenson used his TV time for "fireside" chats directed to the man at home, and delivered from the privacy of the broadcasting studio without the distraction of shouting crowds. General Eisenhower, on the other hand, usually was on TV when he was addressing a night-time rally in one part of the country or another.

The Democratic nominee used the airplane much more than he did the old-fashioned railroad train "whistle stop" technique and, indeed, it was not until the final two weeks of the campaign that Governor Stevenson set off by train for an intensive series of rear platform appearances from Chicago to the East Coast and back again.

● ●

ELECTION RESULTS

On November 3, 1952, America elected General of the Army Dwight D. Eisenhower as its thirty-fourth president. Eisenhower won decisive majorities in both the popular and electoral votes, even in the Democratic "Solid South." The victory appeared to be a personal triumph for Eisenhower, as the Republican Party was unable to translate his landslide into massive gains in either the House or Senate. Eisenhower's popularity delivered the Republican Party its first return to the White House in twenty years, but left the political balance of the nation uncertain.

NOVEMBER 5, 1952
EISENHOWER WINS IN A LANDSLIDE; TAKES NEW YORK; IVES ELECTED; REPUBLICANS GAIN IN CONGRESS

RACE IS CONCEDED

Virginia and Florida Go to the General as Do Illinois and Ohio

SWEEP IS NATION-WIDE

Victor Calls for Unity and Thanks Governor for Pledging Support

By ARTHUR KROCK

Gen. Dwight D. Eisenhower was elected President of the United States yesterday in an electoral vote landslide and with an emphatic popular majority that probably will give his party a small margin of control in the House of Representatives but may leave the Senate as it is—forty-nine Democrats, forty-seven Republicans and one independent.

Senator Richard M. Nixon of California was elected Vice President.

The Democratic Presidential candidate, Gov. Adlai E. Stevenson of Illinois, shortly after midnight conceded his defeat by a record turnout of American voters.

At 4 A. M. today the Republican candidate had carried states with a total of 431 electors, or 165 more than the 266 required for the selection of a President. The Democratic candidate seemed sure of 69, with 31 doubtful in Kentucky, Louisiana and Tennessee.

General Eisenhower's landslide victory, both in electoral and popular votes, was nation-wide in its pattern, extending from New England—where Massachusetts and Rhode Island broke their Democratic voting habits of many years—down the Eastern seaboard to Maryland, Virginia and Florida and westward to almost every state between the coasts, including California.

General Wins Illinois

The Republican candidate took Illinois, Governor Stevenson's home state. In South Carolina, though he lost its electors on a technicality, he won a majority of the voters. And, completing the first successful Republican invasion of the States of the former Confederacy, the General carried Texas and broke the one-party system in the South.

The personal popularity that enabled him to defeat Senator Robert A. Taft of Ohio in the Republican primaries in Texas, and present him with the issue on which he defeated the Senator for the Republican nomination, crushed the regular Democratic organization of Texas

1952 POPULAR VOTE

STATE	TOTAL VOTE	DWIGHT D. EISENHOWER (REPUBLICAN)		ADLAI E. STEVENSON (DEMOCRAT)		VINCENT HALLINAN (PROGRESSIVE)		STUART HAMBLEN (PROHIBITION)	
		VOTES	%	VOTES	%	VOTES	%	VOTES	%
Alabama	426,120	149,231	35.0	275,075	64.6	—	0.0	1,814	0.4
Arizona	260,570	152,042	58.3	108,528	41.7	—	0.0	—	0.0
Arkansas	404,800	177,155	43.8	226,300	55.9	—	0.0	886	0.2
California	5,141,849	2,897,310	56.3	2,197,548	42.7	24,106	0.5	15,653	0.3
Colorado	630,103	379,782	60.3	245,504	39.0	1,919	0.3	—	0.0
Connecticut	1,096,911	611,012	55.7	481,649	43.9	1,466	0.1	—	0.0
Delaware	174,025	90,059	51.8	83,315	47.9	155	0.1	234	0.1
Florida	989,337	544,036	55.0	444,950	45.0	—	0.0	—	0.0
Georgia	655,785	198,961	30.3	456,823	69.7	—	0.0	—	0.0
Idaho	276,254	180,707	65.4	95,081	34.4	443	0.2	—	0.0
Illinois	4,481,058	2,457,327	54.8	2,013,920	44.9	—	0.0	—	0.0
Indiana	1,955,049	1,136,259	58.1	801,530	41.0	1,085	0.1	15,335	0.8
Iowa	1,268,773	808,906	63.8	451,513	35.6	5,085	0.4	2,882	0.2
Kansas	896,166	616,302	68.8	273,296	30.5	—	0.0	6,038	0.7
Kentucky	993,148	495,029	49.8	495,729	49.9	336	0.0	1,161	0.1
Louisiana	651,952	306,925	47.1	345,027	52.9	—	0.0	—	0.0
Maine	351,786	232,353	66.0	118,806	33.8	332	0.1	—	0.0
Maryland	902,074	499,424	55.4	395,337	43.8	7,313	0.8	—	0.0
Massachusetts	2,383,398	1,292,325	54.2	1,083,525	45.5	4,636	0.2	886	0.0
Michigan	2,798,592	1,551,529	55.4	1,230,657	44.0	3,922	0.1	10,331	0.4
Minnesota	1,379,483	763,211	55.3	608,458	44.1	2,666	0.2	2,147	0.2
Mississippi	285,532	112,966	39.6	172,566	60.4	—	0.0	—	0.0
Missouri	1,892,062	959,429	50.7	929,830	49.1	987	0.1	885	0.0
Montana	265,037	157,394	59.4	106,213	40.1	723	0.3	548	0.2
Nebraska	609,660	421,603	69.2	188,057	30.8	—	0.0	—	0.0
Nevada	82,190	50,502	61.4	31,688	38.6	—	0.0	—	0.0
New Hampshire	272,950	166,287	60.9	106,663	39.1	—	0.0	—	0.0
New Jersey	2,418,554	1,373,613	56.8	1,015,902	42.0	5,589	0.2	989	0.0
New Mexico	238,608	132,170	55.4	105,661	44.3	225	0.1	297	0.1
New York	7,128,239	3,952,813	55.5	3,104,601	43.6	64,211	0.9	—	0.0
North Carolina	1,210,910	558,107	46.1	652,803	53.9	—	0.0	—	0.0
North Dakota	270,127	191,712	71.0	76,694	28.4	344	0.1	302	0.1
Ohio	3,700,758	2,100,391	56.8	1,600,367	43.2	—	0.0	—	0.0
Oklahoma	948,984	518,045	54.6	430,939	45.4	—	0.0	—	0.0
Oregon	695,059	420,815	60.5	270,579	38.9	3,665	0.5	—	0.0
Pennsylvania	4,580,969	2,415,789	52.7	2,146,269	46.9	4,222	0.1	8,951	0.2
Rhode Island	414,498	210,935	50.9	203,293	49.0	187	0.0	—	0.0
South Carolina[1]	341,087	9,793	2.9	173,004	50.7	—	0.0	1	0.0
South Dakota	294,283	203,857	69.3	90,426	30.7	—	0.0	—	0.0
Tennessee	892,553	446,147	50.0	443,710	49.7	885	0.1	1,432	0.2
Texas	2,075,946	1,102,878	53.1	969,228	46.7	294	0.0	1,983	0.1
Utah	329,554	194,190	58.9	135,364	41.1	—	0.0	—	0.0
Vermont	153,557	109,717	71.5	43,355	28.2	282	0.2	—	0.0
Virginia	619,689	349,037	56.3	268,677	43.4	311	0.1	—	0.0
Washington	1,102,708	599,107	54.3	492,845	44.7	2,460	0.2	—	0.0
West Virginia	873,548	419,970	48.1	453,578	51.9	—	0.0	—	0.0
Wisconsin	1,607,370	979,744	61.0	622,175	38.7	2,174	0.1	—	0.0
Wyoming	129,253	81,049	62.7	47,934	37.1	—	0.0	194	0.2
TOTALS	61,550,918	33,777,945	54.9	27,314,992	44.4	140,023	0.2	72,949	0.1

1. There were two separate slates of electors pledged to Eisenhower in South Carolina that could not legally be combined: Republican, 9,793; Independent slate, 158,289. Had these two been combined Eisenhower would have totaled 168,082 in the state and 33,936,234 nationally.

OTHER VOTES	%	PLURALITY	
—	0.0	125,844	D
—	0.0	43,514	R
459	0.1	49,145	D
7,232	0.1	699,762	R
2,898	0.5	134,278	R
2,784	0.3	129,363	R
262	0.2	6,744	R
351	0.0	99,086	R
1	0.0	257,862	D
23	0.0	85,626	R
9,811	0.2	443,407	R
840	0.0	334,729	R
387	0.0	357,393	R
530	0.1	343,006	R
893	0.1	700	D
—	0.0	38,102	D
295	0.1	113,547	R
—	0.0	104,087	R
2,026	0.1	208,800	R
2,153	0.1	320,872	R
3,001	0.2	154,753	R
—	0.0	59,600	D
931	0.0	29,599	R
159	0.1	51,181	R
—	0.0	233,546	R
—	0.0	18,814	R
—	0.0	59,624	R
22,461	0.9	357,711	R
255	0.1	26,509	R
6,614	0.1	848,212	R
—	0.0	94,696	D
1,075	0.4	115,018	R
—	0.0	500,024	R
—	0.0	87,106	R
—	0.0	150,236	R
5,738	0.1	269,520	R
83	0.0	7,642	R
158,289	46.4	4,922	D
—	0.0	113,431	R
379	0.0	2,437	R
1,563	0.1	133,650	R
—	0.0	58,826	R
203	0.1	66,362	R
1,664	0.3	80,360	R
8,296	0.8	106,262	R
—	0.0	33,608	D
3,277	0.2	357,569	R
76	0.1	33,115	R
245,009	**0.4**	**6,462,953**	**R**

that was led by Speaker Sam Rayburn of the House of Representatives and had the blessing of former Vice President John N. Garner.

The tide that bore General Eisenhower to the White House, though it did not give him a comfortable working majority in either the national House or the Senate (the Democrats may still nominally control the machinery of that branch), probably increased the number of Republican governors beyond the present twenty-five.

"My fellow citizens have made their choice and I gladly accept it," said Governor Stevenson at 1:46 A. M., Eastern standard time, and he asked all citizens to unite behind the President-elect. The defeated candidate said he had sent a telegram of congratulation to General Eisenhower.

At 2:05 A.M., from the Grand Ballroom of the Commodore Hotel, General Eisenhower said he recognized the weight of his new responsibilities and that he would not give "short weight" in their execution. He also urged "unity" and announced he had sent a telegram of thanks to the Democratic candidate for his promise of support. . . .

On the over-all issue of the record of the Roosevelt-Truman Administrations, including the New Deal and Fair Deal programs, that the President insisted was "all Stevenson had to run on," the result of the election will be taken by the Republicans as repudiation of Mr. Truman.

This undoubtedly will be the basis of the proposals to Congress that President-elect Eisenhower will make and that Congress will sustain, if it is controlled by the Republicans.

At midnight that control seemed possible but not certain. The Democrats lost two Senate seats to the Republicans in Connecticut—those of Mr. Benton and the late Brien McMahon—and that of Herbert R. O'Connor in Maryland.

The Republicans held the seats of Senator H. Alexander Smith of New Jersey, John W. Bricker of Ohio, and Irving M. Ives of New York, in addition to those of Messrs. McCarthy and Jenner. But final returns may disclose that the Democrats have taken the seat held by Senator Henry Cabot Lodge Jr. of Massachusetts by electing Representative John F. Kennedy to his place.

THE PRESIDENTIAL ELECTION OF 1960

KENNEDY GAINS A NARROW WIN FOR THE "NEW FRONTIER"

American politics turned vigorously toward the future in the presidential election of 1960. The two major candidates had both been born in the twentieth century, the first such match in the nation's history, and both had fought in the Second World War, the first such competition between veterans of that conflict in international politics.

The candidates competed in a new world. America's post-war political predominance was being challenged. Western Europe had moved toward an autonomous economic and political union. The Soviet Union had stabilized its empire in Eastern Europe and demonstrated its technological abilities, beating the United States into space exploration with the launch of Sputnik, the Earth's first artificial satellite. The traditional dominance of the West was now challenged by the Communist takeover of Cuba under Fidel Castro, the new independence of African nations, and the rise of Communist China as a great power.

The United States was also changing. The population had grown more than 18 percent in a decade, the largest increase in fifty years, most of it in the swelling suburbs where nearly 50 million children of the "baby boom" crowded nurseries and classrooms. Education levels increased considerably, with high school graduates rising from a third to more than two-fifths, and college graduates now more than a tenth, of the population. Americans were also moving—to the South and West, which would soon gain 16 electoral votes, shifting power. Adding to that movement were the two new states of the Union, Alaska and Hawaii, the first additions in nearly half a century.

Racial issues, long neglected, came to prominence. School desegregation, mandated by the Supreme Court in 1954, met resistance in the South, sometimes led by local officials. African Americans expanded their efforts toward equality with a boycott of segregated buses in Montgomery, Alabama, eventually leading to desegregation of public transit and the emergence of a new national leader, Rev. Martin Luther King Jr. Two new civil rights acts, although weak, brought the federal government into the conflicts. In

Source: AP Images

Sen. John F. Kennedy speaks to a crowd of several thousand at the Alamo while campaigning in San Antonio, Texas, on Monday, September 12, 1960.

February 1960 the civil rights movement further widened its scope, as students conducted "sit-ins" at lunch counters reserved for whites and insisted on equal service.

The political parties also were changing. Television and suburbanization altered campaigning. Voter coalitions still bore the imprint of the New Deal, but as economic prosperity spread, the middle class expanded and union membership declined, diminishing the Democrats' working-class base. Yet that prosperity was shaky, as the nation suffered three recessions during eight years of Republican government. The last, in 1958, led to large Democratic gains in the congressional elections: 49 seats in the House and 17 in the Senate. Partisan conflict between the branches of the national government soon became even sharper in the presidential election. Beyond the parties, unforeseen social conflicts made the decade of the 1960s one of the most tumultuous and fabled periods in American history.

THE PARTIES AND THE CANDIDATES

With Dwight D. Eisenhower concluding his presidency, Democratic prospects for victory attracted many candidates into the race. The most glamorous was the young

1960 ELECTORAL VOTE

STATE	ELECTORAL VOTES	KENNEDY	NIXON	BYRD	STATE	ELECTORAL VOTES	KENNEDY	NIXON	BYRD
Alabama	(11)	5	–	6	Montana	(4)	–	4	–
Alaska	(3)	–	3	–	Nebraska	(6)	–	6	–
Arizona	(4)	–	4	–	Nevada	(3)	3	–	–
Arkansas	(8)	8	–	–	New Hampshire	(4)	–	4	–
California	(32)	–	32	–	New Jersey	(16)	16	–	–
Colorado	(6)	–	6	–	New Mexico	(4)	4	–	–
Connecticut	(8)	8	–	–	New York	(45)	45	–	–
Delaware	(3)	3	–	–	North Carolina	(14)	14	–	–
Florida	(10)	–	10	–	North Dakota	(4)	–	4	–
Georgia	(12)	12	–	–	Ohio	(25)	–	25	–
Hawaii	(3)	3	–	–	Oklahoma	(8)	–	7	1
Idaho	(4)	–	4	–	Oregon	(6)	–	6	–
Illinois	(27)	27	–	–	Pennsylvania	(32)	32	–	–
Indiana	(13)	–	13	–	Rhode Island	(4)	4	–	–
Iowa	(10)	–	10	–	South Carolina	(8)	8	–	–
Kansas	(8)	–	8	–	South Dakota	(4)	–	4	–
Kentucky	(10)	–	10	–	Tennessee	(11)	–	11	–
Louisiana	(10)	10	–	–	Texas	(24)	24	–	–
Maine	(5)	–	5	–	Utah	(4)	–	4	–
Maryland	(9)	9	–	–	Vermont	(3)	–	3	–
Massachusetts	(16)	16	–	–	Virginia	(12)	–	12	–
Michigan	(20)	20	–	–	Washington	(9)	–	9	–
Minnesota	(11)	11	–	–	West Virginia	(8)	8	–	–
Mississippi	(8)	–	–	8	Wisconsin	(12)	–	12	–
Missouri	(13)	13	–	–	Wyoming	(3)	–	3	–
					TOTALS	(537)	303	219	15

John F. Kennedy, a war hero, handsome, rich, and now in his second term as senator from Massachusetts. Kennedy, after narrowly losing an open convention contest for the vice-presidential nomination in 1956, embarked on a quest for organizational backing while preparing to enter the 1960 presidential primaries.

Other major aspirants included Minnesota senator Hubert Humphrey, leading the party's liberal wing; Lyndon Johnson of Texas, already legendary for his legislative mastery as Senate majority leader; Missouri senator Stuart Symington, a defense expert and the choice of former president Harry Truman; Adlai Stevenson, the party's nominee in the two previous elections, who appeared hospitable to a draft; and a host of favorite sons.

Kennedy needed to soothe the qualms of party leaders who feared that the voters would not accept a Catholic candidate. To prove his broad popularity, he entered most primaries, but only Humphrey took up the challenge. In the Wisconsin primary, Kennedy won handily with more than 56 percent of the tallies, but observers downplayed the results, pointing to his relative weakness among Protestant voters.

To answer that argument, Kennedy turned to the primary in West Virginia, a state overwhelmingly Protestant in population. Spending lavishly, Kennedy called for religious tolerance. He asked voters: "Is anyone going to tell me that I lost this primary forty-two years ago when I was baptized?" His pleas were accepted, as he won an overwhelming 61 percent to 39 percent victory over Humphrey, who then withdrew and later endorsed Stevenson.

Kennedy went on to win all seven of the primaries he entered and began to accumulate support from the industrial states and the big city machines. Despite his onward march to the nomination, however, Kennedy still drew opposition from older party leaders. Eleanor Roosevelt encouraged the Democrats to draft Stevenson. Less than two weeks before the party conclave in early July, Truman challenged the front-runner. Listing ten other Democrats whom he considered more capable, Truman disdainfully advised Kennedy: "Senator, are you certain that you're quite ready for the country or the country is ready for you in the role of President in January 1961? . . . May I urge you to be patient?"

As the party convened in Los Angeles, the outcome was still in doubt, with the opposing candidates seeking a deadlock. Johnson challenged Kennedy to a debate before the Texas and Massachusetts delegations, an occasion that Kennedy wittily turned to his own advantage. Stevenson, defying precedent, came to the convention hall and aroused a fervent demonstration. That ardor was further stoked by the formal presentation of his candidacy by Minnesota senator Eugene McCarthy, pleading with the delegates, "Do not reject this man who made us all proud to be called Democrats."

The delegates were moved emotionally, but held to their commitments. At the very end of the first and only presidential ballot, Wyoming switched its vote to unanimous support of Kennedy, resulting in a slender majority of 806 among the 1,521 delegates. In later negotiations, Johnson surprisingly accepted the offer of the vice-presidential nomination, unifying the party for the tough fall campaign.

The Democratic platform promised a more active government, with pledges to increase defense spending, achieve a 5 percent annual growth in the economy, increase minimum wages, and end the immigration quota system. Civil rights issues occasioned dispute from southern delegations, but the convention endorsed sit-ins as "peaceful demonstrations for first-class citizenship," promised abolition of literacy tests and poll taxes as voting requirements, and endorsed a three-year deadline for the onset of desegregation in all schools.

Accepting the nomination, Kennedy—the youngest presidential candidate of the twentieth century—tried to turn his party's heritage to a "New Frontier":

Franklin Roosevelt's New Deal promised security and succor to those in need. But the New Frontier of which I speak is not a set of promises—it is a set of challenges. It sums up not what I intend to offer the American people, but what I intend to ask of them. It appeals to their pride, not their pocketbook—it holds out the promise of more sacrifice instead of more security.

But I tell you the New Frontier is here, whether we seek it or not. Beyond that frontier are uncharted areas of science and space, unsolved problems of peace and war, unconquered pockets of ignorance and prejudice, unanswered questions of poverty and surplus. . . .

The times demand invention, innovation, imagination, decision. I am asking each of you to be new pioneers on that New Frontier. My call is to the young in heart, regardless of age—to the stout in spirit, regardless of party. . . .

All mankind waits upon our decision. A whole world looks to see what we will do. We cannot fail their trust; we cannot fail to try.

The Republican choice was far simpler. Early on, Vice President Richard Nixon became the favored candidate, claiming the mantle of succession from President Eisenhower, who retained his great personal popularity. Nixon had been unusually active for a vice president, gaining attention as an administration spokesman on foreign policy. Particularly notable was the so-called kitchen debate with Soviet leader Nikita Khrushchev at a 1959 exhibition of American consumer goods in Moscow, where Nixon trumpeted the merits of U.S. capitalism.

Nixon had planned a vigorous nomination campaign, but soon lacked any viable opponents. More conservative Republicans looked to Arizona senator Barry Goldwater, who declined to run. More liberal factions hoped that Nelson Rockefeller, recently elected governor of New York, would enter the race, but Rockefeller unequivocally withdrew in December 1959.

Winning every primary without opposition and backed by all party leaders, Nixon was assured of nomination. But he still worried about a "Draft Rockefeller" movement that began after U.S. foreign policy reverses. To win Rockefeller's endorsement, Nixon met secretly in the governor's New York apartment two days before the convention opened in late July in Chicago. In a "compact of Fifth Avenue," the vice president agreed to fourteen amendments proposed by Rockefeller to the tentative party platform; the most important were promises of vigorous actions on civil rights and national defense.

Conservatives were upset, seeing a surrender to Rockefeller, but Nixon toured the state delegations, quelled the rebellion, and united the party behind his candidacy. Winning all but 10 of the 1,331 delegate votes, he became the first incumbent vice president to be nominated for president since Martin Van Buren in the election of 1836. The convention then ratified Nixon's selection for running mate, U.S. ambassador to the United Nations Henry Cabot Lodge Jr., a former Massachusetts senator (defeated by Kennedy in 1952).

As it happened, the two wallflowers of 1960 would be the most active contestants in the Republican nomination dance four years later. Goldwater backed Nixon in a convention speech but, looking to the future, lectured his supporters: "Let's grow up, conservatives. . . . If we want to take this party back—and I think we can someday—let's get to work." For his part, Rockefeller declined an offer to join the ticket; he did introduce the presidential nominee's acceptance speech, making a distracting slip by misstating the middle initial in Nixon's name.

Aside from the limited amendments forced by Rockefeller, the party platform broke no new ground; instead, the Republicans relied on the record of the two Eisenhower administrations. After promising to campaign in all fifty states, an innovative tactic, Nixon set a more idealistic tone in his acceptance speech. He challenged his party and the national television audience:

> When Mr. Khrushchev says our grandchildren will live under communism, let us say his grandchildren will live in freedom. . . .
>
> Let us make it clear to them that our aim in helping them is not merely to stop communism, but that in the great American tradition of concern for those less fortunate we welcome the opportunity to work with people everywhere in helping them to achieve their aspirations for a life of human dignity. . . .
>
> My fellow Americans, it means sacrifice—not the grim sacrifice of desperation but the rewarding sacrifice of choice which lifts us out of the humdrum life in which we live and gives us the supreme satisfaction which comes from working together in a cause greater than ourselves, greater than our Nation, as great as the whole world itself.

> We have the resources, the resources to wage a winning war against poverty, misery and disease wherever it exists in the world. And upon the next President of the United States will rest the responsibility to inspire and to lead the forces of freedom toward this goal.

THE CAMPAIGN

Kennedy and Nixon resembled each other in several ways—in age, political careers, even the rhetoric of their acceptance speeches. But more significant were their differences—Kennedy was well-born, sophisticated, eastern, and Catholic; Nixon was self-made, combative, Californian, and Quaker. The election outcome would depend considerably on voters' judgments of their personal characteristics and abilities. But their basic differences went deeper than individual traits, as evidenced in their basic campaign stances: Kennedy had to challenge the record of the Republican administration, and Nixon had to defend its accomplishments.

From the beginning of the contest, with Nixon holding a small lead in opinion surveys, the nominees knew the race would be close. Their campaign strategies built on the parties' past. Kennedy sought to mobilize the nation's continuing Democratic majority, forging an electoral victory from the industrial states and the party's eroding southern base. Nixon needed to maintain Eisenhower's personal coalition, persuade independents to join the smaller Republican base, and extend the party's reach into the ranks of disaffected white southerners.

Setting new records for financial cost, the campaigns emphasized television advertising and incessant air travel between enthusiastic rallies. In a nostalgic recreation of the past, Kennedy and Nixon also conducted whistle-stop train trips in California and the Midwest. Their efforts continued to the last minute, with Nixon conducting a four-hour national telethon as Kennedy spoke up to midnight to enraptured crowds in New England. Despite a knee injury that kept him hospitalized for two weeks, Nixon fulfilled his pledge to visit every state, but perhaps lost the final decisive votes in competitive large states by going to Alaska on the last weekend before the balloting.

Although the two candidates shared many ideas, the close competition—and some mutual disdain—led to sharp personal attacks and exaggeration of their differences. On foreign policy, Nixon and Kennedy regularly compared their claims to be "the leader of the free world." Nixon asserted his presumed experience in the Eisenhower White House. The Democratic candidate responded by citing the alleged failures of the administration, criticizing a claimed "missile gap" in national defense, and its policies toward Cuba and China. Domestically, Nixon pointed to economic growth under the Republicans, while Kennedy emphasized the onset of a new recession. Each attacked his opponent in harsh terms. Nixon denigrated the Democrat as "ignorant," "an instrument of national disparagement," "dangerously irresponsible," and "frighteningly foolish." Kennedy responded by characterizing the vice president as "naïve," "complacent," and "a man whose political philosophy seemed to shift from month to month."

The confrontation became direct and dramatic in a series of four televised debates, the first in American politics—and the only joint appearances until the institutionalization of debates in 1976. Seventy million Americans watched the debates, a larger number than the eventual turnout. The candidates presented the themes of their overall campaigns—Kennedy vowing "to get the country moving again," and Nixon emphasizing his experience and record.

Kennedy began with an advocacy of activist government:

In the election of 1960, and with the world around us, the question is whether the world will exist half-slave or half-free. . . . If we do well here, if we meet our obligations, if we're moving ahead, then I think freedom will be secure around the world. If we fail, then freedom fails. . . . I should make it very clear that I do not think we're doing enough, that I am not satisfied as an American with the progress that we're making. . . . I don't believe in big government, but I believe in effective governmental action. And I think that's the only way the United States is going to maintain its freedom. It's the only way that we're going to move ahead. I think we can do a better job.

Nixon's response conceded much ground:

The things that Senator Kennedy has said many of us can agree with. . . . And I subscribe completely to the spirit that Senator Kennedy has expressed tonight, the spirit that the United States should move ahead. Where, then, do we disagree? I think we disagree on the implication of his remarks tonight and on the statements that he has made on many occasions during this campaign to the effect that the United States has been standing still. . . . When we compare [the Truman and Eisenhower administrations], I think we find that America has been moving ahead. . . . I believe that we have

the secret for progress, we know the way to progress. . . . But on the other hand, when we look at various programs that he offers, they do not seem to be new.

There would be much more that night and in the following dialogues—a profusion of data, issues as significant as nuclear arms and as small as islands off the coast of China, presentations of personality, and even a debate about scheduling an additional debate. The most important aspect of the discussions was that they occurred at all, giving the electorate the opportunity to compare the candidates directly—at the same time, at the same place, dealing with the same questions.

The political effect was clearly to Kennedy's advantage. Simply by being on the same stage, he showed himself the equal of Nixon, and he gained an edge by dint of his fuller preparation, command of the substantive material, and even his more robust physical appearance at the first debate, when Nixon still was affected by his hospitalization. Surveys indicated that most viewers thought Kennedy "won" the debates—particularly the first confrontation (although radio listeners were split), but that few votes were actually changed, Kennedy gaining a small edge. For Kennedy, it was sufficient to show himself as no less qualified than Nixon. That would be enough to rally the natural Democratic majority to his side.

Beyond the words of debate, the campaign was affected by the emotions of religion and race. Kennedy's Catholic faith continued to draw attention from the media, opposition from some voters, particularly in the South, and expressions of antagonism from some notable Protestant clergy. To resolve the question, Kennedy accepted an invitation to speak to the Houston Ministerial Association, surely not a friendly audience. His speech became a historic statement on the proper place of religion in politics, as he declared:

I believe in an America where the separation of church and state is absolute—where no Catholic prelate would tell the President (should he be a Catholic) how to act and no Protestant minister would tell his parishioners for whom to vote. . . .

Contrary to common newspaper usage, I am not the Catholic candidate for President. I am the Democratic Party's candidate for President, who happens to be a Catholic. I do not speak for my church on public matters—and the church does not speak for me. . . .

But if this election is decided on the basis that 40,000,000 Americans lost their chance of being President on the day they were baptized, then it is the whole nation that will be the loser in the eyes of Catholics and non-Catholics around the world, in the eyes of history, and in the eyes of our own people.

Kennedy won plaudits from the press and from Nixon and possibly some votes from ambivalent Protestants, despite the distribution of 20 million anti-Catholic broadsides. Probably more important was the opposite effect: overwhelming Catholic support stimulated by the frequent repetitions of Kennedy's forceful speech in television broadcasts and ads in northern states.

Race had become a major political factor with the civil rights movement now challenging all forms of segregation. Republicans were torn between their historic commitment to racial equality and their perceived new opportunities in the white South. Their vice-presidential candidate, Ambassador Lodge, tried to appeal to black voters with a promise that a Nixon administration would include a Negro in the president's cabinet, but that promise was quickly withdrawn. (Kennedy did not make the same pledge, but he appointed Robert C. Weaver to head the Housing and Home Finance Agency, which in the Johnson administration became a cabinet department and made Weaver the first African American cabinet member.)

Kennedy did reiterate the party's platform pledges and praised the protests of black students. Late in the campaign, he made a more evocative gesture, when King was imprisoned in Georgia for a traffic violation. Kennedy made a sympathetic call to King's wife, and his brother called the presiding Georgia magistrate on King's behalf. When King was released, their actions kindled enthusiasm and high turnout among northern African Americans, a crucial voting bloc.

THE ELECTION RESULTS

The candidates had fought hard, but to an apparent draw. Opinion analysts and pundits alike were unsure of the outcome, and their uncertainty was reflected in the actual votes.

In the first returns, from New England and the rest of the Northeast, Kennedy ran up large majorities, and his aides began to celebrate an apparent landslide victory. But, as reports came in from the South and the West, their mood changed with the discouraging evidence of an anti-Catholic surge. Without the aid of modern exit polls, they and the nation could only wait for the slow counting of the ballots. The next morning the critical vote of Illinois fell to Kennedy, aided by late but overwhelming support from the Democratic machine in Chicago.

Nationally, 69 million voted, an increase of 10 percent over the 1956 presidential election and setting a mark for electoral participation that stood for the rest of the century. Kennedy's popular vote margin was almost invisible, 49.7 percent to Nixon's 49.5 percent, a numerical margin of less than 120,000 votes. In electoral votes, Kennedy did better, with a clear majority of 303 of the new total of 537 to Nixon's 219. But Kennedy carried only 22 of the 50 states, including 5 (with 63 electoral votes) won by less than one percentage point.

The election results were further confused (and remain so to this day) by returns from the South. Segregationists, controlling the election machinery, listed "free" or unpledged electors under the traditional Democratic label for all of Mississippi's 8 slots and 6 of Alabama's 11. Their hope was that the free electors would hold the balance of power in a deadlocked national election. Frustrated by Kennedy's majority, they cast their votes for Sen. Harry Byrd of Virginia, a leading foe of school desegregation.

Nixon, as the sitting vice president, presided over the official count of the electoral vote in January. By then, the only dispute concerned Hawaii, which had reported two sets of returns. Ruefully, if graciously, Nixon ruled in favor of the later report, which gave Kennedy the state by the thinnest margin, a mere 115 popular votes.

The narrow Kennedy victory was the final echo of the Democrats' erstwhile dominant coalition. Although one of six voters had switched from Eisenhower to Kennedy, the party's presidential vote was not a triumph, but a stand-off. It lost 2 of the 7 megastates—Ohio and California—and slipped close to defeat in other previous strongholds. Moreover, population movements that would be reflected in the next election were predominantly away from the states voting Democratic. In the growing South, with Lyndon Johnson's heft, the ticket still carried 6 states of the former Confederacy, but the Solid South of yore was gone. For the next half century, until 2008, Democratic candidates from the North would carry a southern state only once.

In the overall electorate, Democrats still led in party loyalties, the basis for the party's recapture of the White House and retention of control of Congress, even with the loss of 20 House and 2 Senate seats. But the victory was not only razor-thin, but fragile as well. Catholics had given Kennedy 80 percent of their vote, providing the critical margin in the industrial states. But the return to their ancestral party eroded by the end of the decade. Protestant defections were more numerous. Although less strategically important in 1960 because of the geographical concentration, the change among white southern Protestants persisted in later contests, turning the region strongly Republican.

The new president charted a new national course in his stirring Inaugural Address, while cautioning, "All this will not be finished in the first 100 days. Nor will it be finished in the first 1,000 days, nor in the life of this Administration, nor even perhaps in our lifetime on this planet. But let us begin."

A new politics, much of it unforeseen, soon developed. Europe became further divided with construction of the Berlin Wall, and the world came close to nuclear destruction in the Cuban missile crisis. Racial conflict became violent with attacks on civil rights demonstrators in Alabama, but racial conciliation appeared possible with the biracial march on Washington.

Kennedy's admonition proved prescient. His administration lasted barely more than a thousand days, ending with his assassination in 1963. The hopes enlivened in the election of 1960 wilted with the tragedy of his death.

THE NEW POLITICAL ERA

America faced new challenges as it neared the 1960 election. Domestically, the nation was split over the issue of race. In *Brown v. Board of Education* (1954) the Supreme Court had declared school segregation unconstitutional, but integration was resisted fiercely. Overseas, the Soviet menace had grown, threatening U.S. military and technological dominance. The launch of the satellite Sputnik demonstrated Soviet superiority in the space race, a massive blow to American national pride.

SEPTEMBER 25, 1957
PRESIDENT SENDS TROOPS TO LITTLE ROCK, FEDERALIZES ARKANSAS NATIONAL GUARD; TELLS NATION HE ACTED TO AVOID ANARCHY

EISENHOWER ON AIR

Says School Defiance Has Gravely Harmed Prestige of U. S.

By ANTHONY LEWIS

Special to The New York Times.

WASHINGTON, Sept. 24—President Eisenhower sent Federal troops to Little Rock, Ark., today to open the way for the admission of nine Negro pupils to Central High School.

Earlier, the President federalized the Arkansas National Guard and authorized calling the Guard and regular Federal forces to remove obstructions to justice in Little Rock school integration.

His history-making action was based on a formal finding that his "cease and desist" proclamation, issued last night, had not been obeyed. Mobs of pro-segragationists still gathered in the vicinity of Central High School this morning.

Tonight, from the White House, President Eisenhower told the nation in a speech for radio and television that he had acted to prevent "mob rule" and "anarchy."

Historic Decision

The President's decision to send troops to Little Rock was reached at his vacation headquarters in Newport, R.I. It was one of historic importance politically, socially, constitutionally. For the first time since the Reconstruction days that followed the Civil War, the Federal Government was using its ultimate power to compel equal treatment of the Negro in the South.

He said violent defiance of Federal Court orders in Little Rock had done grave harm to "the prestige and influence, and indeed to the safety, of our nation and the world." He called on the people of Arkansas and the South to "preserve and respect the law even when they disagree with it."

Guardsmen Withdrawn

Action quickly followed the President's orders. During the day and night 1,000 members of the 101st Airborne Division were flown to Little Rock. Charles E. Wilson, Secretary of the Defense, ordered into Federal service all 10,000 members of the Arkansas National Guard.

Today's events were the climax of three weeks of skirmishing between the Federal Government and Gov. Orval E. Faubus of Arkansas. It was three weeks ago this morning that the Governor first ordered National Guard troops to Central High School to preserve order. The nine Negro students were prevented from entering the school.

The Guardsmen were gone yesterday, withdrawn by Governor Faubus as the result of a Federal Court order. But a shrieking mob compelled the nine children to withdraw from the school.

President Eisenhower yesterday cleared the way for full use of his powers with a proclamation commanding the mob in Little Rock to "disperse."

OCTOBER 5, 1957
SOVIET FIRES EARTH SATELLITE INTO SPACE; IT IS CIRCLING THE GLOBE AT 18,000 M.P.H.; SPHERE TRACKED IN 4 CROSSINGS OVER U. S.

OCTOBER 10, 1957
EDITORIAL
POLITICS OF THE SPUTNIK

It is becoming increasingly evident that the main purpose of the sputnik, the man-made moon launched by the Soviets, is political rather than scientific. This political purpose is to give new impact to the Soviet "rocket diplomacy" to compel the United States to deal with the Soviets separately and directly over the heads of our allies as one way of breaking up our alliances.

Such a separate Russian-American deal, designed to open the doors to further Communist advances, has been urged by the Soviets ever since the war. It was implicit in all Soviet proposals on disarmament and the settlement of other world problems, aimed at getting the United States out of Europe and Asia, and most recently out of the Middle East. It has now been broached anew and even more bluntly by Party Chief Khrushchev in his interview with James Reston of this newspaper and in other talks, all hinged to the sputnik.

The Soviet success in launching this satellite into space, Mr. Khrushchev warns, demonstrates Soviet "superiority" not only in science but also in "terrible and pitiless" atomic missiles capable of reaching any part of the world. Since the United States is the only other power now possessing atomic missiles, Mr. Khrushchev holds that the major responsibility for peace rests on Moscow and Washington, irrespective of the interests of other major nations. Consequently, Soviet Russia and the United States should agree between them to bring such satellites and all pilotless missiles under international control. Finally, in a warning remarkable even for the outspoken Mr. Khrushchev, he declares that the two major powers, meaning Soviet Russia and the United States, will either have to talk things out or fight them out. Lending weight to his words he proclaims his conviction that in such a fight "capitalism" would perish and communism triumph.

Even discounting Mr. Khrushchev's well-known addiction to hyperbole, the pressure he seeks to exert on the United States is clear. But it should not change American policy, which does not court surrender. As President Eisenhower and Secretary Dulles emphasize, the Western powers have already proposed international control of outer-space missiles at the London talks, a proposal the Soviets have thus far failed to accept.

The United States is willing to take up Mr. Khrushchev's own proposal to the point of joining in the organization of working groups to study the technical problems involved even outside of other disarmament problems and before a general disarmament convention has been concluded. But our Government continues to insist that such studies and any negotiations on such control must be conducted not between the United States and Soviet Russia but on a many-nation basis and within the United Nations, and that any agreement must be within the framework of a general armament reduction and control pact. The relief expressed in London and Paris over the American position and their quick endorsement of it show both the purpose and the danger of the Soviet proposal. The same realization of the dangers involved in any bilateral talks behind our allies' backs led to the rejection of the Soviet bid for a visit to Washington by Marshal Zhukov.

It is reassuring to hear President Eisenhower declare that neither the Soviet moon nor the Soviet rocket machinery has impaired our national security and that, though he wished that our own military missiles program were "further ahead," it continued to have top priority. But whether this Presidential reassurance, and especially Mr. Eisenhower's explanation of why we fell behind the Soviets in launching an earth satellite, will really satisfy the country is doubtful. The military missiles program has been subjected to recent curtailments in expenditures and development, and the satellite program, conducted at bargain-basement rates as a purely scientific experiment, reveals an unexpected naïveté in Washington as to the political and propagandistic implications of such a feat. It is not too late to remedy the situation, and it must be expected that both Washington and the country will now wake up to necessities of the new age of space that has dawned upon us.

* *

The Front-runners

The 1960 contest began with the entrance of two front-runners into the New Hampshire primaries. John Kennedy, the young senator from Massachusetts, entered first, preempting suggestions that he accept the secondary position of vice president. Richard Nixon, the incumbent vice president followed, entering as the heir-apparent to President Dwight Eisenhower. Both stormed to early victories in the New Hampshire primaries, but still faced grave challenges to unite their parties.

JANUARY 3, 1960
KENNEDY IN RACE; BARS SECOND SPOT IN ANY SITUATION

Formal Announcement Cites Confidence He Will Win Election as President

CHALLENGES SYMINGTON

Insists All Aspirants Should Be Willing to Test Their Strength in Primaries

By RUSSELL BAKER

Special to The New York Times.

WASHINGTON, Jan. 2—Senator John F. Kennedy made it official today.

He told a news conference that he was a candidate for the Democratic Presidential nomination and was convinced that he could win both the nomination and the election.

At the same time Democratic leaders who believe that his following can be consolidated behind the Democratic ticket if Mr. Kennedy is given the Vice-Presidential nomination were given a sober warning.

If he is rejected for top place on the ticket, the Senator said, he will refuse to accept the Vice-Presidential nomination "under any condition."

'Not Subject to Change'

This decision, he added, "will not be subject to change under any condition."

The 42-year-old Massachusetts Democrat, first serious Roman Catholic contender for the Presidency since

Alfred E. Smith ran in 1928, delivered his long-expected announcement to a crowded news conference in the Senate Caucus Room.

Of the many Democratic contenders, Senator Hubert H. Humphrey of Minnesota is the only other who has announced his candidacy for the Presidential nomination.

Regarding religion, Mr. Kennedy said:

"I would think that there is really only one issue involved in the whole question of a candidate's religion— that is, does a candidate believe in the Constitution, does he believe in the First Amendment, does he believe in the separation of church and state. When the candidate gives his views on that question, and I think I have given my views fully, I think the subject is exhausted."

Audience Applauds

An audience of about 300 supporters and friends applauded various answers to the reporters, giving the session the flavor of a political rally. Mrs. Kennedy also attended the conference.

Mr. Kennedy has been openly campaigning for the Democratic nomination for months. Thus today's ceremonial announcement came as no surprise.

At present the Senator is the acknowledged front-runner in the crowded field of Democratic contenders. But the large number of serious candidates and favorite sons threatens to prevent him building a strong lead.

Questioned about Governor Rockefeller's withdrawal from contention for the Republican nomination, Mr. Kennedy said that he had been surprised. "In some ways I think it makes Mr. Nixon's problem more difficult," he said.

He did not elaborate although many Democrats are trying to use the Rockefeller withdrawal to depict Vice President Nixon as the candidate of the Republican bosses.

What attracted the most attention here today, however, was the firmness with which Mr. Kennedy rejected the possibility of the Vice-Presidential nomination. Statements of this type are a standard feature of every announcement of candidacy, but Mr. Kennedy's categorical notice that he would not be available was considered unusual.

"I am a candidate for the Presidency," he said, "and if I fail to achieve that nomination, then I shall return to the Senate." The duties of the Vice-Presidency are limited, he noted, to presiding over the Senate, to voting in case of ties in Senatorial roll-calls "and to watching the health of the President."

JANUARY 10, 1960
EDITORIAL
VICE PRESIDENT NIXON ON HIS 47TH BIRTHDAY
By JAMES RESTON

WASHINGTON, Jan. 9—Vice President Nixon was 47 today, and considering what's ahead in 1960, even Herblock ought to be nice to him this week-end.

Mr. Nixon is not likely to forget his forty-eighth year, coming up, for he is on the verge of a shattering experience, win or lose. For ten long months he will be the principal target of politicians who hate him as much as any man is hated in American political life today.

His opponents have been out of power for eight years, gathering their frustrations all the time, and they must beat him or face the prospect of perhaps eight more years in opposition. For middle-aged men, this comes close to being a political lifetime.

Nixon's Advantages

The Vice President goes into this with many advantages. He has no opponent for the time being and therefore does not have to exhaust himself in the primary elections, as Adlai Stevenson did in 1956. He has the President behind him, tossing him birthday presents like the mission to settle the steel strike. He has all the information and brains of the Administration at his disposal. His opponent for the Presidency will have none of these.

Nevertheless, from now on, he must talk and travel, travel and talk, eat rubber chicken until it comes out of his ears, defend Ezra Taft Benson, be bright and intelligent on a hundred different subjects, wheedle campaign funds out of fat cats, sweet-talk the President, tolerate reporters (which is not easy) and tickle the vanity of thousands of boobs—all in an atmosphere of too much noise, smoke and booze.

There is a popular theory that Nixon is hard as nails, but like most political theories, it is only half true. Physically he is strong. He has been over the course for a long time and knows all the tricks and techniques. He is sustained by a curious fatalism which is equal to his ambition, but he can dish it out better than he can take it.

The Hard Way

This is not the kind of natural man political Washington loves, with a sense of humor and a sense of history. He has few close personal friends to sustain him. He is seldom at ease, even in the clubby atmosphere of the Senate.

Accordingly, even the most casual political meeting or encounter with a reporter seems to be a problem that must be carefully analyzed and executed.

He is a strange combination of confidence and uncertainty. He has done every job given to him and done it well. He was a good Representative and Senator. He has been an effective, if sometimes ruthless campaigner. He has demonstrated in his trips abroad that he can use a professional staff, and follow policy advice as well as any man in the Government. And yet, at 47, he still seems to have no inner serenity, and he is not likely to get it in his forty-eighth year, when for most of the time he will even be denied the refuge of his own home and family.

If the Republicans, who are betting everything on him, want to give him a present for his birthday, they ought to get him some better candidates for Congress.

For, while his dream is the Presidency, his nightmare is that he should have to exercise the terrible responsibilities of that office with a Congress controlled by his Democratic enemies.

Eisenhower could do it. He is a natural man, who blurts out what he thinks, who never seems to be holding back in private conversation.

Even the Democrats who think he is a terrible President insist he is a wonderful human being. So they cooperate with him enough to keep things going.

In an era of divided government—it is almost a mathematical impossibility for the Democrats to lose the Senate in the 1960 election—this is Nixon's primary problem. For he has to win not only the Presidency but the personal confidence of his colleagues in the Congress, including the Democrats, and at 47 that is going to be quite a job.

MARCH 3, 1960
KENNEDY, NIXON BOTH SET MARKS

Senator Gets 42,969 Votes in New Hampshire—Vice President Gains 65,077

By JOHN H. FENTON

Special to The New York Times.

CONCORD, N.H., March 9—Senator John F. Kennedy emerged today from the New Hampshire primary with the endorsement of 42,969 Democrats who hope to see him win the Presidential nomination.

This gave him a strong hand for continuing with his next primary in Wisconsin April 5.

At the same time 65,077 Republicans similarly made known their preference for Vice President Nixon as their candidate in the first of sixteen primaries in the nation this year.

Both men set individual records on the basis of unofficial complete returns. How the total vote compares with

the record of 136,000 set in 1952 will be known when the official results are announced Friday by the Secretary of State's office.

Senator Kennedy also substantially narrowed the traditional gap of two-to-one Republican superiority in this state. The margin yesterday was about 3 to 2.

The consensus of observers was that Senator Kennedy had benefited chiefly from the heavy turnout, which was in considerable measure due to improved party organizations.

• •

PRELUDE TO THE DEMOCRATIC NOMINATIONS

The Democratic Party met in Los Angeles to write the party platform and select its candidates for the 1960 election. Within the party's tenuous coalition, the early actions of the convention signaled a transition of power from southern conservatives to northern liberals. As Democrats adopted—over southern resistance—the strongest civil rights platform seen in any campaign, Sen. Lyndon Johnson of Texas held his regional allies loyal to the party.

JULY 13, 1960
PLATFORM WINS AFTER CLASHES ON CIVIL RIGHTS

SOUTH THE LOSER

Democrats Pledge to End Discrimination—Ask Big Budget

By W. H. LAWRENCE

Special to The New York Times.

LOS ANGELES, July 12—The Democratic National Convention overrode Southern protests tonight to adopt a "big-budget" platform that included the strongest civil-rights plank in party history.

The civil rights pledge to utilize Federal powers to end all forms of discrimination because of race, creed or color was aimed at attracting to the Democratic ticket the largest possible Northern Negro vote in November.

Although ten Southern states dissented, they did not threaten a walkout. However, there were warnings that the strong language might endanger Democratic victories below the Mason-Dixon Line.

Ready for Nomination

Approval of the platform by voice vote cleared the way for the convention to nominate tomorrow its Presidential candidate.

All signs still pointed to an early-ballot victory for Senator John F. Kennedy of Massachusetts. This remained true despite eleventh-hour efforts for Senator Lyndon B. Johnson of Texas, Adlai E. Stevenson of Illinois, and Senator Stuart Symington of Missouri.

JULY 13, 1960
10 SOUTHERN STATES WAGE BITTER FIGHT

By CLAUDE SITTON

Special to The New York Times.

LOS ANGELES, July 12—Ten Southern states fought in vain tonight to prevent the Democratic National Convention from adopting the toughest civil rights platform plank in party history.

Six of the region's orators mounted the flag-bedecked platform to support a minority report from the Platform Committee that damned the proposals as an effort to bring about "government-enforced social equality."

To a mixed chorus of boos and cheers, they warned that the plank might cost the party's Presidential nominee the support of the South in the November elections. Then they returned to their seats with never a threat to walk out of the convention as some of the region's delegations did in 1948, an action that triggered the abortive Dixiecrat revolt.

Following a round of speeches in support of the civil rights proposals, the convention adopted them by voice vote. The Southerners did not press for a roll-call because as one of their leaders said, "we don't want the world to know how badly we are beaten."

The provisions were termed a "calculated effort which is being made by the radicals of both political parties" to force the South to desert the Democrats.

As to recommendations of Federal economic aid, the report declared:

"We the undersigned are here to say that the states of the South will not be bribed with 'technical and financial assistance,' held out as bait in this platform, into sacrificing their children upon the altar of political expediency."

Then the Southerners asked:

"Will the delegates to this convention lead their party to defeat with the halter of a platform framed upon the insistence of a racial wing of our party—a platform pledging our party to the support of legislation which not twice but three times has been rejected by this very party?"

THE DEMOCRATIC NOMINEES

The contest for the Democratic presidential nomination centered on two candidates, front-runner John Kennedy and Lyndon Johnson, the Senate majority leader. Kennedy had won seven primaries, emerging as the clear popular favorite, especially among liberals, while conservatives embraced Johnson. Kennedy scored a narrow first-ballot nomination and then stunned the party by selecting Johnson as his vice-presidential running mate. Rumors circulated that the offer to Johnson was intended to be merely a gesture, but the Texan had accepted at the last minute, forcing JFK's endorsement.

JULY 14, 1960
KENNEDY NOMINATED ON THE FIRST BALLOT; OVERWHELMS JOHNSON BY 806 VOTES TO 409

LONG DRIVE WINS

Wyoming's Vote Puts Bostonian Over Top Before Acclamation

By W. H. LAWRENCE

Special to The New York Times.

LOS ANGELES, Thursday, July 14—Senator John F. Kennedy smashed his way to a first-ballot Presidential nomination at the Democratic National Convention last night and won the right to oppose Vice President Nixon in November.

The 43-year-old Massachusetts Senator overwhelmed his opposition, piling up 806 votes to 409 ballots for his nearest rival, Senator Lyndon B. Johnson of Texas, the Senate majority leader. Senator Kennedy's victory came just before 11 o'clock last night [2 A. M. Thursday, New York time].

Then the convention made it unanimous on motion of Gov. James T. Blair Jr. of Missouri, who had placed Senator Stuart Symington of Missouri in nomination.

'We Shall Win'

Senator Kennedy, appearing before the shouting convention early today, pledged he would carry the fight to the country in the fall "and we shall win."

He thanked his defeated rivals for their generosity and appealed to all of their backers to keep the party strong and united in a tremendously important election. He spoke directly of Senators Johnson and Symington and the favorite sons, but made no reference to Adlai E. Stevenson.

The third session of the national convention adjourned after his speech. The next session will convene at 5 P. M. today.

Little Wyoming, well down the roll-call, provided the decisive fifteen votes that gave victory to Senator Kennedy. Two favorite-son states, Minnesota and New Jersey, waited in vain to give the on-rushing Kennedy bandwagon the final shove.

When Wyoming came in with its vote, the Kennedy total had mounted to 765 votes, or four more than the 761 votes required for nomination.

It was a tremendous victory for Senator Kennedy. Mr. Johnson, the Senate majority leader, had fought desperately to reverse a Kennedy tide that had been running for months. But Senator Johnson quickly telephoned his congratulations to Senator Kennedy and forecast his election in November.

Senator Kennedy, who chose the tough preferential primary road to victory, had demonstrated to the party's big state leaders that he could win votes.

He reasoned that only through the primaries could he, as a Roman Catholic, remove the lingering fear of party leaders that he was destined for the same kind of defeat suffered by former Gov. Alfred E. Smith of New York, a Catholic, in 1928.

The convention will assemble today to ratify Senator Kennedy's choice of a Vice-Presidential running mate. Key names under consideration are those of Senator Symington, Gov. Orville L. Freeman of Minnesota and Senator Henry M. Jackson of Washington.

JULY 15, 1960
JOHNSON IS NOMINATED FOR VICE PRESIDENT; KENNEDY PICKS HIM TO PLACATE THE SOUTH

CHOICE A SURPRISE

Senator Is Selected By Acclamation—Calls for Unity

By W. H. LAWRENCE

Special to The New York Times.

LOS ANGELES, July 14—Senator Lyndon B. Johnson of Texas was nominated for Vice President tonight by the Democratic National Convention as Senator John F. Kennedy's running mate.

Senator Johnson's was the only name placed in nomination. At 9:10 P. M. [12:10 A. M. Friday New York time] the convention suspended its rules and nominated him by acclamation. On a voice vote the roar of ayes far exceeded in volume the negative votes.

The Kennedy-Johnson ticket was ready to do battle with the Republican ticket, which will be headed by Vice President Nixon and will be chosen at the Republican National Convention opening July 25 in Chicago.

Kennedy's Choice

Senator Johnson was nominated on the recommendation of the Massachusetts Senator. Senator Kennedy overrode protests by labor and Northern liberals in the surprise move in naming the Senate majority leader for Vice President. The Texan's acceptance of second place was equally surprising.

Senator Kennedy, a Roman Catholic, moved boldly to win party unity and new strength below the Mason-Dixon Line by choosing the Texan, a Protestant, for his running mate.

The Presidential nominee is 43 years old, and his running mate is 51.

Until yesterday, they were bitter rivals for the Presidency. Senator Kennedy smashed to a first-ballot victory, polling 806 votes to 409 for Senator Johnson.

Convention Ends Today

Tomorrow, the two will accept their nominations formally at an open-air rally in the Coliseum, which seats more than 100,000 persons. That event formally ends the convention.

The Johnson choice was far from universally popular, but it satisfied the overwhelming majority of the delegates. As practical politicians, most leaders believed that Senator Johnson would add more strength to the Democratic ticket in the South than he would hurt it in the North. The choice was particularly offensive to leaders of Americans for Democratic Action. Negro leaders were divided, some favoring and some opposing Senator Johnson.

JULY 17, 1960
EDITORIAL
KENNEDY AND JOHNSON

The Democratic ticket of Kennedy and Johnson is a formidable one, probably the strongest vote-getting combination possible within the party, and certainly composed of two of the shrewdest political strategists in this nation.

Supremely "balanced" in the name of party unity, it is a coldly logical ticket—so logical that almost no one expected it would turn out in exactly this way. Senator Kennedy, whose appeal was directed primarily to the liberal, urban, industrialized centers of the North, deliberately chose as his running-mate the majority leader,

candidate of the conservative elements of the party in the South. While the Democratic left wing is unhappy over Mr. Johnson's selection as blurring the liberal aura of both the Kennedy nomination and the party platform, Mr. Johnson's presence on the ticket may have the practical effect of keeping Texas and other Southern and border states in the Democratic column next November.

The fact is that on matters of public policy the two nominees are not at opposite ends of the political spectrum, as their popular image has been frequently, though erroneously, painted—most recently by some of the very liberals who deserted Mr. Stevenson in favor of Mr. Kennedy. The junior Senator from Massachusetts is—platform or no platform—a middle-of-the-roader with a distinctly liberal cast, while the senior Senator from Texas is a middle-of-the-roader with a slightly conservative one. It is as much nonsense to think of John Kennedy as a flaming liberal—in fact it is difficult to think of this smoothly pragmatic young man as flaming at all—as it is nonsense to think of Lyndon Johnson as a dark reactionary.

Both are essentially political animals, just as Mr. Nixon is; but this does not mean that they are without political courage. Mr. Kennedy has, in fact, a laudable record of independence of judgment as displayed during his years in Congress; and if he failed on the major issue of McCarthy—as did so many of his colleagues—he has spoken up with admirable forthrightness on many other issues of lesser importance. For all his youth and attractiveness, his quality of cool detachment may make him a less sympathetic figure than many previous candidates, both successful and unsuccessful; but he is clearly a man of decision, perspicacity, energy and intelligence—all of which are qualities highly desirable in the White House.

As Vice President, Senator Johnson would merely shift his seat in the Senate from the floor to the rostrum. Mr. Johnson has, in fact, nothing to lose in this election. He is certain to be re-elected majority leader if he is defeated for Vice President; if not, he will surely be in practice his own majority leader, acting from the Vice President's chair. Senator Johnson is a man of great ability, more interested in political effectiveness than in political philosophy, but not without ideas. He was one of the first Senators to recognize the need for greater American concern over the problems of space exploration; he was more responsible than any other man for getting not one but two civil rights bills through the Congress; he has strongly supported mutual security, though he has not shown a detailed interest in the intricacies of foreign policy. He is essentially a political manager; and that will doubtless be the job to which he will continue to devote himself on Capitol Hill whether or not he becomes Vice President of the United States.

• •

Prelude to the Republican Nominations

The Republican Party met several weeks after the Democrats. Vice President Richard Nixon was the clear choice for president, but the platform was in dispute. Two leading figures, New York governor Nelson Rockefeller and Arizona senator Barry Goldwater, represented vastly different ideologies within the party. To avoid a disruptive convention fight, Nixon compromised on the party platform to appease Rockefeller, considered the more powerful rival.

JULY 2, 1960
ROCKEFELLER HINTS PLATFORM FIGHT; G.O.P. IS ALARMED
Threat of Floor Battle Over Foreign Policy Imperils Nixon Hopes for Unity
By LEO EGAN
Special to The New York Times.

CHICAGO, July 22—The tension between Vice President Nixon and Governor Rockefeller on the eve of the Republican National Convention began to alarm some leading Republicans today.

Their concern was touched off by new pressures brought by Mr. Rockefeller to get a party platform to his liking.

Some of the Governor's supporters were suggesting privately that Mr. Rockefeller might upset Mr. Nixon's hopes for a "peace and harmony" convention by leading a floor fight to seek modifications of the Platform Committee's recommendations.

Although not convinced that Mr. Rockefeller would actually do so, some of Mr. Nixon's supporters were reported considering an appeal to President Eisenhower to mediate the differences between the Vice President and the New York Governor.

An Accord Held Possible

Reports were current here tonight that Mr. Nixon and Mr. Rockefeller may have some direct contacts over the week-end in an effort to arrive at an understanding.

There has been no direct contact between the two for a period of two weeks. They have been in touch with each other through representatives.

The convention opens here Monday. Its principal committees, including the platform group, have been at work this week.

JULY 24, 1960
SECRET NIXON-ROCKEFELLER TALKS DRAFT A BASIC PLATFORM ACCORD; RULE OUT GOVERNOR FOR 2D PLACE

8-HOUR MEETING

Vice President Takes Initiative in Setting Up Session Here

By WILLIAM M. BLAIR.

Special to The New York Times.

CHICAGO, July 23—Vice President Nixon and Governor Rockefeller of New York have fashioned the core of the Republican platform in an extraordinary face-to-face meeting.

They produced a set of "basic positions" on major foreign and domestic affairs during their eight-hour night conference in the Governor's Fifth Avenue apartment in New York last night and early today.

The results of their meeting were embodied in a long statement issued in Mr. Rockefeller's name and subsequently subscribed to by Mr. Nixon.

Words of Agreement

Mr. Rockefeller said the statement constituted "the basic positions for which I have been fighting." Mr. Nixon said it "defines our areas of agreement."

The ambiguity of the language in the Governor's statement indicated that he and Mr. Nixon still had differences over details of policies and how to put those policies into effect. This was later confirmed by Mr. Nixon in Washington.

[The Republican Platform Committee declared unanimously late Saturday night, according to The Associated Press, that while it welcomed suggestions such as those from Governor Rockefeller and Vice President Nixon, the committee and the convention would write the platform.].

The agreement removed several obstacles confronting platform drafters but immediately caused trouble in the panel writing a civil rights plank. Southerners and conservatives on the civil rights subcommittee protested that Mr. Nixon had abandoned his "moderate" position and bowed to Mr. Rockefeller's "ultra-liberal" stand.

JULY 24, 1960
EDITORIAL
THE TRUCE OF FIFTH AVENUE, OR MORNINGSIDE REVISITED

By JAMES RESTON

CHICAGO, July 23—Gov. Nelson Rockefeller of New York has been appeased by Vice President Nixon but unless he changes his mind at the last minute he has not been captured. He has influenced and improved the Republican platform but he has not joined the Republican ticket. A short-run compromise has avoided

a dramatic attack by Rockefeller in the convention before a vast television audience, but in the long run a compromise was probably not enough either for Mr. Nixon or Mr. Rockefeller.

What wins elections are the votes of the states in the electoral college, not the words in the party platform.

Senator Kennedy captured Senator Johnson as the Democratic Vice-Presidential nominee in Los Angeles, and in the process probably captured the twenty-four electoral college votes of Texas and the votes of several other Southern states.

The Vice President did very well by accepting some platform language that may mean something or nothing. He was bold enough and self-effacing enough to make the first personal move to arrange a reconciliation and this was not easy, because he was caught between President Eisenhower on the right and Governor Rockefeller on the left. But this was not enough.

For what Mr. Nixon really wanted was not Rockefeller but New York's forty-five electoral votes, not merely Rockefeller's words but Rockefeller's votes among the anti-Kennedy Democrats and independents. His hope was that a reconciliation on the platform would lead to a Nixon-Rockefeller alliance, but all he got was a truce.

The Words vs. the Spirit

The Republican Convention will take the words of the Rockefeller communiqué of today, even with the knowledge that they were drafted here in Chicago by Emmet Hughes, one of Governor Rockefeller's aides.

They will do so to avoid letting Rockefeller dramatize the party conflict before the whole nation on the convention floor, but it does not follow that they are any more eager today than they were yesterday to "lead toward the formation of confederations in the North Atlantic community" or do many of the other things Governor Rockefeller put into the communiqué.

Thus neither the words of the Republican platform nor the words of the Democratic platform represent the true spirit of the two parties. Both platforms reach leftward beyond the candidates' grasp, to the dismay of the Southern Democrats and the Northern conservatives.

The candidates have been reconciled, but the split in both parties remains, and even the personal reconciliations are different. For the Kennedy-Johnson reconciliation brings both to the center of political action in the campaign, whereas the Nixon-Rockefeller conciliation leaves Rockefeller as the lonesome end out of the main scrimmage.

• •

THE REPUBLICAN NOMINATIONS

The Republican Party quickly nominated Richard Nixon for president. Nixon then selected Henry Cabot Lodge as his vice-presidential running mate. Lodge had served as a senator from Massachusetts before being defeated for reelection by John Kennedy in 1952. He then served as the U. S. ambassador to the United Nations. His nomination completed the candidacies of four men from the Senate, pointing to the rising importance of foreign policy in national politics.

JULY 28, 1960
NIXON IS GIVEN NOMINATION BY ACCLAMATION AFTER GOLDWATER GETS 10 LOUISIANA VOTES; CANDIDATE PICKS LODGE FOR SECOND PLACE

UNITY IS STRESSED

Goldwater Withdraws and Asks Backing for the Nominee

By W. H. LAWRENCE

Special to The New York Times.

CHICAGO, Thursday, July 28—Vice President Richard M. Nixon swept to a first-ballot Republican Presidential nomination last night and the right to face Democratic Senator John F. Kennedy in the November election.

Early today, Mr. Nixon chose Henry Cabot Lodge, chief United States delegate to the United Nations, as his Vice-Presidential running mate.

Mr. Nixon received 1,321 votes on the polling of state delegations. Senator Barry Goldwater of Arizona received ten votes, cast by members of the twenty-six-vote Louisiana delegation even after the Arizonan had asked withdrawal of his name from consideration.

At the end of the roll-call, Louisiana moved to make Mr. Nixon's choice unanimous, but balked at changing its ten votes from the Goldwater to the Nixon column without a poll. When the roll-call vote was announced as 1,321 to 10, the Arizona delegation then moved to make the nomination unanimous, and this was done by acclamation.

Goldwater Asks Unity

The convention decision pits the 47-year-old Vice President against the 43-year-old Senator from Massachusetts. Mr. Nixon is the first Vice President in the history of the modern two-party system to win a Presidential nomination in his own right.

Senator Goldwater made the dramatic appearance of the night, calling upon all conservatives to back Mr. Nixon in November and avoid any party split or stay-at-home nonvoting attitude that would help Democrats "dedicated to the destruction of this country."

Withdrawing his own name from consideration for the Presidency, the Arizona Senator, an avowed conservative, said he had been campaigning for Mr. Nixon's nomination for the last six years and would fight for his election in November.

Lecture to Conservatives

"Let us put our shoulders to the wheel of Dick Nixon and push him over across the line," Senator Goldwater said.

He lectured conservatives sternly, telling them they must "grow up" and get to work "if we want to take this party back some day—and I think we can."

JULY 29, 1960
EDITORIAL
THE VICE-PRESIDENCY

In American politics a formula often employed in choosing a candidate for the Vice-Presidency has been to "balance" the ticket ideologically, in the hope of appealing simultaneously to voters holding opposite points of view. With this formula in mind, Mr. Nixon was offered advice from various quarters in Chicago. One group would have had him choose a candidate from the border states, to offset and soften the civil rights sections of the party's platform. Another group recommended the choice of a conservative like Senator Goldwater. A third group suggested a Middle Westerner, either to balance the strongly internationalist position taken in the platform or to strengthen the party's appeal in the farm belt.

Mr. Nixon has taken none of this advice. In Henry Cabot Lodge he has chosen—and the convention has promptly ratified his choice—an urbanite, a liberal and an internationalist.

Mr. Lodge belongs clearly among the "modernists" in the spectrum of varying views which represent the composite thinking of the Republican party. He is a man of courage, wit and resourcefulness who served creditably in the Senate and, more recently, and with more distinction, in view of the larger opportunity, as United States Ambassador to the United Nations. No doubt his success in the latter role was a strong consideration in determining his choice for the Vice-Presidential nomination, since he has handled with shrewdness and skill his end of the continuing debate with the spokesmen of Soviet Russia and since American relations with Soviet Russia seem certain to play a prominent part in this year's election campaign.

As the saying goes, Mr. Lodge has "stood up" to the Russians. But he has been no mere fist-pounder. He has sought diligently and in good faith to reach agreement where agreement of any kind was possible. His experience and his character bring strength to his party's ticket.

THE DEBATES

In a major campaign innovation, John Kennedy and Richard Nixon met four times in televised debates. The joint appearances began cordially, but grew progressively more contentious as election day approached. The debates provided voters a rare glimpse into the candidates' competing ideologies and personalities, but the forums would not recur for nearly two decades.

Republican vice president Richard M. Nixon listens as Sen. John F. Kennedy, the Democratic presidential nominee, makes a point during a live broadcast from a New York television studio of their fourth presidential debate on Oct. 21, 1960. The candidates' respective performances in this debate are often credited with helping lift Kennedy to victory in the general election.

Source: AP Images

SEPTEMBER 27, 1960
EXCHANGE IS CALM

Sharp Retorts Are Few as Candidates Meet Face to Face
By RUSSELL BAKER
Special to The New York Times.

CHICAGO. Sept. 26—Vice President Nixon and Senator John F. Kennedy argued genteelly tonight in history's first nationally televised debate between Presidential candidates.

The two men, confronting each other in a Chicago television studio, centered their argument on which candidate and which party offered the nation the best means for spurring United States growth in an era of international peril. . . .

In one of the sharper exchanges of the hour-long encounter, Mr. Nixon charged that the Democratic domestic program advanced by Senator Kennedy would cost the taxpayer from $13,200,000,000 to $18,000,000,000.

This meant, Mr. Nixon contended, that "either he will have to raise taxes or you have to unbalance the budget."

Unbalancing the budget, he went on, would mean another period of inflation and a consequent "blow" to the country's aged living on pension income.

"That," declared Senator Kennedy, in one of the evening's few shows of incipient heat, "is wholly wrong, wholly in error." Mr. Nixon, he said, was attempting to create the impression that he was "in favor of unbalancing the budget."

In fact, Mr. Kennedy contended, many of his programs for such things as medical care for the aged, natural resources development, Federal assistance to school construction and teachers salaries could be financed without undue burden on the taxpayer if his policies for increasing the rate of economic growth were adopted.

"I don't believe in big government, but I believe in effective government," Mr. Kennedy said. "I think we can do a better job. I think we are going to have to do a better job."

OCTOBER 8, 1960
EXCHANGES SHARP

Senator Is Accused of 'Woolly Thinking'—He, Too, Is Tough

By RUSSELL BAKER

Special to The New York Times.

WASHINGTON, Oct, 7—Vice President Nixon and Senator John F. Kennedy raised the campaign temperature tonight, clashing sharply on foreign policy and civil rights in the second of their nation-wide television debates.

The question of who won will have to await the surveys of voters, but the equally nagging question for Republicans—of how Mr. Nixon would "project" after his unhappy appearance in the first debate—was answered immediately. The Vice President did not have the thin, emaciated appearance that worried Republicans across the nation during the first debate.

One of the high points of tonight's debate was a direct conflict between the Presidential candidates over policy for dealing with the islands of Quemoy and Matsu off the Chinese mainland.

Criticizes Vagueness

Mr. Kennedy took the position that the islands were militarily worthless and, lying virtually in a harbor on the Communist mainland, were indefensible.

Moreover, he said, Administration vagueness about whether the islands would be defended in case of Communist attack created a dangerous uncertainty for the Chinese about this country's intentions. While Taiwan (Formosa) should certainly be defended, he indicated, he favored a pull-back from Quemoy and Matsu by the Chinese Nationalists.

Mr. Nixon denounced this as "the same kind of woolly thinking that led to disaster in Korea." He insisted that the islands should be held. "These two islands are in the area of freedom," he said. To give them up, he argued, would only encourage the Communists to press their drive on Taiwan.

The question was not of "two tiny pieces of real estate," he said, but a matter of principle.

> At one point, in a voice oozing sarcasm, Mr. Kennedy said: 'I always have difficulty recognizing my positions when they're stated by the Vice President.'

OCTOBER 14, 1960
EXCHANGE BITTER

Vice President Takes a Softer Position on Defending Islands

By RUSSELL BAKER

Senator John F. Kennedy and Vice President Nixon bitterly accused each other before a national television audience last night of advocating policies on Quemoy and Matsu that would lead to war.

While the rhetorical temperature of the third debate was torrid, the actual policy difference between the two Presidential candidates appeared to have narrowed considerably. Mr. Nixon pulled back from the strong position he took last week.

Debate over Quemoy and Matsu, which both candidates have decided to make a major issue of the campaign, dominated the program.

It was not entirely a foreign policy fight, however. In other exchanges the candidates clashed on such domestic issues as labor legislation, farm policy, spending, the costs of their respective proposals, economic growth and the 27½ per cent depletion allowance given oil and gas producers.

Arbitration Disputed

The clash on labor arose from Mr. Nixon's assertion that Senator Kennedy favored compulsory arbitration of major disputes. Mr. Kennedy denied vehemently that this was his position.

Last week the Vice President said that defending the two islands, situated four and five miles off the Chinese mainland, was a matter of "principle" because no territory "in the area of freedom" should be surrendered.

In last night's hour-long debate he was much less categorical. He suggested that Quemoy and Matsu would be defended if an attack upon them were "a prelude to an attack on Formosa [Taiwan]." This is essentially the position taken by the Eisenhower Administration since 1954.

Senator Kennedy sought to remind the audience that this was not the position that Mr. Nixon took in their television debate last Friday. Mr. Kennedy, who favors defending Taiwan against Communist attack, said "Mr. Nixon suggests the United States should go to war if these two islands are attacked."

If a Communist attack were aimed at Taiwan, Mr. Kennedy said, the question of Quemoy and Matsu would be academic because the country would be at war in any event, honoring its commitment to Taiwan.

'Extending Commitment'

"He's indicating that we should fight for these islands come what may, because they are, to quote his words, 'in the area of freedom,'" Mr. Kennedy said. "He didn't take that position on Tibet. He didn't take that position on Hungary * * * He's extending the Administration's commitment."

Throughout the hour, the candidates reached a pitch of acrimony unmatched in either of their two previous encounters. Time and again the nation's living rooms were filled with such phrases as "I resent," "He simply doesn't know what he's talking about" and "that's untrue."

At one point, in a voice oozing sarcasm, Mr. Kennedy said:

"I always have difficulty recognizing my positions when they're stated by the Vice President."

Mr. Nixon, countering the Senator's complaints of misrepresentation, announced that he would issue a "white paper" after the program documenting Mr. Kennedy's position in Mr. Kennedy's own language.

OCTOBER 22, 1960
CHARGES TRADED

Most Heated Dispute Concerns Methods of Dealing With Castro

By RUSSELL BAKER

Vice President Nixon and Senator John F. Kennedy clashed before a national television audience last night over United States policy toward Cuba and the Chinese offshore islands of Quemoy and Matsu.

In one of the sharpest exchanges of their fourth debate, which seemed comparatively tepid after the last two meetings, Mr. Nixon called Senator Kennedy's proposals for dealing with Premier Fidel Castro's regime in Cuba "probably the most dangerously irresponsible that he's made in the course of this campaign."

If carried out, the Vice President said, his rival's policies would probably cost this country "all our friends in Latin America," lead to its condemnation in the United Nations and produce a "civil war" in Cuba, with the Soviet Union probably involved.

Mr. Kennedy replied that the Nixon proposal for "quarantining" Cuba through economic sanctions would be useless because the Administration did not have the cooperation of other Latin-American and European states in the effort to put economic pressure on the Castro Government.

Debate Nuclear Tests

These were the other major points as the candidates discussed foreign policy in the hour-long program:

• Nuclear testing. Mr. Nixon proposed making a decision before Jan. 1 for resuming nuclear testing underground unless Moscow indicated it was ready to move toward agreement. Senator Kennedy proposed "one last effort" after the next President takes office to reach a testing agreement with the Russians. If that failed, he said, tests should be resumed underground or in outer space.

• United States prestige. Mr. Nixon, accusing Senator Kennedy of contributing to a decline in American prestige, said his opponent was "dead wrong" in picturing the country as "standing still." Diplomatically, in relative military strength and in economic strength, Mr. Kennedy replied, this country is "standing still."

- Summit meetings. Mr. Nixon said that there should be no further meetings with Premier Khrushchev unless there was reasonable assurance that the Premier was willing to negotiate seriously on agenda points on which there was some likelihood of agreement. Mr. Kennedy said he would not participate in a summit conference unless there was some indication that agreement was possible on Berlin, outer space, general disarmament or nuclear testing.

• •

Unsettled Bases

Traditional party bases fractured during the 1960 election, sending the candidates deeper into "enemy territory." The solid Democratic South showed cracks, partially because of the civil rights issue and partially because of hostility toward Kennedy's Catholicism. In a parallel shift, the once-Republican Northeast showed unusual enthusiasm for the region's native son.

AUGUST 21, 1960
NIXON TRIP SOUTH DISTURBS HIS FOES
Welcome Clouds Democratic Outlook—North Carolina Held No Longer 'Safe'
Special to The New York Times.

RALEIGH, N.C., Aug. 20—The success of Vice President Nixon's first campaign appearance in the South has raised a cloud of doubt over Democratic hopes in the region.

The Republican Presidential candidate and his wife, in a four-hour visit to Greensboro, saw or were seen by some 15,000 persons. The populous Piedmont section gave him an enthusiastic welcome.

Democrats readily conceded that North Carolina was no longer "safe" for Mr. Nixon's opponent, Senator John F. Kennedy. They look with concern on other Southern states as well.

This state has not voted Republican in a Presidential race since it favored former President Hoover over Alfred E. Smith in 1928. A growing conservative trend has been noticeable in national elections, however. Adlai E. Stevenson carried the state against President Eisenhower by no more than 15,000 votes in 1956.

The Nixon welcome, some observers said, destroyed a popular theory that General Eisenhower's showing in 1952 and 1956 represented nothing more than support for a national hero.

Pro Nixon sentiment extends far beyond the group that packed Greensboro's War Memorial Coliseum Wednesday night for "doughnuts and coffee with Pat and Dick." This opinion was voiced by political leaders, editors and the man in the street following the Vice President's departure.

"He made a good impression here," asserted a Greensboro shopkeeper, who declined to have his name used. "I like Nixon for one reason: He's got guts. He's going to tell that louse over there in Russia where to go."

A housewife, Mrs. Robert L. Jones of Greensboro, commented that "my husband is a Democrat but I think he's going to vote Republican."

She and a friend, Mrs. Jan Christopher, agreed that everyone they had talked to was "real pleased" with Mr. Nixon's speech.

William D. Snider, associate editor of The Greensboro Daily News, called the Vice President "articulate and well-informed." He added:

"On any question he provides so many alternatives that his listeners can choose the one they like best. He is a sort of political 'Readers Digest.' "

A Burlington resident, Delmar R. Kirkendall, said he favored Mr. Kennedy.

"But a lot of folks think the Pope will be running things if he gets elected," he added.

Most people with whom the campaign was discussed in a two-day swing through the Piedmont cited the Senator's Roman Catholic faith as the chief issue.

"I hate to say it," observed a Greensboro lawyer, who asked that he not be identified, "but I believe it's worse than when Al Smith ran—and we don't have Tammany and prohibition to worry about." He said he would vote for Mr. Kennedy.

SEPTEMBER 3, 1960
KENNEDY CANVASSES NEW ENGLAND AREA; GREETED BY THRONGS

By W. H. LAWRENCE

Special to The New York Times.

PORTLAND, Me., Sept. 2—Senator John F. Kennedy barnstormed across New England today. He advocated protection for the textile and shoe industries as part of a broad program of economic revival.

The Democratic Presidential nominee thereby indicated some deviation from the free-trade policies that have dominated his party's thinking since the earliest days of President Roosevelt's New Deal.

His thrust into normally Republican New Hampshire and Maine was labeled by him as the beginning of a hard, wide-ranging campaign. Now that Congress has adjourned it will continue almost without let-up until the election on Nov. 8.

Tries to Counter G. O. P.

As a New Englander, the Massachusetts Senator was attempting to stir Democratic enthusiasm in a Republican area. Thus he hoped to set up a counter-irritant to manifestations favorable to Vice President Nixon in sections of the usually Democratic South.

His speeches to enthusiastic crowds were brief and sectional for the most part, with only occasional passages of national interest.

To an airport rally at Manchester, N.H., he sounded the protectionist note for the textile and shoe industries. These have been slumping in this area because of both foreign competition and the movement of factories to the South, where cheaper labor and power are available. He discarded a prepared text in which he had listed "full use of valuable weapons against excessive imports." Instead he declared flatly:

"We can protect our textile and shoe industries." On the northernmost tip of Maine, at Presque Isle, a crowd of several thousand stayed to hear Senator Kennedy despite the three heavy rainstorms that preceded his arrival.

Maine politicians were astounded. Senator Edmund S. Muskie, Maine Democrat, called it the biggest political crowd in the history of Aroostook County.

Here the Senator proclaimed the "basic issue" of the campaign, one that transcended both parties, to be whether the "future" would belong to the Communist world and the "past" would belong to the United States and its allies.

It was to reverse this trend toward the Soviet Union, he declared, that he found it necessary to criticize what he called weaknesses of the Eisenhower Administration in its foreign and national security policies. He cited a recent Gallup poll of ten foreign countries where he said a majority indicated a belief that by 1970 the Soviet Union would be stronger than the United States in science and in military strength.

"That is what we are fighting against," Senator Kennedy said.

Maine newsmen estimated the Presque Isle crowd at 8,000 to 9,000.

The next stop, Bangor, attracted a crowd of more than 5,000 to the fairgrounds despite threatening skies and the rain that fell while Senator Kennedy was speaking.

The enthusiasm of the crowds moved him to remark that he was happy to leave behind the "dust" of Washington, an obvious reference to his pleasure in the fact that the reconvened session of the Congress had quit.

In Portland, Senator Kennedy drew a flood-lighted stadium crowd of 5,000 to 6,000, according to police estimates. Maine newsmen said Vice President Nixon's crowd in the same stadium Aug. 13 totaled about 3,500.

Catholicism

Religion became a major focus of the 1960 campaign, along with substantive issues such as civil rights and foreign policy. Kennedy, the first Catholic nominee since 1928, was battered by defamatory campaign flyers insinuating that his loyalty as president would be to the pope, rather than to America. Kennedy responded most forcefully in Houston, Texas, before a hostile ministerial conference. Many observers expected the final vote to hinge on religious divisions.

SEPTEMBER 14, 1960
EDITORIAL
THE RELIGIOUS ISSUE

The issue of Senator John F. Kennedy's Roman Catholic religion threatens to dominate the Presidential campaign; and if it does, the harm will be irreparable to this country at home and abroad.

The discussion has been rising in crescendo ever since last fall, when Mr. Kennedy's nomination became increasingly likely. The more that has been published about the question, the more it has been discussed. It has, we trust, now reached its climax; and in view of Mr. Kennedy's frank and forthright answers it will, we hope, now fade away. There are, as Mr. Kennedy so correctly pointed out, "far more critical issues in the 1960 election * * * and they are not religious issues."

Yet Senator Kennedy has recognized from the outset that there are legitimate questions rising not from bigotry nor bias but from an honest attempt to appraise his personal position as an individual in the light of the political position frequently attributed to the hierarchy of his church as an institution. As a recent statement of a group of one hundred churchmen and scholars declared, "The bearing of the religious views of any candidate of any party upon his decisions in public office is a public matter."

Mr. Kennedy frames the legitimate question this way, and we do not think it could be framed in better terms: "Would you, as President of the United States, be responsive in any way to ecclesiastical pressures or obligations of any kind that might in any fashion influence or interfere with your conduct of that office in the national interest?" And Mr. Kennedy replies: "I have answered that question many times. My answer was, and is, 'No.' "

He has stated unequivocally: "I believe in an America where separation of church and state is absolute."

He has stated: "I believe in an America where * * * no church or church school is granted any public funds or political preference," and as recently as this year he has voted accordingly.

He has stated: "I am flatly opposed to appointment of an Ambassador to the Vatican."

He has stated, on the question of extending birth-control aid abroad: "I would not think it wise for the United States to refuse assistance to a country which is pursuing a policy it feels to be in its own best interest." This is a better statement on the subject than President Eisenhower's.

He has stated: "I believe in freedom of conscience," and in the propagation by "any faith without any limitations by the power of the state or encouragement by the power of the state."

He has stated, and his record as a Senator substantiates him: "No one can direct me in the fulfillment of my duties as a public official under the United States Constitution."

Finally, he has stated: "I do not speak for my church on public matters—and the church does not speak for me."

What more could Senator Kennedy possibly say to clarify his divorcement from any real or imputed political stand of the Catholic Church in this or any other country? How could he be more explicit or more positive? Why is he not right in insisting that to oppose him as a Catholic would now be to establish an arbitrary religious test for the Presidency that not only is disregarded for every other public office, including Chief Justice, Senator, Governor, but also is directly violative of Article VI of the Constitution of the United States and the most basic principles on which our democracy rests?

In the light of his own statements Senator Kennedy's religious affiliation is irrelevant to his fitness for the Presidency. No American will be doing his duty if he votes against him because he is a Catholic, exactly as no American will be doing his duty if he votes for him because he is a Catholic.

OCTOBER 16, 1960
VAST ANTI-CATHOLIC DRIVE IS SLATED BEFORE ELECTION
By JOHN WICKLEIN

Many conservative Protestant churchmen are planning mass distribution of anti-Catholic literature in the last ten days of the Presidential campaign in a bid to defeat Senator John F. Kennedy. The mailings and handouts will be spurred by sermons and rallies on Reformation Sunday, Oct. 30, when Protestant feeling is at its highest.

"Five days before the election," said Harvey H. Springer, the "cowboy evangelist" of the Rockies, "I'm releasing 1,500,000 volunteer workers to call on voters and give them our literature on Kennedy. I have a secret little letter that I think is going to defeat him."

His optimism is matched only by his enthusiasm for his goal: to keep any Roman Catholic from being elected President of the United States—ever.

Many Protestants Irked

Others in the religious mail campaign are more selective. But their object now is similar: to keep a specific Catholic, the Democratic nominee, from entering the White House next January.

The recent public retreat of the Rev. Dr. Norman Vincent Peale from the religious issue appeared to have turned the tide against those who wished to use Mr. Kennedy's Catholicism politically.

But the furor over Dr. Peale angered many militant Protestants. It turned them from public statements to a quietly determined drive to saturate the country with literature on the issue "before it is too late."

The distributions are being planned and carried out not by political but by religious organizations, both genuine and spurious, all of which have some basis in Protestantism.

The size and sponsorship of the literature drive became apparent in interviews in the last three weeks here and in Washington, Minneapolis, Dallas, Los Angeles and San Francisco, and telephone interviews reaching into other parts of the country.

144 Producers of Literature

Persons questioned, including religious executives, "church and state" group leaders, politicians, mailers of "hate" literature and officials of the Department of Justice, disclosed a total of 144 producers of anti-Catholic literature in the campaign.

Estimates by the Fair Campaign Practices Committee and statements by the mailers themselves put the number of pieces in the tens of millions and the cost of distribution at hundreds of thousands of dollars.

* *

LAST MINUTE PREDICTIONS

As the campaign drew to a close, little was certain. Opinion polls seemed to indicate a Kennedy victory, but the margins were slight. With the electorate closely balanced between the two candidates, experts could only speculate about the eventual outcome. The day before the balloting, the nation held its breath in anticipation, then voted in record numbers.

NOVEMBER 8, 1960
3 OF 4 MAJOR ELECTION POLLS GIVE KENNEDY THE EDGE IN CLOSE VOTE
By CHARLES GRUTZNER

Three of four major professional samplings of voter preferences indicate that Senator John F. Kennedy will win the Presidential election today. The fourth nation-wide poll, which had Senator Kennedy in the lead Friday, reported yesterday that a week-end shift in straw votes had given Vice President Nixon a slight edge.

If these straw votes are an accurate indication of how the political wind is blowing, the popular vote will be the closest in decades. But the pollsters say that there may be a wide margin in the Electoral College because several of the largest states may be wafted into either the Democratic or Republican column by the merest zephyr.

The Kraft, Gallup and Princeton Research Service polls give Senator Kennedy, the Democratic candidate, a margin of from 1 to 4 per cent.

The Roper poll, which had given Senator Kennedy a 1 per cent advantage Friday, gave Vice President Nixon, the Republican nominee, a 2 per cent lead yesterday. This poll reported that 4 per cent of those interviewed had still listed themselves as undecided.

Noting that the undecided percentage was twice as great as Mr. Nixon's apparent margin, Elmo Roper, who directs the poll, said:

"It can go either way. This has been the most volatile campaign since we began taking samplings in 1936. I have never seen the lead change hands so many times."

The other professional pollsters also said that they had never seen a Presidential campaign with so many imponderables. There was general agreement that the element most difficult to assess was how many voters would be influenced by Senator Kennedy's Roman Catholic faith. The pollsters said that their sampling of "representative voters" might not reflect the hidden vote hinging on that question.

• •

ELECTION RESULTS

The election was still unresolved the day after votes were cast. Kennedy held a seemingly insurmountable lead in the Electoral College, but the popular vote was so close that neither candidate declared the race over. Nixon conceded only after the last votes were counted. Kennedy then claimed the presidency, but in a reserved manner, reflecting the narrow victory.

NOVEMBER 9, 1960
KENNEDY IS APPARENT VICTOR; LEAD CUT IN TWO KEY STATES; DEMOCRATS RETAIN CONGRESS
MARGIN NARROW

California and Illinois Give a Setback to Senator's Outlook

By JAMES RESTON

Senator John F. Kennedy of Massachusetts, the cool young Democratic leader of a new generation of American politicians, appeared yesterday to have won election as the thirty-fifth President of the United States.

Vice President Nixon of California appeared on television at 3:20 o'clock this morning to say that "if the present trend continues, Senator Kennedy is going to be the next President of the United States."

However, after both the Vice President and Senator Kennedy had about agreed with the television audience that it was all over and time to go to bed, the trend that had favored Senator Kennedy East of the Mississippi River began to veer toward the Vice President in the key Middle Western state of Illinois and in and beyond the Rockies.

In California, with half the voting districts uncounted, Senator Kennedy's lead was cut to just under 100,000 at 5 o'clock, this morning. While the reports indicated that the Democratic nominee would retain his lead there, some of the officials in key voting districts stopped counting the votes until later in the day, throwing the thirty-two electoral votes of California in doubt until the count could be completed.

1960 POPULAR VOTE

STATE	TOTAL VOTE	JOHN F. KENNEDY (DEMOCRAT) VOTES	%	RICHARD M. NIXON (REPUBLICAN) VOTES	%	ERIC HASS (SOCIALIST LABOR) VOTES	%	(UNPLEDGED) VOTES	%
Alabama	570,225	324,050	56.8	237,981	41.7	—	0.0	—	0.0
Alaska	60,762	29,809	49.1	30,953	50.9	—	0.0	—	0.0
Arizona	398,491	176,781	44.4	221,241	55.5	469	0.1	—	0.0
Arkansas	428,509	215,049	50.2	184,508	43.1	—	0.0	—	0.0
California	6,506,578	3,224,099	49.6	3,259,722	50.1	1,051	0.0	—	0.0
Colorado	736,236	330,629	44.9	402,242	54.6	2,803	0.4	—	0.0
Connecticut	1,222,883	657,055	53.7	565,813	46.3	—	0.0	—	0.0
Delaware	196,683	99,590	50.6	96,373	49.0	82	0.0	—	0.0
Florida	1,544,176	748,700	48.5	795,476	51.5	—	0.0	—	0.0
Georgia	733,349	458,638	62.5	274,472	37.4	—	0.0	—	0.0
Hawaii	184,705	92,410	50.0	92,295	50.0	—	0.0	—	0.0
Idaho	300,450	138,853	46.2	161,597	53.8	—	0.0	—	0.0
Illinois	4,757,409	2,377,846	50.0	2,368,988	49.8	10,560	0.2	—	0.0
Indiana	2,135,360	952,358	44.6	1,175,120	55.0	1,136	0.1	—	0.0
Iowa	1,273,810	550,565	43.2	722,381	56.7	230	0.0	—	0.0
Kansas	928,825	363,213	39.1	561,474	60.4	—	0.0	—	0.0
Kentucky	1,124,462	521,855	46.4	602,607	53.6	—	0.0	—	0.0
Louisiana	807,891	407,339	50.4	230,980	28.6	—	0.0	—	0.0
Maine	421,767	181,159	43.0	240,608	57.0	—	0.0	—	0.0
Maryland	1,055,349	565,808	53.6	489,538	46.4	—	0.0	—	0.0
Massachusetts	2,469,480	1,487,174	60.2	976,750	39.6	3,892	0.2	—	0.0
Michigan	3,318,097	1,687,269	50.9	1,620,428	48.8	1,718	0.1	—	0.0
Minnesota	1,541,887	779,933	50.6	757,915	49.2	962	0.1	—	0.0
Mississippi[1]	298,171	108,362	36.3	73,561	24.7	—	0.0	116,248	39.0
Missouri	1,934,422	972,201	50.3	962,221	49.7	—	0.0	—	0.0
Montana	277,579	134,891	48.6	141,841	51.1	—	0.0	—	0.0
Nebraska	613,095	232,542	37.9	380,553	62.1	—	0.0	—	0.0
Nevada	107,267	54,880	51.2	52,387	48.8	—	0.0	—	0.0
New Hampshire	295,761	137,772	46.6	157,989	53.4	—	0.0	—	0.0
New Jersey	2,773,111	1,385,415	50.0	1,363,324	49.2	4,262	0.2	—	0.0
New Mexico	311,107	156,027	50.2	153,733	49.4	570	0.2	—	0.0
New York	7,291,079	3,830,085	52.5	3,446,419	47.3	—	0.0	—	0.0
North Carolina	1,368,556	713,136	52.1	655,420	47.9	—	0.0	—	0.0
North Dakota	278,431	123,963	44.5	154,310	55.4	—	0.0	—	0.0
Ohio	4,161,859	1,944,248	46.7	2,217,611	53.3	—	0.0	—	0.0
Oklahoma	903,150	370,111	41.0	533,039	59.0	—	0.0	—	0.0
Oregon	776,421	367,402	47.3	408,060	52.6	—	0.0	—	0.0
Pennsylvania	5,006,541	2,556,282	51.1	2,439,956	48.7	7,185	0.1	—	0.0
Rhode Island	405,535	258,032	63.6	147,502	36.4	—	0.0	—	0.0
South Carolina	386,688	198,129	51.2	188,558	48.8	—	0.0	—	0.0
South Dakota	306,487	128,070	41.8	178,417	58.2	—	0.0	—	0.0
Tennessee	1,051,792	481,453	45.8	556,577	52.9	—	0.0	—	0.0
Texas	2,311,084	1,167,567	50.5	1,121,310	48.5	—	0.0	—	0.0
Utah	374,709	169,248	45.2	205,361	54.8	—	0.0	—	0.0
Vermont	167,324	69,186	41.3	98,131	58.6	—	0.0	—	0.0
Virginia	771,449	362,327	47.0	404,521	52.4	397	0.1	—	0.0
Washington	1,241,572	599,298	48.3	629,273	50.7	10,895	0.9	—	0.0
West Virginia	837,781	441,786	52.7	395,995	47.3	—	0.0	—	0.0
Wisconsin	1,729,082	830,805	48.0	895,175	51.8	1,310	0.1	—	0.0
Wyoming	140,782	63,331	45.0	77,451	55.0	—	0.0	—	0.0
TOTALS	**68,838,219**	**34,226,731**	**49.7**	**34,108,157**	**49.5**	**47,522**	**0.1**	**116,248**	**0.2**

1. Votes for unpledged electors who carried the state and cast electoral votes for Harry F. Byrd (D-Va.).

OTHER VOTES	%	PLURALITY	
8,194	1.4	86,069	D
—	0.0	1,144	R
—	0.0	44,460	R
28,952	6.8	30,541	D
21,706	0.3	35,623	R
562	0.1	71,613	R
15	0.0	91,242	D
638	0.3	3,217	D
—	0.0	46,776	R
239	0.0	184,166	D
—	0.0	115	D
—	0.0	22,744	R
15	0.0	8,858	D
6,746	0.3	222,762	R
634	0.0	171,816	R
4,138	0.4	198,261	R
—	0.0	80,752	R
169,572	21.0	176,359	D
—	0.0	59,449	R
3	0.0	76,270	D
1,664	0.1	510,424	D
8,682	0.3	66,841	D
3,077	0.2	22,018	D
—	0.0	7,886	U
—	0.0	9,980	D
847	0.3	6,950	R
—	0.0	148,011	R
—	0.0	2,493	D
—	0.0	20,217	R
20,110	0.7	22,091	D
777	0.2	2,294	D
14,575	0.2	383,666	D
—	0.0	57,716	D
158	0.1	30,347	R
—	0.0	273,363	R
—	0.0	162,928	R
959	0.1	40,658	R
3,118	0.1	116,326	D
1	0.0	110,530	D
1	0.0	9,571	D
—	0.0	50,347	R
13,762	1.3	75,124	R
22,207	1.0	46,257	D
100	0.0	36,113	R
7	0.0	28,945	R
4,204	0.5	42,194	R
2,106	0.2	29,975	R
—	0.0	45,791	D
1,792	0.1	64,370	R
—	0.0	14,120	R
339,561	**0.5**	**118,574**	**D**

NOVEMBER 10, 1960
KENNEDY'S VICTORY WON BY CLOSE MARGIN; HE PROMISES FIGHT FOR WORLD FREEDOM; EISENHOWER OFFERS 'ORDERLY TRANSITION'

RESULTS DELAYED

Popular Vote Almost Even—300–185 Is Electoral Tally

By JAMES RESTON

Senator John F. Kennedy of Massachusetts finally won the 1960 Presidential election from Vice President Nixon by the astonishing margin of less than two votes per voting precinct.

Senator Kennedy's electoral vote total stood yesterday at 300, just thirty-one more than the 269 needed for election. The Vice President's total was 185. Fifty-two additional electoral votes, including California's thirty-two, were still in doubt last night.

But the popular vote was a different story. The two candidates ran virtually even. Senator Kennedy's lead last night was little more than 300,000 in a total tabulated vote of about 66,000,000 cast in 165,826 precincts.

That was a plurality for the Senator of less than one-half of 1 per cent of the total vote—the smallest percentage difference between the popular vote of two Presidential candidates since 1880, when James A. Garfield outran Gen. Winfield Scott Hancock by 7,000 votes in a total of almost 9,000,000.

End Divided Government

Nevertheless, yesterday's voting radically altered the political balance of power in America in favor of the Democrats and put them in a commanding position in the Federal and state capitals unknown since the heyday of Franklin D. Roosevelt.

They regained control of the White House for the first time since 1952 and thus ended divided government in Washington. They retained control of the Senate and the House of Representatives, although with slightly reduced margins. And they increased their hold on the state governorships by one, bringing the Democratic margin to 34–16.

The President-elect is the first Roman Catholic ever to win the nation's highest office. The only other member of his church nominated for President was Alfred E. Smith, who was defeated by Herbert Hoover in 1928.

NOVEMBER 10, 1960
EDITORIAL
THE PRESIDENTIAL ELECTION

The Presidential election of 1960 will go down as one of the closest in American history and one of the least predictable. And in its political results it may yet go down as one of the more interesting.

We note here a number of significant points: (1) The amount of ticket-splitting in this election—though nothing new in American politics—was nevertheless notable and represents a healthy skepticism on the part of the voter. In state after state, heavy majorities for one Presidential candidate or the other bore no necessary relationship to the outcome of contests further down the ticket. While some of this ticket-splitting can be explained on the reprehensible grounds of religious prejudice (working both ways), much of it is surely attributable to a commendable independence of party affiliation. Most notable example near at hand was in New Jersey, where Senator Clifford P. Case, the Republican candidate, won by a majority of more than 335,000 while Mr. Kennedy carried the state by 20,000. Democratic Senator Paul Douglas won overwhelmingly in Illinois, while the Presidential race was in doubt almost to the last minute.

(2) Some of the more persistent geographic clichés of American politics may be gradually becoming obsolescent. Again the "solid South" has lost its solidity, with the Republicans retaining their 1956 foothold in Florida, Virginia and Tennessee, not to mention the normally Democratic border state of Kentucky, or the near-miss in South Carolina. None of the Republican-held House seats from the South—two in Virginia, one in Florida, one in Texas, etc.—was lost. While religious prejudice surely held down the Kennedy vote in the South (as it built it up elsewhere), the fact remains that firm establishment of a two-party system in some areas where it did not exist or was extremely weak before is a growing and hopeful possibility.

(3) The universal drop in Vice President Nixon's strength from that shown by President Eisenhower in 1952 and 1956 proves—if any proof were needed—how greatly the Republicans depended in the last two elections on the personality of Mr. Eisenhower. Mr. Nixon was running on the Eisenhower record, he had the active (but belated) support of Mr. Eisenhower in the campaign, he was intimately identified with Mr. Eisenhower—yet the Eisenhower magic did not rub off on him even though he did do much better than many of his detractors had expected. Where Mr. Nixon's defeat leaves the principles of the Republican party is a nice question. Would he have won if he had taken a more frankly conservative line à la Goldwater? We doubt it. Would he have won if he had taken a more frankly liberal line à la Rockefeller? We doubt that too. Which way should the G.O.P. turn now that it has lost the drawing power of the Eisenhower personality? That question will be debated from now until 1964.

(4) The most striking fact in this election is, of course, the extraordinary closeness of the popular vote. It is astonishing that the difference between the two parties should come down to a few hundred thousand ballots out of so many millions. As between the two principal parties alone, it is certainly the closest election in nearly a century.

While we supported Mr. Kennedy, we think it is a good thing that the election was so close. It should serve as a restraining force, as a reminder to the Kennedy Administration that it should proceed with caution and that it has no mandate to embark on drastic changes of policy, either foreign or domestic. We do not think that extreme moves in any direction have ever been in Mr. Kennedy's mind (or we would not have supported him); but the electoral results emphasize the necessity of restraint, without any suggestion of crippling the new President in his formulation of policy.

We are sure that Democrats and Republicans alike will sympathize with this young President-elect as he now faces the gigantic problems of the next four years, will gladly say farewell to the confusions and exaggerations of the political campaign, and will close ranks behind the man chosen to serve as next President of the United States.

THE INAUGURATION

As John F. Kennedy took the presidential oath of office on January 20, 1961, he delivered what is considered one of the great presidential inauguration speeches. Proclaiming, "Ask not what your country can do for you, but what you can do for your country," JFK promised to usher in a new era of hope and achievement in America. No one could imagine how little time the president would have to accomplish his goals.

JANUARY 21, 1961

KENNEDY SWORN IN, ASKS 'GLOBAL ALLIANCE' AGAINST TYRANNY, WANT, DISEASE AND WAR; REPUBLICANS AND DIPLOMATS HAIL ADDRESS

NATION EXHORTED

Inaugural Says U.S. Will 'Pay Any Price' to Keep Freedom

By W. H. LAWRENCE

Special to The New York Times

WASHINGTON, Jan. 20—John Fitzgerald Kennedy assumed the Presidency today with a call for "a grand and global alliance" to combat tyranny, poverty, disease and war.

In his Inaugural Address, he served notice on the world that the United States was ready to "pay any price, bear any burden, meet any hardship, support any friend, oppose any foe to assure the survival and the success of liberty."

But the nation is also ready, he said, to resume negotiations with the Soviet Union to ease and, if possible, remove world tensions.

"Let us begin anew," Mr. Kennedy declared. "Let us never negotiate out of fear. But let us never fear to negotiate."

Asks Aid of Countrymen

He called on his fellow-citizens to join his Administration's endeavor:

"Ask not what your country can do for you—ask what you can do for your country."

At 12:51 P. M., he was sworn by Chief Justice Earl Warren as the nation's thirty-fifth President, the first Roman Catholic to hold the office.

Ten minutes earlier, Lyndon Baines Johnson of Texas took the oath as Vice President. It was administered by Sam Rayburn, Speaker of the House of Representatives.

At 43 years of age, the youngest man ever elected to the Presidency, Mr. Kennedy took over the power vested for eight years in Dwight D. Eisenhower, who, at 70, was the oldest White House occupant.

" President Kennedy has accepted the challenge and responsibility he so eagerly sought with a pledge of energy, a demand for sacrifice, and a promise of hope that must have inspired all who heard him in this country and in every land of freedom. "

JANUARY 21, 1961
EDITORIAL
'THE TORCH HAS BEEN PASSED'

With the inauguration yesterday of John Fitzgerald Kennedy as thirty-fifth President of the United States, a new generation is taking over the direction of affairs of our country, a new generation "born in this century, tempered by war, disciplined by a cold and bitter peace, proud of our ancient heritage—and unwilling to witness or permit the slow undoing of those human rights to which this nation has always been committed."

In the eloquent words of a superb inaugural address distinguished for its style and brevity as well as for its meaty content, President Kennedy has accepted the challenge and responsibility he so eagerly sought with a pledge of energy, a demand for sacrifice, and a promise of hope that must have inspired all who heard him in this country and in every land of freedom. Speaking almost exclusively on the position of the United States in the world today, President Kennedy revealed his preoccupation with the universal threat to liberty throughout the globe; and he set the tone of his new Administration in foreign affairs, a tone of firmness but not of defiance, of dignity but not of pride, of generosity but not of servility, of reason but not of self-righteousness.

To our old allies of Europe and the Commonwealth, to our new friends of Asia and Africa, to the republics of Latin America and to the United Nations as a whole, President Kennedy said sensible and friendly things without falling into platitudes. His offer to "begin anew" in an attempt to find a common ground on which to negotiate with the Communist world "before the dark powers of destruction unleashed by science engulf all humanity" could not be misunderstood by the Kremlin, nor could his plea that "for the first time" both sides formulate serious proposals for the inspection and control of arms.

With this new generation, a new approach, new ideas and new problems, President Kennedy's Administration opens a new chapter in the history of the American people. He and his associates—and all America—are facing a new world, as different from that of Franklin Roosevelt's day as Roosevelt's of 1933 was from Wilson's before the First World War. Through his words and his demeanor at the inaugural ceremony—which for all its minor mishaps had about it a simple grandeur—the young President bespoke a quiet confidence in himself and in his countrymen, justified, we believe, by the facts of the present and by the indications of the future. It is not the fatness of the land that gives us this hope, but the strength and the character of our people, who, when shown the way, will be capable of the effort and the sacrifice necessary to preserve freedom, defend liberty and extend help to the miserable and the hungry who populate half the globe.

THE PRESIDENTIAL ELECTION OF 1964

JOHNSON TRIUMPHS AND LOOKS TOWARD THE "GREAT SOCIETY"

The presidential election of 1964 bore witness to the transformation of American politics. The contest between Democratic president Lyndon Johnson and Republican senator Barry Goldwater marked the fading of the New Deal consensus on active government involvement in economic management and the postwar consensus on international alliances. Ideological divisions between the parties replaced centrist bargaining over common policy goals. Race became a new cleavage in the electorate as the Republican Party marched south in search of new votes from white segregationists and African Americans became a new foundation of the Democratic Party.

The world now bore more dangers for the United States, previously confident of its dominance. The Soviet Union was resurgent; it had defied the young Kennedy administration by building the Berlin Wall in 1961 to solidify its control of Eastern Europe. A year later, it installed its missiles and nuclear weapons in Cuba, posing a direct threat to the United States and bringing the superpowers close to mutual annihilation in the Cuban missile crisis. Toward the end of the 1964 presidential campaign, China exploded its own atomic bomb, becoming an unpredictable fifth nuclear power and enlarging communism's military threat.

Domestic violence also disturbed the peaceful, sometimes even tepid, American political environment. On November 22, 1963, trauma assailed the nation when President John Kennedy was assassinated by a lone gunman. The sudden death of the young, glamorous leader shocked the world. Vice President Lyndon Johnson assumed power and the Kennedy mantle effectively, but scars remained through years of memories, regrets, and conspiracy investigations.

Once unloosed, the scourge of violence became a continuing political reality. It appeared in the forceful repressions of southern demonstrations for racial equality and the murder of civil rights workers, most wrenchingly the torture and death of three young activists in Mississippi. Racial violence spread northward in black protests against alleged police misconduct, leading to five deaths in Harlem and extensive property

Jacqueline Kennedy, her children Caroline and John Jr., and Attorney General Robert Kennedy follow the late President John F. Kennedy's casket at St. Matthew's Cathedral after a funeral mass on November 25, 1963.

damage in other cities. Many more deaths—but far distant from America—were presaged by an apparent attack on U.S. battleships in the Gulf of Tonkin in Vietnam. Responding to a request from President Johnson, Congress—in three days, with only two dissenting votes—authorized him "to take all necessary steps, including the use of armed force" against North Vietnam. That hazy justification eventually brought 56,000 American deaths, eight years of national conflict, and a changed politics.

THE PARTIES AND THE CANDIDATES

The turn to ideological politics in America was particularly apparent in the Republican Party. Arizona senator Barry Goldwater led the field with his call for a rightward turn, articulated in his book, *The Conscience of a Conservative*. Rejecting the moderation of Dwight Eisenhower and Richard Nixon, Goldwater cast off the party's previous adoption of the welfare state, called for a more assertive and nationalistic

1964 ELECTORAL VOTE

STATE	ELECTORAL VOTES	JOHNSON	GOLDWATER	STATE	ELECTORAL VOTES	JOHNSON	GOLDWATER
Alabama	(10)	–	10	Missouri	(12)	12	–
Alaska	(3)	3	–	Montana	(4)	4	–
Arizona	(5)	–	5	Nebraska	(5)	5	–
Arkansas	(6)	6	–	Nevada	(3)	3	–
California	(40)	40	–	New Hampshire	(4)	4	–
Colorado	(6)	6	–	New Jersey	(17)	17	–
Connecticut	(8)	8	–	New Mexico	(4)	4	–
Delaware	(3)	3	–	New York	(43)	43	–
District of Columbia	(3)	3	–	North Carolina	(13)	13	–
				North Dakota	(4)	4	–
Florida	(14)	14	–	Ohio	(26)	26	–
Georgia	(12)	–	12	Oklahoma	(8)	8	–
Hawaii	(4)	4	–	Oregon	(6)	6	–
Idaho	(4)	4	–	Pennsylvania	(29)	29	–
Illinois	(26)	26	–	Rhode Island	(4)	4	–
Indiana	(13)	13	–	South Carolina	(8)	–	8
Iowa	(9)	9	–	South Dakota	(4)	4	–
Kansas	(7)	7	–	Tennessee	(11)	11	–
Kentucky	(9)	9	–	Texas	(25)	25	–
Louisiana	(10)	–	10	Utah	(4)	4	–
Maine	(4)	4	–	Vermont	(3)	3	–
Maryland	(10)	10	–	Virginia	(12)	12	–
Massachusetts	(14)	14	–	Washington	(9)	9	–
Michigan	(21)	21	–	West Virginia	(7)	7	–
Minnesota	(10)	10	–	Wisconsin	(12)	12	–
Mississippi	(7)	–	7	Wyoming	(3)	3	–
				TOTALS	**(538)**	**486**	**52**

foreign policy, raised the possibility of using nuclear weapons, and questioned the federal government's efforts toward state desegregation. Conservatives, attracted by a candidacy offering "a choice, not an echo," organized to take over state conventions and to mobilize their fervent minority for the primaries.

The moderate forces that had controlled the party for decades were uneasy over the Goldwater challenge to their domination, but lacked a candidate of comparable appeal. Nixon claimed to have retired from politics, having lost the presidential race in 1960 and a race for governor of California two years later. Henry Cabot Lodge, the vice-presidential candidate in 1960, was the U.S. ambassador to Vietnam;

he drew some attention when he won the New Hampshire primary on write-in votes. Lodge also bested Maine senator Margaret Chase Smith, the first notable woman to run for president. But the Lodge boomlet soon faded, as he lost a write-in challenge to Gov. William Scranton in Pennsylvania and the only contest he officially entered, Oregon, to New York governor Nelson Rockefeller.

Rockefeller was the most prominent moderate aspirant, but he lacked opportunities to contest Goldwater directly. The conservative senator, accumulating most of his delegates by taking over local and state organizations, officially entered nine primaries, winning but four against minor opposition.

The only true contest with Rockefeller came at the end of the primary season, in California. At the last moment, Goldwater carried the state narrowly, with 51.6 percent of the vote. The outcome may have resulted from the birth of a child to Rockefeller's second wife just days before the primary vote, reviving disdain for the couple's premarital relationship and messy divorces.

At the convention in San Francisco in mid-July, the moderates made a futile attempt to consolidate their forces behind Scranton. At the least, they hoped to influence the party platform. But the purist conservatives were in no mood for compromise. By successive 2 to 1 votes, the delegates rejected amendments to condemn political extremism, to strengthen the civil rights plank, and to deny local military commanders authority to use tactical nuclear weapons. Rockefeller was vociferously booed while speaking on the first issue, presenting an unappealing picture to the television audience. Goldwater was then nominated on the first ballot, with 883 of 1,308 votes, the opposition coming almost entirely from the Northeast. The new presidential candidate further provoked these dissidents by his selection of a running mate, Rep. William Miller of New York, the acerbic and conservative chair of the Republican National Committee.

The platform and the candidates swerved the party to the right. The party program combined harsh criticism of the Democratic administration with pledges of major changes in policy. On foreign policy, Republicans declared, "This Administration has sought accommodations with Communism without adequate safeguards and compensating gains for freedom . . . and in general pursued a risky path such as began at Munich a quarter century ago." Republicans would insist on "continued military superiority for the United States." On civil rights, the party did promise "full implementation and faithful execution" of existing statutes, while rebuking the Democrats, who had "exploited interracial tensions by extravagant campaign promises . . . encouraging disorderly and lawless elements"; instead, the Republicans emphasized that the elimination of discrimination "is a matter of heart, conscience, and education, as well as of equal rights under law." On economic policy, the party stood on the individualist principle that "Every person has the right to govern himself, to fix his own goals, and to make his own way with a minimum of governmental interference" and therefore advocated a $5 billion cut in federal expenditures and a reduction in individual and corporate taxes.

Goldwater went even further in his acceptance speech, an uncompromising call to a conservative crusade:

> The good Lord raised this mighty Republic to be a home for the brave and to flourish as the land of the free—not to stagnate in the swampland of collectivism, not to cringe before the bully of communism.

> Those who seek to live your lives for you, to take your liberties in return for relieving you of yours, those who elevate the state and downgrade the citizen must see ultimately a world in which earthly power can be substituted for divine will, and this Nation was founded upon the rejection of that notion and upon the acceptance of God as the author of freedom.

> Today, as then, but more urgently and more broadly than then, the task of preserving and enlarging freedom at home and safeguarding it from the forces of tyranny abroad is great enough to challenge all our resources and to require all our strength. Anyone who joins us in all sincerity, we welcome. Those who do not care for our cause, we don't expect to enter our ranks in any case. And let our Republicanism, so focused and so dedicated, not be made fuzzy and futile by unthinking and stupid labels.

> I would remind you that extremism in the defense of liberty is no vice. And let me remind you also that moderation in the pursuit of justice is no virtue.

Goldwater drew ecstatic admiration from his immediate audience, but his apparent defense of extremists provided plentiful grist for the Democrats' mill.

Meeting late in August in Atlantic City, the Democratic convention was completely dominated by Johnson, stage-managed in a manner resembling the Miss America pageants annually held at the beach resort. Johnson achieved this dominance by his sure command of power, first in consoling the nation after the shock of Kennedy's assassination, then in transcending his predecessor in legislative achievement.

Johnson began the transition with the first words of his stirring address to Congress and the nation the day after Kennedy's state funeral: "All I have I would have given gladly not to be standing here today. The greatest leader of our time has been struck down by the foulest deed of our time. . . . No words are sad enough to express our sense of loss. No words are strong enough to express our determination to continue the forward thrust of America that he began."

Then the new leader became specific, calling on Congress to "eloquently honor President Kennedy's memory" by passing the civil rights bill initiated by his predecessor but still legislatively moribund. In his Texas accent, Johnson marked the end of official southern resistance to racial justice: "We have talked long enough in this country about equal rights. We have talked for one hundred years or more. It is time now to write the next chapter, and to write it in the books of law." Through a filibuster of fifty-seven days, Johnson kept pressure on the Senate and achieved, despite Goldwater's nay vote, a strong law banning segregation in schools and public accommodations and outlawing discrimination in voting and employment.

Johnson's reach went beyond Kennedy's fallen grasp. He proposed legislation initiating Medicare and the "war on poverty." He set out a campaign vision of the "Great Society," an effort to make "the American city a place where future generations will come, not only to live, but to live the good life," to restore the countryside to a place where Americans "walk with beauty or wonder at nature," and to improve education so that "every young mind is set free to scan the farthest reaches of thought and imagination." Johnson's advocacy of activist government, endorsed in the lengthy details of the party platform, cast a sharp contrast to Goldwater's program of individual freedom in a polity of limited power.

The Democratic convention enthusiastically renominated Johnson without dissent or even a formal roll call of the more than 5,000 delegates and alternates. But trouble did appear. Some white southerners agreed with Johnson's dour forecast when he signed the civil rights law: "We have lost the South for a generation." Efforts to enforce a loyalty oath on dissident factions led to walkouts by the Mississippi and Alabama delegations. Even more contentious were the protests of a largely black group, the Mississippi Freedom Democratic Party, which contested the violence and discriminatory practices that had kept blacks from participating in their state's nominating process. Party leaders, especially Sen. Hubert Humphrey, won the convention's endorsement of a compromise to seat two blacks and to make the others "honored guests" of the convention. Although neither Mississippi group accepted the proposal, the effort prevented an open fight.

The only significant decision for Democrats was the vice-presidential nomination. Johnson wanted to be his own man and to stand independent of the Kennedy heritage and mystique. In the spring, he declared that he had ruled out any running mate who held a cabinet position, a clumsy way to block a possible movement toward Attorney General Robert Kennedy, the fallen president's brother. For months, Johnson kept his own counsel on the vice-presidential selection. Humphrey campaigned quietly for the designation, canvassing political leaders and encouraging private communications to the president. Johnson still toyed with the aspirants, even holding mock job interviews in the White House. Finally, on the night of his own selection, he came to the convention to personally endorse Humphrey, who was immediately approved by acclamation.

Johnson's maneuvering had led to Kennedy's resignation from the cabinet and to his effort to develop a new political base by running for senator from New York. But Kennedy certainly could not be barred from a major role at the convention. After the party ticket had been securely ratified, he came to the rostrum to present a tribute to his brother. Finally free to express their emotions, the delegates cheered Kennedy for more than twenty minutes, as he stolidly repeated his opening salutation, "Mr. Chairman, Mr. Chairman." Thousands cried at the loss of John Kennedy, many would still remember their loss when Robert Kennedy became a candidate in his own right in 1968, and many would cry again when he too became the victim of political assassination.

THE CAMPAIGN

Democrats began the campaign with great advantages—the voters' desire for stability after Kennedy's assassination, Johnson's accomplishments, impressive economic growth throughout their term in office, and the absence of immediate international crisis. These advantages increased during the fall, to the point that election bettors could find no takers for Goldwater, even at 8–1 odds.

Goldwater unwillingly abetted the Democratic campaign. He had voted against popular programs such as the nuclear weapons test ban treaty, Medicare, federal aid to education, the national wilderness program, and the civil rights act. Prone to exaggeration and casual flippancies, he had suggested making Social Security voluntary, allowing states to maintain segregated schools, physically separating the Northeast from the continent and letting it "float out to sea," American withdrawal from the United Nations, and ending progressive income tax rates. Most worrisome, he seemed ready to use nuclear weapons, hypothetically to deter a Soviet attack in Europe and actually in Vietnam.

By raising the fear of nuclear war, he provided Democrats the opportunity to produce the most famous television advertisement in political history. The "Daisy" ad—actually broadcast in paid time only once but repeated numberless times on the news—showed an adorable young girl pulling petals from a daisy as she counted in a erratic sequence resembling the countdown to a missile launch. Then, the camera came in close to the girl's startled face and a nuclear explosion filled the screen as Johnson, unseen, spoke: "These are the stakes! To make a world in which all of God's children can live, or to go into the dark. We must either love each other, or we must die." Another voice then delivered the political point: "Vote for President Johnson on November 3. The stakes are too high for you to stay home."

The Johnson campaign stressed Goldwater's vulnerabilities. The Democratic platform craftily included the moderate planks defeated at the Republican convention, including condemnation of "extremism, whether from the Right or Left." Attacks on the stump forced Goldwater to devote much of his own effort to refutations, explanations, and endorsements, tepidly by former President Eisenhower and Governor Rockefeller, forcefully by Nixon and celebrity Ronald Reagan.

Goldwater turned more aggressive on a new issue, law and order. Along with rising crime rates and the urban disorders of the summer, voters evidenced concerns over blacks' new militancy. George Wallace, the segregationist governor of Alabama, had shown the potency of this appeal when he won surprising support in the Democratic primaries in Indiana, Maryland, and Wisconsin before dropping his unorganized effort. Goldwater attempted to pick up the discontent in ads implicating the Johnson administration in "Graft! Swindles! Juvenile Delinquency! Crime! Riots!" and insisting, "The leadership of this nation has a clear and immediate challenge to go to work effectively and to go to work immediately to restore proper respect for law and order in this land—and not just prior to election day either."

With Johnson holding a wide lead in opinion surveys, there was little excitement, but much rancor, in the competition. Goldwater hoped, as The New York Times reported, that his clear ideological stand would enliven "hidden" conservative support, particularly in the South, and that the electorate would be moved by "subtle impulses, many of which voters would not discuss candidly with pollsters," such as Johnson's alleged corruption, law and order, and an unvoiced concern with race. The senator made more explicit appeals on policy issues, pledging a 25 percent reduction in income taxes and an end to the military draft. Abandoned by many Republican moderates, he could hardly compensate when he gained the preference of black militant Malcolm X, who found that with Goldwater "black people at least know what they are dealing with."

Johnson disregarded all criticisms in his own campaign efforts. For the most part, he held to his public duties, using the public attention accorded an incumbent president to emphasize the administration's record. Sensing a coming landslide, Johnson found reasons for official visits to all parts of the nation and left the attacks to Humphrey and to the Democrats clambering to grasp his coattails. Unions and blacks mobilized their ranks, seeing Goldwater as a dangerous enemy to racial advancement and to organized labor.

Johnson's self-portrait as an able leader amid tumult was reinforced late in the campaign, when three world events came simultaneously: the Chinese nuclear test, the ousting of Soviet premier Nikita Khrushchev, and the election of a Labour government in Great Britain. Johnson calmly assured the nation that the United States had no reason to fear these changes—if he remained president. The international developments diverted attention from a possible embarrassment, the arrest of Walter Jenkins, a White House aide, on charges of homosexual immorality.

Traditional alliances shattered. Goldwater, doing his campaign "hunting in the pond where the ducks are," as he put it, met enthusiastic crowds in the South, and won new Republican support from white Democratic officials, including South Carolina senator Strom Thurmond, the former Dixiecrat candidate for president, and implicitly from Wallace. In the opposite direction, Johnson won endorsements from northeastern business leaders and, uniquely in electoral history, from a majority of the nation's newspapers, including traditionally Republican publications such as the Saturday Evening Post and the Hearst and Cowles newspaper chains. Urging a "resounding victory" for Johnson and Humphrey, The Times expressed many commentators' discontent with the Republican candidates, fearing that they "would divide the United States from its allies . . . would represent a triumph for the radical right [and] . . . a retrogression from the domestic policies that during the past generation have brought this country to its present state of prosperity."

Eventually, the campaign deteriorated to an exchange of slogans. Goldwater's messages always concluded, "In Your Heart You Know He's Right." Democrats derisively amended the appeal to either "In Your Heart You Know He's Far Right" or "In Your Heart You Know He's Nuts." The election of 1964 did present a clear ideological choice, but it was hardly an inspiring model of civil democratic dialogue.

THE ELECTION RESULTS

As accurately predicted in opinion surveys, Johnson won a landslide victory on November 3. The Democratic candidate carried 44 states and the District of Columbia, newly enrolled in the Electoral College, gaining an overwhelming margin of 486 of the 538 total electoral votes.

In the popular tally, Johnson won more than 43 million votes (61.1 percent), a margin of 16 million over Goldwater (38.5 percent). He achieved more votes and a greater plurality than any previous candidate, and the largest percentage of the total vote in all competitive U.S. elections, past or future. His triumph matched that of his political hero, Franklin Roosevelt, who in 1936 gained a slightly greater percentage of the two-party vote.

Although overwhelming, the Johnson landslide still carried worrisome implications for the Democrats. In a historic reversal, Goldwater carried five states of the Deep South (as well as his home state of Arizona), a clear reflection of white opposition to the Democrats' commitment to the African American movement. In Alabama, Johnson was not even on the ballot, as a slate of "free electors" had captured the Democratic label.

The racial transformation in the region could also be seen in the congressional results. Democrats gained 38 seats in the House and 2 in the Senate, bringing them two-thirds dominance in both chambers, but Republicans competed now throughout the South and broke through to win seats in Alabama, Georgia, and Mississippi. Countervailing trends could be found in the slow increase in black voting in the South and the large increase in black Democratic allegiance in the North, both of which accelerated in later elections. A new pattern began to emerge in American politics, and it soon completely reversed traditional electoral geography.

Nationally, the decisive election results were plain to see. Contrary to the beliefs of Goldwater enthusiasts, there was no hidden conservative vote that could be brought to the polls by a candidate who rejected the party's moderate policies. Despite a degree of unease throughout the country, a racial "backlash" was insufficient to overcome voters' concerns on domestic and foreign issues or to alter the established pattern of a Democratic majority. Johnson stood as a successful incumbent inheriting the glow of a martyred president, as the advocate of spreading prosperity and improving social conditions, as the keeper of apparent peace. In these conditions, a Democratic victory was always probable; Goldwater's erratic campaign and impulsive behavior made the result inevitable.

For Johnson, the win brought him more than the election; he could legitimately claim a mandate for himself and his program. He had been elected in his own right, gaining strong majorities in Congress, with Republicans reduced to a vanquished and quarrelsome opposition. The Great Society loomed ahead, not just as a vision, but as a feasible goal for this acclaimed and able president. But events—in Vietnam and the cities of America—soon challenged the promises of the election of 1964.

• •

JFK Assassination

President John F. Kennedy was assassinated on November 22, 1963, while his motorcade drove through Dallas, Texas. The loss of the popular president brought Vice President Lyndon Johnson to the nation's highest office. Johnson, regarded as more conservative than his predecessor, was less popular within the Democratic Party. As the nation mourned, the parties pondered the impact of Johnson's ascendency on the upcoming 1964 electoral battle.

NOVEMBER 23, 1963
KENNEDY IS KILLED BY SNIPER AS HE RIDES IN CAR IN DALLAS; JOHNSON SWORN IN ON PLANE
TEXAN ASKS UNITY

Congressional Chiefs of 2 Parties Give Promise of Aid

By FELIX BELAIR Jr.

Special to The New York Times

WASHINGTON, Nov. 22—Lyndon B. Johnson returned to a stunned capital this evening to assume the duties of the Presidency.

The new President asked for and received from Congressional leaders of both parties their "united support in the face of the tragedy which has befallen our country." He said it was "more essential than ever before that this country be united."

Partisan differences disappeared in the chorus of assurances with which the Congressional leaders responded.

Lyndon B. Johnson is sworn in as president in the cabin of Air Force One. Jacqueline Kennedy stands at his side while Judge Sarah T. Hughes, a Kennedy appointee to the federal court, administers the oath. In background, from left are, Jack Valenti, administrative assistant to Johnson; Rep. Albert Thomas, D-Tex.; Lady Bird Johnson; and Rep. Jack Brooks, D-Tex.

Source: LBJ Library photo by Cecil Stoughton

Mr. Johnson was described by those who talked with him as "stunned and shaken" by the assassination of President Kennedy.

Discusses U. S. Security

But he moved quickly from problems of national security and foreign policy to funeral arrangements for Mr. Kennedy.

Across the street from the West Wing of the White House, the President conferred with officials in his old Vice Presidential offices in the Executive Office Building.

Senator George A. Smathers, Democrat of Florida, a personal friend of the dead President, was one of those who described Mr. Johnson as shaken.

"Everyone is," he added. "But the President is the more so because he was right there when the tragedy occurred."

While flying to Washington aboard the Presidential plane, Mr. Johnson arranged for a meeting with Cabinet members to ask that they remain at their posts. He made the same request of staff members in the executive office.

NOVEMBER 23, 1963
PARTIES' OUTLOOK FOR '64 CONFUSED

Republican Prospects Rise—Johnson Faces Possible Fight Against Liberals

By WARREN WEAVER Jr.

Special to The New York Times

WASHINGTON, Nov. 22—President Kennedy's assassination threw the American political scene into turmoil today.

It removed at a single blow the man who would have been nominated for a second term in the White House by acclamation nine months from now.

> " Now, following the tragedy in Texas, there seemed to be only questions, thrust so suddenly on the minds of political leaders of both parties that there were few answers. "

It elevated into the Presidency and the leadership of the Democratic party an older, more conservative man still emerging from his Southern heritage.

It increased immeasurably for the leaders of the Republican party prospects of electing a President next November.

The shock of the President's death stilled the official voices of politics in the capital. But so profound was the potential effect on the Government and leadership that private consideration could not be silenced.

Before, there had been facts and strong probabilities on the national political scene: The President would run again. He would be stronger in some states, weaker in the South. He would run with Lyndon B. Johnson again. He would debate his opponent. He would be favored to win.

Now, following the tragedy in Texas, there seemed to be only questions, thrust so suddenly on the minds of political leaders of both parties that there were few answers. These were some of the questions:

Questions Raised

Will President Johnson be able to insure his own nomination next August, on the basis of an inherited nine months in the White House?

Will liberal elements in the Democratic party make any attempt to dislodge Mr. Johnson in favor of a candidate more to their liking?

Could Mr. Johnson, running as the first Southern Presidential candidate of this century, win support in the South despite his espousal of the civil rights cause?

What influence will the political motivation of the assassin, if any, have on the great wave of public revulsion against the act? Will the people turn against left-wing or right-wing extremists—or both?

How will the immediate prospect of fierce two-party competition in next year's Presidential election influence Republican leaders in their choice of a candidate?

Despite the many questions raised, one political consequence seemed clear in the hushed, almost ashamed, assessments that observers undertook this evening: The death of the President gave new life to Republican hopes.

Whatever political liabilities might have encumbered him, John F. Kennedy was an incumbent President, one whose person and personality had been impressed on the American electorate.

All Changed Now

Republican leaders knew this. While they loudly scored what they saw as his weaknesses, they saw Mr. Kennedy as a figure to be reckoned with politically. Their candidate would almost surely be the underdog.

Now, in the flash of a gunshot, all that is changed. The Republican Presidential candidate, whoever he may be, will be running against a man with nine months in the White House—or none at all—instead of nearly four years of unremitting public exposure.

When the first shock of the tragedy has subsided and politicians talk again, they are sure to feel that the Republicans face a new, more favorable course next year. And this is likely to affect their choice of a candidate considerably.

Republican leaders have been saying for months that one of the powerful factors favoring the nomination of Senator Barry Goldwater of Arizona was the prevailing belief that President Kennedy would win anyway. Next year, they said, could be the one to gamble with a controversial candidate.

But now, they may reason, it may not be a time for Republican gambling. It may instead be a time to put a Republican candidate of the broadest possible appeal into the lists to challenge President Johnson or another Democratic nominee.

This conviction, if it became strong enough, could move Republican leaders strongly toward a candidate like Richard M. Nixon, or even Thomas E. Dewey.

LEADING CONTENDERS

President Lyndon Johnson took over John Kennedy's administration as well as his two major political problems, civil rights and the conflict in Vietnam. The new president quickly proved an adept executive, solidifying his leadership and his candidacy in the upcoming election. The opposition Republican Party seemed poised to nominate Sen. Barry Goldwater. Known for his outspoken conservatism, Goldwater sought a new direction for American politics by challenging the policies of the previous thirty years.

MAY 22, 1964
JOHNSON'S FIRST 6 MONTHS: POPULARITY AND PROBLEMS
By TOM WICKER

Special to The New York Times

WASHINGTON, May 21—As President Johnson completed his sixth month in office today, he stood high in all the popularity polls, dominated the national political outlook, and was heavily favored to win the election next Nov. 3. He was firmly in command of the Administration.

Only half a year after the assassination of President Kennedy elevated Mr. Johnson from the Vice-Presidency to the White House, he has a substantial record of achievement at home, and has not been heavily challenged or set back in affairs abroad.

Both at home and abroad, however, the President is still confronted with the two major problems that disturbed the last year of Mr. Kennedy's life.

Rights Problems Persist

In the United States, evidence is mounting that the civil rights crisis threatens not only social but political stability, and that its effects have reached into almost every state and section. Both Negro and white moderates—like Mr. Johnson—seem to have only a tenuous command of the situation, and in Congress there is no resolution of the bitter Senate debate on the Kennedy-Johnson civil rights bill.

In South Vietnam, most signs point to a deteriorating situation in the guerrilla warfare between the Vietcong, the Communist forces, and the Government troops with their United States advisers and support. The President asked this week for an increased United States commitment of military and economic assistance to South Vietnam, and there appears to be no immediate threat of a debacle such as the French suffered a decade ago at Dienbienphu.

Neither, however, does there appear to be hope of immediate or even reasonably quick success in ridding South Vietnam of the Communist threat. In neighboring Laos, Thailand and Cambodia, also, Communist influence is advancing by varying degrees, rounding out a picture of a hard-pressed United States position in Southeast Asia.

His Only Major Worries

These two problems—civil rights and South Vietnam—appear to many of Mr. Johnson's supporters and opponents to be the most likely—perhaps the only—areas in which he might suffer sizable setbacks between now and the Presidential election. Without such setbacks, few opponents and virtually no supporters believe that he can be defeated in November.

JUNE 8, 1964
EDITORIAL
GOLDWATER LEAD

Nomination in Sight

It was a political week.

As it ended, two questions were being asked: First, can Senator Goldwater be stopped? Second, can any Republican beat President Johnson?

The question of whether Mr. Goldwater can be stopped took on new urgency last week as a result of his victory in the California primary. It was a narrow victory—51 per cent of the vote for Senator Goldwater to 49 per cent for Governor Rockefeller. And much of the vote for the Governor was regarded not as pro-Rockefeller but anti-Goldwater—a further indication that he does not have broad support in the party rank and file.

Nevertheless, the Senator's actual and prospective delegate strength after California has put him so close to the nomination that only a coordinated effort by all the other elements in the party—the moderates, the Eastern liberals, the vaguely defined "Eisenhower Republicans"—might withhold it from him. There was speculation about the possibility of such a coalition when former President Eisenhower acted yesterday to hold the Republican convention open for Governor Scranton of Pennsylvania.

The question of whether President Johnson can be beaten arises because of his broadly based strength in the country. Mr. Johnson last week was again busily engaged in "nonpolitical" campaigning, emphasizing the potent themes of prosperity, peace, and American power.

The consensus is that unless the President's position is undercut either by a disaster in Southeast Asia, a civil rights explosion at home, or both, it is going to be hard for any Republican to beat him in November. But the concern among many Republicans is that a ticket headed by Senator Goldwater might go down to such disastrous defeat as to leave the party a shambles.

Victory in California

Despite computer-based forecasts even before some of the polls had closed, the California primary Tuesday was a cliff-hanger. The lead see-sawed back and forth well into the following morning as the returns came in. In the end, it was Goldwater strength in populous Los Angeles County that proved decisive. The final tally: Goldwater, 1,089,133; Rockefeller, 1,030,180. They were the only Presidential aspirants on the ballot and write-ins were not permitted.

In the campaign, Governor Rockefeller had sought to make the California primary a testing ground between the right and moderate wings of the Republican party. It took on something of that complexion when Ambassador Lodge's campaign managers urged his supporters to vote for Governor Rockefeller. Their strategy was dictated less by political ideology, however, than by recognition that if Senator Goldwater won in California, neither Mr. Lodge nor anyone else would have much chance for the nomination. Presumably some supporters of Richard Nixon and Governor Scranton also voted for Governor Rockefeller for the same reason.

An aspect of a right vs. moderate struggle had also been lent to the campaign by a statement by former President Eisenhower the week before last. The general set forth a series of Republican principles which most observers felt fit every prospective nominee except Senator Goldwater. But the impact was largely vitiated when General Eisenhower, on the eve of the primary, said that to read an anti-Goldwater implication into his statement was a "complete misinterpretation."

'Meandering Stream'

Thus the California primary—the first Senator Goldwater has won against any real opposition—was not regarded as a clear-cut test of moderate vs. right-wing sentiment in the G.O.P. rank and file. Certainly, there seemed few persons inclined to agree with Senator Goldwater's statement that the vote was "a victory for the mainstream of Republican thinking." ("All I can say is that we've got a meandering stream," Governor Rockefeller retorted.)

Civil Rights Act of 1964

When Congress passed the Civil Rights Act of 1964, the landmark legislation revealed the contrast between the prospective presidential candidates. Sen. Barry Goldwater futilely voted against the measure, declaring it an unconstitutional infringement of states' rights. President Lyndon Johnson signed it into law with gusto, while expressing private concerns over voter reactions in the South.

JUNE 19, 1964
GOLDWATER SAYS HE'LL VOTE 'NO' ON THE RIGHTS MEASURE

After Visiting Eisenhower to Explain His Stand, Arizonan Tells Senate in Speech Parts of Bill Are Unconstitutional

By CHARLES MOHR

Special to The New York Times

WASHINGTON, June 18—After a flying trip to Gettysburg to explain his reasons to former President Dwight D. Eisenhower, Senator Barry Goldwater told the Senate to-night that he would vote against the civil rights bill.

He said that the public accommodations and fair employment sections of the bill "fly in the face of the Constitution" and would lead to the "creation of a police state."

The Senate galleries were almost full and about half the 100 Senators were on the floor when Mr. Goldwater spoke. His colleagues gave a respectful hearing to Mr. Goldwater, who is the front-runner for the Republican Presidential nomination.

"If my vote is misconstrued, let it be, and let me suffer its consequences," the Arizona Senator said.

[Gov. William W. Scranton of Pennsylvania, a rival for the Republican nomination, urged Mr. Goldwater to repudiate his opposition to the civil rights bill.]

Tonight it was difficult to assess the consequences of Mr. Goldwater's speech, particularly whether his intention to vote against the great majority of his fellow Republicans would cause a reduction in his commanding lead for the nomination.

Mr. Goldwater slipped out of Washington unnoticed today in a private airplane and flew to Gettysburg, where he conferred with General Eisenhower at 2 P.M.

He undertook the trip to explain to General Eisenhower his reasons for opposing the civil rights bill. The conversation was almost wholly on this subject.

Mr. Goldwater's only comment was, "We see each other about once a month and this was just one of those meetings."

After his Senate speech explaining why he planned to vote "no" on final passage of the bill tomorrow, he was asked if he thought his stand would lose him delegates to the Republican National Convention, opening July 13 in San Francisco.

His back already turned, the conservative Senator, who was walking to an elevator, merely shrugged his shoulders expressively.

Opposed to Segregation

Mr. Goldwater said twice that he was "unalterably opposed to discrimination or segregation on the basis of race, color or creed, or any other basis."

However, he attacked the bill's public accommodations section, which would prohibit discrimination in such businesses as hotels and restaurants, and the fair employment practices section, which would prohibit discrimination in hiring. He termed these sections a "grave threat to the very essence of our basic system of government."

Mr. Goldwater said the two sections were unconstitutional and threatened a "constitutional republic in which 50 sovereign states have reserved to themselves and to the people those powers not specifically granted to the central government."

Although he said his basic objection was constitutional, he added the argument that genuine enforcement would "require the creation of a Federal police force of mammoth proportions" and might create an "informer" psychology in the national life.

He said that his vote would be "reluctantly cast" and that he had hoped that the bill would have been altered enough by amendments to permit a vote for it. He said he realized "fully that the Federal Government has a responsibility in the field of civil rights" and that he could have supported the bill without the two sections to which he objected.

JULY 3, 1964
PRESIDENT SIGNS CIVIL RIGHTS BILL; BIDS ALL BACK IT

Approves Sweeping Measure 5 Hours After Passage in House by 289–126 Vote

ASKS END OF INJUSTICE

Johnson Urges Closing of 'Springs of Racial Poison'—Maps Enforcement

By E. W. KENWORTHY

Special to The New York Times

WASHINGTON, July 2—President Johnson signed the Civil Rights Act of 1964 to-night.

It is the most far-reaching civil Rights law since Reconstruction days. The President announced steps to implement it and called on all Americans to help "eliminate the last vestiges of injustice in America."

"Let us close the springs of racial poison," he said in a short television address.

The President signed the bill in the East Room of the White House before television cameras shortly before 7 o'clock. That was about five hours after the House of Representatives had completed Congressional action on the sweeping bill.

Among other things, it prohibits discrimination in places of public accommodation, publicly owned facilities, employment and union membership and Federally aided programs.

Adopts Senate's Changes

The House approved, by a vote of 289 to 126, the changes that the Senate had made. All provisions of the measure became effective with President Johnson's signature except the one prohibiting discrimination in employment and union membership. This one goes into effect a year from now.

In announcing his implementation program, the President said he was, as had been previously indicated by White House sources, appointing former Gov. LeRoy Collins of Florida as director of the new Community Relations Service. Mr. Collins is now president of the National Association of Broadcasters.

Among other implementation steps, the President said he would name an advisory commission to help Mr. Collins resolve disputes arising under the bill. He will also ask Congress, Mr. Johnson said, for a supplemental appropriation to finance initial operations under the new law.

Surrounded by the leaders of both parties in both houses, who had labored to frame and pass the bill, President Johnson began his address to the nation by recalling that 188 years ago this week, "a small band of valiant men began a struggle for freedom" with the writing of the Declaration of Independence.

That struggle, he said, was a "turning point in history," and the ideals proclaimed in the Declaration of Independence still shape the struggles "of men who hunger for freedom."

Nevertheless, he declared, though Americans believe all men are created equal and have inalienable rights, many in America are denied equal treatment and do not enjoy those rights, or the blessings of liberty, "not because of their own failures, but because of the color of their skins."

The reasons, the President said, can be understood "without rancor or hatred" because they are deeply embedded in history, tradition and the nature of man.

"But it cannot continue," the President said with great earnestness.

Treatment Forbidden

The Constitution, the principles of freedom and morality all forbid such unequal treatment, he declared.

"And the law I will sign to-night forbids it," he said.

The President then sought to set fears at rest and to correct misapprehensions by stating that the new law would not restrict anyone's freedom "so long as he respects the rights of others," and would not give special treatment to any citizen.

"It does say that those who are equal before God shall now be equal in the polling booths, in the classrooms, in the factories, and in hotels, restaurants, movie theaters, and other places that provide service to the public."

· ·

THE CHANGING REPUBLICAN PARTY

The Republican Party argued over its platform for the 1964 campaign. Gov. Nelson Rockefeller, failing again in his bid for the nomination, led the moderates who sought to amend the platform. As he spoke in behalf of a declaration against "extremism," Rockefeller was booed into silence at the convention. Sen. Barry Goldwater, crafting a conservative platform that exposed the party's cleavages, proved his dominance.

JULY 15, 1964
PLATFORM VOTED

Negro Bloc Questions Arizonan's Fitness—Rockefeller Booed

By TOM WICKER
Special to The New York Times

SAN FRANCISCO, Wednesday, July 15—The Republican National Convention sounded a thunderous "no" last night to the proposition that it should condemn the John Birch Society. Then the delegates defeated a proposal to broaden the civil rights plank of the party platform.

The roll-call vote on the civil rights question was 897 to 409, with delegates from 26 states and territories voting solidly against the broadening amendment.

Delegates supporting Senator Barry Goldwater of Arizona stayed in their seats past midnight to defeat a third proposal by proponents of Gov. William W. Scranton

of Pennsylvania. It would have reaffirmed the principle of Presidential control of nuclear weapons.

The session, which ran more than eight hours, adjourned in a state of exhaustion at 12:36 A.M., after having adopted the platform by voice vote.

Rockefeller Hooted

But the high point of an unruly evening came earlier.

Spectators in the galleries and some delegates almost drowned out Governor Rockefeller with boos when he spoke strongly for a platform amendment that would have repudiated the right-wing Birch Society and other extremist groups.

Then the extremism amendment was easily defeated on a standing vote, divided roughly between the supporters of Senator Goldwater and Governor Scranton.

That vote, and the roll-call that followed on civil rights, established what everyone knew—that this convention is overwhelmingly for Senator Goldwater for President, and for the platform that was written for his campaign against President Johnson this fall.

The extremism amendment was the first offered by Scranton forces in a final platform fight, intended to salvage a partial victory from the convention.

Nothing could have better demonstrated the hopelessness of the effort more than the howling response to Governor Rockefeller's speech.

The Governor, interrupted at every pause with a chorus of boos and catcalls, stood patiently during most of the outbursts. Finally, he snapped:

"Some of you don't like to hear it, ladies and gentlemen—but it's the truth!"

That only brought more boos.

JULY 15, 1964
GOLDWATER SEES A TREND TO RIGHT

Says Defeat of 3 Liberal Amendments Is Reflecting Conservative Majority

By CHARLES MOHR

Special to The New York Times

SAN FRANCISCO, July 14—Senator Barry Goldwater said tonight that the defeat of liberal efforts to amend the Republican platform showed that "The Republican convention is reflecting the conservative majority in the Republican party."

Mr. Goldwater was commenting, through an aide who read his statement, on the defeat of liberal attempts to alter the platform on the subject of civil rights, extremism and Presidential control of nuclear weapons.

Earlier today Mr. Goldwater said that the Democrats could not "do more harm" to him than his Republican enemies had.

But he also said the conservatives had at last won control of the party from the Eastern liberal wing and that the party platform was a "true representation of the Republican party" of today.

Mr. Goldwater was in such good humor today that he bubbled like a glass of California champagne.

He told a breakfast caucus of the 18-member Oregon delegation that he was still looking for delegates all the time and then joked:

"I sometimes think there may be some delegates under my bed. But I look there and it's just the same old people."

• •

REPUBLICAN NOMINATION

The 1964 Republican convention in San Francisco nominated Barry Goldwater on the first ballot, pairing him with New York representative William Miller. Championing the bold platform as a "strong voice, not just an echo," Goldwater and Miller charged into an uphill battle for the presidency.

JULY 16, 1964

GOLDWATER IS NOMINATED ON FIRST BALLOT; HE CALLS JOHNSON 'BIGGEST FAKER IN U.S.'; SELECTS REP. MILLER AS HIS RUNNING MATE

VOTE IS 883 TO 214

Scranton Plea to Make It Unanimous Is Then Approved

By TOM WICKER

Special to The New York Times

SAN FRANCISCO, July 15—Barry Morris Goldwater, the champion of a new American conservatism, was nominated for President tonight by the 28th Republican National Convention.

The Arizona Senator, the 20th man in the line of Republican nominees that began with John C. Frémont and Abraham Lincoln, needed only one ballot to win the nomination and crush the moderate forces that had controlled his party for a quarter-century.

The only serious challenger was Gov. William W. Scranton of Pennsylvania.

At the conclusion of the ballot he appeared on the platform to move for the unanimous nomination of Senator Goldwater. The convention then adopted by acclamation a resolution making it so.

The count of the first ballot stood as follows for the two leading contenders:

Goldwater	883
Scranton	214

Will Accept Today

Senator Goldwater did not appear at the convention, which adjourned at 11:11 P.M. Pacific daylight time (2:11 A.M., Thursday, New York time). He will accept the nomination tomorrow, after his choice for Vice President, Representative William E. Miller of New York, is duly nominated.

There was never any contest from the moment Senator Everett McKinley Dirksen concluded his nominating speech for Senator Goldwater and set off a wild demonstration that thundered through the Cow Palace for 29 minutes.

Those placed in nomination besides Senator Goldwater and Governor Scranton, were Governor Rockefeller, Gov. George Romney of Michigan, Senator Margaret Chase Smith of Maine, Senator Hiram Fong of Hawaii, former Representative Walter H. Judd of Minnesota and Henry Cabot Lodge, who sent a message of withdrawal.

Not Serious Contenders

None was regarded as a serious candidate. Governor Rockefeller was placed in nomination to keep delegates from Oregon and other states, committed to him, from swinging to the Goldwater camp.

From the moment Mrs. C. Douglass Buck of Delaware began calling the roll, after 33 nominating and second speeches, Senator Goldwater sprang into a lead he never lost. The first state, Alabama, gave him its 20 votes and the total grew steadily.

JULY 16, 1964

SCORNFUL ATTACK

Senator Charges That President Changed Civil Rights Stand

By CHARLES MOHR

Special to The New York Times

SAN FRANCISCO, July 15—Senator Barry Goldwater accused President Johnson today of being "the biggest faker in the United States" and the "phoniest individual who ever came around."

The Arizona Republican made his extemporaneous remarks on his way to a service elevator in a back hall of the Mark Hopkins Hotel after addressing a "captive nations" rally.

A reporter asked him if the Republican National Convention's refusal to strengthen its civil rights plank would not give the Democrats a good issue in November.

The Senator's head snapped around. With an edge of scorn in his voice, he said:

"After Lyndon Johnson—the biggest faker in the United States? He opposed civil rights until this year. Let them make an issue of it. I'll recite the thousands of words he has spoken down the years against abolishing the poll tax and F.E.P.C. [Fair Employment Practices Commission]. He's the phoniest individual who ever came around."

Plans 'Vigorous Campaign'

Later in the day, after his nomination, Senator Goldwater told a news conference that he intended to wage a "vigorous campaign" but assumed that it would not be a campaign of personal attack.

He added that he expected President Johnson also to wage a vigorous campaign.

The Senator said he hoped the campaign would give the American people "time to think, and I hope that I'm the better salesman."

· ·

DEMOCRATIC CONVENTION

As if symbolizing the distance between the parties, Democrats met on the East Coast of the nation in Atlantic City. United on their liberal platform, the delegates happily awaited Johnson's decision on his vice-presidential running mate. Johnson selected Minnesota senator Hubert Humphrey, proclaiming, with subtle reference to his own tragic succession to the White House, that Humphrey was "best qualified to assume the office of President of the United States should that day come." Further invoking Kennedy's memory, Texas governor John Connally, also wounded during the attack on Kennedy, formally made the nomination.

AUGUST 27, 1964
DEMOCRATIC TICKET: JOHNSON AND HUMPHREY; BOTH NOMINATED BY ROARING ACCLAMATION; PRESIDENT AT SCENE, BREAKING A TRADITION
JOYOUS WELCOME

Hall Erupts in Sound as Suspense Over Ticket Is Ended

By TOM WICKER

Special to The New York Times

ATLANTIC CITY, Thursday, Aug. 27—Lyndon Baines Johnson of Texas, the man who took over the Presidency last Nov. 22 in the shattering hour of John F. Kennedy's assassination, was nominated for a term of his own last night by the 34th Democratic National Convention.

Then Mr. Johnson did what he loves to do. He smashed precedent by going before a turbulent and happy gathering of more than 5,000 delegates and alternates to name Senator Hubert H. Humphrey of Minnesota as his choice for the Vice-Presidential nomination.

The happy Democrats, and thousands of spectators jammed into Convention Hall, cheered wildly for both Mr. Johnson and Mr. Humphrey.

It also was Governor Connally who nominated Mr. Johnson in his first abortive bid for the Presidency, at the Chicago convention in 1956.

Gov. Edmund G. Brown of California shared the nominating process, and was followed by seven seconding speakers.

Roared Into Effect

The delegates whooped the nomination into effect with a roar. Speaker of the House John W. McCormack of Massachusetts, the permanent chairman, confirmed it with a bang of his huge gavel.

The nomination set off an enthusiastic demonstration. All over the hall banners waved, balloons soared toward the lofty curved ceiling, bands played in an ear-splitting cacophony, the great organ bellowed and men struggled through the jammed aisles, screaming at the top of their lungs.

When it was quieted with much gaveling, Mr. Johnson came to the platform and set off another booming demonstration.

He stood quietly through it, smiling, waving and nodding once or twice to friends. His wife and two daughters stood with him through the thunderous ovation.

As if to symbolize his grip on this convention, Mr. Johnson himself gaveled the delegates to order.

In his opening greeting, he included a friendly salutation to "columnists and commentators." That brought a laugh, in recollection of the Republicans' anger at the press at their convention in San Francisco.

Mr. Johnson also asked with a smile: "Did we really need all of these lights on?" That recalled his economy drive which included darkening many lights in the White House.

He said he and his party would begin tonight "the march toward an overwhelming victory for our party and for our nation."

Then he paid high tribute to President Kennedy, to the platform the Democrats had written under his close direction, and to the officers and delegates of the convention. He said the Credentials Committee had found a "fair answer" to the thorny Mississippi and Alabama seating disputes.

Then Mr. Johnson reached what he said was his "obligation under a very old American tradition," the recommendation of a Vice-Presidential candidate.

Mr. Johnson said he could make such a recommendation after his wide consultations with other Democrats and after "long prayerful consideration and private thought."

His "single guide," he said, had been "to find a man best qualified to assume the office of President of the United States should that day come."

Tested in Politics

The man he had found, he continued, had been tested in politics, had had long experience in public life and knew the problems of both the world and the nation.

"This is not a sectional choice," Mr. Johnson said. "This is not merely a way to balance the ticket. This is simply the best man in America for the job."

Stretching the suspense as far as it would go, the President held the name in reserve to the end. His man, he said, would make the Vice-Presidency an "important instrument of the executive" and help "carry America around the world."

His confidence in his choice, Mr. Johnson said, was not his alone but "represents the opinion of the great majority in the Democratic Party."

As if sorry to share his secret, Mr. Johnson said slowly: "I hope that you will choose as the next Vice President of the United States my long . . . my longtime. . . ." At this point laughter broke out in the hall at the lengths to which the President was carrying the suspense. " . . . My trusted colleague . . . Senator Hubert Humphrey of Minnesota!"

The name of the state was drowned in a mighty roar. As the delegates and spectators loosed their enthusiasm and vocal chords again, Senator and Mrs. Humphrey and their children came forward to join the Johnson family. Other Democrats joined the throng while the demonstration roared on.

During the demonstration that followed Mr. Johnson's nomination, his wife and two daughters, Lynda Bird and Luci Baines, sat in a special box high above the uproar. They received an ovation of their own when they appeared in the hall just before Mr. McCormack convened the session.

Late in the evening, Mrs. Humphrey joined them and also received the tribute of the crowd.

GOLDWATER CONSERVATISM

Senator Goldwater focused his campaign for president on ideological conservatism, rejecting the liberal revolution begun by Franklin Roosevelt in 1932. Equating liberalism with socialism, Goldwater charged that it had eroded American morality and individualism. His new perspective repelled many voters, but initiated a philosophical argument that would continue for decades.

JULY 19, 1964
GOLDWATER—HIS PERSONALITY AND HIS BELIEFS

By CHARLES MOHR

Special to The New York Times

PHOENIX, Ariz., July 18—Most voters may have already formed opinions about the new Republican Presidential nominee, Barry Goldwater, and those opinions are generally of the strongest nature.

But Senator Goldwater can be expected to surprise both his critics and his fans in the coming campaign—to implant nagging doubts concerning the images that individual voters hold of him.

The reason is that Mr. Goldwater is a strangely contradictory personality, a man who can seem different from day to day and even from hour to hour.

Some persons who regard him as a right-wing ogre will at times be irresistibly attracted by the warmth of his personality or by the almost deferential modesty with which he can sometimes advance an opinion—as though he were turning its validity over in his own mind.

But at other times they may be left nearly breathless by the force and aggressiveness with which he can advance a highly controversial idea.

Even conservatives may find this a rather surprising campaign. Mr. Goldwater is not the spokesman for a broadly understood general philosophy as much as he is the prophet of a uniquely individualistic structure of his own gospel.

He ignores many issues that interest most conservatives, notably the asserted menace of internal Communist subversion.

More attention has been given to Mr. Goldwater's foreign policy views and he, himself, usually gives them priority in speeches. But it is his view of American Government that appears to be the most basic part of his conservative philosophy and the part least elusive of understanding by a liberal.

Mr. Goldwater believes that it is too late to repeal the social welfare legislation that is the legacy of the New Deal. But he would like to change the criteria for future governmental action.

He believes that before the Federal Government begins to act to solve a problem that it must first be clearly demonstrated that a problem exists. Secondly, it must be determined if the will, finances and ability to solve the problem cannot be found at the state or local level. Then only can the Federal Government act.

The burden of proof—of the necessity and of the appropriateness—of legislation would be on the Federal Government.

Mr. Goldwater also believes that the state and local governments must not only be given freedom to act but, more basically, freedom not to act.

He contends that local governments are a valuable laboratory of democracy and a convenient filing case for folly. He likes multiple solutions for difficult problems so that, as he says, mistakes can be buried locally, and successes can be propagated nationally through the force of their success.

Mr. Goldwater does not have the ability mercilessly to exploit an idea as a demagogue might. His speeches often take on a highly moralistic tone, but are spoken in the manner of a gruff old captain reading from the Book of Common Prayer as he buries someone at sea.

Many slightly baffled audiences have heard him chide Americans for their preoccupation with "material wealth." It is not precisely what they expect since Mr. Goldwater on other occasions is the leading champion of the rights of property among American politicians.

The Politician

But the thing about Mr. Goldwater as a politician is that he can express a point of view in ways so different as to change the very content of the idea.

The Senator has told audiences that he opposes medicare because it would weaken the sense of responsibility of children for their aged parents. To some listeners this idea is extraordinary enough in itself.

However, Mr. Goldwater has sometimes gone on to express the idea this way: "I'm against medicare because I don't want to see the Federal Government destroy the American family."

On at least two occasions—before the Commonwealth Club of California and in Columbus, Ga.—Mr. Goldwater has given extremely lucid and compelling statements of the conservative creed.

But once in Nogales, Ariz., he said he opposed the liberals, such as President Johnson, because "They want to take us back to the days of monarchy, dictatorship and one-man rule."

Thus Mr. Goldwater has an unquestioned ability to be a forceful and immensely likeable advocate for an idea and, at the same time, has a certain tendency to excess in language. In a long campaign, the fact is that neither characteristic may become dominant and the public view of Mr. Goldwater may vary from day to day depending on his delivery and his mood.

SEPTEMBER 8, 1964
GOLDWATER TAX PLAN ASKS A 25% CUT OVER 5 YEARS

By CHARLES MOHR

Special to The New York Times

PHOENIX, Ariz., Sept. 7—If elected President, Senator Barry Goldwater would attempt to reduce income taxes by 25 per cent over a five-year period and to stabilize Federal Government expenditures at roughly present levels, a source close to the Republican Presidential candidate said today.

Mr. Goldwater, who spent much of the day filming an informal network television show at his home here, will make a major speech on tax policy tomorrow night at Los Angeles.

[In a Labor Day address in South Bend, Ind., the Senator's running mate, William E. Miller, warned that the policies of the Administration would flood the United States with foreign labor and goods.]

The source familiar with Mr. Goldwater's thinking said he guessed that no tax cut could be proposed until the fiscal year 1967, beginning July 1, 1966, if Mr. Goldwater were elected President.

Mr. Goldwater first broached the idea of what he calls "automatic" annual income-tax cuts in a Labor Day statement that was released Saturday.

His views evolved after consultation with such "conservative" and non-Keynesian economists as Dr. Warren Nutter of the University of Virginia and Dr. Milton Friedman of the University of Chicago, the source told newsmen here.

Mr. Goldwater's hope for a series of tax cuts—or rebates—is based, the source said, on the theory that the gross national product or "national income" is steadily rising and will steadily generate more tax revenue.

If Federal expenditures can be stabilized, Mr. Goldwater is said to believe, a resulting excess in revenue over expenditure can be returned to individual and corporate taxpayers over a period of years.

The source said that Mr. Goldwater was thinking in terms of an annual 5 per cent reduction over a period of five years. This would not be a reduction of 5 per cent in the tax rate itself but, rather, in the amount of tax paid.

One area, the source indicated, where Mr. Goldwater might try to reduce Federal spending would be in the space program, especially by slowing down investment in the Apollo manned moon landing, which is now aimed at completion in this decade.

Generally, however, the Republican nominee is said to be thinking less of eliminating programs than of putting a stringent brake on initiating new Federal programs and of subjecting proposals for such programs to "the closest scrutiny" to see that they were "completely justified."

The source said that Mr. Goldwater's tax proposal was "tied in with a program of, if not reducing, at least holding Federal expenditures at a constant level."

SEPTEMBER 11, 1964
GOLDWATER LINKS THE WELFARE STATE TO RISE IN CRIME

By CHARLES MOHR

Special to The New York Times

MINNEAPOLIS, Sept 10—Senator Barry Goldwater linked welfare state social theories to rising crime rates today. Such theories, the Republican Presidential candidate said, encourage the idea that have-nots can take from the haves.

In what appeared to be an appeal to the small town, rural America where much of Mr. Goldwater's strength is said to be, the Senator deplored what he called "the degradation we see going on in the large cities of the East completely dominated by the Democratic party."

In his speech at a rally here, Mr. Goldwater, as he has been doing consistently, condemned lawlessness and disorder on American streets.

But for the first time the conservative Arizonian sought to relate this to liberal social welfare attitudes.

"If it is entirely proper," he said, "for government to take from some to give to others, then won't some be led to believe that they can rightfully take from anyone who has more than they?"

He criticized what he called "the assumption by the state of the obligation to keep men in a style to which demagogues encourage them."

And he declared:

"This can never again be truly a nation of law and order until it is again fully a nation of individual responsible citizens."

Mr. Goldwater quoted a report by the Federal Bureau of Investigation that he said showed a 15 per cent rise in the crime rate in the first six months of the year and then deplored youth riots in Oregon and New Hampshire and "gang rape in California."

He said:

"Vote to continue this present Administration in power and you will have voted to end the Federal system with its checks and balances—you will have voted instead a form of Federal tyranny" over jobs, schools and possibly prayers.

He asked: "Do you want your children to live in a collectivized ant heap or in the open spaces of freedom?"

Mr. Goldwater, who voted against the Civil Rights Act of 1964, appeared to allude to that fact when he said: "I charge, with a sincerely heavy heart, that the more the Federal government has attempted to legislate morality, the more it actually has incited hatreds and violence."

· ·

VIETNAM

As the battle for the presidency raged at home, the United States battled Communists abroad, particularly in Vietnam. In August 1964 the USS *Maddox* was involved in what became known as the "Gulf of Tonkin incident," prompting Congress to authorize the president to "take all actions necessary" to safeguard American interests in the area. Vietnam became a political issue during the campaign, with Johnson displaying his powers as commander in chief and Goldwater declaring the U.S. response insufficient.

AUGUST 4, 1964
JOHNSON DIRECTS NAVY TO DESTROY ANY NEW RAIDERS
2d Destroyer and Air Cover Ordered in Gulf of Tonkin After Maddox Attack
HANOI TO GET PROTEST
Communist Regime Charge of Raids by U.S. Forces Termed Groundless
By EDWIN L. DALE Jr.
Special to The New York Times

WASHINGTON, Aug. 3—President Johnson has directed the Navy to shoot to destroy attackers in any future incident in the Gulf of Tonkin off North Vietnam.

In orders issued yesterday and announced today, the President also added a second destroyer to the patrol in the gulf and instructed the Navy to provide an air patrol over the destroyers.

The orders followed the unsuccessful attack yesterday on the destroyer Maddox by three North Vietnamese torpedo boats. The Maddox drove off the attackers and damaged them, but did not follow up to sink them.

One of the boats, the Navy said, was left dead in the water. An air search today failed to produce any trace of it, leaving authorities uncertain whether it sank or was towed away.

Channel for Protest

The State Department announced that a formal protest would be made over the incident. It was understood that the protest would be directed to North Vietnam, probably through the three-nation International Control Commission for Indochina. The United States does not have diplomatic relations with North Vietnam.

President Johnson disclosed this morning his orders to the Navy. He called newsmen into his office, read a brief statement and refused to answer questions. He said the orders were issued yesterday. The statement said:

"I have instructed the Navy:

"1. To continue the patrols in the Gulf of Tonkin off the coast of North Vietnam,

"2. To double the force by adding an additional destroyer to the one already on patrol,

"3. To provide a combat air patrol over the destroyers, and

"4. To issue orders to the commanders of the combat aircraft and the two destroyers, (a) To attack any force which attacks them in international waters, and (b) To attack with the objective not only of driving off the force but of destroying it."

In another development affecting North Vietnam, the State Department denied as "without foundation" Hanoi's charge of two separate United States attacks on North Vietnamese territory.

AUGUST 11, 1964
GOLDWATER CALLS FOR DRIVE TO FINISH WAR IN VIETNAM
Implies Johnson Did Not Go Far Enough in Air Attacks on Reds—Bids U.S. Seek 'Peace Through Preparedness'
By CHARLES MOHR
Special to The New York Times

WASHINGTON, Aug. 10—Senator Barry Goldwater indicated today that he believed President Johnson had not gone far enough in last week's air attacks on North Vietnam.

Mr. Goldwater said that the nation must "prosecute the war in Vietnam with the object of ending it" and that "taking strong action simply to return to the status quo is not worthy of our sacrifices" or the national ideals.

The Republican Presidential candidate said he believed he must point out that the President's action had been no more than "a response, an incident, not a program or a new policy; a tactical reaction, not a new winning strategy."

Mr. Goldwater also asserted that the guerrilla war in South Vietnam "would never have occurred had the enemy really believed that we would have moved in."

The Arizona Senator made these remarks in a speech to about 1,500 persons at the national convention of the National Association of Counties. It was his first major speech since he was nominated last month.

The audience of officials and employees of county governments applauded Mr. Goldwater four or five times during his speech.

Striking a theme of "peace through preparedness," Mr. Goldwater accused the Democratic Administration of having shown an "utter disregard" for the development of new weapons systems. He asserted that unless present defense policies and plans were changed that the United States' deliverable nuclear capacity may be cut by 90 per cent.

On the subject of the Vietnam crisis and the attacks of Communist torpedo boats on United States destroyers, Mr. Goldwater said:

"I charge that our policies have become so involved, so twisted with diplomatic red tape that the enemy might well have wondered if we would accept their attacks at sea on the same basis that we have been accepting their attacks on land."

He said that, "before anyone gets the wrong idea," he wanted to say he supported the President's firm action, but he called it no more than a response.

"Yes," said Mr. Goldwater, "all of us support the President in this strong, right action. No—we will not let this one action obscure a multitude of other needed actions."

He said that support of the President's action would not be allowed to "silence our basic criticism."

This criticism he said, is that "the war in Vietnam—and let's call it what it is, a war—is being fought under policies that obscure our purposes, confuse our allies, particularly the Vietnamese, and encourage the enemy to prolong the fighting."

Mr. Goldwater said that to prosecute the war in South Vietnam with the object of "ending" it "does not mean the use of military power alone."

"We have," he said, "vast resources of economic, political and psychological power which have not even been tapped in our Vietnamese strategy.

"These, I suggest, can be the peaceful means of waging war on war itself, and all I say is, let's use them."

Mr. Goldwater said that World War I, World War II and the Korean War would not have taken place if enemies had not thought that the United States was too weak to fight or lacked the will to fight.

Mr. Goldwater, who is a major general in the Air Force Reserve and a strong believer in strategic strength, said that appropriations for strategic deterrent forces were "hardly half of what they were three fiscal years ago."

He then made his assertion that ability to deliver nuclear weapons may be cut 90 per cent by the next decade. He did not amplify this, but in previous speeches Mr. Goldwater has made similar remarks and explained them the following way.

He has remarked that 90 per cent of the megatons of power of United States nuclear weapons are now carried by strategic bombers and that, therefore, when bombers are phased out there will be a marked reduction in delivery capability.

Mr. Goldwater smiled, and evoked a laugh, when he said that Sir Winston Churchill "once was called an extremist—and that's quite a popular word around today—because he spoke up for Britain's defense at a time when appeasement was popular."

On the subject of extremism, Mr. Goldwater advised the men in the audience to ask themselves if they wanted their wives to be "extremely faithful to you or just moderately faithful."

He said, in a reference to his wife, Margaret, "I've told Peggy what I'd prefer."

Mr. Goldwater, who spoke a little after 11 A.M., spent most of the day at his apartment, press aides said.

• •

NUCLEAR WEAPONS

The Johnson and Goldwater campaigns clashed throughout the fall months over the use and control of nuclear weapons, the issue gaining prominence after China detonated its first nuclear weapon in October. Goldwater encouraged decentralized control of nuclear weapons, allowing emergency usage by field commanders. Johnson warned that Goldwater's "casual" approach risked future nuclear conflicts. His attacks culminated in the notorious "Daisy" ad, implying that only Johnson could avoid nuclear war.

OCTOBER 5, 1964
EDITORIAL
THE ISSUE: NUCLEAR CONTROL

Immediately after both parties had finished drafting their platforms and nominating their Presidential candidates, this newspaper announced its belief that the interests of the people of the United States and indeed of the world would be best served by an emphatic electoral victory for the Johnson-Humphrey ticket and an equally strong rejection of the kind of policy and thinking for which Senator Goldwater and Representative Miller stand. Developments in the first month of the campaign have reinforced our belief in the correctness of that conclusion.

In a series of editorials, of which this is the first, we shall attempt to appraise the positions of the rival candidates on the major campaign issues. The logical starting point is the control of nuclear weapons, the issue that has stirred the fiercest controversy and the one with the most fateful implications for national and world survival.

This issue has two very different facets: (1) Should military commanders share with the President the authority to order the use of any part of the American atomic arsenal; and (2) which candidate is better fitted to exercise the judgment on when to use these awesome arms and on how to reduce the danger that they will ever have to be used?

On the diffusion of control, the obscurity with which Mr. Goldwater so often states his position resulted in wide initial belief that he favored delegating authority to field commanders to use tactical atomic weapons in battle. However, he now emphasizes that his sole purpose is to place a stock of "small conventional nuclear weapons" under control of the NATO Supreme Commander in Europe. President Johnson ridicules the idea that any nuclear arms can be considered "conventional," and warns that escalation of an atomic conflict would leave 100 million Americans and 100 million Russians dead in the first exchange.

Unanswered in the debate are authoritative reports that contingency plans already in existence do empower United States military chiefs to employ nuclear weapons in specified situations of extreme emergency. But it is plain that, to the extent such plans do exist, they involve rigorous limitations not contained in the Goldwater proposal. Suggestions for sharing weapons control with our European allies as a means of increasing Atlantic unity have, of course, long been under discussion. However, they contemplate keeping decision in the civilian heads of government, not the military.

We subscribe to Mr. Johnson's assertion that no President can divest himself of the responsibility for controlling a force of such devastating destructive power. The insensitivity to the danger of atomic holocaust Mr. Goldwater reveals in describing even the smallest nuclear weapons as "conventional" fortifies our conviction that he is not the man to put in charge of decisions that will determine mankind's fate.

The Goldwater campaign has turned into an attempt to lull away fears that his combination of bellicosity and rashness will multiply the peril of total war. But no mass infusion of televised tranquilizers can banish memory of his impetuous demand that the Marines be sent into Cuba to force Castro to restore Guantanamo's water or the airiness with which he discussed the possible use of atomic weapons to "defoliate" Communist supply trails in Vietnam.

He voted against the partial nuclear test-ban treaty, and he believes this country can achieve "total victory" over Communism by coupling military strength with ultimatums—a policy reflected in his casual observation that the way to negotiate with Communist China was to tell it our troops would "blow up a bridge, or something" if Peking did not stop helping the Viet-cong.

In his ten months in the White House Mr. Johnson has maintained a wise balance between military resolution and restraint. He has shown an awareness of the complexity of current international relationships, the need for flexibility as well as firmness in United States policy and, above all, the importance of endeavoring to contain conflict, rather than expand it. We have reservations about some of his specific actions, but we have no reservations in recognizing him as an infinitely more dependable custodian of the peace than his Republican rival.

· ·

Election Results

Lyndon Johnson was elected to a full term as president in a landslide. The final vote provided the largest margin of victory in electoral history, giving Johnson and his Great Society programs a clear mandate over Barry Goldwater's conservatism. Offered two distinct alternatives, the nation chose Johnson and liberalism—for a while.

1964 POPULAR VOTE

STATE	TOTAL VOTE	LYNDON B. JOHNSON (DEMOCRAT) VOTES	%	BARRY M. GOLDWATER (REPUBLICAN) VOTES	%	ERIC HASS (SOCIALIST LABOR) VOTES	%	CLIFTON DeBERRY (SOCIALIST WORKERS) VOTES	%
Alabama[1]	689,818	—	0.0	479,085	69.5	—	0.0	—	0.0
Alaska	67,259	44,329	65.9	22,930	34.1	—	0.0	—	0.0
Arizona	480,770	237,753	49.5	242,535	50.4	482	0.1	—	0.0
Arkansas	560,426	314,197	56.1	243,264	43.4	—	0.0	—	0.0
California	7,057,586	4,171,877	59.1	2,879,108	40.8	489	0.0	378	0.0
Colorado	776,986	476,024	61.3	296,767	38.2	302	0.0	2,537	0.3
Connecticut	1,218,578	826,269	67.8	390,996	32.1	—	0.0	—	0.0
Delaware	201,320	122,704	60.9	78,078	38.8	113	0.1	—	0.0
Dist. of Col.	198,597	169,796	85.5	28,801	14.5	—	0.0	—	0.0
Florida	1,854,481	948,540	51.1	905,941	48.9	—	0.0	—	0.0
Georgia	1,139,335	522,556	45.9	616,584	54.1	—	0.0	—	0.0
Hawaii	207,271	163,249	78.8	44,022	21.2	—	0.0	—	0.0
Idaho	292,477	148,920	50.9	143,557	49.1	—	0.0	—	0.0
Illinois	4,702,841	2,796,833	59.5	1,905,946	40.5	—	0.0	—	0.0
Indiana	2,091,606	1,170,848	56.0	911,118	43.6	1,374	0.1	—	0.0
Iowa	1,184,539	733,030	61.9	449,148	37.9	182	0.0	159	0.0
Kansas	857,901	464,028	54.1	386,579	45.1	1,901	0.2	—	0.0
Kentucky	1,046,105	669,659	64.0	372,977	35.7	—	0.0	—	0.0
Louisiana	896,293	387,068	43.2	509,225	56.8	—	0.0	—	0.0
Maine	380,965	262,264	68.8	118,701	31.2	—	0.0	—	0.0
Maryland	1,116,457	730,912	65.5	385,495	34.5	—	0.0	—	0.0
Massachusetts	2,344,798	1,786,422	76.2	549,727	23.4	4,755	0.2	—	0.0
Michigan	3,203,102	2,136,615	66.7	1,060,152	33.1	1,704	0.1	3,817	0.1
Minnesota	1,554,462	991,117	63.8	559,624	36.0	2,544	0.2	1,177	0.1
Mississippi	409,146	52,618	12.9	356,528	87.1	—	0.0	—	0.0
Missouri	1,817,879	1,164,344	64.0	653,535	36.0	—	0.0	—	0.0
Montana	278,628	164,246	58.9	113,032	40.6	—	0.0	332	0.1
Nebraska	584,154	307,307	52.6	276,847	47.4	—	0.0	—	0.0
Nevada	135,433	79,339	58.6	56,094	41.4	—	0.0	—	0.0
New Hampshire	288,093	184,064	63.9	104,029	36.1	—	0.0	—	0.0
New Jersey	2,847,663	1,868,231	65.6	964,174	33.9	7,075	0.2	8,183	0.3
New Mexico	328,645	194,015	59.0	132,838	40.4	1,217	0.4	—	0.0
New York	7,166,275	4,913,102	68.6	2,243,559	31.3	6,118	0.1	3,228	0.0
North Carolina	1,424,983	800,139	56.2	624,844	43.8	—	0.0	—	0.0
North Dakota	258,389	149,784	58.0	108,207	41.9	—	0.0	224	0.1
Ohio	3,969,196	2,498,331	62.9	1,470,865	37.1	—	0.0	—	0.0
Oklahoma	932,499	519,834	55.7	412,665	44.3	—	0.0	—	0.0
Oregon	786,305	501,017	63.7	282,779	36.0	—	0.0	—	0.0
Pennsylvania	4,822,690	3,130,954	64.9	1,673,657	34.7	5,092	0.1	10,456	0.2
Rhode Island	390,091	315,463	80.9	74,615	19.1	—	0.0	—	0.0
South Carolina	524,779	215,723	41.1	309,048	58.9	—	0.0	—	0.0
South Dakota	293,118	163,010	55.6	130,108	44.4	—	0.0	—	0.0
Tennessee	1,143,946	634,947	55.5	508,965	44.5	—	0.0	—	0.0
Texas	2,626,811	1,663,185	63.3	958,566	36.5	—	0.0	—	0.0
Utah	401,413	219,628	54.7	181,785	45.3	—	0.0	—	0.0
Vermont	163,089	108,127	66.3	54,942	33.7	—	0.0	—	0.0
Virginia	1,042,267	558,038	53.5	481,334	46.2	2,895	0.3	—	0.0
Washington	1,258,556	779,881	62.0	470,366	37.4	7,772	0.6	537	0.0
West Virginia	792,040	538,087	67.9	253,953	32.1	—	0.0	—	0.0
Wisconsin	1,691,815	1,050,424	62.1	638,495	37.7	1,204	0.1	1,692	0.1
Wyoming	142,716	80,718	56.6	61,998	43.4	—	0.0	—	0.0
TOTALS	**70,644,592**	**43,129,566**	**61.1**	**27,178,188**	**38.5**	**45,219**	**0.1**	**32,720**	**0.0**

1. Plurality of 268,353 votes is calculated on the basis of Goldwater's vote and the 210,732 votes cast for the unpledged Democratic elector ticket.

OTHER VOTES	%	PLURALITY	
210,732	30.5	268,353	R
—	0.0	21,399	D
—	0.0	4,782	R
2,965	0.5	70,933	D
5,734	0.1	1,292,769	D
1,356	0.2	179,257	D
1,313	0.1	435,273	D
425	0.2	44,626	D
—	0.0	140,995	D
—	0.0	42,599	D
195	0.0	94,028	R
—	0.0	119,227	D
—	0.0	5,363	D
62	0.0	890,887	D
8,266	0.4	259,730	D
2,020	0.2	283,882	D
5,393	0.6	77,449	D
3,469	0.3	296,682	D
—	0.0	122,157	R
—	0.0	143,563	D
50	0.0	345,417	D
3,894	0.2	1,236,695	D
814	0.0	1,076,463	D
—	0.0	431,493	D
—	0.0	303,910	R
—	0.0	510,809	D
1,018	0.4	51,214	D
—	0.0	30,460	D
—	0.0	23,245	D
—	0.0	80,035	D
—	0.0	904,057	D
575	0.2	61,177	D
268	0.0	2,669,543	D
—	0.0	175,295	D
174	0.1	41,577	D
—	0.0	1,027,466	D
—	0.0	107,169	D
2,509	0.3	218,238	D
2,531	0.1	1,457,297	D
13	0.0	240,848	D
8	0.0	93,325	R
—	0.0	32,902	D
34	0.0	125,982	D
5,060	0.2	704,619	D
—	0.0	37,843	D
20	0.0	53,185	D
—	0.0	76,704	D
—	0.0	309,515	D
—	0.0	284,134	D
—	0.0	411,929	D
—	0.0	18,720	D
258,899	0.4	15,951,378	D

NOVEMBER 4, 1964
JOHNSON SWAMPS GOLDWATER AND KENNEDY BEATS KEATING; DEMOCRATS WIN LEGISLATURE

TURNOUT IS HEAVY

President Expected to Get 60% of Vote, With 44 States

By TOM WICKER

Lyndon Baines Johnson of Texas compiled one of the greatest landslide victories in American history yesterday to win a four-year term of his own as the 36th President of the United States.

Senator Hubert H. Humphrey of Minnesota, Mr. Johnson's running mate on the Democratic ticket, was carried into office as Vice President.

Mr. Johnson's triumph, giving him the "loud and clear" national mandate he had said he wanted, brought 44 states and the District of Columbia, with 486 electoral votes, into the Democratic column.

Senator Barry Goldwater, the Republican candidate, who sought to offer the people "a choice, not an echo" with a strongly conservative campaign, won only five states in the Deep South and gained a narrow victory in his home state of Arizona. Carrying it gave him a total of 52 electoral votes.

Senator Plans Statement

A heavy voter turnout favored the more numerous Democrats.

In Austin, Tex., Mr. Johnson appeared in the Municipal Auditorium to say that his victory was "a tribute to men and women of all parties."

"It is a mandate for unity, for a Government that serves no special interest," he said.

The election meant, he said, that "our nation should forget our petty differences and stand united before all the world."

Mr. Goldwater did not concede. A spokesman announced that the Senator would make no statement until 10 A.M. to-day in Phoenix.

Johnson Carries Texas

But the totals were not the only marks of the massive Democratic victory. Traditionally Republican states were bowled over like tenpins—Vermont, Indiana, Kansas, Nebraska, Wyoming, among others.

Former Attorney General Robert F. Kennedy, riding Mr. Johnson's long coattails, overwhelmed Senator Kenneth B. Keating in New York.

But ticket splitting was widespread. And in the South, Georgia went Republican; never in its history had it done so. Into the Goldwater column, too, went Mississippi, Alabama, Louisiana and South Carolina—all part of the once solidly Democratic South.

But Mr. Johnson carried the rest of the South, including Virginia, Tennessee and Florida—states that went Republican in 1960. He carried his home state of Texas by a large margin and won a majority of the popular vote in the Old Confederacy.

Nationwide, the President's popular vote margin apparently would reach 60 per cent or more. His popular vote plurality had risen early this morning to more than 13 million.

The President was clearly carrying into office with him a heavily Democratic Congress, with a substantially bigger majority in the House.

The vote poured in, through the high-speed counting system of the Network Election Service, at such a rate that the leading television broadcasters were calling it a Johnson victory about 9 P.M.

But the only time the Republican candidate ever was in front was early yesterday morning when Dixville Notch, N. H., traditionally the earliest-reporting precinct in the nation, gave him eight votes to none for Mr. Johnson.

After that, in the President's own slogan, it was "L.B.J. all the way."

. . . .

REALIGNMENT?

The landslide outcome of the 1964 presidential race signaled critical movements within the electorate. Goldwater brought political ideology to the forefront of politics, recruiting conservatives into the Republican Party. Conservative white Democrats particularly heeded this call, fragmenting the once-solid Democratic South. In future elections, this movement of voters altered the balance of power in American politics.

Rejected is the thesis that the challenges of an era of dynamic, relentless change in domestic and foreign affairs can be met by dismantling the Federal Government or by shaking a nuclear fist at the rest of the world.

NOVEMBER 4, 1964
EDITORIAL
THE JOHNSON LANDSLIDE

The American people have given emphatic notice that they want to move forward constructively along the road of international understanding and domestic progress. Their overwhelming vote for the Johnson-Humphrey ticket reflects popular attachment to the policies of moderate liberalism that have prevailed through more than three decades of Democratic and Republican rule and that have contributed so notably to national prosperity and security.

Rejected is the thesis that the challenges of an era of dynamic, relentless change in domestic and foreign affairs can be met by dismantling the Federal Government or by shaking a nuclear fist at the rest of the world. No more decisive rebuke could have been administered to the right-wing extremists whose command of the Republican national machinery plunged that great party onto its destructive course.

The tragedy of this election, as President Johnson emphasized in his televised talk on Election eve, was that the sterility of the choice offered by the opposition prevented any meaningful discussion of the real issues that confront the United States.

Indisputably, however, the landslide does attest to support for the President as a leader who can be trusted with sole control over weapons capable of destroying all mankind. The assurance that maximum restraint will continue to govern the exercise of that fateful power will be greeted with relief in every land. So will the knowledge that the United States has reaffirmed its intent of seeking cooperative relations with every country that wants to join in building a world of peace and abundance.

The path to that kind of world remains ill-charted. In both West and East, alliances are disordered; the situation in South Vietnam is abysmal; the power struggle in the Kremlin makes hazardous any forecast of Soviet intentions; Peking's bomb has vastly increased the peril of nuclear proliferation. Yet the strong mandate for flexibility of approach now given to the man in the White House offers some hope, in contrast to the despair that would have been engendered throughout the world—especially among America's allies—by a Goldwater victory.

Domestically, the voters have made it plain that they endorse the pledges of equality in law guaranteed to all Americans by the Civil Rights Act and that they believe the law's firm enforcement will quell civil strife, not incite it. The real obligation in the next four years will be to speed progress toward better schools, better homes, better jobs and all the other ingredients of the "Great Society," whose cloudy outlines were sketched by Mr. Johnson during the campaign. America has the means to provide full opportunity for all its citizens, Negro and white; it still lacks practical programs for translating those means into actuality.

For the Republican party, the results border on catastrophe. In 1960 it came within an eyelash of winning the Presidency; this year it suffered the most sweeping repudiation any major party has had in this century. Dashed into defeat with the Goldwater-Miller ticket were many estimable candidates for lesser office, whose voices will be gravely missed in the determination of balanced public policy.

The primary fault, of course, rests with the right-wing coalition that insisted on a revolutionary break with the centrist tradition of American politics and sought to fashion an electoral victory out of the fears, hates and frustrations of disaffected citizens. But this group could never have gained the ascendancy if so many of the party's moderates and liberals had not defaulted in the bitter primary campaign that preceded Senator Goldwater's nomination at San Francisco. The great task for the G.O.P. now will be to move back into the sunlight of modernism and evict from positions of party power those who would condemn it permanently to a role of ineffectuality and reaction. The country needs a vital two-party system, but it cannot have it if one party stands only for disaster.

NOVEMBER 4, 1964
SOUTH REVERSES VOTING PATTERNS

Goldwater Makes Inroads, but More Electoral Votes Go to the President

BY JOHN HERBERS

Special to The New York Times

ATLANTA, Nov. 3—President Johnson carried a majority of Southern states tonight by turning the normal voting patterns inside out.

The rural Deep South, solidly Democratic in the past, voted for Senator Barry Goldwater of Arizona on the Republican ticket. The states on the border of the region, which had gone Republican in recent Presidential elections, returned to the Democrats.

But so strong was the Goldwater tide in the Deep South that seven Republican Congressional candidates rode to victory on the Senator's coattails from districts that had been Democratic since Reconstruction.

The Republicans made their biggest gains in Alabama, where five candidates for Congress defeated Democratic opponents.

President Johnson carried Virginia, North Carolina, Florida, Tennessee, Arkansas and Texas with a total of 81 electoral votes. Senator Goldwater carried Louisiana, Mississippi, Alabama, Georgia and South Carolina with a total of 47 electoral votes.

South Carolina and Mississippi had not voted for Republican Presidents since Reconstruction.

In Alabama, voters marked a straight Republican ticket, dumping three incumbent Congressmen and defeating two other Democratic candidates.

Only Representative Armistead Seldon in Alabama escaped the Republican sweep. Representative George Grant, who had been in the House since 1938, was unseated in the Second District; Representative Kenneth Roberts was defeated in the Fourth and Representative George Huddleston lost his seat in the Sixth.

In Mississippi, the lone Republican candidates for Congress, Prentiss Walker, a political unknown, staged a tremendous upset over Representative Arthur Winstead, a conservative Democrat who has been in Congress since 1942.

And in South Georgia, Howard H. Callaway, a Goldwater Republican, unseated Representative Garland T. Byrd, the Democratic incumbent.

Despite Senator Goldwater's strong showing in the Deep South, the results clearly demonstrated that a Presidential candidate can no longer carry the South on the civil rights issue alone.

In virtually every state the voting followed this pattern:

The urban and suburban areas which had been building Republican strength in recent years voted Democratic, partly on the basis of a rising Negro vote.

The rural "Black Belt," which previously had shunned the two-party system and voted Democratic, gave its votes to Senator Goldwater, almost purely on the race issue.

THE PRESIDENTIAL ELECTION OF 1968

NIXON GAINS THE PRESIDENCY AMID VIETNAM WAR, CIVIL DISORDER

Death haunted the presidential election of 1968. Death came first in the assassination of President John Kennedy in 1963, which made Lyndon Johnson the sitting president. Violence erupted in the nation's black urban neighborhoods, beginning with Watts in Los Angeles in 1965 and spreading across the country to Detroit, Newark, and hundreds of other cities. Death spread like a virus from Asia when American intervention in Vietnam against Communist guerrillas and regular troops from North Vietnam ended the lives of 36,000 American soldiers there by the end of the year. Murder removed the nation's moral leader, the Reverend Martin Luther King Jr., which led to more urban slaughter. Assassination then took Sen. Robert Kennedy, ending his promising possibility of national reconciliation.

The mayhem also brought political losses. Four years earlier, Johnson had won an overwhelming popular mandate, bringing the Democrats to two-thirds majorities in Congress and total control of the national government. His ambitious program, the Great Society, rivaled the New Deal in its scope and achievements, including the War on Poverty, Medicare and Medicaid, the Voting Rights Act, Head Start and other federal programs supporting public and university education, the end of discriminatory ethnic quotas in immigration, and new initiatives in highway safety, environmental protection, and government support of the arts.

But the escalating war in Vietnam ended Johnson's legislative mastery. Unable to provide a convincing rationale for American involvement, he was also unable to develop a consistent and winning strategy. Beyond its political traumas, the war's economic costs reduced the budgetary resources for the new programs while stimulating inflation in the general economy. Opposition to the U.S. military action split the Democrats and drew public support to the Republicans, bringing them gains in the congressional elections of 1966 of 47 House seats, 3 Senate seats, and 8 new governorships.

Source: AP Images/George Brich

Sen. Robert F. Kennedy is seen during a campaign tour through Oxnard, Calif., on June 1, 1968. He was assassinated four days later, moments after winning the California primary.

Despite the nation's widespread prosperity, the Democratic coalition evidenced the waning of the broad voter alliance that had been dominant since the time of Franklin Roosevelt. As Johnson himself had foretold, the party's support of black civil rights ended its traditional support in the white South. In the North, antipoverty programs through community action groups drew opposition from urban party organizations, and affirmative action on behalf of racial minorities fostered a backlash among the white working class and Catholics who had been the party's foundation since the New Deal.

Race became a major political cleavage, displacing the previous alignments along lines of social class. The civil rights movement seemed threatening to many whites as it changed its methods and goals, shifting from nonviolent resistance to gain political rights to a call for "black power" and economic advantage. Cultural clashes added to whites' racial and economic discontents, as the new life styles, sexual freedom, and seemingly unpatriotic attitudes of war protesters, blacks, and young "hippies" shocked believers in traditional values.

1968 ELECTORAL VOTE

STATE	ELECTORAL VOTES	NIXON	HUMPHREY	WALLACE	STATE	ELECTORAL VOTES	NIXON	HUMPHREY	WALLACE
Alabama	(10)	–	–	10	Montana	(4)	4	–	–
Alaska	(3)	3	–	–	Nebraska	(5)	5	–	–
Arizona	(5)	5	–	–	Nevada	(3)	3	–	–
Arkansas	(6)	–	–	6	New Hampshire	(4)	4	–	–
California	(40)	40	–	–					
Colorado	(6)	6	–	–	New Jersey	(17)	17	–	–
Connecticut	(8)	–	8	–	New Mexico	(4)	4	–	–
Delaware	(3)	3	–	–	New York	(43)	–	43	–
District of Columbia	(3)	–	3	–	North Carolina	(13)	12	–	1
					North Dakota	(4)	4	–	–
Florida	(14)	14	–	–	Ohio	(26)	26	–	–
Georgia	(12)	–	–	12	Oklahoma	(8)	8	–	–
Hawaii	(4)	–	4	–	Oregon	(6)	6	–	–
Idaho	(4)	4	–	–	Pennsylvania	(29)	–	29	–
Illinois	(26)	26	–	–	Rhode Island	(4)	–	4	–
Indiana	(13)	13	–	–	South Carolina	(8)	8	–	–
Iowa	(9)	9	–	–	South Dakota	(4)	4	–	–
Kansas	(7)	7	–	–	Tennessee	(11)	11	–	–
Kentucky	(9)	9	–	–	Texas	(25)	–	25	–
Louisiana	(10)	–	–	10	Utah	(4)	4	–	–
Maine	(4)	–	4	–	Vermont	(3)	3	–	–
Maryland	(10)	–	10	–	Virginia	(12)	12	–	–
Massachusetts	(14)	–	14	–	Washington	(9)	–	9	–
Michigan	(21)	–	21	–	West Virginia	(7)	–	7	–
Minnesota	(10)	–	10	–	Wisconsin	(12)	12	–	–
Mississippi	(7)	–	–	7	Wyoming	(3)	3	–	–
Missouri	(12)	12	–	–					
					TOTALS	**(538)**	**301**	**191**	**46**

New government programs, race, novel life styles, a debilitating war: any of these influences alone would create turmoil in the presidential election. Combined, in a time of literal death, they made 1968 a wrenching year of violent political change.

THE PARTIES AND THE CANDIDATES

The Republican nomination contest, though strongly affected by the national torments, proceeded calmly and tradition- ally. Abandoning the ideological conservatism of the 1964

election, the party moved toward moderation and concen- trated on developing a more effective organization.

Former vice president Richard Nixon, defeated for presi- dent in 1960 and California governor in 1962, returned to politics from his new home in New York, and quickly became the front-runner. A likely moderate opponent, Michigan governor George Romney, dropped out even before the New Hampshire primary, ridiculed for his admission that he had been "brainwashed" in Pentagon briefings on Vietnam.

Other possibilities—incumbent governors Nelson Rocke- feller of New York and Ronald Reagan in California—were coy. Rockefeller assembled a campaign, then abjured interest in the presidency on March 21, only to return to the fray after six weeks, too late to actively contest state primaries. Reagan traveled to meet Republican leaders, but formally claimed to be no more than a favorite son, openly entering the competition only as the convention met in Miami Beach in early August. Nixon, holding his votes against the divided opponents, won a slim majority of 692 of the 1,333 total delegates on the first ballot before a tide of vote switches. In a surprise selection, Maryland governor Spiro Agnew was named for vice president. Outside of the convention, violence flared again, killing three Miami rioters.

The party platform was uncontroversial: moderate, extensive, and simple to write. Condemning the "Johnson-Humphrey administration," it warned that "lawlessness is crumbling the foundations of American society," and promised, even-handedly but ambiguously, "decisive action to quell civil disorder" as well as "a relentless attack on economic and social injustice in any form." On the central issue, the war, Republicans derisively concluded, "The Administration's Vietnam policy has failed—militarily, politically, diplomatically and with relation to our own people." New leadership, the party claimed, would provide a new strategy—"a progressive de-Americanization of the war, both military and civilian"—that would result, if not in victory in Vietnam, at least in Republican victory in the election.

The Democratic candidate seemed obvious: Lyndon Johnson would be renominated for a full second term. (Having served only one year of Kennedy's tenure, Johnson was not barred by the Twenty-second Amendment to the Constitution limiting presidents to two terms.) Antiwar activists, however, were determined to oppose the president. After soliciting other possibilities, they persuaded Minnesota senator Eugene McCarthy to enter the race.

McCarthy was hardly a dynamic challenger. Reserved, wittily caustic, intellectual—actually a published poet—he nevertheless articulated the fervor of war opponents, as evidenced by the young canvassers who cut their long hair and shaved their beards to appear "clean for Gene" as they campaigned in New Hampshire, the first state primary. Their cause gained momentum with news from the battlefields. On January 30, a date corresponding to the Chinese lunar new year, Vietnamese Communists launched the Tet offensive, attacking major cities, defeating scattered U.S. units, and breaching the wall surrounding the U.S. Embassy. Although the offensive itself was repulsed with heavy enemy casualties, Tet marked a psychological Communist victory, contradicting Johnson's optimistic

forecasts of victory. Both the news media, publicly, and the president's closest advisers, confidentially, concluded that the United States must leave the war and bring home the half million American troops.

That message was heard in New Hampshire. McCarthy rode the doleful war news to a surprising showing, gaining 42 percent of the primary vote, while Johnson, even with advantages of an incumbent president, fell short of an absolute majority. Counting Republican write-in votes, McCarthy virtually tied the president, and he won the most delegates. The demonstrated strength of the antiwar movement had an immediate impact on the presidential race. Four days later, New York senator Robert Kennedy, brother of the former president, entered the contest and quickly won both strong endorsements from elements of the New Deal coalition and scorn from the McCarthy camp.

Then the race became completely chaotic. Johnson went on national television to announce a change in his war strategy—a reduction in American bombing and a readiness to attend peace negotiations. At the end of his talk, he added a decision omitted from the advance text:

> I have concluded that I should not permit the Presidency to become involved in the partisan divisions that are developing in this political year. . . . I do not believe that I should devote an hour or a day of my time to any personal partisan causes or to any duties other than the awesome duties of this office—the Presidency of your country. Accordingly, I shall not seek, and I will not accept, the nomination of my party for another term as your President.

Johnson's astonishing withdrawal transformed the Democratic competition. Vice President Hubert Humphrey soon declared his own candidacy, but stayed out of the primaries, basing his effort on the powerful state party organizations, remaining urban machines, and favorite son entrants. McCarthy gained an advantage from the renewed focus on the war and beat Johnson, still listed on the ballot, in the Wisconsin primary. Kennedy, starting very late, jumped into full-time campaigning and drew large crowds of both whites and blacks while preparing for direct clashes with McCarthy in the remaining states. Where both appeared on the ballot, Kennedy won four contests, McCarthy only one. Overshadowing the political contest came King's assassination on April 4, bringing new urban rebellions and the deaths of thirty-seven rioters in the nation's capital.

The final and vital Democratic contest came on June 4 in California. Kennedy carried the Golden State by 5 percent, nearly 150,000 votes. Kennedy now was the only antiwar candidate who might win the nomination. As he left the victory celebration, the senator passed through the hotel kitchen, where he was shot by a disgruntled Palestinian-born gunman. Kennedy died the next day.

Humphrey, who had stayed outside of the primaries, continued to accumulate delegates in state party conventions, while Kennedy's bereaved supporters attempted to rally support behind a new protest aspirant, Sen. George McGovern of South Dakota. As the Democrats met in Chicago in late August, Humphrey's nomination was likely; a stormy convention was certain.

Humphrey, Johnson, and party regulars controlled the proceedings. They made limited concessions to insurgent delegates, abolishing the "unit rule," by which a majority of a state delegation could cast all of its convention votes, and seating a racially integrated delegation from Mississippi. In the rest of seventeen credentials contests, however, the convention seated the Humphrey delegations, despite evidence of high-handed procedures in many states. (For the future, the convention established a party commission to write new rules that would soon transform the nominating process, moving the presidential decision from convention bargaining to state primaries.)

The regulars also dominated the platform. Generally liberal in tone, the long declaration praised the record of Democratic administrations and Johnson's programs, but omitted virtually any personal mention of the president. Rejecting an antiwar minority report urging a halt in American bombing, it pledged only to stop all bombing of North Vietnam when this action would not endanger the lives of troops in the field; and cautioned that this action should take into account the response from Hanoi.

As the convention's heated debates continued, overt violence spread in the surrounding streets, bringing clashes between antiwar protesters and law enforcement officers. Protesters vociferously demonstrated at the delegates' hotels, openly smoked illegal marijuana, and taunted the 20,000 police and national guardsmen encircling their encampment on the Chicago lakeshore. On the night of the presidential nomination, a "police riot" brought aggressive wrath on the dissidents. Observing fearfully at their hotels, delegates could smell tear gas from the street, hear the shouting and the sirens, and see the injured demonstrators and law enforcement officers under treatment in the hotel lobbies.

Disruption also intruded within the convention amphitheater, where 5,600 delegates and alternates spent long hours angrily debating in crowded aisles. Placing McGovern in nomination, Sen. Abraham Ribicoff of Connecticut condemned the "Gestapo tactics in the streets of Chicago." Seated directly in front of the rostrum, Chicago mayor Richard Daley could be clearly seen on television mouthing a salacious epithet.

After a desperate and futile effort to invoke the Kennedy legacy by drafting the family's last surviving brother, Massachusetts senator Edward Kennedy, the convention came to its presidential selection. Humphrey was the easy winner on the first ballot, with 1,759 votes of the 2,622 total; McCarthy gained 601, and McGovern 146. For vice president, Humphrey and the delegates chose Sen. Edmund Muskie of Maine. Civil rights activist Julian Bond of Georgia was also presented, but withdrew because he was under the legal age of thirty-five.

Democrats left Chicago divided and despairing. Many still mourned their fallen leaders, and few were aroused by Humphrey's call for a "politics of joy." President Johnson, the triumphant leader of 1964, now had little support within his own party and did not even dare to come to the convention for a valedictory address.

To further roil the election, a new party appeared. Alabama governor George Wallace created the American Independent Party after achieving national attention for his opposition to racial desegregation of schools and the extension of voting rights to African Americans. Contemptuously finding "not a dime's worth of difference" between the two major parties, Wallace expressed a belligerent and populist stance, bewailing the state of the nation: "Law enforcement agencies and officers are hampered by arbitrary and unreasonable restrictions imposed by a beguiled judiciary; crime runs rampant through the nation; . . . welfare rolls and costs soar to astronomical heights; our great American institutions of learning are in chaos; living costs rise ever higher as do taxes; . . . disciples of dissent and disorder are rewarded for their disruptive actions at the expense our law-abiding, God fearing, hard working citizenry."

Wallace proposed to solve these problems by increasing police power, returning power to the states, reversing civil rights laws, and subjecting federal judges to election and reconfirmation. On Vietnam, he threatened military escalation, exemplified in his selection of a running mate, Curtis LeMay, a former Air Force chief of staff. His advocacy of an emphatic military policy, including possible use of nuclear weapons, evoked comparison to the mad bomber in the classic film, *Dr. Strangelove.*

THE CAMPAIGN

The violence of fiction mixed with the violence of fact in the election. Vietnam, civil disorder, and race dominated the campaign.

Strategically, Republicans and Democrats faced the problems of a three-party election. They could not simply engage in a direct confrontation; rather, they had to deal with Wallace's candidacy and try to turn his insurgency to their own advantage.

Humphrey began the campaign in the worst position. Attacked on his left by the antiwar movement, on his right by Nixon, and on the far right by Wallace, he had to carry the burden of the Johnson record, without the ability to change the administration's policies and with no firm base of support.

Nixon, on the other hand, began with great advantages. His party was essentially united behind his candidacy, renewed organizationally by a new and innovative national chairman, Ray Bliss of Ohio, and free of the ideological extremism of the previous Goldwater crusade. He also benefited from a $25 million treasury—more than twice that of Humphrey—and a focused strategy. Nixon paced himself, giving only two formal speeches each day and making controlled appearances on television, where he would give prepared answers to selected and sympathetic questioners.

The Republican candidate could present himself as a centrist in comparison to Humphrey's liberalism and Wallace's populism. Out of power, he could concentrate on the failings of the Johnson administration while leaving his own policy proposals as vague as assurances of concern for "the forgotten Americans" or his "secret plan" to end the war. A principal aim of his campaign was to skim off some of the Wallace voters, but they were not a coherent group, comprising white southerners and the white working class in the North. Nixon could not match Wallace's overtly racist appeals, but he did seek to cut into the governor's vote by frequent appearances in the South and by opposing "forced integration." In the rest of the nation, he concentrated on suburban areas in his campaign stops and paralleled Wallace in an emphasis on "law and order," criticizing judges for preferring "the criminal forces over the peace forces."

Wallace in many ways had the easiest choices. Gaining large crowds and sizable contributions, he was able to overcome substantial legal obstacles to win a slot on the ballots of all states. A rousing speaker, he delighted his audiences with his scorn of the "pointy-headed" bureaucrats and intellectuals who were allegedly ruining the country. He contemptuously invoked a violent response to potential protesters: "Any demonstrator who lies down in front of my presidential limousine, it will be the last one he lies down in front of."

Although unlikely to win outright in November, Wallace did initially gain close to 20 percent of the national vote in the early polls, a showing that potentially could prevent either Nixon or Humphrey from gaining an electoral majority. The governor relished that possibility and looked forward to then negotiating a "covenant" with one of the major candidates, receiving policy—and surely personal—favors in exchange for the votes of his electors. That covenant, he insisted, would be certified by a national telecast.

In October the tide began to turn toward the Democrats. Labor unions launched a major effort to bring members back to their party loyalties. In 4 million phone calls, they stressed Wallace's anti-union record, sidestepping white workers' racial resentments. On the central issue, Vietnam, Humphrey moved to free himself from Johnson. Gambling diminishing funds on a half-hour national telecast on the last day of September, he distanced himself from the administration and promised, "As President, I would stop the bombing of the North as an acceptable risk for peace," and "would move . . . toward de-Americanization of the war" within a year; he also offered an immediate cease-fire in the conflict. Humphrey's strategy paid off. His campaign prospered, as he gained money, liberal and union endorsements, and northern votes in opinion polls.

No national television debates were held, as Nixon rejected overtures from the Humphrey camp to engage in a direct, two-person confrontation. In the absence of debates, newspaper endorsements could potentially affect the close contest. Nixon gained far more support than Humphrey in the print media. He won the backing of daily papers with a circulation of 36 million readers, compared to 10 million circulation for the pro-Humphrey press—a sharp change from 1964, when a majority of newspapers supported the Democratic ticket. *The New York Times* bucked the trend, endorsing Humphrey's effort "to press forward with the liberal effort to achieve more social justice and to respond to the unending pressures for change." It dismissed Nixon as "a *status quo* candidate who, in effect, puts order ahead of justice, price stability ahead of full employment, and peace of mind—and the pocketbooks—of the affluent ahead of reform in the slums."

As election day neared, new dramatic developments came from the peace negotiations in Paris, with leaked reports of progress toward a reduction of hostilities. Only five days before the U.S. vote, President Johnson announced a total and unconditional halt in the bombing of North Vietnam and the scheduled opening one day after the election of formal peace talks that would include the American-allied government in South Vietnam and the Communist Vietcong. Nixon and Wallace reluctantly supported Johnson's decision, and observers expected that Humphrey would benefit from the last-minute progress toward peace.

The next day brought a sharp reversal. Despite earlier confidential acceptance of the plan, the South Vietnam president denigrated the Johnson plan as only a "unilateral" action of the United States and rejected participation in the talks if the Vietcong were included. Postelection reports found that persons close to Nixon had encouraged the South Vietnam government to reject the Johnson plan in anticipation of a better deal from a Nixon administration. There was no evidence that Nixon himself was a party to the reversal, but the confusion did mean that Humphrey lost a possibly decisive gain.

The only certainty was that the killing in Vietnam would continue. Peace talks eventually resumed under awkward arrangements to seat delegations at separate tables. They dragged on for four more years, and before America left Vietnam, death came there to 22,000 more of its military personnel.

THE ELECTION RESULTS

The outcome of the contest was unsure both before and after citizens cast their votes. In their final surveys, pollsters agreed that the election would be close, but made conflicting predictions of a Nixon or a Humphrey victory. Total turnout was 73 million, an increase of 3 million from 1964, but a smaller percentage of the eligible electorate.

The actual vote did show a close contest, which was not fully resolved for a day after the polling. In the end, Nixon narrowly won the popular vote, amassing 43.4 percent, 510,000 more than Humphrey's 42.7 percent and Wallace's 13.5 percent. The electoral vote was more decisive. Nixon won 32 states for a clear majority of 301 votes of the new total of 538, avoiding the potential crises of a bargain with Wallace or selection in the House of Representatives. Humphrey trailed with 191 from 13 states and the District of Columbia, while Wallace carried only 46 from 5 racially polarized states of the Deep South.

Nixon's victory was real, but modest. Compared to his losing run in 1960, he drew 3 million fewer votes, dropped by six percentage points, and ended up with the lowest winning percentage of any successful candidate since Woodrow Wilson in 1912. Nixon's flaccidity was also shown in the

congressional results, where Republicans gained only 4 seats in the House and 5 in the Senate, leaving them with minorities in both chambers. For the first presidential election since 1848, the nation would have a divided government.

But Democrats, aside from the congressional results, could take no satisfaction from the election tally. Their presidential vote had declined by more than a quarter in only four years, their percentage by nearly a fifth. They carried only Texas in their erstwhile loyal South and declined in the industrial states, losing 3 states decisive for Kennedy in 1960: Illinois, Missouri, and New Jersey.

Wallace failed to realize his dream of becoming the king-maker, but his vote was critical to the result. Later research showed that Wallace hurt Nixon. Without Wallace in the race, Nixon would have received two-thirds of the governor's votes, resulting in a national Republican landslide. Wallace's effect differed, however, by region. In the South, his third of the regional vote prevented a Nixon sweep of Dixie. In the North, Wallace's support shrank considerably during the campaign as union and working class voters returned to the Democrats. Enough Wallace support remained to make the difference in the close states, where small additional shifts might have thrown these states to Humphrey, resulting in a deadlock in the Electoral College.

Combined, the Nixon and Wallace votes constituted a repudiation of the Johnson administration. Contrary to later rationalizations, Humphrey did not lose because of defections from the antiwar movement; these votes returned to him after he pledged to halt the bombing. Humphrey lost because social trends, racial conflicts, and the political conditions of the time had fractured the established Democratic majority coalition.

Discontent with the war clearly was of major importance, but the public wanted only change, not necessarily immediate withdrawal from Vietnam, and was prepared to await Nixon's "secret plan." For the future, the more significant portent was the emerging realignment of the parties. Democrats were losing support among the middle class, union members, Catholics, white southerners, and advocates of law and order, traditional morality, and reflexive patriotism. They were gaining among African Americans, professionals, the college educated, and residents of the Northeast.

The presidential election of 1968 marked a major transition in the nation's electoral patterns. The New Deal coalition was weakened, perhaps ended. The Republicans were on the verge of creating a majority that would win all but one of six presidential elections in the next twenty years. Fresh candidates and issues would still arise in American politics, as the world's oldest democracy continued to peacefully transfer power to its elected leaders.

But after 1968 U.S. politics remained troubled. The scourge of violence continued through and after the election year. Antiwar demonstrations increased, punctuated by disruptions at subsequent conventions, tear gas attacks on protesters at the Pentagon, and the fatal shooting of four students by national guardsmen at Kent State University. In later assassination attempts, Wallace was paralyzed, President Gerald Ford dodged two gun attacks, and President Ronald Reagan suffered significant injuries. Ballots still remained the way Americans chose their leaders, but now bullets too were unwelcome weapons in the electoral process.

• •

CRISES OF THE LATE 1960S

Major conflicts that seethed throughout President Lyndon Johnson's second term dominated the 1968 presidential campaign. Civil rights demonstrations escalated to racial disruptions during the summer months each year. Crime grew rampant. The war in Vietnam continued, swelling during the unexpected Tet offensive. Bloody violence at home and abroad dimmed the optimism of most Americans.

AUGUST 14, 1965
2,000 TROOPS ENTER LOS ANGELES ON THIRD DAY OF NEGRO RIOTING; 4 DIE AS FIRES AND LOOTING GROW

By PETER BART
Special to The New York Times

LOS ANGELES, Saturday, Aug. 14—Two thousand heavily armed National Guardsmen moved into Los Angeles last night to battle rioters in the burning and looted Negro area.

The Guardsmen were under orders to use rifles, machine guns, tear gas and bayonets in support of a battered contingent of 900 policemen and deputy sheriffs.

Four persons were killed in the rioting yesterday, including three Negroes and a police officer. Thirty-three police officers had been injured, 75 civilians seriously injured, and 249 rioters had been arrested. This morning violence spread to white areas.

Gangs of Negroes appeared last night in various parts of Los Angeles County, up to 20 miles from the riot scene. One group of about 25 Negroes started tossing rocks in San Pedro in the harbor area, while another group appeared, in Pecoima [sic], a Negro community in the San Fernando Valley. Police units dispersed these groups.

Gun Fire Exchanged

The National Guardsmen were being brought into the riot zone early this morning in small convoys led by jeeps with machine guns mounted on them. The convoys contained one or two troop carriers. One Guard unit opened machine-gun fire for 10-minutes on a gang of Negroes who then fled down the street. One Guardsman said the rioters fired with pistols and at least one rifle. No one was apparently hit. The Guardsmen continued to penetrate the riot area.

"They've got weapons and ammo," one Guard spokesman said. "It's going to be like Vietnam."

Indications in other areas were that the Negroes were dispersing in the face of the reinforcements and were reforming in other areas.

JANUARY 31, 1968
NATION IS WARNED UNREST IN CITIES IMPERILS SYSTEM

Advisory Unit Calls Failure to Solve Issue Greatest Threat Since Civil War

AUTHORS 'PESSIMISTIC'

Report Says Abdication at Lower Levels Challenges Federal Political Setup

By BEN A. FRANKLIN

Special to The New York Times

WASHINGTON, Jan. 30—The failure of government to prevent rioting, despair and "threatened anarchy" in the nation's large cities has brought the Federal system to the brink of its greatest crisis since the Civil War, a Government study commission declared today.

In a report its authors characterized as "pessimistic," the Advisory Commission on Intergovernmental Relations said the historic American system of plural government—local, state and national—was in danger.

The abdication or inability of the states, of city government, and of the Federal Government, singly or jointly, to hold back the deterioration of urban life, the commission said, raises the prospect of pervasive Federal dominance in the name of security.

14-Page Preamble

In a strongly worded 14-page preamble to its ninth annual report to the President and Congress, the commission warned that Federal authority over governmental responsibilities that had traditionally been those of states, counties and cities might be—might have to be—greatly expanded to maintain law and order. It said many cities were "seething" with racial and class revolt and that many were near public bankruptcy.

"The manner of meeting these challenges," the commission declared, "will largely determine the fate of the American political system; it will determine if we can maintain a form of government marked by partnership and wholesome competition among national, state and local

levels, or if instead—in the face of threatened anarchy—we must sacrifice political diversity as the price of the authoritative action required for the nation's survival." . . .

In an interview, the commission's staff director, William G. Colman, singled out the rapidly growing number of suburban voters in the country as "the leadership potential." Both Mr. Colman and the report spoke encouragingly of efforts to form urban-suburban "metro" governments.

"When the question is raised on the survival of our cities—and some of them are on the verge of bankruptcy—the answer always comes back to the Federal Government," Mr. Colman said. "But these problems are all bound up in archaic and restrictive state constitutions and state legislatures, the very areas of government where suburban people now have or are getting control. There must be leadership from the suburban environment if we are to meet these problems without altering our system of government."

The report attributed much of the inaction on urban needs to local and state failures to end "repressive restrictions" on welfare, housing and education funds and on zoning and planning policies that have created "the 'white noose' of the suburbs" around the teeming poor of the central cities.

Asked to justify the "Civil War analogy" of the report, another commission staff official, Eugene R. Elkins, explained it by saying "then it was a matter of some states pulling out of the Union—now it's a matter of the Federal system going down the drain altogether."

FEBRUARY 8, 1968
EDITORIAL
AFTER THE TET OFFENSIVE

The Administration's organized optimism over the "failure" of the Vietcong's Tet offensive is unfortunately ill-founded. It compounds the harm already done by

what has been a rude if temporary setback to both the political and military position of the United States in Vietnam.

The United States Command may be right, as all Americans hope, in its assertion that Government control has been restored in almost all the invaded cities and towns. But major street fighting has entered its second week in Saigon, and in Dalat as well. General Westmoreland's intelligence chief says that the enemy has the capability to mount new urban attacks equal to those against 35 population centers last week. The expanded fighting in Saigon could be its precursor.

Moreover, it still is not certain that the Marine fortress at Khesanh is the chief Communist objective. It may yet turn out that Khesanh was the diversion for the urban attacks, rather than the reverse, or that the enemy is still weighing his choice. And even if the military side of the Communist "general offensive" achieves little against American power—as is to be expected—the more serious political, administrative and psychological effects have yet to be assessed.

The administrative structure of the new South Vietnamese Government in 26 of the 44 provincial capitals seems to have been the main target of the Vietcong's countrywide assault. The damage done to the redevelopment program and Saigon's control of the provinces will not be quickly repaired.

The psychological damage, too, is tremendous. Secretary McNamara has said that the people of the cities and towns of South Vietnam, surprised and impressed by the Vietcong incursions, have been "dealt a heavy blow." Exposure of the inability of the allied forces to shield the country's urban centers, long isolated from the fighting war, has certainly made the blow even heavier. Furthermore, in many instances it is proving to be exceedingly painful to be rescued. The casualties and rubble produced by the heavy weapons of the American and South Vietnamese forces unquestionably leave a legacy of bitterness.

The political consequences are likely to be mixed. While Secretary McNamara believes that the Vietcong, their brutality exposed, are retreating from the cities "with less support than when they entered," the Saigon Government and its Army have been exposed in all their weakness.

The failure of the population to warn the Government forces of the substantial Vietcong infiltration that preceded the urban attacks does not prove, however, that the people of South Vietnam are pro-Communist. The Vietcong's expectation of a popular uprising was disappointed and its exhortations to revolt proved futile.

What this suggests is that South Vietnam's towns and cities are characterized neither by a Marxist "revolutionary situation" that would favor the Vietcong nor by widespread support for the Saigon regime which normally governs them. The two armed factions that are contesting power in what remains essentially a civil war, despite North Vietnamese and American intervention, probably both represent minorities in a population whose majority is war weary and apathetic.

Politically as well as militarily, stalemate increasingly appears as the unavoidable outcome of the Vietnam struggle. Neither side is entitled any longer to illusions about military victory, nor is there evidence that either side is achieving political ascendancy. A negotiated settlement seeking a political accommodation under international supervision remains the alternative to a prolonged war of attrition, a war that neither side can win.

- -

NIXON'S BID

Richard Nixon, vice president under President Dwight Eisenhower, surprised the nation when he surged to the front of the Republican field in 1968. Reinventing himself after his 1960 loss to John F. Kennedy, Nixon faced two major opponents, Gov. Nelson Rockefeller of New York and Gov. Ronald Reagan of California. Neither became an official candidate until late in the primary season, leaving Nixon the only active campaigner. Nixon seized the opportunity, courting his rivals' bases of support and winning all but one of the primaries he entered.

MARCH 24, 1968
NIXON TO START QUIET COURTSHIP OF MODERATE WING OF G.O.P.

By ROBERT B. SEMPLE, Jr.

Special to the New York Times

WASHINGTON, March 23—Richard M. Nixon will shortly begin a quiet courtship of Republican liberals and moderates who were unexpectedly deprived of a Presidential hopeful this week when Governor Rockefeller decided not to make a fight for the nomination.

Campaigning in Wisconsin Thursday and yesterday, the former Vice President let it be known that he would seek appointments with all Republican Governors over the next two months. He planned to make an intensive canvass of Congressional leaders and hoped to confer with Mr. Rockefeller in a few days.

The New York Governor will return from Puerto Rico at midweek. According to aides, Mr. Nixon's motives are threefold. He is eager to strengthen his ties with a wing of the party that has been lukewarm toward his candidacy. He wants to begin preliminary discussions about a party platform and thus avoid a repetition of the embarrassing confrontation with the liberals and Mr. Rockefeller that occurred in 1960. And he is eager to build the kind of party unity he thinks essential to victory over the Democrats in November.

Deterrent to Rockefeller

Also implicit in the effort is an apparent desire on the part of Nixon strategists to guard against Mr. Rockefeller's possible re-entry into the race.

Although the men around Mr. Nixon do not now think Mr. Rockefeller will change his mind, it is clear that a successful Nixon courtship of the moderates and liberals would diminish the chances that the Governor would reappear as an active challenger, either on his own decision or through a draft.

MAY 29, 1968
NIXON IS A STRONG WINNER

ROCKEFELLER LAGS

Reagan Runs Second but Trails Badly—Winner Jubilant

By LAWRENCE E. DAVIES

Special to The New York Times

PORTLAND, Ore., May 28—Richard M. Nixon rode to a more commanding victory in the Oregon Republican Presidential primary today than his campaign managers or rivals had projected for him.

The former Vice President soundly defeated his only opponent on the ballot, Gov. Ronald Reagan of California, who did not personally campaign. Governor Rockefeller of New York, who was not on the ballot, ran third with write-in votes.

With 1,518 of 2,599 precincts reporting, the vote was:

Nixon	85,303	71%
Reagan	26,147	22%
Rockefeller	8,041	7%

Mr. Nixon, when he was commanding 74 per cent of the votes, declared, "The chances of my now being derailed are pretty well eliminated."

"I expect some phone calls tonight," he continued, "some from Republicans who believe 'Now is the time to get on the train before it leaves the station.'"

"This big win," he said, "will help in making some of the fence-sitters move over."

A jubilant Mr. Nixon, addressing a cheering crowd at his Portland campaign headquarters, took a crack at Governor Rockefeller's poor showing.

He said that he had been on a journey that he thought might be over "a rocky road—it wasn't."

SEARCH FOR A DEMOCRATIC FRONT-RUNNER

President Johnson, eligible to run for reelection because he had not served a full first term, was uncertain whether to seek further tenure. Despite a long-standing tradition of not challenging an incumbent party member, rival Democrats viewed Johnson as a weak candidate susceptible to defeat. In the first-in-the-nation New Hampshire primary, he won only a tepid victory over Sen. Eugene McCarthy of Minnesota. Four days later, a more fearsome long-term rival, New York senator Robert Kennedy, joined the race. With dwindling popularity, failing health, and increasing Democratic opposition, Johnson shocked the nation April 1 by dropping out of the presidential contest, leaving the party nomination uncertain.

MARCH 13, 1968
EDITORIAL
NEW HAMPSHIRE PRIMARY

Senator Eugene McCarthy's remarkable vote in the New Hampshire primary is a warning to the Johnson Administration and a testament to the efforts of the students and other citizens who enlisted in his campaign for peace.

The size of the protest vote is the crucial question for New Hampshire Democrats. Senator McCarthy was not a candidate in the conventional sense because, as a practical matter, he cannot prevent President Johnson's renomination. But his strong showing—well above the 30 per cent that most observers had anticipated—is an indicator of popular dissatisfaction with the war and with the drift of Administration policy. It is true that he had the advantage of being listed on the ballot, while the President's name had to be written in.

The Johnson campaign, however, had the support of Governor King and the party organization. It featured intensive and intemperate advertising aimed at showing that a vote for Senator McCarthy was a vote against backing up American troops in Vietnam. No possible political outcome could justify the moral squalor of this appeal. The large McCarthy vote is a rebuke to these political tactics.

MARCH 15, 1968
EDITORIAL
ENTER ROBERT KENNEDY

The apparent resolve of Senator Robert F. Kennedy to seek the Democratic Presidential nomination remakes the national political scene. Until now, President Johnson's renomination had seemed assured. He faced in Senator Eugene McCarthy's candidacy a moral challenge and a political embarrassment but not a mortal threat. Now, although the political realities continue strongly to favor Mr. Johnson, his renomination can no longer be taken for granted.

Senator Kennedy's decision significantly widens the range of choice for Democratic party members and, indirectly, for all voters. He is his party's most exciting and most controversial figure. Since he has long had serious differences with President Johnson over the course of the war in Vietnam and the priorities to be assigned to the nation's urban and racial problems, it is healthy for democracy that he present his beliefs to the voters in such a way that they can make a clear and deliberate choice.

The timing of Senator Kennedy's entry into the lists reflects a political calculation directly arising from Mr. McCarthy's impressive showing in the New Hampshire primary. Mr. Kennedy, who now looks something like a hitchhiker on another man's work and courage, would have been in a much stronger moral and political position today if he had acted affirmatively three months ago. As it is, if both he and Senator McCarthy remain in the race, they will divide the anti-Johnson vote in the Oregon and California primaries, thereby strengthening not only

Mr. Johnson but also, indirectly, the Republican candidacy of Richard M. Nixon. But in the many states where delegates are chosen by convention, Mr. Kennedy's candidacy is a welcome gain for the "peace Democrats," as he has appeal to some voters and support from state party organizations that Senator McCarthy probably could not reach.

On balance, and under the changed circumstances, President Johnson has to decide whether he can maintain his aloof "above politics" position until the Democratic convention meets in August. It is arithmetically possible for him to achieve renomination if he holds together the Southern delegates and those from such machine-controlled states as Illinois and Pennsylvania. But to start off a re-election campaign having been repudiated in most of the states which have primaries would be a severe psychological handicap. Mr. Johnson may have to carry his case to the Democratic voters whose acquiescence he has been taking for granted.

APRIL 1, 1968
JOHNSON SAYS HE WON'T RUN;

SURPRISE DECISION

President Steps Aside in Unity Bid—Says 'House' Is Divided

By TOM WICKER

Special to The New York Times

WASHINGTON, March 31—Lyndon Baines Johnson announced tonight: "I shall not seek and I will not accept the nomination of my party as your President."

Later, at a White House news conference, he said his decision was "completely irrevocable."

The President told his nationwide television audience:

"What we have won when all our people were united must not be lost in partisanship. I have concluded that I should not permit the Presidency to become involved in partisan decisions."

Mr. Johnson, acknowledging that there was "division in the American house," withdrew in the name of national unity, which he said was "the ultimate strength of our country."

"With American sons in the field far away," he said, "with the American future under challenge right here at home, with our hopes and the world's hopes for peace in the balance every day, I do not believe that I should devote an hour or a day of my time to any personal partisan causes or to any duties other than the awesome duties of this office, the Presidency of your country."

Humphrey Race Possible

Mr. Johnson left Senator Robert F. Kennedy of New York and Senator Eugene J. McCarthy of Minnesota as the only two declared candidates for the Democratic Presidential nomination.

Vice President Humphrey, however, will be widely expected to seek the nomination now that his friend and political benefactor, Mr. Johnson, is out of the field. Mr. Humphrey indicated that he would have a statement on his plans tomorrow.

The President informed Mr. Humphrey of his decision during a conference at the latter's apartment in southwest Washington today before the Vice President flew to Mexico City. There, he will represent the United States at the signing of a treaty for a Latin-American nuclear-free zone.

Surprise to Aides

If Mr. Humphrey should become a candidate, he would find most of the primaries foreclosed to him. Only those in the District of Columbia, New Jersey and South Dakota remain open.

Therefore, he would have to rely on collecting delegates in states without primaries and on White House support if he were to head off Mr. Kennedy and Mr. McCarthy.

KING ASSASSINATED

Just days after President Johnson left the Democratic race, the political terrain shifted again. On April 5, 1968, an assassin fatally shot Martin Luther King Jr., the nation's leading spokesman for civil rights. Johnson urged calm, futilely attempting to hold back the erupting violence. Politics again focused on the issues of civil rights and lawlessness. King's death deprived the nation of a cherished calming voice, leaving citizens shocked, angry, and frustrated.

APRIL 5, 1968
MARTIN LUTHER KING IS SLAIN IN MEMPHIS; A WHITE IS SUSPECTED; JOHNSON URGES CALM
GUARD CALLED OUT
Curfew Is Ordered in Memphis, but Fires and Looting Erupt
By EARL CALDWELL
Special to The New York Times

MEMPHIS, Friday, April 5—The Rev. Dr. Martin Luther King Jr., who preached nonviolence and racial brotherhood, was fatally shot here last night by a distant gunman who then raced away and escaped.

Four thousand National Guard troops were ordered into Memphis by Gov. Buford Ellington after the 39-year-old Nobel Prize-winning civil rights leader died.

A curfew was imposed on the shocked city of 550,000 inhabitants, 40 per cent of whom are Negro.

But the police said the tragedy had been followed by incidents that included sporadic shooting, fires, bricks and bottles thrown at policemen, and looting that started in Negro districts and then spread over the city. . . .

Dr. King's mourning associates sought to calm the people they met by recalling his messages of peace, but there was widespread concern by law enforcement officers here and elsewhere over potential reactions.

In a television broadcast after the curfew was ordered here, Mr. Holloman said, "rioting has broken out in parts of the city" and "looting is rampant."

APRIL 7, 1968
EDITORIAL
RACE CRISIS
A Mood of Tension and Violence

WASHINGTON—Within hours after Martin Luther King was struck down at the Lorraine Hotel in Memphis, the Negro ghettos in many parts of the country exploded. The assassination of the apostle of nonviolence had brought the fears of a long, hot summer to frightening reality—months early.

Pleas for calm, for the need now more than ever to follow Dr. King's teachings came from his friends and followers—the Rev. Ralph Abernathy, his successor at the Southern Christian Leadership Conference, Roy Wilkins of the N.A.A.C.P., Whitney Young of the Urban League, and others. But the ghetto-dwellers did not listen to them. The voice which seemed to express the mood and the temper was that of Stokely Carmichael, the young black militant. He went into the streets of the nation's capital, proclaiming, "White America has declared war on black America!"

Rioting Builds

In more than 40 cities across the country, young Negroes took to the streets. Some were there—ironically in light of Dr. King's life and work—in an almost gleeful mood as they rampaged, burning, breaking and looting. At first, the police in most cities acted with restraint and forbearance. But the violence mounted into a second night on Friday, and into Saturday. The National Guard was called out to quell the rioters and restore order in Detroit, Chicago, Memphis and elsewhere.

One of most destructive outbreaks came in the shadow of the Capitol and the White House. The young rioters burned and looted not only in the Negro ghettos but also in the downtown areas. Friday afternoon, President Johnson declared a state of domestic violence and disorder in Washington and called out Federal troops; but they were only partially successful in calming the city. There were sporadic outbreaks in Washington and around the nation all day yesterday, with thousands under arrest, at least 18 dead by nightfall and an uncounted number injured.

As the rioting continued, there was the critical question of what can be done now, not just to stop this outbreak, but to prevent another. The first step, almost everyone agreed, was apprehension of Dr. King's killer if possible.

Attorney General Ramsey Clark was guiding Federal agents in that task; he said yesterday that he expected an early solution.

From all sides there were also demands that the nation must take affirmative steps to end the conditions that Dr. King was fighting against—inequality and poverty, hatred and bigotry.

Until last Thursday night, President Johnson had shown not the slightest indication of acting on or really even listening to Dr. King's demands, in his planned spring and summer poor people's campaign in Washington for "jobs or income now" for the nation's underclass.

As long as the war in Vietnam continues to drain away $20- or $30-billion a year—even if Mr. Johnson finally gets his 10 per cent Federal income tax surcharge—there will be no room in the Federal budget for the overdue and now (thanks to Dr. King's murder) self-evident urgency to act sweepingly on Dr. King's noble dream for America.

• •

KENNEDY ASSASSINATED

Tribulations mounted for the Democrats. After President Johnson withdrew from the race, Sen. Robert Kennedy dominated Sen. Eugene McCarthy, his only active rival. Vice President Hubert Humphrey had not entered the contest until Johnson withdrew and was unable to get his name on primary ballots. Kennedy surged ahead, anticipating a heated convention contest against Humphrey for the nomination. Then disaster struck again. Kennedy was assassinated upon leaving his California victory party, adding further turmoil, and blood, to the 1968 campaign.

APRIL 14, 1968
KENNEDY LEADING 2 RIVALS IN POLL

Gallup Finds 35% in Party Support Him—Humphrey Gets 31%, McCarthy 23

Special to The New York Times

PRINCETON, N.J., April 13—Senator Robert F. Kennedy leads both Vice President Humphrey and Senator Eugene J. McCarthy in the first full-scale survey of Democratic voters by the Gallup Poll since President Johnson's withdrawal from the Presidential race.

In the latest poll, Mr. Kennedy wins the support of 35 per cent of Democrats, with Mr. Humphrey, who has not officially announced his candidacy, not far behind

with 31 per cent of the vote. Mr. McCarthy wins the support of 23 per cent of the Democrats polled on their choice for the party's Presidential nomination.

The following question was asked of a national sample of rank-and-file Democrats in a survey completed three days ago:

"Suppose the choice for President in the Democratic convention narrows down to Senator Robert Kennedy,

Senator Eugene McCarthy and Vice President Hubert Humphrey. Which ONE would you prefer to have the Democratic convention select?"

Here are the views of Democrats in this survey based on a three-way race:

Kennedy	35%
Humphrey	31
McCarthy	23
Undecided	11

Further indication of the relative strength of the three Democratic candidates is disclosed in answers to questions based on a two-way race for the nomination.

With the choice limited to just two men—Mr. Kennedy and Mr. McCarthy—a fairly tight contest is seen, with Mr. Kennedy winning the support of 46 per cent of Democrats to 37 per cent for Mr. McCarthy. A large proportion of Democrats are undecided, as is shown by the following table:

Kennedy	46%
McCarthy	37
Undecided	17

When the choice is limited to Mr. Kennedy and Mr. Humphrey, the result is another close race, with Mr. Kennedy gaining the support of 45 per cent of the Democrats to 41 per cent for Mr. Humphrey, as follows:

Kennedy	45%
Humphrey	41
Undecided	14

In a final two-way test, Mr. Humphrey defeats Mr. McCarthy, as is shown by the following tabulation:

Humphrey	48%
McCarthy	37
Undecided	15

JUNE 5, 1968

KENNEDY SHOT AND GRAVELY WOUNDED AFTER WINNING CALIFORNIA PRIMARY; SUSPECT SEIZED IN LOS ANGELES HOTEL

CONDITION 'STABLE'

Aide Reports Senator Is 'Breathing Well'—Last Rites Given

By WARREN WEAVER Jr.

Special to The New York Times

LOS ANGELES, Wednesday, June 5—Senator Robert F. Kennedy was shot and critically wounded by an unidentified gunman this morning just after he made his victory speech in the California primary election.

Moments after the shots were fired, the New York Senator lay on the cement floor of a kitchen corridor outside the ballroom of the Ambassador Hotel while crowds of screaming and wailing supporters crowded around him.

On his arrival at Good Samaritan Hospital a spokesman described Senator Kennedy's condition as "stable." He was described as breathing but not apparently conscious.

Frank Mankiewicz, Senator Kennedy's press aide, was quoted as saying, at 4:15 A.M.: "He is breathing well and has good heart. I would not expect he is conscious."

Shot Twice In Head

Mr. Mankiewicz said the Senator had been shot twice in the head—once in the forehead and once near the right ear. He was transferred to Good Samaritan Hospital after a brief stop at General Receiving Hospital.

The Rev. Thomas Peacha said he had administered the last rites of the Roman Catholic Church in the hospital's emergency room. This is normal procedure when a Catholic has been possibly seriously injured. . . .

Mr. Kennedy had just won a major victory in his campaign for the Democratic Presidential nomination. His short victory speech, full of quiet jokes about his dog and his family, closed with these words: "On to Chicago and let's win there."

JUNE 6, 1968
KENNEDY IS DEAD, VICTIM OF ASSASSIN;

SURGERY IN VAIN

President Calls Death Tragedy, Proclaims a Day of Mourning

By GLADWIN HILL

Special to The New York Times

LOS ANGELES, Thursday, June 6—Senator Robert F. Kennedy, the brother of a murdered President, died at 1:44 A.M. today of an assassin's shots.

The New York Senator was wounded more than 20 hours earlier, moments after he had made his victory statement in the California primary.

At his side when he died today in Good Samaritan Hospital were his wife, Ethel; his sisters, Mrs. Stephen Smith and Mrs. Patricia Lawford; his brother-in-law, Stephen Smith; and his sister-in-law, Mrs. John F. Kennedy, whose husband was assassinated 4½ years ago in Dallas.

In Washington, President Johnson issued a statement calling the death a tragedy. He proclaimed next Sunday a national day of mourning.

. . . .

THE REPUBLICAN CONVENTION

Meeting in Miami, the Republican Party prepared to nominate Richard Nixon for president. Two challengers, Gov. Nelson Rockefeller and Gov. Ronald Reagan, attempted to unite in opposition, but the party rallied behind Nixon, nominating him easily on the first ballot. He then surprised the convention by selecting Spiro Agnew, governor of Maryland, as his running mate.

AUGUST 4, 1968
NIXON'S 2 RIVALS STRIVING TO BLOCK HIM ON FIRST VOTE

Rockefeller and Reagan Are Taking Charge of Drives at G.O.P. Convention

ALL 3 MEN CONFIDENT

Californian Is Said to Plan Strong Pro-War Speech—Session On Tomorrow

By TOM WICKER

Special to The New York Times

MIAMI BEACH, Aug. 3—Nelson Rockefeller of New York and Ronald Reagan of California came here today to take personal charge of their parallel campaigns to deny first-ballot nomination to Richard M. Nixon at the Republican National Convention.

If they can achieve that, both Governors and their lieutenants believe, Mr. Nixon will be stopped, and someone else will be nominated for President in the balloting scheduled for Wednesday night. Rockefeller men say that it will be the New York liberal; Mr. Reagan's backers are sure it will be the California conservative.

Meanwhile, Nixon and Rockefeller forces in the platform committee joined cause in an effort to incorporate a peace-oriented plank on the Vietnam issue. They were opposed by conservatives supporting Mr. Reagan.

Mr. Nixon's spokesmen continued to claim an early victory for the former Vice President. His floor manager, Representative Rogers C. B. Morton of Maryland, went further.

'We're Going to Win'

"We're going to win it on the first ballot," he said. "I'm not going to sit around there all night."

Thus, as the delegates and party leaders gathered here for the opening convention session at 10 A.M. Monday, the big question was Mr. Nixon's first-ballot strength.

His staff continued to claim at least 700 delegates, although conceding that some might not swing to his column until the second or third ballot. To nominate, 667 are needed.

Reagan Camp's Strategy

The Rockefeller-Nixon forces sought a more "dovish" statement of the party position on the war.

The strategy of the Reagan men was believed to be to create an issue that would allow the California Governor to go before the convention and make a fighting speech that would enhance his chances for the nomination. They could do this by offering a substitute Vietnam plank when the platform comes up for adoption Tuesday night.

In every other respect, the convention was shaping up as a three-cornered struggle, with Mr. Rockefeller and Mr. Reagan—controlling the two largest state delegations, but representing opposite wings of the party—tacitly cooperating in the prime problem of stopping Mr. Nixon's nomination drive.

Both sides reached back to the Republican National Convention of 1940 for a model of how they expected things to go here. At that convention, held in Philadelphia, Thomas E. Dewey of New York held a lead over Robert A. Taft of Ohio and Wendell L. Willkie of Indiana for the first three ballots; then Mr. Willkie surged ahead on the fourth ballot and was nominated on the sixth.

AUGUST 8, 1968
NIXON IS NOMINATED ON THE FIRST BALLOT;

ORIGINAL VOTE 692

But Convention Then Makes It Unanimous on Plea by Reagan

By TOM WICKER

Special to The New York Times

MIAMI BEACH, Thursday, Aug. 8—Richard Milhous Nixon, the "old pro" of American politics, was nominated for President today on the first ballot at the Republican National Convention.

Mr. Nixon, only the eighth man to be renominated by the Republicans after having lost one Presidential election, triumphed over a determined "stop Nixon" drive waged from the left by Governor Rockefeller of New York and from the right by Governor Ronald Reagan of California.

Just as the Nixon forces had steadfastly contended during a week of maneuvering at this 29th Republican National Convention, the 55-year-old former Vice President, who was also the party's nominee in 1960, proved to have the 667 votes needed for nomination "buttoned up."

The first-ballot count, before the convention made the nomination unanimous, was as follows:

Nixon	692
Rockefeller	277
Reagan	182
Others	182

2 Big States Lost

Mr. Nixon's nomination came at the end of an almost interminable evening of oratory and demonstrations, in which 12 candidates were nominated and seconded; two withdrew before the balloting began at 1:17 A.M.

As the roll-call of the states proceeded, Mr. Nixon's lead mounted steadily—even though the two largest states went elsewhere. California cast 86 votes for Governor Reagan and New York gave 88 of its 92 to Governor Rockefeller.

Wisconsin, whose 30 delegates were won by Mr. Nixon in the state primary last April, put the former Vice President over the top, giving him three votes more than the 667 he had needed.

At the completion of the roll-call, Mr. Nixon had 692 votes and the switching began with Minnesota; it had cast only 9 of its 26 votes for Mr. Nixon, but it switched all to him. One by one, the rest of the states began to fall in line.

A cheer went up when Ohio finally cast 58 votes for Mr. Nixon. Gov. James A. Rhodes had held out as a favorite son, taking 55 Ohio votes on the official roll-call.

Within minutes of the clinching votes, Governor Reagan appeared on the platform.

Reagan Barred at First

Mr. Ford, citing the convention rules, would not immediately let Mr. Reagan come to the rostrum, however.

While Mr. Reagan was waiting, the one-time front runner and a favorite son here, Gov. George Romney of Michigan, also switched his state's 48 votes to Mr. Nixon.

Meanwhile, New York representatives were trying to get recognition, apparently under instructions to move that the nomination be made unanimous. The delegation chairman Charles Schoeneck, finally shouted into the public address system that New York so moved.

Mr. Ford, however, continued to recognize the delegations one by one, rather than entertaining a motion for unanimity.

Ultimately, he entertained a motion from Virginia to suspend the rules. It was shouted through and Mr. Reagan was allowed to come to the platform, where he received an ovation.

Reagan Gets Unanimity

"This nation cannot survive four more years of the kind of policies that have been guiding us," he said.

Then he "proudly" moved that the convention declare itself unanimously behind Mr. Nixon—which it did with a roar.

AUGUST 9, 1968
NIXON SELECTS AGNEW AS HIS RUNNING MATE AND WINS APPROVAL AFTER FIGHT ON FLOOR; REBELS PUT DOWN

Fail in Effort to Have Convention Choose Romney Instead

By TOM WICKER
Special to The New York Times

MIAMI BEACH, Aug. 8—Richard M. Nixon accepted tonight the nomination of a Republican party that was surprised and to a large extent unhappy over his choice of Gov. Spiro T. Agnew of Maryland as his running mate.

Mr. Agnew was approved by the delegates on a roll-call vote in which Gov. George Romney of Michigan received 186 votes and 26 other delegates withheld their votes from the Marylander. Mr. Agnew got 1,128 votes.

Mr. Nixon, addressing a packed and cheering convention hall, pledged that his "first priority foreign policy objective" would be "to bring an honorable end to the war in Vietnam."

His Domestic Policy

Turning to domestic policy. Mr. Nixon promised a tough approach to crime and lawlessness, criticized the courts for going too far "to weaken the peace forces against the criminal forces" and pledged to maintain law and order.

Taking note of the battle over Mr. Agnew's nomination, Mr. Nixon said it had been a healthy thing for the party and that even after spirited contests for President and Vice President, Republicans "stand united before the nation tonight."

Hoped for Unity

Mr. Nixon's aides said he had selected Mr. Agnew as his running mate in the belief that the Maryland Governor would help unite the party. The result was the opposite.

All day long, after the choice was announced, the delegates seethed and grumbled, particularly those in the moderate wing of the party and from the big urban states, who believed a Southern-oriented ticket could not win this fall.

When the convention was called to order at 7:30 P.M., a major revolt against Mr. Nixon's choice might have been set off had not Mayor Lindsay of New York seconded Mr. Agnew's nomination and firmly refused to have anything to do with the dissidents.

Whether the unrest was deep enough to have major effect on the Nixon-Agnew ticket's prospects remained to be seen.

THE DEMOCRATIC CONVENTION

Meeting in Chicago, the Democratic Party worried about major conflicts both within and outside of the convention hall. Several thousand national guardsmen patrolled the streets, attempting to impose order on the city while masses of antiwar activists attempted to disrupt the convention. The Chicago police barricaded, gassed, and beat protesters into submission. Inside the convention, the battles were less bloody but equally hostile. Nevertheless, Vice President Humphrey was nominated on the first ballot and chose Maine senator Edmund Muskie to join him in championing a platform that supported Johnson's Vietnam policy.

AUGUST 29, 1968
NOMINATED ON THE FIRST BALLOT PLANK ON VIETNAM IS APPROVED;

VICTOR GETS 1,761

Vote Taken Amid Boos For Chicago Police Tactics in Street

By TOM WICKER

Special to The New York Times

CHICAGO, Thursday Aug. 29—While a pitched battle between the police and thousands of young antiwar demonstrators raged in the streets of Chicago, the Democratic National Convention nominated Hubert H. Humphrey for President last night, on a platform reflecting his and President Johnson's views on the war in Vietnam.

Mr. Humphrey, after a day of bandwagon shifts to his candidacy, and a night of turmoil in the convention hall, won nomination on the first ballot over challenges by Senator Eugene J. McCarthy of Minnesota and George S. McGovern of South Dakota.

The count at the end of the first ballot was:

Humphrey	1,761¾
McCarthy	601
McGovern	146½
Phillips	67½
Others	32¾

Violence Draws Attention

There was never a moment's suspense in the balloting, and throughout a turbulent evening, the delegates and spectators paid less attention to the proceedings than to television and radio reports of widespread violence in the streets of Chicago, and to stringent security measures within the International Amphitheatre.

Repeated denunciations of Mayor Richard J. Daley from convention speakers and repeated efforts to get an adjournment or recess were ignored by convention officials and Mr. Daley.

He sat through it all, usually grinning and always guarded by plainclothes security men, until just before the roll call. Then he left the hall. A few miles away, the young demonstrators were being clubbed, kicked and gassed by the Chicago police, who turned back a march on the convention hall.

Watched From Hotels

Most of the violence took place across Michigan Avenue from the convention headquarters hotel, the Conrad Hilton, in full view of delegates' wives and others watching from its windows.

From the convention rostrum, Senator Abraham A. Ribicoff of Connecticut, denounced "Gestapo tactics in the streets of Chicago."

Julian Bond, the Negro insurgent leader from Georgia, in announcing his delegation's votes, spoke of "atrocities" in the city.

Wire services reported that Mr. Humphrey had chosen Senator Edmund S. Muskie of Maine for Vice President. Mr. Humphrey's staff denied that a decision had been made, although they would not rule out Mr. Muskie, 54 years old, a Roman Catholic of Polish extraction.

Even the roll-call of the states that nominated Mr. Humphrey could begin only over the protests of New Hampshire, Wisconsin and Mr. Conyers, all of whom moved for a recess or adjournment because of the surrounding violence and the pandemonium in the hall.

Vote Begins Amid Boos

Representative Carl Albert of Oklahoma, the chairman, ignored all the motions and ordered the roll-call to begin amid a huge chorus of boos.

When Illinois's turn came to vote, the huge old amphitheater rocked with the sounds of boos and jeers, and the recording secretary had to ask for a restatement of its vote—112 votes for Mr. Humphrey.

Early in the evening, even Mr. Humphrey got a whiff of tear gas when it was wafted through his window at the Hilton, from the street fighting below.

Mr. McCarthy saw some of the violence from his window and called it "very bad." Later, it was reported at the convention hall, he visited a hospital where some of his young supporters, wounded in the streets, were being treated.

At one point, the police broke into the McCarthy suite at the Hilton, searching for someone throwing objects out of the hotel windows.

Mr. McGovern described the fighting as a "blood bath" that "made me sick to my stomach." He said he had "seen nothing like it since the films of Nazi Germany."

Pennsylvania Does It

Nevertheless, when Pennsylvania cast the votes that put Mr. Humphrey in nomination, the convention hall broke into a demonstration on his behalf that was loud and apparently happy. Mrs. Humphrey, watching from a box with her family, received congratulations with a gracious smile.

The day's events, moving swiftly toward Mr. Humphrey's nomination, began this morning with Edward M. Kennedy's disavowal of a draft movement in his behalf.

In an emotional afternoon debate, the delegates sealed the grip of Mr. Humphrey and Mr. Johnson on this convention by adopting a Vietnam plank drawn to the President's specifications.

They defeated by a comfortable margin a substitute proposal critical of much of the President's policy and supported by backers of Mr. McGovern, Mr. McCarthy and the "draft Ted" movement.

AUGUST 29, 1968
POLICE BATTLE DEMONSTRATORS IN STREETS

HUNDRED INJURED

178 Are Arrested as Guardsmen Join in Using Tear Gas

By J. ANTHONY LUKAS

Special to The New York Times

CHICAGO, Thursday, Aug. 29—The police and National Guardsmen battled young protesters in downtown Chicago last night as the week-long demonstrations against the Democratic National Convention reached a violent and tumultuous climax.

About 100 persons, including 25 policemen, were injured and at least 178 were arrested as the security forces chased down the demonstrators. The protesting young people had broken out of Grant Park on the shore of Lake Michigan in an attempt to reach the International Amphitheatre where the Democrats were meeting, four miles away.

The police and Guardsmen used clubs, rifle butts, tear gas and Chemical Mace on virtually anything moving along Michigan Avenue and the narrow streets of the Loop area.

Uneasy Calm

Shortly after midnight, an uneasy calm ruled the city. However, 1,000 National Guardsmen were moved back in front of the Conrad Hilton Hotel to guard it against more than 5,000 demonstrators who had drifted back into Grant Park.

The crowd in front of the hotel was growing, booing vociferously every time new votes for Vice President Humphrey were broadcast from the convention hall.

The events in the streets stirred anger among some delegates at the convention. In a nominating speech Senator Abraham A. Ribicoff of Connecticut told the delegates that if Senator George S. McGovern were President, "we would not have these Gestapo tactics in the streets of Chicago."

When Mayor Richard J. Daley of Chicago and other Illinois delegates rose shouting angrily, Mr. Ribicoff said, "How hard it is to accept the truth."

Crushed Against Windows

Even elderly bystanders were caught in the police onslaught. At one point, the police turned on several dozen persons standing quietly behind police barriers in front of the Conrad Hilton Hotel watching the demonstrators across the street

For no reason that could be immediately determined, the blue-helmeted policemen charged the barriers, crushing the spectators against the windows of the Haymarket Inn, a restaurant in the hotel. Finally the window gave

way, sending screaming middle-aged women and children backward through the broken shards of glass.

The police then ran into the restaurant and beat some of the victims who had fallen through the windows and arrested them.

At the same time, other policemen outside on the broad, tree-lined avenue were clubbing the young demonstrators repeatedly under television lights and in full view of delegates' wives looking out the hotel's windows.

Afterward, newsmen saw 30 shoes, women's purses and torn pieces of clothing lying with shattered glass on the sidewalk and street outside the hotel and for two blocks in each direction.

WALLACE

Alabama governor George Wallace entered the presidential race as the head of the American Independent Party, which he had created. Wallace campaigned on a populist platform, mainly opposing civil rights and racial integration, while also championing law and order policies and tax reductions. For his running mate, Wallace selected Curtis LeMay, a retired Air Force general known for his stated willingness to employ nuclear weapons. Their candidacies, never likely to win the election, unsettled the two major parties. Eventually, Wallace and LeMay won 5 states and nearly 14 percent of the popular vote.

SEPTEMBER 1, 1968
BY TRIAL AND ERROR, WALLACE SHAPES HIS PLATFORM
By BEN A. FRANKLIN
Special to The New York Times

LOUISVILLE, Ky., Aug. 31—Behind the rustic segregationist rhetoric of his boisterous third party Presidential campaign, former Governor George C. Wallace of Alabama is shaping, by trial and error, the platform for his American Independent party that goes beyond his main themes of resegregation and "law and order."

If an idea goes over well with the huge audiences Mr. Wallace has been drawing across the country, it becomes part of the campaign and a Wallace "issue" is born.

Based on his speeches and news conference comments during a 10-day, cross-country campaign and fund-raising tour that ended here today, Mr. Wallace's published platform—a document that he says will be drawn from

"some things I have said"—is likely to be a mild surprise to his critics.

Audiences Understand Him

Generally, the critics have regarded him as a "one-issue" candidate, preoccupied with race and with suppressing urban disorder, and with a secondary objective of jailing Communists and ending "treasonous" dissent on college campuses concerning Vietnam.

The new proposals in the Wallace platform may not be a total surprise, however, because even in his newly developed material—on Federal tax policy, for example—Mr. Wallace's audiences clearly understand him to be talking about race.

He does not discuss the Vietnam war without linking its prolongation "directly" with slum and campus uprisings by "anarchists and communists." To his listeners, that joins frustrations about the war, at least indirectly, with hostility on the race issue, and interviews in the last week at rallies confirm it.

Since a pledge to bring a return to legally sanctioned racial segregation—if the citizens of a local government want it—remains pre-eminently the main thrust of Mr. Wallace's "Stand Up for America" campaign, the rest of his material, including the new tax reform package, also appears linked to it.

Near Deafening Roars

Last night in Louisville's Freedom Hall, the auditorium at the state fair grounds, Mr. Wallace attracted nearly 14,000 persons from Kentucky and some from Indiana and Ohio to a rally reported to be the largest political gathering ever assembled there.

The nearly deafening roars he got from his audience last night—and from others nearly as large across the nation—by denouncing Federal school desegregation and equal employment guidelines and the Open Housing Act appear to be confirmation that when he repeats and repeats that he is "not talking about race," his listeners hear him talking segregation.

The loudest cheers from his white audience last night came from men in shirt sleeves waving Confederate flags so furiously that when Mr. Wallace remarked that "you are Southerners here in Kentucky," he drew a thunderous roar. So did his tax proposal.

Among other things, the candidate is now developing what started as a transient annoyance with philanthropic foundations into a "major" income tax reduction plan, which he insists can be enacted "even in wartime" and despite inflationary pressures.

He is emphasizing the appeal to "the working man" in calling for a repeal of the Federal tax exemption granted "multibillion-dollar foundations," and an increase in individual taxpayer exemptions from $600 to $1,000, with the revenue taken from the foundations.

'Over-Educated Folks'

Mr. Wallace does not say so directly, but many of the largest tax-free foundations are deeply involved in supporting programs to advance the educational and occupational opportunities of Negroes.

In his words, they are "full of over-educated, ivory tower folks who want to tax the working man to pay people not to work and not to burn our cities down." In the idiom of the Wallace campaign, that means to pay Negroes.

OCTOBER 14, 1968
GEN. LEMAY JOINS WALLACE'S TICKET AS RUNNING MATE

Says He Would Use Nuclear Bomb, but Rules It Out as Unnecessary in Vietnam

EX-GOVERNOR IS UPSET

Declares Former Air Force Chief 'Prefers Not to Use Any Sort of Weapon'

By WALTER RUGABER

Special to The New York Times

PITTSBURGH, Oct. 3—Gen. Curtis E. LeMay, the former Air Force Chief of Staff, became George C. Wallace's Vice-Presidential running mate today and promptly dropped some political bombs in the third-party campaign.

"If I found it necessary [in the Vietnam war]," the general said, "I would use anything that we could dream up, including nuclear weapons, if it was necessary." But he added, "I don't think it's necessary in this case or this war to use it."

Mr. Wallace, who has taken great pains to assure audiences in his Presidential bid that he would use only conventional weapons in Vietnam, appeared markedly perturbed by all the general's talk of nuclear bombs.

As his campaign plane left Pittsburgh for stops in Indianapolis and Toledo, the former Alabama Governor insisted to reporters aboard that the general also flatly ruled out a nuclear war in Vietnam.

An Angry Response

The general was presented by Mr. Wallace at a nationally televised news conference in the Pittsburgh Hilton Hotel.

When Jack Nelson, southern correspondent of The Los Angeles Times, asked Mr. Wallace whether he agreed with the general's position, the Alabamian, obviously nettled, snapped back:

"What you're doing, Mr. Nelson, is typical of The Los Angeles Times. You're trying to say that if the time ever came that it was necessary to use any sort of weapon in the vital interests of our national security, you wouldn't use them.

"All General LeMay has said—and I know you fellows better than he does because I've had to deal with you—he said that if the security of the country depended on the use of any weapon in the future he would use it. But he said he prefers not to use any sort of weapon. He prefers to negotiate."

Mr. Nelson again asked whether Mr. Wallace agreed with his new running mate, and Mr. Wallace replied that "we can win and defend in Vietnam without the use of nuclear weapons."

Referring to his work with the Strategic Air Command, General LeMay said:

"We hoped we could prevent war. I think we can. So my desire is not to use any weapons. But once the time comes that you have to fight, I would use any weapon that we have in the arsenal that is necessary. I do not believe nuclear weapons are necessary in Vietnam.

"But I'm certainly not going to stand up here and tell our enemies that I advocate that under all circumstances I'm not going to use nuclear weapons. We might as well bury them out at Fort Knox with the gold."

• •

THE CAMPAIGN

Presidential candidates Nixon and Humphrey attempted to distinguish their appeals during the 1968 campaign. Democrat Humphrey emphasized social and economic issues, while weakly endorsing the Johnson administration's policy in Vietnam. Nixon, the Republican candidate, emphasized law and order issues, attacking the Johnson administration as weak on crime and unable to win in Vietnam. Drawing close to the election, Nixon held a slim lead.

SEPTEMBER 9, 1968
HUMPHREY TERMS CAMPAIGN A POLL ON HUMAN RIGHTS

Charges Nixon and Wallace Strive to Exploit Fears Aroused by This Issue

'FATEFUL CHOICE' SEEN

Nominee Tells B'nai B'rith Nation Must Back Justice and Wider Opportunity

By MAX FRANKEL

Special to The New York Times

WASHINGTON, Sept. 8—Hubert H. Humphrey defined the 1968 campaign today as a "referendum on human rights" and charged that Richard M. Nixon and George C. Wallace were in competition against him, trying to exploit "the fears and hates aroused by this issue."

Unfolding the tactics that he has been planning since he became the Democratic nominee for President 10 days ago, the Vice President said that social peace in the nation required not a retreat from the programs of the past but efforts to create more opportunity and justice, more education and more jobs.

And he forcefully challenged Mr. Nixon's commitment to those objectives.

His Republican opponent is a fair and just man and no racist, Mr. Humphrey said.

Joining of Forces Scored

But Mr. Nixon and his party have chosen "to join forces with the most reactionary elements in American society," he charged, by openly competing with Mr. Wallace for the votes of those who would halt progress toward full opportunity and by deliberately ignoring the demands of "left-out Americans."

If they succeed on the basis of such a campaign, he said, the tension and violence and separation of the races across the land will only grow worse.

He recognizes the "short-run political dangers" of defining the issue in this way, the Vice President added, but he is taking the risk because he sees the election as "a fateful choice."

Choice Is Outlined

"The choice is simply this," Mr. Humphrey asserted in defining his view of the central question of the campaign.

"Shall we, as a nation, move forward toward one society of opportunity and justice or shall we move instead toward a fractured and separated society, black against white, rich against poor, comfortable against left-out?"

Mr. Nixon looks backward on this question, Mr. Humphrey charged, because he has made common cause with the conservatives of the Old South.

SEPTEMBER 30, 1968
NIXON URGES FOUR STEPS TO CURB NATION'S CRIME

By E. W. KENWORTHY

Special to The New York Times

KEY BISCAYNE, Fla., Sept. 29—Although law enforcement is primarily a local responsibility, Richard M. Nixon said today, a president is obligated to provide a "public climate with regard to law."

In a radio address over the national network of the Mutual Broadcasting System, the Republican Presidential nominee attributed the increase in crime and violence largely to what he asserted was the failure of the Johnson Administration to create such a climate.

Mr. Nixon pledged himself to restore this climate of respect for law and also to take a number of steps intended to curb crime and help prevent it. These steps included:

¶ The establishment of a Cabinet-level "National Law Enforcement Council," with advisory authority akin to that of the National Security Council and the Council of Economic Advisers. This council, he said, would "coordinate Federal policy on the control and prevention of crime."

¶ The establishment of a National Academy of Law Enforcement to provide the local police with training "in the most sophisticated, modern methods" of law enforcement, and also with information about the social sciences and community relations.

¶ The promotion of nationwide "town hall conferences on crime prevention and control."

¶ The establishment of a National Coordinating Center "to marshal the efforts of independent groups and institutions."

Mr. Nixon said the National Academy of Law Enforcement "would not in any sense be a Federal police force."

The purpose of the "town meetings" and the National Coordinating Center, he said, would be "to bring all of the energies of our people to bear" through "a massive educational effort, directed especially at the young and innocent."

He cited narcotics addiction as an area for such community effort by churches, schools, mass media, business and industry.

Mr. Nixon has decided to reserve for radio any statements on what he calls "substantive" matters. He does so in the belief that regular rallies, where people come to shout and applaud, are not adapted to serious exposition, and that television audiences are distracted by the picture of the candidate. Also, he does not like to read over television.

The Administration, he said, likes to place the blame for the increase in crime and violence on poverty, but "poverty is only one contributing factor."

Declaring that the crime rate during the depression of the thirties was at "an all-time low" and that there now is crime in the suburbs as well as the slums, Mr. Nixon said that the principal blame should be laid to a failure in leadership.

The Administration of which Hubert Humphrey is a part, he declared, "has failed in energy, failed in will, failed in purpose."

He scored Mr. Clark, as he does in almost every speech, for saying "there is no wave of crime in this country," and charged him with failure to apply fully the authority granted by Congress to use wire-tapping in the investigation of specific crimes.

Deplores 'Red Tape'

"The whole Federal effort is handcuffed by red tape," Mr. Nixon said, adding: "Let us recognize we are in a war, and let us mobilize all of our forces. Let us resolve that the wave of crime and violence will not be the wave of the future."

Also, as in virtually every stump speech, he rejected any connection between "stressing the need for order" and "being secretly anti-Negro."

Ghetto dwellers are not only victims of lawlessness, he said, but also of loan sharks and narcotics peddlers.

Finally, he repeated today his standard criticism of some Supreme Court decisions on procedural safeguards for the accused—decisions that he asserts "have tipped the balance against the peace forces in this country and strengthened the criminal forces."

"It is the Court's duty to protect legitimate rights," he declared, "but not to raise unreasonable obstacles to enforcement of the law.

Vietnam

Vietnam weighed heavily on the minds of voters weary of the war. Vice President Humphrey, suffering with the administration as the battles dragged on, took a more dovish position in the last month of the campaign. Nixon, benefiting from public frustration, claimed a "secret plan" for winning the war "honorably" without revealing any details. The tables turned just days before the election, with Johnson ceasing the bombing campaign and North Vietnam agreeing to peace talks. The administration's success was short-lived: when South Vietnam refused to attend the talks, the war issue festered as the polls opened.

OCTOBER 8, 1968
NIXON SUGGESTS HE COULD ACHIEVE PEACE IN VIETNAM

Indicates He Might Be Able to Agree to a Settlement Johnson Cannot Accept

SAIGON ROLE MENTIONED

Candidate Links Prospects to Bigger Fighting Share for South Vietnamese

By E. W. KENWORTHY

Special to The New York Times

WASHINGTON, Oct. 7—Richard M. Nixon hinted today that if the military situation in Vietnam improved and if the South Vietnamese shouldered more of the fighting, a Nixon Administration might be able to agree to peace terms that the Johnson Administration could not accept now.

In an hour-long question-and-answer session at the ninth annual conference of the United Press International editors and publishers in Washington this afternoon,

Mr. Nixon went beyond his standard reply when asked to outline his plans for bringing about the peace he promises.

Always before, he has said that he hopes that the negotiations in Paris will succeed and that while the prospects for success do not look too bright, he will say nothing to jeopardize the talks or to lead the North Vietnamese to believe they can get better terms from him than from the Johnson Administration.

President Lyndon B. Johnson listens to a tape recording from his son-in-law Capt. Charles Robb at the White House on July 31, 1968. Robb was a U.S. Marine Corps company commander in Vietnam. Images such as this suggested the toll that managing the war took on Johnson.

Source: AP Images/Jack Kightlinger

Situation in January

Today, however, he said his self-imposed silence on detailed discussion of his peace program was not simply a matter of not harming the negotiations.

It was necessary, the Republican Presidential candidate said, to keep in mind the situation that might prevail in January.

"We might be able to agree to much more then than we can do now," he said, adding that this might be possible especially if South Vietnamese forces were assuming a larger share of the fighting.

In answer to questions of what kind of a peace he wanted and what he meant by "an honorable end to the war," Mr. Nixon said that he favored a "generous" peace; that he had no wish to destroy North Vietnam or conquer it, and that he was, in fact, willing to help rebuild it.

But any settlement, he said, must provide for the territorial and political integrity of South Vietnam.

NOVEMBER 1, 1968
ATTACKS ON NORTH VIETNAM HALT TODAY; JOHNSON SAYS WIDER TALKS BEGIN NOV. 6

PEACE CALLED AIM

Saigon and N.L.F. Can Join in the Enlarged Paris Discussions

By NEIL SHEEHAN

Special to The New York Times

WASHINGTON, Oct. 31—President Johnson announced tonight that he was ordering a complete halt to all American air, naval and artillery bombardment of North Vietnam as of 8 A.M. Friday, Eastern standard time (9 P.M., Vietnam time).

"I have reached this decision on the basis of the developments in the Paris talks," the President said, "and I have reached it in the belief that this action can lead to progress toward a peaceful settlement of the Vietnamese war."

"What we now expect—what we have a right to expect," the President said in a television broadcast, "are prompt, productive, serious and intensive negotiations in an atmosphere that is conducive to progress."

NOVEMBER 1, 1968
HUMPHREY HAILS DECISION AS WISE

Asserts 'Vast Majority' Will Support It—Aides Look for Campaign Upturn

By R. W. APPLE Jr.

Special to The New York Times

BATTLE CREEK, Mich., Oct. 31—Vice President Humphrey reacted cautiously but with scarcely concealed exuberance tonight to the news that President Johnson had ordered a halt in the bombing of North Vietnam.

"I've been hoping for months that it would happen," he said, "for months."

Standing on the ramp of his campaign plane at Newark Airport, Mr. Humphrey said that he fully supported Mr. Johnson's "very wise and prudent" decision and was sure "the vast majority of the American people will also support it."

Displays Good Spirits

Asked whether he thought the breakthrough would help his Presidential campaign, the Vice President replied:

"This is going to help people. I don't think it has much to do with the candidates as such. I suggest that you just look at the President's message and then study it."

But Mr. Humphrey then walked back to the press plane, past the spotlights that had been set up on the runway, and demonstrated that he was in the best spirits imaginable.

He hectored his press secretary, Norman Sherman, for not producing quickly enough a transcript of his remarks, joked with reporters, and made a "my-lips-are-sealed" gesture when asked about the possible political implications of Mr. Johnson's statement.

He also insisted that he had received no word earlier this week that President Johnson had succeeded in arranging a halt in the bombing.

"I had a very firm agreement with the President that I would not involve myself too deeply in the intelligence details of the thing," Mr. Humphrey said. "I didn't want to."

The Vice President's staff argued, without much real conviction, that Mr. Humphrey's race for the White House had been helped by the news.

They cited, for example, the report of New Jersey Democrats today that Mr. Humphrey was likely to lose the state by 100,000 to 150,000 votes unless there was some dramatic, last-minute progress toward world peace.

NOVEMBER 2, 1968
THIEU SAYS SAIGON CANNOT JOIN PARIS TALKS UNDER PRESENT PLAN;

N.L.F. IS TOP ISSUE

South Vietnam Bars Any Separate Seat for the Vietcong

By GENE ROBERTS

Special to The New York Times

SAIGON, South Vietnam, Saturday, Nov. 2—President Nguyen Van Thieu said this morning that his Government would not attend peace talks in Paris until the North Vietnamese agreed to negotiate without the participation of the National Liberation Front as a separate delegation.

President Thieu said that because three key conditions had not yet been met by Hanoi, "The Government of South Vietnam deeply regrets not to be able to participate in the present exploratory talks." The talks are scheduled to begin next Wednesday.

[The White House declined to comment on reports of Mr. Thieu's speech. Other Washington sources said there would be no United States reaction until officials had thoroughly studied the remarks.]

Assembly Enthusiastic

Speaking to a wildly enthusiastic joint session of the National Assembly, President Thieu outlined the three conditions that he said Hanoi must meet.

Specifically, Mr. Thieu called on the North Vietnamese Government to pledge publicly that it advocated serious peace talks and that such discussions would be an "entirely new phase of talks, not just a continuation of the present exploratory talks between the United States and North Vietnam."

The most important point raised by Mr. Thieu, however, was one demanding that North Vietnam appear alone at the bargaining table and not "bring along representatives of the National Liberation Front as a separate delegation."

Coalition Regime Opposed

"This would just be another trick toward a coalition government with the Communists in South Vietnam," the President said.

NOVEMBER 3, 1968
DEMOCRATS FEAR SAIGON'S BOYCOTT MAY COST VOTES

Find Possibility of Damage Instead of Profit From Halt in the Bombing

By WARREN WEAVER Jr.

Special to The New York Times

WASHINGTON, Nov. 2—Democrats who had been hoping to realize a modest political profit from the bombing halt in North Vietnam began wondering today whether the ensuing international controversy might not instead cost them votes next Tuesday.

The refusal of South Vietnam to participate in the Paris talks on the war announced by President Johnson two days ago raised the possibility among politicians of

both parties that the apparent breakthrough toward peace might backfire and hurt, rather than help, Vice President Humphrey's closing drive for the Presidency.

Thinly veiled Republican suggestions that the President's announcement on Thursday had been motivated by a desire to influence the election moved a step closer to open charges today as Richard M. Nixon, the party's Presidential nominee, campaigned through Texas.

Assurances Reported

In Austin, a Nixon aide told United Press International that the President assured the candidate two days ago that all parties to the expanded Paris talks were in agreement before the public announcement of the bombing halt was made.

As a result of the new developments, the Republican adviser said, Mr. Nixon fears that the military and diplomatic situation in Vietnam would be jeopardized and, further, would cast doubt on President Johnson's "credibility in stopping the bombing."

Mr. Nixon had confined his original reaction to the President's announcement to an expression of hope that the move would bring some progress in the Paris talks. He said that he and his running mate, Gov. Spiro T. Agnew of Maryland, would not say anything more lest they endanger improved prospects for peace.

- -

ELECTION RESULTS

With a bare margin of victory, Richard Nixon became the thirty-seventh president, reversing his narrow loss in the 1960 election. Nixon won a personal victory, but the vote left many challenges unsettled. Nixon entered the White House facing a Democratic Congress and with few votes from the urban areas he had hoped to calm. His presidency began with calls for unity and anxious hopes that the country would resolve domestic discord and a bloody foreign war.

> " Richard Milhous Nixon emerged the victor yesterday in one of the closest and most tumultuous Presidential campaigns in history and set himself the task of reuniting the nation. "

NOVEMBER 7, 1968
NIXON WINS BY A THIN MARGIN, PLEADS FOR REUNITED NATION
ELECTOR VOTE 287

Lead in Popular Tally May Be Smaller Than Kennedy's in '60

By MAX FRANKEL.

Richard Milhous Nixon emerged the victor yesterday in one of the closest and most tumultuous Presidential campaigns in history and set himself the task of reuniting the nation.

Elected over Hubert H. Humphrey by the barest of margins—only four one-hundredths of a percentage point in the popular vote—and confronted by a Congress in control of the Democrats, the President-elect said it "will be the great objective of this Administration at the outset to bring the American people together."

He pledged, as the 37th President, to form "an open Administration, open to new ideas, open to men and women of both parties, open to critics as well as those who support us" so as to bridge the gap between the generations and the races.

Details Left for Later

But after an exhausting and tense night of awaiting the verdict at the Waldorf-Astoria Hotel here, Mr. Nixon and his closest aides were not yet prepared to suggest how they

1968 POPULAR VOTE

STATE	TOTAL VOTE	RICHARD M. NIXON (REPUBLICAN)		HUBERT H. HUMPHREY (DEMOCRAT)		GEORGE C. WALLACE (AMERICAN INDEPENDENT)		HENNING A. BLOMEN (SOCIALIST LABOR)	
		VOTES	%	VOTES	%	VOTES	%	VOTES	%
Alabama	1,049,922	146,923	14.0	196,579	18.7	691,425	65.9	—	0.0
Alaska	83,035	37,600	45.3	35,411	42.6	10,024	12.1	—	0.0
Arizona	486,936	266,721	54.8	170,514	35.0	46,573	9.6	75	0.0
Arkansas	619,969	190,759	30.8	188,228	30.4	240,982	38.9	—	0.0
California	7,251,587	3,467,664	47.8	3,244,318	44.7	487,270	6.7	341	0.0
Colorado	811,199	409,345	50.5	335,174	41.3	60,813	7.5	3,016	0.4
Connecticut	1,256,232	556,721	44.3	621,561	49.5	76,650	6.1	—	0.0
Delaware	214,367	96,714	45.1	89,194	41.6	28,459	13.3	—	0.0
Dist. of Col.	170,578	31,012	18.2	139,566	81.8	—	0.0	—	0.0
Florida	2,187,805	886,804	40.5	676,794	30.9	624,207	28.5	—	0.0
Georgia	1,250,266	380,111	30.4	334,440	26.7	535,550	42.8	—	0.0
Hawaii	236,218	91,425	38.7	141,324	59.8	3,469	1.5	—	0.0
Idaho	291,183	165,369	56.8	89,273	30.7	36,541	12.5	—	0.0
Illinois	4,619,749	2,174,774	47.1	2,039,814	44.2	390,958	8.5	13,878	0.3
Indiana	2,123,597	1,067,885	50.3	806,659	38.0	243,108	11.4	—	0.0
Iowa	1,167,931	619,106	53.0	476,699	40.8	66,422	5.7	241	0.0
Kansas	872,783	478,674	54.8	302,996	34.7	88,921	10.2	—	0.0
Kentucky	1,055,893	462,411	43.8	397,541	37.6	193,098	18.3	—	0.0
Louisiana	1,097,450	257,535	23.5	309,615	28.2	530,300	48.3	—	0.0
Maine	392,936	169,254	43.1	217,312	55.3	6,370	1.6	—	0.0
Maryland	1,235,039	517,995	41.9	538,310	43.6	178,734	14.5	—	0.0
Massachusetts	2,331,752	766,844	32.9	1,469,218	63.0	87,088	3.7	6,180	0.3
Michigan	3,306,250	1,370,665	41.5	1,593,082	48.2	331,968	10.0	1,762	0.1
Minnesota	1,588,506	658,643	41.5	857,738	54.0	68,931	4.3	285	0.0
Mississippi	654,509	88,516	13.5	150,644	23.0	415,349	63.5	—	0.0
Missouri	1,809,502	811,932	44.9	791,444	43.7	206,126	11.4	—	0.0
Montana	274,404	138,835	50.6	114,117	41.6	20,015	7.3	—	0.0
Nebraska	536,851	321,163	59.8	170,784	31.8	44,904	8.4	—	0.0
Nevada	154,218	73,188	47.5	60,598	39.3	20,432	13.2	—	0.0
New Hampshire	297,298	154,903	52.1	130,589	43.9	11,173	3.8	—	0.0
New Jersey	2,875,395	1,325,467	46.1	1,264,206	44.0	262,187	9.1	6,784	0.2
New Mexico	327,350	169,692	51.8	130,081	39.7	25,737	7.9	—	0.0
New York	6,791,688	3,007,932	44.3	3,378,470	49.7	358,864	5.3	8,432	0.1
North Carolina	1,587,493	627,192	39.5	464,113	29.2	496,188	31.3	—	0.0
North Dakota	247,882	138,669	55.9	94,769	38.2	14,244	5.7	—	0.0
Ohio	3,959,698	1,791,014	45.2	1,700,586	42.9	467,495	11.8	120	0.0
Oklahoma	943,086	449,697	47.7	301,658	32.0	191,731	20.3	—	0.0
Oregon	819,622	408,433	49.8	358,866	43.8	49,683	6.1	—	0.0
Pennsylvania	4,747,928	2,090,017	44.0	2,259,405	47.6	378,582	8.0	4,977	0.1
Rhode Island	385,000	122,359	31.8	246,518	64.0	15,678	4.1	—	0.0
South Carolina	666,978	254,062	38.1	197,486	29.6	215,430	32.3	—	0.0
South Dakota	281,264	149,841	53.3	118,023	42.0	13,400	4.8	—	0.0
Tennessee	1,248,617	472,592	37.8	351,233	28.1	424,792	34.0	—	0.0
Texas	3,079,216	1,227,844	39.9	1,266,804	41.1	584,269	19.0	—	0.0
Utah	422,568	238,728	56.5	156,665	37.1	26,906	6.4	—	0.0
Vermont	161,404	85,142	52.8	70,255	43.5	5,104	3.2	—	0.0
Virginia	1,361,491	590,319	43.4	442,387	32.5	321,833	23.6	4,671	0.3
Washington	1,304,281	588,510	45.1	616,037	47.2	96,990	7.4	488	0.0
West Virginia	754,206	307,555	40.8	374,091	49.6	72,560	9.6	—	0.0
Wisconsin	1,691,538	809,997	47.9	748,804	44.3	127,835	7.6	1,338	0.1
Wyoming	127,205	70,927	55.8	45,173	35.5	11,105	8.7	—	0.0
TOTALS	73,211,875	31,785,480	43.4	31,275,166	42.7	9,906,473	13.5	52,588	0.1

OTHER VOTES	%	PLURALITY	
14,995	1.4	494,846	A
—	0.0	2,189	R
3,053	0.6	96,207	R
—	0.0	50,223	A
51,994	0.7	223,346	R
2,851	0.4	74,171	R
1,300	0.1	64,840	D
—	0.0	7,520	R
—	0.0	108,554	D
—	0.0	210,010	R
165	0.0	155,439	A
—	0.0	49,899	D
—	0.0	76,096	R
325	0.0	134,960	R
5,945	0.3	261,226	R
5,463	0.5	142,407	R
2,192	0.3	175,678	R
2,843	0.3	64,870	R
—	0.0	220,685	A
—	0.0	48,058	D
—	0.0	20,315	D
2,422	0.1	702,374	D
8,773	0.3	222,417	D
2,909	0.2	199,095	D
—	0.0	264,705	A
—	0.0	20,488	R
1,437	0.5	24,718	R
—	0.0	150,379	R
—	0.0	12,590	R
633	0.2	24,314	R
16,751	0.6	61,261	R
1,840	0.6	39,611	R
37,990	0.6	370,538	D
—	0.0	131,004	R
200	0.1	43,900	R
483	0.0	90,428	R
—	0.0	148,039	R
2,640	0.3	49,567	R
14,947	0.3	169,388	D
445	0.1	124,159	D
—	0.0	38,632	R
—	0.0	31,818	R
—	0.0	47,800	R
299	0.0	38,960	D
269	0.1	82,063	R
903	0.6	14,887	R
2,281	0.2	147,932	R
2,256	0.2	27,527	D
—	0.0	66,536	D
3,564	0.2	61,193	R
—	0.0	25,754	R
192,168	**0.3**	**510,314**	**R**

intended to organize themselves and to approach these objectives. The Republican victor expressed admiration for his opponent's challenge and reiterated his desire to help President Johnson achieve peace in Vietnam between now and Inauguration Day on Jan. 20.

The verdict of an electorate that appeared to number 73 million could not be discerned until mid-morning because Mr. Nixon and Mr. Humphrey finished in a virtual tie in the popular vote, just as Mr. Nixon and John F. Kennedy did in 1960.

With 94 per cent of the nation's election precincts reporting, Mr. Nixon's total stood last evening at 29,726,409 votes to Mr. Humphrey's 29,677,152. The margin of 49,257 was even smaller than Mr. Kennedy's margin of 112,803.

Meaning Hard to Find

When translated into the determining electoral votes of the states, these returns proved even more difficult to read, and the result in two states—Alaska and Missouri—was still not final last night. But the unofficial returns from elsewhere gave Mr. Nixon a minimum of 287 electoral votes, 17 more than the 270 required for election. Mr. Humphrey won 191.

Because of the tightness of the race, the third-party challenger, George C. Wallace, came close to realizing his minimum objective of denying victory to the major-party candidates and then somehow forcing a bargain for his support on one of them. Although he did not do nearly as well as he had hoped and as others had feared, he received 9,291,807 votes or 13.3 per cent of the total, and the 45 electoral votes of Alabama, Georgia, Louisiana, Mississippi and Arkansas.

Mr. Wallace's support ranged from 1 per cent in Hawaii to 65 per cent in his home state of Alabama, and his presence on the ballot in all 50 states unquestionably influenced the outcome in many of them. But there was no certain way of determining whether Mr. Nixon or Mr. Humphrey was the beneficiary of the third-party split-offs.

Mr. Humphrey's narrow victory in states such as Texas was probably due to Mr. Wallace's strong showing there, Conversely, Mr. Wallace's drain-off in traditional Democratic strongholds, such as New Jersey, probably helped Mr. Nixon.

NOVEMBER 7, 1968
EDITORIAL
THE NIXON VICTORY

Richard M. Nixon, bringing to a climax an amazing personal comeback, has been elected President of the United States eight years after he first sought the office. A Republican, he joins Thomas Jefferson and Andrew Jackson, those patristic heroes of the Democratic party, as one of only three men in the nation's history to be elected to the White House after having been defeated in a previous try for the Presidency.

Mr. Nixon's victory was in many respects an exciting re-run of the 1960 election with a different ending. It was particularly remarkable that despite the distorting effects of a third candidate in the race, the popular vote of the two major party nominees divided almost evenly across the country.

In the end, Mr. Nixon did achieve a plurality in the popular vote and a clear majority in the Electoral College which place his victory beyond cavil or dispute. The nation can be profoundly grateful that the voters have reached an indisputable decision. There is to be no further delay before the result is actually known and accepted; nor is there any occasion for what could have been ignominious dickering with the third-party candidate, George C. Wallace.

* * *

Many difficulties confront the President-elect as he approaches his new responsibilities. Since the Democrats have retained control of House and Senate, Mr. Nixon will have to make special efforts to enlist bipartisan cooperation if he is to make any headway with his domestic program. Even more serious and fundamental, however, is the fact that Mr. Nixon appears to have won office with only negligible support from Negro voters. He will have to move promptly and persuasively to win their confidence, for without it he cannot achieve that national reconciliation which is his avowed purpose. In his news conference yesterday, Mr. Nixon wisely stressed that "the great objective of this administration [is] to bring the American people together. . . . We want to bridge the gap between the races."

In foreign affairs, the first priority is to establish a secure relationship between the incoming and outgoing Administrations in the management of the Paris peace negotiations. Next in importance is the early ratification of the nuclear nonproliferation treaty. Now that the campaign has ended, we hope that Mr. Nixon will encourage speedy Senate action.

* * *

This newspaper did not support Mr. Nixon, but we have always recognized that he is an intelligent, able man who is essentially a moderate, responsible conservative on most issues. His long years in national politics have given him the political skills which are a necessary part of a successful President's equipment. His wide lead in the public opinion polls until very recently enabled him to wage a campaign which has left few personal wounds or partisan animosities. His service as Vice President has acquainted him with the routines of the Presidential office and with the scope of its authority, experience which should stand him in good stead as he begins to shoulder the burdens which will pass to him in full measure on January 20.

THE CONGRESSIONAL ELECTIONS OF 1974

WATERGATE SCANDAL YIELDS LARGE DEMOCRATIC GAINS IN CONGRESS

The congressional elections of 1974 marked a political repudiation of the overreaching administration of President Richard Nixon. The Republican president had averted a constitutional crisis when he resigned rather than face certain impeachment and removal from office amid the Watergate scandal. The voters added their own repudiation by giving the Democrats commanding control of both houses of Congress, leading to a presidential victory in 1976 and continuing legislative majorities for the next two decades.

Until the Watergate revelations and Nixon's fall, the Republican Party appeared poised to forge a dominant national coalition. Nixon had been narrowly elected president in 1968 amid the bitter controversies over the Vietnam War, the turmoil of clashing life styles, and racial conflict in the South and northern cities. Once in office, he had reduced American involvement in Vietnam, opened new international contacts, and began new domestic programs on the environment and social welfare. That record had led to Nixon's overwhelming reelection in 1972, when he won nearly 61 percent of the popular vote and carried every state but Massachusetts.

But Nixon's triumph soon faded, as searching investigations revealed deep stains in his character. His personal flaws magnified the party's problems arising from deteriorating economic conditions and institutional clashes between the president and the Democratic Congress. The combination precipitated the Republicans' steep decline in the elections of 1974, altering the course of national politics for the rest of the century.

SETTING OF THE ELECTIONS

The controversies over Watergate and constitutional powers played out amid deteriorating national economic conditions. Nixon's second term, begun in good times, was severely disrupted in October 1973 by war in the Middle East, when Egypt and Syria attacked Israel on Yom Kippur, the most holy day of the Jewish people. After initial successes, the invading

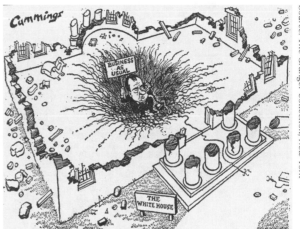

Cartoonist Michael Cummings in 1973 depicts the damage to the administration of President Richard Nixon resulting from the Watergate scandal.

armies were repulsed and came close to total extermination. Nixon provided both military and diplomatic support for Israel, while also putting U.S. forces on nuclear alert, an action seen by some observers as a means to divert attention from the spreading Watergate investigations.

The Arab states compensated for their defeat by commissioning a different weapon—oil. The Organization of Petroleum Exporting Countries (OPEC) lowered oil production and embargoed its shipment to the United States and other countries that had aided Israel. Heavily dependent on oil imports, the United States immediately felt the effects of the embargo. The world price of oil soon quadrupled, leading to an increase of more than 40 percent in the cost of gasoline at the pump. Price, however, was not the biggest problem for Americans. Whatever the cost (even 55 cents per gallon!), gas seemed unavailable. Drivers waited for hours, often futilely, in long lines of cars until rationing was imposed, restricting fill-ups to alternate days. To save energy, the federal government acted in ways that changed American life styles. Highway speed limits

1974 MIDTERM ELECTION RESULTS

HOUSE

ELECTION YEAR	CONGRESS	MEMBERS ELECTED			GAINS/LOSSES	
		DEM.	REP.	MISC.	DEM.	REP.
1974	94th	291	144	–	+43	–57

SENATE

ELECTION YEAR	CONGRESS	MEMBERS ELECTED			GAINS/LOSSES	
		DEM.	REP.	MISC.	DEM.	REP.
1974	94th	61	38	–	+3	–3

were lowered to 55 miles per hour, daylight savings time was extended to the entire year, Christmas lighting was curtailed, and production of large cars declined.

The increase in oil prices brought wider effects in the economy. The stock market plunged, losing 45 percent of its value over two years. The broader economy contracted, going from vigorous growth to actual decline. Both inflation and unemployment climbed—combining in a new measure, a "misery index," of close to 20 percent by the time of the congressional balloting. Sensing their opportunity, Democrats recruited a field of attractive candidates and financed their campaigns well, spending more money on behalf of their challengers than on incumbents, who seemed secure in their seats.

The threatening economic conditions provoked partisan conflict. At the same time, the Democratic Congress and the Republican president clashed sharply on larger issues. More than the usual policy differences, these disputes involved basic controversies over the constitutional powers of the legislative and executive branches.

One dispute concerned spending in the federal budget. Nixon had claimed the authority to withhold money appropriated by Congress. In a major reform of the budgetary process, Congress removed that authority. If Nixon or any future president wanted to end spending on a program, the new law required congressional action to rescind the previous appropriations. Unless both the House and Senate passed a rescission bill within forty-five days, the president would have to spend the money.

The bitter aftermath of Vietnam led to divisions on a still more vital issue: the constitutional powers of the president in foreign policy. Now seeing U.S. involvement in the war as a mistake caused by presidential deception, Congress passed the War Powers Act, which required congressional approval for the use of military force abroad for more than sixty days,

even without a formal declaration of war. Nixon vetoed the law, but Congress repassed it in November 1973. Later presidents would still insist that they had constitutional power as commander in chief to deploy American troops, and the act led to vigorous debate in subsequent conflicts, particularly the U.S. interventions in the Balkans by President Bill Clinton and in Iraq by Presidents George H. W. Bush and George W. Bush.

The impeachment crisis was the defining event of the 1974 congressional elections, assuring Democratic victories. The crisis had begun two years earlier, during the presidential election campaign, with a puzzling break-in at the Democratic National Committee's offices in the Watergate complex in Washington. After the election, investigative reporters of the *Washington Post* drew connections between the burglars and the Nixon administration, soon leading to appointment of a special prosecutor and a televised inquiry by a Senate committee. The hearings produced dramatic revelations of apparent crimes in the executive branch and the existence of a taping system in the Oval Office that recorded all of the president's conversations.

The White House tried a variety of means to thwart the investigations, including convictions and guilty pleas by the original criminals, resignation of Nixon's top aides, resignation of Vice President Spiro Agnew on unrelated corruption charges, repeated presidential denial of any involvement in the break-in or the subsequent cover-up, and resistance to releasing the White House tapes. When a grand jury indicted his aides for the cover-up, Nixon was also secretly named as an unindicted co-conspirator. As the courts ruled that the president must surrender the White House tapes, Nixon conducted his "Saturday Night Massacre," firing the attorney general, the deputy attorney general, and the special prosecutor.

The dismissals brought public outrage at Nixon's bald assertion of power, quickly resulting in introduction of a resolution of impeachment and lengthy investigations behind closed doors by the Judiciary Committee of the House of Representatives, chaired by Rep. Peter Rodino of New Jersey. Rodino conducted a cautious and confidential investigation, emphasizing a bipartisan approach to win the backing of Republicans and conservative southern Democrats.

The House inquiry provided details on Nixon's impeachable conduct. Before and after the break-in, Nixon was involved in perjury, obstruction of justice, bribery, disruption of protest rallies, and investigations of his opponents' finances, medical records, and sex lives. He and his collaborators spied on their opponents; burglarized offices; employed the IRS, FBI, CIA, and Justice Department to violate opponents' constitutional rights; and engaged in an extensive cover-up of these and other actions. In all, the president had attempted a virtual coup d'état to subvert the Constitution and the basic democratic processes of the United States.

At the end of July 1974, the committee held thirty-six hours of public hearings over six days, concluding that Nixon's conduct "warrants impeachment and trial, and removal from office." Three specific counts accused the president of obstruction of justice in the investigation of the Watergate crimes, a series of abuses of power and violations of citizens' constitutional rights, and subversion of the constitutional separation of powers. In the critical vote, all Democrats and seven of seventeen Republicans joined in a decisive 28–10 vote to urge Nixon's impeachment by the House of Representatives.

The committee's condemnation severely weakened Nixon's hold on his office. His position grew still more tenuous as his approval rating in opinion polls dropped below 25 percent. But, before the full House could act on the impeachment, the White House tapes, now fully opened by court order, proved that Nixon had participated actively in the illegal activities and had lied in his previous denials. These revelations guaranteed impeachment in the House and conviction in the Senate. With Republicans—including the conservative leader, Sen. Barry Goldwater, and the party's national chair and future president, George H. W. Bush—leading the refrain, a national chorus of protest convinced Nixon to leave office voluntarily. Congress had achieved the only removal from office of a president in American history, a peaceful resolution to a severe constitutional crisis.

Republicans still saw some opportunities. As Nixon left Washington, they hoped that the new president, Gerald Ford, had correctly assured the nation that "our long national nightmare is over." But Ford soon undermined the party cause. A month after Nixon's resignation, trying to awake into a brighter day undimmed by Nixon's shadow, Ford gave the exiled president a full pardon "for all offenses against the United States which he, Richard Nixon, has committed or may have committed" during his years as president.

Public opinion, stimulated by Democratic attacks, condemned this unmovable barrier to further prosecution of Nixon. Ford's press secretary resigned in protest, and some critics, although lacking any evidence, even saw the pardon as a corrupt bargain. Regardless of the evidence, and even after Ford came to the House for unprecedented sworn testimony, the Nixon pardon became a heavy burden to the party in 1974. Two years later, it also became the margin of defeat in Ford's bid for election to the presidency.

ELECTION RESULTS AND EFFECTS

With the advantage gained by Nixon's troubles, Democrats made strong advances in House elections. They added 48 seats to their 1972 representation to reach a total of 291, their highest tally since the days of Franklin Roosevelt (except for their quickly eroded landslide of 1964). They also won 4 new seats in the Senate, reaching a strong majority of 61 seats. Notably, the previous advantage of incumbency declined. Although 88 percent of officeholders seeking reelection were returned to Congress, 92 first-termers were elected to the House, more than in any contest since 1949, along with 11 new senators.

The impeachment controversy had a direct impact on the election results, most clearly in the contests involving members of the House Judiciary Committee, the only legislators who cast formal votes on the issue. Of the Nixon loyalists who voted against each article of impeachment, four were defeated and five reelected, but with decreased margins from their past candidacies. Those who voted to impeach Nixon did far better: all the Democrats and all but one Republican were reelected.

The election's effects went beyond the immediate balloting. Fewer Americans voted, and the public became more cynical toward politics and politicians. Nearly 80 percent of Americans in 1964 had trusted "the government in Washington to do what is right," and a clear majority still held to that belief in 1972, despite the traumas of Vietnam. But Watergate led to a sharp decline in public confidence: by the end of the impeachment proceedings, only a third of citizens still trusted the national government, and that sour mood continued for decades.

The institutional conflicts that had characterized the previous Congress continued after the elections. With their large majorities in hand, Democrats saw the prospect of "legislative government," but they could not overcome the strengths of the presidential office, even with a weakened chief executive, Gerald Ford, in charge. Attempts to rewrite American energy policy or to combat recession through new tax cuts were turned back by Ford, the president winning on all but eight attempts to override thirty-seven vetoes. Deadlocks between the institutions prevented action on national health insurance, welfare revision, Social Security and Medicare, and energy programs.

Some restrictions on intelligence operations and use of American troops in the waning days of the Vietnam conflict were enacted, but they did little to restrict the president's constitutional powers. Congress did reform its own structure, centralizing power in the hands of party leaders. Democrats also successfully overrode Ford's vetoes on bills to raise spending on education, health and welfare programs, and public works.

With the national government often deadlocked, institutional disputes added to partisan rancor. For the next thirty-five years, the constitutional separation of Congress and the president reinforced the conflicts of Republicans and Democrats. In only ten of those years did the same party control the presidency and both houses of Congress. Even those short periods evidenced fragility within the parties and the growing conflict between them, as they drew further apart on their programs and more hostile to one another. The long-term effects of the congressional elections of 1974 provided little reason for national celebration.

• •

THE IMPERIAL PRESIDENCY

Although he was elected president in 1968 with a minority of the popular vote, Richard Nixon vigorously asserted his executive powers. His active presidency revived tensions between the branches of government that had become dormant during united Democratic control. Dealing with a growing financial crisis and the ongoing war in Vietnam, Nixon broadened the powers of the president, attempting to lead domestic and foreign policy while openly defying acts of Congress he opposed. Congress, still held by the Democrats, resisted the forceful president.

JUNE 5, 1969
PRESIDENT'S SPEECH STIRS RESENTMENT IN CONGRESS
By JOHN W. FINNEY
Special to The New York Times

WASHINGTON, June 4—President Nixon's attack on military critics today appeared to have abbreviated, if not terminated, the Administration's period of good feelings on Capitol Hill. Since the Administration took office, probably no Nixon speech or statement has stirred up such an adverse reaction as the President's national defense speech at the Air Force Academy in Colorado.

Within the prevailing centrist coalition in the Senate, Democrats were openly outraged and Republicans were privately distressed over what they regarded as the "hard line" in the speech and the Presidential suggestions that military critics in Congress were either isolationists or unilateral disarmers.

Personal Criticism

For the first time since the President took office, some Democrats voiced personal criticism of Mr. Nixon.

In varying ways, Senator J. W. Fulbright of Arkansas and Senator Albert Gore of Tennessee suggested that "the old Nixon" had reappeared in the speech.

"It sounded like the old Nixon I used to know," commented Senator Gore, who served with Mr. Nixon in the House and the Senate.

Senator Fulbright protested that Mr. Nixon had indulged in "a form of demagoguery that was very fashionable in the time of his old colleague, Joe McCarthy."

Complaining that the President was attempting to depict military critics as unpatriotic, Senator Fulbright observed to reporters:

"I think it is essentially an un-American approach to attempt to stifle discussion of legitimate problems."

OCTOBER 16, 1970
PRESIDENT IS MEETING DELAY ON PROPOSED REFORMS

By JOHN HERBERS

Special to the New York Times

WASHINGTON, Oct. 15—Last Jan. 6, the Nixon Administration announced a pilot project of storefront "postal academies" that would use the employees and resources of the post offices to give high school dropouts remedial education, counseling and part-time jobs.

Beginning in May, the academies were set up in Chicago, Detroit, Atlanta, San Francisco, Washington and Newark. By Sept. 17, the Administration expressed pleasure with the beginning. But only 312 youths had been enrolled and the evaluation that would decide whether the project would become a nationwide antipoverty effort had not been made by today.

The story of the postal academies is illustrative of the problems of most of the major reforms and innovations in the domestic area promised by the Administration in its first 20 months in office, according to a survey of the executive agencies and of Congress.

President Nixon has proposed more domestic change than either his Democratic critics or conservative supporters had expected. There have been important breakthroughs, such as reforms in Selective Service, restructuring of the Post Office Department and feeding the poor.

But because of budget restraints against inflation, resistance in Congress and in the executive bureaucracy, and difficulty in filling key administrative posts, most reforms and innovations have been frustrated or are still in the formative stage.

AUGUST 16, 1971
NIXON ORDERS 90-DAY WAGE-PRICE FREEZE. ASKS TAX CUTS, NEW JOBS IN BROAD PLAN:

SPEAKS TO NATION

Urges Business Aid to Bolster Economy—Budget Slashed

By JAMES M. NAUGHTON

Special to The New York Times

WASHINGTON, Aug. 15—President Nixon charted a new economic course tonight by ordering a 90-day freeze on wages and prices, requesting Federal tax cuts and making a broad range of domestic and international moves designed to strengthen the dollar.

In a 20-minute address, telecast and broadcast nationally, the President appealed to Americans to join him in creating new jobs, curtailing inflation and restoring confidence in the economy through "the most comprehensive new economic policy to be undertaken in this nation in four decades."

Some of the measures Mr. Nixon can impose temporarily himself and he asked for tolerance as he does.

Others require Congressional approval and—although he proposed some policies that his critics on Capitol Hill have been urging upon him—will doubtless face long scrutiny before they take effect.

2 Tax Reductions

Mr. Nixon imposed a ceiling on all prices, rents, wages and salaries—and asked corporations to do the same voluntarily on stockholder dividends—under authority granted to him last year by Congress but ignored by the White House until tonight.

NOVEMBER 28, 1971
PRESIDENT, AFTER 3 YEARS, IS STILL BALKED BY CONGRESS

He Holds Sway on Foreign Affairs but Has Been Frustrated by Legislators in Hopes for Domestic Program

By ROBERT B. SEMPLE Jr.

Special to The New York Times

WASHINGTON, Nov. 27—President Nixon and Congress are approaching the end of the third year of their troubled and occasionally turbulent relationship in much the same way they began it—with the President in command of foreign policy, the field that most engages his energies, but frustrated and on the defensive in domestic matters.

In recent days, for example, Mr. Nixon has temporarily salvaged the foreign aid program and has fended off renewed Congressional efforts to reduce the number of American troops in Europe and to withdraw American forces from Vietnam by a "date certain." Thus he has kept intact the flexibility he regards as essential to his own conduct of diplomacy.

On the domestic scene, however, Congress has not only treated with indifference the "six great goals" enunciated in Mr. Nixon's State of the Union Message last winter, but has also approved a variety of proposals he does not want and did not ask for.

The two most unwelcome gifts from the Democratic-controlled Congress, from the President's point of view, came this week. One was an amendment to Mr. Nixon's own tax bill that would allow any citizen to earmark $1 of his tax payments for a political contribution, a move that has been condemned by Republicans as a means of refinancing a debt-ridden Democratic party. The second was a provision in a bill extending the antipoverty program, that would provide for a multibillion-dollar system of day-care centers, a move that budget-conscious Republicans have described as too costly.

As things now stand the President may be forced to veto both bills, unless the unwelcome provisions can be removed by parliamentary maneuvering before the measures reach his desk.

To students here of the relationship between the President and Congress, this peculiar pattern of Presidential control of foreign policy and frequent Presidential defeat in the domestic arena, telescoped and dramatized by the event of this week, has been symptomatic of the entire Nixon Presidency. The question is: Why?

Some observers believe they have found the root of Mr. Nixon's problems in what they regard as his "amateurish" Congressional relations, broadly defined as the business of caring and feeding Congressional foes and allies, consulting them, catering to their egos and remaining ever alert to their patronage requirements.

NIXON REELECTED

President Nixon ran for reelection in 1972, seeking a new mandate and expansion of Republican ranks in Congress. Before election day, scandals began to emerge, foremost among them a foiled break-in at the Democratic campaign headquarters located in the Watergate complex in Washington. Links between the burglars and the Republican Party surfaced, although the crime drew only limited immediate attention. Nixon won a landslide electoral victory, but some observers remained wary of the Republican Party.

JUNE 19, 1972
DEMOCRATIC RAID TIED TO REALTOR

Alleged Leader Said to Have G.O.P. Links and to Have Aided C.I.A. on Cuba

By TAD SZULC

Special to The New York Times

WASHINGTON, June 18—The apparent leader of five men arrested yesterday for breaking into the headquarters of the Democratic National Committee here was identified today as an affluent Miami real estate man with important Republican party links in Florida.

He was also said to have been one of the top planners of the Central Intelligence Agency's abortive invasion of Cuba in 1961.

Five men were arrested at gunpoint in the raid. The police said that they possessed sophisticated eavesdropping devices and photographic equipment.

NOVEMBER 1, 1972
THE WATERGATE MYSTERY

By WALTER RUGABER

Special to The New York Times

WASHINGTON, Oct. 31—Despite 19 weeks of intensive investigation, sensational disclosure, and heated political debate, the dimensions of the Watergate affair are far from fixed.

A Federal grand jury has charged seven men—three of them associated with President Nixon's campaign organization, the White House, or both—with rigging the Watergate offices of the Democratic National Committee.

Senator George McGovern has charged, and various unnamed Democrats and unidentified Federal investigators have been quoted as suggesting that the eavesdropping was part of a broader Republican-directed espionage and sabotage effort.

A number of documents and witnesses—not fully rebutted by the Republicans—have indicated that at least some of the money used to spy on the Democrats was diverted from Nixon campaign funds.

The Republicans have said that there was no high-level involvement, no "secret fund" and no massive spying

campaign sanctioned by them. The Justice Department has said there is no evidence to incriminate anyone other than those indicted.

There has been no public indication that either the President or any of his close advisers played roles in or had advance knowledge of an illegal assault upon the opposition party.

The staff of the House Banking and Currency Committee, headed by Representative Wright Patman, Democrat of Texas, raised new questions in a report today about the possible violations of the campaign finances, banking, and tax laws in connection with several contributions to the Nixon re-election committee.

It was reported, for example, that "at least $30,000 was channeled to the committee from a bank in Luxembourg. There was little new information in the report about the Watergate case, however.

NOVEMBER 8, 1972
NIXON ELECTED IN LANDSLIDE; M'GOVERN IS BEATEN IN STATE; DEMOCRATS RETAIN CONGRESS
MARGIN ABOUT 60%

Massachusetts Is Only State to Give Vote to the Dakotan

By MAX FRANKEL

Richard Milhous Nixon won re-election by a huge majority yesterday, perhaps the largest ever given a President.

Mr. Nixon scored a stunning personal triumph in all sections of the country, sweeping New York and most other bastions of Democratic strength.

He was gathering more than 60 per cent of the nation's ballots and more than 500 electoral votes. He lost only Massachusetts and the District of Columbia.

The victory was reminiscent of the landslide triumphs of Franklin D. Roosevelt in 1936 and Lyndon B. Johnson in 1964, although it could fall just short of their record proportions.

Tickets Are Split

Despite this drubbing of George Stanley McGovern, the Democratic challenger, the voters split their tickets in record numbers to leave the Democrats in Congress and a majority of the nation's governorships, Mr. Nixon thus became the first two-term President to face an opposition Congress at both inaugurals.

The turnout of the voters appeared to be unusually low, despite jams at many polling places. Projections indicated a total vote of 76 million out of a voting-age population of 139.6 million, or only about 54 per cent. If accurate, that would be the lowest proportion since 51.4 per cent in 1948. The percentage had been over 60 per cent in every election since then.

NOVEMBER 8, 1972
EDITORIAL
CONFIDENCE LIMITED

It is still impossible to tell with certainty the partisan complexion of the 93rd Congress, but it is evident that despite President Nixon's landslide victory, it will remain in the hands of the Democrats. Interpreted broadly, the over-all results suggest strongly that it was Senator George McGovern personally who went down to defeat, not the Democratic party.

Reasons for the nation's record-breaking resort to ticket-splitting will no doubt be adduced for months to come, as analysts work over the statistics, but some implications seem obvious from the start. One is that while issues were evidently not of decisive importance in the voting for President, they were important enough on the Congressional level to keep Mr. Nixon's coattails too short for effective riding—at least as far as the Senate is concerned.

A probable contributing factor in the outcome was what has been called the penance vote. Democrats who

defected to vote for the President were nevertheless firm enough in their commitment to the party to make up for the major unorthodoxy by being ultra loyal everywhere else on the ticket. If on analysis this turns out to have been the case, the significance will not be lost in the inevitable intra-party struggle to come.

It will be used, rather, as a sign that those of the party's supporters who abandoned its standard-bearer—without officially embracing Mr. Nixon as, for example, John Connally did—still consider themselves in good standing and are by no means ready to turn the party over to the forces that dominated the McGovern convention last July.

Not least, the results indicate that if many voters would not entrust Mr. McGovern with the Presidency, neither were they sure enough of Mr. Nixon's virtues to offer him a second term freed of the restraints of an opposition Congress. The nation gave him, in short, a very big vote of rather limited confidence.

• •

NIXON'S CRISIS

Amid growing concern, the Senate opened public hearings into the Watergate scandal, uncovering potentially damning evidence of Richard Nixon's involvement. The president asserted his innocence, but his refusal to cooperate with the hearings, televised daily, tainted his public image. As faith in the president declined, Nixon's difficulties intensified. The economy overheated, threatening a downturn. War broke out between Israel and its Arab neighbors, who levied oil sanctions on the United States for its assistance to Israel. Oil scarcity further damaged the ailing economy, bringing record gas prices and further deepening Nixon's woes.

MAY 17, 1973
SENATE'S INQUIRY WILL BEGIN TODAY

Ervin Foresees 'Startling Revelations' on Watergate

By WALTER RUGABER

Special to The New York Times

WASHINGTON, May 16—A wide-ranging and potentially epic investigation of the reported effort last year to subvert the Presidential election campaign begins tomorrow on Capitol Hill.

The Senate Watergate committee, a seven-member panel under Sam J. Ervin Jr., Democrat of North Carolina, is scheduled to hear its first public testimony at 10 A.M. in the Caucus Room of the Old Senate Office Building.

The sessions could have a broad impact on the way American campaigns are financed and run, on the future of many prominent political leaders, and on the immediate fortunes of Richard Nixon.

They begin exactly 11 months after the Watergate affair first arose with the arrest of five obscure men who had broken into the Democratic headquarters in an elaborate eavesdropping operation.

The 76-year-old committee chairman said today at a news conference in Brunswick, Me., that he expected "some startling revelations" from the long inquiry.

Most sources expect a relatively slow start. They predict a painstaking effort to piece together the more obscure parts of the complex scandal as well as to question the political personalities involved.

The hearing to be televised nationally in at least the initial stages will run off and on throughout the summer. Some officials think the sessions will run into the fall as well. Senator Ervin said he hoped that the inquiry could be completed by the end of the year.

MAY 30, 1973
ADMINISTRATION IS ATTACKED ON ECONOMIC MANAGEMENT

Salomon Partner Says Economy Is 'Veering Out of Control'

By H. ERICH HEINEMANN

One of Wall Street's leading economists launched a blistering attack yesterday on the Nixon Administration's management of the national economy.

Speaking at the annual meeting of the New York Society of Security Analysts, Henry Kaufman—partner and economist of Salomon Brothers—said that the economy was "veering out of control."

This was largely due, Mr. Kaufman asserted, to Washington's drive to stimulate business for "near-term social and political objectives," presumably including, although he did not say so, President Nixon's re-election last fall.

"The massive fiscal and monetary stimulation during the latest economic expansion," Mr. Kaufman said, "is without parallel in the post-World War II period." It occurred, he said, "against a backdrop that actually warranted only moderate expansion if sustainable economic growth was to be achieved."

Mr. Kaufman has been a leader among the business forecasters who have been warning for many months that the inflation and business boom of 1973 could give way to a recession and rising unemployment in 1974.

JULY 27, 1973
NIXON CONTESTS SUBPOENAS, KEEPS TAPES; HEARING SET AUG. 7 ON HISTORIC CHALLENGE
COURT ACTION DUE
Aide Asserts President Will Abide by Ruling of Supreme Court
By R. W. APPLE Jr.
Special to The New York Times

WASHINGTON, July 26—President Nixon refused today to comply with subpoenas requiring him to furnish to the Senate Watergate committee and the special prosecutor tape recordings of his conversations about the Watergate case.

Chief Judge John J. Sirica of the United States District Court immediately ordered Mr. Nixon to explain by Aug. 7 why he should not be compelled to release the tapes to the prosecutor, Archibald Cox. And the committee, in an unprecedented action, voted to go to court next week to secure the recordings.

The day's dramatic events intensified a historic constitutional struggle, compared by some participants to Marbury v. Madison, the landmark case in 1803 that established the principle of judicial review.

Gerald L. Warren, the deputy White House press secretary, said, "The President, just as in any other matter, would abide by a definitive decision of the highest court."

Hints Are Clarified

That statement, a clarification of earlier hints in the same vein by Mr. Warren, apparently means that if the Supreme Court rejects Mr. Nixon's argument that the separation of the powers precludes him from turning over the tape recordings, he will then release them.

It also apparently eliminates the possibility that Mr. Nixon, faced with an adverse Supreme Court ruling but unwilling to comply, might leave Congress no alternative but impeachment if it wanted to gain access to the tapes.

The President made his position known in carefully drafted letters, amounting to informal legal briefs, that were delivered early this morning to Judge Sirica and to Senator Sam J. Ervin Jr. of North Carolina, the committee chairman.

With former White House aide John D. Ehrlichman waiting at the witness table and the nation watching by television, the committee voted quickly and unanimously to sue the President—something no Congressional committee has ever done in the history of the Republic.

"I think this litigation is essential if we are to determine whether the President is above the law," said Senator Ervin gravely, "and whether the President is immune from all of the duties and responsibilities in matters of this kind which devolve upon all the other mortals who dwell in this land."

OCTOBER 7, 1973
ARABS AND ISRAELIS BATTLE ON TWO FRONTS; EGYPTIANS BRIDGE SUEZ; AIR DUELS INTENSE
SYRIANS IN CLASH
Fighting Along Canal and Golan Heights Goes On All Night
By ROBERT D. McFADDEN

The heaviest fighting in the Middle East since the 1967 war erupted yesterday on Israel's front lines with Egypt along the Suez Canal and Syria in the Golan heights.

Official announcements by Israel and Egypt agreed that Egyptians forces had crossed the Suez Canal and established footholds in the Israeli-occupied Sinai Peninsula.

A military communiqué issued in Cairo asserted that Egyptian forces had captured most of the eastern bank of the 100-mile canal. An Israeli military communiqué said the Egyptians had attempted to cross the canal at several points by helicopters and small boats and had succeeded in laying down pontoon bridges at two points. Armored forces were pouring across them into Sinai, it said.

Fighting All Night

A communiqué issued early today in Tel Aviv said fighting had raged all night along the canal's eastern bank and along the entire cease-fire line with Syria

Each side accused the other of having started the fighting. But military observers posted by the United Nations reported crossings by Egyptian forces at five points along the Suez, and said Syrians had attacked in the Golan heights at two points.

OCTOBER 22, 1973
4 MORE ARAB GOVERNMENTS BAR OIL SUPPLIES FOR U.S.

By RICHARD EDER

Special to The New York Times

BEIRUT, Lebanon, Oct. 21—Four Persian Gulf oil producers—Kuwait, Qatar, Bahrain and Dubai—today announced a total embargo of oil to the United States.

The announcements made the cutoff of Arab oil to the United States theoretically complete. Of the 17 million barrels of crude and heating oil and refinery products used by the United States each day, approximately 6 per cent has been imported from the Arab states.

At the same time, the Netherlands, which has been accused by the Arabs of being pro-Israel, was the object of reprisals today. Iraq announced the nationalization of

Dutch oil holdings in the country. Previously Iraq had nationalized American holdings.

Not even the Arab producers themselves believe that the use of the oil weapon against the United States will have much immediate effect, although if maintained for a long period it could present serious problems. There is, for example, no simple way to prevent oil sold to European countries from finding its way to the United States.

Today's moves completed a second phase of Arab governments' decision to use oil to put pressure on the United States to abandon or reduce its support of Israel.

• •

AGNEW'S DOWNFALL

President Nixon's struggle with the Watergate break-in was only one of several major scandals roiling his administration. In early August the attorney general opened investigations of Vice President Spiro Agnew's involvement in a corruption scheme involving extortion, bribery, and tax evasion. The scandal soon forced Agnew to resign, further damaging the Nixon camp. Seeking to restore his standing, Nixon quickly nominated Gerald Ford, the moderate, soft-spoken Republican House minority leader, to succeed to the vice presidency.

AUGUST 7, 1973

AGNEW IS UNDER U.S. INVESTIGATION IN 'POSSIBLE' CRIMINAL VIOLATIONS; INNOCENT OF WRONGDOING, HE SAYS

CASE IN BALTIMORE

It Is Reportedly Linked to an Alleged Scheme Involving Kickbacks

By R.W. APPLE Jr.

Special to The New York Times

WASHINGTON, Tuesday Aug. 7—Vice President Agnew announced last night that he had been informed that he was under investigation for possible violations of criminal law.

In a terse, late-night statement issued through his press secretary, Marsh Thomson, the Vice President declared:

"I have been informed that I am under investigation for possible violations of the criminal statutes. I will make no further comment until the investigation has been completed, other than to say that I am innocent of any wrongdoing, that I have confidence in the criminal justice system of the United State and that I am equally confident my innocence will be affirmed."

A spokesperson for Mr. Agnew later confirmed that the investigation was being conducted by the United States Attorney in Baltimore, George Beall, the younger brother of Senator J. Glenn Beall Jr., a Republican.

OCTOBER 11, 1973

AGNEW QUITS VICE PRESIDENCY AND ADMITS TAX EVASION IN '67; NIXON CONSULTS ON SUCCESSOR

Agnew Plea Ends 65 Days of Insisting on Innocence

By BEN A. FRANKLIN

Special to The New York Times

BALTIMORE, Oct. 10—Vice President Agnew ended today 65 days of defiant insistence that he was innocent of any wrongdoing by pleading no contest to a charge of cheating the Government of $13,551.47 on his Federal income tax payment for 1967, his first year as Governor of Maryland. Then he resigned his Federal office.

At a dramatic, surprise appearance here before the United States District Court Judge Walter E. Hoffman after two days of secret negotiations, Mr. Agnew was confronted in open court by Attorney General Elliot L. Richardson.

The Attorney General said in a prepared statement that the Government's evidence against the former Vice President went far beyond the six-year-old tax violation. But he said that "critical national interests"—the avoidance of the "serious and permanent scars" upon the nation that would have been inflicted in months or years of a criminal prosecution of a sitting Vice President together with the new and allied dispute over newsmen's sources—justified the agreement with Mr. Agnew. Judge Hoffman then approved the agreement.

Under it, Mr. Agnew in a 40-minute court appearance waived all his rights as a defendant—the right to be indicted and to an arraignment—and was sentenced on the spot to pay a $10,000 fine and to three years of probation. He was admonished by Judge Hoffman to violate no state or Federal laws on pain of having his avoidance of a prison term reconsidered.

A long list of other charges, involving perhaps $100,000 in payoffs by Maryland contractors favored by Mr. Agnew in the award of state contracts, was dropped.

But the charges, and the evidence to support them, were made public later by United States Attorney George Beall. The Justice Department, Mr. Richardson made clear in court, had insisted on that in bargaining with Mr. Agnew.

OCTOBER 13, 1973
GERALD FORD NAMED BY NIXON AS THE SUCCESSOR TO AGNEW
CHOICE IS PRAISED BY BOTH PARTIES

Widespread Enthusiasm Is Expressed in Congress—Fast Confirmation Seen

By RICHARD L. MADDEN

Special to The New York Times

WASHINGTON, Oct.12—Congressional Democrats and Republicans received President Nixon's choice of Gerald R. Ford to be Vice President with widespread enthusiasm tonight.

The reaction indicated that the nomination of Mr. Ford of Michigan, who has been the House Republican leader since 1965, would be confirmed relatively quickly by both houses, barring some unforeseen development.

However, it was expected that the Senate would take more time than the House in considering the nomination.

"My own feeling is Gerry will probably be confirmed," said Speaker Carl Albert of Oklahoma, he added:

"I think I was the first in Congress to tell the President that Gerry would be the easiest candidate to sell to the House. He's a very fine man to work with. I think he earned this."

. . . .

THE SATURDAY NIGHT MASSACRE

The courts entered the Watergate fray, ruling that Nixon must turn over the tapes of White House conversations to investigators. When the president refused to do so, the lead investigator, Archibald Cox, prepared to return to court to force him to comply. Nixon responded by ordering Cox's dismissal. Attorney General Elliot Richardson refused to obey the order and instead resigned his position. Nixon then either dismissed or forced the resignation of several other top officials until he found a member of the Justice Department, Robert Bork, willing to carry out his order to fire Cox. Public reaction erupted in opposition to the president's drastic actions, weakening his tenuous grip on power and raising the prospect of his removal from office.

OCTOBER 21, 1973
NIXON DISCHARGES COX FOR DEFIANCE; ABOLISHES WATERGATE TASK FORCE; RICHARDSON AND RUCKELSHAUS OUT
OUTCRY IN HOUSE

Impeaching Nixon Is Openly Discussed by Leadership

By RICHARD L. MADDEN

Special to The New York Times

WASHINGTON, Oct. 20—For the first time tonight, members of the Democratic and Republican leadership of the House of Representatives began talking publicly and seriously about impeaching President Nixon.

Within minutes after the White House announced a drastic shake-up of the Justice Department, House leaders acknowledged that resolutions calling for impeachment would be pouring into the House when Congress reconvened after the Veteran's Day holiday.

Representative John J. McFall of California, the Democratic whip, said that the House "must now go ahead and seriously consider beginning impeachment."

Representative John B. Anderson of Illinois, the Chairman of the House Republican Conference, said that it was "very difficult" to forecast the outcome, but predicted that "obviously, impeachment resolutions are going to be raining down like hailstones."

OCTOBER 21, 1973
BORK TAKES OVER

Duties of Prosecutor Are Shifted Back to Justice Dept.

By DOUGLAS E. KNEELAND

Special to The New York Times

WASHINGTON, Oct. 20—President Nixon, reacting angrily tonight to refusals to obey his orders, dismissed the special Watergate prosecutor, Archibald Cox, abolished Mr. Cox's office, accepted the resignation of Elliot L. Richardson, the Attorney General, and discharged William D. Ruckelshaus, the Deputy Attorney General.

The President's dramatic action edged the nation closer to the constitutional confrontation he said he was trying to avoid.

Senior members of both parties in the House of Representatives were reported to be seriously discussing impeachment of the President because of his refusal to obey an order by the United States Court of Appeals that he turn over to the courts tape recordings of the conversations about the Watergate case, and because of Mr. Nixon's dismissal of Mr. Cox.

The President announced that he had abolished the Watergate prosecutor's office as of 8 o'clock tonight and that the duties of that office had been transferred back to the Department of Justice, where his spokesman said they would be "carried out with thoroughness and vigor."

Events Listed

These were the events that led to the confrontation between the President and Congress and the Government's top law enforcement officers:

Mr. Cox said in a televised news conference that he would return to Federal court in defiance of the President's orders to seek a decision that Mr. Nixon had violated a ruling that the tapes must be turned over to the courts.

Attorney General Richardson, after being told by the President that Mr. Cox must be dismissed, resigned.

Deputy Attorney General Ruckelshaus was ordered by Mr. Nixon to discharge Mr. Cox. Mr. Ruckelshaus refused and was dismissed immediately.

The President informed Robert H. Bork, the Solicitor General, that under the law he was the acting Attorney General and must get rid of Mr. Cox and the special Watergate force.

Mr. Bork discharged Mr. Cox and had the Federal Bureau of Investigation seal off the offices of the special prosecutor, which Mr. Cox had put in a building away from the Department of Justice to symbolize his independence. Some members of the Cox staff were still inside at the time.

The F.B.I. also sealed off the offices of Mr. Richardson and Mr. Ruckelshaus.

Mr. Richardson had no comment tonight, but he scheduled a news conference for Monday. Mr. Ruckelshaus said, "I'm going fishing tomorrow."

Mr. Cox's reaction was brief: "Whether we shall continue to be a government of laws and not of men is now for Congress and ultimately the American people [to decide]," he said.

OCTOBER 22, 1973
PUBLIC REACTS STRONGLY TO COX OUSTER

By MAURICE CARROLL

Half a block from the White House yesterday, James Goodnow stationed himself on the sidewalk in front of the Treasury Building along with two large cartons full of imitation straw hats bearing "Impeach Nixon" labels.

Only a few of the 72 hats were left after half an hour in which he distributed them to anyone donating to his "committee to Impeach the President," Mr. Goodnow said.

His was one of the more bizarre manifestations of an outpouring of public interest that followed the President's ouster of his Watergate prosecutor.

Politicians spoke out. So did some clergymen. There were protest rallies on some college campuses, including one by about 300 students at Columbia. The telephone switchboards buzzed busily at newspaper and television-station offices.

No White House Report

At the White House, the obvious focal point of attention for matters Presidential, the press office said there would be no immediate report on incoming messages of support for or disagreement with Mr. Nixon.

The Washington Western Union office, while declining to provide specific numbers, said that the volume of messages for the White House was "well above" the 300 received on a normal day.

• •

REINING IN THE PRESIDENT

As tensions between President Nixon and Congress rose, legislators fought back, using their established constitutional powers to constrain the president. To limit the president's ability to commit the nation to war without its approval, Congress passed the War Powers Resolution. Nixon promptly vetoed the resolution, leading to a dramatic override of his action by the House and Senate. Later, asserting its power of the purse, Congress passed the Budget and Impoundment Control Act of 1974, limiting the president's ability to unilaterally withhold spending money appropriated by the legislative branch.

NOVEMBER 5, 1973
EDITORIAL
CONSTITUTIONAL TEST

Another test of the nation's ability to reverse the trend toward executive usurpation of constitutional rights and procedures is scheduled for Wednesday, when the House is expected to vote on the question of overriding a Presidential veto of the war powers bill.

In vetoing the war powers legislation that had received overwhelming support in both houses, Mr. Nixon called the bill "both unconstitutional and dangerous," adding that it posed "a serious challenge to the wisdom of the Founding Fathers." On the contrary, it is the President who has challenged the essential role the Founding Fathers assigned to Congress in war-making decisions.

It is the Nixon doctrine of unlimited Presidential authority to initiate military actions overseas that poses the real threat to American institutions. In a nuclear age it is more important than ever that no man should be granted sole responsibility for steps which, as Secretary Kissinger emphasized during the Middle East crisis, could lead to "unparalleled catastrophe."

The war powers bill represents a careful, conscientious effort by members of both parties in both houses of Congress, after three years of study and debate, to restore the constitutional system of checks and balances to the war-making process. The bill does not limit the President's valid prerogatives—indeed, it may grant him greater freedom than the Founding Fathers intended to act in emergencies they could not have foreseen.

Nevertheless, by requiring the President to report promptly to Congress on any emergency action and by mandating affirmative Congressional approval for any commitment of forces beyond sixty days, the bill preserves the evident intent of the Constitution. It reasserts an essential restraint on Presidential authority that has been dangerously dissipated.

A House vote to override the Nixon veto would provide a welcome sign that the Congress, like the Sirica court, is determined to preserve its independence and authority. It would help to restore the country's shaken faith in the integrity of the constitutional processes.

NOVEMBER 8, 1973
HOUSE AND SENATE OVERRIDE VETO BY NIXON ON CURB OF WAR POWERS; BACKERS OF BILL WIN 3-YEAR FIGHT

TROOP USE LIMITED

Vote Asserts Control of Congress Over Combat Abroad

By RICHARD L. MADDEN

Special to The New York Times

WASHINGTON, Nov. 7—The House and the Senate, dealing President Nixon what appeared to be the worst legislative setback of his five years in office, today overrode his veto of a measure aimed at limiting Presidential power to commit the armed forces to hostilities abroad without Congressional approval.

The House voted first—284 to 135, or only four votes more than the required two-thirds of those present and voting—to override the veto. The Senate followed suit nearly four hours later by a vote of 75 to 18, or 13 more than the required two-thirds.

It was the first time in nine attempts this year that both houses had overridden a veto and the first time legislation has become law over the President's veto since Congress overrode a Nixon veto of a water-pollution-control measure in October, 1972.

First Such Action

Supporters of the measure, who had waged a three-year effort to enact it into law, said it was the first time in history that Congress had spelled out the war-making powers of Congress and the President.

The White House said in a statement that Mr. Nixon felt the Congressional action today "seriously undermines this nation's ability to act decisively and convincingly in times of international crisis." It declined, however, to say what the President planned to do as a result of the overriding of his veto.

With the veto overridden, the war-powers measure—couched in the form of a joint resolution, which in Congress has the same status as a bill—immediately became a law. It contains the following provisions:

The President would be required to report to Congress in writing within 48 hours after the commitment of armed forces to combat abroad.

The combat action would have to end in 60 days unless Congress authorized the commitment, but this deadline could be extended for 30 days if the President certified it was necessary for safe withdrawal of the forces.

Within that 60-day or 90-day period Congress could order an immediate removal of the forces by adopting a concurrent resolution, which is not subject to a Presidential veto.

The Nixon Administration had previously been stung by the legislative branch through such actions as the Senate's rejection of two nominees for the Supreme Court, Clement F. Haynsworth Jr. and G. Harrold Carswell, and the Congressional decision to end the program to develop a United States supersonic transport.

But the votes today were regarded as a rebuke of potentially greater significance because they dealt directly with the President's interpretation of his Constitutional authority.

Beyond reflecting the low political estate to which President Nixon has fallen, the Congressional action represented the most aggressive assertion of independence and power by the legislative branch against the executive branch in many years.

JULY 28, 1974
PRESIDENT IS MORE YIELDING IN CLASHES WITH CONGRESS

By JOHN HERBERS

WASHINGTON, July 28—While the impeachment drive against President Nixon has been attracting widespread attention, a related development has gone virtually unnoticed: That Mr. Nixon has made important concessions of authority to the Congress that must decide whether he remains in office.

This trend has been under way for several months, but there have been recent actions such as the following that go to the heart of the struggle for power between the legislative and executive branches.

A few days ago, Mr. Nixon quietly reversed himself and agreed to permit Kenneth Rush, his counselor for economic policy, to testify before Congressional committees. He had been strongly opposed to such a step, high Administration sources said, because he had felt that he must preserve the long-asserted Presidential prerogative that White House aides are not subject to the same Congressional scrutiny as are Cabinet officers and others whose appointments are confirmed by the Senate.

The effort that Mr. Nixon undertook early in 1973 to impound at will funds appropriated by Congress and to end by Executive order some programs established by Congress has now been abandoned. The President also signed legislation providing for Congressional review of impoundments that may be necessary for the economy or other reasons.

Congressional authorities have noted that the Administration is more cooperative in providing Congress with information and access to officials of the executive branch than it was.

And the President himself in the last two to three months has consulted Congressional leaders of both parties more often on the wider range of issues than was his practice. Over the last few weeks, when the President was in Washington, there was a steady stream of Senators and Representatives into the White House, and he frequently entertained members of Congress aboard the Presidential yacht Sequoia.

A little more than a year ago, Mr. Nixon was challenging Congress for power on a broad front. In addition to impoundment and restrictions on Congressional access to information and aides, he was attempting to reshape areas of the Government without Congressional authority and to effect important foreign and domestic policies without Congressional participation. Congressional leaders were fighting back.

Now, according to a number of authorities, the balance of power is close to where it was under the previous Presidents and there are no indications of further new challenges from the White House.

· ·

TWO BRANCHES AGAINST THE PRESIDENT

Public opinion turned sharply against President Nixon and his administration following the "Saturday Night Massacre," but he held firm in his defiance. When the Supreme Court ordered the White House tapes released, Nixon finally acquiesced to the revelation of his personal involvement in the Watergate scandal. On Capitol Hill, a long investigation in the House of Representatives, highlighted by public hearings, led to three counts of impeachment against the beleaguered president, making him the second president to that point in American history to face removal from office. The combined resistance of the judicial and legislative branches doomed the overreaching president.

JULY 25, 1974
NIXON MUST SURRENDER TAPES, SUPREME COURT RULES, 8 TO 0; HE PLEDGES FULL COMPLIANCE

House Committee Begins Debate on Impeachment

OPINIONS BY BURGER

Name of President Is Left in Indictment as Co-Conspirator

By WARREN WEAVER, Jr.

Special to The New York Times

WASHINGTON, July 24—The Supreme Court ruled today, 8 to 0, that President Nixon must provide potential evidence for the criminal trial of his former-subordinates, rejected flatly the President's contention that he had absolute authority to withhold such material.

Eight hours later in California, the President announced through his attorney that he would accept the high court ruling and comply fully. Until today, White House spokesmen had strongly indicated that Mr. Nixon might choose to defy the Justices.

64 Conversations Cited

As a result of the historic Court decision, announced by Chief Justice Warren E. Burger in a tense, packed chamber, the President will surrender tape recordings and other data involving 64 White House conversations for use in the Watergate cover-up trial, and possibly in impeachment proceedings as well.

In a broader perspective, the Supreme Court reaffirmed with today's ruling its position, carved out in the early days of the republic, that the judicial branch decides what the law is and the executive branch is bound by that determination.

Not since its refusal in 1952 to permit President Truman to seize the nation's steel mills, had the Supreme Court dealt so serious a blow to a President who read broader powers into his constitutional mandate than the Court was willing to recognize.

JULY 25, 1974
2 CHARGES LISTED

Obstruction of Justice and Other Abuses of Power Alleged

By JAMES M. NAUGHTON

Special to The New York Times

WASHINGTON, July 24—The House Judiciary Committee began historic final deliberations tonight on the possible impeachment of President Nixon without waiting to determine whether new evidence might emerge as a result of a Supreme Court judgment earlier today.

Barely eight hours after a unanimous Court ruled that the President must obey subpoenas for Watergate trial evidence and shortly after the White House announced that Mr. Nixon would do so, the Judiciary Committee began debating whether to recommend a Senate trial of the President himself for alleged misconduct in office.

2 Republicans Ask Delay

The committee's two senior Republicans—Representative Edward Hutchinson of Michigan and Representative Robert McClory of Illinois—urged a delay in the deliberations so that the committee could receive new evidence from the additional tapes.

But Democratic committee leaders pressed ahead, on national television, with the second Presidential impeachment in history, one in which two articles charging obstruction of justice and other alleged abuses of Presidential authority were presented.

> " The House Judiciary Committee voted tonight, 27 to 11, to recommend the impeachment of President Nixon on a charge that he personally engaged in a 'course of conduct' designed to obstruct justice in the Watergate case. "

JULY 28, 1974
HOUSE PANEL, 27–11, ASKS IMPEACHMENT OF NIXON FOR OBSTRUCTION OF JUSTICE
A HISTORIC CHARGE

6 Republicans Join 21 Democrats in Vote for Resolution

By JAMES M. NAUGHTON

Special to The New York Times

WASHINGTON, July 27—The House Judiciary Committee voted tonight, 27 to 11, to recommend the impeachment of President Nixon on a charge that he personally engaged in a "course of conduct" designed to obstruct justice in the Watergate case.

This historic charge, the first to be lodged against a President by a House investigating body since 1868, set in motion the constitutional process by which Mr. Nixon could ultimately be stripped of his office.

The charge became official when, at 5 minutes and 21 seconds after 7 o'clock tonight, Peter W. Rodino Jr., the committee's Democratic chairman, his head bobbing gently, said "Aye," and ended the committee's decisive roll-call. He then adjourned the deliberations until 10:30 A.M. Monday.

The margin of the vote, with six of the committee's Republicans joining all 21 Democrats in adoption of the resolution, seemed certain to set a pattern for debate in the full House next month on the charge.

NIXON RESIGNS

Richard Nixon became the first president to resign his office, turning the position over to his appointed vice president, Gerald Ford. Riddled by scandal and a loss of public trust, Nixon squandered one of the greatest electoral victories in presidential history. The failure of his administration damaged the Republican Party in subsequent elections and shrank trust in government for decades. Attempting to avoid further public drama over the issue, President Ford pardoned Nixon, freeing the nation from the Watergate saga, but fatally damaging his own chances of election in 1976.

Richard Nixon bids farewell to his cabinet, aides, and staff as he resigns the presidency on August 9, 1974. Nixon hoped the country could begin "a process of healing" with his departure.

Source: National Archives and Records Administration

AUGUST 9, 1974
NIXON RESIGNS

HE URGES A TIME OF 'HEALING'; FORD WILL TAKE OFFICE TODAY

The 37th President Is First to Quit Post

By JOHN HERBERS

Special to The New York Times

WASHINGTON, Aug. 8—Richard Milhous Nixon, the 37th President of the United States, announced tonight that he had given up his long and arduous fight to remain in office and would resign, effective at noon tomorrow.

At that hour, Gerald Rudolph Ford, whom Mr. Nixon nominated for Vice President last Oct. 12, will be sworn in as the 38th President, to serve out the 895 days remaining in Mr. Nixon's second term.

Less than two years after his landslide re-election victory, Mr. Nixon, in a conciliatory address on national television, said that he was leaving not with a sense of bitterness but with a hope that his departure would start a "process of healing that is so desperately needed in America."

He spoke of regret for any "injuries" done "in the course of the events that led to this decision." He acknowledged that some of his judgments had been wrong.

The 61-year-old Mr. Nixon, appearing calm and resigned to his fate as a victim of the Watergate scandal, become the first President in the history of the Republic to resign from office. Only 10 months earlier Spiro Agnew resigned the Vice-Presidency.

Speaks of Pain at Yielding Post

Mr. Nixon, speaking from the Oval Office, where his successor will be sworn in tomorrow, may well have delivered his most effective speech since the Watergate scandals began to swamp his Administration in early 1973.

In tone and content, the 15-minute address was in sharp contrast to his frequently combative language of the past, especially his first "farewell" appearance—that of 1962, when he announced he was retiring from politics after losing the California governorship race and declared that the news media would not have "Nixon to kick around" anymore.

Yet he spoke tonight of how painful it was for him to give up the office.

"I would have preferred to carry through to the finish whatever the personal agony it would have involved, and my family unanimously urged me to do so," he said.

AUGUST 9, 1974
EDITORIAL
THE NIXON RESIGNATION

The resignation of Richard M. Nixon, 37th President of the United States and the first to leave office under threat of impeachment, comes as a tragic climax to the sordid history of misuse of the Presidential office that has been unfolding before the eyes of a shocked American public for the last two years.

Twice elevated to the nation's Chief Magistracy by electoral majorities that viewed him as an exemplar of stern rectitude in public life, Mr. Nixon announced last night his intention to resign following the production of incontrovertible evidence that he has indeed been criminally guilty of obstruction of justice and abuse of the powers of his great office. Although the only reason he offered was erosion of his "political base" in Congress, he decided to step down from the Presidency only when it had become unmistakably clear within the last few days that the new and additional evidence he himself made public had insured an overwhelming vote of impeachment in the House of Representatives and his almost certain conviction by the Senate. His resignation at this point was to forestall and frustrate the constitutional procedure which had begun earlier this year and was steadily moving forward to its inexorable end.

The forced departure of Richard M. Nixon from the Presidency—for that is what it was even though his resignation is nominally an act of his own volition—is in a larger sense a reaffirmation of the strength of the United States and of the structure of American democracy.

For the events that have been exposed under the generic name of "Watergate," including the disgrace of former Vice President Spiro T. Agnew and culminating in Mr. Nixon's resignation, represented a profound subversion of American democratic institutions, an attempt to seize and consolidate control—not by arms but by a far more effective and penetrating method of subtle accretion of political power in the Executive Office. This is really what was going on at the pinnacle of government, in the White House itself; and this, along with all his other violations of law, is what Richard M. Nixon resolutely refused to acknowledge—or even refer to—in his muted appeal to the American people over the airwaves last night. We who have been among his most persistent critics take no joy in his personal disaster; but all Americans who maintain their belief in a government of laws rather than of men must be thankful that it has survived this extraordinary trauma with resolution and with honor.

SEPTEMBER 9, 1974
FORD GIVES PARDON TO NIXON, WHO REGRETS 'MY MISTAKES'
NO CONDITIONS SET
Action Taken to Spare Nation and Ex-Chief, President Asserts
By JOHN HERBERS
Special to The New York Times

WASHINGTON, Sept. 8—President Ford granted former President Richard M. Nixon an unconditional pardon today for all Federal crimes that he "committed or may have committed or taken part in" while in office, an act Mr. Ford said was intended to spare Mr. Nixon and the nation further punishment in the Watergate scandals.

Mr. Nixon, in San Clemente, Calif., accepted the pardon, which exempts him from indictment and trial for, among other things, his role in the cover-up of the Watergate burglary. He issued a statement saying that he could now see he was "wrong in not acting more decisively and more forthrightly in dealing with Watergate."

'Act of Mercy'

Phillip W. Buchen, the White House counsel, who advised Mr. Ford on the legal aspects of the pardon, said the "act of mercy" on the President's part was done without making any demands on Mr. Nixon and without asking the advice of the Watergate special prosecutor, Leon Jaworski, who had the legal responsibility to prosecute the case.

Dangers Seen in Delay

Mr. Buchen said that, at the President's request, he had asked Mr. Jaworski how long it would be, in the event Mr. Nixon was indicted, before he could be brought to trial and that Mr. Jaworski had replied it would be at least nine months or more, because of the enormous amount of publicity the charges against Mr. Nixon had received when the House Judiciary Committee recommended impeachment.

This was one reason Mr. Ford cited for granting the pardon, saying he had concluded that "many months and perhaps more years will have to pass before Richard Nixon could obtain a fair trial by jury in any jurisdiction of the United States under governing decisions of the Supreme Court."

"During this long period of delay and potential litigation, ugly passions would again be aroused, our people would again be polarized in their opinions, and the credibility of our free institutions of government would again be challenged at home and abroad," Mr. Ford said in a 10-minute statement that he read this morning in the Oval Office upon signing the pardon.

. . . .

WATERGATE'S LEGACY

Just three months after Richard Nixon's resignation, voters returned to the polls to elect a new Congress with Watergate still on their minds, along with parlous economic conditions. Across the nation, Republicans suffered for Nixon's failures as the Democratic Party made massive gains in Congress. Two years later, voters removed Gerald Ford from office as well, a consequence of his pardon of Nixon. The conservative revolution Nixon seemed to inaugurate in 1968 was derailed, leaving the movement in need of a new champion.

NOVEMBER 6, 1974
CAREY WINS, 16-YEAR G.O.P. RULE ENDS; DEMOCRATS PILE UP CONGRESS GAINS; MRS. GRASSO VICTOR; JAVITS RENAMED
Senate and House Margins Are Substantially Enlarged
By JAMES M. NAUGHTON

Democrats swept yesterday toward domination of the next Congress as voters across the nation apparently blamed Republicans for the Watergate scandal and for economic disruption.

With 34 Senate seats and all 435 House districts at stake, the Democrats were substantially enlarging the majorities by which they already control the Congress.

Three Democrats captured Senate seats now held by Republicans in Florida, Colorado and Kentucky. A Democrat appeared to be on the verge of election to the Senate from Vermont for the first time in more than a century. And Democrats were in close, indefinite contests for Republican-held Senate seats in North Dakota, Utah and New Hampshire.

In the House, the Democrats picked up at least 22 Republican seats in states as disparate as Massachusetts, New Jersey, North Carolina, Texas, Virginia, Indiana and Colorado. Republicans were considered potential losers in as many as 25 more House districts they now control.

This would give the Democrats a two-thirds majority in the House, enough to override Presidential vetoes.

The outcome was a stinging rebuke to the Republican party, its worst showing in a Congressional election in a decade.

> Voters in every region, ethnic group and economic classification switched in about the same proportion to Democratic candidates for the House of Representatives in yesterday's election, according to analyses of the vote and major political polls.

NOVEMBER 7, 1974
WIDE VOTER SHIFT FROM G.O.P. SHOWN
Survey Indicates About 8% in All Regions Switched to Democratic Candidates
By DAVID E. ROSENBAUM

Voters in every region, ethnic group and economic classification switched in about the same proportion to Democratic candidates for the House of Representatives in yesterday's election, according to analyses of the vote and major political polls.

One survey showed that about 8 per cent of the voters in the North, South, East, and West, of those in high-, middle-,

and low-income brackets, of Jews, Protestants and Roman Catholics and of professionals and laborers who voted for Republican Congressional candidates two years ago voted Democratic yesterday.

If, as this survey projected, it turns out that 60 per cent of the total vote for House candidates went to the Democrats, it would be a record for one party in this century.

A number of other conclusions can be drawn from the NBC poll, a comparison of the views of members of the 93d and 94th Congresses by CBS News and an inspection of the returns in various states. Among the conclusions are the following:

While voters across the country are deeply concerned about the state of the economy, the Watergate scandal appeared to be a greater factor than the economy in the switch of votes from Republican to Democratic candidates.

Because House races are the nearest thing to a national referendum in a non-Presidential election year, political experts drew some significance from the 8 per cent shift in Democratic candidates.

But the experts cautioned that yesterday's vote appeared to be a negative one—against Republicans rather than for Democrats.

"People would be making a mistake if they saw this Democratic landslide as meaning anything for 1976," said I. A. Lewis, director of the N.B.C. poll.

NOVEMBER 3, 1976
CARTER VICTOR IN TIGHT RACE; FORD LOSES NEW YORK STATE; DEMOCRATS RETAIN CONGRESS
GEORGIAN WINS SOUTH

Northern Industrial States Provide Rest of Margin in the Electoral Vote

By R.W. APPLE Jr.

Jimmy Carter won the nation's Bicentennial Presidential election yesterday, narrowly defeating President Ford by sweeping his native South and adding enough Northern industrial states to give him a bare electoral majority.

Three of the closely contested battleground states slipped into Mr. Carter's column shortly after midnight—New York, Pennsylvania and Texas. The President-designate lost New Jersey and Michigan, Mr. Ford's home state, while Ohio, Illinois and California were still up for grabs.

New York teetered between the rivals for hours, contrary to all expectations, before delivering a small majority to Mr. Carter—a majority that gave the Democrat a bonanza of 41 electoral votes.

When Mr. Carter finally carried Hawaii by a far narrower margin than customary for Democratic candidates in that Democratic stronghold, it gave the Georgian 272 electoral votes in 23 states, two more than a majority. Mr. Ford had 160 electoral votes in 23 states, and five states were still in doubt.

A Southern Victor

Mr. Carter was the first man from the Deep South to be elected President in a century and a quarter, and Mr. Ford, the nation's first appointive President, was the first incumbent to lose a Presidential election since Herbert Hoover.

THE PRESIDENTIAL ELECTION OF 1980

REAGAN, IN A LANDSLIDE, SETS A CONSERVATIVE REPUBLICAN DIRECTION

The nation was in a sour mood as it prepared for the presidential election of 1980. Four successive presidents had left the White House in distress: John Kennedy dying by assassination, Lyndon Johnson withdrawing in the face of enraged political opposition, Richard Nixon resigning in disgrace, and Gerald Ford suffering electoral defeat. The ebullient prosperity of the 1960s had been followed by the stagflation and decreasing incomes of the 1970s. Three-fourths of the nation thought the country was "on the wrong track." Angry at these conditions, disappointed in the presidential candidates, and frustrated by events abroad, Americans prepared for a negative election in a darkening world.

The political effect was a turn toward more conservative candidates—incumbent Democratic president Jimmy Carter and Republican Ronald Reagan—more conservative values, and a clear conservative victory for Reagan, which reshaped the nation's electoral alignments and policy agenda.

Carter had narrowly won the 1976 election, held in the wake of Nixon's near impeachment, by gaining slim margins in the popular vote (50.1 percent) and the Electoral College count (297–240). Troubles soon mounted. Contrary to theoretical expectations, the economy suffered from the twin ills of high inflation and growing unemployment, which combined for a "misery index" of nearly 20 percent, with Americans' woes further worsened by interest rates upwards of 16 percent.

The bad economic news was both caused by and worsened by setbacks in world events, centering on the Middle East. In his first two years as president, Carter had a spectacular success in the region, personally brokering negotiations that led to peace between Israel and Egypt. But that accomplishment had less impact on U.S. politics than another transformation of the region, a revolution in Iran led by militant Muslim clerics, who soon severely cut production in the country's huge oil industry. Consequent shortages not only raised the world price of oil 150 percent, but also forced

Source: The Granger Collection, New York

In his official campaign poster for the presidential election of 1980, Ronald Reagan set a new course for American politics.

Americans to wait hours at gas stations, costing them time, money, and their political patience.

Reacting to the oil price increase, President Carter retreated for ten days of isolated talks, asked for the resignation of the entire cabinet, and actually replaced five members. In a major televised address, he then asked Americans to join in an energy conservation effort to resolve their "crisis of confidence." In fact, Americans did begin to conserve energy, but Carter was personally derided as responsible for a quite different problem, a "crisis of competence."

1980 ELECTORAL VOTE

STATE	ELECTORAL VOTES	REAGAN	CARTER	STATE	ELECTORAL VOTES	REAGAN	CARTER
Alabama	(9)	9	–	Montana	(4)	4	–
Alaska	(3)	3	–	Nebraska	(5)	5	–
Arizona	(6)	6	–	Nevada	(3)	3	–
Arkansas	(6)	6	–	New Hampshire	(4)	4	–
California	(45)	45	–	New Jersey	(17)	17	–
Colorado	(7)	7	–	New Mexico	(4)	4	–
Connecticut	(8)	8	–	New York	(41)	41	–
Delaware	(3)	3	–	North Carolina	(13)	13	–
District of Columbia	(3)	–	3	North Dakota	(3)	3	–
Florida	(17)	17	–	Ohio	(25)	25	–
Georgia	(12)	–	12	Oklahoma	(8)	8	–
Hawaii	(4)	–	4	Oregon	(6)	6	–
Idaho	(4)	4	–	Pennsylvania	(27)	27	–
Illinois	(26)	26	–	Rhode Island	(4)	–	4
Indiana	(13)	13	–	South Carolina	(8)	8	–
Iowa	(8)	8	–	South Dakota	(4)	4	–
Kansas	(7)	7	–	Tennessee	(10)	10	–
Kentucky	(9)	9	–	Texas	(26)	26	–
Louisiana	(10)	10	–	Utah	(4)	4	–
Maine	(4)	4	–	Vermont	(3)	3	–
Maryland	(10)	–	10	Virginia	(12)	12	–
Massachusetts	(14)	14	–	Washington	(9)	9	–
Michigan	(21)	21	–	West Virginia	(6)	–	6
Minnesota	(10)	–	10	Wisconsin	(11)	11	–
Mississippi	(7)	7	–	Wyoming	(3)	3	–
Missouri	(12)	12	–				
				TOTALS	**(538)**	**489**	**49**

The president's burden became still heavier early in the election year, when the Soviet Union invaded Afghanistan, further destabilizing and further eroding American influence in the region. Carter reacted by imposing economic sanctions on the Soviet Union and by canceling U.S. participation in the summer Olympic Games in Moscow. But Carter's indignant reaction had little effect on the invaders, while it disappointed the athletes and deprived others of entertainment and the psychological satisfaction of possible American athletic successes.

Adding insult to these injuries, Iranian militants stormed the U.S. embassy in Tehran, occupied the building, and made hostages of sixty American diplomatic personnel on November 4, 1979—exactly one year before the next U.S. presidential election. Although eight hostages were soon released, the fate of the others became the emotional focus of the campaign. Efforts to end the American humiliation extended over 444 days of diplomatic negotiations, private cabals, economic sanctions, armed intervention, and the empathetic display of yellow ribbons across America. None succeeded during the campaign; the captives won release only in the first minutes after the inauguration of the new president.

Americans had lost prosperity, military dominance, the freedom of the road, and the chance to see their athletes participate in the Olympics. The hostage crisis replaced their traditional optimism and capability with frustration and shame. Citizens seemed hopeless and helpless. But they still could wield one definitive power—their votes.

THE PARTIES AND THE CANDIDATES

The 1980 election was the first contest to show the full effect of changes in the nominating process. Democrats, after the traumas of the 1968 convention, had led the change in party rules, resulting in the unusual selections of George McGovern in 1972 and Carter in 1976. The effects were less evident in the more cautious Republican Party, where they were also slowed by the presence of incumbent presidents in the two previous nomination decisions.

In 1980 the system was fully in place, creating a new structure in both parties. Nominations would no longer depend on bargaining among formal party leaders or be decided at the party nominating conventions. Instead, they would be determined by direct presidential primaries. Scarcely a dozen years earlier, primaries had been held in only seventeen states, selecting about a third of the delegates—and neither presidential candidate owed his victory to the contests. By 1980 the primaries had spread to thirty-seven states and territories, choosing three-fourths of the delegates—and both candidates depended on them for their nominations.

All primaries, however, were not equal. Those held early in the campaign schedule had disproportionate influence, creating "momentum" for the first winners. Unlike delegates at the traditional conventions, primary voters had only one chance to consider their choices and no opportunity for extended deliberation. Often, voters would find that these choices were quite limited, because alternative candidates had already left—or had never entered—the race for lack of money or lack of votes in the first trials. The strange result was that both parties fielded candidates who were neither the consistent preference of their own partisans nor nationally popular. Yet, one would inevitably be the next president.

As the opposition party, the Republicans drew the most candidates. The leading contender was Ronald Reagan. A former governor of California, Reagan had been campaigning for the Republican nomination for a dozen years, and had left his state office after two terms to devote himself to a full-time effort. By his constant campaigning, he became the favorite of the party activists and the leader in most polls of Republican voters, but he sometimes trailed former president Ford, who refrained from an active campaign.

The avowed Republican aspirants included one liberal, Rep. John Anderson of Illinois; two moderates, Senate party leader Howard Baker and former congressman and national party chairman George H. W. Bush; and three conservatives. By dividing the opposition, the large field worked to Reagan's advantage.

But in the first test of these candidates, Bush surprisingly won the Iowa caucuses and declared that he now had "the big Mo"—momentum—on his side. Bush's advantage was short-lived. In New Hampshire, Reagan won attention by inviting all of the candidates to join a televised debate scheduled as only a two-man event. When Bush blocked the others' participation, Reagan appeared intrepid and generous—while borrowing a line from a Spencer Tracy movie—declaring, "I am paying for this microphone."

The Californian went on to win the primary, gaining half of the state vote. During the next ten days, four of the candidates dropped out, even though only 6 percent of the Republican electorate had voted. Anderson continued for three weeks, but withdrew after defeat in his home state; he then launched an independent candidacy. Ford hinted that he was open to a draft, and polls showed him besting Reagan by 2–1 among Republicans. But Ford lacked the money, the organization, and the time to enter primaries. His support, however broad, had become irrelevant in the new nominating structure.

Reagan rolled through most of the remaining primaries, winning overwhelmingly in the South and West, where delegates were generally distributed on a "winner-take-all" basis (including in Bush's adopted state of Texas). Bush's challenge was soon reduced to a few outposts of moderate Republicanism in eastern states and Michigan, but those states' rules for allocating delegates still gave Reagan a substantial share. Within two months of the opening of the contest, Reagan had sealed his nomination.

When Republicans convened in Detroit in mid-July, Reagan had already won three-fourths of the delegates; and when the roll was called, he received all but 55 of 1,994 total votes. The only question facing the convention was the vice-presidential selection. As delegates awaited Reagan's lead, media commentators circulated an odd rumor that Ford was seeking the running-mate slot and that he would function as "co-president" in a prospective Reagan administration. The plan was sufficiently serious to lead to direct meetings between Reagan and Ford but ultimately fell apart. To end the speculation, Reagan came to the convention after midnight to announce his selection of Bush, his former rival, for vice president.

The platform marked a clear turn toward conservative ideology in the Republican Party. It called for a 30 percent reduction in income tax rates and major cuts in federal programs to achieve a balanced budget. At the same time, the party proposed a large increase in military expenditures to achieve nuclear superiority over the Soviet Union. A new focus on social issues came in support of a constitutional amendment to bar abortion, a promise to appoint "pro-life" federal judges, and a reversal of the party's past support of an equal rights amendment to bar discrimination based on sex.

In his acceptance speech, Reagan articulated the new ideological direction. Emphasizing "a community of values embodied in these words: family, work, neighborhood, peace and freedom," he attacked the Carter administration's record of "a disintegrating economy, a weakened defense and an energy policy based on the sharing of scarcity." Vowing, "I will not stand by and watch this great country destroy itself under mediocre leadership," Reagan ended with a personal prayer to the most important leader, "Divine Providence," who "placed this land, this island of freedom, here as a refuge for all those people in the world who yearn to breathe freely."

The Democrats, with an incumbent president, might have expected a traditionally uncontroversial renomination. But Carter's failings brought unease and opposition. In late 1979 the president's popularity rating was below 30 percent, and he trailed Ford in trial heats for the next year's contest. His vulnerability brought an early but weak challenge from Jerry Brown, the Democratic governor of California.

Carter's significant opponent was Sen. Edward Kennedy of Massachusetts. The last surviving brother of the late president, Kennedy carried the mystique of the family heritage, the support of many groups in the traditional Democratic coalition disturbed by Carter's centrist policies, and a 2 to 1 lead in opinion polls of Democratic voters. But Kennedy also carried a great personal burden. In 1969 he had driven recklessly on Chappaquiddick Island in Massachusetts, resulting in the drowning death of a female companion. The incident raised questions about Kennedy's sexual morality and his reaction to crisis, which voters would need to weigh against his strong electoral appeal.

Events worked to Carter's benefit. The takeover of the American Embassy in Tehran came just as Kennedy was preparing his entrance to the nominating contest. As the nation's leader, Carter gained immense support in the crisis, doubling his popularity rating. This "rally 'round the flag" continued with the Soviet invasion of Afghanistan, but then began a consistent decline. The downward trend halted briefly in April, when the U.S. military attempted but failed to rescue the hostages, and then resumed its decline. By the time of the Democratic convention in mid-August, Carter's ratings were again at their nadir.

But the new rules of nomination made these trends irrelevant. The decisive primaries had been held at the beginning of the year, when Carter still appeared strong. With early victories in New Hampshire, Florida, and Illinois, Carter made his renomination inevitable. Although Kennedy came back to win contests in the East and California, the new rules provided for proportional division of the delegates, accumulating convention support for Carter even as he lost the later primaries and public approval.

When the Democrats convened in New York, the Kennedy forces were outnumbered but still defiant. In a final desperate maneuver, they proposed a change in the rules to release delegates from their pledges and create an open convention. But this attempt to return power to the delegates ran against the thrust of the presumed democratic character of selection in the primaries and was certainly unacceptable to Carter. On the critical vote of the convention, the proposed rule change was defeated by a vote of 1,936 to 1,390.

Kennedy formally withdrew at that point, but he and his supporters still fought to change the party platform. By voice vote, the delegates added more liberal promises to the party program, constituting implicit criticism of the president, including a commitment to control unemployment, an extensive jobs program, and restriction of high interest rates. Kennedy himself came to the convention to endorse the amendments. Met with intense emotional support from the delegates, Kennedy concluded his speech with the promise of a future challenge: "For all those whose cares have been our concern, the work goes on, the cause endures, the hope still lives, and the dream shall never die."

Carter was then renominated, 2,123–1,150, and Vice President Walter Mondale was endorsed for a second term without opposition. Carter's acceptance speech combined a plea for party unity with attacks on Reagan. Although Kennedy briefly appeared on the podium during the closing celebrations, he barely acknowledged Carter, his party's chosen leader.

Adding to the Democrats' problems, ten days later John Anderson formally launched his National Unity Campaign. Selecting former Wisconsin governor Patrick Lucey, a Democrat, for vice president, Anderson attempted a cross-partisan appeal. His platform was conservative on economic issues but liberal on social issues. The most notable plank was his energy program, which included a 50-cent a gallon tax on gasoline and a requirement than new cars meet a tough economy standard of 40 miles per gallon.

THE CAMPAIGN

The voters found the presidential choices unacceptable. Unique in academic studies, a near-majority of the electorate could find nothing they liked in *either* of the major candidates. The alternatives were seen, according to one wag, worse than the proverbial "lesser of two evils," but only "the evil of two lessers." Unhappy with the flawed Republican and Democratic candidates as the fall campaign opened, a fifth of survey respondents said they would vote for Anderson. The voters' discontent continued over the fall months, evident in large shifts in their intentions, with many remaining undecided until the last days.

Carter began his campaign with a positive emphasis on his own claimed accomplishments. But that strategy could not work with an electorate that held a strongly negative view of his administration. He hunkered down in the White House to present an image of a hard-working chief executive, spent little time on the hustings until the final weeks, and did not give a single major policy address. His campaign switched to attacks on Reagan's philosophy and personal characteristics. Carter's advocates no longer asked, as they had in 1976, "Why Not the Best?" Instead, they defensively argued, "It could be worse."

Reagan had problems of his own. By opening his campaign in Philadelphia, Mississippi, where three civil rights workers had been murdered in 1964, he seemed either indifferent or callous toward blacks. He was prone to careless statements that raised questions about his fitness for the presidency, such as his apparent doubts about the theory of evolution. Most worrisome was his assertive foreign policy and his emotive disdain for the Soviet Union, making many voters fearful that Reagan would bring war to the United States. Reagan tried to quiet these qualms by television ads stressing his experience as governor and by adopting a moderate tone in his speeches, delivered calmly and humorously with the skill of a former professional actor.

Televised debates became a permanent feature of presidential politics in 1980, under the sponsorship of the League of Women Voters, which offered the candidates a series of four meetings. The invitation also went to Anderson, using the League's own standard that included any candidate who gained 15 percent or more in public opinion polls. Reagan quickly accepted, but Carter refused to appear with Anderson, believing he would take votes from the Democratic ticket.

Reagan made the most of his opportunity in the two-man debate, which reached 50 million viewers. In contrast to the fears agitated by the Carter campaign, the governor presented himself well, coming across as reasonable, informed, still conservative, but not extreme. He rallied Republicans who might have defected to Anderson and now seemed an acceptable alternative to the absent and inadequate president. After the debate, Reagan reversed the race, taking the lead in surveys, while Anderson continued to decline.

The campaign then became increasingly nasty. Carter depicted Reagan as a threat to the social welfare programs of the New Deal and dangerous to the world if invested with the power of the presidency. Reagan portrayed Carter as deceptive, incompetent, and childish in his attacks. The candidates did agree that they would benefit from a direct two-man debate. When the league withdrew the invitation to Anderson, the major candidates took the stage before a television audience of 100 million only a week before the balloting.

The candidates stressed the themes of their campaigns. Carter relied on his experience, attacked Reagan on social programs, and tried to rally Democratic loyalties:

> I think this debate on Social Security, Medicare, national health insurance typifies, as vividly any other subject tonight, the basic historical differences between the Democratic Party and Republican Party. . . . So, it is good for the American people to remember that there is a sharp basic historical difference between Governor Reagan and me on these crucial issues—also, between the two parties that we represent.

Reagan turned the argument to Carter's record, asking the voters to make an easy retrospective judgment:

> I think when you make that decision, it might be well if you would ask yourself, are you better off than you were four years ago? Is it easier for you to go and buy things in the stores than it was four years ago? Is there more or less unemployment in the country than there was four years ago? Is America as respected throughout the world as it was? Do you feel that our security is as safe, that we're as strong as we were four years ago? . . . This country doesn't have to be in the shape that it is in.

As voters came to their final choices at the end of a volatile campaign, the Iranian hostage crisis regained the spotlight. Now at war with Iraq, Iran indicated it was willing to free the American diplomats. It conditioned this willingness on the release of Iranian assets and purchased weapons that the United States had seized. Both parties had worried about such an "October surprise." Republicans feared that Carter would find some way to get the hostages back and boost his popularity. Democrats feared that Reagan's advisers had arranged a deal with the Iranians, to delay release of the hostages until after the election.

A settlement appeared near, and President Carter ended his campaign the Sunday before the election to return to Washington to supervise the negotiations. Although the outlines of a pact were evident, the administration could not get detailed agreement as the Iranians delayed and added conditions. The aborted compact provided voters a final indicator of the Carter administration's impotence.

THE ELECTION RESULTS

As the election neared, opinion surveys—including that of *The New York Times,* working in tandem with CBS News— indicated a close race, amid signs of a movement toward Reagan. That trend proved to be decisive. A tenth of those inclined to vote for Carter stayed home; only 5 percent of Reagan's base abstained. A very high proportion—one out of seven—of the actual voters decided their votes in the last two days, according to exit polls. When these procrastinators actually entered their voting booths, they decisively chose Reagan, by a margin of 51 percent to 29 percent.

That final surge gave Reagan a tidal wave of support, a majority of the total popular vote (50.7 percent), while Carter wallowed in the lowest percentage (41.0 percent) of an incumbent president since Herbert Hoover in 1932. Anderson took most of the remaining vote, but his once-threatening candidacy had been reduced from one in five voters to one in sixteen. What remained of his support did not affect the outcome, as his ballots were drawn about equally from those who otherwise would have voted for either Carter or Reagan.

In the Electoral College, Reagan totally submerged Carter, 489–49. Carter did even worse than Hoover on this count, carrying only 6 states and the District of Columbia. In his victory, Reagan solidified the shift of the South to the Republican column. From 1980 to 2004, the party would win 68 of 77 contests among states of the former Confederacy. With particularly large gains in the plains and mountain states, along with strong victories in the growing megastates of California, Florida, and Texas, Reagan moved the party toward a coalition that might provide an unassailable Republican "lock" on the Electoral College. For the next quarter of a century, no Democrat would be able both to open that lock and win a majority of the popular vote.

Reagan's triumph created the possibility of a new Republican majority in presidential elections. But it was only a possibility, dependent on the new president's record in office. Although turnout had increased by 5 million votes, the turnout

rate continued to drop, demonstrating only limited enthusiasm for Reagan personally. His popular vote was a bare majority, not a ringing endorsement, and he lacked a popular majority in 19 of the states he carried. The election had been decided on negative evaluations of Carter, not positive support for Reagan; two-fifths of both the electorate and Reagan voters said their vote was principally in opposition to the other candidate.

There was no conservative mandate in these results. Republicans did gain 33 seats in the House and a striking 12 in the Senate, but much of their gain could be attributed to the waning of the earlier antipathy to Nixon. Although Republicans now narrowly controlled the Senate, the continuing Democratic majority in the House restricted any Reagan claim of an ideological triumph. Similarly, opinion surveys evidenced neither a shift toward conservatism in the public's thinking nor a new preference for Reagan's policy positions. The voters had decisively rejected Carter; they had not yet embraced Reagan.

Nevertheless, ideology did affect the election through limited partisan realignment of the voters. Carter lost votes among all groups, but the ticket's most dispiriting results were the defection of a third of Democrats and three-fourths of conservatives; among his party's conservatives, Carter barely carried a majority. The Democratic lead in partisan identification still held, but was diluted by ideological appeals. A new group, "Reagan Democrats," had emerged and would become a critical faction in coming elections.

Even with overall stability in public sentiment, the political agenda was moving to the right. Conservatives now controlled a disciplined Republican Party, their program reinforced by an ideological network of journals, think tanks, evangelical churches, and financial backers. Whatever its dynamics, the election did give Reagan the power of the presidency and, with it, the opportunity to move public opinion.

Reagan did not receive a mandate, but he moved quickly and skillfully to reshape the political landscape. In his inaugural address, he stated his conservative credo: "In the present crisis, government is not the solution to our problem; government is the problem." He soon won a 25 percent reduction of income tax rates and cuts in major federal programs. At the same time, he achieved a large increase in military spending to bolster harsh confrontations with the Soviet Union. His endorsement of traditionalist values—even as it came from the nation's first divorced president—brought new emphasis on social issues such as abortion and crime. The "Reagan Revolution" was not predetermined by the election of 1980, but it defined the American agenda for the next quarter of a century.

DISMAL BEGINNINGS

The 1980s began poorly for the United States. The nation struggled with an energy crisis and a stagnating economy that combined rising unemployment and inflation. Iranian students stormed the American Embassy in Tehran, seizing hostages. The Soviet Union remained a menacing nuclear threat. President Jimmy Carter seemed impotent in confronting these challenges, sapping the pride and optimism of the country.

JANUARY 31, 1980
EDITORIAL
THE PEASHOOTER WAR ON INFLATION

With the Consumer Price Index rising at an astounding rate of 13 percent and no relief in sight, the Carter Administration is still not willing to lead the nation in an all-out fight against inflation. There is no other way to construe the weak and limited anti-inflation plan the President set before the nation this week in his annual Budget Message and Economic Report.

It is true that the budgets are speculative documents. And it is true that this budget, in a narrow, fiscal policy sense, makes a stab against inflation. Federal tax and spending policies are to shift toward greater restraint during the next 18 months—moves designed to generate a mild recession and to knock some of the inflation out of the private economy. The new budget counts on huge tax increases to suck some $40 billion out of the economy, primarily through higher Social Security taxes, the windfall tax on oil and the further escalation of incomes into higher tax brackets as a result of inflation.

But while Mr. Carter's decision to take a recession in an election year may be unusual, it was hardly a bold and imaginative anti-inflationary move. He had virtually no choice, not with inflation still flying. The Administration, like almost everyone else, thought the recession was coming last year. But the economy was more resilient than expected. Despite whopping increases in oil prices, consumers kept on spending and the economy kept on growing, if slowly. In 1974, when OPEC first boosted prices, a far smaller drain on the economy generated a remarkably different result, the worst recession since the Depression.

With the next recession still playing hide-and-seek and inflation running high, Mr. Carter could scarcely have suggested an election-year tax cut. For one thing, he had repeatedly promised to balance the Federal budget by the end of his first term. He must already explain why he will

miss by $16 billion, if not more. Second, he might have made room for a tax cut by reducing domestic spending, but that would have been politically dangerous given the challenge on the left from Senator Kennedy. And there was another reason Mr. Carter could not lightly cut taxes: the sudden likelihood that defense spending will jump in the wake of the Soviet invasion of Afghanistan.

The resulting Carter policy means that the Administration is well protected if the long-awaited recession turns out worse than expected. It could still cut taxes quickly. But the White House has not guarded well against inflation, especially not if its rate turns out to be worse than expected. And given the weakness of the Carter attack, just such inflation is likely.

A recession alone—unless it is very deep and very long—cannot defeat inflation. Even the steep drop of 1974 produced only a temporary dip in the inflation rate. The expected drop in output of one percent this year would do far less to moderate prices.

An effective anti-inflation policy is unlikely without a dramatic reduction in the nation's dependence on expensive foreign oil. It also needs an incomes policy that induces people to absorb the rises in energy costs. It should include a Presidential commitment to resist the inflationary requests for economic protection from special interest groups, be they farmers or steelworkers. So far, Mr. Carter does not seem to be thinking along such lines. The new Economic Report speaks of using the voluntary wage-price controls to hold back the spillover of energy prices. What voluntary controls? Several months after the original guidelines have expired, President Carter still has not erected a new set in their place.

The nation should be at war against inflation. The President is still toying with a peashooter.

NOVEMBER 7, 1980
IRAN'S CIVIL GOVERNMENT OUT; HOSTAGES FACE DEATH THREAT; OIL EXPORTS BELIEVED HALTED

STUDENTS WARN U.S.

Ayatollah Instructs Secret Revolutionary Council to Form a Cabinet

By JOHN KIFNER

Special to The New York Times

TEHERAN, Iran, Nov. 6—Prime Minister Mehdi Bazargan's provisional revolutionary Government dissolved today, conceding power to the Islamic authority of Ayatollah Ruhollah Khomeini.

The United States had been counting on Mr. Bazargan's Government to insure the safety of 60 or so American hostages seized Sunday at the American Embassy. The Government's abrupt collapse, after months of frustration and impotence, appeared to further dampen the already dim hopes for a negotiated release of the hostages.

Militant Islamic students holding the embassy said today that they would kill the hostages if the United States used military force in a rescue attempt. The students are demanding that the United States hand over Shah Mohammed Riza Pahlevi, who is undergoing medical treatment in New York City.

[In Washington, President Carter met with his foreign policy advisers and decided to maintain a nonprovocative posture toward Iran in the hope that the hostages would eventually be freed by Iranian religious authorities. And at the United Nations, a Palestine Liberation Organization spokesman said that Yasir Arafat, head of the guerrilla group, was sending a delegation to Teheran to "secure the safety of the Americans" and others held hostage.]

- -

LEADING CONTENDERS

President Jimmy Carter faced an unusually strong challenge for renomination from Sen. Edward Kennedy, brother of the assassinated president, John Kennedy, while perennial Republican contender Ronald Reagan fended off George H. W. Bush and the inactive former president, Gerald Ford. Reagan seized the momentum from his rivals by orchestrating an early debate, leading to a string of primary victories. Carter benefited briefly from an attempt to rescue the Iranian hostages. Even though it failed, it momentarily mobilized public sentiment behind the commander in chief. With their radically different approaches, neither Carter nor Reagan won broad public support, leaving the voters unexcited about the election.

FEBRUARY 25, 1980
A REPORTER'S NOTEBOOK: GRAND OLD PANDEMONIUM

By FRANCIS X. CLINES

Special to The New York Times

NASHUA, N.H., Feb. 24—In a raucous release of anger and glee, the Republicans who would be President dashed their 11th commandment to the floor of a high school gymnasium last night as New Hampshire voters laughed and booed in the bleachers, relishing the sight of a Grand Old Party finding room in its heart for rowdiness.

For months, the candidates had paid homage to the commandment: Thou shalt not speak ill of another Republican. But in a memorably unrehearsed encounter in an otherwise packaged campaign year, they shouted and elbowed for debating room and produced their most impassioned moment so far.

Four of the candidates were reduced to standing on the podium and miming their messages to the people as the moderator, having limited the gymnasium confrontation to a "debate" between the two front-runners, then tried to silence the objections of one of these two, Ronald Reagan.

Voices in the Chaos

"Turn Mr. Reagan's microphone off," the moderator, Jon Breen, the executive editor of The Nashua Telegraph, shouted as Mr. Reagan, the former Governor of California, sought to invite the four candidates standing mute behind him to join the colloquy with George Bush.

"Get 'em chairs!" a woman in a blue smock bellowed from the bleachers, her protest knifing through the din to the podium under the basketball scoreboard.

"Let them speak!" came another cry.

Socially, the room became a shambles, with 2,000 people clamoring to give their viewpoints. Politically, it became an imbroglio that produced the finest moment thus far in New Hampshire for Mr. Reagan, who had paid $3,500 to rent the hall and would not yield to the newspaper editor.

"I am paying for this microphone," Mr. Reagan declared with a glare of fury that brought cheers from the crowd.

"I realize some effort has been made to embarrass them," he said apologetically to the four, who could only shrug and wait and gesture supplicatingly to the crowd.

They did this rather well and it seemed an interesting footnote in American political history, poignant silence on the hustings.

The remaining candidate, George Bush, the former diplomat, Congressman and Director of Central Intelligence whose commercials have been broadcasting the message, "There's no problem that Americans can't solve," sat there with no solution in sight. He preferred a confrontation with Mr. Reagan alone.

Before the night was over he got that format along with the stated enmity of the four who had stood mute and eventually stalked off, with Mr. Anderson waving an exaggerated message of phooey at the editor and Mr. Bush.

APRIL 25, 1980
U.S. ATTEMPT TO RESCUE IRAN HOSTAGES FAILS; 8 DIE AS PLANES COLLIDE DURING WITHDRAWAL

ACCIDENT ON GROUND

No Clashes Occur During Mission in Desert Area, White House Says

By BERNARD GWERTZMAN

Special to The New York Times

WASHINGTON, Friday, April 25—The White House announced early this morning that the United States had attempted to rescue the American hostages in Teheran but that the effort failed and eight American crewmen died in Iran after the attempt was called off.

Giving only few details of the rescue attempt, the White House said that President Carter "has ordered the cancellation of an operation in Iran that was under way to prepare for a rescue of our hostages."

"The mission was terminated because of equipment failure," the White House said in a statement issued at 1 A.M.

"During the subsequent withdrawal, there was a collision between our aircraft on the ground at a remote desert location in Iran," the statement said.

Many Questions Unanswered

It said that there were no hostilities, but that eight crewmen were killed and "others were injured in the accident."

The White House said that the injured were successfully airlifted from Iran and were expected to recover.

The news came suddenly and raised many questions that White House spokesmen were unable to answer. They said that additional details would be provided later today.

It was the first known attempt by the United States to rescue the hostages, who have been in confinement since Nov. 4. The incident raised concern over the well-being of the hostages since the Islamic militants have threatened to kill the Americans if force was attempted to free them.

The White House statement said that the mission "was not motivated by hostility toward Iran or the Iranian people and there were no Iranian casualties."

Talk of Military Action

In the last two weeks Mr. Carter has talked about possible military action against Iran if economic and political sanctions just initiated with the nation's allies failed to achieve results. But Mr. Carter said that he was thinking in terms of moves to block Iran's harbors. In fact, it was reported on Wednesday that Hamilton Jordan, the White

House Chief of Staff, had told senior aides at a meeting Tuesday that Mr. Carter had ruled out any rescue attempts as being unworkable.

The White House statement said that President Carter "accepts full responsibility for the decision to attempt the rescue." Anticipating a possible uproar in Iran, a statement said that "the United States continues to hold the Government of Iran responsible for the safety of the American hostages."

"The United States remains determined to obtain their safe release at the earliest possible date," the statement said.

MAY 15, 1980
REAGAN AND CARTER NEAR PRESIDENTIAL NOMINATIONS
By ADAM CLYMER

Despite some soft spots and an evident lack of enthusiasm from the voters, Ronald Reagan and President Carter each advanced to more than nine-tenths of the way to their party's Presidential nominations Tuesday by winning the primaries in Maryland and Nebraska.

Only one victory was overwhelming—Mr. Reagan's 78 percent landslide in Nebraska. Mr. Carter beat Senator Edward M. Kennedy by the same margin, 47 percent to 38 percent, in both states, and Mr. Reagan's 48-to-41 percent edge over George Bush in Maryland earned him only a 15-to-15 split in delegates from that state because Mr. Bush carried five of the state's eight Congressional districts

Mr. Carter's victories in the two states brought his delegate total to 1,533 won or clearly projected from incomplete

caucus processes, according to the New York Times count, with 1,666 needed for the Democratic nomination.

Mr. Reagan's successes took him to 937 of the 998 delegates needed for the Republican nomination, with a good chance that conventions next weekend and primaries next Tuesday in Michigan and Oregon would get him over the top.

Dwindling Hopes

Their foes pinned their dwindling hopes on achieving a string of victories in the remaining primaries, changing the minds of some of the delegates who have already been chosen, and reversing the directions of the Carter and Reagan bandwagons in caucuses and conventions.

> The sharp contrast of these approaches—one candidate selling himself as confident that he knows the solution, another portraying his approach as one of persistence in the face of complexity—is a basic theme of the developing race for the Presidency.

TWO STRATEGIES, ONE RESULT

Before the formal nominations, the electorate reacted apathetically to both the incumbent president, Jimmy Carter, and the challenger, former governor Ronald Reagan of California. Carter intellectualized national issues as complex problems, requiring careful thought and patience. Reagan explained the nation's ills as simple failures of the administration, requiring only fortitude and quick action to resolve. Weary Americans viewed both of the polarizing candidates with skepticism and indifference.

APRIL 14, 1980
CARTER RIDDLES VS. REAGAN SIMPLE ANSWERS

By ADAM CLYMER

Special to The New York Times

GREENSBURG, Pa., April 11—Ronald Reagan campaigns across the country, drawing ovations by saying that the nation's most troubling problems—inflation, energy, the hostages in Iran, even the decline of the family—can be solved, and solved simply.

President Carter, the man he expects to run against in November, contends that these problems and others can be dealt with, but only over time. If there were "any quick or painless solutions, they would have been implemented long ago," he said in his March 14 speech on inflation.

The sharp contrast of these approaches—one candidate selling himself as confident that he knows the solution, another portraying his approach as one of persistence in the face of complexity—is a basic theme of the developing race for the Presidency. And it unfolds across an unsettled national yearning "for getting a system that seems out of control under control," in the words of a leading Democratic poll taker, Peter Hart.

The counterattacks are also developing. Jody Powell, Mr. Carter's press secretary, hit one key theme yesterday when he said Mr. Reagan presents "a fallacious and terribly simplistic view of the world" and offers "simple-minded theories."

APRIL 18, 1980
POLL FINDS REAGAN-CARTER CHOICE UNSATISFACTORY TO HALF OF PUBLIC

By ADAM CLYMER

To half of the American public, President Carter and Ronald Reagan, who is rapidly gaining ground on Mr. Carter, represent an unsatisfactory choice for President, the latest New York Times/CBS News Poll shows.

The dissatisfied half of the public is more educated, more Eastern, younger, calls itself more liberal and has a higher income than the half that regards the Carter-Reagan choice as good enough. And while many supporters of other candidates are in the dissatisfied group, it also includes a third of those who say that they would vote for Mr. Carter and a fourth of those who would vote for Mr. Reagan.

The former Governor of California has caught up with Mr. Carter and is now the only Presidential candidate viewed by more of the public favorably rather than unfavorably, the poll shows.

Many Signs of Weakness

The high level of dissatisfaction with the seeming Presidential alternatives seven months before the election appears unusual. However, opinions may not have crystallized this early in previous elections because it has been decades since both nominations appeared so firmly in hand this early.

The somewhat greater level of dissatisfaction among Mr. Carter's potential voters is one of many indications of weakness that the poll, taken from April 10 through April 14, found in the President's political position. Support for his handling of the Iranian hostage crisis fell sharply in a month, and one out of six Americans says that he or she does not expect the hostages to return safely.

But while Mr. Carter lost no significant ground to Senator Edward M. Kennedy since March in preferences for the Democratic nomination, the ominous message to Mr. Carter's campaign is that in a month he has lost a clear lead over Mr. Reagan among registered voters who say that they are following the campaign.

The former California Governor is now clearly ahead, 48 to 40 percent, in that group, among whom likely voters tend to be found. In March, Mr. Carter led this segment of the population, 51 percent to 39 percent, with the others undecided.

THE REPUBLICAN CONVENTION

The Republican Party met in Detroit in mid-July in a convention that was more of a campaign rally than a decisive party meeting. The presidential nomination had already been determined by the primaries, leaving only the platform and the selection of a vice-presidential candidate on the table. Ronald Reagan, basking in his party's support, initially courted Gerald Ford as his running mate but then stunned the country by selecting his chief rival, George H. W. Bush. Reagan proposed major changes in public policy of the magnitude of Franklin Delano Roosevelt's New Deal a generation earlier, but in the opposite ideological direction.

JULY 15, 1980
REAGAN IS PROMISING A CRUSADE TO MAKE NATION 'GREAT AGAIN'

CONVENTION OPENS IN DETROIT

Ford, in Blistering Speech, Assails President, Charging That He Has Sold America Short

By HEDRICK SMITH

Special to The New York Times

DETROIT, July 14—In an obviously buoyant mood, Ronald Regan arrived in this Republican convention city today to claim the Presidential nomination he has sought three times in 12 years, but he let former President Gerald R. Ford lead the Republican assault on President Carter.

The former California Governor, responding to chanting partisans in Detroit's jammed, festooned Renaissance Center, declared that his fall campaign would be "a crusade to make America great again."

And he took a humorous poke at Mr. Carter, saying that in a recent dream the President had asked him why he wanted Mr. Carter's job.

"I told him I didn't want his job," Mr. Reagan joshed. "I want to be President." The Reagan crowd erupted into laughter.

Ford Attack on Carter

But Mr. Ford delivered a far more blistering attack on President Carter at the Republican convention's first night session, calling Mr. Carter a leader who had "sold America short" and who had "given up on the Presidency," an evident allusion to the President's "crisis of confidence" speech a year ago.

And Mr. Ford, celebrating his 67th birthday tonight, teased his fellow Republicans with a couple of hints that revived talk of his possibly joining Mr. Reagan on the Republican ticket this fall, just 24 hours after he said flatly that "under no circumstances" would he be the candidate for the Vice Presidency.

Mr. Reagan was reliably reported by well-placed sources, even before the former President's remarks tonight, to be planning another effort to talk Mr. Ford into taking the No. 2 spot on his ticket when the two men meet tomorrow.

At one point, remarking that he did not want to be sidelined as an elder statesman, Mr. Ford quipped, "I am not ready to quit yet." Moments later, he went further, saying that when the Republicans "field the team for Governor Reagan, count me in." Both remarks, despite their vagueness, brought cheers and applause from the crowded hall. The delegates also took fire several times at his sallies against President Carter.

"By his own statistics, Mr. Carter has failed," Mr. Ford said in his speech to the convention. "We cannot take four more years like the last four. We cannot stand four more years of soaring inflation, sky-high interest rates, rising unemployment and shrinking take-home pay. We cannot stake our [survival] on four more years of weak and wavering leadership and lagging defense. We dare not fall another four years behind with dangerous dependence on foreign energy."

"You've heard all Carter's alibis," Mr. Ford said in his fiery address. "Inflation cannot be controlled. The world has changed. We can no longer protect our diplomats in foreign capitals, nor our working men on Detroit's assembly lines. We must lower our expectations. We must be realistic. We must prudently retreat. Baloney."

Former president Gerald Ford lends his support to Ronald Reagan and running mate George Bush, in Peoria, on November 3, 1980, the final day of campaigning before the 1980 election.

Source: AP Images

JULY 17, 1980
REAGAN WINS NOMINATION AND CHOOSES BUSH AS RUNNING MATE AFTER TALKS WITH FORD FAIL

DRAMATIC ABOUTFACE

Till Last Minute Delegates Expected Ex-President to Take No. 2 Spot

By HEDRICK SMITH

Special to The New York Times

DETROIT, Thursday July 17—A jubilant Republican Party formally proclaimed Ronald Regan as its nominee last night and then heard this morning, after one of the most dramatic aboutfaces of recent convention politics, that George Bush would be his Vice-Presidential running mate.

Up until the last moment, the delegates had been expecting that former President Gerald R. Ford would bow to Mr. Reagan's entreaties to join the ticket. But Mr. Reagan broke precedent by going to the hall himself to announce that Mr. Ford had declined and that he had chosen Mr. Bush, the former Texas Congressman who had been his most dogged rival in the primaries.

After 24 hours of negotiations with Mr. Ford over the possible conditions of his serving as Vice President in a Reagan administration, Mr. Reagan told the national convention that the two men had "gone over this and over this

and over this and he and I have come to the conclusion, and he believes deeply that he can be of more value as the former President, campaigning his heart out, as he has promised to do, and not as a member of the ticket."

Announcement by Reagan

Then very quickly, and with a taut smile on his face, Mr. Reagan announced that he had chosen Mr. Bush as his running mate, "a man we all know and a man who was a candidate, a man who has great experience in government, and a man who told me that he can enthusiastically support the platform across the board."

Although many had said that the only item of suspense in the Republican convention would be Mr. Reagan's choice of a running mate, none had expected it to unfold so unpredictably as in the 24 hours before Mr. Reagan announced his choice of Mr. Bush.

Inside the convention hall, it was a day of personal but predicted triumph for Mr. Reagan. For he finally claimed the Presidential nomination that he had sought first in 1968 and again unsuccessfully in 1976 before routing all his adversaries this year and winning an overwhelming triumph and, ultimately, nomination.

JULY 20, 1980
EDITORIAL
FRANKLIN DELANO REAGAN

It is conventional at political conventions for Presidential nominees to align themselves eagerly with the Past Heroes of their parties. Thus there was something audacious, even brilliant, in the way Ronald Reagan ended the 1980 Republican Convention. The hero he chose was— Franklin Roosevelt.

The words Mr. Reagan quoted, denouncing waste in government, came from F.D.R.'s famous 1932 acceptance speech promising a "new deal for the American people." The new Republican nominee knows how effective that speech and campaign were; Ronald Reagan started his political life as a New Deal Democrat. Mr. Reagan also knows how ephemeral the Roosevelt pledges of frugality were. So why recall all that now? There's no end of good reasons.

Citing F.D.R. on frugality suggests that Mr. Reagan has been consistent in his lifelong political philosophy. He may have renounced the Democratic Party. But, as he told Bill Moyers last May, "I have often thought the party changed much more than I did." And if Ronald Reagan casts himself as the latter-day equivalent of Franklin Roosevelt, guess which part Jimmy Carter is meant to play. Finally, most ambitiously, by using F.D.R. as a model, Mr. Reagan suggests that he is not content to be the darling of narrow ideology. On the contrary, he suggests that there will be a tidal change, 1932-like, in the way Americans vote, and that he aspires to lead it.

Moving toward the center was surely the first priority of the convention. Such outreach has always been Chairman Bill Brock's theme; he and others expressed it to the convention. Think, also, of the speeches not made, by people like Phyllis Schlafly whom liberals and moderates love to hate. Room was found on the program for all of Mr. Reagan's primary rivals except arch-conservative Phillip Crane. The only way Senator Jesse Helms finally made it to the platform was by threatening to contest the Vice-Presidential nomination.

Is Mr. Reagan the darling of the right? It was hard to divine that from Senator Paul Laxalt's nominating speech, praising the candidate's term as Governor of California as a veritable Great Society of aid for schools, minorities and the handicapped. And Mr. Reagan was anything but ideologically rigid when it came to choosing his running mate. The pursuit of his 1976 adversary, Gerald Ford, demonstrated a clear Reagan willingness to reach out. So did the ultimate choice of George Bush. So did the effort to kidnap Franklin Roosevelt.

But for all Mr. Reagan's audacity and moderation, what most endures after the convention is a question. Like Henry Kissinger's disappointing speech early in the week, Mr. Reagan's speech gave a passionate recital of America's troubles, and heatedly denounced Jimmy Carter for not solving them. But what does Mr. Reagan propose? To cut taxes and cut government—while increasing defense spending. Those general ideas may be worthy but they do not hold back the nuclear arms race, lower the price of imported oil or chase the Soviets out of Afghanistan.

As an example, recall what Mr. Reagan said Thursday night about Iran: "Incredibly, more than 50 of our fellow Americans have been held captive for over eight months by a dictatorial foreign power that holds us up to ridicule before the world." True enough, but what would he do about it? Bomb Iran flat? Send Ramsey Clark back to Teheran? Mr. Reagan does not say. He denounces Jimmy Carter for practicing "trust me" government. But so far, about the only alteration Mr. Reagan has proposed is the person to whom the pronoun refers.

THE DEMOCRATIC CONVENTION

The Democratic Party met in New York City in August facing severe controversy amid new convention procedures. Sen. Edward Kennedy had gained momentum late in the campaign, but his gathering charge could not overcome the defensive position established by the incumbent's dominance in the early primaries. Unable to change the rules to his benefit, Kennedy withdrew, while winning some concessions to make the party platform more liberal. Carter accepted the nomination, renominated Walter Mondale as vice president, and quickly moved to counter Ronald Reagan's appeal. As the convention adjourned, Democrats remained divided and unclear on their policy alternatives.

AUGUST 12, 1980
DEMOCRATS BACK CARTER ON NOMINATION RULE; KENNEDY WITHDRAWS FROM PRESIDENTIAL RACE

CALL TO PRESIDENT

The Senator Apparently Surprised His Family by Dropping Out

By B. DRUMMOND AYRES Jr.

Senator Edward M. Kennedy apparently surprised even close members of his family and staff last night when he announced he was pulling out of the race for the Democratic Presidential nomination.

"It wasn't something that had been tried out before, that had really been laid out as an option," a close campaign aide said. "Some suggestions had been made earlier about what he might say, but I don't believe that was one of them."

The fact that Mr. Kennedy's political director, Paul Kirk, told reporters just after the rules fight was settled that the Senator would not withdraw was evidence of the apparent surprise in the Kennedy circle.

Later, a Kennedy aide, who asked not to be identified, said the Massachusetts Democrat decided to quit the race in the wake of almost 10 months of nonstop campaigning, after watching the results of the rules fight on television with close family members and aides. The aide said the group, which gathered to munch on a cold supper buffet in the Senator's suite at the Waldorf Astoria Hotel, included his wife, Joan, a sister, Jean Smith, as well as several speech writers and long-time Senate office assistants.

Call to the President

The results of the vote on the rules fight were discussed in a general manner when the balloting was over, the aide reported, then the Senator announced to the gathering that he was going to call President Carter and withdraw.

The Senator's aides refused flatly late last night to discuss whether he might support Mr. Carter in his race against Ronald Reagan, the Republican nominee. One aide said privately, however, that the degree of support might well depend upon the ultimate shape of the platform, which is to be discussed today.

AUGUST 15, 1980
PRESIDENT, ACCEPTING NOMINATION, ASSAILS G.O.P. PROGRAM AS 'FANTASY'; HAILS 'VALIANT' KENNEDY CAMPAIGN

MONDALE ON TICKET

Carter, Vowing a Victory, Asserts the Voters Will Face 'Stark Choice'

By HEDRICK SMITH

President Carter, in a battling partisan mood as he accepted his party's nomination for a second term, declared last night that the 1980 election offered voters "a stark choice" between rival visions of America and vowed, "We are going to beat the Republicans in November."

Evoking the fighting campaign tactics of Harry S. Truman, another underdog Democratic President, in the 1948 campaign, Mr. Carter sharply attacked the arms and tax policies of Ronald Reagan, his Republican rival, as "irresponsible" and "outrageous." The Republicans, he charged, offer a "fantasy America" of "simple solutions—simple and wrong."

The President made a dramatic spotlit entry into the darkened hall for the finale of the party's 38th National Convention. And with a dramatic appeal for party unity, he reached out to Senator Edward M. Kennedy, his vanquished rival, to join the political combat ahead.

Tribute to Kennedy

"Ted, you're a tough competitor and a superb campaigner—and I can attest to that," he said in his remarks. "I reach out tonight to you and those who supported you in your valiant and passionate campaign."

"Ted, your party needs—and I need you. And I need your idealism and your dedication working for us. There is no doubt that even greater service lies ahead of you—and we are grateful to you and to your strong partnership

now in the larger cause to which your own life has been dedicated."

Senator Kennedy provided the political capstone of the evening by setting aside the rivalry of the primary campaign and the divisions of the convention to join the President on the podium for the traditional show of party unity. He had watched the President's speech in his suite at the Waldorf-Astoria Hotel.

Senator Joins Carter

As other political leaders were introduced, the crowd started chanting, "We want Ted," and when he appeared, it gave a tremendous roar. The Senator, his face somber, shook hands with Mr. Carter, Vice President Mondale and other leaders. He waved to the crowd and left after three minutes, but the cheers brought him back.

As the Senator started to leave the second time, the President took a pace or two with him. Mr. Kennedy reached out and appeared to touch him on the shoulder. As the Senator walked off the platform, the 23-minute demonstration died out, and the convention closed at 11:50 P.M.

Before the President's address, the delegates went through the ritual roll-call renomination of Walter F. Mondale as Mr. Carter's Vice-Presidential running mate.

AUGUST 15, 1980
EDITORIAL
PRESIDENT CARTER'S FIGHT AT THE GARDEN

When it comes to convention politics, at a minimum, Jimmy Carter knows how to play tough. This week, the President faced—and faced down—the possibility that the Democrats in Madison Square Garden might erupt on prime time and bitter Kennedy supporters might walk out. Last night, as he accepted his party's nomination, he came out swinging at Ronald Reagan every bit as hard as Edward Kennedy did on Tuesday.

En route to that dramatic moment, he faced a dual battle over the party platform. First, his forces had to try to neutralize, or defeat, challenges to platform planks dealing with the economy and women's rights, among others. Then the President was confronted with a new rule requiring nominees to state in writing what they think of the platform. The Carter forces were unduly stubborn as they traversed this mine field, antagonizing some people needlessly. But in the end, Mr. Carter seems to have come

out about right. The platform and the President's positions give the Democrats at least a semblance of unity that seemed unlikely just a few days ago.

The principal argument was over Senator Kennedy's proposal of a $12 billion Federal jobs program to help offset the effects of recession. There is a mythic faith in the idea that such a strategy would accomplish its goal. But a huge Federal outlay at this troubled point would inevitably misfire. The jobs would come on stream too late to put a floor under the recession. The expenditure would swell the Federal deficit too much for the shaky money markets to absorb without a rapid run-up of interest rates. The result would not be massive hiring but massive disappointment.

The President quite rightly said no to the plank. But what he said yes to is not clear. In his statement on the platform, he embraced the "spirit and aims" of the jobs proposal and promised a sweeping revitalization program to lower unemployment and lift the economy without inflaming inflation. He has had almost four years of failure in managing the economy, and so this promise has to be viewed skeptically. But, for now, the President has been at least politically successful in substituting an as-yet undefined "black box" for a misguided jobs program without driving Senator Kennedy and his supporters out of the Garden.

• •

THE THIRD CANDIDATE: JOHN ANDERSON

Illinois representative John Anderson joined the presidential race as an independent candidate after losing the Republican nomination to Reagan. More liberal than Reagan and more conservative than Carter, Anderson offered a choice between two unpopular candidates, but struggled to construct a serious third-party option. An often-repeated joke—when confronted with a gunman demanding them to choose between Carter or Reagan, voters would answer "shoot"—pointed to the lackluster appeal of the main party candidates and Anderson's modest hope as more attractive than either. Selecting Wisconsin governor Patrick Lucey, a Democrat, as his running mate, Anderson won a position on the ballot in all fifty states, making him a legally viable candidate, but he ultimately failed to convince the public that his campaign was anything but a sideshow.

APRIL 25, 1980
ANDERSON DECLARES AS INDEPENDENT, VOWING TO DRAW MANY NEW VOTERS
By WARREN WEAVER Jr.

Special to The New York Times

WASHINGTON, April 24—John B. Anderson declared his independent candidacy today in the 1980 race for the Presidency, promising to attract millions of new voters into the political process and to raise issues that he said the major parties' contenders would avoid.

"Our nation needs a choice in November," Mr. Anderson said in his announcement. "Not just a choice among candidates. I mean a choice, of course, for the nation. I want to offer that choice."

By dropping out of the Republican competition and proposing a well-financed national campaign on his own, the Illinois Congressman injected a new, unpredictable element into the expected contest between President Carter and Ronald Reagan, the leading candidates of their parties.

Even if Mr. Anderson does not reach his goal of carrying enough states to win the election, he could draw enough votes from either the Democratic or the Republican candidate to elect the other. Or he could carry enough states to deprive any candidate of an electoral-vote majority and force the Presidential choice into the House of Representatives.

Mr. Anderson said that he was abandoning his Republican race because it was clear he could not win a majority of the party's delegates, and he released the delegates he had acquired—59, according to a count by The New York Times. Mr. Anderson had competed in six primaries, none of which he won.

Democratic leaders fear that Mr. Anderson will divert enough liberal and moderate votes from Mr. Carter to assure victory for Mr. Reagan. At the same time, Republicans believe that the independent may weaken prospects for their candidates for Congress and state and local offices if moderate Republicans who desert the head of the ticket then fail to vote for the party's other candidates.

Mr. Anderson promised, if elected, a "national unity" administration composed of leaders of both parties, one that could work with a Republican or Democratic Congress. He said that he would consider "men and women of both parties and independents" when selecting his running mate later in the campaign.

AUGUST 26, 1980
ANDERSON CHOOSES LUCEY FOR HIS TICKET

Praises Ex-Wisconsin Governor as Qualified for the White House

By WARREN WEAVER Jr.

Special to The New York Times

WASHINGTON, Aug. 25—John B. Anderson today formally named Patrick J. Lucey, a Democrat, as the Vice-Presidential candidate of his independent "national unity" campaign, saying he considered the former Governor of Wisconsin "magnificently" qualified to become President.

"Pat Lucey and I very deeply believe," the Congressman said at a news conference, "that this nation faces its most serious challenge since the Second World War and that the nominees of the traditional parties offer neither new ideas nor credible leadership to the American people."

"I am proud to stand here today with John Anderson," Mr. Lucey, a Democrat, responded, "because I think he's right for America."

Seeking Broader Support

The announcement was timed to help promote broader public support for the Anderson campaign at a time when national polls are being taken that will determine whether the independent will participate in a series of Presidential debates sponsored by the League of Women Voters.

Mr. Lucey was the deputy manager of Senator Edward M. Kennedy's Presidential campaign, and his presence on the Anderson ticket is designed to attract supporters of the Senator who cannot accept President Carter as the Democratic nominee.

The Vice-Presidential candidate told the reporters that he expected to devote some of his campaign effort to attempting to obtain a larger share of the labor vote for Mr. Anderson. In his two terms as Governor in 1971–77, he was strongly supported by unions in Wisconsin.

Mr. Lucey will bring a measure of religious and ethnic balance to the independent ticket. He is Roman Catholic of Irish decent; Mr. Anderson is an evangelical Protestant whose father was born in Sweden. Both men have wives of Greek descent.

Matter of Prominence

Asked if he enjoyed enough national prominence to help the ticket significantly, Mr. Lucey replied that, "much of that problem is being solved here this afternoon," as television cameras and scores of reporters recorded the announcement ceremony.

Sees Effect on Congressmen

The new Vice Presidential candidate said Mr. Anderson had agreed that there was "room for some independence on issues" between the two. He said that he differed from Mr. Anderson on national health insurance and labor legislation; he noted that the Presidential candidate "is not wedded to every view he's ever held."

OCTOBER 26, 1980
EDITORIAL
A VOTE FOR ANDERSON IS . . .

The first concerns John Anderson. In Nietzsche's words, he is someone who only shook the tree when the fruit was ripe—but look at the size of the tree he shook. Against all odds, Mr. Anderson got on the ballot in every state. He wrote a platform that the parties might envy. He has campaigned with distinction.

But he remains a marginal candidate who has never won an election outside rural Illinois or managed anything larger than his staff. He has no practical hope of winning, and if he did, he might not be so appealing. It

is far easier to demonstrate boldness to a narrow following than to please the broad coalition required to win. If Mr. Anderson's candidacy has any effect now, it will be as a spoiler in a few close states. Nonetheless, many people of liberal instinct are still drawn to him. They want to protest against the major parties, as Arthur Schlesinger has put it, for "imposing such ridiculous alternatives." That is, send 'em a message. But what message? The clear prospect is that in 1984, neither Mr. Carter nor Mr. Reagan, who will be nearly 74, will try again. The predictable candidates will be men like George Bush and Howard Baker, Walter Mondale and Ted Kennedy, hardly "ridiculous alternatives." A vote for Anderson will end up looking like a quaint aberration.

Even so, Mr. Anderson gives some people a way to say "Shoot." Certain that Jimmy Carter has failed, they are determined to punish him. Though they cannot bring themselves to vote for Mr. Reagan, they profess to see no difference in a Carter-Reagan choice. But there is a difference. And for responsible citizens, there is, finally, no refuge from the second choice:

Carter or Reagan?

- -

REAGAN'S CONSERVATISM

Ronald Reagan's candidacy united a new political alliance, blending economic conservatives with social conservatives, two groups with little obvious overlap. While advocating large increases in defense spending, Reagan proposed cuts in nearly all other government spending and a matching cut in taxes. Tangentially attached to these economic plans were strong appeals to religious conservatives, including promises to ban abortion, restore school prayer, and promote "moral values." The Reagan coalition had been born.

APRIL 13, 1980
RONALD REAGAN'S ECONOMIC POLICY
By STEVEN RATTNER

WASHINGTON

The Ronald Reagan of 1980 is a particularly instructive candidate, replete with lessons in politics and economics. He has provided a vivid demonstration of the conflicts within Republican circles between the traditional conservatism and a newer set of views. He is a campaigning example of the politics of moderation as a mechanism for improving a candidate's electability. And he displays an awareness of the advantages of the politics of generalities when it comes to policy positions.

In his generalities, the former California Governor has held close to the anti-Federal Government conservative instincts he has embodied through most of his two-decade public career. The message is a simple one: The nation's economic problems—particularly inflation—are the fault of spend-too-much, tax-too-much, regulate-too-much policies. His prescription for the solution is equally simple: Clip Washington's wings in all three areas.

"Government exists to protect us from each other," Mr. Reagan has said over and over again in the campaign. "Where Government has gone beyond its limits is in deciding to protect us from ourselves."

Mr. Reagan himself has argued that he is being no more general than any other candidate, but his advisers concede that the front-runner has chosen a non-specific stance as the surest way to maintain his position at the head of the pack.

Some political experts believe he lost the Presidential nomination in 1976 because of his instantly controversial contention that $90 billion could be cut from the Federal budget without reducing spending on defense, Social Security or Medicare. This time around, he is taking no such chances. His aides, who a month or so [ago] were talking of a major economic statement this spring, now suggest that after the Republican convention is more likely.

The generalities persist, even when unresolved contradictions lurk beneath them. He argues, for example, that many Government programs should be transferred back to the states, particularly welfare and education programs. How the tax system would be readjusted to account for this switch, however, remains a mystery.

Part of the speaking in generalities reflects the taking of a more moderate line, as Mr. Reagan works to convince skeptical analysts that he can broaden his support beyond his typical base. His days of advocating highly controversial changes such as making Social Security voluntary seem to be behind him.

From the start of the 1980 campaign, he has added to his standard anti-Government stance a new brand of Republican theory known to most as "supply-side economics."

That view has been represented to Mr. Reagan principally by Representative Jack Kemp of Buffalo and Jude Wanniski, a New Jersey economic consultant. It holds that taxes are now so high that a cut will generate a new upsurge of economic activity that will produce more revenues for the Federal Government than were lost by the original cut. The theory is set out in the Laffer Curve, named after Arthur Laffer, an economics professor at the University of Southern California and sometime adviser to the Reagan campaign.

As for Mr. Reagan's other economic views, he has spoken in a quiet voice for eliminating the minimum wage and with somewhat more volume for at least establishing a lower minimum for the young and for halting additional increases in the adult minimum.

Ironically, Mr. Reagan loves to toss statistics into his anti-Government speeches and one other emerging difficulty is that his statistics often turn out to be wrong.

He has contended, for example, that Alaska's oil potential is greater than the reserves of Saudi Arabia, that General Motors has 23,300 employees filling out Government paperwork and that the Federal Government has increased by 131,000 employees in the past three years. Not one of those contentions is accurate.

"I think it's a problem," said Senator Paul Laxalt of Nevada, his campaign chairman. "It's going to have to be met and it's going to have to be met factually."

APRIL 21, 1980
CONSERVATIVES EMBRACE REAGAN ON SOCIAL ISSUES
By DAVID E. ROSENBAUM
Special to The New York Times

WASHINGTON, April 20—At stop after stop on Ronald Reagan's campaign, from stark airport runways to fancy hotel ballrooms, there is a recurring theme to the questions that are put to him: How does he feel about "abortion on demand"? What would he do to promote "Christian schools"? Will he promise to pick a running mate who shares his views on "family issues"?

The questions reflect a phenomenon that experienced political analysts, including members of Mr. Reagan's own staff, find difficult to assess.

The former California Governor has won the enthusiastic support of activists on the right wing of the Republican party, of the leaders of the antiabortion movement and of several fundamentalist ministers who have a large following on radio and television.

There is no doubt that many Americans identify with those people and those causes, as the repeated questions to Mr. Reagan indicate. But what is unclear is just how many do and how they translate into votes.

'Potential' Vote Power

"I expect there's a potential source of some vote power there, but I don't know that it's ever been demonstrated," said David Keene, who worked for Mr. Reagan in 1976 and is political director of George Bush's campaign this year.

Senator Paul Laxalt of Nevada, the chairman of Mr. Reagan's campaign committee and one of his closest advisers, agreed. "I hope they can turn out the votes, but I don't know," he said in an interview. "It's never been tried before."

The issues have changed since Barry Goldwater in 1964 and George C. Wallace in 1968 tried to mobilize conservative sentiment. No longer are conservatives talking about fluoridation of the water, as they did during the Goldwater race, or displaying the overt racism that was found among many Wallace supporters. This year, what the conservatives ask is a return to what they call traditional moral values.

Mr. Reagan's staff advisers say that he listens to the leaders of conservative and religious organizations but is not dominated by them. "It's a group of people that Reagan's not going to ignore, but they're certainly not going to dictate to him," said Martin Anderson, one of his principal issues advisers.

Nonetheless, some of the spokesmen for those organizations say they believe that their groups are the foundation on which the Reagan candidacy is built and that his campaign is bound to fail if he strays from their principles.

GUNS, BUTTER, AND HOSTAGES

Three issues dominated the 1980 campaign: the stagnating economy, future defense policy, and the Americans held hostage in Iran. Ronald Reagan battered Jimmy Carter for the continuing economic malaise, offering novel, yet untested solutions. Carter stood by his policies, while attacking Reagan for his defense proposals and accusing him of risking war with his aggressive stances. These issues receded as negotiations with Iran developed in late October. The negotiations ultimately lingered past election day, a final indication of Carter's failure to achieve decisive action.

OCTOBER 20, 1980
REAGAN AND CARTER EXCHANGE CHARGES ON ELECTION FEARS

President Contends Victory by Foe Could Lead to a War—Rival Assails 'Mean' Campaign

By ADAM CLYMER

Ronald Reagan and President Carter exchanged political attacks at 2,000-mile range yesterday, with Mr. Carter saying Mr. Reagan's election could lead to war and his challenger calling that charge "beneath decency."

Mr. Carter and Mr. Reagan were seeking to exploit two key developing issues in the Presidential campaign. Mr. Carter's aides have long acknowledged that the Democrats want to play on growing concerns that Mr. Reagan, the Republican nominee, could get the United States into a war, a fear noted by 35 percent of those surveyed in the last New York Times/CBS News Poll.

Meanwhile, the Reagan side says that its polls are showing a rising number of Americans concerned that Mr. Carter's campaigning is mean or nasty, and the Reagan camp is trying to make the most of the opportunity that presents.

Salvo From the President

The President began the latest exchange when he told a labor audience in Los Angeles Monday that in this election "you will determine what kind of life you and your families will have, whether this nation will make progress or go backward, and whether we have peace or war."

Mr. Reagan replied sharply yesterday in Pensacola, Fla. "I think it is inconceivable that anyone, and particularly a President of the United States, would imply," he said, "that

any person in this country would want war, and that's what he's charging and I think it's unforgivable."

Mr. Carter said yesterday in a television interview in Los Angeles that he had not meant to say Mr. Reagan was a "warmonger," but added, "in eight or 10 different instances in recent years, he has called for the use of American military force to address problems that arise diplomatically between nations."

He said Mr. Reagan had called for a blockade of Cuba and for using American forces in Lebanon and off the western coast of South America. "I don't know what he would do if he were in the Oval Office, but if you judge by his past highly rhetorical calls for the use of American military forces in these altercations, it is disturbing," the President commented.

The charge that Mr. Reagan's election would, or could, lead to war has been an element in Mr. Carter's campaign oratory since the day after the Democratic National Convention ended. On Aug. 15, the President said that one of the critical questions voters would be asking as they decided whom to vote for was: "Will my son die in war or will we continue an era of peace."

Growth of Public Concern

Then on Sept. 2, in Independence, Mo., Mr. Carter listed a series of important ways in which "Governor Reagan is different from me." The first of them was: "I believe in peace."

OCTOBER 25, 1980
POCKETBOOK ISSUES STRESSED

By HOWELL RAINES

Special to The New York Times

ARLINGTON, Va., Oct. 24—Ronald Reagan delivered a broad, harshly worded attack on President Carter's economic policies tonight in an attempt to concentrate public attention on pocketbook issues rather than on the hostage situation in Iran in the remaining 10 days of the Presidential campaign.

In a half-hour address broadcast on the ABC television network, the Republican Presidential candidate said that Mr. Carter's economic policies had failed "on a scale so vast in dimensions, so broad, with effects so devastating, that it is virtually without parallel in American history."

Mr. Reagan pledged, if elected, to provide a "humane economy" that, through tax cuts, reduced Government spending and decreased regulation of business, would result in increased prosperity for the average American.

Mr. Reagan's speech was timed to coincide with the release of the Consumer Price Index for September, which Mr. Reagan's advisers had accurately predicted would rise and raise further questions about Mr. Carter's economic policies.

There were no new proposals in Mr. Reagan's speech, but its broadcast at a cost of $150,000 to an estimated audience of 10 million to 12 million people was central to the strategy that the Reagan campaign has adopted to counter the increasing speculation that the 52 American hostages in Iran might be released before the Nov. 4 election to Mr. Carter's political benefit.

"We're not going to talk about the hostages," Lyn Nofziger, Mr. Reagan's press secretary, said today in expressing that strategy. "We're going to talk about the economy." The Reagan plan is based on the premise that feeding speculation about the hostages diverts attention from the economic figures that Mr. Reagan's advisers regard as the President's greatest political weakness.

Mr. Reagan's aides sought to take maximum advantage of today's news by hinting that the index would have gone even higher had the Carter Administration not manipulated the economic figures. But the Republican candidate himself avoided such accusations. Instead, Mr. Reagan held to the attack lines that he has used in countless stump speeches and elaborated the economic plan introduced earlier in the campaign under a new slogan—"the humane economy."

Directed at Average Voter

"What our nation needs, what the American people want, is a humane economy, one that sees them not as interchangeable parts to whom unemployment is a 'temporary inconvenience,' but as individual human beings and members of families with feelings, hopes and dreams," Mr. Reagan said, making reference to the President's recent reference to the "temporary inconveniences and transient problems" of the economy.

"Yes, the mighty music of American economic progress has been all but silenced by four years of Mr. Carter's failures," Mr. Reagan asserted. He contrasted Mr. Carter's 1976 campaign promise to bring inflation down to 4 percent a year with the rise in consumer prices since he took office.

"Mr. Carter has blamed OPEC for inflation," he added. "He's blamed the American people for inflation. He's blamed the Federal Reserve Board for inflation. The symbol of this Administration is a finger pointing at someone else."

Mr. Reagan said he would produce the "humane economy" through an eight-step program anchored by a cut in Government spending and a reduction in personal income taxes coupled with increased depreciation allowances for business.

NOVEMBER 3, 1980
CAMPAIGN TIGHTROPE

Iran's Action May Not Give President A Definite Advantage Against Reagan

News Analysis

By HEDRICK SMITH

Special to The New York Times

WASHINGTON, Nov. 2—In its anxious homestretch drive to catch up with and overtake Ronald Reagan in the Presidential race, the Carter campaign had been hoping for a breakthrough on the hostage situation in Iran. But now that Iran's move has come, it may not be the clear-cut boost the President wanted.

In advance, Democrats and Republicans alike had said that the political impact of a move by Iran would depend on the speed and terms of the hostage release, for polls showed a public wary of an unfavorable deal on election eve.

Afterward, the first assessment from Secretary of State Edmund S. Muskie was that Iran had set "harsh terms that would require negotiations," and others forecast that it would take a week or more to settle the terms.

"It's not the triumphal return of the hostages," commented one senior Reagan aide. "They're not going to get the hostages back by the election on Tuesday. It'll be too inconclusive to have a major impact on the election."

Shift in Public Attention

For White House strategists, the diplomatic moves were politically helpful because the news from Iran shifted public attention off Mr. Reagan's momentum in the wake of last Tuesday's Presidential debate and gave the President a more favorable platform to address the nation as its leader in an international crisis.

"Reagan was going to have the better of the next 48 hours because he had had the better of the last three days," said a Democrat close to the White House, "and the hostage thing has taken people's attention away from him for at least 24 hours."

But it posed a diplomatic and political dilemma for Mr. Carter that made it hard for him to achieve either the diplomatic breakthrough that has eluded him for so long or the political gains that he needs in the 11th hour of a campaign in which several national polls show him trailing Mr. Reagan by one to five percentage points.

As Mr. Muskie observed on national television, for diplomatic reasons the Carter Administration has to avoid too negative a response for fear of playing into the hands of Iranian militants and undercutting more moderate leaders working for the hostage release.

Warnings by Bush and Ford

On the other hand, while Ronald Reagan himself remained virtually silent on the question, the Republicans had primed George Bush, their Vice-Presidential nominee, and former President Gerald R. Ford to carry the warning that Mr. Carter would be in political jeopardy if he were to accept terms that the American public saw as unfavorable or humiliating.

"The sale of arms to Iran or even the delivery of arms they paid for would put us in the quagmire of the Middle East and it would be worse than the experience we had in Vietnam," Mr. Ford told a television audience.

"There are certain terms, clearly, the United States must not and cannot pay," Mr. Bush said. Like Mr. Muskie, he found piecemeal release of the hostages, one of the Iranian proposals, to be unacceptable. And he questioned how the Administration could pledge to return the assets of the late Shah of Iran when that was a matter for the courts.

The President, alert to the political liabilities of appearing either too soft or too opportunistic for electoral purposes called the Iranian move "significant" and "positive," worthy of diplomatic exploration. But he vowed not to be swayed in his decisions by the political calendar and pledged not to compromise "our national honor."

Privately, aides were saying that for Mr. Carter now, "the best politics is not to act political." They were evidently mindful of polls showing that the public is suspicious that the hostage issue may be manipulated and is opposed to American cooperation with Iran.

THE SECOND DEBATE

The second television debate vividly displayed the conflicts of the 1980 campaign. President Carter met Ronald Reagan just one week before election day, after winning a late concession to bar independent John B. Anderson from the proceedings. The debate exemplified the major candidates' strategies. Carter attacked Reagan heatedly; the Republican defended himself coolly. The president's detailed policy analyses crashed against Reagan's personable demeanor. Inconclusive, the debate still left the electorate to make a choice between two moderately acceptable candidates, but with neither representing the full hopes of the country.

OCTOBER 26, 1980
EDITORIAL
AT THE END OF THE ALLEY

The old joke still applies. Someone chases a voter down an alley, points a gun to his head and demands an answer: "Carter or Reagan?" After thinking for a moment, the voter replies, "Shoot." Since we recalled the joke during the primary season last March, it has traveled around the world and onto television, for it turns out to be not merely a joke but the story of the 1980 campaign.

To many voters, the whole year has been a succession of squirms to avoid the inevitable. Would George Bush offer a way out, after winning in Iowa? Would Howard Baker get rolling in New Hampshire, or Ted Kennedy after New York?

Would Jerry Ford run, after all? Might the Democratic convention still be "open"? Could John Anderson be transformed into an independent contender?

No. The caucuses and primaries and conventions have come and gone and so have the escape hatches. And, like much of the public, we still don't like the choice. Polls suggest that perhaps one voter in five is still saying "Shoot." But now, with only nine days left, there is no more escape, even into sardonic humor. Someone will be elected President. Responsible citizens have to choose and the harder the choice, the more they ought to try to make it.

OCTOBER 29, 1980
CARTER AND REAGAN DISPUTE VIEWS ON ARMS POLICY, ECONOMY AND IRAN IN A BROAD DEBATE BEFORE NATION

THEMES REINFORCED

President Stresses a Risk of War—Rival Offers an Image of Reason

By ADAM CLYMER

Special to The New York Times

CLEVELAND, Oct. 28—President Carter and Ronald Reagan each sought in a 90-minute debate tonight to reinforce the dominant themes of eight weeks of often desultory campaigning.

Mr. Carter hammered on the themes of arms control and the risk of war, while his challenger repeatedly denounced the President's economic record.

With one week left in a tight race for the White House, Mr. Carter appealed to the traditional elements of the Democratic constituency—blacks, Southerners, union

members and admirers of the late Hubert H. Humphrey, the defeated Democratic candidate of 1968.

Mr. Reagan sought, with equal determination, to emphasize an image of reasonableness, and to deflect Mr. Carter's continual charges that the Californian's past statements contradicted his present policy.

Contrast in Styles

Mr. Carter's focus on detail contrasted with Mr. Reagan's more relaxed, more genial manner in the only campaign confrontation between the two this fall. But there were sharp differences offered.

Mr. Carter returned again and again to the theme that nuclear policy was "the most important crucial difference in this election campaign" and said that his opponent had an "extremely dangerous and belligerent" attitude on that matter.

Mr. Reagan said that the President had allowed the country's economic position to deteriorate and suggested that voters ask themselves:

"Are you better off than you were four years ago?"

John B. Anderson, the independent candidate who was not invited to the Cleveland confrontation, attended electronically. On a cable network news show, he responded to the questions posed to his rivals, and, like them, made many of the same points that featured in his campaign speeches. He called the positions of both his opponents on taxes "irresponsible," and he said of his rivals for the Presidency, "I have become convinced there really is no significant difference between them on whether we can fight a limited nuclear war. There is no such thing as limited nuclear war."

Emotional Arguments Used

For each candidate, this debate seemed the culmination of a long, long road toward the White House. The confrontation had the potential to settle a quest that began for Mr. Reagan at least as early as 1968, and for Mr. Carter no later than 1974.

Beyond the details cited by Mr. Reagan and Mr. Carter, each used emotional argument often. Mr. Reagan asked rhetorical questions such as "Is America as respected throughout the world as it was four years ago?" and promised, as

he does repeatedly on the stump, to "take government off the backs of the great people of our country."

Mr. Carter, whose continuing focus was on war and peace, as his campaign has stressed, emphasized how a President must make "lonely decisions" and how he was sure that from what he had learned in four years "I think I'm a much wiser man."

While Mr. Reagan insisted that he was a man of peace, who knew that the "use of force is always and only a last resort," Mr. Carter assailed him for comments on many issues that implied bellicosity. "Habitually Governor Reagan has advocated the injection of military power into troubled areas," he said. Mr. Reagan's argument was that American power has weakened in Mr. Carter's term, inviting a war. Mr. Carter said it had got stronger since he replaced Republican Presidents.

On the economy, Mr. Carter said his Administration had created nine million new jobs and said that the inflation rate was now 7 percent. Mr. Reagan argued that inflation was at 12 percent, "because the government is living too well." This was an area where Mr. Carter stressed his appeal to Democrats, and blacks, arguing they had been the beneficiaries of job programs in his term. Mr. Reagan snapped back that unemployment among blacks in Detroit was now 56 percent.

Each side had a predictable, immediate reaction. Jody Powell, Mr. Carter's press secretary, said that the debate gave the voters "a better understanding of the two candidates and a better feel for the sharper differences between them."

Mr. Reagan's running mate, George Bush, said of Mr. Reagan, "He was Presidential. He stood there and he took this continued pummeling and was just great."

⚬ ⚬

ELECTION RESULTS

On November 4, 1980, Ronald Reagan vanquished Jimmy Carter to become the 40th president of the United States. Despite polls predicting a close race, Reagan dismantled the Democratic majority and assembled a new Republican coalition that would hold for the next two decades. Despite the landslide, the Republican victory provided no mandate for a revolution in government. The margin of victory was widely perceived as a sound defeat of Carter, rather than a surge towards conservatism. But Reagan moved quickly to counter this limited interpretation, using the presidency to reinvent American government.

NOVEMBER 5, 1980
REAGAN EASILY BEATS CARTER; REPUBLICANS GAIN IN CONGRESS

PRESIDENT CONCEDES

Republican Gains Victories in All Areas and Vows to Act on Economy

By HEDRICK SMITH

Ronald Wilson Reagan, riding a tide of economic discontent against Jimmy Carter and promising "to put America back to work again," was elected the nation's 40th President yesterday with a sweep of surprising victories in the East, South and the crucial battlegrounds of the Middle West.

At 69 years of age, the former California Governor became the oldest person ever elected to the White House. He built a stunning electoral landslide by taking away Mr. Carter's Southern base, smashing his expected strength in the East, and taking command of the Middle West, which both sides had designated as the main testing ground. The entire West was his, as expected.

Mr. Carter, who labored hard for a comeback re-election victory similar to that of Harry S. Truman in 1948, instead became the first elected incumbent President since Herbert Hoover in 1932 to go down to defeat at the polls.

Concession by Carter

Despite pre-election polls that had forecast a fairly close election, the rout was so pervasive and so quickly apparent that Mr. Carter made the earliest concession statement of a major Presidential candidate since 1904 when Alton B. Parker bowed to Theodore Roosevelt.

At 9:50 P.M., Mr. Carter appeared with his wife, Rosalynn, before supporters at the ballroom of the Sheraton Washington Hotel and disclosed that an hour earlier he had telephoned Mr. Reagan to concede and to pledge cooperation for the transition to new leadership.

"The people of the United States have made their choice and, of course, I accept that decision," he said. "I can't stand here tonight and say it doesn't hurt."

At a celebration in the Century Plaza Hotel in Los Angeles, Mr. Reagan claimed his victory and said: "There's never been a more humbling moment in my life. I give you my sacred oath that I will do my utmost to justify your faith."

With 73 percent of the popular vote counted, Mr. Reagan had 31,404,169 votes, or 50 percent to 26,295,331 or 42 percent, for Mr. Carter, with John B. Anderson, the independent, drawing 3,862,679 or 6 percent of the national total.

Mr. Reagan also suggested that enough Congressional candidates might ride the coattails of his broad sweep to give Republicans a chance to "have control of one house of Congress for the first time in a quarter of a century."

The Republicans picked up Senate seats in New Hampshire, Indiana, Washington, Iowa, Alabama, Florida and South Dakota and were leading in Idaho. Going into the election, the Senate had 58 Democrats, 41 Republicans and one independent. The Republicans also appeared likely to gain at least 20 seats in the House, nowhere nearly enough to dislodge the Democratic majority.

In the Presidential race, Mr. Carter managed six victories—in Georgia, Rhode Island, West Virginia, Maryland, Minnesota and the District of Columbia—for 45 electoral votes. But everywhere else the news was bad for him. By early this morning, Mr. Reagan had won 39 states with 444 electoral votes, and more were leaning his way.

In the South, the states of Texas, Florida, Mississippi, Louisiana, Virginia, South Carolina, North Carolina, Tennessee and Kentucky fell to the Reagan forces, an almost total rejection of the President by his home region. In the Middle West, the former California Governor took Ohio, Illinois and Michigan, three states on which Mr. Carter had pinned heavy hopes, as well as most others.

But Mr. Reagan's showing was even more startling in the East. He took New York and Pennsylvania, always vital bases for Democrats, as well as New Jersey, Connecticut and several smaller states.

A New York Times/CBS News poll of more than 10,000 voters as they left the polls indicated that the predominant motivation among voters was the conviction that it was time for a change. The biggest issue in their minds was the nation's economy, especially inflation.

"The Iranian thing reminded people of all their frustration," Robert S. Strauss, the Carter campaign chairman, said. "They just poured down on him. I don't think there's anything anyone could have done differently."

1980 POPULAR VOTE

STATE	TOTAL VOTE	RONALD REAGAN (REPUBLICAN) VOTES	%	JIMMY CARTER (DEMOCRAT) VOTES	%	JOHN B. ANDERSON (INDEPENDENT) VOTES	%	ED CLARK (LIBERTARIAN) VOTES	%
Alabama	1,341,929	654,192	48.8	636,730	47.4	16,481	1.2	13,318	1.0
Alaska	158,445	86,112	54.3	41,842	26.4	11,155	7.0	18,479	11.7
Arizona	873,945	529,688	60.6	246,843	28.2	76,952	8.8	18,784	2.1
Arkansas	837,582	403,164	48.1	398,041	47.5	22,468	2.7	8,970	1.1
California	8,587,063	4,524,858	52.7	3,083,661	35.9	739,833	8.6	148,434	1.7
Colorado	1,184,415	652,264	55.1	367,973	31.1	130,633	11.0	25,744	2.2
Connecticut	1,406,285	677,210	48.2	541,732	38.5	171,807	12.2	8,570	0.6
Delaware	235,900	111,252	47.2	105,754	44.8	16,288	6.9	1,974	0.8
Dist. of Col.	175,237	23,545	13.4	131,113	74.8	16,337	9.3	1,114	0.6
Florida	3,686,930	2,046,951	55.5	1,419,475	38.5	189,692	5.1	30,524	0.8
Georgia	1,596,695	654,168	41.0	890,733	55.8	36,055	2.3	15,627	1.0
Hawaii	303,287	130,112	42.9	135,879	44.8	32,021	10.6	3,269	1.1
Idaho	437,431	290,699	66.5	110,192	25.2	27,058	6.2	8,425	1.9
Illinois	4,749,721	2,358,049	49.6	1,981,413	41.7	346,754	7.3	38,939	0.8
Indiana	2,242,033	1,255,656	56.0	844,197	37.7	111,639	5.0	19,627	0.9
Iowa	1,317,661	676,026	51.3	508,672	38.6	115,633	8.8	13,123	1.0
Kansas	979,795	566,812	57.9	326,150	33.3	68,231	7.0	14,470	1.5
Kentucky	1,294,627	635,274	49.1	616,417	47.6	31,127	2.4	5,531	0.4
Louisiana	1,548,591	792,853	51.2	708,453	45.7	26,345	1.7	8,240	0.5
Maine	523,011	238,522	45.6	220,974	42.3	53,327	10.2	5,119	1.0
Maryland	1,540,496	680,606	44.2	726,161	47.1	119,537	7.8	14,192	0.9
Massachusetts[1]	2,522,890	1,057,631	41.9	1,053,802	41.7	382,539	15.2	22,038	0.9
Michigan	3,909,725	1,915,225	49.0	1,661,532	42.5	275,223	7.0	41,597	1.1
Minnesota	2,051,980	873,268	42.6	954,174	46.5	174,990	8.5	31,592	1.5
Mississippi	892,620	441,089	49.4	429,281	48.1	12,036	1.3	5,465	0.6
Missouri	2,099,824	1,074,181	51.2	931,182	44.3	77,920	3.7	14,422	0.7
Montana	363,952	206,814	56.8	118,032	32.4	29,281	8.0	9,825	2.7
Nebraska	640,854	419,937	65.5	166,851	26.0	44,993	7.0	9,073	1.4
Nevada	247,885	155,017	62.5	66,666	26.9	17,651	7.1	4,358	1.8
New Hampshire	383,990	221,705	57.7	108,864	28.4	49,693	12.9	2,064	0.5
New Jersey	2,975,684	1,546,557	52.0	1,147,364	38.6	234,632	7.9	20,652	0.7
New Mexico	456,971	250,779	54.9	167,826	36.7	29,459	6.4	4,365	1.0
New York	6,201,959	2,893,831	46.7	2,728,372	44.0	467,801	7.5	52,648	0.8
North Carolina	1,855,833	915,018	49.3	875,635	47.2	52,800	2.8	9,677	0.5
North Dakota	301,545	193,695	64.2	79,189	26.3	23,640	7.8	3,743	1.2
Ohio	4,283,603	2,206,545	51.5	1,752,414	40.9	254,472	5.9	49,033	1.1
Oklahoma	1,149,708	695,570	60.5	402,026	35.0	38,284	3.3	13,828	1.2
Oregon	1,181,516	571,044	48.3	456,890	38.7	112,389	9.5	25,838	2.2
Pennsylvania	4,561,501	2,261,872	49.6	1,937,540	42.5	292,921	6.4	33,263	0.7
Rhode Island	416,072	154,793	37.2	198,342	47.7	59,819	14.4	2,458	0.6
South Carolina	894,071	441,841	49.4	430,385	48.1	14,153	1.6	5,139	0.6
South Dakota	327,703	198,343	60.5	103,855	31.7	21,431	6.5	3,824	1.2
Tennessee	1,617,616	787,761	48.7	783,051	48.4	35,991	2.2	7,116	0.4
Texas	4,541,636	2,510,705	55.3	1,881,147	41.4	111,613	2.5	37,643	0.8
Utah	604,222	439,687	72.8	124,266	20.6	30,284	5.0	7,226	1.2
Vermont	213,299	94,628	44.4	81,952	38.4	31,761	14.9	1,900	0.9
Virginia	1,866,032	989,609	53.0	752,174	40.3	95,418	5.1	12,821	0.7
Washington	1,742,394	865,244	49.7	650,193	37.3	185,073	10.6	29,213	1.7
West Virginia	737,715	334,206	45.3	367,462	49.8	31,691	4.3	4,356	0.6
Wisconsin	2,273,221	1,088,845	47.9	981,584	43.2	160,657	7.1	29,135	1.3
Wyoming	176,713	110,700	62.6	49,427	28.0	12,072	6.8	4,514	2.6
TOTALS	**86,513,813**	**43,904,153**	**50.7**	**35,483,883**	**41.0**	**5,720,060**	**6.6**	**921,299**	**1.1**

1. Figures from Clerk of the House of Representatives, *Statistics of the Congressional and Presidential Election* (Washington, D.C.: U.S. Government Printing Office, 1980); *Massachusetts Election Statistics, 1980.*

OTHER VOTES	%	PLURALITY	
21,208	1.6	17,462	R
857	0.5	44,270	R
1,678	0.2	282,845	R
4,939	0.6	5,123	R
90,277	1.1	1,441,197	R
7,801	0.7	284,291	R
6,966	0.5	135,478	R
632	0.3	5,498	R
3,128	1.8	107,568	D
288	0.0	627,476	R
112	0.0	236,565	D
2,006	0.7	5,767	D
1,057	0.2	180,507	R
24,566	0.5	376,636	R
10,914	0.5	411,459	R
4,207	0.3	167,354	R
4,132	0.4	240,662	R
6,278	0.5	18,857	R
12,700	0.8	84,400	R
5,069	1.0	17,548	R
—	0.0	45,555	D
6,880	0.3	3,829	R
16,148	0.4	253,693	R
17,956	0.9	80,906	D
4,749	0.5	11,808	R
2,119	0.1	142,999	R
—	0.0	88,782	R
—	0.0	253,086	R
4,193	1.7	88,351	R
1,664	0.4	112,841	R
26,479	0.9	399,193	R
4,542	1.0	82,953	R
59,307	1.0	165,459	R
2,703	0.1	39,383	R
1,278	0.4	114,506	R
21,139	0.5	454,131	R
—	0.0	293,544	R
15,355	1.3	114,154	R
35,905	0.8	324,332	R
660	0.2	43,549	D
2,553	0.3	11,456	R
250	0.1	94,488	R
3,697	0.2	4,710	R
528	0.0	629,558	R
2,759	0.5	315,421	R
3,058	1.4	12,676	R
16,010	0.9	237,435	R
12,671	0.7	215,051	R
—	0.0	33,256	D
13,000	0.6	107,261	R
—	0.0	61,273	R
484,418	**0.6**	**8,420,270**	**R**

"It was really a referendum on leadership," countered Richard Wirthlin, the Reagan pollster. "The Presidential debate did not have a tremendous influence on the vote, but it strengthened Reagan's credibility for taking Carter on as sharply as we did in the last five days and drive home the attack on the economy."

The Times/CBS News survey revealed a general collapse of the traditional coalition that has elected Democratic Presidents since the New Deal. It showed Mr. Carter running behind his 1976 performance not only in the South but also among such groups as blue-collar workers, Roman Catholics and Jews.

NOVEMBER 5, 1980
THE COLLAPSE OF A COALITION

Carter Failed in Groups That Backed Him in '76

News Analysis

By ADAM CLYMER

The old Democratic coalition deserted President Carter yesterday, with defections reminiscent of the defeat of George McGovern in 1972.

Roman Catholics went against the President, he gained little better than a split among voters from union households, and his margins among Jews, liberals and low-income voters fell well below the percentages that Democrats usually get. That was the message from a New York Times/CBS News Poll of more than 10,000 voters leaving polling booths across the nation yesterday.

And Mr. Carter neither repeated the unusual strength he showed in 1976 among such predominately Republican groups as white Protestants, nor made the compensating gains he had counted on among blacks or the teachers who had turned out in force to help him win this year's Democratic nomination. In fact, teachers went for Ronald Reagan.

The poll proved the Carter campaign correct in an analysis it made early. All summer long the Carter camp had said that if it could make Mr. Reagan the issue the President could win, but that he risked defeat if he became the issue.

On Election Day, Mr. Carter was the issue. One of the most frequently cited reasons for voting—it came entirely from the Republican's supporters—was: "It's time for a change."

This referendum focused on the economy. In 1976, Mr. Carter attacked President Ford on inflation and unemployment and got three-fourths of the votes of those who felt that they were worse off financially than they had been the year before. This year, he got only a fourth of them. Democrats and independents who felt that they were worse off were particularly likely to punish Mr. Carter with their votes. Moreover, two-thirds of the voters yesterday cited economic problems such as unemployment, taxes and inflation as a key reason for their vote.

> " It needs to be emphasized, and without disrespect, that Mr. Carter lost this election even more than Mr. Reagan won it. The American people recoiled all year from having to choose either. "

NOVEMBER 5, 1980
EDITORIAL
PRESIDENT REAGAN, AND OTHER MESSAGES

Ronald Reagan deserves more than congratulations on his decisive victory. He is to be admired for persistence in his 12-year quest; for an impressive, almost always good-humored campaign; and for his skill in reuniting Republicans while tapping the discontent of Democrats and independents. We salute him and George Bush as they turn to the burdens that will quickly follow today's glory.

For more than reasons of ceremony, we extend a tribute, too, to President Carter and Walter Mondale. Their failures were undeniable but they were not failures of the spirit. They will leave a record that includes major achievements. Jimmy Carter flew the banners of human rights abroad and of equal opportunity at home. He learned to understand the world as it is. He was defeated not by a better program but by the widespread feeling that his best efforts were not good enough.

It needs to be emphasized, and without disrespect, that Mr. Carter lost this election even more than Mr. Reagan won it. The American people recoiled all year from having to choose either. And they did not lightly turn against yet another incumbent. Consider: the last man to serve out two terms in the White House was Dwight Eisenhower; no American younger than 30 can now remember an eight-year Presidency.

The President-elect would be wise to ask why a public inclined to stability voted out another leader; the explanation should shape his course. Americans voted against Mr. Carter not because he sponsored a complicated arms treaty or ambiguous Middle East peace; they turned him out because in a time of economic stress, he gave them no firm sense of direction.

And even many people who voted for the President were not so much for Mr. Carter as against Mr. Reagan. They resisted the Republican not because he promised an impossible mix of big tax cuts and higher defense budgets, but because in a complicated world, he often sounded nostalgic and naïve. The choice was all the harder because the candidates hammered only at each other's insufficiencies. Even in the great debate, they ducked the hard issues; this morning's "mandate" has little policy content.

The voters understood all too well, we think, that neither man really knows what to do about the economy, the debilitating cycles of ever higher inflation and stagnation. Yet that is the issue, above all, to which the next Administration must devote itself. Without a stable economy, there can be no significant social development or effective defense and diplomacy. And only sustained and extraordinary political leadership will produce a stable economy.

On one crucial problem after another, a whole generation of leaders has now failed the nation. Once the confetti is swept up and the bunting packed away, it is the people's resentment of those failures that should haunt the nation's new leaders over the next four years.

The Reagan Years Begin

Ronald Reagan's inauguration became one of the most storied in American history, as the new president declared, "Government isn't the solution to our problems, government is the problem!" He then immediately froze all federal hiring, carrying out a campaign promise to limit government upon assuming office. Capping the inaugural spectacle came the release of the Iranian hostages, ending the American humiliation. Although negotiated previously by the departing president, Jimmy Carter, the release immediately portrayed Reagan as an active, strong leader.

JANUARY 21, 1981
REAGAN TAKES OATH AS 40TH PRESIDENT; PROMISES AN 'ERA OF NATIONAL RENEWAL' MINUTES LATER, 52 U.S. HOSTAGES IN IRAN FLY TO FREEDOM AFTER 444-DAY ORDEAL
FREEZE SET ON HIRING
Californian Stresses Need to Restrict Government and Buoy Economy
By STEVEN R. WEISMAN

Special to The New York Times

WASHINGTON, Jan. 20—Ronald Wilson Reagan of California, promising "an era of national renewal," became the 40th President of the United States today as 52 Americans held hostage in Iran were heading toward freedom.

The hostages, whose 14 months of captivity had been a central focus of the Presidential contest last year, took off from Teheran in two Boeing 727 airplanes at 12:25 P.M. Eastern standard time, the very moment that Mr. Reagan was concluding his solemn Inaugural Address at the United States Capitol.

The new President's speech, however, made no reference at all to the long-awaited release of the hostages, emphasizing instead the need to limit the powers of the Federal Government, and to bring an end to unemployment and inflation.

'Government Is the Problem'

Promising to begin immediately to deal with "an economic affliction of great proportions," Mr. Reagan declared: "In this present crisis, government is not the solution to our problem; government is the problem." And in keeping with this statement, the President issued orders for a hiring "freeze" as his first official act.

Wearing a charcoal gray club coat, striped trousers and dove gray vest and tie, Mr. Reagan took his oath of office at 11:57 A.M. in the first inaugural ceremony ever enacted on the western front of the United States Capitol. The site was chosen to stress the symbolism of Mr. Reagan's addressing his words to the West, the region that served as his base in his three Presidential campaigns in 1968, 1976, and 1980.

Oldest to Assume Presidency

The ceremony today, filled with patriotic music, the firing of cannons and the pealing of bells, marked the transfer of the Presidency back to the Republicans after the four-year term of Jimmy Carter, a Democrat, as well as the culmination of the remarkable career of a conservative former two-term Governor of California who had started out as a baseball announcer and motion picture star.

At the age of 69, Mr. Reagan also became the oldest man to assume the Presidency, and in five months he will become the oldest man to serve in the office.

Mr. Carter, looking haggard and worn after spending two largely sleepless nights trying to resolve the hostage crisis as the final chapter of his Presidency, flew from Washington after the inaugural ceremony to Plains, Ga., his hometown. He was scheduled to fly to West Germany early tomorrow to greet the hostages personally at the invitation of the man who defeated him for re-election, Mr. Reagan.

Mr. Reagan's briskly delivered speech, lasting 20 minutes, touched on the themes that had characterized his Presidential campaign, particularly its populist invocation of the wisdom of "we, the people," and its stern warning to "the enemies of freedom, those who are potential adversaries," that the United States stood ready to act "to preserve our national security."

"Those who say that we are in a time when there are no heroes, they just don't know where to look," Mr. Reagan said, employing an almost conversational style rather than flights of rhetoric. He spoke of "professionals, industrialists, shopkeepers, clerks, cabbies and truck drivers" and of "individuals and families who pay taxes to support the Government and whose voluntary gifts support church, charity, culture, art and education."

"I have used the words 'they' and 'their' in speaking of these heroes," Mr. Reagan said. "I could say 'you' and 'your' because I am addressing the heroes of whom I speak—you, the citizens of this blessed land. Your dreams, your hopes, your goals are going to be the dreams, the hopes and the goals of this Administration, so help me God."

At another point, Mr. Reagan said: "We must act today in order to preserve tomorrow. And let there be no misunderstanding—we are going to begin to act beginning today."

The clouds that covered the sky at dawn moved south during the morning, and the winter sun broke through in the inaugural ceremony, sending the temperature to 56 degrees and making it one of the warmest inaugural days on record.

With his hand on a family Bible once used by his mother and held by his wife, Nancy, Mr. Reagan repeated the oath of office administered by Warren Earl Burger, Chief Justice of the United States. He said:

"I, Ronald Wilson Reagan, do solemnly swear that I will faithfully execute the office of the President of the United States, and will to the best of my ability, preserve, protect and defend the Constitution of the United States, so help me God."

THE PRESIDENTIAL ELECTION OF 1992

CLINTON WINS THE WHITE HOUSE IN A THREE-CANDIDATE RACE

As election year 1992 opened, President George H. W. Bush accurately reported, "In the past 12 months, the world has known changes of almost biblical proportions." And, he boasted, "Communism died this year. . . . The biggest thing that has happened in the world in my life, in our lives, is this: By the grace of God, America won the Cold War."

The president's rhetorical crowing might be excused by the truth of his claim. In fact, America's contest of nearly half a century with the Soviet Union had ended, leaving the United States the dominant military and political power of the world. The infamous Berlin Wall had fallen, the satellite countries of Eastern Europe had been freed, and the Soviet Union itself had disappeared, split into separate independent states.

In the same year, the United States had beaten another, if less formidable foe, the Iraqi regime of Saddam Hussein. In early 1991 Bush had reversed Iraq's invasion of oil-rich Kuwait, its neighbor in the Persian Gulf. Firmly declaring "this aggression will not stand," the president had organized a worldwide coalition that overwhelmed the invaders in the four-day military triumph of "Operation Desert Storm." Bush's popularity soared to the highest level ever recorded, achieving almost 90 percent approval in opinion polls.

Surely, this record would lead to the reelection of the triumphant president. Many potential Democratic candidates drew that lesson from Bush's combined victories over Iraq and communism and decided not to run. Ironically, the effect of the president's mastery in international affairs removed his advantage on issues of foreign policy from the election agenda. Without threats from its long-term Soviet adversary and with the military sway evident in the Gulf War, Americans could turn their attention to domestic concerns.

And here the news was not favorable to the incumbent Republican president. The overall economy had stagnated during the Bush administration, average incomes had dropped, and taxes had increased. By the time of the election, unemployment had grown to almost 8 percent, leading four-fifths

Source: AP Images

On October 16, 1992, the second of Ross Perot's thirty-minute commercials aired. The program, "Solutions: Balancing the Budget, Reforming Government," was part of the billionaire third-party candidate's attention-getting campaign which, for a time, posed a serious threat in the competition for votes.

of the electorate to evaluate national conditions as "not so good" or "poor." Within eight months of the Gulf War, Bush's approval rating had dropped to a bare majority. Approval of his economic policies, never high, was even worse, a calamitous 25 percent one year before the election. His eventual Democratic opponent, Arkansas governor Bill Clinton, managed to shift the focus to his own campaign slogan, "It's the economy, stupid."

Both major party candidates had to face an additional uncertainty—the independent candidacy of H. Ross Perot of Texas, a self-made billionaire. With imaginative populist attacks on government institutions and the loss of jobs to foreign nations, Perot became the wild card in the election. His likely vote varied greatly over the course of the campaign—he even led in national polls at one point—making the race both more entertaining and less predictable. The eventual distribution of his support could tip the balance toward either Bush or Clinton or throw the decision to the House of Representatives.

1992 ELECTORAL VOTE

STATE	ELECTORAL VOTES	CLINTON	BUSH	STATE	ELECTORAL VOTES	CLINTON	BUSH
Alabama	(9)	–	9	Montana	(3)	3	–
Alaska	(3)	–	3	Nebraska	(5)	–	5
Arizona	(8)	–	8	Nevada	(4)	4	–
Arkansas	(6)	6	–	New Hampshire	(4)	4	–
California	(54)	54	–	New Jersey	(15)	15	–
Colorado	(8)	8	–	New Mexico	(5)	5	–
Connecticut	(8)	8	–	New York	(33)	33	–
Delaware	(3)	3	–	North Carolina	(14)	–	14
District of Columbia	(3)	3	–	North Dakota	(3)	–	3
Florida	(25)	–	25	Ohio	(21)	21	–
Georgia	(13)	13	–	Oklahoma	(8)	–	8
Hawaii	(4)	4	–	Oregon	(7)	7	–
Idaho	(4)	–	4	Pennsylvania	(23)	23	–
Illinois	(22)	22	–	Rhode Island	(4)	4	–
Indiana	(12)	–	12	South Carolina	(8)	–	8
Iowa	(7)	7	–	South Dakota	(3)	–	3
Kansas	(6)	–	6	Tennessee	(11)	11	–
Kentucky	(8)	8	–	Texas	(32)	–	32
Louisiana	(9)	9	–	Utah	(5)	–	5
Maine	(4)	4	–	Vermont	(3)	3	–
Maryland	(10)	10	–	Virginia	(13)	–	13
Massachusetts	(12)	12	–	Washington	(11)	11	–
Michigan	(18)	18	–	West Virginia	(5)	5	–
Minnesota	(10)	10	–	Wisconsin	(11)	11	–
Mississippi	(7)	–	7	Wyoming	(3)	–	3
Missouri	(11)	11	–				
				TOTALS	(538)	370	168

THE PARTIES AND THE CANDIDATES

Neither Bush nor Clinton had a clear path to his party's presidential nomination. Neither achieved strong personal popularity. But both won the early state contests, gaining the critical momentum that "reforms" in the nominating process encouraged. Both then achieved ritualistic coronations at their party conventions. Perot followed a different and meandering course, essentially crowning himself as the leader of a national insurgency.

In the Democratic Party, the most prominent leaders, such as New York governor Mario Cuomo and New Jersey senator Bill Bradley, chose to stay out of the race, overawed by Bush's successes and transient popularity. Those who did enter were more intrepid but less imposing—including Sen. Paul Tsongas of Massachusetts, Sen. Tom Harkin of Iowa, and former California governor Jerry Brown, who was running for the third time.

Among the diminished band of aspirants, Arkansas governor Bill Clinton gained the most notice. In six terms of two years each, Clinton had developed a record of economic development, school improvement, and racial harmony. He had become the chair of the Democratic Leadership Council, a group of prominent moderates, many from the South.

They hoped that centrist economic programs would end the Republican presidential dominance, which had given their opponents victories in five of the last six elections. Running as a "new Democrat," Clinton took an early lead in opinion polls and financial contributions.

The first contest, as usual, was in New Hampshire. There, Clinton's status as front-runner met obstacles raised by questions about his personal character. Clinton countered reports of marital infidelity—based on news stories of a twelve-year affair with a cocktail waitress—with a confessional televised interview immediately after the Super Bowl, in tandem with his wife, Hillary Rodham Clinton. Then, only a week before the primary vote, came accusations that he had used dubious tactics to avoid the Vietnam draft. The governor offered various explanations to defend his actions, again using a televised interview, this time alone.

In the New Hampshire vote, Tsongas came in first, with 33 percent, and Clinton gained close to 25 percent. Yet Clinton was exultant about his second-place finish and convinced the media that he deserved his self-designation, "the Comeback Kid." Clinton's claim set the stage for the following weeks' primaries, conducted largely in the South, where he won all seven contested states. Four weeks after New Hampshire, victories over Tsongas in Illinois and Brown in Michigan assured his nomination. Clinton ended the primaries with 52 percent of the total 20 million votes cast (a significant drop from 1988), with strength evident among the traditional party groups, the white working class and African Americans.

The Democratic convention, held in New York in mid-July, was programmed as a rally for the fall campaign. Clinton was formally nominated by a roll call vote by 3,372 of the 4,288 total delegates. Sen. Albert Gore Jr. of Tennessee was selected for vice president to exemplify the party's appeal to youth and its renewed attention to the South. Women were featured in what the party hoped would be the "Year of the Woman." The platform took a moderate economic stance, with less stress than in the past on government welfare programs. In his acceptance speech, Clinton pointed the way to a recapture of "Reagan Democrats" with an appeal to "those who do the work, pay the taxes, raise the kids and play by the rules . . . the hard-working Americans who make up our forgotten middle class."

Republicans, contrary to tradition, experienced a contest against their incumbent president. Running as the heir of Ronald Reagan, Bush had won the hearts of party activists in 1988 with a tough stand on taxes, vowing: "Congress will push me to raise taxes, and I'll say no, and they'll push, and I'll say no, and they'll push again, and I'll say, to them, 'Read my lips: no new taxes.' " But, in fact, faced with a rising federal budget deficit, he did strike a deal with Congress in 1990 to raise taxes by $150 billion.

That decision, combined with the poor economic conditions, caused unease in the party. Patrick Buchanan, an articulate journalist, tried to harness the discontent by entering the Republican primaries. He astonished the press by gaining 37 percent of the vote in New Hampshire, to Bush's 53 percent. Despite that setback, Bush was clearly in control, eventually winning all of the thirty-eight state primaries and accumulating nearly three-fourths of the 12.7 million votes. At the formal convention in Houston in mid-August, he received the votes of all but 18 of the 2,200 delegates. Vice President Dan Quayle, a frequent target of ridicule, was renominated without a roll call.

Looking to the campaign, Bush worried most about the possible defection of conservatives, their concerns already voiced by Buchanan. To rally their support, the platform adamantly took rightist views on "family values"—defined as "faith in God, hard work, service to others and limited government." More specifically, the party platform promoted a constitutional amendment to bar abortion and opposed gay marriage and child adoption; it favored prayer in the schools, parental choice of private schools, and gun ownership. In a further effort to mollify conservative dissidents, Buchanan was given a prime speaking spot to define the election as a "cultural war" against "the agenda Clinton & Clinton would impose on America—abortion on demand, a litmus test for the Supreme Court, homosexual rights, discrimination against religious schools, women in combat—that's change, all right. But it is not the kind of change America wants."

In his acceptance speech, Bush made his own appeal. He apologized for the tax increase he had supported two years earlier, promising never to repeat his error, extolled his foreign policy record, and blamed the Democratic Congress for the nation's ills. He then reinforced the Republican's attempted moralistic appeals:

> Sure, we must change, but some values are timeless. I believe in families that stick together, fathers who stick around. I happen to believe very deeply in the worth of each individual human being, born or unborn. I believe in teaching our kids the difference between what's wrong and what's right, teaching them respect for hard work and to love their neighbors. I believe that America will always have a special place in God's heart, as long as He has a special place in ours.

And then there was Ross Perot, sometimes a candidate and sometimes not. In February, interviewed on television by Larry King, the Texas billionaire had first declined interest in the presidency, then said he would run if supporters could place his name on the ballot in all fifty states. As that effort proceeded, with Perot high in opinion polls, he created a professional campaign organization for his movement, United We Stand America. But as he drew more attention, Perot also drew more criticism, falling rapidly in public estimation.

Then, on the last day of the Democratic convention, Perot suddenly withdrew, finding Clinton an acceptable advocate of change in national policy, while also complaining about alleged Republican smears of his family. Six weeks later, he was back, but without benefit of any party convention or nomination. As his running mate, he selected James Stockdale, a retired Navy admiral who had gained attention by surviving as a prisoner of war in Vietnam. The gyrations of the Perot candidacy provided the background music for the cacophony of the election campaign.

THE CAMPAIGN

The campaign was odd. Beginning as a two-man race, it became a three-way contest on the first of October, when Perot returned. In contrast to electoral tradition, all of the three candidates came from states of the former Confederacy, the only such contest in American history. The regional lineup testified to the rising influence of the South, with its 147 competitive electoral votes.

The major party candidates developed consistent themes. On the positive side, Bush presented his foreign policy successes and attempted to show his concern over the economic slide, buoyed by late encouraging indicators of revival. Clinton presented himself as a different kind of Democrat. He pledged a middle class tax cut and "an end to welfare as we know it," and he endorsed the death penalty and gun ownership. To show his independence from militant blacks, he used an appearance at the NAACP Convention to denounce the anti-white language of Sister Souljah, a provocative rap singer.

But more negative than positive, the campaigns were rife with criticisms of the principal candidates. Clinton concentrated on Bush's economic policies. Particularly effective were television ads that contrasted Bush's previous optimism with current conditions. In one ad, a Bush quote, "I'm not prepared to say we are in recession," was followed by a statistic, the "March 1992 jobless rate hits a six-year high." Another recalled Bush's 1988 promise, "You will be better off four years from now than you are today," and then rhetorically asked, "Well, it's four years later. How're you doing?" That negative

portrait of Bush as distant from the economic realities facing average Americans was underscored by reports of a Bush visit to a supermarket, where he seemed astonished at the use of barcodes at the checkout counter.

For their part, Republicans found much to criticize about Clinton. They sought to raise doubts about his personal character, as exemplified by his avoidance of the draft and his changing explanations of his behavior during the Vietnam War—in contrast to Bush's heroism as a World War II pilot. Clinton's integrity was also questioned in a clever ad showing two candidates, with their faces obscured, taking opposite positions on a series of issues. At the end, the faces were revealed by the narrator, "One of these candidates is Bill Clinton. Unfortunately, so is the other"—as Clinton futilely pleaded, "There is a simple explanation for why this happened."

Going beyond the commercials, Bush and Clinton developed new campaign techniques. Through the use of cell phones, 1-800 phone numbers, and computers, the campaigns were able to run integrated national campaigns. With news reports giving little time to their speeches, the candidates opted for longer interviews on talk shows, the fluffy morning news programs, satellite connections to local stations, comedy shows, and the growing medium of cable television. They also turned to nonpolitical outlets, such as the youth-oriented MTV, most ostentatiously when Clinton came to a late night program, playing the saxophone while wearing "shades."

For all their efforts, the Republican and Democratic campaigns had little impact on voter preferences for most of the fall. Once the conventions were over, Clinton held a persistent lead of close to 10 percent in surveys. Clinton was regarded marginally more favorably than critically, and Bush the opposite, but little changed. That stability was reflected in finances. The major candidates had close to equal money for their efforts—$55 million each in federal funds, which were at least doubled by party contributions and expenditures.

This inertia disappeared when Perot came back. Although Perot had been officially out of the race since July, his organization had continued its efforts, gaining him a spot on all fifty state ballots. Both Bush and Clinton had sought his support, sending representatives to plead their cases. Ultimately, Perot rejected both camps, explaining, "I thought both political parties would address the problems that face the nation. We gave them a chance. They didn't do it."

Perot brought innovation in techniques and uncertainty about the results. Spending $62 million of his own money, he went beyond the customary spot ads to present a series of 30-minute "infomercials," in which he provided tutorials on the national economy. Using detailed charts and a straightforward presentation, he argued that increasing budget deficits threatened to destroy the United States. Instead, he urged, "If you want a candidate who comes from the people, rather than at the people, let your vote say so. If you want to reduce our four trillion dollar national debt, let your vote say so. Look at the issues. Look at the facts. Look at all three candidates and then—Vote Your Conscience."

Televised debates were now an institutionalized part of the presidential campaign, arranged by the unofficial Commission on Presidential Debates. But the Bush campaign was wary and delayed its acceptance of the challenge. The debates were finally scheduled for an intense eight-day period in mid-October, including the Perot ticket, under varying formats for three presidential and one vice-presidential meeting.

The debates demonstrated the candidates' strengths and weaknesses to 100 million viewers. Bush emphasized his experience in the presidency, but appeared to lack the common touch. Clinton empathized with voters' economic concerns, but had been inconsistent on many issues. Perot presented himself as a plain-spoken citizen and businessman, but seemed quirky and blunt. The television audience agreed that Bush did the worst in these performances, with Clinton and Perot splitting the winners' honors.

As the election neared, Clinton still held a significant, if diminishing, lead in surveys, and Bush hoped that voters' last-minute qualms about Clinton would keep Republicans in power. Perot had clearly benefited most from the debates; his favorable ratings increased markedly, his prospective vote rose sharply to nearly 20 percent, and he became the choice of those voters who gave priority to the issue of the national budget deficit. The uncertainties of a three-man race would be resolved only when voters finally cast their ballots.

The Election Results

With voters showing unprecedented interest in the campaign and atypical satisfaction with the choice of candidates, turnout rose considerably, to 104.4 million, the highest in any American election to that date. More than a tenth of the ballots were cast by first-time voters, both young and old. The total vote increased 14 percent over the 1988 tally, reaching the highest level of participation since the close 1960 contest between John Kennedy and Richard Nixon.

Bill Clinton won the presidency, carrying a 43.0 percent plurality of the popular vote, garnering a margin of nearly 6 million votes over Bush's 37.4 percent. The president's support declined markedly from his first election, a loss of nearly 10 million popular votes and sixteen percentage points. His fall was almost as bad as Herbert Hoover's in the midst of

the Great Depression and far worse than the 1840 decline of Martin Van Buren, the last incumbent vice president to be elected directly to the White House. Perot amassed nearly 19 percent of the total vote, the largest of any third-party candidate in the eighty years since Theodore Roosevelt ran in 1912.

Clinton carried 32 states and swept Bush in the Electoral College, 370–168; Perot was shut out. With a ticket of two native sons, the Democrats were again able to crack the South, winning four states, while carrying all but one northern state from the Atlantic Ocean to the west bank of the Mississippi River, as well as those on the Pacific coast.

Although impressive geographically, the Democrat's victory was less substantial than it appeared on the map. Clinton actually won a lower percentage of the popular vote than Michael Dukakis did in 1988. He gained an absolute majority of the vote only in his home state of Arkansas, in contrast to ten for Dukakis (both carried the District of Columbia). The regional bases of the two candidates were similar, the votes typically showing a shift of less than 7 percent toward the Democrats across most states. With a large vote for Perot, that shift created an inflated landslide in electoral votes. But the party victory was shallow. In the congressional elections, Democrats actually lost 9 seats in the House and gained only 1 in the Senate, leaving the party with majorities of 258 to 176 and 57 to 43.

For the longer term, the 1992 election showed no significant shifts in either party's electoral coalitions. Republicans had achieved virtual parity with the Democrats in the Reagan years, and they remained more loyal to their party in 1992 than Democrats did. Clinton gained votes for the Democrats consistently among most demographic groups, and his moderate stance produced notable gains among new voters and previous defectors such as independents, men, southern whites, and born-again Christians.

Ross Perot, for all the sound and fury of his interrupted campaigns, had little impact. Although his large vote denied Clinton absolute majorities in the nation and individual states, it did not actually decide the outcome. Postelection polls showed that the Perot voters, if confined to a choice between Bush and Clinton, would have abstained or split their votes evenly. Rather than an upheaval in the political landscape, Perot created only a passing tremor. Disdaining political parties, Perot proved unable or unwilling to transform his fleeting faction into a true movement. Running again in 1996 under the banner of the futile Reform Party, he won only 8 percent of the vote, then disappeared from politics.

Clinton had won the presidency less on his own merits than on discontent with the incumbent and national economic conditions. His election authorized no specific policy directions; it was a mandate only to be different from George Bush. As he took the oath of office in January, Clinton foresaw "a spring reborn in the world's oldest democracy that brings forth the vision and courage to reinvent America." But warmer weather brought a mixed harvest.

Clinton eventually presided over an exuberant economy that resulted in a sharp drop in poverty and the largest increase in job creation in American history. His tax program provided relief for low-income workers and marginally increased rates for the wealthy. He advanced the causes of women, racial minorities, and gays. Abroad, the United States maintained its dominance, and NATO expanded into the former Soviet satellite nations of Eastern Europe.

But he suffered failures in his efforts to revive the activist government typical of Democrats. A comprehensive program of universal health care, developed by Hillary Clinton, never came to a vote in Congress, and an energy program to reduce oil consumption failed. Although Clinton's presidency interrupted the Reagan transformation, many of his successes resembled Republican programs, including NAFTA, the North American Free Trade Agreement; a federal budget surplus after program cuts; deregulation of banks; expansion of the death penalty; and severe restrictions on welfare programs. Clinton easily won reelection in 1996, but his impact on the course of American politics remained ambiguous and debatable for many years.

- -

A NEW WORLD

The 1992 election followed four years of incredible change in world affairs. After fifty years of cold war, the American and Soviet superpowers ended their epic struggle. First, an infamous symbol of the Soviet empire crumbled when the wall dividing East Berlin from West Berlin was torn down. Two years later, the United States galvanized world support behind the liberation of Kuwait from Iraqi invasion and led the forces that achieved a stunning and rapid military victory. Then, just eleven months before the 1992 election, the Soviet Union itself collapsed, leaving the United States as the sole superpower in the world.

NOVEMBER 10, 1989
EAST GERMANY OPENS FRONTIER TO THE WEST FOR MIGRATION OR TRAVEL; THOUSANDS CROSS

A JUBILANT HORDE

Berlin Wall Is Rushed by Easterners as Travel Limits Are Lifted

By SERGE SCHMEMANN

Special to The New York Times

EAST BERLIN, Friday, Nov. 10—East Germany on Thursday lifted restrictions on emigration or travel to the West, and within hours tens of thousands of East and West Berliners swarmed across the infamous Berlin Wall for a boisterous celebration.

Border guards at Bornholmer Strasse crossing, Checkpoint Charlie and several other crossings abandoned all efforts to check credentials, even though the new regulations said East Germans would still need passports and permission to get across. Some guards smiled and took snapshots, assuring passers-by that they were just recording a historic event.

The extraordinary breach of what had been the most infamous stretch of the Iron Curtain marked the culmination of an extraordinary month that has seen the virtual transformation of East Germany under the dual pressures of unceasing flight and continuing demonstrations. It also marked a breach of a wall that had become the premier symbol of Stalinist oppression and of the divisions of Europe and Germany into hostile camps after World War II.

An Effort to Stem a Tide

The immediate reason for the decision was evidently a recognition by East Germany's embattled authorities that they could not stem the outward tide by opening the door a crack and hoping that rapid liberalization at home would end the urge to flee. They now seemed to hope that an open door would quickly let out those who were determined to leave, and give pause to those who had doubted the sincerity of the Government's pledge of profound change.

FEBRUARY 28, 1991
BUSH HALTS OFFENSIVE COMBAT; KUWAIT FREED, IRAQIS CRUSHED

MILITARY AIMS MET

Firing Ending After 100 Hours of Ground War, President Declares

By ANDREW ROSENTHAL

Special to The New York Times

WASHINGTON, Thursday, Feb. 28—Declaring that "Kuwait is liberated" and Iraq's army defeated, President Bush ordered allied forces on Wednesday night to suspend offensive military operations against President Saddam Hussein's isolated and battered army.

Mr. Bush said the suspension, which began at midnight Eastern time, would continue as long as Iraq did not attack allied forces or launch missile attacks on any other country. In an address from the Oval Office that was televised around the world at 9 P.M. Eastern time, he called on Mr. Hussein to send his commanders to meet with allied officers in the war zone within 48 hours to settle the military terms of a permanent cease-fire.

For such a cease-fire to be approved, he said, Iraq must comply with all 12 United Nations resolutions concerning Kuwait, including measures calling for Iraq to void its annexation of the territory and agree in principle to pay reparations to Kuwait and other countries. Iraq must also free all prisoners of war and detained Kuwaiti citizens, and give the allies the location of all land and sea mines that Iraq had laid in the region, Mr. Bush said.

No Official Word From Iraq

Administration officials said they had received no authoritative response from the Iraqi Government. At the United Nations, Soviet diplomats said Iraq had submitted a letter signaling its willingness to comply with all 12 resolutions adopted by the Security Council. But the letter did not say whether Baghdad was willing to comply with the rest of Mr. Bush's demands, including the freeing of Kuwaiti civilians seized in recent days.

Pentagon officials said this morning there were no reports of renewed Iraqi attacks on allied positions.

Speaking in a solemn voice, President Bush said: "This war is now behind us. Ahead of us is the difficult task of securing a potentially historic peace."

He seemed to invite the citizens of Iraq to overthrow the man who had defied the assembled military and political power of the international alliance. "Coalition forces fought this war only as a last resort," Mr. Bush said, "and I look forward to the day when Iraq is led by people prepared to live in peace with their neighbors."

DECEMBER 26, 1991
GORBACHEV, LAST SOVIET LEADER, RESIGNS; U.S. RECOGNIZES REPUBLICS' INDEPENDENCE

Communist Flag is Removed; Yeltsin Gets Nuclear Controls

By FRANCIS X. CLINES

Special to the New York Times

MOSCOW, Dec. 25—Mikhail S. Gorbachev, the trailblazer of the Soviet Union's retreat from the cold war and the spark for the democratic reforms that ended 70 years of Communist tyranny, told a weary, anxious nation tonight that he was resigning as President and closing out the union.

"I hereby discontinue my activities at the post of President of the Union of Soviet Socialist Republics," declared the 60-year-old politician, the last leader of a totalitarian empire that was undone across the six years and nine months of his stewardship.

Mr. Gorbachev made no attempt in his brief, leanly worded television address to mask his bitter regret and concern at being forced from office by the creation of the new Commonwealth of Independent States, composed of 11 former republics of the collapsed Soviet empire under the informal lead of President Boris N. Yeltsin of Russia.

'A New World'

Within hours of Mr. Gorbachev's resignation, Western and other nations began recognition of Russia and the other former republics.

"We're now living in a new world," Mr. Gorbachev declared in recognizing the rich history of his tenure. "An end has been put to the cold war and to the arms race, as well as to the mad militarization of the country, which has crippled our economy, public attitudes and morals. The threat of nuclear war has been removed."

Mr. Gorbachev's moment of farewell was stark. Kremlin guards were preparing to lower the red union flag for the last time. In minutes, Mr. Gorbachev would sign over the nuclear missile launching codes for safeguarding to Mr. Yeltsin, his rival and successor as the dominant politician of this agonized land.

• •

The Contenders

Despite the emergence of the United States as the world's only superpower, the national mood was anything but confident as the 1992 presidential campaign got under way. The domestic economy sputtered, driving more people into unemployment, lowering retail spending, and limiting the wages of those still at work. In this troubled atmosphere, President George H. W. Bush faced an unusually strong reelection challenge for an incumbent, fending off conservative Republican Patrick Buchanan in the primaries. On the Democratic side, Arkansas governor William Jefferson Clinton campaigned for the nomination against Sen. Paul Tsongas and a host of other competitors. The early races provided challenges to Bush and Clinton, but Super Tuesday propelled them into the lead and their eventual nominations, in what was for both parties a dour race.

FEBRUARY 19, 1992
BUSH JARRED IN FIRST PRIMARY; TSONGAS WINS DEMOCRATIC VOTE
BUCHANAN AT 40%
Clinton Finishes Strong, Taking 2d and Poised for Drive in South
By ROBIN TONER
Special to The New York Times

BEDFORD, N.H., Feb. 18—President Bush received a jarring political message in the New Hampshire primary today, scoring a less-than-impressive victory over Patrick J. Buchanan, the conservative commentator.

With 99 percent of the precincts reporting, Mr. Bush had 58 percent of the vote and Mr. Buchanan 40 percent.

On the Democratic side, also with 99 percent of the vote counted, former Senator Paul E. Tsongas of Massachusetts was the winner with 35 percent. Gov. Bill Clinton of Arkansas was comfortably in second place at 26 percent and in a position to take his resilient candidacy on to the string of primaries in his native South.

The Democratic results left the race for the nomination unsettled, and seemed likely to fuel talk of another candidate's entering the race. The Bush-Buchanan battle also brought Mr. Clinton some relief by taking him out of the glare of the political spotlight, where he has been trapped for the last two weeks in the debate over his draft status during the Vietnam War.

Clinton Looks Ahead

Reflecting Democratic glee over the President's showing, Governor Clinton said, "In November, we will win a great victory against Pat Buchanan."

Mr. Bush, in a statement tonight, said his opponents in both parties had "reaped the harvest of discontent with the pace of New Hampshire's economy" and added, "I understand the message of dissatisfaction."

The signal to Mr. Bush was unmistakable. Even though Mr. Buchanan's support represented more than 63,000 actual votes, it amounted to a roar of anger from those who voted in the Republican primary, and it showed the power of a "send a message" campaign against him in times of economic distress.

Mr. Bush now faces a galvanized Buchanan campaign in one state after another, with the battle to be joined on March 3, when the Buchanan forces hope to make another stand in Georgia. Down the road, Mr. Bush will confront a Democratic Party that has now been given a road map of his vulnerabilities.

MARCH 11, 1992
CLINTON TAKES FLORIDA EASILY, SWEEPING PRIMARIES IN SOUTH; PROTEST VOTES STILL DOG BUSH
TSONGAS SET BACK
Former Senator Salvages Victories in the North, Capturing 3 States
By ROBIN TONER
Special to The New York Times

MIAMI, March 10—Gov. Bill Clinton of Arkansas dominated former Senator Paul E. Tsongas today in the biggest test so far of the primary season, winning a string of victories in his native South, including a decisive triumph in Florida.

The Super Tuesday primaries and caucuses, held in 11 states, gave Mr. Clinton a powerful lift in his drive for the Democratic Presidential nomination as the race moves on to the March 17 contests in Illinois and Michigan. For Mr. Tsongas, those contests now become critical as he seeks to repair the damage caused by his heavy losses across the South, most tellingly in Florida, the one Southern state where he had hoped to hold the line.

In Florida, with more than 95 percent of the votes counted, Mr. Clinton had 52 percent to 34 percent for Mr. Tsongas. In Texas, with more than 90 percent counted, Mr. Clinton had 66 percent to 19 percent for Mr. Tsongas.

Warning for a President

On the Republican side, President Bush won commandingly across the region, with about two-thirds or more of the vote everywhere. But the President was once again given a warning for the November election, that even in Bush strongholds like Texas and Florida, a sizable minority of Republican voters would vote against him. Patrick J. Buchanan, the conservative commentator, won a third of the vote in Florida, a little less than a quarter in Texas and had similar backing in most other states.

Projected results tonight showed that Mr. Clinton was reaching the one-third mark in the race for the Democratic nomination, with more than 670 delegates, including the Democratic National Committee members, governors and former elected officials, or super delegates, who have declared their support for him. He needs 2,145 delegates to win the nomination.

Uncommitted Delegates

Mr. Tsongas follows with at least 340 delegates, but there are more delegates, some 350 in all, who are not committed to any Democratic candidate, including those who were selected previously for Senators Tom Harkin of Iowa and Bob Kerrey of Nebraska, who have both dropped out of the race.

For the President, as expected, Super Tuesday produced an enormous crop of delegates, at least 360, bringing his total to at least 566. He needs 1,105 to be nominated. Mr. Buchanan added only about 25 delegates to his total, now about 45 delegates.

EARLY, PERSISTENT ATTACKS

The negativity and scandals of the 1992 campaign began early, even before the parties made their nominations. Governor Clinton came under immediate scrutiny for a variety of scandals, including alleged marital infidelities and charges that he had dodged the Vietnam draft. President Bush was attacked for being out of touch with average Americans, particularly after *The New York Times* published an article depicting the president's supposed amazement at the checkout scanners used at supermarkets. Other news outlets later contested the depiction, but *The Times* supported its published account. By mid-February the 1992 campaign had already adopted a negative tone, to the dismay of voters, journalists, and candidates alike.

JANUARY 28, 1992
EDITORIAL
LEERS, SMEARS AND GOVERNOR CLINTON

At times, voters can legitimately ask about a political candidate's financial, sexual or other personal conduct; it can bear on one's capacity for public service. At other times any such inquiry amounts to no more than leers, smears or smug moralizing.

So far at least, Gov. Bill Clinton of Arkansas and his wife have found a reasonable place to draw a line between the two, responding to the first curiosity while resisting the second. In a televised interview Sunday night, Mr. Clinton, an early front-runner for the Democratic Presidential nomination, responded to stories, some of which have burdened his long years in office, alleging extramarital affairs.

He and his wife, Hillary, acknowledge they have had problems but say they are now together, committed—and determined to limit further discussion of their private lives. They make a plausible case; there can be some preserve of privacy, even for politicians.

Ordinarily the public does not need to endure accounts of public officials' peccadilloes, but sometimes indiscretions disclose more than gossip. For a public servant to flaunt behavior many voters abhor—by no means established in the Clinton case—could imply a recklessness and audacity that deserves to be weighed at the ballot box. That's why responsible news organizations as well as scandal sheets have inquired into rumors in Arkansas.

For lack of satisfactory evidence, most journalists declined to publish stories about Mr. Clinton's personal life. Then Gennifer Flowers, a former state employee, paid by a supermarket tabloid, contended she had a longstanding affair with the Governor. She rehearsed the accusations yesterday on television.

In his response Sunday, Governor Clinton "acknowledged wrongdoing. I have acknowledged causing pain in my marriage." He won't provide detail and he need not, unless it develops that his private conduct arguably touches his public performance or fitness for office.

"Anybody who's listening gets the drift of it," he said, "and let's get on and get back to the real problems of this country." To which Hillary Clinton added sensibly, "If that's not enough for people, then heck, don't vote for him."

Mr. Clinton describes Gennifer Flowers as no more than a friendly acquaintance. Because the tape recordings she so far proffers don't appear to refute that characterization, there seems to be little basis for demanding further comment from the Clintons.

Nor do other candidates have to open themselves to questions like "Have you ever had an affair?" merely because they offer themselves for public service. There's a line, albeit rough and constantly redefining itself, between idle curiosity and responsible attention. The Clintons appear to have found it.

FEBRUARY 5, 1992
BUSH ENCOUNTERS THE SUPERMARKET, AMAZED

By ANDREW ROSENTHAL

Special to The New York Times

ORLANDO, Fla., Feb. 4—As President Bush travels the country in search of re-election, he seems unable to escape a central problem: This career politician, who has lived the cloistered life of a top Washington bureaucrat for decades, is having trouble presenting himself to the electorate as a man in touch with middle-class life.

Today, for instance, he emerged from 11 years in Washington's choicest executive mansions to confront the modern supermarket.

Visiting the exhibition hall of the National Grocers Association convention here, Mr. Bush lingered at the mock-up of a checkout lane. He signed his name on an electronic pad used to detect check forgeries.

"If some guy came in and spelled George Bush differently, could you catch it?" the President asked. "Yes," he was told, and he shook his head in wonder.

Then he grabbed a quart of milk, a light bulb and a bag of candy and ran them over an electronic scanner. The look of wonder flickered across his face again as he saw the item and price registered on the cash register screen.

"This is for checking out?" asked Mr. Bush. "I just took a tour through the exhibits here," he told the grocers later. "Amazed by some of the technology."

Marlin Fitzwater, the White House spokesman, assured reporters that he had seen the President in a grocery store. A year or so ago. In Kennebunkport.

Some grocery stores began using electronic scanners as early as 1976, and the devices have been in general use in American supermarkets for a decade.

FEBRUARY 17, 1992
GODZILLA VS. KING KONG

LESLIE H. GELB

Croatians, Outer Mongolians and British soccer fans need look no further than campaign '92 in the United States as they struggle to master the techniques of democracy.

Democratic Consultant: Let's get away from the smears and back to issues confronting the middle class.

Republican Consultant: Right, Clinton roomed with the Vietcong when he was at Oxford.

Press to Governor Clinton: There are reports that you roomed with the Vietcong at Oxford when you were dodging the draft.

Mr. Clinton: Those are lousy anti-middle class lies. I may have talked with a VC or been friendly with one or two. But I never slept with one. I mean, how dumb do you think the American people are?

Headline: Clinton Denies Sleeping With Vietcong.

●

Democrat: We need to be talking about good middle-class jobs, jobs, jobs.

Republican: Jeffrey Dahmer is a registered Democrat.

Press to Democrat: It has been charged that Jeffrey Dahmer is a registered Democrat. Is there any truth to that?

Democrat: It's not our fault if this guy registered as a Democrat. Maybe he was middle class and agreed with us on the issues. And we don't know for a fact how he registered. But it's not our fault. Middle class.

Headline: Democrats Disavow Dahmer's Support.

●

Democrat: Our candidates are offering concrete middle-class proposals on health, education and the economy. Mr. Bush just isn't dealing with the pain of the middle class.

Republican: Mario Cuomo went to Willie Horton's bar mitzvah.

Press to Governor Cuomo: We have information that you attended Willie Horton's bar something.

Mr. Cuomo: His what?

Press: Horton's confirmation party.

Mr. Cuomo: Oh. I see. We all see, profoundly and tragically. Another attack on the Italians and other minorities. Why is it always the Italians? Was Hitler an Italian? Is Jeffrey Dahmer an Italian? What about the great Italians—Judge Sirica, Joe DiMaggio, St. Augustine, Mario Proccacino? Does anyone ever talk about them? I'm not saying who I think is behind this anti-Italian, anti-minorities, anti-welfare smear campaign. But we would not be surprised to hear just those kinds of dubious statements being made in the salons of Little Rock, Ark. I'm not pointing fingers. But you don't hear about Italians being draft dodgers, do you?

Headline: Cuomo Reconsidering Presidential Bid. Dodges Charges About Italian Links to Willie Horton.

•

Democrat: Republicans have shafted the middle class for over a decade now. Under Republican Administrations, the rich got richer and the middle class and the poor got poorer.

Republican: There you go again: class warfare, anti-free market, anti-American. The Commies have lost out everywhere in the world but in the Democrat Party, head-quartered in Washington D.C.

Press to Democratic Party Chairman: What's your answer to that?

Party Chairman: We were for some of the poor some of the time before 1992. Now we're for the middle-class poor and all the other middle classes all of the time.

Headline: Democrats Consider Relocating Headquarters in Peoria, Some Say.

•

Democrat: O.K. O.K. Saddam Hussein is still in power. Right there in Baghdad. And where was George Herbert Walker Bush 10 years ago when America's supermarkets installed price-scanners? Up there in Kennebunkport, in his plush vacation resort, guzzling gas in his motorboat and not paying taxes in Texas. This shows we're for the middle class and health care for all, except rich Republicans with yachts and plush resorts. Saddam Hussein and the middle class—that's what we're against and for.

Republican: There you go again. Tax and spend and smear and tax. You Democrats dare attack the President who led us in the Great Desert War while the Democrat Party of Washington D.C. cowered in its bunker in Congress, Washington D.C.?

TV Talk-Show Host: Let's stay with this substantive discussion on foreign affairs. What about Japan?

Democrat: John F. Kennedy, Lyndon Johnson and Jimmy Carter didn't vomit when they went to Japan.

Republican: Hirohito was a Democrat.

Democrat: He was not.

Republican: Was too.

> " For the umpteenth time, H. Ross Perot is insisting that he does not want to be President. But by opening the door a tiny crack to his possible candidacy in this election year, the Texas billionaire is attracting telephone calls, letters and money to his Dallas office—all urging him to run. "

THE UNPREDICTABLE, BUT APPEALING PEROT

Attracting attention outside of the major parties, H. Ross Perot, a billionaire Texan, threatened to run as an independent candidate for president. After he informally entered the race, voters became intrigued by Perot, who gained considerable media attention and public support. With his flamboyant personality and willingness to spend large amounts of his own money, he competed closely with the major party candidates in national polls and earned a place on the ballot in all fifty states. Despite the support, Perot resisted formally entering the race while the primaries were fought.

MARCH 7, 1992
BILLIONAIRE IN TEXAS IS ATTRACTING CALLS TO RUN, AND $5 DONATIONS
By DORON P. LEVIN

For the umpteenth time, H. Ross Perot is insisting that he does not want to be President. But by opening the door a tiny crack to his possible candidacy in this election year, the Texas billionaire is attracting telephone calls, letters and money to his Dallas office—all urging him to run.

Call it just one more sign of voter disaffection with Washington politics as usual. In any case, Mr. Perot will probably not be appearing in television commercials, kissing babies or standing in front of an American flag, bemoaning the Federal deficit.

"I'm not going to be one of these people who hires handlers and image makers," Mr. Perot said. "What you see is what you get."

Theoretically, anyone from any state who wishes to support him as an independent candidate still has enough time to sign a petition calling for his name to be placed on the Presidential ballot. The earliest deadline is in Texas on May 11.

Mr. Perot's "candidacy," if it could even be called that, grew out of his appearance on the CNN program "Larry King Live" on Feb. 20. Since selling the data processing company he founded to the General Motors Corporation in 1984 for $2.5 billion, Mr. Perot has frequently spoken out publicly in favor of political and economic change.

Mr. King and callers questioned Mr. Perot about why he does not run for political office if he feels so strongly that the nation's economy and education system need fixing.

After stating several times during the talk show that he was not interested in becoming a politician, Mr. Perot, 61 years old, finally hedged his refusal. "If voters in all 50 states put me on the ballot—not 48 or 49 states, but all 50—I will agree to run," he said. He also said he would not accept more than $5 from each supporter.

A week after appearing on the talk show Mr. Perot's secretary, Sally Bell, said that she had received calls from people in 46 states promising support, as well as many $5 contributions.

APRIL 26, 1992
POLL SHOWS PEROT GAINING STRENGTH TO RIVAL CLINTON'S
FIFTH OF VOTERS BACK HIM

But Few Are Able to Say if Texan Is Liberal or a Conservative—38% Support Bush
By ROBIN TONER

Riding a wave of discontent with politics-as-usual, Ross Perot is now the preferred Presidential alternative of more than a fifth of the registered voters, putting him just behind Gov. Bill Clinton, according to the latest New York Times/CBS News Poll.

More than two-thirds of registered voters admitted knowing little about Mr. Perot, who has not yet officially entered the race but is considering an independent candidacy. More than half in the new survey were unable to describe him as a liberal, a conservative or a moderate. But the Texas businessman is increasingly seen as an option by voters dissatisfied with Mr. Clinton, the likely Democratic nominee, and President Bush, the poll showed.

Asked how they would vote if the election were held today, 23 percent of registered voters said they would back Mr. Perot, 28 percent Mr. Clinton and 38 percent Mr. Bush. A month ago, Mr. Perot was at 16 percent, Mr. Clinton at 31 percent and Mr. Bush at 44 percent.

THE DEMOCRATIC CONVENTION

The Democratic Party met in New York City in mid-July, thirsty for the presidency after twelve years of Republican rule. The party adopted a more moderate platform than in the past, moving away from the liberal positions of their losing bids in the three previous elections. Nominating Bill Clinton and his running mate, Tennessee senator Al Gore Jr., the Democrats portrayed themselves as a moderate, united party, fighting for the middle classes and a stronger economy. Their electoral prospects boomed on the last day of the convention, when independent Ross Perot shocked the nation by withdrawing from the race.

JULY 15, 1992
DEMOCRATS, EMPHASIZING UNITY, EMBRACE A MODERATE PLATFORM
APPEAL TO WOMEN

Abortion Rights Stressed In Effort to Harness Anger at Bush

By R. W. APPLE Jr.

With the last challenge to Bill Clinton's hegemony fading, the least contentious, most confident Democratic National Convention in years adopted a platform last night fashioned to match the moderate prescription for victory that he has championed.

Seeking to capitalize on the national mood of discontent with Washington and distaste for politics, the 10,000-word document pledged "a revolution in government."

Madison Square Garden rang with denunciations of President Bush, who was accused by orator after orator of breaking promises. The Democrats sought to project an image of unity between blacks and whites, mayors and governors and senators, men and women, and to highlight their support for abortion rights.

Clinton Takes the Lead

Mr. Clinton's formal nomination was still 24 hours away and his crucial speech to the delegates still 48. But the Arkansas Governor took the lead in his party's appeal to women, many of whom resent Mr. Bush's opposition to abortion, telling women's groups in a speech yesterday, "It makes a difference whether the President believes in a woman's right to choose, and I do."

Six Republican supporters of Mr. Clinton's stand made a convention appearance later, with one of them, Kathy Taylor, telling the delegates that "women's right to choose

hangs by a thread." The first real exuberance of the week followed, with hundreds of "Pro-Choice Pro-Clinton" signs dancing above the heads of the crowd.

Clearly exhilarated by the sunny mood at the convention, by his rising standing in the polls and by the relative lack of acrimony in the party, the prospective nominee said his chances for November looked good. But he conceded that "it's not going to be easy" to win against an experienced incumbent President and a billionaire independent, Ross Perot.

The Democratic platform, in a sharp departure from the party's practice since the New Deal, de-emphasizes government intervention as the principal solution for social and political problems, speaking often of market forces and personal responsibility. It mentions "law and order," a phrase Democrats once derided, and to overcome the party's reputation for foreign-policy softness, it argues that the nation "must be prepared to use military force decisively when necessary to defend our vital interests."

Long Parade of Speakers

Nonetheless, it has many liberal planks, including those for broader child care, civil rights for homosexuals, higher taxes on the wealthy and higher spending on public works and the environment—enough to sharply differentiate it from the platform the Republicans will adopt.

JULY 17, 1992
PEROT QUITS RACE, LEAVING TWO-MAN FIELD; CLINTON VOWS CHANGE AND 'NEW COVENANT' AS HE AND BUSH COURT ABANDONED VOTERS

Democratic Team Opens by Appealing to Middle Class

By GWEN IFILL

Gov. Bill Clinton and his running mate, Senator Al Gore, opened their general election campaign last night with a stern attack on President Bush's economic policies and a vision for a Democratic administration that would have as its priorities jobs, health care, AIDS research, the environment and political reform.

In an address intended to dispel the impression that he has character flaws that might disqualify him from the Presidency, the Arkansas Governor spoke of his background as a fatherless child and of his vision of a government based on the values of community, responsibility and compassion.

"I end tonight where it all began for me," Mr. Clinton concluded his speech, evoking the small-town virtues of his birthplace, Hope, Ark. "I still believe in a place called Hope."

Then the balloons fell and the delegates waved banners, celebrating with the quadrennial burst of unity and enthusiasm that Democrats display whenever they feel the Presidency is within reach once again. Along with their nominee, they chanted, "We can do it!"

At the conclusion of his acceptance speech, Mr. Gore took an additional turn around the podium, dancing arm in arm with his wife, Tipper.

Mr. Clinton accused the Bush Administration of giving lip service to those values for political purposes but forgetting them when it came to governing. "Frankly, I'm fed up with politicians in Washington lecturing the rest of us about 'family values,'" he said. "Our families have values. But our government doesn't."

Mr. Clinton asserted a Democratic claim to the issues that the Republicans have monopolized for three elections, even citing passages from the Pledge of Allegiance as if in a defiant challenge to President Bush to use patriotism against him in the manner the Republicans employed so successfully with former Gov. Michael S. Dukakis, the 1988 nominee.

"In the name of those who do the work, pay the taxes, raise the kids and play by the rules—in the name of the hard-working Americans who make up our forgotten middle class—I proudly accept your nomination," Mr. Clinton said. "I am a product of that middle class. And when I am your President, you will be forgotten no more."

JULY 17, 1992
PEROT SAYS DEMOCRATIC SURGE REDUCED PROSPECT OF VICTORY

By STEVEN A. HOLMES

Special to The New York Times

DALLAS, July 16—In halting his campaign before it ever formally began, Ross Perot explained today that the Democratic Party had become so much stronger recently that he no longer believed he could win the election at the polls in November.

Instead, he said, he feared that a three-way contest would have to be decided in January by the House of Representatives, a prospect he called disruptive to the country.

"When we started in early summer," Mr. Perot said at a news conference here, "there was a climate there where we could win outright. The Democratic Party has revitalized itself. They've done a brilliant job, in my opinion, in coming back."

A Series of Setbacks

But officials of the Texan's campaign said the Democrats' resurgence was only one reason for Mr. Perot's decision. In recent weeks the Perot camp has suffered unfavorable news articles about Mr. Perot's history and style as a business executive, setbacks in public opinion polls and fundamental arguments over the direction of the campaign—discord that culminated in the resignation on Wednesday of Edward J. Rollins, the campaign co-manager.

Morton H. Meyerson, one of Mr. Perot's most trusted business associates and friends, who also serves as a "senior adviser" to the campaign, said today that Mr. Perot had been surprised at the intensity of the scrutiny he was receiving and of the attacks leveled at him by political opponents.

"I think he visualized the difficulties of the task," Mr. Meyerson said. "I don't think that he quite realized the tension, the pulling and tugging and the extraneous ideas that come out about a Presidential candidate. I think he thought it would be on a slightly higher plane."

Disappointed Supporters

Regardless of Mr. Perot's reasons or prospects for success, his announcement disappointed, even infuriated, many supporters. Volunteers at local Perot campaign headquarters across the nation, having been roused to action just weeks or months ago, said they felt betrayed.

Nor did Mr. Perot offer them much guidance on what to do next. He declined to endorse either President Bush or Gov. Bill Clinton of Arkansas. He urged followers to continue circulating petitions to get his name onto state ballots, saying that this would let the Republican and Democratic parties know who the disaffected voters are. And he suggested that his backers might want to stay together as a voting bloc to influence the political process.

"That's up to them," he said of the volunteers. "They would make that decision."

If some supporters accused Mr. Perot of a failure of courage, he angrily rejected the idea. A reporter asked him what he would say to those who would consider him a quitter, a man unable to take the heat of a political campaign.

"People can say anything they want to say," Mr. Perot said, affixing the questioner with a cold stare. "I am trying to do what's right for my country. Now that probably makes me odd in your eyes, but that's what I'm trying to do."

• •

THE REPUBLICAN CONVENTION

The Republican Party met to rally around President Bush in his home state of Texas, to heal fractures within the party, and to protect their presidential reign. While praising the accomplishments of the previous four years, the party also attempted to appease its right wing by writing socially and economically conservative policies into the party platform and by giving Patrick Buchanan a prominent speaking role to pursue what he called the "culture wars" in America. Seeking to atone for his betrayal of his 1988 promise of "no new taxes," Bush apologized and promised broad tax cuts upon his reelection.

AUGUST 19, 1992
REPUBLICANS ASSAIL CLINTON AS RADICAL AND BIG SPENDER AND ASSERT BUSH STRENGTHS
THEMES FOR FALL

President Promises New Faces in Cabinet if He Wins Second Term

By ANDREW ROSENTHAL

Special to The New York Times

HOUSTON, Aug. 18—The Republicans pressed their lacerating attack on Gov. Bill Clinton and the Democrats in Congress at their National Convention today, as speaker after speaker portrayed Mr. Clinton as a radical liberal who would coddle criminals, disarm America and break the economy with higher taxes and more Government spending.

President Bush worked in his hotel room with his advisers to devise an acceptance speech intended to restore the credibility of the "read my lips" candidate's economic promises. As if previewing his themes, Mr. Bush promised in interviews to put new faces in his Cabinet in a second term, restore economic growth and take a tougher line with Congress.

An Image of Diversity

This produced a wave of reports across the Astrodome that the three men widely regarded as the architects of Mr. Bush's unpopular economic policies—Treasury Secretary Nicholas F. Brady; the budget director, Richard G. Darman; and the chief White House economist, Michael J. Boskin—would be offered as sacrifices after the election.

In the Astrodome, there was no mention of Mr. Bush's broken promise not to raise taxes; apologies were left for the President himself to make on Thursday night. And the night's speeches were a dutiful effort to make the case for Mr. Bush's domestic policies that lacked the full-throated conservatism of Patrick J. Buchanan's speech the previous night or the nostalgic fire of Ronald Reagan's.

A parade of public officials representing minorities, the disabled and even abortion rights advocates took the stage to paint a picture of diversity and to praise President Bush and hammer away at the Republican themes for the fall campaign: Mr. Bush won the cold war and the war against Iraq, he represents "family values" and he is a skilled diplomat.

But behind the scenes, Republican strategists—driven by the conviction that religion and cultural divides are still powerful tools—unapologetically proclaimed their intention to follow Patrick J. Buchanan's declaration of a religious and cultural war with the Democrats.

AUGUST 21, 1992
BUSH PROMISES ACROSS-THE-BOARD TAX CUT AND AN ECONOMIC REVIVAL IN A SECOND TERM
Stresses Global Experience And Question of 'Character'
By ROBIN TONER
Special to The New York Times

HOUSTON, Aug. 20—President Bush tonight appealed for a second term with a promise of new, across-the-board tax cuts next year, a pledge to control Government spending and an attack on his opponent, Gov. Bill Clinton, as a throwback to failed Democratic policies at home and abroad.

Mr. Bush, accepting his party's nomination here before 2,210 delegates in the Houston Astrodome, presented himself as a tested leader on the world stage who was now committed to waging the struggle for economic revival at home.

He proudly claimed credit for helping usher in the sweeping changes of the last four years, from the unification of Germany to the commencement of Arab-Israeli peace talks, from the easing of conflict in Central America to the collapse of the Soviet Union.

"The world changes for which we've sacrificed for a generation have finally come to pass," Mr. Bush said, "and with them a rare and unprecedented opportunity to pass the sweet cup of prosperity around our American table."

Admits Erring On Taxes

He apologized for breaking his "no new taxes" pledge of 1988, but he cast his acceptance of the 1990 budget agreement, which included new taxes, as a one-time error. Seeking to reclaim the Republicans' political advantage as the party of fiscal restraint, Mr. Bush declared, "Who do you trust in this election? The candidate who raised taxes one time and regrets it, or the other candidate, who raised taxes and fees 128 times, and enjoyed it every time?"

This speech, capping the final night of the 35th Republican National Convention, did not reach the emotional heights that Mr. Bush attained in 1988, when his acceptance speech was widely hailed as the "speech of a lifetime." Mr. Bush was forced onto the defensive by an ailing economy, and he went into great detail blaming a "gridlock Democratic Congress" for blunting the promise of his current term.

But this partisan audience and his beaming advisers clearly thought he had succeeded in the essential chore of softening up Mr. Clinton and his poll ratings before the long slog through September and October. For that reason, the 58-minute address veered sharply from the visionary tone of its opening passage to the routine battering of a typical campaign speech.

Promises to Propose Cuts

On balance, Mr. Bush seemed to have more energy for defending his record and for assailing his opponents than for laying down a roadmap for a second term.

In promising to call for new across-the-board reductions in taxes when Congress returns next year, Mr. Bush said he would insure that they were tied to spending reductions so they did not increase the deficit. The President said he would propose several actions to cut spending, including vetoing any appropriations bill that exceeded his budget request and pushing for a cap on mandatory spending programs like Medicare, Medicaid and veterans' benefits.

PEROT RETURNS

After withdrawing from the presidential contest in mid-July, Ross Perot announced a surprising return to the race only five weeks before the election. To regain his momentum and to vie with the major party candidates, Perot spent lavishly on 30-minute television infomercials that brought his economic plans directly to the people. Focusing almost completely on the economy and national deficit, Perot proposed innovative plans to restructure the American government. Opinion polls registered support for Perot's ideas, but his sudden change of mind created skepticism among voters deterred by his earlier exit and third-party status.

OCTOBER 2, 1992
PEROT RE-ENTERS THE CAMPAIGN, SAYING BUSH AND CLINTON FAIL TO ADDRESS GOVERNMENT 'MESS'

FACES LAG IN POLLS

Negotiators for Parties Report Agreement on Series of Debates

By ROBIN TONER

Special to The New York Times

DALLAS, Oct. 1—Ross Perot jumped back into the race for the Presidency today, instantly creating new risks, opportunities and uncertainties for Gov. Bill Clinton and President Bush in the final 33 days before Election Day.

Mr. Perot, who bolted from the race in July, asserted he was reactivating his independent campaign at the plea of his supporters. "I thought that both political parties would address the problems that face the nation," he said. "We gave them a chance. They didn't do it."

Despite new polls showing his support vastly diminished, Mr. Perot dismissed the notion that he could function only as a spoiler or that he was motivated by animosity toward Mr. Bush.

Playing Familiar Themes

He presented his candidacy as a de facto nomination from the grass roots, declaring: "I would like to thank the American people. By choosing me as your candidate, you have given me the highest honor I could ever receive."

With his running mate, retired Vice Adm. James B. Stockdale, at his side, Mr. Perot struck many of the same themes that he rode to sudden political prominence last spring, assailing a "Government in gridlock" that has let the deficit and other critical national needs go unresolved.

"The American people are good," he said, "but they have a Government that is a mess. Everybody in Washington makes excuses. Nobody takes responsibility even when they have direct responsibility."

Slapping at News Media

The Perot camp declared that it expected Mr. Perot to be included in upcoming Presidential debates, and both Bush and Clinton campaigns said they were willing to do so. Negotiators said tonight that they had reached a tentative agreement on the debates. Officials close to the negotiations said there would be three debates, with the first one on Oct. 11.

In a remarkably combative news conference for an announcement day, Mr. Perot, a Texas billionaire, also lambasted the news media for investigating his past and his political practices and asserted that he would keep his campaign focused solely on the issues he wanted to highlight.

OCTOBER 7, 1992
PEROT CHARTS POOR ECONOMY IN 30-MINUTE TV TALK

By KEVIN SACK

Special to The New York Times

DALLAS, Oct. 6—Using an unusual purchase of 30 minutes of television time, Ross Perot took viewers on a graphic tour of America's faltering economy tonight and asked them to choose a President "who will do it, not just talk about it."

Armed with more than two dozen charts and a metal pointer, Mr. Perot used virtually his entire presentation to dissect the causes of the recession. The independent Presidential candidate heaped scorn on both political parties, contended that government had lost touch with the people, and blamed short-sighted policies for the country's indebtedness.

"We got into trickle-down economics and it didn't trickle," Mr. Perot said.

Throughout the taped presentation, the camera never veered from Mr. Perot, who was seated at a desk backed by a simple bookcase. While conventional campaign advertisements often use poignant visuals or indignant charges to capture attention, Mr. Perot relied on his most dependable political asset—his gift for plain talk and homespun anecdotes.

Solution to Come Later

Government leaders, he said, "assume we are major dumb." In the 1980's, "we were just like little boys playing with money," he said.

- -

NEW CAMPAIGN TECHNIQUES

Using a variety of new technologies and television formats, political campaigns evolved in 1992. Ross Perot began his campaign with an appearance on *Larry King Live* and ushered in an era when candidates appeared on "soft" television shows outside of the typical political programs. Bill Clinton continued this trend, playing his saxophone on Arsenio Hall's show and appearing on Phil Donahue's talk show. President Bush took advantage of the popularity of 1-800 telephone numbers by offering free copies of his economic plan to anyone who called.

JUNE 5, 1992
WHISTLE-STOPS A LA 1992: ARSENIO, LARRY AND PHIL

By ELIZABETH KOLBERT

He wore cheap sunglasses. He blew the saxophone. He explained that he really wanted to inhale; he just didn't know how.

With his Secret Service entourage sitting stiffly in the front row, Gov. Bill Clinton chatted with Arsenio Hall Wednesday night about his mistakes, his faults and his ideas for America's future. It was not the kind of television performance Presidential candidates typically give, but it is not likely to be the last.

In a year when "conventional politicians" travel only in disguise, Presidential candidates are rushing as never before to address voters through unconventional forums like late-night interview programs and television call-in shows. Ross Perot launched his independent campaign on a by-now famous installment of "Larry King Live." During the New York primary campaign, Mr. Clinton and his opponent, Edmund G. Brown Jr., the former governor of California, put in appearances on the Phil Donahue show. And after Governor Clinton won the California primary, he stayed in the state an extra day to tape Arsenio Hall, then went to Little Rock, Ark., to do Mr. King's call-in show via satellite.

Decline of Network News

Politicians and media analysts agree that the rise of the talk show in political culture reflects broader trends, most significantly the declining influence of the network news shows.

"These types of programs have become much more important as a source of information for people," said Frank Greer, a top adviser to Mr. Clinton. "Ten years ago, these programs didn't have the audience or the impact that they have now."

Appearing on the talk-show circuit presents several advantages for candidates. It allows them to speak directly to viewers, and in a relatively informal setting. And it allows them to present their case without having to answer many specific questions.

SEPTEMBER 12, 1992
BUSH'S TOLL-FREE NUMBER: GOOD CALL OR POLITICAL 911?
By ELIZABETH KOLBERT

It is too early to tell whether it will do much for President Bush, but it definitely ushered in a new era of respectability for 800 numbers.

On Thursday night, Mr. Bush purchased five minutes of prime time on four networks—ABC, NBC, CBS and CNN—to inform the viewing public about his "Agenda for American Renewal," as he titled his economic plans. The commercial, taped in the Oval Office, showed a serious-looking President sitting on his desk and speaking directly into the camera.

"At this pivotal point in history we're faced with two very different philosophies, two very different agendas and a very real choice," Mr. Bush said at the end of the advertisement. Then an 800-number appeared on the screen for viewers to call to receive a free copy of his plans.

OCTOBER 7, 1992
CLINTON AND GORE RETURN TO THE CALL-IN
By GWEN IFILL
Special to The New York Times

NASHVILLE, Oct. 6—Gov. Bill Clinton and Senator Al Gore returned to the television talk-show circuit Monday night and today, moving their joint campaign from the old-fashioned handshaking of a bus trip to the newfangled discourse of viewer call-ins.

Often, as was the case on "Larry King Live" on Monday night, the occasion was comfortable: Mr. Gore wore blue jeans, Mr. Clinton's mother called to say hello from Las Vegas, Nev., the broadcast originated from a livestock arena.

Other times the candidates, who are looking for what Mr. Clinton called the "unfiltered" forum of live television, stumbled into lively encounters. For example,

Mr. Clinton entered the ring today with Phil Donahue, sparring with the talk-show host in the pattern of heated exchange that the two perfected during a spring appearance on the show.

Clinton Challenged

They talked about health care and jobs policy and free trade. But Mr. Clinton, who completed a bus tour in Florida before flying here this afternoon, grew most lively and irritated when Mr. Donahue or viewers of the call-in portions of the program challenged him on his military history, opposition to the Vietnam War and his arms-length relationship with the Rev. Jesse Jackson.

THE ECONOMY

The dominant issues of the 1992 election were the state of the national economy and the candidates' competing plans to spur it to full recovery. Even when President Bush tried to broaden the debate to include foreign affairs and family values, areas where he thought he could dominate his rivals, the public drew the conversation back to the economy. Clinton's campaign motto, "It's the economy, stupid," implored his staff to remember this. The three candidates had starkly different views on the health of the economy, as well as what, if anything, the government should do to improve it.

SEPTEMBER 13, 1992
SKIPPING AHEAD

On the Economy, Bush Tries to Keep Focus on the Future
By DAVID E. ROSENBAUM

"THE ECONOMY, STUPID."

That sign on the wall of Bill Clinton's headquarters in Little Rock is a reminder to the campaign staff. Stick to the basics. Avoid diversions.

The economic slump of the last four years is George Bush's chief weakness and Mr. Clinton's greatest strength. Few people doubt that if the election turns on that issue, the Governor of Arkansas will be the next President of the United States. The most recent New York Times/CBS News Poll, in late August, found that 77 percent of registered voters disapproved of the way Mr. Bush had dealt with the economy, compared with only 17 percent who approved.

So everywhere he goes nowadays, Mr. Clinton fans the flames, reminding voters that economic growth under President Bush has been slower than in any other Presidential term since World War II, and that more businesses have failed and fewer jobs have been created. He talks about how incomes have dropped while unemployment has risen, how American wages are lower than those in a dozen other countries and how the gap between the rich and the poor has widened significantly.

"Labor has been devalued for a dozen years," Mr. Clinton said in Cromwell, Conn., last week in a typical stump speech. "We have stayed too long with trickle-down economics, and we have paid a terrible price for it."

For a time, the Bush camp believed that the best strategy was to change the subject, to try to get the public to focus on other issues like foreign policy and family values and crime. But when James A. Baker 3d took over the Bush campaign after the Republican National Convention last

month, he decided the President had to confront the economic issue head-on. Mr. Baker just tried to make a subtle change in the lens. Instead of focusing on the state of the economy now or in the last four years, Mr. Baker would like voters to concentrate on what the economy should be in the next four years and even in the next century. He wants them to see Mr. Bush as reliable and trustworthy, Mr. Clinton as rash and irresponsible.

That was what the President's speech on Thursday to the Detroit Economic Club was about. He broke little new substantive ground. But for the first time in his Presidency—more than three and a half years after he took office, 26 months after the recession began and just 53 days before the election—Mr. Bush cast his views on the economy in terms of themes and principles, hopes and dreams, instead of random legislative proposals.

First he talked about why the economy had gone sour. It was caused, he said, by "profound changes now at work in our economy," listing items like layoffs in the defense industry, the staggering debts accumulated by companies and households in the 1980's and the shaky banking system.

Then he talked about his desire "to keep tax rates low and make them lower, to keep money sound, to limit government spending and regulations and to open the way for greater competition and freer trade."

And he spoke of "the mirage that my opponent offers of a government that accumulates capital by taxing it and borrowing it from the people and then redistributing it according to some industrial policy."

Only time will tell whether Mr. Bush can succeed in getting voters to compare the candidates' economic visions rather than to think just about his economic record. Over the years, incumbent Presidents have generally been judged on their records. In the last half century, the only Presidential election years when the economy was as bad as it is now were 1960 and 1980, and both times the incumbent party was voted out of office.

Mr. Bush and Mr. Clinton have hedged on what is perhaps the central economic question facing the next President: how to reduce the enormous budget deficit. That would almost certainly require raising most people's taxes or cutting popular government programs, stands no candidate wants to take.

But if voters do look at the future, the choices will be clear. The two candidates this year have strikingly different views of how the economy should be handled in the years ahead.

Mr. Bush wants the Government basically to leave the free market alone. Mr. Clinton believes the Government should take an active role in directing the nation's economy.

Mr. Bush believes wealthy Americans are taxed too much. Mr. Clinton would raise their taxes.

Mr. Bush would cut social programs and public works to the bone. Mr. Clinton would expand Government spending in many areas and would invest in capital projects like roads and bridges, transportation systems and communications networks.

Mr. Bush would loosen and abolish Government rules and restraints on businesses. Mr. Clinton wants new regulations on business to protect the environment and to force energy conservation.

Mr. Bush's ideas about medical care and job training are based on tax incentives. Mr. Clinton would require employers to provide medical insurance and training to their employees or pay money to the Government to do the job for them.

Mr. Bush favors free trade at almost all costs. Mr. Clinton is increasingly taking the view that the United States should be tougher on its trading partners.

Rightly or wrongly, the Bush camp believes that if voters examine those differences, they will come down on the President's side. "We're trying to focus on some of the key differences that separate us from Bill Clinton," a senior Administration official said in Detroit just before Mr. Bush's speech Thursday. "Goals are important in terms of giving a country a sense of direction."

OCTOBER 17, 1992
IN HALF-HOUR, PEROT DETAILS PLAN FOR CUTTING DEFICIT

By STEVEN A. HOLMES

Special to The New York Times

DALLAS, Oct. 16—With his campaign for President still lagging far behind his Republican and Democratic rivals, Ross Perot took to the airwaves tonight to lay out his plans for eliminating the Federal budget deficit and radically changing Federal elections laws.

Using a half-hour block of time he bought from NBC for $150,000, the Dallas billionaire detailed a $754 billion package of tax increases, spending cuts and additional Federal spending that he said would produce a Federal budget surplus in six years and would spur economic growth. The format of tonight's show was similar to his last 30-minute broadcast last week when he detailed what he saw as the problems wrought by the $4 trillion national debt.

Mr. Perot has often spoken of the "shared sacrifices" that his plans would require of Americans, but this was the first time he has publicly discussed just how painful those sacrifices might be.

Seated at a polished wood table, Mr. Perot used a stack of more than 20 hand-held charts to illustrate his points. This time, however, the writing on his charts was much larger, in response, he said, to viewer complaints about the small-sized print on his charts in his last program.

'This One Does Add Up'

In providing specifics of his deficit-reduction package Mr. Perot chastised both President Bush and Gov. Bill Clinton for what he said were, in essence, bogus plans for ending Federal red ink.

"The Wall Street Journal asked the President and Governor Clinton after they looked at their economic plans and said, 'Can either one of you folks add?'" Mr. Perot said during the broadcast. "This one does add up. It is real."

Almost all of the proposals outlined by Mr. Perot tonight are in his book, "United We Stand: How We Can

Take Back Our Country." But tonight was the first time the independent candidate had presented his plan in person and in his own folksy style. By choosing to present the plan on his own 30-minute program, and by refraining, as he did Thursday night, to speak of it in any detail in the Presidential debates, Mr. Perot has, so far, avoided having to answer questions about it.

Under his plan, Mr. Perot would cut Federal spending on optional programs by $315 billion and automatic spending that benefits certain classes of people, like the elderly or the poor, by $268 billion. He would raise taxes on individuals by $293 billion and on businesses by $49 billion. Changes in benefit programs, including higher Medicare premiums and increased taxes on benefits for some Social Security recipients, would produce an additional savings of $268 billion, Mr. Perot said.

To spur the economy, Mr. Perot proposed increasing Federal spending by $109 billion and cutting certain taxes, including some capital gains taxes, by $62 billion.

- -

The Debates

The three candidates met in three debates in October. For the first time, the vice-presidential candidates also held a debate. Throughout the presidential confrontations, President Bush presented himself as the only candidate with sufficient leadership experience to run the country, but he was continually attacked for his failure to improve the national economy. Clinton acted as the front-runner, avoiding strong policy stances, deflecting criticisms of his personal character, and promising change. Perot, delivering humorous one-liners and quips, attempted to appear as a viable candidate, while stressing his outsider status and business skills. As the debates drew to a close, Clinton solidified his lead in national opinion polls.

OCTOBER 12, 1992
BUSH STRESSES HIS EXPERIENCE BUT 2 RIVALS CITE ECONOMIC LAG
FIRST OF 3 DEBATES
Bush and Clinton Tangle Over Antiwar Role—Perot Adds Color
By R. W. APPLE Jr.

In the long-awaited first debate of the 1992 Presidential campaign, with his Presidency in jeopardy, George Bush asked the American people last night for more time to right the economy, but his economic stewardship drew withering fire from Bill Clinton and Ross Perot.

White House officials said later that if he was re-elected Mr. Bush planned to dismiss his three top economic advisers, as demanded for months by Republican conservatives outraged over tax increases. They are Nicholas F. Brady, the Treasury Secretary; Richard G. Darman, the budget director; and Michael J. Boskin, the top White House economist.

Trailing badly in the national polls and in most big states, the President promised to make James A. Baker 3d, the former Secretary of State who now heads his campaign, the overseer of all domestic programs once Election Day had passed. It was an effort to suggest that he understood the urgency of American economic problems, something many voters doubt, but it also suggested that Mr. Baker, not Mr. Bush, was the man who gets things done.

Renews Attack on Clinton

"Jim Baker is going to put together the economic program for the President," said Marlin Fitzwater, the White House spokesman. "That means we'll be getting a new economic team."

Focusing on foreign policy, the President depicted himself as the only candidate with enough experience to handle the pressures of the Oval Office, and he questioned the "judgment and character" of Mr. Clinton, his Democratic rival.

He renewed his attacks on Mr. Clinton's role in antiwar demonstrations abroad during the Vietnam era, contending that the Democrat's actions raised grave questions about his fitness to serve as Commander in Chief.

Mr. Clinton, mild-mannered in most exchanges, answered sharply, accusing Mr. Bush of unfairly maligning his patriotism. He recalled the unsubstantiated charges of the late Joseph R. McCarthy and pointedly reminded the President that his father, the late Senator Prescott Bush of Connecticut, had been one of McCarthy's early foes.

A Vivid Perot

During the debate, held at Washington University in the St. Louis suburb of Clayton, Mo., and televised nationally, Mr. Bush sought to identify Governor Clinton of Arkansas, his Democratic opponent, with the liberals whose economic programs have proved unpopular with American voters in the past, like Walter F. Mondale, Michael S. Dukakis and Jimmy Carter.

Both the major-party nominees did their best to ignore Mr. Perot, their independent rival, but he was nevertheless a bright, sparky presence in the 90-minute debate, full of pithy one-liners and self-deprecation. He seemed to have a good time, making fun of his big ears, telling the audience he was "not playing Lawrence Welk music tonight" and responding, when Mr. Bush touted his Presidential experience, that "I don't have any experience in running up a $4 trillion debt."

Mr. Perot may have gone some way toward regaining at least a bit of the credibility he lost when he abruptly walked away from the race in July. His vivid performance suggested what a power he might have been had he stayed in, but he had little specific to say except on his plan to help reduce the deficit by raising taxes on gasoline by 50 cents over five years.

OCTOBER 16, 1992
ISSUES, NOT ATTACKS, DOMINATE AS AUDIENCE GUIDES 2D DEBATE
FOCUS ON ECONOMY
Few Chances for Bush to Score Needed Points on Character Issue
By ROBIN TONER

The three Presidential candidates engaged in an earnest town-meeting exchange last night that became a forum for airing the nation's domestic woes during President Bush's Administration.

Mr. Bush defended his record and his sensitivity to the suffering of the recession. "Of course, you feel it when you're President of the United States," he said.

But he asserted that a Clinton Presidency would mean huge new taxes rather than a growing economy. "Governor Clinton's program wants to tax more and spend more," Mr. Bush said. "I don't believe that's the way to do it."

Governor Clinton, however, quickly dismissed the charge.

It was a night in which there were a few sweeping promises. Ross Perot, the independent candidate, promised he would serve only one term and would not take compensation for the $200,000-a-year job. Mr. Clinton promised to propose a universal health-care plan in the first 100 days of his Presidency.

Thrives on Format

Mr. Clinton, who seemed to thrive on the town-meeting format that he had used throughout his primary campaign, presented himself as a man with long years of experience in dealing with the problems of ordinary people. He also asserted that the blame for these problems clearly rested with the "failed economic theory" of the Republicans.

Mr. Perot once again sharply criticized the "gridlock" in Washington, casting the two parties as mired in a cycle of blame that produced only economic drift and decline. "It's not the Republicans' fault, of course, and it's not the Democrats' fault," he said. "Somewhere out there there's an extraterrestrial that's doing this to us, I guess."

At the start of the program and in his closing statement, Mr. Bush tried to move the debate to the issue of character and trust, which he said should be a paramount consideration for voters when they choose a President, and suggested that Mr. Clinton did not pass the test. He asked the voters which President they would prefer in the event of an international crisis.

As for Mr. Clinton, at one point he looked at Mr. Bush and said: "I'm not interested in his character. I want to change the character of the Presidency."

Little New Ground

But in general, it was a night that broke little new substantive ground and offered Mr. Bush few opportunities for the dramatic strokes that his strategists think he needs to come back from a clear deficit in the public opinion polls.

Mr. Clinton, for his part, seemed clearly content to avoid confrontations and follow a no-risk strategy befitting a front-runner. He pointedly turned away from opportunities to respond to Mr. Bush's probing attacks on his character and to take on the President over his handling of Iraq.

The 90-minute debate, held on the campus of the University of Richmond, opened the candidates to questions from an audience of 209 people selected by the Gallup Organization to represent uncommitted voters. Carole Simpson, of ABC News, was the moderator. The questioners were relentlessly focused on issues, from gun control to free trade, from health care to urban woes.

OCTOBER 20, 1992
BUSH PUSHES HARD IN 3D DEBATE BUT FOES PUT HIM ON DEFENSIVE
CLINTON ATTACKED
Governor and Perot Cite Troubles in Economy—No Clear Victor
By ROBIN TONER

The last of the three Presidential debates ended last night with President Bush still on the defensive about his first-term record and laboring to revive his campaign by warning that Gov. Bill Clinton lacked the leadership, the record and the character to be President.

In their most spirited, direct exchange yet, Mr. Bush assailed Mr. Clinton's record in Arkansas, his economic proposals and what Mr. Bush asserted was a habit of trying to have it both ways on issue after issue.

Mr. Clinton, responding to the President's attacks, hammered Mr. Bush's economic stewardship and resurrected his broken pledge from 1988: "I really can't believe Mr. Bush is still trying to make trust an issue after 'read my lips.'"

Focus on Iraq Conflict

The Democratic Governor also joined with Ross Perot, the independent candidate, in opening a withering critique of Mr. Bush's handling of events leading to the conflict with Iraq.

Mr. Bush, who entered this debate with a clear and persistent deficit in public opinion polls, gave his most aggressive performance yet but did not appear to deliver the devastating blow to Mr. Clinton that Republicans had hoped for.

Mr. Bush contended, repeatedly, that Mr. Clinton was a throwback to Democratic big-government and tax-and-spend policies that were abhorrent to the voters. "Mr. and Mrs. America, when you hear him say we're going to tax only the rich, watch your wallet because his figures don't add up, and he's going to sock it right to the middle-class taxpayer and lower, if he's going to pay for all the spending programs he proposes," Mr. Bush declared.

Bush Chided on Baker

In one of the sharpest exchanges of the evening, Mr. Clinton criticized the President for initially saying that James A. Baker 3d, the White House chief of staff and former Secretary of State, would return to the foreign-policy post and days later saying that Mr. Baker would be in charge of the economy.

"I'll make some news in the third debate," Mr. Clinton said. "The person responsible for economic policy in my administration will be Bill Clinton."

Mr. Bush responded hotly: "That's what worries me. He's going to be responsible."

And striking a persistent theme from last night—reminiscent of the Republican attack against Gov. Michael S. Dukakis in 1988—he added that Mr. Clinton "would do for the United States what he's done to Arkansas."

Defending His State

That remark prompted Mr. Clinton to interrupt "to defend the honor of my state" and defend his record.

But Mr. Clinton also delivered a biting critique of Mr. Bush's economic stewardship, saying that the President's "trickle-down economics" had been a failure. He defended his accomplishments as Governor and presented himself repeatedly as a man committed to easing the lot of the middle class.

"We're a low-spending, low-tax-burden" state, he said. "We dramatically increased investment, and our jobs are growing. I wish America had had that record."

In a sharp response to Mr. Bush's assertion that he had repeatedly waffled on important issues, Mr. Clinton reminded the national television audience that Mr. Bush had once described Ronald Reagan's economic proposals as "voodoo economics" only to embrace them when he joined the ticket in 1980.

Direct Attacks Avoided

Both Mr. Bush and Mr. Clinton avoided direct attacks on Mr. Perot, reflecting the belief of strategists in both camps that many of the Texas billionaire's supporters would drift away in the final days and be up for grabs.

And Mr. Perot, who remains mired in a distant third place in the public opinion polls, used his closing statement to urge voters to disregard the pundits who say he is not electable.

"You got to stop letting these people tell you who to vote for," he said. "You got to stop letting these folks in the press tell you you're throwing your vote away."

Mr. Perot also returned to one of his strongest appeals. "Who would you give your pension fund and your savings account to manage?" he asked.

A CBS News Poll of 553 registered voters taken immediately after the debate found the race virtually unchanged since the previous CBS Poll taken over the weekend. The new poll, with a margin of sampling error of plus or minus five percentage points, found Mr. Clinton with 48 percent, Mr. Bush with 33 percent and Mr. Perot with 16 percent.

Mr. Clinton shattered the Republicans' political base with a promise of change to an electorate clearly discontented with President Bush.

ELECTION RESULTS

On November 3, 1992, American voters swept William Jefferson Clinton into the White House. Clinton unseated George H. W. Bush by a huge electoral margin, 370–168, but fell far short of a popular majority, gaining 43 percent of the national vote. Independent H. Ross Perot had fractured the vote, as he drew 19 percent of the popular vote, one point higher than originally reported, without winning a single electoral vote. The election granted Clinton the presidency, but gave him a fragile mandate. The country prepared for a new leader, but remained uncertain of its future.

NOVEMBER 4, 1992
CLINTON CAPTURES PRESIDENCY WITH HUGE ELECTORAL MARGIN; WINS A DEMOCRATIC CONGRESS

BUSH PLEDGES HELP

Governor Given an Edge of 43% to 38%, With Perot Getting 18%

By ROBIN TONER

Gov. Bill Clinton of Arkansas was elected the 42d President of the United States yesterday, breaking a 12-year Republican hold on the White House.

Mr. Clinton shattered the Republicans' political base with a promise of change to an electorate clearly discontented with President Bush.

Ross Perot, the Texas billionaire who roiled this race throughout, finished third, drawing roughly equally from both major party candidates, according to Voter Research & Surveys, the television polling consortium. His share of the popular vote had the potential to exceed any third-party candidate's in more than half a century.

Faithful Are Won Back

The President-elect, capping an astonishing political comeback for the Democrats over the last 18 months, ran strongly in all regions of the country and among many groups that were key to the Republicans' dominance of the 1980's: Catholics, suburbanites, independents, moderates and the Democrats who crossed party lines in the 1980's to vote for Ronald Reagan and Mr. Bush.

The Governor from Arkansas won such big, closely contested states as Michigan, Missouri, Pennsylvania, New Jersey and Illinois. As polls closed across the nation, networks announced projected winners based on voter surveys. It was Ohio that put him over the top shortly before 11 P.M., followed closely by California. Based on those projections, Mr. Bush prevailed in his adopted state of Texas and other pockets of Republican states around the country.

With 83 percent of the nation's precincts reporting by 3 A.M. today, Mr. Clinton had 43 percent to 38 percent for Mr. Bush and 18 percent for Mr. Perot.

A state-by-state breakdown of those returns gave the President-elect more than 345 electoral votes, a commanding victory in the Electoral College, which requires 270 for election. His victory also provided coattails for Democrats

running for Congress in the face of tough Republican challenges: Democrats, who control both chambers, appeared likely to gain in the Senate and suffer manageable losses in the House.

'With High Hopes'

In a victory speech to a joyous crowd in Little Rock, Mr. Clinton declared, "On this day, with high hopes and brave hearts, in massive numbers, the American people have voted to make a new beginning."

He described the election as a "clarion call" to deal with a host of domestic problems too long ignored and to "bring our nation together." He paid tribute to the voters he had met along the campaign trail, saying they had simply demanded that "we want our future back." The President-elect, who looked euphoric and seemed to savor every cheer, added, "I intend to give it to you."

He also hailed his longtime rival, Mr. Bush, for "his lifetime of public service" and the "grace with which he conceded this election."

"Not very long ago I received a telephone call from President Bush," the President-elect said. "It was a generous and forthcoming telephone call, of real congratulations and an offer to work with me in keeping our democracy running in an effective and important transition."

The crowd hailed the victor repeatedly with cries of "We love you, Bill," especially when he paid tribute to his home state, the object of Republican ridicule throughout the campaign.

Mr. Clinton credited much of his success to his wife, Hillary, who was also a target of Republican attacks. The Clintons and their daughter, Chelsea, were joined by Vice President-elect Al Gore and his family, creating once again the tableau of youth and generational change that they projected throughout the campaign. Mr. Gore and Mr. Clinton embraced in jubilant bear hug.

1992 POPULAR VOTE

STATE	TOTAL VOTE	BILL CLINTON (DEMOCRAT) VOTES	%	GEORGE BUSH (REPUBLICAN) VOTES	%	ROSS PEROT (INDEPENDENT) VOTES	%	ANDRE V. MARROU (LIBERTARIAN) VOTES	%
Alabama	1,688,060	690,080	40.9	804,283	47.6	183,109	10.8	5,737	0.3
Alaska	258,506	78,294	30.3	102,000	39.5	73,481	28.4	1,378	0.5
Arizona	1,486,975	543,050	36.5	572,086	38.5	353,741	23.8	6,759	0.5
Arkansas	950,653	505,823	53.2	337,324	35.5	99,132	10.4	1,261	0.1
California	11,131,721	5,121,325	46.0	3,630,574	32.6	2,296,006	20.6	48,139	0.4
Colorado	1,569,180	629,681	40.1	562,850	35.9	366,010	23.3	8,669	0.6
Connecticut	1,616,332	682,318	42.2	578,313	35.8	348,771	21.6	5,391	0.3
Delaware	289,735	126,054	43.5	102,313	35.3	59,213	20.4	935	0.3
Dist. of Col.	227,572	192,619	84.6	20,698	9.1	9,681	4.3	467	0.2
Florida	5,314,392	2,072,698	39.0	2,173,310	40.9	1,053,067	19.8	15,079	0.3
Georgia	2,321,125	1,008,966	43.5	995,252	42.9	309,657	13.3	7,110	0.3
Hawaii	372,842	179,310	48.1	136,822	36.7	53,003	14.2	1,119	0.3
Idaho	482,142	137,013	28.4	202,645	42.0	130,395	27.0	1,167	0.2
Illinois	5,050,157	2,453,350	48.6	1,734,096	34.3	840,515	16.6	9,218	0.2
Indiana	2,305,871	848,420	36.8	989,375	42.9	455,934	19.8	7,936	0.3
Iowa	1,354,607	586,353	43.3	504,891	37.3	253,468	18.7	1,076	0.1
Kansas	1,157,335	390,434	33.7	449,951	38.9	312,358	27.0	4,314	0.4
Kentucky	1,492,900	665,104	44.6	617,178	41.3	203,944	13.7	4,513	0.3
Louisiana	1,790,017	815,971	45.6	733,386	41.0	211,478	11.8	3,155	0.2
Maine	679,499	263,420	38.8	206,504	30.4	206,820	30.4	1,681	0.2
Maryland	1,985,046	988,571	49.8	707,094	35.6	281,414	14.2	4,715	0.2
Massachusetts	2,773,700	1,318,662	47.5	805,049	29.0	630,731	22.7	9,024	0.3
Michigan	4,274,673	1,871,182	43.8	1,554,940	36.4	824,813	19.3	10,175	0.2
Minnesota	2,347,948	1,020,997	43.5	747,841	31.9	562,506	24.0	3,374	0.1
Mississippi	981,793	400,258	40.8	487,793	49.7	85,626	8.7	2,154	0.2
Missouri	2,391,565	1,053,873	44.1	811,159	33.9	518,741	21.7	7,497	0.3
Montana	410,611	154,507	37.6	144,207	35.1	107,225	26.1	986	0.2
Nebraska	737,546	216,864	29.4	343,678	46.6	174,104	23.6	1,340	0.2
Nevada	506,318	189,148	37.4	175,828	34.7	132,580	26.2	1,835	0.4
New Hampshire	537,943	209,040	38.9	202,484	37.6	121,337	22.6	3,548	0.7
New Jersey	3,343,594	1,436,206	43.0	1,356,865	40.6	521,829	15.6	6,822	0.2
New Mexico	569,986	261,617	45.9	212,824	37.3	91,895	16.1	1,615	0.3
New York	6,926,925	3,444,450	49.7	2,346,649	33.9	1,090,721	15.7	13,451	0.2
North Carolina	2,611,850	1,114,042	42.7	1,134,661	43.4	357,864	13.7	5,171	0.2
North Dakota	308,133	99,168	32.2	136,244	44.2	71,084	23.1	416	0.1
Ohio	4,939,967	1,984,942	40.2	1,894,310	38.3	1,036,426	21.0	7,252	0.1
Oklahoma	1,390,359	473,066	34.0	592,929	42.6	319,878	23.0	4,486	0.3
Oregon	1,462,643	621,314	42.5	475,757	32.5	354,091	24.2	4,277	0.3
Pennsylvania	4,959,810	2,239,164	45.1	1,791,841	36.1	902,667	18.2	21,477	0.4
Rhode Island	453,477	213,299	47.0	131,601	29.0	105,045	23.2	571	0.1
South Carolina	1,202,527	479,514	39.9	577,507	48.0	138,872	11.5	2,719	0.2
South Dakota	336,254	124,888	37.1	136,718	40.7	73,295	21.8	814	0.2
Tennessee	1,982,638	933,521	47.1	841,300	42.4	199,968	10.1	1,847	0.1
Texas	6,154,018	2,281,815	37.1	2,496,071	40.6	1,354,781	22.0	19,699	0.3
Utah	743,999	183,429	24.7	322,632	43.4	203,400	27.3	1,900	0.3
Vermont	289,701	133,592	46.1	88,122	30.4	65,991	22.8	501	0.2
Virginia	2,558,665	1,038,650	40.6	1,150,517	45.0	348,639	13.6	5,730	0.2
Washington	2,288,230	993,037	43.4	731,234	32.0	541,780	23.7	7,533	0.3
West Virginia	683,762	331,001	48.4	241,974	35.4	108,829	15.9	1,873	0.3
Wisconsin	2,531,114	1,041,066	41.1	930,855	36.8	544,479	21.5	2,877	0.1
Wyoming	200,598	68,160	34.0	79,347	39.6	51,263	25.6	844	0.4
TOTALS	104,425,014	44,909,326	43.0	39,103,882	37.4	19,741,657	18.9	291,627	0.3

OTHER VOTES	%	PLURALITY	
4,851	0.3	114,203	R
3,353	1.3	23,706	R
11,339	0.8	29,036	R
7,113	0.7	168,499	D
35,677	0.3	1,490,751	D
1,970	0.1	66,831	D
1,539	0.1	104,005	D
1,220	0.4	23,741	D
4,107	1.8	171,921	D
238		100,612	R
140		13,714	D
2,588	0.7	42,488	D
10,922	2.3	65,632	R
12,978	0.3	719,254	D
4,206	0.2	140,955	R
8,819	0.7	81,462	D
278		59,517	R
2,161	0.1	47,926	D
26,027	1.5	82,585	D
1,074	0.2	56,600	D
3,252	0.2	281,477	D
10,234	0.4	513,613	D
13,563	0.3	316,242	D
13,230	0.6	273,156	D
5,962	0.6	87,535	R
295		242,714	D
3,686	0.9	10,300	D
1,560	0.2	126,814	R
6,927	1.4	13,320	D
1,534	0.3	6,556	D
21,872	0.7	79,341	D
2,035	0.4	48,793	D
31,654	0.5	1,097,801	D
112		20,619	R
1,221	0.4	37,076	R
17,037	0.3	90,632	D
—		119,863	R
7,204	0.5	145,557	D
4,661	0.1	447,323	D
2,961	0.7	81,698	D
3,915	0.3	97,993	R
539	0.2	11,830	R
6,002	0.3	92,221	D
1,652		214,256	R
32,638	4.4	119,232	R
1,495	0.5	45,470	D
15,129	0.6	111,867	R
14,646	0.6	261,803	D
85		89,027	D
11,837	0.5	110,211	D
984	0.5	11,187	R
378,522	**0.4**	**5,805,444**	**D**

NOVEMBER 4, 1992
EDITORIAL
A MONUMENTAL, FRAGILE MANDATE

The American public thundered yesterday for, above all, change.

Yes, voters endorsed Bill Clinton both for his positive program and his dignity in facing down nasty negative attacks. Yes, the voters brought joy to Democrats long out of power and relief to millions worried that Republicans would pack the Supreme Court for years to come. But the public said more than that:

The vote was a relentless rejection of Mr. Bush's Presidency. A White House aide got it almost precisely right last week: "Basically, things are pretty steady. Sixty percent of the people didn't want to re-elect him nine months ago, and 60 percent don't want to re-elect him today."

The surprising number of votes for Ross Perot demonstrated an eagerness for change that transcended Mr. Clinton's appeal. Nearly one voter in five chose the candidate ("I'm Ross and you're the boss") of no party at all.

Polls showed that many voters were choosing the candidate least disliked. All three candidates, including Mr. Clinton, drew remarkably high unfavorable ratings.

Finally, by their numbers, the voters sent a reverberating message. The tide that swept into all those church basements and school auditoriums embodied public impatience, even anger, over the course of the economy and Government.

What all that adds up to is an Electoral College victory of monumental but tenuous proportion. The test now will be how quickly President-elect Clinton can convert his mandate into momentum.

If he is to avoid the fate of Jimmy Carter, the last Democrat to follow a failed Republican Administration, he'll have to set out a short list of clear goals—and work fast to meet them, before the political concrete dries.

Mr. Bush's rejection appeared, from exit polls, to be devastating. Women voted against him by twice the margin of men. Two of five 1988 Bush voters abandoned the President this year. For every first-time voter who voted for Mr. Bush, two voted for Mr. Clinton.

Just how far Mr. Clinton has come can be judged by recalling a graph on page 1 of USA Today on May 28. Who would win the Electoral College? A long red bar indicated "Bush 190." Another one said "Perot 128." A tiny red strip said "Clinton 6." "Ho, ho, ho," analysts hooted. "Bill Clinton's been marginalized."

Ho, ho, ho. A little-known underdog, splattered and battered by controversy in the campaign's earliest days, defended himself with dignity, offered a promising, even inspiring program—and persevered.

The exit polls showed wide support for his domestic ideas. Among people concerned about health care, education and the environment, for instance, he won overwhelming majorities. Having won that support, can he make it last?

Armadas of special interests, armed with rich, sophisticated PAC's, lie in wait. And members of Congress who once could be rallied by legendary leaders like Sam Rayburn and Lyndon Johnson now heed no discipline but their own.

That means the President-elect needs a short list of immediate goals. The four most urgent, consistent with his long-term program, are: Jobs and infrastructure, especially for people in deteriorating cities. . . . Immediate stimulus for the sluggish economy, perhaps through a one-year-only tax credit for investment in infrastructure. . . . Reform of the health care system that now costs so much yet excludes so many. . . . Flushing out the sewer of campaign finance.

Still and all, after 12 years in the wilderness, the Democrats are entitled to celebrate first. And there's good reason for bipartisan satisfaction as well. Through 13 arduous months, Bill Clinton has urged racial tolerance, social justice and national unity. Much as Americans thirst for steady economic management, those could be the most important goals of all.

President George Bush, right, shakes hands with President-elect Bill Clinton at the White House prior to an Oval Office meeting in Washington, D.C., on November 18, 1992.

Source: AP Images/Marcy Nighswander

THE CONGRESSIONAL ELECTIONS OF 1994

REPUBLICANS, OFFERING A "CONTRACT WITH AMERICA," DOMINATE CONGRESS

After forty years as the minority party in the House of Representatives, Republicans overturned the political system with a sweeping victory in 1994. Armed with renewed control of the Senate and presidential victories in 2000 and 2004, Republicans easily dominated American politics for a dozen years.

The 1994 elections brought the greatest turnover in Congress in nearly fifty years. Republicans defeated 34 incumbents, lost none of their own sitting members, netted 52 new seats, and won a 230 to 204 majority in the House, while also adding 8 seats in the Senate for a 53 to 47 majority. Overall, the party's candidates won more than 52 percent of the total ballots—its first national majority since 1946. Their prizes included triumphs over the Democratic Speaker of the House and four committee chairs.

The results came in a sweep of popular votes, turnout increasing to 70 million, 36 percent of the eligible electorate. In the House contests, the Republicans won 36.6 million votes in 1994, gaining 9 million votes over its tally in the last congressional elections, the largest midterm-to-midterm increase in one party's vote total in the nation's history. Democratic House candidates, on the other hand, lost almost a million votes over the period.

The Republican tide was impressive even beyond the numbers. For decades, incumbents had been gaining electoral invulnerability. Challengers faced ever-lengthening odds as House districts became larger, campaign expenses rose, district gerrymandering became more sophisticated, and sitting legislators granted themselves more privileges. In the previous two decades, the average party turnover in House elections had fallen to only 12, making the 1994 upheaval stunningly impressive.

Particularly significant was the regional cast of the Republican victory. Although the party gained across the country, its success was especially notable in the South. The party that arose to counter southern slavery and secession

President Bill Clinton, flanked by House speaker Newt Gingrich, left, and Senate Majority Leader Bob Dole of Kansas, gestures prior to the start of a bipartisan meeting with members of Congress to discuss the legislative agenda, Thursday, January 5, 1995, in the White House Cabinet Room.

took 16 House seats and 2 Senate seats from Democrats in the southern states, outpolling the opposition in every southern state but Mississippi. After the results were fully tallied, for the first time in U.S. history except during Reconstruction, Republicans held a majority of seats from the former Confederacy, with margins of 64 to 61 in the House and 13 to 9 in the Senate, including the seat of Richard Shelby of Alabama, who switched to the GOP after the election.

SETTING OF THE ELECTIONS

The party victory developed unique campaign strategies, established a new national agenda, and extended sharp partisan conflict.

The Republican triumph was founded in a basic strategic change among its membership in the House, led by Rep. Newt Gingrich of Georgia. Seemingly doomed to a perpetual minority, the party had been led by moderates who cooperated with the Democratic majority to maintain some influence

1994 MIDTERM ELECTION RESULTS

HOUSE

		MEMBERS ELECTED			GAINS/LOSSES	
ELECTION YEAR	CONGRESS	DEM.	REP.	MISC.	DEM.	REP.
1994	104th	204	230	1	−52	+52

SENATE

		MEMBERS ELECTED			GAINS/LOSSES	
ELECTION YEAR	CONGRESS	DEM.	REP.	MISC.	DEM.	REP.
1994	104th	47	53	–	−8	+8[1]

1. Sen. Richard Shelby (Ala.) switched from the Democratic to the Republican Party the day after the election, bringing the total Republican gain to nine.

over the course of legislation. Gingrich and other conservatives took a different and more combative approach, drawing sharp lines between the parties as they emphasized strong ideological positions. A series of minor scandals in Congress provided a favorable environment for their attacks.

Gingrich successfully moved the legislative party toward philosophic conservatism, reflecting his own intellectual bent after earning a Ph.D. in history. Only four years after entering the House, he founded the Conservative Opportunity Society to promote new policies for the party. He then won party contests to become the Republicans' minority whip and its moving force in 1989, its formal leader in 1994, and, after that year's elections, Speaker of the House.

As Bill Clinton became president in 1993, the ascendant Republican conservatives were ready to do battle. Clinton came to the White House without benefit of an electoral mandate, winning the three-man contest of 1992 with only 43 percent of the popular vote. As his personal popularity eroded, Clinton's legislative proposals actually strengthened the Republicans. His first executive action was a controversial effort to permit homosexuals to serve in the military. He won approval of his tax program and budget by a one-vote margin, without support from a single Republican. One accomplishment, the North American Free Trade Agreement (NAFTA), split the Democrats, with a majority of the party's legislators opposed. His main domestic proposal, comprehensive health insurance, spurred a legislative and television assault, which eventually killed the proposal without its ever reaching the floor in either chamber. Party lines, in keeping with the Gingrich strategy, were sharply drawn—almost three-fourths of roll call votes divided the parties.

To forward the party program, Gingrich had assumed leadership of GOPAC, a Republican political action committee. The organization recruited potential future candidates and provided training in campaign techniques, lessons in election rhetoric, and funding. In the 1994 contests, the national Republican organizations joined a coordinated financial effort, giving party candidates a big advantage in campaign funds, outspending the Democrats by $150 million to $78 million. Other money came from contributions to individual candidates, spending by sympathetic interest groups, such as the National Rifle Association and Christian conservatives, and from donations by incumbent Republicans with cash to spare in their own campaign coffers. The party also gained from congressional redistricting after the 1990 Census, which enabled state legislatures to construct district lines favorable to Republican candidates, often by jamming black voters into a few Democratic districts and leaving the other seats favorable to the GOP.

As the congressional elections neared, Republicans tied Democrats to Clinton's unpopular programs, while emphasizing their own party unity behind a common program. In late September 1994 they dramatized this approach by presenting a manifesto, titled "Contract with America," which most Republican members and candidates signed. Unveiled at an outdoor ceremony at the Capitol and advertised through popular publications such as *TV Guide,* the contract pledged the party to an 18-point program, developed through focus-group research, that centered on economic issues. It included government reform measures to be passed on the first day of Republican House control and ten statutes to be voted on in the first hundred days of the party's takeover.

The government reform proposals included independent auditing of internal expenditures, reductions in the number of House committees, term limits on committee chair positions, open committee meetings, and requiring a two-thirds vote for approval of tax increases. The promised statutes included a constitutional amendment to limit tax increases; reductions in existing income taxes and federal mandates on state government spending; harsher criminal penalties and extension of capital punishment; reform of social welfare to cut spending, require recipients to work, and end payments after five years; revisions in Social Security; and a constitutional amendment to impose a 12-year term limit on congressional service in both the House and Senate.

Beyond policies, the Republican campaign also stoked resentment of politicians, particularly Democratic incumbents. As *New York Times* reporter Robin Toner described the party's television appeals, "A life in politics, in fact, is sometimes presented as no less a social problem than a life in crime. . . . Contempt of Congress is not a crime in the ads of 1994; it is a core strategy." That resentment brought early retirement, voluntary or forced, to scores of officials, and opportunities for new politicians to display their claimed virtues or reveal their hidden flaws.

THE RESULTS AND EFFECTS

The Republican landslide affected American politics directly for the next dozen years, with implications through the present. The Republicans maintained steady margins of control in both houses until 2006, except for a brief hiatus in 2001. With that control, they institutionalized the "Reagan Revolution," even with Clinton as president, and pushed it still more during George W. Bush's two terms.

The vote overturned past concepts and past voter behavior. Incumbents thought they could protect their seats by the construction of uncompetitive districts and by amassing early campaign bankrolls; in fact, many were scared into retirement or defeated by dedicated challengers. Congressional elections were conventionally treated as a series of localized personal contests, but Republican strategists nationalized the race into a partisan choice between Clinton and their own programs. In the vote itself, Republicans achieved more than a normal midterm gain, building an enlarged coalition for the party rather than for individual candidates, by winning large shifts among white voters, particularly men, southerners, born-again Christians, and former supporters of Ross Perot.

Under Gingrich's leadership, the House—and, to a lesser degree, the Senate—became an exemplar of the theory of party responsibility, with Republicans defining their victories as mandates, standing for an explicit program, and then putting that program into effect. Exemplifying the practice of the theory, Republican legislators supported their party, on average, on nearly 90 percent of floor votes after the congressional elections. Their cohesion was even more striking on issues specified in the Contract with America. There, Republicans voted unanimously on most of the items, with defections, on average, limited to only a single "nay."

United, the Republicans eventually saw most of their program wishes become policy realities. They did not accomplish their proposed constitutional amendments—term limits failed in the House, and a mandatory balanced budget was defeated in the Senate. Some items were vetoed by Clinton, and some were compromised in the less ardent Senate. Yet, overall, most of the contract was implemented. The Republicans accomplished virtually all they promised in regard to congressional reform, unfunded mandates, and welfare, as well as substantial elements of their program in regard to crime, defense, and Social Security. Initially defeated on major economic issues, they later achieved many of these goals, including a balanced budget agreement in place of a constitutional amendment and a reduction in capital gains taxes.

On these questions, as indeed on the general range of American government, Republicans won the greatest victory of all: they set the agenda for the United States, and the Democratic president eventually followed their lead. For example, Clinton first vetoed welfare reform, signed a second bill, and then took credit for the legislation in his reelection campaign.

Gingrich moved Congress toward a parliamentary system of party control. As they organized the House, the Republicans centralized power in the hands of the Speaker, abolished institutionalized caucuses of constituency interests, and distributed chairmanships on the basis of loyalty to the party program rather than seniority. The Republican leadership employed instruments of party discipline to achieve its goals. It insisted that committees report party bills, even when opposed by the chairman, and used rewards and punishments to secure loyalty. The rewards included committee assignments, campaign contributions, and disposition of individual members' bills. Many of these structural changes in the House were later adopted by both the Senate and the Democrats, perhaps most significantly the rotation of committee chairmanships, curbing the past antiparty influence of seniority.

But the American system is not actually a parliamentary government. The reality of separated institutions and checks and balances quickly limited the effects of the 1994 elections.

Flush with power, perhaps dizzy with success, the Republicans challenged Clinton by refusing to enact the federal budget unless he accepted the large tax reductions and expenditure cuts they proposed in health, education, welfare, and environmental programs. Clinton vetoed the budget bill, and, when funds ran out, the president shut down all nonessential services, resulting in the closure of government installations and nonpayment of benefits and contracts, providing a vivid display of the important services provided by the federal government. After five days, Congress passed a temporary funding bill, but continued resistance from Republicans resulted in another presidential veto and another shutdown for three weeks during the Christmas and New Year periods. Finally, Gingrich and his party relented, the Senate took a more active role, and Congress passed a budget with most Clinton programs intact. Clinton had demonstrated the power and independence of the executive branch and put himself on the road to reelection in 1996. Republicans kept control of Congress in those elections, but made no significant gains. The revolution had stalled.

Another confrontation came in 1998. Investigations of President Clinton by an independent counsel of the Justice Department revealed that Clinton had engaged in an extramarital affair with a White House intern. In a lurid report to Congress, immediately released to the public on compact disc, the prosecutor presented charges of perjury and obstruction of justice. After the fall elections, the lame-duck House hurriedly conducted hearings and passed two articles of impeachment against Clinton. In sharp partisan divisions, all but four Republicans voted for the indictments, and all but five Democrats voted against. The Senate later rejected both charges, on votes of 45 to 55 and 50 to 50, well short of the two-thirds vote needed for conviction.

The impeachment effort damaged the Republicans considerably. Clinton maintained high job approval ratings in opinion polls throughout the controversy, even though the public deplored his private conduct. The party lost its moral luster when both Gingrich and his chosen successor resigned their seats upon revelations of their own marital infidelities. When the voters had their say, Republicans unexpectedly lost 5 seats in the House and gained no seats in the Senate, contrary to historical patterns.

The whirlwind of the 1994 election had spent its force. The Republican majority elected that year had made major changes in procedures and policies, but no longer had its dynamic leadership or political energy. Although clinging to power in three more legislative elections, 2000 through 2004, the party soon suffered its own downward turn on the wheel of party fortune. In 2006 Democrats returned to majority control of both the House and Senate, providing the foundation for the party's audacious success in the presidential election of 2008.

● ●

THE CONSERVATIVE MOVEMENT

Following the 1992 electoral defeat of President George H. W. Bush, the conservative branch of the Republican Party looked to renew the philosophy and standing of the GOP. Allied with aggressive commentators on talk radio, they recalled their heyday under Ronald Reagan and looked forward to a seismic shift in national politics.

JANUARY 24, 1993
CONFERRING ON FUTURE, CONSERVATIVES LONG FOR THE PAST
By RICHARD L. BERKE
Special to The New York Times

WASHINGTON, Jan. 23—In their first major gathering since the election last November, many prominent conservatives vowed today to stage a comeback even as some spoke almost in awe of President Clinton's political skills.

As if they had already put the Bush Administration out of their minds, speakers at what was billed as a "Conservative Summit" spoke longingly about bringing back the era of Ronald Reagan. The gathering here was sponsored by the National Review Institute, an offshoot of the conservative magazine.

In his welcoming comments, John O'Sullivan, editor of The National Review, drew hearty cheers from several hundred participants when he said, "We're not at the beginning of the Clinton years, but at the mid-point of the Bush-Clinton years."

Bill Harris, who ran the Republican National Convention last summer, which was widely attacked as having a program dominated by the right wing, acknowledged the failure: "We did not stand for anything in 1992. We did not articulate for the American people a clear vision of what we believed in."

Grim Assessments

Frank Luntz, a poll taker for Ross Perot's independent campaign last year, declared: "George Bush's election in 1988 was a historical aberration." In advice that sounded similar to what Stan Greenberg, Mr. Clinton's poll taker, told the Democratic Party earlier this week about appealing to Mr. Perot's supporters, Mr. Luntz said, "If we lose the Perot constituency, we will be out of power at least until the year 2000."

But the first three speakers did not criticize Mr. Bush or his campaign, because one, Jack F. Kemp, was his Housing Secretary, and the others, Caspar W. Weinberger, the former Defense Secretary, and Elliott Abrams, a former Assistant Secretary of State, were pardoned by him in December for their involvement in the Iran-contra affair.

Mr. Weinberger, who was greeted with a standing ovation, said he feared that Mr. Clinton would drastically cut the military and leave the nation unprepared for conflicts like the Persian Gulf war.

"What I worry about is that the new President will keep his campaign promises," Mr. Weinberger said. "As long as he's violating them, I think we're all right." Joining several other speakers in a call for party inclusiveness, he said, "What I do fear is if we break up into splinter groups, or if we try to narrow rather than broaden the base of the people we have to attract."

Mr. Kemp, already the favorite of many conservatives to lead the Republican ticket in 1996, expanded on the theme that the conservative movement must be more open to differing viewpoints. "Our movement cannot be sustained simply on opposing what liberals want to do and telling people they cannot be a part of this great cause," he said. "There are many men and women who are by definition conservatives who do not yet call themselves conservatives because they want to know if conservatives really care."

Donald J. Devine, who headed the Office of Personnel Management under Mr. Reagan, sounded less optimistic as he warned that with Mr. Clinton in office conservatives have far to go.

'Shrewdest Political Analyst'

"The bad news is that Bill Clinton is probably the shrewdest political analyst that's been in the White House since William McKinley, and we should recognize that," he said. "Ninety-nine point nine percent of every conservative Republican I talk to thinks that Bill Clinton's going to be Carter 2. He's going to go out, build Government, increase taxes, increase spending, and he's going to have the same fate. And if he does, we're going to be fine."

But, Mr. Devine said, "My nightmare is that Bill Clinton can solve the deficit problem" and cut back Government "and do it using our rhetoric."

For all the longing for the Reagan years, some speakers emphasized that the conservative movement would have to start anew.

"The Reagan voter, the more educated, affluent and more religious, make up a decreasing share of the voters," Mr. Luntz said. "The Reagan coalition is dead."

. . . .

FRACTURING POLITICS

Bill Clinton assumed the presidency with the Democratic Party in control of both chambers of Congress. But the new administration faced great difficulty in passing its programs. Rousing conservative sentiments, congressional Republicans rejected compromise on the president's major initiatives. Bitter partisan conflicts erupted over the budget, trade pacts with Mexico and Canada, health care reform, and gay rights. Despite Democratic control, the united Republican lawmakers became the loudest voices in Washington.

AUGUST 11, 1993
PRESIDENT SIGNS BUDGET BILL, THEN TURNS TO NEXT BATTLES

By GWEN IFILL

Special to The New York Times

WASHINGTON, Aug. 10—Rolling out all the imperial trappings of the executive branch onto the South Lawn of the White House, President Clinton today signed the budget bill for which he had fought so hard and scolded Republicans in Congress, saying they had shown "partisan bitterness and rancor" in last week's narrow victory.

Even before the music from the red-suited Marine Band faded today, Mr. Clinton and his aides turned to the battles ahead, predicting bipartisan victories on trade and health care issues and challenging the Republicans who have opposed them.

"This country has begun to take responsibility for itself," Mr. Clinton said.

"I say to those members who took a big chance in voting for this, with all the rhetoric that was thrown against them, if you go home and look your people in the eye and tell them you were willing to put your job on the line so that they can keep their jobs, I think they will understand and reward you with re-election."

Implicit in Mr. Clinton's remarks and explicit in the interpretation offered by his advisers was the belief in the White House that the Administration can gain the upper hand if it beats Republicans to the punch in describing what it hopes to accomplish on the next critical issues.

Thinking Positive

White House officials, acknowledging that they had lost a public relations war while gaining a legislative victory, planned to appeal to voters by promoting the benefits of health care changes and predicting job growth if the North American Free Trade Agreement is enacted. Nafta involves the United States, Canada and Mexico.

"Politically, they'll reinforce each other," said David R. Gergen, the counselor to the President who has been helping plot the next stage of the White House image battle.

"If you're being asked in a tough district to go home and talk about Nafta and you also have health care, you've got something that's very positive to say."

JUNE 17, 1994
G.O.P. IN THE HOUSE IS TRYING TO BLOCK HEALTH CARE BILL
GINGRICH LEADING FIGHT
He Says Republicans Should Oppose Any Plan to Widen Support for Proposal

By ADAM CLYMER

Special to The New York Times

WASHINGTON, June 16—At the urging of Representative Newt Gingrich, their deputy leader, House Republicans are trying to keep health care legislation from reaching the floor in a form that could pass.

Despite criticism from Democrats and even from one Republican who accused him of putting partisan politics first, Mr. Gingrich said today that Republicans should vote against amendments that might broaden the support for a bill that the House Ways and Means Committee is considering.

A few hours later, Republican committee members followed that prescription; all 14 opposed an amendment to

soften the bill's impact on small businesses by providing tax credits to offset their new insurance costs.

But Mr. Gingrich's hardball strategy backfired when previously divided Democrats closed ranks and voted unanimously for a series of amendments, even though some made clear that they did not like them and might alter some later. Several said Mr. Gingrich's move had unified them.

Mr. Gingrich's comments confirmed in part accusations of obstructionism that Democrats had leveled at Republican leaders, saying they were muzzling moderates in their party and blocking compromise on any health care bill. But the Democrats had never provided specifics.

"It's becoming clearer and clearer that they are interested in frustrating action," Representative Richard A. Gephardt of Missouri, the House majority leader, said today. Although Republicans have often said they desired bipartisan cooperation, he said, "their real intention is to, unfortunately, not do anything." He said Republicans were acting like "robots."

In an interview today, Mr. Gingrich, of Georgia, responded, "I think it is very sad to see Gephardt reduced to a Clinton level of dishonesty." He said that Republicans had repeatedly offered to work with Democrats on health care legislation but that "what they mean by bipartisan is us caving in." He said members of his party were resisting "selling out your principles to pass one bill."

Mr. Gingrich said he had told Republican members of the Ways and Means Committee that "they should do what they think is effective in minimizing the prospect that the Gibbons bill will pass." The committee's bill was proposed by its acting chairman, Representative Sam M. Gibbons of Florida.

The Gibbons bill would seek to provide health insurance for all Americans by requiring employers to pay most of the cost of premiums for their workers and by creating a new form of Medicare, the existing health program for the elderly, to include the unemployed and others not reached through employment.

"There is no point in improving it so it will pass," Mr. Gingrich said. "It's a bad bill, and it's wrong." He said the bill would cause "bigger government, bigger bureaucracy and higher taxes for worse health care."

Mr. Gingrich, who is all but certain to become minority leader after the November elections, confirmed a complaint made on Wednesday by Representative Fred Grandy, Republican of Iowa. In a meeting of the committee, Mr. Grandy said Mr. Gingrich had urged that an amendment suggested by Mr. Grandy not be offered because the taxes it involved might be used as an issue against Republican candidates.

Mr. Grandy agreed not to propose the amendment in the committee meeting, but he said today, "To see health care pre-empted by politics, even in the short run, is unsettling."

* *

THE RISE OF NEWT GINGRICH

Georgia representative Newt Gingrich, a former history professor serving as minority whip, the second most powerful member of the minority party in the House, led the Republican revolution of 1994. Gingrich rejected policy compromises with Democrats, spurning the tactics Republicans had long used in dealing with the Democratic majority. His allies viewed him as principled and loyal to his beliefs; his opponents viewed him as a recklessly partisan politician.

OCTOBER 27, 1994
WITH FIERY WORDS, GINGRICH BUILDS HIS KINGDOM

By KATHARINE Q. SEELYE

Special to The New York Times

TULLAHOMA, Tenn.—Already, they call him Mr. Speaker. And he answers.

Not until the wee hours of Nov. 9 will Representative Newt Gingrich learn whether the country has elected enough Republicans to elevate him from minority whip to Speaker of the House and put him third in the line of Presidential succession.

But the Republicans are confident that even if they fail to win a majority, they will at least take effective control. And the silver-thatched Georgia firebrand makes clear as he hopscotches around the country—he has visited 125 Congressional districts, including the one that includes this Tennessee town, to drum up support for the foot soldiers in his pending revolution—that either way he expects to rule the roost.

"We'll be either the strongest Republican minority since 1954," he told a group of Atlanta business owners over breakfast the other day, "or we're going to be the majority. Our working assumption is that we'll be a majority. If we're a minority, we're going to move in exactly the same direction."

He was less cautious on Rush Limbaugh's syndicated radio program: "The odds are at least 2–1 we'll be the majority," he asserted, citing newspaper polls that show a majority of respondents saying they plan to vote Republican.

But whether his new title is minority leader or House Speaker, this one-man intifada, an Army brat who "grew up surrounded by infantry" and has devoted himself more to ferocious partisanship than to advancing legislation, already views himself in a new light.

"I've been seen as a partisan," he said in an interview, "and I am a partisan, obviously, because, a) I've been trapped in the House, which is a very partisan environment, for my entire public career in Washington, and, b) because under Reagan and Bush, it was their job to do the vision and it was my job to be a partisan soldier. That era is over."

In the new era, Mr. Gingrich remains the partisan but gets to do the vision thing too. His goal: to reshape national policy, or, in his immodest phrases, "renew American civilization" and "redirect the fate of the human race."

His remedies range from requiring students to do two hours of homework a night to overhauling the welfare state to asserting America's primacy in the world. "America is the most successful society in the history of the human race," he told an audience here. "We need to say that, frankly, we don't intend to learn much about being like Haiti, but we sure do wish Haitians would learn a lot about being like Americans."

But a revolution is not a dinner party, as Mao said and Mr. Gingrich is finding out. As a long-distance guest on the Limbaugh program, he spoke by telephone from the cramped back room of a restaurant in Augusta, Ga., just off the kitchen, where he was pinned between a metal rack of the day's breads and a glass refrigerator holding vats of mayonnaise.

During a break, he suddenly appeared overwhelmed by the size of his task.

"This is really hard, making this happen, educating, re-educating, over and over, making a mistake, having to re-analyze," he said, his hand cupped over the phone. "I'm trying to educate a nation in the skills of self-government."

He went on: "Starting Nov. 9th, if I'm Speaker—we have to live this. We will have a much bigger burden. People really want to know where we go. Every day we have to be that transformation, not just talk it, and we will make mistakes and I'm very worried about how to do it."

His Republican allies seem less daunted, saying Mr. Gingrich has almost single-handedly revitalized the party's dispirited ranks and set the terms of the national debate with his "contract with America," the platform on which more than 350 Republican candidates for the House have pledged to run.

"He is chief cheerleader, chief fund-raiser, chief recruiter and chief message developer," said Representative Bill Paxon, a New York Republican who is chairman of the National Republican Congressional Committee.

William Kristol, a Republican strategist, added, "Newt really has set the agenda for this campaign, more than Clinton" or any Democrat. Still, he said, Mr. Gingrich spends hours on the phone obsessing about "how to govern."

At the same time, critics of Mr. Gingrich, who have been appalled at his ability as minority whip to thwart legislation, worry that if he becomes Speaker the partisanship will only intensify.

"No one has poisoned the well of public discourse in this country more than Newt," said former Representative Ben Jones, his Democratic challenger at home in Atlanta. "Most of us are trying to fix these problems, and he's done everything in his power to prevent progress."

Asked if Mr. Gingrich might change, Mr. Jones scoffed: "All you have to do is turn on the TV. He accuses his opponents of using 'Stalinist' tactics, of being 'enemies of normal Americans' and says when he gets control of the House, he will use subpoena power against them. That's the kind of rhetoric we heard in the 1950's from Joe McCarthy, and he's already got more power than McCarthy."

Representative Mike Synar, Democrat of Oklahoma, who considers Mr. Gingrich a friend, says he is "a control freak."

"Newt is dangerous because he's smart, he's articulate and he's in control of his party," added Mr. Synar, who lost his own bid for re-election. "There is no dissension, and his principles and philosophy are as flexible as necessary."

House Speaker Newt Gingrich of Georgia holds up his *Contract With America* and a paperback best seller list during his usual Monday meeting with reporters, January 30, 1995, on Capitol Hill.

Source: AP Images/John Duricka

THE CONTRACT WITH AMERICA

As the 1994 midterm elections neared, the Republican Party, led by House Minority Whip Newt Gingrich, offered the voters a "Contract with America." In it, Gingrich presented a list of new policies, promising their enactment in the first hundred days of a Republican-controlled Congress. Democrats attacked the contract as fiscally irresponsible and a return to "Reaganomics." They argued it would help the wealthy while ignoring the poor and middle class.

SEPTEMBER 28, 1994
REPUBLICANS OFFER VOTERS A DEAL FOR TAKEOVER OF HOUSE

By DAVID E. ROSENBAUM

Special to The New York Times

WASHINGTON, Sept. 27—With flags waving, a band playing and a bank of television cameras rolling, Republican candidates for the House of Representatives mustered on the steps of the Capitol today to sign a list of tax cuts and other measures that they promised to press in their first 100 days if they win control of the House in November. They called it their "contract with America."

In a way, it was a throwback to the Reagan era with pledges of deep reductions in taxes for individuals and companies, a stronger military and a constitutional amendment requiring a balanced Federal budget. In Reagan fashion, there was little mention of exactly where Government spending would be cut so that the lower taxes would not worsen the budget deficit.

But the 10-point list of promises made today differed with the Reagan policies in one important respect. The social issues like abortion, gun control, school prayer and flag-burning that dominated Republican dogma in the 1980's were ignored.

Democrats derided the Republicans as fiscally irresponsible.

"All told," said Representative Richard A. Gephardt of Missouri, the House majority leader, "their contract would blow a hole in the Federal budget of roughly $1 trillion."

But Representative Newt Gingrich of Georgia, who is in line to be Republican leader in the next Congress and Speaker of the House if Republicans are in the majority, was not fazed by Democratic accusations that Republicans sought a free lunch—lower taxes with no way to pay for them.

He quoted Franklin D. Roosevelt: "We have nothing to fear but fear itself." He quoted Ronald Reagan: "We have every right to dream heroic dreams; after all, we are Americans." And he said that while it might be a heroic dream to think the budget could be balanced, it could be accomplished through "tremendous creativity and new effort."

The rally on the steps off the West Front of the Capitol had the flavor of a political convention. A band of retired military musicians played Sousa marches and college fight songs. Hundreds of miniature American flags were passed out. Candidates wore large name tags, and some waved placards. Eventually, more than 300 Republican candidates, incumbents and challengers alike, filed past a table covered with red, white and blue bunting and signed their "contract with America."

The contract resembled a party platform: a constitutional amendment requiring a balanced budget in five years and a three-fifths vote of both houses of Congress to raise taxes; a tax credit of $500 per child, regardless of the parents' income; a tax reduction for married couples; tax-free savings accounts; lower taxes for middle- and upper-income Social Security beneficiaries; tax breaks to help Americans buy insurance to cover long-term medical care; lower capital gains tax rates; more favorable depreciation rules for businesses; term limits for members of Congress; more applications of the death penalty; cuts in spending on welfare; a stronger military, and much, much more.

Adding to the festivities was a large fund-raising event tonight, similar to those held during party conventions, where the Republican candidates hoped to pocket donations from the very lobbyists and political action committees that they criticize in the abstract.

A net of 40 seats would have to swing from Democrats to Republicans for them to win control of the House in the November election. The morning line is that Republicans may well pick up 25 to 30 seats but are not likely to reach 40.

• •

A Disenchanted Electorate

As the 1994 election neared, bitter fighting between the two major parties further inflamed the frustrations of the American public. Two years earlier, nearly one-fifth of the electorate had voted for third party candidate Ross Perot in the presidential race; many seemed ready to do the same for Congress, but lacked such an option. Trust in government and in elected officials plummeted, as voters had little hope that their representatives would provide positive change. In this environment, Republicans continued to trumpet their "Contract with America," portraying their party as the better alternative to entrenched Democrats.

NOVEMBER 3, 1994
VOTERS DISGUSTED WITH POLITICIANS AS ELECTION NEARS
A FEELING OF PESSIMISM
Poll Shows the Most Profound Sense of Alienation Among the Public Since 1979
By KATHARINE Q. SEELYE

Heading into Tuesday's election, voters are profoundly alienated from their elected representatives and from the political process and confess to a deepening powerlessness and pessimism over the future of the nation, according to the latest New York Times/CBS News Poll.

Disgust with Congress is near the recorded high, and more than 60 percent of those polled were unable to name an elected official they admired.

The public has not appeared so disconsolate since 1979, when the nation was gripped by economic stagnation and Americans were taken hostage in Iran. Now people say they are frustrated and cynical and feel that life has veered out of control.

"I don't feel the people of this country have any control over what's going on, even if we voted-in the person we wanted," said Debra Flesher, a 35-year-old mother of four in Greenfield, Ind.

"The country is so big and there are so many issues and everyone has a different point of view," she added. "It's hard to have a safe neighborhood anymore. Even the media doesn't have control because bad is what sells. Like the Simpson case—that's what people want to see."

Mrs. Flesher was one of the respondents who agreed to a follow-up interview after taking part in the nationwide telephone poll of 1,429 adults, taken Oct. 29 through Nov. 1. The poll has a margin of sampling error of plus or minus three percentage points.

Asked about "the way things are going in the United States," 43 percent said they expect things to be worse five years from now. And most people fear that the next generation will be worse off than they are.

In the poll, crime emerged as a stark symbol of fear and powerlessness. Twenty-three percent of those surveyed identified crime as "the most important problem facing this country today." Economic concerns ranked second, with 18 percent calling them the nation's most pressing problem. Health care, which ranked second in September, has plunged to fifth place, tied with drugs.

Other sources of anxiety that emerged include a fear by a quarter of Americans that some close relative will lose his job in the next year, and a concern by 4 of 10 about their safety, saying there is an area within a mile of their homes where they would be afraid to walk at night.

Most voters hold fickle if not contradictory notions about Congress. But their overall regard for the institution continues to plummet, with the number who disapprove up 10 percentage points since September.

Three-fourths of the people surveyed disapproved of the job Congress is doing, just about the same level as disapproved in July 1992, when disgust with Congress peaked at news of the House bank scandal. Only 20 percent said they approved of the job Congress was doing.

Voters still gave their own representatives a break, compared with the rest of Congress, but anger at their elected officials is mounting.

The last two months of campaigning have clearly soured the electorate; the number of those who disapprove of their own representatives has doubled to 33 percent since September. At no time since The Times and CBS News started asking this question in 1977 have voters registered greater complaints about their own representatives.

Fifty-six percent approve of their elected officials, but only about a third think their own representatives deserve re-election. When asked about Congress as a whole, only 12 percent think most members of Congress deserve re-election, while 82 percent want Congress to start from scratch with all new people. Yet more than half said that even if all new people were elected, the Government would not work any better.

- -

Republicans today declared a political revolution, promised to balance the Federal budget and generally reveled in winning control of both the House and the Senate for the first time in 40 years.

ELECTION RESULTS

The Republican revolution of 1994 swept the party into power in the House and Senate, while also winning important governorships throughout the nation. The message was clear: Americans were demanding change, exemplified by the Republicans' "Contract with America." President Clinton and the new leaders of Congress promised to work together, but doubts remained whether the bitter politics of the 1994 elections could be left behind.

NOVEMBER 10, 1994
G.O.P. CELEBRATES ITS SWEEP TO POWER; CLINTON VOWS TO FIND COMMON GROUND

Committee Chairmanships Are Sure Spoils of Victory

By ADAM CLYMER

Special to The New York Times

WASHINGTON, Nov. 9—Republicans today declared a political revolution, promised to balance the Federal budget and generally reveled in winning control of both the House and the Senate for the first time in 40 years.

The depth of their victory was sounded by the fact that no sitting Republican governor, senator or representative was defeated.

Behaving more like striped-pants diplomats than the cranky, feuding politicians who had exchanged insults in the final days of the campaign, President Clinton and the Republican Congressional leaders, Senator Bob Dole of Kansas and Representative Newt Gingrich of Georgia, promised to look for areas where they could work together.

President Clinton told a White House news conference, "I am going to do my dead level best" to work with Republicans, and identified welfare reform as an area where "I think we will get an agreement."

Representative Gingrich, in line to become Speaker in a House where not one member has ever served under a Republican, said in an interview that he hoped his party could find a way to deal with Mr. Clinton and "package some things he can sign while he is vetoing others." He identified welfare reform, allowing the President to veto specific spending items and not just entire bills, and increasing the tax benefits for parents with children as matters that "fit rhetorically" with the President's aims.

Senator Dole, who will be Senate majority leader again, said he had called the President to tell him, "I wanted to let you know right up front that we want to work together where we can." But he offered fewer specifics, saying he would work with Mr. Clinton to secure approval of the new international trade agreement, but that he expected Mr. Clinton to explain the pact to the nation.

With eight of the House races not yet decided, the Republican landslide produced a gain of at least 49 Representatives—for a total of 227, to 199 for the Democrats and one independent. The Democratic casualties included the Speaker of the House, Thomas S. Foley, the former Ways and Means chairman, Dan Rostenkowski, and the Judiciary chairman, Jack Brooks.

In the Senate, Republicans won eight additional seats, and their edge went to 53–46 when Senator Richard C. Shelby of Alabama, who was elected eight years ago as a Democrat but who votes with Republicans on major issues, made an anticlimactic announcement this morning that Southern conservatives were no longer welcome in the Democratic party and joined the new majority. The California Senate race between the Democratic incumbent, Dianne Feinstein, and the Republican Michael Huffington, remained undecided today, although Ms. Feinstein claimed victory.

• •

ONE HUNDRED DAYS AND BEYOND

Following the 1994 midterm elections, the new Republican majority in Congress began to address the promises of the "Contract with America" by crafting legislation that sought to redefine the programs of the federal government. During their first one hundred days in office, a majority of House members adopted most of the Republican proposals, but the more cautious Senate and the even more recalcitrant Democratic president delayed action. As months passed, few of the contract's items were enacted into actual laws, leaving House Republicans eager for action but short of results.

JANUARY 27, 1995
HOUSE APPROVES BILL TO MANDATE BALANCED BUDGET

A CONSERVATIVE VICTORY

Amendment Is Expected to Face a Close Vote When It Goes to the Senate

By MICHAEL WINES

Special to The New York Times

WASHINGTON, Jan. 26—The House of Representatives voted tonight to amend the Constitution for the 28th time in 203 years, to prohibit the Federal Government from spending more money than it takes in.

The vote was 300 to 132, with 3 Democrats not voting. That is 12 more than the 288 votes, or two-thirds of the House members who were present, that is required to adopt a constitutional amendment. Two Indiana Republicans, Representatives John Hostettler and Mark E. Souder, voted against the measure; 72 Democrats supported it.

The measure now goes to the Senate, which is considering an identical proposal and where the amendment's fate is widely said to hang by no more than a vote or two.

Should the Senate approve it as well, the amendment will go directly to the state legislatures; if 38 vote to ratify, it will become part of the Constitution.

The House action was a triumph for conservatives and especially for Speaker Newt Gingrich of Georgia, who seized control of the chamber for his party with a campaign promoting a budget amendment as the ultimate cure for the Government's improvidence and bloat.

Chants of "Newt! Newt! Newt!" rang from the Republican side of the chamber as Mr. Gingrich assumed command of the big wood-and-marble rostrum at the front of the House to oversee the final votes. And they broke into whoops and cheers when the tally reached the necessary two-thirds.

FEBRUARY 2, 1995
CONGRESS LIMITS FEDERAL ORDERS COSTLY TO STATES

By JOHN H. CUSHMAN Jr.

Special to The New York Times

WASHINGTON, Feb. 1—The House of Representatives brought a prolonged debate to its foregone conclusion today and overwhelmingly passed legislation making it harder for Congress to impose new requirements on the states and cities without providing Federal money to pay for them.

The legislation, which passed the Senate in similar form last week and has President Clinton's endorsement, is the first major step in what the new Republican majority in Congress is promising will be a steady shift of power from Washington back to the local governments.

"This is really the first debate we have had on the New Federalism," said Representative William F. Clinger, Republican of Pennsylvania, as the debate ended. It had

consumed most of three weeks, including several nights when the House worked past midnight as Republicans fought off Democratic amendments. The bill was finally passed in a bipartisan vote of 360 to 74.

It was the second piece of the Republicans' campaign manifesto, the Contract With America, to have been approved by both chambers of Congress, each winning bipartisan support. President Clinton has already signed the first, which eliminated Congress's exemption from 11 Federal labor laws.

But the third such proposal to pass the House, which would amend the Constitution to require a balanced Federal budget, is far from the day of decision in the Senate, where debate continued inconclusively today.

FEBRUARY 10, 1995
REPUBLICANS ADVANCE PROPOSAL TO REPLACE THE WELFARE SYSTEM

Seek to Cut Aid to Teen-Age Mothers and Aliens

By ROBERT PEAR

Special to The New York Times

WASHINGTON, Feb. 9—House Republican leaders moved today to undo more than a half-century of social welfare policy by proposing to eliminate the right of poor women and children to receive cash assistance from the Government.

In place of the welfare program established 60 years ago as part of the Social Security Act, Republicans said they wanted to make a lump sum payment of $15.3 billion a year, which the states could use "in any manner reasonably calculated" to assist needy families with children. This represents the amount spent in 1994; there would be no allowance for inflation. Benefits would no longer be automatically available to people who met certain criteria.

Republican leaders reaffirmed their commitment to the most hotly debated features of their proposal, which would deny cash assistance to hundreds of thousands of unmarried teen-age mothers and to most immigrants, including legal aliens.

These provisions, fleshed out today with new detail by Representative E. Clay Shaw Jr., Republican of Florida, immediately encountered a barrage of criticism from some Republicans, from opponents of abortion and from liberal defenders of child welfare programs.

In a speech at the United States Chamber of Commerce, Mr. Shaw, who is chairman of the Ways and Means Subcommittee on Human Resources, said the Republican proposal embodied "tough love," using hard measures to save poor people from a life of dependence on the dole.

The subcommittee will begin voting on welfare legislation next week. House Speaker Newt Gingrich, Republican of Georgia, has promised a floor vote on the bill by mid-April, as part of the Contract With America. The Senate appears likely to support major changes to require welfare recipients to work. But Senator Bob Dole, the Republican floor leader, predicted last month that neither teen-age mothers nor legal immigrants would be cut from the rolls.

FEBRUARY 13, 1995
G.O.P. FACING SOME OBSTACLES AFTER FAST START

By DAVID E. ROSENBAUM

Special to The New York Times

WASHINGTON, Feb. 12—First, they changed the rules of the House. Then they passed the balanced-budget amendment. Then came restrictions on unfinanced requirements on the states.

This last week, the Republicans rammed through the House of Representatives a measure that would give the President a line-item veto and began passing bills to crack down on criminals.

On the surface, it looks as if the Republicans, controlling the House for the first time in 40 years, are having no more trouble with their Contract With America than a shopper crossing items off a grocery list.

But the ease of the last seven weeks may be illusory.

The first sign is that the balanced-budget amendment, the centerpiece of the contract, has become stalled in the Senate. At the end of last week, it was not clear whether the

Republicans could muster the two-thirds majority needed for approval unless they agreed to remove Social Security from the calculations.

As a practical matter, exempting Social Security would probably mean the death of the amendment, which the House passed easily last month. Balancing the budget by 2002, as the amendment would require, would be difficult in the best of circumstances. It would probably be impossible without counting the nearly $700 billion by which Social Security revenues are expected to exceed Social Security spending over the next seven years.

The prospect of giving the President a line-item veto, enabling him to revoke specific parts of a spending bill without vetoing the entire legislation, is also clouded in the Senate, where Congressional prerogatives are guarded more jealously than they are in the House.

JUNE 8, 1995
WITH FIRST VETO, CLINTON REJECTS BUDGET-CUT BILL
New Offensive Opened Against the G.O.P.

By ALISON MITCHELL

WASHINGTON, June 7—President Clinton vetoed his first bill today, striking down a plan to cut $16.4 billion in spending this year and marking a new phase in his confrontation with the Republican-controlled Congress.

During a Rose Garden ceremony honoring high schools for combating drug use, Mr. Clinton repeatedly struck a lectern for emphasis as he said the bill, which Republicans had offered as a down-payment on their promise to balance the Federal budget in seven years, would strike at an array of education programs while providing new money for building projects.

"I cannot in good conscience sign a bill that cuts education to save pet Congressional projects," Mr. Clinton said, as the invited guests applauded. "That is old politics. It is wrong. It wasn't a good policy when we were increasing spending on everything. It is a terrible policy if you're going to cut education to put pork back in."

Republican leaders said they could not muster the two-thirds majority in each house to override the veto, and would reopen negotiations with the White House to seek a compromise.

Mr. Clinton also challenged Congress to resolve the differences between its versions and send him a bill to sign that would give a President the power to veto individual items within bills. In exchange, he pledged that if this year he was given the power called for in the Republicans' Contract With America, he would not use it to kill individual tax provisions, only spending items. But he said he still held out the right to veto entire tax cut proposals.

Mr. Clinton's veto, the first of many he has threatened in recent months, puts his relationship with Congress into a new period of testing. There are inherent political risks and benefits for each side depending on how they maneuver in the coming months over future budget cuts as well as changes in foreign aid, environmental legislation and welfare, among other proposals.

AUGUST 20, 1995
EDITORIAL
THE CONTRACT, PARTLY FULFILLED

By the most common yardstick—legislation passed—the Republican takeover of Congress has not yet amounted to much. Only two parts of the Contract With America have been signed into law. No tax has been cut. Government spending continues to rise. But the impact of Newt Gingrich and friends goes well beyond a litany of votes. They have turned political debate around on nearly every important issue.

Before November, Congress debated how much more it would spend to put welfare enrollees to work. Now it debates how much less it will spend. Before November, politicians debated whether to cut off public services to illegal aliens. Now they debate whether to cut off legal immigrants as well. Congress used to debate which technology and national service programs to create. Now liberals declare victory if they keep existing programs alive. The Republicans' cramped vision of limited government has won, for now.

Nevertheless, the Republicans deserve some credit, especially for tackling problems from which the Democrats cowered. They have adopted a plan to balance the budget—too quickly for this page's tastes—and will deliver a proposal next month to slow the growth of Medicare. This takes real political courage. Medicare's popularity among the elderly makes it an uninviting target. But the program is headed toward bankruptcy.

The trouble with the G.O.P. is its tendency to steer every reasonable idea toward excess. The Republicans pledge to reform needlessly costly health, safety and environmental rules. But their alternative is destructive legislation that would cripple the Government's ability to enforce prudent rules.

They vow to return many other programs to the states to administer. This is a sensible idea applied to programs that provide valued services to local residents. But when applied to welfare, which helps only the poor and provides no immediate benefit to middle-class taxpayers, the Republicans invite states to send benefits tumbling, thereby driving the poor into someone else's lap.

Republicans talk a lot about cutting waste from the Federal budget. What this really means is cutting programs that cater to the needy. Low-income families absorbed about 60 percent of the budget cuts for the current year, even though they benefit from only about 12 percent of total discretionary spending. The G.O.P.'s seven-year plan calls for cutting entitlements for the poor by about 45 percent, even though the poor account for only 25 percent of total entitlement spending. By contrast, corporate subsidies and middle-class entitlements like Social Security were not nicked.

The excesses and hypocrisy subtract from what is perhaps the most important lesson of the last eight months of legislating. A year ago, pundits sat around wondering whether either party could govern and whether Congress was destined to remain an unorganizable collection of 535 political entrepreneurs. In the House, Speaker Newt Gingrich has shown that a majority party, under aggressive and decisive leaders, can execute a disciplined agenda.

Fortunately, the Senate has shown that it can rein in the excesses of the House. It has turned aside the balanced budget amendment and stalled the line item veto and welfare reform. President Clinton has shown that a well-aimed veto can make him relevant. An extreme G.O.P. agenda threatens at every turn. But perhaps the Senate and President can block or fix most of what is bad.

* *

The Government Shutdown

The Republican Congress and Democratic president fought throughout 1995. In November these clashes climaxed with an impasse over the federal budget, as Republicans demanded steep reductions in spending and President Clinton vetoed their legislation. Unwilling to compromise, the two sides allowed government funding to expire. Without appropriated funds, the mighty United States government shut down. Twice, once for two weeks and then again for five weeks, all nonessential services were shuttered. Ultimately, public opinion shifted in favor of the president, forced the Republicans to back down, and delivered a huge victory to Clinton.

NOVEMBER 14, 1995
PRESIDENT VETOES STOPGAP BUDGET; SHUTDOWN LOOMS
LATE MEETING FAILS
Irresponsibility Charged as Agencies Prepare to Close Today
By ADAM CLYMER

WASHINGTON, Tuesday, Nov. 14—President Clinton on Monday vetoed two bills intended to keep the Government in business as he and Republican leaders exchanged accusations of partisan irresponsibility and much of the Government prepared to shut down later today.

A last-ditch effort to reach agreement ended shortly before midnight without any progress between Mr. Clinton and Republican leaders. While Bob Dole of Kansas, the Senate majority leader, called the 90-minute session "constructive," he said, "We went around and around, but we

don't have an agreement." Senator Thomas A. Daschle of South Dakota, the Democratic leader, was even more emphatic, saying, "No progress was made."

While other Republicans will meet with Administration officials later today, the failure to agree meant that about 800,000 Federal workers will be furloughed after reporting to work this morning.

Shortly before the meeting began at 10 P.M. Monday, Mr. Clinton vetoed a two-week extension of spending authority for the Federal Government, complaining of its reductions in spending: "We don't need these cuts to balance the budget. And we do not need big cuts in education and the environment to balance the budget."

On Monday morning, President Clinton vetoed a four-week extension of the Government's authority to borrow money. He asserted that provisions attached to it would set back three decades of environmental and public health protection as part "of an overall back-door effort by the Congressional Republicans to impose their priorities on our nation." He said they should "drop their extreme proposals." Later, he said the Republican budget "violates our values."

Speaker Newt Gingrich replied by saying, "We were elected to change politics as usual." He continued, "We were elected to get rid of all the phony promises and the phony excuses and to be honest with the American people." He attacked the Administration for "harsh rhetoric," contending that "they say that wanting to balance the budget is the act of a terrorist" and that "it's extremist to want honesty in the welfare rolls." He said Mr. Clinton had vetoed the bill "so they can play political games."

Republicans delayed delivering the stopgap spending measure, or continuing resolution, until late Monday night so he could not reject it in time for the evening television news, Republican Congressional aides said. That measure is needed because Congress has sent only 4 of the 13 regular spending bills to him, and he has vetoed one of them.

> " Nearly half the civilian functions of the Federal Government ground to a sputtering halt today as President Clinton and the Republican-controlled Congress remained deadlocked over spending priorities. "

NOVEMBER 15, 1995
FEDERAL WORKERS GO HOME AS BUDGET IMPASSE STIFFENS
Any Resolution Appears to Be Days Away
By TODD S. PURDUM

WASHINGTON, Nov. 14—Nearly half the civilian functions of the Federal Government ground to a sputtering halt today as President Clinton and the Republican-controlled Congress remained deadlocked over spending priorities and appeared to push off any possible resolution until at least the end of the week.

It was a day of dueling televised oratory, fitful negotiations and mutual accusations of bad faith, and the price was the closing of Government offices, parks, museums and laboratories and the furloughing of some 800,000 employees, who reported for work only to be sent home, their desks eerily empty and their suites dark by midmorning. Vital functions, from mail delivery to air traffic control, continued uninterrupted.

Nevertheless, thousands of Americans who needed Government services that seemed vital to them—locating tax records, applying for Social Security benefits, obtaining passports—found themselves frustrated and sometimes furious because of a battle in Washington that most did not profess to understand.

"We are at an impasse," Leon E. Panetta, the White House chief of staff, told reporters late this afternoon, after his second meetings of the day with Congressional budget leaders on Capitol Hill. "I believe we are looking at a situation in which they are going to continue to try to put their budget together, send it to the President and the President will veto that budget."

Late Monday, Mr. Clinton vetoed a stopgap spending measure that would have kept the Government running until the end of the month because, he said, the Republicans had attached unacceptable conditions and cuts in programs he favors.

At midafternoon, Mr. Clinton appeared in the White House briefing room to accuse the Republicans of putting "ideology ahead of common sense and shared values." He said he vetoed the temporary spending measure, and another that would have extended the Government's borrowing authority until mid-December, "because America can never accept under pressure what it would not accept in free and open debate." He vowed to "continue to fight for the right kind of balanced budget," and added, "It is my solemn responsibility to stand against a budget plan that is bad for America."

He had no sooner finished speaking than an angry Speaker Newt Gingrich accused him of "deliberate misrepresentation" and "a phony argument about fantasy cuts." And Senator Bob Dole of Kansas, the majority leader, said Mr. Clinton "didn't make it any easier" to get an agreement to keep the Government running. Both sides said they could not predict when the shutdown, the fifth since 1981 but apparently the most serious, would end.

DECEMBER 17, 1995
ACT II OF FEDERAL SHUTDOWN: SOME SEE POLITICS OF ABSURD
By FRANCIS X. CLINES

WASHINGTON, Dec. 16—Cpl. Yamashita Johnson locked the door of the National Gallery of Art at noon sharp today, leaving Karen Rose fuming on the street in esthetic deprivation, while Joan Phillips delighted inside at the windfall of being among the final gallery visitors to the Vermeer supershow.

"It's grandstanding," said Ms. Phillips, speaking of the politicians, not the paintings, as she sympathized with Ms. Rose and other citizens locked outside the museum, normally open until 5 P.M. "You can't really shut down the Government," she said as the gallery crowd thinned down to a precious few savoring the unhurried serenity of Vermeer. "These politicians are grandstanding."

On the street, Ms. Rose, who had timed her drive perfectly from Orlando, Fla., to Rhode Island for her afternoon tickets to the Winslow Homer show here, was furious. "It's just this great big drama the pols are trying to create," she insisted, gesturing angrily down Constitution Avenue toward the Capitol. "O.K., so I miss this show, but the real problem will be Monday when people can't talk to the Social Security Administration and other things like that."

Measuring the first hours of the renewed shutdown was almost a metaphysical task on a quiet weekend day. But the Americans inconvenienced by the Congress and White House—even though their numbers were few—were noteworthy for the similarity of their complaints. They said the underlying issue seemed to be a matter of politicians preferring to cry wolf, rather than uncle, in their chronic budget crises.

"It's just political theater, and I had enough of it in their first performance," said Robert Untreberger, who journeyed from Philadelphia for a weekend visit to the Washington Mall museums and found himself with enough idle time to wonder at the state of national politics.

JANUARY 5, 1996
SPLIT AND BRUISED IN POLLS, G.O.P. WEIGHS NEW TACTICS
By ROBIN TONER

WASHINGTON, Jan. 4—As the partial Government shutdown limps toward its fourth week, Republicans on Capitol Hill have begun the search for an exit strategy, some way of breaking what looks increasingly like a stalemate that has badly shaken their unity.

But the Senate and the House approach this task with sharp differences in tactics, style and political position. The center of gravity in the House is the freshmen, cheerfully immune to the polls, happy with their reputation as unpolitical politicians and convinced of their historic mission to balance the budget in seven years.

That conviction has immensely complicated the task of the House Republican leadership as it searches for a way to move beyond a dangerous status quo for the party: inconclusive budget talks and a Government shutdown for which Republicans are widely blamed.

Many of the freshmen continued to insist today that the only way to keep the heat on the White House was to keep the Government sharply curtailed. "We got snookered once by the President, and I don't think we should get snookered twice," said Representative Ray LaHood, Republican of Illinois, referring to the failure to reach agreement after a Government shutdown in November. "The best way to hold his feet to the fire is by causing a lot of anxiety and heartburn by keeping the Government shut down."

In contrast, the Senate had already abandoned that ground; Senator Bob Dole, the majority leader, pushed through a measure on Tuesday night to reopen the Government, saying Federal workers were unfairly "caught in the middle." The measure was quickly denounced by many conservatives, including some in the House, and it was just as quickly bottled up on the House floor. But it reflected the complicated political and institutional imperatives of the Senate, and Mr. Dole's own uneasiness with the hard-line, confrontational politics of the House.

JANUARY 6, 1996
CONGRESS VOTES TO RETURN 760,000 TO FEDERAL PAYROLL AND RESUME SOME SERVICES
STEP IS TEMPORARY
Clinton Quickly Agrees to a Temporary End to the Shutdown
By ADAM CLYMER

WASHINGTON, Saturday, Jan. 6—Congress voted on Friday to put 760,000 Federal workers back on the payroll for three weeks and to resume politically visible Government operations, from the national parks and medical research to payments for veterans' pensions, through September, and President Clinton approved the temporary end of the shutdown just after midnight.

Congress approved three bills returning workers to their jobs and reopening closed programs to varying degrees. The White House said early today that Mr. Clinton had signed legislation to finance certain Federal programs, to return furloughed Federal employees to work at full pay and to reinstate pay for those employees who remained at their jobs.

The vote came after Representative John R. Kasich, the Ohio Republican and chairman of the House Budget Committee, and other Republican leaders had spent much of Friday morning convincing dubious Republican freshmen that they were not giving up a vital advantage, which some had said was their only tool to force concessions from President Clinton. "We're not anywhere near raising a white flag," Mr. Kasich said.

While 12 Republican freshmen voted no, 60 voted yes and one did not vote. The measure was passed by the House, 401 to 17. The Senate passed the measure on a voice vote.

Republicans insisted that the partial reopening would enable them to refocus public attention away from sad stories about the effects of the 21-day partial Government shutdown, and toward President Clinton and what they called his refusal to propose a Federal budget that would be balanced within seven years.

Before heading for the White House and a meeting with the President, Speaker Newt Gingrich told reporters, "Frankly, the House Republican Conference has no faith that the President is negotiating in good faith and has no faith that the President will in fact ever provide a balanced budget."

• •

FALLOUT

Political battles between President Clinton and the Republican Congress elected in 1994 were ongoing. The 1996 election continued the clash, as Americans reelected both Clinton and the Republican Congress. The Republican Party had gained national parity with the Democrats, but neither had clear control of the government in a new era of partisan bitterness. During Clinton's second term, Congress opened investigations into his involvement in scandals including campaign finance irregularities, real estate dealings, and allegations of sexual misconduct with a White House intern.

NOVEMBER 6, 1996
CLINTON ELECTED TO A 2D TERM WITH SOLID MARGINS ACROSS U.S.; G.O.P. KEEPS HOLD ON CONGRESS

Democrats Fail to Reverse Right's Capitol Hill Gains

By DAVID E. ROSENBAUM

With close races all across the country, Republicans retained control of the Senate and the House in yesterday's elections.

The votes in several states were still in doubt early today, but Republicans were guaranteed of having at least 51 Senate seats in the next Congress. And around 2 A.M., Speaker Newt Gingrich proclaimed that his party had retained control of the House.

The Republicans won in the Senate by holding most of their own seats and picking up at least two seats in states where popular Democratic Senators are retiring.

In one of the most compelling political contests of the year, Senator John Kerry of Massachusetts was re-elected. All other Democratic incumbents who were running also won.

But only one Republican Senator lost, and Republican newcomers won in Nebraska and Alabama, replacing retiring Democrats.

Republicans began Election Day with a 53-to-47 advantage and thus could afford to lose a net of two seats and still have a majority in the 100-member Senate.

Among the Republican Senators who were re-elected were Jesse Helms of North Carolina and Strom Thurmond of South Carolina.

In North Carolina, where Senator Helms, a Republican, was challenged by Harvey B. Gantt, a black architect who is the former Mayor of Charlotte, a survey of voters showed that more than 80 percent of those who voted were white and that three-fifths of them voted for Mr. Helms. Mr. Gantt was winning more than 90 percent of the much smaller black vote.

"I can guarantee you one thing," Mr. Helms said in a victory speech. "There's going to be six more years of torment for Ted Kennedy and all those other liberals."

NOVEMBER 7, 1996
EDITORIAL
THE ROAD AHEAD

Pessimists looking at this week's election results will conclude that the voters have no idea what they really want—Gingrich conservatism, Clintonesque post-liberalism, or just plain gridlock between the Republican Congress and Democratic White House. But the American people actually seem to have sent a pretty clear message. They think the country is going in the right direction, toward a leaner but still active Federal Government. The challenge now is whether the President and Congress can build on that rough consensus and move the country forward.

President Clinton must take the lead. For the last two years he has been an artful defensive strategist, allowing the Republican Congress to expose its worst excesses and offering himself as a safer, more moderate alternative. But

1997 cannot be a replay of 1995. For all their errors, the Republicans seized intellectual leadership in Washington over the last two years, capturing the nation's attention and dictating the policy debate's terms. Now Mr. Clinton must set the agenda and force Congress to respond to his legislative initiatives.

There can be no question about his mandate. The American people express their clearest opinion about what they want government to do through their choice of chief executive. In his campaign Mr. Clinton described a Government that is efficient and cost-conscious but nonetheless uses its powers to improve schools, preserve our natural resources and protect the weak and the ostracized. It is his duty to follow through.

The nation's bipartisan political center now embraces a middle-class, suburban outlook that supports government activism on issues like education and environment, backs gun control and abortion, worries more about balanced budgets than tax cuts and demands the campaign-finance reform for which it once hopelessly yearned. Mr. Clinton is much closer to the public on these matters than a Republican leadership that is frozen in place by its Southern base and its fear of Ralph Reed. The President can take the initiative by building coalitions between his own party and moderate Republicans who think outside the Gingrich-Lott guidelines. Mr. Clinton must also take a bipartisan approach to Medicare reform that assures Republicans they will be protected from the kind of hyperpolitical assault he made himself during the last campaign.

Mr. Clinton's greatest, and loneliest, challenge will be to salvage the nation's commitment to the poor and helpless. He and many other Democrats are obligated to build a humane replacement for the welfare system they helped destroy. Most Americans are now wary of expensive social programs, and resent any aid to the poor that smacks of giveaways. But they did not shun Mr. Clinton's own campaign message of a generalized commitment to aiding the poor, protecting the children and giving minorities a chance to help themselves. Using the bounce of his victory, the President can fashion a new social agenda that reconnects the safety net while assuring middle America that all citizens, including the poor, will be required to take responsibility for their lives and work for their living.

The most threatening obstacle to this sort of second Clinton Administration is the long string of ongoing investigations into Mr. Clinton's past conduct. The Republican Congress will want to begin another inquiry into new questions about Mr. Clinton's campaign fund-raising. But the last four years should certainly have taught the President that stonewalling and covering up can be much more damning than the original offense.

This time Mr. Clinton must voluntarily open up his campaign-finance records, explain what a top Democratic fund-raiser with ties to Indonesian business magnates was doing in the Oval Office, and whom that man met during dozens of trips to the White House this year. If Mr. Clinton finds aides who have broken the law or compromised their ability to serve, now is the time to dismiss them.

The election results are a disappointment to those who had hoped that Mr. Clinton's seemingly inevitable re-election would be coupled with Democratic control in Congress and a return to the New Deal tradition that was repudiated in 1994. There is not going to be a going back. That does not mean that America is stumbling into a new century of heartless self-preoccupation. The path seems open to a new policy synthesis, a tougher yet still inclusive social contract. But Bill Clinton is going to have to show us how to get there.

THE PRESIDENTIAL ELECTION OF 2000

BUSH TAKES POWER AFTER THE SUPREME COURT ENDS CONTEST

On November 7, 2000, the United States chose a new president. But who was it?

The answer was unknown after Americans cast 105 million ballots. It remained in dispute for five weeks of counting and recounting the ballots, street demonstrations, and legal wrangling. Ultimately, the election was decided by a single vote—cast not by a citizen in the voting booth but by a justice in the U.S. Supreme Court.

In the end, Republican George W. Bush, governor of Texas, was named the new president. Son of a former president, he trailed Democrat Albert E. Gore Jr. by more than half a million popular votes, but defeated Gore by the barest possible margin in the Electoral College after snaring the votes of Florida in a controversial decision that bitterly divided Republicans and Democrats.

Precedents for Bush's success existed only in the nineteenth century. In 1824 John Quincy Adams was installed by the House of Representatives after an overwhelming loss in the popular vote; a trailing Republican (Rutherford B. Hayes in 1876) came to power through the disputed electoral vote of Florida; and another Republican candidate (Benjamin Harrison in 1888) achieved office without either a majority or a plurality of the popular vote.

The electoral outcome abounded in ironies and anomalies. The small tally for minor left-wing candidate Ralph Nader drained enough votes from Gore to give power to Bush. A nation that largely ignored issues of national security in the election would soon face the shock of terrorist attacks on its homeland, two wars abroad, and deep internal divisions.

The stage for these strange events was set by the eight-year presidency of Bill Clinton (1993–2001). Attempting to recast the Democratic Party's New Deal heritage, Clinton had adopted more moderate economic programs, even accepting typical Republican policies such as welfare reform and declaring, "The era of big government is over." By 2000 the U.S. economic record during his tenure was hugely positive. Although foreign policy had become less important in the post-Soviet world, Clinton also had notable successes

President George W. Bush talks to his father, former president Bush, as he sits at his desk in the Oval Office for the first time on Inauguration Day, January 20, 2001.

promoting accords in the Middle East and Northern Ireland and resolving civil wars in the Balkans.

Although Clinton's popularity was understandably high, his personal standing did little to bolster his party. He won two terms without capturing a popular majority. Two years after his first inauguration, Republicans won control of Congress in the cyclonic election of 1994 and held power in both chambers for the rest of Clinton's tenure. On the mass level, Republican partisanship maintained the near-parity with Democrats achieved in the Reagan years.

Reports of intimate escapades and marital infidelity had dogged Clinton throughout his career, even threatening to end his first campaign for the presidency. In 1998 his problems mounted when an affair with a White House intern became public in official, almost pornographic, revelations. In an atmosphere of intense partisanship, the House of Representatives passed two articles of impeachment against Clinton (similar to criminal indictments) on charges of perjury and obstruction of justice. Acting as a trial court, the Senate acquitted the president on both counts. Clinton survived and maintained his favorable opinion ratings, but the accumulated dirt still clogged Democratic wheels in the election of 2000.

2000 ELECTORAL VOTE

STATE	ELECTORAL VOTES	BUSH	GORE	STATE	ELECTORAL VOTES	BUSH	GORE
Alabama	(9)	9	–	Montana	(3)	3	–
Alaska	(3)	3	–	Nebraska	(5)	5	–
Arizona	(8)	8	–	Nevada	(4)	4	–
Arkansas	(6)	6	–	New Hampshire	(4)	4	–
California	(54)	–	54	New Jersey	(15)	–	15
Colorado	(8)	8	–	New Mexico	(5)	–	5
Connecticut	(8)	–	8	New York	(33)	–	33
Delaware	(3)	–	3	North Carolina	(14)	14	–
District of Columbia	(3)	–	2	North Dakota	(3)	3	–
Florida	(25)	25	–	Ohio	(21)	21	–
Georgia	(13)	13	–	Oklahoma	(8)	8	–
Hawaii	(4)	–	4	Oregon	(7)	–	7
Idaho	(4)	4	–	Pennsylvania	(23)	–	23
Illinois	(22)	–	22	Rhode Island	(4)	–	4
Indiana	(12)	12	–	South Carolina	(8)	8	–
Iowa	(7)	–	7	South Dakota	(3)	3	–
Kansas	(6)	6	–	Tennessee	(11)	11	–
Kentucky	(8)	8	–	Texas	(32)	32	–
Louisiana	(9)	9	–	Utah	(5)	5	–
Maine	(4)	–	4	Vermont	(3)	–	3
Maryland	(10)	–	10	Virginia	(13)	13	–
Massachusetts	(12)	–	12	Washington	(11)	–	11
Michigan	(18)	–	18	West Virginia	(5)	5	–
Minnesota	(10)	–	10	Wisconsin	(11)	–	11
Mississippi	(7)	7	–	Wyoming	(3)	3	–
Missouri	(11)	11	–				
				TOTALS	(538)	271	266

THE PARTIES AND THE CANDIDATES

In contrast to its intense ending, election year 2000 began quietly. The major party nominations were settled quickly, within five weeks of primary votes, in favor of early front-runners. With the country confident, prosperous, and at peace, the outlook was for a relatively unexciting contest between two seemingly moderate candidates. The reality turned out to be far different.

Early decisions on the nominations were virtually certain because of changes in the schedule of state primaries. Seeking to gain influence in the choice of presidential candidates, many states had moved the dates of their contests to the early months. This process of "front-loading" meant that virtually half of the convention delegates would be chosen by the first week of March—a sharp change from earlier years, when less than a fifth would be selected by that date.

The schedule worked to the advantage of a candidate who was already in the public eye and could accumulate campaign funds early. For the Republicans, that candidate was George W. Bush, son of former president George H. W. Bush. As governor of Texas, the younger Bush had presided over a standard Republican program of limited taxes and social conservatism, while showing support of educational reform and concern for Hispanic immigrants. His reelection in 1998, generally a bad year for Republicans, also gave promise of electoral appeal to a party eager to reclaim the White House. Party officials began lining up behind him.

Bush's greatest asset was money. Raising record sums, Bush declined federal funds for his nomination campaign, the first candidate to spurn the support provided under the campaign finance reforms of 1974. Although twelve potential candidates had entered the nomination race in 1999, six of them soon withdrew for lack of funds. The most intriguing possibility was Elizabeth Dole, the first woman ever to launch a significant presidential effort, but she too found the money wells dry.

By the new year, the only serious challenger to Bush was Arizona senator John McCain. (Billionaire Steve Forbes could match Bush financially, but lacked other qualifications.) Although an economic conservative, McCain had also shown an independent streak and had the attraction of being a war hero. With limited money, he turned to a ground campaign, stubbornly pleading his case in town hall forums in the first primary state, New Hampshire. Drawing large support from independents and crossover Democrats, McCain shredded the nomination script by decisively beating Bush in the state primary, 49 percent to 30 percent.

Having ignored McCain before the New Hampshire contest, the Bush forces now turned to a full attack on him in South Carolina, presenting McCain as a renegade from the party, a defender of government welfare programs, and, in some smear attacks, as a supporter of homosexuality and the father of an illegitimate black child. Bush won the state decisively, 53 percent to 42 percent, although McCain recovered briefly with a win in Michigan.

The critical primaries came on March 7, when eleven front-loaded states voted. Drawing two-thirds of the Republican faithful, Bush carried seven contests, including the major states of California, New York, and Ohio. McCain withdrew two days later, and Bush then swept all of the remaining states, amassing 63 percent of the total 17 million votes.

The Democratic nomination followed a parallel path. There, the front-runner was Al Gore, the incumbent vice president. Other Democrats considered a race, then decided to avoid a fight that Gore seemed certain to win. Only one Democrat proved willing to challenge him, former senator Bill Bradley of New Jersey.

Bradley provided the unusual combination of the renown of a former professional basketball star, the intellect of a Rhodes scholar and serious author, and the insight of a policy innovator. Unexpectedly, he also had money, his treasury

almost as full as Gore's. But he could not break through. After a futile effort in the Iowa caucuses, he narrowly lost the critical New Hampshire primary, as Gore carried the state 50 percent to 46 percent. On the same decisive day that Bush sealed his nomination, Gore won all of the eleven primaries. Bradley withdrew two days later. Gore went on to win every Democratic contest and 76 percent of the 14 million Democratic votes.

With the presidential nominations settled in record time, each candidate looked to his party convention to boost him ahead in a race that was very close in opinion surveys. In the ritualistic nominating roll calls, each won unanimous endorsement, Bush by 2,066 Republicans, Gore by 4,339 Democrats.

As the out party, the Republicans met first. At their convention in Philadelphia, July 31 to August 3, they attempted to move to the moderate center of public opinion. They drew a verbal portrait of Bush as a "compassionate conservative" and a television picture of a diverse party, giving much formal attention and camera coverage to the women and the few African Americans in attendance. To shore up his own qualifications, Bush selected an experienced Washington hand for the vice-presidential slot—Richard Cheney, former White House chief of staff and secretary of defense.

Initiating his presidential bid, Bush held to the theme. He criticized Clinton and Gore in a rhetorical refrain, "They had their chance. They have not led. We will." Then he moved toward a moderate credo: "Big government is not the answer, but the alternative to bureaucracy is not indifference." He endorsed new programs of federal standards for public schools and private retirement plans to supplement the Social Security program, along with tax reductions. But he received the most applause when he returned to more common Republican themes, such as elimination of inheritance taxes and a ban on late-term abortions. Looking back to Clinton's sex scandal and forward to his presidential inauguration, he pledged, "I will swear to not only uphold the laws of our land, I will swear to uphold the honor and dignity of the office to which I have been elected, so help me God." Bush left Philadelphia amid the enthusiasm of Republicans and with the comfort of a widening lead in opinion polls.

Two weeks later, convening in Los Angeles, the Democrats recovered. Even before the delegates met, Gore won plaudits with his pathbreaking vice-presidential selection of Connecticut senator Joseph Lieberman, the first Jew on a national ticket. Furthermore, Lieberman's strong religious views and moral sternness distanced the Democrats from Clinton's bawdiness.

Gore faced a delicate choice between running on the Clinton record, a mix of policy success and personal misbehavior, or establishing an autonomous identity. While Clinton held the limelight of the convention on its first days, Gore moved toward a distinct appeal in his acceptance speech (initiated with a long passionate kiss with his wife).

Gore minimized the economic prosperity that was his greatest asset, conceding: "This election is not an award for past performance. I'm not asking you to vote for me on the basis of the economy we have. Tonight I ask for your support on the basis of the better, fairer, more prosperous America we can build together. . . . We're electing a new president. And I stand here tonight as my own man." The vice president then appealed to Americans disturbed that "powerful forces and powerful interests stand in your way, and the odds seem stacked against you, even as you do what's right for you and your family." He proposed new programs of universal health coverage and college tuition tax credits, while also promising to pay off the national debt and maintain abortion rights.

Their convention boosted the Democrats. Gore's personal ratings became highly favorable, and the opinion polls indicated that he had completely eliminated Bush's lead. A close vote between the major parties loomed on the horizon. But there were also two small threatening clouds in the electoral sky.

One was the Reform Party, a remnant of Ross Perot's independent presidential bids in 1992 and 1996. After internal wrangling that led to two competing conventions, Patrick Buchanan—formerly a Republican challenger to Bush's father—became the official Reform Party candidate, receiving more than $12 million in federal funding. On the left side of the political spectrum, Ralph Nader led the Green Party on a platform attacking corporate dominance of the nation's economy and political institutions. The famous consumer advocate certainly did not expect to win, but he did hope to gain 5 percent of the vote, which would give him federal funding for the next presidential election. Although Buchanan and Nader agreed on little but their protectionist trade policies, neither admired George Bush. For both, ironically, their only significant effect on the election of 2000 was to drag the Republican candidate over the last steps into the White House.

The Campaign

Voters were interested in the campaign, yet complacent. Times were good, jobs were plentiful, there were budget surpluses for the federal government, and the world was apparently safe for the United States.

Issue differences between the parties lessened as Bush moderated customary Republican positions. The nominee dropped the party's previous call for abolition of the Department of Education, instead supporting new federal spending to bolster school performance. He also favored an extension of Medicare to cover prescription costs, and gave little attention to the usual "wedge" issues of abortion, homosexuality, and crime. Bush—ironically, as it turned out—argued for a limited U.S. role in international affairs and against efforts at "nation-building."

Gore portrayed himself as a "new" Democrat, practiced in "reinventing government." But a basic philosophic difference between the parties and their leaders remained. Republicans' instincts still led them first to seek solutions through private actions or through the marketplace, while Democrats consistently looked for governmental solutions. That difference was evident on fundamental questions such as allocation of the windfall surpluses in the federal budget: Bush sought a huge, across-the-board cut in taxes, and Gore proposed a panoply of new government programs and tax cuts. In a specific illustration, providing funds for Social Security, Bush would encourage individuals to invest part of their tax payments in private investment accounts, but Gore would transfer other government funds into the Social Security trust fund. This philosophical difference could be seen even in the intimate question of teenage pregnancy, where Republicans relied on individual morality, sexual abstinence by adolescents, and Democrats supported sex education programs, which might include distribution of condoms in public schools.

Voters' ambivalence made the race a dead heat right up to election day. That closeness was reinforced by the parties' coherent ideological support—the Republicans had few self-identified liberals in their ranks, and the Democrats had few self-identified conservatives. Nor was there any overriding campaign issue that either Gore or Bush could turn to his advantage.

Although voters clearly liked their prosperity, they gave Gore little credit for Clinton's economic record. And, rather than appeal to the past, the vice president hurt his own cause by turning the election away from an advantageous retrospective evaluation of the Clinton administration to an uncertain prospective choice based on future expectations, where Bush's program might be as convincing to the voters as Gore's. If the election came down to only a choice of the manager of a consensual agenda, Bush's individual qualities might well be more attractive.

Gore's neglect of the economic issue reflected his more general quandary about the incumbent president. The voters' mixed verdict on Clinton paralleled their overall evaluations on America's direction. They strongly agreed that the country was "generally on the right track," but also predominantly saw its "moral climate off on the wrong track." Given these conflicting attitudes, Gore hesitated to claim Clinton's heritage or to have the president campaign for him.

As voters examined the actual candidates, they focused on different qualities. Gore was preferred on most policy issues, while Bush was rated more highly on personal qualities. Gore's individual strengths among the electorate were his experience and intelligence, while Bush's strengths were his strong leadership and honesty. These differing portrayals were reinforced by the three television debates, and even more so by media commentaries that criticized Gore for excessive attention to policy details and Bush for factual inaccuracies. How much the debates influenced the voters was, however, unclear. Although viewers more often considered Gore the "winner," the political effect was to convert a narrow Bush deficit in the opinion polls into a narrow Bush lead. But neither candidate could achieve anything more than a statistical draw.

The continuing, and agonizing, closeness of the race led to still more frenzied efforts. The candidates and the parties spent considerably more than the $75 million provided in federal funds. The Republicans also spent $45 million, and the Democrats $35 million, in television advertising. Adding the funding of independent groups and the congressional races, the total political outlay in 2000 was estimated at $3 billion for all campaigns. New means of reaching voters included informal interviews on talk shows, particularly programs oriented to women such as *Oprah* and *Rosie O'Donnell*, and late-night comedy. The Internet had its first significant impact on national politics, employing interactive Web sites, e-mail communication with supporters, and full coverage of the conventions and campaign events.

In the final days, the Nader vote became potentially critical, threatening to drain enough protest votes from Gore to make Bush a narrow winner. (Buchanan by now drew neither attention nor support, but his name on the ballot had a controversial effect in Florida.) Nader, scorning both major candidates, persisted in his effort to win 5 percent of the national vote, thereby gaining federal funding. Desperate to win, some Gore voters used Internet mail to propose trades, in which Nader backers would vote for Gore in close states while Gore backers would reciprocate by voting for Nader in safe states. The scheme fell apart because such trades were unenforceable and possibly illegal, but the proposal testified to the new reach of the Internet and to the anxiety of the electorate.

THE ELECTION RESULTS?

The evident closeness of the race brought 9 million new voters to the polls compared to 1996, but the turnout was only barely above that in 1992. Gore increased the Democratic tally over the previous election by 3.5 million votes, amassing the highest total of any Democratic candidate in history. But Bush did far better, adding 11 million Republican ballots. The final count was 48.4 percent for Gore, 47.9 percent for Bush, a sliver of 2.7 percent for Nader, and a trace 0.4 percent for Buchanan. Surveys indicated that the nonvoters favored Gore by a 3 to 2 margin—but their opinions literally did not count.

Even though the winner of the election was unknown until December 12, the voting pattern was evident in one day. Despite the predictions of journalistic pundits and academic scholars, Gore had lost the victory that the incumbent party in a time of prosperity and peace could expect. He did well among voters who focused on the economic record, but that factor had less importance than in previous elections. Its reduced advantage for Gore was overcome by support for Bush derived from his tax-cut program, the voters' favorable impressions of his personal qualities, and defections based on Clinton's perceived immorality.

Both candidates won overwhelmingly among their own partisans, but Bush won more of the former Perot voters than Gore. Bush also gained significantly among independents, white Protestants, Catholics, Hispanics, and men, turning the fabled "gender gap" into a net gain for the Republicans. Gore retained traditional Democratic strength among African Americans, Jews, the poor, and union members. He did win the popular vote—but this year the election would be decided by a different count.

Geography was also decisive. In carrying the preponderance of states (30, including Florida), Bush changed the landscape of American politics. He swept the interior of the nation, including all states in the South, and the border, plains, and mountain states, other than a hairbreadth loss in New Mexico. Gore won in only 20 states and the District of Columbia, almost all on the geographical fringes of the nation, and he lost 14 states that Clinton had carried previously, including his home state of Tennessee. Reflecting the sharp geographical divisions, the vote varied considerably among the nation's regions and states. Gore won as much as two-thirds of the votes in New England, but fewer than one in three in the mountain states.

Bush ultimately won because of the determining tally in the Electoral College. In 2000 the Electoral College outcome provided a rare instance of the conflict between "large states" and "small states" that the framers of the Constitution tried to resolve. Their compromise gives disproportionate weight to smaller states because each state, in addition to the votes allocated on the basis of population, receives two electoral votes reflecting its equal suffrage in the Senate. Gore did well in the largest states, carrying six of nine, an advantage of 165 to 78 in the electoral count, but Bush carried 13 of the 19 smallest states for 54 votes to Gore's 23. The Texan's dominance in these small states exactly compensated for his loss of the single largest state, California, even though he accumulated a million fewer votes than Gore in the combined totals of these states.

Yet, even with these structural advantages, Bush won the presidency only by securing Florida's 25 electoral votes and a bare majority of 271 to 267 in the Electoral College. That became the ultimate story of the election of 2000.

On election night, Gore appeared to be the presidential winner, after reports from exit polls gave him the votes of Pennsylvania, Michigan, and then the final edge in Florida. As more returns came in, however, the media quickly recanted their predictions, and a long electronic night followed. After midnight, broadcasters now declared Bush the winner in Florida and the next president. Gore accepted the judgment and called Bush to concede. But, as the sun rose, further reports found Florida again uncertain, and Gore retracted his concession.

In the following weeks, the nation focused on the counting and recounting of the Florida ballots. The framework for that long and controversial process, however, had been set in earlier decisions that consistently structured the ballot count in Bush's favor.

The first structuring element was the distribution of the vote for the minor candidates. Buchanan, as a conservative candidate, might have taken votes from Bush, but his campaign had collapsed, aiding the Republicans. At the other end of the spectrum, however, Nader had mounted a more serious challenge, and surveys indicated that Gore was preferred over Bush by two-thirds of Nader's voters. In Florida alone, if Nader were not on the ballot, this shift would have given Gore a convincing victory in the state by a margin of 25,000—and the presidency.

Nader aside, the political structure of Florida favored Bush. The co-chairs of his state campaign were Gov. Jeb Bush, the candidate's brother, and Katherine Harris, the secretary of state, in charge of administering the election. The legislature was controlled in both chambers by Republicans. Before and after election day, all of these partisan groups would use their powers to advance George W. Bush toward the White House.

The Republican advantage began with the enrollment of voters. Harris led an effort to remove ineligible persons from the registration lists. While such purging was normal, Harris's effort was particularly vigorous—and often flawed—in counties with large African American and Democratic enrollments, and in regard to ex-felons, ineligible to vote in Florida, who were disproportionately black and potentially Democratic.

Moreover, Democratic counties had older and less reliable voting machines, increasing the likelihood of long waiting times and inaccurate counts.

A different ballot problem existed in Palm Beach County, under a Democratic supervisor of elections. To include all of the presidential candidates on a single page, she created a "butterfly ballot," on which all the candidates were listed in two columns, next to a single set of "punch holes" between the two columns. The arrangement confused some voters about the appropriate way to record their votes. With the Buchanan "hole" immediately next to Gore's name, many erroneously voted for the Reform candidate, giving him 3,400 ballots, quadruple his tally in any other county, or they voted for both Buchanan and Gore, which invalidated the ballot. Together with another ballot snafu in the Democratic stronghold of Jacksonville, Gore was estimated to have lost as many as 20,000 votes.

And then the recounting began. As Bush's margin in the state dropped, at one point to only 154 votes, Secretary Harris twice attempted to end the counting, and twice the Florida Supreme Court—where Democratic appointees held a majority—intervened to prolong the process, as the local election judges became bleary-eyed in their examination of individual ballots. Upon Lieberman's charitable urging, absentee military ballots—favoring Bush—were accepted, although many were late and improperly certified. Even before the counts could be completed, the governor and Harris certified Bush as the winner, while the legislature contemplated bypassing the popular vote and choosing the electors itself. Outside of the counting rooms, street demonstrators rallied in support of each camp, and Republican protesters forced suspension of the recount in Miami. Later newspaper and academic analyses were divided, but tended to the conclusion that Gore would have won the state if every eligible vote had been cast and counted as originally intended. A year after the election, confusion was still evident to a reporter for *The New York Times*, who concluded, "Mr. Bush's victory in the most fouled-up, disputed and wrenching presidential election in American history was so breathtakingly narrow that there is no way of knowing with absolute precision who got the most votes."

Finally, the Bush camp appealed its case to the U.S. Supreme Court, which decided the election in the case of *Bush v. Gore*. The Court found that Florida's electoral administration was too erratic to provide equal protection to all voters and stopped the ongoing recount. Then, five justices, all appointed by Republican presidents, refused to allow further efforts, ruling that a decision had to made within two hours, midnight of December 12, to comply with the deadline set by a federal statute of 1887 for an unchallengeable certification.

The four dissenters did not accept the December 12 deadline. They would have allowed the Florida authorities to try to set a uniform standard for the recounts and conclude the process before the eventual electors met on December 18, or before Congress was to officially count the electoral vote on January 6, 2001.

Gore accepted the decision the next day, and Democrats discouraged any effort to overturn the result when Congress formally received the electoral vote. Ironically, the Supreme Court's intervention was probably unnecessary. In the congressional elections, Republicans had kept control of the House of Representatives, 221–212, and in a majority of the state delegations (while dropping to a 50–50 split in the Senate). Leaving the choice of the president to the House and vice president to the Senate, as provided by the Constitution, would still have brought Bush the victory. More strangely, Lieberman might have been chosen as vice president, with Gore, as presiding officer, casting the decisive tie-breaker in the upper chamber.

The end of the complicated election of 2000 was a commonplace repetition of American political ritual. The voters peacefully accepted an outcome that most of them had opposed. George W. Bush was inaugurated as president, and the earth did not move. Although favored only by a minority, he promised to be "a uniter, not a divider," and even his opponents wished him well.

But the Bush presidency turned out to be quite different from these expectations. Although a minority president, Bush envisaged a permanent Republican national majority as enduring as his party's dominance of the early twentieth century. Even without an electoral mandate, Bush achieved much of his policy agenda. Entering the White House in a time of peace, he led the nation into two wars and threatened others. Gaining power by criticizing the excesses of the Clinton administration, he expanded the powers of the presidency beyond the limits of statutes and into areas of doubtful constitutional legitimacy.

As Bush openly took office in Washington, another political leader—Osama bin Laden—secretly plotted another course. On September 11, 2001, the earth did shake. The United States then took a diverging road—and, to paraphrase Robert Frost, that would make all the difference.

· ·

THE POLITICAL CLIMATE

The 2000 election began in an unusual political climate. Foreign policy had receded from national concern with the United States apparently the world's sole superpower. Domestically, President Bill Clinton had maintained high overall approval ratings, buoyed by the greatest economic boom in fifty years. Jobs were abundant, and incomes and consumer spending soared. But Clinton also became mired in sex scandals, leading to his impeachment by the House and eventual acquittal by the Senate just a year before the election. Economic prosperity normally produces great gains for the incumbent party, but the nation was uncertain if it could endorse one tainted by scandal.

FEBRUARY 13, 1999
CLINTON ACQUITTED DECISIVELY: NO MAJORITY FOR EITHER CHARGE
CENSURE IS BARRED
But Rebuke From Both Sides of Aisle Dilutes President's Victory
By ALISON MITCHELL

WASHINGTON, Feb. 12—The Senate today acquitted President Clinton on two articles of impeachment, falling short of even a majority vote on either of the charges against him: perjury and obstruction of justice.

After a harrowing year of scandal and investigation, the five-week-long Senate trial of the President—only the second in the 210-year history of the Republic—culminated shortly after noon when the roll calls began that would determine Mr. Clinton's fate.

"Is respondent William Jefferson Clinton guilty or not guilty?" asked Chief Justice William H. Rehnquist, in his gold-striped black robe. In a hushed chamber, with senators standing one by one to pronounce Mr. Clinton "guilty" or "not guilty," the Senate rejected the charge of perjury, 55 to 45, with 10 Republicans voting against conviction.

It then split 50–50 on a second article accusing Mr. Clinton of obstruction of justice in concealing his affair with Monica S. Lewinsky. Five Republicans broke ranks on the obstruction-of-justice charge. No Democrats voted to convict on either charge, and it would have taken a dozen of them, and all 55 Republicans, to reach the two-thirds majority of 67 senators required for conviction.

Chief Justice Rehnquist announced the acquittal of the nation's 42d President at 12:39 P.M. "It is therefore ordered and adjudged that the said William Jefferson Clinton be, and he hereby is, acquitted of the charges in the said articles," he said. Almost immediately, the mood in the Senate lightened.

As required by the Senate's impeachment rules, Secretary of State Madeleine K. Albright was formally notified of the Senate's judgment.

Mr. Clinton responded by once again declaring himself "profoundly sorry" for his actions and words that had thrown the nation into a 13-month ordeal. "Now I ask all Americans, and I hope all Americans here in Washington and throughout our land, will re-dedicate ourselves to the work of serving our nation and building our future together," he said in a brief appearance in the White House Rose Garden.

DECEMBER 4, 1999
234,000 NEW JOBS IN NOVEMBER KEPT ECONOMY HUMMING
STOCK PRICES UP SHARPLY
Expectations of a Slowing Fail To Materialize—Analysts Now See Strong Growth
By LOUIS UCHITELLE

The tireless national economy kept spinning out new jobs in November, assuring robust economic growth in the final months of the American Century.

Not only that, but people also worked longer hours, the Labor Department reported yesterday. The combination of more people employed—a hefty 234,000 more—and more time on the job for everyone gave rise to forecasts that in the fourth quarter the economy would keep up its spectacular growth.

"We were expecting the economy to slow more quickly, with the help of a stock market decline," said Chris Varvares, a partner in Macroeconomic Advisers in St. Louis, which is forecasting an annual growth rate of nearly 5 percent, or almost as much as the 5.5 percent in the third quarter. "But we are getting a revving up, not a slowing, and we are certainly not going through a stock market decline."

Stock prices shot up yesterday, in reaction to two numbers in the report: the job growth and the average hourly wage for ordinary workers. That wage rose only 2 cents, to $13.41. The combination of healthy economic growth and modest wage gains suggests the likelihood of little inflationary pressure.

The Clinton administration hailed the job report as a milestone. With the 234,000 new jobs in November, job creation during the president's nearly seven years in office passed the 20 million mark, reaching 20,043,000, an achievement that mainly reflects the strong economy but also the administration's economic policies, officials said.

Labor Secretary Alexis M. Herman called the achievement historic—and indeed there has been no other seven-year period in which so many jobs have been created.

THE CONTENDERS

Quick nominations were expected in both parties for the 2000 presidential contest. Republican governor George W. Bush of Texas and Democratic vice president Al Gore appeared poised to seize their parties' leadership. Unexpectedly, insurgent runs by Republican senator John McCain of Arizona, and a former senator, Democrat Bill Bradley of New Jersey, initially blocked their paths to the nominations. Despite showing early promise, the two challengers were ultimately rebuffed in the primaries, setting the stage for what would become a long and epic battle for the presidency.

FEBRUARY 2, 2000
MCCAIN ROMPS IN FIRST PRIMARY; GORE WINS, EDGING OUT BRADLEY
RESULT STUNS BUSH
Arizonan's Margin Built On Independent Vote in New Hampshire
By RICHARD L. BERKE

MANCHESTER, N.H., Wednesday, Feb. 2—Senator John McCain swamped Gov. George W. Bush Tuesday in the New Hampshire Republican primary, piling up the widest margin here since Ronald Reagan defeated Mr. Bush's father 20 years ago.

"Thank you. Thank you. Thank you. Thank you," an elated Mr. McCain told a raucous crowd of supporters last night as he embraced a victory that his advisers hope is the first step to blocking Mr. Bush's once seemingly unstoppable march to the nomination.

Mr. McCain's triumph was particularly exceptional because surveys of voters Tuesday found it was built not only on a core of independents but also on wide and deep support among faithful Republicans whom the Bush campaign considered its most reliable voters.

Now, as the race turns to Delaware, South Carolina, and then to Michigan and Arizona, Republican strategists say the question is whether Mr. McCain can propel his victory margin of 18 percentage points into a genuine challenge to Mr. Bush. For months, the Texas governor has been widely viewed as the front-runner because of his towering financial advantage and his vast endorsements from elected Republicans, even before his victory in the Iowa caucuses last week.

While Mr. McCain and Mr. Bush have sparred for weeks over the size of their tax-cut proposals and the depth of their opposition to abortion, the surveys of voters found that the most crucial factor among the Arizona senator's backers was that they viewed him as a candidate of unshakable character who was willing to stand up for his convictions.

FEBRUARY 2, 2000
TOUGH FIGHT AHEAD
Vice President Claims a Victory but Faces Key Contests in March
By ADAM CLYMER

MANCHESTER, N.H., Feb. 1—Vice President Al Gore held off a strong challenge by former Senator Bill Bradley in the New Hampshire primary today, but both candidates vowed a long, tough fight for the Democratic presidential nomination.

Tonight's tight result, despite a solid victory for Mr. Gore in the Iowa caucuses eight days ago, means that Mr. Gore has to face the critical month of March, when more than half the party's delegates to the Democratic National Convention will be elected on the first two Tuesdays, with a dead serious fight ahead.

Mr. Bradley, in a quasi-concession speech in which he congratulated Mr. Gore without using the words victory or defeat, said, "We have made a remarkable turnaround, but there is still a tough fight ahead."

Minutes later, Mr. Gore replied, "We have just begun to fight." He called Mr. Bradley "a tough competitor who made us fight for every vote." He told cheering supporters in Manchester that they had overcome a Bradley lead maintained for 14 weeks, and promised to lead them "all the way to victory in November."

Those brief speeches, given before Mr. Bradley left for Hartford and Mr. Gore flew to New York, displayed the edge the two have shown each other that has become increasingly obvious in recent weeks, and is likely to become even plainer.

One critical reason the fight will be rough is that Mr. Bradley got a substantial majority of votes from those who decided on their candidate in the last few days, when Mr. Bradley was most combative. He will have that information, from a poll of today's voters, to push him toward more confrontations in the weeks ahead.

MARCH 8, 2000
GORE AND BUSH TRIUMPH NATIONWIDE, PUTTING NOMINATIONS IN THEIR GRASP
New York and California Give Crucial Support to Texan
By RICHARD L. BERKE

Gov. George W. Bush and Vice President Al Gore crushed their rivals from ocean to ocean yesterday in powerful displays that assured them their parties' nominations.

After claiming the two biggest electoral powerhouses, California and New York, which account for more than 40 percent of the delegates chosen yesterday, Mr. Bush and Mr. Gore immediately turned to each other—and to firing the first salvos of the more than eight-month general election campaign that lies ahead.

Mr. Bush laid out several themes for the general election in a combative speech that was devoted not to his challenger, Senator John McCain, but to lambasting Mr. Gore. "He is the candidate of the status quo in Washington, D.C., and he has a tough case to make in the general election," Mr. Bush said to supporters in Austin, Tex.

At a boisterous rally in Nashville earlier in the evening, Mr. Gore did not mention Mr. Bush by name but called on the Republican nominee to debate him twice a week and to spurn unregulated soft money donations.

"I will challenge the Republican nominee to hold joint open meetings with me," he said, "to make this contest of ideas and not insults, a campaign conducted in full daylight and not through secretly funded special interest attack ads or smear telephone calls from the extremist right wing."

Mr. Gore's opponent, former Senator Bill Bradley of New Jersey, did not win one state, a defeat so pronounced that his advisers said it was only a matter of days before he withdraws. And Mr. McCain said he would retreat to the mountains of Arizona to "take stock of our losses" and decide whether to proceed.

MARCH 9, 2000
GORE AND BUSH SET FOR A FIERY RACE THAT STARTS NOW
Shunning Any Letup, Both Camps Vow a Preconvention Push
By RICHARD L. BERKE

Strategists for Vice President Al Gore and Gov. George W. Bush said yesterday that there would be no letup from the primary season as they move quickly to define each other on the stump and on the air in an unusually frenetic five-month run up to their parties' nominating conventions.

Both campaigns recalled how Bob Dole in 1996 and Michael S. Dukakis in 1988 lay dormant in the summer before the general election, allowing their rivals to gain the upper hand through television or oratorical barrages. This time, officials on both sides said, that will not happen.

The sheer competitiveness of the race—early polls show Mr. Gore and Mr. Bush running neck and neck—also seems to be driving each candidate to be engaged earlier and more forcefully than in past campaigns. Even if the candidates wanted to lie low, strategists on both sides said, they could not because of the proliferation of coverage on the Internet and on cable television.

"There will be a continued focus on message each and every day," said Karl Rove, Mr. Bush's chief strategist. "Virtually every day, Bush will be somewhere in a position to comment on something of significance."

Christopher Lehane, a spokesman for Mr. Gore, put it this way: "Strap on your seat belt. The roller coaster ride has just begun. If people think the pace has been intense up to this point, they haven't seen anything yet."

● ●

THE REPUBLICAN CONVENTION

The Republican Party met in Philadelphia to nominate George W. Bush for president and former defense secretary Dick Cheney for vice president. Precisely controlled, the convention projected a united and mainly positive message. The party endorsed the conservative direction of previous Republican platforms, but also incorporated several policies Bush termed "compassionate conservatism," an attempt to moderate the party's image. While criticizing the Clinton administration, Bush focused on upbeat and patriotic themes in his appeal to the general electorate.

AUGUST 1, 2000
REPUBLICANS OPEN CONVENTION, EMPHASIZING UNITY
Platform Strives to Reach Right and Center
By ROBIN TONER

PHILADELPHIA, July 31—The Republican National Convention today approved a platform intended to both reassure the party's conservative base and signal to the broader electorate that the party had been transformed by Gov. George W. Bush's bid for the center.

Gov. Tommy G. Thompson of Wisconsin, the chairman of the platform committee, hailed the document's "positive, uplifting" tone and described it to the delegates as a platform that "every Republican can be proud of, and one that will carry George Bush to the White House."

But the effort to satisfy moderate and conservative constituencies alike, and help ensure a peaceful convention, carried political risks of its own. Democrats and their allies quickly seized on the most conservative parts of the platform, like its call for a ban on abortion, as evidence that little had changed in the Republican Party beyond rhetoric and imagery.

"We're going to use the platform like we're going to use George Bush's record in Texas and Dick Cheney's voting record—to show the American people that this is still the same old Republican Party," said Jenny Backus, a spokeswoman for the Democratic National Committee.

The document approved today had been carefully managed by Mr. Bush's allies, and much of it bears his unmistakable mark. It incorporates his policy proposals, and his language, on a set of issues at the heart of his campaign, from education to tax cuts, from health care to immigration. In keeping with his theme of "compassionate conservatism," it declares that "for every American, there must be a ladder of opportunity, and for those most in need, a safety net of care."

Governor Thompson and other Bush allies worked hard over weeks of private and public meetings to ensure that the platform process was free of the divisiveness of prior years and did not distract from the upbeat message of the convention and the campaign.

They chose to fight conservatives on some issues—notably the governor's education plan—that they felt were imperative to underscore the idea that Mr. Bush was "a different kind of Republican." But they removed the abortion issue from contention early on, declaring that they did not want the plank to change, even though Mr. Bush says his personal position is less restrictive.

AUGUST 4, 2000
BUSH, ACCEPTING G.O.P. NOMINATION, PLEDGES TO 'USE THESE GOOD TIMES FOR GREAT GOALS'

AN UPBEAT THEME

Says Clinton and Gore Have Had a Chance but 'Have Not Led'

By R. W. APPLE Jr.

PHILADELPHIA, Aug. 3—Introducing himself to a nation that barely knows him, Gov. George W. Bush of Texas pledged tonight to "confront the hard issues—threats to our national security, threats to our health and retirement security" that he said the Clinton administration had consistently ducked.

At a jubilant final session of the Republican National Convention, Mr. Bush argued that "times of plenty" were times to solve major problems, not to relax. With that, he sought to cut the ground from beneath his Democratic rival, Vice President Al Gore, whose strongest electoral argument is his association with the prosperity of the last eight years.

His parents and many other members of his large family were in the V.I.P. seats to hear Mr. Bush offer this curt verdict on Bill Clinton's and Al Gore's time in the White House:

"Our current president embodied the potential of a generation. So many talents. So much charm. Such great skill. But in the end, to what end? So much promise, to no great purpose."

Mr. Bush accused the vice president of indulging in "the politics of the roadblock, the philosophy of the stop sign." He turned Franklin D. Roosevelt's famous first inaugural address around and aimed it squarely at Mr. Gore, charging that "the only thing he has to offer is fear itself."

He mocked Mr. Gore by saying, "I do not need to take your pulse before I know my own mind. I do not reinvent myself at every turn. I am not running in borrowed clothes." Yet Mr. Bush has been successively moderate, conservative and moderate again, as the imperatives of the nominating campaign dictated.

In a further, more indirect, thrust at the president he hopes to succeed, the Republican nominee quoted the poet Robert Frost, remembered by older Americans for his appearance at John F. Kennedy's inaugural four decades ago, on the need to "occupy the land with character." Few if any of the thousands who filled the First Union Center here and few of those watching on television can have missed the allusion to Mr. Clinton's sexual involvement with an intern, which led to his impeachment.

"This administration had its chance," Governor Bush asserted. "They have not led. We will."

But as he had pledged, many of Mr. Bush's words were upbeat. "Tonight we vow to our nation: We will seize this moment of American promise," he said. "We will use these good times for great goals."

Except for tonight's gibes and Wednesday night's hard-edged speech by Dick Cheney, his running mate, Mr. Bush and his party have tried all week to avoid the kind of sniping—to say nothing of the internal bickering—they know the American electorate detests.

They succeeded, but not without cost; lacking debate or drama, the convention experienced considerable trouble in attracting TV viewers. Many preferred Regis Philbin or "Friends" to the Republicans' voter-friendly show.

AUGUST 5, 2000
BOWING TO THE MIDDLE, KEEPING TO THE RIGHT

By ALISON MITCHELL

PHILADELPHIA, Aug. 4—With his convention speech, Gov. George W. Bush created a synthesis new to Republican politics: conservative policies described in ways that his campaign believes swing voters will love.

So his $1.3 trillion, 10-year tax cut—more sweeping than Congressional Republicans ever tried to push through—became an effort to bring "common sense and fairness to the tax code." His plan to divert some

Social Security payroll taxes to private investment accounts amounted to giving "American workers security and independence that no politician can ever take away."

The language was positively Clintonian, but as many conservatives were quick to note, Mr. Bush had not actually changed any of the Republican Party's core principles—from its opposition to abortion, to its support for large tax cuts, to its backing of a vast missile defense system, to its search for conservative Supreme Court justices.

"He has packaged the traditional conservative positions with completely new covering," said Marshall Wittmann, a policy analyst at the Heritage Foundation. "It's not necessarily a new Republicanism in quite the way that Clinton was a new Democrat."

This synthesis is central to Mr. Bush's effort to assemble a winning coalition. The Bush campaign wants to hold its conservative base through its policy proposals, and then pick up the moderate middle through Mr. Bush's conciliatory language and willingness to speak about issues that Democrats long dominated.

The question for the fall campaign is whether Mr. Bush can convincingly keep up his balancing act as the Democrats try to home in on the details of policy proposals and his record back in Texas.

Where Mr. Bush describes a tax cut that helps people at the bottom of the economic ladder, the Democrats see a tax cut that helps the rich. While Mr. Bush promises to strengthen Social Security, the Democrats say he could reduce retirement benefits. For all the time Mr. Bush spent delivering policy addresses this spring, a number of his proposals lack specifics.

And Mr. Bush's record does not always square with his rhetoric. The man who showcased minorities all across his convention is, after all, the same candidate who, when he needed to recover from a defeat in the New Hampshire primaries, began his comeback campaign at a South Carolina university that banned interracial dating.

"An informed voter is their worst nightmare," Douglas Hattaway, a Gore spokesman, said of the Bush campaign. The Democrats have already begun a barrage of ads trying to challenge Mr. Bush's commitment on issues like the environment.

• •

THE DEMOCRATIC CONVENTION

The Democrats met in Los Angeles to watch President Bill Clinton pass the torch to Vice President Al Gore as the party's leader and to mark the pioneering nomination of a Jew, Sen. Joseph Lieberman of Connecticut, for vice president. Moving past minor fractures in party unity, Gore sought to portray himself as independent of Clinton's moral failures, but partially responsible for the economic success of his administration. This delicate balance became a theme of his campaign.

AUGUST 15, 2000
GORE AND LIEBERMAN VOICE POPULIST THEMES
By KATHARINE Q. SEELYE

ST. LOUIS, Aug. 14—Without even a nod to President Clinton, who delivered his valedictory speech to Democrats in Los Angeles tonight, Vice President Al Gore struck populist themes today in two appearances and pledged to "stand up for what's right" for the country.

Mr. Gore was introduced at a humid open-air rally here tonight within view of the city's landmark Gateway Arch by his running mate, Senator Joseph I.

Lieberman, as a "decent and honest" man. But neither referred to the president, whose administration's policies they have both generally supported and want to perpetuate, but whose private behavior they have both criticized.

After the rally, Mr. Gore relaxed with his wife, Tipper, Mr. Lieberman, and his wife, Hadassah, in a hotel room as he listened to Mr. Clinton's speech.

"I thought it was a great speech," he said. "I appreciate the generous and kind words he said about me."

After the speech, he called Mr. Clinton and thanked him, a White House aide said.

Asked how he reacted to the "adulation" heaped on Mr. Clinton, Mr. Gore said, "Appropriate and what you would think would happen."

How could he expect in his own speech on Thursday night to top Mr. Clinton's? Mr. Gore's wife shot reporters an exasperated look as he blew past the question.

While Mr. Lieberman flew on to Los Angeles tonight, Mr. Gore will meet Mr. Clinton in Michigan on Tuesday for a symbolic "passing of the torch," a ceremony that Gore aides hope will help shift the attention from Mr. Clinton.

At the rally here, Mr. Gore focused on his many pledges—to improve education, move toward universal health-care coverage, raise the minimum wage and enact anti-hate-crimes legislation. He framed the election as a choice between middle-class families and special interests like drug and insurance companies.

"It all comes down to this," he declared to several hundred people here. "Which side are you on?"

"On one side there are working families, middle-class families, and they face a lot of obstacles; and on other side there are a lot of powerful interests who misuse the campaign finance system to wield more influence than they should," he declared. "We need campaign finance reform to give democracy back to you."

"It also makes a world of difference who you've got in the White House," he said. "I have never hesitated to take on the powerful, to take on the ones that find ways to make the system work for them, even if it comes as a disadvantage to most people."

"I believe that when the big drug companies say that they're opposed to a prescription drug benefit, that shouldn't rule the day in the Congress and in our nation," he said. "We ought to have people who are willing to fight hard enough to overcome that and do what's right for the people of this country. That's what I'm all about; that's what this campaign is all about."

In an earlier appearance today in Independence, Mo., Mr. Gore gave a flash preview of his coming convention speech, plunging into details of how he would shore up Medicare and Social Security and suggesting that his Republican opponent, Gov. George W. Bush, was hiding behind generalities on his tax-cut proposal that Mr. Gore argued would cut benefits and hurt other programs.

Mr. Gore is hoping that his detail-laden speech on Thursday, when he accepts the Democratic nomination for president, will accomplish a couple of things: give him a political mandate to follow the course he is proposing, and portray the Republicans as speaking vaguely because their positions are unpopular.

"To give generalities and not give the specifics—that's not the best way to elevate our democracy," he said today in Independence.

Mr. Gore's advisers say these detailed discussions, while not exciting, address the concerns of ordinary Americans and play to Mr. Gore's strengths, including his grasp of policy, and at the same time suggest that Mr. Bush is unprepared to grapple with such basic issues.

AUGUST 16, 2000
SOME DISCONTENT AT CENTRIST THEME OF GORE'S TICKET
UNEASE ON PARTY'S LEFT
Lieberman Confers With Black Caucus to Seek to Allay Its Concerns About Him
By JAMES DAO
and KEVIN SACK

LOS ANGELES, Aug. 15—Faced with an undercurrent of grumbling about the centrist tone of its ticket and platform, the Democratic Party devoted much of its convention today to reassuring its liberal base, sending its vice-presidential candidate, Senator Joseph I. Lieberman, before black delegates to declare his unequivocal support for affirmative action.

"I was for affirmative action, am for affirmative action and will be for affirmative action," Mr. Lieberman, who has been critical of racial preference programs, told the convention's Black Caucus. Immediately afterward, Representative Maxine Waters, a Los Angeles Democrat who had voiced strong doubts about Mr. Lieberman this weekend, declared that she would support him wholeheartedly.

But other leading liberals continued to express doubts here today about Mr. Gore himself. "The most important thing to me is that Gore is not emotionally in touch with the party's base," Mayor Willie L. Brown Jr. of San Francisco said in an interview. "If he's smart, he'll go to a black church every Sunday from now until Election Day."

It is difficult to gauge the depth of discontent among black voters, union members and other core Democrats with the ticket and its agenda. But Mr. Gore's selection of Mr. Lieberman, a Connecticut senator who has staked out centrist positions not only on affirmative action, but also on school vouchers, military spending and Social Security, seems to have crystallized their worries that Mr. Gore is taking them for granted.

The Gore campaign moved swiftly today to address these worries, dispatching two black cabinet secretaries, Transportation Secretary Rodney Slater and Labor Secretary Alexis M. Herman, and other prominent black Democrats to declare their strong support for Mr. Lieberman.

At the same time, the list of convention speakers tonight was almost a who's who of leaders from the party's liberal wing, including two union presidents, a prominent environmentalist, gay rights and abortion rights leaders, former Senator Bill Bradley and the Rev. Jesse Jackson.

In his speech tonight, Mr. Jackson alluded to the party's fault lines, saying, "Within our party we can fight for the right to do what's right. We can change, we can challenge, we can agree to disagree, we can agree to be agreeable. But we are family."

Discontent among core Democrats poses a potentially significant problem for Mr. Gore because black voters and union members are among the party's largest and most loyal constituencies. And while some of those voters might defect to Ralph Nader, the Green Party candidate, the Democrats' greater fear is that some base voters will stay home on Election Day, making it difficult to win swing states like Michigan and Georgia.

"People are saying, 'We don't see the Democrats standing for us,'" said Senator Paul Wellstone, of Minnesota, a leader of the party's liberal wing. "It is a hurdle to overcome. And the vice president needs to do it soon."

AUGUST 18, 2000
GORE, IN DEBUT AS A PRESIDENTIAL NOMINEE, SAYS 'I STAND HERE TONIGHT AS MY OWN MAN'
REJOINDER TO G.O.P.

Vow to Enact Tax Cuts—Seeks to Speak for 'Working Families'

By R. W. APPLE Jr.

LOS ANGELES, Aug. 17—A deputy no more, Vice President Al Gore made his debut as the Democratic presidential nominee tonight with a vow to work for all Americans, "especially those who need a voice, those who need a champion, those who need to be lifted up so they are never left behind."

Speaking to the Democratic National Convention that nominated him on Wednesday night and to the nation beyond, Mr. Gore said, "I stand here tonight as my own man"—a clear rejoinder to the Republicans who have sought to picture him as a cut-rate version of President Clinton.

The vice president told a whooping crowd at the Staples Center on the fringe of downtown Los Angeles that he would give working families "a full range of targeted tax cuts," including an early end to the so-called marriage penalty and a reform of the federal estate tax. But his proposals stopped well short of those made by his Republican rival, Gov. George W. Bush of Texas.

In a pointed reference to Mr. Bush's promise to cut federal income taxes by more than $1.3 trillion over 10 years, Mr. Gore said, "I will not go along with a huge tax cut for the wealthy at the expense of everyone else and wreck our good economy in the process."

In what sounded like a subtle attempt to distance himself from Mr. Clinton, he promised, "I will never let you down." And he was careful to confine his criticism of the opposition to policies rather than personalities.

Trailing Mr. Bush in the polls, faced with an uphill fight in the Midwestern and Mid-Atlantic swing states that will decide the outcome, Mr. Gore seemed to be laying the groundwork for a fall campaign in which he would identify himself as the friend of the little guy and Mr. Bush as the candidate of the rich, powerful and influential.

"Together let's make sure that our prosperity enriches not just the few, but all working families," the vice president declared.

Again and again, he spoke of unspecified "powerful forces" and "powerful interests," which he implicitly identified with the Republicans, standing in the way of working men and women. It was reminiscent of Theodore Roosevelt's denunciation of "the malefactors of great wealth" in 1907 and Franklin D. Roosevelt's castigation of "economic royalists" during the New Deal.

"I'm happy that the stock market has boomed and so many businesses and new enterprises have done well," Mr. Gore said. "This country is richer and stronger. But my focus is on working families—people trying to make house payments and car payments, working overtime to save for college and do right by their kids."

The economy is in many ways Mr. Gore's greatest asset on the stump. Given its strength, he should be doing much better, by normal standards. Candidates of parties that hold the White House usually fare well when the economy is strong and the country is involved in no foreign war.

But the vice president has been unable to generate the kind of electricity that follows Mr. Clinton everywhere. And Mr. Clinton's speech on Monday night did nothing to light a fire for his protégé. "All he did was, he made a good case for Clinton," said Gerald Rafshoon, Jimmy Carter's image-maker.

Even in this most important hour of Mr. Gore's career, the shadow of Mr. Clinton fell across his path. It was disclosed in Washington that a new grand jury has been convened to consider whether the president should be indicted after leaving office for having lied under oath about his affair with a White House intern.

· ·

THIRD PARTIES

Third parties, although common in presidential contests, usually attract little fanfare, little media attention, and relatively few votes. In 2000, with the election hinging upon a few thousand votes in battleground states, two minor candidates, Ralph Nader of the Green Party and Pat Buchanan of Ross Perot's Reform Party, received attention from both the media and public. By drawing just a few thousand votes from the major contenders, these two candidates had the potential to tip the election either way.

OCTOBER 29, 2000
WHAT MAKES RALPH (AND PAT) RUN?
By SAM HOWE VERHOVEK

SEATTLE

There is no obvious ideological line that connects Ralph Nader to H. Ross Perot, Robert M. LaFollette, George C. Wallace, Theodore Roosevelt, John B. Anderson, Eugene V. Debs, Strom Thurmond and many of the other independent and third-party candidates who have mounted notable campaigns for the presidency in the course of American history. But comparing the issues these candidates ran on is not the only way to assess just what it is they were trying to appeal to in the electorate. And to many historians, there is at least one prism through which they appear remarkably similar.

"Looking at these things in only a left-to-right way sort of misses the point," said Bruce J. Schulman, director of

American Studies at Boston University. "Third-party candidates almost always have talked about trying to purify the system in some way. They talk about the existing system as hopelessly corrupt; they say you need to clean it up one way or the other. So you can look at these things not so much as left versus right, but clean versus dirty."

Indeed, many of these candidates have somehow invoked an image of purity, a sense that they were fighting a system that is corrupt to the core, and Mr. Nader, the consumer advocate and Green Party presidential nominee, fits firmly into this tradition. It has frequently been the two-party system itself that these candidates have cast as the villain, thus, of course, offering the rationale for a new party.

"The belief that the political system is corrupt fuels all the third-party candidates in our political history," said Zachary Karabell, author of "The Last Campaign: How Harry Truman Won the 1948 Election" (Knopf), a contest in which Mr. Thurmond, the states' rights "Dixiecrat" candidate and Henry A. Wallace, the Progressive Party nominee who wrote "Toward World Peace," occupied an important place on the stage, though each got only 2.4 percent of the vote.

"They may not have used the exact phrase, but both Wallace and Thurmond would certainly have referred to the two major parties as Republicrats, " said Mr. Karabell, using the term Mr. Nader has repeatedly voiced in this campaign to persuade voters that there is little difference between Vice President Al Gore and Gov. George W. Bush of Texas (whom he has also called "Gush and Bore"). And Mr. Nader's construction that the major-party candidates are "Tweedledum and Tweedledee" is also not new in American politics.

In almost all cases, whether they were arguing against civil rights or for economic rights, these candidates have hearkened back to the founding fathers and invoked a time of purer ideals and thoughts. The phrase "sweeping the rascals out" dates to the 1870's, when a breakaway group of liberal Republicans ran against what they depicted as the corruption of the age. The populist People's Party Platform of 1892 bemoaned that corruption "dominates the ballot box, the legislatures, the Congress" and "touches even the ermine of the bench."

And it's surely no coincidence that Mr. Perot, who captured 18.9 percent of the vote for the Reform Party in 1992, one of the most successful showings of a third-party candidate in history, often vowed to "clean out the stables" if the American people sent him to the White House. Images of corruption were a part of the Perot playbook. When he went to Valley Forge, Pa., to launch his second run for the presidency, in 1996, he denounced the two-party system and vowed to "kill that little snake this time."

While George Wallace's and Mr. Thurmond's campaigns are often depicted in the negative—as against civil rights—the candidates themselves told fellow Southerners that they were battling oppressive forces in the nation's capital out to dictate their way of life.

Of course, an obvious question comes to mind: why haven't any of these candidates been more successful? No third-party candidate has ever won (Mr. Roosevelt, the ex-president who ran as the "Bull Moose" Progressive Party candidate in 1912, came closest, with 27.4 percent of the vote).

And with the exception of the Republican Party, which came to crowd out the Whigs as the pre-eminent challenger to the Democrats, no third party seems to have ever really survived. And now, Mr. Perot's Reform Party is clearly teetering: its nominee, Patrick J. Buchanan, seems unlikely to get much traction in this presidential race.

One reason for the failure of third parties is that however messy the two-party system is, a major party almost always finds a way to co-opt at least some of the themes offered by any third party that generate appeal. By the time of the New Deal, for example, Democrats had appropriated some of the planks of Mr. LaFollette, the Wisconsin senator who got 16.6 percent of the vote as the Progressive nominee in 1924. Republicans like Richard M. Nixon defused Mr. Wallace's appeal and made inroads into the once solidly Democratic South.

But there may be an even simpler reason why so many third parties have had trouble catching on permanently.

"They're Jeremiahs, talking about purging the Republic of sin and corruption," said David M. Kennedy, a Stanford University history professor and the author of "Freedom From Fear: The American People in Depression and War, 1929–1945" (Oxford University), which won the Pulitzer Prize for history this year. "What all these movements have so strikingly in common is that they're anti-establishment. They position themselves as outsiders who really in a sense don't make any serious argument about wanting to become an established party. They're outside the traditional framework, so sometimes they're not built to last, even in their own minds."

Mr. Nader and many of his supporters might dispute that, arguing that the main goal of his candidacy at this point is not to win but to capture the 5 percent of the vote needed to qualify for federal funds in the next presidential election cycle and thus build up the Green Party as an enduring force.

Still, a large part of Mr. Nader's appeal is clearly the notion of where he fits on the clean-versus-dirty spectrum. In interviews in Portland, Ore., last week, where support for Mr. Nader is strong, many voters described him as incorruptible or virtuous, or said they were following their "conscience." "I just trust Nader," said Danielle DeDee, a sales clerk at a craft gallery. "He seems so honest. I mean, look at his lifestyle. He lives on, like, what, $25,000 a year? He gives away something like 80 percent of his money."

Many Democrats, of course, are furious with Mr. Nader, and Vice President Gore went so far as to depict him as a pawn, unwitting or not, of big business. In doing so, Mr. Gore was trying to cloak himself in the purer-than-thou mantle that has often been worn by the third-party candidates.

"If the big oil companies and chemical manufacturers and the other big polluters were able to communicate a message to this state, they would say vote for George Bush or, in any case, vote for Ralph Nader," Mr. Gore told a crowd in Wisconsin last week. "They would say whatever you do, don't vote for Al Gore."

• •

THE CAMPAIGN

From September through early November 2000, George W. Bush and Al Gore battled fiercely for the presidency, focusing public attention on their three debates. Opinion polls portrayed an extremely tight race, with a few battleground states likely to determine the eventual winner. Voters emphasized the two candidates' individual qualities, with no single issue dominating the campaign. Bush attempted to demonstrate his competency for office, to counter voters' concern over his inexperience, while Gore battled to appear trustworthy, to offset public doubts about his personality. As the polls opened, the outcome remained uncertain.

SEPTEMBER 17, 2000
GROUND SHIFTS IN FIGHT TO GAIN ELECTORAL EDGE
Close Race Gets Fierce in 10 Crucial States
By ADAM CLYMER

WASHINGTON, Sept. 16—Vice President Al Gore, who has erased Gov. George W. Bush's lead in most national polls, has also edged ahead of him in the battle for electoral votes, according to independent and partisan analysts. But despite the postconvention trend in Mr. Gore's favor, enough states are either tossups or held so narrowly that the race remains fiercely competitive.

The overall picture is almost a mirror image of how things looked before the Republican National Convention, when Mr. Bush held a slim but decided lead in the Electoral College.

But major states that had leaned Mr. Bush's way, like Florida, Michigan, Missouri and Wisconsin, have since become tossups, according to strategists in both campaigns, as well as postconvention polls and political scientists interviewed around the country. Similarly, earlier tossup states like Minnesota, New Jersey and Pennsylvania are now leaning toward Mr. Gore.

OCTOBER 4, 2000
BUSH AND GORE STAKE OUT DIFFERENCES IN FIRST DEBATE
Blunt Encounter Offers a Clash In Priorities
By RICHARD L. BERKE

BOSTON, Oct. 3—Vice President Al Gore and Gov. George W. Bush presented starkly different stands on issues ranging from taxes to abortion to oil drilling tonight as Mr. Gore repeatedly cast Mr. Bush as a friend of the rich and Mr. Bush upbraided his rival as a Washington insider with big promises and few accomplishments.

In the first debate of the 2000 presidential campaign, at the University of Massachusetts, Mr. Bush and Mr. Gore engaged in blunt condemnations of each other's proposals. Even when attacking, they smiled their way through the 90-minute encounter. They steered clear of personal criticisms until the final few minutes, when Mr. Bush questioned the vice president's credibility and his involvement in the campaign fund-raising scandals of 1996.

Neither candidate mentioned President Clinton, but from the opening of the debate to its last moments, Mr. Bush criticized the vice president as part of an administration that squandered its opportunities to make progress on issues like prescription drugs and Social Security.

Portraying himself as governor of a large state who effectively reached out to Republicans and Democrats alike, Mr. Bush assailed Mr. Gore as deeply entrenched in a poll-driven Washington culture that had little to show for itself.

In doing so, he addressed persistent criticism that he was unprepared for the presidency.

"I fully recognize I'm not of Washington," Mr. Bush said. "I'm from Texas. And he's got a lot of experience. But so do I. And I've been the chief executive officer of the second biggest state in the union. I've had a proud record of working with both Republicans and Democrats, which is what our nation needs."

Tonight was the first opportunity for tens of millions of Americans to assess the contenders for more than a flash in a television commercial or on the evening news.

Besides being the most watched single event of the campaign thus far, with an estimated audience of 75 million, the confrontation took on even greater significance because the contest is disturbingly close: just 35 days before the election, most polls show the race in a statistical dead heat.

In delivering their pitches, both contenders offered distinct philosophies as to how they would approach governing and the presidency. Mr. Gore spoke of proposals that would help Americans at every income level and embraced views favored by liberals, like abortion rights and protecting the environment.

Mr. Bush unabashedly referred to conservative principles and underscored his party's long-held tenets that the federal government is too powerful and that the military needs to be strengthened. But his muted response to questions about abortion made it clear that he, like Mr. Gore, was making his case to the sliver of swing voters likely to determine the outcome of the race.

Mr. Bush said his opponent had accomplished little in his eight years in office. "Look," he said, "let's forget all the politics and all the finger-pointing and get some positive things done on Medicare and prescription drugs and Social Security."

Mr. Gore, not wanting to invoke Mr. Clinton, refrained from aggressively defending the administration, instead turning his fire on Mr. Bush.

In a phrase he repeated again and again, Mr. Gore asserted that the Texas governor's tax plan was tilted to the rich. "He would spend more money on tax cuts for the wealthiest 1 percent than all of the new spending that he proposes for education, health care, prescription drugs and national defense all combined," Mr. Gore said. "Now, I think those are wrong priorities." He mentioned the "wealthiest 1 percent" 10 times during the debate.

In response, Mr. Bush said tartly said that the vice president was guilty of "fuzzy math" and trying to "scare" the people with inaccurate depictions of his proposals. "This man is running on 'Medi-scare,'" Mr. Bush said after Mr. Gore asserted that under the governor's Medicare prescription drug plan "95 percent of all seniors" would get no assistance for four or five years.

OCTOBER 22, 2000
FOCUSING ON THE FEW, BLIND TO THE MANY
By RICHARD L. BERKE

SAGINAW, Mich.

In the cliffhanger that is the 2000 race for president, the drama should be palpable. Suspense should be building because, with just 16 days left, either Vice President Al Gore or Gov. George W. Bush could take the White House.

Why, then, in the tightest presidential contest in decades, do people seem more at the edge of boredom than at the edge of their seats?

The audience for the three presidential debates fell sharply from most other campaigns, and was no better than four years ago—when the race was something of a dud. Ratings were down on the national conventions. And voting experts project that despite the closeness of the race, turnout at the polls will not likely surpass 1996, and may dip further.

It may be the candidates' own fault. Both Mr. Bush and Mr. Gore have so narrow-casted their message to a sliver of voters in swing states crucial for an electoral college victory that they have deserted the rest. Meanwhile, those in the sights of the candidates—in fierce battlegrounds like here in Michigan—seem to yearn for candidates who can stir more passion.

Rather than talk about the merits of Mr. Gore and Mr. Bush, two patrons at Dawn Donuts in Saginaw ("101 Delicious Varieties"), a Democrat and a Republican, lamented last week about how they missed a politician like Ronald Reagan.

"I didn't like him," said John Anguiano, 65, the Democrat, who explained that he never voted for Mr. Reagan, "But he was a good politician because he was a good actor. He knew how to smile."

Personality aside, the problem for many people may not be a paucity of issues, but the issues that the candidates chose to discuss. More and more, the nominees are focusing on those few million undecided voters who, if they choose to vote at all, may decide the election. So even if the race is climactic, that may not be enough to make voting relevant to a wider audience. It may be similar to how some people view movie stars: they like to gossip about them but do not bother to see their movies.

"People have increasingly come to see the election as a kind of drama but one that doesn't have some direct affect on their lives," said Neal Gabler, author of "Life, the Movie: How Entertainment Conquered Reality." (Knopf, 1998.) "There's a very interesting distinction: You can be a political junkie but not vote. That's a new phenomenon."

The wider public may also feel neglected because, as Curtis B. Gans, director of the Center for the Study of the American Electorate, put it: "There's a broad mass of the American people who are not involved in most of the issues at stake. The candidates are not talking to a lot of people."

The prescription drug and Medicare proposals that are so in the forefront of the campaign, for example, are designed to appeal to the crucial block of elderly voters. No wonder young people tell pollsters they feel even more alienated from the process this year. Other segments of the population feel downright left out: When was the last time one of the candidates made a speech on issues near and dear to big city dwellers?

Yet factors unique to the current campaign—namely the nominees themselves—are also driving the lack of engagement.

An obvious explanation is that in blissful economic times, voters never have much taste for politics. That is especially true when no war-and-peace issues are brewing. In 1960, voters seemed riveted by the presidential campaign not because the economy was in the tank (it wasn't) but because there were weighty matters at stake. Somehow, the tussle over whether Mr. Gore or Mr. Bush would offer more generous prescription drug benefits does not seem on par with the space race or the missile gap.

"I held out hope that the debates might energize the public and that the closeness of the race would come together," said Tom Patterson, a government professor at Harvard University and co-director of Harvard University "Vanishing Voter" project. Instead, he said, "We're seeing an accelerated movement away from politics."

· ·

An Election Without a Winner

On November 8, 2000, the nation awoke without knowing who would be its forty-third president. The national popular vote was clear; Al Gore won more votes than his Republican rival George W. Bush, but the Electoral College result was uncertain. The decisive state would be Florida, where the vote was so close that it could not be called for either candidate. Although Bush initially held a slight lead, the ultimate outcome hinged on the formal counting and recounting of the ballots. That task dragged on for days, then weeks, as the parties disputed the recount procedures. With the most powerful position on the planet at stake, neither candidate was prepared to yield.

NOVEMBER 8, 2000
BUSH AND GORE VIE FOR AN EDGE WITH NARROW ELECTORAL SPLIT

FLORIDA IS PIVOTAL

Long Night of Seesawing Tallies for Governor and Vice President

By Richard L. Berke

The outcome of the presidential race between Gov. George W. Bush and Vice President Al Gore balanced early this morning on no more than a few thousand votes in the closely contested state of Florida.

Shortly after 2 A.M., Mr. Bush appeared to have won Florida, and several news organizations, including The New York Times, declared that he had captured the White House. Aides to Mr. Gore said he was preparing his concession speech, while Mr. Bush expected to announce his victory.

But later in the morning, as the count in Florida neared an end, the narrow margin that Mr. Bush had achieved unexpectedly evaporated, and state officials said they might have to count the overseas absentee ballots before they could be certain of the result.

By 4 this morning, the candidates were separated by only the barest of margins in the popular and electoral votes as the electorate seemed agonizingly split between Mr. Gore and Mr. Bush.

Mr. Bush was able to claim much of the South, while Mr. Gore captured the largest states on both coasts. But the two divided a patchwork of Midwestern states that are crucial for victory.

Mr. Bush, the governor of Texas who presented himself as an antidote to the scandals of the Clinton years and pledged to reach across the partisan divide and restore dignity to the White House, swept the south and won a patchwork of states in the Middle West. Mr. Gore claimed the largest states on the two coasts but fell just short of victory.

It appeared to be the narrowest electoral margin since 1916, when Woodrow Wilson drew 277 votes from the Electoral College and Charles E. Hughes won 254. When the final tally is in, it may even turn out to be the closest since 1876, when Rutherford B. Hayes beat Samuel J. Tilden by a single electoral vote.

 For the first time in more than a century, the winner of a presidential election remained unknown a full day after the polls closed, as Gov. George W. Bush of Texas and Vice President Al Gore dispatched teams of lawyers to Florida yesterday to wrangle over the handful of votes upon which their White House dreams now rest.

NOVEMBER 9, 2000
BUSH BARELY AHEAD OF GORE IN FLORIDA AS RECOUNT HOLDS KEY TO THE ELECTION

TALLY DUE TODAY

Vice President Clings to Slim Edge in Popular Vote Nationwide

By RICHARD L. BERKE

For the first time in more than a century, the winner of a presidential election remained unknown a full day after the polls closed, as Gov. George W. Bush of Texas and Vice President Al Gore dispatched teams of lawyers to Florida yesterday to wrangle over the handful of votes upon which their White House dreams now rest.

The fate of the two rivals appeared to ride on the verdict in Florida, where an incomplete vote count had Mr. Bush leading Mr. Gore by 1,784 votes, an extraordinarily narrow margin in a nationwide race in which more than 96 million people voted. His lead in Florida was three one-hundredths of 1 percent of the votes cast.

Green Party presidential candidate Ralph Nader addresses a campaign rally in Washington on November 5, 2000. During an earlier appearance on "Meet The Press," Nader had said his candidacy's potential cost to Democratic presidential nominee Vice President Al Gore wouldn't stop him asking for votes. Many Democrats expressed anger at Nader during and after the controversial election.

Source: AP Images

The Florida secretary of state said she would probably declare a winner by the close of business today after a recount of nearly six million votes and the tallying of absentee ballots. But it was far from certain that the matter would be resolved swiftly.

Even if Florida's 25 electoral votes are delivered to Mr. Bush, Democrats suggested that they would pursue complaints about voting irregularities. Some Democrats in Palm Beach called for a new election in the county, saying the punch-card ballot was so perplexing that people mistakenly voted for Patrick J. Buchanan, the Reform Party candidate, instead of Mr. Gore. In addition, election officials in other states with close outcomes, like Iowa and Wisconsin, said they were bracing for challenges.

With Mr. Gore clinging to the slimmest popular vote margin in modern times, and Mr. Bush grasping for a bare majority of electoral votes to pull him over the top, both candidates were no doubt wondering if, had they done things a bit differently, they might now be mulling over choices for their Cabinet, not mulling over their job prospects.

Still dazed by the events since Tuesday, an official at the Gore headquarters in Nashville proclaimed breathlessly last night, "We have just reached the twilight zone of American politics."

NOVEMBER 9, 2000
ANGRY DEMOCRATS, FEARING NADER COST THEM PRESIDENTIAL RACE, THREATEN TO RETALIATE

By JAMES DAO

WASHINGTON, Nov. 8—Liberal Democrats today angrily threatened retribution against Ralph Nader and his Green Party allies if Vice President Al Gore was declared the loser in the too-close-to-call presidential election.

Mr. Nader won just 3 percent of the nationwide vote, but his totals in the closely contested states of Florida, Oregon and New Hampshire were well above the margins there between Mr. Gore and Gov. George W. Bush. Pre-election polling around the country had found that if Mr. Nader were not in the race, perhaps half his supporters would back Mr. Gore; others had said they did not know what they would do in the event of a Nader-less race, though some said they would vote for Mr. Bush.

With the race hanging in the balance today as ballots were counted in Oregon, recounted in Florida and studied in New Hampshire, where Mr. Bush was already declared the winner, staunch Democrats and their liberal allies attacked Mr. Nader for having refused to bow out of the race weeks ago.

Regardless of the outcome, they said, Mr. Nader's once-stellar reputation among liberals has been permanently tarnished, his ability to raise money and to work with Democrats forever damaged.

"His standing has been severely diminished by his actions," said Amy Isaacs, national director of Americans for Democratic Action. "People basically view him as having been on a narcissistic, self-serving, Sancho Panza, windmill-tilting excursion."

Senator Joseph R. Biden Jr. of Delaware, echoing the sentiments of several other Democrats on Capitol Hill, said: "Ralph Nader is not going to be welcome anywhere near the corridors. Nader cost us the election."

Other Democrats argued that if Mr. Bush won the election, Mr. Nader should be held responsible for jeopardizing the well-being of gays and lesbians, minorities and the poor, women and organized labor.

"Because of him and his activities, there is a possibility that the people we represent can be harmed, can be hurt, that our agenda that we fought for may not take place," said Gerald McEntee, president of the American Federation of State, County and Municipal Employees and chairman of the A.F.L.-C.I.O.'s political committee.

And Kate Michelman, president of the National Abortion and Reproductive Rights Action League, said Mr. Nader had infuriated many liberal women by having effectively helped an anti-abortion candidate, Mr. Bush.

"He may pay a price," Ms. Michelman said. "He has damaged his own credibility by so willfully dismissing, so cavalierly dismissing, this major concern of many, many voters."

NOVEMBER 12, 2000
BUSH SUES TO HALT HAND RECOUNT IN FLORIDA

HEARING ON MONDAY

Palm Beach Tally Starts as G.O.P. Cites Risk of Flaws in Process

By DAVID FIRESTONE
and MICHAEL COOPER

TALLAHASSEE, Fla. Nov. 11—The disputed presidential election in Florida moved into the federal courts today, when Gov. George W. Bush's campaign filed suit to block the manual recount of ballots sought by Vice President Al Gore. The campaign cited the "potential for mischief" and said the process was inherently less fair and more subjective than counting by machine.

The announcement, by James A. Baker III, came a day after the Republicans criticized the Democrats for threatening to take the ballot issue to court, a step that the Republicans said would lead to endless wrangling in a number of states.

But Mr. Baker contended this morning that the Democrats had effectively started the legal battle because

their supporters—though not the Gore campaign itself—had already filed state lawsuits in Florida.

The suit was filed as workers in Palm Beach County began a manual recount of thousands of ballots, examining each one for signs of partly punched holes. The recount in Volusia County was postponed until Sunday morning, though officials said it was because they were still studying write-in ballots, not because of the Bush campaign's lawsuit. Officials in both counties said they would proceed with their recount unless they received a federal court order telling them not to.

NOVEMBER 12, 2000
2 CAMPS CLASH VOTE BY VOTE, SCRAP BY SCRAP

By DON VAN NATTA Jr.

and RICK BRAGG

WEST PALM BEACH, Fla., Sunday, Nov. 12—A Palm Beach County elections board decided this morning to hold a manual recount of all ballots cast in the presidential election on Tuesday.

A hand recount of more than 4,000 votes, or 1 percent of the total cast, located 33 additional votes for Vice President Al Gore and 14 additional votes for Gov. George W. Bush.

An election commissioner said the difference, if applied to the entire county, could sway the battle for Florida's 25 electoral votes. The new count would narrow Mr. Bush's statewide lead to about 300 votes.

The extraordinary motion for the recount was made by Commissioner Carol Roberts of Palm Beach County shortly before 2 A.M. today at the county government building.

"I have instructed the board to conduct a manual recount of all the votes in Palm Beach County," Ms. Roberts said.

Lawyers here said they believed it would be the first time in American history that a county would do a full manual recount in a presidential election.

The election commissioners will meet Monday at 10 A.M. to discuss planning for the manual recount.

Mark Wallace, a lawyer for the Bush campaign, argued strenuously against the recount, saying it was inappropriate under the circumstances. Waiting for today's count, Mr. Wallace said, was "painful, uncertain and bizarre."

The painstaking process of counting votes by hand in a presidential election so close that every vote actually could count led to constant partisan challenges during the day over exactly what constituted a vote.

Teams of Democrats, Republicans and election officials argued over whether the ballots were actually perforated or just dented, and then argued over exactly what the policy was and whether it had changed as the day had worn on.

Again and again, the counting stopped when the two sides accused each other of miscounting and misinterpreting the ballots.

What should have been a simple question—whether or not a vote was cast when a hole was punched in a piece of paper—was complicated because the hole was not punched through cleanly and left a hanging or torn piece, known as a chad.

Democrats accused Republicans of discarding ballots that should not have been set aside. Republicans accused Democrats of including ballots that had dimples, not hanging chads. Mistrust seemed to grind the process even slower.

"We can't keep stopping when you all raise your hands," said Charles Burton, a county judge who is the chairman of the Palm Beach County canvassing committee, according to a pool report by a reporter who was in the room. "This will never work."

• •

ELECTION BY COURT

The 2000 election moved from ballot boxes to administrative recounts and finally into the courts. Democrat Al Gore requested a manual recount of ballots in four disputed Florida counties. Republican George W. Bush sued to prevent a new tally, seeking quick certification of his narrow victory by Florida officials supporting his candidacy. The Florida Supreme Court, siding with Gore, endorsed the recount, 4–3, even as time grew short before the formal vote of the Electoral College. Bush then appealed to the U.S. Supreme Court. The nine justices, in a controversial 5–4 vote largely along partisan lines, stopped the recount, ended the election, and secured the presidency for Bush. The next day, Gore accepted the verdict.

2000 POPULAR VOTE

STATE	TOTAL VOTE	GEORGE W. BUSH (REPUBLICAN) VOTES	%	AL GORE (DEMOCRAT) VOTES	%	RALPH NADER (GREEN) VOTES	%	PATRICK J. BUCHANAN (REFORM) VOTES	%
Alabama	1,666,272	941,173	56.5	692,611	41.6	18,323	1.1	6,351	0.4
Alaska	285,560	167,398	58.6	79,004	27.7	28,747	10.1	5,192	1.8
Arizona	1,532,016	781,652	51.0	685,341	44.7	45,645	3.0	12,373	0.8
Arkansas	921,781	472,940	51.3	422,768	45.9	13,421	1.5	7,358	0.8
California	10,965,856	4,567,429	41.7	5,861,203	53.4	418,707	3.8	44,987	0.4
Colorado	1,741,368	883,748	50.8	738,227	42.4	91,434	5.3	10,465	0.6
Connecticut	1,459,525	561,094	38.4	816,015	55.9	64,452	4.4	4,731	0.3
Delaware	327,622	137,288	41.9	180,068	55.0	8,307	2.5	777	0.2
Dist. of Col.	201,894	18,073	9.0	171,923	85.2	10,576	5.2	—	0.0
Florida	5,963,110	2,912,790	48.8	2,912,253	48.8	97,488	1.6	17,484	0.3
Georgia	2,596,645	1,419,720	54.7	1,116,230	43.0	13,273	0.5	10,926	0.4
Hawaii	367,951	137,845	37.5	205,286	55.8	21,623	5.9	1,071	0.3
Idaho	501,621	336,937	67.2	138,637	27.6	12,292	2.5	7,615	1.5
Illinois	4,742,123	2,019,421	42.6	2,589,026	54.6	103,759	2.2	16,106	0.3
Indiana	2,199,302	1,245,836	56.6	901,980	41.0	18,531	0.8	16,959	0.8
Iowa	1,315,563	634,373	48.2	638,517	48.5	29,374	2.2	5,731	0.4
Kansas	1,072,218	622,332	58.0	399,276	37.2	36,086	3.4	7,370	0.7
Kentucky	1,544,187	872,492	56.5	638,898	41.4	23,192	1.5	4,173	0.3
Louisiana	1,765,656	927,871	52.6	792,344	44.9	20,473	1.2	14,356	0.8
Maine	651,817	286,616	44.0	319,951	49.1	37,127	5.7	4,443	0.7
Maryland	2,020,480	813,797	40.3	1,140,782	56.5	53,768	2.7	4,248	0.2
Massachusetts	2,702,984	878,502	32.5	1,616,487	59.8	173,564	6.4	11,149	0.4
Michigan	4,232,711	1,953,139	46.1	2,170,418	51.3	84,165	2.0	2,061	0.0
Minnesota	2,438,685	1,109,659	45.5	1,168,266	47.9	126,696	5.2	22,166	0.9
Mississippi	994,184	572,844	57.6	404,614	40.7	8,122	0.8	2,265	0.2
Missouri	2,359,892	1,189,924	50.4	1,111,138	47.1	38,515	1.6	9,818	0.4
Montana	410,997	240,178	58.4	137,126	33.4	24,437	5.9	5,697	1.4
Nebraska	697,019	433,862	62.2	231,780	33.3	24,540	3.5	3,646	0.5
Nevada	608,970	301,575	49.5	279,978	46.0	15,008	2.5	4,747	0.8
New Hampshire	569,081	273,559	48.1	266,348	46.8	22,198	3.9	2,615	0.5
New Jersey	3,187,226	1,284,173	40.3	1,788,850	56.1	94,554	3.0	6,989	0.2
New Mexico	598,605	286,417	47.8	286,783	47.9	21,251	3.6	1,392	0.2
New York	6,821,999	2,403,374	35.2	4,107,697	60.2	244,030	3.6	31,599	0.5
North Carolina	2,911,262	1,631,163	56.0	1,257,692	43.2	—	0.0	8,874	0.3
North Dakota	288,256	174,852	60.7	95,284	33.1	9,486	3.3	7,288	2.5
Ohio	4,701,998	2,350,363	50.0	2,183,628	46.4	117,799	2.5	26,721	0.6
Oklahoma	1,234,229	744,337	60.3	474,276	38.4	—	0.0	9,014	0.7
Oregon	1,533,968	713,577	46.5	720,342	47.0	77,357	5.0	7,063	0.5
Pennsylvania	4,913,119	2,281,127	46.4	2,485,967	50.6	103,392	2.1	16,023	0.3
Rhode Island	409,047	130,555	31.9	249,508	61.0	25,052	6.1	2,273	0.6
South Carolina	1,382,717	785,937	56.8	565,561	40.9	20,200	1.5	3,519	0.3
South Dakota	316,269	190,700	60.3	118,804	37.6	—	0.0	3,322	1.1
Tennessee	2,076,181	1,061,949	51.1	981,720	47.3	19,781	1.0	4,250	0.2
Texas	6,407,637	3,799,639	59.3	2,433,746	38.0	137,994	2.2	12,394	0.2
Utah	770,754	515,096	66.8	203,053	26.3	35,850	4.7	9,319	1.2
Vermont	294,308	119,775	40.7	149,022	50.6	20,374	6.9	2,192	0.7
Virginia	2,739,447	1,437,490	52.5	1,217,290	44.4	59,398	2.2	5,455	0.2
Washington	2,487,433	1,108,864	44.6	1,247,652	50.2	103,002	4.1	7,171	0.3
West Virginia	648,124	336,475	51.9	295,497	45.6	10,680	1.6	3,169	0.5
Wisconsin	2,598,607	1,237,279	47.6	1,242,987	47.8	94,070	3.6	11,446	0.4
Wyoming	218,351	147,947	67.8	60,481	27.7	4,625	2.1	2,724	1.2
TOTALS	**105,396,627**	**50,455,156**	**47.9**	**50,992,335**	**48.4**	**2,882,738**	**2.7**	**449,077**	**0.4**

OTHER VOTES	%	PLURALITY	
7,814	0.5	248,562	R
5,219	1.8	88,394	R
7,005	0.5	96,311	R
5,294	0.6	50,172	R
75,530	0.7	1,293,774	D
17,494	1.0	145,521	R
13,233	0.9	254,921	D
1,182	0.4	42,780	D
1,322	0.7	153,850	D
23,095	0.4	537	R
36,496	1.4	303,490	R
2,126	0.6	67,441	D
6,140	1.2	198,300	R
13,811	0.3	569,605	D
15,996	0.7	343,856	R
7,568	0.6	4,144	D
7,154	0.7	223,056	R
5,432	0.4	233,594	R
10,612	0.6	135,527	R
3,680	0.6	33,335	D
7,885	0.4	326,985	D
23,282	0.9	737,985	D
22,928	0.5	217,279	D
11,898	0.5	58,607	D
6,339	0.6	168,230	R
10,497	0.4	78,786	R
3,559	0.9	103,052	R
3,191	0.5	202,082	R
7,662	1.3	21,597	R
4,361	0.8	7,211	R
12,660	0.4	504,677	D
2,762	0.5	366	D
35,299	0.5	1,704,323	D
13,533	0.5	373,471	R
1,346	0.5	79,568	R
23,484	0.5	166,735	R
6,602	0.5	270,061	R
15,629	1.0	6,765	D
26,610	0.5	204,840	D
1,659	0.4	118,953	D
7,500	0.5	220,376	R
3,443	1.1	71,896	R
8,481	0.4	80,229	R
23,864	0.4	1,365,893	R
7,436	1.0	312,043	R
2,945	1.0	29,247	D
19,814	0.7	220,200	R
20,744	0.8	138,788	D
2,303	0.4	40,978	R
12,825	0.5	5,708	D
2,574	1.2	87,466	R
617,321	0.6	537,179	D

DECEMBER 9, 2000
FLORIDA COURT BACKS RECOUNT; BUSH APPEALING TO U.S. JUSTICES

A 4-TO-3 DECISION

Statewide Tally Set for Uncounted Votes—Deadline Tomorrow

By DAVID FIRESTONE

TALLAHASSEE, Fla., Dec. 8—Vice President Al Gore's flagging presidential hopes were suddenly jolted back to life this afternoon when a bitterly divided Florida Supreme Court ordered an immediate manual recount of thousands of ballots across the state.

Wielding its power with a force that neither candidate had fully anticipated, a four-member majority of the seven-member court suddenly erased the growing sense of inevitability that had developed around Gov. George W. Bush and set loose what could turn out to be days of confusion and disorder.

A judge ordered tonight that the recount of the largest pool of those ballots begin at 8 A.M. Saturday and that all recounts conclude by 2 P.M. Sunday.

Within an hour of the Supreme Court opinion, election officials around Florida mobilized for a hastily organized recount of ballots on which no vote for president had been officially recorded. In reversing a lower court's decision on Monday that had rejected the Gore campaign's request for a manual recount of disputed ballots, the State Supreme Court said the recount had to go beyond the two counties whose ballots Mr. Gore had contested and include all the so-called undervotes—a number estimated at more than 45,000.

Just as quickly, lawyers for Governor Bush rushed to the United States Supreme Court to stop the count, filing a request for a stay with Justice Anthony M. Kennedy 31 days after the election, and simultaneously demanding an emergency hearing from the United States Court of Appeals for the 11th Circuit in Atlanta.

In a nine-page request for an injunction from the court of appeals, the lawyers said Mr. Bush would "suffer irreparable injury as a result of the unconstitutional Florida manual recounts," and requested the court prevent any manual recounts from being included in certified vote tabulations.

James A. Baker III, Mr. Bush's representative in Tallahassee, said the opinion was flawed and disappointing, and suggested it might disenfranchise Florida's voters.

> " Lawyers and aides for Vice President Al Gore, who had been ruddy and full-throated all morning as the counting of more than 45,000 ballots began, were suddenly the ones looking ashen. Members of Gov. George W. Bush's legal team, who had been in the same position on Friday, were now the ones exchanging high-fives. "

DECEMBER 10, 2000
SUPREME COURT, SPLIT 5-4, HALTS FLORIDA COUNT IN BLOW TO GORE
TALLY IS CUT SHORT

Democrats Look Ashen as Republicans Praise the Legal System

By DAVID FIRESTONE

TALLAHASSEE, Fla., Dec. 9—As abruptly as the world seemed to change at 4 P.M. on Friday, it did so again at 2:45 P.M. today when the United States Supreme Court halted the hand count that the Florida Supreme Court had ordered. Judges and election officials, who had begun counting ballots shortly after dawn today across Florida, started packing them up and waiting to see if the ground would shake once more.

Lawyers and aides for Vice President Al Gore, who had been ruddy and full-throated all morning as the counting of more than 45,000 ballots began, were suddenly the ones looking ashen. Members of Gov. George W. Bush's legal team, who had been in the same position on Friday, were now the ones exchanging high-fives. Democrats began quoting dissenting justices, while Republicans praised the wisdom of the nation's legal system.

David Boies, Mr. Gore's chief lawyer here, was eating lunch with friends at a restaurant near the Capitol when the news came over the television. He jumped up from his table, incredulous, and shouted, "What is the irreparable harm?" The reference was to the successful claim the Bush lawyers had made to the United States Supreme Court, convincing the justices that they should stop the recount because of the harm it was doing to their client.

No longer the bristling and scolding figure he was the day before, James A. Baker III, Mr. Bush's representative here, told reporters how pleased he and Mr. Bush were that one Supreme Court had overruled another.

"It's one day you're up, one day you're down," said Mr. Baker, suddenly smiling and relaxed, bearing no complaints about the legal system.

DECEMBER 13, 2000
EDITORIAL
THE COURT RULES FOR MR. BUSH

The United States Supreme Court has brought the presidential election to a conclusion in favor of Gov. George W. Bush, but its decision to bar a recount in Florida comes at considerable cost to the public trust and the tradition of fair elections. Our national history bears the comforting lesson that the American people's confidence in the rule of law and the stability of their institutions will not be damaged in the long run. It is incumbent on citizens and elected officials alike to respect the authority of the ruling and the legitimacy of the new presidency whether or not they agree with the court's legal reasoning. In the

short term, Mr. Bush and Vice President Al Gore bear great responsibility for bringing the nation together in spirit if not in immediate political agreement. Mr. Bush needs to be gracious and unifying in victory, and Vice President Gore must master the difficult task of placing the national need for continuity ahead of any bitterness he may feel.

The five weeks since the election have seen the writing of an entirely unexpected chapter in the nation's political history. This will long be remembered as an election decided by a conservative Supreme Court in favor of a conservative candidate while the ballots that could have brought a different outcome went uncounted in Florida. The court overruled the Florida Supreme Court by saying that the recount it ordered was inconsistent with the equal protection and due process provisions of the federal Constitution, and that state election laws afforded no more time to conduct a full recount under uniform standards. These days will also be recorded as a time of struggle between the nation's highest federal court and a Southern state supreme court that, in a reversal of the old states' rights routine, showed the greater sensitivity to protecting the franchise. Finally, these will be remembered as days of bitterness between Republicans and Democrats. We will not know for some time whether that bitterness will usher in a period of ruinous conflict capable of tying up Congress and hobbling a new presidency.

The resolution depends greatly on what the nation sees as it begins to examine the man who upon the stroke of a ruling from an ideologically divided court stands to become its 43rd president. Mr. Bush faces first the task of speaking healing words to a nation that cast 300,000 more popular votes for his rival. He must define himself in full public view with a fast-track transition and with efforts to soothe the wounds of an election that tested both the nation's patience and its laws. In truth, there is nothing in the Texas governor's public record to guarantee that he can unite an electorate and a Congress so evenly divided between two parties that have not fully shed their battle armor. But the grand theme of presidential history has to do with ordinary men exceeding expectations, quite often by curbing the vengeful or triumphalist elements within their own parties.

Just as John F. Kennedy carried a piece of note paper reminding him of the narrowness of his victory in 1960, Mr. Bush should keep in mind the more complicated numbers of this election. Vice President Gore got more popular votes nationally and probably in Florida as well. Mr. Bush's title to the office comes through the electoral count and through appropriate legal procedures that settled in his favor the official result of a messy Florida election. Die-hards may want to keep arguing this outcome for four years, and that makes it doubly important for Mr. Bush to reach out to the broader constituency.

* *

THE UNITED STATES ATTACKED

Just eight months into the George W. Bush presidency, the world changed. On September 11, 2001, terrorists in hijacked commercial airliners destroyed the World Trade Center in New York City and damaged the Pentagon near Washington, D.C., while being thwarted in another attack by a fourth plane that crashed in rural Pennsylvania. In an instant, the assaults transformed the United States and the Bush presidency. No longer able to focus on domestic concerns, President Bush turned to foreign policy, declaring a "war on terrorism" that led to the invasion of Afghanistan in 2001 and ultimately to the invasion of Iraq in 2003.

SEPTEMBER 12, 2001
U.S. ATTACKED
HIJACKED JETS DESTROY TWIN TOWERS AND HIT PENTAGON IN DAY OF TERROR
A CREEPING HORROR
Buildings Burn and Fall as Onlookers Search for Elusive Safety
By N. R. KLEINFIELD

It kept getting worse.

The horror arrived in episodic bursts of chilling disbelief, signified first by trembling floors, sharp eruptions, cracked windows. There was the actual unfathomable realization of a gaping, flaming hole in first one of the tall towers, and then the same thing all over again in its twin. There was the merciless sight of bodies helplessly tumbling out, some of them in flames.

Finally, the mighty towers themselves were reduced to nothing. Dense plumes of smoke raced through the downtown avenues, coursing between the buildings, shaped like tornadoes on their sides.

Every sound was cause for alarm. A plane appeared overhead. Was another one coming? No, it was a fighter jet. But was it friend or enemy? People scrambled for their lives, but they didn't know where to go. Should they go north, south, east, west? Stay outside, go indoors? People hid beneath cars and each other. Some contemplated jumping into the river.

For those trying to flee the very epicenter of the collapsing World Trade Center towers, the most horrid thought of all finally dawned on them: nowhere was safe.

For several panic-stricken hours yesterday morning, people in Lower Manhattan witnessed the inexpressible, the incomprehensible, the unthinkable. "I don't know what the gates of hell look like, but it's got to be like this," said John Maloney, a security director for an Internet firm in the trade center. "I'm a combat veteran, Vietnam, and I never saw anything like this."

SEPTEMBER 12, 2001
A SOMBER BUSH SAYS TERRORISM CANNOT PREVAIL

By ELISABETH BUMILLER

with DAVID E. SANGER

WASHINGTON, Sept. 11—President Bush vowed tonight to retaliate against those responsible for today's attacks on New York and Washington, declaring that he would "make no distinction between the terrorists who committed these acts and those who harbor them." "These acts of mass murder were intended to frighten our nation into chaos and retreat, but they have failed," the president said in his first speech to the nation from the Oval Office. "Our country is strong. Terrorist acts can shake the foundation of our biggest buildings, but they cannot touch the foundation of America."

His speech came after a day of trauma that seems destined to define his presidency. Seeking to at once calm the nation and declare his determination to exact retribution, he told a country numbed by repeated scenes of carnage that "these acts shattered steel, but they cannot dent the steel of American resolve."

Mr. Bush spoke only hours after returning from a zigzag course across the country, as his Secret Service and military security teams moved him from Florida, where he woke up this morning expecting to press for his education bill, to command posts in Louisiana and Nebraska before it was determined the attacks had probably ended and he could safely return to the capital.

It was a sign of the catastrophic nature of the events that the White House kept his whereabouts secret during much of the day as he was shuttled about on Air Force One, with an escort of F-16's and F-15's.

Tonight, he looked tense and drawn, as he declared that "today our nation saw evil, the very worst of human nature."

"The search is under way for those who are behind these evil acts," Mr. Bush said. "I have directed the full resources of our intelligence and law enforcement communities to find those responsible and to bring them to justice."

His mention of the terrorists and the countries they operate from were the closest the White House would come to assigning blame for the attacks. Intelligence officials said they strongly believed that Osama bin Laden's terrorist organization was behind the attacks. But Afghanistan and administration officials insisted there was no hard evidence to connect Mr. bin Laden to today's attacks.

One of his national security officials said tonight, "I have never seen the president so angry or so determined."

Mr. Bush asked the country to pray tonight, for the thousands who are dead, "for the children whose worlds have been shattered, for all whose sense of safety and security has been threatened." He quoted from the 23rd Psalm: "Even though I walk through the valley of the shadow of death, I fear no evil, for you are with me."

OCTOBER 8, 2001
U.S. AND BRITAIN STRIKE AFGHANISTAN, AIMING AT BASES AND TERRORIST CAMPS; BUSH WARNS 'TALIBAN WILL PAY A PRICE'

Bomb and Missile Attacks—Bin Laden Issues Threat

By PATRICK E. TYLER

WASHINGTON, Oct 7—Striking at night from aircraft carriers and distant bases, the United States and Britain launched a powerful barrage of cruise missiles and long-range bombers against Afghanistan today to try to destroy the terrorist training camps of Osama bin Laden's Qaeda network and the Taliban government that has protected it.

"On my orders, the United States military has begun strikes," President Bush said in a televised statement from the White House at 1 P.M., just more than half an hour after the first explosions were reported in Kabul, the Afghan capital.

"These carefully targeted actions are designed to disrupt the use of Afghanistan as a terrorist base of operations and to attack the military capability of the Taliban regime," Mr. Bush said.

The Taliban was warned, he said, to meet America's demands to surrender Mr. bin Laden, stop supporting terrorism and release foreign aid workers they hold. "None of these demands were met," he said. "And now, the Taliban will pay a price."

"Today we focus on Afghanistan," he added, but "the battle is broader." Alluding to the Sept. 11 terror attacks that destroyed the World Trade Center, damaged the Pentagon and killed more than 5,000 people, Mr. Bush again warned that nations that sponsor or protect "outlaws and killers of innocents" will "take that lonely path at their own peril."

The skies over Kabul lit up with flashes, and thunderous explosions rumbled through the night, witnesses said. The Taliban fired antiaircraft guns into the dark sky, and their tracers could be seen by residents of the capital and around the cities of Kandahar and Jalalabad, strongholds of the radical Islamic regime.

Mr. Bush's statement was followed by one from Prime Minister Tony Blair of Britain. Both leaders emphasized that the military campaign was not "a war with Islam," as Mr. Blair asserted, though no Muslim country took part directly in the attacks and many refused to allow offensive operations to be staged from their territory.

Mr. Bush said "we are the friends of almost a billion" people worldwide "who practice the Islamic faith."

THE PRESIDENTIAL ELECTION OF 2008

OBAMA FELLS A RACIAL BARRIER IN DECISIVE VICTORY

The election of 2008 marked the significant steps in a reconstruction of American politics. Illinois senator Barack Obama became the nation's first African American president, and two women conducted the first significant campaigns for national office. New technology turned electioneering techniques toward a twenty-first century reliance on computers and the Internet. In winning the contest, Democrats achieved major changes in the electoral map and gained new support among large voter groups. From the winning candidate to precinct canvassers, 2008 will be known as a year of American electoral transformation.

Entering the election year, the prospects were dim for the incumbent Republicans, bringing expectations of a Democratic victory. George W. Bush had entered the White House in 2000 without a plurality of the popular vote and only after a contentious Supreme Court ruling awarded him Florida's disputed electoral votes. The terrorist attacks on the United States on September 11, 2001, made Bush, in his own words, a "war president," who vigorously extended executive power to combat the attackers and led the nation into war in Afghanistan and then Iraq. Continuing public concern over terrorism enabled Bush to narrowly win reelection in 2004, defeating Democratic senator John Kerry with a thin majority of the popular vote and a 286 to 252 electoral vote margin.

Once reelected, Bush and his party fell precipitously in public standing. The war in Iraq had been justified as necessary to eliminate weapons of mass destruction, but no such weapons were found. Instead of the promised quick victory, the American invaders faced civil war, widespread destruction, insurgent guerrillas, and the deaths of four thousand troops. At home, the president squandered his reelection victory in a failed attempt to privatize Social Security, the prized core of the national welfare state. When Hurricane Katrina ravaged New Orleans, the administration was perceived as both incompetent and uncaring. The combined record brought rebuke at the polls, when Democrats in 2006 took control of both the House and the Senate, ending twelve years of Republican legislative dominance.

President Barack Obama and his wife, Michelle, walk during the inaugural parade in Washington, D.C., on Tuesday, January 20, 2009.

As 2008 opened, the political environment became still more foreboding for Republicans. Housing values fell sharply, mortgage credit shrank, and foreclosures mounted. The country entered a recession that eventually became its most serious economic crisis since the Great Depression of the 1930s. Although a troop increase calmed the turmoil in Iraq and reduced military casualties considerably, public opinion had turned irrevocably against the war. Abuses of civil liberties—including unauthorized wiretapping and political prosecutions in the United States and torture of prisoners of war abroad—brought public protests and judicial checks.

2008 ELECTORAL VOTE

STATE	ELECTORAL VOTES	OBAMA	McCAIN	STATE	ELECTORAL VOTES	OBAMA	McCAIN
Alabama	(9)	–	9	Montana	(3)	–	3
Alaska	(3)	–	3	Nebraska	(5)	1	4
Arizona	(10)	–	10	Nevada	(5)	5	–
Arkansas	(6)	–	6	New Hampshire	(4)	4	–
California	(55)	55	–	New Jersey	(15)	15	–
Colorado	(9)	9	–	New Mexico	(5)	5	–
Connecticut	(7)	7	–	New York	(31)	31	–
Delaware	(3)	3	–	North Carolina	(15)	15	–
District of Columbia	(3)	3	–	North Dakota	(3)	–	3
Florida	(27)	27	–	Ohio	(20)	20	–
Georgia	(15)	–	15	Oklahoma	(7)	–	7
Hawaii	(4)	4	–	Oregon	(7)	7	–
Idaho	(4)	–	4	Pennsylvania	(21)	21	–
Illinois	(21)	21	–	Rhode Island	(4)	4	–
Indiana	(11)	11	–	South Carolina	(8)	–	8
Iowa	(7)	7	–	South Dakota	(3)	–	3
Kansas	(6)	–	6	Tennessee	(11)	–	11
Kentucky	(8)	–	8	Texas	(34)	–	34
Louisiana	(9)	–	9	Utah	(5)	–	5
Maine	(4)	4	–	Vermont	(3)	3	–
Maryland	(10)	10	–	Virginia	(13)	13	–
Massachusetts	(12)	12	–	Washington	(11)	11	–
Michigan	(17)	17	–	West Virginia	(5)	–	5
Minnesota	(10)	10	–	Wisconsin	(10)	10	–
Mississippi	(6)	–	6	Wyoming	(3)	–	3
Missouri	(11)	–	11				
				TOTALS	**(538)**	**365**	**173**

Bush had a bare majority approving his job performance as he began his second term, but his standing in polls was in the low thirties at the beginning of 2008. By election day, he had fallen to the lowest approval rating, and highest disapproval, ever recorded in opinion polls, even worse than Richard Nixon at the time of his forced departure from the White House in 1974 under threat of impeachment.

Americans were eager for change; more than three-fourths of those polled believed the country was on the "wrong track." Change was already inevitable because of the candidates. For the first time in more than half a century, since 1952, neither the incumbent president nor incumbent vice president was to be on the ballot. Both major parties undertook open and passionate contests to choose their candidates, followed by an intense, expensive, and ideological fall campaign. Then, a new person, a man, or a woman, or someone with a racial identity different from all previous presidents would come to power.

THE PARTIES AND THE CANDIDATES

The parties followed different courses in their presidential nominations. Since the major changes in party procedures in the 1970s, the choice of candidates had been determined largely through state primaries, with the nominations typically foreclosed after a few early contests. That pattern had encouraged states to "front-load," to move their primaries to dates early in the calendar year to accomplish two goals: to gain greater attention from the contenders and the media and to have greater influence on the presidential selections.

The same pattern developed early in 2008. Iowa and New Hampshire insisted on their standing as the first states to conduct, respectively, a caucus and a primary; they even contemplated moving their contests to late 2007 to maintain their priority. Other states tried to get some of the action. Among Democrats, to bring more ethnic diversity to the process, Nevada and South Carolina were permitted to hold their own caucus and primary early in the year. Florida and Michigan flouted party rules by moving their contests to January. More than twenty states stayed within the formal rules, but scheduled their nominating contests for a single day, February 5. It appeared likely that the presidential selections would be settled on that "Super Tuesday," nine months before the final national vote. The effects of these developments were quite different in the two major parties' races.

Ten candidates entered the Republican race. The early leader was Arizona senator John McCain. Basically conservative, McCain had earned wide respect for his independence, openness, and relative moderation while unsuccessfully seeking the party nomination in 2000. In 2008 he turned more toward the conservative wing, supporting Bush on most issues, vigorously backing the Iraq occupation, and attempting to repair a breach with religious fundamentalists. Although he was the most prominent candidate, his campaign faltered amid organizational and financial disarray.

The other major Republican candidates included Mitt Romney, former governor of Massachusetts; Rudy Giuliani, the heroic mayor of New York at the time of the 9/11 attacks; former senator Fred Thompson, who had become a noted television actor; and Mike Huckabee, governor of Arkansas and an ordained Baptist minister. Despite their diverse backgrounds, they all presented themselves as conservatives, even changing their views on social issues to court the right wing, as Romney did on abortion and Giuliani on gun control.

In the first contest, Iowa, Romney, although well-financed from his personal fortune, met unexpected defeat from Huckabee, who had energized the large number of evangelical Christians, some of them concerned about Romney's Mormon religion. Many commentators now assumed McCain had been eliminated, but the Arizonan changed his tactics to rely on intimate town-hall meetings. He won a rebound victory in New Hampshire, lost in Michigan to Romney (whose father had been governor of that state), and then led the field

in conservative South Carolina, dashing Huckabee's chances. Giuliani, who had led opinion polls, kept away from these contests, relying on Florida, with its large number of former New Yorkers. When McCain won the state in late January, his path was clear. McCain swept the Super Tuesday contests and essentially clinched the Republican nomination on February 5. He had successfully followed the established pattern.

The Democratic contest was quite different. The leading candidate was Sen. Hillary Clinton of New York. After eight years as first lady, she moved to New York and developed an independent political appeal, winning its Senate seat in 2000, as her husband, Bill Clinton, was finishing his presidential term. In 2006 she gained a smashing reelection. Clinton added personal prestige, large financial resources, and the backing of the party establishment to her inspiring appeal as the first serious woman candidate for the White House.

Seven other candidates vied to become the alternative to Clinton's seemingly inevitable nomination. They included John Edwards, the party's vice-presidential nominee in the previous election; New Mexico governor Bill Richardson, who had held two cabinet positions; and accomplished senators Joe Biden of Delaware and Chris Dodd of Connecticut. The most intriguing alternative was a younger senator, Barack Obama of Illinois. Only forty-six and still in his first senatorial term, Obama had drawn attention for his early opposition to the Iraq war and his eloquent keynote address to the Democratic convention in 2004. Most striking was his heritage: a black man, the child of an interracial marriage, Obama was the first member of his race and his generation to make a credible try for the presidency. Although dismissed by most Democratic leaders as too young and untried, Obama proved to be a master campaign strategist and an inspiration to millions, particularly younger and African American voters.

Obama leapt to the front of the line in the Iowa caucuses, scoring a surprising victory for an African American in a state with few minority voters. By the end of January, all the other contenders but Clinton had dropped out, making the race a direct two-person contest. During January, Clinton rebounded by rallying women to gain her own surprising win in New Hampshire. They fought to a draw in the Nevada caucus, but Obama moved blacks to register and vote in South Carolina, where he won overwhelmingly and ended Edwards's fading hopes to be the compromise choice. In the same month, Michigan and Florida held primaries unauthorized by the Democratic rules. Clinton won both (with no other candidates even listed on the Michigan ballot or campaigning in Florida), but the party's national committee refused to accept the states' delegates.

The battleground was now set for a decisive confrontation on Super Tuesday, February 5, when twenty-three states and territories would select their delegates, including the megastates of California, New York, and Illinois. The basic premises of the Clinton strategy had been that these contests would decide the nomination and that she would sweep the field on the basis of her prominence, party contacts, treasury, and experienced campaign management. In reality, the foundation of the strategy was shaky. The campaign was riven with conflicts, its managers were confused, and profligate spending had depleted its funds to the point that Senator Clinton had to lend the campaign $13 million of her own money.

Nor did the strategy work. On Super Tuesday, Clinton and Obama split the vote. Clinton won 9 of 16 primaries, including the big prizes of California and New York. Obama countered with significant showings in most states and with wins in six of the seven areas choosing delegates in party caucuses. With a broader appeal, he more than offset the losses in California and New York with wins in Illinois and Georgia. When all the results were in, Obama had netted 17 more delegates than Clinton.

They battled for the next four months, meeting in twenty television debates, with Obama steadily moving toward the nomination. He benefited from a national strategy, having organized in almost all states and the territories, while Clinton had not planned beyond the concluding victories she expected on Super Tuesday. As a result, Obama compiled a streak of 11 straight victories in February, ranging from 3 delegates in the Virgin Islands caucus to a net gain of 25 in the Virginia primary. Notably, he benefited from the early mobilization of enthusiastic supporters and won all of the five constituencies choosing delegates in caucuses, contests that Clinton had virtually ignored.

The competition then turned to the larger and industrial states, where Clinton was better positioned because of her support among working class voters. But Clinton still fell short. The party rules provided for proportional division of delegates rather than a "winner-take-all" allocation. The effect was to dilute Clinton's victories, so that she netted an advantage of only 7 delegates among the 577 selected in 7 states during March and April. The race was effectively over in the first week of May, when Obama won decisively in North Carolina and almost carried Indiana, although Clinton persevered to carry four of the remaining six primaries. The final nail in her electoral coffin came in the last weekend of the primary season, when the Democratic National Committee voted to seat only half of the delegates chosen in the renegade Michigan and Florida primaries, a net gain for Clinton of 24 delegates, a paltry consolation prize.

The Democrats, in effect, had conducted a national presidential primary stretched over five months, giving voters in every area the opportunity to cast meaningful ballots. The turnout was an astonishing 37 million votes, better than 60 percent of the tally for Kerry in the 2004 general election. In the end, Obama won a bare plurality of the popular vote in the Democratic contests, and a winning margin of 127 among the 3,434 pledged delegates. His victory was sealed by his lead of 463 to 257 among the "superdelegates," the party officials and officeholders who were automatically allotted a fifth of the convention seats. Originally included to provide experience and potential negotiating skills, these established politicians at first had favored Clinton. As Obama aroused popular enthusiasm, spurred new party enrollments, and carried 31 of the 51 Electoral College constituencies, the superdelegates fell in line with their constituents, guaranteeing Obama's nomination.

The two parties held their conventions late in the summer, the Democrats in Denver in the week before Labor Day, the Republicans the following week. The late dates had been selected to allow the candidates to continue raising money as long as possible before receiving federal campaign subsidies, which prohibited further fund-raising after the formal convention nominations. Obama, however, rejected the subsidies in order to continue raising funds—vast funds as it happened—free of federal restrictions. Although McCain accepted the funds, his campaign fell behind Obama's in financial resources in the fall competition. Eventually, in television advertising alone, Obama and the Democrats would spend nearly $175 million, almost doubling the McCain and Republican Party's combined outlay of $92 million.

Both conventions were rousing party rallies. After extensive investigations, Obama chose Senator Biden as his running mate, a popular choice within the party except among a remnant of Clinton backers. Obama came to Denver with a nominal delegate lead of 2,229 to 1,896. There, he won a rousing endorsement from Clinton, who dramatically moved his nomination from the floor in the middle of the evening television network news programs. Accepting his designation before a crowd of eighty thousand in the Denver Broncos' football stadium, the Democratic candidate attacked the Bush administration, tied John McCain to its failures, and ended with a rhetorical variation on "change," his central electoral appeal:

> America, we cannot turn back. Not with so much
> work to be done. Not with so many children to
> educate, and so many veterans to care for. Not with
> an economy to fix and cities to rebuild and farms

to save. Not with so many families to protect and so many lives to mend. America, we cannot turn back. We cannot walk alone. At this moment, in this election, we must pledge once more to march into the future.

As Democrats left Denver, they were heady with the expectation of victory. On the eve of his own party's convention, McCain quickly deflated their joyful balloons by announcing his surprising choice of Alaska governor Sarah Palin for the Republican vice-presidential nomination. The selection rekindled the enthusiasm of party conservatives. Meeting in St. Paul, the party rallied behind McCain, cheering speeches by his former opponents as well as one by Sen. Joseph Lieberman, the 2000 Democratic candidate for vice president, while President Bush was shunted to a brief videotaped spot outside of prime time. McCain ended the convention with an emotional invocation of his patriotism and service:

> My country saved me, and I cannot forget it. And I will fight for her for as long as I draw breath. . . . I'm going to fight for my cause every day as your President. I'm going to make sure every American has every reason to thank God, as I thank Him: that I'm an American, a proud citizen of the greatest country on earth, and with hard work, strong faith and a little courage, great things are always within our reach. Fight with me.

THE CAMPAIGN

The long nomination contests set a clear choice before the electorate. McCain and Obama were different in virtually every respect. They were of two different generations, twenty-five years apart in age. Nor would any voter miss the difference between a white and a biracial candidate. Their lives also had been sharply distinct—the Republican a scion of a family of military leaders and himself a distinguished veteran of the Vietnam War, the Democrat abandoned by his foreign father and raised by an unconventional mother before achieving notable academic and professional successes. McCain had been a national legislator for more than twenty-five years, Obama for less than four. They disagreed on most issues, ranging from economic policy to the Iraq war.

Crammed into two months after the late conventions, the contest was intense. With such different candidates in a time of great national stress, the race drew the interest of 90 percent of the voters, stimulated by cable television, the 24/7 news cycle, text messaging, and the Internet, with its innumerable sites, from individual blogs to social networks such as YouTube and Facebook. Dramatic events regularly disrupted past patterns, further increasing candidate anxiety and voter interest.

The Palin nomination was the first major event of the fall campaign. Initially, her selection appeared to be a brilliant stroke, a bold and unconventional choice of a woman who might appeal to former loyalists of Hillary Clinton. Palin was a conservative who would rally those on the right still skeptical of McCain's reputed moderation, and she was a state executive with some claims as a reformer of political ethics. She delivered a rousing acceptance speech at the Republican convention and drew large, energetic crowds and ecstatic comments from right-wing commentators. Suddenly, the race tightened, with McCain either tied with or ahead of Obama in the polls.

Soon, however, the glamour faded. Televised interviews showed that Palin had little knowledge of most policy issues, particularly foreign policy. Admiration turned to ridicule in news media and television comedy, as when she claimed expertise in international affairs because of Alaska's proximity to Russia. Intensive investigations also raised questions about her character, including her spending $150,000 of party funds for campaign clothing. Ultimately, Palin probably harmed the Republican prospects. Three out of five voters considered her not qualified to step in as president, while only one of six had the same dour judgment of Democrat Joe Biden.

More serious matters came quickly to dominate the election race. The U.S. financial system, already weak, seemed to be on the verge of collapse. Losses from bad home mortgages spread through the web of financial institutions—banks, brokers, investors, lenders, and borrowers. A torrent of dire economic news changed the electoral frame. Inflation spiked, in response to record high prices for oil, with gasoline selling above $4 a gallon. At the same time, unemployment grew to a five-year high. One financial catastrophe followed another, leading to large losses in the values of U.S. stocks, which dropped more than 25 percent from the time of the nominating conventions to election day.

Voters were frightened by the serious threats to their job prospects, life styles, savings, and future retirement pensions. The political stakes also rose, as the Bush administration proposed that Congress provide the huge sum of $700 billion to rescue the financial system and give the secretary of the Treasury virtually unlimited power to spend this money. The credit crisis and the proposed legislation made the economy the predominant issue in the presidential election, stressed by 63 percent of the electorate, a greater focus on one issue than had ever been recorded in opinion surveys.

That focus inevitably helped the Democrats, always more trusted on these issues, and harmed the Republicans, who bore the burdens of the Bush record. The candidates' reactions magnified these effects. Obama, while calmly indicating reserved acceptance of the rescue plan, also tried to turn the crisis to his advantage by blaming the "failed economic philosophy" of both McCain and Bush. McCain fumbled the opportunity, however limited, to gain support. He veered from attempted reassurance to a failed attempt to craft a legislative solution to a suggested suspension of the campaign and the scheduled television debates.

The television debates went ahead as planned—three between the presidential candidates and one between vice-presidential nominees Biden and Palin. Each drew an audience of 60 million to 75 million viewers; most watched, uncharacteristically, was the confrontation of Biden and Palin

The first debate, between Obama and McCain, came as Congress was considering the financial rescue plan and inevitably focused on the economy. Next was the vice-presidential clash, where Palin's folksy manner and language made her more likeable to some, more bizarre to others. The presidential candidates returned to economic and other issues in a town-hall format, including questions gathered through YouTube videos. They concluded three weeks before the election in a face-to-face, but barely civil, discussion, strangely focused on "Joe the plumber," a working-class McCain supporter who had conducted a street colloquy with Obama on tax policy.

Whatever the format, the debates showed the clear differences between the candidates and between the parties. Although policy issues formed the framework of the debates, the essential political point was to win votes, not to define positions on programs. On this criterion, Obama clearly predominated. In a year of voter discontent, the television confrontations favored the Democrat by reinforcing the basic narrative of the campaigns, Obama's stress on change, McCain's on experience. For Obama, the greatest benefit of the debates—and of the lengthy campaign—was simple exposure. He began his presidential quest with limited public recognition, an exotic and unconventional background, a thin record in office, and the inescapable but politically charged identity of a black man. The debates and the months on the stump made him both familiar and comfortable to the electorate. Polls showed the effects. After each of the debates, presidential and vice-presidential, the national audience deemed the Democrat the "winner."

As the race reached its final weeks, Obama had a consistent lead, averaging close to 7 percent in a blizzard of polls. The candidates campaigned vigorously; Obama flew 80,000 miles, and McCain logged 70,000. They and their running mates made personal appearances in most of the country, in contrast to previous elections, when the contenders concentrated their attention on a very few "battleground" states. The diffusion of the campaigns owed much to Obama's strategy to challenge Republicans in their previous redoubts and to his immense treasury, which enabled him to implement that strategy.

The outcome would depend on the quality of the candidates' campaign organizations. The Obama campaign proved its mettle, conducting probably the most effective effort in any modern election, combining the techniques Obama learned as a local community organizer with the older effective practices of Chicago ward politics. Primarily using the Internet rather than traditional events, the year-long campaign raised $750 million from nearly 4 million contributors, the median contribution below $200. In this effort, the candidate's organization developed an e-mail list of 13 million addresses and sent a billion messages to the list, sponsored 35,000 volunteer groups, 3.2 million Facebook enrollments, and 3 million phone calls to spur turnout in the last four days before the election. Just as plane travel and television transformed electioneering in the twentieth century, the Obama campaign created a new politics for the twenty-first.

THE ELECTION RESULTS

On November 4 Barack Obama won a decisive victory over McCain. *The New York Times* expressed the drama and the historical importance of the election in its front page election report. OBAMA, declared its inch-high bold type banner headline—the single word conveying deep emotion and deep significance.

Obama gained a margin of 9 million in the popular ballot count (53.5 percent of the two-party vote), and better than two-thirds of the electoral votes (365 to 173). He became only the second Democrat (Lyndon Johnson was the first) since Franklin Roosevelt to win a decisive majority of the total popular vote. And Obama outshone all but three of his party's nominees throughout American history, including Woodrow Wilson, Harry Truman, John Kennedy, and Bill Clinton. In the post–New Deal period, he also out-performed every first-term Republican winner except Dwight Eisenhower.

In winning the electoral vote, Obama forged new paths across the states of the Union. In the two most recent contests,

Democrats had restricted their efforts to electoral fortresses in the Northeast, parts of the Midwest, and the Pacific coast. To win the White House with this minimalist strategy, they needed victories in almost all of these states, neglecting wide swathes of the nation. By losing just one state in these critical areas—Florida in 2000 and Ohio in 2004—they also lost the national electoral count.

Obama changed the Democratic strategy, extending the contest to more states and to more areas, often Republican strongholds, within these states. His ample funds enabled him to implement what became a winning strategy on election day. The Illinois senator won a majority of the states, 28, and the District of Columbia. Holding all of the 20 constituencies won by John Kerry in 2004, he added 9 states carried by Bush to his own tally (as well as a single electoral vote from Nebraska). Sweeping the Midwest, including 3 states won by Bush in 2004, carrying 3 of the former Confederate states in the South, and mobilizing new voters to win 3 of the 8 Rocky Mountain domains, Obama won a national victory.

The exciting presidential election induced more than 130 million Americans to cast ballots, a noticeable rise of some 8 million in the absolute turnout numbers. Proportionate participation, however, increased only slightly from 2004, with about 62 percent of eligible citizens casting votes in 2008.

Turnout varied considerably among the states, expanding mostly because of the registration drives by the Obama campaign that focused on youths, African Americans, and Latinos. Expectations of high turnout had come from this large number of new registrants and from the heavy participation in early and absentee voting before election day itself. More than 30 million ballots were cast before the official opening of the polls, comprising close to a quarter of the total vote, an increase of at least 5 million since 2004. The increased turnout led to Obama victories in previous Republican bailiwicks in the South, mountain states, and Indiana.

Obama's mandate in 2008, in contrast to Bush in the two previous elections, was decisive, a 7 percent margin in the two-party vote. He increased the Democratic vote by 10 million votes (a 17 percent increase) over John Kerry's losing tally in 2004. McCain not only lost the election; he also lost votes, garnering 3 million fewer than the Republican president's previous tally (a 4 percent decline).

Obama scored well across most demographic categories, according to exit polls. He won new support for the Democratic ticket, compared to Kerry in 2004, in virtually every demographic and affinity group, as defined by sex, race, age, religion, education, income, family status, residence, and region. Democratic losses were confined to the oldest voters, small town residents, and southern white evangelicals. Particularly striking were his large majorities—far greater than Kerry's—among younger voters, African Americans, and Latinos. Although Obama did not achieve a majority among white voters as a whole, he still did better than Kerry among most groups of whites. Despite fears of a racial backlash, the first black nominee for president won a broad victory.

Building on his impressive victory, Obama had the potential to create a new Democratic majority coalition. The Democrats built a wider geographical base for the party, reaching into the West and the modernizing states of the South. The demographic foundation of a new party majority also was laid. The groups that voted for Obama will grow in relative size in future years, including blacks, Latinos, the college-educated, secularists, and metropolitan residents. Inevitably, too, those now young and more Democratic will replace contemporary aging Republicans. Yet, the presidential vote, in itself, meant only a repudiation of the Bush administration. The emergence of a long-term Democratic majority was possible, but not guaranteed.

The election of 2008 did carry one enduring significance. Obama's victory culminated the long struggle of African Americans for political equality. For whites it was also a time of personal liberation, a redeeming renunciation of the shame of racism. As he took the oath of office before millions of hopeful Americans, Obama could see the Lincoln Memorial where, only forty-five years earlier, Martin Luther King Jr. had dreamed that someday the nation's children would be judged "not by the color of their skin but by the content of their character." In the figure of a child only two years old at the time, that dream became real on January 20, 2009. As Obama himself had expressed the nation's pride: "If there is anyone out there who still doubts that America is a place where all things are possible; who still wonders if the dream of our founders is alive in our time; who still questions the power of our democracy, tonight is your answer."

THE BUSH LEGACY

In the early years of the twenty-first century, the Republican Party dominated government, holding unified control of Congress and firmly following President George W. Bush's leadership. By the middle of his second term, the party's power had waned. Bush's public approval plummeted, with the nation losing faith in his domestic programs and his war policies in Iraq and Afghanistan. Congressional Republicans also lost support through an unsavory string of sex and corruption scandals. In 2006 voters delivered a sharp rebuke to the party, returning control of both chambers of Congress to the Democrats for the first time in twelve years. As the 2008 presidential contest approached, *The Times* editorialized on Bush's perceived failures and the declining state of the economy. Public evaluations on these criteria looked likely to dominate the election campaign.

NOVEMBER 8, 2006
ON WAVE OF VOTER UNREST, DEMOCRATS TAKE CONTROL OF HOUSE
By CARL HULSE

Democrats rode voter unrest over Congressional misconduct and the war in Iraq back to power in the House on Tuesday night, ending 12 years of Republican rule by persuading voters it was time to change course in Washington.

Led by a string of victories in the Northeast and Midwest, Democrats gained at least 21 seats, 6 more than the 15 required to install Representative Nancy Pelosi of California as the first woman to become speaker of the House. Assuming they hold on to enough of their incumbent seats elsewhere, Democrats will hold the House majority for the first time since 1994.

"Today, the American people have stated loud and clear that they want a new direction for our country," said an ebullient Representative Louise M. Slaughter, Democrat of New York, who is in line to become the chairwoman of the House Rules Committee in the new Democratic regime.

Republicans were dogged by scandal throughout the campaign, and it cost them dearly. They lost seats in Ohio, Pennsylvania, Texas and Florida as the direct result of criminal cases and other misconduct. Exit polls showed that corruption weighed heavily on the minds of voters.

But public dissatisfaction with the Iraq war and other issues was clear. Three Republican incumbents were defeated in conservative Indiana and another in Kentucky. Two moderate Republicans were ousted in New Hampshire and at least one more in Connecticut. New York, with Democrats leading the top of the ticket, gave the party at least two more seats. Democratic gains mounted as votes were counted in the West.

The White House acknowledged that the once overwhelming Republican majority in the House had slipped away.

JANUARY 2, 2008
EDITORIAL
THE ECONOMY AND THE NEW YEAR

As 2008 begins, house prices are still skidding, bank losses are still mounting, oil is again flirting with $100 a barrel and consumers are buying less as prices rise. To many, the wheels appear to be coming off the economy.

To others, including President Bush and his aides, the economy is fundamentally sound and resilient.

Obviously, both camps cannot be right. Unfortunately, the preponderance of evidence is grim.

When Mr. Bush says the economy is strong, he is generally referring to rising wages, low unemployment and what he calls healthy economic growth. But wages have either fallen or failed to outpace inflation during most of his tenure. Job creation is now slowing from a pace that has long been subpar. Economic growth is also braking, if not contracting. In any event, growth during the Bush years has not been healthy; rather, it has been abnormally lopsided. Corporate profits have soared (until recently) and the rich have become richer, while most Americans have treaded water or lost ground, their troubling circumstances masked by an unprecedented borrowing binge, now exacting its toll.

Hoping for the best is facile if not paired with preparation for the worst. Perhaps more than anything, a lack of preparation makes it hard to believe Mr. Bush's assurances that all will be well. The administration has operated in a state of economic denial for years: conducting wars while cutting taxes, piling up debt, neglecting to regulate the financial sector even as it went on a lending binge, and ignoring the pain that was sure to come when consumers, bankers and investors sobered up.

Given that record, it is no surprise that Mr. Bush is now refusing to acknowledge the seriousness of the problems he has helped create. Americans don't need more denial. They need an unvarnished appraisal of the nation's economy—including the politics and ideology that has driven it to this point. That is the only real hope for starting to turn things around.

- -

THE PRIMARIES

The 2008 presidential primaries opened the election cycle earlier than ever as states fought to gain prominence by moving their contests forward on the calendar. Both the Democrats and Republicans had clear front-runners heading into the opening contest in Iowa—former Massachusetts governor Mitt Romney for the Republicans and New York senator Hillary Clinton for the Democrats—but both lost. Emerging from the back of the Republican field, Arizona senator John McCain went on to win subsequent primaries in a surprising comeback, eventually sealing his nomination. Among Democrats, Senator Clinton battled back from her initial loss to Illinois senator Barack Obama, evening the nomination battle with a victory in New Hampshire, and setting up an epic clash for the party's mantle.

JANUARY 4, 2008
OBAMA TAKES IOWA IN A BIG TURNOUT AS CLINTON FALTERS; HUCKABEE VICTOR
By ADAM NAGOURNEY

DES MOINES—Senator Barack Obama of Illinois, a first-term Democratic senator trying to become the nation's first African-American president, rolled to victory in the Iowa caucuses on Thursday night, lifted by a record turnout of voters who embraced his promise of change.

The victory by Mr. Obama, 46, amounted to a startling setback for Senator Hillary Rodham Clinton, 60, of New York, who just months ago presented herself as the front-runner for the Democratic presidential nomination. The result left uncertain the prospects for John Edwards, a former senator from North Carolina, who had staked his second bid for the White House on winning Iowa.

Mrs. Clinton and Mr. Edwards, who edged her out for second place by less than a percentage point, both vowed to stay in the race.

"They said this day would never come," Mr. Obama said as he claimed his victory at a packed rally in downtown Des Moines.

On the Republican side, Mike Huckabee, the former governor of Arkansas who was barely a blip on the national scene just two months ago, defeated Mitt Romney, a former Massachusetts governor, delivering a serious setback to Mr. Romney's high-spending campaign and putting pressure on Mr. Romney to win in New Hampshire next Tuesday.

Mr. Huckabee, a Baptist minister, was carried in large part by evangelical voters, who helped him withstand

extensive spending by Mr. Romney on television advertising and a get-out-the-vote effort.

"Tonight we proved that American politics is still in the hands of ordinary folks like you," said Mr. Huckabee, who ran on a platform that combined economic populism with an appeal to social conservatives.

JANUARY 9, 2008
CLINTON IS VICTOR, TURNING BACK OBAMA; MCCAIN ALSO TRIUMPHS
By PATRICK HEALY
and MICHAEL COOPER

MANCHESTER, N.H.—Senator Hillary Rodham Clinton of New York rode a wave of female support to a surprise victory over Senator Barack Obama in the New Hampshire Democratic primary on Tuesday night. In the Republican primary, Senator John McCain of Arizona revived his presidential bid with a Lazarus-like victory.

The success of Mrs. Clinton and Mr. McCain followed their third- and fourth-place finishes in the Iowa caucuses last week. Mrs. Clinton's victory came after her advisers had lowered expectations with talk of missteps in strategy and concern about Mr. Obama's momentum after his first-place finish in Iowa. Her team is now planning to add advisers and undertake a huge fund-raising drive to prepare for a tough and expensive fight with Mr. Obama in

the Democratic nominating contests over the next four weeks.

Mr. McCain had pursued a meticulous and dogged turnaround effort: his second bid for the White House was in tatters last summer because of weak fund-raising and a blurred political message, leading him to fire senior advisers and refocus his energy on New Hampshire.

The New Hampshire results foreshadow a historic free-for-all for both the Democratic and Republican presidential nominations in the weeks to come. Mr. McCain's victory dealt another serious blow to Mitt Romney, the former governor of neighboring Massachusetts. Mr. Romney campaigned hard and spent heavily as he sought wins in Iowa and New Hampshire, only to come up short in both states.

FEBRUARY 6, 2008
SUPPORT DIVIDED, TOP DEMOCRATS TRADE VICTORIES
By PATRICK HEALY

Senators Hillary Rodham Clinton and Barack Obama carved up the nation in the 22-state nominating contest on Tuesday, leaving the Democratic presidential nomination more elusive than ever. Mrs. Clinton won California, Massachusetts, New Jersey and her home state, New York, while Mr. Obama took Connecticut, Georgia, Minnesota and his base in Illinois.

It was a night of drama as millions of Democrats cleaved sharply between two candidates offering them a historic first: The opportunity to nominate a woman or an African-American to lead their party's effort to reclaim the White House. Yet it was also a night when neither Mr. Obama nor Mrs. Clinton could decisively lay claim—or even secure an edge—to the nomination, assuring an electoral fight that will unfold for weeks to come.

In remarks to their supporters in Manhattan and Chicago, Mrs. Clinton and Mr. Obama smiled broadly but were relatively low key in their assessments of the night, as if they knew that their state-by-state successes did not add up to the grand prize of Democratic standard-bearer. Both sounded a little tired at times, already exhausted by campaigning and fund-raising, with only more of both ahead.

The results and exit polls showed formidable strengths for each candidate, with Mr. Obama gaining appeal with white voters—particularly white men—and Mrs. Clinton solidifying her support among Hispanics. Mrs. Clinton won Democratic primaries in states that her party rarely carries in a general election, like Arkansas—where she served as first lady—as well as Oklahoma and Tennessee.

FEBRUARY 6, 2008
MCCAIN GAINS WIDE SUPPORT; HUCKABEE WINS IN STATES IN SOUTH
By MICHAEL COOPER

Senator John McCain of Arizona won the most states and appeared poised to win the most delegates on Tuesday with impressive primary victories in the delegate-rich states of California, New York and Illinois. Mike Huckabee, the former Arkansas governor, revived his candidacy with victories across the South.

Their strong showings posed a serious challenge to the candidacy of Mitt Romney, the former Massachusetts governor, who vowed to press on with his campaign after winning in Montana, North Dakota, Minnesota, Massachusetts, Utah and Alaska. He pinned his hopes on further strong showings in the West, and hoped to be able to still pick up delegates in California, whose delegates are awarded to the winner of each Congressional district.

As voters in 21 states made their choice for the Republican presidential nomination, several of Mr. McCain's victories came in states that award all their delegates to the statewide winner, including New York, New Jersey, Connecticut and Delaware, allowing him to proclaim himself the favorite.

"Tonight, I think we must get used to the idea that we are the Republican Party front-runner for the nomination of president of the United States," Mr. McCain said to cheers on Tuesday night in Phoenix, after winning his home state, Arizona. "And I don't really mind it one bit."

If Mr. McCain failed to sweep the contests that followed his big win last week in Florida or to knock his rivals out of contention, his victories in the delegate-heavy Northeast and in Oklahoma were a sweet reward for his resurgent candidacy. Eight years ago, he had his presidential hopes dashed when he lost a coast-to-coast swath of nominating contests that were held that year in March, and which effectively ended his campaign.

FEBRUARY 8, 2008
ROMNEY IS OUT, MCCAIN EMERGES AS GOP CHOICE
By ELISABETH BUMILLER
and DAVID D. KIRKPATRICK

WASHINGTON—Senator John McCain all but captured the Republican presidential nomination on Thursday after Mitt Romney withdrew from the race, saying the war in Iraq and the terrorist threat made it imperative that the party unite.

In a dramatic announcement before a convention of stunned and largely unhappy conservatives, Mr. Romney said that he wanted to fight on but that taking his campaign all the way to the Republican convention in September would delay a national campaign against Senator Hillary Rodham Clinton or Senator Barack Obama, the two remaining Democratic contenders. Mr. Romney described both as weak on national security.

"They would retreat, declare defeat, and the consequences of that would be devastating," Mr. Romney, a former governor of Massachusetts, told a crowd that broke into chants of "Mitt, Mitt, Mitt."

Staying in the race, he said, "would make it easier for Senator Clinton or Obama to win."

Mr. Romney, who spent tens of millions of dollars of his fortune on the race, added, "Frankly, in this time of war, I simply cannot let my campaign be a part of aiding the surrender to terror."

Mr. McCain stepped forward two hours later before the same gathering to try to make peace with a group deeply skeptical of him, if not outright hostile. In a moment that will long be remembered by Republicans, he was greeted with jeers as well as cheers.

OBAMA V. CLINTON

For five months, Democrats struggled to select a clear winner in the extended race between Obama and Clinton. Growing bitter and inflammatory, the candidates sparred on issues and credentials, yet remained locked tightly in the delegate count in a sequence of primaries throughout the nation. Obama developed momentum through late February and March, then faltered before accruing a slight, but sufficient, lead to capture the nomination outright in early June.

FEBRUARY 7, 2008
OBAMA AND CLINTON BRACE FOR A LONG-DISTANCE RUN
By PATRICK HEALY

With no breakout winner in Tuesday's Democratic primaries, Senators Hillary Rodham Clinton and Barack Obama on Wednesday began fortifying for a drawn-out nomination fight, with Mrs. Clinton disclosing that she had lent her campaign $5 million while Mr. Obama raised $3 million online in a single day and rejected calls for more debates.

While Mr. McCain moved far ahead in the total number of nominating delegates, with 689 compared with 156 for Mike Huckabee and 133 for Mr. Romney, Mr. Obama and Mrs. Clinton were in a narrower and more complicated delegate battle, with both camps claiming a lead based on their own analysis of Tuesday's vote.

Mrs. Clinton had the overall lead of delegates and so-called superdelegates—Democrats who are governors, senators and party leaders, according to an analysis by The New York Times. Mrs. Clinton had 892 delegates and

Mr. Obama 716; the Democratic nomination requires support from 2,025 delegates. The Times counts only delegates that have been officially selected and are bound by their preferences.

The narrow margin in delegates, and the growing likelihood that it will remain close, prompted concern on Wednesday from the chairman of the Democratic Party, Howard Dean, who said Tuesday night that Mr. Obama and Mrs. Clinton should avoid taking the nominating fight all the way to the party convention in August.

"I think we will have a nominee sometime in the middle of March or April," Mr. Dean said Wednesday on the NY1 cable news channel, "but if we don't, then we're going to have to get the candidates together and make some kind of an arrangement. Because I don't think we can afford to have a brokered convention; that would not be good news for either party."

FEBRUARY 20, 2008
OBAMA EXTENDS STREAK TO 10 AND MAKES INROADS AMONG WOMEN
By PATRICK HEALY
and JEFF ZELENY

Senator Barack Obama decisively beat Senator Hillary Rodham Clinton in the Wisconsin primary and the Hawaii caucuses on Tuesday night, accelerating his momentum ahead of crucial primaries in Ohio and Texas and cutting into Mrs. Clinton's support among women and union members.

With the two rivals now battling state by state over margins of victory and allotment of delegates, surveys of

voters leaving the Wisconsin polls showed Mr. Obama, of Illinois, making new inroads with those two groups as well as middle-age voters and continuing to win support from white men and younger voters—a performance that yielded grim tidings for Mrs. Clinton, of New York.

On the Republican side, Senator John McCain of Arizona won a commanding victory over Mike Huckabee in the Wisconsin contest and led by a wide margin in Washington

State. All but assured of his party's nomination, Mr. McCain immediately went after Mr. Obama during a rally in Ohio, deriding "eloquent but empty" calls for change.

For Mr. Obama, Hawaii was his 10th consecutive victory, a streak in which he has not only run up big margins in many states but also pulled votes from once-stalwart supporters of Mrs. Clinton, like low- and middle-income people and women.

Mrs. Clinton wasted no time in signaling that she would now take a tougher line against Mr. Obama—a recognition, her advisers said, that she must act to alter the course of the campaign and define Mr. Obama on her terms.

MAY 10, 2008
FOR FIRST TIME, MORE SUPERDELEGATES FAVOR OBAMA
By JOHN M. BRODER

The trump card Senator Hillary Rodham Clinton held in her faltering bid for president—her support among the superdelegates who can control the fate of the Democratic nomination—began slipping from her grasp on Friday as Senator Barack Obama moved into the lead on this front, with uncommitted delegates declaring their allegiance to him as others deserted her.

Mrs. Clinton publicly vowed to fight on for the nomination while campaigning on Friday in Oregon. But a new, more conciliatory tone crept into her stump speeches, as she shied away from the more spirited attacks on Mr. Obama that characterized her recent primary battles, instead engaging him more gently on the issues while aiming her fire on Senator John McCain of Arizona, the presumptive Republican nominee.

The superdelegate movement toward Mr. Obama, of Illinois—giving him a net gain of six on Friday alone, with more expected—increased the pressure on Mrs. Clinton, of New York, to at least refrain from divisive remarks, particularly after her comments on Wednesday that lower-income white voters would not support Mr. Obama if he became the Democratic nominee. Aides now say she regrets the comments.

Democratic officials said what had been a trickle of superdelegates declaring for Mr. Obama was turning into a steady stream in the wake of Tuesday's primaries, when Mrs. Clinton lost by 14 percentage points in North Carolina and narrowly won Indiana. Mr. Obama is just 166 delegates away from the 2,025 delegates needed to secure the nomination.

MAY 21, 2008
OBAMA DECLARES BID "WITHIN REACH" AFTER 2 PRIMARIES
By ADAM NAGOURNEY
and JEFF ZELENY

Senator Barack Obama took a big step toward becoming the Democratic presidential nominee on Tuesday, amassing enough additional delegates to claim an all but insurmountable advantage in his race against Senator Hillary Rodham Clinton.

While Mrs. Clinton's campaign continued to make a case that she could prevail, Mr. Obama seized on the results from Democratic contests in Kentucky and Oregon to move into a new phase of the campaign in which he will face different challenges. Those include bringing disaffected Clinton supporters into his camp; winning over elements of the Democratic coalition like working-class whites, Hispanics and Jews; and fending off attacks from Senator John McCain, the presumptive Republican nominee, especially on national security.

Mr. Obama won easily in Oregon. But his obstacles were underlined by a lopsided defeat in Kentucky, where just half of the Democratic voters said in exit polls that they would back him in the general election this fall.

Under the rules used by Democrats, the split decision was enough for Mr. Obama to secure a majority of the delegates up for grabs in primaries and caucuses.

His campaign has portrayed success in winning those pledged delegates as the most important yardstick for judging the will of Democratic voters, and has encouraged superdelegates—elected officials and party leaders who have an automatic vote at the convention—to fall in line accordingly.

JUNE 4, 2008
OBAMA CLINCHES NOMINATION; FIRST BLACK CANDIDATE TO LEAD A MAJOR PARTY TICKET
By JEFF ZELENY

Senator Barack Obama claimed the Democratic presidential nomination on Tuesday evening, prevailing through an epic battle with Senator Hillary Rodham Clinton in a primary campaign that inspired millions of voters from every corner of America to demand change in Washington.

A last-minute rush of Democratic superdelegates, as well as the results from the final primaries, in Montana and South Dakota, pushed Mr. Obama over the threshold of winning the 2,118 delegates needed to be nominated at the party's convention in August. The victory for Mr. Obama, the son of a black Kenyan father and a white Kansan mother, broke racial barriers and represented a remarkable rise for a man who just four years ago served in the Illinois Senate.

"You chose to listen not to your doubts or your fears, but to your greatest hopes and highest aspirations," Mr. Obama told supporters at a rally in St. Paul. "Tonight, we mark the end of one historic journey with the beginning of another—a journey that will bring a new and better day to America. Because of you, tonight I can stand here and say that I will be the Democratic nominee for president of the United States of America."

Mrs. Clinton paid tribute to Mr. Obama, but she did not leave the race. "This has been a long campaign and I will be making no decisions tonight," Mrs. Clinton told supporters in New York. She said she would be speaking with party officials about her next move.

In a combative speech, she again presented her case that she was the stronger candidate and argued that she had won the popular vote, a notion disputed by the Obama campaign.

"I want the nearly 18 million Americans who voted for me to be respected," she said in New York to loud cheers.

But she paid homage to Mr. Obama's accomplishments, saying, "It has been an honor to contest the primaries with him, just as it is an honor to call him my friend."

· ·

RACE AND POLITICS

As the first black candidate to compete for a major party nomination, Obama invoked questions of race from the beginning. Obama's minister, Jeremiah Wright, enflamed the issue by repeated denunciations of the United States as a racist country. Obama strongly repudiated Wright's words, expounding his full view most forcefully in mid-March. His widely acclaimed speech implored the nation to confront race honestly as a deep cleavage in American politics.

MARCH 19, 2008
OBAMA URGES U.S. TO GRAPPLE WITH RACE ISSUE
By JEFF ZELENY

PHILADELPHIA—Senator Barack Obama delivered a sweeping assessment of race in America on Tuesday, bluntly confronting the divisions between black and white as he sought to dispel the furor over inflammatory statements by his former pastor.

Mr. Obama again condemned the more incendiary remarks of the pastor, the Rev. Jeremiah A. Wright Jr. But, drawing on his experiences as the son of a white mother and a black father, Mr. Obama went on to try to explain to white voters the anger and frustration behind Mr. Wright's words and to urge blacks to understand the sources of the racial fears and resentments among whites.

While his immediate political goal was to tamp down any doubts that his association with Mr. Wright has caused among voters as he battles for the Democratic presidential nomination, Mr. Obama also sought to link his theme of understanding and reconciliation to more concrete issues at stake in the election as the economy weakens.

"The fact is," he said, "that the comments that have been made and the issues that have surfaced over the last few weeks reflect the complexities of race in this country that we've never really worked through—a part of our Union that we have yet to perfect.

"And if we walk away now," he continued, "if we simply retreat into our respective corners, we will never be able to come together and solve challenges like health care, or education, or the need to find good jobs for every American."

After running a campaign that in many ways tried not to be defined by race, Mr. Obama placed himself squarely in the middle of the debate over how to address it, a living bridge between whites and blacks still divided by the legacy of slavery and all that came after it.

His language reached at times for the inspiration and idealism of the civil rights movement, but for the most part addressed the politics of race in straightforward terms that seemed intended to keep the discussion grounded in the realities of the moment.

"It's a racial stalemate we've been stuck in for years," Mr. Obama said. "Contrary to the claims of some of my critics, black and white, I have never been so naïve as to believe that we can get beyond our racial divisions in a single election cycle, or with a single candidacy—particularly a candidacy as imperfect as my own."

For Mr. Obama, who is engaged in an intense fight for his party's nomination with Senator Hillary Rodham Clinton, the 37-minute speech five weeks before the Pennsylvania primary was an attempt to realign his campaign after a turbulent two weeks. Images of Mr. Wright, replayed again and again on television, threatened to damage a coalition of black and white voters that Mr. Obama has been trying to forge.

"I can no more disown him than I can disown my white grandmother," he said, "a woman who helped raise me, a woman who sacrificed again and again for me, a woman who loves me as much as she loves anything in this world, but a woman who once confessed her fear of black men who passed by her on the street, and who on more than one occasion has uttered racial or ethnic stereotypes that made me cringe."

● ●

THE DEMOCRATIC CONVENTION

The Democrats met in Denver over four days in late August. Added to the customary chores of nominating the ticket and adopting a platform was the task of mending a party torn by the long and competitive primary battle. Speeches from Sen. Edward Kennedy, Senator Clinton, and former president Bill Clinton marked the changing of the guard with Obama's nomination. Selecting Sen. Joe Biden of Delaware as his running mate, Obama focused on winning support from Republicans and independents still uncertain of his personal character and his policy directions. Culminating with Obama's acceptance speech before a massive stadium audience, the convention launched the Democrats' campaign message, a portrayal of a party of change and hope.

AUGUST 26, 2008
APPEALS EVOKING AMERICAN DREAM RALLY DEMOCRATS
By ADAM NAGOURNEY

DENVER—Senator Edward M. Kennedy, struggling with brain cancer, arrived on Monday night at the Democratic National Convention in a triumphant appearance that evoked 50 years of party history as Democrats gathered to nominate Senator Barack Obama for president.

Mr. Kennedy's appearance wiped away, at least for the evening, some of the tension that continued to plague the party in the wake of the primary fight between Mr. Obama and Senator Hillary Rodham Clinton. It also represented an effort by the Obama campaign to claim the Kennedy mantle, and it set the stage for the second part of what was designed to be an emotionally powerful two-act evening: an appearance later by Michelle Obama, who began a weeklong effort to present her husband—and his entire family—as embodiments of the American dream.

As elaborately choreographed as the evening was, with a series of speeches carefully screened by the Obama campaign, it was marked by an event that no one was sure until the very last moment would happen, given the severity of Mr. Kennedy's illness. He arrived at the convention site here shortly before dusk, accompanied by a flock of family members. He walked a few halting steps to a waiting golf cart, which drove him into the arena.

After a speech by his niece Caroline Kennedy and a video tribute, Mr. Kennedy walked slowly to the lectern, limping slightly, with his wife, Victoria, who kissed him and left him there. His white head of hair was noticeably thinned in the back; throughout the speech, he stared straight ahead to the front of the room. The crowd, many of them wiping tears from their eyes, cheered for close to two minutes until he settled them down.

"My fellow Democrats, my fellow Americans, it is so wonderful to be here," said Mr. Kennedy, his voice booming across the hall. "And nothing—nothing—is going to keep me away from this special gathering tonight."

A stool that had been slipped behind him went unused during his 10-minute speech. And while Mr. Kennedy spoke slowly and at times haltingly, his voice was firm and he was in command of this moment, gesturing and sounding very much like the man who enraptured the party's convention 28 years ago.

"There is a new wave of change all around us," he said, "and if we set our compass true, we will reach our destination—not merely victory for our party, but renewal for our nation. And this November, the torch will be passed again to a new generation of Americans.

"So with Barack Obama, and for you and for me, our country will be committed to his cause."

In an invocation of his parting remarks to the 1980 convention, when he promised that "the dream will never die" as he ceded the presidential nomination to Jimmy Carter, Mr. Kennedy declared, "The work begins anew, the hope rises again, and the dream lives on."

AUGUST 27, 2008
CLINTON RALLIES HER TROOPS TO FIGHT FOR OBAMA

By PATRICK HEALY

JILL ABRAMSON, MARK LEIBOVICH AND JIM RUTENBERG CONTRIBUTED REPORTING.

With her husband looking on tenderly and her supporters watching with tears in their eyes, Senator Hillary Rodham Clinton deferred her own dreams on Tuesday night and delivered an emphatic plea at the Democratic National Convention to unite behind her rival, Senator Barack Obama, no matter what ill will lingered.

Mrs. Clinton, who was once certain that she would win the Democratic nomination this year, also took steps on Tuesday—deliberate steps, aides said—to keep the door open to a future bid for the presidency. She rallied supporters in her speech, and, at an earlier event with 3,000 women, described her passion about her own campaign. And her aides limited input on the speech from Obama advisers, while seeking advice from her former strategist, Mark Penn, a loathed figure in the Obama camp.

But the main task for Mrs. Clinton at the convention—reaffirming her support for Mr. Obama in soaring and unconditional language—dominated her 23-minute speech, and she betrayed none of the anger and disappointment that she still feels, friends say, and that has especially haunted her husband.

Declaring herself to be "a proud supporter of Barack Obama," Mrs. Clinton urged Democrats to put aside their loyalty to her and unite behind Mr. Obama—or risk continuing Bush administration policies under the presumptive Republican nominee, Senator John McCain.

"Whether you voted for me, or voted for Barack, the time is now to unite as a single party with a single purpose," Mrs. Clinton said, beaming as the convention hall burst into applause. "And you haven't worked so hard over the last 18 months, or endured the last eight years, to suffer through more failed leadership."

AUGUST 28, 2008
HERALDING NEW COURSE, DEMOCRATS NOMINATE OBAMA
By ADAM NAGOURNEY; KITTY BENNETT, JOHN M. BRODER AND JANET ELDER CONTRIBUTED REPORTING.

Barack Hussein Obama, a freshman senator who defeated the first family of Democratic Party politics with a call for a fundamentally new course in politics, was nominated by his party on Wednesday to be the 44th president of the United States.

The unanimous vote made Mr. Obama the first African-American to become a major party nominee for president. It brought to an end an often-bitter two-year political struggle for the nomination with Senator Hillary Rodham Clinton of New York, who, standing on a packed convention floor electric with anticipation, moved to halt the roll call in progress so that the convention could nominate Mr. Obama by acclamation. That it did with a succession of loud roars, followed by a swirl of dancing, embracing, high-fiving and chants of "Yes, we can."

In an effort to fully ease the lingering animosity from the primary season, former President Bill Clinton, in a speech that had been anxiously awaited by Mr. Obama's aides given the uncomfortable relations between the two men, offered an enthusiastic and unstinting endorsement of Mr. Obama's credentials to be president. Mr. Clinton's message, like the messenger, was greeted rapturously in the hall.

"Last night Hillary told us in no uncertain terms that she is going to do everything she can to elect Barack Obama," Mr. Clinton said. "That makes two of us."

Mr. Clinton proceeded to do precisely what Mr. Obama's campaign was looking for him to do: attest to Mr. Obama's readiness to be president, after a campaign largely based on Mrs. Clinton's contention that he was not.

"I say to you: Barack Obama is ready to lead America and restore American leadership in the world," Mr. Clinton said. "Barack Obama is ready to preserve, protect and defend the Constitution of the United States. Barack Obama is ready to be president of the United States."

Senator Joseph R. Biden Jr. of Delaware, Mr. Obama's choice for vice president, accepted the nomination with a speech in which he spoke frequently, and earnestly, of his blue-collar background, in effect offering himself as a validator for Mr. Obama among some voters who have been reluctant to embrace the Democratic presidential nominee.

He then turned to Senator John McCain, the likely Republican nominee, signaling how he would go after him in the campaign ahead. He referred to Mr. McCain as a friend— "I know you hear that phrase a lot in politics; I mean it," he said—and then proceeded to offer a long and systematic case about why Mr. McCain should not be president.

"The choice in this election is clear," Mr. Biden said. "These times require more than a good soldier. They require a wise leader," he said, a leader who can deliver "the change that everybody knows we need."

His 21-minute address completed, Mr. Biden was joined on stage by his wife, Jill, who told the crowd they were about to be joined by an unscheduled guest. The crowd exploded as Mr. Obama walked around the corner.

"If I'm not mistaken, Hillary Clinton rocked the house last night," he said, gazing up at where Mr. and Mrs. Clinton were watching the proceedings and leading the crowd in applause. "And President Clinton reminded us of what it's like when you have a president who actually puts people first. Thank you."

AUGUST 29, 2008
OBAMA TAKES THE FIGHT TO MCCAIN

By ADAM NAGOURNEY and JEFF ZELENY

DENVER—Barack Obama accepted the Democratic Party presidential nomination on Thursday, declaring that the "American promise has been threatened" by eight years under President Bush and that John McCain represented a continuation of policies that undermined the nation's economy and imperiled its standing around the world.

The speech by Senator Obama, in front of an audience of nearly 80,000 people on a warm night in a football stadium refashioned into a vast political stage for television viewers, left little doubt how he intended to press his campaign against Mr. McCain this fall.

In cutting language, and to cheers that echoed across the stadium, he linked Mr. McCain to what he described as the "failed policies of George W. Bush" and—reflecting what has been a central theme of his campaign since he entered the race—"the broken politics in Washington."

"America, we are better than these last eight years," he said. "We are a better country than this."

But Mr. Obama went beyond attacking Mr. McCain by linking him to Mr. Bush and his policies. In the course of a 42-minute speech that ended with a booming display of fireworks and a shower of confetti, he offered searing and far-reaching attacks on his presumptive Republican opponent, repeatedly portraying him as the face of the old way of politics and failed Republican policies.

He said Mr. McCain was out of touch with the problems of everyday Americans. "It's not because John McCain doesn't care," he said. "It's because John McCain doesn't get it."

Senator John McCain astonished the political world on Friday by naming Sarah Palin, a little-known governor of Alaska and self-described 'hockey mom' with almost no foreign policy experience, as his running mate on the Republican presidential ticket.

THE REPUBLICAN CONVENTION

Seizing attention immediately after the close of the Democratic convention, John McCain selected Sarah Palin, governor of Alaska, as his party's vice-presidential candidate. Palin was little-known on the national stage prior to the convention, but it quickly introduced her to the nation. In a convention most notable for the absence of the sitting president, Palin's acceptance speech reignited the Republican base and added credibility to McCain's candidacy in the eyes of conservatives. Taking the stage the following evening, McCain worked to build support for the beleaguered party by focusing on his experience and patriotism.

On August 29, 2008, presumptive Republican presidential nominee Sen. John McCain, left, introduced his vice-presidential running mate, Alaska governor Sarah Palin, in Dayton, Ohio.

Source: AP Images

AUGUST 30, 2008
ALASKAN IS MCCAIN'S CHOICE; FIRST WOMAN ON G.O.P. TICKET

By MICHAEL COOPER and ELISABETH BUMILLER

DAYTON, Ohio—Senator John McCain astonished the political world on Friday by naming Sarah Palin, a little-known governor of Alaska and self-described "hockey mom" with almost no foreign policy experience, as his running mate on the Republican presidential ticket.

Ms. Palin, 44, a social conservative, former union member and mother of five who has been governor for two years, was on none of the widely discussed McCain campaign short lists for vice president. In selecting her, Mr. McCain reached far outside the Washington Beltway in an election year in which the Democratic presidential candidate, Senator Barack Obama, is running on a platform of change.

"She's not from these parts, and she's not from Washington, but when you get to know her, you're going to be as impressed as I am," Mr. McCain told a midday rally of 15,000 people in a basketball arena here shortly before Ms. Palin, with her husband and four of her children, strode out onto the stage.

Within moments, Ms. Palin made an explicit appeal to the disappointed supporters of Senator Hillary Rodham Clinton by praising not only Mrs. Clinton but also another woman who has been on a major presidential ticket, Geraldine A. Ferraro, Walter F. Mondale's Democratic running mate in 1984.

"Hillary left 18 million cracks in the highest, hardest glass ceiling in America, but it turns out the women of America aren't finished yet, and we can shatter that glass ceiling once and for all," Ms. Palin said to huge applause.

SEPTEMBER 4, 2008
PALIN ASSAILS CRITICS AND ELECTRIFIES PARTY
By ELISABETH BUMILLER and MICHAEL COOPER

ST. PAUL—Gov. Sarah Palin of Alaska introduced herself to America before a roaring crowd at the Republican National Convention on Wednesday night as "just your average hockey mom" who was as qualified as the Democratic nominee, Senator Barack Obama, to be president of the United States.

"Before I became governor of the great state of Alaska, I was mayor of my hometown," Ms. Palin told the delegates in a speech that sought to eviscerate Mr. Obama, as delegates waved signs that said "I love hockey moms." "And since our opponents in this presidential election seem to look down on that experience, let me explain to them what the job involves. I guess a small-town mayor is sort of like a 'community organizer,' except that you have actual responsibilities."

As the crowd cheered its approval, Ms. Palin went on: "I might add that in small towns we don't quite know what to make of a candidate who lavishes praise on working people when they are listening, and then talks about how bitterly they cling to their religion and guns when those people aren't listening."

Ms. Palin was referring to Mr. Obama's experience as a community organizer in Chicago before he served in the Illinois legislature and was elected to the United States Senate in 2004 as well as comments he made at a fundraiser in California about bitter rural voters who "cling" to guns and religion.

"I'm not a member of the permanent political establishment," Ms. Palin said in her remarks, which took aim at the news media as the crowd began lustily booing the press. "And I've learned quickly, these past few days, that if you're not a member in good standing of the Washington elite, then some in the media consider a candidate unqualified for that reason alone. But here's a little news flash for all those reporters and commentators: I'm not going to Washington to seek their good opinion; I'm going to Washington to serve the people of this country."

Ms. Palin spent the first part of her speech introducing her family one by one to the crowd, including her husband, Todd. "We met in high school, and two decades and five children later he's still my guy," Ms. Palin said.

Ms. Palin also displayed humor in one of her biggest lines of the night when she said that "the difference between a hockey mom and a pit bull" was "lipstick."

Ms. Palin's speech was the big draw of a convention night notable for not a single mention from the stage of the unpopular president, George W. Bush, who addressed the delegates Tuesday via satellite from the White House after the hurricane forced him to cancel his appearance.

SEPTEMBER 5, 2008
MCCAIN VOWS TO END 'PARTISAN RANCOR'
By ADAM NAGOURNEY and MICHAEL COOPER

ST. PAUL—Senator John McCain accepted the Republican presidential nomination Thursday with a pledge to move the nation beyond "partisan rancor" and narrow self-interest in a speech in which he markedly toned down the blistering attacks on Senator Barack Obama that had filled the first nights of his convention.

Standing in the center of an arena here, surrounded by thousands of Republican delegates, Mr. McCain firmly signaled that he intended to seize the mantle of change Mr. Obama claimed in his own unlikely bid for his party's nomination.

Mr. McCain suggested that his choice of Gov. Sarah Palin of Alaska as his running mate gave him the license to run as an outsider against Washington, even though he has served in Congress for more than 25 years.

"Let me just offer an advance warning to the old, big-spending, do-nothing, me-first-country-second crowd: Change is coming," Mr. McCain said.

With his speech, Mr. McCain laid out the broad outlines of his general election campaign. He sought to move from a convention marked by an intense effort to reassure the party base to an appeal to a broader general election audience that polling suggests has turned sharply on Republicans and President Bush. He invoked, in one of the most emotional moments of the night, his struggles as a prisoner of war in Vietnam.

Mr. McCain also returned to what has been his signature theme as a candidate, including in his unsuccessful 2000 campaign: that he is a politician prepared to defy his own party. He used the word "fight" 43 times in the course of the speech, as he sought to present himself as the insurgent he was known as before the primaries, when he veered to the right.

"Stand up, stand up, stand up and fight," he said at the end of his speech. "Nothing is inevitable here. We're Americans, and we never give up. We never quit. We never hide from history. We make history."

SARAH PALIN

Sarah Palin, the Republican vice-presidential candidate, garnered an unusual amount of attention throughout the campaign. Relatively unknown, Palin stormed onto the electoral stage with an electrifying speech at the Republican convention, but then declined media appearances after news of potential scandals broke. With voters keen to learn more, she lost luster in some television interviews, due to awkward prepared statements or rambling responses. Her standing deteriorated further after spoofs on popular late-night comedy programs. Palin's candidacy polarized the electorate, drawing fervent supporters and fierce detractors.

SEPTEMBER 2, 2008
PALIN DAUGHTER'S PREGNANCY INTERRUPTS G.O.P. CONVENTION SCRIPT
By MONICA DAVEY

ST. PAUL—Just days after Gov. Sarah Palin was named as Senator John McCain's running mate, Ms. Palin made an unlikely announcement of her own on Monday: Her daughter Bristol, 17 and unmarried, was five months pregnant.

As Americans began learning this week about Ms. Palin—Alaskan hunter, hockey mom, former beauty queen, corruption fighter, and governor they knew little about—they were also piecing together a portrait of her family life and all its complications.

Ms. Palin had once supported the candidate who ran against her own stepmother-in-law for mayor of her town, Wasilla. She was being investigated over claims that she had put pressure on an underling to fire her sister's former husband from his job as a state trooper. And she had waited until she was seven months pregnant to make public news that she was expecting a fifth child this year, a pregnancy that was complicated by Down syndrome.

If anything, the still-unfolding story of Ms. Palin, 44, and her family eclipsed whatever other message anyone may have hoped to send from the Republican National Convention here on Monday. It was a narrative worthy of a Lifetime television drama (which, perhaps fittingly, is sponsoring a string of events aimed at women here this week).

Like so many here, Ted Boyatt, 20, a delegate from Maryville, Tenn., seemed stunned by Ms. Palin's announcement and its awkward timing.

"It seems like the whole script has just been knocked out of balance," Mr. Boyatt said. "We had it on paper," he said of the convention agenda, "and in the blink of an eye it all went out the window."

SEPTEMBER 17, 2008
SNL'S GOALS: FUNNY AND EVENHANDED

By BRIAN STELTER

For the staff of a comedy show, the people behind "Saturday Night Live" certainly care a lot about fairness.

Speaking at a Manhattan event sponsored by the Museum of the Moving Image on Monday night, the cast members Seth Meyers and Amy Poehler answered questions about their much discussed sketch, broadcast by NBC on Saturday, that featured Ms. Poehler as Senator Hillary Rodham Clinton, the former Democratic presidential candidate, and Tina Fey as Gov. Sarah Palin, the Republican vice presidential candidate.

"The trick with all of these people is to try to come out as fair and evenhanded as possible," said Mr. Meyers, also the head writer for "SNL." He added that the inclusion of Ms. Poehler's Clinton character "made it safer to mention things about Sarah Palin without making it seem like an attack piece."

Among the jokes:

Mrs. Clinton: "I believe that diplomacy should be the cornerstone of any foreign policy."

Ms. Palin: "And I can see Russia from my house."

Ms. Clinton: "I believe global warming is caused by man."

Ms. Palin: "And I believe it's just God hugging us closer."

Saturday's episode, which opened with the Palin sketch, was the highest-rated edition of the show since 2002, according to Nielsen's preliminary ratings. Additionally, the Palin sketch has been viewed more than five million times on YouTube.com and nbc.com. The cast members said changes had been made to it up until the final minutes before the broadcast.

"The Palin people were happy with it as well, which was the weird thing," Mr. Meyers said.

SEPTEMBER 26, 2008
A QUESTION REPRISED, BUT THE WORDS COME NONE TOO EASILY FOR PALIN

By ALESSANDRA STANLEY

Her first interview, with the ABC News anchor Charles Gibson, was too hard. The second, with Sean Hannity on the Fox News Channel, was too soft. The third, however, did not turn out to be just right for Gov. Sarah Palin of Alaska.

On the "CBS Evening News" on Thursday, Katie Couric asked Ms. Palin, Senator John McCain's running mate, what she meant when she cited Alaska's proximity to Russia as foreign affairs experience. Ms. Palin could have anticipated the question—the topic of their interview, pegged to her visit to the United Nations, was foreign affairs. Yet Ms. Palin's answer was surprisingly wobbly: her words tumbled out fast and choppily, like an outboard motor loosened from the stern.

"That Alaska has a very narrow maritime border between a foreign country, Russia, and on our other side, the land—boundary that we have with—Canada," she replied. She mentioned the jokes made at her expense and seemed for a moment at a loss for the word "caricature."

"It—it's funny that a comment like that was—kind of made to—cari—I don't know, you know? Reporters—"

Ms. Couric stepped in. "Mocked?" Ms. Palin looked relieved and even grateful for the help. "Yeah, mocked, I guess that's the word, yeah."

Ms. Couric pressed her again to explain the geographic point. "Well, it certainly does," Ms. Palin said, "because our, our next-door neighbors are foreign countries, they're in the state that I am the executive of."

Ms. Couric asked the governor if she had ever been involved in negotiations, for example, with her Russian neighbors.

"We have trade missions back and forth," Ms. Palin said. "We—we do—it's very important when you consider even national security issues with Russia as Putin rears his head and comes into the airspace of the United States of America, where—where do they go? It's Alaska. It's just right over the border."

Ms. Palin, looking at Ms. Couric intently, kept on going. "It is from Alaska that we send those out to make sure that an eye is being kept on this very powerful nation, Russia, because they are right there. They are right next to—to our state."

That exchange was so startling it ricocheted across the Internet several hours before it appeared on CBS and was picked up by rival networks.

Ms. Couric asked her questions firmly but gently, careful not to seem flippant or condescending. But she ended on a "gotcha" moment. After Ms. Palin attacked Senator Barack Obama for saying he would meet with leaders of Syria and Iran without preconditions, Ms. Couric reminded the governor that she recently met with former Secretary of State Henry Kissinger, who supports direct diplomacy with both countries. "Are you saying Henry Kissinger is naïve?" Ms. Couric asked. Ms. Palin replied, "I've never heard Henry Kissinger say, 'Yeah, I'll meet with these leaders without preconditions being met.' "

After the interview, Ms. Couric faced the camera and added a postscript. "Incidentally, we confirmed Henry Kissinger's position following our interview," she said, explaining that Mr. Kissinger supports talks "without preconditions."

- -

The Economic Collapse

Shortly after the conventions, the strained U.S. economy cracked and began to collapse. Failures in home mortgages precipitated a series of economic declines, including frozen credit markets, bankrupt finance companies, rising unemployment, and declining consumer spending. The international finance system wavered on the brink of disaster. As President Bush and the Democratic Congress frantically pieced together a stimulus package to prevent a full depression, the state of the economy became the dominant focus of the election.

SEPTEMBER 15, 2008
NATION'S FINANCIAL INDUSTRY GRIPPED BY FEAR
By BEN WHITE and JENNY ANDERSON

Fear and greed are the stuff that Wall Street is made of. But inside the great banking houses, those high temples of capitalism, fear came to the fore this weekend.

As Lehman Brothers, one of oldest names on Wall Street, filed for bankruptcy protection, anxiety over the bank's fate—and over what might happen next—gripped the nation's financial industry. By Sunday night, Merrill Lynch, under mounting pressure, had reached a deal to sell itself to Bank of America for $29 a share or about $50 billion, according to people with knowledge of the deal.

Dinner parties were canceled. Weekend getaways were postponed. All of Wall Street, it seemed, was on high alert.

In skyscrapers across Manhattan, banking executives were holed up inside their headquarters, within cocoons of soft rugs and wood-paneled walls, desperately trying to assess their company's exposure to the stricken Lehman. It was, by all accounts, a day unlike anything Wall Street had ever seen.

SEPTEMBER 16, 2008
WALL ST. IN WORST LOSS SINCE '01 DESPITE REASSURANCES BY BUSH
By STEPHEN LABATON

WASHINGTON—In another unnerving day for Wall Street, investors suffered their worst losses since the terrorist attacks of 2001, and government officials raced to prevent the financial crisis from spreading.

Trading opened sharply down Monday morning, and the mood later turned even gloomier, despite efforts by President Bush and Treasury Secretary Henry M. Paulson Jr., in separate appearances at the White House, to reassure markets that Wall Street's deepening problems would not weaken an already anemic economy.

Amid worries that the bankruptcy of Lehman Brothers and the sale of Merrill Lynch over the weekend might not be enough to stop the downward spiral, stocks fell sharply in the last half hour of trading. By the end of the day, the Dow Jones industrial average had dropped 504.48 points, or 4.4 percent, as a record volume of more than 8 billion shares traded hands on the New York Stock Exchange. It was the biggest decline since Sept. 17, 2001—the day the

index reopened after the 9/11 terrorist attacks—when it fell 7 percent, or 684.81 points.

A concern hanging over the market is the fate of other financial companies, most notably the American International Group, one of the world's largest insurers. After the Fed rebuffed a request by the company for a $40 billion temporary loan, federal and state officials worked on Monday to stabilize A.I.G., with the State of New York relaxing rules to allow the company to borrow as much as $20 billion in much-needed cash, while the New York Federal Reserve Bank was engaged in talks with JPMorgan Chase and Goldman Sachs on a $75 billion loan for the insurer.

Market participants fear that without a cash infusion for A.I.G., losses on its financial insurance contracts could cause a ripple effect that would damage other companies. Shares of A.I.G., already battered in recent weeks, plunged another 60 percent on Monday, closing at $4.76. Last year, the company had traded as high as $72.

SEPTEMBER 21, 2008
ADMINISTRATION IS SEEKING $700 BILLION FOR WALL STREET
By DAVID M. HERSZENHORN

WASHINGTON—The Bush administration on Saturday formally proposed a vast bailout of financial institutions in the United States, requesting unfettered authority for the Treasury Department to buy up to $700 billion in distressed mortgage-related assets from the private firms.

The proposal, not quite three pages long, was stunning for its stark simplicity. It would raise the national debt ceiling to $11.3 trillion. And it would place no restrictions on the administration other than requiring semiannual reports to Congress, granting the Treasury secretary unprecedented power to buy and resell mortgage debt.

"This is a big package, because it was a big problem," President Bush said Saturday at a White House news conference, after meeting with President Álvaro Uribe of Colombia. "I will tell our citizens and continue to remind them that the risk of doing nothing far outweighs the risk of the package, and that, over time, we're going to get a lot of the money back."

After a week of stomach-flipping turmoil in the financial system, and with officials still on edge about how global markets will respond, the delivery of the administration's plan set the stage for a four-day brawl in Congress. Democratic leaders have pledged to approve a bill but say it must also include tangible help for ordinary Americans in the form of an economic stimulus package.

Staff members from Treasury and the House Financial Services and Senate banking committees immediately began meeting on Capitol Hill and were expected to work through the weekend. Congressional leaders are hoping to recess at the end of the week for the fall elections, after approving the bailout and a budget measure to keep the government running.

With Congressional Republicans warning that the bailout could be slowed by efforts to tack on additional provisions, Democratic leaders said they would insist on a requirement that the administration use its new role, as the owner of large amounts of mortgage debt, to help hundreds of thousands of troubled borrowers at risk of losing their homes to foreclosure.

"It's clear that the administration has requested that Congress authorize, in very short order, sweeping and unprecedented powers for the Treasury secretary," the House speaker, Nancy Pelosi of California, said in a statement. "Democrats will work with the administration to ensure that our response to events in the financial markets is swift, but we must insulate Main Street from Wall Street and keep people in their homes."

THE DEBATES

The first debate between John McCain and Barack Obama paralleled Congress's debates over the economic collapse, with the candidates clashing over how to best revive the economy and handle foreign policy. Although McCain and Obama drew a large audience, the most watched debate was the next one, between the vice-presidential candidates, with voters eager to see Sarah Palin perform. Over the next month, the presidential candidates sparred twice more, drawing increasingly sharp distinctions between their economic proposals, while revealing their differing experience and temperament. The final debate, three weeks before election day, brought "Joe the plumber" into the American political lexicon, as Obama and McCain invoked an Ohio tradesman in arguments over tax policy.

SEPTEMBER 27, 2008
RIVALS DISPLAY STARK CONTRASTS IN CLASHES ON WAR AND ECONOMY
By ADAM NAGOURNEY and JEFF ZELENY

From the economy to foreign affairs to the way they carried themselves on stage, Senators John McCain and Barack Obama offered a dramatic contrast to the nation in their first presidential debate on Friday night, mixing disdain and often caustic remarks as they set out sharply different views of how they would manage the country and confront America's adversaries abroad.

The two men met for 90 minutes against the backdrop of the nation's worst financial crisis since the Great Depression and intensive negotiations in Congress over a $700 billion bailout plan for Wall Street.

Despite repeated prodding, Mr. McCain and Mr. Obama refused to point to any major adjustments they would need to make to their governing agendas—like scaling back promised tax reductions or spending programs—to accommodate what both men said could be very tough economic times for the next president.

For the first 40 minutes, Mr. Obama repeatedly sought to link Mr. McCain to President Bush, and suggested that it was policies of excessive deregulation that led to the financial crisis and mounting economic problems the nation faces now.

"We also have to recognize that this is a final verdict on eight years of failed economic policies promoted by George Bush, supported by Senator McCain—the theory that basically says that we can shred regulations and consumer protections and give more and more to the most and somehow prosperity will trickle down," Mr. Obama said. "It hasn't worked, and I think that the fundamentals of the economy have to be measured by whether or not the middle class is getting a fair shake."

Mr. McCain became more animated during the second part of the debate, when it shifted to the advertised topic: foreign policy and national security. The two men offered strong and fundamentally different arguments about the wisdom of going to war against Iraq—which Mr. McCain supported and Mr. Obama opposed—as well as how to deal with Iran.

More than anything, Mr. McCain seemed intent on presenting Mr. Obama as green and inexperienced, a risky choice during a difficult time. Again and again, sounding almost like a professor talking down to a new student, he talked about having to explain foreign policy to Mr. Obama and repeatedly invoked his 30 years of history on national security (even though Mr. McCa]in, in the kind of misstep that no doubt would have been used by Republicans against Mr. Obama, mangled the name of the Iranian president, Mahmoud Ahmadinejad, and he stumbled over the name of Pakistan's newly inaugurated president, calling him "Qadari." His name is actually Asif Ali Zardari.).

"I don't think I need any on-the-job training," Mr. McCain said in the closing moments of the debate. "I'm ready to go at it right now."

But Mr. Obama seemed calm and in control and seemed to hold his own on foreign policy, the subject on which Mr. McCain was assumed to hold a natural advantage. Mr. Obama talked in detail about foreign countries and their leaders, as if trying to assure the audience that he could hold his own on the world stage. He raised his own questions about Mr. McCain's judgment in supporting the Iraq war.

"You like to pretend like the war started in 2007—you talk about the surge. The war started in 2003," Mr. Obama said. "At the time, when the war started, you said it was going to be quick and easy. You said we knew where the weapons of mass destruction were. You were wrong. You said that we were going to be greeted as liberators. You were wrong."

There were no obvious game-changing moments—big mistakes, or the kind of sound bites that dominate the news for days—in the course of the 90-minute debate, held at the University of Mississippi in Oxford. Still, the debate served as a reminder of just how different these two men would be as president as they appeared for their first extended session together before a huge audience, including many Americans who are just beginning to focus on this long-lasting race.

OCTOBER 3, 2008
CORDIAL BUT POINTED, PALIN AND BIDEN FACE OFF

By PATRICK HEALY

Gov. Sarah Palin used a steady grin, folksy manner and carefully scripted talking points to punch politely and persist politically at the vice-presidential debate on Thursday night, turning in a performance that her rival, Senator Joseph R. Biden Jr., sought to undermine with cordially delivered but pointed criticism.

If the issues and positions were familiar to many viewers—on taxes and the economy, energy and oil, same-sex marriage, Iraq and Afghanistan—it was Ms. Palin's debut in a nationally televised debate that made for unusual theater. And Ms. Palin, a former small-town mayor, was unlike any other running mate in recent memory, using phrases like "heck of a lot" and "Main Streeters like me" to appeal to working-class and middle-class voters who feel abandoned by Washington.

Mr. Biden, a six-term senator who has twice sought the presidency, remained forceful and composed against an opponent who proved difficult to attack, given that she is a newcomer and a woman in an arena long dominated by men.

Focusing his attacks on the Republican presidential nominee, Senator John McCain, Mr. Biden only occasionally lost patience with Ms. Palin's debating tactics, as when she used Mr. Biden's words against him.

In the only vice-presidential debate of the campaign, at Washington University in St. Louis, Ms. Palin exceeded expectations in this highly anticipated face-off, though those expectations were low after she had stumbled in recent television interviews. She succeeded by not failing in any obvious way. She mostly reverted to and repeated talking points, like referring to Mr. McCain as a "maverick" and the Republican ticket as a "team of mavericks," while not necessarily quelling doubts among voters about her depth of knowledge.

Instead Ms. Palin emphasized her down-home qualities and her membership in the middle class, a group that she and Mr. Biden sparred over repeatedly during their 90-minute encounter.

"Go to a kids' soccer game on Saturday and turn to any parent there on the sideline and ask them, 'How are you feeling about the economy?' " Ms. Palin said. "And I'll betcha you're going to hear some fear in that parent's voice, fear regarding the few investments that some of us have in the stock market—did we just take a major hit with those investments?"

Mr. Biden, standing at a lectern a few feet from Ms. Palin's, replied with one of his characteristic strategies in the debate: portraying Mr. McCain as unaware or unmoved by voters' problems and as an ally of the deeply unpopular President Bush.

"It was two Mondays ago John McCain said at 9 o'clock in the morning that the fundamentals of the economy were strong," Mr. Biden said. "Eleven o'clock that same day, two Mondays ago, John McCain said that we have an economic crisis. That doesn't make John McCain a bad guy, but it does point out he's out of touch. Those folks on the sidelines knew that two months ago."

Rarely has a vice-presidential showdown been packed with such political importance. Ms. Palin's unsteady performances in recent interviews turned this debate into can't-miss television, but they have also raised questions—from conservatives, among others—about the soundness of Mr. McCain's judgment in picking a relative newcomer as his running mate. Recent polls have suggested that his shifting statements on the economic bailout talks in Washington have not reassured some of these conservatives, raising the stakes for Ms. Palin to deliver steady, informed answers and repartee in the debate.

OCTOBER 17, 2008
CANDIDATES CLASH OVER CHARACTER AND POLICY
By JIM RUTENBERG

Senator John McCain used the final debate of the presidential election on Wednesday night to raise persistent and pointed questions about Senator Barack Obama's character, judgment and policy prescriptions in a session that was by far the most spirited and combative of their encounters this fall.

At times showing anger and at others a methodical determination to make all his points, Mr. McCain pressed his Democratic rival on taxes, spending, the tone of the campaign and his association with the former Weather Underground leader William Ayers, using nearly every argument at his disposal in an effort to alter the course of a contest that has increasingly gone Mr. Obama's way.

But Mr. Obama maintained a placid and at times bemused demeanor—if at times appearing to work at it—as he parried the attacks and pressed his consistent line that Mr. McCain would represent a continuation of President Bush's unpopular policies, especially on the economy.

That set the backdrop for one of the sharpest exchanges of the evening, when, in response to Mr. Obama's statement that Mr. McCain had repeatedly supported Mr. Bush's economic policies, Mr. McCain fairly leaped out of his chair to say: "Senator Obama, I am not President Bush. If you wanted to run against President Bush, you should have run four years ago."

Acknowledging Mr. McCain had his differences with Mr. Bush, Mr. Obama replied, "The fact of the matter is that if I occasionally mistake your policies for George Bush's policies, it's because on the core economic issues that matter to the American people—on tax policy, on energy policy, on spending priorities—you have been a vigorous supporter of President Bush."

Seizing on an encounter in Ohio this week with a voter—Joe Wurzelbacher, a plumber—who told Mr. Obama that he feared that his tax policies would punish him as a small-business owner, Mr. McCain pressed his attack on Mr. Obama as a tax-and-spend liberal. Mr. Obama's plan would raise taxes on filers earning more than $250,000 a year, a category that includes some small businesses, but would cut taxes on households earning less than $200,000 a year.

Seeking to suggest that Mr. Obama would hurt the economy and many entrepreneurs, Mr. McCain said, "The whole premise behind Senator Obama's plans are class warfare—let's spread the wealth around," repeating a phrase Mr. Obama had used to Mr. Wurzelbacher in explaining the rationale for his upper-income tax increase.

"Why would you want to do that—anyone, anyone in America—when we have such a tough time, when these small-business people like Joe the Plumber are going to create jobs unless you take that money from him and spread the wealth around," Mr. McCain said.

The plumber came up directly or indirectly 24 times during the debate, an Everyman symbol of the divide between the candidates on how best to address the economy.

As he has done in previous encounters, Mr. Obama looked into the camera and repeated his plan: "Now, the conversation I had with Joe the Plumber, what I essentially said to him was, five years ago, when you weren't in the position to buy your business, you needed a tax cut then. And what I want to do is to make sure that the plumber, the nurse, the firefighter, the teacher, the young entrepreneur who doesn't yet have money, I want to give them a tax break now."

Campaigning 2.0

Major changes in campaign techniques came about in the 2008 election. One innovation was the Obama campaign's successful effort to raise massive amounts of money by online solicitation of relatively small contributions from millions of donors. Rejecting public financing, Obama accumulated twice the money available to McCain. That funding paid for novel campaign methods over the Internet, providing direct contact between the candidate and grassroots supporters and portending a new era of presidential electioneering.

OCTOBER 20, 2008
OBAMA'S SEPTEMBER SUCCESS RECASTS THE CAMPAIGN FUND-RAISING LANDSCAPE
By MICHAEL LUO

Senator Barack Obama's announcement on Sunday of his record-shattering $150 million fund-raising total for September underscored just how much his campaign has upended standards for raising money in presidential campaigns.

His campaign has now raised more than $600 million, almost equaling what all the candidates from both major parties collected in private donations in 2004.

It is a remarkable ascent to previously unimagined financial heights—Mr. Obama's September total more than doubled the record $66 million he collected in August—that has been cheered by some and decried by others concerned about the influence of money in politics. The impact on the way presidential campaigns are financed is likely to be profound, potentially providing an epitaph on the tombstone of the existing public finance system.

NOVEMBER 3, 2008
CAMPAIGNS IN A WEB 2.0 WORLD
By DAVID CARR AND BRIAN STELTER

Shortly after 9 A.M. on Oct. 19, Colin Powell endorsed Barack Obama for president during the taping of "Meet the Press" on NBC. Within minutes, the video was on the Web.

But the clip was not rushed onto YouTube; it was MSNBC.com, the network's sister entity online, that showed the video hours before television viewers on the West Coast could watch the interview for themselves.

Old media, apparently, can learn new media tricks. Not since 1960, when John F. Kennedy won in part because of the increasingly popular medium of television, has changing technology had such an impact on the political campaigns and the organizations covering them.

For many viewers, the 2008 election has become a kind of hybrid in which the dividing line between online and off, broadcast and cable, pop culture and civic culture, has been all but obliterated.

Many of the media outlets influencing the 2008 election simply were not around in 2004. YouTube did not exist, and Facebook barely reached beyond the Ivy League. There was no Huffington Post to encourage citizen reporters, so Mr. Obama's comment about voters clinging to guns or religion may have passed unnoticed. These sites and countless others have redefined how many Americans get their political news.

When viewers settle in Tuesday night to watch the election returns, they will also check text messages for alerts, browse the Web for exit poll results and watch videos distributed by the campaigns. And many folks will let go of the mouse only to pick up the remote and sample an array of cable channels with election coverage—from Comedy Central to BBC America.

But as NBC's decision to release the Powell clip early shows, the networks and their newspaper counterparts have not simply waited to be overtaken. Instead, they have made specific efforts to engage audiences with interactive features, allowing their content to be used in unanticipated ways, and in many efforts, breaking out of the boundaries of the morning paper and the evening newscast.

"Old media outlets—the networks, the newspapers— learned a lot of lessons from the last cycle and didn't allow others to own the online space this time," said Rick Klein, the senior political reporter for ABC News.

NOVEMBER 4, 2008
THE '08 CAMPAIGN: SEA CHANGE FOR POLITICS AS WE KNOW IT
By ADAM NAGOURNEY

The 2008 race for the White House that comes to an end on Tuesday fundamentally upended the way presidential campaigns are fought in this country, a legacy that has almost been lost with all the attention being paid to the battle between Senators John McCain and Barack Obama.

It has rewritten the rules on how to reach voters, raise money, organize supporters, manage the news media, track and mold public opinion, and wage—and withstand— political attacks, including many carried by blogs that did not exist four years ago. It has challenged the consensus view of the American electoral battleground, suggesting that Democrats can at a minimum be competitive in states and regions that had long been Republican strongholds.

The size and makeup of the electorate could be changed because of efforts by Democrats to register and turn out new black, Hispanic and young voters. This shift may have long-lasting ramifications for what the parties do to build enduring coalitions, especially if intensive and technologically-driven voter turnout programs succeed in getting more people to the polls. Mr. McCain's advisers expect a record-shattering turnout of 130 million people, many being brought into the political process for the first time.

"I think we'll be analyzing this election for years as a seminal, transformative race," said Mark McKinnon, a senior adviser to President Bush's campaigns in 2000 and 2004. "The year campaigns leveraged the Internet in ways never imagined. The year we went to warp speed. The year the paradigm got turned upside down and truly became bottom up instead of top down."

To a considerable extent, Republicans and Democrats say, this is a result of the way that the Obama campaign sought to understand and harness the Internet (and other forms of so-called new media) to organize supporters and to reach voters who no longer rely primarily on information from newspapers and television. The platforms included YouTube, which did not exist in 2004, and the cellphone text messages that the campaign was sending out to supporters on Monday to remind them to vote.

President Obama

On November 4 the nation voted decisively for Barack Obama, giving him a 365 to 173 Electoral College victory. The first African American elected president, Obama brought the Democrats back to the White House after eight years and increased party majorities in both the House and Senate. Obama's nationwide campaign strategy led to gains across the country, even in areas and demographic groups previously considered Republican strongholds. Taking office eleven weeks later, Obama represented a historic change in American race relations and stirred hopes that a more active government would meet the evident problems of the nation.

NOVEMBER 5, 2008
OBAMA
RACIAL BARRIAR FALLS IN DECISIVE VICTORY
By ADAM NAGOURNEY

Barack Hussein Obama was elected the 44th president of the United States on Tuesday, sweeping away the last racial barrier in American politics with ease as the country chose him as its first black chief executive.

The election of Mr. Obama amounted to a national catharsis—a repudiation of a historically unpopular Republican president and his economic and foreign policies, and an embrace of Mr. Obama's call for a change in the direction and the tone of the country.

But it was just as much a strikingly symbolic moment in the evolution of the nation's fraught racial history, a breakthrough that would have seemed unthinkable just two years ago.

Mr. Obama, 47, a first-term senator from Illinois, defeated Senator John McCain of Arizona, 72, a former prisoner of war who was making his second bid for the presidency.

To the very end, Mr. McCain's campaign was eclipsed by an opponent who was nothing short of a phenomenon, drawing huge crowds epitomized by the tens of thousands of people who turned out to hear Mr. Obama's victory speech in Grant Park in Chicago.

Mr. McCain also fought the headwinds of a relentlessly hostile political environment, weighted down with the baggage left to him by President Bush and an economic collapse that took place in the middle of the general election campaign.

"If there is anyone out there who still doubts that America is a place where all things are possible, who still wonders if the dream of our founders is alive in our time, who still questions the power of our democracy, tonight is your answer," said Mr. Obama, standing before a huge wooden lectern with a row of American flags at his back, casting his eyes to a crowd that stretched far into the Chicago night.

"It's been a long time coming," the president-elect added, "but tonight, because of what we did on this date in this election at this defining moment, change has come to America."

Mr. McCain delivered his concession speech under clear skies on the lush lawn of the Arizona Biltmore, in Phoenix, where he and his wife had held their wedding reception. The crowd reacted with scattered boos as he offered his congratulations to Mr. Obama and saluted the historical significance of the moment.

"This is a historic election, and I recognize the significance it has for African-Americans and for the special pride that must be theirs tonight," Mr. McCain said, adding, "We both realize that we have come a long way from the injustices that once stained our nation's reputation."

Not only did Mr. Obama capture the presidency, but he led his party to sharp gains in Congress. This puts Democrats in control of the House, the Senate and the White House for the first time since 1995, when Bill Clinton was in office.

2008 POPULAR VOTE

STATE	TOTAL VOTE	BARACK OBAMA (DEMOCRAT) VOTES	%	JOHN McCAIN (REPUBLICAN) VOTES	%
Alabama	2,099,819	813,479	38.7	1,266,546	60.3
Alaska	326,197	123,594	37.9	193,841	59.4
Arizona	2,293,475	1,034,707	45.1	1,230,111	53.6
Arkansas	1,086,617	422,310	38.9	638,017	58.7
California	13,561,900	8,274,473	61.0	5,011,781	37.0
Colorado	2,401,349	1,288,568	53.7	1,073,584	44.7
Connecticut	1,648,560	1,000,994	60.7	628,873	38.1
Delaware	412,412	255,459	61.9	152,374	36.9
District of Columbia	265,853	245,800	92.5	17,367	6.5
Florida	8,390,744	4,282,074	51.0	4,045,624	48.2
Georgia	3,924,440	1,844,137	47.0	2,048,744	52.2
Hawaii	453,568	325,871	71.8	120,566	26.6
Idaho	655,032	236,440	36.1	403,012	61.5
Illinois	5,523,051	3,419,673	61.9	2,031,527	36.8
Indiana	2,751,054	1,374,039	49.9	1,345,648	48.9
Iowa	1,537,123	828,940	53.9	682,379	44.4
Kansas	1,235,872	514,765	41.7	699,655	56.6
Kentucky	1,826,508	751,985	41.2	1,048,462	57.4
Louisiana	1,960,761	782,989	39.9	1,148,275	58.6
Maine	731,163	421,923	57.7	295,273	40.4
Maryland	2,630,947	1,628,995	61.9	959,694	36.5
Massachusetts	3,080,985	1,904,097	61.8	1,108,854	36.0
Michigan	5,001,766	2,872,579	57.4	2,048,639	41.0
Minnesota	2,910,369	1,573,354	54.1	1,275,409	43.8
Mississippi	1,289,865	554,662	43.0	724,597	56.2
Missouri	2,925,205	1,441,911	49.3	1,445,814	49.4
Montana	490,109	231,667	47.3	242,763	49.5
Nebraska	801,281	333,319	41.6	452,979	56.5
Nevada	967,848	533,736	55.1	412,827	42.7
New Hampshire	710,970	384,826	54.1	316,534	44.5
New Jersey	3,868,237	2,215,422	57.3	1,613,207	41.7
New Mexico	830,158	472,422	56.9	346,832	41.8
New York	7,594,813	4,769,700	62.8	2,742,298	36.1
North Carolina	4,310,789	2,142,651	49.7	2,128,474	49.4
North Dakota	316,621	141,278	44.6	168,601	53.3
Ohio	5,698,260	2,933,388	51.5	2,674,491	46.9
Oklahoma	1,462,661	502,496	34.4	960,165	65.6
Oregon	1,827,864	1,037,291	56.7	738,475	40.4
Pennsylvania	5,991,064	3,276,363	54.7	2,651,812	44.3
Rhode Island	469,767	296,571	63.1	165,391	35.2
South Carolina	1,920,969	862,449	44.9	1,034,896	53.9
South Dakota	381,975	170,924	44.7	203,054	53.2
Tennessee	2,599,749	1,087,437	41.8	1,479,178	56.9
Texas	8,077,795	3,528,633	43.7	4,479,328	55.5
Utah	952,370	327,670	34.4	596,030	62.6
Vermont	325,046	219,262	67.5	98,974	30.4
Virginia	3,723,260	1,959,532	52.6	1,725,005	46.3
Washington	3,036,878	1,750,848	57.7	1,229,216	40.5
West Virginia	714,246	304,127	42.6	398,061	55.7
Wisconsin	2,983,417	1,677,211	56.2	1,262,393	42.3
Wyoming	254,658	82,868	32.5	164,958	64.8
TOTALS	131,235,440	69,459,909	52.9	59,930,608	45.7

OTHER VOTES	%	PLURALITY	
19,794	0.9	453,067	R
8,762	2.7	70,247	R
28,657	1.2	195,404	R
26,290	2.4	215,707	R
275,646	2.0	3,262,692	D
39,197	1.6	214,984	D
18,693	1.1	372,121	D
4,579	1.1	103,085	D
2,686	1.0	228,433	D
63,046	0.8	236,450	D
31,559	0.8	204,607	R
7,131	1.6	205,305	D
15,580	2.4	166,572	R
71,851	1.3	1,388,146	D
31,367	1.1	28,391	D
25,804	1.7	146,561	D
21,452	1.7	184,890	R
26,061	1.4	296,477	R
29,497	1.5	365,286	R
13,967	1.9	126,650	D
42,258	1.6	669,301	D
68,034	2.2	795,243	D
80,548	1.6	823,940	D
61,606	2.1	297,945	D
10,606	0.8	169,935	R
37,480	1.3	3,903	R
15,679	3.2	11,096	R
14,983	1.9	119,660	R
21,285	2.2	120,909	D
9,610	1.4	68,292	D
39,608	1.0	602,215	D
10,904	1.3	125,590	D
82,815	1.1	2,027,402	D
39,664	0.9	14,177	D
6,742	2.1	27,323	R
90,381	1.6	258,897	D
0	—	457,669	R
52,098	2.9	298,816	D
62,889	1.0	624,551	D
7,805	1.7	131,180	D
23,624	1.2	172,447	R
7,997	2.1	32,130	R
33,134	1.3	391,741	R
69,834	0.9	950,695	R
28,670	3.0	268,360	R
6,810	2.1	120,288	D
38,723	1.0	234,527	D
56,814	1.9	521,632	D
12,058	1.7	93,934	R
43,813	1.5	414,818	D
6,832	2.7	82,090	R
1,844,923	**1.4**	**9,529,301**	**D**

NOVEMBER 5, 2008
NO TIME FOR LAURELS; NOW THE HARD PART
By PETER BAKER

WASHINGTON—No president since before Barack Obama was born has ascended to the Oval Office confronted by the accumulation of seismic challenges awaiting him. Historians grasping for parallels point to Abraham Lincoln taking office as the nation was collapsing into Civil War, or Franklin D. Roosevelt arriving in Washington in the throes of the Great Depression.

The task facing Mr. Obama does not rise to those levels, but that these are the comparisons most often cited sobers even Democrats rejoicing at their return to power. On the shoulders of a 47-year-old first-term senator, with the power of inspiration yet no real executive experience, now falls the responsibility of prosecuting two wars, protecting the nation from terrorist threat and stitching back together a shredded economy.

Given the depth of these issues, Mr. Obama has little choice but to "put your arm around chaos," in the words of Leon E. Panetta, the former White House chief of staff who has been advising his transition team.

"You better damn well do the tough stuff up front, because if you think you can delay the tough decisions and tiptoe past the graveyard, you're in for a lot of trouble," Mr. Panetta said. "Make the decisions that involve pain and sacrifice up front."

What kind of decision maker and leader Mr. Obama will be remains unclear even to many of his supporters. Will he be willing to use his political capital and act boldly, or will he move cautiously and risk being paralyzed by competing demands from within his own party? His performance under the harsh lights of the campaign trail suggests a figure with remarkable coolness and confidence under enormous pressure, yet also one who rarely veers off the methodical path he lays out.

> "Mr. Obama, the son of a black man from Kenya and a white woman from Kansas, inherited a White House built partly by slaves and a nation in crisis at home and abroad."

JANUARY 21, 2009
OBAMA TAKES OATH, AND NATION IN CRISIS EMBRACES THE MOMENT

By PETER BAKER

WASHINGTON—Barack Hussein Obama was sworn in as the 44th president of the United States on Tuesday and promised to "begin again the work of remaking America" on a day of celebration that climaxed a once-inconceivable journey for the man and his country.

Mr. Obama, the son of a black man from Kenya and a white woman from Kansas, inherited a White House built partly by slaves and a nation in crisis at home and abroad. The moment captured the imagination of much of the world as more than a million flag-waving people bore witness while Mr. Obama recited the oath with his hand on the same Bible that Abraham Lincoln used at his inauguration 148 years ago.

Beyond the politics of the occasion, the sight of a black man climbing the highest peak electrified people across racial, generational and partisan lines. Mr. Obama largely left it to others to mark the history explicitly, making only passing reference to his own barrier-breaking role in his 18-minute Inaugural Address, noting how improbable it might seem that "a man whose father less than 60 years ago might not have been served at a local restaurant can now stand before you to take a most sacred oath."

But confronted by the worst economic situation in decades, two overseas wars and the continuing threat of Islamic terrorism, Mr. Obama sobered the celebration with a grim assessment of the state of a nation rocked by home foreclosures, shuttered businesses, lost jobs, costly health care, failing schools, energy dependence and the threat of climate change. Signaling a sharp and immediate break with the presidency of George W. Bush, he vowed to usher in a "new era of responsibility" and restore tarnished American ideals.

"Today, I say to you that the challenges we face are real," Mr. Obama said in the address, delivered from the west front of the Capitol. "They are serious and they are many. They will not be met easily or in a short span of time. But know this, America, they will be met."

The vast crowd that thronged the Mall on a frigid but bright winter day was the largest to attend an inauguration in decades, if not ever. Many then lined Pennsylvania Avenue for a parade that continued well past nightfall on a day that was not expected to end for Mr. Obama until late in the night with the last of 10 inaugural balls.

Mr. Bush left the national stage quietly, doing nothing to upstage his successor. After hosting the Obamas for coffee at the White House and attending the ceremony at the Capitol, Mr. Bush hugged Mr. Obama, then left through the Rotunda to head back to Texas. "Come on, Laura, we're going home," he was overheard telling Mrs. Bush.

In his address, Mr. Obama praised Mr. Bush "for his service to our nation as well as the generosity and cooperation he has shown throughout this transition." But he also offered implicit criticism, condemning what he called "our collective failure to make hard choices and prepare the nation for a new age."

He went on to assure the rest of the world that change had come. "To all other peoples and governments who are watching today," Mr. Obama said, "from the grandest capitals to the small village where my father was born, know that America is a friend of each nation and every man, woman and child who seeks a future of peace and dignity, and that we are ready to lead once more."

INDEX

Page numbers in italics refer to illustrations. Tables are indicated with t following the page number.